Basic Psychology

Third Edition

Basic Psychology

Third Edition

HENRY GLEITMAN
UNIVERSITY OF PENNSYLVANIA

W · W · NORTON & COMPANY · NEW YORK · LONDON

Composition by New England Typographic Service, Inc.
Manufacturing by R. R. Donnelley & Sons Company.
Book design by Antonina Krass.

Library of Congress Cataloging-in-Publication Data

Gleitman, Henry.
    Basic psychology / Henry Gleitman.
        p.   cm.
    Includes bibliographical references and index.
    1. Psychology.   I. Title.
BF121.G27   1992
150—dc20   91-39818

ISBN 0-393-96242-3 (paper)

W. W. Norton & Company, Inc., 500 Fifth Avenue, New York, N.Y. 10110

W. W. Norton & Company, Ltd., 10 Coptic Street, London WC1A 1PU

1 2 3 4 5 6 7 8 9 0

To Ellen, Claire, David, and Philip

The Contents in Brief

Introduction

Contents

look at psychology's intellectual history, for a number of the field's endeavors are hard to explain unless one points to the paths that led up to them. Why did Thorndike study cats in puzzle boxes? Why did his conclusions have such an important effect on American psychology? Why were they challenged by Köhler and Tolman? It still pays to take a serious look at the work of such pioneers before turning to the present. Much as a river's water is clearer when it is taken from its source, so issues that have become more and more complex as detail has been piled upon detail become plainer and more evident when traced back to their origin.

GENERAL ORGANIZATION

The most obvious difference between this and the previous editions is the explanation of the coverage of the topics of social psychology and personality. The first is now treated in two chapters (one on social cognition and emotion, the other on social action); the second is considerably enlarged, with a consideration of four different theoretical approaches to personality theory. Further changes represent updatings (in some cases, major updatings) of the subject matter that are best described within an outline of the overall structure of the book. After a short introductory section, the book is divided into five parts that reflect the perspectives from which most psychological phenomena can be regarded: Action, Cognition, Social Behavior, Development, and Individual Differences. In brief outline, they cover the following topics:

Part I: Action

This part focuses on overt behavior and its physiological basis. It begins by considering the biological underpinnings of human and animal action, leading to a discussion of the nervous system and its operation (Chapter 1) and some phenomena of motivation (Chapter 2). It then asks how organisms can modify their behavior to adapt to new circumstances, a topic which leads to a discussion of classical and instrumental conditioning and modern behavior theory (Chapter 3).

In Chapter 1 (Biological Bases of Behavior) there is an increased emphasis on neurotransmitter processes at the synapse and on modern work on recovery of nervous function. Chapter 2 (Motivation) now includes sections on feeding disorders and drug addiction. Chapter 3 (Learning) stresses recent developments in animal learning, including work on contingency and modern cognitive approaches to classical and instrumental conditioning.

Part II: Cognition

This part deals with knowledge and how it is gained and used. It begins by asking how the senses provide us with information about the world outside (Chapter 4) and how this information is organized and interpreted to lead to the perception of objects and events (Chapter 5). Further questions concern the way this knowledge is stored in memory and retrieved when needed (Chapter 6), the way it is organized through thinking (Chapter 7), and the way knowledge is communicated to others through the medium of language (Chapter 8).

Many of the things in this part reflect a greater concern with recent information-processing approaches. In Chapter 5 (Perception), the organization has been changed to give more prominence to some modern approaches to pattern recognition. Chapter 6 (Memory) highlights the changes in outlook from the stage theories of the sixties to the modern emphasis on encoding and retrieval and such current concerns as the role of schemas in memory and the difference between explicit and implicit memory. Chapter 7 (Thinking) includes new material on artificial intelligence, on reasoning, and on the role of framing in decision making. Chapter 8 (Language), written by Lila Gleitman and myself, deals with language structure and processing as well as with language acquisition and includes a discussion of recent work on sensitive periods in language learning.

Part III: Social Behavior

This part concerns our interactions with others. It begins with a discussion of built-in social tendencies in humans and animals, a topic to which ethology and evolutionary theory have made major contributions (Chapter 9). It proceeds by taking up the first influential attempt to understand how childhood affects human socialization by considering Freud and psychoanalytic concepts (Chapter 10), thus paving the way for the discussion of modern approaches to social development taken up later in the section on development. It then turns to modern social psychology, considering how people try to understand the social situation in which they find themselves, how they interpret their own internal states and emotions, and how they interact with others (Chapters 11 and 12).

There have been several changes in this section. Chapter 9 (The Biological Basis of Social Behavior) includes an expanded section on primate social behavior, as well as an expanded discussion of the relevance of sociobiological theories to human concerns. Like its counterpart in the previous edition, Chapter 10 (The Individual and Society: The Contributions of Sigmund Freud) discusses the contributions of psychoanalytic and related views to our conceptions of socialization. Two chapters are now devoted to issues in modern social psychology. Chapter 11 (Social Cognition and Emotion) focuses on the way individuals interpret social events and includes discussions of attitudes and attitude change, attribution, impressions of others, and the interpretation of one's own internal states. Chapter 12 (Social Interaction) deals with the way individuals deal with others and includes discussions of social exchange, attraction and love, conformity, obedience, and crowd behavior.

Part IV: Development

This section contains two chapters on development. Chapter 13 (Physical and Cognitive Development) has an enlarged discussion of recent, post-Piagetian approaches to mental growth. Chapter 14 (Social Development) is updated with expanded discussions of such topics as moral development, empathy, sex, and gender.

Part V: Individual Differences

This part begins with a chapter on mental testing in general and intelligence testing in particular (Chapter 15) and then continues with a chapter on personality assessment and theory (Chapter 16). It continues by looking at several varieties of psychopathology and asking how they arise (Chapter 17) and concludes by examining various methods of treatment and therapy (Chapter 18).

Chapter 15 (Intelligence) has been updated by a discussion of some relatively recent test instruments, such as the *Kaufman Assessment Battery for Children.* Chapter 16 (Personality) is a considerably enlarged treatment. It begins with a discussion of personality assessment and discusses trait theory as one of four theoretical approaches to personality, with particular attention to the trait-situation controversy and recent attempts to look for biological and genetic bases of personality differences. It continues by taking up three other theoretical approaches to personality—the psychodynamic, behavioral, and humanistic. Both Chapter 17 (Psychopathology) and Chapter 18 (Treatment of Psychopathology) have been updated to include modern developments, such as the two-syndrome hypothesis of schizophrenia, new work on panic disorder, and new approaches to the evaluation of treatment outcome.

THE READER AND THE BOOK

It is sometimes said that students in the introductory course want to learn about things that are relevant to themselves and to their own lives. But why should this be a problem? When you come right down to it, there is something odd about the idea that psychology is *not* relevant to anyone's particular life history—specialist and nonspecialist alike. Psychology deals with the nature of human experiences and behavior, about the hows and whys of what we do, think, and feel. Everyone has perceived, learned, remembered, and forgotten, has been angry and afraid and been in love, has given into group pressure and been independent. In short, everyone has experienced most of the phenomena that psychology tries to explain. This being so, psychology cannot fail to be relevant.

It surely is relevant, but its relevance has to be pointed out. I've tried to do so by a liberal use of examples from ordinary experience and a frequent resort to metaphors of one kind or another, in the hope that in doing so I would show the direct relation of many psychological phenomena to the reader's own life.

In these attempts, the most important guide has been my own experience as a classroom teacher. There is little doubt that one of the best ways of learning something is to teach it, for in trying to explain it to others, you first have to clarify it to yourself. This holds for the subject matter of every course I have ever taught, but most especially for the introductory course. Students in an advanced course will come at you with tough and searching questions; they want to know about the evidence that bears on a theory of, say, color vision or language acquisition and about how that evidence was obtained. But students in an introductory course ask the toughest questions of all. They ask why anyone would ever want to know about color vision (or language acquisition or whatever) in the first place. And they also ask what any one topic has to do with any other. They ask such questions because they—unlike the advanced students—have not as yet accepted the premises of the field. They wonder whether the emperor is really wearing any clothes. As a result, they made me ask myself afresh what the field of psychology is all about—what the emperor's clothes are really like when you look at them more closely.

This book as well as its predecessor grew out of my attempts to answer such questions over the years in which I taught the introductory course, to answer them not only to satisfy the students but also to satisfy myself.

SUPPLEMENTARY MATERIALS

To help serve the needs of students, instructors, and teaching assistants, several supplementary materials are available with this text.

1. *For the student:*

There is a complete *Study Guide,* prepared by two of my colleagues and collaborators, John Jonides of the University of Michigan and Paul Rozin of the University of Pennsylvania. This *Study Guide,* a revised version of the guide the same authors wrote for the first, second, and third editions of *Psychology,* should prove very useful to students who want some help and guidance in mastering the material in the text. Moreover, for every chapter, it provides experiments and observational studies that students can carry out on their own to get some first-hand experience with psychology's subject matter.

2. *For the instructor:*

There is an *Instructor's Manual,* prepared by Christine Massey of Swarthmore College, Hilary Schmidt of New Jersey Medical School and the Monell Institute, Alan Silberberg of American University, and myself, which offers specific suggestions for every textbook chapter, including discussion topics, demonstrations, and a bibliography. The manual also includes an annotated film and media guide prepared by James B. Maas and Brian P. Schilling both of Cornell University.

John Jonides of the University of Michigan and Paul Cornwell of Pennsylvania State University, with the help of Tibor Palfai of Syracuse University, have prepared a *Test-Item File,* which includes questions for all chapters plus the statistical appendix. A proportion of these questions have been statistically analyzed at Syracuse and Pennsylvania State Universities; the resulting data are included in the printed *Test-Item File.* Of course, this *Test-Item File* is available on diskette in MS-DOS, Apple II, and Macintosh formats.

I have also prepared a set of *Classroom Demonstrations* with the collaboration of Paul Rozin and Lila Gleitman, both of the University of Pennsylvania. Included are materials necessary to perform about twenty-five in-class experiments covering a range of phenomena, from the speed of the nervous impulse, through the Stroop effect, to a demonstration of sex stereotypes. Slides, transparencies, student worksheets, data summaries, and detailed instructions for the instructor are included. These demonstrations are adapted from those that I and my collaborators have used in our own teaching.

ACKNOWLEDGMENTS

There remains the pleasant task of thanking the many friends and colleagues who helped me so greatly in the various phases of writing this book and its immediate predecessors. Some read parts of the manuscript and gave valuable advice and criticism. Others talked to me at length about various issues in the field that I then saw more clearly. I am very grateful to them all. These many helpers, and the main areas in which they advised me, are as follows:

Biological Foundations

Elizabeth Adkins-Regan, *Cornell University;* Dorothy Cheney, *University of Pennsylvania;* Steven Fluharty, *University of Pennsylvania;* Douglas G. Mook, *University of Virginia;* Paul Rozin, *University of Pennsylvania;* Jonathan I. Schull, *Haverford College;* Robert Seyfarth, *University of Pennsylvania;* Peter Shizgall, *Concordia University;* Edward M. Stricker, *University of Pittsburgh.*

Learning

Ruth Colwill, *Brown University;* Paula Durlach, *McMaster University;* Werner Honig, *Dalhousie University;* Robert Rescorla, *University of Pennsylvania.*

Sensation and Perception

Linda Bartoshuk, *Yale University;* Leo M. Hurvich, *University of Pennsylvania;* Dorothea Jameson, *University of Pennsylvania;* R. Duncan Luce, *University of California, Irvine;* Jacob Nachmias, *University of Pennsylvania;* Brian Wandell, *Stanford University.*

Cognition

Robert G. Crowder, *Yale University;* Lila R. Gleitman, *University of Pennsylvania;* John Jonides, *University of Michigan;* Michael McCloskey, *John Hopkins University;* Douglas Medin, *University of Michigan;* Morris Moscovitch, *University of Toronto;* Daniel Reisberg, *Reed College.*

Language

Barbara Landau, *University of California, Irvine;* Anne Lederer, *University of Pennsylvania;* Elissa Newport, *University of Rochester;* Ruth Ostrin, *Medical Research Council,* Cambridge, England; Ted Suppala, *University of Rochester.*

Social Psychology

Phoebe C. Ellsworth, *University of Michigan;* Alan Fridlund, *University of California, Santa Barbara;* Clark R. McCauley, *Bryn Mawr College;* Dennis Regan, *Cornell University;* John Sabini, *University of Pennsylvania;* R. Lance Shotland, *Pennsylvania State University.*

Development

Renée Baillargeon, *University of Illinois;* Adele Diamond, *University of Pennsylvania;* Susan Scanlon Jones, *Indiana University;* Philip J. Kellman, *Swarthmore College;* Robert Schoenberg, *University of Pennsylvania;* Elizabeth Spelke, *Cornell University.*

Intelligence

Jonathan Baron, *University of Pennsylvania.*

Personality

Hal Bertilson, *Saint Joseph's University;* Nathan Brody, *Wesleyan University;* Peter Gay, *Yale University;* Lewis R. Goldberg, *University of Oregon, Eugene.*

Psychopathology

Lyn Y. Abramson, *University of Wisconsin;* Lauren Alloy, *Temple University;* Sue Mineka, *Northwestern University;* Rena Repetti, *University of California, Los Angeles;* Ingrid I. Waldron, *University of Pennsylvania.*

General advice on topic coverage

Thomas Critchfield, *Illinois State University;* Mark Fineman, *Southern Connecticut State University;* Murray Goddard, *University of New Brunswick, St. John;* Robert Stern, *Pennsylvania State University;* Toni Strand, *Ohio State University;* David Thomas, *Oklahoma State University;* Lori Van Wallandael, *University of North Carolina, Charlotte.*

To state in detail how each of these persons helped me is impossible. But I do want to express special thanks to a few whose comments helped me to see whole topics in a new light for this edition. I owe special thanks to Ruth Colwill, Paula Durlach, Werner Honig, and Robert Rescorla, whose wise counsel and comments helped me understand how recent developments in the field of animal learning have given new life to many issues of its past; to Dorothy Cheney and Robert Seyfarth, who gave me valuable insights into empirical and theoretical issues in modern ethology; to Michael McCloskey and Douglas Medin, who provided unfailingly good advice in the areas of perception and cognition; to Robert Crowder, whose incisive comments on memory were invaluable; to Daniel Reisberg, who gave me important insights into new developments in the fields of memory and thinking and whose help went far beyond the bounds of collegial duty; to Jonathan Baron, Phoebe Ellsworth, and Rick McCauley, whose discussions of thinking, social processes, and intelligence helped me consider many aspects of these areas from a new perspective; to Adele Diamond, Susan Scanlon Jones, and Philip Kellman, who helped me to see the developmental forest as well as its trees; to Nathan Brody, whose many discussions and insightful comments on the personality chapter I found invaluable; and to Lauren Alloy, whose comments and advice on facts and theories in the field of psychopathology were indispensable.

Yet another kind of thanks goes to Neil Macmillan who wrote "Statistics: The Collection, Organization, and Interpretation of Data," an appendix for *Basic Psychology,* with a fine sense of balance between the demands of the subject matter and the demands of expositional clarity.

Four persons contributed in a special way: Lyn Abramson, John Jonides, Paul Rozin, and John Sabini. All four are distinguished scientists as well as dedicated teachers with considerable experience in the introductory course. They served as an editorial advisory group who counseled me on all aspects of this edition, sharing their knowledge of the subject matter as well as their experience in communicating it to beginning students. Lyn Abramson was particularly helpful in discussions of individual differences and psychopathology. John Jonides provided sharp criticisms and new perspectives, especially in the area of cognition. As always, Paul Rozin helped me see many facets of the field in a new way, especially its biological aspects. John Sabini shared his wide-ranging scholarly perspective, which was of particular help in the areas related to social processes.

In thanking all these persons I take particular pleasure from the fact that about half of them were once undergraduate and/or graduate students of mine. I find something reassuring in the reflection that those I once taught are now teaching me, though it's almost certain that I learn much more from them now than they ever learned from me.

To one person I owe a special debt: my wife, friend, and collaborator, Lila R. Gleitman. She read virtually all the chapters of this manuscript and did what she always does to the things I do and think and write about—she makes them better. Much better. I can't thank her enough.

Several persons helped on this edition or its immediate predecessor in still other ways. Kathy Hirsh-Pasek took photographs of her children to add to those illustrating previous developmental chapters. Further thanks go to a number of persons at my publisher's, W. W. Norton: To Antonia Krass who designed the inside of the book; to Hugh O'Neill who saw to the cover; to Dolores Bego who executed the drawings and illustrations; to Amy Cherry and JoAnn Schambier who did the photo and art research, and to Claire Gleitman and Libby Miles who participated in that endeavor; to Ruth Mandel who lent her sharp artistic eye; to Hank Smith who provided helpful and generous editorial advice and encouragement; to Roberta Flechner for her ability to arrange the layouts so as to fit the many pieces of the puzzle into a seamless whole; and to Roy Tedoff who managed the production of the book and whose experience and wisdom helped us to get the book we really wanted. I owe still further thanks to Jane Carter, who served as manuscript editor of this edition and combined a fine sense and judgment for the overall whole with the ability to attend to the multifarious details involved in producing this text.

My final thanks go to three other persons at Norton. One is its president, Donald Lamm. I met him over twenty-five years ago when he first gave me the idea to write this book. We have both aged (somewhat) in the interim, but he is still the same sharp-eyed critic that he was twenty-five years ago—his ideas are as brilliant (and often as outrageous) as ever, his puns as bad as ever, and my esteem and affection for him as great as ever.

The other two persons at Norton I want to thank are my two editors, Cathy Wick and Sandy Lifland, who worked on this edition and its most immediate predecessor, the third edition of *Psychology.* Cathy's invaluable experience with the needs of a broad spectrum of the academic community, her untiring efforts to keep the whole project under control and on time, and her willingness to extend herself both personally and professionally, make her an editor of great skill and tact. Sandy's enormous sensitivity coupled with her extraordinary judgment and competence, make her, too, an editor and a person to be cherished. Both she and Cathy were a pleasure to work with.

H. G.

Merion, Pennsylvania
October 1991

Basic Psychology

Third Edition

Introduction

What is psychology? It is a field of inquiry that is sometimes defined as the science of mind, sometimes as the science of behavior. It concerns itself with how and why organisms do what they do: Why wolves howl at the moon and sons rebel against their fathers; why birds sing and moths fly into the flame; why we remember how to ride a bicycle twenty years after the last try; why humans speak and make love and war. All of these are behaviors, and psychology is the science that studies them all.

THE SCOPE OF PSYCHOLOGY

The phenomena that psychology takes as its province cover an enormous range. Some border on biology, others touch on social sciences such as anthropology and sociology. Some concern behavior in animals, many others pertain to behavior in humans. Some are about conscious experience, others focus on what people do regardless of what they may think or feel inside. Some involve humans or animals in isolation, others concern what they do when they are in groups. A few examples will give an initial sense of the scope of the subject matter.

Electrically Triggered Images

Consider the relation between biological mechanisms and psychological phenomena. Some investigators have developed a technique of electrically stimulating the brains of human patients who were about to undergo brain surgery. Such operations are generally conducted under local rather than general anesthesia. As a result, the patients are conscious and their reports may guide the neurosurgeon in the course of the operation.

These and other procedures have shown that different parts of the brain have different psychological functions. For example, when stimulated in certain portions of the brain, patients have visual experiences—they see streaks of color or flickering lights. When stimulated in other regions they hear clicks or buzzes. Stimulation in still other areas produces an involuntary movement of some part of the body (Penfield and Roberts, 1959; Penfield, 1975).

Related findings come from studies that look at the rate at which blood flows through different parts of the brain. When any part of the body is especially active, more blood will flow to it—to deliver oxygen and nutrients, and carry away waste products—and the brain is no exception. The question is whether the blood flow pattern depends on what the patient does. The answer is yes. When the patient reads silently, certain regions of the brain receive more blood (and are thus presumably more active) than do others. A different blood flow pattern is found when the person reads aloud, yet another when he watches a moving light, and so on (Lassen, Ingvar, and Skinhoj, 1978).

Ambiguous Sights and Sounds

Many psychological phenomena are much further removed from issues that might be settled by biological or medical investigations. To study these, one proceeds at the psychological level alone. An example is the perception of ambiguous visual patterns. Consider the photograph (opposite) of a vase created for Queen Elizabeth on the occasion of her Silver Jubilee. It is usually seen as a vase, but it can also be seen as the profiles of the queen and her consort, Prince Philip.

The way ambiguous figures are perceived often depends on what we have seen just before. Take the figure below, which can be seen as either a rat or an amiable gentleman with glasses. If we are first shown an unambiguous figure of a rat, the ambiguous picture will be seen as a rat. If we are first exposed to an unambiguous face, the ambiguous figure will be perceived as a face.

What holds for visual patterns also holds for language. Many utterances are ambiguous. If presented out of context, they can be understood in several different ways. An example is the following sentence:

The mayor ordered the police to stop drinking.

This sentence may be a command to enforce sobriety among the population at large. It may also be a call to end drunkenness among the police force. Just how it is understood depends on the context. A prior discussion of panhandlers and skid row probably would lead to the first interpretation; a comment about alcoholism among city employees is likely to lead to the second.

Reversible figure *Photograph of a vase celebrating the twenty-fifth year of the reign of Queen Elizabeth in 1977. Depending on how the picture is perceptually organized, we see either the vase or the profile of Queen Elizabeth and Prince Philip. (Courtesy of Kaiser Porcelain Ltd.)*

Perceptual bias *(A) An ambiguous form that can be seen either as (B) a rat or (C) a man with glasses. (After Bugelski and Alampay, 1961)*

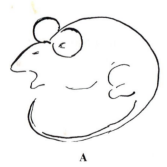

A

B

C

The visual cliff (A) An infant is placed on the center board that is laid over a heavy sheet of glass and his mother calls to him. If he is on the "deep" side, he will not crawl across the apparent cliff. (Courtesy of Richard D. Walk) (B) A similar reaction in a kitten. (Courtesy of William Vandivert)

The Perceptual World of Infants

Phenomena of the sort we've just discussed document the enormous effect of prior experience on what we see and do. But this does not mean that all psychological accomplishments are acquired by past experience. Some seem to be part of the innate equipment that all of us bring into the world when we are born. An example is the infant's reaction to heights.

Crawling infants seem to be remarkably successful in noticing the precipices of everyday life. A demonstration is provided by the so-called *visual cliff*. This consists of a large glass table, which is divided in half by a wooden center board. On one side of the board, a checkerboard pattern is attached directly to the underside of the glass; on the other side, the same pattern is placed on the floor three feet below. To adults, this arrangement looks like a sudden drop-off in the center of the table. Six-month-old infants seem to see it in much the same way. When the infant is placed on the center board and called by his mother, his response depends on where she is when she beckons. When she is on the shallow side, he quickly crawls to her. But when she calls from the apparent precipice, discretion wins out over valor and the infant stays where he is.

This result suggests that, to some extent at least, the perception of depth is not learned through experience, but is built into our system at the very start.

Displays

Thus far, all our examples have dealt with individuals in isolation. But much of the subject matter of psychology is inherently social. This holds for animals no less than humans. For virtually all animals interact with others of their species, whether as mates, parents, offspring, or competitors.

In animals, many social interactions depend on largely innate forms of communication. An example is courtship in birds. Many species of birds have evolved elaborate rituals whereby one sex—usually the male—woos the other. Just what this wooing consists of depends on the species. Some males court by making themselves conspicuous: The peacock spreads his magnificent tail feathers, the blue bird of paradise displays his plumage while hanging upside down from a branch, and the red frigate bird inflates his red throat pouch. Other males take a more romantic approach: The bower bird builds a special cabin that

A

B

C

Courting birds Birds have evolved many diverse patterns of courtship behavior that are essentially built-in and characteristic of a particular species. (A) The peacock displays his tail feathers. (Photograph by Keith Gunnar/Bruce Coleman) (B) The blue bird of paradise shows off his plumage while hanging upside down from a branch. (Photograph by B. Castes/Bruce Coleman) (C) The frigate bird puffs up his red throat pouch. (Photograph by William E. Ferguson)

he decorates with colored fruit and flowers. The males of other species offer gifts. In all cases, the fundamental message is the same: "I am a male, healthy, and willing peacock (or bird of paradise, or frigate bird, or whatever), and hope that your intentions are similar to mine."

Such social communications are based on built-in signals called *displays,* which are specific to a particular species. They are ways by which one individual informs another of his current intentions. Some are mating displays, as in the case of courtship displays. Others are threats ("Back off or else!"; see the photo of the male mandrill below). Still others are attempts at appeasement ("Don't hurt me. I am harmless!"). Some built-in displays form the foundation of emotional expression in humans. An example is the smile, a response found in all babies, even those born blind who couldn't have learned it by imitation. It is often considered a signal by which humans tell each other: "Be good to me. I wish you well."

Complex Social Behavior in Humans

Human social interactions are generally much more subtle and flexible than those of animals. Male peacocks have just one way of going courting: They spread their tail feathers and hope for the best. Human males and females are much more complex, in courtship and many other social interactions. They try one approach, and if it fails, they will try another and yet another. If these fail too, the partners will do their best to save the other's face. For much of human so-

Displays (A) Threat display of the male mandrill, a large West African baboon. (Photograph by George H. Harrison/Grant Heilman) (B) The human smile. (Photograph by Suzanne Szasz)

A

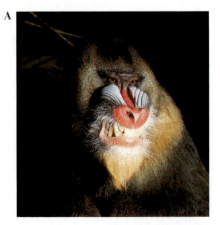

B

Panic   *Richard Bosman, 1982. (Collection of Robert H. Helmick; courtesy Brooke Alexander, New York)*

cial life is based on the individual's rational appraisal of how another person will respond to his own actions: "If I do this . . . he will think this . . . then I will have to do this . . . ," and so on. Such subtleties are beyond the peacock. If his usual courtship ritual fails, he has no alternate strategy. He won't try to build bowers or offer flowers; all he can do is to display his tail feathers again and again.

While human social behavior has a strong element of rationality, there are some apparent exceptions in which we seem to act with little thought or reason. This is especially likely when we are in large groups. Under some circumstances, people in crowds behave differently than they do when alone. An example is panic. When someone shouts "Fire" in a tightly packed auditorium, the resulting stampede may claim many more victims than the fire itself would have. At the turn of the century, a Chicago theater fire claimed over six hundred victims, many of whom were smothered or trampled to death by the frantic mass behind them. In the words of a survivor, "The heel prints on the dead faces mutely testified to the cruel fact that human animals stricken by terror are as mad and ruthless as stampeding cattle" (Brown, 1965). The task for psychology is to try to understand why the crowd acted differently from the way each of its members would have acted alone.

A SCIENCE OF MANY FACES

These illustrations document the enormous range of psychology, whose territory borders on the biological sciences at one end and touches on the social sciences at the other. This broad range makes psychology a field of multiple perspectives, a science of many faces.

Given the many-faceted character of psychology, it is not surprising that those who have contributed to it came from many quarters. Some had the proper title of psychologist with appropriate university appointments in that discipline, including two of its founding fathers, Wilhelm Wundt of Germany and William James of the United States. But psychology was not built by psychologists alone. Far from it. Among its architects are philosophers, beginning with Plato and Aristotle and continuing to our own time. Physicists and physiologists played important roles and still do. Physicians contributed greatly, as did specialists in many other disciplines, including anthropology, and more recently, linguistics and computer science. Psychology, the field of many faces, is by its very nature a field of many origins.

In presenting the subject matter of psychology as it is today, we must try to do justice to this many-sidedness. In an attempt to achieve that, this book has been organized around five topics that emphasize somewhat different perspectives on the field as a whole: ***action, cognition, social behavior, development,*** and ***individual differences.***

Wilhelm Wundt (1832–1920) (Courtesy *Historical Pictures Service, Chicago*)

THE TASK OF PSYCHOLOGY

Psychology is sometimes popularly regarded as a field that concentrates on the secret inner lives of individual persons—why Mary hates her mother and why George is so shy with girls. But questions of this sort are really not psychology's main concern. To be sure, there is an applied branch of psychology that deals with various adjustment problems, but it is only a special part of the field. The primary questions psychology asks are of a more general sort. Its purpose is not to describe the distinctive characteristics of a particular individual. Its main goal is to get at the facts that are general for all of humankind.

The reason is simple. Psychology is a science and, like all other sciences, it looks for *general principles*—underlying uniformities that different events have in common. A single event as such means little; what counts is what any one event—or object or person—shares with others. Ultimately of course, psychology—again, like all other sciences—hopes to find a route back to understand the individual event. It tries to discover, say, some general principles of adolescent conflict or parent-child relations to explain why George is so shy and why Mary is so bitter about her mother. Once such explanations are found, they may lead to practical applications: to help counsel and guide, and perhaps to effect desirable changes. But, at least initially, the science's main concern is with the discovery of the general principles.

Is there any field of endeavor whose primary interest is in individual persons, with the unique George and Mary who are like no other persons who ever lived or ever will live? One such field is literature. The great novelists and playwrights have given us portraits of living, breathing individuals who exist in a particular time and place. There is nothing abstract and general about the agonies of a Hamlet or the murderous ambition of a Macbeth. These are concrete, particular individuals, with special loves and fears that are peculiarly theirs. But from these particulars, Shakespeare gives us a glimpse of what is common to all humanity, what Hamlet and Macbeth share with all of us. Both science and art have something to say about human nature, but they go about it from different directions. Science tries to discover general principles and then to apply them to the individual case. Art focuses on the particular instance and then uses this to illuminate what is universal in us all.

William James (1842–1910) (Courtesy *The Warder Collection*)

Science and art are complementary. To gain insight into our own nature we need both. Consider Hamlet's description:

> What a piece of work is a man, how noble in reason, how infinite in faculties; in form and moving how express and admirable, in action like an angel, in apprehension like a god: the beauty of the world, the paragon of animals! (*Hamlet,* Act II, scene ii).

To understand and appreciate this "piece of work" is a task too huge for any one field of human endeavor, whether art, philosophy, or science. What we will try to do here is to sketch psychology's own attempts toward this end, to show what we have come to know and how we have come to know it. And perhaps even more important, how much we have not learned as yet.

PART I

Action

The study of mind has many aspects. We may ask what human beings know, we may ask what they want, and we may ask what they do. Much of psychology is an attempt to answer the last question: What is it that humans do and why do they do it? In this section we will deal with the approach to mind that grows out of an interest in what all animals do, an approach that emphasizes behavior as the basic subject matter of psychology. We will focus on the particular version of this approach that is based on the notion that mind can be understood as a reflex machine. We shall see how the reflex notion has led to impressive achievements in our understanding of the structure and function of the nervous system, and how this notion has been modified to encompass the phenomena of motivation and of learning in animals and humans.

CHAPTER 1

Biological Bases of Behavior

The ancients, no less than we, wondered why men and beasts behave as they do. What is it that leads to animal movement, impels the crab to crawl, the tiger to spring? Prescientific man could only answer *animistically:* There is some inner spirit in the creature that impels it to move, each creature in its own fashion. Today we know that any question about bodily movement must inevitably call for some reference to the nervous system; for to us it is quite clear that the nervous system is the apparatus which most directly determines and organizes an organism's reactions to the world in which it lives.

Modern advances in the study of this system have given us insights into its functioning that would have amazed the scientists who lived a century ago, let alone the ancients. Some of the new techniques allow us to observe the operations of small components of individual nerve cells (see Figure 1.1). Others permit us to eavesdrop on the workings of living human brains without seriously disturbing their owners (see Figure 1.2A and B). Our advances have been considerable. But to understand them more fully, we will take a look at some of the historical origins of our current conceptions.

We will soon ask many detailed questions about the structure and function of the nervous system—the apparatus that underlies human and animal action. But before we do so, we must ask a more general question: Broadly speaking, what must such a system accomplish?

1.1   Observing the nervous system through a microscope   *A nerve cell in the spinal cord. (Photograph by Michael Abbey/Photo Researchers)*

THE ORGANISM AS MACHINE

In modern times this question was first raised seriously by the French philosopher René Descartes (1596–1650), and his answer provides the broad outline within which we think about such matters even now. Descartes lived in a period that saw the beginning of the science of mechanics. Kepler and Galileo were beginning to develop ideas about the movements of the heavenly bodies which some thirty years later led to Newton's *Principia.* Radically new views of the universe were being put forth. There were laws of nature that determined the fall of

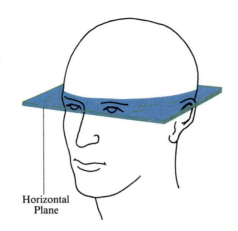
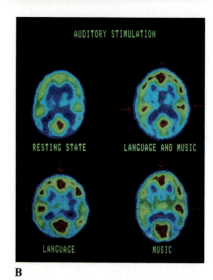

1.2 Observing the living brain with PET scans *(A) The horizontal plane of the brain used in taking the PET (Positron Emission Tomography) scan. (B) Four PET scans taken while the subject rests, listens to someone talk, listens to music, or both. These scans indicate the degree of metabolic activity in different parts of the brain, viewed in horizontal cross-section as shown in the diagram with the front of the head on top. Red indicates the most intense activity and blue the least. Listening to speech activates the left side of the brain, listening to music activates the right side, and listening to both activates both sides. (PET scans taken by Dr. John Mazziotta, UCLA School of Medicine, et al./Science Photo Library/Photo Researchers)*

Horizontal Plane

A

B

stones and the motions of planets: rigid, precise, and immutable. The universe was run by a system of pushes and pulls originally set in motion by God, the Great Watchmaker. At a more lowly level, these natural laws were mirrored in the workings of ingenious mechanical contrivances that were all the rage in the wealthy homes of Europe: clocks with cuckoos that would call the hour, water-driven gargoyles with nodding heads, statues in the king's garden that would bow to the visitor who stepped on a hidden spring. The action of a lever, the release of a spring—these could explain the operation of such devices. Could human thought and action be explained in similar mechanical terms?

Descartes and the Reflex Concept

To Descartes all action, whether human or animal, was essentially a response to some event in the outside world. His human machine would work as follows. Something from the outside excites one of the senses. This transmits the excitation upward to the brain, which then relays the excitation downward to a muscle. The excitation from the senses thus eventually leads to a contraction of a muscle and thereby to a reaction to the external event which started the whole sequence. In effect, the energy from the outside is *reflected* back by the nervous system to the animal's muscles—the term *reflex* finds its origin in this conception (Figure 1.3).

Conceived thus, human doings could be regarded as the doings of a machine. But there was a problem. The same external event produces one reaction today and another tomorrow. The sight of food leads to reaching movements, but only when we are hungry. In short, the excitation from one of the senses will excite a nerve leading to one muscle on one occasion, but on another occasion it will excite a different nerve that may move an entirely different muscle. This means that Descartes's mechanism must have a central switching system, supervised by some operator who sits in the middle to decide what incoming pipe to connect with which pipe leading to the outside.

To describe these behavioral options mechanically was very difficult. Descartes was deeply religious, and he was extremely concerned over the theological implications of his argument should he bring it to its ultimate conclusion. In addition he was prudent—Galileo had difficulties with the Inquisition because his scientific beliefs threatened the doctrines of the Church. So Descartes proposed

René Descartes *(Courtesy National Library of Medicine)*

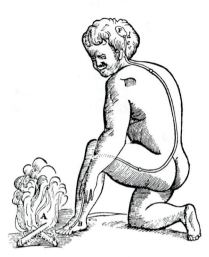

1.3   Reflex action as envisaged by Descartes   *In this sketch by Descartes, the heat from the fire, A, starts a chain of processes that begins at the affected spot of the skin, B, and continues up the nerve tube until a pore of a cavity, F, is opened. Descartes believed that this opening allowed a gas-like substance in the cavity to enter the nerve tube and eventually travel to the muscles which pull the foot from the fire. While the figure shows that Descartes anticipated the basic idea of reflex action, it also indicates that he did not realize the anatomical distinction between sensory and motor nerves. (From Descartes, 1662)*

that human mental processes were only semiautomatic. To handle the switching function he provided a soul (operating through a particular structure in the brain), which would affect the choice of possible nervous pathways.

Descartes shrank from taking the last step in his own argument, the reduction of human beings to the status of machines. Animals might be machines, but humans were more than mere robots. Later thinkers went further. They felt that the laws of the physical universe could ultimately explain all action, whether human or animal, so that a scientific account required no further "ghost in the machine"—that is, no reference to the soul. They ruthlessly extended Descartes's logic to human beings, arguing that humans differ from animals only in being more finely constructed mechanisms.

The Basic Nervous Functions: Reception, Integration, Reaction

Psychologists today agree with Descartes that much of behavior can be understood as reactions to outside events: The environment poses a question and the organism answers it. This approach, like Descartes's, must lead to a tripartite classification of nervous functions: *reception* through the senses, *reaction* from the muscles and glands, and a *conduction* and *integration* system that mediates between these two functions.

As here conceived, the chain of events that leads to action typically begins outside of the organism. A particular physical energy impinges upon some part of the organism sensitive to it. This event we call a *stimulus* (a term that derives from the name of a wooden implement with a nail at one end used by Roman farmers some two thousand years ago to goad their sluggish oxen). The stimulus excites *receptors,* specialized structures capable of translating some physical energy into a nervous impulse. Once a receptor is stimulated, the excitation is conducted farther into the nervous system. Bundles of nerve fibers that conduct excitation toward the brain or spinal cord are called *afferent nerves* (from the Latin, *affere,* "to bring to"). These fibers transmit their message still farther, in the simplest case, to other fibers that go directly to the *effectors,* the muscles and glands that are the organs of action. Nerve fibers that lead to the effectors are called *efferent nerves* (from the Latin, *effere,* "to bring forth").

The transmission path from receptors to effectors is usually more circuitous than this, however. The afferent fibers often bring their messages to intermediate nerve cells, or *interneurons,* in the brain or spinal cord. These interneurons may transmit the message to the efferent nerve cells or send it on to yet other interneurons. Typically, many thousands of such interneurons have been "consulted" before the command to action is finally issued and sent down the path of the efferent nerve fibers.

We now turn to a more detailed discussion of the nervous system. We will deal with progressively larger units of analysis, first discussing the smallest functional and structural units of nervous activity (the nerve impulse and the nerve cell), then the interaction among different nerve cells (the synapse), and finally, the functional plan of the major structures of the nervous system.

NERVE CELL AND NERVE IMPULSE

Neuroscientists know that the basic unit of nervous function is the *nerve impulse,* the firing of an individual nerve cell, or *neuron.* Our discussion begins with a brief look at the anatomy of the neuron.

The Neuron

The neuron is the simplest element of nervous action. It is a single cell, with three subdivisions: the **dendrites,** the **cell body,** and the **axon** (see Figure 1.4). The dendrites are usually branched, sometimes enormously so. The axon may extend for a very long distance, and its end may fork out into several end branches. Impulses from other cells are received by the dendrites; the axon transmits the impulse to yet other neurons or to effector organs such as muscles and glands. Thus, the dendrites are the receptive units of the neuron, while the axon endings may be regarded as its effector apparatus.

Many axons are surrounded by a **myelin sheath,** a tube mainly composed of fatty tissue that surrounds the axon and insulates it from other axons. The tube is not continuous but consists of a number of elongated segments, with small uncoated gaps, the so-called **nodes of Ranvier,** between each segment.

A few details about neurons will give a feeling for their size and number. The diameter of an individual neuron is very small; cell bodies vary from 5 to about 100 microns in diameter (1 micron = 1/1,000 millimeter). Dendrites are typically short; say, a few hundred microns. The axons of motor neurons can be very long; some extend from the head to the base of the spinal cord, others from the spinal cord to the fingers and toes. To get a sense of the relative physical proportions of the cell body to the axon in a motor neuron, visualize a basketball attached to a garden hose that stretches the whole fourteen-mile length of Manhattan Island. The total number of neurons in the human nervous system has been estimated to be as high as a 1,000 billion (Nauta and Feirtag, 1986). While this number may seem prodigious, it is somewhat sobering to realize that there is no way of getting more; a neuron, once lost, can't be replaced.*

The gap between the axon terminals of one neuron and the dendrites and cell body of another is called the synapse; this is the gap that has to be crossed for one neuron to stimulate the next. Such junctions often involve many more than two cells, especially in the brain, where a typical neuron may give and receive signals from 1,000 to 10,000 other neurons.

* Though some recent findings sound a more optimistic note, at least for male songbirds. Their brains shrink in the winter (when they don't sing) and expand in the spring (when they do). This annual increase in brain size is partially caused by the formation of new neurons during the spring which replace old neurons that die off in the fall (Nottebohm, 1987).

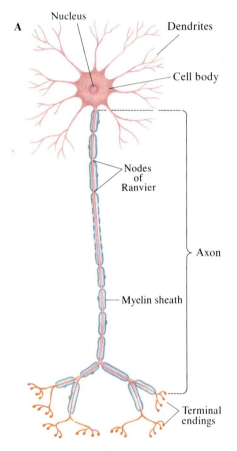

1.4   The neuron   *(A) A schematic diagram of the main parts of a "typical" neuron. Part of the cell is myelinated; that is, its axon is covered with a segmented, insulating sheath. (After Katz, 1952) (B) Highly magnified nerve cell in the human brain showing cell body and several dendrites. The long diagonal bands are branches from other nerve cells. (Nilsson, 1974)*

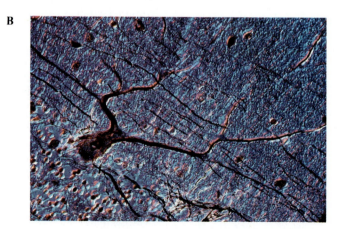

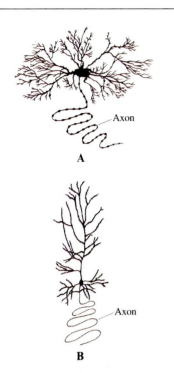

A

B

C

1.5 Different kinds of neurons (A) A motor neuron of the human spinal cord. (B) A neuron in the human cerebral cortex, the part of the brain concerned with such higher mental functions as perception and planning. (After Kolb and Whishaw, 1980). (C) A specialized neuron in the cerebellum, a part of the brain which controls motor coordination. This kind of cell has been said to gather impulses from as many as 80,000 other neurons. The photomicrograph is from the cerebellum of a 12-month-old infant. It has been stained by a special chemical that shows the extent of the branching of the cell's dendrites. (© Guigoz/Dr. A. Privat/ Petit Format/Science Source/Photo Researchers)

Different kinds of neurons are specialized for different tasks. We will mention only a few of the varieties. Some neurons are attached to specialized *receptor cells* that can respond to various external energies, such as pressure, chemical changes, light, and so on. These receptor cells can translate (more technically, *transduce*) such physical stimuli into electrical changes, which will then trigger a nervous impulse in other neurons. Receptor cells are like money changers, exchanging the various energies impinging from the other world into the only currency acceptable within the nervous system—the nervous impulse.

Neurons that convey impulses from receptors toward the rest of the nervous system are called *sensory neurons.* Sometimes the receptor is a specialized part of the sensory neuron; an example is the neurons that are responsible for sensing pressure on the skin. But in many cases, transduction and transmission are separate functions that are entrusted to different cells. In vision and hearing, there are receptor cells which transduce optic stimulation and air pressures into electrical changes in the cell. These changes in the receptors trigger impulses in sensory neurons that then transmit their information to other neurons in the nervous system.

Other neurons have axons that terminate in effector cells. An important example is the *motor neurons* that activate the *skeletal musculature,* the muscles that control the skeleton, such as those of the arms and legs. The cell bodies of the motor neurons are in the spinal cord or brain, and their long axons have terminal branches whose final tips contact individual muscle cells. When a motor neuron fires, a chemical event is produced at its axon tips which causes the muscle fibers to contract.

In complex organisms, the vast majority of nerve cells are *interneurons,* which have a functional position that is between sensory neurons and motor neurons. Interneurons come in many shapes and forms. They usually show considerable branching, which produces an enormous number of synaptic contacts (see Figure 1.5).

The Electrical Activity of the Neuron

The biological function of a neuron is to receive and transmit impulses. How does it perform this function? The scientific understanding of the underlying electrical events required several advances in scientific instrumentation. One of these was the development of ever finer *microelectrodes,* some of which have tips tapered to a diameter of 1 micron. Such electrodes can pick up currents from within a neuron without squashing the cell they are supposed to study. Equally important was the development of the *oscilloscope,* a device whose electrical response is amplified by vacuum tubes that send forth a stream of electrons that are swept across a fluorescent screen, leaving a glowing line in their wake. The pattern on the screen indicates what happened electrically during the entire (very brief) interval of the cell's activity. Yet another contribution was made by evolution, which provided the squid, an animal that contains several axons with giant diameters up to 1 millimeter—a great convenience for electrophysiological work on the nervous impulse.

THE RESTING POTENTIAL

Figure 1.6 shows a microelectrode that is inserted on the inside of an axon while the other records from the surface of the fiber. In this manner one can record the *electrical potential* (the voltage) across the cell membrane. One fact emerges immediately. There is a difference in potential between the inside and the outside of

1.6 Recording the impulse *A schematic drawing of how the impulse is recorded. One electrode is inserted into the axon; the other records from the axon's outside. (After Carlson, 1986, p. 36)*

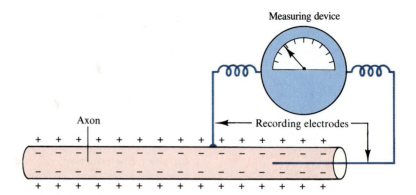

Measuring device

Recording electrodes

Axon

the fiber when the cell is at "rest" (that is, not firing). The inside is electrically negative with respect to the outside. This *resting potential* is about −70 millivolts relative to the outside of the cell. This means that in its normal state the cell membrane is *polarized.* Its outside and inside are like the electrical poles of a miniature battery, with the outside positive and the inside negative.

THE ACTION POTENTIAL

What happens when the neuron is aroused from rest? To find out, the surface of the fiber is stimulated by means of a third microelectrode which applies a brief electrical pulse. This pulse reduces the potential across the membrane for a brief instant. If the pulse is weak, nothing further will happen; there is no impulse. If the strength of the pulse is slowly increased, the resting potential drops still more, but there is still no impulse. This continues until the pulse is strong enough to decrease the potential to a critical point, the *threshold* (about 55 millivolts in mammals).

Now a new phenomenon occurs. The potential suddenly collapses; in fact, it overshoots the zero mark and for a brief moment the axon interior becomes positive relative to the outside. This brief flare lasts about 1 millisecond and quickly subsides. The potential then returns to the resting state. This entire sequence of electrical events is called the *action potential* (Figure 1.7).

The action potential is recorded from only one small region of the axon. What happens elsewhere in the fiber? Consider Figure 1.8. An *adequate stimulus*—that is, one that is above threshold—is applied to point *A* and the potential is measured at points *A, B,* and *C.* At first, an action potential is observed at *A;* at that

1.7 The action potential *Action potential recorded from the squid giant axon. (After Hodgkin and Huxley, 1939)*

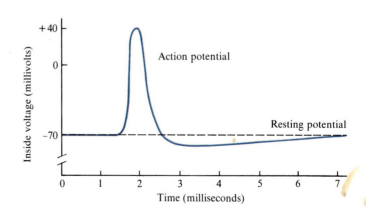

Action potential

Resting potential

Inside voltage (millivolts)

+40

0

−70

0   1   2   3   4   5   6   7

Time (milliseconds)

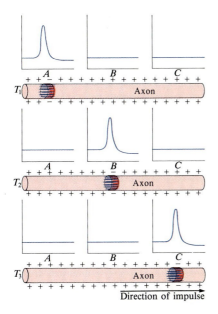

1.8 The action potential as it travels along the axon *The axon is shown at three different moments in time—T₁, T₂, and T₃—after the application of a stimulus. The electrical potential is shown at three different points along the axon —A, B, and C. (After Carlson, 1986, p. 47)*

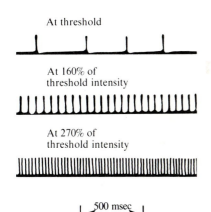

At threshold

At 160% of
threshold intensity

At 270% of
threshold intensity

|← 500 msec →|

1.9 Stimulus intensity and firing frequency *Responses of a crab axon to three levels of current intensity. The time scale is relatively slow. As a result, the action potentials show up as single vertical lines or "spikes." Note that while increasing the current intensity has no effect on the height of the spikes (the all-or-none law) it leads to a marked increase in the frequency of spikes per second. (After Eccles, 1973)*

time *B* and *C* are still at rest. A bit later, *A* returns to normal, while *B* shows the action potential. Still later, *B* returns to normal but an action potential is found at *C*. (Of course, these time intervals are exceedingly brief.) The change in potential is evidently infectious; each region sets off its neighbor much as a spark travels along a fuse.

These phenomena are produced by a number of physical and chemical interactions at the cell membrane. The neuron is enclosed in a very thin membrane, which serves as a gatekeeper to the cell governing the entrance and exit of various particles. The particles are *ions,* atoms or molecules that have gained or lost electrons, thus acquiring a negative or positive charge. The action potential is produced by a rush of positively charged ions (specifically, sodium ions) from outside the membrane, which creates an excess of positively charged particles inside. This reversal of polarization produces electric currents that flow toward neighboring regions of the membrane and set off the same effect in them. The end result is the propagation of the impulse along the entire region of the axon.

All-or-none law One point should be stressed. The electrical response of the axon—that is, the action potential—is unaffected by the intensity of the stimulus, once the stimulus is at threshold level or above. Increasing the stimulus value above this level will not increase the intensity of the action potential or affect its speed of conduction to other points in the fiber. This phenomenon is sometimes referred to as the *all-or-none law* of axon reaction. The all-or-none law clearly implies that the stimulus does not provide the energy for the nervous impulse. It serves as a trigger and no more. Given that the trigger is pulled hard enough, pulling yet harder has no effect. Like a gun, a neuron either fires or does not fire. It knows no in-between.*

Stimulus intensity We have seen that the axon obeys the all-or-none law. It appears that stimulus intensity has no effect once threshold is passed. Does this law make sense? Much of our everyday experience seems to deny it. We can obviously tell the difference between the buzz of a mosquito and the roar of a jet plane, even though both sounds are above threshold. How can we square such facts with the all-or-none law?

In many cases what happens is that the more intense stimulus excites a *greater number of neurons.* This is precisely what we should expect, for we know that different neurons vary enormously in their thresholds. Thus, a strong stimulus will stimulate more neurons than a weak stimulus. The weak stimulus will stimulate all neurons whose thresholds are below a given level; the strong stimulus will stimulate all of those, plus others whose threshold is higher.

While remaining strictly obedient to the all-or-none law, however, the individual neuron is nevertheless affected by stimulus intensity. This becomes apparent when we apply a continuous stimulus for somewhat longer intervals. Now we obtain not one impulse but a whole volley. We notice that the size of the action potentials remains the same whatever the stimulus intensity. What changes instead is the *impulse frequency.* The stronger the stimulus, the more *often* the axon will fire. This effect holds until we reach a maximum rate of firing, after which further increases in intensity have no effect (see Figure 1.9). Different neurons have different maximum rates; the highest in man is of the order of 1,000 impulses per second.

---

* The all-or-none law holds for the action potential—that is, for conduction along the axon. As we will see shortly, the situation is different at the dendrites and cell body, where potentials are graded, being built up or lowered in a continuous rather than an all-or-none fashion.

Interaction among nerve cells   *An isolated nerve cell, magnified 20,000 times. The cell body is in contact with other cells through numerous extensions. The figure illustrates how nerve fibers cross each other to form an elaborate network. (Nilsson, 1974)*

INTERACTION AMONG NERVE CELLS

In a way, the neurons of our nervous system are like 1,000 billion speakers, endlessly prattling and chattering to one another. But each of them has only one word with which to tell its story, the one and only word it can utter. It can choose only whether to speak its word or keep silent, and whether to speak it often or more rarely. Looked at in isolation, the individual speakers seem like imbeciles with a one-word vocabulary, babbling and being babbled at. But when taken as a whole, this gibbering becomes somehow harmonious. The trick is in the integration of the individual messages, the interplay of the separate components. The really interesting question for psychology, then, is not how a neuron manages to produce its word, but rather how it can talk to others and how it can listen.

The Reflex

To study the interactions among different neurons, we begin with the simplest illustration of such interactions—the *reflex.* Descartes had pointed out that some of our actions are automatic—controlled by mechanical principles and not by the "will." Later progress in neuropsychology was made by studying animal motion that persists after the brain is gone. (What farmer had not seen a chicken running around the barnyard after its head was cut off?) Around 1750, the Scottish physician Whytt showed that such movements are reflexes controlled by the spinal cord. He found that a decapitated frog will jerk its leg away from a pinprick; but when deprived of *both* brain and spinal cord it no longer responded. Presumably, the frog's leg movement depended on the spinal cord.

Today we can list a host of reflexes, built-in response patterns executed automatically, without thought and without will. Some of these reflexes are controlled by the spinal cord, some by other neural structures. Examples include vomiting, the rhythmic contraction of the intestines (peristalsis), erection of the penis, blushing, limb flexion in withdrawal from pain, sucking in newborns—the catalog is very large.

Can we classify these reflexes in any sensible fashion? One distinction concerns the number of steps in the *reflex arc*—the reflex pathway that leads from stimulus to response. Some reflexes represent a chain of only two components, as in the case of an afferent neuron which contacts a motor neuron directly. More typically the chain is longer, and one or more interneurons are interposed between the afferent and efferent ends.

Inferring the Synapse

Until the turn of the century, most neurologists believed that the reflex pathway was across a long and essentially continuous strand of nervous tissue. The notion of the *synapse,* a gap between neurons across which they must communicate, is relatively modern. The critical studies which established the existence of the synapse and its role in nerve interaction were performed at the turn of the century by the English physiologist Sir Charles Sherrington (1857–1952). Sherrington's work was conducted at the level of behavior rather than that of electrophysiology. What he observed directly was reflex action in dogs, cats, and monkeys. How the synapse worked, he inferred.

Sherrington set out to study the *simple reflex,* that is, the reflex considered in splendid neurological isolation, unaffected by activities elsewhere in the nervous

Sir Charles Sherrington   *(Courtesy National Library of Medicine)*

system. Of course he was well aware that such simplicity does not really exist, for even the lowliest spinal reflex is modified by higher centers in the spinal cord or the brain. An itch in your side will initiate a scratch reflex, but if you are the catchman in a trapeze act you will probably inhibit it. To remove the effect of higher centers, Sherrington used the **spinal animal,** usually a dog, whose spinal cord had been completely severed in the neck region. This cut all connections between the body (from the neck down) and the brain, so that spinal reflexes could be studied pure.

EXCITATION

Sherrington's method was simple. He applied mild electric shocks to some point on the spinal animal's skin and observed whether this stimulus evoked a particular reflex response (see Figure 1.10). His results indicated that there had to be conduction across at least two neurons—a sensory neuron from the skin receptor and a motor neuron that activates muscle fibers. Sherrington asked whether conduction across neurons had the same characteristics as conduction within neurons. He discovered that it did not.

One line of evidence came from **temporal summation.** Sherrington showed that while one stimulus below threshold will not elicit the reflex, two or more of them (all equally subthreshold) may do so if presented in succession. The important point was that such temporal summation effects occurred even when the individual stimuli were spaced at intervals of up to half a second or thereabouts. But summation over such comparatively long time intervals does not occur within an individual axon fiber. The fact that temporal summation takes place anyway suggests that the summation process occurs somewhere else, presumably at the crossover point between neurons. The differences between conduction in reflex arcs and conduction in individual nerve fibers point to different mechanisms operating at the synaptic junction.

Sherrington supposed that there is some kind of excitatory process (presumably caused by the liberation of a then still undiscovered chemical substance from the ends of the axon) which accumulates at the synapse and builds up until it reaches a level high enough (the threshold level) to trigger the next neuron into action. This hypothesis clearly accounts for temporal summation. Every time cell *A* fires, a tiny amount of the excitatory substance is liberated into the synaptic gap between cell *A* and cell *B*. With enough repetitions of the stimulus, the total quantity of what Sherrington called the **central excitatory state** exceeds the threshold of cell *B* which then fires (see Figure 1.11A).

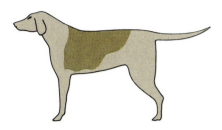

1.10 Saddle-shaped area of spinal dog *When a stimulus whose strength is above threshold is applied at any point in the "saddle," the animal will perform a scratching movement. (After Sherrington, 1906)*

1.11 Arguments for synaptic transmission *(A) Temporal summation. A subthreshold stimulus will not elicit the reflex but two or more stimuli will if presented successively at intervals of up to half a second. This indicates that the effects of the first stimulus were somehow stored and added to the effects of the second. (B) Spatial summation. Subthreshold stimuli applied to different points in the saddle area will not evoke a reflex if presented separately, but they will if presented simultaneously. This indicates that the excitatory effects from different regions are all funneled into the same common path.*

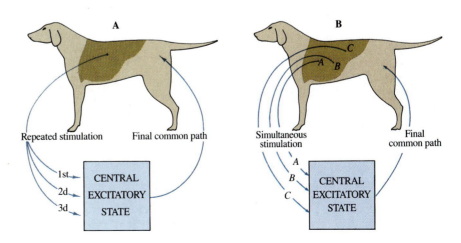

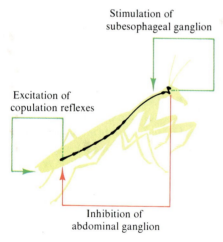

1.12   An example of muscle antagonists
The figure shows how the members of an antagonistic muscle pair (biceps and triceps) oppose each other in flexing and extending the forearm.

1.13   The disinhibitory mechanism in the praying mantis   *Excitation of the abdominal ganglion leads to copulatory movements in the male. But the sight of the moving female stimulates the subesophageal ganglion in the male's head. This in turn inhibits the abdominal ganglion so that copulation stops. Decapitation severs the subesophageal ganglion. The result is disinhibition and copulation resumes. Here, as in later diagrams, green indicates excitation and red inhibition. (Roeder, 1967)*

Further evidence for Sherrington's general approach derives from the phenomenon of **spatial summation,** which highlights the fact that several neurons may funnel in upon one output. Consider two fairly adjacent points on a dog's flank, *A* and *B,* such that stimulating either of them alone will elicit a particular reflex if the stimulus is intense enough. Sherrington showed that subthreshold stimulation at *both* points will yield the reflex, even though this same weak stimulation would not suffice for either of these points in isolation. This indicates that two groups of nerve fibers converge upon one neural output—the **final common path.** At this juncture, the several converging neurons generate excitatory processes whose effects summate (see Figure 1.11B).

INHIBITION

So far it would appear that neurons either vote "aye," thus adding to the central excitatory state at the synapse, or else abstain altogether. However, some neurons may signal "nay" and set up an inhibitory effect, actively opposing and preventing excitation.

One of the clearest demonstrations of such an effect is the phenomenon of **reciprocal inhibition.** Skeletal muscles typically come in antagonistic pairs—flexor and extensor (see Figure 1.12). What happens to the flexor muscle when the extensor is excited and conversely? Patently, the antagonists must not both contract at the same time, like wrestlers straining against each other. For maximum mechanical efficiency, the force of the excited muscle should encounter no opposition whatever from its antagonist.

Using a spinal animal, Sherrington provided an experimental demonstration. He found that stimulation of a sensory site that caused the flexor to contract had a further effect. It also caused the extensor to relax so that it actually became limp —limper in fact than it was in the normal resting state. Sherrington concluded that this unusually low level of muscular contraction could only be explained by assuming that there was a counteracting process that nullifies the excitatory messages to the muscle fibers—**inhibition.**

These facts suggest that a neuron can receive both excitatory and inhibitory messages. The two processes summate algebraically; they pull in opposite directions and thus have opposite signs (with excitation positive, inhibition negative). Whether an efferent neuron fires (and thus activates a muscle fiber) depends upon many other neurons that form a synapse with it. Each of these cells gives a positive or negative signal or remains neutral and thereby determines whether the excitatory threshold of the efferent neuron is reached, and therefore, whether it fires or does not.

DISINHIBITION

Impulses that have an inhibitory effect may derive from centers higher up than the spinal cord. The inhibitory effect of such brain centers is often discovered directly, by noting an *increase* in the strength of a reflex after the influence of this higher center is removed. Such an effect is called **disinhibition.** A classic example is spinal reflexes in frogs, which are more vigorous when all brain structures have been removed.

A rather ghoulish instance of disinhibition is provided by the love life of the praying mantis (see Figure 1.13). The female mantis is a rapacious killer. She seizes and devours any small creature unfortunate enough to move across her field of vision. Since the male mantis is smaller than the female, he too may qualify as food. This cannibalism is quite puzzling. How can the mantis survive as a species given a behavior tendency that counteracts successful fertilization?

According to one hypothesis, the female's predatory pattern is triggered almost exclusively by moving visual stimuli. The courting male's behavior is delicately attuned to this fact. As soon as he sees her he becomes absolutely immobile. Whenever she looks away for a moment he stalks her ever so slowly, but immediately freezes as soon as her eyes wheel back toward him—an inhibitory effect upon overall reflex activity. When close enough to her, he suddenly leaps upon her back and begins to copulate. Once squarely upon the female's back he is reasonably safe (her normal killer reflexes are elicited only by moving visual stimuli and he is mostly out of sight). But the dangers he must surmount to reach this place of safety are enormous. He must not miss her when he jumps; he must not slip while upon her. Should he fall, he will surely be grasped and eaten. Fairly often he does lose his balance, but even then all love's labour is not lost—for his genes, if not for him. The female commences to eat her fallen mate from the head on down. In almost all instances, the abdomen of the male now starts vigorous copulatory movements that are often successfully completed. Clearly, the male performs his evolutionary duty whatever his own private fate. But what is the mechanism?

It appears that the intact male's copulatory reflexes are inhibited by the subesophageal ganglion, located in his head. When this nerve cluster is removed, the animal will engage in endless copulatory movements even when no female is present. The same thing happens if the female chances to seize her mate and eat him. She first chews off his head and with it the subesophageal ganglion, thus disinhibiting the male's copulatory pattern which now resumes in full force—proof positive that love can survive beyond the grave (Roeder, 1935).*

The Synaptic Mechanism

Sherrington could only guess at the specific physical mechanism that governs transmission at the synapse, but he did sketch some general guidelines. There had to be excitatory and inhibitory processes, accumulating over time, pooling effects from various neural inputs and adding algebraically. But what was their nature?

SYNAPTIC TRANSMISSION

Sherrington and some of his contemporaries guessed that neurons communicate with their neighbors by means of some chemical substance that is released when the impulse reaches the end of the axon. The proof came in 1920 when Otto Loewi performed a crucial experiment. He dissected two frogs, removed their hearts, and placed each of the two hearts in separate, fluid-filled jars in which they kept on beating. One of the hearts still had the so-called vagus nerve attached to it; this nerve inhibits the heart muscle and slows down the heartbeat. Loewi electrically stimulated the vagus nerve for half an hour or so. All this time the other heart stayed in its own jar, and beat at its own, more rapid pace. After a while, Loewi took the fluid from the jar that held the first heart (whose beat had been slowed down by the vagus nerve) and poured it into the jar in which the second heart was kept. Almost immediately that second heart slowed down as well. The implication was clear. The stimulation of the vagus nerve liberated (at a region we now know acts just like a synapse) some substance whose effect on the heart muscle is to inhibit its function (see Figure 1.14). Loewi called that substance "vagus stuff." We now call it *acetylcholine* (usually abbreviated ACh), the

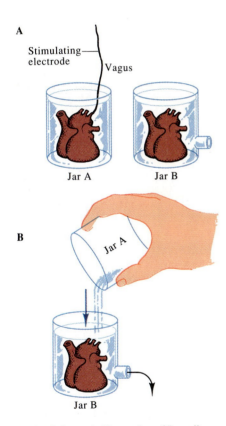

1.14 Schematic illustration of Loewi's discovery of the action of neurotransmitters *The hearts in two jars, A and B, are beating. (A) The vagus nerve that is still attached to the heart in jar A is stimulated, thus inhibiting its muscle and slowing down its heartbeat. (B) After an interval, the fluid in jar B is replaced by the fluid from jar A. The heart in jar B will now slow down almost immediately. (After Groves and Rebec, 1988)*

* A more recent study suggests that this cannibalistic pattern may only occur under artificial conditions of captivity and when the female is virtually starved. Under more natural circumstances, males seem to manage to mate quite successfully without losing their heads in the process. But even if induced artificially, the phenomenon is an interesting if macabre illustration of the effect of disinhibition (Liske and Davis, 1984).

first of a hundred or more substances now identified as **neurotransmitters** (Loewi, 1960; Eccles, 1982).

Loewi's experiment had only shown that the transmission of the neural message involves a chemical substance. We now know quite a bit more about the way in which this transmission occurs in actual neurons. Let's begin by distinguishing between the **presynaptic neuron** and the **postsynaptic neuron.** The presynaptic neuron sends the neural message; the postsynaptic neuron is the one the message is directed to. The process begins in tiny knobs of the axon terminals of the presynaptic neuron. Within these swellings are numerous tiny sacs, or **vesicles,** which contain chemical substances called neurotransmitters. When the presynaptic neuron fires, the vesicles in its axon knobs release their transmitter load into the synaptic gap that separates the two cells. The transmitter molecules diffuse across this gap and come to rest upon the dendrite or cell body of the postsynaptic cell (see Figure 1.15A and B).

Once across the synaptic gap, how do transmitters perform their transmitting function? They do so by activating specialized receptor molecules in the postsynaptic membrane. When one of these receptors is activated, it opens or closes certain ion gates in the membrane. For example, some neurotransmitters open the gates to sodium ions. As these sodium ions enter the postsynaptic cell, that cell's resting potential is *decreased* (see Figure 1.15C and D). (We'll consider inhibitory effects shortly.) As more and more transmitter molecules are hurled across the synaptic gap, they activate more and more receptors, which drops the resting potential of the postsynaptic cell further and further. When the drop gets large enough, the cell's threshold is reached, the action potential is triggered, and the impulse will now speed down the second cell's axon.

The changes in potentials in the dendrites and cell body which are produced by the transmitters are quite different from the action potential in the axon. For unlike the action potential, they are **graded** rather than all-or-none. They can be small or they can be large because the small changes will add up as the presynaptic neuron keeps on firing and more and more transmitter molecules affect the postsynaptic cell (temporal summation). They will also add up in space. Most neurons receive

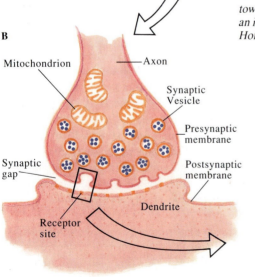

A

Neuron A

Impulse

Neuron B

B

Mitochondrion

Axon

Synaptic Vesicle

Presynaptic membrane

Synaptic gap

Postsynaptic membrane

Dendrite

Receptor site

1.15 Schematic view of synaptic transmission *(A) Neuron A transmits a message through synaptic contact with Neuron B. (B) The events in the axon knob (the mitochondria shown in the figure are structures that help to produce the energy the neuron requires for its functioning). (C) The vesicle is released, and neurotransmitter molecules stream toward the postsynaptic membrane. (D) Transmitter molecules settle on the receptor site, an ion channel opens, and sodium ions (Na^+) stream in. (After Bloom, Lazerson, and Hofstadter, 1988)*

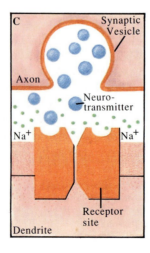

C

Synaptic Vesicle

Axon

Neuro-transmitter

Na^+ Na^+

Receptor site

Dendrite

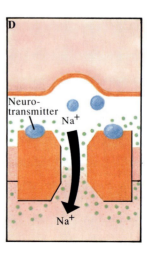

D

Neuro-transmitter

Na^+

Na^+

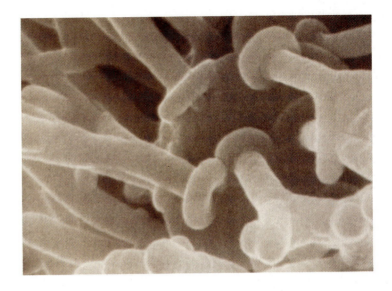

The synapse *Electron micrograph of synaptic knobs, the tiny swellings of the axon terminals that contain the vesicles. (Here magnified 11,250 times.) (Lewis et al., 1969)*

inputs from a great many presynaptic cells—in the brain, often from a thousand or more (spatial summation). As a result, transmitter molecules will arrive at several different regions of the postsynaptic membrane, and their effects will summate.

A similar mechanism accounts for inhibition. At some synapses, the presynaptic cell liberates transmitter substances that produce an *increase* in the resting potential of the postsynaptic neuron. As a result, a larger drop in resting potential will now be necessary to set off the action potential in the postsynaptic cell. Since most neurons make synaptic connections with neurons that excite them as well as others that inhibit them, the response of a given postsynaptic cell depends on a final tally of the various excitatory and inhibitory effects that act upon it. If the net value is excitatory (and if this value exceeds the threshold), the cell will fire.

What happens to the transmitter molecules after they have affected the postsynaptic neuron? It wouldn't do just to leave them where they are, for they might continue to exert their effect long after the presynaptic neuron had stopped firing. Or they might wander off and trigger impulses at other synapses that they were never meant to affect. There are two mechanisms that prevent such false messages from being sent. Some transmitters are inactivated shortly after they've been discharged by a special "cleanup" enzyme that breaks them up into their chemical components. Others are removed from the synaptic cleft by *reuptake,* a process whereby they are, so to speak, sucked back into the presynaptic neuron.

NEUROTRANSMITTERS

On the face of it, one might think that the nervous system only needs two transmitters: one excitatory and the other inhibitory. But nature, as so often, turns out to be exceedingly generous, for in actual fact there are a great number of different transmitter substances. About a hundred or so have been isolated thus far, and many more are sure to be discovered within the next decade.

We will mention just a few of these neurotransmitters here. One is Loewi's "vagus stuff," or *acetylcholine (ACh)*, which is released at many synapses and at the junction between motor neurons and muscle fibers (a junction that is a kind of synapse) and makes the fibers contract. Others include *serotonin (5HT), norepinephrine (NE),* and *dopamine (DA)* to which we will refer in later discussions of drug effects and certain mental disorders. For now, we only want to note that neurons differ in the transmitters they release as well as the transmitters that affect them. Thus neurons sensitive to dopamine will not respond to serotonin and

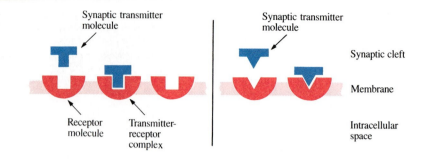

Synaptic transmitter molecule

Synaptic transmitter molecule

Synaptic cleft

Membrane

Receptor molecule

Transmitter-receptor complex

Intracellular space

1.16 Lock-and-key model of synaptic transmission *Transmitter molecules will only affect the postsynaptic membrane if their shape fits the shape of certain receptor molecules in that membrane much as a key has to fit into a lock. The diagram shows two kinds of transmitters and their appropriate receptors. (From Rosenzweig and Leiman, 1982)*

vice versa. It is as if different neurons speak different languages. Some speak "Do-paminese," others speak "Serotonese," and so on.

An attempt to understand these differences in chemical responsiveness is the so-called ***lock-and-key model*** of transmitter action. This theory proposes that transmitter molecules will only affect the postsynaptic membrane if their shape fits into certain synaptic receptor molecules much as a key must fit into a lock (see Figure 1.16). But the mere fact that a given molecule fits into the receptor is not enough to qualify it as a transmitter. The key must not just fit into the lock; it must also turn it. In the language of neurophysiology, the transmitter molecule must produce the changes in membrane potential that correspond to excitatory and inhibitory processes.

POISONS, DRUGS, AND NEUROTRANSMITTER ACTIVITY

The fact that communication between neurons depends on different neurotransmitter substances has wide implications for many aspects of psychological functioning. One is the effect of various drugs that enhance or impede the activity of transmitters at the synapse. Drugs that enhance this activity are technically called ***agonists,*** a term borrowed from Greek drama in which the agonist is the name for the hero. Drugs that impede a transmitter's action are ***antagonists,*** a term that refers to whoever opposes the hero (so to speak, the villain).

Many such drugs operate by increasing or decreasing the amount of available transmitter substance. Some agonists enhance a transmitter effect by blocking its reuptake, or by counteracting the cleanup enzyme, or by increasing the availability of some ***precursor*** (a substance required for the transmitter's chemical manufacture). Antagonists impede transmitter action through the same mechanisms operating in reverse: speeding up reuptake, augmenting cleanup enzymes, and decreasing available precursors. Still other drugs affect the synaptic receptors. Some are agonists that activate the receptors by mimicking the transmitter's action, much as a false passkey opens a lock. Others are antagonists that prevent the transmitter effect by binding themselves to the synaptic receptor and blocking off the transmitter, thus serving as a kind of putty in the synaptic lock.

Acetylcholine and curare An example of such a blocking action is provided by ***curare,*** a substance discovered by certain South American Indians who dipped their arrows in a plant extract that contained it, with deadly effect on animal prey and human enemies. Curare blocks the action of acetylcholine at the synaptic junctions between motor neurons and muscle fibers. The result is total paralysis and eventual death by suffocation since the victim is unable to breathe.

Dopamine and schizophrenia The transmitter blockade produced by curare leads to catastrophic results. But other blockades may be beneficial. An example is the effect of various ***antipsychotic drugs*** such as ***chlorpromazine*** on the symp-

Curare and paralysis *Certain South American Indians used curare-tipped arrows to immobilize and kill animal prey and human enemies. This Cofan man from Colombia is using a blowgun to hunt. (Photograph by B. Malkin/Anthro-Photo File)*

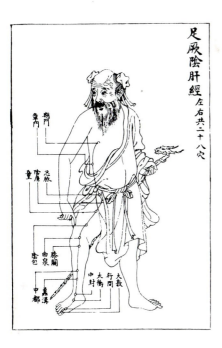

1.17 Acupuncture *Acupuncture is a complex system of treatment that grew up in ancient China and was based on the idea that disease is a disturbance in the balance of certain vital energies which were thought to circulate in certain channels. Their balance was to be restored by manipulating metal needles at special points along these channels. The figure is from a seventeenth-century Chinese treatise and illustrates the liver tract with twenty-eight special points. (From Blakemore, 1977, p. 42)*

toms of schizophrenia, a serious mental disorder that afflicts about 1 percent of the population. In its more extreme forms, schizophrenia is characterized by delusions (believing what isn't so, such as conspiracies and persecution), hallucinations (perceiving what isn't there, such as hearing voices), or bizarre mannerisms and unusual postures that may be maintained for many hours. According to one hypothesis, schizophrenia is produced by an oversensitivity to the transmitter dopamine. Neurons that liberate dopamine have an arousing function in many parts of the brain. Adherents of the dopamine hypothesis believe that people who are overly responsive to this transmitter will be continually overaroused, which may ultimately lead to the symptoms of schizophrenia. One of the arguments for this theory comes from the fact that chlorpromazine, which blocks the effect of dopamine, has a pronounced effect in alleviating schizophrenic symptoms. While the dopamine hypothesis of schizophrenia is still a matter of dispute, many investigators do agree that disturbances in transmitter function play a role in the production of this and other mental disorders (see Chapter 17 for further discussion).

ENDORPHINS

Neurotransmitters have been implicated in yet another psychological process: the alleviation of pain (Bolles and Fanselow, 1982).

The alleviation of pain   There is little doubt that the perception of pain can be alleviated or even abolished by psychological means that serve as an *analgesic* (a pain reliever). There are many stories of athletes or soldiers at war who suffer injuries but don't feel the pain until the game or the battle is over. Related effects have been produced in the laboratory. Thus rats subjected to various forms of stress, such as being forced to swim in cold water, become less sensitive to pain (Bodnar, Kelly, Brutus, and Glusman, 1980). Similar results have been shown in humans. Paradoxically enough, mild electric shock to the back or limbs can serve as an analgesic. So can acupuncture, an ancient Chinese treatment in which needles are inserted in various parts of the body (see Figure 1.17; Mann et al., 1973). In all these cases, the question is why.

The answer seems to be a matter of brain chemistry. It's long been known that the experience of pain can be dulled or entirely eliminated by various drugs, such as morphine and other opiates. These drugs are typically applied from the outside. But on occasion, the brain can be its own pharmacist. For when assailed by various kinds of stress (one of which is extremely painful stimulation), the brain can sometimes produce its own brand of opiates, which it then administers to itself. These are the so-called *endorphins*, a group of neurotransmitters that are secreted by certain neurons within the brain. They do this by stimulating yet other neurons, which in their turn disrupt messages from the pain receptors sent up to the brain by a spinal cord tract. Regular opiates such as morphine are chemically very similar to the endorphins and will therefore activate the same pain-inhibiting neurons (though, in fact, some of the brain's own endorphins are considerably more powerful than the artificially produced morphines dispensed by physicians; Snyder and Childers, 1979; Bloom, 1983).

23

Placebos   Many investigators believe that the endorphins play a similar role in the pain reduction produced by a ***placebo,*** a chemically inert substance that the patient believes will help him, such as the old family doctor's little sugar pill.

To prove that the endorphins are involved in these and similar instances in which pain is reduced by "psychological" means, investigators turned to ***naloxone.*** This is a drug known to inhibit the effect of morphine and other opiates; it is generally given to addicts who have overdosed on heroin (which of course is yet another opiate). A number of studies have shown that naloxone also blocks the pain alleviation produced by acupuncture (Mayer et al., 1976). The same holds for placebos dispensed to patients who believe they are taking a pain killer. In one such study, patients were given a placebo after having a wisdom tooth extracted. This helped some of the patients, but had no effect when the patients were given naloxone in addition to the placebo (Levine, Gordon, and Fields, 1979). Some more recent studies have shown that while naloxone attenuates such placebo effects it does not abolish them completely. This indicates that there are some avenues to pain relief that do not involve the endorphin system (Watkins and Mayer, 1982; Grevert and Goldstein, 1985). An example is hypnosis, which is sometimes used as a means of surgical anesthesia. The mechanisms that produce this pain relief are still unknown, but they evidently do not involve endorphins since the analgesic effect of hypnosis is not abolished by naloxone (Mayer, 1979).

INTERACTION THROUGH THE BLOODSTREAM: THE ENDOCRINE SYSTEM

Thus far, we have considered the one primary instrument of communication within the body: the nervous system. But there is another organ system that serves a similar function: the ***endocrine glands*** (see Figure 1.18 and Table 1.1). Various endocrine glands (for example, the pancreas, adrenal glands, and pituitary) release their ***hormone*** secretions directly into the bloodstream and thus exert effects upon structures often far removed from their biochemical birthplace. As an example, take the ***pituitary gland.*** One of its components secretes a hormone that tells the kidney to decrease the amount of water excreted in the urine, a useful mechanism when the body is short of water (see Chapter 2).*

On the face of it, the integration that the endocrine glands give us seems to be very different from that which is provided by the nervous system. In the nervous system, messages are sent to particular addresses through highly specific channels. In contrast, the chemical messengers employed by the endocrine system travel indiscriminately to all parts of the body until they finally reach the one organ that is their destination. But at bottom, the two communication systems have a good deal in common, for ultimately they both use chemical substances to transmit information. In the nervous system, these are the neurotransmitters that excite or inhibit the postsynaptic cell; in the endocrine system, they are the hormones that affect specially sensitive cells in the target organ. To be sure, there is an enormous difference in the distance these messengers have to travel. In the case of the neurotransmitters, it is the synaptic cleft, which is less than 1/10,000 mm wide; in the case of the endocrine system, it may be half the length of the en-

---

* In addition to the endocrine glands, there are also ***duct glands*** (for example, salivary and tear glands), which have ducts that channel their secretions to the proper region of application.

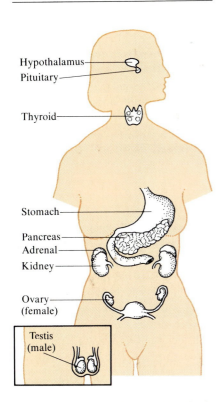

1.18 *Location of major endocrine glands and hypothalamus*

Table 1.1   THE MAIN ENDOCRINE GLANDS AND THEIR FUNCTIONS

Gland	Functions of the released hormones
Anterior pituitary	Often called the body's master gland because it triggers hormone secretion in many of the other endocrine glands.
Posterior pituitary	Prevents loss of water through kidney.
Thyroid	Affects metabolic rate.
Islet cells in pancreas	Affects utilization of glucose.
Adrenal cortex	Various effects on metabolism; some effects on sexual behavior.
Adrenal medulla	Increases sugar output of liver; stimulates various internal organs in the same direction as the sympathetic branch of the ANS (e.g., accelerates heart rate).
Ovaries	One set of hormones (estrogen) produces female sex characteristics and is relevant to sexual behavior. Another hormone (progesterone) prepares uterus for implantation of embryo.
Testes	Produces male sex characteristics. Relevant to sexual arousal.

tire body. But the fact that in both cases the medium of their message is chemical leads to a number of important similarities. Thus, several substances turn out to serve both as hormones and as neurotransmitters. For example, norepinephrine is the transmitter released by certain neurons that make blood vessels constrict; it is also one of the hormones secreted by the adrenal gland and has similar results.

THE MAIN STRUCTURES OF THE NERVOUS SYSTEM

Our general approach has been to move from the simple to the increasingly complex. We first looked at the operation of the smallest functional unit of the nervous system, the neuron, and then considered the way in which two or more neurons may interact. We now turn to a third and still more complex level of analysis to discuss the function of large aggregates of neurons. What can we say about the function of those clumps of nervous tissue, each made up of millions of neurons, which comprise the gross structures of the brain and spinal cord?

The Peripheral Nervous System

Taken as a whole, the human nervous system consists of a fine network of fibers that gradually merge into larger and larger branches which converge upon a central trunk line, like the tributaries of a stream. This system is composed of the central and peripheral nervous systems (see Figure 1.19). The ***central nervous system*** (usually abbreviated ***CNS***) is made up of the brain and spinal cord. The ***peripheral system,*** as its name implies, comprises all nervous structures that are outside of the CNS.

Anatomists distinguish between two divisions of the peripheral nervous system —the somatic and the autonomic. The ***somatic division*** is primarily concerned with the control of the skeletal musculature and the transmission of information from the sense organs. It consists of various nerves that branch off from the CNS —efferent fibers to the muscles and afferent fibers from the skin, the joints, and the special senses. The ***autonomic nervous system (ANS)*** serves the many visceral structures that are concerned with the basic life processes, such as the heart, the blood vessels, the digestive systems, the genital organs, and so on.

The Central Nervous System

The central nervous system can be described as a long tube that is very much thickened at its front end. The portion of the tube below the skull is the ***spinal cord,*** while the portion located in the skull is the ***brain stem.*** Two structures are attached to the brain stem. One is the pair of ***cerebral hemispheres,*** which are very large and envelop the central tube completely; the other is the ***cerebellum*** (literally, "little brain"), which is located lower down and is much smaller (see Figure 1.20).

Neuroanatomists find it convenient to consider the brain in terms of three major subdivisions: the ***hindbrain, midbrain,*** and ***forebrain*** (see Figures 1.20 and 1.21).

THE HINDBRAIN

The hindbrain includes the medulla and the cerebellum. The ***medulla*** is the part of the brain stem closest to the spinal cord; it helps to control some vital bodily functions such as heartbeat, circulation, and respiration. The ***cerebellum*** is a deeply convoluted structure that controls bodily balance and muscular coordination. It functions as a specialized computer whose 30 billion or more neurons integrate the enormous amount of information from the muscles, joints, and tendons of the body that are required both for ordinary walking and for the skilled, automatic movements of athletes and piano players.

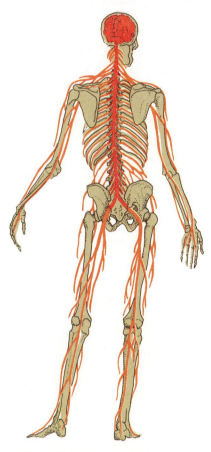

1.19   Central and peripheral nervous system   *The central nervous system (in red) and the peripheral nervous system (in orange). (After Bloom, Lazerson, and Hofstadter, 1988, p. 19)*

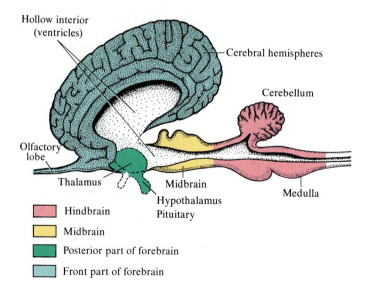

Hollow interior (ventricles)
Cerebral hemispheres
Cerebellum
Olfactory lobe
Thalamus
Midbrain
Hypothalamus
Pituitary
Medulla

■ Hindbrain
■ Midbrain
■ Posterior part of forebrain
■ Front part of forebrain

1.20   The central nervous system   *This diagram is a highly schematic representation of the main parts of the brain. (After Lickley, 1919)*

A

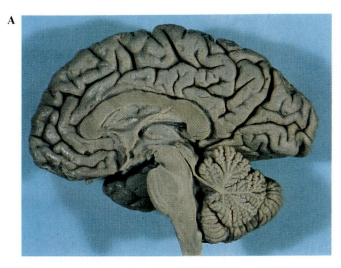

B

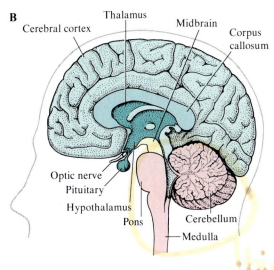

1.21 *The human brain* (A) A photo-graph of the brain cut lengthwise. (Photograph by Biophoto Associates, Photo Researchers) (B) A diagram of the brain, cut lengthwise. The colors are analogous to those used in Figure 1.20 to indicate hindbrain (pink), midbrain (yellow), between-brain (dark green), and forebrain (light green). (After Keeton, 1980)

THE MIDBRAIN

The midbrain contains several neural centers that act as lower level control centers for some motor reactions and that also have some limited auditory and visual functions (such as controlling eye movements). Of particular interest is a rather diffuse structure known as the *reticular formation,* which extends through the entire length of the brain stem from medulla to thalamus but is particularly prominent in the midbrain region. One of its functions is to serve as a general activator whose excitation arouses other parts of the brain, particularly the cerebral hemispheres. Its deactivation seems related to sleep. We will return to these issues in a later section (see Chapter 2).

FOREBRAIN: THALAMUS AND HYPOTHALAMUS

Two of the forebrain structures represent the topmost region of the brain stem. They are the thalamus and the hypothalamus. The *thalamus* is a large system of various centers that serves as a kind of reception area to the cerebral hemispheres. Fibers from the eyes, the ears, the skin, and some motor centers, pass their information to the thalamus, which then forwards it upward to the cerebral cortex. The *hypothalamus* is intimately involved in the control of behavior patterns that stem from the basic biological urges (e.g., feeding, drinking, maintaining an appropriate temperature, sexual activity, and so forth; see Chapter 2).

FOREBRAIN: CEREBRAL HEMISPHERES

We finally turn to the structures that have traditionally been regarded as the functional summit of the behaving organism (or at least, of the thinking organism): the *cerebral hemispheres.* Anatomists usually distinguish several large parts within each hemisphere, called *lobes.* There are four such lobes, each named for the cranial bone nearest to it: the *frontal, parietal, occipital,* and *temporal.*

The outer layer of the cerebral hemispheres is called the *cerebral cortex,* and it is this region rather than the hemispheres as a whole that is thought to represent the pinnacle of neural integration. The cells in the cortex are densely packed and intricately interconnected; they are therefore capable of the most complex synaptic interconnections. While the cortex is only about 3 mm thick, it comprises a substantial proportion of the entire human brain. This is because the cerebral

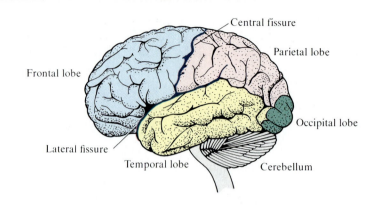

1.22   The cerebral hemispheres, side view

hemispheres are deeply folded and convoluted. Thus crumpled up, the cerebral surface that can be packed into the cranial cavity is very much increased (see Figure 1.22). The cortex is generally believed to be critical for the so-called "higher mental processes" (thinking, many aspects of memory, planned and voluntary action) and is the most recent to emerge in the course of evolution. Fish have none at all, reptiles and birds have but a poor beginning, while in mammals there is considerable enlargement, especially in the primates.

FOREBRAIN: SUBCORTICAL STRUCTURES

A word or two should be added about several structures located in the subcortical regions of the cerebral hemispheres. One important group of structures are the **basal ganglia,** which are located near the base of the cortex and relay commands that coordinate large muscle movements.

Another set of important structures is located near the center of the cerebral hemispheres, in a region that borders on the brain stem (see Figures 1.23 and 1.24). These are often grouped together under the term **limbic system** (from *limbique,* "bordering"). Many limbic subsystems are part of what (in evolutionary terms) is an older unit, sometimes called the "old cortex." The limbic system has

1.23   The limbic system *A schematic diagram of the limbic system (in blue) shown in the side view. (After Russell, 1961)*

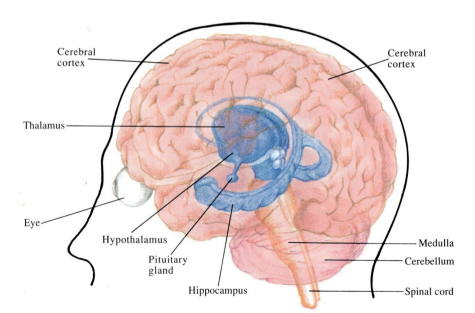

1.24   Important structures of the limbic system *Thalamus, hypothalamus, and hippocampus as if seen through transparent hemisphere. (After Bloom, Lazerson, and Hofstadter, 1988)*

close anatomical ties with the hypothalamus and is involved in the control of emotional and motivational activities. We will later take a closer look at one particular limbic structure, the *hippocampus,* which plays an important role in various aspects of learning and memory (see Chapter 6).

THE CEREBRAL CORTEX

We now turn to the cerebral cortex, the part of the nervous system that allows us to be intelligent. For without a cortex there can be no planning, no complex sequence of motor movements, no perception of organized form, and no speech—in short, no semblance of anything that we call human.

Projection Areas

Among the first discoveries in the study of cortical function was the existence of the so-called *projection areas.* These serve as receiving stations for sensory information or as dispatching centers for motor commands. *Sensory projection areas* are those regions of the cortex where the messages that come from the various senses (usually through some other relay stations) are first received. *Motor projection areas* are those from which directives that ultimately go to the muscles are issued. The term *projection* is here used in a geometrical sense: motor and sensory areas of the body are projected (mapped) onto particular regions of the cortex, resulting in a rough topographical correspondence between the location in the body and the location of the receiving or dispatching center in the cortex.

MOTOR AREAS

The discovery of the cortical motor areas occurred when several physiologists opened the skull of a lightly anesthetized dog and then applied mild electric currents to various portions of its cerebral cortex. They discovered a region in the frontal lobe that controls movement. Stimulating a given point led to motion of the forelimb, stimulating another point led to motion of the trunk, and so forth. Exciting the left hemisphere led to movements on the right side of the body; exciting the right hemisphere caused movements on the left. This made good anatomical sense because most of the major efferent pathways from the brain cross over to the opposite side just as they leave the hindbrain.

Similar studies were conducted on human subjects by the Canadian neurosurgeon, Wilder Penfield. The stimulation was administered in the course of a brain operation. As already mentioned, such operations are usually administered under local rather than general anesthesia and patients are therefore able to report their experiences. Electrical stimulation applied to the open brain produces no pain. While pain receptors are located throughout the body and send their messages upward to the brain, the brain itself contains no such receptors.

The results of Penfield's studies showed that the cortical motor area in humans is in a region of the frontal lobe that is quite similar to that found in dogs. Stimulation there led to movement of some parts of the body, much to the surprise of patients who had no sense of "willing" the action, or of "performing it themselves." Systematic exploration showed that for each portion of the motor cortex, there was a corresponding part of the body that moved when its cortical counterpart was stimulated, with each hemisphere controlling the side of the body opposite to it. The results are sometimes expressed graphically by drawing a "motor

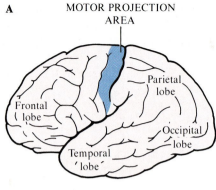

A

MOTOR PROJECTION
AREA

Frontal lobe

Parietal lobe

Temporal lobe

Occipital lobe

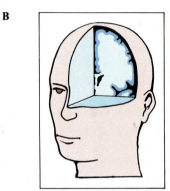

B

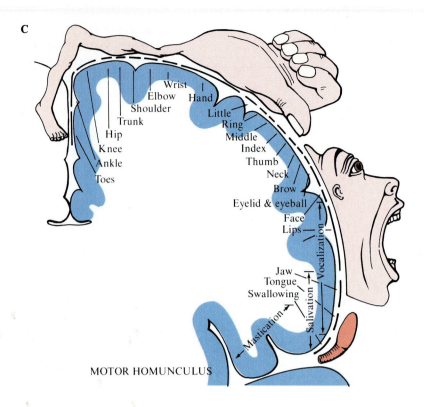

C

Wrist
Elbow
Shoulder
Trunk
Hip
Knee
Ankle
Toes

Hand
Little
Ring
Middle
Index
Thumb
Neck
Brow
Eyelid & eyeball
Face
Lips

Vocalization

Jaw
Tongue
Swallowing

Salivation

Mastication

MOTOR HOMUNCULUS

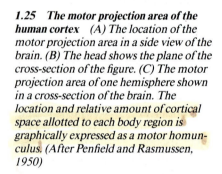

1.25   The motor projection area of the human cortex   *(A) The location of the motor projection area in a side view of the brain. (B) The head shows the plane of the cross-section of the figure. (C) The motor projection area of one hemisphere shown in a cross-section of the brain. The location and relative amount of cortical space allotted to each body region is graphically expressed as a motor homunculus. (After Penfield and Rasmussen, 1950)*

homunculus," a schema of the body as it is represented in the motor projection area (Figure 1.25).

Inspection of the motor homunculus shows that equal areas of the body do not receive equal cortical space. Instead, parts of the body that are very mobile and capable of precisely tuned movement (for instance, the fingers, the tongue) are assigned greater cortical space compared to those employed for movements that are more gross and undifferentiated (for instance, the shoulder). What matters is evidently function, the extent and complexity of use (Penfield and Rasmussen, 1950).

Some related findings with various animals fit neatly into this picture. For example, consider the cortical representations of the forepaw in dogs and raccoons. Unlike the dog, the raccoon is a "manual" creature which explores the world with its forepaws; neatly enough, the forepaw cortical area in raccoons dwarfs its counterpart in dogs (Welker, Johnson, and Pubols, 1964).

SENSORY AREAS

Analogous stimulation methods have demonstrated the existence of cortical sensory areas. The **somatosensory area** is located in the parietal lobes. Patients stimulated at a particular point of this area report a tingling sensation somewhere on the opposite side of their bodies. (Less frequently, they will report experiences of cold, warmth, or of movement.) Again, we find a neat topographic projection. Each part of the body's surface is mapped onto a particular part of the cortical somatosensory area but again with an unequal assignment of cortical space. The parts of the body that are most sensitive to touch, such as the index finger and the tongue, enjoy a disproportionately larger cortical space allocation. And again we find a crossover effect. Each part of the body is mapped onto the hemisphere that is on the side that's opposite to it: the right thumb onto the left hemisphere, the left shoulder onto the right hemisphere, and so on.

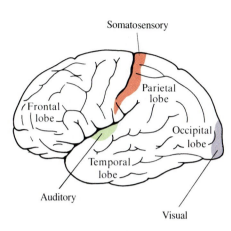

1.26 Sensory projection areas of the human cortex *The location of the somatosensory, auditory, and visual projection areas in the brain. (After Cobb, 1941)*

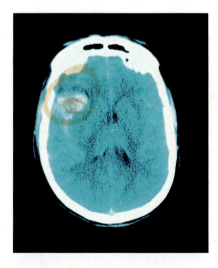

CAT scan *The CAT scan shows a subarachnoid hemorrhage, resulting from a ruptured blood vessel. The hemorrhage is the light area over the right side of the brain (left on image). It looks white because there was considerable bleeding; blood absorbs more radiation than ordinary brain tissue (Courtesy Radiography Dept., Royal Victoria Infirmary, Newcastle-upon-Tyre. Photo by Simon Fraser/Science Photo Library/Photo Researchers, Inc.)*

Similar projection areas exist for vision and for hearing and are located in the occipital and temporal lobes respectively (Figure 1.26). Patients who are stimulated in the visual projection area report optical experiences, vivid enough, but with little form and meaning—flickering lights, formless colors, streaks. Stimulated in the auditory area, patients hear things, but again the sensation is rather meaningless and chaotic—clicks, buzzes, booms, hums. Some psychologists might argue that here we have "pure" visual and auditory input, the crude, raw materials of sensation, which are then shaped and interpreted as the excitation is transmitted to other areas of the brain.

Association Areas

Less than one-quarter of the human cortex is devoted to the projection zones. The remaining regions are the **association areas,** which are implicated in such higher mental functions as planning, perceiving, remembering, thinking, and speech.* Most of the evidence comes from studies of human patients who have incurred damage (technically, **lesions**) through tumors, hemorrhage, or blockage of cerebral blood vessels (popularly known as a stroke), or accident. Further evidence comes from a comparison of the anatomy of the cortex found in different mammals. In the rat, the bulk of the cortex is taken up by projection zones. In the cat, proportionally more cortical space is devoted to the association areas. The proportion is greater yet in monkeys, and it is greatest of all in humans.

METHODS FOR STUDYING LOCALIZATION

The traditional interpretation of the effect of lesions in association areas is that they impair the organization of messages that come from the sensory projection areas or that go to the motor projection areas. But just how do we know exactly where the lesions are? To be sure, their exact location will eventually be known through an autopsy, but both the physician (and no doubt the patient) would surely prefer to get an answer while the patient is still alive. Standard X-rays are of some help, but they only reveal very gross pathologies. Fortunately, several modern techniques have been developed that provide us with a much more precise picture of the anatomical structure of a living patient's brain.

One such technique is the so-called **CAT scan** (an abbreviation for **Computerized Axial Tomography**). It employs a narrow beam of X-rays that is aimed through the patient's head and hits a detector on the opposite side. This beam slowly moves in a circular arc around the patient's head, and the detector moves along with it. Different brain tissues vary in density, and will therefore block the X-rays to different degrees. A computer eventually constructs a composite picture based on the X-ray views from all the different angles.

A more recent development allows neurologists and psychologists to look into a living brain and observe some aspects of its functioning. This is the **PET scan** (or, to give it its full name, **Positron Emission Tomography**), which utilizes the fact that brain tissue, like all other living tissue, uses more fuel the more active it is. The person is injected with a radioactive sugar that resembles glucose (the only metabolic fuel the brain can use). Active cells of the brain will take up this substance, which will then signal its presence by emitting subatomic particles. The greater the emission in a given region of the brain, the greater its metabolic activity. The resulting PET scan can tell the physician that a certain region of the brain

---

* The term grew out of earlier belief that these are the regions where neural messages from the different senses meet and become associated.

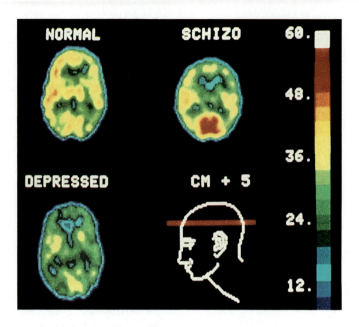

1.27   PET scans and disorders   The scans show the difference in metabolic levels in normal, schizophrenic, and depressed individuals. Red indicates highest metabolic activity, with yellow next, followed by green, and then blue. During depression, for example, brain activity is considerably reduced, especially in the frontal areas. (NIH/SPL/Photo Researchers)

is abnormally active or inactive and may suggest a tumor, a lesion, or a psychological disorder (see Figure 1.27). PET scans are also useful tools in studying localization of function in normal persons. For example, they will show varying degrees of activity in the general region of the visual projection area depending on the complexity of the scene that is being viewed (see Figure 1.28).

DISORDERS OF ACTION

We've seen how modern neuropsychologists can determine the precise location of cerebral lesions. The next question is what these lesions tell us about the functions of the cortical association areas.

Some lesions produce ***apraxias*** (Greek, "inability to act"), which are serious disturbances in the initiation or organization of voluntary action. In some apraxias, the patient is unable to perform certain well-known actions such as saluting or waving goodbye when asked to do so. In others, actions that normal persons regard as quite simple and unitary become fragmented and disorganized. When asked to light a cigarette, the patient may strike a match against a matchbox, and then strike it again and again after it is already burning; or he may light the match and then put it into his mouth. These deficits are in no sense the result of a motor paralysis, for the patient can readily perform each constituent of the

1.28   PET scan and visual stimulation   These scans show the difference in metabolic brain activity depending on whether the patient's eyes were closed, or whether he was viewing a simple or complex scene. (Photograph by Dr. John Mazziotta et al./Photo Researchers)

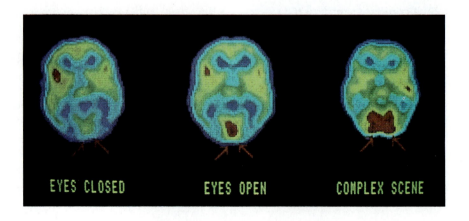

action in isolation. His problem is in initiating the sequence or in selecting the right components and fitting them together (Luria, 1966; Kolb and Whishaw, 1990).

Apraxia is evidently some impairment of a neurological system that organizes individual movements into coherent, larger actions, and also initiates them. The association region whose lesion leads to apraxia is perhaps analogous to the command post of a regiment that draws up the battle plan and orders an attack. If the command post falls and no other takes its place, there can be no organized attack, even though the individual soldiers are still able to fire their guns and throw their hand grenades. There is considerable debate over just where this neural command post is localized, or for that matter, whether there is one such center or several (Geschwind, 1975; Kolb and Milner, 1981).

DISORDERS OF PERCEPTION AND ATTENTION

In several other disorders caused by lesions in certain cortical association areas, the patient suffers a disruption in the way he perceives the world or attends to it.

One such disorder is ***agnosia*** (Greek, "without knowledge"). Whereas apraxia represents a disrupted organization of action, agnosia is characterized by a disorganization of various aspects of the sensory world. In visual agnosia, patients can see, but they are often unable to recognize what they see. They may have 20/20 vision, but they nevertheless suffer a kind of "psychic blindness." Some of these patients can perceive each separate detail of a picture, but they are unable to identify the picture as a whole. When shown a drawing of a telephone, one such patient painstakingly identified several parts and then ventured an appropriate guess: "A dial . . . numbers . . . of course, it's a watch or some sort of machine!" (Luria, 1966, p. 139; see Figure 1.29).

In some agnosias (technically known as ***prosopagnosias,*** from the Greek *proso,* "face"), the primary difficulty is in recognizing faces. Some of these patients are unable to distinguish familiar faces from others; others are even unable to recognize that a face *is* a face. When walking in the street, one such patient would pat the tops of fire hydrants which he thought were the heads of little children. On one occasion he mistook his wife's head for a hat (Sacks, 1985).

DISORDERS OF LANGUAGE

Certain lesions of cortical association lead to serious disruptions of the most distinctively human of all human activities—the production and comprehension of speech. Disorders of this kind are called ***aphasias*** (Greek, "lack of speech"). In right-handers, they are almost always produced by lesions in certain cortical areas of the left hemisphere.

Expressive aphasia   In one form of aphasia, the patient's primary difficulty is with the production of speech. This is ***expressive aphasia,*** which is essentially a language apraxia. In extreme cases, a patient with this disorder becomes virtually unable to utter or to write a word. Less extremely, a few words or phrases survive. These may be routine expressions such as "hello" or emotional outbursts such as "damn it!" In still less severe cases, only a part of the normal spoken vocabulary is lost, but the patient's speech becomes fragmented, as finding and articulating each word requires a special effort. The result is a staccato, spoken telegram: "Here . . . head . . . operation . . . here . . . speech . . . none . . . talking . . . what . . . illness" (Luria, 1966, p. 406).

The similarity to the apraxias we have discussed before is very striking. There is no paralysis of speech muscles, for the patient is perfectly able to move lips and tongue. What is impaired is the ability to organize and plan these movements

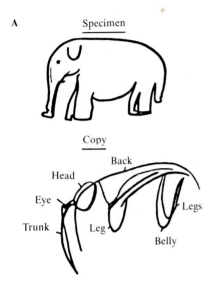

Specimen

Copy

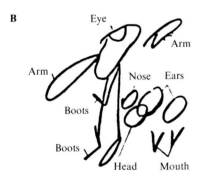

1.29   Drawings by a patient with visual agnosia   *(A) Trying to copy an elephant. (B) Production when asked to draw a man. (From Luria, 1966)*

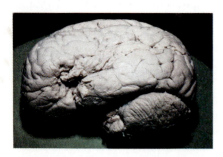

1.30 Tan's brain *The embalmed brain of Broca's famous aphasic patient "Tan," so-called because this was the only syllable he was able to utter. Note the area of damage on the lower side of the left frontal lobe, now known as Broca's area. (Photograph by M. Sakka, courtesy Musée de l' Homme et Musée Dupuytren, Paris)*

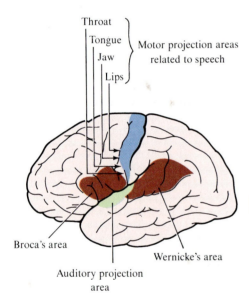

1.31 Broca's and Wernicke's areas *The diagram shows the two association areas most relevant to language. Destruction of Broca's area generally leads to expressive aphasia; destruction of Wernicke's area leads to receptive aphasia. Note the proximity to the relevant projection areas: Broca's area is closest to the regions that control the speech muscles, while Wernicke's area borders on the auditory projection zone.*

into a unified sequence, the ability to synthesize individual movements so as to form a word or to put one word after another so as to create a coherent sentence.

Expressive aphasias of the kind described here are generally produced by lesions in a region of the left frontal lobe called ***Broca's area*** (after a French physician, Paul Broca, who first noted its relation to speech in 1861; see Figures 1.30 and 1.31). This is an association area that borders on the part of the motor projection zone that controls the various speech muscles (jaw, tongue, lips, larynx, and so on) and presumably plays an important role in orchestrating their separate functions.

Receptive aphasia In expressive aphasia, patients generally understand what they hear but cannot answer. In another form of aphasia, the patient's problem is that they don't understand when they are spoken to, though they usually answer anyway. This condition is called ***receptive aphasia,*** which amounts to a kind of language agnosia. Unlike patients with expressive aphasia, those with receptive aphasia talk very freely and very fast, but while they utter many words, they say very little. The sentences they produce are reasonably grammatical, but they are largely composed of the little filler words that provide little information. A typical example is, "I was over the other one, and then after they had been in the department, I was in this one" (Geschwind, 1970, p. 904).

Receptive aphasia is usually associated with left-hemisphere lesions (in right-handed people) in various association areas of the temporal and parietal lobes. Many authorities believe that the crucial locus is ***Wernicke's area.*** Wernicke's area is a region that borders on the auditory projection zone and is named after a nineteenth-century neurologist who first described receptive aphasias (see Figure 1.31).

One Brain or Two?

Anatomically, the two hemispheres appear to be quite similar, but there is abundant evidence that their functions are by no means identical. This asymmetry of function is called ***lateralization,*** and its manifestations include such diverse phenomena as language, spatial organization, and handedness—the superior dexterity of one hand over the other (Springer and Deutsch, 1981).

We have already seen that in right-handers aphasia is usually associated with lesions in the left hemisphere. At first, neuroscientists interpreted this fact to mean that one hemisphere is *dominant* over the other. As a result, they called the (right-hander's) right hemisphere the "minor hemisphere," for they believed that it is essentially a lesser version of the left hemisphere, a hemisphere that lacks language functions, has less capacity for fine motor control, and so forth.

Later evidence has rescued the right hemisphere from this poor relation status, for it now appears that it has some important functions of its own. Right-handers with lesions in the right hemisphere often suffer from various difficulties in the comprehension of various aspects of space and form; they concentrate on details but cannot grasp the overall pattern. Some have trouble recognizing faces. Some have great difficulties in dressing themselves; they put their arms in a pants leg or put a shirt on backwards (Bogen, 1969).

The results are more ambiguous for the 12 percent or so of the population that is left-handed (and also generally left-footed, and to a lesser extent, left-eyed and left-eared as well; Porac and Coren, 1981). Somewhat more than half of the left-handers have speech predominantly lateralized in the left hemisphere; in the rest, language is usually represented in both hemispheres. But overall, there seems to be less lateralization in left-handers than in right-handers, so that the functional

Throat
Tongue
Jaw   Motor projection areas
Lips   related to speech

Broca's area
Auditory projection area
Wernicke's area

capabilities of the left-handers' two hemispheres are more on a par. Thus, in left-handers, aphasia may often be produced by lesions to either hemisphere. But by the same token, left-handed aphasics have a greater chance for ultimate recovery, for the intact hemisphere is better able to take over the responsibilities formerly assigned to the hemisphere that suffered damage (Brain, 1965; Springer and Deutsch, 1981).

EVIDENCE FROM SPLIT BRAINS

Some of the most persuasive evidence about the different functions of the two cerebral hemispheres comes from studies originated by Nobel laureate Roger Sperry using persons with *split brains* (Sperry, 1974, 1982). These are people whose *corpus callosum* has been surgically severed. The corpus callosum is a massive bundle of nerve fibers that interconnects the two hemispheres so that they can pool their information and function as a harmonious whole. This neurological bridge (and some other subsidiary ones) is sometimes cut in cases of severe epilepsy so that the seizure will not spread from one hemisphere to the other (Bogen, Fisher, and Vogel, 1965; Wilson et al., 1977). Once confined to a smaller cortical area, the seizures are less severe and less frequent. The operation clearly relieves suffering, but it has a side effect—the two hemispheres of the split brain become functionally isolated from each other and in some ways act as two separate brains (Gazzaniga, 1967; see Figure 1.32).

The effect of the split-brain operation is best demonstrated by setting a task that poses a question to one hemisphere and requires the answer from the other (see Figure 1.33). One method is to show a picture so that the neural message only reaches one hemisphere. This is done by flashing the picture for a fraction of a second to either the right or the left side of the patient's field of vision. The anatomical pathways of the visual system are such that if the picture is flashed to the right, it is projected to the left hemisphere; if presented to the left, it is projected

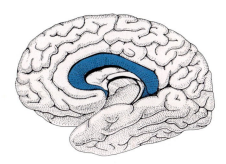

1.32 The split brain *To control epilepsy, neurosurgeons sometimes sever the two hemispheres. This is accomplished by cutting the corpus callosum (in blue) and a few other connective tracts. The corpus callosum is shown here in a lateral cross-section.*

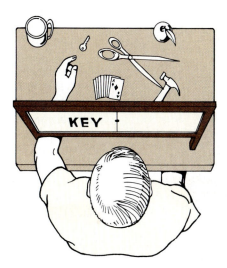

1.33 A setup sometimes used in split-brain studies *The subject fixates a center dot and then sees a picture or a word on the right or left side of the dot. He may be asked to respond verbally, by reading the word or naming the picture. He may also be asked to respond without words, for example, by picking out a named object from among a group spread out on a table and hidden from view, so that it can only be identified by touch. (After Gazzaniga, 1967)*

Left visual field

Right visual field

Retina

Optic chiasma

Thalamus

Left visual cortex

Right visual cortex

Corpus callosum

1.34 The visual pathway *The visual pathway is so arranged that all points in the right visual field send their information to the left hemisphere; all those in the left field send theirs to the right hemisphere. Information from one hemisphere is transmitted to the other by way of the corpus callosum.*

to the right hemisphere (see Figure 1.34). The patient's job is merely to say what he sees. When the picture is on the right, he can easily do so, for the information is transmitted to the same hemisphere that can formulate a spoken answer—the left hemisphere (which as we've seen is the site of language knowledge and of speech). The situation is different when the picture is flashed on the left. Now the visual image is sent to the right hemisphere, but this hemisphere can neither provide a spoken reply, nor can it relay the information to the left hemisphere, which has the language capacity, because the bridge between the two has been cut (Gazzaniga, 1967).

This is not to say that the right hemisphere has no understanding of what it's been shown. One patient was unexpectedly shown a picture of a nude girl. When this picture was flashed to the left hemisphere, the patient laughed and correctly described what she had seen. When the same picture was presented to the right hemisphere, she said that she saw nothing, but immediately afterward she smiled slyly and began to chuckle. When asked what was so funny, she said, "I don't know . . . nothing . . . oh—that funny machine" (Gazzaniga, 1970, p. 106). The right hemisphere knew what it was laughing at. The left hemisphere heard the laughter but could only guess at the cause, for *it* didn't see what the right hemisphere had looked at.

The split-brain studies give further proof that language is the province of the left hemisphere. But this doesn't mean that the right hemisphere has no language capacity at all. When a right-handed patient is asked to name a picture that is flashed to the left side (that is, to the right hemisphere), he sometimes makes a haphazard guess. But immediately afterwards, he often frowns or shakes his head. The right hemisphere evidently has some—limited—ability to understand what it hears. It sees the pictured object, and while it cannot produce the correct name—say, "ashtray"—it knows enough to understand that the name it just came up with—say, "coffeepot," couldn't possibly be right (Gazzaniga, 1967).

Further documentation of right-hemisphere language abilities comes from studies which show that split-brain patients can understand short written words flashed to the right hemisphere, and can tell whether a small string of letters, such as *house* and *pouse,* is or is not an English word (Zaidel, 1976, 1983; for some alternative interpretations, see Gazzaniga, 1983; Levy, 1983).

LATERALIZATION IN NORMAL SUBJECTS

All the evidence for lateralization we've discussed thus far has come from patients with neurological deficits: some with lesions in one or another hemisphere, others with a severed corpus callosum. Can lateralization be demonstrated in normal populations? There is evidence that it can.

One approach is to try to observe the operation of the two hemispheres by looking in at the cortex from the outside. In recent years, neuroscientists have developed a number of techniques for doing so. One such tool is the PET scan we discussed earlier, which assesses the activity of different brain regions by measuring their metabolic action. A similar logic underlies the *rCBF (regional cerebral blood flow)* technique, which measures the blood flow in different cortical areas while the subject is engaged in various mental operations. Here the idea is that an increase in the activity of brain cells in a certain part of the cortex will call for an increase in the amount of blood supplied to that region. To determine the distribution of blood flow in the cortex, a mildly radioactive (but harmless) gas is injected into an artery (or is inhaled) and special radiation counters are placed at various points on the subject's skull. The subject is fully conscious and is asked to perform various tasks: to speak, read, follow a moving light, and so on. The distribution of counter readings at the various points on the skull will then give an

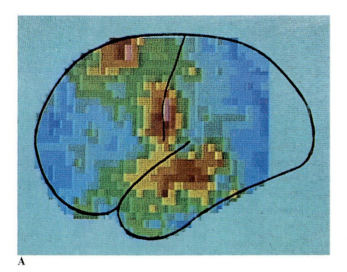

A

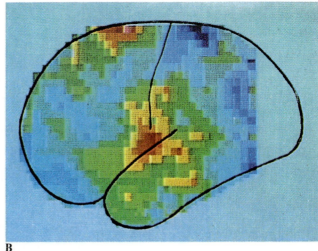

B

1.35 Cerebral blood flow in right and left hemispheres during speech *Blood-flow maps obtained with the rCBF technique while subjects were speaking. In these maps, the brain surface was divided into squares, and a computer averaged the blood flow in each square. The rate of flow is indicated by the color, with green indicating average blood flow, shades of blue indicating flow rates below average, and shades of red flow rates above average. (A) left hemisphere. Note that maximum blood flow occurred in the lower portion of the motor and somatosensory areas (the regions that control movement of the mouth, tongue, and larynx, or receive sensory input from them), the auditory projection area, and Broca's area. (B) Right hemisphere. There is considerably less activity in these regions. (Courtesy of Niels. A. Lassen)*

index of the rate at which blood flows through a given region (Ingvar and Lassen, 1979).

The results of such studies provide a graphic proof that different cortical regions become activated during different tasks. In particular, they document the asymmetry of hemispheric functions. Figure 1.35 shows the rate of blood flow in the two hemispheres while subjects were speaking. In the left hemisphere, the blood flow was more extensive in areas where one would expect it to be: the lower portions of the motor and somatosensory cortex (which control and receive sensory information from the mouth, tongue, and larynx), the auditory projection zone, and Broca's area. In the right hemisphere, the activity was much less, especially in the mouth and auditory areas (Lassen, Ingvar, and Skinhoj, 1978).

TWO MODES OF MENTAL FUNCTIONING

The preceding discussion indicates that language and spatial organization are usually handled in two different areas of the brain. Some psychologists believe that this difference in localization goes along with a distinction between two fundamentally different modes of thought: one that involves words, the other spatial processes. This distinction is certainly in line with everyday observation. We often think in words—about scientific problems, about politics, about who likes whom; the list is endless. But we also mentally manipulate the world with little benefit of language—as when we visualize our living room with rearranged furniture or when we work a jigsaw puzzle. Many problems can be solved by either mode. We may find our way to a friend's home by referring to a mental map, or by memorizing a verbal sequence such as "first right turn after the third traffic light." But the two modes are somehow not intersubstitutable. How a corkscrew works is hard to describe in words; the pros and cons of a political two-party system are impossible to get across without them.

Recovery from Brain Injury

As we've seen, much of our knowledge of the brain comes from an analysis of the effects of various cerebral lesions. We now ask how people recover from cerebral injury and by what mechanisms they do so. It is self-evident that this topic is of great medical and general interest. But in addition, the facts about recovery have considerable scientific importance, for they throw yet further light on how the human brain works.

REPAIR FROM WITHIN

Recovery from cerebral lesions varies enormously. Consider aphasia. In some cases, there is considerable recovery; for example, a stroke patient with aphasia may regain normal fluency and comprehension after a couple of months, though a certain difficulty in finding words (sometimes called *anomia*) usually remains. When shown a picture of a key, the patient may be unable to think of its name and say, "I know what it does . . . you use it to open a door" (Kolb and Whishaw, 1990). But in other cases, the recovery is considerably less, and the prospects for improvements are not too bright; if the individual has not recovered a year or so after the brain injury, the hopes for further gains are relatively small.

How can we explain these great variations in the degree to which patients recover from brain damage?

Recovery of damaged but living neurons   A critical factor is whether some—or even all—of the neurons in the affected area were damaged rather than being destroyed outright. If so, many of the symptoms may be reversible. An example of such a reversible condition is the damage produced by the pressure brought on by the swelling following a head injury, an infection, or a tumor. If these conditions are removed, for example by draining some cerebral fluid to relieve cranial pressure, the damaged neurons may recover and the patient's symptoms will become less severe or even disappear entirely (Moscovitch and Rozin, 1989).

Sprouting of collaterals   The outlook is much less favorable when neurons have been destroyed. For as we've seen, there is no replacement warranty for dead neurons; a neuron lost is lost forever. But even so, some possibilities of improvement remain. One possibility is the formation of new connections. The axons of some healthy neurons adjacent to the damaged cells will grow new branches, called *collateral sprouts,* which may eventually attach themselves to the synapses left vacant by the cells lost through injury (Veraa and Grafstein, 1981). Consider the effects of a certain lesion in the hypothalamus of a rat. In the first few days after the lesion, the animal just lies on its belly, unable to stand, let alone walk around, but after a few weeks there is recovery (Golani, Wolgin, and Teitelbaum, 1979). Some authors believe that some of the axons cut by this lesion gradually sprout new collateral branches that fill in for cells that were permanently destroyed. As a result, a smaller number of neurons can now do the work formerly done by many (Stricker and Zigmond, 1976).

Substitution of function   Another factor that can produce recovery is that the function of the damaged regions is taken over by other parts of the brain. This seems to occur in certain cases of recovery from aphasia; here the right hemisphere comes to perform some of the tasks originally handled by the left. Evidence comes from patients who show nearly complete recovery of language function subsequent to left-hemisphere lesions; in most of these cases, there is an increase in the blood flow to the right hemisphere (Knopman et al., 1984, cited in Rosenzweig and Leiman, 1989).

REPAIR FROM WITHOUT

Thus far, we've talked about cases in which the nervous system manages to repair itself, at least to some extent. Is there a way in which we can help that repair along?

We've seen that the brain cannot replace dead neurons. But there are some recent animal studies which suggest that someday neurologists may be able to provide some such replacement by transplanting neural tissue from outside. Thus far, this work is still in the early experimental stages, but initial results give some grounds for hope (Fine, 1986).

One group of such studies is of potential relevance to *Alzheimer's disease*, which afflicts 5 to 10 percent of all persons over age sixty-five (Gelman, 1989). This devastating disease is characterized by a progressive decline in intellectual functioning that begins with serious memory problems, continues with increasing disorientation, and culminates in total physical and mental helplessness. While Alzheimer's disease leads to degenerative changes throughout the brain, the worst destruction seems to befall a pathway of acetylcholine-releasing neurons that have their origin in a region at the base of the forebrain and extend to many cortical association areas as well as to the hippocampus (a structure that is important for memory). When enough of these cells are dead or dying, the cortical and hippocampal regions to which they project are no longer activated. As a result, there is loss of memory and cognitive functioning (see Figure 1.36; Coyle, Price, and DeLong, 1983, p. 1187).

Can degenerative changes of this sort be reversed by brain transplants? They can in rats, at least to some extent. Some investigators worked on rats that had been subjected to lesions in acetylcholine-releasing pathways analogous to those destroyed in Alzheimer patients. Others used animals of a fairly advanced age (in rats, this is about two years of age). Both the lesioned and the aged rats showed substantial impairments on various tests of memory and spatial learning. Initially they couldn't learn certain simple mazes, or retain what they had learned from one occasion to the next. But after appropriate brain transplants, there was significant improvement (Björklund and Stenevi, 1984; Gage and Björklund, 1986).

Just how do these brain grafts lead to recovery? There are probably several answers. In part, the transplanted tissue may provide new cells for the host brain; in part, the graft may stimulate some of the host's intact neurons to release more transmitter substances; finally, the grafted tissue may encourage axon sprouting (Freed, de Medicacelli, and Wyatt, 1985).

What are the chances that these or similar techniques can be applied to human patients? As of yet, we can't say. There are obvious technological hurdles. But it's worth noting that if and when the transplantation techniques are ready for clinical application, there will be some serious ethical problems as well, because the most probable donors would be aborted human fetuses.

To sum up, while we know much more about the brain than we did only a decade or two ago, medical technology is as yet unable to do much to aid the recovery of the injured brain. But it looks as if we're on the threshold of a new era of progress in this crucial area. Considering that our population is aging at an ever-increasing rate, with a concomitant increase in the proportion of persons with degenerative brain disorders, that era can come none too soon.

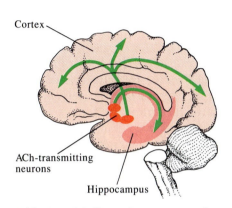

1.36 Acetylcholine pathways apparently involved in Alzheimer's disease *Acetylcholine-transmitting neurons located in regions at the base of the forebrain activate many regions of the cortex as well as the hippocampus. The degeneration of these neurons may be a major cause of Alzheimer's disease. (After Coyle, Price, and Delong, 1983)*

SOME PROBLEMS IN LOCALIZING BRAIN FUNCTION

The preceding discussion has sketched some recent advances in our understanding of localization of function in the human brain. But the picture is not as neat as we have presented it thus far, for there are various problems of both method and interpretation that complicate the analysis of any correlation between anatomical site and psychological function.

One problem is anatomical. Most of our knowledge of human cerebral function comes from the study of lesions. But the exact locus of a lesion is hard to determine while a patient is alive. The results are sometimes ambiguous even if postmortem inspection is possible. There may be other lesions elsewhere in the brain in addition to those the neurologist considers critical. Did those others contribute to the disorder?

Another problem is that the relevant functional disturbance is often accompanied by others. Which disorder was caused by which lesion? Neuropsychologists have described lesions as cruel experiments performed by nature, but nature is not a scientist and her experiments are rarely neat and precise. None of these difficulties is insurmountable. One way of coping with many of them is to study a large number of patients all of whom share one lesion but not others. If they all show a similar loss of function, it is very likely that the relevant anatomical loss is the one shared by all.

Suppose we have overcome the difficulties in specifying the precise anatomical locus that corresponds to a particular psychological effect. Does this mean that we have localized a function? Not necessarily, for we must first be sure that we understand what the underlying function really is. Sometimes this is fairly clear, as in lesions of sensory projection areas which cause defects in vision or hearing. In other cases, the explanation is less obvious. For example, certain studies have shown that stimulation of certain regions of the temporal lobes in some epileptic patients leads to vivid recollections of past events (Penfield and Roberts, 1959). This result is fascinating, but we won't be able to explain it until we know more about memory as such (or perhaps about epilepsy, for the result may be specific to patients with this disorder). In summary, psychology and neurophysiology go hand in hand. To claim that psychology will not progress until we know more about the brain is to assert only half the truth because the search for a neurophysiological underpinning necessarily requires some knowledge of what it is an underpinning of.

SUMMARY

1. Since Descartes, many scientists have tried to explain human and animal movement within the framework of the *reflex* concept: A stimulus excites a sense organ, which transmits excitation upward to the spinal cord or brain, which in turn relays the excitation downward to a muscle or gland and thus produces action. Descartes's general classification of nervous function is still with us as we distinguish between *reception, integration,* and *reaction.*

2. Later investigators showed that the smallest unit of the nervous system is the *neuron,* whose primary anatomical subdivisions are the *dendrites, cell body,* and *axon.*

3. The main function of a neuron is to produce a *nerve impulse.* This is an electrochemical disturbance that is propagated along the membrane of the axon. This occurs when the cell's normal *resting potential* is disrupted by a stimulus whose intensity exceeds the *threshold.* This stimulus produces a brief depolarization of the cell, which leads to an *action potential.* The action potential obeys the *all-or-none law:* Once threshold is reached, further increases of stimulus intensity have no effect on its magnitude. But the nervous system can nevertheless distinguish between different intensities of stimuli all of which are above threshold. One means is *frequency:* The more intense the stimulus, the more often the neuron fires.

4. To understand how neurons communicate, investigators have studied *reflex action,* which is necessarily based on the activity of several neurons. Results of studies with *spinal dogs* led Sherrington to infer the processes that underlie conduction across the *synapse,* the gap between the axon of one neuron and the dendrites and cell body of the next. Conduc-

tion within neurons was shown to obey different laws than conduction between neurons (that is, across the synapse). Evidence included the phenomena of *spatial* and *temporal summation.* Sherrington concluded that the excitation from several neurons funnels into a common reservoir to produce a *central excitatory state.*

5. Further studies argued for a *central inhibitory state.* Evidence came from *reciprocal inhibition* found in antagonistic muscles. Further work showed that a reflex can be activated either by increasing excitation or by decreasing inhibition. An example of the latter is the *disinhibition* produced by the destruction of higher centers which inhibit the reflex.

6. Sherrington's inferences of synaptic functions have been confirmed by modern electrical and chemical studies. Today we know that transmission across the synapse is accomplished by *neurotransmitters,* chemical substances that are liberated at the axon terminals of one neuron and exert excitatory or inhibitory effects on the dendrites and cell body of another. These transmitters cross the *synaptic gap* and affect *receptor molecules* located on the *postsynaptic membrane.* This creates *graded potentials* that summate and spread. When they reach threshold value, they produce an action potential in the axon of the second neuron.

7. Important examples of neurotransmitters include *acetylcholine, norepinephrine* and *dopamine.* Of special interest is a group of neurotransmitters called *endorphins* whose activity serves to alleviate pain.

8. In addition to the nervous system, there is another group of organs whose function is to serve as an instrument of communication within the body. This is the *endocrine system,* whose glands secrete their *hormones* directly into the bloodstream, which will eventually carry them to various target organs.

9. A crude anatomical outline of the vertebrate nervous system starts out with the distinction between the *peripheral (somatic* and *autonomic)* and *central nervous systems.* The central nervous system consists of the *spinal cord* and the *brain.* Important parts of the brain are the *hindbrain* (including *medulla* and *cerebellum*), *midbrain* (including the *reticular formation*) and *forebrain* (including *thalamus, hypothalamus, cerebral hemispheres,* and *cerebral cortex*). Of special interest is a group of subcortical structures of the forebrain called the *limbic system.*

10. The *cerebral cortex* is generally believed to underlie the most complex aspects of behavior. The *projection areas* of the cortex act as receiving stations for sensory information or as dispatching centers for motor commands. The remaining regions of the cortex are called *association areas.* Their function concerns such higher mental processes as planning, remembering, thinking, and speech.

11. A number of modern neurological tools, including the *CAT scan* and the *PET scan,* make it possible to diagnose and study lesions in the brains of living patients. Certain lesions of association areas lead to *apraxia,* a serious disturbance in the organization of voluntary action. Other lesions produce *agnosia,* a disorganization of perception and recognition. Still others cause *aphasia,* a profound disruption of language function, which may involve speech production, speech comprehension, or both.

12. In many ways, the two hemispheres are mirror images of each other. But to some extent, their function is not symmetrical. In most right-handers, the left hemisphere handles the bulk of the language functions, while the right hemisphere is more relevant to spatial comprehension. One source of evidence for this difference in hemispheric function, or *lateralization,* comes from the study of *split-brain patients* in whom the main connection between the two hemispheres, the *corpus callosum,* has been surgically cut. Direct observation of the operation of the two hemispheres can be obtained by measuring different rates of blood flow in the two hemispheres.

13. Recovery from cerebral lesions varies considerably from one patient to another. Some recovery is produced by *collateral sprouting,* whereby healthy neurons adjacent to the region of injury will grow new branches. In addition, some functions of the damaged regions are sometimes taken over by other, undamaged, parts of the brain. Recent work on the transplanting of neural tissue offers some hope that neurobiologists may ultimately provide some replacement for damaged tissue.

CHAPTER 2

Motivation

In this chapter, we will examine some of the simple motives that human beings share with other animals. These motives steer our behavior in certain directions rather than others; toward food, say, rather than toward shelter.

Our main concern will be with motives that are essentially unlearned and that pertain to the individual alone rather than to his interaction with others. Examples are hunger and thirst, the desire for safety, the need for rest. We will later take up two other kinds of motives. One concerns desires that are acquired through learning, such as the need to achieve, to attain prestige, or to amass possessions (see Chapters 11, 12, and 14). The other group is no less biologically based than hunger and thirst, but it involves motives that transcend the individual alone and focus on his relations with other persons, such as sex, filial love, and aggression (see Chapter 9).

MOTIVATION AS DIRECTION

Most human and animal actions are directed. We don't simply walk, reach, shrink, or flee; we walk and reach *toward* some objects, shrink and flee *away* from others. The objects that are approached or withdrawn from may be in the organism's here and now, as when a kitten jumps toward a rolling ball. But often enough, the object exists in an as yet unrealized future. The hawk circles in the sky in search of prey, but there is none in sight as yet. In such a case, an inner motive (a purpose, a desire) leads to actions that bring the hawk closer to its food.

Directed action seems difficult to reconcile with Descartes's notion of humans and animals as reflex machines, however complex their internal wiring. This problem is most pronounced for actions that are directed toward some future goal, for it is hard to see how an automaton can be imbued with purpose or desire. But difficulties arise even in the simplest case in which the direction is toward (or away from) an immediately present object. Consider the kitten reaching for the ball. What matters is not whether this flexor muscle is contracted or that extensor muscle relaxed, but rather whether the overall pattern of muscular activity gets

Motivation as directed action Cast adrift on a raft for weeks, the few survivors of a shipwreck direct all their efforts toward a nearby ship that might bring rescue. (The Wreck of the Medusa by Theodore Gericault, 1819; courtesy the Louvre)

the creature closer to the final end state—near the ball. The kitten may swipe at the ball with its right paw or its left, it may crouch more on one side or the other —all that matters is that, whatever the specific motor response, it will be toward the ball. Descartes's statues walked out and bowed when a visitor stepped on a hidden spring, but did they bow *to* the visitor? Suppose the visitor were to push the spring and then jump quickly to the left. The statue would surely lumber through its prescribed routine exactly as before, in stony disregard of the altered circumstance.

It is evident that a simple automaton is incapable of directed action. Can the machine be modified to overcome this lack? The answer is yes.

Control Systems

Modern engineers have developed an immense technology based on machines that control their own activities and are in that sense directed. The basic principle upon which these devices are built is the notion of a *feedback system.* When a machine is in operation it performs some kind of action which may be mechanical, electrical, thermal, or whatever, but which in all cases engenders some changes in the external environment. If these changes in turn influence the further operation of the machine—if they feed back upon the machine—we have a control system based on feedback.

In *positive feedback systems,* the feedback strengthens the very response that produced it. The result is an ever-increasing level of activity. A technological example is a rocket that homes in on airplanes. It is designed to increase its velocity the closer it gets to its target.

Of greater relevance to our present concern is *negative feedback* in which the feedback stops, or even reverses, the original response of the machine that produced the environmental change. Negative feedback underlies a large number of industrial devices called *servomechanisms* that can maintain themselves in a particular state. A simple example is the system that controls most home furnaces. A

2.1 Negative feedback *In negative feedback systems, the feedback stops or reverses the action that produces it. A sensing device indicates the level of a certain stimulus. If that level exceeds a certain setpoint, the action stops. The effect is self-regulation.*

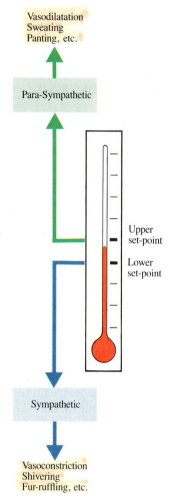

2.2 Reflexive temperature regulation in mammals *When the temperature deviates from an internal setpoint, various reflexive reactions will occur to restore the temperature to this setpoint.*

complish this? The most direct control is exerted by the autonomic nervous system (ANS), which sends commands to the *glands* and to the *smooth muscles** of the viscera (internal organs) and the blood vessels. The ANS has two divisions: the *sympathetic* and the *parasympathetic*. These two divisions often act as antagonists. Thus, the excitation of the sympathetic division leads to an acceleration of heart rate and inhibition of peristalsis (rhythmic contractions) of the intestines. Parasympathetic activation has effects that are the very opposite: cardiac deceleration and stimulation of peristalsis. This same antagonism is seen in temperature regulation. The sympathetic division acts to counteract cold; it triggers vasoconstriction, shivering, and fur-ruffling. In contrast, the parasympathetic helps to cool the body when it is overheated; it stimulates panting, sweating, and vasodilatation (see Figure 2.2; see also Figure 2.11, p. 56). We'll have more to say about the tug-of-war between the two autonomic divisions when we discuss fear and rage. For now, we merely note that the autonomic nervous system is an important agent in directing the control of the internal environment.

SENSING THE INTERNAL ENVIRONMENT: THE HYPOTHALAMUS

The sympathetic and parasympathetic divisions control the various reflexive levers that help to maintain the internal environment. But what governs *them*? A crucial center is the hypothalamus (see Figure 2.3), which contains its own thermometer: receptor cells that respond to the temperature of the body fluids in which the brain is bathed. These thermoreceptors are hooked up to the reflex controls so as to yield negative feedback—a hypothalamic thermostat. If this is so, one should be able to fool the hypothalamus by changing its temperature independently of the temperature of the skin and body; a hot hypothalamus should then cause sweating, regardless of the actual body temperature. This is just what happens. When a cat's anterior hypothalamus is heated by a warm wire, there is panting and vasodilatation despite the fact that the cat's body temperature may be well below normal (Magoun et al., 1938). The effect is analogous to what happens when hot air is directed at a home thermostat. The furnace will shut itself off, even though the house is actually freezing.

Vasoconstriction and vasodilatation are involuntary reflexes, more in the domain of physiology than that of behavior. Does the hypothalamic feedback device have similar effects upon actions that reach out into the external world (for instance, wearing a fur coat)? Indeed it does. As one example, consider a study that utilized the fact that rats in a cold chamber will press a bar for a brief burst of heat (Weiss and Laties, 1961). The question was whether rats that had learned this skill in a cold environment would bar-press for heat if one cooled their brains rather than their bodies. The test was to run cold liquid through a very thin U-shaped tube implanted in the anterior hypothalamus (Satinoff, 1964). The rats turned on the heat lamp when their brains were cooled even though the outside temperature was reasonably neutral.

THIRST

What holds for temperature holds for most other homeostatic regulations as well. An example is the body's water supply. The organism continually loses water—primarily through the kidneys, but also through the respiratory system, the sweat glands, the digestive tract, and occasionally, by hemorrhage.

---

* The individual fibers of these muscles look smooth when observed under a microscope, in contrast to the fibers of the skeletal muscles, which look striped.

How does the system act to offset these losses? One set of reactions is entirely internal. Thus, a loss of water volume leads to a secretion of the so-called ***antidiuretic hormone (ADH)*** by the pituitary gland. ADH instructs the kidneys to reabsorb more of the water that passes through them. As a result, less water is passed out of the body in the urine.

But as with temperature regulation, internal readjustments can only restore the bodily balance up to a point. ADH can protect the body against further water loss, but it cannot bring back what was lost already. Eventually, the corrective measures must involve some behavior by which the organism reaches out into the external world so as to readjust its internal environment. This behavior is drinking—in humans, an average of two to three quarts of water per day.

How does the organism know that it lacks water? Most modern investigators believe that the stimuli that produce drinking are intimately tied up with the body's general fluid system. Some arise from within the veins that contain receptors which detect drops in blood pressure set off by lowered fluid volume (Stricker, 1973). Other receptors are located within the hypothalamus and respond to a chemical messenger produced by the kidneys which signals a decrease of the body's water level (Epstein, Fitzsimons, and Rolls, 1970). Still other cells in the brain respond to the salt concentration of the body fluids and initiate drinking whenever this concentration rises above some critical level.

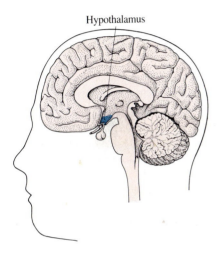

Hypothalamus

2.3 The hypothalamus *Cross-section of the human brain with the hypothalamus indicated in blue. (After Keeton, 1980)*

HUNGER

All animals have to eat and much of their lives revolve around food—searching for it, hunting it, ingesting it, and doing their best not to become food for others. There is no doubt that feeding, like drinking, is ultimately in the service of homeostasis, for no matter what food an animal eats or how he gets it, the ultimate biological consequence is always the same—to maintain appropriate nutrient supplies in the internal environment. But what are the actual mechanisms that determine whether humans and animals eat or stop eating? To put it another way, what is hunger and what is satiety?

The Signals for Feeding

There are numerous signals that control food intake. Among the most important of these are stimuli that arise from within the animal's own body and somehow inform the brain of the current state of the nutrient supplies. That some such messages are sent is certain. Without them, neither humans nor animals would be able to control their food intake, and they generally do. If food is freely available, they usually tend to eat just about the right amount to keep a roughly constant weight as adults. What is regulated is calorie intake rather than the total volume of food that is eaten. This was demonstrated in a study in which the experimenter varied the calorie level of the diet he fed to rats by adulterating their food with nonnutritive cellulose. The more diluted the food, the more of it was eaten, in a quantity roughly adequate to keep the total calorie content constant (Adolph, 1947).

RECEPTORS IN THE BRAIN

How does the animal manage to adjust its food intake to its calorie needs? From the start, investigators focused on ***glucose*** (or blood sugar), which is the major source of energy for bodily tissues. They believed that somewhere in the body are receptors that detect changes in the way this metabolic fuel is utilized.

Many authors believe that some of the relevant receptors are in the brain itself, most likely the hypothalamus. These ***glucoreceptors*** are thought to sense the amount of glucose that is available for metabolic use (Mayer, 1955). Evidence comes from studies in which the hypothalamus was injected with a chemical that made its cells unable to respond to glucose. The result was ravenous eating. This treatment presumably silenced the glucoreceptors whose failure to fire was then interpreted as a fuel deficiency, which led to feeding (Miselis and Epstein, 1970).

RECEPTORS IN THE STOMACH AND INTESTINES

Why does an animal stop eating? The receptors in the brain can't be the only reason. For they respond to fuel deficiency in the bloodstream, and this deficiency will not be corrected until after the meal has been at least partially digested. Yet, humans and animals will terminate a meal much before that. What tells them that it's time to stop?

Common sense suggests that feeding stops when the stomach is full. This is true enough, but it is only part of the story, for animals will stop eating even when their stomach is only partially full. This will only happen, however, if they have ingested a nutritious substance. If the stomach is filled with an equal volume of nonnutritive bulk, the animal will continue to eat. This suggests that the stomach walls contain receptors that are sensitive to the nutrients dissolved in the digestive juices. They signal the brain that nutrient supplies to the internal environment are on their way as food is about to enter the intestines. The result is satiety (Deutsch, Puerto, and Wang, 1978).

Further satiety signals come from the ***duodenum,*** the first part of the small intestine. When food passes out of the stomach into the intestines, the duodenum begins to release a hormone from its mucous lining. There is good evidence that this hormone—***cholecystokinin,*** or ***CCK***—sends "stop eating" messages to the brain (Gibbs and Smith, 1984). When CCK is injected into the abdominal cavity of hungry rats and dogs, they stop feeding; when it is administered to people, it produces a sense that they've had enough (Stacher, Bauer, and Steinringer, 1979).

SIGNALS FROM THE LIVER

Yet another source of information about the body's nutrient levels comes from the organ that acts as the manager of the body's food metabolism—the liver.

Immediately after a meal, glucose is plentiful. Since the body can't use it all, much of it is converted into other forms and put in storage. One such conversion goes on in the liver, where glucose is turned into ***glycogen*** (often called animal starch). Glycogen cannot be used up as a metabolic fuel. This is fine right after a meal, but eventually the stored energy has to be tapped. At that time, the chemical reaction goes the other way. Now the glycogen is turned into usable glucose.

Several recent studies suggest that the liver contains receptors that can sense in which direction the metabolic transaction goes, from glucose cash to glycogen deposits, or vice versa. If the balance tips toward glycogen manufacture, the receptors signal satiety and the animal stops eating. If the balance tips toward glucose production, the receptors signal hunger and the animal eats (Figure 2.4). The evidence that this happens in the liver comes from hungry dogs that were injected with glucose. If the injection was into the vein that goes directly to the liver, the dogs stopped eating. If the injection was anywhere else, there was no comparable effect (Russek, 1971; Friedman and Stricker, 1976).

SIGNALS FROM THE OUTSIDE

The self-regulation of food intake is remarkable, but it is not perfect. Humans and animals eat to maintain nutritive homeostasis; put another way, they eat be-

GLUCOSE ➡ GLYCOGEN

↓

LIVER RECEPTORS

↓

DON'T EAT!

GLUCOSE ⬅ GLYCOGEN

↓

LIVER RECEPTORS

↓

EAT!

2.4   The relation between the glucose-glycogen balance in the liver and eating

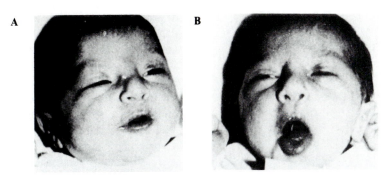

2.5   The response of newborn human babies to different tastes *Drops of different solutions were placed on the infants' lips and tongue to record their reaction to (A) a sweet taste (sugar solution) and (B) a bitter taste (quinine solution). (From Steiner, 1977; photographs courtesy of Jacob Steiner)*

cause they are hungry. But they sometimes eat because they like the taste of a particular food. We eat dessert even though we may be full; our hunger is gone, but not our appetite.

Such facts show that eating is not solely determined by stimuli that come from within the body. For these are supplemented by various external signals. We clearly do not eat for calories alone. Taste—and also smell and texture—is a powerful determinant of food intake for humans as well as animals. Some taste preferences are built into the nervous system. An example is the response to sweet and bitter tastes. When a human newborn's mouth is moistened with a sweet solution (say, sugar water), the infant's facial expression suggests pleasure; when the solution is bitter (say, quinine water), the newborn screws his face into a grimace and turns away (Steiner, 1974; see Figures 2.5A and B). This selectional bias makes good biological sense, for it leads to the best nutritional bet: In general, sweet substances have more nutritional value than others. In contrast, bitter tastes are found in many poisonous plants. Occasionally, the nutritional bet is lost: Saccharin is sweet and is generally preferred to less sweet substances, but it contains no calories whatsoever.

But palatability is not the only external signal for eating. Other signals are determined through learning. The expected mealtime is one example; the company of fellow eaters is another. A hen who has had her fill of grain will eagerly resume her meal if joined by other hens who are still hungry (Bayer, 1929).

Hypothalamic Control Centers

We have seen that there are many different signals for food intake. It was natural to suppose that these various messages are all integrated at one point in the nervous system where a final decision is made to eat or not to eat. The natural candidate for such a "feeding center" was the hypothalamus, which was already known to house controls for temperature regulation and water balance and which gave evidence of containing glucoreceptors. Psychophysiologists soon devised a theory of hypothalamic control of feeding that was analogous to the temperature system. It postulates two antagonistic centers, one corresponding to hunger, the other to satiety.

DUAL-CENTER THEORY

According to dual-center theory, the hypothalamus contains an "on" and an "off" command post for eating. Two anatomical regions are implicated. One is located in the *lateral region* of the hypothalamus; it was said to function as a "hunger center" whose activation leads to food search and eating. The other is the *ventromedial region* which was thought to be a "satiety center" whose stimulation stops eating.

To buttress their claims about the functions of these regions, dual-center theorists pointed to the effects of lesions. Rats whose lateral hypothalamus has been

A

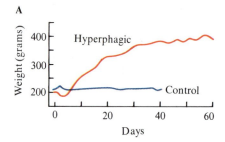

B

2.6 Hyperphagia (A) Curve showing the weight gain of hyperphagic rats after an operation creating a hypothalamic lesion. The weight eventually stabilizes at a new level. (After Teitelbaum, 1955) (B) Photograph of a rat several months after the operation. This rat weighed over 1,000 grams. (Courtesy Neal E. Miller, Rockefeller University)

destroyed suffer from ***aphagia*** (Greek, "no eating"). They refuse to eat and drink and will starve to death unless forcibly tube-fed for weeks (Teitelbaum and Stellar, 1954). Interestingly enough, eventually there is some recovery of function. After a few weeks the animals begin to eat again, especially if tempted by such delectables as eggnog (Teitelbaum and Epstein, 1962).

The reverse occurs after lesions to the ventromedial region. Animals with such lesions suffer from ***hyperphagia*** (Greek, "excess eating"). They eat voraciously and keep on eating. If the lesion is large enough, they may become veritable mountains of rat obesity, finally reaching weights that are some three times as great as their preoperative levels (see Figure 2.6). Tumors in this hypothalamic region (although very rare) have the same effects on humans (Miller, Bailey, and Stevenson, 1950; Teitelbaum, 1955, 1961).

While ventromedial lesions lead to rapid weight gain, this levels off in a month or two, after which the animal's weight remains stable at a new (and of course much greater) level. Once this new weight is reached, the animal eats enough to maintain it but no more (Hoebel and Teitelbaum, 1976). This suggests that the lesion produced an upward shift in the ***setpoint*** for weight regulation—the point that defines a kind of target value that determines food intake.

Details aside, dual-center theorists regard the two hypothalamic regions as mutually inhibitory centers, of which one serves as an on-switch for eating, the other as an off-switch. These switches are in turn activated by a number of internal and external signals. All of these signals act upon the feeding centers—some to trigger eating, others to inhibit it. Whether the organism eats will then depend on the summed value of them all: the level of various available nutrients in the bloodstream, satiety signals from the stomach, food palatability, learned factors, and so on (Stellar, 1954).

DUAL CENTERS RECONSIDERED

The dual-center theory of feeding has held center stage for several decades. But it has been seriously questioned in recent years. The main grounds concern the effects of hypothalamic lesions. Some critics believe that some of the effects of these lesions are not directly on behavior, but rather on food metabolism (Stricker and Zigmond, 1976).

An example of this approach is a reanalysis of the effects of ventromedial lesions. According to the dual-center view, rats with such lesions overeat because of damage to some off-switch for feeding. But an alternative interpretation lays the blame on a disruption of fat metabolism.

Under normal conditions, animals store some of their unused nutrients in the form of fats. This tendency to save for later use can sometimes go too far, however. One effect of ventromedial lesions is that they produce an overreaction of certain branches of the parasympathetic system. This in turn increases the proportion of usable nutrients, especially glucose, that are turned into fat and cached away as adipose tissue. The trouble is that so much is stored that not enough is left over to serve as metabolic fuel. As a result, the animal stays hungry; it has to eat more to get the fuel that it needs. But since most of what it eats is turned into fat and stored away, the process continues and the animal has to keep on eating. It is in the position of a rich miser who has buried all of his possessions and has therefore no money to live on.

Evidence in favor of this general approach comes from studies which show that animals with ventromedial lesions get fatter than normal animals even when both groups are fed the identical amount. Whether such results are a decisive disproof of the dual-center theory is still a matter of debate (Friedman and Stricker, 1976).

The transmission of food preferences
People (and, of course, other animals) differ in their food preferences. Some preferences are essentially built-in: gazelles eat grass, lions eat gazelles. But many other food preferences are acquired through learning, in humans by cultural transmission. (Photograph by Suzanne Szasz)

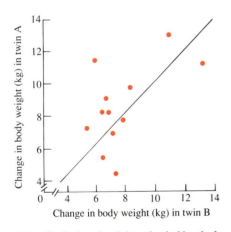

2.7 Similarity of weight gains in identical twins Weight gains for twelve pairs of identical twins after 100 days of the same degree of overfeeding. Each point represents one twin pair, with the weight gain of twin A plotted on the vertical axis and the weight gain of twin B plotted on the horizontal axis. Weight gains are plotted in kilograms (1 kg = 2.2 lbs). The closer the points are to the diagonal line, the more similar the weight gains of the twins are to each other. (After Bouchard et al., 1990)

Obesity

Both homeostatic and nonhomeostatic determinants of food intake are relevant to a problem partially created by the affluence of modern society which prior eras would have suffered only too gladly: obesity. Obesity is sometimes defined as a body weight that exceeds the average for a given height by 20 percent. Judged by this criterion, about one-third of all Americans are obese. Most of them would rather be slim, and their wistful desires offer a ready market for a vast number of diet foods and fads. In part, the reason is health (at least it is sometimes said to be). But more important are social standards of physical attractiveness. There are no corpulent matinee idols, no fat sex goddesses (Stunkard, 1975).

Most authorities agree that there are several reasons why people become fat. In some cases, the cause is a bodily condition. In others, it is a matter of eating too much.

BODILY FACTORS IN OBESITY

Most of us take it for granted that body weight is a simple function of calorie intake and energy expenditure. To some extent this is undoubtedly true, but it is not the whole story. For there is good evidence that a number of constitutional factors can predispose one person to get fat, even if she eats no more (and exercises no less) than her next-door neighbor.

Metabolic efficiency One reason may be a more proficient digestive apparatus; the person who manages to digest a larger proportion of the food she ingests will necessarily put on more weight than her digestively less efficient fellows. Another reason may be a different metabolic level; the less nutrient fuel is burnt up, the more is left for fatty storage. These constitutional differences may help to explain why some people gain weight much more readily than others (Sims, 1986).

Some recent studies suggest that such constitutional differences in metabolic efficiency depend partially on genetic makeup. One was a study on the effects of overeating on twelve pairs of identical male twins. Each of these men was overfed by about 1,000 excess calories per day above the amount required to maintain his initial weight. The activities of each subject were kept as constant as possible, and there was very little exercise. This regimen continued for a period of 100 days. Needless to say, all twenty-four men gained weight, but the amount they gained varied substantially: from about ten to thirty pounds. A further difference concerned the parts of the body where the newly gained weight was deposited. For some subjects, it was the abdomen; for others, it was the thighs and buttocks. The important finding was that the amount each person gained was very similar to the weight gain of his twin (see Figure 2.7). Similarly for the location on the body where the weight was gained. If one gained in the abdomen, so did his twin; if another deposited the fat in his thighs and buttocks, his twin did too. These findings are a strong indication that people differ in the efficiency with which their bodily machinery handles excess calories, and that this metabolic pattern is probably inherited (Bouchard et al., 1990).

Fat cells in the body Another bodily factor concerns the fat cells in the body. In obese people, their number is some three times larger than in normal people (Hirsch and Knittle, 1970). To the obese person, these cells are an adipose albatross that cannot be removed. If a fat person diets, the fat cells will shrink in size, but their total number will remain unchanged. Some investigators suspect that the brain receives some signals that urge further eating until the shrunken fat cells are again refilled. If this is so, the once-fat can never truly escape their obese past. They may rigorously diet until they become as lean as a friend who was never fat, but their urge to eat will always be greater.

Some authors believe that the number of fat cells in the body is fixed sometime in early life, and is partly determined by genetic constitution and partly by feeding patterns in early childhood (Knittle and Hirsch, 1968). Others feel that additional fat cells can be added in adolescence and adulthood. If this is so, it is yet another argument against repeated bouts of dieting followed by gradual regaining of the lost weight, for every weight gain generates additional fat cells that can never be lost (Sjöström, 1980).

BEHAVIORAL FACTORS

In some persons, obesity is evidently produced by a bodily condition. But for many others, the cause lies in behavior: They simply eat too much. The question is why. It is virtually certain that there is no one answer, for chronic overeating has not one cause but many.

The externality hypothesis Some years ago, a number of investigators subscribed to the **externality hypothesis,** which held that obese people are comparatively unresponsive to their own internal hunger state but are much more susceptible to signals from without (Schachter and Rodin, 1974). One line of evidence came from studies in which people were asked how hungry they are. In normal subjects, the response depended on the time since their last meal. But in obese people, there was no such correlation between the subjective experience of hunger and the deprivation interval. Further evidence came from experiments that seemed to show that obese subjects are rather finicky when it comes to food. If offered a fine grade of vanilla ice cream, they eat more than normal subjects. But if offered vanilla ice cream that has been adulterated with bitter-tasting quinine, they eat *less* of this mixture than do normal subjects (Nisbett, 1968; see Figure 2.8).

According to some advocates of the externality hypothesis, this discrepancy in the sensitivity to external and internal cues for eating might be a contributing cause of obesity. Since he is presumably rather insensitive to his internal body state, the obese person will eat even though his body needs no further calories as long as there are enough external cues that prompt him on. And in food-rich twentieth-century America, such cues are certainly plentiful (Schachter, 1971).

The restrained-eating hypothesis More recent studies have thrown doubt on the externality hypothesis. To begin with, the evidence for the greater sensitivity of obese persons to external cues turns out to be rather inconsistent. But to the extent that this oversensitivity does exist, its explanation may be quite different from what it was originally; it may be an *effect* of the obesity rather than its cause (Nisbett, 1972; Rodin, 1980, 1981).

In our society many people who are overweight consciously try to restrain their eating. After all, obesity is a social liability, so they make resolutions, go on diets, buy low-calorie foods, and do what they can to clamp a lid on their intense desire to eat. But the clamp is hard to maintain, for any external stimulus for eating will threaten the dieter's resolve. In effect, there is "disinhibition" of eating restraint (Herman and Polivy, 1980).

An interesting demonstration of the disinhibition of eating is provided by a study of "restrained" and "unrestrained" eaters. Persons judged as restrained said they were on a diet or expressed concerns about their weight. The subjects participated in what was described as an experiment on the perception of tastes. Initially, some subjects had to taste (and consume) one or two 8 oz. milk shakes,

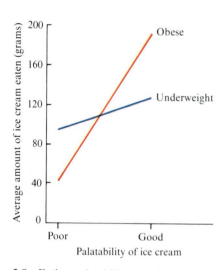

2.8   Eating, palatability, and obesity
In the experiment, obese and underweight subjects were given the opportunity to eat ice cream. If the ice cream tasted good, the obese subjects ate more than the underweight ones. The reverse was true if the ice cream did not taste good. (After Nisbett, 1968)

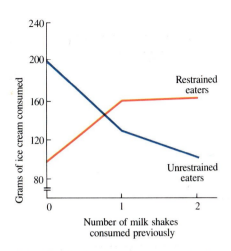

2.9   The diet-busting effect in restrained eaters   *In the experiment, restrained (red) and unrestrained eaters (blue) were asked to consume 0, 1, or 2 milk shakes in what they thought was an experiment on taste perception. They were later asked to judge the taste of ice cream and allowed to sample as much of it as they wished. The figure shows that restrained eaters ate considerably more ice cream if they had previously consumed one or more milk shakes previously. (After Herman and Mack, 1975)*

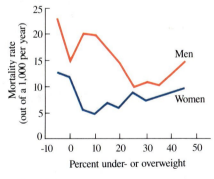

2.10   Relation of obesity to mortality   *The figure presents the mortality rate in a sample of 5,209 persons in Massachusetts for men and women from 45 to 74 years old between 1948 and 1964. The percent overweight is calculated by reference to mean weights for a given height. The figure shows that overweight does not increase the overall mortality risk, at least not for overweight percentages that are less than 50. (From Andres, 1980)*

while control subjects tasted none. After this, the subjects were asked to judge the taste of ice cream. While performing this task, they were left alone with an unlimited supply of ice cream. How much would they eat? Unrestrained eaters ate a sensible, homeostatically appropriate amount: The more milk shakes they previously had consumed, the less ice cream they ate in the subsequent test. But the exact opposite was true of the restrained eaters. The more milk shakes they previously consumed the more ice cream they ate now. The prior exposure disinhibited their restraint and led to a motivational collapse—a phenomenon all too familiar to would-be dieters which some investigators have dubbed the "what the hell" diet-busting effect (Herman and Mack, 1975; see Figure 2.9).

The setpoint hypothesis   The restrained-eating hypothesis tries to explain some of the effects of obesity. But it has little to say about its cause. One possibility is that people differ in their setpoints for weight. If so, then many a person who is fat by the standards of official what-your-weight-should-be tables may weigh just the right amount considering his own particular setpoint. If he starves himself, he'll drop to a weight level below that level. But in the long run he probably won't stay there, for there'll always be a tendency to go back to the setpoint weight (Nisbett, 1972). Some authors point out that the tendency to maintain a given body weight affects energy expenditure as well as caloric intake. Thus when obese persons starve themselves, they don't lose anywhere as much weight as they should on the assumption (known to all dieters) that 3,500 calories equals one pound. The reason is that their body compensates for the calorie loss by a drastic reduction in metabolism (Keesey and Powley, 1986).

THE TREATMENT OF OBESITY

What can be done to help people who are overweight? Everyone knows that it's relatively easy to lose weight over the short run; the problem is to keep it off for good. Can it be done? Some authors are optimists and believe that obesity is a behavioral problem that can be remedied by retraining people to develop self-control and acquire appropriate habits of diet and exercise. Other authorities are more pessimistic, for they believe that weight depends largely on a person's setpoint, which he can't escape from in the long run. Attempts at treatment include psychoanalysis, various forms of behavior therapy (techniques for modifying the individual's behavior by the systematic use of certain principles of learning; see Chapters 3 and 18), and self-help groups (for example, Weight Watchers International). There is considerable dispute over the extent to which any of these methods leads to long-term changes although there is some suggestion that the self-help groups do a fairly good job, especially for those who are only mildly overweight (Booth, 1980; Stuart and Mitchell, 1980; Stunkard, 1980; Wilson, 1980).

At this point it is difficult to decide whether the optimists have a better case than the pessimists. Thus far, the outcomes of the various procedures have not been studied systematically enough. For all we know, more effective treatment methods may be developed in the future. But suppose the pessimists turn out to be correct—suppose that there is a setpoint which decrees that weight is fate. If so, can we offer any hope to those who are overweight?

To begin with, one may question the widely held belief that being overweight is necessarily a disorder. It is often asserted that being overweight is a health hazard, and that over one-third of the U.S. population are too heavy (U.S. Public Health Service, 1966). But apart from cases of gross obesity, the relation between overweight and life expectancy is still a matter of debate (Fitzgerald, 1981; see Figure 2.10). Some authors argue that for the great majority of individuals, obesity is a social and aesthetic problem, rather than a problem of physical health. (This is especially so for women, who are much more likely to regard themselves as over-weight than are men; Gray, 1977; Fallon and Rozin, 1985). Seen in this light, being slender is a social ideal, but we should not forget that it is an ideal of *our* society. Other cultures set different standards. The women painted by Rubens, Matisse, and Renoir were considered beautiful by their contemporaries; today they would be considered overweight. But does it really make sense to aspire to the body form of a fashion model if it is not one's own and perhaps can't be?

Many people who regard themselves as overweight try to become lithe and slender but often fail anyway. Perhaps the best advice to them is to accept themselves as they are.

Anorexia and Bulimia

In some cases, the concern about being thin may be so extreme that it leads to certain eating disorders whose health hazards are much more serious than those produced by being somewhat overweight. One such condition is **anorexia nervosa,** which afflicts about 1 in 200 young women of the middle and upper classes in our society. Where the obese person is too fat and almost always eats too much, the anorexic is too thin (often dangerously so) and eats much too little. There are some cases of anorexia (literally "lack of appetite") that are caused by various organic conditions; for example, in cancer patients undergoing chemotherapy which produces nausea and various food aversions. In contrast, anorexia nervosa is not produced by any known organic pathology but is at least in part brought on by psychological factors. Its defining feature is "the relentless pursuit of thinness through self-starvation, even unto death" (Bruch, 1973, p. 4).

Anorexics are intensely and continually preoccupied by the fear of becoming fat. They eat only low-calorie food, if they eat at all. In addition, they often engage in strenuous exercise, often for many hours each day. Of course, this regimen leads to extreme weight loss, sometimes reaching levels that are less than 50 percent of the statistical ideal. Further symptoms include the cessation of menstruation, hyperactivity, sleep disorders, and avoidance of sex. In perhaps 10 percent of the cases, the end result of this self-starvation is death. What leads to anorexia nervosa? Many investigators believe that it is produced by fears of being sexually unattractive, fears of sex, or rebellion against the parents. Others argue that the problem involves hormonal disturbances, as shown by the fact that anorexics have unusually low levels of reproductive and growth hormones. As yet, we don't know whether the hormonal imbalances are an effect rather than the cause of the psychological problems and the self-starvation diet. But it is very likely that the psychological factors—including the cultural obsession with slimness—are major contributors (Logue, 1986).

Another eating disorder is **bulimia,** which is characterized by repeated eating binges that are often followed by attempts to purge the calories just consumed by self-induced vomiting or laxatives. Unlike anorexics, bulimics are of roughly normal weight, but their repeated binge-and-purge bouts can lead to a variety of problems. To begin with, many bulimics suffer considerable depression after a binge. In addition, the repeated binges may produce disruptions of the electrolyte balance that may ultimately lead to cardiac, kidney, and urinary infections. Bulimia is fairly common among current college students (in one survey, it was found in 19 percent of the women and 5 percent of the men). The binge-and-purge cycle is a perfect expression of our contradictory attitudes toward food and eating. On the one hand, there are the easily available high-calorie foods that we are continually urged to buy ("Treat yourself to a _____ . You deserve it!"); on the other hand, we are constantly reminded that to be sexually attractive we must be thin (Logue, 1986).

A

B

C

Changing conceptions of the relation between body weight and attractiveness
An underlying cause of many eating disorders in Western women is their belief that being slender is beautiful. But is it? It depends. (A) The Venus of Willendorf, *a prehistoric statuette, unearthed near Willendorf, Austria, that was sculpted some 30,000 years ago. Some archeologists believe that it depicts a fertility goddess; others, that it represents the female erotic ideal of the ice age. (Courtesy Naturhistorisches Museum, Wien) (B)* The Three Graces, *painted by the Flemish master Peter Paul Rubens in 1639. (Courtesy Museo del Prado) (C) Paulina Porizkova, a model in the 1980s. (Photograph by M. Carrard/Gamma-Liaison)*

FEAR AND RAGE

Thus far, our emphasis has been on motives that are largely based on internal, homeostatic controls, in which there is a disruption of the internal environment and the organism performs some action that ultimately restores its internal balance. But there are a number of motives that do not fit this pattern. Sex is one example. While internal states such as hormone levels play an important role, the desire is essentially aroused (as it were, "turned on") by external stimuli of various kinds; homeostatic imbalances have nothing to do with it. We will discuss this in a later chapter that deals with motives that are primarily social (see Chapter 9). Here we will consider another example of a motive that is instigated from without rather than within: the reaction to intense threat, which results in attempts to escape or to fight back in self-defense and is often accompanied by the violent emotions of rage and fear.

Threat and the Autonomic Nervous System

What are some of the biological mechanisms that underlie these intense reactions? We'll begin our discussion by looking at the functions of the autonomic nervous system. We have previously seen how the interaction of sympathetic and parasympathetic excitations permits adjustments of the visceral machinery in the control of temperature. But the opposition between the two autonomic branches is more fundamental yet. According to the American physiologist Walter B. Cannon (1871–1945), they serve two broad and rather different functions. The ***parasympathetic system*** handles the *vegetative* functions of ordinary life: the conservation of bodily resources, reproduction, and the disposal of wastes. In effect, these reflect an organism's operations during times of peace—a lowered heart

Walter Cannon   (Courtesy National Library of Medicine)

2.11 The sympathetic and parasympathetic branches of the autonomic nervous system   *The parasympathetic system (shown in red) facilitates the vegetative functions of the organism: It slows the heart and lungs, stimulates digestive functions, permits sexual activity, and so on. In contrast, the sympathetic system (shown in blue) helps to place the organism on an emergency basis: It accelerates heart and lung actions, liberates nutrient fuels for muscular effort, and inhibits digestive and sexual functions.*

Note that the fibers of the sympathetic system are interconnected through a chain of ganglionic fibers outside of the spinal cord. As a result, sympathetic activation has a somewhat diffuse character; any sympathetic excitation tends to affect all of the viscera rather than just some. This is in contrast to the parasympathetic system whose action is more specific. (After Cannon, 1929)

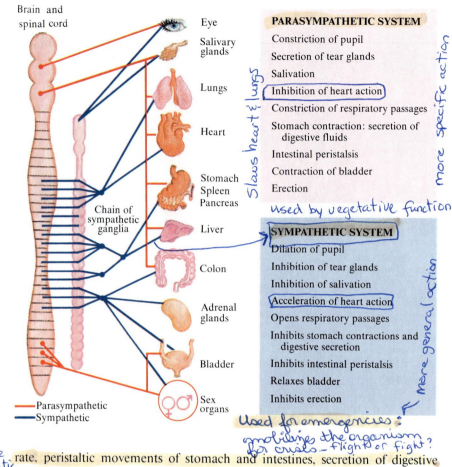

Brain and spinal cord

Eye
Salivary glands
Lungs
Heart
Stomach
Spleen
Pancreas
Liver
Colon
Adrenal glands
Bladder
Sex organs

Chain of sympathetic ganglia

— Parasympathetic
— Sympathetic

PARASYMPATHETIC SYSTEM
Constriction of pupil
Secretion of tear glands
Salivation
Inhibition of heart action
Constriction of respiratory passages
Stomach contraction: secretion of digestive fluids
Intestinal peristalsis
Contraction of bladder
Erection

SYMPATHETIC SYSTEM
Dilation of pupil
Inhibition of tear glands
Inhibition of salivation
Acceleration of heart action
Opens respiratory passages
Inhibits stomach contractions and digestive secretion
Inhibits intestinal peristalsis
Relaxes bladder
Inhibits erection

[handwritten margin notes: From within / Fear and rage / Motives → internal Homeost. → action = Restore Homeostic balance / Reestore / Control / From external environment / • Sex (aroused by ext. stym.) / • reaction to intense threat / escape / fight / Crisis → emergency reaction / autonomic response to fear (pulse rate, resp. etc.) / Slows heart & lungs / used by vegetative function / more specific action / More general action / Used for emergencies: mobilizes the organism for crisis — flight or fight?]

rate, peristaltic movements of stomach and intestines, secretion of digestive glands. In contrast, the **sympathetic system** has an *activating* function. It summons the body's resources and gets the organism ready for vigorous action (Cannon, 1929).

As an example of this opposition, consider the role of the two autonomic divisions in governing the delivery of nutrient fuels and oxygen as well as the removal of waste products to and from the musculature. Parasympathetic excitation slows down the heart rate and reduces blood pressure. Sympathetic excitation has the opposite effect and also inhibits digestion and sexual activity. In addition, it stimulates the inner core of the adrenal gland, the so-called **adrenal medulla,** to pour epinephrine (adrenaline) and norepinephrine into the bloodstream. These have essentially the same effects as sympathetic stimulation—they accelerate the heart rate, speed up metabolism, and so on. As a result, the sympathetic effects are amplified yet further (see Figure 2.11).

THE EMERGENCY REACTION

Cannon pointed out that intense sympathetic arousal has a special function. It serves as an **emergency reaction** that mobilizes the organism for a crisis—for flight or fight.

Consider a grazing zebra, placidly maintaining homeostasis by nibbling at the grass and vasodilatating in the hot African sun. Suddenly it sees a lion approaching rapidly. The vegetative functions must now take second place, for if the zebra does not escape it will have no internal environment left to regulate. The violent exertions of the skeletal musculature require the total support of the entire bodily machinery, and this support is provided by intense sympathetic activation. There is more nutrient fuel for the muscles which is now delivered more rapidly. At the same time, waste products are removed more quickly and all unessential organic

2.12   Sympathetic emergency reaction
A cat's terrified response to a frightening encounter. (Photograph by Walter Chandoha)

activities are brought to a halt. If the zebra does not escape, it is not because its sympathetic system did not try.

Cannon produced considerable evidence suggesting that a similar autonomic reaction occurs when the pattern is one of attack rather than of flight. A cat about to do battle with a dog shows accelerated heartbeat, piloerection (its hair standing on end—normally a heat-conserving device), and pupillary dilation—all signs of diffuse sympathetic arousal, signs that the body is girding itself for violent muscular effort (Figure 2.12).

Cannon emphasized the biological utility of the autonomic reaction, but his principle cannot tell us which choice the animal will make—whether it will choose fight or flight. This depends in part upon built-in predispositions, in part upon the specific situation. For example, a rat first tries to escape, but fights when finally cornered. Emergency situations may produce still different reactions from those we have already seen. Some animals become paralyzed by fright and stand immobile—an adaptive reaction since predators are more likely to detect a prey that is in motion. Other animals have even more exotic means of self-protection. Some species of fish pale when frightened, which makes them harder to spot against the sandy ocean bottom. This effect is produced by the direct action of epinephrine upon various pigmented substances in the animal's skin (Odiorne, 1957).

Bodily concomitants of intense emotion are of course found also in humans. In fear, our hearts pound, our palms sweat, and we sometimes shiver—all sympathetic activities. It is hardly surprising that such autonomic responses (for example, pulse rate, respiration, and the so-called galvanic skin response) are often used as indicators of emotional states. The *galvanic skin response (GSR)* is a particularly favored measure. It is a drop in the electrical resistance of the skin, particularly of the palm (related to, but not identical with, the activity of the sweat glands), that is a sensitive index of general arousal.

CENTRAL CONTROLS

The autonomic nervous system is by no means as autonomous as its name implies, rather it is largely guided by other neural centers. Some of these are among the oldest and most primitive portions of the cerebral cortex. These primitive cortical structures, together with parts of the hypothalamus and some surrounding regions, comprise the so-called *limbic system,* which is intimately involved in the control of the emotional reactions to situations that call for flight, defense, or attack (see Figure 2.13). Electrical stimulation of certain portions of the limbic

2.13   The limbic system   *The brain is pictured here as if the hemispheres were essentially transparent. One of the structures particularly relevant to emotional reactions is the amygdala, a walnut-sized structure that has been implicated in the production of aggressive behavior and fear reactions. (After Bloom, Lazerson, and Hofstadter, 1988)*

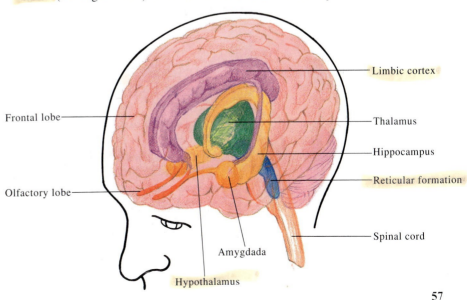

Limbic cortex

Thalamus

Hippocampus

Reticular formation

Spinal cord

Frontal lobe

Olfactory lobe

Amygdada

Hypothalamus

system transforms a purring cat into a spitting, hissing Halloween figure. Stimulation of the same region in humans often produces feelings of great anxiety or of rage, as in a patient who said that she suddenly wanted to tear things to pieces and to slap the experimenter's face (Magnus and Lammers, 1956; King, 1961; Flynn et al., 1970).

Psychologically there seem to be different kinds of attack, and they are evidently initiated by different control centers. In cats, the stimulation of one hypothalamic region produces predatory attack: quiet stalking followed by a quick, deadly pounce. The stimulation of another region leads to the Halloween pattern: a counterattack in self-defense (probably related to what in humans is called rage). When this rage pattern is triggered, the cat ignores a nearby mouse and will spring viciously at the experimenter, by whom it presumably feels attacked. (Egger and Flynn, 1963; Clemente and Chase, 1973). The lion who pounces on the zebra is probably not at all enraged but is merely engaged in the prosaic business of food gathering. (Whether the zebra is comforted by the fact that the lion is not angry at it is another question.)

Disruptive Effects of Autonomic Arousal

Our preceding discussion emphasized the biological value of the emergency system. But strong autonomic arousal can also be disruptive and even harmful to the organism. This negative side of the matter is especially clear in humans. In our day-to-day lives we rarely encounter emergencies that call for violent physical effort. But our biological nature has not changed just because our modern world contains no sabertooth tigers. We still have the same emergency system that served our primitive ancestors, and its bodily consequences may take serious tolls.

The disruptive effect of fear and anger upon digestion or upon sexual behavior is a matter of common knowledge. During periods of marked anxiety there are often complaints of constipation or other digestive ills. The same holds for impotence or frigidity. This is hardly surprising, since digestive functions and many aspects of sexual activity (for example, erection) are largely controlled by the parasympathetic system and are thus inhibited by intense sympathetic arousal. Moreover, the aftereffects of emotional arousal can sometimes be more permanent, causing profound and long-lasting bodily harm. Various disorders such as peptic ulcer, colitis, asthma, and hypertension can often be traced back to emotional patterns in the patient's life and are then considered psychophysiological disorders in which a psychological cause produces a bodily effect (see Chapter 17).

SLEEP AND WAKING

Thus far, our main concern has been with the *directive* function of motives. This direction can be primarily imposed from within, as in the case of the homeostatic motives such as thirst and hunger. It can also be initiated by stimulus conditions from the outside, as in fear and rage. Either way, the effects on behavior are readily described in terms of a negative feedback system. In the case of homeostatic motives, the organism acts so as to change the state of the internal environment; it eats or drinks until its water balance or nutrient levels are restored. In the case of rage and fear, it acts to change the conditions of the external environment that prompted the disturbance. The cat runs away to remove *itself* from a barking dog, or it hisses and scratches in a frantic attempt to remove the *dog*.

Motives have another function in addition to direction. They *arouse* the organism, which then becomes increasingly alert and vigorous. A given motive will thus act like both the tuner and the volume control of a radio. A thirsty animal seeks water rather than food or a sexual partner. And the thirstier it is, the more intensely it will pursue its goal. Psychologists have used various terms to describe this facet of motivation. Some call it **activation;** others prefer the term **drive.** They all agree that increased drive states generally lead to increased behavioral vigor. Thus, rats will run faster to water the longer they have been water-deprived.

We will now look at some of the biological mechanisms of activation as we consider its two extremes. One is a state of intense waking arousal, perhaps best typified by fear and rage. The other is sleep.

Waking

In a sense, we may consider the sympathetic branch of the autonomic nervous system as an arousal system for the more primitive physiological processes of the body. Similar arousal systems operate to alert the brain. They activate the cortex so that it is fully responsive to incoming messages. In effect, they awaken the brain.

One of the most important of these is the *reticular activating system* or **RAS.** This neurological system has its origin in the upper portion of the reticular formation, a network of interconnected cells that extends throughout the brain stem and has branches that ascend to much of the rest of the brain (Figure 2.14). Sleeping cats whose RAS is electrically stimulated will awaken; cats whose RAS is destroyed are somnolent for weeks (Lindsley, 1960). RAS activity not only leads to awakening but it also produces increasing levels of arousal once awake. Stimulation of the RAS in waking monkeys jolts them into an alert state of attention in which they look around expectantly.

What triggers the RAS? One factor is sensory stimulation. On the face of it, this is hardly surprising, for we all know that sleep comes more readily when it is quiet and dark. But the neurological chain of events that explains why intense stimuli lead to awakening is fairly complex. Oddly enough, the direct input from the sensory pathways to the cortex is not the primary cause of wakefulness. In one study, the investigators severed virtually all of the sensory tracts to the cortex in cats (Lindsley et al., 1950). When the cats were asleep the experimenters presented a loud tone and the cats woke up. But how could this be, if the path from ear to cortex was cut so that the cortex was isolated from any auditory input? The answer is that there is another, indirect pathway that leads through the RAS. All of the sensory pathways to the cortex send collateral side branches to the RAS. The information the RAS receives in this manner is very meager and unspecific; it amounts to no more than a statement that a sensory message is on its way up to the cortex without any further indication of what that message might be. But this is enough for the RAS which now functions as a general alarm. It arouses the cortex which can then interpret the specific signals sent over the direct sensory pathway. In effect, the RAS is like a four-year-old who has just been handed a telegram while his mother is asleep. The child cannot read but he awakens his mother who can.

Sensory stimulation is not the only source of RAS activation. Another comes from the cortex itself. There are descending fibers from the cortex that may excite the RAS which will then activate the cortex more fully. This circuit—cortex to RAS to cortex—probably plays an important role in many phenomena of sleep and waking. We sometimes have trouble in falling asleep because we "can't shut off our thoughts." Here cortical activity triggers the RAS which activates the cor-

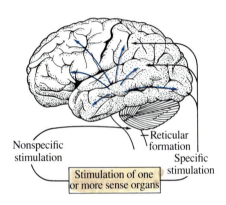

2.14 The reticular activating system
The figure indicates the location and function of the reticular structures in the hind- and midbrain. When a sense organ is stimulated, its message is relayed to a particular region of the cortex, typically a projection area. The sensory stimulation also triggers the reticular system which then arouses the cortex. As a result, the areas of the brain that receive the specific sensory message are sufficiently activated so that they can interpret it.
(After French, 1957)

Nonspecific stimulation

Reticular formation

Specific stimulation

Stimulation of one or more sense organs

tex which again excites the RAS and so on. The importance of cortical activation of the RAS is also shown by the fact that some stimuli are more likely to wake us than others, regardless of their intensity—a baby's cry, the smell of fire, the sound of one's own name.

Sleep

The primary focus of this chapter is on motivation, and thus on the direction and activation of behavior that motives bring about. In this context, sleep is of considerable interest because it seems to represent the very opposite of arousal. But it has a more direct relevance as well. The desire for sleep is one of the most powerful of motives; if kept awake long enough, the urge to sleep will eventually take precedence over most other motives (which is one of the reasons jailers sometimes use enforced sleeplessness to force confessions out of prisoners). What can we say about this state in which most of us spend a third of our lives?

SLEEP AND BRAIN ACTIVITY

Sleep cannot be observed from within, since it is by definition a condition of which the sleeper is unaware. We must perforce study it from without. One way of doing this is by observing what the brain does while its owner is asleep.

Eavesdropping on the brain of waking or sleeping subjects is made possible by the fact that the language of the nervous system is electrical. When electrodes are placed at various points on the skull, they pick up the electrical changes that are produced by the summed activity of the millions of nerve cells in the cerebral cortex that is just underneath. In absolute terms these changes are very small; they are therefore fed to a highly sensitive amplifier whose output in turn activates a series of pens. These pens trace their position on a long roll of paper that moves at a constant speed (see Figure 2.15). The resulting record is an *electroencephalogram,* or EEG, a picture of voltage changes over time occurring in the brain.

Figure 2.16 shows an EEG record. It begins with the subject in a relaxed state, with eyes closed, and "not thinking about anything in particular." The record shows *alpha waves,* a rather regular waxing and waning of electrical potential, at some eight to twelve cycles per second. This alpha rhythm is very characteristic of this state (awake but resting), and is found in most mammals. When the subject attends to some stimulus with open eyes, or when he is involved in active thought (for instance, mental arithmetic) with his eyes closed, the picture changes. Now the alpha rhythm is *blocked;* the voltage is lower, the frequency is much higher, and the pattern of ups and downs is nearly random.

THE STAGES OF SLEEP

Several decades of work involving continuous, all-night recordings of EEGs and other measures have shown that there are several stages of sleep and that these vary in depth. Just prior to sleep, there tends to be an accentuated alpha rhythm. As the subject becomes drowsy, the alpha comes and goes; there are increasingly long stretches during which the pattern is random. The subject is now in a light,

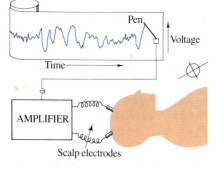

2.15 Schematic diagram of EEG recording *A number of scalp electrodes are placed on a subject's head. At any one time, there are small differences in the electrical potential (that is, the voltage) between any two of these electrodes. These differences are magnified by an amplifier and are then used to activate a recording pen. The greater the voltage difference, the larger the pen's deflection. Since the voltage fluctuates, the pen goes up and down, thus tracing a so-called brain wave on the moving paper. The number of such waves per second is the EEG frequency.*

2.16 Alpha waves and alpha blocking *(After Guyton, 1981)*

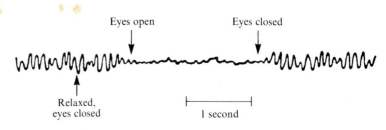

(Stage 1)   (Stage 2)   (Stage 3)   (Stage 4)   Dreaming

2.17 The stages of sleep *The figure shows EEG records taken from the frontal lobe of the brain, during waking, quiet sleep, and active sleep. (Courtesy of William C. Dement)*

dozing sleep, from which she is easily awakened (Stage 1 in Figure 2.17). Over the course of the next hour she drifts into deeper and deeper stages, in which the EEGs are characterized by the complete absence of alpha and by waves of increasingly higher voltage and much lower frequency (Stages 2 through 4 in Figure 2.17). In the last stages, the waves are very slow. They occur about once every second and are some five times greater in amplitude than those of the alpha rhythm. At this point the sleeper is virtually immobile and will take a few seconds to awaken, mumbling incoherently, even if shaken or shouted at. During the course of the night, the sleeper's descent repeats itself several times. She drops from dozing to deep, slow-wave sleep, reascends to Stage 1, drops back to slow-wave sleep, and so on for some four or five cycles.

The oscillations between different sleep stages are not merely changes in depth. When the sleeper reascends into Stage 1, he seems to enter a qualitatively different state entirely. This state is sometimes called ***active sleep*** to distinguish it from the ***quiet sleep*** found during the other stages. Active sleep is a paradoxical condition with contradictory aspects. In some ways it is as deep as sleep ever gets. The sleeper's general body musculature is more flaccid and he is less sensitive to external stimulation (Williams, Tepas, and Morlock, 1962). But judged by some other criteria, the level of arousal during active sleep is almost as high as during alert wakefulness. One sign is the EEG, which in humans is rather similar to that found in waking (Jouvet, 1967). Another is the appearance of dreams (of which more later), which are found in active rather than quiet sleep and during which we often feel as if we were active and thoroughly awake.

Of particular interest are the sleeper's eye movements which can be recorded by means of electrodes attached next to each eye. During quiet sleep, the eyes drift slowly and no longer move in tandem. But during active sleep a different pattern suddenly appears. The eyes move rapidly and in unison behind closed lids, as if the sleeper were looking at some object outside. These jerky, rapid eye movements (REMs) are one of the most striking features of active sleep, which is often called ***REM sleep.*** Young human adults enter this stage about four times each night (Figure 2.18).

Non-REM   REM

A

Eye movements

B

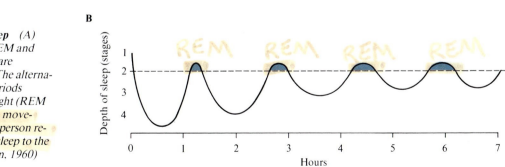

2.18 REM and non-REM sleep *(A) Eye movements during non-REM and REM sleep. The REM periods are associated with dreaming. (B) The alternation of non-REM and REM periods throughout the course of the night (REM periods are in color). Rapid eye movements and dreams begin as the person repeatedly emerges from deeper sleep to the level of Stage 1. (After Kleitman, 1960)*

REM sleep was discovered fairly recently, but its discoverers almost immediately related it to a phenomenon surely known to humans since prehistoric times: dreaming.

Dreaming and REM sleep   When sleeping subjects are awakened during REM sleep, they generally report a dream: a series of episodes that seemed real at the time. Not so for quiet (that is, non-REM) sleep. When awakened from quiet sleep, subjects may say that they were thinking about something, but they rarely relate the kind of inner drama we call a dream (Cartwright, 1977). Further evidence links the duration of the dream events to the length of the REM period. Subjects who are awakened five minutes after the onset of REM tend to describe shorter dreams than subjects awakened fifteen minutes after the REM period begins. This result argues against the popular notion that dreams are virtually instantaneous, no matter how long they take to relate when later recalled. In actual fact, the dream seems to take just about as long as the dream episode might have been in real life (Dement and Kleitman, 1957; Dement and Wolpert, 1958).

These findings suggest that the average adult dreams for about one and a half hours every night, the time spent in REM sleep. How can we square this statement with the fact that in everyday life many people seem to experience dreams only occasionally, and that some deny that they ever dream? The answer is that dreams are generally forgotten within minutes after they have occurred. In one study, subjects were awakened either during REM sleep or five minutes after a REM period had ended. In the first condition, detailed dream narratives were obtained on 85 percent of the narratives; in the second, there were none (Wolpert and Trosman, 1958).

Do dreams have a function?   The ancients believed that dreams have a prophetic function. In our own time, several theorists have argued that their function is related to the sleeper's personal problems. The most influential account was that of Sigmund Freud, who maintained that during dreams a whole host of primitive and forbidden impulses—mostly concerning sex and aggression—start to break through the barriers we erect against them while awake. The result is a compromise. The prohibited materials emerge, but only in a heavily masked and censored form. Freud believed that this explains why our dreams are so often strange and senseless. According to Freud, they are only odd on the outside. If we look beneath the surface, we can recognize the disguised meaning, the hidden, unacceptable wishes that are cleverly masked and lie underneath (Freud, 1900).

During the last thirty years, more and more evidence has come up that has thrown considerable doubt on Freud's dream theory (for details, see Chapter 10). Today, many authors believe that dreams don't have the complex functions that Freud (let alone the ancients) maintained. In their view, the dream is simply a reflection of the brain's aroused state during active sleep. During this period, the cerebral cortex is active, and its activity is manifested in conscious experience— the dream. But this dream experience necessarily has a special form. The cortex may be active, but it is largely shut off from sensory input. Under the circumstances, its activity is not constrained by the demands of external reality. Memory images become more prominent than they are in waking life, for they do not have to compete with the insistent here and now provided by the senses. The recent experiences of the day are evoked most readily, and they will then arouse a host of previous memories and intermingle with them. The cortex is sufficiently active to connect and interpret these raw materials so that we experience a running, inner narrative. But this is often accomplished in a primitive, disjointed way; perhaps the cortex is not active enough to provide more than a crude organization (Hobson, 1988).

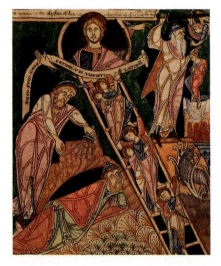

Jacob's Dream   *Dreams have often been regarded as a gateway between everyday reality and a more spiritual existence. An example is the biblical patriarch Jacob, who dreamed of angels descending and ascending a ladder between heaven and earth. (From the Lambeth Bible, England, twelfth century; courtesy of the Lambeth Palace Library)*

WHAT DIFFERENT MOTIVES HAVE IN COMMON

The preceding sections have dealt with a number of motives that impel to action—hunger, thirst, fear, and so on. Some such as hunger are in the service of homeostasis and serve to maintain the internal environment. Others such as fear and rage are triggered by stimuli in the environment and are relevant to self-preservation. Still others, such as the craving for drugs, are acquired and ultimately deleterious but are no less compelling for all that. For a few others—the main example is sleep—the function is still unknown. These various motives are clearly very different, as are the goals toward which they steer the organism—food, water, escape from threat, a dose of heroin, a good night's sleep. But despite the differences between them, is there something that all these motives and these goals have in common?

Level of Stimulation

A number of theorists have suggested that all—or at least most—motives can be described as a search for some *optimum level of arousal* or of general stimulation. One of the early controversies in the area was over the question of what this optimum level is.

According to the drive-reduction theory proposed by Clark L. Hull some fifty years ago, the optimum level of arousal that organisms seek is essentially zero. Hull and his students were impressed by the fact that many motives seem directed at the reduction of some internal state of bodily tension which if continued would lead to injury or even death. Examples are food deprivation, water deprivation, pain, and so on. Hull believed that this is true for all motives. In his view, all built-in rewards produce some reduction of bodily tension (or, as he called it, of drive). This position amounts to the assertion that what we normally call pleasure is at bottom nothing else but the reduction of pain or discomfort. According to this view, what organisms strive for is the absolute minimum of all arousal and stimulation, a biopsychological version of the Eastern search for *Nirvana* (Hull, 1943).

Seeking stimulation   People have invented many activities to experience the paradoxical joy of fear and danger. (A) Some of these activities induce excitement but are known to be safe in reality, such as riding on roller coasters. (B) Others are more dangerous but provide greater thrills, such as skydiving. (C) In yet other activities the fear and danger are experienced vicariously, as in watching horror movies. The figure shows a woman attacked by a shark in the 1975 film Jaws. *(Photographs by Georg Gerster, Comstock; Guy Sauvage, Agence Vandystadt/Photo Researchers; movie still courtesy of the Kobal Collection).*

A

B

C

2.19 Curiosity and manipulation Young rhesus monkeys trying to open a latch. The monkeys received no special reward for their labors but learned to open the devices just "for the fun of it." (After Harlow, 1950; photograph courtesy of University of Wisconsin Primate Laboratory)

Hull's drive-reduction theory suggests that, in general, organisms seek minimum levels of stimulation, preferring peace and quiet to states of tension and arousal. But, in fact, this does not seem to be true. For there is little doubt that some experiences are actively sought after. One example is the taste of sweets or erotic stimulation. These are both felt to be positive pleasures rather than the mere removal of some irritant. One example concerns saccharin, a sweet substance that has no nutritive value and thus no effect on the bodily tension and deficit that underlies hunger. But rats and other animals will nevertheless drink a saccharine solution avidly (Sheffield and Roby, 1950).

Such evidence suggests that drive reduction is not the only goal. Similar conclusions emerge from work on curiosity and manipulation. Monkeys will go through considerable lengths to puzzle out how to open latches that are attached to a wooden board (see Figure 2.19). But when the latches are unlocked, nothing opens, because the latches never closed anything in the first place. Since unlatching gets the animal nothing, the response was presumably its own reward. In this regard, monkeys acted much like human beings, who in countless ways indicate that they often do things as ends in themselves, rather than as means to other ends.

According to Hull's theory, organisms always seek to diminish their level of arousal. But as we have seen, the evidence says otherwise. To be sure, we do try to reduce arousal if our arousal level is unduly high, as in intense hunger or fear or pain. But in many other cases we apparently try to increase it. This suggests that there is an above-zero optimum level of arousal. If we are above this optimum (for example, in pain), we try to reduce arousal. But if we are below it, we seek stimulation to ascend beyond it. This optimum undoubtedly varies from time to time and from person to person. According to some authors, some people are "sensation seekers" who generally look for stimulation, while others prefer a quieter existence (Zuckerman, 1979; see Chapter 16).

Drugs and Addiction

The normal ways of coping with an arousal level that is too high or too low are by actively coping with the world outside. If we are overaroused, we move toward quiescence: we still our hunger, escape from pain, or go to sleep. If we are underaroused, we seek stimulation. In some cases, this may reach rather high-pitched levels—by prolonged sex play, by watching an effective horror movie, by riding on a roller coaster. But there is another way to create a drastic change of arousal. We can use drugs that artificially give us a "high" or a "low."

SOME DRUGS THAT CHANGE AROUSAL LEVEL

Our own interest concerns two major classes of drugs that have powerful psychological effects: those that act as behavioral *depressants* and those that act as *stimulants.*

Let's begin with the depressants. They include various sedatives (for example, barbiturates), alcohol, and the opiates (opium, heroin, and morphine).* Their general effect is to depress the activity of all the neurons in the central nervous system. On the face of it that may seem surprising since all of us have seen loud and aggressive drunks who seem anything but lethargic or depressed. The paradox is resolved if we recognize that their hyperexcitability is a case of disinhibition. At the first stage of inebriation (or at low doses of alcohol ingestion), the depression hits inhibitory synapses in the brain before it affects the excitatory ones. The usual constraints are relaxed, and the individual may engage in activities that he normally might not. But with further alcohol ingestion, the depressive effects will hit all of the cerebral centers. Now the excitement produced by disinhibition will give way to a general slowdown of activity. Attention and memory will blur, and bodily movement and speech will become increasingly uncoordinated, until finally the person will become completely incapacitated and lose consciousness.

The behavioral stimulants, which include amphetamine and cocaine, boost behavioral activity and can lead to an intense elevation of mood—a euphoric "rush" or "high" accompanied by feelings of enormous energy and increased self-esteem. This is especially so for cocaine, which some turn-of-the-century physicians (including Sigmund Freud) regarded as a miracle drug that produced boundless energy, exhilaration, and euphoria with no untoward side effects. This is unfortunately far from true, for the initial euphoria is bought at a considerable cost, for as we now know, amphetamines and cocaine often produce addictions that eventually become the user's primary focus in life. In addition, repeated use of cocaine (and amphetamines) can lead to extremely irrational states that resemble certain kinds of schizophrenia, in which there are delusions of persecution, irrational fears, and hallucinations (Siegel, 1984).

TOLERANCE AND WITHDRAWAL

In many individuals, repeated drug use leads to *addiction.* One result is an increased *tolerance* for the drug, especially for the opiates, so that the addict requires ever-larger doses to obtain the same effect.

A second consequence of addiction goes hand in hand with increased tolerance. When the drug is withheld, there are *withdrawal symptoms.* In general, these are the precise opposite of the effects produced by the drug itself. Thus heroin users deprived of their drug feel hyperexcitable; they are extremely irritable, are restless and anxious, and suffer from insomnia. Similarly for the behavioral stimulants. The cocaine or amphetamine user's manic energy and elation give rise to severe emotional depression coupled with profound fatigue when the drug is withdrawn (Julien, 1985; Volpicelli, 1989).

By its very nature, addiction tends to be self-perpetuating. To begin with, the addict wants to regain the intense pleasure of his drug-induced euphoria (which will become harder and harder because of his increased tolerance). Even more important, perhaps, is the fact that the addict (especially the opiate addict) wants

---

* Strictly speaking, the opiates belong to a separate class. For unlike alcohol and other sedatives, they serve as narcotics (that is, pain relievers) and act on separate opiate receptors. In addition, one of their number—heroin—seems to be able to produce an unusually intense euphoric "rush," sometimes likened to intense sexual excitement, when taken intravenously.

65

to escape the pangs of drug withdrawal. To dull those pains, he has to take another dose of the drug. And so on.

Further factors that underlie addiction are various social and psychological problems—in the family, at the workplace, or whatever (Alexander and Hadaway, 1982). Such problems often existed before the drug use began. But they can only be worsened by the addiction, and another dose or another drink is a way of escaping them for a while (and making them even more serious in the long run).

The Opponent-Process Theory of Motivation

What accounts for the phenomena of drug use and drug addiction? Some suggestions come from the ***opponent-process theory,*** which offers a broad outline of how many motives are acquired.* Opponent-process theory emphasizes the fundamental opposition of the various emotional feelings associated with pain and pleasure (such as fear and terror on the one hand, and joy and euphoria on the other). Its basic premise is that the nervous system has a general tendency to counteract any deviation from normalcy. If there is too much of a swing to one pole of the pain-pleasure dimension, say toward joy and ecstasy, an opponent process is called into play that tilts the balance toward the negative side. Conversely, if the initial swing is toward terror or revulsion, there will be an opponent process toward the positive side. The net effect is that there will be an attenuation of the emotional state one happens to be in, so that ecstasy becomes mild pleasure and terror loses some of its force. A further assumption of this theory is that repetitions of the initial emotional state will produce an increase in the power of the opponent process that is its antagonist (Solomon and Corbit, 1974; Solomon, 1980).

Opponent-process theory tries to account for some of the phenomena of drug addiction we have just discussed. Consider tolerance and withdrawal effects. According to the theory, the emotional reaction produced by a behavioral stimulant such as amphetamine produces an opponent process that pulls in the opposite direction. The more often the drug is taken, the stronger this opponent process becomes. The result is increased tolerance so that ever larger doses of the drug are required to produce an emotional high. The effect of the opponent process is revealed more starkly when the drug is withheld and there is no further pull toward the positive side of the emotional spectrum. Now all that remains is the opponent process whose strength has increased with every dose. This pulls the reaction in the opposite direction, resulting in the anguish of withdrawal (Solomon, 1980).

Some critics point to a problem with this interpretation. It essentially explains addiction as a way of escaping from the withdrawal symptoms. But in so doing it ignores how the addiction began in the first place. What made the addict start to take heroin in the first place, and take it frequently enough and at large enough doses to lead to tolerance and withdrawal? In addition, the critics deny that the withdrawal distress—while certainly unpleasant—is really as unbearable as it is sometimes said to be. According to this view, the drug must continue to produce some positive pleasure, rather than just the alleviation of withdrawal pain (Wise and Bozarth, 1987).

Self-stimulation

Thus far, we have discussed what the various motives that humans and animals strive to satisfy have in common psychologically. Another approach to this issue

Self-stimulation in rats *The rat feels the stimulation of a pulse lasting less than a second. (Courtesy of Dr. M. E. Olds)*

* The term *opponent process* was originally used in the field of color vision where it designates neural processes that pull in opposite directions (see Chapter 4, pp. 135–37).

has been through studies of the brain processes that come into play when an organism is rewarded. A number of investigators have asked whether there is a special region of the brain whose activation gives rise to what humans call "pleasure," a so-called "pleasure center" that is triggered whenever a motive is satisfied, regardless of which motive it is. They have tried to answer this question by studying the rewarding effects of electrical stimulation of various regions in the brain.

This general area of investigation was opened up in 1954 when James Olds and Peter Milner discovered that rats would learn to press a lever to give themselves a brief burst of electrical stimulation in certain regions of the limbic system (Olds and Milner, 1954). Similar rewarding effects of self-stimulation have been demonstrated in a wide variety of animals, including cats, dogs, dolphins, monkeys, and human beings. To obtain it, rats will press a lever at rates up to 7,000 presses per hour for hours on end. When forced to opt between food and self-stimulation, hungry rats will typically opt for self-stimulation, even though it literally brings starvation (Spies, 1965).

The pleasure center hypothesis runs into a number of problems, however (Gallistel, 1983). One is the fact that the same rats who initially responded with such wild frenzy will ignore the lever altogether when put back in the experimental chamber after an interval of an hour or less. But they will resume their wild pressing if first given a few free brief electric pulses. It seems as if something in the brain has to be "primed" in order to reinstate the desire for the brain stimulation (see Figure 2.20). It appears that self-stimulation has several functions. It serves as a reward. But it also starts a positive feedback cycle in which every stimulation strengthens the tendency to get yet another stimulation, and so on. These two functions apparently have two different physiological underpinnings. (For discussion, see Deutsch, 1960; Gallistel, 1973, 1983; Stellar and Stellar, 1985).

In this regard, the effect of self-stimulation may be similar to the effect of many natural rewards. When we start to eat, the first taste increases our desire for more food rather than decreasing it. In sexual behavior, this effect is even more striking. Each stimulation heightens the desire for further stimulation as sexual passion mounts to a higher and higher pitch. Of course, the positive feedback system is shut off eventually; feeding is finally stopped by satiety signals from the stomach and elsewhere, and sexual passion subsides with orgasm. The priming effect may well be just another instance of this general phenomenon. The difference is that the poor (or perhaps enviable) rat with a self-stimulating electrode in its head has no shut-off mechanism. There is no satiety signal and no orgasm, and so the rat keeps on self-stimulating and self-stimulating until the experimenter finally tears it away from the lever or it falls to the ground in sheer exhaustion.

The Nature of Motives

To sum up, during the past fifty years, there has been enormous progress in our understanding of the psychology and physiology of the biological motives. But as yet, there is no agreement on one mechanism that explains their action. It may be that such a unitary mechanism doesn't really exist (although advocates of a general pleasure center would probably disagree). Like all scientists, psychologists are much happier when they get neat explanations, and one underlying mechanism would be so much neater than many different ones. But nature did not design organisms to make psychologists happy. And it may well have provided multiple mechanisms rather than just one.

A final point: This chapter was concerned with a number of built-in motives—the biological goals we must seek in order to survive. But whenever we looked at a motive in detail (as in the case of human food selection), we saw that the specific

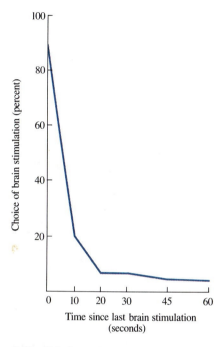

2.20 Priming and rewarding brain stimulation *Very thirsty rats were given a choice between two arms of a maze: one led to brain stimulation, the other to water. This choice was made either immediately after a burst of brain stimulation or from 10 to 60 seconds after stimulation. The figure shows that the animals were much more likely to ignore their thirst and choose brain stimulation if they had been primed with such stimulation shortly before the choice. (Data from Deutsch, Adams, and Metzner, 1964)*

nature of these goals depends not only on our biology but also on what we have learned and have been taught. Just what we drink is not only a matter of our water balance: except for Count Dracula, few of us drink blood. By the same token, we have to maintain certain nutrient levels, but this doesn't mean that we'd be satisfied with a diet of grasshoppers. Similar concerns apply to what we fear and hate, or how we behave in sexual matters and when, where, and with whom. In all these cases, experience builds upon biology and gives form to the built-in basics with which we start. We learn—from the experience of our own lifetime, and through culture, from the lifetime of hundreds of prior generations.

Evolution gave us a set of built-in, biological goals and a few built-in mechanisms for attaining them. Learning provides the way to modify these goals and to find ever more complex means to achieve them. We turn next to the mechanisms by which such learning occurs in humans and animals.

SUMMARY

1. Most human and animal actions are motivated. *Motives* have a two-fold function: They *direct* behavior toward or away from some goal. They also serve to *activate* the organism, which becomes more aroused the greater the strength of the motive.

2. The biological basis of directed action is *negative feedback* in which the system "feeds back" upon itself to stop its own action. Built-in negative feedback is responsible for many reactions that maintain the stability of the organism's internal environment or *homeostasis*. Special cells in the hypothalamus sense various aspects of the body's internal state. An example is temperature. If this is above or below certain *setpoints*, a number of self-regulatory reflexes controlled by the sympathetic and parasympathetic divisions of the autonomic nervous system are triggered (for example, shivering). In addition, directed, voluntary acts (such as putting on a sweater) are brought into play.

3. Similar homeostatic mechanisms underlie a number of other biological motives. An example is *thirst*. Water losses are partially offset by reflex mechanisms, including the secretion of the *antidiuretic hormone* (ADH), which instructs the kidneys to reabsorb more of the water that passes through them. In addition, the organism readjusts its own internal environment by directed action—drinking.

4. The biological motive that has been studied most extensively is *hunger*. Many of the signals for feeding and satiety come from the internal environment. Feeding signals include nutrient levels in the bloodstream (which probably affect *glucoreceptors* in the brain) and metabolic processes in the liver (especially the *glucose-glycogen* balance). Satiety signals include messages from receptors in the stomach and the small intestine (particularly a satiety hormone, *cholecystokinin*, or *CCK*). Other feeding and satiety signals are external, including the *palatability* of the food.

5. Many authors believe that the control of feeding is lodged in two antagonistic centers in the hypothalamus whose excitation gives rise to hunger and satiety respectively. As evidence, they point to the effect of lesions. Destruction of the supposed hunger center leads to *aphagia*, a complete refusal to eat. Destruction of the supposed satiety center produces *hyperphagia*, a vast increase in food intake.

6. A feeding-related disorder is *obesity*. Some cases are produced by various constitutional factors, including genetically based metabolic efficiency and an overabundance of fat cells. Others are the result of various behavioral factors. According to the *externality hypothesis*, overweight people are comparatively insensitive to internal hunger signals and oversensitive to external ones such as palatability. An alternative is the *setpoint hypothesis*, which asserts that overweight people have a higher internal setpoint for weight.

7. Other eating disorders are *anorexia nervosa* in which there is a pattern of relentless self-starvation, sometimes to the point of death, and *bulimia*, which is characterized by repeated binge-and-purge bouts.

8. In contrast to thirst and hunger, which are largely based on homeostatic factors from within, a number of motives are instigated from without. An example is the intense reaction to external threat. Its biological mechanisms include the operations of the *autonomic nervous system.* This consists of two antagonistic branches. One is the *parasympathetic nervous system,* which serves the vegetative functions of everyday life, such as digestion and reproduction. It slows down the heart rate and reduces blood pressure. The other is the *sympathetic nervous system,* which activates the body and mobilizes its resources. It increases the available metabolic fuels and accelerates their utilization by increasing the heart rate and respiration. Intense sympathetic activity can be regarded as an *emergency reaction,* which underlies the overt reactions of *fight* or *flight* and their usual emotional concomitants, rage or fear. The sympathetic emergency reaction is not always adaptive. It can produce temporary disruptions of digestive and sexual functions, and can also lead to more permanent psychophysiological disorders.

9. While the sympathetic system arouses the more primitive physiological processes of the body, a structure in the brain stem, the *reticular activating system,* or *RAS,* arouses the brain. The RAS awakens the cortex and is opposed by an antagonistic system which leads to sleep.

10. During sleep, brain activity changes as shown by the *electroencephalogram* or *EEG.* Each night, we oscillate between two kinds of sleep. One is *quiet sleep,* during which the cortex is relatively inactive. The other is *active sleep,* characterized by considerable cortical activity and *rapid eye movements* or *REMs,* a pattern of internal activity which is experienced as *dreams.*

11. According to *drive-reduction theory,* all built-in motives act to reduce stimulation and arousal. Today most authors believe instead that organisms strive for an *optimum level of arousal.* If below this optimum, they try to increase arousal by various means.

12. One way of coping with an arousal level that is too high or too low is by the use of drugs. Some drugs act as *depressants,* including alcohol and the opiates. Others such as the *amphetamines* and *cocaine* act as *stimulants.* In many individuals, repeated drug use leads to *addiction,* accompanied by increased *tolerance* and *withdrawal effects* if the drug is withheld. The *opponent-process theory of motivation* tries to explain these and many other phenomena by arguing that all shifts of arousal level produce a counteracting process that acts to moderate the ups and downs. When the original instigator of the shift is removed, the opponent process is revealed more clearly, as in withdrawal effects.

13. Work on the rewarding effects of certain regions of the brain has led to speculations about possible *pleasure centers* in the brain. A problem with the pleasure center hypothesis is the fact that self-stimulation requires some *priming.*

CHAPTER 3

Learning

Thus far, our discussion has centered on the built-in facets of human and animal behavior, the general neural equipment that provides the underpinning for everything we do, and the specific, innate feedback systems that underlie directed action. But much of what we do and are goes beyond what nature gave us. It is acquired through experience in our lifetime. People learn—to grasp a baby bottle, to eat with knife and fork, to read and write, to love or hate their neighbors, and eventually, to face death. In animals, the role of learning may be less dramatic, but it is enormously important even so.

What can psychology tell us about the processes whereby organisms learn? Many investigators have tried to reconcile the phenomena of learning with the reflex-machine conception that goes back to Descartes. The adherents of this approach, whose modern exponents are sometimes called *behavior theorists,* argued that the organism's *prewired* repertory of behaviors is supplemented by continual *rewirings* that are produced by experience. Some of these rewirings consist of new connections between stimuli. Thus, the sight of the mother's face may come to signify the taste of milk. Other rewirings involve new connections between acts and their consequences, as when a toddler learns that touching a hot radiator is followed by a painful burn. The behavior theorists set themselves the task of discovering how such rewirings come about.

The behavior theorists' interest in the learning process was admirably suited to the intellectual climate during the first part of this century, especially in the United States. For here was a society that was deeply committed to the individual's efforts to improve himself by pushing himself on to greater efforts and acquiring new skills—in numerous public schools and colleges, night classes for recent immigrants, dance classes for the shy, courses for those who wanted to "win friends and influence people," and martial-arts classes for those less interested in winning friends than in defeating enemies. There was—and in many ways, still is—an enormous faith in the near-limitless malleability of human beings, who were thought to be almost infinitely perfectible by proper changes in their environment, especially through education. Under the circumstances, it was hardly surprising that learning became (and still is) one of the paramount concerns of American psychology.

How should the learning process be studied? At least initially, most behavior theorists felt that there are some basic laws that come into play, regardless of what is learned or who does the learning—be it a dog learning to sit on command or a college student learning integral calculus. This early conception was very influential. It led to the view that at bottom even the most involved learned activities are made up of simpler ones, much as complex chemical compounds are made up of simpler atoms. Given this belief, it was only natural that the early investigators concentrated their efforts on trying to understand learning in simple situations and in (relatively) simpler creatures like dogs, rats, and pigeons. By so doing, they hoped to strip the learning process down to its bare essence so that its basic laws might be revealed.

As we will see, some of the beliefs of the early behavior theorists had to be modified in the light of later discoveries. They never succeeded in finding *one* set of laws that underlie *all* phenomena of learning in *all* organisms, including humans. But even so, their search led to the major discoveries that form the basis of much of what we know today. It is to these that we now turn.

HABITUATION

The simplest of all forms of learning is **habituation.** This is a decline in the tendency to respond to stimuli that have become familiar due to repeated exposure. A sudden noise usually startles us—an adaptive reaction, for sudden and unfamiliar stimuli often spell danger. But suppose the same noise is repeated over and over again. The second time, the startle will be diminished, the third time it will hardly be evoked, and after that, it will be ignored altogether. Our startle response has become habituated. Much the same holds for many other everyday events. We have become so accustomed to the ticking of a clock in the living room that we are utterly unaware of it until it finally stops. By the same token, city dwellers become completely habituated to the noise of traffic but are kept awake by the crickets when they take a vacation in the country.

Habituation is found at virtually all levels of the animal kingdom. Mammals, birds, fish, insects, and snails perform various escape reactions when they first encounter a novel stimulus, but after several repetitions they come to ignore it. Thus marine snails initially withdraw their gills at the slightest touch, but they will stop responding after repeated stimulation. Similarly, male Siamese fighting fish adopt a striking fighting posture upon encountering another male of their own species (or when looking into a mirror), but after several such encounters they become less and less aggressive and eventually hold their peace (Figler, 1972; Peeke, 1984).

What is the adaptive significance of habituation? One of its major benefits is that it narrows down the range of stimuli that elicit escape reactions. After all, organisms have to eat and drink and mate to survive, and they can't do so if they spend all their time running away from imaginary enemies. Habituation allows them to ignore the familiar and focus their emergency reactions on things that are new and may signal dangers (Wyers, Peeke, and Herz, 1973; Shalter, 1984).

CLASSICAL CONDITIONING

In habituation, an organism learns to recognize an event as familiar, but he doesn't learn anything about the relation between that event and any other circumstances. Such learned relationships are called **associations.** There's little

Habituation in Siamese fighting fish
Male Siamese fighting fish adopt a fighting posture when they see another male, but after a while they habituate to his presence. (Photograph by Toni Angermeyer/Photo Researchers)

Ivan Petrovich Pavlov *(Courtesy Sovfoto)*

doubt that much of what we learn consists of various associations between events: between thunder and lightning, between the nipple and food, between the sound of a thumping motor and a large automobile repair bill. The importance of associations in human learning and thinking has been emphasized since the days of the Greek philosophers, but the experimental study of associations did not begin until the end of the nineteenth century. A major step in this direction was the work on conditioning performed by the great Russian scientist, Ivan P. Pavlov (1849–1936).

Pavlov and the Conditioned Reflex

Ivan Petrovich Pavlov had already earned the Nobel Prize for his work on digestion before he embarked upon the study of conditioning which was to gain him even greater fame. His initial interest was in the built-in nervous control of the various digestive reflexes in dogs; most important to us, the secretion of saliva. He surgically diverted one of the ducts of the salivary gland, thus channeling part of the salivary flow through a special tube to the outside of the animal's body where it could be easily measured and analyzed. Pavlov demonstrated that salivation was produced by several innate reflexes, one of which prepares the food for digestion. This is triggered by food (especially dry food) placed in the mouth.

In the course of Pavlov's work a new fact emerged. The salivary reflex could be set off by stimuli which at first were totally neutral. Dogs that had been in the laboratory for a while would soon salivate to a whole host of stimuli that had no such effect on their uninitiated fellows. Not only the taste and touch of the meat in the mouth, but its mere sight, the sight of the dish in which it was placed, the sight of the person who usually brought it, even that person's footsteps—eventually all of these might produce salivation. Pavlov soon decided to study such effects in their own right, for he recognized that they provided a means of extending the reflex concept to embrace learned as well as innate reactions. The approach was simple enough. Instead of waiting for accidental events in each animal's history, the experimenter would provide those events himself. Thus he would repeatedly sound a buzzer and always follow it with food. Later he observed what happened when the buzzer was sounded and no food was given (Pavlov, 1927; Figure 3.1).

The fundamental finding was simple: Repeated buzzer-food pairings led to salivation when the buzzer was presented alone (that is, unaccompanied by food) on occasional test trials. To explain this, Pavlov proposed a distinction between unconditioned and conditioned reflexes. *Unconditioned reflexes* he held to be essentially inborn and innate; these are unconditionally elicited by the appropriate stimulus regardless of the animal's history. An example is food in the

3.1 Apparatus for salivary conditioning The figure shows an early version of Pavlov's apparatus for classical conditioning of the salivary response. The dog was held in a harness, sounds or lights functioned as conditioned stimuli, while meat powder in a dish served as the unconditioned stimulus. The conditioned response was assessed with the aid of a tube connected to an opening in one of the animal's salivary glands. (After Yerkes and Morgulis, 1909)

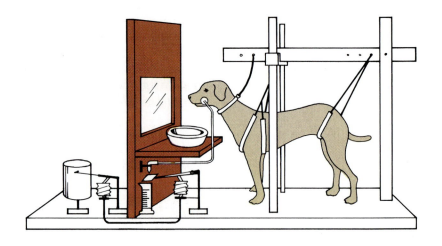

CS - conditioned stimulus
US - Unconditioned stim.
CR - Conditioned response
UR - unconditioned response

BEFORE TRAINING

US (food in mouth) ⟶ UR (salivation) *Kinborn*

CS (e.g., tone) ⟶ No relevant response

TRAINING

CS (tone) + US (food in mouth)   X several trials

AFTER TRAINING (that is, conditioning)

CS (tone) ⟶ CR (salivation)

3.2   Relationships between CS, US, CR, and UR in classical conditioning

mouth, which unconditionally elicits salivation. In contrast, **conditioned reflexes were acquired, and thus they were conditional upon the animal's past experience,** and according to Pavlov, based upon newly formed connections in the brain. (A stricter translation might have been "unconditional reflex" and "conditional reflex" respectively.)

According to Pavlov, every unconditioned reflex is based upon a (presumably built-in) connection between an **unconditioned stimulus (US)** and an **unconditioned response (UR).** In Pavlov's laboratory, these were food in the mouth (the US) and salivation (UR). The corresponding terms for the conditioned reflex are **conditioned stimulus (CS)** and **conditioned response (CR).** Here CS would be an initially neutral stimulus, that is, some stimulus (here, the buzzer) that does not elicit the CR without prior conditioning. The CR (here again, salivation) is the response elicited by the CS after some such pairings of CS and US. These various relationships are summarized in Figure 3.2 and constitute the basis of what is now known as **classical conditioning.***

The Major Phenomena of Classical Conditioning

Pavlov saw conditioning as a way of extending the reflex concept into the realm of learning. Later workers (especially in the United States) were not as convinced as he that the so-called conditioned reflex is in fact some kind of reflex, even one that is modified. As a result, they substituted the more neutral term "response" for "reflex," as in "unconditioned response." But until quite recently, most of them shared Pavlov's conviction that conditioning was essentially a change in what the animal does, and so, like he, they focused on the acquisition of the conditioned response. As we will see, later workers came to see conditioning in rather different ways than Pavlov did. But we will begin by describing his empirical discoveries with a minimum of editorial comment, for these findings laid the foundations for all subsequent theories of classical conditioning and indeed of much of learning generally.

ACQUISITION OF CONDITIONED RESPONSES

Pavlov noted that the tendency of the CS to elicit the CR goes up the more often the CS and the US have been paired together. Clearly then, presenting the US to-

---

* The adjective *classical* is used, in part, as dutiful tribute to Pavlov's eminence and historical priority, and in part, to distinguish this form of conditioning from *instrumental conditioning* to which we will turn later.

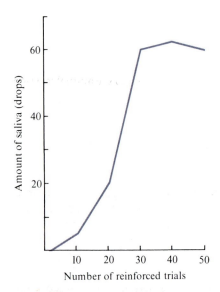

3.3 Learning curve in classical conditioning *The figure shows the increase in the amount of saliva secreted (the CR) as reinforced trials proceed. The CS was a tone, the US was meat powder, and the strength of the CR was measured by the number of drops of saliva secreted by the dog during a thirty-second period in which the CS was presented alone. (Data from Anrep, 1920)*

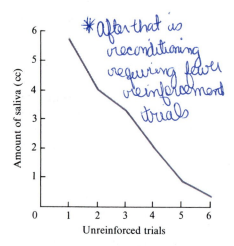

*After that is reconditioning requiring fewer reinforcement trials

3.4 Extinction of a classically conditioned response *The figure shows the decrease in the amount of saliva secreted (the CR) with increasing number of extinction trials—that is, trials on which CS is presented without US. (After Pavlov, 1928)*

gether with (or more typically, subsequent to) the CS is a critical operation in classical conditioning. Such a pairing is said to *reinforce* the connection; trials on which the US occurs and on which it is omitted are called *reinforced* and *unreinforced trials* respectively.

The effect of repeated reinforcements is shown in Figure 3.3, a typical *learning curve* in which magnitude of CR is plotted against successive test trials. In this and other conditioning curves, the general trend is very clear and unsurprising: Response strength increases with the number of reinforced trials (the first measured on the x-axis, the second on the y-axis). Response strength can be measured in several ways. One is response *amplitude:* here, the amount of saliva secreted when presented with CS (which increases with increasing number of CS-US pairings). Another is response *latency:* the time from the onset of CS to the CR (which decreases with increasing number of CS-US pairings).

Once the CS-US relation is solidly established, the CS can serve to condition yet further stimuli. To give one example, Pavlov first conditioned a dog to salivate to the beat of a metronome, using meat powder as the US. After many such pairings, he presented the animal with a black square followed by the metronome beat, but without ever introducing the food. Eventually the sight of the black square alone was enough to produce salivation. This phenomenon is called *higher-order conditioning.* In the present case, conditioning was of the second order. The metronome which served as the CS in first-order conditioning functioned as the US for a second-order conditioned response. In effect, the black square had become a signal for the metronome, which in turn signaled the appearance of food.

EXTINCTION

The adaptive value of conditioning is self-evident. A zebra's chance of future survival is enhanced by conditioning: There's much to be gained by a conditioned fear reaction to a place from which a lion has pounced some time before (assuming, of course, that the zebra managed to survive the CS-US pairing in the first place). On the other hand, it would be rather inefficient if a connection once established could never be undone. The lion may change its lair and its former prowling place may now be perfectly safe for grazing.

Pavlov showed that in fact a conditioned reaction can be undone. He demonstrated that the conditioned response will gradually disappear if the CS is repeatedly presented without being reinforced by the US; in his terms, the CS-US link undergoes *experimental extinction.* Figure 3.4 presents an extinction curve from a salivary extinction experiment. As usual, response strength is measured along the y-axis, while the x-axis indicates the number of extinction trials (that is, trials without reinforcement). As extinction trials proceed, the salivary flow dries up. In effect, the dog has learned that the CS is no longer a signal for food.

A conditioned response that has been extinguished can be resurrected. One means is through *reconditioning,* that is, by presenting further reinforced trials. Typically, reconditioning requires fewer reinforced trials to bring the CR to its former strength than were necessary during the initial conditioning session, even if extinction trials had been continued until the animal stopped responding altogether. The conditioned response was evidently not really abolished by extinction but instead was somehow masked.

The fact that the conditioned response is only masked rather than abolished by extinction is also shown by the phenomenon of *spontaneous recovery.* An extinguished CR will usually reappear after a rest interval during which the animal is left to its own devices. The interpretation of this effect is still a matter of debate.

According to a recent analysis, the animal gradually loses interest in the CS as extinction proceeds and no longer looks or listens to it. After an interval away from the situation, it attends to the CS once again and therefore resumes responding (Robbins, 1990).

GENERALIZATION

So far our discussion has been confined to situations in which the animal is tested with the *identical* stimulus that had served as the CS during training. But of course in the real world the stimuli are never really identical. The master's voice may signal food, but the exact intonation will surely vary from one occasion to another. Can the dog still use whatever it has learned before? If it can't, its conditioned response will be of little benefit. In fact, animals do respond to stimuli other than the original CS, so long as these are sufficiently similar.

This phenomenon is called ***stimulus generalization.*** A dog may be conditioned to respond to a tone of 1,000 hertz (cycles per second); nevertheless, the CR will be obtained not just with that tone, but also with tones of different frequencies, like 900 or 1,100 hertz. But the CR evoked by such new stimuli will show a ***generalization decrement;*** it will be weaker than the CR elicited by the original CS. The greater the difference between the new stimulus and the original CS, the larger this decrement will be. The resulting curve is called a ***generalization gradient*** (see Figure 3.5).

DISCRIMINATION

Stimulus generalization is not always beneficial. A kitten may be similar to a tiger; but a man who generalizes from one to the other is likely to be sorry. What he must do instead is discriminate.

The phenomenon of ***discrimination*** is readily demonstrated in the laboratory. A dog is first conditioned to salivate to a CS, for example, a black square (CS$^+$). After the CR is well established, reinforced trials with the black square are randomly interspersed with nonreinforced trials with another stimulus, say, a gray square (CS$^-$). This continues until the animal discriminates perfectly, always salivating to CS$^+$, the reinforced stimulus, and never to CS$^-$, the nonreinforced stimulus. Of course the dog does not reach this final point immediately. During the early trials it will be confused, or more precisely, it will generalize rather than discriminate. It will tend to salivate to CS$^-$ (which, after all, is quite similar to CS$^+$); by the same token, it will often fail to salivate when presented with CS$^+$. Such errors gradually become fewer and fewer until perfect discrimination is finally achieved. Not surprisingly, the discrimination gets harder and harder the more similar the two stimuli are. As similarity increases, the tendency to respond to CS$^+$ will increasingly generalize to CS$^-$, while the tendency not to respond to CS$^-$ will increasingly generalize to CS$^+$. As a result, the dog will require many trials before it finally responds without errors.

One might think that the difficulty in forming discrimination is that the animal has trouble telling the two stimuli apart. But that is generally not the reason. The dog's problem is not that it can't form a sensory discrimination between CS$^+$ and CS$^-$. What is at fault is not its eyesight, for it can distinguish between the dark-gray and light-gray squares visually. Its difficulty is in discovering and remembering which stimulus is *right,* which goes with the US and which does not. Eventually the animal learns, but this doesn't mean that it has learned to see the stimuli differently. What it has learned is their significance; it now knows which stimulus is which.

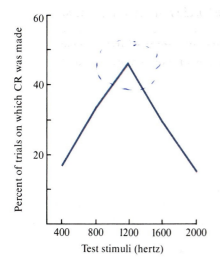

3.5 Generalization gradient of a classically conditioned response *The figure shows the generalization of a conditioned blinking response in rabbits. The CS was a tone of 1,200 hertz and the US was electric shock. After the conditioned response to the original CS was well established, generalization was measured by presenting various test stimuli, ranging from 400 hertz to 2,000 hertz and noting the percent of the trials on which the animals gave the CR. The figure shows the results, averaged over several testing sessions. (After Moore, 1972)*

Extensions of Classical Conditioning

Thus far, our discussion has been largely restricted to the laboratory phenomena that Pavlov looked at: dogs salivating to buzzers, lights, and metronomes. Needless to say, conditioning would be of little interest if it only applied to those phenomena. But in actual fact, its scope is very much larger than that.

To begin with, classical conditioning has been found in a large variety of animal species other than dogs, including ants and anteaters, cats and cockroaches, pigeons and people. Any number of reaction patterns have been classically conditioned in animals. Thus, crabs have been conditioned to twitch their tail spines, fish to thrash about, and octopuses to change color. Responses conditioned in laboratory studies with humans include the galvanic skin response (where the US is typically a loud noise or electric shock) and the blink-reaction of the eyelid (where the US consists of a puff of air on the open eye; Kimble, 1961).

Nor is classical conditioning restricted to the laboratory, for there is little doubt that it plays a considerable role in our everyday life. Many of our internal feelings and urges are probably the result of classical conditioning. We tend to feel hungry at mealtimes and less so during the times between; this is so even if we fast a whole day. Another example is sexual arousal. This is often produced by a partner's special word or gesture whose erotic meaning is very private and is surely learned.

CONDITIONED FEAR

Of special importance is the role of classical conditioning in the formation of various emotional reactions, especially those concerned with fear. A common consequence of a conditioned fear reaction is *response suppression.* The CS will evoke fear, which in turn will suppress whatever other activities the animal is currently engaged in. This is the basis of a widely used technique to study fear conditioning, the *conditioned emotional response (CER)* procedure. A hungry rat is first taught to press a lever for an occasional food reward. After a few training sessions, the rat will press at a steady rate. Now classical conditioning can start. While the animal is pressing, a CS is presented—a light or a tone that will stay on for, say, three minutes. At the end of that period, the CS terminates and there is a mild, brief electric shock (the US). Some twenty minutes later, the same CS-US sequence is repeated. After this, there is another twenty-minute interval during which neither the CS nor the US are presented, followed by yet another CS-US sequence, and so on (Estes and Skinner, 1941; Kamin, 1965). After twelve such trials, the response is completely suppressed (see Figure 3.6).

It is a plausible guess that many adult fears are based upon classical conditioning, acquired in much the same way that fear is acquired in the laboratory. These fears may be relatively mild or very intense (if intense enough, they are called *phobias*). They may be acquired in early childhood or during particular traumatic episodes in later life. An example is an Air Force pilot who bailed out of his plane but whose parachute failed to open until the last five seconds before he hit the ground. In such traumatic episodes, conditioning apparently occurs in a

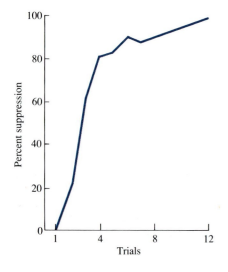

3.6 Response suppression *A rat is trained to press a lever at a steady rate to gain food. The figure plots the extent to which this response is suppressed after successive presentations of a 3-minute light CS that is immediately followed by electric shock. After 12 such trials, suppression is at 100 percent, and the animal doesn't respond at all during the 3 minutes when the CS is presented. (Data from Kamin, 1969)*

single trial. This seems reasonable enough, for it would certainly be unadaptive if the pilot had to bail out on ten separate occasions, each time barely escaping death, before he finally developed a conditioned fear reaction (Sarnoff, 1957).

INSTRUMENTAL CONDITIONING

Habituation and classical conditioning are two of the main forms of simple learning. Another is *instrumental conditioning* (which is also called *operant conditioning* or *instrumental learning*). An example of instrumental conditioning comes from the zoo. When a seal learns to turn a somersault to get a fish from the zoo attendant, it has learned an *instrumental response.* The response is instrumental in that it leads to a sought-after effect—in this case, the fish.

There are some important differences between instrumental and classical conditioning. The most important is the fact that in instrumental learning, reinforcement (that is, reward) depends upon the proper response. For the seal the rules of the game are simple: no somersault, no fish. This is not true for classical conditioning. There the US is presented regardless of what the animal does. Another difference concerns response selection. In instrumental learning, the response must be selected from a sometimes very large set of alternatives. The seal's job is to select the somersault from among the numerous other things a seal could possibly do. Not so in classical conditioning. There the response is forced, for the US unconditionally evokes it.

We could loosely summarize the difference between the two procedures by a rough description of what is learned in each. In classical conditioning the animal must learn about the relation between two stimuli, the CS and the US: Given CS, US will follow. In instrumental learning, the animal has to learn the relation between a response and a reward: Given this response, there will be reinforcement. But such statements are only crude descriptions. To get beyond them, we must discuss instrumental learning in more detail.

Thorndike and the Law of Effect

The experimental study of instrumental learning began a decade or two before Pavlov. It was an indirect consequence of the debate over the doctrine of evolution. Darwin's theory was buttressed by impressive demonstrations of continuity in the bodily structures of many species, both living and extinct. But his opponents could argue that such evidence was not enough. To them the essential distinction between humans and beasts was elsewhere: in the human ability to think and reason, an ability that animals did not share. To answer this point it became critical to find proof of mental as well as of bodily continuity.

For evidence, the Darwinians turned to animal behavior. At first, the method was largely anecdotal. Several British naturalists (including Darwin himself) collected stories about the intellectual achievements of various animals as related by presumably reliable informants. Taken at face value, the results painted a flattering picture of animal intellect, as in accounts of cunning cats scattering bread crumbs on the lawn to entice the birds (Romanes, 1882). But even if such observations could be trusted (and they probably could not), they did not prove that the animals' performances were achieved in the way a human might achieve the same thing: by reason and understanding. To be sure of that, one would have to study the animals' learning processes from start to finish. To see a circus seal blow a melody on a set of toy trumpets is one thing; to conclude from this observation that it has musical understanding is quite another.

Edward L. Thorndike (Courtesy The Granger Collection)

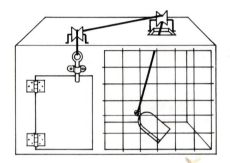

3.7 Puzzle box *This box is much like those used by Thorndike. The animal steps on a treadle which is attached to a rope, thereby releasing a latch that locks the door. (After Thorndike, 1911)*

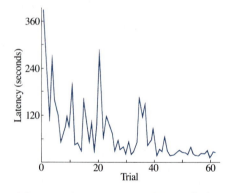

3.8 Learning curve of one of Thorndike's cats *To get out of the box, the cat had to move a wooden handle from a vertical to a horizontal position. The figure shows the gradual decline in the animal's response latency (the time it takes to get out of the box). Note that the learning curve is by no means smooth but has rather marked fluctuations. This is a common feature of the learning curves of individual subjects. Smooth learning curves are generally produced by averaging the results of many individual subjects. (After Thorndike, 1898)*

There was clearly a need for controlled experimental procedures whereby the entire course of learning could be carefully scrutinized. That method was provided in 1898 by Edward L. Thorndike (1874–1949) in a brilliant doctoral dissertation that became one of the classic documents of American psychology (Thorndike, 1898).

CATS IN A PUZZLE BOX

Thorndike's method was to set up a problem for the animal. To gain reward the creature had to perform some particular action determined by the experimenter. Much of this work was done on hungry cats. The animal was placed in a so-called **puzzle box,** an enclosure from which it could escape only by performing some simple action that would unlatch the door, such as pulling a loop or wire or pressing a lever (Figure 3.7). Once outside, the animal was rewarded with a small portion of food and then placed back into the box for another trial. This procedure was repeated until the task was mastered.

On the first trial, the typical cat struggled valiantly; it clawed at the bars, it bit, it struck out in all directions, it meowed, and it howled. This continued for several minutes until the animal finally hit upon the correct response by pure accident. Subsequent trials brought gradual improvement. The mad scramble became shorter and the animal took less and less time to perform the correct response. By the time the training sessions were completed the cat's behavior was almost unrecognizable from what it had been at the start. Placed in the box, it immediately approached the wire loop, yanked it with businesslike dispatch, and quickly hurried through the open door to enjoy its well-deserved reward. The cat had certainly learned.

How had it learned? If one merely observed its final performance one might credit the cat with reason or understanding, but Thorndike argued that the problem was solved in a very different way. For proof he examined the learning curves. Plotting the time required on each trial (that is, the response *latency*) over the whole course of training, he usually found a curve that declined quite gradually (Figure 3.8). Had the animals "understood" the solution at some point during training, the curves should have shown a sudden drop with little change thereafter (for one would hardly expect further errors once understanding was reached).

THE LAW OF EFFECT

Thorndike proposed that what the animal had learned was best described as an increase in the strength of the correct response. Initially, the cat has the tendency to perform a large set of responses, perhaps because of prior learning, perhaps because of built-in predispositions. As it happens, virtually all of these lead to failure. As trials proceed, the strength of the incorrect responses gradually weakens. In contrast, the correct response, which at first is weak, increasingly grows in strength. In Thorndike's terms, the correct response is gradually "stamped in" while futile ones are correspondingly stamped out. The improvements in the learning curves "represent the wearing smooth of a path in the brain, not the decisions of a rational consciousness" (Thorndike, 1911).

According to Thorndike, some responses get strengthened and others weakened as learning proceeds. But what produces these different effects? Thorndike's answer was a bold formulation called the **law of effect.** The relevant features of his analysis are schematized in Figure 3.9, which indicates the tendency to perform the various responses, whether correct (R_c) or incorrect (R_1, R_2, R_3, etc.). The critical question is how the correct response gets strengthened until it finally overwhelms the incorrect ones that are at first so dominant. Thorndike's pro-

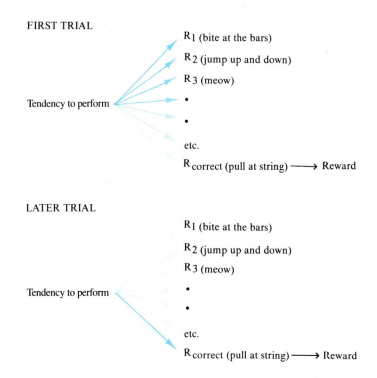

FIRST TRIAL

Tendency to perform

R₁ (bite at the bars)
R₂ (jump up and down)
R₃ (meow)
·
·
etc.
R correct (pull at string) ⟶ Reward

LATER TRIAL

Tendency to perform

R₁ (bite at the bars)
R₂ (jump up and down)
R₃ (meow)
·
·
etc.
R correct (pull at string) ⟶ Reward

3.9 The law of effect *The figure is a schematic presentation of Thorndike's theory of instrumental learning. On the first trial, the tendency to perform various incorrect responses (biting the bars, jumping up and down) is very strong, while the tendency to perform the correct response (pulling the string) is weak or nonexistent. As trials proceed, the strength of these responses change. The incorrect responses become weaker and weaker, for none of these responses is immediately followed by reward. In contrast, there is a progressive strengthening of the correct response because this is followed more or less immediately by reward.*

posal, the law of effect, held that the consequences (that is, the effect) of a response determine whether the tendency to perform it is strengthened or weakened. If the response is followed by reward, it will be strengthened; if it is followed by the absence of reward (or worse yet, by punishment) it will be weakened. There was no need to postulate any further intellectual processes in the animal, no need to assume that the animal noticed a connection between act and consequence, no need to believe that it was trying to attain some goal. If the animal made a response and reward followed shortly, that response was more likely to be performed at a subsequent time.

Skinner and Operant Behavior

Thorndike initiated the experimental study of instrumental behavior, but the psychologist who shaped the way in which most modern behavior theorists think about the subject is B. F. Skinner (1904–1990). Unlike Thorndike who believed that classical and instrumental conditioning are much alike, Skinner was one of the first theorists to insist on a sharp distinction between classical and instrumental conditioning. In classical conditioning, the animal's behavior is *elicited* by the CS; to that extent, the salivation is set off from the outside. But Skinner insisted that in instrumental conditioning the organism is much less at the mercy of the external situation. Its reactions are *emitted* from within, as if they were what we ordinarily call *voluntary.* Skinner called these instrumental responses **operants;** they operate on the environment to bring about some change that leads to reward. Like Thorndike, Skinner believed in the law of effect, insisting that the tendency to emit these operants is strengthened or weakened by its consequences (Skinner, 1938).

Behavior theorists have always searched for ever-simpler situations in the hope that the true laws of learning will show up there. An early example is the ***runway*** in which the animal has to run from one end of an alley to the other, with response strength measured by the time it takes to traverse the path. Skinner's way

B. F. Skinner *(Photograph by Nina Leen, Life Magazine, © Time Inc.)*

A

B

3.10   Animals in operant chambers
(A) A rat trained to press a lever for water reinforcement. (Photograph by Mike Salisbury) (B) A pigeon pecking at a lighted key for food reinforcement. Reinforcement consists of a few seconds' access to a grain feeder which is located just below the key. (Photograph by Susan M. Hogue)

of simplifying the study of operant behavior was to create a situation in which the same instrumental response could be performed repeatedly. The most common example is the experimental chamber (popularly called the Skinner box), in which a rat presses a lever or a pigeon pecks at a lighted key (Figure 3.10). In these situations, the animal remains in the presence of the lever or key for, say, an hour at a time, pressing and pecking at whatever rate it chooses. All of the animal's responses are automatically recorded; stimuli and reinforcements are presented automatically by automatic programming devices. The measure of response strength is *response rate,* that is, the number of responses per unit time.

The Major Phenomena of Instrumental Conditioning

Many of the phenomena of instrumental learning parallel those of classical conditioning. Consider *reinforcement.* In classical conditioning, the term refers to an operation (establishing a CS-US contingency) that strengthens the CR. In the context of instrumental learning, reinforcement refers to an analogous operation: having the response followed by a condition that the animal "prefers." This may be the presentation of something "good," such as grain to a hungry pigeon. The grain is an example of an *appetitive stimulus* (a stimulus for which the animal so to speak "has an appetite"). In Thorndike's terms, it is something that the animal does everything to attain and nothing to prevent. Reinforcement may also be the termination or prevention of something "bad," such as the cessation of an electric shock. Such a shock is an example of an *aversive stimulus,* one that the animal does everything to avoid and nothing to attain.

At a more technical level, we can also distinguish between *positive reinforcement* and *negative reinforcement.* Positive reinforcement refers to conditions in which the response produces an appetitive stimulus—a rat presses a lever to get food. Negative reinforcement refers to conditions in which the instrumental response eliminates or prevents an aversive stimulus—a rat jumping over a barrier to escape an electric shock.

As in classical conditioning, the probability of responding increases with an increasing number of reinforcements. And, again as in classical conditioning, the response suffers *extinction* when reinforcement is withdrawn.

GENERALIZATION AND DISCRIMINATION

The instrumental response is not elicited by external stimuli but is, in Skinner's terms, emitted from within. But this doesn't mean that such stimuli have no ef-

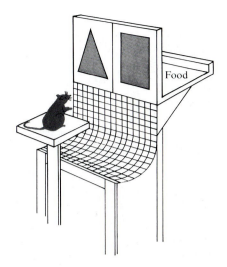

3.11 Studying discriminative stimuli with the jumping stand *The rat has to jump to one of two cards, say, a triangle or a square, behind which is a ledge that contains food. If the choice is correct, the card gives way and the animal gets to the food. If the choice is incorrect, the card stays in place, the rat bumps its nose and falls into the net below. (After Lashley, 1930)*

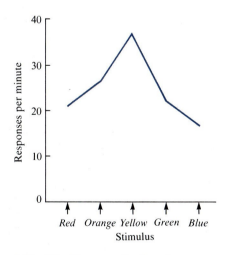

3.12 Stimulus generalization of an instrumental response *Pigeons were originally reinforced to peck at a yellow light. When later tested with lights of various colors, they showed a standard generalization gradient, pecking more vigorously at colors more similar to yellow (such as green and orange) than at colors farther removed (such as red and blue). Prior to being reinforced on the yellow key, their tendency to peck was minimal and roughly equal for all colors. (After Reynolds, 1968)*

fect. They do exert considerable control over behavior, for they serve as ***discriminative stimuli.*** Suppose a pigeon is trained to hop on a treadle to get some grain. When green light is on, hopping on the treadle will pay off. But when a red light is on, the treadle-hopping response will be of no avail, for the pigeon gets no access to the food container. Under these circumstances, the green light becomes a positive discriminative stimulus and the red light a negative one (here indicated by S$^+$ and S$^-$ respectively). The pigeon will hop in the presence of the first and not when presented with the second. But this discrimination is made in an instrumental and not a classical conditioning context. The green light doesn't signal food the way a CS$^+$ might in Pavlov's laboratory. Instead, it signals a particular relationship between the instrumental response and the reinforcer, telling the pigeon as it were "If you hop now, you'll get food." Conversely for the red light, the S$^-$ tells the animal that there's no point in going through the treadle-hopping business right now.

A variety of techniques have been used to study the role of discriminated stimuli in affecting learned instrumental behaviors. Many of the results mirror those of generalization and discrimination in classical conditioning (see Figure 3.11).

An example is the study of stimulus generalization using operant techniques. Figure 3.12 shows a typical stimulus generalization gradient for color in pigeons. The animals were trained to peck at a key illuminated with yellow light, after which they were tested with lights of varying wavelengths. The resulting gradient is orderly. As the test light became less similar to the original S$^+$, the pigeons were less inclined to peck at it (Guttman and Kalish, 1956).

SHAPING

How does an animal learn the particular instrumental response that will lead to reinforcement? The law of effect tells us that once that response has been made, then reinforcement will act to strengthen it. But what happens if that response isn't ever made in the first place? As it happens, pecking and lever pressing are fairly easy as such responses go; many animals hit upon them of their own accord. But we can make the response much more difficult. For example, we could set the rat's lever so high on the wall that it must stretch up on its hindlegs to depress it. Now the animal may never make the response on its own. But it can learn this response and even ones more outlandish if its behavior is suitably shaped. This is accomplished by the method of ***successive approximations.***

Take the problem of the elevated lever. The first step is to train the animal to approach the tray in which the food is delivered whenever the food-dispensing mechanism gives off its characteristic click. At random intervals, the click sounds and a food pellet drops into the tray; this continues until the rat shows that it is properly trained by running to pick up its pellet as soon as it hears the click. Shaping can now begin. We might first reinforce the animal for walking into the general area where the lever is located. As soon as it is there, it hears the click and devours the pellet. Very soon it will hover around the neighborhood of the lever. We next reinforce it for facing the lever, then for stretching its body upward, then for touching the lever with its paws, and so on until we finally complete its education by reinforcing it for pressing the lever down. The guiding principle throughout is immediacy of reinforcement. If we want to reinforce the rat for standing up on its hindlegs we must do it the instant after the response; even a one-second wait may be too long, for by then the rat may have fallen back on all fours and if we reinforce it then we will reinforce the wrong response.

By means of this technique, animals have been trained to perform exceedingly complex response chains. Pigeons have been trained to play Ping-Pong and dogs to plunk out four-note tunes on a toy piano. Such successes encouraged some enterprising psychologists to develop live advertising exhibits, featuring such stars as "Priscilla, the Fastidious Pig" to promote the sale of certain farm feeds (Bre-

3.13 Animals in show business (A) A pig trained by means of operant techniques to push a market cart. The animal was first reinforced for putting its front feet up on the handle, until it could raise up on the handle, and push the cart while walking on its hind feet. (B) A rabbit trained to get up in a firetruck, pull a lever a fixed number of times, and stay in the truck for a fixed interval so as to get reinforced. (Photographs courtesy of Animal Behavior Enterprises)

land and Breland, 1951). Priscilla turned on the radio, ate breakfast at a kitchen table, picked up dirty clothes and dropped them in a hamper, vacuumed the floor, and finally selected the sponsor's feed in preference to Brand X—a convincing tribute to the sponsor and to the power of reinforcement (Figure 3.13).

CONDITIONED REINFORCEMENT

So far, our examples of reinforcement have included food or water or termination of electric shock, whose capacity to reinforce responses is presumably based upon built-in mechanisms of various kinds. But instrumental learning is not always reinforced by events of such immediate biological consequence. For example, piano teachers rarely reinforce their pupils with food or the cessation of electric shock; a nod or the comment "good" is all that is required. How does the Thorndikian approach explain why the word *good* is reinforcing?

The answer is that a stimulus will acquire reinforcing properties if it is repeatedly paired with a primary reinforcer. It will then provide **conditioned reinforcement** if administered after a response has been made.

Numerous experiments give evidence that neutral stimuli can acquire reinforcing properties. For example, chimpanzees were first trained to insert poker chips into a vending machine to acquire grapes. Having learned this, they then learned to operate another device which delivered poker chips (Cowles, 1937; see Figure 3.14). Examples of this kind indicate that the critical factor in establishing a stimulus as a conditioned reinforcer is its association with primary reinforcement. It is then not surprising that the effect increases the more frequently the two have been paired. As we might also expect, a conditioned reinforcer will gradually lose its powers if it is repeatedly unaccompanied by some primary reinforcement. All of this argues that conditioned reinforcement is established by a process that is akin to, if not identical with, classical conditioning. The conditioned reinforcer serves as a CS that signals some motivationally significant US.

If conditioned reinforcers are so readily extinguished in the laboratory, why do they seem so much more permanent in human life? Nods do not lose their reinforcing value just because they haven't been paired with any primary reinforcer for a month or more. In part, the answer may be that the nod or the smile has

3.14 Conditioned reinforcement in chimpanzees A chimpanzee using a token to obtain food after working to obtain tokens. (Courtesy Yerkes Regional Primate Research Center of Emory University)

enormous generality. It is associated not with one but with many different desirable outcomes. Even if extinguished in one context, it would still be maintained in countless others.

DELAY OF REINFORCEMENT

According to the law of effect, a response will be strengthened if it is followed by a reward. But the mere fact that a reward will follow is not enough. In general, the reward must follow rather quickly, for a reinforcer becomes less and less effective the longer its presentation is delayed after the response is made.

The relation between the delay and the effectiveness of a reward has been experimentally studied in various ways. One experimenter trained several groups of rats to press a lever which was withdrawn from the box immediately after the correct response. Food was delivered after different delays of reinforcement ranging from 0 to 30 seconds for the various groups. Learning was clearly faster the shorter the interval. These results are summarized in Figure 3.15, which shows the declining effectiveness of reinforcement with increasing delay. Note that in this study there was no learning at all when the interval was as large as 30 seconds; in instrumental learning, late is sometimes no better than never (Perin, 1943).

To what extent does the delay of reward principle apply to humans? It depends upon which aspects of human behavior we consider. At one level there is an enormous gap between what we see in the rat and what we know of ourselves. Rats and humans live according to different time scales entirely. Reinforcement may come months or even years after an action and still have effect, because humans can relate their present to their past by all sorts of symbolic devices. A politician wins a close election, looks carefully at the returns, and realizes that a speech he gave a month ago turned the tide. Unlike the rat, humans can transcend the here and now.

SCHEDULES OF REINFORCEMENT

So far, we've primarily dealt with cases in which reinforcement follows the response every time it is made. But outside of the laboratory, this arrangement is surely the exception and not the rule. The fisherman does not hook a fish with every cast, and even a star tennis player occasionally loses a match to one of her less accomplished rivals. All of these are cases of **partial reinforcement,** in which a response is reinforced only some of the time.

One way of studying phenomena of this kind is in the operant situation. Here reinforcement can easily be *scheduled* in different ways—after every response, after some number of responses, after some interval, and so on. The **schedule of reinforcement** is simply the rule set up by the experimenter which determines the occasions on which a response is reinforced.

Ratio schedules One example of such a rule is the so-called **fixed-ratio schedule** (abbreviated FR 2, FR 4, FR 50, as the case may be) in which the subject has to produce a specified number of responses for every reward, like a factory worker paid by piecework. Such schedules can generate very high rates of responding but to get the organism to that level requires some finesse. The trick is to increase the ratio very gradually, beginning with continuous reinforcement and slowly stepping up the requirement. By such procedures, pigeons (and probably factory workers) have been led to perform at schedules as high as FR 500.

When the fixed ratio gets high enough, a new pattern develops. Following a reinforcement, the pigeon will pause for a while before it starts to peck again. The

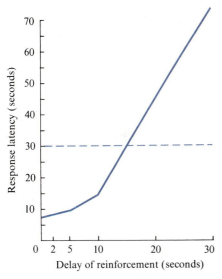

3.15   The effect of a delay in reinforcement   *The graph shows the response latency for rats pressing a lever after 50 trials on which they received a food reward following a delay of 0, 2, 5, 10, or 30 seconds. The dotted line indicates the animals' average latency at the very first trial. It is clear that animals trained with delays up to 10 seconds improved over trials, and the shorter the delay the greater was their improvement. But animals trained with a delay of 30 seconds did not improve; on the contrary, their performance was markedly worse after 50 trials than it was initially. (Data from Perin, 1943)*

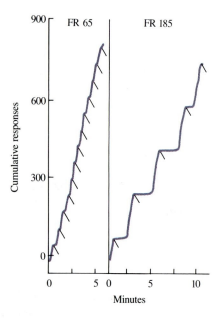

3.16   Performance on two fixed-ratio schedules   *The figure records the pigeon's cumulative responses—how many key pecks it has made after 5 minutes in the operant chamber, after 10 minutes, and so on. The steeper the record, the faster the response rate. The left-hand panel shows performance on FR 65, the right on FR 185. The small diagonal slashes indicate times when the animal received reinforcement. Note the characteristic pause after the fixed ratio has been run off, and that the duration of this pause increases with increasing ratios. (Adapted from Ferster and Skinner, 1957)*

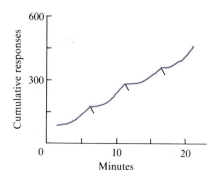

higher the ratio, the longer the pause (see Figure 3.16). In a way, the pigeon is like a student who has just finished one term paper and has to write another. It is very hard to start again, but once the first page is written, the next ones come more readily. In part, this effect is the result of a discrimination. A peck (or a page) is only reinforced if it is preceded by other pecks (or pages). Not having pecked before is then a stimulus associated with lack of reinforcement, an S⁻ which inhibits the response. The pause following reinforcement can be eliminated by changing the schedule to a ***variable ratio (VR).*** In VR schedules, reinforcement still comes after a certain number of responses but that number varies irregularly, averaging out to a particular ratio (for example VR 50). Now there is no way whereby the pigeon can know which of its pecks will bring reward. It might be the first, the tenth, or the hundredth peck following the last reinforcement. Since the number of prior pecks is no longer a clue, the pause disappears. A glance at a gambling casino gives proof that VR schedules affect humans much as they do pigeons. The slot machines are set to pay off occasionally, just enough to maintain the high rate of behavior that keeps the casino lucrative to its owners and not to its clients.

Interval schedules   Ratio schedules are based on *numbers* of responses. Another set of schedules is defined by intervals of *time.* In a ***fixed-interval schedule (FI),*** the animal is reinforced for the first response performed after a certain interval has passed following the last reinforcement, but it is not reinforced for any response performed before then. For example, if the interval is two minutes (FI 2), the pigeon may peck all it wants after a reinforcement, but all its work is of no avail until the two minutes are up. After this, the first peck will be rewarded and the cycle will start all over again. An example of an FI schedule in ordinary life is our mail delivery, which comes once a day (FI 24 hours).

After an animal has been on an FI schedule for a while, it shows a characteristic response pattern. Immediately after reinforcement, its response is very low, but this rate will gradually pick up and get faster and faster as the end of the interval approaches (see Figure 3.17).

The animal's response rate will become very stable and uniform if the animal is put on a ***variable-interval schedule (VI)*** (see Figure 3.18). This differs from an FI schedule in that the interval varies irregularly around some average period, say four minutes (VI 4). Unpleasant examples of such schedules in ordinary life involve aversive stimuli such as surprise quizzes in the classrooms and speed traps on the highway.

Partial reinforcement and extinction   Some of the most dramatic effects of partial reinforcement are seen during subsequent extinction. The basic fact can be stated very simply: A response will be much harder to extinguish if it was acquired during partial rather than continuous reinforcement. This phenomenon is often called the ***partial-reinforcement effect*** (Humphreys, 1939).

A good illustration is provided by an experiment in which several rats were trained on a runway for food (Weinstock, 1954). All animals received the same number of trials but not the same number of reinforcements. One group was reinforced on every trial, another only on 30 percent of the trials. Figure 3.19 shows what happened to these two groups during extinction. The rats reinforced 100 percent of the time gave up very much sooner than their partially reinforced

3.17   Performance on a fixed-interval schedule   *This figure shows the cumulative record of a pigeon's performance on a fixed-interval schedule, FI 5. The small diagonal slashes are reinforcements. Note the scalloped shape that is characteristic of performance on FI after the animal has been on that schedule for a few sessions. (After Ferster and Skinner, 1957)*

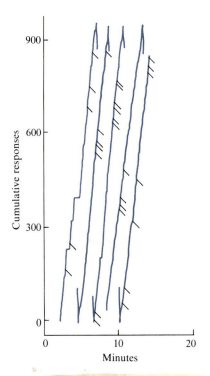

3.18 Performance on a variable-ratio schedule *This figure shows the cumulative record of a pigeon's performance on a variable ratio, VR 173. Again, the small slashes indicate reinforcements. As the record shows, response rates are very high and there are no pauses after reinforcement. (After Ferster and Skinner, 1957)*

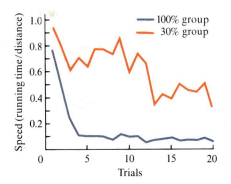

fellows. Numerous other experiments have given substantially the same result, on all manner of subjects, including humans.

On the face of it, the partial-reinforcement effect is paradoxical. If the strength of an instrumental response increases with increasing reinforcements, we should expect that groups reinforced 100 percent of the time would continue to respond for longer than those reinforced only partially. In fact, the very opposite is true. The question is why? Speaking loosely, we might suggest that the partially reinforced rat has come to expect that reward may occur even after several unrewarded trials; it has learned that "if you don't succeed, try and try again." In contrast, the rat reinforced 100 percent of the time has never encountered unreinforced trials before. If this interpretation of the partial-reinforcement effect is correct, we would expect an irregular sequence of reinforcements to be harder to extinguish than a regular one, even if the proportion of reinforcements is the same in both cases. This is precisely what happens. Thus ratio schedules engender greater resistance to extinction if they are variable rather than fixed.

To see the partial-reinforcement effect in action, consider a simple problem in child rearing. Many parents find that their six-month-old does not want to go to sleep; put into his crib at night, he howls his vehement protests until he is lifted out again. Sooner or later his parents resolve that this has to stop. The baby is put back in the crib, and the wails begin. The parents stay firm for a while but eventually they weaken (after all, the baby might be sick). Brought out of his crib, the baby gurgles happily, and the process of partial reinforcement has begun. Next time, the parents will have an even harder time. According to one study (and to common sense), the answer is consistent nonreinforcement. Two determined parents plotted an extinction curve for their twenty-one-month-old child's bedtime tantrums. One day they simply decided to put their little tyrant to bed and then leave the bedroom and not go back. On the first occasion, the child howled for forty-five minutes; the next few times the cries were much diminished, until finally after ten such "trials," the child went to sleep smiling and with no complaints at all (Williams, 1959).

AVERSIVE CONDITIONING

So far, our discussion of instrumental learning has largely centered on cases where reinforcement is positive, of the kind we normally call reward. But there is another class of events that is no less relevant to instrumental learning than is reward; it represents the opposite side of the coin—the stick rather than the carrot, punishment rather than reward. These are ***aversive stimuli,*** such as swats on the rear for infants and electric shock for laboratory rats. There is little doubt that both organisms learn whatever they must to minimize such unpleasantries, to get as few shocks, swats, and insulting reproofs as they possibly can.

Punishment Psychologists distinguish between several kinds of instrumental learning that depend on the use of aversive stimuli. The most familiar from everyday life is ***punishment training.*** Here, a response is followed by an aversive stimulus, which will then tend to suppress the response on subsequent occasions. One factor that determines the resulting response suppression is the extent to which reinforcement is delayed, which we've already discussed in the context of

3.19 The partial-reinforcement effect *The figure shows runway speeds during extinction of two groups of rats. One group had previously been reinforced on every trial; the other had only been reinforced on 30 percent of the trials. The figure shows that the group trained under full reinforcement (in blue) stops running considerably before the group that was trained under partial reinforcement (in red). (After Weinstock, 1954)*

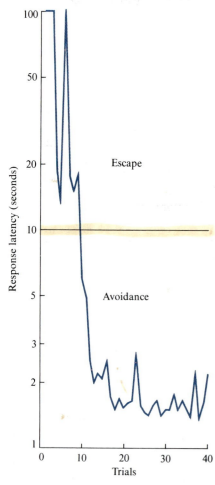

3.20   The course of avoidance learning in a dog   *The figure shows response latencies of one animal in a shuttle box (where latency is the time from the onset of CS to the animal's response). A warning stimulus indicated that shock would begin 10 seconds after the onset of the signal. For the first nine trials the dog escaped. It jumped over the hurdle after the shock began. From the tenth trial on, the dog avoided: It jumped before its 10 seconds of grace were up. The jumping speed increased even after this point until the animal jumped with an average latency of about 1½ seconds. (Latency is plotted on a logarithmic scale. This compresses the time scale so as to put greater emphasis on differences between the shorter response latencies.) (After Solomon and Wynne, 1953)*

reward. Consider a cat that has developed the unfortunate habit of using a large indoor plant as its private bathroom. The irate owner discovers the misdeed an hour or so later, and swats the cat severely when he sees it in the kitchen. It's hardly surprising that the punishment will not produce the hoped for hygienic result, for the animal has no way of connecting the crime with the punishment. For punishment to have its desired effect, it must be administered shortly after the unwanted response was performed. While humans are much better than cats at linking events that are separated in time, they too are subject to the delay of reinforcement principle. The young child who steals a cookie is more likely to refrain from further thefts if punished immediately than if told "Just wait until your father comes home."

Escape and avoidance   Aversive stimuli can weaken response tendencies (as in punishment training), but they can also be used to strengthen them. This happens in *escape* and *avoidance learning.* In escape learning, the response stops some aversive event that has already begun. In avoidance learning, the subject can forestall it altogether. An example of escape learning is when a rat learns to press a lever to get rid of an electric shock. An example of avoidance learning is when a dog learns to jump over a hurdle in a **shuttle box** when it hears a tone that signals impending shock; if it jumps within some grace period, it will manage to avoid the shock entirely (see Figure 3.20).

Aversive reinforcement and the law of effect   Both punishment training and escape learning readily fit into the Thorndike-Skinner conception of instrumental learning. Punishment training simply represents the opposite side of the law of effect: Where appetitive stimuli strengthen the response that precedes them, aversive stimuli weaken it. The interpretation of escape learning is even easier: The response is followed by the termination of an aversive stimulus, a termination which then serves as a reward.

The interpretation of avoidance learning is more difficult. Consider a dog who jumps back and forth over a hurdle to avoid shock. What is the reinforcement? It is not the *cessation* of shock as it is in escape learning, for the animal doesn't get shocked to begin with. Could it be the *absence of shock*? This too won't work, for *not* receiving punishment can only be a source of satisfaction if punishment has been threatened. (After all, most of us spend our entire lives without being drowned, beaten, or otherwise put to bodily harm, but we don't therefore regard ourselves as being in a state of perpetual bliss.) It's not absence of shock as such that is the reward. It is rather the *absence of shock (or any other aversive event) when shock is expected.*

Avoidance learning in human life   An enormous amount of ordinary human activity involves avoidance. We stop at red lights to avoid getting traffic tickets, pay bills to avoid interest charges, carry umbrellas to avoid getting wet, and devise excuses to avoid having lunch with a bore. We probably perform dozens of such learned avoidance responses each day, and most of them are perfectly useful and adaptive (Schwartz, 1989).

But some avoidance learning is essentially maladaptive and is often based on more potent aversive stimuli than a boring lunch. An extreme example is phobias. As already mentioned, some people have intense fears of various situations —heights, open spaces, dogs, elevators, and so on. As a result, they will develop elaborate patterns to avoid getting into these situations. In some cases, the phobia may be caused by traumatic experiences in the past as in the case of a woman who was trapped for several hours in a swaying elevator stuck between the fortieth and forty-first floor of an office building, and never used an elevator thereafter. Such an avoidance reaction is of little future use, for elevators ordinarily function perfectly well. But the trouble is that the avoidance response is self-perpetuating. It will not extinguish even if the aversive stimulus is no longer there. The reason is that the person (or animal) will not stay in the previously dangerous situation long enough to discover whether the danger is indeed still there. The woman who avoids elevators will never find out that they are now perfectly safe, for she won't ever use them again—a rather inconvenient behavior pattern if her own office happens to be above the forty-first floor.

Avoidance learning   *No doubt the infant will soon learn to avoid the flame.* (Photograph by Erika Stone)

Edward C. Tolman   (Courtesy Psychology Department, University of California, Berkeley)

COGNITIVE LEARNING

To the early behavior theorists, the essential thing about classical and instrumental conditioning was that both procedures modify action. This held for classical conditioning, which Pavlov saw as a rather primitive and mechanical extension of reflex action whereby the elicitation of certain responses (the UR's) is passed from one set of stimuli (the US's) to another (the CS's). It also held for instrumental conditioning, which Thorndike and Skinner regarded as the strengthening of certain responses by the mechanical effect of reinforcement.

From the earliest days of behavior theory, however, there was an alternative view that asserted that what really matters when animals (and humans) learn is that they acquire new *knowledge.* One of the most prominent exponents of this view was Edward C. Tolman (1886–1959), who argued that in both classical and instrumental conditioning an animal gains various bits of knowledge, or ***cognitions.*** These bits of knowledge are organized so that they can be utilized when needed. This is very different from asserting that the animal acquires a tendency to perform a certain response. As Tolman saw it, the response an animal acquires in the course of a learning experiment is only an index that a given cognition has been gained. It is an indispensable measuring stick, but it is not what is being measured. Rather the essence of what is learned is something within an animal, a private event that will only become public when the animal acts upon its newly acquired knowledge. Today such cognitions are often called ***representations,*** which correspond to (represent) certain events or relations between events in the animal's world (Dickinson, 1987).

Evidence that animals acquire cognitions came from a number of experiments designed to determine whether instrumental learning can occur without the performance of the relevant response. Many early behavior theorists had claimed that performance is an indispensable ingredient for instrumental learning, insisting that the animal "learns by doing" and in no other way. Several studies, however, suggest that this is not the case. For example, rats have been ferried from one end of a large room to another in transparent trolley cars. Later tests showed that they had learned something about the general features of the room even though they had not performed any relevant responses during their trolley-car ride (Gleitman, 1963). They had acquired what Tolman called a "cognitive map" that represents what is where and what leads to what (Tolman, 1948).

A Cognitive View of Classical Conditioning

The cognitive approach has had considerable impact on current conceptions of animal learning and may well be the dominant position in the field today. One of its effects was a reinterpretation of classical conditioning. Pavlov believed that the essential feature of classical conditioning is the newly achieved ability of one stimulus to elicit a response that was originally evoked by another. But some current investigators have a different interpretation. They believe that the animal ac-

Conditioning is more efficient when CS precedes UCS but declines when interval between CS - UCS increases beyond optimal interval.

Temporal relation of CS and UCS.

Contingency measure whether CS - UCS are based on variation of interval between two stimuli

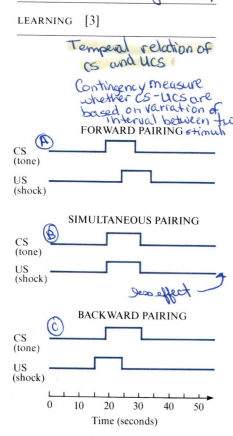

FORWARD PAIRING

CS (tone)

US (shock)

Ⓐ

SIMULTANEOUS PAIRING

CS (tone)

US (shock)

Ⓑ

less effect

BACKWARD PAIRING

CS (tone)

US (shock)

Ⓒ

Time (seconds)
0 10 20 30 40 50

3.21 Some temporal relationships in classical conditioning

quires a representation about the relation between the two stimulus events. Instead of substituting for the US, the CS becomes a sign that the US will follow (Tolman, 1932; Rescorla, 1988).

TEMPORAL RELATIONS BETWEEN THE CS AND THE US

It appears that what is learned in classical conditioning is an association between two events: the CS and the US. But how is this association acquired? In line with many philosophers who had thought about association, Pavlov believed that a necessary condition is temporal *contiguity,* that is, togetherness in time. As we will see, the answer is not quite as simple as that.

One way of finding out whether the CS-US association is based on contiguity in time is to vary the interval between the two stimuli as well as the order in which they are presented. A number of procedures do just that. In some, the CS precedes the US *(forward pairing),* in others it follows the US *(backward pairing),* and in yet others the two stimuli are presented at the same time *(simultaneous pairing).* (See Figure 3.21.)

The general results of these procedures are as follows: Conditioning is best when the CS *precedes* the US by some optimum interval that is generally rather short (see Figure 3.22).* Presenting the CS and the US simultaneously is generally much less effective, and the backward procedure is even worse. On the other hand, the effectiveness of forward pairing declines rapidly when the CS-US interval increases beyond the optimum interval (Rescorla, 1988, p. 337).

How can we make sense of these facts? A reasonable suggestion is that the CS serves a signaling function: It prepares the organism for a US that is to come. Let us consider forward, simultaneous, and backward pairing in this light by likening the subject's situation to that of a driver setting out upon an unfamiliar road. Suppose our driver wants to go from Denver to Salt Lake City and that some 150 miles out of Denver there is a dangerous hairpin turn over a ravine. How should the driver be warned of the impending curve? Presumably there will be a sign, "Hairpin Turn," which should obviously appear just a bit before the turn (analogous to forward pairing with a short CS-US interval). If the interval is too long it will be almost impossible to connect the sign with that which it signifies. We will lose some of our faith in the Highway Department if it sets up the sign, "Hairpin Turn," just outside the Denver city limits while the turn itself is three hours away (forward pairing with a long CS-US interval). Our faith will be really shaken if we see the sign prominently displayed just at the sharpest bend of the turn (simultaneous pairing). We finally begin to suspect a degree of malevolence if we discover the sign innocently placed on the road a hundred feet or so beyond the turn (backward pairing), though we should probably be grateful that we did not find it at the bottom of the ravine.

* The precise value of that optimum interval depends on the particulars of the situation; it usually varies from about half a second to about ten seconds. In one form of classical conditioning, learned taste aversion, the optimum CS-US is very much longer and may be of the order of an hour or more. This phenomenon poses obvious difficulties for a contiguity theory of conditioning—and much else besides—and will be discussed in a later section (see p. 97).

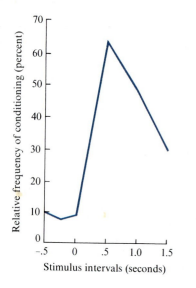

Relative frequency of conditioning (percent)
70
60
50
40
30
20
10
0

Stimulus intervals (seconds)
-.5 0 .5 1.0 1.5

3.22 The CS-US interval in classical conditioning *The figure shows the results of a study on the effectiveness of various CS-US intervals in humans. The CR was a finger withdrawal response, the CS a tone, and the US an electric shock. The time between CS and US is plotted on the horizontal axis. Negative intervals mean that the US was presented before the CS (backward pairing), a zero interval means that the two stimuli were presented simultaneously, and a positive interval means that the CS began before the US (forward pairing). The vertical axis indicates the degree of conditioning. (After Spooner and Kellogg, 1947)*

Table 3.1 CONTINGENCY IN
CLASSICAL CONDITIONING

Three tables illustrating three different CS/US contingency arrangements in a hypothetical experiment in which the CS is a tone and the US is meat powder. Each table presents a different tone/meat contingency based on twenty trials. The column labeled p *shows the probabilities that meat will occur under a particular stimulus condition.*

Meat contingent upon tone

	Meat	No Meat	*p*
Tone	8	2	.80
No Tone	2	8	.20

Meat contingent upon absence of tone

	Meat	No Meat	*p*
Tone	3	7	.30
No Tone	7	3	.70

Meat and tone independent

	Meat	No Meat	*p*
Tone	5	5	.50
No Tone	5	5	.50

It would seem that in classical conditioning an organism learns that one stimulus is a signal for another. The next task is to describe just what such a sign relationship between two events consists of.

Consider a dog in Pavlov's laboratory who is exposed to several presentations of a beating metronome followed by some food powder. The poor beast doesn't know that he is supposed to form a CS-US connection. All he knows is that every once in a while food appears. There are all sorts of stimuli in the laboratory situation. Of course he hears the metronome, but he also hears doors slamming, and a babble of (Russian) voices in the background, and he feels the strap of the conditioning harness. How does he discover that it is the metronome that is the signal for food rather than the scores of other stimuli that he was also exposed to? After all, no one told him that metronome beats are Professor Pavlov's favorite conditioned stimuli.

A useful way of trying to understand what happens is to think of the animal as an amateur scientist. Like all scientists, the dog wants to predict important events. (When his human counterparts succeed, they publish; when the dog succeeds, he salivates.) How can he predict when food will appear? He might decide to rely on mere contiguity and salivate to any stimulus that occurs along with food presentation. But if so, he'd have to salivate whenever he was strapped in his harness or whenever he heard voices, for these stimuli were generally present when he was fed. But if the dog had any scientific talent at all, he would realize that the harness and the voices are very poor food predictors. To be sure, they occur when food is given, but they occur just as frequently when it is not. To continue in his scientific quest, the dog would look for an event that occurs when food appears and that does not occur when food is absent. The metronome beat is the one stimulus that fulfills *both* of these conditions, for it never beats in the intervals between trials when food is not presented. Science (or rather classical conditioning) has triumphed, and the dog is ready to announce his findings by salivating when the CS is presented and at no other times.

Contingency versus contiguity The preceding account is a fanciful statement of an influential analysis of classical conditioning developed by Robert Rescorla (Rescorla, 1967). According to Rescorla, classical conditioning depends not only on CS-US pairings but also on pairings in which the absence of CS goes along with the *absence of US.* These two experiences—metronome/meat, and no metronome/no meat—allow the dog to discover that the occurrence of the US is **contingent** (that is, dependent) upon the occurrence of the CS. According to Rescorla, conditioning does not occur because the US is contiguous with the CS but rather because it is contingent upon the CS. By determining this contingency, the animal can forecast what is going to happen next.

To determine if getting meat is contingent upon the metronome, the animal must somehow compute two probabilities: the probability of getting meat when the metronome is sounded and the probability of getting meat when it is not. If the first probability is greater than the second, then getting meat is contingent upon the metronome. If it is smaller than the second, getting meat is contingent upon the absence of the tone. Such a negative contingency is analogous to the relation between a sunny sky and rain—rain is more likely when the sun is *not* shining. An important final possibility is that the two probabilities are identical. If so, there is no contingency, and the two events are independent (see Table 3.1).

If this line of thinking is correct, it follows that temporal contiguity as such will not produce conditioning. For according to this view, conditioning will only occur if the probability of a US when the CS is present is greater than the probability of a US when the CS is absent. To prove his point, Rescorla exposed rats to

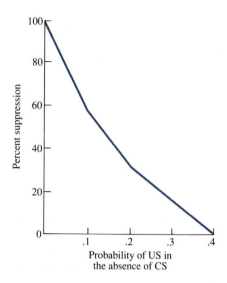

3.23   Contingency in classical conditioning   *The figure shows the results of fear conditioning as a function of contingency. The probability of the US in the presence of the CS was always .40, but the probability of the US in the absence of the CS varied from 0 to .40. Conditioning was measured by the degree of response suppression. (After Rescorla, 1966)*

various combinations of a tone CS and a shock US in a conditioned suppression experiment. In one set of conditions, the probability of receiving a shock when the tone was sounded was always the same (about .40). What varied was the probability that a shock would occur when no tone was sounded. The results were clear-cut. If the likelihood of a shock when the tone was on was the same as the likelihood of a shock when the tone was off, there was no conditioning. But if the likelihood of a shock was smaller when the tone was off than when it was on, conditioning did take place. The greater the difference in these probabilities, the stronger the level of conditioning the animal achieved (see Figure 3.23). The critical factor is evidently not contiguity, because the sheer number of CS-US pairings was identical for all groups. What mattered is whether the tone became an informative signal that told the animal that shock was more likely now than at other times (Rescorla, 1967, 1988).

The absence of contingency   What happens when there is no contingency whatsoever? On the face of it, there is nothing to learn. But in a situation in which there is fear and danger (for example, electric shock) the animal does learn something after all: It can never feel safe at any time.

Consider two situations. In one, there is a CS that signals that shock is likely to follow. When the CS appears, the animal will become more fearful. But there is a compensation. When there is no CS, the animal can relax, for now shock is less likely. The absence of the CS has become a ***safety signal.***

The situation is quite different when there is no stimulus that predicts when shock will occur. Now the animal is worse off than it is when there is a CS-US contingency, for it now has good reason to be afraid at all times. This unpleasant state of affairs is mirrored by a number of harmful physiological consequences. For example, rats who are exposed to unsignaled electric shock are much more likely to develop stomach ulcers than rats who receive just as many shocks, but with a signal that predicts their occurrence (Seligman, 1968; Weiss, 1970, 1977).

BLOCKING

We've seen that an animal in a conditioning experiment can be likened to a scientist who tries to predict something in the world around him. To predict the occurrence of the US, the animal must discover a contingency between this US and some other stimulus event (the CS). Such a contingency is a necessary requirement without which conditioning will not occur. But as it turns out, contingency alone is not sufficient. Animals don't pay equal attention to everything in the world around them; they have various prejudices about what is important and what is not. In this regard, they are no different from ourselves.

Suppose prior experience makes us believe that one given event causes another. This may make us ignore some other aspects of the situation that are no less important. Consider the early biologists who asked themselves where maggots come from. Whenever they saw rotting meat, they saw maggots, and they never saw maggots anywhere else. As a result, they assumed that the maggots' appearance was contingent upon the rotting meat (which they took as proof for the theory that life is generated spontaneously). Once having discovered a contingency (which fit in with their prior beliefs), they were blinded to other contingencies that were also present—such as the fact that the meat had been lying around for a while (so flies could lay their eggs in it). Something similar holds for animals in classical conditioning laboratories. If they've already found a stimulus that signals the appearance of the US, they don't attend to other stimuli that are additional signals but provide no further information. The old stimuli overshadow the recognition of the new, much as a scientist's old theory prejudices her to further facts.

The effect of prior experience on attention was demonstrated by a study in which rats first received a series of trials during which a sound was followed by shock. Not surprisingly, this sound became a CS for conditioned fear. In a later series of trials, the shock was preceded by *two* stimuli that were presented simultaneously: one was the same sound that had previously served as a CS for shock, the other was a light. After this, they were tested with the light alone to see whether this would produce a conditioned fear reaction. The results showed that the animals were completely undisturbed by the light. What had happened? The answer is that the light did not provide any new information. The sound already told the animals about the impending shock, and so they never paid attention to the light. As a result, they never connected the light with the shock, an effect technically known as ***blocking*** (Kamin, 1969).

A Cognitive View of Instrumental Conditioning

We have seen that what is learned in classical conditioning is a representation about the relation between two stimulus events, the CS and the US. There is reason to believe that a similar cognitive account applies to instrumental conditioning. As with classical conditioning, this interpretation goes back to Tolman. Thorndike and Skinner had argued that instrumental learning involves the strengthening of a particular response, such as pressing a bar in a Skinner box. In contrast, Tolman believed that the animal acquires an internal representation of the relation between the response and the reinforcer that followed it: It learns *that the bar* led to a food pellet. In effect, it acquires an association between an act and its outcome. This act-outcome representation might or might not be used on a later occasion, depending on the circumstances, such as the animal's needs and motives (Tolman, 1932).

EVIDENCE FOR ACT-OUTCOME ASSOCIATIONS

Early evidence that animals do acquire act-outcome cognitions of this sort comes from a study in which rats were run in an enclosed maze that had a black end box on one side and a white one on the other (see Figure 3.24). Both ends contained food, and the animals chose indifferently between them on several trials. Subsequently, the animals were placed into each box by hand without actually running the maze. In one end box they now found food as before; in the other they were shocked. After all this, the animals were again allowed to run down the original maze. Now virtually all of them chose the side away from the end box in which they had been shocked. Clearly, the rats had learned which turn led to which box, but this cognition led to selective action only after the two boxes had acquired

3.24   Proving that rats learn what leads to where   (I) Floor plan of a maze in the first phase of an experiment during which rats could learn that a left turn leads to end box A, a right turn to end box B. (II) The second phase of the experiment in which the two end boxes were detached from the rest of the maze and the animals were shocked in one of them, say, A. (III) In the third phase of the experiment, the animals were returned to the original situation. If they could put the two experiences together, then, having learned that a left turn led to A and that A led to shock, they should turn right—that is, away from shock. The results showed that they did. (After Tolman and Gleitman, 1949)

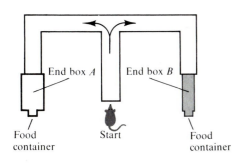

Food container   Start   Food container

I

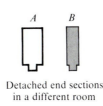

A   B

Detached end sections in a different room

II

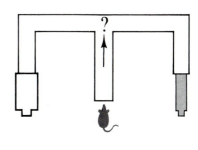

III

3.33   The same-different problem   *(After Premack and Premack, 1972)*

Having matched to sample on only three prior problems, Sarah and a few other animals readily handled new problems, performing perfectly on the very first trial. Even more impressive is the fact that Sarah learned to use two special tokens to indicate *same* and *different*. She was first shown two identical objects, such as two cups, and was then given a token whose intended meaning was *same.* Her task was to place this *same* token between the two cups. She was then presented with two different objects, such as a cup and a spoon, was given yet another token intended to mean *different,* and was required to place this *different* token between the cup and the spoon. After several such trials, she was tested with several pairs of items, some identical and some different, had to decide whether to place the *same* or the *different* token between them, and did so correctly (see Figure 3.33).

Such accomplishments show that chimpanzees can develop a way of thinking about the world that goes beyond the specific perceptual relations of the concrete moment. They can of course respond to these concrete relationships, for example, the relationship between, say, red and red, circle and circle, A-flat and A-flat. But chimpanzees can also deal with some *higher-order relationships,* the relations that hold between the various concrete relationships. They can therefore recognize that the relation between red and red is identical to that between circle and circle, and for that matter between hippopotamus and hippopotamus—that in all of these the relation is *sameness*.

TAKING STOCK

What is the upshot of the scientific study of animal learning that began with the studies of Pavlov and Thorndike some ninety years ago? It is clear that they and their intellectual descendants have discovered many vital phenomena of learning. Whether the principles they uncovered in their study of habituation, classical conditioning, and instrumental conditioning underlie all forms of learning is still a matter of debate. For certain complex intellectual achievements in animals and humans such as insightful understanding, abstract concepts, and—especially—human language may well be acquired in some different ways. But there is no question that the study of how CS-US and response-reinforcer relations are acquired and represented in animals will give important clues about the fundamental nature of some rock-bottom learning processes that are found in both humans and animals.

When we began our discussion, our initial focus was on *action,* on how classical and instrumental conditioning change what animals *do:* how Pavlov's dogs came to salivate at ticking metronomes they had never heard before, how Thorndike's cats came to perform all sorts of novel tricks. But as we saw, these changes of overt behavior are only one aspect of what has happened to these animals— they are the consequence of having learned rather than its essence. For unlike

Pavlov and Thorndike, who focused on the overt behavior, modern investigators of animal learning have shown that at bottom classical and instrumental conditioning (and many other forms of learning too) depend on *cognition*. Rats—and dogs and pigeons—learn what events predict what other events and what actions produce what outcomes. These and other phenomena make it clear that psychological functions involve not just what animals and humans do, but also what they *know*.

Psychology must necessarily deal with both action and knowledge. In our discussion of animal learning we have straddled them both, for the field represents a kind of a bridge between these two major concerns. We will now cross the bridge completely and move on to the study of cognition as a topic in its own right.

SUMMARY

1. The simplest of all forms of learning is *habituation,* a decline in the tendency to respond to stimuli that have become familiar through repeated exposure.

2. In habituation the organism learns that it has encountered a stimulus before. In *classical conditioning,* first studied by I. P. Pavlov, it learns about the *association* between one stimulus and another. Prior to conditioning, an *unconditioned stimulus* or *US* (such as food) elicits an *unconditioned response* or *UR* (such as salivation). After repeated pairings of the US with a *conditioned stimulus* or *CS* (such as a buzzer), this CS alone will evoke a *conditioned response* or *CR* (here again, salivation) that is often similar to the UR.

3. The strength of conditioning is assessed by the readiness with which the CS elicits the CR. This strength increases with the number of *reinforced trials,* that is, pairings of the CS and the US. When a CS-US relation is well established, the CS can be paired with a second neutral stimulus to produce *higher-order conditioning.*

4. Nonreinforced trials, during which the CS is presented without the US, lead to *extinction,* a decreased tendency of the CS to evoke the CR. According to some authors, the CR is masked rather than abolished by extinction, as shown by the phenomenon of *spontaneous recovery.*

5. The CR is elicited not only by the CS but also by stimuli that are similar to it. This effect, *stimulus generalization,* increases the greater the similarity between the CS and the new stimulus. To train the animal to respond to the CS but not to other stimuli, one stimulus (CS^+) is presented with the US, while another (CS^-) is presented without the US. The more similar the CS^+ is to the CS^-, the more difficult this *discrimination* will be.

6. Classical conditioning can involve many responses other than salivation, for example, conditioning of fear as assessed by the *conditioned emotional response (CER)* procedure.

7. In classical conditioning, the US is presented regardless of whether the animal performs the CR or not. In another form of simple learning, *instrumental conditioning* (or *operant conditioning*), something analogous to the US, reward or *reinforcement,* is only delivered upon performance of the appropriate instrumental response.

8. An early study of instrumental conditioning was conducted by E. L. Thorndike using cats that learned to perform an arbitrary response to escape from a *puzzle box.* As Thorndike saw it, what the animals learned involved no understanding but was rather based on a gradual strengthening of the correct response and a weakening of the incorrect one. To account for this, he proposed his *law of effect,* which states that the tendency to perform a response is strengthened if it is followed by a reward (reinforcement) and weakened if it is not.

9. During the past sixty years or so, the major figure in the study of instrumental conditioning has been B. F. Skinner, who was one of the first theorists to insist on a sharp distinction between classical conditioning in which the CR is *elicited* by the CS, and instrumental (which he called *operant*) conditioning in which the instrumental response, or *operant,* is *emitted* from within. Operants are strengthened by *reinforcement,* but their acquisition may require some initial *shaping* by the method of *successive approximations.*

10. While some reinforcers are stimuli whose reinforcing power is unlearned, others are *conditioned reinforcers* that acquire their reinforcing power from prior pairings with stimuli that already have that capacity. One of the factors that determines the strength of instrumental conditioning is the *delay of reinforcement:* The shorter the interval between the response and the reinforcement, the stronger the response will be.

11. During *partial reinforcement,* the response is reinforced only some of the time. Responses that were originally learned under partial reinforcement are harder to extinguish than those learned when the response was always reinforced. The rule that determines the occasions under which reinforcement is given is a *schedule of reinforcement.* In *ratio schedules,* reinforcement comes after a number of responses, which may be fixed or variable. In *interval schedules,* the animal is reinforced for the first response made after a given interval since the last reinforcement, which again can be fixed or variable.

12. Reinforcement can be provided by the presentation of *appetitive stimuli,* or by the termination or prevention of *aversive stimuli.* Aversive stimuli can weaken or strengthen instrumental responses, depending on the relation between the aversive stimulus and the response. In *punishment training,* the response is followed by an aversive stimulus; as a result, the animal learns *not* to perform it. In *escape learning,* the response stops an aversive stimulus that has already begun; in *avoidance training,* it averts it altogether.

13. Pavlov, Thorndike, and Skinner believed that the essential aspect of both classical and instrumental conditioning is that they modify *action. Cognitive theorists* such as Köhler, Tolman, and, more recently, Rescorla believe that what really matters when humans and animals learn is that they acquire new bits of knowledge or *cognitions.* According to many theorists, what is learned in classical conditioning is an association about two events, the CS and the US, such that the CS serves as a signal for the US. One line of evidence comes from studies of the effect of the CS-US interval. The general finding is that conditioning is more effective when the CS precedes the US by some optimum interval, which is typically rather short.

14. A number of investigators have asked how the animal learns that the CS is a signal for the US. The evidence shows that CS-US pairings alone will not suffice; there must also be trials on which the absence of CS goes along with the absence of US. This allows the animal to discover that the US is *contingent* (depends) upon the CS.

15. Unlike Thorndike and Skinner who argue that instrumental learning involves the strengthening of an instrumental response, cognitive theorists believe that it is based on an association between an act and its outcome. Evidence for this view comes from studies in which animals are trained to perform two responses that lead to two different outcomes, after which one of the outcomes is made less desirable. Subsequent tests indicate that the animals have learned which response led to what.

16. Contingency is crucial in instrumental conditioning just as it is in classical conditioning. In instrumental conditioning, the relevant contingency is between a response and an outcome. When there is no such contingency, the organism learns that it has no *response control.* Threatening conditions in which there is no response control may engender *learned helplessness,* which often generalizes to other situations.

17. According to Pavlov, Skinner, and other early behavior theorists, the connections established by classical and instrumental conditioning are essentially *arbitrary.* This view is challenged by the fact that certain CS's are more readily associated with some US's than with others, as shown by studies of *learned taste aversions* in rats. These studies suggest that animals are biologically "prepared" to learn certain relations more readily than others.

18. Cognitive theorists point out that animals are capable of rather complex cognitions. Evidence comes from work on spatial memory in rats and chimpanzees which shows that these animals can acquire rather elaborate *cognitive maps.* Further work concerns the ability to abstract *conceptual* relationships. Early evidence came from Köhler's studies of *insightful learning* in chimpanzees, who showed wide and appropriate transfer when later tested in novel situations. Later work showed that monkeys acquire *learning sets* and learn to learn when solving discrimination problems. Another example is provided by chimpanzees who can acquire certain *higher-order* concepts such as "same-different."

PART II

Cognition

The approach to mental life we have considered thus far emphasizes action, whether natively given or modified by learning. It is an approach that asks what organisms do and how they do it. We now turn to another approach to mental functioning that asks what organisms know and how they come to know it.

Both humans and many animals are capable of knowledge, though in our own species, knowing (or cognition*) is vastly more refined. We know about the world directly around us,* perceiving *objects and events that are in our here and now, like the rose that we can see and smell. We also know about events in our past at least some of which are stored in our* memory *and can be retrieved at some later time; the rose may fade, but we can recall what it looked like when it was still in bloom. Our knowledge can be transformed and manipulated by* thinking; *we can somehow sift and analyze our experiences to emerge with new and often abstract notions, so that we can think of the faded rose petals as but one stage in a reproductive cycle which in turn reflects the procession of the seasons. Finally, we can communicate our knowledge to others by the use of* language, *a uniquely human capacity which allows us to accumulate knowledge across the generations, each building upon the discoveries of the preceding.*

CHAPTER 4

Sensory Processes

To survive, we must know the world around us. For most objects in the world are charged with meaning. Some are food, others are mates, still others are mortal enemies. The ability to distinguish between these—say, between a log and a crocodile—is literally a matter of life and death. To make these distinctions, we have to use our senses. We must do our best to see, hear, and smell the crocodile so that we can recognize it for what it is before it sees, hears, smells, and (especially) tastes and touches us.

THE ORIGINS OF KNOWLEDGE

The study of sensory experience grows out of an ancient question: Where does human knowledge come from? Most philosophers in the past subscribed to one of two opposed positions. The *empiricists* maintained that all knowledge is acquired through experience. In contrast, the *nativists* argued that many aspects of our knowledge are based on innately given characteristics of the human mind (or, as we would now say, of the brain).

The Empiricist View

A major proponent of the empiricist position was the English philosopher John Locke (1632–1704). Locke maintained that all knowledge comes through the senses. There are no innate ideas; at birth, the human mind is a blank tablet, a *tabula rasa,* upon which experience leaves its marks.

> Let us suppose the mind to be, as we say, a white paper void of all characters, without any ideas:—How comes it to be furnished? Whence comes it by that vast store which the busy and boundless fancy of man has painted on it with an almost endless variety? Whence has it all the materials of reason and knowledge? To this I answer, in one word, from *experience.* In that all our knowledge is founded; and from that it ultimately derives itself (Locke, 1690).

John Locke *(Courtesy National Library of Medicine)*

Locke's view fit in well with the emerging liberalism that was the dominant sentiment of the rising middle classes during the eighteenth century. The merchants and manufacturers of Western Europe had little use for the hereditary privileges of a landed aristocracy or the divine right of kings to govern (and worse, to tax) as they chose. Under the circumstances, they readily grasped at any doctrine that proclaimed the essential equality of all men. If all men enter life with a *tabula rasa,* then all distinctions among them must be due entirely to a difference in their environments.

DISTAL AND PROXIMAL STIMULI

Given the assumption that all knowledge comes through the senses, it was natural enough to ask about the kind of knowledge that the senses can give us. What is the information that the senses receive? Consider vision. We look at a tree some distance away. Light reflected from the tree's outer surface enters through the pupil of the eye, is gathered by the lens, and is cast as an image upon the photosensitive region at the rear of the eye called the ***retina.*** The stimuli that are involved in this visual sequence can be described in either of two ways. We can talk about the ***distal stimulus,*** an object or event in the world outside, such as the tree. (This is typically at some distance from the perceiver, hence the term *distal.*) We can also talk about the ***proximal stimulus,*** the pattern of stimulus energies that takes its origin at the distal stimulus and finally impinges on a sensory surface of the organism (hence, the term *proximal.*). In our example, this proximal stimulus would be the optical image the tree casts on the retina. As perceivers, our interest obviously centers upon the distal stimulus, the real object in the world outside. We want to know about the tree, not its retinal image. Our interest is in the tree's real size, its distance away from us, the kinds of leaves it has, and so on. But we can only learn about the distal stimulus through the proximal stimuli to which it gives rise. There is no way of really seeing the tree out there without a retinal image of the tree. The same holds for the other senses. We can only smell a rotten egg (the distal stimulus) because of hydrogen sulfide molecules suspended in the air which flows over the sensory cells in our nasal cavities (the proximal stimulus).

If the senses are the only portals we have to the world outside, the proximal stimuli are the only messengers that are allowed to pass information through them. Such heirs of Locke as Bishop George Berkeley (1685–1753) were quick to show that this fact has enormous consequences. For one thing, the sensory information provided by the proximal stimulus seems to lack many of the qualities that presumably characterize the external object (that is, the distal stimulus) to which this information refers.

Berkeley pointed out that we cannot tell the size of the physical object from the size of its retinal image. Our tree might be a miniature plant nearby or a giant one in the distance. By the same token, we cannot tell whether an object is in motion or at rest from its retinal image alone, for motion of the image may be caused by motion of the external object or by movements of the observer's eye. It appears that the knowledge that comes by way of the retinal image is very meager (see Figure 4.1).

SENSATIONS

Considerations of this sort led later empiricists to assume that the raw materials out of which knowledge is constructed are ***sensations.*** These are the primitive experiences that the senses give us and upon which we must then build. Green and brown are examples of visual sensations. An example of an auditory sensation

Bishop George Berkeley *(Detail from* The Bermuda Group *by John Smibert; courtesy Yale University Art Gallery, gift of Isaac Lothrop of Plymouth, Mass.)*

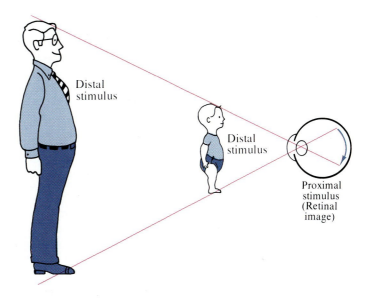

4.1 Distal and proximal stimuli *The baby in diapers and his father are distal stimuli, real objects in the world outside. The proximal stimuli they give rise to are the images they cast on the retina. In the example, the baby is one-third the size of his father. But since the father is three times farther removed from the observer's eye than the baby, the size of the retinal image he casts is the same as the one cast by the baby.*

would be a loud A-flat. An example of a gustatory (that is, taste) sensation would be a bitter taste. According to the empiricists, our perceptual experience is ultimately composed of such sensations—a mosaic of colored patches, tones of different pitch and loudness, sweets and sours, and so on.

Can this description possibly do justice to the richness of our perceptual world? The fact is that we do see trees (and innumerable other objects) and not mere patches of green and brown. While Bishop Berkeley might argue that our vision cannot inform us about depth or true size, in actual life we seem to have little difficulty in telling how far an object is away from us. (Were it otherwise, every automobile would become a wreck within minutes of leaving the showroom.) And we can in fact perceive the true size of an object. After all, even Berkeley would have had little trouble in distinguishing between a tiger in the distance and a kitten close by.

How did the empiricists reconcile these facts with their assumptions about the nature of sensation? Their answer was learning.

THE ROLE OF ASSOCIATION

The empiricists assumed that the organized character and the meaningfulness of our perceptual world are achieved by prior experience. The key to this accomplishment was held to be ***association,*** the process whereby one sensation is linked to another. The basic idea was very simple: If two sensations occur together often enough, eventually one of them will evoke the idea of the other. According to the empiricists, this associative linkage is the cement that binds the separate components of the perceptual world to each other.*

An example is provided by the various ***distance cues.*** Some of these had been noted by the painters of the Renaissance who discovered several techniques for rendering a three-dimensional world on a two-dimensional canvas. Among them was ***linear perspective***—objects appear to be farther away as they decrease in size

---

* It is obvious that the notion of association is at the root of many of the theories of learning we have described in previous chapters. For instance, Pavlov's conceptions of classical conditioning are in many ways derived from the views of the early associationists.

4.2 The use of linear perspective in Renaissance art The School of Athens by Raphael, 1509–1511. (Stanze di Raffaello, Vatican; courtesy Scala/Art Resource)

Immanuel Kant (Courtesy National Library of Medicine)

(Figure 4.2). To an empiricist, the explanation is a matter of prior association. Visual cues of perspective generally precede reaching or walking; eventually, the visual cue alone will produce the memory of the appropriate movement and thus the experience of depth.

The Nativist Rejoinder

The major theoretical alternative to the empiricist conception is *nativism,* which asserts that many aspects of perceptual experience are part of our natural endowment and do not depend on learning. This general position has a long ancestry with roots that go back as far as Plato. In more recent times, the more influential nativist rejoinder to empiricism came from the German philosopher Immanuel Kant (1724–1804). Kant argued that knowledge cannot come from sensory input alone; there must also be certain preexisting "categories" according to which this sensory material is ordered and organized. Examples are space, time, and causality—categories which, according to Kant, are *a priori,* built into the mind (or, as we would now say, into the nervous system). In Kant's view, there is no way in which we can see the world except in terms of these categories. It is as if we looked at the world through colored spectacles that we could never take off; if they were red, then redness would necessarily be part of everything we see. According to Kant, what experience does is to provide the sensory input that is then ordered according to the *a priori* categories. But the categories themselves, and the way in which they order the sensory information, are natively given.

PSYCHOPHYSICS

The dispute between empiricists and nativists focused attention on the role of the senses and prodded later investigators into efforts to discover just how these senses function. The question they were concerned with can be stated very simply: What is the chain of events that begins with a stimulus and leads up to reports such as "a bitter taste," a "dull pressure," or a "brightish green"? The details of this sequence are obviously very different for the different senses. Vision differs from hearing, and both differ from taste—in the stimuli that normally excite them, in their receptors, in the qualities of their sensations. Even so, we can analyze the path from stimulus to sensory experience in quite similar ways, whatever the particular sense may be.

In all cases, one can crudely distinguish three steps in the sequence. First, there is the proximal stimulus. Second, there is the neural chain of events that this stimulus gives rise to. The stimulus is converted (technically, *transduced*) into an electrical signal, which is then translated into the only language that all neurons understand, the nerve impulse.* Once converted in this manner, the message is transmitted further and often is modified by other parts of the nervous system. Third, there is some sort of psychological response to the message, often in the form of a conscious, sensory experience (or sensation).

The sensory sequence can be looked at from several points of view. One concerns the *psychophysical* relations between some property of the (physical) stimulus and the (psychological) sensory experience it ultimately gives rise to, quite apart from the intervening neural steps. Another approach concerns the *psychophysiology.* Here the questions concern the neural consequences of a given stimulus input—how it affects the receptors and the neural structures higher up in the brain. For now, we will confine our discussion to psychophysical matters, leaving psychophysiological issues for later on.

The object of *psychophysics* is to relate the characteristics of physical stimuli to attributes of the sensory experience they produce. There are a variety of stimuli to which the human organism is sensitive. They include chemicals suspended in air or dissolved in water, temperature changes on the skin, pressure on the skin or within various parts of the body, pressure in the form of sound waves, and electromagnetic radiations within the visible spectrum. In each case, the sensory system will not respond unless the stimulus energy is above some critical level of intensity, the so-called *absolute threshold.*

The range of stimuli to which a given sensory system reacts is actually quite limited. Human sight is restricted to the visible spectrum and human hearing to sound waves between 20 and 20,000 hertz (that is, cycles per second). But there are many organisms that respond to different ranges of stimulation and thus see and hear a world different from ours. Many insects see ultraviolet light, while dogs and cats hear sound waves of much higher frequency than we can. The bat has carried high-frequency hearing to a point of exquisite perfection. As it glides through the night it emits high-pitched screams of about 100,000 hertz which are used as a kind of sonar. They bounce off small objects in the air such as insects, echo back to the bat, and thus enable it to locate its prey.

Measuring Sensory Intensity

Measuring the magnitude of a stimulus is in principle easy enough. We measure the physical stimulus energy—in pounds, in degrees centigrade, in footcandles, in decibels, or whatever. But matters become more difficult when we try to assess *psychological intensity,* the magnitude of a sensation rather than that of a stimulus.

Gustav Theodor Fechner (1801–1887), the founder of psychophysics, believed that sensations cannot be measured directly. In his view, sensations and the stim-

Gustav Theodor Fechner (Courtesy National Library of Medicine)

---

* This is typically a two-stage affair. The transduction process produces a graded potential in specialized receptor cells, which in their turn trigger a nerve impulse in other neurons.

uli that produce them belong to two totally different realms—to use the terms many philosophers employ, that of the body and that of the mind. If this is so, how can one possibly describe them by reference to the same yardstick? Fechner argued that while sensations can't be compared to physical stimuli, they can at least be compared to each other. A subject can compare two of his own sensations and judge whether the two are the same or are different.

Consider the sensation of visual brightness produced by a patch of light projected on a certain part of the eye. We can ask, what is the minimal amount by which the original light intensity of the patch must be increased so that the subject experiences a sensation of brightness *just* greater than the one he had before? This amount is called the ***difference threshold.*** It produces a ***just-noticeable difference,*** or ***j.n.d.*** The j.n.d. is a psychological entity, for it describes a subject's ability to discriminate. But it is expressed in the units of the physical stimulus that produced it. (In our example, this would be millilamberts, a unit of illumination.) Fechner had found an indirect means to relate sensory magnitude to the physical intensity of the stimulus.

Before proceeding we should note that the absolute threshold may be considered as a special case of a difference threshold. Here the question is how much stimulus energy must be added to a zero stimulus before the subject can tell the difference between the old stimulus ("I see nothing") and the new ("Now I see it").

THE WEBER FRACTION

To Fechner, measuring j.n.d.'s was only the means to a larger goal—the formulation of a general law relating stimulus intensity to sensory magnitude. He believed that such a law could be built upon an empirical generalization first proposed by the German physiologist E. H. Weber (1795–1878) in 1834. Weber proposed that the size of the difference threshold is a constant ratio of the standard stimulus. Suppose that we can just tell the difference between 100 and 102 candles burning in an otherwise unilluminated room. If Weber is right, we would be able to just distinguish between 200 and 204 candles, 400 and 408, and so forth. Fechner was so impressed with this relationship that he referred to it as ***Weber's law,*** a label by which we still know it. Put algebraically, Weber's law is usually written as

$$\frac{\Delta I}{I} = C$$

where ΔI is the increment in stimulus intensity (that is, the j.n.d.) to a stimulus of intensity I (that is, the standard stimulus) required to produce a just-noticeable increase, and where C is a constant. The fraction $\Delta I / I$ is often referred to as the ***Weber fraction.***

Fechner and his successors performed numerous studies to determine whether Weber's law holds for all of the sensory modalities. In a rough sort of way, the answer seems to be yes, at least for much of the normal range of stimulus intensity within each sense. The nervous system is evidently geared to notice relative differences rather than absolute ones.

Weber's law allows us to compare the sensitivity of different sensory modalities. Suppose we want to know whether the eye is more sensitive than the ear. How can we tell? We certainly cannot compare j.n.d.'s for brightness and for loudness. To mention only one problem, the values will be in different units—millilamberts for the first, decibels for the second. The problem is circumvented by utilizing the Weber fractions for the two modalities. Being fractions, they are dimensionless and can therefore be used to compare the sensitivity of different senses. If $\Delta I / I$ is small, the discriminating power of the sense modality is great;

E. H. Weber   (Courtesy National Library of Medicine)

Table 4.1 REPRESENTATIVE VALUES FOR THE WEBER FRACTION FOR THE DIFFERENT SENSES

Sensory modality	Weber fraction ($\Delta I/I$)
Vision (brightness, white light)	.08
Audition (loudness, noise)	.05
Touch (vibration at fingertip)	.04
Kinesthesis (lifted weights)	.02
Taste (table salt)	.08
Smell (butyl alcohol)	.07

SOURCE: Teghtsoonian, 1971, and Cain, 1977.

proportionally little must be added to the standard for a difference to be observed. The opposite holds when $\Delta I/I$ is large. It turns out that we are keener in discriminating weight than smell; the Weber fraction for the first is 1/50, for the second it is only 1/14. Weber fractions for other sense modalities are presented in Table 4.1.

FECHNER'S LAW

Weber's law indicated that the more intense the stimulus, the more stimulus intensity has to be increased before the subject notices a change. By making a number of further assumptions, Fechner generalized Weber's finding to express a broader relationship between sensory and physical intensity. The result was *Fechner's law,* which states that the strength of a sensation grows as the logarithm of stimulus intensity,

$$S = k \log I$$

where S stands for psychological (that is, subjective) magnitude, I for stimulus intensity, and k is a constant that depends on the value of the Weber fraction.

This law has been challenged on several grounds which are beyond the scope of this book. For our purposes, it is sufficient to note that a logarithmic law such as Fechner's makes good biological sense. The range of stimulus intensities to which we are sensitive is enormous. We can hear sounds as weak as the ticking of a watch twenty feet away and as loud as a pneumatic drill operating right next to us. Our nervous system has to have a mechanism to compress this huge range into some manageable scope, and this is precisely what a logarithmic transformation does for us.

Detection and Decision

The goal of psychophysics is to chart the relationships between a subject's responses and various characteristics of the physical stimulus. But are these physical characteristics the only factors that determine what the subject does or says? What about her expectations or wishes? The early psychophysicists believed that such factors could be largely disregarded. But a more recent approach to psychophysical measurement insists that they cannot. This is *signal detection theory,* a very influential way of thinking about the way people make decisions.

RESPONSE BIAS

To understand how beliefs and attitudes come into play in a psychophysical experiment, consider a study of absolute thresholds. On every trial, the harried subject is forced into a decision. Is a stimulus there or isn't it? The decision is often difficult, for at times the stimulus is so weak that the subjects may be quite uncertain of their judgment. Under the circumstances, their *response bias* will necessarily exert an effect. Such a response bias is a preference for one response over another (here "yes" or "no"), quite apart from the nature of the stimuli. Thus, some subjects will approach the task with a free-and-easy attitude, cheerfully offering "yes" judgments whenever they are in doubt. Others will take a more conservative line and will never respond with a "yes" unless they are quite certain. This will produce a difference in obtained thresholds that will necessarily be lower for the subjects who are more liberal with their "yes" responses. But this only reflects a difference in response bias, not in sensory sensitivity. Both groups of subjects can presumably hear or see or feel the stimuli equally well. They only differ in their willingness to report a stimulus when they are unsure.

SIGNAL DETECTION

Such considerations make it clear that thresholds obtained with traditional techniques reflect two factors. One is sensitivity—how well the subject can hear or see the stimulus. The other is response bias—how readily the subject is willing to say "yes, I heard" when he is not certain. How can these two factors be separated?

The early psychophysicists tried to cope with this problem by using only subjects who were highly trained observers. In absolute threshold studies, such subjects were models of conservatism; they would never say "yes" unless they were completely certain. To maintain this attitude, the experimenters threw in an occasional "catch trial" on which there was no stimulus at all (Woodworth, 1938).

Signal detection theory has developed a more systematic way of dealing with response bias. To begin with, it has provided a somewhat different testing procedure, the so-called *detection experiment,* in which catch trials are part of the regular procedure rather than just an occasional check to keep the subjects on their toes (Green and Swets, 1966).

One version of this procedure is related to the measurement of the absolute threshold. Here the question is whether the subject can detect the presence of a stimulus. We take a fairly weak stimulus and present it on half the trials. On the other half of the trials (interspersed in random order), we present no stimulus at all. We will now look at two kinds of errors. One is a *miss,* not reporting a stimulus when one is present. The other is a *false alarm,* reporting a stimulus when in fact none is present. By the same token, there are two different kinds of correct responses: reporting a stimulus when it is actually there (a *hit*) and not reporting one when none is present (a *correct negative*) (see Table 4.2).

THE PAYOFF MATRIX

The detection experiment can tell us what factors underlie response bias. One such factor is differential payoff. Suppose we (literally) pay a subject for every hit and correct negative but penalize him for every miss and false alarm according to a prescribed schedule of gains and losses called a *payoff matrix.* Thus the subject might gain 10 cents for every hit and 5 cents for every correct negative, while losing 10 cents for every miss and only 1 cent for every false alarm. Such a payoff matrix will lead to a bias toward "yes" judgments (Table 4.3). Suppose there are, say, fifty trials on which the subject has no sensory information on the basis of which she can decide whether the stimulus is present or not. If she consistently says "yes," she will on the average be correct on twenty-five trials (thus collecting $2.50) and wrong on the other twenty-five (thus losing $0.25) for a net gain of $2.25. In contrast, consistent "no" judgments will lead to a net loss (+ $1.25 for the correct negatives and − $2.50 for the false alarms).

Table 4.2   THE FOUR POSSIBLE OUTCOMES OF THE DETECTION EXPERIMENT

	Responds "yes"	Responds "no"
Stimulus present	Hit	Miss
Stimulus absent	False alarm	Correct negative

Table 4.3   PAYOFF MATRIX THAT WILL PRODUCE A "YES" BIAS

	Subject says "yes"	Subject says "no"
Stimulus present	+ 10¢	− 10¢
Stimulus absent	− 1¢	+ 5¢

If the stimulus is presented on half of the trials, the payoff bias can be calculated easily by comparing the sum of the values under the *Says "yes"* column with the sum under the *Says "no"* column. In this example, these sums are + 9¢ and − 5¢ respectively. Under the circumstances, the subject will do well to adopt a liberal criterion and give a "yes" judgment whenever she is in doubt.

Illustrations of the effect of payoff matrices abound in real life. There the differential payoff is usually reckoned in units larger than pennies. Consider a team of radiologists poring over an X-ray to look for a tiny spot that indicates the start of a malignant tumor. What are the penalties for error here? If the physicians decide there is no spot when there actually is one, their miss may cost the patient's life. If they decide that they see a spot when in fact there is none, their false alarm has other costs, such as the dangers of more elaborate clinical tests, let alone those of an operation. What the physicians ultimately decide will depend, both on what their eyes tell them as they inspect the X-ray and also on the relative costs of the two possible errors they may commit.

The preceding discussion showed that the subject's responses are jointly determined by his sensitivity to the stimulus and his response bias. The detection experiment provides a means for measuring these two factors separately. The details of this procedure are beyond the scope of this book; suffice it to say that it is based on a calculation that utilizes the percentage of both hits and false alarms.

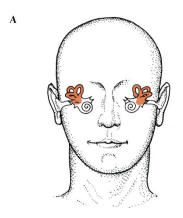

A

AN OVERVIEW OF THE SENSES

The development of psychophysical methods, coupled with various physiological techniques, gave psychology a powerful set of tools with which to study the various senses. Our primary focus will be on just one sense, which we will consider in detail: vision. But we will first look briefly at several other sensory systems that provide us with information about various aspects of the world and about our own position within it.

Kinesthesis and the Vestibular Sense

One group of senses informs the organism about its own movements and its orientation in space. Skeletal movement is sensed through **kinesthesis,** a collective term for information that comes from receptors in the muscles, tendons, and joints. Another group of receptors signals the rotation of the head. These are the receptors in the **semicircular canals,** which are located within the so-called **vestibules** of the inner ear (Figure 4.3). The three canals contain a viscous liquid that moves when the head rotates. This motion bends hair cells that are located at one end of each canal. When bent, these hair cells give rise to nervous impulses. The sum total of the impulses from each of the canals provides information about the nature and extent of the head's rotation.

One vital function of the semicircular canal system is to provide a firm base for vision. As we walk through the world, our head moves continually. To compensate for this endless rocking, the eyes have to move accordingly. This adjustment is accomplished by a reflex system which automatically cancels each rotation of the head by an equal and opposite motion of the eyes. These eye movements are initiated by messages from the three semicircular canals which are relayed to the appropriate muscles of each eye. Thus, the visual system is effectively stable, operating as if it rested on a solid tripod.

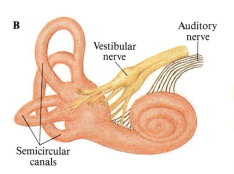

4.3 The vestibular sense *(A) The location of the inner ears, which are embedded in bone on both sides of the skull. The vestibules are indicated in orange. The rest of the inner ear is devoted to the sense of hearing. (After Krech and Crutchfield, 1958) (B) Close-up of the vestibular apparatus. (After Kalat, 1984, p. 139)*

B

Auditory nerve

Vestibular nerve

Semicircular canals

115

The Skin Senses

Stimulation of the skin informs the organism of what is directly adjacent to its own body. Not surprisingly, skin sensitivity is especially acute in those parts of the body that are most relevant to exploring the world that surrounds us directly: the hands and fingers, the lips and tongue. These sensitivities are reflected in the organization of the cortical projection area for bodily sensations. As we have seen, the allocation of cortical space is quite unequal, with a heavy emphasis on such sensitive regions as face, mouth, and fingers (see Chapter 1).

How many skin senses are there? Aristotle believed that all of the sensations from the skin could be subsumed under just one rubric, that of touch. But today most investigators believe that there are at least four different skin sensations: *pressure, warmth, cold,* and *pain.* How are these different sensory experiences coded by the nervous system? Here, as in the study of many other senses, the first line of inquiry was an influential proposal by the German physiologist Johannes Müller (1801–1858): If the sensory qualities are different, see whether there are different receptors that underlie them.

Are there different receptors that correspond to these different sensations? The answer is a qualified yes. There is good reason to believe that various sensations of pressure are produced by a number of different specialized receptors in the skin (see Figure 4.4). Some of these receptors are wrapped around hair follicles in the skin and sense movements of the hair. Others are capsules that are easily bent by slight deformations of the skin. Some of these capsules respond to continued vibration; others react to sudden movement across the skin, still others sense steady indentation. It's clear that there is not one touch receptor but several.

Less is known about the underlying receptor systems for temperature and pain. Some of these experiences are probably signaled by free nerve endings in the skin that have no specialized end organs. These free nerve endings have been thought to provide information about cold and pain, but some of them may also be additional pressure receptors (Sherrick and Cholewiak, 1986).

Pain in particular has been the subject of much controversy. Some investigators believe that there are specialized pain receptors which are activated by tissue injury and produce an unpleasant sensation. Others hold that pain results from the overstimulation of any skin receptor. But whatever its receptor basis, there is little doubt that pain has a vital biological function. It warns the organism of po-

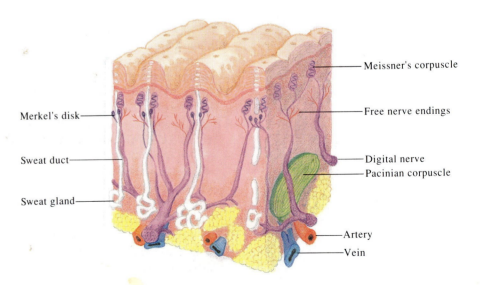

4.4   A cross-section through the skin   *The figure shows a number of structures that serve as receptors in hairless skin; for example, on the fingertips and palms. (After Carlson, 1986, p. 257)*

Meissner's corpuscle

Free nerve endings

Merkel's disk

Sweat duct

Digital nerve

Pacinian corpuscle

Sweat gland

Artery

Vein

tential harm. This point is vividly brought home by persons who have a congenital insensitivity to pain. On the face of it, the inability to experience this unpleasant sensation might seem to be a blessing, but nothing could be further from the truth. People who lack pain sensitivity often sustain extensive burns and bruises, especially in childhood; they never receive the first signals of danger so they don't withdraw the affected body parts. As a child, one such patient bit off the tip of her tongue while chewing food and sustained serious burns when kneeling on a hot radiator (Sternbach, 1963; Melzack, 1973; for a discussion of how the nervous system alleviates pain, see Chapter 1, p. 23).

The Sense of Taste

The sense of taste has a simple function. It acts as a gatekeeper for the organism's digestive system by providing information about the substances that may or may not be ingested. Its task is to keep poisons out and usher foodstuffs in. In most land-dwelling mammals, this function is performed by specialized receptor organs, the *taste buds*, which are sensitive to chemicals dissolved in water. The average person possesses about 10,000 such taste buds, located mostly in the tongue but also in other regions of the mouth. Fibers from these receptors convey the message to the brain, first to the medulla and then further up to the thalamus and cortex.

TASTE SENSATIONS

Most investigators believe that there are four basic taste qualities: *sour, sweet, salty,* and *bitter.* In their view, all other taste sensations are produced by a mixture of these primary qualities. Thus, grapefruit tastes sour and bitter, while lemonade tastes sweet and sour. What are the stimuli that produce these four basic qualities? As yet, we don't have a full answer. We do know that the salty taste is usually produced by inorganic molecules dissolved in water and the sour taste by acids. The story is more complicated for sweet and bitter sensations. Both are generally produced by complex organic molecules, but as yet there are no clear-cut rules that predict the resulting taste sensation. For example, "sweet" is produced by various sugars, but also by saccharin, a chemical compound that is structurally very different from sugar. Additional problems are posed by effects of concentration. Some substances, such as saccharin, that taste sweet in low concentrations taste bitter when their concentration is increased.

TASTE AND SENSORY INTERACTION

The sense of taste provides an illustration of a pervasive principle that holds for most (perhaps all) of the other senses and that we will here call *sensory interaction.* It describes the fact that a sensory system's response to any given stimulus rarely depends on that stimulus alone. It is also affected by other stimuli that impinge, or have recently impinged, upon that system.

One kind of sensory interaction occurs over time. Suppose one taste stimulus is presented continuously for fifteen seconds or more. The result will be *adaptation,* a phenomenon that is found in virtually all sensory systems. If the tongue is continually stimulated with the identical taste stimulus, sensitivity to that taste will quickly decline. For example, after continuous exposure to a quinine solution, the quinine will taste less and less bitter and may finally appear to be completely tasteless. This adaptation process is reversible, however. If the mouth is rinsed out and left unstimulated for, say, a minute, the original taste sensitivity will be restored in full.

In another form of interaction, the adaptation to one taste quality may lead to the enhancement of another, an effect that is sometimes regarded as a form of contrast. For example, adaptation to sugar makes an acid taste even sourer than before (Kuznicki and McCutcheon, 1979). A related effect is the change in the taste of ordinary tap water after prior adaptation to various substances. Adaptation to a salty solution will make water taste sour or bitter; adaptation to one that's sweet will make it taste bitter (McBurney and Shick, 1971).

The Sense of Smell

Thus far, our discussion has centered on the sensory systems that tell us about objects and events close to home: the movements and position of our own body, what we feel with our skin, and what we put in our mouth. But we clearly receive information from much farther off. We have three main receptive systems that enlarge our world by responding to stimuli at a distance: smell, hearing, and vision.

THE OLFACTORY STIMULUS

Smell, or to use the more technical term, *olfaction,* provides information about chemicals suspended in air that excite receptors located in a small area at the top of our nasal cavity, the *olfactory epithelium* (see Figure 4.5). There is still considerable debate about the nature of the chemicals that act as effective olfactory stimuli ("odorants") and the way in which they set off the olfactory receptors. Several classification schemes exist for describing all odors by reference to a number of primary smell sensations, for example, *fragrant* (rose), *spicy* (cinnamon), and *putrid* (rotten eggs). But as yet, there is no agreement about the underlying principle that makes certain chemicals arouse one of these olfactory experiences rather than another. At present, the best guess is that olfactory quality is not coded by particular receptors—with, say, one group of receptors responding to stimuli we call fragrant and another receptor group responding to stimuli we describe as putrid. Instead, the relevant sensory code for quality is probably a *pattern* of excitation across different receptor groups.

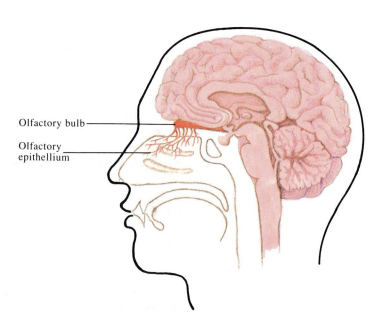

Olfactory bulb

Olfactory epithellium

4.5   The olfactory apparatus   *Chemicals suspended in the air that flows through the nasal passages stimulate receptors in the olfactory epithelium which relay their information to a structure in the forebrain, the olfactory bulb. (After Amoore et al., 1964; Carlson, 1986)*

SMELL AS A DISTANCE SENSE

As a distance sense, smell plays a relatively minor part for humans. It is clearly less important to us than it is to many other species. In this regard we are similar to our primate cousins and to birds, in that these animals all left the odor-impregnated ground to move up into the trees, an environment in which other senses, especially vision, became more critical. In contrast, smell is of vital importance to many ground dwellers such as dogs. For them, it furnishes a guide to food and to receptive mates, and it may give warning against certain natural enemies. Modern psychophysical methods allow us to determine just how much more sensitive the dog's nose is compared to our own; it turns out that the ratio in sensitivities is about a thousand to one (Marshall and Moulton, 1981; Cain, 1988).

Compared to dogs and most other land-dwelling animals, we are evidently olfactory incompetents. But that doesn't mean that smell is of no relevance to human life. It does warn us of impending danger, as when we sniff escaping gas; it greatly adds to our enjoyment of food; and it provides the basis of the perfume and deodorant industries. Smell also plays a role in identifying other persons. In one study, a psychologist asked men and women to wear T-shirts for twenty-four hours without taking a shower or using perfumes or deodorants. After twenty-four hours, each (unwashed) T-shirt was sealed in a separate bag. Every subject was then asked to sniff the contents of three of these bags without looking inside. One contained his or her T-shirt, a second the T-shirt worn by another man, a third the T-shirt worn by another woman. About three-quarters of the subjects were able to identify their own T-shirt based only on its odor, and could also correctly identify which of the other T-shirts had been worn by a man or by a woman (Russell, 1976; McBurney, Levine, and Cavanaugh, 1977). This sensitivity to human odors starts in the nursery. Thus babies apparently respond to the odor of their own mother's breast and underarm in preference to the odors of a strange mother (Russell, 1976; Cernoch and Porter, 1985).

PHEROMONES

In many species, olfaction has a function beyond those we have discussed thus far. It represents a primitive form of communication. Certain animals secrete special chemical substances called *pheromones* that trigger particular reactions in other members of their own kind. Some pheromones affect reproductive behavior. In many mammals, the female secretes a chemical (often in the urine) that signals that she is sexually receptive. In some species, the male sends chemical return messages to the female. For example, boars apparently secrete a pheromone that renders the sow immobile so that she stands rigid during mating (Michael and Keverne, 1968).

Other pheromones signal alarm. It appears that some animals can smell danger. They can smell a substance secreted by members of their own species who have been frightened. Thus rats who suffer an electric shock in an experimental chamber seem to exude a chemical that induces fear in other rats that are exposed to the air from that same chamber (Valenta and Rigby, 1968).

Are there pheromones in humans? There may be some vestigial remains. One line of evidence concerns the development of *menstrual synchrony.* Women who live together, for example, in college dormitories, tend to develop menstrual cycles that roughly coincide with each other, even though their periods had been very different at the start of the school year (McClintock, 1971). Some recent studies suggest that this synchrony is primed by olfactory cues. Female subjects exposed to the body odor of a "donor" woman gradually shifted their menstrual cycles toward that of the donor, even though the subjects and the donors never saw each other (Russell, Switz, and Thompson, 1980).

A

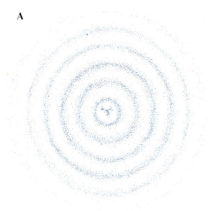

B   Wavelength

Amplitude

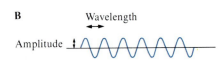

4.6   The stimulus for hearing   *(A) The figure depicts a momentarily frozen field of vibration in air. An insect vibrating its wings rapidly leads to waves of compression in the surrounding air. These waves travel in all directions like ripples in a pond into which a stone has been thrown. (B) The corresponding wave pattern is shown in simplified form. The amplitude of the wave is the height of each crest; the wavelength is the distance between successive crests. (From Gibson, 1966)*

Hearing

The sense of hearing, or *audition,* is a close relative of other receptive senses that react to mechanical pressure, such as the vestibular sense or touch. Like these, hearing is a response to pressure, but with a difference—it informs us of pressure changes in the world that may take place many meters away. In effect, then, hearing is feeling at a distance.

SOUND

What is the stimulus for hearing? Outside in the world there is some physical movement which disturbs the air medium in which it occurs. This may be an animal scurrying through the underbrush or a rock dropping from a cliff or a set of vibrating vocal cords. The air particles directly adjacent to the movement are agitated, push particles that are ahead of them, and then return to their original position. Each individual air particle moves back and forth just a tiny bit, but this is enough to set up a series of successive pressure variations in the air medium. These travel in a wave form analogous to the ripples set up by a stone thrown into a pond. When these *sound waves* hit our ears, they initiate a set of further mechanical pressure changes which ultimately trigger the auditory receptors. These initiate various further neural responses in the brain which ultimately lead to an experience of something that is heard rather than felt.

Sound waves can vary in both *amplitude* and *wavelength.* Amplitude refers to the height of a wave crest: the greater the intensity of the vibration, the higher this crest will be. Wavelength is simply the distance between successive crests. Sound waves are generally described by their *frequency,* which is the number of waves per second. Since the speed of sound is constant within any given medium, frequency is inversely proportional to wavelength (Figure 4.6).

Both amplitude and frequency are physical dimensions. Our brain translates these into the psychological dimensions of *loudness* and *pitch.* Roughly speaking, a sound will appear to be louder as its amplitude increases and will appear more high-pitched as its frequency goes up.

Amplitude and loudness   The range of amplitudes to which humans can respond is enormous. Investigators have found it convenient to use a scale which compresses this unwieldy range into a more convenient form. To this end, they developed a logarithmic scale that describes sound intensities in *decibels* (Table 4.4). Perceived loudness doubles every time the physical intensity (that is, the amplitude) goes up by 10 decibels. The physical stimulus intensity rises more steeply, increasing by a factor of 10 every 20 decibels (Stevens, 1955).

Table 4.4   INTENSITY LEVELS OF VARIOUS COMMON SOUNDS

Sound	Intensity level (decibels)
Manned spacecraft launching (from 150 feet)	180
Loudest rock band on record	160
Pain threshold (approximate)	140
Loud thunder; average rock band	120
Shouting	100
Noisy automobile	80
Normal conversation	60
Quiet office	40
Whisper	20
Rustling of leaves	10
Threshold of hearing	0

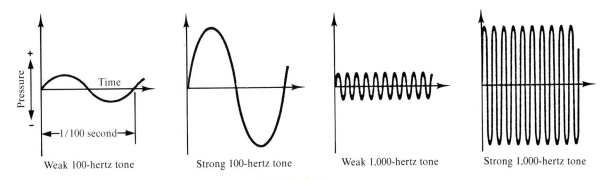

| Weak 100-hertz tone | Strong 100-hertz tone | Weak 1,000-hertz tone | Strong 1,000-hertz tone |

4.7 Simple wave forms vary in frequency and amplitude *Simple sound waves can be graphically expressed by plotting air-pressure change over time. The result is a so-called sine curve. These curves show the sine waves for a weak and a strong 100-hertz tone (relatively low in pitch) and a strong and a weak 1,000-hertz tone (comparatively high pitch). (After Thompson, 1973)*

Frequency and pitch The frequency of a sound wave is generally measured in *hertz* (H$_z$), or waves per second (so-called after the nineteenth-century German physicist Heinrich Hertz). Young adults can hear tones as low as 20 hertz and as high as 20,000 hertz, with maximal sensitivity to a middle region in between. As people get older, their sensitivity to sound declines, especially at the higher frequencies (see Figure 4.7).

GATHERING THE PROXIMAL STIMULUS

Most of the ear is made up of various anatomical structures whose function is to gather the proximal stimulus—they conduct and amplify sound waves so that they can affect the auditory receptors (Figure 4.8). Sound waves collected by the outer ear are funneled toward a taut membrane which they cause to vibrate. This is the *eardrum* which transmits its vibrations across an air-filled cavity, the *middle ear,* to another membrane, the *oval window,* that separates the middle from the *inner ear.* This transmission is accomplished by way of a mechanical bridge built of three small bones that are collectively known as the *ossicles.* The vibrations of the eardrum move the first ossicle, which then moves the second, which in turn moves the third, which completes the chain by imparting the vibratory pattern to the oval window to which it is attached. The movements of the oval window set up waves in a fluid which fills the *cochlea,* a coiled tube in the inner ear which contains the auditory receptors.

Why did nature choose such a roundabout method of sound transmission? The major reason is that the cochlear medium is a fluid which like all liquids is harder to set into motion than air. To overcome this difficulty, the physical stimulus must be amplified. This amplification is provided by various features of the middle-ear organization. One involves the relative sizes of the eardrum and of that portion of the oval window moved by the ossicles; the first is about twenty times larger than the second. The result is the transformation of a fairly weak force that acts on the entire eardrum into a much stronger pressure that is concentrated upon the (much smaller) oval window.

4.8 The human ear *Air enters through the outer ear and stimulates the eardrum which sets the ossicles in the middle ear in motion. These in turn transmit their vibration to the membrane of the oval window which causes movement of the fluid in the cochlea of the inner ear. Note that the semicircular canals are anatomically parts of the inner ear. (After Lindsay and Norman, 1977)*

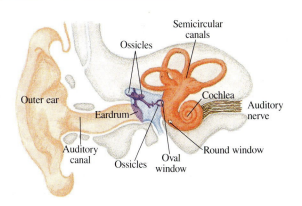

4.9 Detailed structure of the middle ear and the cochlea *(A) Movement of the fluid within the cochlea deforms the basilar membrane and stimulates the hair cells that serve as the auditory receptors. (After Lindsay and Norman, 1977) (B) Cross-section of the cochlea showing the basilar membrane and the hair cell receptors. (After Coren and Ward, 1989)*

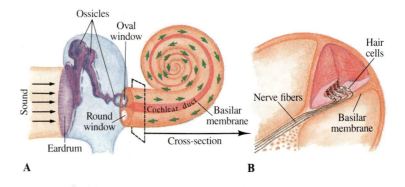

A   B

TRANSDUCTION IN THE COCHLEA

Throughout most of its length the cochlea is divided into an upper and lower section by several structures including the **basilar membrane.** The auditory receptors are so-called **hair cells** which are lodged between the basilar membrane and other membranes above it. Motion of the oval window produces pressure changes in the cochlear fluid which in turn lead to vibrations of the basilar membrane. As the basilar membrane vibrates, its deformations bend the hair cells and provide the immediate stimulus for their activity (Figure 4.9).

How does the activity of the auditory receptors lead to the sensory properties of auditory experience? Much of the work in the area has focused upon the perception of **pitch,** the sensory quality that depends upon the frequency of the stimulating sound wave.

Basilar place and pitch According to the **place theory** of pitch, first proposed by Hermann von Helmholtz (1821–1894), different parts of the basilar membrane are responsive to different sound frequencies. In Helmholtz's view, the nervous system will then interpret the excitations from different basilar places as different pitches. The stimulation of receptors at one end of the membrane will lead to the experience of a high tone, while that of receptors at the other end leads to the sensation of a low tone.

Today we know that Helmholtz was correct at least in part. The classical studies were performed by Georg von Békésy (1899–1972) whose work on auditory function won him the Nobel Prize in 1961. Some of Békésy's experiments used cochleas taken from fresh human cadavers. Békésy removed part of the cochlear wall so that he could observe the basilar membrane through a microscope when the oval window was vibrated by an electrically powered piston. He found that such stimulation led to a wavelike motion of the basilar membrane (Figure 4.10). When he varied the frequency of the vibrating stimulus, the peak of the deformation produced by this wave pattern occurred in different regions of the mem-

4.10 The deformation of the basilar membrane by sound *(A) In this diagram, the membrane is schematically presented as a simple, rectangular sheet. In actuality, of course, it is much thinner and coiled in a spiral shape. (B) The relation between sound frequency and the location of the peak of the basilar membrane's deformation. The peak of the deformation is located at varying distances from the stapes (the third ossicle, which sets the membrane in motion by pushing at the oval window). As the figure shows, the higher the frequency of the sound, the closer to the stapes this peak will be. (After Lindsay and Norman, 1977; Coren and Ward, 1989)*

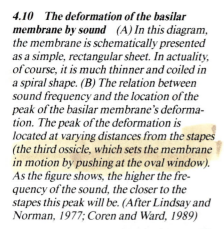

A

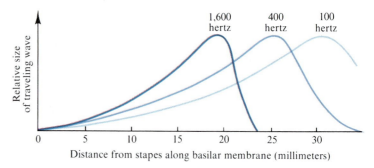

B

Hermann von Helmholtz (1821–1894)
(Courtesy National Library of Medicine)

Georg von Békésy (1899–1972)
(Courtesy Nobel Stiftelsen)

brane: High frequencies corresponded to regions close to the oval window, low ones to regions close to the cochlear tip (Békésy, 1957).

Sound frequency and frequency of neural firing   The place theory of pitch faces a major difficulty. As the frequency of the stimulus gets lower and lower, the deformation pattern it produces gets broader and broader. At very low frequencies (say, below 50 hertz), the wave set up by the tone deforms the entire membrane just about equally so that all receptors will be equally excited. But since we can discriminate low frequencies down to about 20 hertz, the nervous system must have some means for sensing pitch in addition to basilar location.

It is generally believed that this second means for sensing pitch is related to the firing frequency of the auditory nerve. For lower frequencies, the basilar membrane vibrates at the frequency of the stimulus tone and this vibration rate is then directly translated into the appropriate number of neural impulses per second, as evidenced by gross electrical recordings taken from the auditory nerve. The impulse frequency of the auditory output is further relayed to higher centers which somehow interpret it as pitch.

It appears then that pitch perception is based upon two separate mechanisms: higher frequencies are coded by the place of excitation on the basilar membrane, lower frequencies by the frequency of the neural impulses. It is not clear where the one mechanism leaves off and the other takes over. Place of excitation is probably relatively unimportant at frequencies below 500–1,000 hertz and has no role below 50 hertz, while impulse frequency has little or no effect for tones above 5,000 hertz. In all probability, sound frequencies in between are handled by both mechanisms (Green, 1976; Goldstein, 1989).

The Senses: Some Common Principles

In our discussion of the various senses, we have come across many ways in which they differ. We have also encountered a number of important phenomena that are not specific to any one sensory system but are found more generally.

First, in most sense modalities, the processing of external stimulus energies begins with various structures which gather and amplify these physical energies and thereby fashion a "better" proximal stimulus for the receptors to work on. An example is provided by the semicircular canals which contain a liquid that is set in motion by head rotation and then stimulates the hair cell receptors of the vestibular system.

Second, in all sense modalities, the next step involves the receptors which achieve the **transduction** of the physical stimulus energy into an electrical signal. In some sensory systems, particularly hearing and vision, the nature of this transduction process is reasonably well understood. In other systems, such as smell, it is still unknown.

Third, the processing of stimulus input does not stop at the receptor level. There are typically further neural centers at which **coding** occurs. The stimulus information is coded (so to speak, translated) into the various dimensions of sensation that we actually experience. Some of these dimensions involve intensity. In taste, we have more or less bitter; in hearing, we have more or less loud. Other dimensions involve differences in quality. In taste, we have the differences between bitter, sweet, sour, and salty; in hearing, we have differences in pitch.

Fourth, any part of a sensory system is in **interaction** with the rest of that system. This process of interaction pertains both to the immediate past and to present activity in neighboring parts of the system. We considered some examples of sensory interaction in the taste system, including the phenomenon of adaptation (with continued exposure, quinine tastes less bitter).

VISION

We now turn to a detailed discussion of vision, which in humans is the distance sense *par excellence*. The organization of this account will reflect characteristics which are common to most of the senses. We will begin by describing the eye as a structure for gathering the visual stimulus. We will then turn to the transduction of light energies by the visual receptors. After this, we will discuss some interaction processes found in vision. We will finally consider the coding processes that are involved in experiencing a sensory quality—in the case of vision, color.

The Stimulus: Light

Most visual sensations have their point of origin in some external (distal) object. Occasionally, this object will be a light source which *emits* light in its own right; examples (in rather drastically descending order of emission energy) are the sun, an electric light bulb, and a glow worm. All other objects can only give off light if some light source illuminates them. They will then *reflect* some portion of the light cast upon them while absorbing the rest.

The stimulus energy we call light comes from the relatively small band of radiations to which our visual system is sensitive. These radiations travel in a wave form which is somewhat analogous to the pressure waves that are the stimulus for hearing. This radiation can vary in its *intensity,* the amount of radiant energy in unit time, which is a major determinant of perceived brightness (as in two bulbs of different wattage). It can also vary in *wavelength,* the distance between the crests of two successive waves, which is a major determinant of perceived color. The light we ordinarily encounter is made up of a mixture of different wavelengths. The range of wavelengths to which our visual system can respond is the *visible spectrum,* from roughly 400 ("violet") to about 750 ("red") nanometers (1 nanometer = 1 millionth of a millimeter) between successive crests.

Gathering the Stimulus: The Eye

The next stop in the journey from stimulus to visual sensation is the eye. Except for the *retina,* none of its major structures has anything to do with the transduction of the physical stimulus energy into neurological terms. Theirs is a prior function: to fashion a proper proximal stimulus for vision, a sharp retinal image, out of the light that enters from outside.

Let us briefly consider how this task is accomplished. The eye has often been compared to a camera, and in its essentials the analogy holds up well enough (Figure 4.11). Both eye and camera have a *lens* which suitably bends light rays

4.11 Eye and camera *As an accessory apparatus for fashioning a sharp image out of the light that enters from outside, the eye has many similarities to the camera. Both have a lens for bending light rays to project an inverted image upon a light-sensitive surface at the back. In the eye a transparent outer layer, the cornea, participates in this light-bending. The light-sensitive surface in the eye is the retina, whose most sensitive region is the fovea. Both eye and camera have a focusing device; in the eye, the lens can be thickened or flattened. Both have an adjustable iris diaphragm. And both finally are encased in black to minimize the effects of stray light; in the eye this is done by a layer of darkly pigmented tissue, the choroid coat. (Wald, 1950)*

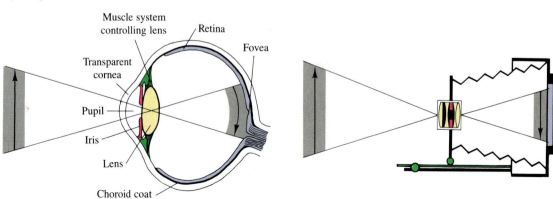

Muscle system
controlling lens

Retina

Fovea

Transparent
cornea

Pupil

Iris

Lens

Choroid coat

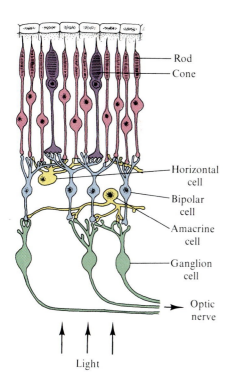

Rod
Cone

Horizontal cell

Bipolar cell

Amacrine cell

Ganglion cell

Optic nerve

Light

4.12 The retina *There are three main retinal layers: the rods and cones, which are the photoreceptors; the bipolar cells; and the ganglion cells whose axons make up the optic nerve. There are also two other kinds of cells, horizontal cells and amacrine cells, that allow for sideways (lateral) interaction. As shown in the diagram the retina contains an anatomical oddity. As it is constructed the photoreceptors are at the very back, the bipolar cells are in between, and the ganglion cells are at the top. As a result, light has to pass through the other layers (they are not opaque so this is possible) to reach the rods and cones whose stimulation starts the visual process. (After Coren and Ward, 1989)*

passing through it and thus projects an image upon a light-sensitive surface behind—the film in the camera, the retina in the eye. Both have a focusing mechanism. In the eye this is accomplished by a set of muscles that changes the shape of the lens. It is flattened for objects at a distance and thickened for objects closer by, a process technically known as **accommodation.** Finally, both camera and eye have a **diaphragm** which governs the amount of entering light. In the eye this function is performed by the **iris,** a smooth, circular muscle which surrounds the pupillary opening and which contracts or dilates under reflex control when the amount of illumination increases or decreases substantially.

The image of an object that falls upon the retina is determined by simple optical geometry. Its size will be inversely proportional to the distance of the object, while its shape will depend on its orientation. Thus, a rectangle viewed at a slant will project as a trapezoid. In addition, the image will be reversed with respect to right and left and will be upside down.

The Visual Receptors

We have arrived at the point where the path from distal object to visual sensation crosses the frontier between optics and psychophysiology—the transformation of the physical stimulus energy into a nervous impulse. We now consider the structures which accomplish this feat: the visual receptor organs in the retina.

The retina is made up of several layers of nerve cells, one of which is the receptor layer. Microscopic inspection shows two kinds of receptor cells, whose names describe their different shapes—the **rods** and the **cones.** The cones are more plentiful in the **fovea,** a small roughly circular region at the center of the retina. While very densely packed in the fovea, they are less and less prevalent the farther out one goes toward the periphery. The opposite is true of the rods; they are completely absent from the fovea and are more frequent in the periphery. In all, there are some 120 million rods and about 6 million cones.

The receptors do not report to the brain directly, but relay their message upward by way of two intermediate neural links—the **bipolar cells** and the **ganglion cells** (Figure 4.12). The bipolar cells are stimulated by the receptors, and they, in their turn, excite the ganglion cells. The axons of these ganglion cells are collected from all over the retina, converging into a bundle of fibers that finally leaves the eyeball as the **optic nerve.** The region where these axons converge contains no receptors and thus cannot give rise to visual sensations; appropriately enough, it is called the **blind spot** (Figure 4.13).

VISUAL ACUITY

One of the most important functions of the visual sense is to enable us to tell one object from another. A minimum precondition for doing so is the ability to distinguish between separate points that are projected on the retina so that we do not

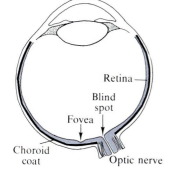

Retina

Blind spot

Fovea

Choroid coat

Optic nerve

4.13 Fovea and blind spot *The fovea is the region on the retina in which the receptors are most densely packed. The blind spot, where the optic nerve leaves the eyeball, is a region where there are no receptors at all. (After Cornsweet, 1970)*

see a blur. The ability to make such distinctions is called *acuity.* Under normal daylight conditions, this is greatest in the fovea, for it is there that the receptors are most closely bunched and thus provide the sharpest optical resolution. To "look at" an object means to move the eyes so that the image of that object falls upon both foveas. In peripheral vision we often see something without quite knowing what it is. To see it clearly, we swivel our eyes so that the image of the as yet unidentified something falls upon the foveal regions where our resolving power is greatest.

THE DUPLEX THEORY OF VISION

The fact that rods and cones differ in structure suggests that they also differ in function. Almost a hundred years ago, this notion led to the development of the *duplex theory of vision,* a theory that by now has the status of established fact. The essential idea is that rods and cones handle different aspects of the visual task. The rods are the receptors for night vision; they operate at low light intensities and lead to *achromatic* (colorless) sensations. The cones serve day vision; they respond at much higher levels of illumination and are responsible for sensations of color. The biological utility of such an arrangement becomes apparent when we consider the enormous range of light intensities encountered by organisms like ourselves who transact their business during both day and night. In humans, the ratio between the stimulus energy at absolute threshold and that transmitted by a momentary glance at the midday sun is 1 to 100,000,000,000. Evolution has evidently provided a biological division of labor, assigning two separate receptor systems to the upper and lower portions of this incredible range.

Several facts provide important evidence in support of the duplex theory. Sensitivity to dim light is much greater in the periphery where rods are prevalent than in the center of the fovea where they are absent. This fact is familiar to sailors who know that the way to detect a faint star in the night sky is to look at it not directly, but to look off at an angle from where they think it might be. The quality of the visual sensation produced by such dim light is invariably achromatic, much like a black-and-white film.

Further evidence for the duplex theory comes from the study of dark adaptation. When we first enter a movie theater from a sunlit street we can barely find our seats, but we gradually adjust and eventually we see rather well. This phenomenon is called *dark adaptation,* an increased sensitivity to light following a period of darkness. The opposite effect occurs after an interval of light exposure. Now the eye becomes *light adapted* and grows insensitive to weaker light intensities.

Dark adaptation can be studied experimentally by measuring absolute thresholds after different periods spent in the dark. One experiment used a test patch of short-wave light that was projected on an area that contains both rods and cones. The most dramatic result is a tremendous increase in sensitivity. After thirty minutes in the dark, the subject can detect a light whose intensity is only 1/100,000 of that which was required before dark adaptation began.

An important further feature of the dark-adaptation curve is its shape. It is discontinuous, reaching a first plateau within five or ten minutes, and then sharply descending once again. This discontinuity further supports the duplex theory. The first portion of the curve represents the dark adaptation of the cones, the second that of the rods. Proof comes from studies that varied the retinal position. If the test patch is projected on a cone-free region well to the side of the fovea, the resulting dark-adaptation curve has no break in it and looks just like the second (that is, the rod-produced) segment of the usual curve. The opposite result is obtained if the test patch is projected entirely within the rod-free fovea. Now we only obtain the first (cone) portion of the adaptation curve (see Figure 4.14).

4.14   The dark adaptation curve as a composite of two separate processes   *The figure shows separate dark adaptation curves for cones and rods. The green curve is for a light patch projected into the rod-free fovea and represents the cone-produced portion of the standard dark adaptation curve. The red curve is for a light patch projected well off the fovea into a cone-free region and represents the rod-produced component of the standard adaptation curve. The blue curve is the characteristic two-part adaptation curve, obtained when the test patch stimulates both rods and cones so that both rod-produced and cone-produced effects come into play. (After Cornsweet, 1970)*

When light hits a visual receptor, its energy eventually triggers a nervous impulse. The first stage of this energy conversion involves a photochemical process. We are again reminded of the camera. In a photographic plate the sensitive elements are grains of silver salt such as silver bromide. When light strikes the film, some of it is absorbed by the silver bromide molecules with the result that the silver is separated from the compound (and eventually becomes visible after several darkroom manipulations). The visual receptors contain several *visual pigments* which perform an analogous function for the eye. One such substance is *rhodopsin,* which serves as the visual pigment for the rods.

Unlike a photographic emulsion, the visual pigments constantly renew themselves. Were it otherwise, a newborn infant would open his eyes, look at the bustling world around him, and never see again—his retina would be bleached forever. The bleached pigments are somehow reconstituted to permit an unbroken succession of further retinal pictures.

Interaction in Time: Adaptation

We now turn to some phenomena which prove that the visual system (as indeed all sensory systems) is much more than the passive observer which Locke had assumed it to be. On the contrary, the visual system actively shapes and transforms the optic input; its components never function in isolation, but constantly interact.

One kind of interaction concerns the relation between what happens now and what happened just before. The general finding is simple: There will be a gradual decline in the reaction to any stimulus that persists unchanged. For example, after continued inspection of a green patch, its greenness will eventually fade away. Similar adaptation phenomena are found in most other sensory systems. Thus, the cold ocean water feels warmer after we have been in it for a while.

What does the organism gain by sensory adaptation? One advantage is the likelihood that stimuli which have been around for a while tend to be safe and of lesser relevance to the organism's survival; under the circumstances, it pays to give them less sensory weight. What is important is change, especially sudden change, for this may well signify food to a predator and death to its potential prey. Adaptation is the sensory system's way of pushing old news off the neurophysiological front page.

Interaction in Space: Contrast

Adaptation effects show that sensory systems respond to change over time. If no such change occurs, the sensory response diminishes. What holds for time, holds for space as well. For here, too, the key word is *change.* In vision (as in some other senses), the response to a stimulus applied to any one region partially depends on how the neighboring regions are stimulated. The greater the difference in stimulation, the greater the sensory effect.

BRIGHTNESS CONTRAST

It has long been known that the appearance of a gray patch depends upon its background. The identical gray will look much brighter on a black background than it will on a white background. This is *brightness contrast,* an effect that increases the greater the intensity difference between two contrasting regions. Thus,

 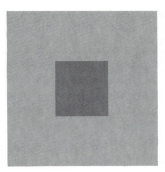  

4.15 Brightness contrast *Four (objectively) identical gray squares on different backgrounds. The lighter the background, the darker the gray squares appear.*

gray appears brighter on black than on dark gray and darker against white than against light gray (see Figure 4.15).

Contrast is also a function of the distance between the two contrasting regions—the smaller that difference, the greater the contrast (see Figure 4.16). This phenomenon gives rise to a number of visual illusions and has been used by some contemporary artists to create some striking effects.

LATERAL INHIBITION

What is the physiological mechanism that underlies spatial interaction? Today we know it is ***lateral inhibition*** (inhibition exerted sideways). This accounts for why neighboring regions in the retina tend to inhibit each other. A simplified version of how this mechanism works is as follows: When any visual receptor is stimulated, it transmits its excitation upward to other cells that eventually relay it to the brain. But this excitation has a further effect. It also stimulates some neurons that extend sideways along the retina. These lateral cells make contact with neighboring cells whose activation they inhibit.

To see how lateral inhibition works, consider the retinal image produced by a gray patch surrounded by a lighter ring (Figure 4.17). For the sake of simplicity, we will only look at two neighboring receptor cells, *A* and *B*. *A* is stimulated by the gray patch and receives a moderate amount of light. *B* is stimulated by the lighter ring and receives much more light. Our primary interest is in the excita-

4.16 The effect of distance between contrasting regions *(A) The white lines in the grid are physically homogeneous, but they don't appear to be—each of the "intersections" seems to contain a gray spot. The uneven appearance of the white strips is caused by contrast. Each strip is surrounded by a black square which contrasts with it and makes it look brighter. But this is not the case at the intersections which only touch upon the black squares at their corners. As a result, there is little contrast in the middle of the intersections. This accounts for the gray spots seen there. (B) The same point is made by the second grid. Here there seem to be whitish spots at the intersections. The explanation is the same. The black lines are bounded by white and thus look darker by contrast. There is less contrast operating on the regions in the middle of the intersections. As a result, they don't appear as dark as the streets, looking like whitish spots. (After Hering, 1920)*

A
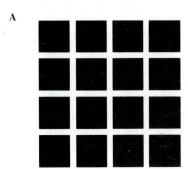

B
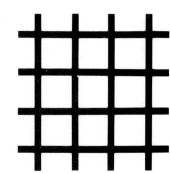

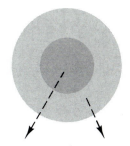

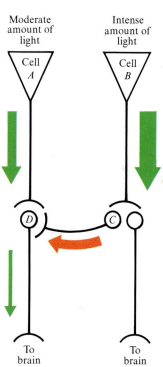

Moderate amount of light   Intense amount of light

Cell *A*   Cell *B*

D   *C*

To brain   To brain

4.17 *Lateral inhibition and contrast*   *Two receptor cells, A and B, are stimulated by neighboring regions of a stimulus. A receives moderate stimulation; B receives an intense amount of light. A's excitation serves to stimulate the next neuron in the visual chain, cell D, which transmits the message further toward the brain. But this transmission is impeded by cell B, whose own intense excitation exerts an inhibitory effect on its neighbors. B excites a lateral cell, C, which exerts an inhibitory effect on cell D. As a result, cell D fires at a reduced rate. (Excitatory effects are shown by green arrows, inhibitory ones by red arrows.)*

tion which cell *A,* the one stimulated by the gray patch, relays upward to the brain. The more cell *A* is stimulated, the more excitation it will relay further, and the brighter the patch will appear to be. The important point is that the excitation from cell *A* will not be passed on unimpeded. On the contrary, some of this excitation will be cancelled by inhibition from neighboring cells. Consider the effect of cell *B,* whose stimulation comes from the lighter ring. That cell is intensely excited. One result of this excitation is that it excites a third cell *C* whose effect is inhibitory and exerted sideways (in short, a lateral inhibitor). The effect of this lateral cell *C* is to block the excitation that *A* sends upward.

Lateral inhibition is the basis of brightness contrast. Let's go back to the three cells in Figure 4.17. The more intensely cell *B* is stimulated, the more it will excite the lateral inhibitor, cell *C.* So a gray patch on a black background looks brighter than it would surrounded by white. Because the black background does not stimulate cell *B,* the lateral inhibitor *C* will not be active. But a white background will stimulate cell *B,* which excites cell *C,* which in turn diminishes the excitation cell *A* sends upward to the brain to inform it of the apparent brightness of the gray patch. The upshot of all this is contrast. The brain gets a visual message that is an exaggeration. What is dark seems darker, what is light seems lighter.

Color

Despite their many differences, the sensory systems of hearing and of vision have some things in common. In both, the relevant stimulus energy is in wave form. And in both, wavelength is related to a qualitative psychological dimension—in one case pitch, in the other color. Much of the research in both domains has revolved around the question of how these sensory qualities are coded. We will here consider only one of these domains, that of color.

CLASSIFYING THE COLOR SENSATIONS

A person with normal color vision can distinguish over seven million different color shades. What are the processes that allow him to make these distinctions? One step in answering this question is to find a classification system that will allow us to describe any one of these millions of colors by reference to a few simple dimensions. In this task we concentrate on what we see and experience, on psychology rather than physics. What we want to classify is our color sensations rather than the physical stimuli that produce them. In doing so, we cannot help but discover something about the way our mind—that is, our nervous system—functions. Whatever order we may find in the classification of our sensations is at least partially imposed by the way in which our nervous system organizes the physical stimuli that impinge upon it.

The dimensions of color   Imagine seven million or so colored paper patches, one for each of the colors we can discriminate. We can classify them according to three perceived dimensions: hue, brightness, and saturation.

Hue is a term whose meaning is close to that of the word *color* as used in everyday life. It is a property of the so-called ***chromatic colors*** (for example, red and blue) but not of the ***achromatic colors*** (that is, black, white, and all of the totally

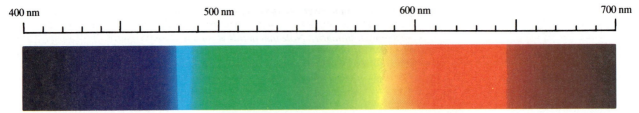

400 nm   500 nm   600 nm   700 nm

4.18   The visible spectrum and the four unique hues   *The visible spectrum consists of light waves from about 360 to 700 nanometers (1 nm = one millionth of a millimeter). White light contains all of these wavelengths. They are bent to different degrees when passed through a prism, yielding the spectrum with the hues shown in the figure. Three of the four unique hues correspond to part of the spectrum: unique blue at about 465 nm, unique green, at about 500 nm, and unique yellow, at about 570 nm. These values vary slightly from person to person. The fourth, unique red—that is, a red which has no apparent tinge of either yellow or blue—is called extraspectral because it is not represented by a single wavelength on the spectrum. It can only be produced by a mixture of wavelengths. (From Ohanian, 1985)*

neutral grays in between). Hue varies with wavelength (Figure 4.18). Thus, **unique blue** (a blue which is judged to have no trace of red or green in it), occurs on the spectrum at about 465 nanometers, **unique green** (which has no blue or yellow) at about 500 nanometers, and **unique yellow** (which has no green or red) at about 570 nanometers.

Brightness varies among both the chromatic and achromatic colors. Thus, ultramarine is darker than light blue and charcoal gray is darker than light gray (Figure 4.19). But the brightness dimension stands out most clearly if we consider achromatic colors alone. These differ in brightness only, while the chromatic colors may also differ in hue (as we have seen) and in saturation (which we will discuss next). Note that white and black represent the top and bottom of the brightness dimension. Thus, white is hueless and maximally bright; black is hueless and minimally bright.

Saturation is the "purity" of a color, the extent to which it is chromatic rather than achromatic. The more gray (or black or white) is mixed with a color, the less saturation it has. Consider the various blue patches in Figure 4.20. All have the same hue (blue). All have the same brightness as a particular, achromatic gray (which is also the same gray with which the blue was mixed to produce the less saturated blue patches, *A, B, C,* and *D*). The patches only differ in one respect: the proportion of blue as opposed to that of gray. The more gray there is, the less the saturation. When the color is entirely gray, saturation is zero. This holds for all colors.

The color circle and the color solid   Some hues appear to be very similar to others. Suppose we only consider the color patches that look most chromatic—that is, those whose saturation is maximal. If we arrange these on the basis of their

A   **B**

4.19   Brightness   *Colors can be arranged according to their brightness. (A) This dimension is most readily recognized when we look at a series of grays, which are totally hueless and vary in brightness only. (B) Chromatic colors can also be classified according to their brightness. The arrows indicate the brightness of the blue and dark green shown here in relation to the series of grays.*

4.20   Saturation   *The four patches A–D are identical in both hue and brightness. They only differ in saturation, which is greatest for A and decreases from A to D. The gray patch, E, on the far right matches all the other patches in brightness; it was mixed with the blue patch A in varying proportions to produce patches B, C, and D.*

A   B   C   D   E

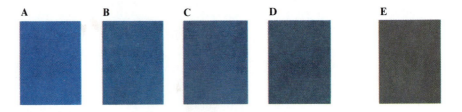

A

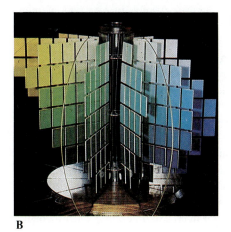

B

4.21 **The color circle and the color solid** *(A) The relationship between maximally saturated hues can be expressed by arranging them in a circle according to their perceptual similarity. Note that in this version of the color circle, the spacing of the hues depends upon their perceptual properties rather than the wavelengths that give rise to them. In particular, the four unique hues are equally spaced, each 90 degrees from the next. (Hurvich, 1981) (B) Every color can be placed within a so-called color solid that is based on the three dimensions of brightness, hue, and saturation. The inside of the solid is shown by taking slices that illustrate variations in hue, brightness, and saturation. (Munsell Color, courtesy of Macbeth, a division of Kollmorgen Corporation)*

perceptual similarity, the result is a circular series, the so-called *color circle,* such that red is followed by orange, orange by yellow, yellow-green, green, blue-green, blue and violet, until the circle finally returns to red. The color circle embodies the perceptual similarities among the different hues. To complete our classificatory schema, we construct the so-called *color solid,* which incorporates the color circle with the other two dimensions of perceived color, brightness, and saturation. Each of our original seven million color patches can be fitted into a unique position in this solid (Figure 4.21). Our classificatory task is thus accomplished.

COLOR MIXTURE

With rare exceptions, the objects in the world around us do not reflect a single wavelength; rather, they reflect different ones, all of which strike the same region of the retina simultaneously. Let us consider the results of some of these mixtures.

Subtractive mixture Before proceeding, we must recognize that the kind of mixture sensory psychologists are interested in is very different from the sort artists employ when they stir pigments together on a palette. Mixing pigments on a palette (or smearing crayons together on a piece of paper) is *subtractive mixture.* In subtractive mixture, one set of wavelengths is subtracted from another set. The easiest demonstration is with colored filters, such as those used in stage lighting, which allow some wavelengths to pass through them while holding others back. Take two such filters, *A* and *B.* Suppose filter *A* allows passage to all light waves between 420 and 520 nanometers but no others. The broad range of light that comes through this filter will be seen as blue. In contrast, filter *B* passes light waves between 480 and 660 nanometers but excludes all others. The band of light waves that comes through this filter will be seen as yellow (Figure 4.22).

4.22 **Subtractive mixture** *In subtractive mixture, the light passed by two filters (or reflected by two mixed pigments) is the band of wavelengths passed by the first minus that region which is subtracted by the second. In the present example, the first filter passes light between 420 and 520 nanometers (a broad-band blue filter), while the second passes light between 480 and 660 nanometers (a broad-band yellow filter). The only light that can pass through both is in the region between 480 and 520 nanometers, which appears green.*

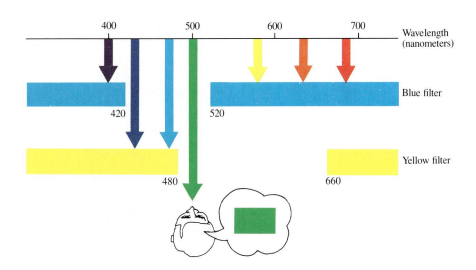

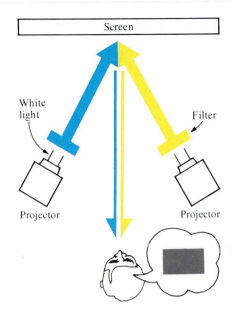

4.23 Additive mixture *In additive mixture, the light passed by two filters (or reflected by two pigments) impinges upon the same region of the retina at the same time. The figure shows two projectors throwing blue and yellow filtered light upon the same portion of the screen from which it is reflected upon the same region of the retina. In contrast to what happens in subtractive mixture, the result of adding these two colors is gray.*

We now ask how we see light that has to pass through *both* filters. Filter *A* (the blue filter) blocks all light above 520 nanometers, while filter *B* (the yellow filter) blocks all light below 480 nanometers. As a result, the only light waves that can pass through this double barricade are those that can slip through the narrow gap between 480 and 520 nanometers, the only interval left unblocked by *both* filters. As it happens, light in this interval is seen as green. Thus, when the mixture is subtractive, mixing blue and yellow will yield green (see Figure 4.22, p. 131).

Thus far we have dealt with filters which let some wavelengths through while blocking others. The same account also applies to artists' pigments. Any pigment reflects only a certain band of wavelengths while absorbing the rest. Suppose we mix pigment *A* (say, blue) to pigment *B* (say, yellow). The result is a form of subtraction. What we will see is the wavelengths reflected by the blue pigment (420 to 520 nanometers) minus the wavelengths absorbed by the yellow pigment (everything below 480 nanometers). The effect is exactly the same as if we had superimposed a blue filter over a yellow one. All that is reflected is light between 480 and 520 nanometers, which is seen as green.

Additive mixture In subtractive mixture, one set of wavelengths is removed from another set. In another kind of mixture, the procedure is the very opposite. This is **additive mixture,** which occurs when different bands of wavelengths stimulate the same retinal region simultaneously. Such additive mixtures can be produced in the laboratory by using filtered light from two different projectors which are focused on the same spot. As a result, the light from each filtered source will be reflected back to the same retinal area (Figure 4.23).

In real life, additive mixture has many uses. One is color television, in which the additive mixture is accomplished by three different sets of photosensitive substances. Another example is provided by the Pointillist painter Georges Seurat. He used dots of different colors that are too close together to be seen separately, especially when the picture is viewed from a distance (Figure 4.24).

A

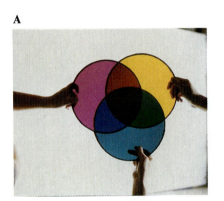

B

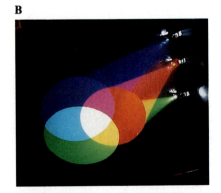

Color mixture *The effect of (A) passing light through several filters (subtractive mixture), and (B) throwing different filtered lights upon the same spot (additive mixture). (Photographs by Fritz Goro/Life Magazine, © Time Warner, Inc.)*

4.24 Additive mixture in Pointillist art *The Channel of Gravelines (1890) by Georges Seurat. A detail of the painting (on the left) shows the separate color daubs which, when viewed from a distance, mix additively. The Pointillists employed this technique instead of mixing pigments to capture the bright appearance of colors outdoors. Pigment mixture is subtractive and darkens the resulting colors. (Courtesy Indianapolis Museum of Art, gift of Mrs. James W. Fesler in memory of Daniel W. and Elizabeth C. Marmon)*

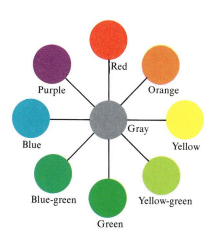

4.25 Complementary hues *Any hue will yield gray if additively mixed (in the correct proportion) with a hue on the opposite side of the color circle. Such hue pairs are complementaries. Some complementary hues are shown here linked by a line across the circle's center. Of particular importance are the two complementary pairs that contain the four unique hues: red-green and blue-yellow.*

COMPLEMENTARY HUES

An important fact about additive color mixture is that every hue has a ***complementary,*** another hue which if mixed with the first in appropriate proportions will produce the color gray. An easy way to find complementaries is by reference to the color circle. Any hue on the circumference will yield gray if mixed (additively) with the hue on the opposite side of the color circle (see Figure 4.25). Of particular interest are the complementary pairs that involve the four ***unique colors,*** red, yellow, green, and blue. Blue and yellow are complementaries that produce gray upon additive mixture; the same holds for red and green. Hues that are not complementary produce mixtures that preserve the hue of their components. Thus, the mixture of red and yellow leads to orange (a yellowish red) while that of blue and red yields a violet (a reddish blue).

At the risk of repetition, note that all of this holds only for additive mixture. When blue and yellow are additively mixed in the right proportions, the observer sees gray. This is in contrast to what happens when the mixture is subtractive, as in drawing a blue crayon over a yellow patch. Now the result is green. The same holds for red and green. Additive mixture of the two yields gray; subtractive mixture will produce a blackish brown.

COLOR ANTAGONISTS

The color-mixture effects we have just described suggest that color complementaries, such as blue and yellow on the one hand, and red and green on the other, are mutually opposed "antagonists" that cancel each other's hue. There are some further phenomena that lead to a similar conclusion.

One such phenomenon is the chromatic counterpart of brightness contrast. In general, any region in the visual field tends to induce its complementary color in adjoining areas. The result is ***simultaneous color contrast.*** For example, a gray

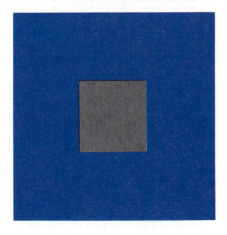

4.26   Color contrast   *The gray patches on the blue and yellow backgrounds are physically identical. But they don't look that way. To begin with, there is a difference in perceived brightness: the patch on the blue looks brighter than the one on the yellow, a result of brightness contrast. There is also a difference in perceived hue, for the patch on the blue looks somewhat yellowish, while that on the yellow looks bluish. This is color contrast, a demonstration that hues tend to induce their antagonists in neighboring areas.*

4.27   Negative afterimage   *Stare at the center of the figure for about a minute or two, and then look at a white piece of paper. Blink once or twice; the negative afterimage will appear within a few seconds showing the rose in its correct colors.*

patch will tend to look bluish if surrounded by yellow, yellowish if surrounded by blue, and so on (see Figure 4.26).

In simultaneous contrast, the complementary relation involves two adjoining regions in space. In a related phenomenon, the contrast is with an immediately preceding stimulus; it is a contrast in time rather than in space. Suppose we stare at a green patch for a while and then look at a white wall. We will see a reddish spot. This is a ***negative afterimage*** (see Figure 4.27). Negative afterimages have the complementary hue and the opposite brightness of the original stimulus (which is why they are called negative). Thus, fixation on a brightly lit red bulb will make us see a dark greenish shape when we subsequently look at a white screen.

Afterimages are caused by events that occur in the retina and associated visual mechanisms. This is why, when the eye moves, the afterimage moves along with it. One reason for the effect is retinal adaptation. When we fixate a white disk on a black background, the pigments in the retinal region that corresponds to the disk will be stimulated more intensely than those in surrounding areas. During subsequent exposure to a homogeneous white surface, the more deeply stimulated regions will respond less vigorously and will thus report a lesser sensory intensity. The result is a dark gray negative afterimage. But peripheral adaptation is probably not the whole story. In addition, there may be a ***rebound phenomenon.*** While the inspection stimulus was still present, the excited regions may well have inhibited an antagonistic process. White held back black, blue inhibited yellow, and so on. When the stimulus is withdrawn, the inhibited processes rebound, like a coiled spring that is suddenly released.

The Physiological Basis of Color Vision

What is the physiological basis of color vision? We will consider this issue by subdividing it into two questions: first, how wavelengths are transduced into receptor activity, and, second, how the receptor output is coded so that it yields the psychological attributes of color, such as the sensory experience of unique blue.

COLOR RECEPTORS

The raw material with which the visual system must begin is light of various intensities. Since we can discriminate among different wavelengths, there must be different receptors (that is, different types of cones) that are somehow differentially attuned to this physical dimension.

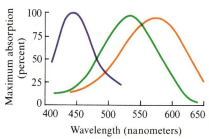

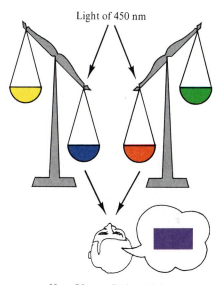

4.28 Sensitivity curves of three different cones in the primate retina *The retinas of humans and monkeys contain three different kinds of cones, each with its own photopigments which differ in their sensitivity to different regions of the spectrum. One absorbs more of the shorter wavelengths (and is thus more sensitive to light in this spectral region), a second more of the middle wavelengths, a third more of the longer ones. The resulting sensitivity curves are shown here. (After MacNichol, 1964)*

Hue: Blue + Red = Violet

4.29 The opponent-process hue systems *The diagram shows how opponent-process theory interprets our response to light of a particular wavelength. In the example, the light is in the short-wave region of the visible spectrum, specifically, 450 nanometers. This will affect both the blue-yellow and the red-green systems. It will tip the blue-yellow balance toward blue, and the red-green balance toward red. The resulting hue will be a mixture of red and blue (that is, violet).*

It turns out that normal human color vision depends on three different kinds of cone elements (which is why it is often called *trichromatic*). While each of these cone types responds to a broad range of wavelengths in the visible spectrum, their sensitivity curves differ in that one cone type is most sensitive to wavelengths in the short-wave region of the spectrum, the second to wavelengths in the middle range, and the third to the longer wavelengths (Bowmaker and Dartnall, 1980; MacNichol, 1986; see Figure 4.28).

The critical fact about all three cone elements is that their sensitivities overlap extensively so that most of the wavelengths of the visible spectrum stimulate each of the three receptor elements. This being so, how can we manage to discriminate different wavelengths? We can, because each receptor element will respond in differing degree depending upon the wavelength of the stimulus light. If the light is from the blue end of the spectrum, there will be maximum output from the cone element whose sensitivity is greatest in the short-wave region. If the light is from the orange end, it will elicit maximum activity from the cone element whose sensitivity is greatest in the long-wave region. As a result, each wavelength will produce a different ratio of the outputs of the three receptor types. Assuming that the nervous system can tell which receptor type is sending which message, wavelength discrimination follows.

COLOR CODING: THE OPPONENT-PROCESS THEORY

The preceding analysis can explain how lights of different wavelengths are discriminated from each other, but it alone cannot account for why these lights *look* the way they do. As we have seen, some colors appear pure or primary (for example, unique blue) while others do not (for example, violet). Furthermore, these primary colors form two complementary and antagonistic pairs (red-green and blue-yellow). To explain phenomena of this kind we must assume some further mechanisms which work on the three receptor outputs and ultimately code them into the sensory qualities we know as color.

A widely accepted approach is the *opponent-process theory* formulated by Leo Hurvich and Dorothea Jameson which dates back to the nineteenth-century psychophysiologist, Ewald Hering. This theory asserts that there are six psychologically primary color qualities—red, green, blue, yellow, black, and white—each of which has a different neural process that corresponds to it. These six processes are not independent, but instead are organized into three opponent-process pairs: red-green, blue-yellow, and black-white. The two members of each pair are antagonists. Excitation of one member automatically inhibits the other (Hurvich and Jameson, 1957).

The two hue systems According to the opponent-process theory, the experience of hue depends upon two of three opponent-process pairs—red-green and blue-yellow. (As we will see, the black-white system is not relevant to perceived hue.) Each of these opponent-process pairs can be likened to a balance scale. If one arm (say, the blue process) goes down, the other arm (its opponent, yellow) necessarily comes up. The hue we actually see depends upon the position of the two balances (Figure 4.29). If the red-green balance is tipped toward red and the blue-yellow balance toward blue (excitation of red and blue with concomitant inhibition of green and yellow), the perceived hue will be violet. This follows, because the resulting hue will be a combination of red and blue, which is seen as violet. If either of the two scales is evenly balanced, it will make no contribution to the hue experience. This will occur when neither of the two antagonists is stimulated, and also when both are stimulated equally and cancel each other out. If both hue systems are in balance, there will be no hue at all and the resulting color will be seen as achromatic (that is, without hue).

Ewald Hering *(Courtesy National Library of Medicine)*

The black-white system The brightness or darkness of a visual experience is determined by the activity of a third pair of antagonists, black and white. Every wavelength contributes to the excitation of the white system, in proportion to its intensity and the sensitivity of daylight vision to this point of the spectrum. The black process is produced by inhibition of the antagonistic white process. This is best exemplified by some phenomena of brightness contrast. A black paper placed against a dark gray background will look not black but a darker shade of gray. We can make it look pitch-black by presenting it against a brilliantly illuminated background. By doing so, we inhibit the white process within the enclosed region, which necessarily enhances the activity of its antagonist.

The relation between color receptors and opponent processes Can we reconcile the fact that there are three elements at the receptor level while there are four chromatic color opponents? Hurvich and Jameson have suggested a neural system that might produce the appropriate opponent-process reactions at some level beyond the receptor elements. The basic idea is that the three receptor elements have both excitatory and inhibitory connections with neurons higher up that correspond to opponent processes, and that one pole of each opponent process will be activated by excitation while its opposite pole will be activated by inhibition. (The details of this proposal are beyond the scope of this book. See Hurvich and Jameson, 1974).

THE PHYSIOLOGICAL BASIS OF OPPONENT PROCESSES

When the theory was first developed, the opponent processes were only an inference, based upon the perceptual phenomena of color vision. Today there is evidence that this inference was close to the neurophysiological mark. The proof comes from single-cell recordings (in the retina or higher up), which show that some neurons behave very much as an opponent-process theory would lead one to expect.

As an example, take a study of single-cell activity in the visual pathway of the rhesus monkey, whose color vision is known to be very similar to ours. Some of its visual cells behave as though they were part of a blue-yellow system. If the retina is stimulated by blue light, these cells fire more rapidly. The opposite holds true if the same area is exposed to yellow light—the firing rate is inhibited (see Figure 4.30). This is exactly what should happen if the underlying color mechanism mirrors the perceptual phenomena. Blue should have one effect and yellow the opposite. Other cells have been discovered that show a similar antagonistic pattern when stimulated by red or by green light (de Valois, 1965).

4.30 Opponent-process cells in the visual system of a monkey *The figure shows the average firing rate of "blue-yellow cells" to light of different wavelengths. These cells are excited by shorter wavelengths and inhibited by longer wavelengths, analogous to the cells in the human system that signal the sensation "blue." As the figure shows, shorter wavelengths lead to firing rates that are above the spontaneous rates obtained when there is no stimulus at all. Longer wavelengths have the opposite effect, depressing the cell's activity below the spontaneous firing rate. (Data from de Valois and de Valois, 1975)*

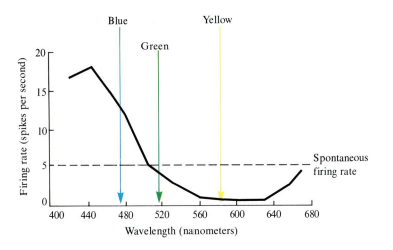

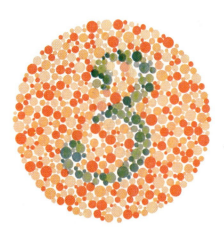

4.31 **Testing for color blindness** *A plate used to test for color blindness. To pick out the number in the plate, an observer has to be able to discriminate certain hues. Persons with normal color vision can do it and will see the number 3. Persons with red-green color blindness cannot do this. (Courtesy American Optical Corporation)*

A small proportion of the total population consists of people who do not respond to color as most others do. Of these the vast majority are men, since many such conditions are inherited and sex-linked. Some form of color defect is found in 8 percent of all males as compared to only .03 percent of females.

Color deficiencies come in various forms, some of which involve a missing visual pigment, others a defective opponent process, and many involve malfunction at both levels (Hurvich, 1981). Most common is a defect in which reds are confused with greens; least common is total color blindness in which no hues can be distinguished at all. Color defects are rarely noticed in everyday life, for color-blind persons ordinarily use color names quite appropriately. They call blood red and dollar bills green, presumably on the basis of other cues such as form and brightness. To determine whether a person has a color defect he or she must be tested under special conditions in which such extraneous cues are eliminated (see Figure 4.31).

How do people with color defects see colors? We may know that a particular person cannot distinguish between red and green, but that does not tell us how these colors look to him. He cannot tell us, for he cannot know what sensory quality is lacking. The question would have remained unanswerable had it not been for a subject who was red-green color blind in one eye and had normal color vision in the other. This subject (who happened to be one of the rare females with a color defect) was able to describe what she saw with the defective eye by using the color language of the normal one. With the color-blind eye she saw only grays, blues, and yellows. Red and green hues were altogether absent, as if one of the opponent-process pairs was missing (Graham and Hsia, 1954).

TAKING STOCK

Let us take stock. We have looked at the way in which the different sensory systems respond to external stimuli, how they transduce the proximal stimulus and convert it into a neural impulse, how they code the incoming message into the various dimensions of our sensory experience, and how activity in any part of a sensory system interacts with the activity of other parts. All of this has led us to some understanding of how we come to see bright yellow-greens and hear high-pitched noises. But it has not yet addressed the question with which we started. How do we come to know about the objects and events outside—not just bright yellow-greens but grassy meadows, not just high-pitched noises but singing birds? That the sensory systems contribute the raw materials for such knowledge is clear enough. But how do we get from the sensory raw materials to a knowledge of the world outside? This question is traditionally dealt with under the heading of *perception,* the topic to which we turn next.

SUMMARY

1. The study of sensory processes grew out of questions about the origin of human knowledge. John Locke and other *empiricists* argued that all knowledge comes through stimuli that excite the senses. We can distinguish two kinds of stimuli. One is the *distal stimulus,* an object or event in the world outside. The other is the *proximal stimulus,* the pattern of physical stimulus energies that impinges on a given sensory surface. The only way to get information about distal stimuli outside is through the proximal stimuli these

give rise to. This leads to theoretical problems, for we perceive many qualities—depth, constant size and shape—that are not given in the proximal stimulus. Empiricists try to overcome such difficulties by asserting that much of perception is built up through learning by *association.* This view has been challenged by *nativists* such as Immanuel Kant who believe that the sensory input is organized according to a number of built-in categories.

2. The path to sensory experience or *sensation* begins with a proximal stimulus. This is *transduced* into a nervous impulse by specialized *receptors,* is usually further modified by other parts of the nervous system, and finally leads to a sensation. One branch of sensory psychology is *psychophysics,* which tries to relate the characteristics of the physical stimulus to both the quality and intensity of the sensory experience.

3. The founder of psychophysics, Gustav T. Fechner, studied sensory intensity by determining the ability of subjects to discriminate between stimulus intensities. Important measures of this ability are the *absolute threshold* and the *difference threshold.* The difference threshold is the change in the intensity of a given stimulus (the so-called *standard* stimulus) that is just large enough to be detected, producing a *just noticeable difference or j.n.d.* According to *Weber's law,* the j.n.d. is a constant fraction of the intensity of the standard stimulus. Fechner generalized Weber's law to express a wider relationship between sensory intensity and physical intensity. This is *Fechner's law,* which states that the strength of a sensation grows as the logarithm of stimulus intensity.

4. A way of disentangling sensory sensitivity and *response bias* is provided by *signal-detection theory.* In a typical *detection experiment,* the stimulus is presented on half of the trials, and absent on the other half. In this procedure, there can be two kinds of errors: *misses* (saying a stimulus is absent when it is present) and *false alarms* (saying it is present when it is absent). Their relative proportion is partially determined by a *payoff matrix.*

5. Different sense modalities have different functions and mechanisms. One group of senses provides information about the body's own movements and location. Skeletal motion is sensed through *kinesthesis,* bodily orientation by the *vestibular organs* located in the *inner ears.*

6. The various *skin senses* inform the organism of what is directly adjacent to its own body. There are at least four different skin sensations: *pressure, warmth, cold,* and *pain.* Whether each of these four is produced by separate receptors is still a matter of debate.

7. The sense of *taste* acts as a gatekeeper to the digestive system. Its receptors are *taste buds* whose stimulation generates the four basic taste qualities of *sour, sweet, salty,* and *bitter.*

8. Smell or *olfaction* is a distance sense that gives information about objects outside of the body. In humans, olfaction is a relatively minor distance sense, but in many animals it is a vital guide to food, mates, and danger. In many species, it permits a primitive form of communication based on *pheromones.*

9. The sense of hearing or *audition* informs us of pressure changes that occur at a distance. Its stimulus is a disturbance of the air that is propagated in the form of *sound waves,* which can vary in *amplitude* and *frequency.*

10. A number of accessory structures help to conduct and amplify sound waves so that they can affect the auditory receptors. Sound waves set up vibrations in the *eardrum* which are then transmitted by the *ossicles* to the *oval window* whose movements create waves in the *cochlea* of the inner ear. Within the cochlea is the *basilar membrane,* which contains the auditory receptors that are stimulated by the membrane's deformation. According to the *place theory,* the sensory experience of pitch is based on the place of the membrane that is stimulated; each place being responsive to a particular wave frequency and generating a particular pitch sensation. According to the *frequency theory,* the stimulus for pitch is the firing frequency of the auditory nerve. Modern theorists believe that both mechanisms operate: Higher frequencies depend upon the place of the basilar membrane, while lower frequencies depend upon neural firing frequency.

11. Vision is our primary distance sense. Its stimulus is light, which can vary in *intensity* and *wavelength.* Many of the structures of the eye, such as the *lens* and the *iris,* serve mainly as accessory devices to fashion a proper proximal stimulus, the *retinal image.* Once

on the retina, the light stimulus is transduced into a neural impulse by the visual receptors, the *rods* and *cones. Visual acuity* is greatest in the *fovea* where the density of the receptors (here, cones) is greatest.

12. According to the *duplex theory of vision,* rods and cones differ in function. The rods operate at low light intensities and lead to colorless sensations. The cones function at much higher illumination levels and are responsible for sensations of color. Further evidence for the duplex theory comes from different *spectral sensitivity curves* and from the study of *dark adaptation.*

13. The first stage in the transformation of light into a neural impulse is a photochemical process that involves the breakdown of various *visual pigments* that are later resynthesized. One such pigment is *rhodopsin,* the photochemically sensitive substance contained by the rods.

14. The various components of the visual system do not operate in isolation but interact constantly. One form of interaction occurs over time, as in various forms of *adaptation.*

15. Interaction also occurs in space, between neighboring regions on the retina. An example is *brightness contrast,* which tends to enhance the distinction between an object and its background. The physiological mechanism that underlies these effects is *lateral inhibition.*

16. Visual sensations have a qualitative character—they vary in color. Color sensations can be ordered by reference to three dimensions: *hue, brightness,* and *saturation.* Colors can be mixed *subtractively* (as in mixing pigments) or *additively* (as in simultaneously stimulating the same region of the retina with two or more stimuli). The results of additive mixture studies show that every hue has a *complementary hue* which, when mixed with the first, yields gray. Two important examples are red and green, and blue and yellow. These two color pairs are color antagonists, a fact shown by the phenomena of the *negative afterimage* and *simultaneous color contrast.*

17. One question about the mechanisms that underlie color vision concerns the way in which the different light waves are transduced into a receptor discharge. There is general agreement that this is done by the joint action of three different cone types, each of which has a somewhat different sensitivity curve.

18. A second question concerns the way the receptor output is coded to produce color quality. A leading approach is the *opponent-process theory* of Hurvich and Jameson. This assumes that there are three neural systems, each of which corresponds to a pair of antagonistic sensory experiences: red-green, blue-yellow, and black-white. The first two determine perceived hue; the third determines perceived brightness. Further evidence for the opponent-process view comes from single-cell recordings of monkeys and some phenomena of *color blindness.*

CHAPTER 5

Perception

In the previous chapter, we discussed some of the simpler attributes of sensory experience, such as red, A-flat, and cold. Locke and Berkeley thought that these experiences were produced by a passive registration of the proximal stimulus energies which impinge upon the senses. But, as we have seen, the eye is more than a camera, the ear more than a microphone, for both sensory systems actively transform their stimulus inputs at the very start of their neurological journey, emphasizing differences and minimizing stimulation that remains unchanged. This active organization of the stimulus input is impressive enough when we consider the experience of simple sensory attributes, but it becomes even more dramatic when we turn to the fundamental problem traditionally associated with the term *perception:* how we come to apprehend the objects and events in the external reality around us; how we come to see, not just a brightish red, but an apple.

THE PROBLEM OF PERCEPTION

What must be explained to understand how we see the apple? Our initial reaction might be that the only problem is the perceptual meaning of the visual input, how it is interpreted as an edible fruit—which grows on trees, which keeps the doctor away, which caused the expulsion from Eden, and so on. But how objects acquire perceptual meaning is by no means the only question, or even the most basic one, for the student of perception. The fundamental issue is not why a given stimulus is seen as a particular kind of object, but rather why it is seen as any object at all. Suppose we show the apple to someone who has never seen any fruit before. He will not know its function, but he will certainly see it as some round, red thing of whose tangible existence he has no doubt—in short, he will perceive it as an object.

How can he accomplish this feat? After all, the apple is a distal stimulus which (at least visually) is known to us only through the proximal stimulus that it projects upon our retina, and this proximal stimulus is two-dimensional and is constantly changing. It gets smaller or larger depending upon our distance from it; it stimulates different regions of the retina; it moves across the retina as we

The problem of perception How do we come to perceive the world as it is—to see the flags as smaller than the boat, to see the wall extending continuously behind the people that block some portion of it from view, and so on? (Claude Monet, Terrace at Sainte-Adresse, 1867; courtesy The Metropolitan Museum of Art, purchased with special contributions and purchase funds given or bequeathed by friends of the Museum, 1967)

move our eyes. Before an observer can decide whether the object he's looking at is an apple (or a baseball or a human head, or whatever), he must somehow perceive the constant properties of this external object despite the continual variations in the proximal stimulus. To do this, he must *organize* the sensory world to which it is exposed into a coherent scene in which there are real objects (such as apples) and events (such as apples that fall from trees). To achieve this organization, he has to answer three important perceptual questions about what he sees (or hears and feels) in the world outside: Where is it? Where is it going? (And most important) What is it?

We will begin our discussion by turning to the first question, which concerns the perception of depth.

THE PERCEPTION OF DEPTH: WHERE IS IT?

Quite apart from the question of *what* an object is (which we'll take up shortly), we have to know where it is located. The object may be a potential mate or a sabertooth tiger, but the perceiver can hardly take appropriate action unless he can also locate the object in the external world.

Much of the work on the problem of visual localization has concentrated on the perception of depth, a topic that has occupied philosophers and scientists for over three hundred years. They have asked: How can we possibly see the world in three dimensions when only two of these dimensions are given in the image that falls upon the eye? This question has led to a search for *depth cues,* features of the stimulus situation which indicate how far the object is from the observer or from other objects in the world.

Binocular Cues

A very important cue to depth comes from the fact that we have two eyes. These look out on the world from two different positions. As a result, they obtain a somewhat different view of any solid object they converge on. This *binocular disparity* inevitably follows from the geometry of the physical situation. Obviously, the disparity becomes less pronounced the farther the object is from the observer. Beyond thirty feet the two eyes receive virtually the same image (Figure 5.1).

5.1 Retinal disparity Two points, A and B, at different distances from the observer, present somewhat different retinal images. The distance between the images on one eye, a_1b_1, is different (disparate) from the distance between them on the other, a_2b_2. This disparity is a powerful cue for depth. (After Hochberg, 1978a)

← 65 millimeters →

141

5.2   Linear perspective as a cue for depth   *(Photograph by Roberta Intrater)*

Binocular disparity alone can induce perceived depth. If we draw or photograph the two different views received by each eye while looking at a nearby object and then separately present each of these views to the appropriate eye, we can obtain a striking impression of depth. To achieve this stereo effect, the two eyes must converge as they would if they were actually looking at the solid object at the given distance.

Monocular Cues

Binocular disparity is a very powerful (and probably innate) determinant of perceived depth. Yet, we can perceive depth even with one eye closed. Even more important, many people who have been blind in one eye from birth see the world in three dimensions. Clearly then, there are other cues for depth perception that come from the image obtained with one eye alone—the ***monocular depth cues.***

Many of the monocular depth cues have been exploited for centuries by artists, and are therefore called ***pictorial cues.*** Examples include ***linear perspective*** (Figure 5.2), ***interposition*** (Figure 5.3), and ***relative size*** (Figure 5.4). In each case, the effect is an optical consequence of the projection of a three-dimensional world upon a flat surface. Objects that are farther away are also inevitably blocked from view by any other opaque object that obstructs their optical path to the eye (interposition). Far-off objects necessarily produce a smaller retinal image than do nearby ones (linear perspective and relative size).

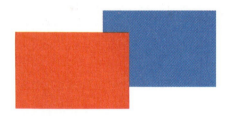

5.3   Interposition   *When one figure interrupts the contour of another figure, it provides a monocular cue for depth. This is interposition. Because of interposition, the red rectangle in the figure is perceived to be in front of the blue one.*

A

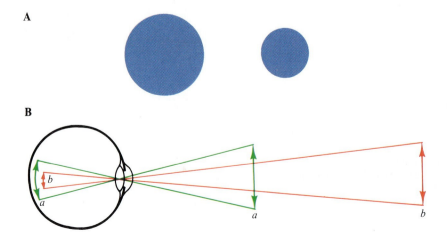

B

5.4   Relative size   *(A) All other things equal, the larger of two otherwise identical figures will seem to be closer than the smaller one. This is a consequence of the simple geometry of vision illustrated in (B). Two equally large objects, a and b, that are at different distances from the observer, will project retinal images of different size.*

A
B

5.5   Texture gradients as cues for depth   Uniformly textured surfaces produce texture gradients that provide information about depth: as the surface recedes, the texture density increases. (A) At a seashore, such gradients may be produced by rocks, or (B) a gannet colony. (Photographs by Hans Wallach and Robert Gillmor/Bruce Coleman)

A very powerful set of pictorial cues is provided by ***texture gradients,*** whose role was emphasized by James J. Gibson, a very influential theorist in the psychology of perception. Such gradients are ultimately produced by perspective. Consider what meets the eye when we look at cobblestones on a road or clumps of grass in a meadow. Gibson pointed out that the retinal projection of such objects must necessarily show a continuous change, a texture gradient, that depends upon the spatial layout of the relevant surfaces (see Figure 5.5). Such texture gradients are powerful determinants of perceived depth. Discontinuities in texture gradients provide information about further spatial relationships between the various textured surfaces. Thus, the abrupt change of texture density in Figure 5.6 produces the impression of a sharp drop, a "visual cliff" (see also p. 144–45; Gibson, J., 1950, 1966).

The Perception of Depth through Motion

Thus far we have encountered situations in which both the observer and the scene observed are stationary. But in real life we are constantly moving through the world we perceive. This motion provides a vital source of visual information

A
B

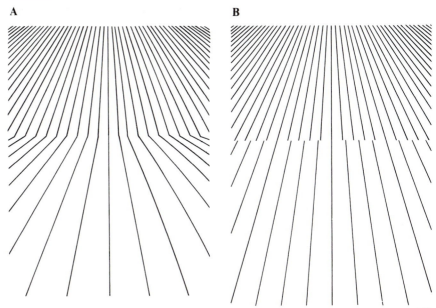

5.6   The effect of changes in texture gradients   Such changes provide important information about spatial arrangements in the world. Examples are (A) an upward tilt at a corner; and (B) a sudden drop. (After Gibson, 1950)

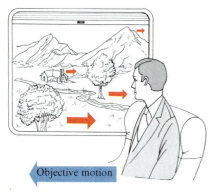

5.7 Motion parallax *When an observer moves relative to a stationary environment, the objects in that environment will be displaced (and will therefore seem to move) relative to him. (The rate of relative displacement is indicated by the thickness of the red arrows. The thicker these arrows, the more quickly the objects seem to move. The observer's movement is indicated by a blue arrow.) (After Coren and Ward, 1989)*

5.8 An infant on the visual cliff *The infant is placed on the centerboard laid across a heavy sheet of glass and her mother calls to her. If the mother is on the "deep" side, the infant pats the glass, but despite this tactual information that all is safe, she refuses to crawl across the apparent cliff. (Photograph by Richard D. Walk)*

about the spatial arrangement of the objects around us, a pattern of cues that once again follows from the optical geometry of the situation.

As we move our heads or bodies from right to left, the images projected by the objects outside will necessarily move across the retina. The apparent relative motion of these objects is an enormously effective depth cue, **motion parallax.** As we move through space, nearby objects seem to move very quickly and in a direction opposite to our own; as an example, consider the trees racing backward as one looks out of a speeding train. Objects farther away also seem to move in the opposite direction, but at a lesser velocity (Helmholtz, 1909; see Figure 5.7).

Innate Factors in Depth Perception

In many organisms, important features of the perception of space are apparently built into the nervous machinery. An example is the localization of sounds in space. One investigator studied this phenomenon in a ten-minute-old baby. The newborn consistently turned her eyes in the direction of a clicking sound, thus demonstrating that some spatial coordination between eye and ear exists prior to learning (Wertheimer, 1961).

There is evidence that some aspects of visual depth perception are also innately given (or come in at such an early age that if they are learned, they must be learned very quickly). The facets of depth that apparently come in first are those that are based on perceived movement, such as motion parallax. Another example is the response to **looming,** a rapid magnification of a form in the visual field that generally signals an impending impact. To study this looming effect experimentally, several investigators have simulated the visual consequence of rapid approach by various means, for example by a rapidly expanding shadow cast on a screen. When exposed to these expanding patterns, crabs flatten out, frogs jump away, and infant monkeys leap to the rear of their cages. Human infants as young as two or three weeks of age blink their eyes as if they sense a coming collision, stiffen, and cry (Schiff, 1965; Ball and Tronick, 1971; Yonas, 1981).

Another demonstration of early (and possibly unlearned) visual depth perception is a classic study by Richard Walk and Eleanor Gibson. They noted that crawling infants are surprisingly (though by no means perfectly) successful in avoiding the precipices of their everyday lives (Walk and Gibson, 1961). The investigators studied infant behavior on the **visual cliff** (see Figure 5.8), which simulates the appearance of a steep edge but is safe enough to mollify the infants' mothers, if not the infants themselves. This device consists of a large glass table, about three feet above the floor, which is divided in half by a wooden centerboard. On one side of the board, a checkerboard pattern is attached directly to the underside of the glass; on the other side, the same pattern is placed on the floor. The apparent drop-off is perceived by adults, in part because of a sudden change in texture density, in part because of motion parallax and binocular disparity. But will six-month-old infants respond to any of these cues? The babies were placed on the centerboard, and their mothers called and beckoned to them. When the mother beckoned from the shallow side, the baby usually crawled quickly to her. But only a very few infants ventured forth when called from across the apparent precipice.

An empiricist might well argue that these findings are inconclusive because the babies had six months of previous experience. Unfortunately, there is no easy way of studying visual cliff behavior in younger infants. You can't very well ask where an infant will crawl to if he cannot get up on his knees. But motor coordination matures much earlier in many species, and various very young animals show appropriate cliff-avoidance as soon as they are old enough to move around

Physical events

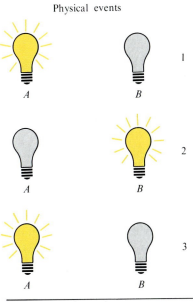

Perceptual experience

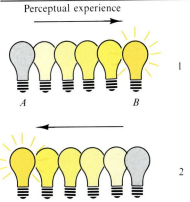

5.9 Stroboscopic movement *The sequence of optical events that produces stroboscopic movement. Light A flashes at time 1, followed by light B at time 2, then back to light A at time 3. If the time intervals are appropriately chosen, the perceptual experience will be of a light moving from left to right and back.*

at all. Kids and lambs were tested as soon as they were able to stand. They never stepped onto the steep side. Chicks tested less than twenty-four hours after hatching gave the same result (Walk and Gibson, E., 1961; Gibson, E., 1969; Walk, 1978).

THE PERCEPTION OF MOVEMENT: WHAT IS IT DOING?

To see a large, unfriendly Doberman in front of you is one thing; to see him bare his teeth and rush directly at you is quite another. We want to know where an object is, but we also want to know what it is doing. Put another way, we want to perceive events as well as objects. The basic ingredient of the perception of events is the perception of movement.

Illusions of Movement

What leads to the perception of movement? One might guess that one sees things move because they produce an image that moves across the retina. But this answer is too simple. For in fact, we sometimes perceive movement even when none occurs on the retina.

STROBOSCOPIC MOVEMENT

Suppose we briefly turn on a light in one location of the visual field, then turn it off, and after an appropriate interval (somewhere between 30 and 200 milliseconds) turn on a second light in a different location. The result is *apparent movement* (sometimes called *stroboscopic movement* or the *phi phenomenon*). The light is seen to travel from one point to another, even though there was no stimulation—let alone movement—in the intervening region (Figure 5.9). This phenomenon is perceptually overwhelming; given the right intervals, it is indistinguishable from real movement. It is an effect that has numerous technological applications, ranging from animated neon signs to motion pictures (Wertheimer, 1912). These results suggest that one stimulus for motion is relative displacement over time. Something is here at one moment and there at the next. If the time intervals are right, the nervous system interprets this as evidence that this something has moved.

INDUCED MOVEMENT

How does the perceptual system react when one of two objects is moving while the other is (physically) stationary? Consider a ball rolling on a billiard table. We see the ball as moving and the table at rest. But why not the other way around? To be sure, the ball is being displaced relative to the table edge, but so is the table edge displaced relative to the ball. One might guess that the reason is learning. Perhaps experience has taught us that balls generally move around while tables stay put. But the evidence indicates that what matters is a more general perceptual relationship between the two stimuli. The object that encloses the other tends to act as a frame which is seen as stationary. Thus, the table serves as a frame against which the ball is seen to move.

In this example, perception and physical reality coincide, for the frame provided by the table is truly stationary. What happens when the objective situation is reversed? In one study subjects were shown a luminous rectangular frame in an

145

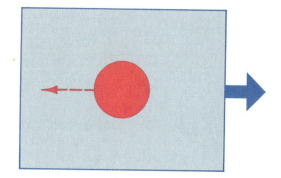

5.10 Induced movement *Subjects in an otherwise dark room see a luminous dot surrounded by a luminous frame. When the frame is moved to the right, subjects perceive the dot moving to the left, even though it is objectively stationary. (Duncker, 1929)*

otherwise dark room. Inside the frame was a luminous dot. In actual fact, the rectangle moved to the right while the dot stayed in place. But the subjects saw something else. They perceived the dot as moving to the left, in the opposite direction of the frame's motion. The physical movement of the frame had induced the perceived movement of the enclosed figure (Figure 5.10).

The *induced movement* effect is familiar from everyday life as well. The moon apparently drifts through the clouds; the base of a bridge seems to float against the flow of the river current. In the second case, there may also be *induced motion of the self.* If the subject stands on the bridge that she perceives as moving, she perceives herself moving along with it. The same effect occurs when sitting in a train that's standing in a station. If a train on the adjacent track pulls out, we tend to feel ourselves moving though in fact we—and the train we're in—are stationary.

FORM PERCEPTION: WHAT IS IT?

We've asked how we see where an object is and where it is going. But we have not dealt with the most important question of all: How do we perceive and recognize *what* that object is?

In vision, our primary means for recognizing an object is through the perception of its form. To be sure, we sometimes rely on color (a violet), and occasionally on size (a toy model of an automobile), but in the vast majority of cases, form is the major avenue for identifying what it is we see. The question is how. How do we recognize the myriad forms and patterns that are present in the world around us—triangles and ellipses, skyscrapers and automobiles, hands and faces?

In trying to answer this question, some investigators asked whether there are some primitive components into which all (or at least most) forms could be analyzed, and if so, what these components are.

Elements of Form

Max Wertheimer (1880–1943), the founder of Gestalt psychology and one of the most influential figures in the psychology of perception. (Courtesy Omikron)

The early empiricists believed that the elementary units out of which all forms are constructed are the simple visual sensations such as patches of color and brightness. In their view, these are gradually pieced together through learning. But modern investigators believe that the elementary building blocks of form are more complex than these early thinkers had supposed. In their view, such units of form as edges and angles are not pieced together through learning, but are instead extracted from the stimulus by processes that are part of our native equipment. Their beliefs are derived from the study of the innate mechanisms of form perception.

5.11 Cartoon pictures of normally arranged and scrambled faces *Newborns spend about as much time looking at each; four-month-olds prefer to look at the normally arranged face. (From Fagan, J.F., 1976).*

No stimulus   Stimulus

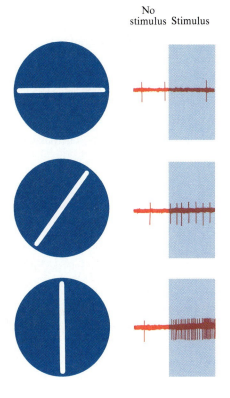

5.12 Feature detectors in the visual system of the cat *The response of a single cortical cell when stimulated by a slit of light in three different orientations. This cell was evidently responsive to the vertical. A horizontal slit led to no response, a tilted slit led to a slight response, while a vertical slit led to a marked increase in firing. (After Hubel, 1963)*

INNATE FACTORS IN FORM PERCEPTION

There is some evidence that at least some aspects of form perception are based on built-in processes. Some of the evidence comes from animals. A one-day-old chick will peck at small spheres in preference to small pyramids, even if kept in darkness from hatching to the time of the test. A prewired preference for round shapes together with the capacity to distinguish them is presumably useful to a creature whose primary foods are grain and seed (Fantz, 1957). Human form perception is less ready-made than the chick's; but even so, the visual world of a newborn infant is not a chaotic jumble of color and light. When a three-day-old infant is presented with a simple form, such as a triangle, its eyes do not move randomly. Photographs of the infant's cornea show that its eyes tend to orient toward those features of the pattern that help to define it, such as its edges and its vertices (Salapatek and Kessen, 1966; Salapatek, 1975).

Of special interest is the infant's early tendency to look at forms that resemble a human face, in preference to others (Fantz, 1961; Freedman, 1971; Fagan, 1976). This tendency is probably based on a preference for certain visual components that comprise a face, such as curved rather than straight contours (Fantz, 1970). Whatever its basis, such a built-in predisposition to look at facelike forms must have considerable survival value in an organism whose period of infantile dependence is so long and so intense (Figure 5.11).

By about three months of age, there is evidence that the infant can recognize something about the mother's face in a photograph. When presented with color slides of their mother or of a strange woman, they preferred to look at the picture of their mother. This indicates that some aspects of the familiar facial pattern were recognized even in a novel, two-dimensional form (Barrera and Maurer, 1981). (For further discussion of infant perception, see Chapter 13.)

FEATURE DETECTORS

All in all, there seems to be good reason to believe that some aspects of form perception are innately given. But what are the mechanisms whereby the nervous system accomplishes this organization of the stimulus input? The last two or three decades have seen some steps toward an answer.

Two physiologists, Nobel prize winners David Hubel and Torsten Wiesel, studied the activity of single cortical cells in response to various visual stimuli. They found some cells that react to some of the elements of visual form—lines or edges or a particular orientation. One such cell might be excited by a thin sliver of light slanted at, say, 45 degrees, regardless of where on the retina the stimulus is presented (see Figure 5.12). This cell is called a **feature detector;** it analyzes the visual input to detect some fairly complex feature (such as orientation) and responds to this feature rather than to other aspects of the stimulus pattern. Hubel and Wiesel have discovered cells that detect even more complex features of visual form. An example is a cell that reacts to right angles (Hubel and Wiesel, 1959, 1979).

Later research has focused on cortical cells that signal other perceptual features. For example, some cells in the cortex are sensitive to binocular disparity (Hubel and Wiesel, 1970; Poggio and Fischer, 1978; Ferster, 1981). Other cells respond to directional movement; they fire if a line moves in one direction but won't fire if it moves in the direction that's opposite (e.g., Barlow and Hill, 1963; Vaultin and Berkeley, 1977).

5.13 Perceptual segregation *(A) A still life. (Photograph by Jeffrey Grosscup) (B) An overlay designating five different segments of the scene shown in (A). To determine what an object is, the perceptual system must first decide what goes with what: does portion B go with A, with C, D, or E? Or with none of them?*

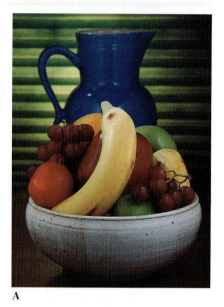

A

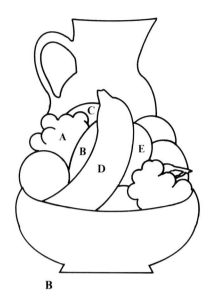

B

5.14 Figure and ground *The first step in seeing a form is to segregate it from its background. The part seen as figure appears to be more cohesive and sharply delineated. The part seen as ground is perceived to be more formless and to extend behind the figure.*

5.15 Reversible figure-ground pattern *The classic example of a reversible figure-ground pattern. It can be seen as either a pair of silhouetted faces or a white vase.*

Perceptual Segregation

Suppose the observer looks at the still life in Figure 5.13A. To make sense of the picture, her perceptual system must somehow group the many visual elements of the scene appropriately. For one thing, it has to determine what is focal (for example, the fruit and the bowl) and what can at least temporarily be relegated to the background (for example, the green shutters, the table, and perhaps the pitcher). But there is still more to be done. Some objects will necessarily be partially occluded by others that stand or lie in front of them. Consider the portions *A, B, C, D,* and *E* of the figure shown in Figure 5.13B. To determine what any given object could possibly be, we must first perform an initial job of segregating the scene into subcomponents: decide whether portion *B* goes with *A* (half an apple combined with some grapes), or with *C* (half an apple with a piece of orange), or with *D* (half an apple with a banana), or finally with *E* (an apple).

This *visual segregation* process is sometimes called *perceptual parsing.* It performs the same function for vision that parsing performs for speech. When someone talks to us, our eardrums are exposed to a sound stream that is essentially unbroken. What hits the ears is a sequence of sounds such as:

Thestudentsaidtheteacherisafool

The listener parses the sound pattern by grouping some sounds together with others, forming units called words:

The student said the teacher is a fool

He may then parse further by grouping the words into larger units called phrases, as in:

The student, said the teacher, is a fool.

In some cases, he may even discover that there are alternate ways of parsing, as in:

The student said, the teacher is a fool.

The important point is that the parsing is not primarily in the stimulus. It is contributed by the listener, for the sound stream itself has no pauses between words and contains no commas. (This is why foreigners often sound as if they speak much faster than we do.) Until at least some basic parsing has been performed, the listener has no hope of comprehending what she has heard. To un-

5.16 Figure-ground reversal in the visual arts *The Trojan War as depicted by Salvador Dali. The scene of wild carnage conceals the image of the Trojan Horse, whose outline follows the gateway to the city. (Courtesy Esquire)*

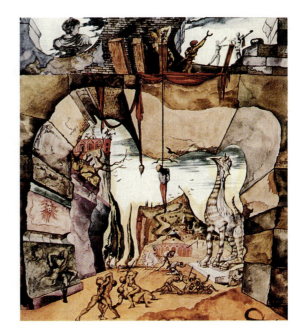

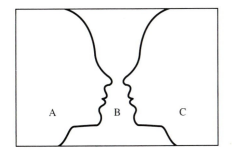

5.17 Fine detail is more readily seen in the figure than the ground *Subjects look at the vase-profiles figure as shown above, and have to determine whether lines that are briefly flashed at points A, B, or C are tilted or vertical. If the vase is seen as figure, they do much better when the stimuli are presented at B than at A or C. If the profiles are seen as figure, they do much better when the lines are presented at A or C rather than at B. (After Weisstein and Wong, 1986)*

derstand the meaning of the word *student,* she must first have segregated it from the surrounding sounds and heard it as a separate word.

What holds for words in speech, also holds for objects in the visual world. Visual segregation (or parsing) is the first step in organizing the world we see.

FIGURE-GROUND

Visual segregation begins with the separation of the object from its setting, so it is seen as a coherent whole that stands out against its background, as a tree stands out against the sky and the clouds. This segregation of *figure* and ***ground*** can be easily seen in two-dimensional pictures. In our still life, the apple is generally perceived as the figure, the tablecloth as the ground. But the same phenomenon also occurs with figures that have no particular meaning. Thus in Figure 5.14, the white splotch appears as the figure, which seems to be more cohesive and articulated than the blue region, which is normally perceived as the ground. This darker ground is seen as relatively formless and as extending behind the figure.

The differentiation between figure and ground is a perceptual achievement that is accomplished by the perceptual system. It is not in the stimulus as such. This point is made strikingly by ***reversible figures,*** in which either of two figure-ground organizations is possible. A classic demonstration is shown in Figure 5.15, which can be seen either as a white vase on a blue background or as two blue profile faces on a white background. This reversibility of figure-ground patterns has fascinated various artists, especially in recent times (see Figure 5.16).

According to one proposal, the figure-ground distinction corresponds to two different kinds of neural processing. One (in regions seen as the figure) involves the analysis of fine detail, while another (in regions seen as the ground) involves a cruder analysis appropriate to the perception of larger areas (Julesz, 1978). To test this hypothesis, subjects were presented with brief exposures to vertical and slightly tilted lines that were flashed on either of three locations of a line drawing of the vase-profile figure (see Figure 5.17). The subjects' task was to judge the orientation of the lines. In accordance with the detail-processing hypothesis, the subjects were much more accurate when the line was projected onto the area the subject happened to see as the figure than when it was projected onto the area they saw as the ground (Weisstein and Wong, 1986).

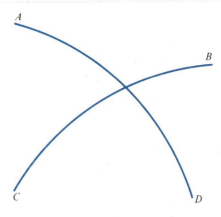

5.18 Good continuation *The line segments in the figure will generally be grouped so that the contours continue smoothly. As a result, segment A will be grouped with D and C with B, rather than A with B and C with D.*

Reversible figure-ground formations demonstrate that the same proximal pattern may give rise to different perceptual organizations. The same conclusion follows from the related phenomenon of perceptual **grouping.** Suppose we look at a collection of dots. We can perceive the pattern in various ways depending upon how we group the dots: as a set of rows, or columns, or diagonals, and so on. In each case, the figural organization is quite different even though the proximal stimulus pattern is always the same.

What determines how a pattern will be organized? Some factors that determine visual grouping were first described by Max Wertheimer, the founder of **Gestalt psychology,** a school of psychology that believes that organization is basic to all mental activity, that much of it is unlearned, and that it reflects the way the brain functions. Wertheimer regarded these grouping factors as the laws of **perceptual organization** (Wertheimer, 1923). A few of these are discussed below.

Proximity The closer two figures are to each other **(proximity)** the more they will tend to be grouped together perceptually. Proximity may operate in time just as it does in space. The obvious example is auditory rhythm: four drum beats with a pause between the second and third will be heard as two pairs. Similarly, these six lines generally will be perceived as three pairs of lines:

Similarity Other things being equal, we tend to group figures according to their **similarity.** Thus, in the figure below, we group blue dots together with blue dots, and red dots together with red dots. As a result, we see rows rather than columns in the left panel, and columns rather than rows in the right panel.

Good continuation Our visual system seems to "prefer" contours that continue smoothly along their original course. This principle of grouping is called **good continuation** (Figure 5.18). Good continuation is a powerful organizational factor that is often used by the military for camouflage. It also helps to camouflage animals against their natural enemies. For example, it helps to conceal various insects from predators who tend to see parts of the insect's body as continuations of the twigs on which it stands.

Closure We often tend to complete figures that have gaps in them. Figure 5.19 is seen as a triangle despite the fact that the sides are incomplete.

A closurelike phenomenon yields **subjective contours.** These are contours that are seen, despite the fact that they don't physically exist (Figure 5.20). Some theorists interpret subjective contours as a special case of good continuation. In their view, the contour is seen to continue along its original path, and, if necessary, jumps a gap or two to achieve the continuation (Kanizsa, 1976).

5.19 Closure *There is a tendency to complete—or close—figures that have a gap in them, as in the incomplete triangle shown here.*

A

B

Good continuation as the basis of camouflage *(A) Here, camouflage is achieved by providing artificial contours that break up the outlines of the soldier's face and body. (Courtesy the United States Government) (B) Good continuation helps to conceal the insect from predators who tend to see parts of the insect's body as continuations of the twigs on which it stands. (Photograph by Farrell Grehan, Photo Researchers)*

Pattern Recognition

Thus far we have considered the first steps in perceiving an object—seeing it as a figure that stands out against its background and whose parts seem to belong together. The next step is to determine *what* that object is. To do this, the organism must match the form of this figure to the form of some other figure it has previously seen and recognize it appropriately. This process is called *pattern recognition.* One of the major problems of the psychology of perception is to determine how this is accomplished.

Humans and animals can recognize a form even when most of its component parts are altered. Consider two similar triangles. It doesn't matter whether they are small, rendered as solids or as line drawings, made up of dots or dashes. The

5.20 Subjective contours *Subjective contours are a special completion phenomenon in which contours are seen even where none exist. In (A), we see a white triangle whose vertices lie on top of the three blue circles. The three sides of this white triangle (which looks brighter than the white background) are clearly visible, even though they don't exist physically. In (B), we see the same effect with blue and white reversed. Here, there is a blue triangle (which looks bluer than the blue background) with subjective blue contours. (Kanizsa, 1976)*

A   B

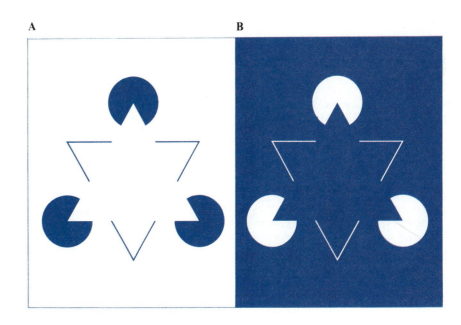

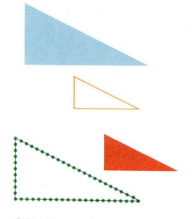

5.21 Form equivalence *The perceived forms remain the same regardless of the parts of which they are composed.*

perceived form remains the same (Figure 5.21). This phenomenon is sometimes called the *transposition of form* or *pattern.* A triangle is a triangle is a triangle, whatever the elements of which it is composed. Similar effects occur in the temporal patterning of sounds. A melody remains the same even when all of its notes are changed by transposing to another key, and the same rhythm will be heard whether played on a kettledrum or a glockenspiel.

Phenomena such as these were among the chief arguments of the Gestalt psychologists who insisted that forms are not perceived by somehow summing up all of the localized sensations that arise from individual retinal points of excitation. They argued instead that a form is perceptually experienced as a *Gestalt,* a whole that is different from the sum of its parts. (The term *Gestalt* is derived from a German word that means "form" or "entire figure.") To recognize that a form is the same as one we have seen before, we must perceive certain relations among its component parts.

A MACHINE MODEL OF PATTERN RECOGNITION

We now turn to a discussion of the mechanisms by which particular patterns are recognized, whether it is the letter *A,* or the face of our grandmother, or a picture of an apple. We will consider the steps in information processing by which the parts are transformed into patterns that we recognize as real objects and events in the world.

Some thirty years ago, an important approach to pattern recognition grew out of the efforts of computer scientists to develop machines that could "read" letters and numerals. Devices of this kind would have numerous practical applications, for example, sorting mail for the postal service or organizing bank records.

Many attempts to design such artificial recognition systems involved a chain of processing steps that began with the analysis of visual features. This approach was partially influenced by the neurophysiological work on feature detectors in the nervous system (see p. 147). Under the circumstances, it seemed reasonable

5.22 A pattern-recognition model *The physical stimulus "T" gives rise to a visual image. This is then analyzed for the presence or absence of various component features, such as vertical or horizontal lines, various corners, and so on. Each feature stimulates the stored letter patterns that contain it. In this example, one of the feature units stimulates the pattern "P," one the pattern "R," and four the pattern "T." As a result, the "T" is more actively excited than the "P" and "R," which leads to the decision that the letter is "T." (After Goldstein, 1984)*

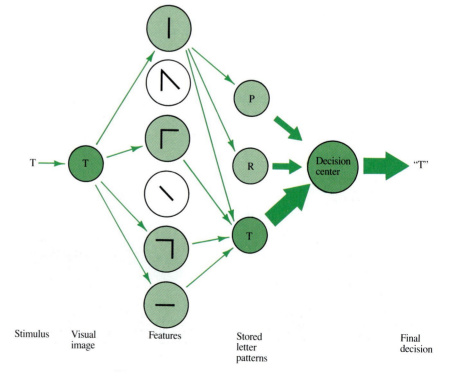

Stimulus   Visual image   Features   Stored letter patterns   Final decision

enough to endow systems of human (or machine) perception with a similar ability to extract elemental properties. A very influential system (or model) of this sort was one proposed by Oliver Selfridge (Selfridge, 1959). Suppose we have a machine that can scan the optical image of a letter. How can it decide that this letter is, say, a *T?* What the machine can do is start out by looking for the presence or absence of certain visual features (for example, horizontal, vertical, or diagonal bars, curves to the right or left, and so on). It can then consult a list stored in its memory in which each capital letter is entered, together with the visual features that define it. By comparing the features in the stimulus with those of the letters on the list, it can reach a decision (see Figure 5.22).

TOP-DOWN PROCESSING

Thus far we have discussed pattern recognition as a ***bottom-up process,*** which starts with component features and gradually builds up to larger units that are, so to speak, at the top. But there are reasons to believe that bottom-up processing is not enough. Pattern recognition often involves ***top-down processes*** in which the chain of events begins with the activation of higher units, which then affect units lower down. Evidence comes from the fact that recognition is often affected by higher-level knowledge and expectations.

One demonstration of top-down processing in perception is provided by so-called ***context effects.*** In some cases, context effects depend on stimuli that are simultaneously present with the affected stimulus. As an example, take the two words shown in Figure 5.23. The two middle "letters" of each word are physically identical, but they are usually seen as an *H* in *THE* and an *A* in *CAT.*

In other cases, the context is provided by experiences in the past (often the immediately preceding past). A good example is provided by ambiguous figures. Consider Figure 5.24A, which can be seen as either an old woman in profile or a young woman whose head is turned slightly away. In one study, subjects were first shown two fairly unambiguous versions of the figure (Figures 5.24B and C). When later presented with the ambiguous figure (Figure 5.24A), they perceived it in line with the ambiguous version they had been shown before (Leeper, 1935).

Similar context effects can make us hear speech sounds where in fact there are none. Something of this sort occurs in everyday life, for when people talk they

THE CAT

5.23   The effect of context on letter recognition   *(After Selfridge, 1955)*

5.24   An ambiguous figure   *(A) This is ambiguous and is just as likely to be seen as a young woman or as an old woman. (B) and (C) are essentially unambiguous, and depict the young woman and old woman respectively. If the subjects are first shown one of the unambiguous figures, they are almost sure to see the ambiguous picture in that fashion later on. (After Boring, 1930; Leeper, 1935)*

A

B

C

sometimes cough or clear their throat so that the speech stream is interrupted. But even so, we usually hear and understand them and never notice that there were physical gaps in their actual physical utterance. In a laboratory demonstration of this phenomenon subjects listened to tape-recorded sentences in which the speech sounds were tampered with, as in the sentence:

The state governors met with their respective legislatures convening in the capital city.

In this sentence the experimenter replaced the middle *s* in the word *legislatures* with a cough-like noise. Yet, virtually none of the subjects even noticed that any speech sound was missing. They somehow restored the deleted speech sound, and "heard" the *s* that was provided by the total context (Warren, 1970).

BIDIRECTIONAL ACTIVATION

Context effects demonstrate that there is some top-down processing. But this hardly means that bottom-up processing is unimportant. On the contrary. After all, if perceptual processing were only in the top-down direction, we would always see what we expect and think about—even if there were no stimulus whatever. To be sure, knowledge and expectations do help us to interpret what we see and hear, but there has to be some sensory basis that confirms these interpretations. As a result, perceptual processing is generally in both directions: from the top down, but also from the bottom up.

PERCEPTUAL PROBLEM SOLVING

Bidirectional activation of the kind just discussed fit in with the belief that much of perception is essentially a form of problem solving in which the observer tries to discover (usually without awareness) what it is that she sees. Seen in this light, the perceptual system generally starts out with both a stimulus and a hypothesis. The perceptual hypothesis represents the top-down aspect of the process. It is tested as the system analyzes the stimulus (the bottom-up aspect) for some appropriate features. If these are found, the perceptual hypothesis gains plausibility and is either accepted or checked for further proof. If such features are not found, then a new hypothesis is considered, which is then tested by searching for yet other features, and so on.

Occasionally, we become consciously aware that some such process operates. This sometimes happens when we are presented with a visual display that initially makes no sense. An example is Figure 5.25. At first glance most observers don't know what to make of it. But as they continue to look at the figure, they develop hypotheses about what it might be (e.g., maybe this part is the leg of some animal, maybe the animal has a spotted hide). If they are lucky, they eventually hit on the correct hypothesis (a Dalmatian dog). When they finally see the dog, the top-down and bottom-up processes meet, and there is a perceptual insight, a visual "Aha!" Here the process of perceptual problem solving was quite conscious. But this is rare, for we usually see cars, trees, and people (and even Dalmatian dogs) without being aware that we are trying to solve any perceptual puzzles. But according to theorists who take the problem-solving approach to perception, much the same kind of thing occurs even then, though at much greater speed and outside of consciousness.

To sum up, perceptual processing must include both bottom-up and top-down processes. Without bottom-up processing, there would be no effect of the exter-

"By George, you're right! I thought there was something familiar about it."
(Drawing by Chas. Addams; © 1957, 1985 The New Yorker Magazine, Inc.)

5.25 Perceptual problem solving *This is a picture of something. What? (Photograph by Ronald James)*

nal stimulus, and we would not perceive but only hallucinate. Without top-down processing, there would be no effect of knowledge and expectation, and we would never be able to guide and interpret what we see.

PERCEPTUAL SELECTION: ATTENTION

We have seen that our perceptual system shapes and organizes the patchwork of different sensations into a coherent whole that has depth, motion, and form, as well as meaning, and is the product of both bottom-up and top-down processing. In part, this organization arises from the fact that not all parts of the perceptual world are given equal weight. We focus on the figure, not on the ground; we are more likely to notice shapes that are moving rather than those that are stationary. Such examples indicate that in addition to its other characteristics, perception is selective. We don't look at all the stimuli that are there to be looked at or focus upon them all. Our ability to take in and interpret the myriad stimulations around us is finite, and so our perceptual system is forced to choose among them. The various ways in which we exercise such choices and perceive selectively are often grouped together under the general label *attention.*

Selection by Physical Orientation

The most direct means of selecting the input is to orient the various sensory systems physically toward one set of stimuli and away from another. The organism does not passively touch, see, or hear; it actively feels, looks, and listens. It turns its head and eyes, converges and accommodates, explores the world with its hands (or paws or lips or prehensile trunk), and if it has the necessary motor endowment, pricks up its ears. These orienting adjustments of the sensory machinery are the external manifestations of attention.

In humans, the major means of physically selecting the stimulus input are movements of the eyes. Peripheral vision informs us that something is going on, say, in the upper left of our field of vision. But our peripheral acuity is not good enough to tell us what it is precisely. To find out, our eyes move so that this region

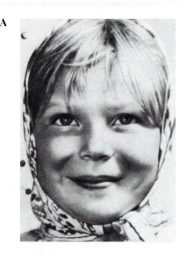

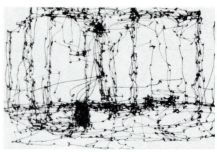

5.26 Eye-movement records when looking at pictures *Both (A) and (B) are pictures that were looked at for 3 and 10 minutes respectively. With each picture is the record of the eye movements during this period. As the records show, most of the eye movements are directed toward the most visually informative regions. As a result, the eye-movement record is a crude mirror of the main contours of the picture. (From Yarbus, 1967)*

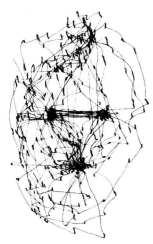

falls into the fovea. A number of investigators have developed techniques for recording eye movements made when looking at pictures. The records show that the subjects glance most frequently at the regions that are visually most informative (see Figure 5.26, from Yarbus, 1967).

These results show that the act of looking is purposeful. People don't scan the world in the wistful hope that their foveas will by chance hit on some interesting bit of visual news. They pick up some information from what they've vaguely seen in the periphery and from their general notions of what the scene is all about. They then move their eyes to check up on what they've seen and to refine their visual knowledge further (Yarbus, 1967; Rayner, 1978; Stark and Ellis, 1981).

Central Selection

Eye movements and other means for changing physical orientation determine the sensory input the perceptual system receives. But selectional control of perception may be by central as well as peripheral means. Such central selectional processes determine whether a particular portion of the sensory input will be dealt with further, and if so, how it will be interpreted.

SELECTIVE LOOKING

A widely used method for studying visual attention is the ***visual search procedure*** in which a subject is briefly shown an array of letters, digits, or other visual forms, and has to indicate as quickly and accurately as she can whether a particular target, for example, an *X,* is or is not present among a number of other letters in the array. The time required to conduct this search increases the larger the number of other letters among which that target is embedded, especially if that target is similar in form to the other letters (e.g., an *X* among other letters that are also angular, such as *H, W,* and *Z*).

Not surprisingly, visual search becomes very much easier if the subject knows where to look. If she is told in advance that if a target is present it will be at, say, the 3 o'clock position from the center of the array, she will look there right away and come up with a quick and appropriate decision. But there are a number of studies that show that prior information about location will help the subject's search even if she does not move her eyes. In such experiments, the subject is first asked to look at a dot on a screen, and to keep her eyes on this ***fixation point.*** Shortly thereafter, an arrow appears for an instant and points to the critical location, after which the array is flashed on. What's crucial in this procedure is that the interval between the appearance of the arrow and the disappearance of the array is too short to permit a voluntary eye movement.* But even so the arrow helps to make the search much easier. It does not affect the *physical* orientation of the eyes; for, given the very brief intervals, the eyes never change position. But it evidently does affect an *internal* selection process, as if the mind's eye moves even though the eyes in the head are stationary (Egeth, Jonides, and Wall, 1972; Eriksen and Hoffman, 1972; Jonides, 1980, 1983).

SELECTIVE LISTENING

A different method for studying selectional attention focuses on listening to speech and is modeled on a phenomenon often observed in real life, the ***cocktail-party effect.*** During conversations at a noisy party, one tunes in on the voice of the person one is talking to. The many other voices are somehow filtered out and are consigned to a background babble. This effect has been studied experimentally by asking subjects to attend to one of two simultaneously presented verbal messages. The usual procedure is ***dichotic presentation.*** The subject wears two earphones and receives different messages through each of them. To guarantee selective attention, the subject is generally asked to ***shadow*** the to-be-attended message. This means that he has to repeat it aloud, word for word, as it comes over the appropriate earphone. Under these conditions, the irrelevant message tends to be shut out almost entirely. The subject can hear speechlike sounds, but notices little else. He is generally unable to recall the message that came by way of the unattended ear. In fact, he often does not even notice if the speaker on the unattended ear shifts into a foreign language or if the tape is suddenly played backward (Cherry, 1953).

THE FILTER THEORY OF ATTENTION

Results of this sort suggested that selective attention acts as a kind of filter. This filter is presumably interposed between the initial sensory registration and later stages of perceptual analysis. If the information is allowed through the attentional filter (that is, if it is fed into the attended ear), it can be further analyzed—recognized, interpreted, and stored in memory. But if it does not pass through, it is simply lost. Early versions of this theory suggested that the filtering effect is all-or-none. Subjects in a dichotic listening experiment were thought to understand no part of the message that entered by way of the unattended ear (Broadbent, 1958).

This all-or-none theory turned out to be false, for there is good evidence that information which has some special significance is registered even if it is carried as part of the unattended message. The best example is the sight or sound of one's own name. No matter how intently we concentrate on the person next to us, we can't help but hear our own name in another conversation held on the other side of the room.

This everyday experience has been documented with the shadowing method. When subjects are forced to repeat a message that comes over one ear, word for word, they are almost completely oblivious to the irrelevant message that is fed into the other ear. But they do take notice when that irrelevant message contains the sound of their own name (Moray, 1959). This result suggests that the attentional filter does not block irrelevant messages completely. It only attenuates it, like a volume control that is turned down but not off. If the item is important enough (or perhaps familiar enough), then it may pass through the filter and be analyzed to some extent (Treisman, 1964).

---

* That interval is usually about 100 ms, while an eye movement takes about 150 to 200 ms to execute.

THE PERCEPTION OF REALITY

Of what use are all the mechanisms of perceptual organization we have considered throughout this chapter, whether innately given or based on learning? The answer is simple enough: They all help us to perceive reality. To be sure, the perceptual system may occasionally lead us astray, as in illusions of depth or movement. But these are fairly rare occasions. By and large, the processes that lead to the perception of depth, movement, and form serve toward the attainment of a larger goal—the perception of the real world outside.

To see the real world is to see the properties of distal objects: their color, form, size, and location, their movement through space, their permanence or transience. But as we have noted before, organisms cannot gain experience about the distal stimulus directly; all information about the external world comes to us from the proximal stimulus patterns that distal objects project upon the senses. The trouble is that the same distal stimulus object can produce many different proximal stimulus patterns. Its retinal image will get larger or smaller depending upon its distance; its retinal shape will change depending upon its slant; the amount of light it projects on the retina will increase or decrease depending on the illumination that falls upon it.

Under the circumstances, it may seem surprising that we ever manage to see the real properties of a distal object. But see them we do. The best proof is provided by the ***perceptual constancies:*** a crow looks black even in sunlight; an elephant looks large even at a distance; and a postcard looks rectangular even though its retinal image is a trapezoid unless it is viewed directly head on. In all of these cases, we manage to transcend the vagaries of the proximal stimulus and react to certain constant attributes of the distal object such as its shape and its size.

Empiricism and Nativism Revisited

How does the organism accomplish this feat? The attempts to answer this question are best understood as part of the continuing debate between the empiricist heirs of Locke on the one hand, and the nativist descendants of Kant on the other.

THE EMPIRICISTS' ANSWER

Empiricists handle the problem by asserting that the sensation produced by a particular stimulus is modified and reinterpreted in the light of what we have learned through past experience. Consider perceived size. People five feet away look just about as tall as those at a fifty-foot distance. This is not merely because we *know* them to be average-sized rather than giants or midgets. The fact is that they really *look* equally tall provided there are cues that indicate their proper distance (Figure 5.27).

A

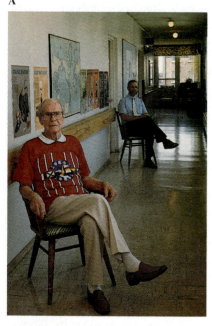

B

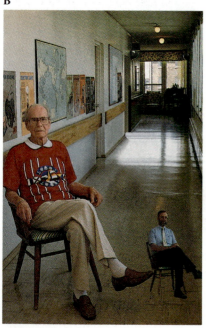

5.27 Perceived size and distance *(A) The actual image of the two men in the picture— which corresponds to the size of their retinal image—is in the ratio of 3 to 1. But this is not the way they are perceived. They look roughly equal in size, but at different distances, with one about three times farther off than the other. In (B) there are no cues that indicate that one man is farther away than the other. On the contrary. The figure was constructed by cutting the more distant man out of the picture, and pasting him next to the other man, with the apparent distance from the viewer equal for the two. Now they look very different in size. (After Boring, 1964; Photograph by Jeffrey Grosscup)*

How can we explain this and similar phenomena? The most influential version of the empiricists' answer was formulated by Hermann von Helmhotz in the late nineteenth century. According to Helmholtz, the perceiver has two sources of information. To begin with, there is the sensation derived from the size of the object on the retina. In addition, there are a number of depth cues that indicate how far away the object is. Prior learning has taught the perceiver a general rule: the farther away things are, the smaller will be the sensation derived from the retinal image. The perceiver can now infer the true size of the object, given its retinal size, its distance, and the learned rule that relates the two. As a result she adjusts her perception of size, shifting it downward if the object is seen as close by and upward if it is seen farther off. Helmholtz of course knew full well that we don't go through any *conscious* calculation of this sort when we look at objects and perceive their size. But he believed that some such process was going on anyway and he therefore called it **unconscious inference** (Helmholtz, 1909).

It's worth noting that the unconscious inference theory is really an early version of the top-down processing hypothesis in perception. Both positions insist that perception is only partially determined by the sensory stimulation, that perception is in part a kind of mental construction, based on various expectations and inferences of which the observer is often unaware. Thus contemporary theorists who argue that perception often involves a form of problem solving hold a view that is in many ways quite similar to that of Helmholtz (e.g., Hochberg, 1981, 1988; Rock, 1977, 1983, 1986).

THE NATIVISTS' ANSWER

The nativists' reply is that the perception of size is directly given. They argue that the stimulus for the perceived size of an object is not the size of the retinal image as such. It is rather some relationship between that size and certain other attributes that pertain to depth.

A very influential modern version of this approach is that of James J. Gibson (1950, 1966, 1979). Gibson believed that such vital characteristics of an object as its size, its shape, and its distance from the observer are signaled by various **higher-order patterns of stimulation** to which the organism is innately sensitive.

As an example, let's return to size. To be sure, the size of the retinal image projected by an object must necessarily vary with its distance from the observer. But Gibson argued that this does not mean that there is no size information in the stimulus that hits the eye. One reason is that objects are usually seen against a background whose elements—leaves, pebbles, clumps of grass, or whatever—provide a texture. Since these elements are generally of about the same size, their size on the retina varies with distance and leads to texture gradients. As we've already seen, these texture gradients provide information about distance. But in addition, they also provide information about the relative size of objects in the world outside. For distance has the same effect on the retinal image of the object as it has on the retinal image of the adjacent texture elements of the object's background. In both cases, the retinal size decreases with increasing distance. As a result, there is a constant ratio between the retinal size cast by the object and the retinal size of its adjacent texture elements. According to Gibson, this ratio provides a higher-order stimulus relationship that remains *invariant* over changes of distance, and we pick up the information provided by this ratio directly, without any intermediate cognitive steps (such as unconscious inference). Gibson called this process **direct perception.** (See Figure 5.28.)

The extent to which higher-order patterns of stimulation (such as the size ratio) provide information about various attributes of the world—of which size is only one—is still a matter of debate. Nor is it clear that perceivers are necessarily sensi-

A

B

5.28 *An invariant relationship that provides information about size* (A) and (B) show a dog at different distances from the observer. The retinal size of the dog varies with distance, but the ratio between the retinal size of the dog and the retinal size of the texture elements made up of the bushes is constant. (Photographs by Jeffrey Grosscup)

This interpretation seems to fit at least some of the size illusions. Thus, the Ponzo illusion is considerably stronger when it is displayed as part of a photograph rather than as a line drawing. This is presumably because depth cues are generally more powerful in a photograph than in a schematic line drawing (Leibowitz, Brislin, Perlmutter, and Hennessy, 1969). Other studies show that the Ponzo illusion is stronger for older than younger children. This makes sense if one assumes that older children have more experience with depth cues, especially as they appear in pictures (Coren and Girgus, 1978).

Illusions are special cases in which reality is misperceived. In ordinary life, such mistakes are rare because our perceptual systems are geared to see the world as it really is—allowing us to bypass the continual fluctuations of the proximal stimulus so that we can grasp the enduring properties of the distal reality outside.

But while illusions are fairly rare, they are exceedingly useful to those who want to understand how perception works. By studying illusions, we can learn about the mechanisms upon which our normal perception of reality is based. Some of these mechanisms are built in; illusory effects such as brightness contrast have shown the way to their discovery. Other mechanisms involve learning and past experience. The perspective illusions just discussed are a case in point. But so, of course, are many other perceptual phenomena (such as the recognition of form) which we have seen to be enormously affected by memory of the past and expectations of the future, for there is a wide region in which it is not quite clear where seeing ends and knowledge begins.

THE REPRESENTATION OF REALITY IN ART

The mechanisms of perceptual organization evolved to serve in the struggle for survival that all organisms must wage. They allow us to see reality as it actually is, so that we can perceive what is out there in the world that we must seek or must avoid. But it is part of our humanity that we have managed to turn these perceptual mechanisms to a use that goes beyond the stark necessities of sheer survival: the representation of reality in art.

The psychology of visual art is yet another illustration of the overlap between seeing and knowing that we've repeatedly encountered in our previous discussions of perceptual phenomena. We will see that an acute awareness of this overlap is found in the artists who try to represent the perceptual world on paper or on canvas.

Seeing and Knowing

5.35   Carved tomb relief of a government official, ca. 2350–2280 B.C.   The conventions of Egyptian art required the main parts of the human body to be represented in its most characteristic view. Thus, heads are shown in profile, arms and legs from the side, but eyes are depicted in full-face view, as are the shoulders and the chest. (Courtesy The Egyptian Museum, Cairo)

Consider Figure 5.35, a tomb relief carved in Egypt some four thousand years ago. Why did the artist depict the figure as he did, with eyes and shoulders in front view and the rest of the body in profile? His fellow Egyptians were surely built as we are. But if so, why didn't he draw them "correctly"?

The answer seems to be that Egyptian artists drew, not what they could see at any one moment or from any one position, but rather what they knew was the most enduring and characteristic attribute of their model. They portrayed the various parts of the human body from the vantage point that shows each form in its most characteristic manner: the front view for the eyes and shoulders, the profile for the nose and feet. The fact that these orientations are incompatible was evidently of no concern; what mattered was that all of the components were represented as the artist knew them to be (Gombrich, 1961).

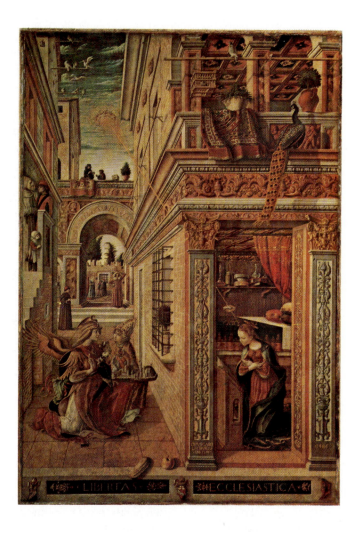

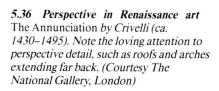

5.36 Perspective in Renaissance art
The Annunciation *by Crivelli (ca. 1430–1495). Note the loving attention to perspective detail, such as roofs and arches extending far back. (Courtesy The National Gallery, London)*

The Renaissance: Scenes through a Window Frame

The illustrations of Egyptian art show the enormous role of the known in the visual representation of the seen. One may argue that this simply reflects the fact that these artists never set themselves the task of mirroring nature as it appears to the eye. Does the artist copy more precisely if his purpose is to do just that?

The most striking examples come from the Renaissance masters who conceived the notion that a picture should look just like a real scene that is viewed through a window from one particular orientation. The painting's frame is then the frame of this window into the artist's world. One major step toward achieving this end was the discovery of the geometrical laws of perspective. This was supplemented by the systematic use of other pictorial cues for depth such as interposition.

In effect, the Renaissance masters seemed to believe that to catch visual reality, one's picture should correspond to the image the model casts on the eye also. This motivated their search for means to portray depth on a flat canvas (see Figure 5.36). The same conception also served as the starting point for such empiricists as Locke and Berkeley, whose concern was with the nature of perception. The empiricists asked how the painters' means of portraying depth—the pictorial cues—could lead to the experience of depth if the image on the eye is two-dimensional.

165

5.37 **Bend in the Epte River, near Giverny** *(1888) by Claude Monet* *Monet, one of the leaders of Impressionism, was engaged in a life-long attempt to catch the fleeting sensations of light in nature. If the painting is viewed from farther back or out of foveal vision, the form becomes clearer and less impressionistic. What is lost is the brilliant shimmer of light and color. The oscillation between these two modes of appearance contributes to the total esthetic effect. (Courtesy Philadelphia Museum of Art: The William L. Elkins Collection)*

The Impressionists: How a Scene Is Perceived

The Renaissance painters tried to represent a scene as it is projected on the eye. Other schools of painting set themselves a different task. Consider the French Impressionists of the late nineteenth century. They tried to recreate certain perceptual experiences that the scene evokes in the observer, the impression it makes rather than the scene itself. One of their concerns was to render color as we see it in broad daylight. Their method was to create a seeming patchwork of different daubs of bright colors (Figure 5.37). These are clearly separate when looked at directly. But when viewed from the proper distance they change appearance, especially in the periphery where acuity is weak. The individual patches now blur together and their colors mix. But when the eyes move again and bring that area of the picture back into the fovea, the mixtures come apart and the individual patches reappear. Some authors believe that this continual alternation between mixed colors and separate dots gives these paintings their special vitality (Jameson and Hurvich, 1975).

This patchwork technique has a further effect. It enlists the beholder as an active participant in the artistic enterprise. Her active involvement starts as soon as she tries to see the picture as a whole rather than as a meaningless jumble of colored patches. This happens when the separate patches blur: when they are viewed from the periphery or from a few steps back. Now the picture suddenly snaps into focus and a whole emerges. This is both similar to and different from what happens in ordinary life. There we move our eyes to bring some part of the world to a region of greater acuity, the fovea. In the museum, we sometimes move our eyes (or our entire body) to bring a picture to a region of lesser acuity, away from the fovea. In either case, active movement leads to the perception of a figural whole (Hochberg, 1978b, 1980).

The Moderns: How a Scene Is Conceived

The Impressionists tried to engender some of the perceptual experiences a scene evokes in the observer. Later generations went further and tried to capture not just how the scene is *perceived* but how it is *conceived;* how it is known as well as seen. Modern art provides many examples, as in Pablo Picasso's still life showing superimposed fragments of a violin (Figure 5.38). Here perception and knowledge are cunningly merged in a sophisticated return to some of the ways of Egyptian artists (Gombrich, 1961).

Some modern artists are not satisfied to add conceptual elements to their visual representations. They want to create ambiguity by setting up visual puzzles that can't be solved. One way is to pit knowledge against visual perception, as in Picasso's faces that are seen in profile and front-face at the same time. Another is to build contradictions within the perceptual scene itself. An example is a painting by the turn-of-the century Italian Giorgio de Chirico (Figure 5.39). One reason for the disturbing quality of this picture is the fact that de Chirico used incompatible perspectives. The structure on the left converges to one horizon, that on the right to a horizon far below the other, while the wagon in the middle does not converge at all. The result is an insoluble visual problem, an eerie world which cannot be put in order.

De Chirico's streets do not look like real streets and Picasso's violins are a far cry from those one sees in a concert hall. In this regard, these modern painters appear quite different from many of their predecessors whose representations were closer to the world as it appears to the perceiver. But we have to realize that no artists, whether Renaissance masters, Impressionists, or moderns, ever try to fool the observer into thinking that he is looking at a real scene. They neither can nor want to hide the fact that their painting is a painting. It may spring to life for a

5.38 **Violin and Grapes** *by Pablo* **Picasso, 1912** *(Courtesy Museum of Modern Art, New York, Mrs. David M. Levy bequest)*

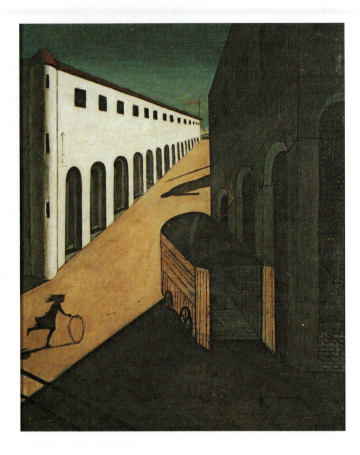

5.39 **Melancholy and Mystery of a Street** *by Georgio de Chirico, 1914   (Private Collection, U.S.A.)*

moment and look like a real person or a real sunset, or it may briefly conjure up a vivid memory of what a face or a violin looks like when viewed from several angles. But whether it emphasizes the seen or the known, it is also recognized as a flat piece of canvas daubed with paint.

According to some authors, this perceptual duality is an important part of the beholder's esthetic experience as he looks at a work of representational art. In a well-known poem by Robert Browning, a duke points to his "last duchess painted on the wall,/Looking as if she were alive." The key words are *as if.* One reason why visual art leads to an esthetic experience may be because it provides us with a halfway mark between seen reality and painted appearance, because it presents a visual *as if* (Hochberg, 1980).

In our discussion of visual art we have taken yet another step across the wide, shadowy region where perception and conception, seeing and knowing merge. In the next chapter we cross the boundary altogether and consider how we remember objects and events that no longer stimulate our senses.

SUMMARY

1. The fundamental problem of *perception* is how we come to apprehend the objects and events in the world around us. In the field of visual perception, the major issues concern the way in which we see *depth, movement,* and *form.*

2. The visual world is seen in three dimensions even though only two of these are given in the image that falls upon the eye. This fact has led to an interest in *depth cues.* Among these are *binocular disparity* and various *monocular cues* such as *interposition* and *perspec-*

tive. Of special interest are *texture gradients,* which are powerful determinants of perceived depth. More important still is the motion of our own heads and bodies. This leads to *motion parallax,* which provides vital information about the distance of objects from each other and from ourselves.

3. Many aspects of depth perception are apparently built into the nervous machinery. Evidence comes from the behavior of very young humans or animals, as in reactions to the *visual cliff.*

4. Retinal displacement alone cannot explain the perception of movement as shown by the phenomena of *apparent movement* and *induced movement.*

5. One issue in the psychology of form perception is whether there are primitive components into which forms can be analyzed, and if so, what these components are. Much of the work on this topic gained impetus from the discovery that some aspects of form seem to be built in as shown by the perceptual achievements of very young humans and animals. Attempts to find the physiological mechanisms that underlie these achievements have concentrated on *feature detectors,* both in the retina and in the brain. These are cells that respond to certain relational aspects of the stimulus, such as edges and corners, as shown by single-cell recordings.

6. Before the perceiver can recognize a form, he must first engage in a process of *visual segregation* and *parse* the visual scene. This involves the segregation of *figure* and *ground.* This is not inherent in the proximal stimulus but is imposed by the perceptual system, as shown by reversible figure-ground patterns. Further segregation produces *perceptual grouping,* which depends upon factors such as *proximity, similarity, good continuation,* and *closure.*

7. A crucial fact in form perception is *transposition of form.* A perceived form may remain the same even if all of its constituent parts are altered. This phenomenon is the keystone of *Gestalt psychology,* a theory that emphasizes the importance of wholes created by the relationship between their parts.

8. An important approach to *pattern recognition* grew out of efforts of computer scientists to develop machines that could identify visual forms such as letters. Most such attempts start with the view that pattern recognition typically involves two kinds of processes. One is *bottom-up processing,* which starts with the stimulus and "works up" by subjecting it to a *feature analysis,* which begins with lower-level units (such as slanted lines) that then activate higher-level units (such as letters and words). The other is *top-down processing,* which is based on expectations and hypotheses and begins with the activation of higher-level units that then activate lower-level ones.

9. Top-down and bottom-up processes typically operate jointly. Top-down processes provide *perceptual hypotheses* that are then tested by bottom-up processes.

10. Perception is selective, for all aspects of a stimulus are not given equal weight. This selection is partially achieved by physical orientation, as in the case of *eye movements.* It is also achieved by a central process, *selective attention.* Methods for studying attention include *selective looking,* as in *visual search,* and *selective listening,* as in *dichotic presentation,* in which one message is *shadowed.*

11. The ultimate function of perceptual organization is to help the organism perceive the outside world as it really is. An illustration is the *constancies* in which the perceiver responds to certain permanent characteristics of the distal object despite various contextual factors—illumination, distance, and orientation—which lead to enormous variations in the proximal stimulus. In *lightness constancy,* the perceiver responds to the object's *reflectance* and tends to ignore the level of illumination that falls upon it. In *size and shape constancy,* the perceiver responds to the actual size and shape of the object more or less regardless of its distance and orientation.

12. Attempts to resolve the discrepancy between what the proximal stimulus gives us and what we actually see go back to two main approaches, the *empiricist* and *nativist.* Empiricists explain this discrepancy by referring to *unconscious inference* based on a learned rule (in the case of size constancy, the rule that farther objects lead to smaller retinal sensa-

tions). Nativists emphasize *invariant higher-order stimulus relationships* that are directly given (in the case of size constancy, invariant size ratios in the retinal image).

13.   The evidence indicates that lightness constancy is in large part based upon the same built-in processes that yield brightness contrast. The verdict is less clear-cut for size and shape constancy, but if those constancies are based on learning, that learning must occur quite early in life. Some of the compensations for distance that produce size constancy sometimes produce misperceptions, as in the case of the *moon illusion.*

14.   The psychology of visual art is a further illustration of the overlap between perception and thinking. The artist represents both what he sees and what he knows. *Renaissance* painters represented scenes seen through a window frame; the *Impressionists* tried to recreate certain perceptual experiences the scene evokes in the beholder; while many modern artists try to represent the scene as it is conceived and thought about.

A cartoonist's view of the problem of seeing versus knowing   (Drawing by Alain; © 1955, 1983 The New Yorker Magazine, Inc.)

CHAPTER 6

Memory

Our discussion of perception, and especially of visual perception, has emphasized the way in which psychological events are organized in space. Locke and Berkeley to the contrary, our perceptual world is not a jumbled mosaic of isolated sensory fragments, but an organized, coherent whole in which every piece relates to every other. We now turn to the subject of *memory* in which organization plays an equally prominent part. Where perception concerns the organization of space, memory—or at least many aspects of memory—concerns organization in time.

Memory is the way in which we record the past and later utilize it so that it can affect the present. It is hard to think of humans (or any animal that is able to learn) without this capacity. Without memory, there would be no then but only a now, no ability to employ skills, no recall of names or recognition of faces, no reference to past days or hours or even seconds. We would be condemned to live in a narrowly circumscribed present, but this present would not even seem to be our own, for there can be no sense of self without memory. Each individual wakes up every morning and never doubts that he is *he* or she is *she.* This feeling of personal identity is necessarily based upon a continuity of memories that links our yesterdays to our todays.

STUDYING MEMORY

The preceding comments underline the overwhelming importance of memory to psychological functioning. To see how psychologists have tried to study this process, we have to make a few preliminary points.

To start with, we should note that any act of remembering implies success at three aspects in the memory process. Consider a person working on a crossword puzzle who is trying to think of an eight-letter word meaning "African anteater." If she comes up with the answer, we can be sure that she succeeded in all three aspects of remembering. The first is *acquisition.* To remember, one must first have learned; the puzzle solver must first have encountered and noted this particular item of zoological exotica. During this acquisition phase, the relevant experi-

The Persistence of Memory *by Salvador Dali. Memory persists, sometimes in distorted form. (Courtesy of Museum of Modern Art)*

ences leave some record in the nervous system, the ***memory trace.*** Next comes ***storage,*** during which the memory traces are squirreled away and held in some more or less enduring form for later use (probably the next crossword puzzle). The final phase is ***retrieval,*** the point at which one "tries to remember," to dredge up this particular memory trace from among all the others we have stored. Many failures to remember are failures of retrieval and not of storage. Our crossword expert may be unable to come up with the correct answer at the time, but when she later sees the solution, she realizes that she'd known it all along: "Of course. It's *Aardvark!"*

The preceding discussion makes it clear that there can be no remembering without prior acquisition. But just what does this acquisition consist of? The subject presumably encountered the word *aardvark* on some previous occasion. But to understand just what she remembered and how, we have to know more than that some such encounter took place. We must also know how the item was ***encoded.*** Taken from computer science, the term *encoding* refers to the form (that is, the code) in which an item of information is stored. In most cases, there are a number of possible codings. The subject might have encoded the word as a sound pattern, or as a particular letter sequence, or in terms of its meaning, or as all of these. What she later remembers will generally reflect this encoding.

Encoding, storage, and retrieval are the three aspects of the memory process. Encoding and retrieval represent the start and the end of this process, and are the two aspects that can be studied more or less directly and that we will focus upon in this chapter.

There are two major methods psychologists employ to study these memory processes. The first is ***recall*** in which the subject is asked to *produce* an item or a set of items. Our anteater illustration is one example of a recall question. Others are "Where did you park your car?" or "What is the name of the boy who sat next to you in the third grade?" The experimental psychologist often tests for the recall of materials learned in the laboratory; this assures that any failures in recall aren't simply failures of original acquisition. The second method is ***recognition.*** A person is shown an item and has to indicate whether she has encountered it before, either in general ("Have you seen this face before?") or in a particular context ("Is this one of the girls who played on your high school field hockey team?"). In the laboratory, the subject is usually asked to pick out the previously learned item from among several false alternatives. Examples are multiple-choice or true-false tests, which obviously put a greater premium on recognition than do essay or short-answer fill-in examinations whose emphasis is on recall.

ENCODING

How are memories formed? We will start our account by considering two major theoretical approaches to memory. We will call the first *stage theory.* This position assumes that there are several different memory systems and regards the main problem of memory as deciding *where* a given memory is stored and how it is transferred from one storage system to another. A second approach is one that we will call the *organizational view.* This approach emphasizes *how* memories are processed and organized. Most investigators currently working in the area accept some mixture of the two approaches, through the more recent organizational view is becoming increasingly dominant in the field.

The Stage Theory of Memory

Memory has often been compared to a storehouse. This conception goes back to the Greek philosophers and to St. Augustine who described the "roomy chambers of memory, where are the treasures of countless images. . . ." This spatial metaphor, which likens memories to objects that are put into storage compartments, held for a while, and then searched for, is a recurrent theme in both ancient and modern thought.

An influential account developed some twenty years ago represents a modern variation on this same spatial metaphor but casts it within the framework of an information processing approach. Unlike Augustine who believed that there is one memorial warehouse, this theory asserts that there are several such storage systems, each with different properties (Broadbent, 1958; Waugh and Norman, 1965; Atkinson and Shiffrin, 1968).

The belief that there are several memory stores comes from the fact that memory may reach back for years but may also concern events that occurred just moments ago. We usually think of memory in terms of a past that is reckoned in hours, days, or years. But a moment's reflection tells us that memory comes into play as soon as the stimulus has disappeared from the scene. An example is a telephone number we look up and retain just long enough to complete the dialing; here the interval between acquisition and retrieval is a matter of mere seconds, but it is a memory all the same.

These simple facts provide the starting points for the stage theory of memory. One of its assertions is that there are several memory systems. Of these, the most important are *short-term memory,* which holds information for fairly short intervals, and *long-term memory,* in which materials are stored for much longer periods, sometimes as long as a lifetime. The second and even more important assertion of the theory is that information enters these two systems in successive stages: To get to the long-term system, information must first pass through the short-term store (see Figure 6.1).

6.1   The relation between the short-term and long-term memory system as envisaged by stage theory   *The figure is a schematic representation of the relation between the two memory systems as stage theory conceived it. Information is encoded, and it enters the short-term store. To enter the long-term store, it must remain in short-term memory for a while. The means for maintaining it there is rehearsal. (Adapted from Waugh and Norman, 1965)*

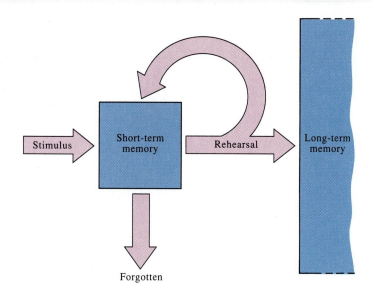

THE CAPACITY OF SHORT-TERM MEMORY

There is reason to believe that memories for relatively recent and remote events differ in some important ways. One difference concerns the relative *storage capacities* of the two postulated memory systems. The capacity of long-term memory is enormous: The size of an average college student's reading vocabulary (about 80,000 words, according to one estimate) is documentation enough. In contrast, the capacity of short-term memory is exceedingly limited.

One way to determine the capacity of short-term memory is by measuring the **memory span,** the number of items an individual can recall after just one presentation. For normal adults, this span is remarkably consistent. If the items are randomly chosen letters or digits, the subject can recall about seven items, give or take about two. This quantity, 7 plus or minus 2, has been called the **magic number,** a widely quoted term originated by George Miller (Miller, 1956). According to Miller, this number represents the holding capacity of the short-term system, the number of items that will fit into its store at any one time. There is some debate about whether this number, 7 plus or minus 2, is really an accurate description of short-term capacity, but all investigators are agreed that this capacity is very small indeed.

SHORT-TERM MEMORY AS A LOADING PLATFORM

What is the relation between short-term and long-term memory? The stage theory of memory asserts that the road into long-term memory necessarily passes through the short-term store. According to this view, short-term memory can be regarded as a loading platform for the huge long-term warehouse.

According to stage theory, some items on the short-term loading platform are transferred into the long-term store by an essentially mechanical process. The longer an item remains in the short-term store, the greater its chance for achieving this transfer. The trouble is that most of the memory packages don't stay on the short-term platform long enough for this to occur, for most of what's in short-term memory is quickly forgotten. While reading the morning newspaper, we briefly note all kinds of extraneous matter; the coffee tastes bitter, a child is crying next door, there is a printer's error on the editorial page. But only a few mo-

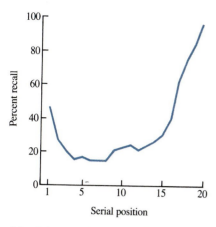

6.2 Primacy and recency effects in free recall *Subjects heard a list of twenty common words presented at a rate of one word per second. Immediately after hearing the list, the subjects were asked to write down as many of the words on the list as they could recall. The results show that the words at the beginning (primacy effect) and at the end (recency effect) were recalled more frequently than those in the middle. (After Murdock, 1962)*

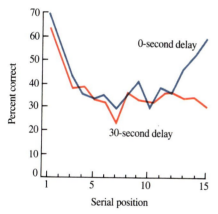

6.3 The recency effect and short-term storage *Subjects heard several fifteen-word lists. In one condition (blue), free recall was tested immediately after they heard the list. In the other condition (red), the recall test was given after a thirty-second delay during which rehearsal was prevented. The long delay left the primacy effect unaffected but abolished the recency effect, indicating that this effect is based on retrieval from short-term storage. (After Glanzer and Cunitz, 1966)*

ments hence these experiences are as if they had never been. They were briefly in short-term memory, but were never transferred to the long-term store.

According to stage theory, one way of increasing the chance that an item will stay in short-term memory long enough to be transferred is ***rehearsal.*** By repeating an item over and over again, a subject will necessarily hold it in short-term memory, which increases the probability that this item will eventually be transferred into the long-term store.

PRIMACY AND RECENCY IN FREE RECALL

These hypotheses about the relations between short- and long-term memory systems fit rather well with certain well-known facts obtained by the method of ***free recall.*** The subject hears a list of unrelated items, such as common English words, presented one at a time and is asked to recall them in any order that she wants to. If the items are presented only once, and if their number exceeds the memory span, the subject cannot possibly produce them all. Under these circumstances, the likelihood that any one item will be recalled depends upon where in the list it was originally presented. Items that were presented at the beginning or the end of the list will be recalled much more often than those that were in the middle. The ***primacy effect*** describes the enhanced recall of items at the beginning; the ***recency effect*** designates the greater recall for those at the end (see Figure 6.2).

Stage theorists believe that the recency effect is produced because the items that were presented at the end of the list are retrieved from short-term memory. These items are generally reported first. They are still clear in the subject's memory because she heard them just a few seconds ago. As a result, she quickly recites them before they disappear from the short-term store. According to stage theory, the recency effect simply reflects this phenomenon: the fact that three or four items are still in the short-term store when the subject begins to recall and that these items are the first she reports.

According to stage theory, the items at the beginning of the list are presumably retrieved from long-term memory. One reason for this interpretation of the primacy effect is that the early items have had more opportunity for rehearsal and thus for transfer into the long-term store. For example, if the first three items are *camera, boat,* and *zebra,* the subject could give her full attention to rehearsing *camera* after hearing it. She would then have to divide her attention between rehearsing *camera* and *boat* after hearing the second item, divide it yet again to rehearse *camera, boat,* and *zebra* after hearing the third, and so on. The more attention a word gets, the more likely that word will make it to the long-term warehouse. Since the attention is greater for the words at the beginning than those that come later on, those first words have a memorial advantage.

To sum up, as stage theory sees it, the items at the beginning of the list benefit from the greater opportunity for rehearsal, which increases their chance to get into long-term memory (the primacy effect). The words at the end of the list benefit from the short time interval between their presentation and recall, which increases the chance that they will still be in short-term memory when the subject begins to report (the recency effect).

Supporting evidence for these interpretations comes from various manipulations of the primacy and recency effects. One important factor is the interval between the last item on the list and the signal to recall. If this interval is increased to thirty seconds (during which the subject performs some mental tasks such as counting backwards so she can't rehearse), the primacy effect remains unchanged but the recency effect is completely abolished. This is just what one would expect if the last items are stored in short-term memory from which forgetting is very rapid (see Figure 6.3). Other procedures diminish the primacy effect. An example

time. Similar results were found when the subjects were asked to guess at the number of syllables. When asked to supply some other words which they thought sounded like the target, the subjects were usually in the correct phonological neighborhood. Presented with the definition "a small Chinese boat" for which the proper answer is *sampan,* subjects who said they almost remembered but not quite, supplied the following as sound-alikes: *Saipan, Saim, Cheyenne,* and *sarong* (Brown and McNeill, 1966; Koriat and Lieblich, 1974).

Implicit Memory

Up to now, we've considered only methods of retrieval that are *explicit,* specifically recall and recognition. In both procedures, the subject is asked a question that refers to her prior experience. She may be tested for recall: "Tell me the name of one of your former high school teachers." Or she may be asked for recognition: "Was Mr. Halberdam one of your former high school teachers?" In either case, the question explicitly refers to the subject's remembered past. But retrieval need not be explicit. An example comes from the performance of well-practiced skills. The pianist is not consciously aware of when and where he learned to finger the keys as he strikes a chord, nor does the golfer consciously remember where and how he perfected his golf swing while swinging the club. To play the chord or hit the ball, both pianist and golfer necessarily retrieve something from memory, but these retrievals are *implicit* rather than explicit, for there is typically no awareness of "remembering" at the time. In consequence, the memory that underlies such retrievals is sometimes called **implicit memory** (Graf and Schacter, 1985; Schacter, 1987).

Implicit memory has been the subject of many laboratory investigations (see Lewandowsky, Dunn, and Kirsner, 1989). In one such study the subjects were shown a number of words after which they were given two tests of memory. The first was a test of explicit memory, in which a standard recognition procedure was employed. The second was a of implicit memory, in which the subjects' task was to identify words that were flashed on a screen for 35 milliseconds. Some of these words were the same as those that had been on the original list. The results of this second test showed **repetition priming:** Words that were on the original list were identified more readily than words that were not. The crucial finding was that this priming effect held even for words that the subjects failed to recognize on the previous test of explicit memory. In short, subjects may have implicit memory for items that they cannot consciously—that is, explicitly—remember (Jacoby and Witherspoon, 1982).

Similar implicit memory effects have been shown using a number of other priming procedures. An example is word completion, in which subjects are presented with a word fragment (such as C_O_O_I_E for CROCODILE) and have to complete it with the first appropriate word that comes to mind. Here priming is indicated by an increased tendency to use words that were shown on a previous list (Jacoby and Dallas, 1981; Tulving, Schacter, and Stark, 1982; Graf and Mandler, 1984).

Retrieval from Active Memory

So far, all our discussions have dealt with retrieval from a passive (that is, long-term) store. The sought-for materials might be words from an experimenter's list, or names of former classmates, or uncommon items in the subject's own vocabulary—in every case, they were generally not in the would-be retriever's consciousness at the time she was asked to recall. They were typically in her passive, not her active memory. Here it makes some intuitive sense to talk of retrieval or of search. Can one talk about retrieval when the items are in active (or short-term)

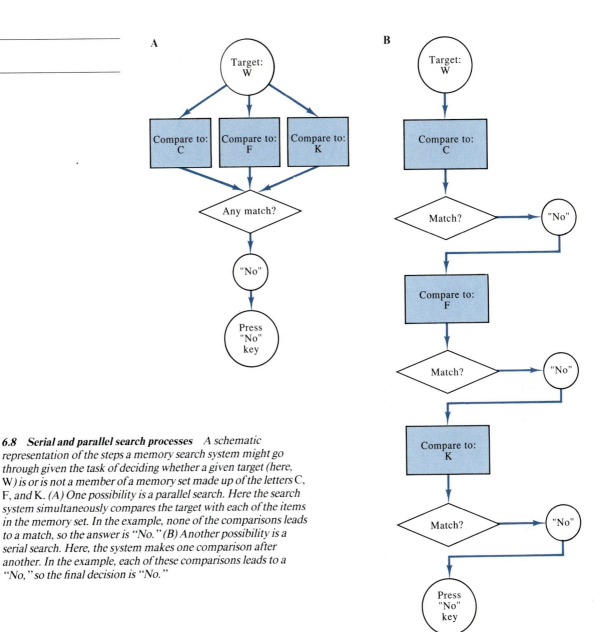

6.8 Serial and parallel search processes *A schematic representation of the steps a memory search system might go through given the task of deciding whether a given target (here, W) is or is not a member of a memory set made up of the letters C, F, and K. (A) One possibility is a parallel search. Here the search system simultaneously compares the target with each of the items in the memory set. In the example, none of the comparisons leads to a match, so the answer is "No." (B) Another possibility is a serial search. Here, the system makes one comparison after another. In the example, each of these comparisons leads to a "No," so the final decision is "No."*

memory—when they are right on the memory workbench and thus, so to speak, in plain view? One might guess that in such cases there is no retrieval process at all, that there is no need for any kind of mental search. But in fact, the situation is not quite so simple. For it turns out that retrieval from active memory is not instantaneous but requires some mental search and comparison.

The evidence comes from a series of elegant experiments by Saul Sternberg. His subjects were first shown a short list of letters, the memory set, which might contain as few as one or as many as seven items. Suppose the memory set was *C, F,* and *M.* The subjects were then shown a single item (e.g., *W*) and had to indicate whether it was or was not a member of that memory set. What are the retrieval processes that allow the subject to accomplish this task? One thing is clear. To decide whether the target item was or was not presented a moment before, it must be compared with the items that are now in active memory. For each comparison, the memory system must decide whether the target stimulus is an adequate match for the trace. How are these comparisons conducted? One possibility is ***parallel search*** (Figure 6.8A). This proposes that the stimulus letter

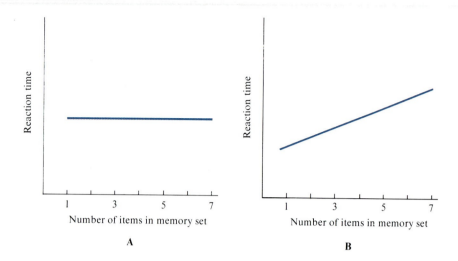

6.9 Predicted results in Sternberg's experiment *(A) If the search through short-term memory is parallel, the time to decide whether a given item is a member of the memory set should be the same regardless of the number of items. If so, the curve that relates reaction time and the size of the memory set would be a horizontal line. The height of this reaction-time function would depend on the time required for processes other than the comparison, such as the time required to recognize the target letter, the time to press the key, and so on. (B) If the search is serial, reaction time must increase with the size of the memory set, since each additional item in the set requires an additional comparison. The slope of the predicted line is the increase in reaction time added by any one comparison.*

W is simultaneously compared to each of the three items in the memory set. The second alternative is ***serial search.*** In serial search the comparisons occur successively. The stimulus W is first compared to C, then to F, and finally to M (Figure 6.8B).

To decide between these alternatives, Sternberg measured the subjects' ***reaction time*** (the time they took to respond) from the moment the target stimulus appeared until they pressed either a "Yes" or a "No" key. To find out whether the search process is conducted serially or in parallel, he determined how reaction time is affected by the number of items in the memory set. Suppose the process is handled in parallel. If so, then the size of the memory set should have no effect, for the various comparisons between the target and the items in memory are assumed to proceed simultaneously (Figure 6.9A).

The results should be quite different if the search is serial, for now the comparisons are assumed to occur one after the other. On the assumption that each comparison takes the same amount of time, reaction time should be a linear function of the size of the memory set (Figure 6.9B).

The results actually obtained fit the hypothesis that the search process is serial: The relation between reaction time and size of memory set is best rendered by a straight line (Figure 6.10). As Sternberg sees it, the slope of this line corresponds to the time it takes to compare the target stimulus to one of the items in the memory set. This slope has generally been found to have a value of about 30 milliseconds. It appears that the search process is serial but is conducted at an exceedingly rapid rate (Sternberg, S., 1969).

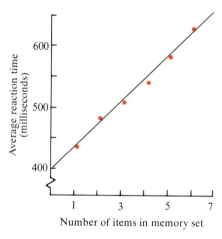

6.10 Actual results of Sternberg's study *The figure shows the actual results of one of Sternberg's experiments. The average reaction time over all trials at a given memory set size is shown by the circles. The results clearly support the prediction made by the serial search hypothesis. (After Sternberg, S., 1970)*

CONCEPTUAL FRAMEWORKS AND REMEMBERING

Remembering depends upon encoding and retrieval. But both of these are affected by still another factor that we've discussed only in passing: what the learner already knows. For all remembering takes place against a backdrop of prior knowledge that necessarily colors whatever enters memory. Without prior knowledge, we could not understand the words we hear, their connection with each other, or their relation to events in the world.

The utilization of prior knowledge in memory is analogous to the effect of top-down processing in perception. As in perception, such top-down effects can be enormously helpful. But again as in perception, our knowledge and expectations can lead us astray. For just as we can misperceive, so we can—and often do—misremember.

Memory Distortions

The most influential experiments on memorial distortions were performed by the British psychologist Frederic Bartlett almost sixty years ago. Bartlett's subjects were asked to reproduce stories taken from the folklore of other cultures; thus, their content and structure were rather strange to Western ears. The reproductions showed many changes from the original. Some parts were subtracted, others were overelaborated, still others were additions that were completely new. In effect, the subjects had built a new story upon the memorial ruins of the original. This memorial reconstruction was generally more consonant with the cultural conceptions of the subjects than with the story they had actually heard. For example, certain supernatural plot elements were reinterpreted along more familiar Western lines.

THE EFFECT OF SCHEMAS AND SCRIPTS

Numerous experiments document Bartlett's claim that memories for events or narratives are strongly affected by the framework of prior knowledge in terms of which they are understood. In one study, subjects were asked to read a description of a home while taking either of two different viewpoints: that of a prospective home buyer or that of a burglar. Later recall showed that the different perspectives affected what was remembered: in the case of the "home buyers," a leaky roof; in the case of the "burglars," a valuable coin collection (Anderson and Pichert, 1978). In another study, subjects who were told about a person's visit to the dentist falsely recalled hearing some details that typically occur in a dentist's office (checking in with the receptionist, looking at a magazine in the waiting room, and so on) even though these were never explicitly mentioned (Bower, Black, and Turner, 1979).

In all these cases, the subjects' memory was affected by their knowledge of the world. They had some ideas of how home buyers, burglars, and dental patients are likely to behave, and they fit their particular recollections into the general outlines of this knowledge. Following Bartlett, many contemporary psychologists describe such conceptual frameworks as *schemas.* As used in this context, the term refers to a general cognitive structure into which data or events can be entered, typically with more attention to the broad brush strokes than to specific details. Many aspects of our experience are redundant: When prospective buyers look at a house they inspect the roof and basement; when patients visit the dentist, they generally check in with a receptionist, and so on. A schema is an effective summary of this redundancy, and can therefore help us interpret and supplement the details of our remembered experience (Schwartz and Reisberg, 1991). A special subcase of a schema is a *script,* which describes a characteristic scenario of behavior in a particular setting, such as a restaurant script (whose sequence includes being seated, looking at the menu, ordering the meal, eating the food, paying the bill, and leaving), or the visit-to-the-dentist script we've considered before (Schank and Abelson, 1977).

EYEWITNESS TESTIMONY

The schema-induced distortions we've discussed thus far were not particularly damaging. To be sure, the subject's memory for the particular details was faulty, but that hardly mattered since she recalled the gist. Under the circumstances, there was no harm done, since our ultimate object is to remember what a statement is all about, not its detailed phrasing. One might even argue that schematized remembering is beneficial since its efficiency lets us package, store, and retrieve more material than we could otherwise manage in an information-cluttered world.

The trouble is that this enhanced efficiency has a down side, for sometimes the details *are* of considerable importance. They are to the student who has to remember a specific chemical formula or the locations of the cranial nerves or the particulars of a novel. And they are to lawyers and judges who are concerned with the accuracy of eyewitness testimony. In all these cases, schematic distortion can have deleterious effects.

Witnesses are sometimes quite confident of various circumstances that fit their assumptions but don't fit the actual facts. An accident occurred months ago, and its details have dimmed over time; as he tries to retrieve this past event the witness may fill in the gaps by an inference of which he is quite unaware.

A series of studies by Elizabeth Loftus and her associates has highlighted this problem of schematized memory processes in eyewitness testimony. An important factor is the way in which recall is questioned. In one study, subjects viewed a brief film segment of a car accident. Immediately afterward they were asked a number of questions that were in either of two forms:

"Did you see the broken headlight?"
or
"Did you see a broken headlight?"

The results showed that subjects who were questioned about *the* headlight were more likely to report having seen one than subjects who were asked about *a* headlight. This was so whether the film actually showed a broken headlight or did not. In effect, the use of the definite article, *the,* makes the query a leading question, one which implies that there really was a broken headlight and that the only issue is whether the subject has noticed it. No such presupposition is made when the indefinite article, *a,* is used (Loftus and Zanni, 1975).

Another study showed that suitable leading questions during a first interrogation may lead to a reinterpretation of a recently witnessed account. When later questioned again, the witness will recall this reinterpretation. Subjects were again shown film segments of a car accident. Shortly afterward some were asked leading questions such as, "Did you see the children getting on the school bus?" A week later, all subjects were asked the direct question, "Did you see a school bus in the film?" In actual fact, there was no school bus. But when compared to controls, subjects who were originally asked the leading question that presupposed the school bus were three to four times more likely to say that they had seen one (Loftus, 1975).

These results are of considerable relevance both to the legal process and to the psychology of memory. To legal scholars they reemphasize the crucial importance of how questions are worded, not only in the courtroom but also in prior interrogations. To students of memory, they underline the fact that remembering is in part a reconstructive process in which we sometimes recreate the past while trying to retrieve it.

The Limits of Distortion

In the last chapter we saw that perception is an active process. It depends on incoming stimuli, but it does not provide a mere copy, for the incoming sensory information is often reshaped and transformed. A similar point applies to memory. It depends on what is stored, but a given act of remembering provides us with more than a frozen slice of the past; it often fills in gaps and reconstructs as we unwittingly try to fit our past into our present (Neisser, 1967).

But these acts of cognitive construction and reconstruction have some limits, in memory as well as in perception. For while there are numerous ways in which a memory can be distorted, such distortions don't always occur. Far from it. After all, we do remember many details of experiences we've been exposed to, and many of those fit into no particular cognitive mold. And even in cases in which various schemas have led to distortions of recall, subsequent tests of recognition show that more is remembered than seems so at first (Alba and Hasher, 1983).

In sum, our memory is neither wholly distorted nor wholly accurate. Memory is again much like perception: Both are affected by processes that work from the top down as well as by those that start from the bottom up. Perception without any bottom-up processing (that is, without any reference to stimuli) would amount to continual hallucination. Memory without bottom-up processing (that is, without any reference to memory traces) would amount to perpetual delusion, a mere will-o'-the-wisp in which the remembered past is continually constructed and reconstructed to fit the schemas of the moment. Both top-down and bottom-up processes operate in both cognitive domains.

VARIETIES OF LONG-TERM MEMORY

We've discussed long-term memory as if it were all of a piece, like a huge warehouse in which all our memories are stored, regardless of their form and content. But during the past twenty years or so, a number of authors have tried to make some further distinctions that may provide some clue as to how this warehouse is arranged.

Generic Memory

One important distinction is between episodic memory and what is sometimes called generic memory. *Episodic memory* is the memory for particular events (episodes) of one's own life: what happened when and where, as when recalling that one ate fried chicken the other night. This contrasts with *generic memory,* which is memory for items of knowledge as such, independent of the particular occasion on which one had acquired them, such as the capital of France, the square root of 9, and the fact that Aaron Burr shot Alexander Hamilton in a duel. In effect, a person's generic memory is the sum total of his acquired knowledge—the meanings of words and symbols, facts about the world, what objects look like, and various general principles, schemas, and scripts.

Most of the studies on memory we have described thus far are primarily about episodic memory. Consider an experiment in which subjects have to memorize a list of nouns such as *submarine, typewriter, elephant,* and so on. When the experimenter tests for later recall, his interest is in what the subjects learned at the time of the experiment—that the list they were presented with included *elephant* and *typewriter* but not *gazelle* and *thermometer.* This is not to say that there were no generic memories that the subjects brought to bear on the tasks. After all, they knew and understood all the words on the list. But the experimenter was not interested in their generic memories. Had she been, she would have asked questions such as "What is an elephant?" (Tulving, 1972).

One of the most important components of generic memory is *semantic memory,* the memory that concerns the meanings of words and concepts. As some authors conceive it, our entire vocabulary is this store: every word, together with its pronunciation, all of its meanings, its relations to objects in the real world, the way it is put together with other words to make phrases and sentences. How do

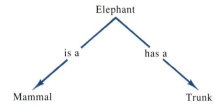

6.11 Network structure in semantic memory models *The figure shows a small section of a semantic memory model, with nodes ("elephant" "mammal" "trunk") connected through associative links. Some networks employ "labeled associations" that indicate the particular relations between the nodes (such as "is a" "has" and so on).*

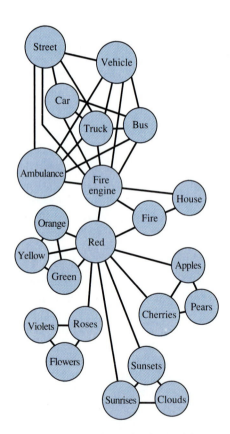

6.12 The spreading activation model *The figure shows a—very small—portion of the semantic network postulated by the spreading activation model. The shorter the path, the stronger the semantic relation. (After Collins and Loftus, 1975, p. 412)*

we ever find any one bit of information in this near-infinity of verbal knowledge? One thing is certain. When we search for an item—say, a synonym for *quiet*—we don't go through all of the items in the semantic store by a serial search. If we did, the hunt might last for days or weeks. The fact that we can come up with *silent* in a second or less shows that we make use of a much more efficient retrieval system. To use a library analogy, the person who takes out a book doesn't have to rummage through all of the volumes on each shelf in order to find the one he wants. He can obtain his book much faster because there is an organized system according to which the books are arranged in the stacks.

A HIERARCHICAL NETWORK

Semantic memory is surely organized, but just what does its organization consist of? Many contemporary theorists believe that this organization is best represented by a ***network model*** in which the words and concepts stored in semantic memory are linked through a complex system of relationships (e.g., Collins and Quillian, 1969; Collins and Loftus, 1975). In such networks, the words and concepts are indicated by ***nodes,*** while the associations between them are indicated by lines or arrows (see Figure 6.11).

An example is the ***spreading activation model*** developed by Collins and Loftus in which semantic relationships are built directly into the network. In this network, shorter arrows between two nodes indicate a closer semantic relationship —based on hierarchical position (as in *vehicle–truck*) or on similarity in meaning (*apple–cherry*) or on well-learned associations (*fire engine–red*). Collins and Loftus proposed that nodes can be activated—again analogous to a similar process in pattern recognition—and that this activation spreads to other nodes. This effect will be greater (and occurs more quickly) for nodes that are nearby than for others that are farther off, for the activation tends to dissipate as it spreads (Collins and Loftus, 1975; see Figure 6.12).

How can this spreading activation hypothesis be tested? One line of evidence came from a study in which broad semantic categories were activated. Subjects were asked to think of a word that begins with a certain letter and belongs to some semantic category. Suppose she is asked for a word that is a *G-fruit.* The experimenter measures the reaction time from the presentation of the category term *fruit* and the response (say, *grapes*). Shortly thereafter the subject gets tested once more. On some occasions, the same category is again called for, though with a different initial letter, as in *S-Fruit.* Now, the time to retrieve a suitable word (say, *strawberries*) is quite a bit shorter than it was the first time. What seems to have happened is that a semantic category is activated and remains that way for a while, like a section in a library that is lit up by a previous user who leaves the lights on when she departs. This part of the library will now become easier to find (Loftus, 1973).

Visual Memory

Important as words and the abstract concepts that underlie them may be, they are not all that we remember. We also seem to have memory systems that preserve some of the characteristic attributes of our senses. The idea is not just that we know that, say, people's waists are between their head and their toes. Of course we do, but that isn't all. We also seem to be able somehow to retrieve this betweenness from a mental image that has some of the characteristics of the original visual experience. As some authors (beginning with Shakespeare) have put it, we see it in "our mind's eye." While similar claims have been made for other senses

188

6.13   Test picture for study of eidetic imagery   This picture from *Alice in Wonderland* was shown for half a minute to elementary schoolchildren, a few of whom seemed to have an eidetic image of it. (Illustrated by Marjorie Torrey)

6.14   Image scanning   Subjects were asked to look mentally at a map of a fictional island and then to imagine a speck zipping from one location to another. (After Kosslyn, Ball, and Reiser, 1978)

—hearing with the mind's ear (composers), feeling with the mind's fingers (blind persons)—our primary concern will be with visual memory.

One question is whether the image is a mental picture from which we can read off information as if it were an actual visual scene outside? By and large, the answer is no. But there are some exceptions. The most striking is *eidetic imagery,* which is characterized by relatively long-lasting and detailed images of visual scenes that can sometimes be scanned and "looked at" as if they had real existence outside. In one study, a group of schoolchildren was shown a picture for thirty seconds. After it was taken away, the subjects were asked whether they could still see anything and, if so, to describe what they saw (Leask, Haber, and Haber, 1969). Evidence for eidetic imagery is contained in the following protocol of a ten-year-old boy, who was looking at a blank easel from which a picture from *Alice in Wonderland* had just been removed (Figure 6.13).

EXPERIMENTER: Do you see something there?
SUBJECT: I see the tree, gray tree with three limbs. I see the cat with stripes around its tail.
EXPERIMENTER: Can you count those stripes?
SUBJECT: Yes (pause). There's about 16.
EXPERIMENTER: You're counting what? Black, white or both?
SUBJECT: Both.
EXPERIMENTER: Tell me what else you see.
SUBJECT: And I can see the flowers on the bottom. There's about three stems but you can see two pairs of flowers. One on the right has green leaves, red flower on bottom with yellow on top. And I can see the girl with a green dress. She's got blond hair and a red hair band and there are some leaves in the upper left-hand corner where the tree is (Haber, 1969, p. 38).

Eidetic imagery is relatively rare. Only 5 percent of tested schoolchildren seem to have it, and the proportion is almost surely smaller in adults. According to one author, this difference between children and adults may only indicate that children tend to rely more on imagery in their thinking, perhaps because their verbal and conceptual memory systems are not as yet sufficiently developed (Kosslyn, 1980, 1984). In any case, there is no reason to believe that this form of imagery is an especially useful form of mental activity. Contrary to popular belief, memory experts don't generally have eidetic imagery (or photographic memory as it is sometimes popularly referred to); their skill is in organizing material in memory, rather than in storing it in picture form.

OTHER FORMS OF VISUAL MEMORY

With the possible exception of eidetic imagery—which as we've seen is a rare and rather elusive phenomenon—visual memory is not a simple reembodiment of stored visual sensation. Our perceptions are not like photographs, and so our visual memories can't be either. But they may nevertheless contain certain pictorial attributes that are also found in visual perception. A number of studies suggest that this is indeed the case.

One line of evidence comes from studies on *image scanning.* In one such study, the subjects were first shown the map of a fictitious island containing various objects: a hut, a well, a tree, a meadow, and so on (see Figure 6.14). After memorizing this map by copying it repeatedly, the subjects performed a reaction time task. The experimenter named two objects on the map (say, the hut and the meadow). The subjects' task was to conjure up a mental image of the entire island and then to imagine a little black speck zipping from the first location to the second. The results showed that their reaction time was directly proportional to the distance between the two points. This result would be no surprise had the subjects scanned a physical map with their *real* eye. That the same holds true when they scan an image with their *mind's* eye is rather remarkable (Kosslyn, Ball, and Reiser, 1978).

FORGETTING

In popular usage, the word *forgetting* is employed as a blanket term whenever memory fails. But as we have seen, memorial failures have many causes. Some arise from faulty storage procedures, while others are produced by conditions at the moment of recall. We now turn to the relation of such failures to the **retention interval** that intervenes between original learning and the time of the test.

At least on the face of it, forgetting increases with retention interval. Yesterday's lesson is fresher today than it will be tomorrow. This fact was well known to Hermann Ebbinghaus (1850–1909), who began the experimental study of human learning by constructing lists of **nonsense syllables**—two consonants with a vowel in between that do not form a word, such as *zup* and *rif*—and then serving as his own subject as he memorized their serial order. He was the first to plot a **forgetting curve** by testing himself at various intervals after learning (using different lists for each interval), and then asking how much effort he had to expend to relearn the list to the level previously achieved. He found that there was a *saving:* Relearning the list took fewer trials than did the original learning. As one might expect, the saving declined as the retention interval increased. The decline was sharpest immediately after learning and became more gradual thereafter (Ebbinghaus, 1885; see Figure 6.15).

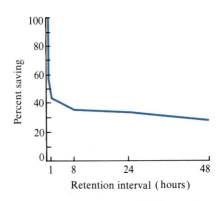

6.15 Forgetting curve *The figure shows retention after various intervals since learning. Retention is here measured in percentage saving, that is, the percent decrease in the number of trials required to relearn the list after an interval of no practice. If the percentage saving is 100 percent, retention is perfect—no trials to relearn are necessary. If the percentage saving is 0 percent, there is no retention at all, for it takes just as many trials to relearn the list as it took to learn it initially. (After Ebbinghaus, 1885)*

Theories of Forgetting

What accounts for the fact that the retention of long-term memories seems to decline the longer the time since learning? There are several theories designed to explain this and related phenomena.

DECAY

The most venerable theory of forgetting holds that memory traces gradually **decay** as time passes, like mountains that are eroded by wind and water. The erosion of memories is presumably caused by normal metabolic processes whose impact wears down the memory trace until it fades and finally disintegrates.

While this theory has considerable intuitive appeal, there is so far little direct evidence in its favor. One study tried to provide an indirect test by varying body temperature. Like most chemical reactions, metabolic processes increase with increasing temperature. If these reactions are responsible for memorial decay, then forgetting should be a function of the body temperature during the retention interval. This prediction has been tested with cold-blooded animals such as the goldfish whose body takes on the temperature of its surroundings. By and large, the results have been in line with the hypothesis: the higher the temperature of the tank in which the fish is kept during the retention interval, the more forgetting takes place (Gleitman and Rozin, as reported in Gleitman, 1971).

But some other findings complicate this picture. There is good evidence that forgetting is determined not simply by the duration of the retention interval, but by what happens during this time. Experiments on human subjects have shown that recall is substantially worse after an interval spent awake than after an equal period while asleep (Jenkins and Dallenbach, 1924). Later studies suggest that the favorable effect of sleep on retention only holds for quiet, slow-wave sleep (Ekstrand, 1972; Ekstrand et al., 1977).

Such results pose difficulties for a theory that assigns all of the blame for forgetting to decay, for they show that time itself does not cause all of the loss. To explain such findings within a theory of decay, one would have to assert that the relevant processes that erode the memory trace are slowed down (or are counteracted) during one or all of the sleep states.

INTERFERENCE

A rather different theory of forgetting is **interference.** According to this view, a forgotten memory is neither lost nor damaged, but is only misplaced among a number of other memories that interfere with the recovery of the one that was sought. Seen in this light, our inability to remember the name of a high school friend is analogous to what happens when a clerk cannot find a letter he received a year ago. The letter is still somewhere in his files, but it has been hopelessly buried in a mass of other letters that he filed both before and since.

Memorial interference is easily demonstrated in the laboratory. A major example is **retroactive inhibition** in which new learning hampers recall of the old. In a typical study, a control group learns some rote material such as a list of nonsense syllables (List A) and is tested after a specified interval. The experimental group learns the same list as the control group and is tested after the same retention interval. But in addition it must also learn a second list (List B) that is interpolated during the retention interval (Table 6.1). The usual result is a marked inferiority in the performance of the experimental group; the interpolated list interferes with (inhibits) the recall of List A.

Table 6.1   RETROACTIVE INHIBITION EXPERIMENT

	Initial period	Retention interval	Test period
Control group	Learns list A	_____	Recalls list A
Experimental group	Learns list A	Learns list B	Recalls list A

A similar effect is **proactive inhibition** in which interference works in a forward (proactive) direction. The usual procedure is to have an experimental group learn List A followed by List B, and then test for recall of List B after a suitable retention interval. The critical comparison is with a control group which learns only List B (Table 6.2). In general, the experimental group does worse on the recall test.

Table 6.2   PROACTIVE INHIBITION EXPERIMENT

	Initial period		Retention interval	Test period
Control group	_____	Learns list B	_____	Recalls list B
Experimental group	Learns list A	Learns list B	_____	Recalls list B

The child's world is in many ways utterly different from the adult's *According to some authors, childhood amnesia is partially produced by the enormous change in the retrieval cues available to the adult. (Photo courtesy of Suzanne Szasz)*

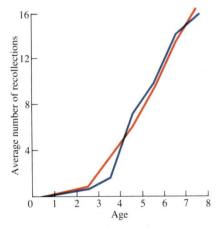

6.16 Number of childhood memories *College students were asked to recall childhood experiences. The figure plots the average number of events recalled as a function of the age at which they occurred for men (blue) and for women (red). Women recall a bit more at the earliest ages, which may reflect the fact that the maturation of girls is generally ahead of that of boys. (Data from Waldfogel, 1948)*

CHANGE OF RETRIEVAL CUES

Decay theory holds that the memory trace gradually fades away, while interference asserts that the trace gets lost among other traces acquired both before and after. There is a further alternative which argues that memorial success or failure is primarily determined by the retrieval cues presented at the time of recall.

Changes in retrieval cues with increasing retention interval We have already seen that a change in retrieval cues disrupts remembering. But can this effect explain why forgetting increases with an increasing retention interval? To maintain the hypothesis that the critical factor is cue alteration, one must assume that such an alteration becomes ever more likely with the passage of time. There are some cases for which this may well be true. Certain memories may have been acquired in a particular locale; over the years the neighborhood changes as some houses are torn down and new ones are built, thus altering the physical cues and thereby decreasing the chance of retrieval.

Childhood amnesia Some authors appeal to the retrieval cue hypothesis to explain the phenomenon of ***childhood amnesia***—the fact that most of us can't recall events of our very early childhood. When college students are asked to report any events they can remember that occurred in early life, the average age of their earliest recollection is about three and a half years (Waldfogel, 1948; Sheingold and Tenney, 1982; see Figure 6.16). One possible cause is a massive change of retrieval cues. The world of the young child is utterly different from the world she will occupy some ten or fifteen years later. It is a world in which tables are hopelessly out of reach, chairs can be climbed upon only with great effort, and adults are giants in size and gods in ability. Whatever memories the child may store at this time are necessarily formed and encoded within this context; thus the appropriate retrieval context is necessarily absent from the adult's environment (Schachtel, 1947; Neisser, 1967).

An alternative hypothesis appeals to encoding differences rather than to changes in retrieval cues. According to some authors, infants and very young children store memories—especially explicit memories—less efficiently than older children and adults. This may be because some relevant neural structures are not yet sufficiently mature (Nadel and Zola-Morgan, 1984). It may also be because these very young children have not yet developed the necessary schemas within which experiences can be explicitly organized, encoded, and rehearsed (White and Pillemer, 1979).

In summary, we must conclude that each of the theories of forgetting proposed thus far can account for some of the aspects of the phenomenon but not all. Interference and change of retrieval cues play a major role, but neither of them can readily explain why forgetting increases with the passage of time. While the evidence for decay is by no means solid, it nevertheless seems reasonable to suppose that some such process does occur and is partially responsible for the effect of the retention interval.

When Forgetting Seems Not to Occur

The fact that there is forgetting doesn't mean that it always occurs. For memory doesn't always fail, even after very long time intervals.

LONG-LASTING SEMANTIC MEMORIES

Some evidence was provided by Harry Bahrick who studied the long-term retention of materials in semantic memory. Bahrick was interested in what people re-

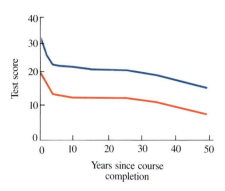

40
30
20
10
0

Test score

0   10   20   30   40   50

Years since course
completion

6.17 Forgetting of a foreign language
The figure displays performance on a Spanish reading comprehension test administered from 0 to 50 years after taking Spanish in high school or college to persons who had previously earned a grade of A (blue) or C (red). (After Bahrick, 1984)

member from what they learned in school. To this end, he gave a Spanish reading comprehension test to nearly 800 persons who had studied Spanish either in high school or in college for three or four years. They were tested at intervals that ranged from one week to fifty years since their last Spanish course. The results showed that quite a bit is forgotten in the first two or three years after learning. But after this, the test performance levels off until much later in life, where aging effects probably account for the bulk of the later memory loss (see Figure 6.17). Educators will probably be gratified by the fact that even after fifty years the test performance reflects how well the language was learned originally. On average, students who had earned an A performed better than those who had received a C, even after half a century had passed (Bahrick, 1984).

The important finding is that some fraction of what had been learned originally remained intact without any further forgetting. In Bahrick's terms, these memories—vocabulary items, idioms, bits of grammar—moved into what he called a ***permastore.*** The semantic memory of an adult contains much information that is essentially permanent. We don't forget the meaning of ordinary words, or the rules of arithmetic, or many individual bits of information. In part, this may be because such materials are extremely well-learned in the first place. But in part, it may be because such items—and hopefully much of what we learn in school—have an inherent structure that protects them from forgetting, a structure that Ebbinghaus's nonsense syllable series certainly lacked (Neisser, 1989).

FLASHBULB MEMORIES

Bahrick's findings concerned semantic memory. Are there some episodic memories that are also essentially immune to forgetting? According to Roger Brown and James Kulik, certain unexpected and emotionally important events produce ***flashbulb memories,*** which are extremely vivid and essentially permanent. They believe that such memories are like a photograph that preserves the scene when a flashbulb is fired. Some of the events that trigger the flash may be private and personal, such as an early morning telephone call that tells of a parent's death. Others may involve news of powerful national import such as the assassination of President Kennedy or the space shuttle disaster. Brown and Kulik found that most people recall where they were at the time they learned of President Kennedy's assassination and also what they did, who told them, and so on. On the face of it, these detailed memories are surprising. That a president's assassination is an important and memorable event is obvious, but why should so many Amer-

Events that have produced flashbulb memories *(A) The attack on Pearl Harbor, (B) after the Kennedy assassination, (C) the space shuttle disaster. (Courtesy the Bettmann Archive)*

A

B

C

icans recall the humdrum circumstances in which they personally found themselves at the time, such as "the weather was cloudy and gray," or "I was carrying a carton of Viceroy cigarettes which I dropped?" According to Brown and Kulik, the reason is that such surprising and emotionally powerful events set off a mental flashbulb that preserves the entire scene along with perfectly mundane and unremarkable details (Brown and Kulik, 1977; see also Pillemer, 1984; McCloskey, Wible, and Cohen, 1988).

The flashbulb hypothesis has been the subject of considerable debate. The main issue is whether such memories are really created by a special mechanism that fixes the circumstances of the moment with a special "flashbulb" clarity. The best guess is that such a special mechanism does not exist. To begin with, there is some debate about the accuracy of these memories; they may be vivid, but that does not mean that they are fully correct (e.g., Neisser, 1982a, 1986; Thompson and Cowan, 1986; McCloskey, Wible, and Cohen, 1988). In addition, much of what was remembered may have been rehearsed in subsequent conversations with others. But if so, what was entered in memory did not depend on a hypothetical flashbulb set off in the head. All in all, there is good reason to doubt the existence of a special flashbulb mechanism.

DISORDERED MEMORIES

Thus far, our discussion has largely centered on people with normal memories. But during the last thirty years, some of the most intriguing questions about human memory have been raised by studies of people with drastic defects in memory functions that are caused by various kinds of damage to the brain (Rozin, 1976b; Cermak, 1979; Squire, 1987; Mayes, 1988).

Anterograde Amnesia

Certain lesions in the human temporal cortex (specifically in the *hippocampus* and other structures near the base of the brain) produce a memory disorder called *anterograde amnesia* (anterograde, "in a forward direction"). In this condition, the patient's deficit is not so much in remembering what he had learned prior to the injury (though he may well have problems even here). His primary difficulty is in learning anything new thereafter. Such lesions can occur in various ways. They are found in certain chronic alcoholic patients who suffer from *Korsakoff syndrome* (named after the Russian physician who first described it). They sometimes accompany senility. In a few instances they are a tragic side effect of neurosurgery such as that undertaken to minimize seizures in severe epilepsy (see Figure 6.18).

A famous example is the case of H.M., whose hippocampal lesion was the result of surgery performed when he was twenty-nine. His memory disorder subsequent to surgery, seemed to fit in well with the idea that short-term and long-term memory represent two distinct memory systems. For example, he had a normal memory span. But he seemed to be incapable of adding any new information to his long-term storage. He could not recognize anyone he had not met before the surgery, no matter how often they met afterward. He was unable to find his way to the new house his family subsequently moved into. When told that his uncle had died he was deeply moved, but then forgot all about it and repeatedly asked when this uncle would come for a visit. On each occasion he was informed once more of his uncle's death and every time his grief was as intense as before; to him, each time he was told was the first.

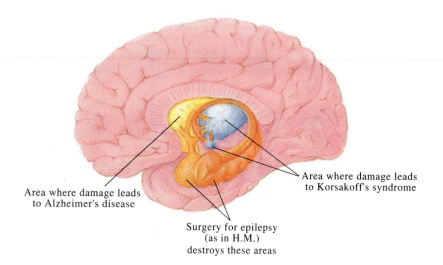

6.18   Regions of the brain where damage can cause memory loss *A cutaway section of the human brain showing regions of the hippocampus and associated structures whose destruction caused H.M.'s massive memory deficits. Patients with Korsakoff's syndrome tend to have lesions in regions that lie higher up, including the thalamus, while patients with Alzheimer's disease show damage in the base of the forebrain. (Adapted from Mishkin and Appenzeller, 1987)*

Area where damage leads to Alzheimer's disease

Area where damage leads to Korsakoff's syndrome

Surgery for epilepsy (as in H.M.) destroys these areas

In the case of H.M. and others like him the primary deficit is a massive impairment in the ability to store any new information. But their memory for what happened before the injury is often quite good, especially for events that happened a year or two previously (Marslen-Wilson and Teuber, 1975). Since they remember the distant past and experience the immediate present, they are often aware that there is a large gap in between. Some of H.M.'s comments give some idea of what such an amnesic state is like:

> Right now, I'm wondering. Have I done or said anything amiss? You see, at this moment everything looks clear to me, but what happened just before? That's what worries me. It's like waking from a dream; I just don't remember. [And on another occasion] . . . Every day is alone in itself, whatever enjoyment I've had, and whatever sorrow I've had. (Milner, 1966; Milner, Corkin, and Teuber, 1968)

Retrograde Amnesia

Various brain injuries may lead to ***retrograde amnesia*** (retrograde, "in a backward direction") in which the patient suffers a loss of memories for some period *prior* to the accident or the stroke. That period may be relatively brief, perhaps a matter of days or weeks. But in some cases, the retrograde amnesia covers a much longer span and may be reckoned in years. Some retrograde effects often go along with anterograde amnesia. Thus H.M. has difficulty remembering events that happened one to three years before his operation, but he has perfectly normal memory for those that occurred before then (Mayes, 1988).

What accounts for the loss of memories for events preceding the cerebral injury? According to some authors, one of the causes is ***trace consolidation.*** This is a hypothetical process by which newly acquired memory traces undergo a gradual change through which they become established (consolidated) ever more firmly. This consolidation effect may be on storage—young traces need time to become more resistant to forgetting, for until then they are as vulnerable as a cement mixture before it has hardened. The effect may also be on retrieval—like a newly acquired library book that will be difficult to find until the librarian takes the time to fill out its card for the catalogue and to file it properly (Weingartner and Parker, 1984).

Whether retrograde amnesia effects can be explained in this manner is still a matter of debate. One trouble is the fact that retrograde amnesia often extends back for several years prior to the injury. If so, consolidation could not explain

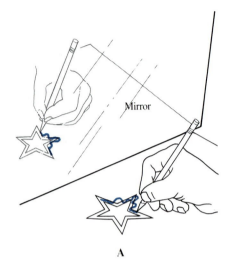

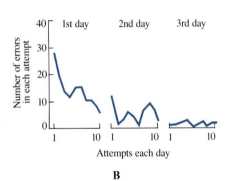

6.19 An example of what amnesics can learn *(A) In mirror drawing subjects have to trace a line between two outlines of a figure while looking at their hand in a mirror. (Kolb and Whishaw, 1990) (B) Initially, this is very difficult, but after some practice subjects get very proficient at it. The same is true for amnesics. The figure shows H.M.'s improvements on this task over a period of three days. (Milner, Corkin, and Teuber, 1968)*

the deficit unless one assumes that it is an exceedingly drawn-out process that may continue for very long time periods (Squire and Cohen, 1979, 1982; Squire, 1987).

Explicit and Implicit Memory Revisited

For quite a while, it was thought that H.M. and other patients with the amnesic syndrome could not acquire any long-term memories at all. But with further study, it turned out that this wasn't true. They can be classically conditioned, they can learn to trace the correct path through a maze, and they can acquire certain skills like mirror-tracing and reading mirror-imaged print. With practice, their performance gets better and better. But each time they are brought back into the experimental situation, they continue to insist that they have never seen the conditioning apparatus or the maze before, and that they don't remember anything at all (Corkin, 1965; Weiskrantz and Warrington, 1979; Cohen and Squire, 1980).

How can we make sense of these findings? Anterograde amnesics are evidently quite competent at retaining skills such as mirror-tracing (they do just about as well as normals, despite their insistence that they don't remember anything about it; see Figure 6.19). On the other hand, they are utterly incompetent at many ordinary long-term memory tasks; for example, they don't recognize an experimenter they have met on twenty different occasions. The one kind of memory is spared; the other is not. What is the essential difference?

Some authors believe that the essential distinction is between what computer scientists call **procedural** and **declarative knowledge.** Procedural knowledge is "knowing how": how to ride a bicycle or how to read mirror writing—areas in which the amnesic's memory is relatively unaffected. According to this view, such skills are essentially programs (that is, procedures) for executing certain motor or mental operations. In contrast, declarative knowledge is "knowing that": that there are three outs in an inning, that raisins are made of grapes, that I had chicken for dinner last Thursday. To know something procedurally does not guarantee that one also knows it declaratively. Professional baseball players "know" the procedures for swinging a bat, but not all of them can explain just what it is that they know. Conversely, most physicists probably know (and can describe) the underlying mechanics of a baseball swing, but few will be able to perform competently when given a bat and asked to hit a ball. Neuroscientists who argue that this distinction explains what amnesics can remember and what they can't also believe that procedural and declarative memories depend on different neural systems (Cohen and Squire, 1980; Squire, 1986).

A somewhat different explanation centers on the distinction between explicit and implicit memory (see p. 182). The memories may be there, but they may be implicit, so that the patient doesn't know that he has them. As a result, he cannot answer questions like "Do you remember?" or "Do you recognize?" when they pertain to events that occurred after he sustained the cerebral damage. Some evidence that the amnesics' deficit concerns explicit but not implicit memory comes from priming procedures. When amnesic patients are shown a number of words and are later asked to recall or recognize them, they fail completely. But the results are quite different when they are presented with fragments of the words and asked to complete them by forming the first words that come to mind. Now there is evidence that something was remembered. The patient who was previously shown ELEPHANT and BOOKCASE will properly complete the fragments _L_P_A_T and B_O_C_S_, even though he will not recognize either word if explicitly asked whether he'd just seen it before (Warrington and Weiskrantz, 1978; Diamond and Rozin, 1984). Interestingly enough, this implicit memory effect will work only if the patient does not connect it with any intentional attempt to retrieve the word from memory. If he is explicitly asked to recall the previously presented words by using the fragments as cues, he will fail again (Graf, Mandler, and Squire, 1984).

As yet, we do not know just what it is about the development of declarative knowledge or of explicit, conscious access that makes them so vulnerable to brain damage? Why is procedural knowledge spared? As we begin to find some answers, it is likely that they will shed light not only on the amnesic disorders but on memory functions in general (Crowder, 1985).

(Cartoon by Abner Dean)

TAKING STOCK

In looking back over this chapter, we are again struck by the intimate relation between the fields of perception, memory, and thinking. It is often unclear where one topic ends and another begins. To give just one example, consider memory search. As we saw, trying to recall the names of one's high school classmates apparently involves many of the same thought processes that are called upon when we try to figure out how to solve a geometry problem. To the extent that this is so, it is clear that much of memory involves thinking. And as we saw previously, the same is also true of perception. For there, too, the perceiver becomes a thinker as he tries to solve perceptual problems and make sense out of ambiguous figures. In the next chapter, we will consider the topic of thinking in its own right.

SUMMARY

1. Any act of remembering implies success in each of three phases: *acquisition,* during which a memory trace is formed and *encoded; storage* over some time interval; and *retrieval,* which may be tested by recognition or recall.

2. The text describes two general approaches to memory: *stage theory* and the *organizational view.* According to the stage theory of memory, there are two main memory systems. One is *short-term memory* in which information is held for fairly short intervals. The other is *long-term memory* in which information is stored for much longer periods. According to stage theory, to get to the long-term memory system, material must first pass through the short-term store.

3. According to stage-theory, an important difference between short-term memory and long-term memory is in their *capacity.* That of long-term memory is enormous; that of short-term memory is very limited as shown by studies of memory span. Since stage theory assumes that the only gateway to long-term memory is through short-term memory, there is an obvious bottleneck. This is overcome by recoding the incoming material into larger *chunks.*

4. The recall of an item heard just before may be from short-term memory or long-term memory. Studies of *free recall* with lists of unrelated items have provided a way of determining from where such items are retrieved. According to stage theory, the *primacy effect* obtained by use of this procedure is associated with long-term memory; the *recency effect* is associated with short-term memory.

5. In the past two decades, there has been a growing emphasis on what the text calls the *organizational view* of memory. Theorists who take this position regard short-term memory not as a depot for recent memories, but rather as the currently activated portion of long-term memory, and call it *active memory* or *working memory.* Another change is an increased emphasis on how the subject encodes and processes incoming material. This includes demonstrations that memory is helped by *chunking* and *organization,* and is further aided by relating the material with what is already known. These general principles of memorial organization underlie *mnemonics,* techniques for helping memory, which include various forms of verbal organization and the use of *visual imagery.*

6. Remembering depends in part upon the presence of appropriate *retrieval cues*. According to the principle of *encoding specificity*, remembering is most likely if the context at the time of retrieval is identical to that present at the time of original encoding. One reason why certain forms of encoding (for example, organization and understanding) are better than others is that they help in later retrieval.

7. Retrieval from long-term memory is often preceded by a process of *memory search*. In some cases, the search reaches a halfway point, where we seem to recall something but not quite, and we experience the *tip-of-the-tongue phenomenon*.

8. Retrieval from active memory has been studied by *reaction time* procedures. The results suggest that this retrieval is based on a *serial* rather than a *parallel search* process. Evidence comes from the relation between reaction time and the number of items in the *memory set*, which shows that each additional item adds a constant time increment.

9. In some cases, the memory that underlies retrieval is *implicit* rather than *explicit*, for there is no awareness of remembering at the time that this memory is utilized. Examples come from the exercise of learned skills, and from *repetition priming*.

10. In many cases, remembering depends on prior knowledge, which affects encoding and later retrieval by relating the incoming material to various conceptual frameworks called *schemas* and *scripts*. The utilization of such frameworks can sometimes lead to *memory distortions* as originally shown by Bartlett. Modern studies of eyewitness testimony have elaborated this point by demonstrating that what is remembered can be seriously affected by building various *presuppositions* into the request for recall.

11. A distinction is often made between two varieties of long-term memory, *episodic* and *generic* memory. An important component of generic memory is *semantic memory*, whose organization has been described by various *network models* and which has been studied by various techniques for assessing memory search, including *memory activation*.

12. Some long-term memory systems seem to be essentially visual. An extreme and rather rare example is *eidetic memory*. More common are other forms of visual memory that are not a simple reembodiment of the original visual impression but preserve some of the pictorial properties of the original. Evidence comes from work on *image scanning*.

13. Other things being equal, forgetting increases the longer the time since learning. This point was first demonstrated by Ebbinghaus who plotted the forgetting of associations between *nonsense syllables*. The causes of forgetting are still a matter of debate. One theory holds that traces gradually *decay* over time, though this view is complicated by the fact that forgetting is greater if the subject is awake rather than asleep during the retention interval. Another view argues that the fundamental cause of forgetting is *interference* produced by other, inappropriate memories. This approach leans heavily on two forms of interference produced in the laboratory, *retroactive* and *proactive inhibition*. Yet another theory asserts that forgetting is primarily caused by *retrieval cue changes* at the time of recall. This position is sometimes used to explain the phenomenon of *childhood amnesia*.

14. Under some circumstances, forgetting doesn't seem to occur. There is evidence that some semantic memories last for a very long time, as in the case of a language learned in school, some remnants of which seem to remain in *permastore*. Other evidence for long-lasting memories are *flashbulb memories*, as in remembering where one was at the time one heard that President Kennedy was assassinated.

15. Certain injuries to the brain, particularly to the *hippocampus* and surrounding regions, can produce disorders of memory. In *anterograde amnesia*, the patient's primary deficit is in the ability to store any new information. In *retrograde amnesia*, the loss is for memories just prior to the injury and is sometimes attributed to a disruption of *trace consolidation*. An important current issue is why patients with severe anterograde amnesia can acquire certain long-term memories (learning a maze, benefiting from seeing a word by later repetition priming) but not others (remembering that they have seen the maze or the word before). According to one hypothesis, the crucial distinction is between *procedural and declarative knowledge;* according to another, it is between *implicit* and *explicit memory* (that is, between remembering and knowing that one remembers).

CHAPTER 7

Thinking

In ordinary language, the word *think* has a wide range of meanings. It may be a synonym for *remembering* (as in "I can't think of her name"), or for *attention* (as in the exhortation "Think!"), or for *belief* (as in "I think sea serpents exist"). It may also refer to a state of vague and undirected reverie as in "I'm thinking of nothing in particular." These many uses suggest that the word has become a blanket term which can cover virtually any psychological process that goes on within the individual and is essentially unobservable from without.

But thinking also has a narrower meaning which is graphically rendered in Rodin's famous statue of "The Thinker." Here, the meaning of thinking is best conveyed by such words as *to reason* or *ponder* or *reflect.* Psychologists who study thinking are mainly interested in this sense of the term. To distinguish it from the others, they refer to ***directed thinking,*** a set of internal activities that are aimed at the solution of a problem, whether it be the discovery of a geometric proof, of the next move in a chess game, or of the reason why the car doesn't start. In all of these activities, the various steps in the internal sequence are directed and dominated by the ultimate goal, the solution of the problem.

THE COMPONENTS OF THOUGHT

An old endeavor in the study of thinking is the search for the elements that make up thought. Some psychologists have proposed that the ultimate constituents of thought are images; others have felt that they are abstract mental structures such as concepts. We will look at both suggestions in turn.

Mental Imagery

One of the oldest proposals is that thought consists of mental images as seen by the mind's eye. According to Berkeley and other British empiricists, all thought is ultimately comprised of such images, which enter and exit from the stage of con-

Thinking   *(Aristotle Contemplating the Bust of Homer, 1653, by Rembrandt; courtesy The Metropolitan Museum of Art, purchased with special funds and gifts of friends of the Museum, 1961)*

sciousness as the laws of association bid them. But later studies have shown that it is very unlikely that thought is the simple kaleidoscope of mental pictures (or sounds and touches) that this view claims it to be. Imagery plays an important role in thinking, but by no means an exclusive one, for much thought goes on without images. Around the turn of the century, several psychologists asked subjects to describe everything that "went through their minds" as they tried to solve various intellectual problems. The solution frequently came without a trace of imagery (and also without words). The subjects reported that when their thought was both wordless and imageless they often had a sense of certain underlying relationships, such as the experience of "this doesn't go with that" or a "feeling of *if* or *but*" (Humphrey, 1951). Mental images are evidently one of the elements of thought. But they are not the only ones.

Abstract Elements

Mental images are in some ways picture-like. There are some constituents of thinking, however, that are not picture-like at all. Unlike images, they are essentially abstract and symbolic. A good example (though by no means the only one) is words.

Consider a picture of a mouse and compare it to the word *mouse.* The picture is in some ways quite different from the real animal. It *represents* a mouse rather than actually being one. But even so, the picture has many similarities to the creature that it represents, for it looks quite a bit like a real mouse. In contrast, take the word *mouse.* This word stands for the same long-tailed, big-eared, and be-whiskered creature that the picture represents. But unlike the picture, the word has no similarity to the mouse whatever. The relation between the sound "mouse" (or the written, five-letter word *mouse*) and the little long-tailed animal that it represents is entirely arbitrary and symbolic.

Many psychologists believe that the kind of thinking that utilizes mental imagery differs from the kind that underlies words and sentences much as pictures differ from words. In their view, the language-related form of thinking is more

A

B

Some representations are picture-like; others are abstract (A) A photograph of Ambroise Vollard, a French art dealer at the turn of the century. (B) A cubist portrait of Monsieur Vollard by Pablo Picasso. Note that while Picasso's rendering is by no means literal, there is still enough of a pictorial similarity to the model that the portrait is still recognizable. While this painting is a picture-like representation, the model's name— Ambroise Vollard—is not. It stands for him, but it is not like him, for both names and words are abstract representations rather than picture-like ones. (Picasso's Portrait of Ambroise Vollard, *1909.* Moscow, Pushkin Museum; courtesy Scala/Art Resource)

symbolic and abstract than the picture-like form that uses imagery. The attempt to describe the components of this more abstract level of thinking is relatively recent, at least for psychologists. But some of the key items of such a description are already in the vocabulary of related disciplines such as logic and linguistics. Examples are the terms *concept* and *proposition.*

CONCEPTS

The term **concept** is generally used to describe a class or category that subsumes a number (sometimes an infinite number) of individual instances. An example is *dwelling,* which includes *hut, house, tent, apartment,* and *igloo.* Other concepts designate qualities or dimensions. Examples are *length* and *age.* Still others are relational, such as *taller than.* Relational concepts don't apply to any one item in isolation. One can't be *taller than* except in relation to something else to which one's height is being compared. (For more detail, see Chapter 8.)

PROPOSITIONS

Concepts describe classes of events or objects or relations between them. They are what we generally think about. In so doing, we tend to combine them in various ways. The British empiricists emphasized one such mental combination: the simple associative train of thought in which one idea leads to another. A more important way of relating concepts is by asserting something about them, for example, "dogs generally bite postmen." Such statements are called **propositions.** They make some assertion that relates a **subject** (the item about which an assertion is made; e.g., *dogs*) and a **predicate** (what is asserted about the subject; e.g., *generally bite postmen*) in a way that can be true or false.

PROBLEM SOLVING

Thus far our concern has been with the elements of which thought is composed. We now turn from the question of *what* to the question of *how.* How does thinking operate as we try to solve the myriad of problems encountered in life, whether trying to fix a broken lawn mower, smoothing over an awkward social situation, or solving an anagram?

Regarded in this context, thinking is an activity. It is something an organism does. Locke, Berkeley, and their many descendants believed that this stream of activity is produced by a chain of associated ideas, each triggered by the one before. The fundamental difficulty of this position is that thinking, like every other activity of the organism, is organized, for the individual items in any activity an organism is engaged in generally do not stand in isolation but take their meaning from the overall structure in which they are embedded.

Consider problem solving. The problem solver goes through a sequence of internal steps, which are organized in a special way: They are directed toward a goal —the solution of the problem. Suppose a taxi driver is trying to decide on the best route from the city to the airport. According to a simple chain-association hypothesis, the initial stimulus ("Get me to the airport in time for a 9:15 flight") triggers various internal responses (such as "superhighway," "crosstown express," etc.) until the correct solution is finally evoked. But this interpretation cannot readily explain why the would-be solutions that come to mind, whether right or wrong, are usually relevant to the problem at hand. Nor can it explain how such potential solutions are accepted or rejected. If they were merely aroused by associative connections, the problem solver would be adrift in a sea of irrelevancies: "Crosstown express" might evoke "uptown local" or "crossword puzzle." Instead, each mental step is determined not just by the step before but by the original problem. This sets the overall direction which dominates all of the later steps and determines how each of them is to be evaluated. The taxi driver considers the superhighway and rejects it as he recalls some road construction along the way, thinks of the crosstown express and dismisses it because of rush-hour traffic, and so on. The original problem acts like a schematic frame, waiting to be filled in by a "fitting" solution. Given this frame, the irrelevant word association "crossword puzzle" never enters his mind.

Hierarchical Organization and Chunking

We have encountered the notion of hierarchical organization while discussing various aspects of memory (see Chapter 6). A similar principle governs directed thinking. To the taxi driver, the idea "take the crosstown express" is a sort of master plan that implies various subsidiary actions: entering from the appropriate one-way street, maneuvering out of the truck lane, following the signs to the airport exit, and so on. To the experienced driver all of these substeps require no further thought, for they are a consequence of hierarchical organization which resembles that of a disciplined army. The colonel who orders his regiment to attack does not have to specify the detailed commands his second lieutenants issue to their platoons. Given the order from above, the subcommands follow (Figure 7.1).

The ability to subsume many details under a larger chunk is one of the crucial features of directed activity, including the internal activity we call thinking. As we shall see, much of the difference between master and apprentice is in the degree to which subcomponents of the activity have been chunked hierarchically. To the master, the substeps have become automatic.

DEVELOPING SKILLS

The role of chunking in directed activity is particularly clear when we study how people become proficient at various skills such as typing, driving a car, or playing golf. In all such activities, becoming skillful depends upon a qualitative change in how the task is performed.

The first experimental study in this area was done about ninety years ago by Bryan and Harter. These psychologists were trying to discover how telegraph operators master their trade. Their subjects were Western Union apprentices whose progress at sending and receiving Morse code messages was charted over a period of about forty weeks. Figure 7.2 plots one student's improvement at receiving, measured in letters per minute. What is interesting about this learning curve is its shape. Following an initial rise, the curve flattens into a *plateau,* after which it may rise again until it reaches another plateau, and so on. According to Bryan and Harter, such plateaus are an indication that the learner gradually transforms his task. At first he merely tracks individual letters, getting progressively faster in doing so as practice proceeds. But with time, the effective units he deals with become larger and larger: first syllables and words, then several words at a time, then simple phrases. The plateau represents the best the learner can do given a unit of a lower level (say, letters); once this lower level is completely mastered, a higher level of organization—a larger chunk—is possible and the learning curve shoots up once more (Bryan and Harter, 1897).

Similar effects are observed in the acquisition of many other skills, such as typing, or driving a car, or playing golf. In all such activities, becoming skillful involves a qualitative change in how the task is performed (Keele, 1982). To the

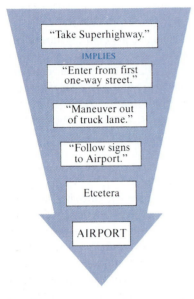

7.1 Hierarchical organization of a plan *Plans have subcomponents which have subcomponents below them, as here illustrated by the taxi driver's task.*

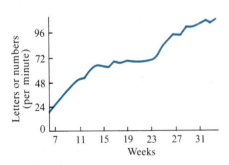

7.2 An apprentice telegrapher's learning curve *The curve plots the number of letters or digits the operator can receive per minute against weeks of practice. Note the plateau in the learning curve. The curve stays level from weeks 15 to 25 and then starts to rise again. According to Bryan and Harter, the new rise indicates the use of larger chunks. (After Bryan and Harter, 1899)*

novice, typing proceeds letter by letter; to the expert, the proper units are much larger, including familiar letter groupings, words, and occasionally phrases. Similarly, the beginning driver laboriously struggles to harmonize clutch, gas pedal, steering wheel, and brake, to the considerable terror of innocent bystanders. After a while, those movements come quite routinely and are subsumed under much higher (though perhaps equally dangerous) chunks of behavior, such as overtaking another car. An even simpler example is dressing. To the small child every article of clothing represents a major intellectual challenge; she beams with pride when she finally gets the knack of tying her shoelaces. To an adult the unit is "getting dressed" and its various components are almost completely submerged within the larger chunk. We decide to dress and before we know it we are almost fully clothed. Somehow our shoes get laced but we never notice, unless the laces break.

AUTOMATIZATION

The automatization of subcomponents in skilled activities, however, has a side effect. Once the plan is set into motion, its execution may be difficult to stop. An example is reading. When we see a billboard on a highway, we can't help but read what it says, whether we want to or not. The forms on the sign proclaim that they are letters and words; this is enough to trigger our automatized reading routines (La Berge, 1975). A striking demonstration of this phenomenon is the so-called *Stroop effect* (Stroop, 1935). Subjects are asked to name the colors in which groups of letters are printed and to do so as quickly as they can (Figure 7.3). In one case, the letter groups are unrelated consonants or vowels. In this condition, the subjects have little trouble. After a little practice, they become very proficient at rattling off the colors, "red, green . . ."

The subjects' task becomes vastly more difficult in a condition in which the letters are grouped into words, specifically color names. Diabolically enough, these are not the names of the colors in which the words are printed. Now the subjects respond much more slowly. They are asked to say "green, red, yellow. . ." But they can't help themselves from reading the words "yellow, black . . ." for reading is an automatized skill. As a result, there is violent response conflict. This conflict persists even after lengthy practice. One way subjects finally manage to overcome it is by learning to unfocus their eyes. By this maneuver, they can still see the colors but can no longer recognize the words (Jensen, 1965).

THE CHUNKING PROCESS

At present we know very little about the mechanisms that underlie the chunking process. Associationists propose that the explanation involves *chaining.* In their view, many skilled acts are highly overpracticed stimulus-response chains in which the first movement provides the kinesthetic stimulus for the second, which produces the stimulus for the third, and so on. This interpretation is almost certainly false. As Karl Lashley pointed out, a trained pianist may reach a rate of sixteen successive finger strokes a second when playing an arpeggio. This speed is too high to allow time for a sensory message to reach the brain and for a motor command to come back to the fingers (Lashley, 1951). We can only conclude that there is a learned neural program that allows the successive finger movements to occur without alternative sensory monitoring, but the nature of the mechanism that underlies this process is still a matter of debate (e.g., Shiffrin and Schneider, 1977; Newell and Rosenbloom, 1981; Logan, 1988).

We may not understand precisely how this complex chunking is acquired, but there is little doubt of its importance. It is hard to imagine any organized, skilled behavior in which this process does not play a role. In Bryan and Harter's words,

A	B
ZYP	RED
QLEKF	BLACK
SUWRG	YELLOW
XCIDB	BLUE
WOPR	RED
ZYP	GREEN
QLEKF	YELLOW
XCIDB	BLACK
SUWRG	BLUE
WOPR	BLACK
SUWRG	RED
ZYP	YELLOW
XCIDB	GREEN
QLEKF	BLUE
WOPR	GREEN
QLEKF	BLUE
WOPR	RED
ZYP	YELLOW
XCIDB	BLACK
SWRG	GREEN

7.3 The Stroop effect *The two lists, (A) and (B), are printed in four colors—red, green, blue, and yellow. To observe the Stroop effect, name the colors (aloud) in which each of the nonsense syllables in list (A) is printed as fast as you can, continuing downward. Then do the same for list (B), calling out the colors in which each of the words of the list is printed, again going from top to bottom. This will very probably be easier for list (A) than for list (B), a demonstration of the Stroop effect.*

NAGMARA

BOLMPER

SLEVO

STIGNIH

TOLUSONI

7.4   Anagrams   *Rearrange the letters on each line to form a word. (For the solution, see p. 208.)*

7.5   Matchstick problem   *Assemble all six matches to form four equilateral triangles, each side of which is equal to the length of one match. (For the solution, see Figure 7.16, p. 209.)*

7.6   Nine-dot problem   *Nine dots are arranged in a square. Connect them by drawing four continuous straight lines without lifting your pencil from the paper. (For the solution, see Figure 7.15, p. 209.)*

"The ability to take league steps in receiving telegraphic messages, in reading, in addition, in mathematical reasoning and in many other fields, plainly depends upon the acquisition of league-stepping habits. . . . The learner must come to do with one stroke of attention what now requires a half a dozen, and presently, in one still more inclusive stroke, what now requires thirty-six." The expert can, if necessary, attend to the lower-level units of his skill, but for the most part these have become automatic. This submergence of lower-level units in the higher chunk frees him to solve new problems. "Automatism is not genius, but it is the hands and feet of genius" (Bryan and Harter, 1899, p. 375).

SEARCHING FOR SOLUTIONS

Psychologists have devised many experimental situations to study human problem solving. Subjects have been asked to decipher anagrams (Figure 7.4), to manipulate various concrete objects so as to produce a desired result (Figure 7.5), or to find the solution to various geometrical problems (Figure 7.6). Considering this variety of tasks, it is hardly surprising that there are differences in the way in which they are attacked; a subject who tries to join nine dots with one continuous line will call upon a somewhat different set of mental skills than one who has to rearrange the letters *STIGNIH* into an English word. The question is whether there is a common thread that runs through all attempts at problem solving, no matter what the particular problem may be. Many psychologists believe that hierarchical organization is such a common feature.

The role of organization in problem solving was highlighted in a classic study by the Gestalt psychologist Karl Duncker, who asked his subjects to "think out loud" while they tried to find the solution (Duncker, 1945). One of Duncker's problems was cast in medical terms:

> Suppose a patient has an inoperable stomach tumor. There are certain rays which can destroy this tumor if their intensity is large enough. At this intensity, however, the rays will also destroy the healthy tissue which surrounds the tumor (e.g., the stomach walls, the abdominal muscles, and so on). How can one destroy the tumor without damaging the healthy tissue through which the rays must travel on their way?

Duncker's subjects typically arrived at the solution in several steps. They first reformulated the problem so as to produce a general plan of attack. This in turn led to more specific would-be solutions. For example, they might look for a tissue-free path to the stomach and so propose to send the rays through the esophagus. (A good idea which unfortunately will not work—rays travel in straight lines and the esophagus is curved.) After exploring several other general approaches and their specific consequences, some subjects finally hit upon the appropriate general plan. They proposed to reduce the intensity of rays on their way through healthy tissue and then turn up this intensity when the rays reach the tumor. This broad restatement of what is needed eventually led to the correct specific means, which was to send several bundles of *weak* rays from various points outside so that they meet at the tumor where their effects will summate (Figure 7.7).

MASTERS AND BEGINNERS

Some people solve certain problems better than others do. One reason is experience; the trained mechanic is more likely to hit on the why and wherefore of automotive failure than is his young apprentice. But what exactly does experience contribute? A major factor is chunking, which plays a similar role in problem solving to that played in the execution of various skills. Experts approach a prob-

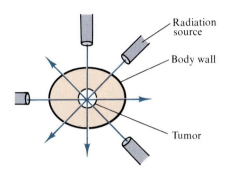

7.7 The solution to the ray-tumor problem *Several weak rays are sent from various points outside so that they will meet at the tumor site. There the radiation of the rays will be intense, for all the effects will summate at this point. But since they are individually weak, the rays will not damage the healthy tissue that surrounds the tumor. (After Duncker, 1945)*

7.8 Memory for chess positions in masters and average players
(A) An actual chess position which was presented for five seconds after which the positions of the pieces had to be reconstructed. Typical performances by masters and average players are shown in (B) and (C) respectively, with errors indicated in red. (After Hearst, 1972)

lem in different ways than beginners. They think in larger units whose components are already contained within them and thus require no further thought.

An interesting demonstration of how chunking makes the master comes from a study of chess players conducted by the Dutch psychologist Adrian de Groot whose findings have been corroborated and extended by several American investigators (de Groot, 1965; Chase and Simon, 1973a, 1973b). The chess world ranks its members according to a ruthlessly objective hierarchy of merit based on a simple record of who beats whom. Grandmasters are at the top, followed by masters, experts, down to Class *D* players at the lower rungs of the chess ladder. De Groot, himself a chess master, posed various chess problems to members of each merit category (including two former world champions) and asked them to select the best move. All of the masters chose continuations that would have won the game, while few of the other players did. But why? De Groot and many later theorists believed that the reason was in the way the players organized the problem. The chess master structures the chess position in terms of broad strategic concepts (e.g., a king-side attack with pawns) from which many of the appropriate moves follow naturally. In effect, the master has a "chess vocabulary" of more and larger chunks. If so, one would expect him to grasp a chess position in a shorter time. This is indeed the case. Players of different ranks were shown chess positions for five seconds each and were then asked to reproduce them a few minutes later. Grandmasters and masters did so with hardly an error; lesser players (including mere experts) performed much more poorly (see Figure 7.8). This is not because the chess masters have better visual memory. When presented with bizarre positions that would hardly ever arise in the course of a well-played game, they recall them no better than novices do. Their superiority is in the conceptual organization of chess, not in the memory for visual patterns as such.

Some later studies have shown that the superiority of the chess masters is not entirely produced by better chunking. They are also better in evaluating chess positions and look further ahead in their mental calculations (Charness, 1981; Holding and Reynolds, 1982; Holding, 1985). But chunking clearly plays a role in this mental skill, just as it does in telegraphy, typing, and various athletic pursuits (e.g., Allard, Graham, and Paarsalu, 1980).

At least in part, the essence of expertise is twofold. To begin with, experts know more than novices. And in addition, they have developed an organization of the relevant subcomponents, which allows them to solve their problems in terms of fewer but vastly larger steps. Whether the skill is reading or typing or playing a musical instrument, its mastery depends on the acquisition of newer and better chunkings.

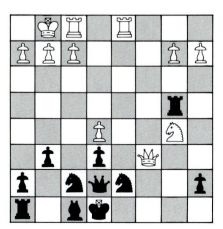

A. Actual position

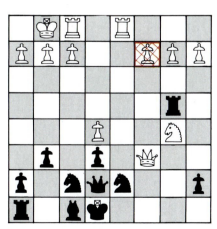

B. Typical master player's performance

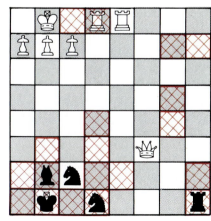

C. Typical average player's performance

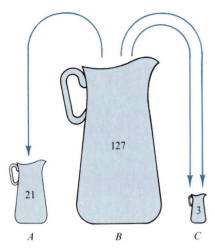

7.9 The standard method for solving the three-container problem *(After Luchins, 1942)*

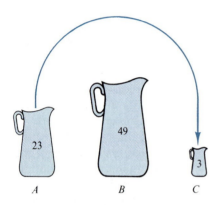

7.10 A simpler method for solving certain three-container problems *(After Luchins, 1942)*

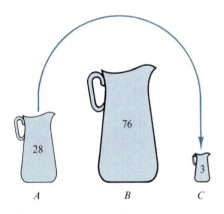

7.11 A case where only the simple method works *(After Luchins, 1942)*

Acquiring the appropriate chunkings is in part a matter of experience. But in part, it is also a matter of talent, for some people can see chunks where the rest of us cannot. When the mathematician Karl Friedrich Gauss was a young boy in grammar school, his teacher asked the class to add all the numbers from 1 to 10. Young Gauss got the answer almost immediately. Unlike his classmates, he did not chug through all of the tedious steps of the summation. He recognized that the series $1 + 2 + 3 \ldots + 10$ can be rewritten as a sum of 5 pairs each of which equals 11. That is, $(5 + 6) + (4 + 7) + (3 + 8) + (2 + 9) + (1 + 10) = 5 \times 11 = 55$ (Wertheimer, 1945). Given this insight, he quickly came up with the correct answer, 55, no doubt to the considerable amazement of the teacher.

Obstacles to Problem Solving

So far, we have primarily dealt with situations in which problem solvers succeed. How can we explain their all too many failures? In many cases, the solution is simply out of reach. The problem solver lacks some necessary informational prerequisites or relevant chunkings—as when a ten-year-old is unable to solve a problem in integral calculus. But failure often occurs even when all the necessary ingredients for solution are known perfectly well, for the would-be problem solver may get stuck in a wrong approach and may not be able to get unstuck. When finally told the answer, his reaction often shows that he was blind rather than ignorant: "How stupid of me. I should have seen it all along." He was victimized by a powerful ***mental set*** that was inappropriate for the problem at hand.

FIXATION

A well-known study shows how mental set can make people rigid. They became ***fixated*** on one approach to the task, which made it hard for them to think of it in any other way. The subjects were presented with a series of problems. They were told that they had three jars of known volume. Their job was to use these to obtain (mentally) an exact quantity of water from a well. In one problem, for example, the subjects had three containers—A, B, and C—which held 21, 127, and 3 quarts respectively. Their task was to use these three jars to obtain 100 quarts. After a while, they hit upon the correct method. This was to fill jar B (127 quarts) completely, and then pour out enough water to fill jar A (21 quarts). After this, they would pour out more water from jar B to fill jar C (3 quarts), empty jar C and fill it again from jar B. The remaining water in jar B was the desired quantity, 100 quarts (see Figure 7.9).

On the next few problems, the numerical values differed (see Table 7.1). But in all cases, the solution could be obtained by the same sequence of arithmetical steps, that is, B − A − 2C. Thus, $163 - 14 - 2 \times 25 = 99; 43 - 18 - 2 \times 10 = 5$, and so on.

Table 7.1   THE THREE-CONTAINER PROBLEM

Desired quantity of water (quarts)	Volume of empty jar (quarts)		
	A	B	C
99	14	163	25
5	18	43	10
21	9	42	6
31	20	59	4

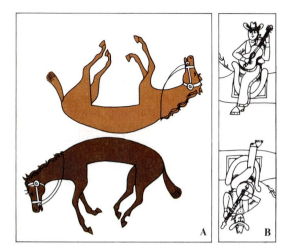

7.12   Horse-and-rider problem   *The task is to place (B) on (A) in such a way that the riders are properly astride the horses. (After Scheerer, Goldstein, and Boring, 1941; for the solution, see Figure 7.17, p. 210.)*

A

B

7.13   Functional fixedness   *(A) The problem is to mount two candles on the wall, given the objects shown. (B) To solve the problem, one has to think of a new function for the box. (After Glucksberg, 1962; photographs by Jeffrey Grosscup)*

After five such problems, the subjects were given two critical tests. The first was a problem that required them to obtain 20 quarts, given jars whose volumes were 23, 49, and 3 quarts. Now most of the subjects showed a mechanization effect produced by the mental set. They dutifully performed the laborious arithmetical labors they had used before, computing $49 - 23 - 2 \times 3 = 20$. They did so, even though there was a simpler method that takes only one step (see Figure 7.10).

Subsequent to this was a second critical problem. The subjects were now asked to obtain 25 quarts, given jars of 28, 76, and 3 quarts. Note that here the only method that will work is the direct one; that is, $28 - 3 = 25$ (see Figure 7.11). But the mental set was so powerful that many subjects failed to solve the problem altogether. They tried the old procedure, which is inappropriate ($76 - 28 - 2 \times 3$ does not equal 25), and so could not hit on an adequate alternative. The set had made them so rigid that they became mentally blind (Luchins, 1942).

Similar effects have been demonstrated in other problem situations. In many of these there is no need to induce the misleading set by instructions or prior practice, for it is usually engendered by the perceptual arrangement of the problem. Examples of such perceptually induced sets are the nine-dot problem (see Figure 7.6, p. 204) and the horse-and-rider problem (see Figure 7.12).

SET AND MOTIVATION

In fairy tales, the hero is sometimes required to solve a riddle or suffer death but, being a fairy-tale hero, he invariably succeeds. In real life, he would have a harder time, for problem solution, unfairly enough, becomes more difficult when the need for it is especially great. This is because of the relation between set and motivation. The greater the motivation toward solution, the stronger are the sets with which the problem is approached. If these sets happen to be appropriate, well and good. But if they are inappropriate, increased motivation will be a hindrance, for sets will then be that much harder to break. Since difficult problems—almost by definition—are problems that tend to engender the wrong set, their solution will be impeded as motivation becomes intense.

Evidence for these assertions comes from several experiments which show that flexibility goes down when motivation becomes intense enough. In one such study, the subjects were posed a practical problem. The problem was to mount two candles on a wall, given only the candles, a box of matches, and some thumbtacks (see Figure 7.13). The solution is to empty one of the boxes, tack it to the wall, and then place the candles upon it. The difficulty of this particular problem

7.17 Solution of the horse-and-rider problem *To solve the horse-and-rider puzzle (see Figure 7.12, p. 207) requires a change of perceptual set. (A) must be rotated 90 degrees so that the two old nags are in the vertical position. One can now see that the head of each (vertical) can join (horizontally) with the hindquarters of the other. The final step is to slide (B) over the middle of (A) and the problem is solved. (After Scheerer, Goldstein, and Boring, 1941)*

only be solved by a 90-degree rotation of the drawing which recombines the fore- and hindquarters of the misshapen horses to form two new animals entirely (see Figure 7.17).

Gestalt psychologists have proposed that this kind of perceptual restructuring lies at the heart of most problem solving in both animals and humans (see Chapter 3). So far, little is known about the mechanisms that underlie the restructuring effect, but there is reason to believe that it is a central phenomenon in the psychology of thinking. (For a contrary view, see Weisberg and Alba, 1981.)

CREATIVE THINKING

The creative thinker is one who generates a solution that is both new and appropriate. At the top of the pyramid are such giants as Archimedes, Descartes, and Newton, whose creations define whole chapters of intellectual history. On another level are the anonymous copywriters who develop new advertising slogans for spray deodorants. But whether great or humble, these real-life achievements are quite similar to those of the problem solver in the psychological laboratory. They represent a conceptual reorganization of what was there before.

According to the creators' own accounts, the critical insights typically occur at unexpected times and places. There is usually a period of intense preparation during which the thinker is totally immersed in the problem and approaches it from all possible angles. But illumination tends not to come then. Quite the contrary. After the initial onslaught fails, there is usually a period of retreat during which the problem is temporarily shelved. Rest or some other activity intervenes, and then suddenly the solution arrives, not at the writer's desk or the composer's piano, but elsewhere entirely—while walking in the woods (Helmholtz), or riding in a carriage (Beethoven, Darwin), or stepping onto a bus (the great mathematician Poincaré), or, in the most celebrated case of all, while sitting in a bathtub (Archimedes; see Figure 7.18).

7.18 Archimedes in his bathtub *A sixteenth-century engraving celebrating a great example of creative restructuring. The Greek scientist Archimedes (287–212 B.C.) tried to determine whether the king's crown was made of solid gold or had been adulterated with silver. Archimedes knew the weight of gold and silver per unit volume but did not know how to measure the volume of a complicated object such as a crown. One day, in his bath, he noticed how the water level rose as he immersed his body. Here was the solution: The crown's volume is determined by the water it displaces. Carried away by his sudden insight, he jumped out of his bath and ran naked through the streets of Syracuse, shouting "Eureka! I have found it!" (Engraving by Walter H. Ryff, courtesy The Granger Collection)*

Such effects have sometimes been attributed to a process of *incubation* (Wallas, 1926). According to this view, a thinker does not ignore the unsolved problem altogether when she turns away from it in baffled frustration; she continues to work on it, but does so "unconsciously." This hypothesis adds little to our understanding, for it merely substitutes one mystery for another. Unless we know the why and wherefore of unconscious thought (whatever that may be), we know no more than we did before.

Many psychologists suspect that such so-called incubation effects are produced by a change in mental set (e.g., Wickelgren, 1974; Anderson, 1990). To find the solution, the problem solver must shake off one or more false approaches. These become increasingly restricting the longer she stays at the task, all the more so since her motivation is very intense. Leaving the problem for awhile may very well break the mental set. As time elapses, the false set may be forgotten, and the drastic change of retrieval cues (to the woods or to the bathtub) will prevent its reinstatement. Once the false set is dropped, there is a chance that the true solution may emerge. Of course, it is only a chance that may come to fruition if one is totally familiar with all the ins and outs of the problem and (especially) if one has the talents of a Beethoven or an Archimedes. Just taking a bath is unfortunately not enough.

ARTIFICIAL INTELLIGENCE: PROBLEM SOLVING BY COMPUTER

The preceding discussion has emphasized the role played by hierarchical organization in thinking. But how does this organization come about? How does the problem solver hit upon the right plan of attack and how does she recognize that it is right when she thinks of it? These questions are as yet unanswered, but there have been some promising leads.

One interesting avenue of research comes from attempts to program computers so as to simulate certain aspects of human thinking. The impetus for this work stems from the belief, held by many psychologists, that humans and computers are similar in one important regard—they are both *information-processing systems.* We have already seen several examples of the information-processing approach in our discussions of perception and memory. When we talk of items that are temporarily activated in working memory, are recoded into fewer and more compact chunks, and are later retrieved by various hierarchical search procedures, we are describing a system in which information is systematically converted from one form into another. There is a formal similarity between this sequence of inferred events in human memory and the actual steps of a computer program that handles the storage, recoding, and retrieval of various materials (such as library titles, tax returns, and so on). In an analogous way, what we call "thinking" may be the systematic manipulation of the hierarchically arranged conceptual chunks stored in our brain.

To be sure, the underlying physical machinery is very different. Computers use hardware made of magnetic cores and transistors, while biological systems are built of neurons. But this difference does not prohibit a similarity in their operations. Two different computers may be built with either electronic tubes or transistors, but they may be fed the same programs even so—and they will both compute the same functions. Similarly—for at least some purposes—it may not matter that digital computers are built of steel and ceramic chips while an organism's mental machinery is built of neurons. To students of *artificial intelligence,* the important point is that both computers and human beings are information-processing systems (Turing, 1950). They therefore regard it as likely that the study of one will help in the understanding of the other.

Solution to the cheap-necklace problem
The obvious (but incorrect) approach to the problem (Figure 7.14, p. 208) is to try to link the four chains together: A to B to C to D and then back to A. The trouble is that this procedure will cost too much. To solve the problem, one has to shift the representation and see that one of the chains (say, A) can provide the connecting links to connect the other three chains. The first step is to destroy a chain by opening all three links in A (at a total cost of 6 cents). The first link is used to connect B and C (creating a 7-link chain), the second to join this new chain with D (making an 11-link chain), and finally the third to join the ends of this 11-link chain together, at a total cost of 9 cents. One of the reasons why this problem is quite difficult is that its solution requires a detour: In order to make a larger chain (that is, the final necklace) one has to destroy one of the smaller ones. (From Wickelgren, 1974)

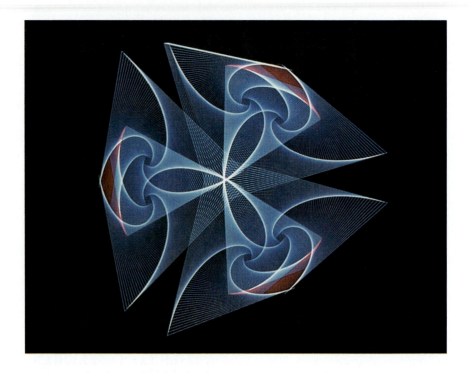

Computer-generated visual design   *By now, computers are used to assist in many human endeavors. The figure shows a computer design generated from a graphic program that incorporates various geometrical algorithms. ("Tri-Vail" © 1968 Melvin L. Prueitt)*

A further advantage of the computer simulation of thought comes from the fact that machines are painfully literal. The program must be spelled out in absolutely precise detail, for the computer will balk if presented with vague or over-generalized instructions. This limitation is a blessing in disguise. It forces the scientist to formulate his notions in completely rigorous and explicit terms.

Algorithms and Heuristics

Several investigators have deliberately forced their "thinking" programs to be as humanlike as possible. The most prominent among these are Allen Newell and Nobel laureate Herbert Simon, who have programmed computers to play chess, to discover and prove theorems in symbolic logic, and to decipher cryptograms. They began by studying how human subjects deal with these problems, discovered their typical strategies by use of the think-aloud technique we discussed earlier, and then incorporated these problem-solving plans into the instructions fed to their computer. Interestingly enough, the computer does fairly well if it attacks these problems as human subjects say they do (Newell and Simon, 1972).

Newell and Simon found it useful to distinguish between two major kinds of solution strategies. One is an ***algorithm,*** a procedure in which all of the operations required to achieve the solution are specified step by step. Examples are the various manipulations of arithmetic. An algorithm guarantees that a solution will be found in time, but this time may be very long in coming. Consider a person working on a crossword puzzle who is trying to find a synonym for "sharp-tongued" that will fit into _c_ _bi_. An algorithm exists: Insert all possible alphabetic combinations into the four empty spaces and check each result against an unabridged dictionary. While this procedure is certain to produce "acerbic," it should appeal to few puzzle solvers, for it will require the inspection of nearly 460,000 possibilities.

In actual practice, crossword puzzles are solved by procedures which, though not as sure, are much less slow. These are ***heuristics,*** which are various tricks and rules of thumb that have often worked in the past and may do so again, such as guessing at a suffix given the word's grammatical class (*ic* is a good bet for an adjective), forming hypotheses on the basis of likely letter sequences in the language (if *c* is the second letter, the first must be an *s* or a vowel), and so on. The various procedures for overcoming obstacles to problem solving which we have discussed before, such as working backwards, finding analogies, and changing the way the problem is represented, are heuristics of a similar sort—they are by no means guaranteed to work, but they often do. The great majority of problems people face are solved by such heuristic procedures rather than by algorithms, for human life is short and human processing capacity is limited. Physicians reach their diagnoses by first considering a few hypotheses that seem most plausible and then testing those. If instead they looked at every possibility, the patient would be dead before being diagnosed.

If the problem is complex enough, even high-speed computers must resort to heuristics (Boden, 1977). Consider the analysis of a chess position some ten moves ahead. The total number of possibilities (based on moves, replies, replies to replies, and so on) has been estimated at an astronomical billion billion billion. Under the circumstances, an algorithm is out of the question. (If the inspection of each possibility takes one-millionth of a second, the inspection of all of them would be completed after 1,000 billion years.) On the other hand, heuristics work remarkably well. Modern chess programs require the computer to search for moves that satisfy certain subgoals such as material superiority (e.g., give a pawn for a queen but not vice versa) and various strategic objectives such as occupation of the center squares (which limits the opponent's mobility). Chess programs that employ heuristics of this sort have become very powerful (Holding, 1985). They combine what is essentially brute force (the ability to search at extremely high speeds) with the ability to evaluate positions. Under the circumstances, it is not surprising that they are closing in on the game's human champions. One such program, Deep Thought, has already defeated several grandmasters (Byrne, 1989).

EXPERT SYSTEMS

A promising new trend in the field of artificial intelligence is the development of **expert systems.** These are problem solving programs with a very narrow scope. They deal only with problems in a highly limited domain, such as some subfield of organic chemistry, law, or medicine. Because they are so specialized, their memory can be stocked with a considerable amount of know-how in their own area.

An example is MYCIN, a computer program designed to assist physicians in the treatment of infectious diseases. MYCIN is not just a stored table that lists drugs to combat this or the other microorganism. It can diagnose, suggest therapies, estimate their effectiveness, and will even explain how it arrived at its decisions if asked. The physician "informs" the computer of the patient's symptoms and of the results of various blood tests and bacterial cultures. The computer will then consult its memory for lists of potentially useful drugs and will then choose among them by following various decision rules (which consider the patient's age, other medications, side effects, and so on) and make a recommendation, indicating the statistical probability of success. If appropriately "instructed," it will add to or modify its rules; for example, it may note that a particular antibiotic ought not to be administered to a patient with a certain allergy (Shortliffe et al., 1973; Duda and Shortliffe, 1983; Buchanan and Shortliffe, 1985).

Is MYCIN intelligent? In a sense, it obviously isn't. Its very strengths are its weaknesses. It "knows" only about infectious diseases. If it is asked about a broken bone or a psychiatric condition, it will be utterly lost. It is a highly specialized expert that may eventually become a valuable though rather limited assistant.

But it is not a model of the human intellect, for it simulates only a few human mental operations. Like other expert systems that are now being developed, MYCIN is meant to be an aid to human intelligence, not a substitute. All the same, its operations may be a microcosm of how the human mind solves some very limited problems and so, in the end, it may provide a genuine contribution to our understanding of the psychology of human thought.

Some Limitations of Artificial Intelligence

Computer simulation has added a new and exciting dimension to the study of cognitive processes. But so far at least, it still has some serious limitations as an approach to human thinking.

WELL-DEFINED AND ILL-DEFINED PROBLEMS

The problems that existing computer programs can handle are *well-defined.* There is a clear-cut way to decide whether a proposed solution is indeed the right one. Examples are algebraic proofs (Are the terms identical on both sides of the equation?), chess problems (Is the opposing king checkmated?), and anagrams (Is the rearranged letter sequence a word that appears in the dictionary?).

In contrast, many of the problems people face in real life are *ill-defined.* Consider an architect who is asked to design a modern college dormitory. Exactly what is a correct solution? Some proposals can obviously be rejected out of hand —for example, if there are no provisions for bathrooms—but there is no definite criterion for what is acceptable. Similarly for many other problem activities, such as completing a sonnet or organizing a lecture or planning a vacation. In all of these cases, the critical first step is to define the problem so that it can be answered and so that the answer can be evaluated. The architect begins by asking questions about the number of students who are to be housed, the facilities that must be included, the surrounding terrain, the available budget—all in an attempt to transform an ill-defined problem into a well-defined one. The progress of human knowledge is often a matter not of problem solution but of problem definition and redefinition. The alchemist looked for a way to change lead into gold; the modern physicist tries to discover the atomic structure of matter.

As of yet, computer programs do not define their own problems. It's by no means clear that computers will ever be able to do so in the way people do.

THE LACK OF COMMON SENSE

Some computer scientists feel that another difference between human and artificial intelligence concerns what is popularly called "common sense"—an understanding of what is relevant and what is not. People possess it, and computers do not. Consider a simple example. Let's assume that you build a computer program to perform some of the functions of a college registrar keeping records of enrollments and grades. In principle it shouldn't be too hard to do so, and in many ways the program will do a much better job than people might; it will never lose an entry, or misfile it. Now let's suppose that you ask this computer a simple question: "How many psychology majors passed Computer Science 101 last semester?" The computer will search its memory and may come up with the answer "None." You become worried and restless and wonder whether psychology majors have some special disability. But if you understand the limitations of most computer programs, you will ask the computer a further question: "How many psychology majors enrolled in Computer Science 101 last semester?" When the computer comes up with the answer "None," you breathe a sigh of relief. But you will look at the computer wonderingly. A human registrar would never have an-

"This one writes some fine lyrics, and the other one has done some beautiful music, but they just don't seem to hit it off as collaborators." (©1978 by Sidney Harris—American Scientist Magazine)

swered the first question as the computer did. He would have understood the point of the question and would have responded relevantly and without extra prompting: "There were no psychology majors enrolled in the course." This is presumably because the human registrar—but not the computer—would immediately realize how misleading the original bare response "None" would be (Joshi, 1983; for a discussion of the problem of relevance, see Sperber and Wilson, 1986).

The problem is that there is an enormous amount of knowledge about the world and its potential relevance to this or other questions that the computer can't possibly have. This certainly applies to expert systems such as MYCIN no less than to our computerized registrar. Suppose MYCIN's patient is a farmer. The program will not "realize" that some farmers are more likely to become infected with certain micro-organisms because they get their water from wells. Of course that knowledge could be added to the program. But that's only the beginning. For MYCIN also recommends against the administration of a certain antibiotic to children under eight. This time, what MYCIN doesn't know is that this is because that particular antibiotic stains developing teeth. A human physician would obviously decide that if the disease is severe enough, cosmetic side effects should be ignored. Here once again, the relevant knowledge can be added to the program. But more and more such exceptions will be encountered, each of which will require the addition of yet another item of knowledge, together with the rules that tell the program when this knowledge is relevant and when it isn't. To give the computer the common sense of a human physician, one would have to give it the entire knowledge of that physician, including the basic sense of values that tells him that death is a worse outcome than dingy teeth.

Computer scientists, who are well aware of the current limitations of Artificial Intelligence, sometimes tell a story about an interchange between an Army general and the Pentagon's main computer in the war room:

COMPUTER: The Russians (or the Chinese, or the Iraqis, or whoever) are coming!
GENERAL: By land or by sea?
COMPUTER: Yes.
GENERAL: Yes what?
COMPUTER: Yes, SIR!!!

The computer can answer questions. But it cannot understand why the questions were asked.

SPATIAL THINKING

Thus far, we have discussed problem solving as if all problems were essentially alike. In some ways, they may well be; for example, they may all be susceptible to mental sets that obstruct their solution. But it's likely that they also differ in some important ways. One difference is in the kinds of thinking that different problems tend to elicit.

Our present interest is in *spatial thinking,* the kind that we use when we want to determine a shortcut between two locations, or when we mentally try to rearrange the furniture in the living room.

Spatial Problem Solving and Imagery

How do people solve spatial problems? One way is by means of mental images. Such images have a picture-like quality that can be an important aid in various thinking tasks. By consulting a mental picture, the traveller can read off shortcuts

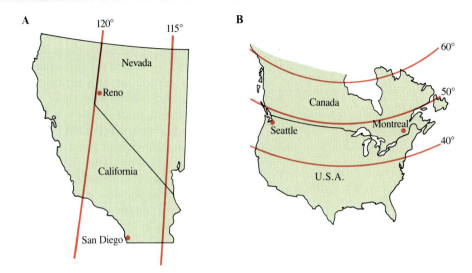

7.19 Conceptual mental maps *Subjects tend to judge San Diego to be west of Reno and Montreal to be north of Seattle. But these judgments are in error. (A) A map of California and Nevada with colored lines of longitude (angular distance from an arbitrary reference point in Greenwich, England) which shows that in fact San Diego is east of Reno. (B) A map of the United States and southern Canada with colored lines of latitude (angular distance from the equator) which shows that Seattle is slightly north of Montreal. (Stevens and Coupe, 1978)*

as he might from an actual map, and the decorator who wants to modify his furniture placement can save wear-and-tear on his back muscles by rearranging his images before moving the actual armchairs and sofas. Evidence for the picture-like aspects of images comes from various laboratory studies. We've already seen that images can be scanned (see Chapter 6). Further demonstrations come from studies on mental maps.

MENTAL MAPS THAT ARE PICTURE-LIKE

Most people have a general conception of the spatial layout of their environment. According to some investigators, part of this geographical knowledge is based on mental maps that have picture-like qualities. In one study, students were asked to estimate the distance between various locations on their university campus—for example, between their dormitory and the gymnasium, or between the student union and the library. It turned out that the subjects were quite accurate in their estimates. But even more interesting was the time it took to provide these estimates. The longer the distance, the longer the estimation time. It was as if the subjects measured distances with a mental ruler on a mental map, much as one might measure the length of a wall with a small ruler. The longer the wall, the more often the ruler would have to be moved from point to point, and the more time the process would take (Jonides and Baum, 1978).

MENTAL MAPS THAT ARE CONCEPTUAL

Some kinds of spatial thinking may refer to picture-like images, but others involve processes that are much more abstract and conceptual. In one study, subjects were asked to indicate the relative locations of two cities. One of the pairs was San Diego, California, and Reno, Nevada. The subjects judged San Diego to be west of Reno, although it actually is farther east. Another pair was Montreal, Canada, and Seattle, Washington. Here the subjects judged Montreal to be farther north, although its actual direction is south of Seattle. These results suggest that the subjects didn't base their answers on picture-like mental maps resembling the real maps shown in Figure 7.19. If they had, they would have said that Reno is west of San Diego. But in fact, they (falsely) asserted the very opposite.

How can we explain the subjects' errors? The most plausible explanation is that their judgments were affected by what they knew about the relative locations of the states or countries that contain the cities about which they were asked (e.g.,

Nevada is east of California and Canada is north of the United States). But this knowledge was symbolic and conceptual rather than picture-like. What the subjects knew about San Diego and Reno can be summarized by the three propositions shown below:

California is west of Nevada.
San Diego is in California.
Reno is in Nevada.

This way of representing spatial knowledge could easily lead to error, for it might suggest that the east-west relation that holds for the states also holds for all the cities within them. This would be true if the larger geographical units (California and Nevada) were conceptual categories such as *bird.* (If we know that owls and robins are birds, it automatically follows that they both have wings, beaks, and feathers.) Of course, states and countries are not at all equivalent to categories such as *bird:* Reno is not *a* Nevada but is *in* Nevada. But even so, most of us often store spatial information in such a rough-and-ready conceptual way. (One hopes that airplane navigators are an exception.) To the extent that we do store some geographical information under category rubrics, our spatial knowledge cannot be exclusively—or even largely—picture-like (Stevens and Coupe, 1978).

REASONING AND DECISION MAKING

How do people reason? For many years, the assumption was that the processes they use are intimately related to the formal laws of logic. Thus, George Boole, a famous nineteenth-century mathematician, entitled his treatise on the laws of logic "An Investigation into the Laws of Thought," with little doubt that the laws that governed the one would also govern the other (Henle, 1962). Today, this belief is no longer held as widely. For by now, there is ample evidence that people are very prone to errors of reasoning. As a result, some psychologists have argued that the laws of logic have more to say about how people *should* think than about how they really *do* think, for in their view humans are not quite as rational as one would like to believe.

Deductive Reasoning

In **deductive reasoning,** the reasoner tries to determine whether certain conclusions can or cannot be drawn—that is, deduced—from a set of initial assertions. The decision as to whether the deduction is valid or not depends entirely on the initial assertions coupled with some basic logical operations such as affirmation, negation, and so on.

A classical example of deductive reasoning is the analysis of **syllogisms,** an enterprise that goes back to Aristotle. Each syllogism contains two premises and a conclusion. The question is whether the conclusion logically follows from the premises (see Figure 7.20). A few examples of such syllogisms (some valid, others invalid) are:

7.20 Syllogistic argument *Insisting upon the execution of the Cheshire Cat, the King of Hearts argued that anything that has a head can be beheaded, including the Cheshire Cat, which at this stage of the story consists of nothing but a head. (Lewis Carroll,* Alice in Wonderland, *p. 55)*

All A are B.
All B are C.
Therefore: All A are C. (valid)

All A are B.
Some B are C.
Therefore: Some A are C. (invalid)

Or, stated in more concrete terms:

>All American Eagles are patriots.
>All patriots are redblooded.
>Therefore: All American Eagles are redblooded. (valid)

To give another example:

>All heavenly angels are accomplished harp players.
>Some accomplished harp players are members of the American musicians' union.
>Therefore: Some heavenly angels are members of the American musicians' union. (invalid)*

Until the nineteenth century, most philosophers were convinced that the ability to evaluate syllogisms of this kind was an essential aspect of human rationality. Under the circumstances, it was a bit disheartening when experimental psychologists demonstrated that subjects make a considerable number of errors on syllogism tasks.

One cause of errors is the subjects' tendency to perform inappropriate logical transformations. They hear the statement "All A are B" and somehow interpret it as if it were symmetrical. As a result, they convert it to: "All A are B and all B are A." Such invalid conversions will then of course lead to invalid judgments (Revlin and Leirer, 1980). An example is "All owls are birds," which of course does not permit the conclusion "All birds are owls."

Inductive Reasoning

In deductive reasoning, we typically go from the general to the particular. We apply some general rule or rules ("All men are mortal") and ask how it applies to a particular case ("John Smith is mortal"). In **inductive reasoning,** this process is reversed. Here we go from the particular to the general. We consider a number of different instances and try to determine—that is, *induce*—what general rule covers them all.

Induction is at the very heart of the scientific enterprise, for the object of science is to determine what different events have in common. To do so, scientists formulate various *hypotheses*—tentative assumptions about what constitutes the general rule from which the individual observations can be derived. Hypotheses are developed by laymen as well as scientists. All of us try to see some general pattern in the world around us, as in trying to explain the behavior of a moody daughter or a troublesome automobile. The hypotheses we come up with may not be particularly profound ("She's a teenager" or "It's a lemon"), but profound or not they are attempts to comprehend an individual case by subsuming it under a more general statement.

What do people do to determine whether their hypotheses are correct? A number of investigators have concluded that there is a powerful **confirmation bias.** By and large, people seek evidence that will confirm their hypotheses, but they only rarely set out to see whether their hypotheses are false.

An illustration is provided by a study in which subjects were presented with the three numbers "2–4–6" and were told that they were an example of a series that conforms to a general rule which the subjects were asked to discover. To do this, they had to generate a three-number series of their own. Every time they pro-

"There it comes again."

(Illustration by Henry Gleitman)

* Note that the validity of the syllogisms only depends on whether the conclusion follows *logically* from the premises. The empirical plausibility of the conclusion (e.g., that the angels of heaven are unionized) has nothing to do with the matter.

duced such a series, the experimenter would tell them whether it did or not fit the rule. The subjects always indicated why they chose a particular series, and after a number of trials they announced their hypothesis. This continued until the subject succeeded or finally gave up.

The rule the experimenter had in mind was exceedingly simple: "Any three numbers in increasing order of magnitude." It was so simple in fact that the subjects took quite a while before they discovered what it was. But the real issue was how they went about their task. All of them soon developed one or another hypothesis. But whenever they did, they almost always generated a series that fit this hypothesis—to confirm it. They very rarely generated a series that was not consistent with their current hypothesis, and would *dis*confirm it.

For example, one subject began with the notion that the rule was: "You start with any number and then add 2 each time." She came up with four successive series: "8–10–12," "14–16–18," "20–22–24," and "1–3–5" and was told each time that they conformed to the experimenter's rule. She then announced her hypothesis, was informed that it was false, and developed a new hypothesis: "The middle number is the average of the other two." To test this hypothesis she first offered "2–6–10" and then "1–50–99." After learning that each of these conformed to the correct rule, she announced her new hypothesis, and was again told that it was false. She continued to formulate new hypotheses, for example, "the difference between the first and second number is equal to the difference between the second and third." She again tested the hypothesis by looking for confirmations, generating the series "3–10–17" and "0–3–6," was again told that each of them conformed to the rule, and again discovered that this hypothesis too was incorrect. Eventually, she did hit on the correct hypothesis. But what is interesting is that she hardly ever tested any of her hypotheses by generating a sequence that was *in*consistent with them. For example, she never tried a sequence such as "2–4–5," a quick way to show that the "add 2" hypothesis was wrong (Wason, 1960, 1968; Wason and Johnson-Laird, 1972).

The confirmation bias shown in the 2–4–6 experiment is a very pervasive phenomenon. It is not restricted to the psychologist's laboratory, for it is also found in the real-world behavior of scientists and engineers. They too tend to seek confirmations of their hypotheses and are disinclined to seek evidence that contradicts them. When Galileo provided visible proof that Jupiter has moons that

The confirmation bias in science *Galileo vainly trying to persuade a group of university professors to look through his telescope. (From a National Theatre production of* Galileo *by Bertolt Brecht; photograph by Zoe Dominic)*

rotate around it, some of his critics were so incensed at this challenge to their geocentric views of the universe that they refused even to *look* through his telescope (Mitroff, 1974; Mahoney, 1976).

There is little doubt that the confirmation bias can be a genuine obstacle to understanding, for in many ways, disconfirmations are more helpful in the search for truth than are confirmations. *One* disconfirmation shows that a hypothesis is false, but countless confirmations cannot really prove that it is true.

What accounts for the confirmation bias? A plausible guess is that humans have a powerful tendency to seek order in the universe. We try to understand what we see and hear, and impose some organization upon it. The organization may not be valid, but it is better than none at all, for without some such organization we would be overwhelmed by an overload of information. But this benefit also has a corresponding cost, for our confirmation bias often condemns us to remain locked within our false beliefs and prejudices (Howard, 1983). Our tendency to come up with plausible hypotheses often serves us well. But we would be better off if we would be more ready to consider their falsity and would heed Oliver Cromwell's advice to a group of clergymen: "I beseech you, in the bowels of Christ, think it possible you may be mistaken."

Decision Making

Deductive reasoning is about certainties: If certain premises are true, then certain conclusions will follow. There are no exceptions. If it is true that John Smith is a man and that all men are mortal, then it inevitably follows that John Smith is mortal. The situation is very different in inductive reasoning, in which we try to find (that is, induce) a general rule when given a number of individual instances. Once this rule is induced, we will then try to apply it to new instances. But in contrast to deductions, inductions can never be certain but only probable. This even holds for Mr. Smith's mortality. For in actual fact, the proposition "All men are mortal" is only an induction. To be sure, this induction is based on all of human history in which every single man who ever lived was ultimately observed to die. That John Smith will be an exception is therefore exceedingly unlikely—in fact, astronomically improbable. But death (or for that matter, taxes) is not an *absolute* certainty in the sense in which deductively arrived truths always are.

In ordinary life, we are usually concerned with probabilities that are much less clear-cut, and evaluating these probabilities is often crucial. Baseball batters have to estimate the likelihood that a pitcher will throw a fast ball; brokers must judge the probability that a certain stock will rise; patients who contemplate elective surgery must do their best to weigh the relevant medical risks. How do people form the relevant probability estimates? And how do they utilize them to decide whether to swing at the pitch, buy the stock, or undergo the surgery? These questions are the province of an area of psychology (and other social sciences) called *decision making.*

COGNITIVE SHORTCUTS FOR ESTIMATING PROBABILITIES

Technically, the probability that a particular event will happen is defined by a ratio: the frequency of that event (for example, the number of times a coin falls "heads") divided by the total number of observations (the number of times the coin is tossed). But in practice we often don't know these frequencies. And even if we do, we often find it difficult to use them properly. According to Amos Tversky and Daniel Kahneman, we instead make use of various heuristics, which as we've seen are rules of thumb, cognitive shortcuts that often serve us well enough. But as Tversky and Kahneman point out, they sometimes lead to serious errors when they are used to estimate likelihoods (Tversky and Kahneman, 1973, 1974).

The representativeness heuristic One such rule of thumb is called the ***representativeness heuristic.*** When people have to make a judgment about the probability that a particular object or event belongs to a certain category, they often do this by comparing the similarity of the particular instance to a prototype of the category (that is, a representative case of that category). As a result, they may seriously misjudge the actual probabilities. A representativeness heuristic often comes into play when we have to make judgments about people. In one study, Kahneman and Tversky presented subjects with the following thumbnail sketch of an individual:

> Jack is a 45-year old man. He is married and has four children. He is generally conservative, careful, and ambitious. He shows no interest in political and social issues and spends most of his time on his many hobbies which include carpentry, sailing, and mathematical puzzles.

One group of subjects was told that this description was drawn at random from a group of seventy engineers and thirty lawyers, and were asked to indicate their judgment of the probability that the person described by the sketch was an engineer. A second group of subjects was given the identical task with only one difference: They were told that the description was drawn at random from a group of seventy lawyers and thirty engineers.

The results showed that both groups estimated that the odds that Jack was an engineer were more than 90 percent. They evidently concluded that the thumbnail sketch described a person with hobbies and interests that were more stereotypical of an engineer than of a lawyer. To that extent Jack seemed more representative of an engineer than of a lawyer. That the subjects took this information into account in making their judgment is not too surprising. What is surprising is that the group that was told that engineers accounted for only 30 percent of all the cases did not take this fact into account at all. It appears that the subjects completely ignored the ***base rate,*** the proportion of the category—here, engineers—that were in the original sample. The concrete description and its similarity to the stereotype overwhelmed all other factors in the estimate (Kahneman and Tversky, 1972, 1973).

The availability heuristic Another rule of thumb used in inductive reasoning is the ***availability heuristic.*** This is a cognitive shortcut for estimating the frequency of certain events by considering how many such events come readily to mind (are currently available to memory). One study involved guesses of how often certain letters appear in different positions in English words. As an example, take the letter *R*. Considering all the words in the language, does it occur more frequently in the first position or in the third position of all the words in the language? Over two-thirds of the subjects said that it is more common in the first than the third position. In actuality the reverse is true. The reason for the errors is availability. The subjects made their judgments by trying to think of words in which *R* is the first letter (e.g., *r*ed, *r*ose, *r*ound) and of words in which it is the third (e.g., er*r*ing, bo*r*ing, ca*r*t, st*r*ong). They then compared the number they managed to generate in each category. But this method leads to a wrong estimate because our memorial dictionary (as well as Webster's) is organized according to the first rather than the third letter in each word. As a result, words that start with an *R* are much more easily retrieved (that is, more available) than those whose third letter is an *R*. As a result, their frequency is seriously overestimated (Tversky and Kahneman, 1973).

The availability heuristic can have serious practical consequences. What are the chances that the stock market will go up tomorrow or that a certain psychiatric patient will commit suicide? The stockbrokers and psychiatrists who have to decide on a particular course of action must base their choice on their estimate of these probabilities. But this estimate is likely to be affected by the availability heuristic. The stockbroker who remembers a few vivid days on which the market went up may overestimate the chances of an upswing; the psychiatrist who remembers one particular patient who unexpectedly slashed his wrists may underestimate the likelihood of eventual recovery of his other patients.

Another example is the assessment of a politician's chances in an election. The people who surround him generally tend to overestimate how well he will do. In part, this may be caused by wishful thinking, but in part it may be another manifestation of the availability heuristic. Evidence comes from statements by the reporters who covered the election campaign of Senator George McGovern, the unsuccessful Democratic candidate for president in 1972. These reporters had spent much of the campaign with McGovern and hardly any with his opponent, the incumbent President Richard Nixon. Senator McGovern lost by a landslide, yet on the night of the election these highly experienced reporters believed that the election would be much closer. The reporters were affected by the enthusiastic crowds of McGovern supporters they had been exposed to. Of course, they knew these were a biased sample, but they couldn't help but be affected anyway. The wildly cheering crowds were much more vivid than the pale statistics of the polls they read (Figure 7.21). This led to an increased availability to memory, which then colored the reporters' estimates of McGovern's national support (Nisbett and Ross, 1980).

7.21 The availability heuristic as a cause of political misjudgment *The photo shows Senator George McGovern surrounded by enthusiastic crowds of supporters during his unsuccessful presidential campaign in 1972. Reporters who covered his campaign mistakenly believed that the election outcome would be much closer than it was. (Photograph by Owen Franken/Stock, Boston)*

BIASES IN JUDGING OUTCOMES: FRAMING

The representativeness and availability heuristics can produce biases in estimates of the probability that some event will occur. Certain other heuristics affect our judgment of the desirability of those events.

One such heuristic is the way the choice is ***framed.*** Consider the following example, in which one group of subjects was presented with this problem:

> Imagine that the U.S. is preparing for the outbreak of an unusual Asian disease, which is expected to kill 600 people. Two alternative programs to combat the disease have been proposed. Assume that the exact scientific estimate of the consequences of the two programs are as follows:
>
> If Program A is adopted, 200 of these people will be saved.
>
> If Program B is adopted, there is 1/3 probability that 600 people will be saved and 2/3 probability that no people will be saved.
>
> Which of the two programs would you favor?

Given this problem 72 percent of the subjects opted for Program A. They preferred the guarantee of 200 lives saved to a one-third chance of saving them all.

The results were quite different for a second group of subjects who were given the same problem but with a different formulation of the two programs, again applied to 600 people. For this group of subjects, the alternatives were:

> If Program A is adopted, 400 people will die.
>
> If Program B is adopted, there is 1/3 probability that nobody will die and 2/3 probability that 600 people will die.

Given this formulation, 78 percent of the subjects chose Program B. To them the certain death of 400 people was less acceptable than a two-thirds probability that all 600 persons would die (Tversky and Kahneman, 1981).

The crucial point here is that the two problems are formally identical. The only difference between them is the way in which the alternative outcomes are framed. In the first case, they are characterized as gains, as "lives saved" (e.g., 200 out of

600). In the second case, they are as characterized losses, as "lives lost" (e.g., 400 out of 600). But these different descriptions obviously have a massive effect. In the first case (gains), they lead to the decision to take a certain gain and avoid any risk. In the second, they lead to the decision to take a risk in order to avoid a certain loss.

The framing process seems to occur in a number of commonplace situations. The most obvious examples concern the marketplace. In these days of paying in plastic, a number of retailers (for example, gas stations) have two prices for the same service or merchandise: one for cash, the other for credit. Retailers generally prefer to describe this price difference as a "cash discount" rather than as a "credit card surcharge." Needless to say, the dollar amount is identical; what differs is which of the two prices is treated as the "normal" reference point. By using the word "discount," the reference standard is the credit card price; as a result, the discount is seen as a gain. Conversely, the term "surcharge" frames the cash price as the reference point; if so, the surcharge is seen as a loss. Since people are more willing to give up gains than to suffer losses, they don't mind paying by credit card and feel that they're getting a bargain if they pay in cash.

A BACKWARD LOOK AT PERCEPTION, MEMORY, AND THINKING

In looking back over the three domains of cognition—perception, memory, and thinking—we can only repeat a note we have struck before. There are no clear boundaries that demark these three domains. In describing perception, we often cross over the border into memory. For the way we perceive familiar objects—let alone such ambiguous figures as the young woman–old woman picture—is based in part on how we perceived them in the past. But perception also shades into thinking. We look at the moon at the horizon, decide that it must be larger than it first appears because it looks farther off, and promptly perceive it in line with this (presumably unconscious) inference. Nor is it clear where memory leaves off and thinking begins. Much of remembering seems like problem solving. We try to recall to whom we lent a certain book, conclude that it has to be Joe, for we know no one else who is interested in the book's topic, and then suddenly have a vivid recollection of the particular occasion on which he borrowed it (and the way he swore that he'd return it right away). But if remembering is sometimes much like thinking, thinking can hardly proceed without reference to the storehouse of memory. Whatever we think about—which route to take on a vacation trip, how to fill out a tax form—requires retrieval of items from various memory systems.

All of this shows that there are no exact boundaries between perception, memory, and thinking. These areas are not sharply separated intellectual domains, with neat lines of demarcation between them. They are simply designations for somewhat different aspects of the general process of cognition. We will now turn to the one aspect of cognition that we have thus far discussed only in passing—language. It, too, is intertwined with the other domains of cognition, but unlike perception, memory, and thinking, which are found in many animals, language is unique to human beings.

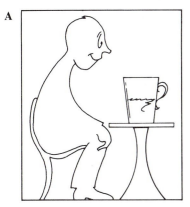

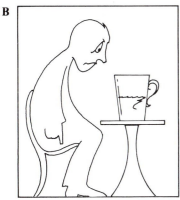

Is the glass half full or half empty? *A hoary version of the framing effect is the contrast between the optimist who regards the glass as half full (a gain) and the pessimist who sees the same glass as half empty (a loss).*

SUMMARY

1. A classical issue in the study of thinking concerns the *elements* that make up thought. According to one view, all thought is necessarily composed of *mental images.* While there is good evidence that some thinking has the picture-like quality of imagery, most psychologists doubt that all thinking is of this kind. They feel that there is another, more abstract and symbolic mode of thinking that involves mental structures such as *concepts* and *propositions.*

2. Considered as an activity, thinking is *directed.* In problem solving, all steps are considered as they fit into the overall structure set up by the task. This structure is typically *hierarchical,* with goals, subordinate subgoals, and so on. This hierarchical structure is not unique to problem solving but may be a general characteristic of any directed activity.

3. Increasing competence at any directed activity goes together with an increase in the degree to which the subcomponents of this activity have become chunked and *automatized.* In learning to send and receive Morse code, as in the attainment of many skills, learning curves exhibit *plateaus,* followed by a later rise, suggesting the acquisition of progressively larger units. Similar chunking seems to occur in many forms of mental activity, including problem solving, and differentiates masters and beginners in many endeavors such as mental calculation, musical composition, and playing chess.

4. Problem solving is not always successful. One reason may be a strong, interfering *mental set,* which makes the subject *rigid* and which is especially hard to overcome under conditions of intense motivation.

5. Investigators of thinking have come up with a few suggestions to overcome obstacles to problem solving. One is *working backwards* from the goal; another is trying to *find an analogy,* yet another is *changing the mental representation* of the problem. Sometimes the solution involves a radical *restructuring* by means of which a misleading set is overcome. Such restructurings may be an important feature of much *creative thinking.* Accounts by prominent writers, composers, and scientists suggest that restructuring often occurs after a period of *incubation.*

6. An influential approach to problem solving comes from work on *artificial intelligence,* which tries to simulate certain aspects of human thinking. A number of solution strategies have been incorporated into several computer programs, including *algorithms* and *heuristics.* Some further extensions feature the use of *expert systems.* Among the limitations of current artificial intelligence programs as an approach to human thinking includes their difficulty in dealing with *ill-defined problems.* Even more important is their lack of *common sense,* a knowledge about many aspects of the world together with an understanding of what is *relevant* to the problem at hand.

7. While the solution of *spatial problems* often depends on mental imagery, it is sometimes based on a more abstract, conceptual form of thinking. Evidence comes from studies which indicate that geographical knowledge is often organized in a conceptual rather than picture-like form.

8. Studies of *deductive reasoning* show that people are prone to various errors in thinking. Errors of reasoning in dealing with *syllogisms* are caused by a number of factors, including the tendency to perform inappropriate logical transformations.

9. In deductive reasoning, the thinker tries to deduce a particular consequence from a general rule or rules. In *inductive reasoning,* the direction is reversed, for here the thinker tries to induce a general rule from particular instances. An initial, tentatively held induction is a *hypothesis.* A number of studies have pointed to a powerful *confirmation bias* that makes subjects seek evidence that will confirm their hypothesis rather than look for evidence that would show their hypothesis to be false.

10. *Decision making* involves the estimation of probabilities and the utilization of these estimates in deciding on a course of action. To make such estimates, people often make use of certain *heuristics.* These are cognitive rules of thumb that often serve us well enough but that may also lead to serious errors. One such rule of thumb is the *representativeness heuristic:* estimating the probability that an object belongs to a category by comparing the object to a prototype of the category while ignoring other factors such as *base rates.* Another rule of thumb is the *availability heuristic:* estimating the frequency of an event by how readily an example of such an event comes to mind.

11. Some heuristics affect the judgment of the desirability of certain events. A major example is the way outcomes are *framed,* which affects whether they are interpreted as gains or as losses.

CHAPTER 8

Language

BY LILA R. GLEITMAN AND HENRY GLEITMAN

When we consider the social forms and physical artifacts of human societies, we are struck by the diversity of cultures in different times and places. Some humans walk on foot, others travel on camels, and still others ride rockets to the moon. But in all communities and all times, humans are alike in having language. This essential connection, between *having language* and *being human,* is one reason why those interested in the nature of human minds have always been particularly intrigued with language.

To philosophers such as Descartes, language was that function which most clearly distinguished between beasts and humans, and was "the sole sign and only certain mark of thought hidden and wrapped up in the body." Descartes held that humans were utterly distinct from the other animals because all humans have language, while no other animals have anything of the sort. But this claim comes up against an immediate objection: There are about 4,000 languages now in use on earth (Comrie, 1987). Obviously, these are different from one another, for the users of one cannot understand the users of another. In what sense, then, can we speak of "language in general" rather than of French or English or Hindi? The answer is that human languages are at bottom much more alike than they seem at first glance to be. For example, all languages convey thought by the same *means:* They all use words and sentences to organize ideas. In contrast, animal communications often have something like words (for instance, a cat can purr happily and hiss angrily), but they never have complicated sentences (such as *I'm going to stop purring and start hissing unless you give me that catnip immediately).*

Another similarity is in the *ideas* human languages can express. When the United Nations ambassador from France makes a speech, numerous translators immediately whisper its equivalent in English, Russian, Arabic, and so on, to the listening ambassadors from other countries. The fact that the French speech can readily be translated suggests that, by and large, the same things that can be said in French can be said in English and Russian as well. This is true despite the fact that the Russian and English listeners may disagree with what the French diplomat is saying. But the translation will allow them to *know* that they disagree, so that they are in a position to stomp out of the room in a rage, or make a counter-

The biblical account of the origin of different languages According to the Bible, all men once spoke a common language. But they built a tall structure, the Tower of Babel, and tried to reach the heavens. To punish them for their pride and folly, God made them unable to understand each other, each group speaking a different language. (Tower of Babel *by Pieter Brueghel, the Elder, c. 1568; courtesy the Kunthistoriches Museum, Vienna)*

speech—which will also be translatable. In our discussion of language, we will use English as our main example. But it is important to keep in mind that what we say about English generally goes for the other human languages as well.

MAJOR PROPERTIES OF HUMAN LANGUAGE

There are five major properties of all human languages that psychology must describe: language is ***creative*** (or ***novel***), it is highly ***structured*** (or ***patterned***), it is ***meaningful,*** it is ***referential*** (that is, it refers to and describes things and events in the real world), and it is ***interpersonal*** or ***communicative*** (involving the thoughts of more than one person at a time).

Language Is Creative

At first glance, language might seem to be merely a complicated habit, a set of acts by ear and mouth that have been learned by memorization and practice. According to this view, the explanation of talking is simple: Each of the memorized speech acts is simply performed whenever the appropriate circumstances arise. Our mothers said *That's a rabbit* when they saw a rabbit. Having observed this, we now say *That's a rabbit* when we see a rabbit. But this position of language as habit is hard to maintain, for speakers can and will utter and understand a great many sentences that they have never uttered or heard before. To see this point, it is only necessary to realize that, in addition to *That's a rabbit,* each of us can also say and understand:

> *That's a rabbit over there.*
> *A rabbit is what I see over there.*
> *Obviously, that's a rabbit.*
> *How clearly I recall that the word for that animal is* rabbit.
> *Well bless my soul, if that isn't a rabbit!*

And so on, with hundreds of other examples. A little child who has memorized all these sentences must be industrious indeed. But the situation is really incredibly more complicated than this, for we can talk about objects and creatures other than rabbits, including aardvarks and Afghans, apples and armies, and proceeding all the way to zebras and Zyzzogetons.

Furthermore, the sheer number of English sentences rules out habit as the explanation for language use. A good estimate of the number of reasonably short (20 words or fewer) English sentences is 10^{30}. Considering the fact that there are only 3×10^9 seconds in a century, a learner memorizing a new sentence every second would have learned only a minute fraction of them in the course of a lifetime. But the fact is that we can all say and understand most of them (Postal, 1968).

In sum, we effortlessly create and interpret new sentences on the spot. Only a very few such as *How are you?*, *What's new?*, and *Have a nice day* are said and heard with any frequency. All the rest are at least partly new—new to the person who says them and new to his listeners as well. To express all the thoughts, we combine a limited—though large—number of words into sentences. Thus language is a system that allows us to reach a limitless end from limited means: Our stock of memorized, meaningful words is finite, but we nevertheless have the capacity to speak of an infinite number of new things and events. We can do so because our language system allows us to combine the old words in novel ways.

Language Is Structured

While language use is creative in the sense that we can and do invent new sentences all the time, it is also restricted: There are unlimited numbers of strings of English words that—accidents aside—we would never utter. For example, we do not say *Is rabbit a that* or *A rabbit that's* even though these are fairly comprehensible ways to say *That's a rabbit*. Speakers construct their utterances in accord with certain abstract principles of language structure. These **structural principles** underlie the way in which we combine words to make up new sentences, and they are honored by every normal individual—without special thought and without any formal training in school. These principles are generally not known consciously, but are *implicit*. Even so, they govern our use of language and allow us to compose and understand boundless new sentences.

We should point out that the structural principles of language (sometimes called **descriptive rules**) have to be distinguished from certain **prescriptive rules** handed down from various authorities about how they think we *ought* to speak or write. Prescriptive rules are the so-called "rules of grammar" that many of us learned painfully at school in the fourth grade (and thankfully forgot in the fifth), such as "Never say ain't" or "A sentence cannot end with a preposition." These recipes for speech and writing often do not conform to the actual facts about natural talking and understanding. For example, most of us have no qualms about ending sentences with a preposition (as in the sentence, *Who did you give the packages to?*) or even two prepositions (as in *What in the world are you up to?*). In some cases it sounds rather odd not to do so, as Winston Churchill pointed out when spoofing this "rule" by insisting that *This is the kind of language up with which I will not put!*

The **structural principles** we will be concerned with in this chapter are those that every normal speaker honors without effort or formal instruction—for example, the principle by which we invariably say *the rabbit* rather than *rabbit the*. It is these regularities that are fundamental to understanding language as a universal human skill. In fact, most human cultures outside of America and Western Europe do not have prescriptions for "proper" speech at all.

The power of an "H" *A scene from the stage version of* My Fair Lady, *in which the cockney flower girl, Eliza (Julie Andrews) is taught by Henry Higgins (Rex Harrison) how to pronounce an "H" the way the British upper classes do. She thus becomes a lady. This shows that following prescriptive rules can sometimes confer important social advantages (Labov, 1970: photograph by Leonard McCombe/LIFE MAGAZINE, © Time Warner, Inc.)*

Language Is Meaningful

Each word in a language expresses a meaningful idea (or concept) about some thing (e.g., *camera* or *rabbit*), action (*run* or *rotate*), abstraction (*justice* or *fun*), quality (*red* or *altruistic*), and so on. The purpose of language is to express all these meanings to others, so we have no choice but to learn a conventional word for each.

But people talk in whole sentences rather than just one word at a time. This is because the grammatical patterns that we discussed in the previous section also contribute to meaningfulness. For example, the words *dogs, cats, bite* express very different meaningful thoughts depending on how they are put together: *Dogs bite cats,* or *Cats bite dogs.*

Language Is Referential

Language users know more than how to put words together into meaningful and grammatical sentences. They also know which words refer to which things, scenes, and events in the world. If a child said *"That's a shoe"* (a sentence whose grammar is impeccable and whose meaning is transparent) but did so while pointing to a rhinoceros, we would not think she had learned English very effectively. This is the problem of ***reference:*** how to use language to describe the world of real things and events—saying *shoe* to make reference to a shoe, but saying *rhinoceros* to refer to a rhinoceros.

Language Is Interpersonal

Many aspects of human language are within the individual and are thus the property of each single human mind. But language is a process that goes beyond the individual, for it is a social activity in which the thoughts of one mind are conveyed to another. To accomplish these social ends, each speaker must know not only the sounds, words, and sentences of his language, but also certain ***principles of conversation.*** These principles govern the way in which language is used appropriately under varying circumstances.

Suppose, for example, that one sees a lion in the parlor and wants to tell a companion about this. It is not enough that both parties speak English. One has to estimate the listener's mental state, capacities, motivations, and relations to oneself in order to speak appropriately. If the companion is a sharpshooter with a revolver, one might say:

Quick, shoot! There is a lion in the parlor.

But if the companion is an artist, one might say:

Quick, draw! Lion of a gorgeous shade of ochre in the parlor.

To a biologist, one might say:

Quick, look! Member of the genus Felis leo *in the parlor.*

And to an enemy,

Lovely morning, isn't it? See you later.

Clearly, what one says about a situation is not just a description of that situation, but depends upon one's knowledge, beliefs, and wishes about the listener. To communicate successfully, then, one must build a mental picture of "the other" to whom speech is addressed (Grice, 1968; Searle, 1969; Clark, H., 1978; Prince, E., 1981; Sperber and Wilson, 1986; Schiffrin, 1988).

THE STRUCTURE OF LANGUAGE

All human languages are organized as a hierarchy of structures. At the bottom of the hierarchy, each language consists of little snippets of sound; and at the other end, of sentences and conversations. We will begin by describing the basic building blocks: the 40 or so phonemes, the 80,000 or so morphemes, and the hundreds of thousands of words.

Phonemes

To speak, we move the various parts of the vocal apparatus from one position to another in a rapid sequence while expelling a column of air up from the lungs and out through the mouth (see Figure 8.1). Each of these movements shapes the column of air from the lungs differently, and thus produces a distinctive speech sound (MacNeilage, 1972). Many of these differences among speech sounds are ignored by the listener. Consider the word *bus,* which can be pronounced with more or less of a hiss in the *s.* This difference is irrelevant to the listener, who interprets what was heard to mean 'a large vehicle' in either case. But some sound distinctions do matter, for they signal differences in meaning. Thus neither *butt* nor *fuss* will be taken to mean 'a large vehicle.' This suggests that the distinctions among *s, f,* and *t* sounds are relevant to speech perception, while the difference in hiss magnitude is not. The distinctions that are perceived to matter are called **phonemes.** They are the perceptual units of which speech is composed (Liberman, 1970; see Figure 8.2, which illustrates the entire hierarchy of linguistic structures).

Children can learn to pronounce a couple of hundred different speech sounds clearly and reliably. But each language restricts itself to using only some of them.

8.1 The human vocal tract *Speech is produced by the air flow from the lungs which passes through the larynx (popularly called the voice box) containing the vocal cords and from there through the oral and nasal cavities which together make up the vocal tract. Different vowels are created by movements of the lips and tongue which change the size and shape of the vocal cavity. Consonants are produced by various articulatory movements which temporarily obstruct the air flow through the vocal tract. For some consonants the air flow is stopped completely. Examples are* p, *where the stoppage is produced by bringing both lips together, and* t, *where it is produced by bringing the tip of the tongue to the back of the upper teeth. Some other consonants are created by blocking the air flow only partially, for example* th *(as in* thick*), produced by bringing the tip of the tongue close to the upper teeth but without actually touching. (After Lieberman, 1975)*

Labels on figure: Palate; Dental consonant region; Nasal cavity; Lips; Tongue; Vocal cords (Larynx); Soft palate; Oral cavity

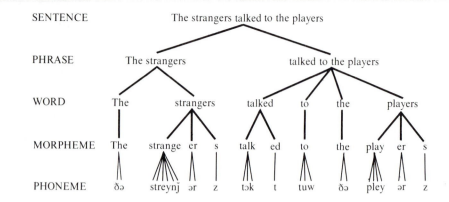

SENTENCE	The strangers talked to the players
PHRASE	The strangers · talked to the players
WORD	The · strangers · talked · to · the · players
MORPHEME	The · strange · er · s · talk · ed · to · the · play · er · s
PHONEME	ðə · streynj · ər · z · tɔk · t · tuw · ðə · pley · ər · z

8.2 The hierarchy of linguistic structures *Every sentence is composed of phrases, which are composed of morphemes (simple units of meaning such as* strange *and the plural* -s*), which in turn are composed of phonemes (the units of speech sound, such as* p *and* ə*). The phonemes are described by symbols from the phonetic alphabet because English spelling is not always true to the sounds of words.*

Noam Chomsky

English uses about forty.* Other languages select differently from among the possible phonemes. For instance, German uses certain gutteral sounds that are never heard in English, and French uses some vowels that are different from the English ones.

As speakers of a language, we have learned the phonemes that constitute its sound elements. But we have learned something further as well—the way these phonemes can be combined into words. Some of these choices are a matter of historical accident. For instance, English happens to have a word *pledge,* composed phonemically of the sounds p-l-e-j. But it does not happen to have a word *medge,* composed of m-e-j. But some of the facts about how phonemes combine in words are systematic rather than accidental choices.

To see this point, consider the task of an advertising executive who tries to find a name for a new breakfast food. She will have to find some sequence of phonemes that has not already been used to mean something else. Will any new arrangement of phonemes do? The answer is no. To begin with, some, such as *gogrps* or *fpibs,* would be hard to pronounce. But even among phoneme sequences that can be pronounced, some seem somehow un-Englishlike. Consider the following possibilities: *Pritos, Glitos,* and *Tlitos.* They can all be pronounced, but one seems wrong: *Tlitos.* English speakers sense intuitively that English words never start with *tl,* even though this sequence is perfectly acceptable in the middle of a word (as in *motley* or *battling*). So the new breakfast food will be marketed as tasty, crunchy *Pritos* or *Glitos.* Either of these two names will do, but *Tlitos* is out of the question.The restriction against *tl*-beginnings is not a restriction on what human tongues and ears can do. For instance, one Northwest Indian language is named *Tlingit,* obviously by people who are perfectly willing to have words begin with *tl.* This shows that the restriction is a structural principle of English specifically. Few of us are conscious of this principle, but we have learned it and similar principles exceedingly well, for we honor them in our actual language use (Chomsky and Halle, 1968).

Morphemes and Words

At the next level of the linguistic hierarchy (see Figure 8.2), fixed sequences of phonemes are joined into morphemes. The ***morphemes*** are the smallest language units that carry bits of meaning. Some words consist of a single morpheme, such as *and, run,* or *strange.* But many morphemes cannot stand alone and must be joined with others to make up a complex word. Examples are *er* (meaning 'one

* The English alphabet provides only twenty-six symbols (letters) to write these forty phonemes, so it often uses the same symbol for more than one. Thus, the letter *O* stands for two different sounds in *hot* and *cold,* an "ah" sound and an "oh" sound. This fact contributes to the difficulty of learning how to read English.

who') and *s* (meaning 'more than one'). When these are joined with the morpheme *strange* (meaning 'alien' or 'odd') into the complex word *strangers* (*strange + er + s*), the meaning becomes correspondingly complex ('ones who are odd or alien'). Each of these morphemes has a fixed position within the word. Thus *er* has to follow *strange* and precede *s*; other orders (such as *erstranges* or *strangeser*) are not allowed (Aranoff, 1976).

The morphemes such as *strange* that carry the main burden of meaning are called **content morphemes.** The morphemes that add details to the meaning but also serve various grammatical purposes (such as the suffix *er* or the connecting word *and*) are called **function morphemes.**

The average speaker of English has acquired about 80,000 morphemes by adulthood (Miller and Gildea, 1987), knows the meaning of each, and how they are positioned within words. If we counted vocabulary by words rather than morphemes, normal people would be credited with several hundred thousand of these, for then *strange, stranger, strangers,* etc., would each count as a separate item.

Phrases and Sentences

Just as a morpheme is an organized grouping of phonemes, and a word is an organized grouping of morphemes, so a **phrase** is an organized grouping of words. Phrases are the building blocks of which sentences are composed. Consider the sentence

The French bottle smells.

This sentence is **ambiguous:** It can be understood in two ways depending on how the words are grouped into phrases; either

(The French bottle) (smells).

or   *(The French) (bottle) (smells).*

Thus by the choice of phrasing (that is, word grouping), the word *bottle* comes out a noun in the first interpretation, so that sentence is telling us something about French bottles. But *bottle* comes out a verb in the next interpretation, in which case the sentence is telling us about what the French put into bottles—namely, smells (that is, perfumes). For another example, see Figure 8.3.

The phrase is thus the unit that organizes words into meaningful groupings within the sentence. Just as for phoneme sequences and morpheme sequences, some phrase sequences (like those we just considered) are acceptable, while others are outlawed; for example, *(The French) (smells) (bottle).*

The term **syntax** (from the Greek, *arranging together*) is the name for the system that arranges (or groups) words together into meaningful phrases and sentences. This topic has been extensively investigated by the American linguist, Noam Chomsky (Chomsky, 1957, 1975, 1980, 1987; for overviews of syntactic theory, see Newmeyer, 1983; Sells, 1985; Radford, 1988).

8.3   How phrase structure can affect meaning   *On being asked what a Mock Turtle is, the Queen tells Alice "It's the thing Mock Turtle Soup is made from."   Needless to say, this is a misanalysis of the phrase* mock turtle soup *as (mock turtle) (soup). It ought to be organized as* (mock) (turtle soup)—*a soup that is not really made out of turtles (and is in fact usually made out of veal). (Lewis Carroll,* Alice in Wonderland, *1865/1969, p. 73)*

THE LINGUISTIC HIERARCHY AND MEANING

We have seen that language consists of a small number of sound units (the forty or so phonemes) organized into fixed sequences (the 80,000 or so morphemes and hundreds of thousands of words), which in turn are organized into the boundless number of sentences. In sum, as we ascend the linguistic ladder there are more and more units at every level. How can the human mind deal with this ever-expanding number of items? There is only one possible answer. We don't learn the billions of sentences in the first place. Instead, we acquire generalizations that allow us to construct any sentence: the structural principles and the principles of conversation.

But why do humans go to the trouble of acquiring language? The answer, of course, is just that it allows us to convey boundless thoughts from one human mind to another human mind. Of primary interest, then, are the higher-level units and patterns of language: the meaningful words, phrases, and sentences. In the following sections, therefore, we will take up the questions of word and sentence meaning in detail.

The Meaning of Words

The question, "What do words mean?" is one of the knottiest in the whole realm of language (see Putnam, 1975; Fodor, 1983; 1988). The subfield that deals with this question, **semantics,** has thus far been able to give only a few, rather tentative answers. As so often, the first step is to eliminate some of the answers that appear to be false.

MEANING AS REFERENCE

One of the oldest approaches to the topic equates word and phrase meaning with **reference.** According to this position, the meaning of a word or phrase is whatever it refers to in the world. Thus this view asserts that words and certain phrases are essentially names. Proper names such as *Steffi Graf, Australia,* and the *Eiffel Tower* are labels for a particular person, place, and object. The reference theory of meaning claims that expressions such as *tennis player, continent,* and *building* function in a similar manner. According to this view, the only difference between such expressions and true proper names is that the former are more general: *tennis player* refers to various male and female players and to champions as well as duffers; *Steffi Graf* refers to one player and no one else.

The reference theory of meaning runs into several difficulties. One is that some words or phrases are perfectly meaningful even though it is hard to know exactly what they refer to. Some of these are abstract expressions such as *justice, infinity,* and *historical inevitability.* One cannot point to a real "infinity" somewhere out there in the world. Others are imaginary, such as *unicorn* and *the crown prince of South Dakota,* which presumably have no real-world referents at all. Yet these expressions do not seem to be "meaningless" or "semantically empty."

A famous example of the distinction between meaning and reference was pointed out by the German philosopher, Gottlob Frege (1892): The expression *the morning star* has one meaning (namely, 'the last star visible in the eastern sky as dawn breaks'), and the expression *the evening star* has quite a different meaning (namely, 'the first star visible in the western sky as the sun sets'). Yet both of these expressions refer to one and the same object in the sky (namely, the planet Venus). Thus two expressions can have different meanings and yet refer to the same thing. It follows that there is a distinction between the meaning of a word or phrase and the things that this word or phrase refers to in the world. The meaning of a word is the idea or concept that it expresses. The referents of the word are all those things in the real (or imaginary) world that fall under that concept.

THE DEFINITIONAL THEORY OF MEANING

Most theories of word meaning assert that only a relative handful of the words in a language describe elementary "simple" concepts. The rest are labels for bundles

Is this the entry for bird in your mental dictionary? **bird** *n. [ME, fr. OE bridd]. Any of a class (Aves) of warm-blooded vertebrates distinguished by having the body more or less completely covered with feathers and the forelimbs modified as wings.*

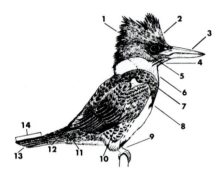

bird 2 (kingfisher): 1 *crest,* 2 *crown,* 3 *bill,* 4 *throat,* 5 *auricular region,* 6 *breast,* 7 *scapulars,* 8 *abdomen,* 9 *tarsus,* 10 *upper wing coverts,* 11 *primaries,* 12 *secondaries,* 13 *rectrix,* 14 *tail (Webster's 9th Collegiate Dictionary)*

Can a white rose be red? *The Queen had ordered the gardeners to plant a red rose bush but they planted a white one by mistake. They're now trying to repair their error by painting the white roses red. On the definitional theory of meaning, this seems reasonable enough. For the expressions* red rose bush *and* white rose bush *differ by only a single feature—red versus white. But if so, why are they so terrified that the Queen will discover what they did? (From Lewis Carroll,* Alice in Wonderland, *1865/1969, p. 62)*

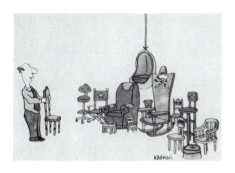

"Attention, everyone! I'd like to introduce the newest member of our family."
(Drawing by Kaufman; © 1977 The New Yorker Magazine, Inc.)

of concepts. Thus the words *feathers, flies, animal, wings* might describe simple concepts, but all of these ideas are bundled together in the (relatively) complex word *bird.* One approach of this kind is the **definitional theory of meaning.** It holds that meanings are analyzable into a set of subcomponents, organized in our minds much as they are in standard dictionaries. This approach starts out with the fact that there are various meaning relationships among different words and phrases. Some words are similar in meaning *(wicked-evil),* others are opposites *(wicked-good),* still others seem virtually unrelated *(wicked-ultramarine).* According to the definitional proposal, these relationships can be explained by assuming that words are **bundles of semantic features** (Katz and Fodor, 1963; Katz, 1972). As an example, take the word *bachelor.* This word clearly has something in common with *uncle, brother, gander,* and *stallion.* As speakers of English, we know that all of these words carry the notion *male.* This point is forcefully made by considering various sentences that most English speakers will regard as odd. Thus, the sentence *My _____ is pregnant* sounds very peculiar if the missing word is any of the members of the bachelor-related group listed below:

	uncle	
	brother	
My	gander	is pregnant.
	stallion	
	bachelor	

Demonstrations of this sort suggest that words like *stallion* and *bachelor* are not simple in meaning, but rather are composed of a number of meaning atoms—the semantic features. For *bachelor,* these might be 'never married,' 'human,' 'adult,' and 'male'; for *stallion,* they would include 'adult,' 'male,' and 'horse.' Words like *stallion* and *bachelor* will be perceived to be related because when an individual looks up the features for each of these words in her mental dictionary, she will find that the meaning atom 'male' is listed for both of them. Taken together, the semantic features constitute a definition of a word. According to this theory, we carry such definitions in our heads as the meanings of words.

THE PROTOTYPE THEORY OF MEANING

The definitional theory faces a problem, for some members of a meaning category appear to exemplify that category better than others do. Thus a German shepherd seems to be a more doglike *dog* than a Pekinese, and an armchair seems to be a better example of the concept of *furniture* than a reading lamp. This seems to be at odds with the analysis we have described thus far, whose aim was to specify the necessary and sufficient attributes that *define* a concept. When a dictionary says that a bachelor is "an adult human male who has never been married," it claims to have said it all. Whatever fits under the umbrella of this definitional feature list is a bachelor. Whatever does not, is not. But if so, how can one bachelor be more bachelorlike (or one dog more doglike) than another?

The question is whether the semantic categories described by words are really as all-or-none as the definitional theory would have it. Several investigators have made a strong case for an alternative view, called the **theory of prototypes** (Rosch, 1973b; Rosch and Mervis, 1975; Smith and Medin, 1981).

The facts that the prototype theory tries to account for can easily be illustrated. Close your eyes and try to imagine a bird. It is pretty safe to guess that you just imagined something like a robin or sparrow, not a buzzard, ostrich, or goose. There is something quintessentially *birdy* about a robin, while a goose does not seem such a good example of a bird. The definitional theory would have considerable trouble explaining why this is so. According to this theory, some feature or features associated with the concept *bird* (such as 'has feathers,' 'lays eggs,' 'flies,' 'chirps') are both necessary and sufficient to pick out all birds and only birds. But

233

8.4 The Smith brothers and their family resemblance *The Smith brothers are related through family resemblance, though no two brothers share all features. The one who has the greatest number of the family attributes is the most prototypical. In the example, it is Brother 9, who has all the family features: brown hair, large ears, large nose, moustache, and eyeglasses. (Courtesy Sharon Armstrong)*

if geese and robins are both said to be birds because they share these necessary and sufficient features, what makes the robin more birdy than the goose?

According to the prototype theory, the answer is that the meaning of many words is described as a whole set of features, no one of which is individually either necessary or sufficient. The concept is then held together by a ***family resemblance structure*** (Wittgenstein, 1953). Consider the way in which members of a family resemble each other. Joe may look like his father to the extent that he has his eyes. His sister Sue may look like her father to the extent that she has his nose. But Joe and Sue may have no feature in common (he has his grandfather's nose and she has Aunt Fanny's eyes), and so the two of them do not look alike at all. But even so, the two are physically related through a family resemblance, for each bears some resemblance to their father (see Figure 8.4).

In sum, a family resemblance structure is like a collection of attributes. Probably no single member of the family will have them all. Nor will any two members of a family have the same ones (except for identical twins). But all will have at least some. Some individuals will have many of the family features. They are often called the "real Johnsons" or "prototypical Smiths." They are the best exemplars of the family resemblance structure because they have, say, the most Johnson-attributes and the least Jones-attributes. Other family members are marginal. They have only the nose or the little freckle behind the left ear.

Many investigators believe that what holds for the Smiths and the Johnsons may hold for many word concepts, such as *bird,* as well. Thus, contrary to our first guess, not all birds fly (ostriches don't fly). And not everything that lays eggs is a bird (giant tortoises lay eggs). Not all birds chirp (crows do not chirp, they caw), and some chirpers (crickets) are not birds. What are we left with from our list of defining features? Nothing but a pile of feathers! But feathers alone do not make something a bird. Hats have feathers too.

According to prototype theorists, birdiness is largely a matter of the total number of bird features a given creature exhibits. No one of these features is necessary and none is sufficient, but animals that have few (such as penguins and ostriches) will be judged to be poor members of the bird family, while those that have many (such as robins) will seem to be exemplary members. According to the theory, these judgments are based on a comparison with an internal ***prototype*** of the concept. Such prototypes represent mental averages of all the various examples of the concept the person has encountered.

Evidence for the prototype view comes from the fact that when people are asked to come up with typical examples of some category, they generally produce instances that are close to the presumed prototype (e.g., *robin* rather than *ostrich*). A related result concerns the time required to verify category membership. Subjects respond more quickly to the sentence *A robin is a bird* than to *An ostrich is a bird* (Rosch et al., 1976; for a related discussion, see Chapter 6).

COMBINING DEFINITIONAL AND PROTOTYPE DESCRIPTIONS

It appears that both the definitional and the prototype approaches to word meaning have something to offer. The prototype view helps us to understand why robins are better birds than ostriches. But the definitional theory explains why an ostrich is nevertheless recognized as a bird (Miller and Johnson-Laird, 1976; Smith and Medin, 1981; Armstrong, Gleitman, and Gleitman, 1983).

Organizing Words into Meaningful Sentences

While individual words describe things, events, and so forth, the word groups that constitute phrases describe the endless varieties of complex categories for which the 80,000 words would be insufficient. Thus, once in a lifetime, we might want

A grammar lesson at the Mad Hatter's Tea Party *The meanings of words change in different linguistic constructions, so grammatical patterns are of great importance for communication.*
March Hare: *"You should say what you mean."*
Alice: *"I do—at least I mean what I say—that's the same thing, you know."*
Hatter: *"Not the same thing a bit! Why, you might just as well say that 'I see what I eat' is the same thing as 'I eat what I see'!"*
March Hare: *"You might just as well say that 'I like what I get' is the same thing as 'I get what I like.' "*
(From Lewis Carroll, Alice in Wonderland, *1865/1969, p. 44)*

to speak of *three of the spotted ostriches on Joe Smith's farm.* We could not possibly memorize enough word items for all such complex categories that we could construct and might want to talk about, so we combine the words together in patterned ways to express our more complex concepts.

Sentence meanings are even more complex. They have to do with the various relations *among* the concepts that we want to express. Basic sentences introduce some concept that they are about (this is called the ***subject of the sentence)*** and then ***propose*** or ***predicate*** something of that concept (called the ***predicate of the sentence***). Thus when we say *The boy hit the ball,* we introduce *the boy* as the subject or topic, and then we propose or predicate of the boy that he *hit the ball.* This is why sentence meanings are often called ***propositions:*** *The boy hit the ball* proposes (of the boy) that he hit the ball.

More generally, a simple proposition is usefully thought about as a sort of miniature drama in which the verb is the action and the nouns are the performers, each playing a different role. In our proposition about *boy-hitting-ball, the boy* is the "doer," *the ball* is the "done-to," and *hit* is the action itself. The job of a listener is much like that of a playgoer. The playgoer must determine which actors are portraying the various roles in the drama, and what the plot (the action) is. Similarly, for each of the millions of heard sentences, the listener must discover exactly who did what to whom (Healy and Miller, 1970). To do so, listeners must first understand the structure of the sentence (Fillmore, 1968; Jackendoff, 1987; Rappaport and Levin, 1988).

PHRASE STRUCTURE

Consider again the simple sentence *The boy hit the ball.* It seems to be naturally organized into two main phrases. One is a ***noun phrase*** *(the boy)* and the other is a ***verb phrase*** *(hit the ball).* Linguists use a ***tree diagram*** (so called because of its

8.5 The structure of the sentence
The boy hit the ball *This tree is called a phrase-structure description, for it shows how the sentence can be analyzed into phrase units. Notice particularly that there are two noun phrases in this sentence: one noun phrase* (the ball) *is part of the verb phrase* (hit the ball); *the other noun phrase* (the boy) *is not part of the verb phrase. A description of this kind also shows the word class types (e.g., noun, verb) of which each phrase consists. Finally, it shows the words of the sentence. Reading these (the bottom row in the tree) from left to right, we get the actual sequence of words in the sentence being described. Thus (in its bottom row) the tree describes the actual words that speakers say and listeners hear.*

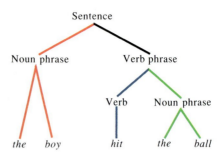

branching appearance) to convey this partitioning of sentences into parts:

The tree diagram notation is a useful way of showing that sentences can be thought of as a hierarchy of structures (see Figure 8.2). Each sentence can be broken down into phrases, which can in turn be broken down into words. The descending branches of the tree correspond to the smaller and smaller units of sentence structure. The whole tree structure is called a **phrase structure description** of the sentence.

Figure 8.5 shows the phrase structure of the example sentence *The boy hit the ball.* At the very top of the tree this description asserts that the example is a sentence; at the bottom it is a string of words, and in between it is a sequence of phrases, subphrases, and word-class names (e.g., *noun* and *verb*).

UNDERSTANDING SIMPLE SENTENCES

What is the point of the formal diagrams of phrase structure as described by linguists and depicted in Figure 8.5? The answer is that if sentences are organized mentally just as they are in these diagrams, the listener can identify the characters in the sentence drama of who-did-what-to-whom by inspecting the subparts of the diagram. Inspecting Figure 8.5, the doer is whoever played this role:

sentence
noun phrase

Looking at this part of the tree in Figure 8.5 (red), we see that *the boy* was the doer. The done-to is whoever played this role:

verb phrase
noun phrase

Looking at this part of the tree in Figure 8.5 (green), we find that *the ball* was the done-to. But what was the action? Whatever occupies this place in the tree:

Looking at this part of the tree (blue), we see that *hit* was the action. Thus the phrase analysis of sentences is more than just a depiction of their parts. It begins to show how mental computations can inform the listener of what the speaker meant by the string of words she uttered. Figure 8.6 shows the structure as the listener would interpret it according to these semantic roles.

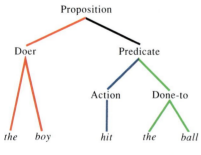

8.6 From structure to meaning *The drama of who-did-what-to-whom as reconstructed by the listener from the structure in Figure 8.5.*

Lewis Carroll's poignant tale of how an animal's mind would be different if it had language   Alice came to a forest where nothing had a name. She met a fawn that walked trustingly by her side: "So they walked together through the wood, Alice with her arms clasped lovingly around the soft neck of the Fawn, till they came out into another open field [where things had names]. And here the Fawn gave a sudden bound into the air, and shook itself free of Alice's arm. 'I'm a Fawn!' it cried out in a voice of delight. 'And dear me! You're a human child!' A sudden look of alarm came into his beautiful brown eyes, and in another moment it had darted away at full speed." (Carroll, Through the Looking Glass, *1871/1946, p. 227).*

THE GROWTH OF LANGUAGE IN THE CHILD

Now that we have surveyed the boundless forms and contents of language, it seems impossible that any save the most brilliant person could possibly learn it. Yet we know that language is as natural and inevitable a part of human nature as chirping is to birds, roaring is to lions, and barking is to dogs. Whatever their talent, their motivation, or their station in life, normal children learn their native tongue to a high level of proficiency during the preschool years. This holds for children reared in poverty on the streets of New York and in the deserts of North Africa as much as it does for British upper-class children reared by nannies and sent to posh nursery schools.

Still, language seems to pose awesome problems for the mere babes who must learn it. It is not even obvious which sounds are relevant and which can be ignored. The infant listening to adults is exposed to an enormous jumble of sounds. Some of these sounds constitute speech, but others are coughs, hums, whistles, and even animal imitations ("and the big cow said 'Mooooooooo' "). How does the learner ever sort through this jumble of noise to discover which of the sounds she hears are speech sounds and which are not?

It is clear that the young language learner is confronted with a confusing welter of sounds and information about the world. But she somehow makes sense out of all this jumble even so. If she is a learner of English, she extracts the general fact that the sound "see" means 'gaze with the eyes'; if she is a learner of Spanish, she extracts the different fact that the same sound "see" (as in "Si!") means 'yes.' The question is how.

Is Language Learning the Acquisition of a Skill?

Language learning is more than mere imitation. It is true that young children say "dog" and not "perro" or "chien" if they are exposed to English, so in this sense they are imitating the language community around them. But the real trick in word learning and use is creative: The word *dog* must apply to new dogs that the learners see. What served as a label for the pet bulldog must apply to the neighborhood poodle as well.

What goes for words goes for sentences too. Young children utter sentences they have never heard before. For instance, a mother may say to her child "I love you, Jane." But in response Jane may say "I hate you, Mommy" or "I'm going to crayon a face on this wall." These sentences are clear, though unwelcome, creative language acts of Jane's. They could not possibly have been learned by imitation.

Another popular hypothesis about language learning is that it is based on explicit *correction* or *reinforcement* by parents. According to this view, grammatical mistakes are immediately pointed out to the young learner, who subsequently avoids them. But in fact, this hypothesis is false (Morgan and Travis, 1989). In actual practice, mistakes in grammar and pronunciation generally go unremarked, as in the following exchange:

> 2-year-old: Mamma isn't boy, he a girl.
> Mother: That's right.

The situation is quite different if the child makes an error of fact. In that case, the mother often does provide a correction:

> 2-year-old: And Walt Disney comes on Tuesday.
> Mother: No, he does not.

(Brown and Hanlon, 1970)

These findings are perfectly reasonable. Parents are out to create socialized and rational beings, not little grammarians, and so they correct errors of conduct and fact, not errors of grammar.

LANGUAGE DEVELOPMENT

As we have just seen, imitation, correction, and reinforcement can't bear too much of the burden in explaining language learning. Children don't come to the task of acquiring their native tongue as little robots who can only notice and copy whatever they hear, whenever they hear it. How then are we to explain the growth of speech and comprehension? We will begin by tracing the child's progress during the first few years of life.

The Social Origins of Language

Infants begin to vocalize from the first moments of life. They cry, coo, and babble. They make sounds such as "ga" and "bagoo" that sound very much like words—except that these babbles have no conventional meaning. This vocaliza-

Social origins of speech   (Photograph by Erika Stone)

tion soon takes on a social quality, for three-month-olds will vocalize more when an adult vocalizes to them (Collis, 1975; Bloom, K., 1988).

Though true speech is absent in the first year of life, prelinguistic children have their own ways of making contact with the minds, emotions, and social behaviors of others. Quite early in life, babies begin to exchange looks, caresses, and touches with caregivers. Several investigators have suggested that these gestures are precursors and organizers of the language development to follow. The idea is that the gesture-and-babble interaction helps children to become linguistically socialized; to realize, for instance, that each participant in a conversation "takes a turn" and responds to the other (Bruner, 1974/1975; Sinclair, 1970, 1973).

Thus language knowledge is essentially social and interpersonal from the beginning. Though the capacity to learn it is built into the individual brain of the child, specific knowledge of a particular language requires social interactions between more than one person at a time. To speak to another, one has to have an idea—no matter how primitive—that the other lives in the same, mutually perceived, world (Bates, 1976; Bates and MacWhinney, 1982).

Infants' Discovery of the Phonemes

We have previously seen that all languages are built out of a few basic sound distinctions: the phonemes. But these linguistic sound atoms vary somewhat from language to language. Thus in English, there is a crucial difference between "l" and "r" (as in *lob* vs. *rob*). Though physically these sounds are quite similar, each of them falls within a different phoneme in English, whose speakers have no trouble producing and perceiving the distinction. In contrast, this distinction has no linguistic significance in Japanese, where "l" and "r" sounds fall within the same phoneme. In consequence, Japanese speakers can neither produce nor perceive a distinction between them. How does the infant learn which sound distinctions are the phonemes of his language?

The answer is that initially infants respond to just about all sound distinctions made in any language. They discover the phonemes of their native tongue by *learning to ignore* the distinctions that don't matter. Their first step in understanding, say, Japanese, is to learn not to become speakers of all the other 4,000 languages on earth (Jusczyk, 1985).

Evidence comes from studies which show that two-month-old babies can distinguish between such sounds as "ba" and "pa," "la" and "ra," and so forth. The experimenters used a version of the habituation method (see Chapter 13; pp. 367–68). The babies were given a pacifier, and whenever they sucked on it the syllable "ba" was broadcast over a loudspeaker. The infants quickly learned that their sucking led to the sound, and they began sucking faster and faster to hear it some more. After awhile, the babies habituated to the "ba" sound and their sucking rate diminished. At this point, the experimenters changed the broadcast sound from "ba" to "pa." The babies now started to suck again at a rapid rate. They had become dishabituated. This result indicates that they could discriminate between the two sounds (see Figure 8.7; Eimas, Siqueland, Jusczyk, and Vigorito, 1971).

Infants in the first year of life are sensitive to just about every contrast that occurs in *any* human language, but their sensitivity to foreign contrasts diminishes significantly by twelve months of age (Werker and Tees, 1984). This is consistent with the idea that infants must be prepared by nature to learn any language on earth. After all, they arrive without a passport that tells them which language they are going to hear. But the diminished sensitivities of twelve-month-olds suggest that babies recalibrate their perceptions just as true speech and un-

A

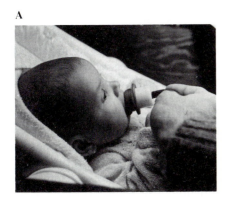

B

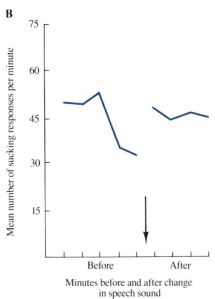

Minutes before and after change in speech sound

8.7 Sucking rate and speech perception in the infant   (A) An infant sucks to hear "pa" or "ba." (Photograph courtesy of Philip Morse, Boston University) (B) The graph shows the sucking rate of four-month-olds to "pa" or "ba." The infants soon become habituated, and the sucking rate drops. When a new stimulus is substituted ("ba" for "pa" and "pa" for "ba"), the infant dishabituates and sucks quickly once again. The point of the shift is indicated by the arrow. (From Eimas, Siqueland, Jusczyk, and Vigorito, 1971) Similar results have been obtained for one-month-olds.

worse for these words. Thus the child now overgeneralizes the use of certain structures. (For an alternative view, see Rumelhart and McClelland, 1986; for discussion, see Pinker and Prince, A., 1988).

Further Stages of Language Learning: Word Meaning

Five-year-olds have a vocabulary of 10,000 to 15,000 words, whereas at fifteen months they had a vocabulary of only about twenty-five words. This means they must be acquiring about ten words a day—every day, every week, every month. It is likely that none of us adults could do as well.

CAREGIVER AIDS TO WORD LEARNING

Part of the explanation for this remarkably rapid learning may come from the quite regular ways in which mothers talk to their children, for syntax often contains useful hints about what a word could mean. Let's return to the problem of learning which word means 'ear' and which means 'rabbit' (see Figure 8.8, p. 241). It turns out that when mothers refer to the whole rabbit, they use simple sentences ("This is a rabbit") and often point to the rabbit at the same time. But when they want to refer to the ear, they first refer to the whole rabbit, and then use such words as *his* in referring to the part: "This is a rabbit; these are his ears" (Shipley, Kuhn, and Madden, 1983).

PERCEPTUAL AND CONCEPTUAL BIASES IN CHILD LEARNERS

Much of the child's word learning is explained by how she is disposed to carve up *(categorize)* the world that she observes. Some ways of conceptualizing experience are natural to humans while others are less natural (Rosch, 1973a; Keil, 1979; Fodor, 1983). Thus the child can learn more easily if she assumes that each word represents some "natural" organization of experience.

Evidence comes from experimental attempts to teach new words to children. The method is to point to a new object and label it with a new (nonsense) word, and then to determine *what else* other than the first sample object the child will apply this new label to. Thus if an experimenter points toward an object and says "That's biff," children will almost always guess that "biff" names the whole object rather than, say, some of its parts, or the material of which it is made, its color, and so forth (Markman and Hutchinson, 1984). This is despite the logical problem that when one points toward an object one simply can't help pointing toward its color (e.g., green) and substance (e.g., plastic or pewter) at the same time. Even more interesting, if one then shows this child other objects that are *shaped just like the original sample object* but differ from it in size or color, the child will take these as more biffs. But the same child will reject, as "not biffs," objects that have *even slightly different shapes.* Evidently, colors and textures are not as salient in the child's perceptual organization as shapes, so the slightest change in the latter will convince the learner that the new item is something wholly different from the one previously called "a biff" (Landau, Smith, and Jones, 1988).

WORD CLASSES AND WORD MEANINGS

Children are disposed to organize the world into overarching categories—things, events, properties, and so forth. But what is more, they appear to believe that language will classify words according to related categories—nouns, verbs, and adjectives—in a way that is consistent with the conceptual categories (Braine, 1976; Pinker, 1984).

(Photograph by Roberta Intrater, 1980)

8.13 Word classes and word meanings
When asked "In this picture can you see any sibbing?" (verb), children pointed to the hands; when asked "Can you see a sib?" (common noun), they pointed to the blue bowl; and when asked "Can you see any sib?" (mass noun), they pointed to the pink confetti. (Adapted from Brown, R., 1957)

This phenomenon was demonstrated in an experiment with three- and four-year-olds in which the experimenter showed children a picture in which a pair of hands seemed to be performing a kneading sort of motion, with a mass of pink confetti-like material that was overflowing a low, striped, container (see Figure 8.13). The children were introduced to the picture in sentences that used nonsense words, but either as verbs ("In this picture can you see *sibbing?*"), common nouns *("Can you see a sib?")*, or mass nouns *("Can you see any sib?").** The children who had been asked to show *sibbing* made kneading motions with their hands, those asked to show *a sib* pointed to the container, and those asked about *any sib* pointed to the confetti (Brown, R., 1957; see also Katz, Baker, and MacNamara, 1974; Carey, 1982). Thus children use their growing knowledge of word classes and their semantic correlates to discover what a new word refers to, even though the scene itself can be interpreted in many ways (Grimshaw, 1981; Pinker, 1989; Gleitman, L., 1990).

LANGUAGE LEARNING IN CHANGED ENVIRONMENTS

Thus far, our focus has been on language development as it proceeds normally. Under these conditions, language seems to emerge in much the same way in virtually all children. They progress from babbling to one-word speech, advance to the two-word telegraphic stage, and eventually graduate to complex sentence forms and meanings. The fact that this progression is so uniform and universal has led many psycholinguists to the view that children are biologically pre-programmed to acquire language. Further evidence for this view stems from studies of language development under certain unusual conditions, when children grow up in environments that are radically different from those in which language development usually proceeds.

Wild Children

There are some remarkable examples of children who wandered (or were abandoned) in the forest, and who survived, reared by bears or wolves. In 1920, some Indian villagers discovered a wolf mother in her den together with four cubs. Two were baby wolves, but the other two were human children, subsequently named Kamala and Amala. No one knows how they got there and why the wolf adopted them. The psycholinguist, Roger Brown, tells us what these children were like:

> Kamala was about eight years old and Amala was only one and one-half. They were thoroughly wolfish in appearance and behavior: Hard callus had developed on their knees and palms from going on all fours. Their teeth were sharp edged. They moved their nostrils sniffing food. They ate raw meat. . . . At night they prowled and sometimes howled. They shunned other children but followed the dog and cat. They slept rolled up together on the floor. . . . Amala died within a year but Kamala lived to be eighteen . . . In time, Kamala learned to walk erect, to wear clothing, and even to speak a few words. (Brown, 1958, p. 100)

---

* A **common** or **count noun** is one that (1) requires a specifier such as *the* or *two* (compare *The dog walks down the street* with the ungrammatical *Dog walks down the street*), and (b) generally refers to the kinds of entities that can be counted (e.g., *One dog, two dogs*). A **mass noun** (1) occurs without a specifier (compare *Water flows through the pipes* with the ungrammatical *A water flows through the pipes*), and (2) generally refers to stuff that can't be counted, e.g., *water, confetti,* or *sand.*

8.14 A modern wild boy *Ramu, a young boy discovered in India in 1976, appears to have been reared by wolves. He was deformed, apparently from lying in cramped positions, as in a den. He could not walk, and drank by lapping with his tongue. His favorite food was raw meat, which he seemed to be able to smell at a distance. After he was found, he lived at the home for destitute children run by Mother Theresa in Lucknow, Uttar Pradesh. He learned to bathe and dress himself, but never learned to speak. He continued to prefer raw meat, and would often sneak out to prey upon fowl in the neighbor's chicken coop. Ramu died at the age of about 10 in February, 1985. (*New York Times, *Feb. 24, 1985; photographs courtesy Wide World Photos)*

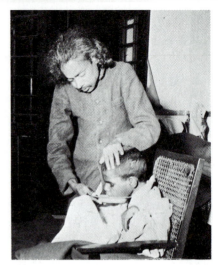

The outcome was much the same for the thirty or so other wild children about whom we have reports. When found, they were all shockingly animal-like. None of them could be rehabilitated so as to use language at all normally, though some, including Kamala, learned to speak a few words (Figure 8.14).

Isolated Children

Kamala and Amala were removed from all human society. Some other children have been raised by humans, but under conditions that were almost unimaginably inhumane, for their parents were either vicious or deranged. Sometimes, such parents will deprive a baby of all human contact. "Isabelle" was hidden away, apparently from early infancy, and given only the minimal attention necessary to sustain her life. Apparently no one spoke to her (in fact, her mother was deaf and did not speak). Isabelle was six years old when discovered. Of course she had no language. But within a year, this girl learned to speak. Her tested intelligence was normal, and she took her place in an ordinary school (Davis, K., 1947; Brown, R., 1958).

Rehabilitation from isolation is not always so successful. A child, "Genie," discovered in California about twenty years ago, was fourteen years old when found. Since about twenty months, apparently, she had lived tied to a chair, was frequently beaten, and never spoken to—but sometimes barked at, for her father said she was no more than a dog. Afterwards, she was taught by psychologists and linguists (Fromkin et al., 1974). But Genie did not become a normal language user. She says many words, and puts them together into meaningful propositions as young children do, such as "No more take wax" and "Another house have dog." Thus she has learned certain basics of language. Yet, even after many years of instruction, Genie did not learn the function words that appear in mature English sentences, nor did she combine propositions together in elaborate sentences (Curtiss, 1977).

Why did Genie not progress to full language learning while Isabelle did? The best guess is that the crucial factor is the age at which language learning began. Genie was discovered after she had reached puberty while Isabelle was only six. As we shall see later, there is some reason to believe there is a ***critical period*** for language learning. If the person has passed this period, language learning proceeds with greater difficulty.

Language without Sound

The work on wild and isolated children argues that a necessary condition for learning language is some social contact with other humans. Our next question concerns the more specific factors of the learner's human environment. What aspects of this environment are essential for language to emerge?

It has sometimes been suggested that an important ingredient is exposure to language sounds. According to this view, language is intrinsically related to the way we organize what we hear. This hypothesis is false. For there is one group of humans that is cut off from auditory-vocal language—the deaf, who cannot hear it. Yet this doesn't mean that they have no language. Most deaf people eventually learn to read and write the language of the surrounding community of hearing persons. But they also have a manual-visual, or *gestural system.* One such system is *American Sign Language* (or *ASL*).

Are gestural systems genuine languages? One indication that they are is that these systems are not derived by translation from the spoken languages around them, but are independently created within and by communities of deaf individuals (Klima, Bellugi, et al., 1979). Further evidence comes from comparing ASL to the structure and development of spoken languages. ASL has hand shapes and positions of which each word is composed, much like the tongue and lip shapes that allow us to fashion the phonemes of spoken language (Stokoe, 1960). It has morphemes and grammatical principles for combining words into sentences that are similar to those of spoken language (Supalla, 1986; see Figure 8.15).

Finally, babies born to deaf users of ASL (whether or not the babies themselves are deaf) pick up the system from these caregivers through informal interaction rather than by explicit instruction, just as we learn our spoken language (Newport and Ashbrook, 1977). And they go through the same steps on the way to adult knowledge as do hearing children learning English. It is hard to avoid the conclusion that ASL and other gestural systems are true languages (Klima, Bellugi et al., 1979; Supalla and Newport, 1978; Newport, 1984).

Thus language does not depend on the auditory-vocal channel. When the usual modes of communication are denied to humans of normal mentality, they come up with an alternative that reproduces the same contents and structures as other language systems. It appears that language is an irrepressible human trait: Deny it to the mouth and it will dart out through the fingers.

Language without a Model

The evidence we have reviewed shows that language emerges despite many environmental deprivations. Still, each case seemed to have one requirement—some adults who knew a language and could impart it to the young. But this must leave

8.15   Some common signs in ASL (A) The sign for tree. One difference between ASL and spoken language is that many of the signed words physically resemble their meanings. This is so for tree, in which the upright forearm stands for the trunk and the outstretched fingers for the branches. But in many cases, such a resemblance is not present. Consider (B) which is the modern sign for help, whose relation to its meaning seems as arbitrary as that between most spoken words and their meanings. Even so, such a relation was once present, as shown in (C), a nineteenth-century sign for help. At that time, the sign was not arbitrary; it consisted of a gesture by the right hand to support the left elbow, as if helping an elderly person cross a street. (B) grew out of (C) by a progressive series of simplifications in which signs tend to move to the body's midline and use shorter, fewer, and more stylized movements. All that remains of (C) is an upward motion of the right palm. (Frishberg, 1975; photographs of and by Ted Supalla)

us puzzled about how language originated in the first place. Is it a cultural artifact (like the internal combustion machine or the game of chess) rather than a basic property of human minds, an invention that happened to take place in prehistoric times? Our bias has been the opposite, for we have argued that humans are biologically predisposed to communicate by language. Is there a better test than those provided by the tragic cases of brutal mistreatment and neglect so far considered?

It certainly would be interesting if we could find a case of mentally normal children living in a socially loving environment but not exposed to language use by the adults around them. Feldman, Goldin-Meadow, and L. Gleitman (1978) found six children who were in such a situation. These children were deaf, and so they were unable to learn spoken language. Both parents of each child were hearing; they did not know ASL and decided not to allow the children to learn a gestural language. This is because they shared the belief (held by some groups of educators) that deaf children can achieve adequate knowledge of spoken language by special training in lip reading and vocalization. The investigators looked at these children before they had acquired any knowledge of English, for a number of prior studies had shown that under these circumstances deaf children will spontaneously gesture in meaningful ways to others (Tervoort, 1961; Fant, 1972). The question was which aspects of communication these youngsters would come up with as they developed.

The results showed that the children invented a sizeable number of pantomimic gestures that the investigators could comprehend. For example, they would flutter their fingers in a downward motion to express *snow,* twist their fingers to express a twist-top *bottle,* and flap their arms to represent *bird* (see Figure 8.16).

The development of this "language" showed many parallels to ordinary language learning: The children gestured one sign at a time in the period (about eighteen months of age) when hearing learners speak one word at a time. At two and three years of age they went on to two- and three-word sentences and so on. And in these basic sentences, the individual gestures were serially ordered by semantic role. This is strong evidence for a rudimentary syntactic organization, just like that of children who hear German or French—or see ASL—produced by adults.

On the other hand, we should not lose sight of severe limitations of these homemade systems. First, they are limited to the elementary basics of language as we know it, with function words and elaborately organized sentences absent (Goldin-Meadow, 1982). And there is a yet more serious limitation that goes back to the social and interpersonal nature of ordinary language use: The parents of these children used gestures to them very rarely, and their sporadic gesturing was in terms of isolated "words" and pointings to things in view, with no syntactic organization (Goldin-Meadow and Mylander, 1983). The result was that social interaction in this medium was quite restricted, for it takes more than one individual—inventive as he or she may be—to make a living language.

In sum, these studies provide us with a fairly pure case of a group of children who were isolated from language stimulation, but not from love and affection. The findings show that the capacity to organize thought using the word and syntax principles of language is a deep-seated property of the human mind, at least in its basics if not in its elaborations. Yet the same studies show us the necessarily in-

A

B

8.16 Self-made signs in a deaf boy never exposed to sign language *A two-sign sequence. (A) The first sign means "eat" or "food." Immediately before, the boy had pointed to a grape. (B) The second sign means "give." The total sequence means "give me the food." (Goldin-Meadow, 1982; drawing courtesy Noel Yovovich)*

terpersonal and interactive nature of human communication, which must become stymied and dysfunctional in the end if there is no "other" with whom it can be used.

Children Deprived of Access to Some of the Meanings

Children usually learn the meanings of words in situations in which they can determine the referents of those words. Thus it is certainly easier to learn the meaning of the word *horse* if that word is said in the presence of a horse. To the extent that referents of the words and sentences help the learner, we should expect blind learners to have significant difficulties in learning a language. For often the mother may be talking of things that are too large, gossamer, or distant for the blind child to feel with her hands (e.g., mountains, clouds, or birds).

In this sense, blind children seem to suffer an environmental deprivation symmetrical with the one previously considered: The isolated deaf children heard no language *forms* from their parents, but they were free to observe all the things and events in the world that language describes. In contrast, blind children hear the language forms from their parents, but they are cut off from some opportunities to observe their referents (and thus, presumably, to acquire word and sentence *meanings*).

All the same, recent evidence shows that blind children learn language as rapidly and as well as sighted children. One striking example is vision-related words like *look* and *see,* which blind children use as early (two-and-a-half to three years of age) and as systematically as sighted children. To be sure, there are some differences in how blind and sighted children understand these words. A young sighted listener, even if her vision is blocked by a blindfold, will tilt her covered eyes upward when asked to "Look up!" This suggests that to the sighted child, looking *must* refer to vision (Figure 8.17A). But a congenitally blind child, when also told to "Look up!," shows that she too has a sensible interpretation of *look,* though a somewhat different one. Keeping her head immobile, the blind youngster reaches upward and searches the space above her body with her hands (Figure 8.17B). Thus each of these children understands *look* differently. But the meanings resemble each other even so. Both children realize that *look* has something to do with perceiving the world by use of the sense organs. The children arrive at meaningful interpretations of words even though their information about the world is often quite different.

This fits with the general picture of language learning as we have discussed it, for all learners—not just blind ones—must (and do!) build their language knowledge from relatively sparse information about referents. Thus one child may see a Great Dane and a poodle when he hears "dog." Another child may be introduced to this same word when seeing a collie and a terrier. Based on these quite different experiences, both children will acquire the same category, as we know from the fact that both will apply it to Chihuahuas and Huskies the first time they see them. In light of this marvelous ability of children to categorize the world in terms that are important to their own perceptual and conceptual lives, perhaps it is not so surprising that the blind child understands *looking* to mean 'exploring with the hands' (Landau and Gleitman, L., 1985; see also Urwin, 1983; Mulford, 1986; Bigelow, 1987).

A

B

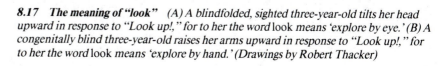

8.17 The meaning of "look" (A) A blindfolded, sighted three-year-old tilts her head upward in response to "Look up!," for to her the word look means 'explore by eye.' (B) A congenitally blind three-year-old raises her arms upward in response to "Look up!," for to her the word look means 'explore by hand.' (Drawings by Robert Thacker)

Before leaving this topic, we should again strike a cautionary note (as we did with the self-invented gesture language of deaf children). Even though blind learners' language forms and word meanings are strikingly like those of sighted children, up until age three they manifest many problems in understanding the particulars of conversations going on around them. This creates significant frustration (sometimes leading to severe behavioral problems) in blind toddlers. This is not surprising. Imagine what it would be like if all your companions were involved in face-to-face conversation, but you were connected to them only by telephone. Like blind children, you would experience confusion about what was being talked about, have trouble identifying the referents of pronouns, and so forth (Landau and Gleitman, 1985).

Helen Keller and her teacher Anne Sullivan *(Photograph courtesy of the American Foundation for the Blind)*

The Case of Helen Keller

The most dramatic and compelling picture of children cut off from contact with a language community comes to us from the case of Helen Keller (1880–1968). At eighteen months, she was a bright toddler, learning her first few words. But she then suffered a devastating illness (never adequately diagnosed) that left her both deaf and blind. Thus Helen, unlike the congenitally deaf and blind children we have discussed (who never experienced hearing or seeing), was aware of suffering a catastrophic loss. She later wrote (speaking of herself in the third person):

> With appalling suddenness she [Helen] moved from light to darkness and became a phantom. . . . Helplessly the family witnessed the baffled intelligence as Phantom's hand stretched out to feel the shapes which she could reach but which meant nothing to her. . . . Nothing was part of anything, and there blazed up in her frequent fierce anger. . . . I remember tears rolling down her cheeks but not the grief. There were no words for that emotion or any other, and consequently they did not register. (Keller, 1955)

Helen thus suffered the double affliction of sudden darkness and silence, and lived the next five years of her life in many ways isolated from the world of other people. But in the end, she entered Radcliffe, studied algebra, Greek, and literature, wrote classic and elegantly crafted books on her life and experiences, became an illustrious educator, and was personally close to many of the important people of her time, including Mark Twain, Eleanor Roosevelt, and Alexander Graham Bell (Lash, 1980).

Helen Keller gave the credit for this triumphant return to life to her great teacher, Anne Sullivan. Sullivan, herself half-blind and raised in appalling conditions in a "poor house," had acquired a partial manual system. It was through this medium that she began to unlock the stifled mind of Helen: She fingerspelled onto her eager pupil's palm. Helen reported her awakening in this famous passage (in which Anne Sullivan is holding one of Helen's hands under a waterspout):

> . . . as the cool stream gushed over one hand, she [Anne Sullivan] spelled into the other the word water. . . . I stood still, my whole attention fixed upon the motions of her fingers. . . . Suddenly I felt a misty consciousness as of something forgotten—a thrill of returning thought; and somehow the mystery of language was revealed to me. . . . Everything had a name, and each name gave birth to a new thought. As we returned to the house every object which I touched seemed to quiver with life. (Quoted in Lash, 1980)

Helen Keller conversing with Eleanor Roosevelt *Helen understood speech by noting the movements of the lips and the vibration of the vocal cords. (Photograph by Larry Morris/New York Times; courtesy of the American Foundation for the Blind)*

What can we learn from Helen Keller's case? It is not as though this child was completely unable to communicate or think before the arrival of Sullivan in her life. In Helen's biography, she underestimated her own status at that time, remembering herself as merely "a wild and destructive little animal." But Anne Sullivan saw something else. Like the deaf children we have described in the previous section, Helen had spontaneously invented many gestures to describe her wants and needs. For instance, "a desire for ice cream was shown by turning the freezer and a little shiver; . . . knotting hair on the back of her head symbolized her mother. . . . If she wanted bread and butter, she imitated the motions of cutting . . . and spreading." Sullivan recognized at least sixty such spontaneous "descriptive gestures" when she first met Helen (Lash, 1980).

So Helen's case is consistent with that of the deaf children we discussed earlier. Isolated from language forms, a human infant begins to invent her own. But Helen's case also reveals the crushing limitations of such a homemade language system for communicating with the surrounding community, which neither knows this idiosyncratic system nor understands its significance. Anne Sullivan, an incredibly sophisticated and talented teacher, differed from the loving but bewildered parents by realizing that language learning has to be natural and communicative. She signed into Helen's palm "as we talk into the baby's ear" (Lash, 1980; see also Chomsky, C., 1984).

Thus Sullivan's success depended not only on exploiting the child's natural disposition to organize language according to deep-seated principles of form and meaning, but on introducing language in the context of its—just as deep-seated —functions for communicating about things, events, and feelings with others (see Bates and MacWhinney, 1982).

LANGUAGE LEARNING WITH CHANGED ENDOWMENTS

We have now shown that language learning proceeds quite successfully despite severe environmental differences and deprivations. This suggests that there is an innate "mental machinery" for language that runs its course undeflected by any but the most radical environmental stresses (such as that suffered by Genie). But what happens if the nature of the learners themselves is changed? To the extent that language learning and use are determined by brain function, changing that brain should have strong effects (Lenneberg, 1967; Menyuk, 1977; Gleitman, L., 1986).

There are many indications that the nature and state of the brain have massive consequences for language functioning. An obvious instance is *aphasia,* as described in Chapter 1. We found there that if there is damage to a certain part of the left hemisphere of the brain *(Broca's area),* the victim loses use of the function words; and if the damage is to another part *(Wernicke's area),* the loss is to the content words (Figure 8.18).

We will turn our attention to quite a different distinction in the mental machinery that learners bring into the task of learning a language. This is their chronological age when they are exposed to linguistic stimulation. As the brains of humans are still growing and developing almost to the time of puberty, there is room to believe that young vs. old learners of a language approach the task equipped with rather different mental apparatus. Does this matter? The fact that Isabelle (who was rehabilitated at age 6) did achieve full language knowledge, while Genie (who was rehabilitated at age 14) did not, lends some initial plausibility to the idea that exposure early in life is necessary for full language learning. We now examine the evidence on this topic more closely.

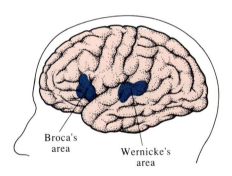

8.18 The language areas of the brain *Certain areas of the cerebral cortex (in most right-handers, in the left hemisphere) are devoted to language functions. These include Broca's area, whose damage produces deficits in speech production, especially of function words (expressive aphasia), and Wernicke's area, whose damage leads to deficits in comprehension of word meanings (receptive aphasia). For more details, see Chapter 1. (After Geschwind, 1972)*

Broca's area

Wernicke's area

THE MEDIUM OF TRANSMISSION FOR CHIMPANZEE COMMUNICATION

Chimpanzee vocal tracts differ from our own, so they cannot literally speak as we do (Hayes, 1952). Several investigators have overcome this obstacle by employing visual systems of various kinds. Some use artificial systems based on colored plastic chips or symbols on a computer screen (Premack, 1976; Rumbaugh, 1977). Others have adopted items from ASL (Gardner and Gardner, 1969; 1975; 1978; Terrace, Petitto, Sanders, and Bever, 1979).

VOCABULARY

Chimpanzees using any of the visual systems just mentioned can acquire a substantial number of "words." Consider Washoe, a chimpanzee introduced to words at about age one year and treated just like a human child, with naps, diapers, and baths. She was taught ASL signs by having her hands physically molded into the desired position; other signs were learned by imitation (Fouts, 1972). After four years, she had learned about 130 signs for objects *(banana, hand),* actions *(bite, tickle),* and action modifiers *(enough, more).* This rate cannot compare with the human child who learns about 10,000 words in this period, but is impressive all the same (for discussion, see Savage-Rumbaugh, Rumbaugh, Smith, and Lawson, 1980).

Also of considerable interest is the finding that some of the chimpanzees use their new acquisitions in naturalistic interactions with their trainers, not just in laboratory tests. Moreover, Washoe appears to be teaching some of her human signs to an adopted chimpanzee baby (Fouts, Hirsch, and Fouts, 1982). If this result holds up, it is a very interesting case of "cultural transmission" by another species.

A

B

Chimpanzees signing A young chimpanzee making the sign for (A) "hug" and (B) "apple." (Terrace, 1979; photograph courtesy Herbert Terrace)

PROPOSITIONAL THOUGHT

Are chimpanzees capable of propositional thought? We know that they have mental representations of various objects and events in the world, for as we just saw, they can be taught words for them. But do they have anything like a notion of this-does-something-to-that?

One line of evidence comes from David Premack's (1976) studies on the concept of causation in chimpanzees. Premack showed his animals pairs of objects. In each pair the second object was the same as the first but had undergone some change. One pair consisted of a whole apple and an apple that was cut in pieces; another pair was a dry towel and a wet towel; a third was an unmarked piece of paper and a piece of paper covered with pencil marks. The chimpanzee's task was to place one of several alternatives between the objects—a knife, a bowl of water, or a pencil. The question was whether the animals would choose the item that caused the change (Figure 8.21). Premack's star pupil, Sarah, performed correctly on 77 percent of the trials, far more than would be expected by chance. Perhaps these animals have some primitive notions of the relation between certain objects, acts, and outcomes—knives cut up things, water wets them, and pencils mark them. To the extent that the apes have these concepts, they have the germs of propositional thought.

SYNTAX

Human speech is characterized by abstract syntactic principles. Can chimpanzees do anything of this sort? Can they organize their signs for *Mama, tickle,* and *Washoe* so as to say either *Mama tickles Washoe* or *Washoe tickles Mama?* The Gardners believe that Washoe has some such ability. As evidence, they refer to

A

B

8.21 A test for propositional thought in chimpanzees *(A) A chimpanzee is shown a whole apple and two halves of an apple. Its task is to place one of three alternatives between them: a pencil, a bowl of water, or a knife. (B) The animal chooses the knife, the instrument which produced the change from the uncut to the cut state. In other trials, when the animals were shown a blank piece of paper and a scribbled-upon piece of paper, in general, they would put the pencil in the middle. When shown a dry sponge and a wet sponge, they chose the bowl of water. (From Premack, 1976; photographs courtesy David Premack)*

apparently novel sequences of signs produced by Washoe on her own. For instance, she once signed *listen eat* on hearing an alarm clock that signals mealtime, and she signed *water bird* upon seeing a duck.

A number of critics feel that such observations prove little or nothing. They are anecdotes that can be interpreted in several ways. Take the sequence *water bird*. On the face of it, its use seems like a remarkable achievement—a chimpanzoid equivalent of a compound noun that presumably means something like *bird that lives in water*. But is this interpretation justified? Or did Washoe merely produce an accidental succession of two signs: *water* (perhaps water was seen just before) and *bird* (because of the duck)? It is hard to believe that she really understood the significance of the order (in English) in which the two words are uttered: a *water-bird* is a bird that lives in water, but *bird-water* is water for a bird. Since all we have is an anecdote, we cannot be sure.

Recent claims for another species, the pygmy chimpanzee, are even stronger. It is claimed that these animals quite often come up with novel combinations of words and that their language knowledge in general is broader than that of common chimpanzees (Savage-Rumbaugh et al., 1986; Savage-Rumbaugh, 1987). But these claims too are quite controversial.

IS IT LANGUAGE?

To sum up, recent years have seen a tremendous growth of scientific interest in the question of whether chimpanzees (and dolphins, gorillas, and other advanced animals) can acquire language. What current evidence supports is that there are some precursors and prerequisites (such as primitive propositional thought) to our language capacities that are observable in trained chimpanzees. However, these very findings have led to great controversy. Some scientists have concluded from them that there is little qualitative difference in this regard between us and these primates—only a difference in degree. Others conclude that the chimpanzees' accomplishments are too sporadic and limited to be of much interest for understanding the minds of either chimpanzees or humans. Many other scientists find no merit at all in calling these chimpanzee behaviors "language" in any useful sense. Their view is that these trained behaviors are no more convincing than the tricks of dancing circus poodles, whose accomplishments are never taken to prove that dogs, like humans, are two-legged animals (Seidenberg and Pettito, 1979).

Whether the chimpanzees' accomplishments should be called *language,* then, seems to depend on one's definition of that term. We can choose to say that trained chimpanzees use language. But in doing so, we have changed the technical meaning of the term so as to exclude from consideration the learning, speech, and comprehension machinery shown by every nonpathological human. Worse, we have even changed the common-sense meaning of the term *language.* For one thing is certain: If any of our children learned or used language the way Washoe or Sarah does, we would be terror-stricken and rush them to the nearest neurologist.

LANGUAGE AND ITS LEARNING

In our survey of language, we emphasized that human communication systems are similar all over the world. To be sure, the words themselves sound different so the speakers of different languages cannot understand each other. Still, every language turned out to consist of a hierarchy of structures that represent a complex interweaving of meaning and form. The effect is that, if we share a language, we can communicate about all the endless social, emotional, and intellectual matters that concern us as humans.

Language is marvelously ornate and intricate—so much so that we must be boggled by the idea that human babies can learn any such thing. And yet they do, as we have seen. In all the nurturant (and even most of the horribly abusive) circumstances in which human babies find themselves, language makes its appearance and flourishes. Our nearest primate cousins even given the utmost in social and linguistic support do not approach the competence and sophistication of the most ordinary three-year-old human child. What makes this learning possible?

We have argued throughout that language is the product of the young human brain, such that virtually any exposure conditions will suffice to guide acquisition of any language in the world. In retrospect, this is scarcely surprising. It would be just as foolish for evolution to have created human bodies without human "programs" to run these bodies as to have created giraffe bodies without giraffe programs or sparrow bodies without sparrow programs.

But we must close by reemphasizing that specific languages must be learned by human babies, even though the capacity to accomplish this is given in large part by nature. This is because the manifestations of the human language capacity are certainly variable, particularly in the sounds of the individual words. To reiterate a point with which we began: Greek children learn Greek, not Urdu or Swahili. For this reason, we have had to view language acquisition as a complex interaction between the child's innate capacities and the social, cognitive, and specifically linguistic supports provided in the environment. Perhaps, in light of the efficiency and sure-handedness with which (as we saw) human babies accomplish this feat, you might feel disposed to buttonhole the next baby you meet in the street to compliment her for being born a human being.

SUMMARY

1. Language has five major properties. It is *creative* or novel: All normal humans can say and understand sentences they have never heard before. It is *structured:* Only certain arrangements of linguistic elements (phonemes, words, and so forth) are allowed. It is *meaningful:* Each word or combination of words expresses a meaningful idea (or concept). It is *referential:* It relates to things, scenes, and events in the extralinguistic world. It is *interpersonal:* It enables us to communicate with other persons.

2. Languages are organized as a hierarchy of structures. The lowest-level units are *phonemes,* the sound elements of language. Each language uses somewhere between twelve and sixty phonemes and has specific arrangements of the phonemes it uses. Each language also has *morphemes,* which are the smallest language units that carry bits of meaning. There are *content morphemes,* which carry the bulk of meaning, and *function morphemes,* which carry the structure of the sentence. *Phrases* are groupings of morphemes that carry more complex meanings than single morphemes and words. Phrases are combined into *sentences* according to the principles of syntax. There are infinitely many phrases and sentences in a language.

3. Word and phrase meaning is not identical to word and phrase reference, for some expressions can refer to the same thing and yet have different meanings. The *definitional theory of meaning* holds that each word describes a bundle of more elementary semantic features. The *prototype theory of meaning* responds to the fact that it is hard to find definitions for all words. The most widely held theory of word meaning today combines the definitional and prototype theories. The definitional part picks out properties that a concept must have. The prototype part concerns the most "typical" properties, the ones that most members of the concept share.

4. Human thought is in terms of whole *propositions,* consisting of a subject or topic, and a *predicate* (that which is said about the subject or topic). The linguistic expression of a

SUMMARY

proposition is a simple sentence, consisting of a *noun phrase* (representing the subject or topic) and a *verb phrase* (representing the predicate). Sentence structures are represented by hierarchical tree diagrams, which show the relations among the phrases and words that make up the full sentences.

5. Language learning is more than skill acquisition, for the learning cannot be described as a habit acquired through imitation and reinforcement.

6. Infants are responsive to linguistic stimulation from birth. For instance, they have been shown to be responsive to differences among just about all the phonemes used in the various languages of the world. Learning a specific language's phoneme structure involves learning not to notice those distinctions not made in one's native language.

7. Most infants begin talking in *one-word sentences* at about one year of age and rapidly acquire a large vocabulary. They seem to have propositional ideas in mind, and some appreciation of syntactic structure, even at this early stage.

8. At about two years of age, children begin using rudimentary *two-word* or *telegraphic sentences* that contain content words but typically omit function morphemes and words. These short sentences have a good deal of structure.

9. Language learning takes place successfully in many radically different environments. It fails only if children are removed from all human company or violently isolated and abused. Even if one is deaf, one learns a language. In this case, the language will probably be a signed (visual-manual) language rather than a spoken (auditory-vocal) one.

10. Children isolated from opportunities to learn the language around them invent some of it for themselves. An example is deaf children not exposed to signed languages who invent pantomimic gestures for words and propositions.

11. In contrast to the cases of changed environmental conditions, which children of normal mentality generally overcome, are cases of changed conditions of mentality. An important case of a "changed brain" that learns a language is the second-language learner who is chronologically older than the usual first-language learner. The less mature brain and the mature brain appear to have different capacities. The finding is that the younger the second-language learner, the more likely he or she is to acquire the new language adequately.

12. Because experimental evidence makes it clear that language learning is based on special properties of the young human brain, we should not expect to find that human language can be fully or even adequately learned by other higher animals such as chimpanzees and dolphins. Nevertheless, chimpanzees have been shown to have rather good word-learning capacities, though nowhere as good as those of a two-and-a-half-year-old human. They also seem to be able to think propositionally to some degree; that is, to think in terms of who-did-what-to-whom. There is little or no credible evidence, however, that chimpanzees can acquire even the rudiments of syntactic principles.

13. Summarizing all the evidence, language learning results from the interaction between a young human brain and various social, cognitive, and specifically linguistic supports provided in the environment. Language is perhaps the central cognitive property whose possession makes us "truly human." If aliens came from another planet but spoke like us, we would probably try to get to know them and understand them—rather than trying to herd them or milk them—even if they looked like cows.

PART III

Social Behavior

In the preceding chapters, we have asked what organisms do, what they want, and what they know. But thus far we have raised these questions in a somewhat limited context, for we have considered the organism as an isolated individual, abstracted from the social world in which it lives. For some psychological questions this approach may be perfectly valid. Robinson Crusoe's visual system was surely no different on his lonely island than back home in London. But many other aspects of behavior are impossible to describe by considering a single organism alone, without reference to its fellows. Consider a male parrot feeding a female in a courtship ritual, a monkey mother clasping her infant closer at a stranger's approach, two stags locking antlers during the rutting season, or the front runner of a band of wild hunting dogs cutting off a fleeing zebra's escape—all of these activities are social by definition. Courtship, sex, parental care, competition, and cooperation are not merely actions. *They are* interactions *in which each participant's behavior is affected by the behavior of the others.*

Social interactions are vital in the lives of most animals: after all, successful reproduction (that is, sex and parental care) is what survival is all about. In humans, the role of social factors is even more powerful than in animals, for our world is fashioned not only by our contemporaries but by generations preceding whose vast cultural heritage structures the very fabric of our lives. Most of our motives are social for they concern other people—the desire to be loved, to be accepted, to be esteemed, perhaps to excel, and in some cases, unhappily, to inflict pain and hurt. The all-importance of social factors extends even to motives that, on the face of it, seem to involve only the isolated organism, motives such as hunger, thirst, and temperature maintenance. These motives as such may pertain primarily to the individual, but the ways in which they are satisfied are enormously affected by the social context in which we live. We eat food that is raised by a complex agricultural technology based on millennia of human discovery, and we eat it, delicately, with knife and fork, according to the etiquette of a long-dead king. Even the isolated Robinson Crusoe was no exception. In Defoe's tale, Crusoe's survival depended upon a few items of valuable debris he managed to salvage from his sunken ship. Thus his existence was not truly solitary: he was still bound to a world of others—by a few nails, a hammer, and a plank or two. Robinson Crusoe was on an island, but even he was not an island entire unto himself.

In the following chapters we will discuss these social factors in some detail, as they bear on our actions, motives, thoughts, and knowledge.

CHAPTER 9

The Biological Basis
of Social Behavior

A classic question posed by philosophers is, "What is the basic social nature of man?" Are greed, competition, and hate (or, for that matter, charity, cooperation, and love) unalterable components of the human makeup, or can they be instilled or nullified by proper training? To answer these questions, we will have to consider not just humankind but some of its animal cousins as well.

Thomas Hobbes   *(Painting by John Michael Wright; courtesy The Granger Collection)*

THE SOCIAL NATURE OF HUMANS AND ANIMALS

Are human beings so built that social interaction is an intrinsic part of their makeup? Or are they essentially solitary creatures who turn to others only because they need them for their own selfish purposes? The English social philosopher Thomas Hobbes (1588–1679) argued for the second of these alternatives. In his view, man is a self-centered brute who, left to his own devices, will seek his own gain regardless of the cost to others. Except for the civilizing constraints imposed by society, men would inevitably be in an eternal "war of all against all." According to Hobbes, this frightening "state of nature" is approximated during times of anarchy and civil war. These were conditions Hobbes knew all too well, for he lived during a time of violent upheavals in England when Stuart royalists battled Cromwell's Puritans, when commoners beheaded their king in a public square, and when pillage, burning, and looting were commonplace. In such a state of nature, man's life is a sorry lot. There are "no Arts; no Letters; no Society; and which is worst of all, continuall fear, and danger of violent death; And the life of man solitary, poore, nasty, brutish, and short" (Hobbes, 1651, p. 186). Hobbes argued that under the circumstances, men had no choice but to protect themselves against their own ugly natures. They did so by entering into a "social contract" to form a collective commonwealth, the State.

Hobbes's psychological starting points are simple enough: Man is by nature asocial and destructively rapacious. Society is a means to chain the brute within. Only when curbed by social fetters does man go beyond his animal nature, does he become truly human. Given this position, the various social motives that bind us to others (such as love and loyalty) presumably are imposed through culture and convention. They are learned, for they could not possibly be part of our intrinsic makeup.

Natural Selection and Survival

During the nineteenth century, Hobbes's doctrine of inherent human aggression and depravity was garbed in the mantle of science. The Industrial Revolution seemed to give ample proof that life is indeed a Hobbesian battle of each against all, whether in the marketplace, in the sweatshops, or in the far-off colonies. Ruthless competition among men was regarded as just one facet of a more general struggle for existence that is waged among all living things. This harsh view of nature had gained great impetus at the start of the nineteenth century when Thomas Malthus announced his famous law of population growth. According to Malthus, human and animal populations grow by geometrical progression (for example, 1, 2, 4, 8, 16, . . .) while the food supply grows arithmetically (for example, 1, 2, 3, 4, 5, . . .). As a result, there is inevitable scarcity and a continual battle for survival.

When Charles Darwin (1809–1882) read Malthus's essay, he finally found the explanatory principle he had been seeking to account for the evolution of living things. He, as others before him, believed that all present-day plants, animals, and even humans, were descended from prior forms. The evidence came from various sources, such as fossil records that showed the gradual transformation from long-extinct species to those now living. But what had produced these changes? Within each species there are individual variations; some horses are faster, others are slower. Many of these variations are part of the animal's hereditary makeup and thus are bequeathed to its descendants. But will an individual animal have descendants? That depends on how it fares in the struggle for existence. As a matter of fact, most organisms don't live long enough to reproduce. Only a few seedlings grow up to be trees; only a few tadpoles achieve froghood. But certain characteristics may make survival a bit more likely. The faster horse is more likely to escape predatory cats than its slower fellow, and it is thus more likely to leave offspring who inherit his swiftness. This process of *natural selection* does not guarantee survival and reproduction; it only increases their likelihood. In consequence, evolutionary change is very gradual and proceeds over eons (Darwin, 1872a).

Charles Darwin   (Painting by J. Collier; courtesy of The National Portrait Gallery, London)

PERSONAL AND GENETIC SURVIVAL

Natural selection leads to the "survival of the fittest." But just what does it mean to be fit? Thus far, our examples of better "fitness" involved attributes that make *personal survival* more likely: the faster horse, the more ferocious cat, and so on. But personal survival as such is not what the evolutionary game is about. The trick is to have reproductive success—to have offspring who will pass one's genes along. A horse that manages to live two or three times longer than any of its fellows but that for some reason or another stays celibate has not survived in an evolutionary sense. Personal survival (at least until sexual maturity) is a prerequisite for *genetic survival,* but it alone is not enough.

Seen in this light, it's clear that "fitness" is determined by all characteristics that enhance reproductive success, whether or not such characteristics contribute

Genetic survival *The peacock's long tail feathers are a cumbersome burden that may decrease his chances of escaping predators and thus his own personal survival. But this is more than offset by his increased chances in attracting a sexual partner, thereby assuring survival of his genes. (Photograph by G. K. Brown, Ardea London Ltd.)*

A woven nest *Many animals have genetically determined behavior patterns characteristic of their species. An example is nest weaving in the thick-billed African weaverbird. (Photo courtesy of Brian M. Rogers/Biofotos)*

to the individual's own personal survival. Consider the magnificent tail feathers of the peacock. His long, cumbersome tail may somewhat *decrease* his chance to escape predators, but it hugely contributes to his evolutionary fitness. The peacock has to compete with his fellow males for access to the peahen; the larger and more magnificent his tail, the more likely she will respond to his sexual overtures. From an evolutionary point of view, the potential gain was evidently greater than the possible loss; as a result, long tail feathers were selected for. Much the same holds for many other characteristics that are of advantage in sexual competition. This is especially so among males (for reasons we'll discuss later on, see pp. 274–75). Some of these characteristics are rather general, such as strength and aggressiveness. Others, such as the brightly colored plumage of many male birds and the large antlers of the stag, are more specialized. But whatever the particulars of a given attribute, its contribution to the animal's fitness is the extent to which it leads to reproductive success.

INHERITED PREDISPOSITIONS TO BEHAVIOR

The inherited characteristics that increase the chance for biological survival (that is, reproduction) may concern bodily structures such as the horse's hooves or the stag's antlers. But Darwin and his successors pointed out that natural selection may also involve behavior. Squirrels bury nuts and beavers construct dams; these behavior patterns are characteristic of the species and depend on the animals' **genes,** the basic units of heredity. Whether these genes are selected for or not depends upon the **adaptive value** (that is, the biological survival value) of the behavior they give rise to. A squirrel who has a genetic predisposition to bury nuts in autumn is presumably more likely to survive the winter than one who doesn't. As a result, it is more likely to have offspring who will inherit the nut-burying gene (or genes). The end product is an increase in the number of nut-burying squirrels.

Granted that behavior can be shaped by evolution, what kind of behavior is most likely to evolve? And, most important to us, what kind of built-in predispositions are most likely to characterize humankind? Many nineteenth-century thinkers answered in Hobbesian terms. They reasoned that man is an animal and that in the bitter struggle for existence all animals are shameless egoists by sheer necessity. At bottom, they are all solitary and selfish, and man is no exception. To the extent that humans act sociably and on occasion even unselfishly—mating, rearing children, living and working with others—they have learned to do so in order to satisfy some self-centered motive such as lust or hunger.

On the face of it, this Hobbesian view seems to fit evolutionary doctrine. But on closer examination, Darwinian theory does not imply anything of the sort. It holds that there is "survival of the fittest," but "fittest" only means most likely to survive and to have offspring; it says nothing about being solitary or selfish. Darwin himself supposed that certain predispositions toward cooperation might well be adaptive and would thus be selected for. We now know that something of this sort is true, for animals as well as human beings. As we shall see, there is considerable evidence that, Hobbes to the contrary, humans and animals are by nature social rather than asocial and that much of their social behavior grows out of natively given predispositions rather than running counter to them.

Built-in Social Behaviors

Most systematic studies of built-in social behavior have been conducted within the domain of **ethology,** a branch of biology that studies animal behavior under natural conditions. Led by the Europeans Konrad Lorenz and Niko Tinbergen, both Nobel Prize winners, ethologists have analyzed many behavior patterns that are characteristic of a particular species and seem to be primarily built-in or in-stinctive. Many of these instinctive, *species-specific* behavior patterns are social; they dictate the way in which creatures interact with others of their own kind. Some involve a positive bond between certain members of the same species—courtship, copulation, care of the young. Others concern reactions of antagonism and strife—the struggle for social dominance, competition for a mate, and dis-pute over territory.

FIXED-ACTION PATTERNS

The early ethologists believed that many species-specific social reactions are based on genetically pre-programmed *fixed-action patterns,* which in turn are elicited by genetically pre-programmed *releasing stimuli.* An example of such a fixed-action pattern is the begging response of newly hatched herring gulls. They beg for food by pecking at the tips of their parents' beaks. The parent will then re-gurgitate some food from its crop and feed it to the young. What is the critical stimulus that "releases" the chick's begging pecks? To find out, Tinbergen offered newly hatched gull chicks various cardboard models of gull heads and observed which ones they pecked at the most. The most successful model was one that was long and thin and had a red patch at its tip (see Figure 9.1). These are the very characteristics of an adult herring gull's beak, but the newly hatched chick has never encountered a parent's beak previously. Tinbergen concluded that evolu-tion had done a good job in pre-programming the chick to respond to certain stimulus features so as to recognize the parent's beak at first sight (Tinbergen, 1951).

Many releasing stimuli are produced by an animal's own behavior. An impor-tant example of such response-produced stimulus releasers are *displays.* Displays produce an appropriate reaction in another animal of the same species and are thus the basis of a primitive, innate communication system. The gull chick's beg-ging peck is an elementary signal whose meaning is genetically given to both chick and parent: "Feed me! Feed me now!" (Tinbergen, 1951).

THE SOCIOBIOLOGICAL APPROACH

The analysis of chick pecking we have just discussed concentrated on the causes of behavior that are in the organism's own past (often the immediately preceding past): the particular stimuli that elicit the behavior, the physiological mecha-nisms that underlie it, and the developmental factors (such as learning) that help to shape it further. But there is another level of causation that precedes the partic-ular organism's own past by countless generations: the animal's own evolution-ary history, which created the built-in bias toward that behavior through natural selection. In the last twenty years, a new branch of biology called *sociobiology* has arisen that focuses on these long-past causes with particular reference to the evo-lutionary basis of various *social* behaviors (Wilson, 1975). Most behavioral scien-tists agree that sociobiology has provided valuable insights about social behavior in animals. What is much more controversial is the sociobiologists' contention that similar analyses can be applied to human social patterns, a topic to which we turn in a later section (see pp. 275–76, 282–83).

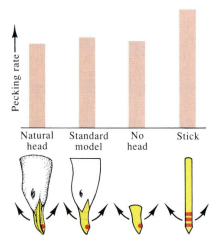

9.1 Stimulus releasers for pecking
The figure indicates the pecking rate of a herring gull chick when presented with various models. As the figure indicates, a flat cardboard model is a bit more effective than a real head and a disembod-ied bill works almost as well. Best of all was a stick with spots on it moving back and forth horizontally. (Adapted from Keeton and Gould, 1986, p. 558)

BIOLOGICAL SOURCES OF AGGRESSION

We will begin our discussion of built-in social patterns by considering the biologi-cal basis of aggression. In humans, some of the causes of aggression are events in the immediate present, such as threats and frustrations that provoke anger and hostility. Other causes stem from the individual's own past and prior learning. Our present concern is with sources that lie in our inherent makeup, the biological roots of aggression that derive from our evolutionary past. To uncover these, we have to study animals as well as humans, for the biological sources of human aggression are often obscured by cultural factors and tradition.

Conflict between Species: Predation and Defense

Most psychobiologists restrict use of the term *aggression* to conflict between members of the same species. When an owl kills a mouse, it has slaughtered for food rather than murdered in hatred. As Lorenz points out, the predator about to pounce upon his prey does not look angry; the dog who is on the verge of catching a rabbit never growls, nor does it have its ears laid back (Lorenz, 1966).

Somewhat closer to true aggression is the counterattack lodged by a prey animal against a predatory enemy. Flocks of birds sometimes *mob* an intruding cat or hawk. A colony of lovebird parrots will fly upon a would-be attacker in a body, flapping their wings furiously and uttering loud, shrill squeaks. In the face of this commotion, the predator often withdraws to look for a less troublesome meal (Dilger, 1962). Defense reactions may also occur when a hunted animal is finally cut off from retreat. Even normally reticent creatures may then become desperate fighters, as in the case of the proverbial cornered rat.

Conflict between Like and Like

There is probably no group among the animal kingdom that has foresworn aggression altogether; fighting has been observed in virtually all species. Fish chase and nip each other; lizards lunge and push; birds attack with wing, beak, and claw; sheep and cows butt heads; deer lock antlers; rats adopt a boxing stance and eye each other warily, until one finally pounces upon the other and begins a furious wrestling match with much kicking and leaping and occasionally serious bites (see Figure 9.2).

Among vertebrates, the male is generally the more aggressive sex. In some mammals, this difference in combativeness is apparent even in childhood play. Young male rhesus monkeys, for instance, engage in more vigorous rough-and-tumble tusslings than do their sisters (Harlow, 1962). A related result concerns the effect of *testosterone,* a male sex hormone. High testosterone levels in the bloodstream accompany increased aggressiveness in males; the reverse holds for decreased levels. This generalization seems to hold over a wide range of species including fish, lizards, turtles, birds, rats and mice, monkeys, and human males (Davis, 1964).

SECURING RESOURCES

What do animals fight about? Their struggles are about scarce *resources*—something valuable in their world that is in short supply. Such a resource may be a food source or a water hole; very often it is a mate. To secure a modicum of such resources many animals stake out a claim to a particular region which they will then defend as their exclusive preserve, their private *territory.*

An example is provided by male songbirds. In the spring, they endlessly patrol their little empires and furiously repel all male intruders who violate their borders. Contrary to the poet's fancy, the male bird who bursts into full-throated song is not giving vent to inexpressible joy, pouring out his "full heart in profuse strains of unpremeditated art." His message is more prosaic. It is a warning to

A

B

9.2 Aggressive fighting Male rats generally fight in fairly stereotyped ways, including (A) a "boxing position" that often escalates into (B) a leaping, biting attack. (From Barnett, 1963)

Aggressive encounter between male bighorn rams (Courtesy Stouffer Productions, Animals Animals)

male trespassers and an invitation to unattached females: "Have territory, will share."

A biological benefit of territoriality is that it secures an adequate supply of resources for the next generation. The songbird who chases his rivals away will probably leave more offspring than the one who doesn't, for his progeny will have a better start in life. Once his claim is staked out he can entice the female, offering his territory as a kind of dowry.

A side effect of territoriality is that it often serves to keep aggression within bounds. Good fences make good neighbors, at least in the sense that they keep the antagonists out of each others' hair (or fins or feathers).

One mechanism whereby territoriality limits combat is rather simple. Once a territory is established, its owner has a kind of home-court advantage in further disputes (Krebs, 1982). On his home ground he is courageous; if he ventures beyond it, he becomes timid and is readily repulsed. As a result, there are few actual conflicts other than occasional border skirmishes. This behavior pattern is utilized by circus trainers who make sure that they are the first to enter the training ring and that the animals come in later. As a result, the ring becomes the trainer's territory and even the great cats are more readily cowed (Hediger, 1968).

LIMITING AGGRESSION

A certain amount of aggression may be biologically adaptive. This is especially so for males who compete for access to females. For example, a more aggressive songbird will conquer a larger and more desirable territory, which will help him attract a mate. In addition, his territory confers further advantages such as more seeds or more worms, which further help his progeny who will get more and better food in their early days as nestlings. As a result, we would expect some selection for aggressiveness. But this holds only up to a point, for while aggression may confer some benefits, it also has its costs. Combat is dangerous and can lead to death or serious injury. In addition, it distracts the animal from other vital pursuits. The male who is continually fighting with his sexual rivals will have little time (let alone energy) left to mate with the female after his competitors have fled. Under the circumstances, natural selection strikes a compromise; there is aggression, but a number of factors keep it firmly in hand. One way of avoiding catastrophic damage to life and limb is to assess the strength of the enemy. If he seems much stronger (or more agile, or better armed) than oneself, the best bet is to proclaim a cease-fire and concede defeat or, better yet, never to start the battle at all (Krebs and Davies, 1987). Another strategy for avoiding the costs of a bloody defeat is found in many species of sheep and deer whose males engage in a

Bull seal threatening an intruder (Photograph by Robert W. Hernández/ Photo Researchers)

9.3 Ritualized fighting *Two South African wildebeest males in a harmless ritualized duel along an invisible but clearly defined mutual border between their territories. (Photograph by Lennard Lee Rue III/Bruce Coleman)*

ritualized form of combat as if under an internal compulsion not to inflict serious wounds (see Figure 9.3).

The limitation on violence appears in a number of ways. Many conflicts are settled by blustering diplomacy before they erupt into actual war. For example, male chimpanzees try to intimidate each other by staring, raising an arm, or uttering fearsome shouts. This approach is found throughout the entire animal kingdom: Whenever possible, try to get your way by threat or bluff rather than by actual fighting. This holds even for creatures as large as elephants and as fierce as tigers. Both these and other creatures make use of ***threat displays,*** a much less costly method for achieving one's aim than actual combat (see Figure 9.4).

In some cases, serious fighting will occur even so, for animals no less than human generals may miscalculate their chances of victory. But some ways of limiting the cost of defeat still remain. In wolves, the loser may "admit defeat" by adopting a special submissive gesture, such as begging like a puppy or rolling on his back. This is an ***appeasement display*** that is functionally equivalent to our white flag of surrender. Unlike some human warriors, the victorious wolf is without rancor. He generally accepts the loser's submission, and all fighting stops (Lorenz, 1966). The adaptive value of such submissive signals is clear enough. They allow today's loser to withdraw from the field of battle so that he can come back in a year or two when he is older, wiser, and when he may very well win a rematch. The evolutionary rule is simple enough: Don't fight unless the probable gains (in reproductive success) outweigh the costs. If you lose and run away (or make an appeasement display), you may live to fight (and copulate) another day.

9.4 Threat displays *(A) Some species threaten by making themselves appear larger and more impressive, as when lizards expand their throat skin fold. (Photograph by Joseph T. Collins/Photo Researchers) (B) Other species threaten by shouting at the top of their lungs, like the howler monkeys, who scream at each other for hours on end. (Photograph by Wolfgang Bayer/Bruce Coleman)*

A

B

DOMINANCE AND SUBMISSION

Animals that live in groups often develop a social order based on ***dominance hierarchies.*** Such hierarchies can be quite complex among troops of primates. For example, in baboons, the dominant male has usually achieved his status through victory in several aggressive encounters. After this, his status is settled for a while, and lower-ranking baboons generally step aside to let the "alpha male" pass, and nervously scatter if he merely stares at them.

Dominance hierarchies may reduce internal friction, but they do not begin to abolish it. Much of an alpha male's life is spent in efforts to maintain his place at the top—harassing his subordinates, approaching them until they back away, staring at them until they look down, and if necessary, attacking them with teeth and nails. In these endeavors, the alpha male often depends on alliances with other males (often his own brothers) who will join him to fight off his rivals and who in turn are supported by him in their future aggressive encounters (Walters and Seyfarth, 1986; see Figure 9.5A).

Why should the animals spend so much time to achieve and maintain dominance? The answer is that rank has considerable privileges. The alpha male has first choice of sleeping site, enjoys easier access to food, and has priority in mating (see Figure 9.5B). Such perquisites undoubtedly make life more pleasant for the alpha male than for his less-fortunate fellows. But even more important may be the long-run evolutionary value of rank, for in terms of genetic survival, the higher-ranking animal is more "fit." Since he has easier access to females, he will presumably leave more offspring (Smith, 1981; Silk, 1986).

Thus far, our primary focus has been on dominance relations among primate males. This followed the initial emphasis of investigators in this area who focused on male-male aggression. To be sure, the males' aggressive encounters are quite obvious, as they fight and strut and bellow. Many authors took this as evidence that the social order among most primates (and by implication, our own) was ultimately based on the political struggles among males. But recent research shows that this conclusion is far off the mark. For in many primate societies, females compete no less than males and develop hierarchies that are often more stable than those of males. Moreover, female rank has important long-term consequences, for mothers tend to bequeath their social rank to their offspring, especially to their daughters (Hrdy and Williams, 1983; Walters and Seyfarth, 1986).

TERRITORIALITY IN HUMANS

Is any of the preceding discussion of animals relevant to human behavior? At least on the surface there are parallels that have led some writers to suppose that concepts such as territoriality, dominance hierarchy, and the like, apply to

9.5   Dominance hierarchies   *(A) The two baboons at the right jointly threaten the larger baboon on the left who could defeat either of them alone but won't risk fighting them both. (Courtesy L. T. Nash, Arizona State University) (B) A dominant male baboon with a harem of females and young. (Courtesy of Bruce Coleman)*

A

B

9.6 Personal space *Relatively even spacing in ring-billed gulls (Photograph by Allan D. Cruikshank © 1978/Photo Researchers)*

humans as well as to animals. There are certainly some aspects of human behavior that resemble territoriality. Even within the home, different members of a family have their private preserves—their own rooms or corners, their places at the dinner table, and so on. Other territorial claims are more temporary, such as a seat in a railroad car, whose possession we mark with a coat, a book, or a briefcase if we have to leave for a while.

A related phenomenon is ***personal space,*** the physical region all around us whose intrusion we guard against. On many New York subways, passengers sit on long benches. Except during rush hour, they will carefully choose their seats so as to leave the greatest possible distance between themselves and their nearest neighbor (Figure 9.6). A desire to maintain some minimum personal space is probably nearly universal, but the physical dimensions seem to depend upon the particular culture. In North America, acquaintances stand about two or three feet apart during a conversation; if one moves closer, the other feels crowded or pushed into an unwanted intimacy. For Latin Americans, the acceptable distance is said to be much less. Under the circumstances, misunderstanding is almost inevitable. The North American regards the Latin American as overly intrusive; the Latin American in turn feels that the North American is unfriendly and cold (Hall, 1959).

How seriously should we take such parallels between humans and animals? The best guess is that while the overt behaviors may sometimes be similar, the underlying mechanisms are not. Territoriality in robins is universal and innately based; but in humans it is enormously affected by learning. For example, there are some societies in which private ownership is relatively unimportant, which certainly suggests that cultural factors play a vital role.

THE BIOLOGICAL BASIS OF LOVE: THE MALE-FEMALE BOND

The preceding discussion has made it clear that there is some biological foundation for strife and conflict. The tendencies toward destruction are kept in bounds by a set of counteracting tendencies such as territoriality and ritualized fighting. As we shall see, they are also controlled and modified by learning, especially during childhood in humans, and their expression is greatly affected by situational factors (see Chapters 11 and 14).

But over and above these various inhibiting checks on aggression, there is a positive force that is just as basic and deeply rooted in the biological makeup of

9.7 Grooming in baboons (Photograph by Mitch Reardon/Photo Researchers)

animals and humans. The poets call it love. Scientists use the more prosaic term *bonding,* the tendency to affiliate with others of one's own kind.

The forces of social attraction are most obvious between mate and mate, and between child and parent. But positive bonds occur even outside of mating and child care. Examples are the social relationships cemented by ***grooming*** in monkeys and apes who sit in pairs while the groomer meticulously picks lice and other vermin out of the groomee's fur (Figure 9.7). The animals evidently like to groom and be groomed over and above considerations of personal hygiene; it is their way of forming a social bond, and it works. Grooming occurs most commonly among kin (brothers and sisters, cousins, and so on), although it may also occur among unrelated animals. But whether they be kin or unrelated, animals who groom most often are also the most closely bonded by other measures of primate togetherness: They sit together, forage for food together, and stick together in alliances against common antagonists (Walters and Seyfarth, 1986).

It has sometimes been suggested that a comparable human practice is small talk, in which we exchange no real information but simply talk for the sake of "relating" to the other person. Other people are part of our universe, and we need them and want their company. Much the same is probably true for our primate cousins. They groom each other, whether or not they have vermin. We talk to each other, whether or not we really have something to say.

Sexual Behavior

In some very primitive organisms, reproduction is asexual; thus amoebas multiply by a process of simple cell division. This form of procreation seems to work well enough, for amoebas are still among us. It appears that contrary to one's first impression, sex is *not* necessary (at least, not for reproduction). But if so, why do the vast majority of animal species reproduce sexually? Perhaps sexual reproduction is more enjoyable than the asexual varieties, but its biological advantage lies elsewhere. It comes from the fact that it assures a greater degree of genetic variability.

An amoeba that splits into two has created two replicas of its former self. Here natural selection has no differences to choose between, for the second amoeba can be neither better nor worse in its adaptation to the environment than the first since the two are genetically identical.

Things are quite different in sexual reproduction. Here specialized cells, ***sperm*** and ***ovum,*** must join to form a fertilized egg, or ***zygote,*** which will then become a new individual. This procedure amounts to a kind of genetic roulette. To begin with, each parent donates only half of the genetic material: Within some limits, it is then mere chance that determines which genes are contained in any one sperm or ovum. Chance enters again to determine which sperm will join with which ovum. As a result, there will be inevitable differences among the offspring. Now natural selection can come into play, perhaps favoring the offspring with the sharper teeth, or the one with the more sexually attractive display, which will then enhance the survival of the gene that produced these attributes.

Sexual Choice

For sexual reproduction to occur, sperm and ovum have to meet in the appointed manner, at the proper time, and in the proper place. Many structures and behavior patterns have evolved to accomplish these ends. Our first concern is with those that underlie sexual choice and determine who mates with whom.

9.8 Advertising one's sex *The comb and wattle of this barred rock rooster proclaim that he is a male. (Photograph by Garry D. McMichael, 1987/Photo Researchers)*

9.9 Courtship rituals *(A) The male bower bird tries to entice the female into an elaborate bower decorated with berries, shells, or whatever else may be available, such as colored clothespins. (B) Grebes engage in a complex aquatic ballet. (C) The male tern courts by feeding the female. (Photographs from left to right by Philip Green; Bob and Clara Calhoun/Bruce Coleman; Jeff Foott/Bruce Coleman)*

ADVERTISING ONE'S SEX

The first job of a would-be sexual partner is to proclaim his or her sex. Many animals have anatomical structures whose function is precisely that, for example, the magnificent tail feathers of the male peacock or the comb and wattle of the rooster (see Figure 9.8).

In humans, structural displays of sex differences are less pronounced, but they are present nonetheless. A possible example is the enlarged female breast whose adipose tissue does not really increase the infant's milk supply. According to some ethologists, it evolved as we became erect and lost our reliance upon smell, a sense which provides the primary information about sex and sexual readiness in many mammals. Under the circumstances, there had to be other ways of displaying one's sex. The prominent breasts of the female may be one such announcement among hairless, "naked apes" (Morris, 1967).

COURTSHIP RITUALS

Advertising one's intentions In many animals, sexual display involves various species-specific behavior patterns, called **courtship rituals.** These are essentially ways of advertising one's amorous intentions. Some of these rituals are mainly a means to exhibit the structural sex differences, as in the male peacock spreading his tail feathers. Others are much more elaborate. Thus penguins bow deeply to each other while rocking from side to side, and certain grebes complete an elaborate aquatic ballet by exchanging gifts of seaweed (Figure 9.9).

Indicating one's species Courtship rituals have a further function. They not only increase the likelihood that boy meets girl, but they virtually guarantee that the two will be of the same species. This is because these rituals are so highly species-specific, as in the case of the gift-exchanging grebes. In effect they are a code, whereby each member of the pair informs the other that he belongs, say, to the duck species *anas platyrhynochos,* rather than to *bucephala clangula* or *tachyeres patachonicus,* or yet another duck species that no self-respecting *anas platyrhynochos* would want to mate with. The effect of such species-specific courtship codes is that they make it more likely that the mating will produce fertile offspring. For contrary to popular view, different species can interbreed if they are related closely enough. But the offspring of such "unnatural" unions is often infertile; an example is the mule, a result of crossing a horse with a donkey. Species-specific courtship rituals have evolved to avoid such reproductive failures.

A

B

C

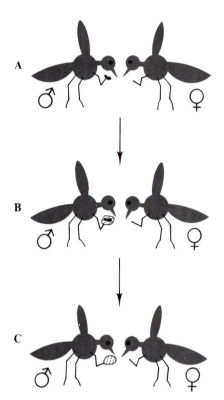

9.10   The evolution of courtship in dancing flies   *(A) In some species, the male catches a prey animal and gives it to the female to eat during copulation; this keeps her busy so she is less likely to eat him. (B) In other species, the male first wraps the prey in a balloon of secreted silk. This keeps the female even busier since she has to unwrap the prey. (C) Finally, in the dancing fly, the male gives the female a ball of silk without anything in it. (After Klopfer, 1974)*

The evolutionary origin of courtship rituals   We've discussed the general function of courtship rituals, but what can we say about the evolutionary history of a particular ritual or display? Displays leave no fossils so there is no direct method for reconstructing their biological past. One possible approach is to compare displays in related species. By noting their similarities and differences, the ethologist tries to reconstruct the evolutionary steps in their history, much as a comparative anatomist charts the family tree of fins, wings, and forelegs.

An example of how this comparative method works when applied to species-specific behaviors is an analysis of an odd courtship ritual in a predatory insect, the dancing fly (Kessel, 1955). At mating time, the male dancing fly secretes a little ball of silk which he brings to the female. She plays with this silk ball while the male mounts her and copulates. How did this ritual arise? The courtship patterns in a number of related species give a clue. Most flies of related species manage with a minimum of precopulatory fuss; the trouble is that the female may decide to eat the male rather than mate with him. However, if she is already eating a small prey animal, the male is safe. Some species have evolved a behavior pattern that capitalizes on this fact. The male catches a small insect and brings it to the female for her to eat while he mates with her. In still other species, the male first wraps the prey in a large silk balloon. This increases his margin of safety, for the female is kept busy unwrapping her present. The dancing fly's ritual is probably the last step in this evolutionary sequence. The male dancing fly wastes no time or energy in catching a prey animal, but simply brings an empty ball of silk, all wrapping and no present. Copulation can now proceed unimpeded since the female is safely occupied—perhaps the first creature in evolutionary history to realize that it is the thought and not the gift that matters (Figure 9.10).

WHO MAKES THE CHOICE

The preceding discussions have centered on the various factors that bring male and female together. But, interestingly enough, the two don't have an equal voice in the ultimate decision. In most species, the female finally decides whether or not to mate. The biological reason is simple—the female shoulders the major cost of reproduction. If she is a bird, she supplies not only the ovum but also the food supply for the developing embryo. If she is a mammal, she carries the embryo within her body and later provides it with milk. In either case, her biological burden is vastly greater than the male's. If a doe's offspring fails to survive, she has lost a whole breeding season. In comparison, the stag's loss is minimal—a few minutes of his time and some easily replaced sperm cells. Under the circumstances, natural selection would favor the female who is particularly choosy about picking the best possible male; that is, the male whose genetic contribution will best ensure their offsprings' survival. From the male's point of view, the female seems coy or "plays hard to get." But in fact this is not just playacting for, to the female, reproduction is a serious business with heavy biological costs (Trivers, 1972).

There are a few interesting exceptions. One example is the sea horse, whose young are carried in a brood pouch by the male. In this animal, the male exhibits greater sexual caution and discrimination than the female. A similar effect is found in the phalarope, an arctic seabird whose eggs are hatched and whose chicks are fed by the male (Figure 9.11). Here a greater part of the biological burden falls on the male, and we should expect a corresponding increase in his sexual choosiness. This is just what happens. Among the phalaropes, the female does the wooing. She is brightly plumaged, and aggressively pursues the dull-colored, coyly careful male (Williams, 1966).

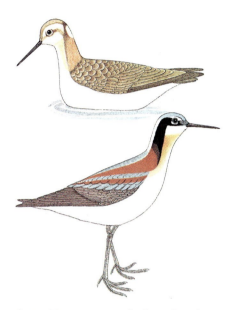

9.11 Plumage pattern in the male and female phalarope *The phalarope male hatches and feeds the chicks. Since he carries a larger share of the biological cost of reproduction, he is more coy and choosy than the female. As the drawing indicates schematically, the female phalarope (bottom) is larger and more colorfully plumaged than the male (top). (Höhn, 1969)*

Reproduction and Timing

Once male and female have met, the next step is to arrange for the union of their respective sperm and ovum. Terrestrial animals have evolved a variety of sexual mechanics to accomplish this end. In general, the male introduces his sperm cells into the genital tract of the female, where the ovum is fertilized. The problem is synchronization. The sperm has to encounter a ready ovum, and the fertilized egg can develop only if it is provided with the appropriate conditions. Under these circumstances, timing is of the essence. In birds and mammals, the timing mechanism depends on a complex feedback system between brain centers and hormones.

ANIMAL SEXUALITY AND HORMONES

Hormonal cycles   Except for some primates, mammals mate only when the female is in heat, or *estrus.* For example, the female rat goes through a fifteen-hour estrus period every four days. At all other times, she will resolutely reject any male's advances. If he nuzzles her or tries to mount, she will kick and bite. But during estrus, the female responds quite differently to the male's approach. She first retreats in small hops, then stops to look back, and wiggles her ears provocatively (McClintock and Adler, 1978). Eventually, she stands still, her back arched, her tail held to the side, in all respects a willing sexual partner.

What accounts for the difference between the female's behavior during estrus and at other times? The crucial fact is a simple matter of reproductive biology. The time of estrus is precisely the time when the female's ova are ripe for fertilization. Evolution has obviously provided a behavioral arrangement that is exactly tuned to reproductive success.

Hormonal changes and behavior   Some hormonal changes affect behavior dramatically. When male rats are castrated, they soon lose all sexual interest and capacity, as do female rats without ovaries. But sexual behavior is quickly restored by appropriate injections of male or female hormones, specifically testosterone and estrogen.

Many investigators believe that behavioral effects of hormones are caused by neurons in the hypothalamus that contain receptors with which certain hormone molecules from the bloodstream combine. When this occurs, it leads to neural changes in the hypothalamus that trigger sexual appetite and behavior. This hypothesis has been tested by injecting minute quantities of various hormones into several regions of the hypothalamus. The total amounts were negligible and could hardly affect the overall hormone concentration in the blood. Will the hypothalamic sexual control system be fooled by the local administration of the hormone, as is its thermostatic counterpart when it is locally cooled or heated (see Chapter 2)? It evidently is. A spayed female cat will go into estrus when estrogen is implanted in her hypothalamus (Harris and Michael, 1964). Analogous effects have been obtained with **androgens** (that is, male hormones) administered to castrated male rats (Davidson, 1969; McEwen et al., 1982; Feder, 1984).

HUMAN SEXUALITY AND HORMONES

The major difference between animal and human sexuality concerns the flexibility of sexual behavior. When does it occur, how, and with whom? Compared to animals, we are much less automatic in our sexual activities, much more varied,

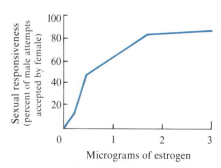

9.12 Estrogen and sexual behavior *The effect of estrogen injections on the sexual responsiveness of female rats was measured by the number of male attempts at mounting that were accepted by the female. The females' ovaries had been removed, so they could not produce estrogen themselves. The hormone was injected daily in the doses shown above. Sexual behavior was measured eight days after hormone treatment began. (After Bermant and Davidson, 1974)*

Birds as monagamous *Birds tend to mate and stay together during a mating season as both parents are needed for successful incubation of their young. Here a black-bowed albatross male courts a female on the nest that will serve as home for their offspring. (Photograph by Robert W. Hernandez/The National Audubon Society Collection/Photo Researchers)*

much more affected by prior experience. Human sexuality is remarkably plastic and can be variously shaped by experience, especially early experience, and by cultural patterns (see Chapters 10 and 14).

The difference between animal and human sexual behavior is especially marked when we consider the effects of hormones. In rats and cats, sexual behavior is highly dependent upon hormone levels; castrated males and spayed females stop copulating a few months after the removal of their gonads (Figure 9.12). In humans, on the other hand, sexual activity may persist for years, even decades, after castration or ovariectomy, provided that the operation was performed after puberty (Bermant and Davidson, 1974).

The liberation from hormonal control is especially clear in human females. To be sure, women are subject to a physiological cycle, but this has relatively little impact on sexual behavior, at least when compared to the profound effects seen in animals. The female rat or cat is chained to an estrus cycle that commands her to be receptive during one period and prevents her from being so at all other times. There are no such fetters on the human female, who is capable of sexual behavior at any time during her cycle and also capable of refusing.

Evolution and Mating Systems

In many species, the male and female part company after copulation and may very well never meet again. But in others, the partners remain together for a breeding season or even longer. In many cases, their arrangement involves **polygyny,** and the resulting family consists of one male, several females, and their various offspring. In a very few others, the mating system is **polyandry,** which works the other way around, with one female and several males. And in still others, the mating pattern is **monogamy,** with a reproductive partnership based on a special, more or less permanent tie between one male and one female.

MATING SYSTEMS IN ANIMALS

What accounts for the different mating systems found in different parts of the animal kingdom? A clue comes from the different patterns found in mammals and birds. Some 90 percent of all birds are monogamous: They mate and stay together throughout a breeding season. In contrast, more than 90 percent of all mammals are polygynous, with one male monopolizing a number of females. Why should this be so?

Sociobiologists seek the answer through some kind of evolutionary economics: The patterns that evolved are such as to maximize each individual's reproductive success. Consider the reproductive problem faced by birds. In many species, successful incubation requires both parents: one who sits upon the eggs, another who forages for food to nourish the bird that's sitting. After hatching, finding food for a nestful of hungry chicks may still require the full-time efforts of both birds. Under the circumstances, monogamy makes reproductive sense for both sexes: The father has to help the mother after she lays her eggs, or else no chicks will survive into adulthood.

The situation is quite different for most mammals. Here there is no incubation problem; since the fetus grows within the mother's womb, she is still able to forage for her own food during the offspring's gestation. In addition, the mother has the exclusive job of feeding the offspring after birth, for only females can secrete the milk on which the infants live. Now the reproductive calculus leads to a different conclusion. The male does not have to invest time and effort in taking care of his offspring; instead, his best bet for maximizing his own reproductive success lies in mating with as many females as he possibly can. To accomplish this, he has

9.13 Sexual dimorphism *Polygynous species tend to be dimorphic. (A) A rocky mountain bull elk rounding up his harem. Note the bull's large antlers and larger size. (Pat and Tom Leeson/Photo Researchers) (B) In Titi monkeys, which are monogamous, males and females are very similar in size and form. (Photograph by Nina Leen/Life Magazine, © Time Warner, Inc.)*

Polygynous tendencies in humans *The archetype of the philandering male is Don Juan, or to use his Italian name, Don Giovanni. In Mozart's opera, Don Giovanni boasts of having seduced 1,975 women of every age and rank, but is eventually punished for his polygynous sins and dragged down to hell. (From a 1989 production of* Don Giovanni, *with Erie Mills and John Cheek, © 1989 Martha Swope)*

to become attractive to females (by developing the most impressive antlers, or whatever), and he has to win in the competition with many other males, all of whom have the identical goal. The end result is polygyny, with one successful male monopolizing a number of females.

There's an interesting anatomical correlate of mating arrangements in the animal kingdom. Almost invariably, polygyny is accompanied by *sexual dimorphism,* a pronounced anatomical difference in the size or bodily structures of the two sexes. The more polygynous the species, the more dimorphic it tends to be, with the males larger and often more ornamented than the females, as shown by the peacock's tail, the stag's antlers, and the male elephant seal's disproportionate size (Figure 9.13A). In contrast, monogamous species such as the gibbon show no such dimorphism (Figure 9.13B).

MATING PATTERNS IN HUMANS

A number of authors have tried to extend this general line of reasoning to account for the evolution of human sexual and mating behavior. They start out with the observation that humans are somewhat dimorphic: On average, the human male is about 10 percent larger than the female. Since such dimorphism is correlated with polygyny in animals, one might expect some similar tendency in humans.

The sociobiological perspective To bolster their case, sociobiologists refer to a number of findings that in their view point in this direction. One is the anthropological evidence. A review of 185 cultures showed that the majority formally allowed polygyny. Only 16 percent of the cultures had monogamous marriage arrangements that permitted only one spouse to each partner (Ford and Beach, 1951). Related findings come from a number of studies of our own culture. These strongly suggest that, on average, men have a greater desire for a variety of sexual partners than do women (Symons, 1979).

Sociobiologists argue that these differences are ultimately rooted in our biological nature. In their view, men want greater sexual variety because for them it is reproductively adaptive: the more women they mate with, the more children they father. In contrast, women are much more cautious in evaluating potential sexual partners and more interested in a stable, familial relationship—a good reproductive strategy since, as we've seen, the biological parental investment of a female is almost always greater than a male's. Such built-in patterns are presumably no longer relevant in a modern world in which birth control techniques have managed to uncouple sex from reproduction. But according to the sociobiologists, these remnants of our biological past are still with us just the same. They were once reproductively adaptive, and they continue to influence our behavior even though their adaptive role is diminished or altogether gone.

The cultural perspective   The sociobiological view has been severely challenged, however. One line of attack concerns the role of culture. Many critics argue that differences in sexual attitudes are a product of society rather than of biological predispositions and reflect a cultural rather than a built-in double standard. In their opinion, polygyny is a natural outgrowth of cultural conditions in which men are dominant and women are perceived as property. As to the differences in men's and women's desire for sexual variety, they regard it as a product of early social training: Boys are taught that many sexual conquests are a proof of "man-liness," while girls are taught to value home and family and to seek a single partner.

Critics of the sociobiological approach have no quarrel with the sociobiologists' efforts to understand animal behavior in an evolutionary perspective. Their critique is aimed at the attempt to extend these concepts to the human level. After all, terms such as *monogamy* have quite a different meaning when applied to, say, geese and humans. In geese, the term describes the fact that two parents stay together for one breeding season to hatch and raise their young; in humans, the term describes an arrangement that only makes sense in the context of a network of social and legal patterns. Evolution may have shaped many of our impulses and desires, but we simply don't know how these in turn have shaped the culture in which humans live and mate and bring up their children. Since this is so, it is rank speculation to assert that the reproductive economics that underlie an elephant seal's attempts to set up a harem are at bottom the same as those that account for the philandering found in some human males (Kitcher, 1985).

THE BIOLOGICAL BASIS OF LOVE: THE PARENT-CHILD BOND

There is another bond of love whose biological foundations are no less basic than those of the male-female tie—the relation between mother and child (and in many animals, the relation between father and child as well). In birds and mammals some kind of parental attachment is almost ubiquitous. In contrast to most fish and reptiles that lay eggs by the hundreds and then abandon them, birds and mammals invest in quality rather than quantity. They have fewer offspring, but they then see to it that most of their brood survives into maturity. They feed them, clean them, shelter them, and protect them during some initial period of dependency. While under this parental umbrella, the young animal can grow and become prepared for the world into which it must soon enter and can acquire some of the skills that will help it survive in that world. This period of initial dependency is longest in animals that live by their wits, such as monkeys and apes, and is longest of all in humans.

The Infant's Attachment to the Mother

In most birds and mammals, the young become strongly attached to their mother. Ducklings follow the mother duck, lambs the mother ewe, and infant monkeys cling tightly to the mother monkey's belly. In each case, separation leads to considerable stress: the young animals give piteous distress calls and

Orangutan mother and child   (Photograph by Roy P. Fontaine/The National Audubon Society Collection/Photo Researchers)

quack, bleat, and keen continuously until the mother returns. The biological function of this attachment is a simple matter of personal survival. This holds for humans as well as animals. For there is little doubt that in our early evolutionary history a motherless infant would probably have died an early death—of exposure, starvation, or predation. There are very few orphanages in nature.

The mechanisms that lead to this attachment will be discussed in a later section (see Chapter 14). For now, we will only say that while some theorists believe that the main factor is the child's discovery that the mother's presence leads to the alleviation of hunger, thirst, and pain, there is strong evidence that the attachment is more basic than that. For the distress shown by the young—whether birds, monkeys, or humans—when they are separated from their mother occurs even when they are perfectly well-fed and housed. It appears that the infant's attachment to its mother is based on more than the satisfaction of the major bodily needs. The infant evidently comes predisposed to seek social stimulation, which is rewarding in and of itself.

The Mother's Attachment to the Infant

For the infant, the function of the mother-child bond is simple personal survival. For the mother, the biological function is again a matter of survival, but for her, the survival is genetic rather than personal, for unless her young survive into adulthood, her own genes will perish. But what are the mechanisms that produce the parents' attachment? Robins and gibbons behave like proper parents: they care for their young and protect them. But they surely don't do this because they realize that their failure to act in this way would lead to genetic extinction. The real reason must lie elsewhere. One possibility is that there are some built-in predispositions toward parental behavior. If such predispositions do exist, they would then be favored by natural selection.

There is good evidence that the young of many animal species have a set of built-in responses that elicit caretaking from the parents. To give only one example, many baby birds open their mouths as wide as they can as soon as the parent arrives at the nest. This "gaping" response is their means of begging for food (see Figure 9.14). Some species of birds have special anatomical signs that help to elicit a proper parental reaction. An example is the Cedar Waxwing, whose bright red mouth lining evidently provides a further signal to the parent: I'm young, hungry, and a Cedar Waxwing!

9.14 Gaping in young birds *The gaping response of the young yellow warbler serves as a built-in signal that elicits the parents' feeding behavior. (Photograph by John Shaw/Bruce Coleman)*

Child care in humans is obviously more complex and flexible than it is in Cedar Waxwings, but it too has biological foundations. The mother-child relation grows out of a number of built-in reaction patterns, of child to mother and mother to child. The human infant begins life with a few relevant reflex patterns, including some that help him find the mother's nipple and suck at it once it is found. He also has an essentially innate signal system through which he tells the mother that he is in distress: he cries. Analogous *distress calls* are found in many animals, for when the young chirp, bleat, mew, or cry, the mother immediately runs to their aid and comforts them.

According to ethologists, evolution has further equipped the infant with a set of stimulus features that function as innate releasers of parental, and especially maternal, feelings. The cues that define "babyness" include a large, protruding forehead, large eyes, an upturned nose, chubby cheeks, and so on. Endowed with these distinctive properties, the baby looks "cute" and "cuddly," something to be picked up, fussed over, and taken care of. The case is similar for the young of various animals who share aspects of the same "baby schema." Various commercial enterprises are devoted to the deliberate manufacture of cuteness. Dolls and Walt

Disney creatures are designed to be babied by children, while certain lap dogs are especially bred to be babied by adults.

Nature has provided the infant with yet another trick to disarm even the stoniest of parental hearts: the smile. In some fashion, smiling may begin within the first month: it is often considered a built-in signal by which humans tell each other. "I wish you well. Be good to me." There is reason to believe that it is innate. Infants who are born blind smile under conditions that also produce smiling in sighted children, as when they hear their mother's voice. They obviously could not have learned this response by imitation.

COMMUNICATING MOTIVES

The preceding discussion has given ample testimony that many animal species exist within a social framework in much the same way that humans do. What one creature does often has a crucial effect on the behavior of another of its own kind. As we have seen, the major means of exerting such social influences is the signaling display.

Expressive Movements: Animal Display

Displays represent a simple mode of communication whereby animals inform each other of what they are most likely to do in the immediate future. The crab waves its claws and the wolf bares its fangs; these threat messages may save both sender and receiver from bodily harm if the message is heeded.

How do ethologists determine what message is conveyed by a given display? Since the sender is an animal, they cannot ask it directly. They can try, however, to infer the message by noting the correlation between a given display and the animal's behavior just before and after its occurrence. For example, if a certain posture is generally followed by attack, then it is usually called a threat display; if it is usually followed by mating, it is probably a courtship signal, and so on.

Some ethologists interpret such correlations between displays and subsequent behavior by assuming that in effect displays communicate the animal's present motive state—its readiness to fight or to mate, its need for food or parental attention, and so forth. For this reason, displays are sometimes said to "express" the animal's inner state and are therefore described as *expressive movements.*

The Expression of Emotions in Humans

In humans, built-in social displays are relegated to a lesser place. After all, we have the much richer communication system provided by human language. But even so, we do possess a set of displays that tell others something about our feelings and needs—our various emotional expressions.

THE UNIVERSALITY OF EMOTIONAL EXPRESSIONS

Humans have a sizable repertory of emotional expressions, most of them conveyed by the face. We smile, laugh, weep, frown, snarl, and grit our teeth. Are any of these expressive patterns our human equivalent of displays? If so, they should be universal to all humans and innately determined (Ekman, 1973; Ekman and Oster, 1979; Fridlund, Ekman, and Oster, 1983).

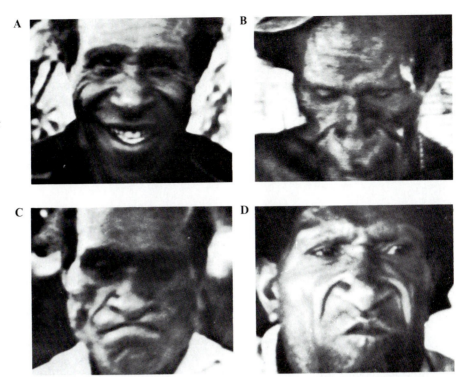

9.15 Attempts to portray emotion by New Guinea tribesmen Acting out emotions appropriate to various situations: (A) "Your friend has come and you are happy" (B) "Your child has died" (C) "You are angry and about to fight" (D) "You see a dead pig that has been lying there for a long time." (© Paul Ekman, 1971)

In one study, American actors posed in photographs to convey such emotions as fear, anger, and happiness. These pictures were then shown to members of different cultures, both literate (Swedes, Japanese, Kenyans) and preliterate (members of an isolated New Guinea tribe barely advanced beyond Stone-Age culture). When asked to identify the portrayed emotion, all groups came up with quite similar judgments. The results were much the same when the procedure was reversed. The New Guinea tribesmen were asked to portray the emotions appropriate to various simple situations such as happiness at the return of a friend, grief at the death of a child, and anger at the start of a fight. Photographs of their performances were then shown to American college students who readily picked out the emotions the tribesmen had tried to convey (see Figure 9.15).

These results indicate that there may be some emotional expressions that are common to all humans. This conclusion fits observations of children born blind. These children cry, smile, and laugh under essentially the same conditions that elicit these reactions in sighted children. In fact, much the same is true even of children born both blind and deaf. It would be hard to argue that these children had *learned* the emotional expressions considering that their sensory avenues of both sight and sound had been blocked off from birth.

At least in part, such built-in expressions may serve a similar function as do animal displays. They act as social signals by which we communicate our inner states to others, a way of saying what we are likely to do next.

THE ROLE OF CULTURE

These findings do not imply that smiling and other emotional expressions are unaffected by cultural conventions. According to some accounts, Melanese chieftains frown fiercely when greeting each other at a festive occasion, and Samurai mothers are said to have smiled upon hearing that their sons had fallen in battle (Klineberg, 1940). But such facts do not disprove the claim that facial expressions are built-in social signals; they only show that such signals can be artificially masked and modified. How and when such artifice comes into play, however, depends on the culture.

Some evidence for this view comes from studies in which American and Japanese subjects were presented with a harrowing documentary film of a primitive puberty rite. As they watched the film, their facial expressions were recorded with a hidden camera. The results showed that when alone, the facial reactions of the Japanese and American subjects were virtually identical. But the results were quite different when the subject watched the film in the company of a white-coated experimenter. Now the Japanese looked more polite and smiled more than the Americans (Ekman, 1977; for further discussion, see Fridlund, 1990).

SELF-SACRIFICE AND ALTRUISM

The preceding pages have provided ample evidence that animals are necessarily social: they fight and compete with each other, mate, reproduce, and communicate. Still further work by ethologists suggests that under certain conditions they may even behave as if they were "unselfish altruists."

It's of course well known that many animals go to considerable lengths to defend their offspring. Various birds have evolved characteristic ways of feigning injury such as dropping one wing and paddling around in circles to draw a predator away from their nests (see Figure 9.16). On the face of it, such acts appear heroically unselfish, for the parents court the danger that the predator will seize them. But here again we come up with the difference between personal and genetic survival. For what seems unselfish from the vantage of the individual looks different from a biological point of view (Wilson, 1975). The mother bird who does not divert a potential attacker may very well live longer because she has played it safe. But from an evolutionary perspective what counts is not her own survival but the survival of her genes. And these are more likely to perish if she flies off to safety; while she hides in the bushes, the marauding cat will eat her chicks. As a result, she will have fewer offspring to whom she can pass on her genes, including the very gene or genes that underlie her maternal indifference. Those of her offspring that do survive will in turn have fewer offspring, and so on, until her genetic attributes disappear.

9.16   A misleading display   In feigning injury, the killdeer, a small American bird, runs and flies erratically from predators that approach its nest, often flopping about as if it has a broken wing. (Photograph by Wayne Lankinen/Bruce Coleman)

Altruism in Animals

Seen in this light, parental self-sacrifice can be understood in evolutionary terms. Can a similar analysis be applied to unselfish acts that benefit individuals who are not one's own children? Such apparently altruistic acts are found in various animal species.* A case in point is the warning signal given off by many species at the approach of a predator (see Figure 9.17). When a robin sees a hawk overhead, it gives an alarm call, a special cry that alerts all members of the flock and impels them to seek cover. This alarm call is based on a built-in, inherited tendency and is essentially unlearned. All robins emit this cry when in danger, and they do so even if raised in complete isolation from their fellows. There is no doubt that this alarm benefits all robins who hear it. They crouch low and hide, so their chances of escape are enhanced. But what does it gain the bird who sounds the alarm? Doesn't it place him in greater danger by increasing the likelihood that the hawk will detect *him?* Why does the robin play the hero instead of quietly stealing away

* In modern biological usage, the term *altruism* is reserved for cases in which the good deed benefits neither the doers nor their own offspring.

and leaving his fellows to their fate? There are several possible factors, each of which may play a role.

ENLIGHTENED SELF-INTEREST

One possibility is that this act of avian heroism is not as unselfish as it seems, for it may well increase the warner's own chance of personal survival in the long run. If a particular robin spies a hawk and remains quiet, there is a greater chance that some bird in the flock will be captured, most likely another bird. But what about tomorrow? A hawk who has seized a prey will probably return to the very same place in search of another meal. And this meal may be the very same robin who originally minded his own business and stayed uninvolved (Trivers, 1971).

KIN SELECTION

There is another alternative. Let us assume that our heroic robin is unlucky, is seized by the hawk, and dies a martyr's death. While this act may have caused the robin to perish as an individual, it may well have served to preserve some of that bird's genes. This may be true even if none of the birds in the flock are the hero's own offspring. They may be relatives who carry some of his genes, brothers and sisters who share half of the same genes, or nieces and nephews who share one-fourth. If so, the alarm call may have saved several relatives who carry the alarm-calling gene and who will pass it on to future generations of robins. From an evolutionary point of view, the alarm call had survival value—if not for the alarm caller or its direct offspring, then for the alarm-calling gene (Hamilton, 1964; Maynard-Smith, 1965).

According to this view, altruistic behavior will evolve if it promotes the survival of the individual's kin. This **kin-selection** hypothesis predicts that unselfish behavior should be more common among relatives than unrelated individuals. There is some evidence that this is indeed the case. Certain deer snort loudly when alarmed, which alerts other deer that are nearby. Groups of does tend to be related; bucks, who disperse when they get old enough, are less likely to be related. The kin-selection hypothesis would then predict that does should be more likely to give the alarm snort than bucks. This is indeed what happens. Similar results have been obtained for various other species (Hirth and McCullough, 1977; Sherman, 1977).

RECIPROCAL ALTRUISM

There is yet another possible mechanism that leads to biologically unselfish acts. Some animals—and we may well be among them—may have a built-in Golden Rule: Do unto others, as you would want them to do unto you (or unto your genes). If an individual helps another and that other later reciprocates, the ultimate upshot is a benefit to both. For example, male baboons sometimes help each other in aggressive encounters, and the one who received help on one occasion is more likely to come to the other's assistance later on (Packer, 1977).

A built-in predisposition toward reciprocity may well be one of the biological foundations of altruism in some animals (and perhaps ourselves as well). If the original unselfish act doesn't exact too great a cost—in energy expended or in danger incurred—then its eventual reciprocation will yield a net benefit to both parties. A tendency toward reciprocal altruism of this kind, however, presupposes relatively stable groups in which individuals recognize one another. It also presupposes some safeguards against "cheating," accepting help without reciprocating. One such safeguard might be a link between a disposition toward altruism and a disposition to punish cheaters (Trivers, 1971).

9.17 Alarm call *Ground squirrels give alarm calls when they sense a nearby predator. Such alarm calls are more likely to be given by females rather than males. The females usually have close relatives living nearby. As a result, their alarm call is more likely to benefit genetically related rather than unrelated individuals, which suggests that it is based on kin selection. (Photograph by Georg D. Lepp/Bio-Tec Images)*

Braving death for an ideal   During the Civil War, a vastly outnumbered group of black Union soldiers attacked an impregnable fortress held by the Confederate forces, suffering enormous casualties. They were willing to die for the abolition of slavery and to show that blacks are just as capable of sacrificing themselves for an ideal as whites are. From the 1989 film Glory, directed by Edward Zwick. (Photo courtesy of Photofest)

Altruism in Humans

There is little doubt that humans are capable of considerable self-sacrifice. Soldiers volunteer for suicide missions, and religious martyrs burn at the stake. In addition to these awesome deeds of heroism are the more common acts of altruism—sharing food and money, offering help, and the like. Can such human acts of altruism be understood in the biological terms that apply to the alarm calls of birds and monkeys?

THE SOCIOBIOLOGISTS' VIEW

According to Edward Wilson, the founder of sociobiology, the answer is yes, at least to some extent. While Wilson emphasizes the enormous variations among human social systems, he notes that there are certain common themes, which he regards as grounded in our genetic heritage. Of these, the most important is kinship. Wilson and other sociobiologists suggest that, by and large, we will be most altruistic to our closest relatives. According to Wilson, the person who risks death in battle or through martyrdom probably helps to ensure the survival of the group of which he is a member—and thus of his own genes, since this group probably includes his own kin. As with the robin, the individual hero may die, but his genes will survive (Wilson, 1975; 1978).

Sociobiologists believe that this position is supported by the fact that kinship is of considerable importance in just about all human societies, as attested to by the elaborate terms used to describe the precise nature of kinship relations: brother, sister, uncle, cousin, second-cousin-once-removed, and so on. At least in our culture, the likelihood that one person will make a sacrifice for another increases the closer the two are genetically related to each other (Essock-Vitale and McGuire, 1985).

SOME PROBLEMS OF FACT AND THEORY

Still, the sociobiological analysis of human altruism is highly controversial. To begin with, studies of different cultures show that the degree to which relatives help each other is not a simple function of their genetic closeness. It often depends much more on whether individuals regard themselves as close and related than on whether they actually are so genetically. Some evidence comes from the study of several cultures in which newly married couples live in the groom's father's household and eventually create an extended family with many brothers, sisters, uncles, aunts, and so on. A young boy in this family will get to know his *paternal* uncles—they will live in the same hut or one nearby. But he won't have much to do with his *maternal* uncles; they stayed behind in his *maternal* grandfather's household. Genetically, he is of course equally close to both, but when questioned about whom he feels closer to (and is more likely to help or be helped by), he immediately says that it is the paternal uncle, whom he has known and lived with all his life (Sahlins, 1976).

Critics of sociobiology feel that these and similar findings show that human social behavior depends crucially on culture. To understand human altruism, we have to understand it in its own social terms. The Polynesian boy who feels close to his paternal but not his maternal uncle is responding to kinship as his culture describes it, rather than as something defined by his genes. The same holds for self-sacrifice. The ancient Romans fell on their swords when defeated not to save their brothers' genes but to save their honor. The early Christians defied death because of a religious belief rather than to maintain a particular gene pool. We cannot comprehend the ancient Romans without considering their concept of honor, nor can we explain the martyrdom of the early Christians without reference to their belief in the hereafter.

To sum up, Wilson and other sociobiologists have argued that human social behaviors such as altruism and self-sacrifice are at bottom biological adaptations that guarantee the survival of the reproductively fittest—in principle no different from the social patterns found in primates and in lower animals. The critics of this view do not deny the powerful influence of biology on human behavior. But they insist that human social behavior is so thoroughly infused by culture—by moral and religious beliefs, by customs, by art—that the analogy to animal behavior is more misleading than informative. This issue is still being hotly debated in current psychological, biological, and anthropological thought, and we cannot solve it here. But we will return to it when we discuss altruistic behavior as it is studied by modern social psychologists (see Chapter 12, pp. 331–34).

ETHOLOGY AND HUMAN NATURE

Over three hundred years have passed since Hobbes described the "war of all against all," which he regarded as the natural state of all mankind. We are still far from having anything that even resembles a definite description of our basic social nature. But at least we know that some of Hobbes's solutions are false or oversimplified. Humans are not built so as to be solitary. Other people are a necessary aspect of our lives, and a tendency to interact with others is built into us at the very outset. What holds for humans holds for most animals as well. The robin is programmed to deal with other robins, the baboon with other baboons. Some of these interactions are peaceful, while others are quarrelsome. What matters is that there is always some intercourse between like and like. This social intercourse is an essential aspect of each creature's existence, as shown by an elaborate repertory of built-in social reactions that govern reproduction, care of offspring, and intraspecies competition at virtually all levels of the animal kingdom. No man is an island; neither is any other animal.

Human martyrdom *A painting of Saint Serapion, a thirteenth-century Christian martyr who was tortured to death by North African Moors to whom he preached Christianity. Can we really attribute the behavior of such martyrs to kin selection or reciprocal altruism? (*Saint Serapion, *by Francisco de Zubarán, 1628, © Wadsworth Atheneum, Hartford, Conn., Ella Gallup Sumner and Mary Catlin Sumner Collection)*

CHAPTER 10

The Individual and Society: The Contributions of Sigmund Freud

In the last chapter, we considered the basic social nature of human beings. We began by considering the effects of our evolutionary past as revealed by various social—and perhaps built-in—dispositions of animals and humans. We now turn to the effects of a much more recent and personal past—our own childhoods. This is the period in which we first encounter the force of society as embodied in the way in which we are reared, in which we are introduced to that web of shared knowledge, of common do's and don'ts, that is called *culture.* This culture necessarily channels and modifies many of the built-in patterns that are part of our biological makeup. To understand human social nature, we must ask how people transmit their culture from one generation to the next. A major figure who asked this question was the founder of psychoanalysis, Sigmund Freud (1856–1939), whose views were to revolutionize all subsequent accounts of what human beings are really like.

Sigmund Freud *(Courtesy National Library of Medicine)*

THE ORIGINS OF PSYCHOANALYTIC THOUGHT

In some ways, Freud can be regarded as a modern Hobbesian. Hobbes had insisted that at bottom men are savage brutes whose natural impulses would inevitably lead to murder, rape, and pillage if left unchecked (see Chapter 9). To curb this beast within, they had formed a social contract in some distant past and subordinated themselves to a larger social unit, the state. Like Hobbes, Freud regarded the basic human instincts as a "seething cauldron" of pleasure seeking that blindly seeks gratification regardless of the consequences. This savage, selfish human nature had to be tamed by civilization.

The Dream of Reason Produces Monsters
An engraving by Francisco Goya (1799) which suggests that the same mind that is capable of reason also produces unknown terrors. (Courtesy National Library of Medicine)

Unlike Hobbes, Freud did not believe that the subjugation of the brute in man was a onetime event in human political history. It occurs in every lifetime, for the social contract is renewed in the childhood of every generation. Another difference concerns the nature of the taming process. According to Hobbes, men's baser instincts are curbed by *external* social sanctions; they want to rob their neighbors but don't do so because they are afraid of the king's men. According to Freud, the restraints of society are incorporated internally during the first few years of childhood. The first curbs on behavior are based on a simple (and quite Hobbesian) fear of direct social consequences—of a scolding or spanking. But eventually the child inhibits his misdeeds because he feels that "they are bad," and not just because he fears that he will be caught and punished. At this point, the taming force of society has become internalized. The king's men are now within us, internalized embodiments of society's dictates whose weapons—the pangs of conscience—are no less powerful for being mental.

According to Freud, the taming process is never fully complete. The forbidden impulses cannot be ruled out of existence. They may be denied for a while, but eventually they will reassert themselves, often through new and devious channels, leading to yet further repressive measures which will probably fail in their turn as well. As a result, there is constant conflict between the demands of instinct and of society, but this war goes on underground, within the individual and usually without his or her own knowledge. As a result, man is divided against himself, and his unconscious conflicts express themselves in thoughts and deeds that appear irrational.

Hysteria and Hypnosis

When Freud began his medical practice, many of his patients suffered from a disorder then called **hysteria.** The symptoms of hysteria presented an apparently helter-skelter catalogue of physical and mental complaints—total or partial blindness or deafness, paralysis or anesthesia of various parts of the body, uncontrollable trembling or convulsive attacks, distortions, and gaps in memory. Except for these symptoms, the patients were in no sense "insane"; they were generally lucid and did not have to be institutionalized. Was there any underlying pattern that could make sense of this confusing array of complaints?

The first clue came with the suspicion that hysterical symptoms are **psychogenic,** the results of some unknown psychological cause rather than the product of organic damage to the nervous system. This hypothesis grew out of the work of Jean Charcot (1825–1893), a French neurologist, who noticed that many of the bodily symptoms of hysteria make no anatomical sense. For example, some patients suffered from anesthesia of the hand but lost no feeling above the wrist. This **glove anesthesia** could not possibly be caused by any nerve injury, since it is known that an injury to any of the relevant nerve trunks must affect a portion of the arm above the wrist (Figure 10.1). This rules out a simple organic interpretation and suggests that glove anesthesia has some psychological basis. While such findings showed that the hysterical symptoms are somehow psychological, this does not mean that they are therefore unreal. The patients weren't simply faking; their symptoms were real enough to them and often caused considerable suffering.

Charcot and other French psychiatrists of the period tried to relate hysteria to **hypnosis.** This is a temporary, trancelike state which can be induced in normal people but which may produce effects that resemble hysterical symptoms. The hypnotized person is exceedingly **suggestible.** If told that he cannot move his arm, he will act as if paralyzed. Similarly for suggestions of blindness, deafness, or anesthesia. If the trance is deep enough, the hypnotist can induce hallucinations

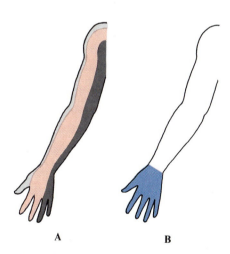

A   B

10.1 Glove anesthesia *(A) Areas of the skin of arms that send sensory information to the brain by way of different nerves. (B) A typical region of anesthesia in a patient with hysteria. If there were a nerve injury (in the spinal cord), the anesthesia would extend the length of the arm, following the nerve distribution shown in (A).*

Charcot demonstrating hypnosis
(Courtesy The Bettmann Archive)

in which the subject "sees" or "hears" imaginary objects. There are also effects on memory. If the subject is asked to forget everything that happened during the trance he generally complies. During this period of **posthypnotic amnesia** he will respond to suggestions planted during the trance. He might, for example, take off his shoes when the hypnotist gives the previously arranged signal. Such characteristics of the hypnotized state, especially those that involve paralysis and sensory deficit, buttressed the suspicion that hypnosis and hysteria were somehow related.

One of Charcot's contemporaries, Hippolyte Bernheim, thought that the link between the two phenomena is suggestion. In his view, the hysterical symptom was caused by suggestion, usually produced under conditions of intense emotional stress. If so, couldn't one fight fire with fire and remove the suggested symptom by a countersuggestion made during hypnosis? Bernheim and his colleagues tried to do just that. There were occasional successes, but in many cases the symptom proved obdurate. Sometimes the hysterical symptoms disappeared upon direct posthypnotic suggestion but were then replaced by others; a patient might regain the use of her legs but lose her sight.

In collaboration with another physician, Josef Breuer (1842–1925), Freud took an important further step. Both men came to believe that removing hysterical symptoms by suggestion is essentially futile; it was an attempt to erase a symptom without dealing with its underlying cause, like trying to cure measles by painting the spots. Their own efforts were based on the notion that hysterical symptoms are a disguised means of keeping certain emotionally charged memories under mental lock and key. When such memories are finally recovered, there is **catharsis,** an explosive release of previously dammed up emotions that has therapeutic effects.

Initially Breuer and Freud probed for these memories while the patients were in a hypnotic trance. One of Breuer's cases was Anna O., a twenty-one-year-old woman who was a walking collection of assorted symptoms: various paralyses, hysterical squints, coughs, occasional disorders of speech, and so on. When hypnotized, she was able to recall certain crucial events in her past that seemed to be at the root of this or the other symptom. Many cf these events dated back to a particularly traumatic period during which she nursed her dying father. An example was a nervous cough which she traced to an occasion at her father's bedside. She heard the sound of dance music coming from a neighbor's house, felt the wish to be there, and was immediately struck by guilt and self-reproach. She covered up her feelings with a nervous cough, and thereafter coughed uncontrollably whenever she heard rhythmic music. The symptom disappeared when the forgotten episode was remembered (Freud and Breuer, 1895).

Resistance and Repression

Eventually Freud abandoned hypnosis altogether, in part because not all patients were readily hypnotized. He found that crucial memories could be recovered even in the normal, waking state through the method of *free association.* The patients are told to say anything that enters their mind, no matter how trivial and unrelated it might seem, or how embarrassing, disagreeable, or indiscreet. Since all ideas are presumably related by an associative network, the emotionally charged "forgotten" memories should be evoked sooner or later. At first, this procedure seemed to work and yielded results similar to those obtained through hypnotic probes. But a new difficulty arose, for it became clear that the patients did not really comply with Freud's request. There was a *resistance* of which the patient was often unaware:

> The patient attempts to escape . . . by every possible means. First he says nothing comes into his head, then that so much comes into his head that he can't grasp any of it. Then we observe that . . . he is giving in to his critical objections, first to this, then to that; he betrays it by the long pauses which occur in his talk. At last he admits that he really cannot say something, he is ashamed to. . . . Or else, he has thought of something but it concerns someone else and not himself. . . . Or else, what he has just thought of is really too unimportant, too stupid and too absurd. . . . So it goes on, with untold variations, to which one continually replies that telling everything really means telling everything (Freud, 1917, p. 289).

Freud noticed that the intensity of resistance was often an important clue to what was really important. When a patient seemed to struggle especially hard to change a topic, to break off a train of thought, she was probably close to the recovery of an emotionally charged memory. Eventually it would come, often to the patient's great surprise. But if this was so, and if the recovery of these memories helped the patient to get better (as both Freud and his patients believed), why then did the patients resist the retrieval of these memories and thus obstruct their own cure? Freud concluded that the observed phenomenon of resistance was the overt manifestation of some powerful force that opposed the recovery of the critical memories into consciousness. Certain experiences in the patient's life—certain acts, impulses, thoughts, or memories—were pushed out of consciousness, were *repressed*.

Freud believed that the repressed material is not really eradicated but remains in the *unconscious.* This is a metaphorical expression which only means that the repressed ideas still exert a powerful effect. Again and again, they push up from below, like a jack-in-the-box, fueled by the biological urges that gave rise to them in the first place or triggered by associations in the here and now. As these repressed ideas well up again, they also bring back anxiety and are therefore pushed down once more. The result is a never-ending unconscious conflict.

The task Freud set for himself was the analysis (as he called it, the *psychoanalysis*) of these conflicts, the discovery of their origins, of their effects in the present, of their removal or alleviation. But he soon came to believe that the same mechanisms which produce the symptoms of psychopathology also operate in normal persons, that his discoveries were not just a contribution to psychiatry, but were a foundation for a general theory of human personality.

Anna O. In the annals of psychoanalysis, Anna O. figures only as a famous case history. But in real life, Anna—or to use her true name, Bertha Pappenheim—was much more than that. After she recovered from her various disorders, she became a distinguished pioneer in the field of social work, as well as a militant and effective champion of women's rights in Eastern Europe.

Inner conflicts as envisaged by Plato The Greek philosopher Plato anticipated Freud's tripartite division of the mind by over two thousand years. In one of his Dialogues, he likened the soul to a chariot with two horses that often pull in opposed directions. The chariot's driver is Reason, the two horses are Spirit (our nobler emotions) and Appetite. This Renaissance medallion depicts Plato's image of the internal conflict.

UNCONSCIOUS CONFLICT

Our sketch of Freud's theory of the nature and development of human personality will concentrate on those aspects that seem to represent the highlights of a complex theoretical formulation that was continually revised and modified during the course of Freud's long career. In this description, we will separate two aspects of Freudian theory. We will begin with the conception of the mechanisms of unconscious conflict. We will then deal with Freud's theory of the origins of these conflicts in the individual's life history and of their relation to the development of sexual identity and morality.

The Antagonists of Inner Conflict

Freud's theories concern the forces whose antagonism produces unconscious conflict and the effects produced when they clash. But who fights whom in unconscious conflict?

When conflict is external, the antagonists are easily identified: David and Goliath, St. George and the Dragon, and so on. But what are the warring forces when the conflict is inside of the individual? In essence, they are different behavior tendencies, such as Anna O's sexually tinged desire to be at a dance and her conflicting reactions of guilt at leaving a dying father. One of the tasks Freud set himself was to classify the tendencies that participate in such conflicts, to see which of them are usually arrayed together and fight on the same side. The eventual result was a threefold classification of conflicting tendencies within the individual, which he regarded as three more or less distinct subsystems of the human personality: the *id,* the *ego,* and the *superego.* In some of Freud's writings, there is a tendency to treat these three systems as if they were three separate persons that inhabit the mind. But this is only a metaphor that must not be taken literally; *id, ego,* and *superego* are just names for three sets of very different reaction patterns. They are not persons in their own right (Freud, 1923).

THE ID

The *id* is the most primitive portion of the personality from which the other two are derived. It contains all of the basic biological urges: to eat, drink, eliminate, be comfortably warm, and, most of all, to gain sexual pleasure.* The id's sole law is the *pleasure principle*—satisfaction now and not later, regardless of circumstances and whatever the cost.

The id's blind strivings for pleasure know no distinction between self and world, between fantasy and reality, between wishing and having. Its insistent urges spill out into reflex motor action, like emptying the bladder when it is full. If that doesn't work, the clamoring for pleasure leads to primitive thoughts of gratification, fantasies that cannot be distinguished from reality.

THE EGO

At birth, the infant is all id. But the id's shrill clamors are soon met by the harsh facts of external reality. Some gratifications come only after a delay. The breast or the bottle are not always present; the infant has to cry to get them.

---

* These urges are sometimes called instincts, but that is a misnomer caused by an unfortunate translation of Freud's original term.

The confrontations between hot desire and cold reality lead to a whole set of new reactions that are meant to reconcile the two. Sometimes the reconciliation is by appropriate action (saying "please"), sometimes by self-imposed delay (going to the bathroom), sometimes by suppression of a forbidden impulse (not touching one's genitals). These various reactions become organized into a new subsystem of the personality—the *ego.* The ego is derived from the id and is essentially still in its service. But unlike the id, the ego obeys the *reality principle.* It tries to satisfy the id (that is, to gain pleasure), but it does so pragmatically, in accordance with the real world and its real demands. As time proceeds, the opposition between need and reality leads to the emergence of more and more skills, all directed to the same end, as well as a whole system of thought and memories that grows up concurrently. Eventually, this entire system becomes capable of looking at itself and now deserves the name Freud gave it, ego or self. Until this point, there was no "I" but only a mass of undifferentiated strivings (appropriately named after the Latin impersonal pronoun *id,* literally "it").

The Furies and the superego *According to Greek mythology, the pangs of guilt, which Freud attributed to the superego, are caused by outside forces—the Furies, who pursue and torment evildoers. (From a scene in Peter Hall's 1981 production of Aeschylus's* Oresteia *at the London National Theatre; photograph by Nobby Clark)*

THE SUPEREGO

The id is not the ego's only master. As the child grows older, a new reaction pattern develops from within the ego that acts as a kind of judge that decides whether the ego has been "good" or "bad." This new mental agency is the *superego* which represents the internalized rules and admonitions of the parents, and through them, of society. Initially, the ego only had to worry about external reality. It might inhibit some id-inspired action, but only to avert some future trouble: You don't steal cookies because you might be caught. But a little later, the forbidden act is suppressed even when there can never be any real punishment. This change occurs because the child starts to act and think as if he himself were the parent who administers praise and reproof. A three-year-old is often seen to slap his own hand as he is about to play with mud or commit some other heinous deed; he sometimes mutters some self-righteous pronouncement like "Dirty. Bad." This is the beginning of the superego, the ego's second master, which praises and punishes just as the parents did. If the ego lives up to the superego's dictates, the reward is pride. But if one of the superego's rules is broken, the superego metes out punishment just as the parents scolded or spanked or withdrew their love. There is then self-reproach and a feeling of guilt.

In summary, Freud's threefold division of the personality is just a way of saying that our thoughts and actions are determined by the interplay of three major factors: our biological drives, the various ways we have learned to satisfy these drives and master the external world, and the commands and prohibitions of society. Freud's contribution is his insistence that the conflicts among these three forces are inside the individual, that they are derived from childhood experiences, and that they are waged without the individual's conscious awareness.

The Nature of Unconscious Conflict

We now turn to Freud's formulation (here drastically simplified) of the rules by which these inner wars are waged. In rough outline, the conflict begins when id-derived urges and various associated memories are pushed underground, are repressed. But the forbidden urges refuse to stay down. They find substitute outlets whose further consequence is a host of additional defenses that are erected to reinforce the original repression, hold off the id-derived flood, and allow the ego to maintain its self-regard (Freud, S., 1917a, 1926; Freud, A., 1946).

What underlies repression? Freud came to believe that the crucial factor is intense *anxiety,* an emotional state akin to fear (see Chapter 2). According to Freud, various forbidden acts become associated with anxiety as the child is scolded or disciplined for performing them. The parents may resort to physical punishment or they may merely register their disapproval with a frown or reprimand; in either case, the child is threatened with the loss of their love and becomes anxious. The next time he is about to, say, finger his penis or pinch his baby brother, he will feel a twinge of anxiety, an internal signal that his parents may leave him and that he will be abandoned and alone.

Since anxiety is intensely unpleasant, the child will do everything he can in order to remove it or to ward it off. If the cause is an external stimulus, the child's reaction is clear. He runs away and thus removes himself from the fear-inducing object. But how can he cope with a danger that comes from within? As before, he will flee from whatever evokes fear or anxiety. But now the flight is from something inside himself. To get rid of anxiety, the child must suppress that which triggers it—the forbidden act.

Freud's concept of repression applies to the thought no less than the deed. We can understand that a four-year-old boy who is punished for kicking his baby brother will refrain from such warlike acts in the future. But why does the boy stop *thinking* about them and why does he fail to remember the crucial incident, as Freud maintains? One answer is that thinking about an act is rather similar to performing it. This is especially so given the young child's limited cognitive abilities. He has not as yet fully mastered the distinction between thought and action. Nor does he know that his father can't really "read his mind," that his thoughts are private and thus immune from parental prosecution. The inhibition therefore applies not just to overt action, but to related thoughts, memories, and wishes.

Repression can be regarded as the primary, initial *mechanism of defense* that protects the individual against anxiety. But repression is often incomplete. Often enough the thoughts and urges that were pushed underground refuse to stay buried and surge up again. But as they do, so does the anxiety with which they are associated. As a result, various further mechanisms of defense are brought into play to reinforce the original dam against the forbidden impulses.

Displacement   One such supplementary defense mechanism is *displacement.* When a geyser is dammed up, its waters usually penetrate other cracks and fissures and eventually gush up elsewhere. According to Freud, the same holds for repressed urges, which tend to find new and often disguised outlets. An example is *displaced aggression,* which develops when fear of retaliation blocks the normal direction of discharge. The child who is reprimanded by her parent turns on her playmate or vents her anger on the innocent household cat. According to many social psychologists, the same mechanism underlies the persecution of minority groups. They become convenient scapegoats for aggressive impulses fueled by social and economic unrest.

Reaction formation   In displacement, the forbidden impulse is rechanneled into a safer course. Certain other mechanisms of defense are attempts to supplement the original repression by blocking off the impulse altogether. An example is *reaction formation* in which the repressed wish is warded off by its diametrical opposite. The young girl who jealously hated her sister and was punished for hostile acts may turn her feelings into the very opposite; she now showers her sister with an exaggerated love and tenderness, a desperate bulwark against aggressive wishes that she cannot accept. But the repressed hostility can still be detected underneath the loving exterior; her love is overly solicitous and stifling, and the sister probably feels smothered by it.

Rationalization *The expression "sour grapes" comes from a fable by Aesop, which tells of a fox who desperately desired some grapes that hung overhead. When the fox discovered that the grapes were so high that he could not reach them, he said that he never really wanted them, for they were much too sour. (From* Baby's Own Aesop *by Walter Crane, engraved and colored by Edmund Evans; reproduced from the print collection of the New York Public Library, Astor, Lenox, and Tilden Foundations)*

Rationalization　In reaction formation, there is an attempt (albeit not too successful) to keep the forbidden wishes at bay. Some other mechanisms represent a different line of defense; the repressed thoughts break through but they are reinterpreted and are not recognized for what they are. One example of this is ***rationalization*** in which the person interprets some of his own feelings or actions in more acceptable terms. The cruel father beats his child mercilessly but is sure that he does so "for the child's own good." Countless atrocities have been committed under the same guise of altruism; heretics have been tortured to save their immortal souls and cities have been razed to protect the world against barbarism. Rationalization is also employed at a more everyday level, as a defense not only against repressed wishes but against any thought that would make the individual feel unworthy and anxious. An example is the sour-grapes phenomenon. The jilted lover tells his friends that he never really cared for his lost love; eventually he believes it himself.

Projection　Another example of a defense mechanism in which cognitive reorganization plays a major role is ***projection.*** Here the forbidden urges well up and are recognized as such. But the person does not realize that these wishes are his own; instead, he attributes them to others. "I desire you" becomes "You desire me," "I hate you" becomes "You hate me"—desperate defenses against repressed sexual or hostile wishes that can no longer be banished from consciousness (Freud, 1911).

Isolation　In yet another defense mechanism, the dangerous memories are allowed back into consciousness; what's held back is their relation to the patient's motives and emotions. The memories themselves are retained, but they are *isolated* (so to speak, compartmentalized) from the feelings that go along with them. This mechanism is sometimes seen in people who have suffered severe distress, such as concentration camp survivors or rape victims. Some of these persons are able to relate their experiences in precise detail but are unable to recall the emotions that accompanied them.

Origins of Unconscious Conflict

Freud believed that the unconscious conflicts he uncovered always referred to certain critical events in the individual's early life. His observations of his patients convinced him that these crucial events are remarkably similar from person to person. He concluded that all human beings go through a largely similar sequence of significant emotional events in their early lives, that some of the most important of these involve sexual urges, and that it is this childhood past that shapes their present (Freud, 1905).

STAGES OF PSYCHOSEXUAL DEVELOPMENT

Freud's theory of psychosexual development emphasizes different stages, each of which is built upon the achievements of those before. (In this regard it resembles Jean Piaget's theory of cognitive growth, which we will take up in Chapter 13.) In Freud's view, the child starts life as a bundle of pleasure-seeking tendencies. Pleasure is obtained by the stimulation of certain zones of the body that are particularly sensitive to touch: the mouth, the anus, and the genitals. Freud called these regions **erogenous zones,** for he believed that the various pleasures associated with each of them have a common element which is sexual.* As the child develops, the relative importance of the zones shifts. Initially, most of the pleasure seeking is through the mouth (the **oral stage**). With the advent of toilet concerns, the emphasis shifts to the anus (the **anal stage**). Still later, there is an increased interest in the pleasure that can be obtained from stimulating the genitals (the **phallic stage**). The culmination of **psychosexual development** is attained in adult sexuality when pleasure involves not just one's own gratification but also the social and bodily satisfaction brought to another person (the **genital stage**).

How does the child move from one stage to the next? In part, it is a matter of physical maturation. For example, bowel control is simply impossible at birth, for the infant lacks the necessary neuromuscular readiness. But there is another element. As the child's bodily maturation proceeds, there is an inevitable change in what the parents allow, prohibit, or demand. Initially, the child nurses, then he is weaned. Initially, he is diapered, then he is toilet trained. Each change automatically produces some frustration and conflict as former ways of gaining pleasure are denied. (For some of Freud's hypotheses about the long-term effects of such conflicts during the anal stage on adult personality, see Chapter 16, pp. 475–76.)

THE OEDIPUS COMPLEX

We now turn to that aspect of the theory of psychosexual development that Freud himself regarded as the most important—the family triangle of love and jealousy and fear that is at the root of internalized morality and out of which grows the child's identification with the parent of the same sex. This is the **Oedipus complex,** named after the mythical king of Thebes who unknowingly committed the two most awful crimes—killing his father and marrying his mother. According to Freud, an analogous family drama is reenacted in the childhood of all men and women. We will take this family drama up separately for men and women, starting with Freud's theory of how genital sexuality emerges in males (Freud, 1905).

First act: Love and hate   At about three or four years of age, the **phallic stage** begins. The young boy becomes increasingly interested in his penis, which becomes a source of both pride and pleasure. He masturbates and this brings satisfaction, but it is not enough. His erotic urges seek an external object. The inevitable choice is his mother (or some mother substitute).

But there is an obstacle—the boy's father. The little boy wants to have his mother all to himself, as a comforter as well as an erotic partner, but this sexual utopia is out of the question. His father is a rival and he is bigger. The little boy wants his father to go away and not come back—in short, to die.

Second act: Fear and renunciation   At this point, a new element enters into the family drama. The little boy begins to fear the father he is jealous of. According to Freud, this is because the boy is sure that the father knows of his son's hostility and that the father will surely answer hate with hate.

With childish logic the little boy suspects that his punishment may be all too horribly appropriate to his crime. The same organ by which he sinned will be the one that is made to suffer. The result is **castration anxiety** which is aggravated by whatever threats the parents may have issued when they saw him masturbate. As a result, the boy tries to push the hostile feelings underground, but they refuse to

---

*One of his arguments for regarding oral and anal stimulation in infancy as ultimately sexual was the fact that such stimulation sometimes precedes (or replaces) sexual intercourse in adulthood.

Oedipus Rex *From a 1955 production directed by Tyrone Guthrie with Douglas Campbell in the title role, at Stratford, Ontario. (Courtesy Billy Rose Theatre Collection, The New York Public Library at Lincoln Center, Astor, Lenox and Tilden Collections)*

stay buried. They return, and the only defense that is left is projection: "I hate father" becomes "Father hates me." This can only increase the boy's fear, which increases his hate, which is again pushed down, comes back up, and leads to yet further projection. This process spirals upward, until the father is finally seen as an overwhelming ogre who threatens to castrate his son.

Third act: Renunciation and final victory As the vicious cycle continues, the little boy's anxiety eventually becomes unbearable. At this point, he throws in the towel, renounces his mother as an erotic object, and more or less renounces genital pleasures, at least for a while. Instead, he *identifies* with his father. He concludes that by becoming like him, he will eventually enjoy an erotic partnership of the kind his father enjoys now, if not with his mother, then at least with someone much like her.

According to Freud, the renunciation of the Oedipal problem is accomplished by the repression of all the urges, feelings, and memories of the family drama. One lasting residue is the superego, the internalized voice of the father admonishing his son from within.

Freud believed that once the tumult of the Oedipal conflict dies down, there is a period of comparative sexual quiet which lasts from about five to twelve years of age. This is the *latency period* during which phallic sexuality lies dormant; boys play only with boys, devote themselves to athletics, and want to have nothing to do with the opposite sex. All of this changes at puberty. The hormone levels rise, the sex organs mature rapidly, and the repressed sexual impulses can no longer be denied. But as these urges come out of their closet, parts of the Oedipal family skeleton come out as well, dragging along many of the fears and conflicts that had been comfortably hidden away for all these years.

According to Freud, this is one of the reasons why adolescence is so often a period of deep emotional turbulence. The boy is now physically mature, and he is strongly attracted to the opposite sex, but this very attraction frightens him and he doesn't know why. Sexual contact with women arouses the unconscious wishes and fears that pertain to mother and father. In healthy individuals, the Oedipus complex has been resolved well enough so that these fears can be overcome without generating still further defenses. The boy can eventually accept himself as a man and achieve *genital sexuality,* in which he loves a woman as herself rather than as some shadowy substitute for his mother and in which his love involves giving as well as taking.

THE ELECTRA COMPLEX

We have traced Freud's account of the male psychosexual odyssey to adult sexuality. What about the female? In Freud's view, she goes through essentially identical oral and anal phases as does the male. And in many ways, the development of her phallic interests (Freud used the same term for both sexes) is symmetrical to the male's. As he focuses his erotic interests on the mother, so she focuses hers upon the father. As he resents and eventually comes to fear the father, so she the mother. In short, there is a female version of the Oedipus complex (sometimes called the *Electra complex* after the Greek tragic heroine who goaded her brother into slaying their mother).

Windows into the Unconscious

Freud arrived at his theory of unconscious conflict by studying the behavior of disturbed individuals, usually hysterics. But he soon concluded that the same clash of unconscious forces that results in neurotic symptoms is also found in the life of normal persons. Their inner conflicts are under control, with less resulting anxiety and no crippling effects, but they are present nonetheless. We will consider two areas to which Freud appealed for evidence: lapses of memory and slips of the tongue in everyday life, and the content of dreams.

ERRORS OF SPEECH AND MEMORY

Freud drew attention to what he called the psychopathology of everyday life, in which we momentarily forget a name that might call up embarrassing memories or in which we suffer a slip of the tongue (a "Freudian slip") that unwittingly reveals an underlying motive (Freud, 1901). Suppressed intentions sometimes emerge to make us become "absentminded" about things we don't really want to do. Freud cites the example of a friend who wrote a letter which he forgot to send off for several days. He finally mailed it, but it was returned by the post office, for there was no address. He addressed it and sent it off again only to have it returned once more because there was no stamp.

This is not to say (though psychoanalytic writers often seem to say it) that all slips of the tongue, all mislayings of objects, and all lapses of memory are *motivated* in Freud's sense. The host who cannot call up a guest's name when he has to introduce him to another guest is unlikely to have some hidden reason for keeping that name out of his consciousness. The name is probably blocked because of simple, and quite unmotivated, memory interference (see Chapter 6).

THE THEORY OF DREAMS

One of Freud's most influential works was his theory of dreams (Freud, 1900). He argued that dreams have a meaning which can be deciphered if one looks deeply enough. In his view, dreams concern the dreamer's past and present, and they arise from unknown regions within. He saw dreams as somewhat analogous to hysterical symptoms. On the surface, they both appear meaningless and bizarre, but they become comprehensible when understood as veiled expressions of an unconscious clash between competing motives.

Freud began with the assumption that at bottom every dream is an attempt at *wish fulfillment.* While awake, a wish is usually not acted upon right away, for there are considerations of both reality (the ego) and morality (the superego) that must be taken into account: "Is it possible?" and "Is it allowed?" But during sleep these restraining forces are drastically weakened and the wish then leads to imme-

An artist's dream *A painting that depicts a dream in which an artist is at a friend's house when the door suddenly opens and a man to whom he was once apprenticed enters, joined by a nude woman who was one of his most beautiful models. Freud would probably have noted the Oedipal theme, considering that the dream featured a former mentor and his nude model. (The frontispiece of* Les rêves et les moyens de les diriger, *by Marquis d'Hervey de Saint Denis, 1867)*

diate thoughts and images of gratification. In some cases the wish fulfillment is simple and direct. Starving explorers dream of sumptuous meals; men stranded in the desert dream of cool mountain streams. According to a Hungarian proverb quoted by Freud, "Pigs dream of acorns and geese dream of maize."

Simple wish-fulfillment dreams are comparatively rare. What about the others, the strange and illogical nightly narratives that are far more usual? Freud argued that the same principle of attempted wish fulfillment could explain these as well. But here a new process comes into play. The underlying wish touches upon some forbidden matters that are associated with anxiety. As a result, various mechanisms of defense are invoked. The wish cannot be expressed directly; it is *censored* and is only allowed to surface in symbolic disguise. The dreamer never experiences the underlying *latent dream* that represents his own hidden wishes and concerns. What he does experience is the carefully laundered version that emerges after the defense mechanisms have done their work—the *manifest dream.* The end product is reminiscent of hysterical symptoms and various pathologies of everyday life. It represents a compromise between forbidden urges and the repressive forces that hold them down. The underlying impulse is censored, but it surreptitiously emerges in a veiled disguise.

In some dreams, the underlying wish finds expression in various displaced forms. There is *symbolism* in which one thing stands for another. Some symbols are widely shared because certain physical, functional, or linguistic similarities are perceived by most people (for example, screwdriver and box for penis and vagina). But there is no simple cipher that can be generally applied. After all, many physical objects are either long and pointed or round and hollow; a pat equation with male and female genitals will be of little use. Most symbolic relationships depend upon the dreamer's own life experience and can only be interpreted by noting his free associations to the dream.

A REEXAMINATION OF FREUDIAN THEORY

Thus far, we have presented Freud's views with a minimum of critical comment. We now shift our perspective to consider some of his assertions in the light of present-day thought and evidence.

By what criteria can one determine whether Freud's assertions are in fact correct? Freud's own criterion was the evidence from the couch. He considered the patient's free associations, his resistances, his slips of the tongue, his dreams, and then tried to weave them into a coherent pattern that somehow made sense of all the parts. But can one really draw conclusions from this kind of clinical evidence alone? Clinical practitioners cannot be totally objective no matter how hard they try. As they listen to a patient, they are more likely to hear and remember those themes that fit in with their own views than those that do not. (This point is especially pertinent to Freud who never took notes during psychoanalytic sessions.) Would a clinician with different biases have remembered the same themes?

The issue goes deeper than objective reportage. Even if the analyst could be an utterly objective observer, he could not possibly avoid affecting that which he observes. His own theoretical preconceptions would be inevitably noticed by his patients, whose dreams and free associations would very likely be colored by them. The trouble is that there is no way of disentangling the effect of the analyst (and of his theories) upon the patient's mental productions (which we want to use as evidence for or against these theories).

Such considerations suggest that if we want to test Freud's assertions, we must look for more objective evidence and must be more rigorous in the way in which we interpret it. We will begin by considering some work that bears on Freud's theories of repression and unconscious defense.

Testing Freud's Theories of Repression and Defense

The fact that we are unaware of many of our own mental processes was by no means unknown to psychologists before Freud arrived on the scene. They knew that we often retrieve material from memory without conscious awareness, and that many mental operations drop out of consciousness as we automatize them by constant practice, such as the way in which we tie our shoelaces (see Ellenberger, 1970). Yet it was Freud's influence that made the term "unconscious" a part of everyday language. In addition, the term "unconscious" meant more to Freud than mental processes of which the individual is unaware. To him, it mostly referred to mental processes—acts, wishes, thoughts, perceptions—that are *kept out* of consciousness by an elaborate system of internal censorship: the mechanisms of defense headed by repression. This notion of repressive forces is the cornerstone of psychoanalytic thought. What is the evidence for unconscious processes in this more narrow, Freudian sense? Our primary concern will be with cases that involve memory and are thus akin to what Freud called repression.

There have been many efforts to produce repression and related effects in the laboratory (see Eriksen and Pierce, 1968). But this task is far from easy. According to psychoanalytic theory, motivated forgetting is a defense against anxiety. One would therefore expect that materials that are associated with anxiety will be recalled less readily than neutral items. But how can the experimenter be sure that the critical material is really anxiety-provoking for the subject?

To cope with this problem, several investigators selected their items to fit each subject's own pattern of anxieties. One way of doing this is by an initial word-association test. The subject is given a list of words; she has to reply to each with the first word that comes to mind. If her reaction to any one stimulus word is unusually slow or if it is accompanied by increased heart rate or a marked galvanic skin response, that word is presumably emotion-arousing for her. Using this method, one experimenter selected a set of neutral and emotional words for each subject (Jacobs, 1955). When these were later used as the responses in a paired-associate task, the subject had more trouble in producing the emotional than the neutral items. One way of explaining the result is to assume that as the emotionally loaded word was about to be retrieved from memory, it triggered anxiety which blocked further efforts at retrieval.

Seen in this light, repression may turn out to be a special case of retrieval failure. We have previously seen that recall is enormously dependent upon the presence of an appropriate retrieval cue. We forget the street names of the city we grew up in, but most of them come back when we revisit the city after many years. The same may hold for memories that Freud said are repressed. Perhaps they are not really held back by some imperious censor; perhaps they are rather misfiled under a hard-to-reach rubric and cannot be retrieved for this reason. One might want to add some further assumptions about the role of anxiety in maintaining this state of affairs. Perhaps anxiety blocks refiling; perhaps it impedes the use of appropriate retrieval cues (Erdelyi and Goldberg, 1979).

Problems of Freud's Dream Theory

The preceding discussion suggests that unconscious conflict and defense are probably genuine phenomena. To this extent, Freud's general position has been upheld. But the verdict has been less favorable on some of his more specific assertions. An example is his theory of dreams.

Stated in the most general terms, Freud's theory asserts that dreams tend to reflect the current emotional preoccupations of the dreamer, including those of which he is unaware, often portrayed in a condensed and symbolic form. This is probably quite true. Thus, patients who await major surgery reveal their fears in what they dream about during the two or three nights before the operation. Their fears are rarely expressed directly; few, if any, of their dreams are about scalpels or operating rooms. The reference is indirect, in condensed and symbolized form, as in dreams about falling from tall ladders or standing on a high, swaying bridge, or about a decrepit machine that needs repair (Breger, Hunter, and Lane, 1971).

Such evidence indicates that dreams may express whatever motives are currently most important. But Freud's theory went much further than this. As we saw, he believed that the manifest dream is a censored and disguised version of

The Nightmare This painting by Henry Fuseli (painted in 1783 and said to have decorated Freud's office) highlights what seems to be one of the difficulties of Freud's dream theory. If all dreams are wish fulfillments, what accounts for nightmares? According to Freud, they are often dreams in which the latent dream is not sufficiently disguised. The forbidden wish is partially recognized, anxiety breaks through, and the sleeper suffers a nightmare. (Courtesy The Detroit Institute of Arts)

the latent dream that lies underneath and represents a wish fulfillment. This conception of dreams has been much criticized. To begin with, there is considerable doubt that all (or even many) dreams are attempts at wish fulfillments, whether disguised or open. In one study, subjects were made extremely thirsty before they went to sleep. Since thirst is hardly a forbidden urge, there is no reason to suppose an internal censorship. However, none of the subjects reported dreams of drinking. Since they were so thirsty, why didn't they gratify themselves in their dreams (Dement and Wolpert, 1958)?

Another problem is the fact that the same urge is sometimes freely expressed in dreams, but heavily disguised on other occasions. Tonight, the sleeper dreams of unabashed sexual intercourse; tomorrow night, she dreams of riding a team of wild horses. For sake of argument, let us agree that riding is a symbol for intercourse. But why should the censor disguise tomorrow what is so freely allowed tonight?

One investigator, C. S. Hall, has come up with a plausible suggestion (Hall, 1953). According to Hall, the dream symbol does not *disguise* an underlying idea; on the contrary, it *expresses* it. In Hall's view, the dream is a rather concrete mental shorthand that embodies a feeling or emotion. Riding a horse, plowing a field, planting a seed—all of these may be concrete renditions of the idea of sexual intercourse. But they are not meant to hide this idea. Their function is much the same as the cartoonist's picture of Uncle Sam or John Bull. These are representations of the United States and of England, but they are certainly not meant as disguises for them. During sleep, more specifically during REM sleep (see Chapter 2), we are incapable of the extreme complexity and abstractness of waking mental life. We are thus reduced to a more concrete and archaic form of thinking. The wishes and fears of our waking life are still present at night, and we dream about them. But the way in which these are now expressed tends to be more primitive, a concrete pictorialization that combines fragments of various waking concerns and serves as a kind of symbolic cartoon.

Biology or Culture?

While many psychologists agree with Freud's thesis that there is unconscious conflict, they are more skeptical of his particular assertions of what these conflicts are. One of their major quarrels is with Freud's insistence that the pattern of these conflicts is biologically based and will therefore be found in essentially the same form in all men and all women.

THE EMPHASIS ON SOCIAL FACTORS

Since Freud believed that the key to emotional development is in biology, he assumed that its progression followed a universal course. In his view, all humans pass through oral, anal, and phallic stages and suffer the conflicts appropriate to each stage. This conception has been challenged by various clinical practitioners, many of whom used Freud's own psychoanalytic methods. These critics felt that Freud had overemphasized biological factors at the expense of social ones. This point was first raised by one of Freud's own students, Alfred Adler (1870–1937). It was later taken up by several like-minded authors who are often grouped together under the loose label *neo-Freudians,* including Erich Fromm (1900–1980), Karen Horney (1885–1952), and H. S. Sullivan (1892–1949).

According to the neo-Freudians, human development cannot be properly understood by focusing on the particular anatomical regions—mouth, anus, genitals—through which the child tries to gratify his instinctual desires. In their view, the important question is how humans relate, or try to relate, to others—whether by dominating, or submitting, or becoming dependent, or whatever. Their description of our inner conflicts is therefore in social terms. Consider the sexual sphere. According to Freud, the neurotic conflict centers on the repression of erotic impulses. According to the neo-Freudian critics, the real difficulty is in the area of interpersonal relationships. Neurosis often leads to sexual symptoms, not because sex is a powerful biological motive that is pushed underground, but rather because it is one of the most sensitive barometers of interpersonal attitudes. The man who can only relate to other people by competing with them may well be unable to find sexual pleasure in his marriage bed; but the sexual malfunction is an *effect* of his neurotic social pattern rather than its *cause.*

The same emphasis on social factors highlights the neo-Freudian explanation for how these conflicts arise in the first place. In contrast to Freud, it denies that these conflicts are biologically ordained; they rather depend upon the specific cultural conditions in which the child is reared. According to the neo-Freudians, the conflicts that Freud observed may have characterized *his* patients, but this does not mean that these same patterns will be found in persons who live at other times and in other places.

THE REJECTION OF CULTURAL ABSOLUTISM

One set of relevant findings came from another discipline, **cultural anthropology,** which concerns itself with the practices and beliefs of different peoples throughout the world. There are evidently considerable variations in these patterns, with accompanying variations in the kind of person who is typical in each setting. Personality characteristics that are typical in our culture are by no means universal, a result that was beautifully tuned to the antibiological bias of the neo-Freudians.

A well-known example concerns cultural variations in the roles that different societies assign to the two sexes. An influential study by the American anthropologist Margaret Mead, "Sex and Temperament," compared the personality traits of men and women in three New Guinea tribes that lived within a hundred-mile radius. Among the Arapesh, both men and women were mild, cooperative, and, so to speak, "maternal" in their attitudes toward each other and especially toward children. Among the neighboring Mundugomor, both sexes were ferociously aggressive and quarrelsome. In yet another tribe, the Tchambuli, the usual sex roles were reversed. The women were the hale and hardy breadwinners who fished and went to market unadorned. While the women managed the worldly affairs, the men gossiped and pranced about, adjusted elaborate hairdos, carved and painted, and practiced intricate dance steps (Mead, 1935, 1937). The neo-Freudians took such findings as a strong argument against the cultural absolutism which regards the patterns of modern Western society as the built-in givens of human nature.

Several anthropologists have criticized Mead's account as an oversimplification. They point out that there are probably some universal sex roles after all; for example, warfare is generally conducted by the men, even among the Tchambuli. They argue that some of the differences between male and female aggressiveness may very well be due to biological factors, for aggression is in part under hormonal control; as androgen levels rise, both human and animal males become more aggressive (see Chapter 9). What culture does is to determine how this aggression is to be channeled and against whom, whether it is to be valued, and how much of it is allowed. (For recent discussions of Mead's work, see Freeman, 1983, 1986; Brady, 1983; Patience and Smith, 1986.)

Critiques of Freud's Theories of Development

It's rather ironic that Freud, whose views of childhood development had such a powerful influence on Western thought, never himself studied children. His theories of early development were mostly based on his adult patients' recollec-

Margaret Mead   (Courtesy The American Museum of Natural History)

Freud at age sixteen with his mother, Amalie Nathanson Freud *Freud was his mother's first-born and her favorite, a fact that may have affected his theory of the human family drama. As he put it, "A man who has been the indisputable favorite of his mother keeps for life the feeling of a conqueror, that confidence of success that often induces real success." (E. Jones, 1954, p. 5; photograph courtesy Mary Evans/Freud copyrights)*

tions, dreams, and free associations. Under the circumstances, it was essential to gather evidence on actual childhood behavior.

Today the study of human development is a flourishing enterprise. We will describe it in some detail in Chapters 13 and 14. For now our concern is with evidence that bears directly on Freud's theories of child development. While some of Freud's broader concepts are still of considerable influence, the verdict has not been too favorable on his more specific hypotheses. (For an overview, see Zigler, Lamb, and Child, 1982.)

The most influential of Freud's assertions about early childhood concerns sexuality and the Oedipus complex. Our major source of information in this area comes from studies of other cultures. On the whole, the evidence was welcome grist to the neo-Freudian mill: The Oedipus conflict is not universal but depends upon cultural variations in the family constellation.

This point was first raised some fifty years ago by the English anthropologist Bronislaw Malinowski on the basis of his observations of the Trobriand Islanders of the Western Pacific (Malinowski, 1927). The family pattern of the Trobriand Islanders is quite different from our own. Among the Trobrianders, the biological father is not the head of the household. He spends time with his children and plays with them, but he exerts no authority. This role is reserved for the mother's brother who acts as a disciplinarian. The Trobriand Islanders thus separate the roles that in Freud's Vienna were played by one and the same person.

According to Freud, this different family pattern should make no difference. There should still be an Oedipus complex in which the father is the hated villain for, after all, it is he who is the little boy's sexual rival. But this did not turn out to be the case. Malinowski saw no signs of friction between sons and fathers, though he did observe a fair amount of hostility directed at the maternal uncle. The same held for dreams and folk tales. The Trobriand Islanders believe that there are prophetic dreams of death; these generally involve the death of the maternal uncle. Similarly there are no myths about evil fathers or stepfathers; again, the villain is typically the mother's brother. If we accept Freud's notion that dreams (and myths) involve unconscious wishes and preoccupations, we are forced to conclude that the Trobriand boy hates his uncle, not his father. In sum, the child has fears and fantasies about the authoritarian figure in his life, the man who bosses him around. This is the father in Freud's Austria, but the uncle on the Trobriand Islands. His fears are not about his mother's lover as such, for the Trobriand boy does not hate the father who plays this role.

FREUD'S CONTRIBUTIONS IN RETROSPECT

We have seen that many of Freud's beliefs have not been confirmed. There are good grounds to doubt Freud's essentially Hobbesian view of human nature. There is little evidence for his general theory of psychosexual development, and there is good reason to believe that he overemphasized biological givens at the expense of cultural factors. We have also seen that Freud can be criticized not just for what he asserted but for the way in which he tried to prove his claims. Many of Freud's theoretical proposals are vague and metaphorical, so that it is not clear how one can decide whether they are right or wrong.

All in all, this is a formidable set of criticisms. But even so, many psychologists would maintain that, wrong as he probably was in any number of particulars, Sigmund Freud must nevertheless be regarded as one of the giants of psychology, one of the few our field has known thus far. There are at least two reasons.

The first concerns one major conception of Freud's that still stands, however much it may have to be modified and reinterpreted—the notion that there is in-

Freud looking at a bust of himself sculpted for his seventy-fifth birthday by O. Nemon (Courtesy Wide World Photos)

ternal conflict of which we are often unaware. Freud was not the first to recognize that we are often torn in opposite directions and that we frequently deceive ourselves about what we want (Ellenberger, 1970). But he was the first for whom this insight was the cornerstone of an entire point of view. Whether his own therapeutic procedure, psychoanalysis, is an appropriate tool to make the unknown known and thus to restore a measure of free choice to the emotionally crippled victims of inner conflict is still debatable (see Chapter 18). But whether his therapy works or not, Freud's contribution remains. He saw that we do not know ourselves, that we are not masters of our own souls. By pointing out how ignorant we are, he set a task for later investigators who may ultimately succeed, so that we may then be able to follow Socrates's deceptively simple prescription for a good life, "Know thyself."

The other major reason why Freud has a lasting place among the greats of intellectual history is the sheer scope of his theoretical conception. His was a view of human nature that was virtually all-embracing. It tried to encompass both rational thought and emotional urges. It conceived of neurotic ailments as a consequence of the same psychological forces that operate in everyday life. It saw humans as biological organisms as well as social beings, as creatures whose present is rooted in their past and who are simultaneously children and adults. Freud's theory has many faults, but it certainly dealt with matters of genuine human significance; it concerned both human beings and their works; it was an account that was about humanity as a whole. To this extent Freud provided a goal for posterity. He showed us the kinds of questions that we have to answer before we can claim to have a full theory of human personality.

We will have reason to come back to Freud's ideas in a number of later chapters, in which we discuss what modern psychology has found out about social development and socialization (Chapter 14), about personality (Chapter 16), about psychopathology and its treatment (Chapters 17 and 18). We'll see that many of his views have not been confirmed, but we'll also see that these views have influenced virtually all thinkers in these areas who have come after him. For Freud was one of those rare intellectual figures who cast his shadow over a whole century. And right or wrong, he provided a guide for posterity by showing us the kinds of questions we must answer before we can claim to have a full theory of human personality.

SUMMARY

1. Sigmund Freud asserted that all persons experience *unconscious conflicts* originating in childhood. His theories grew out of studies of *hysteria,* a *psychogenic* mental disorder whose symptoms are similar to some effects observed in *hypnosis.* Freud proposed that hysterical symptoms are a means of keeping *repressed* thoughts or wishes unconscious. He believed that the symptoms would be eliminated once the repressed materials were recovered and devised a procedure, *psychoanalysis,* directed toward this end.

2. Freud distinguished three subsystems of the human personality. One is the *id,* a blind striving toward biological satisfaction that follows the *pleasure principle.* The second is the *ego,* a system of reactions that tries to reconcile the id-derived needs with the actualities of the world, in accordance with the *reality principle.* A third is the *superego,* which represents the internalized rules of the parents and punishes deviations by feelings of guilt.

3. Internal conflict is initially prompted by *anxiety,* which becomes associated with forbidden thoughts and wishes, usually in childhood. To ward off this anxiety, the child resorts to *repression* and pushes the forbidden materials out of consciousness. Repression is the initial, primary *mechanism of defense* against anxiety. But the repressed materials generally surface again, together with their associated anxiety. To push these thoughts and wishes down again, further, supplementary defense mechanisms come into play, including *displacement, reaction formation, rationalization, projection*, and *isolation.*

4. Freud believed that most adult unconscious conflicts are ultimately sexual in nature and refer back to events during childhood *psychosexual development.* This passes through three main stages that are characterized by the *erogenous zones* through which gratification is obtained: *oral, anal,* and *phallic.* At each stage, socialization thwarts some of these gratifications, as in weaning and toilet training.

5. During the phallic stage, the male child develops the *Oedipus complex.* He directs his sexual urges toward his mother, hates his father as a rival, and comes to dread him as he suffers increasing *castration anxiety.* He finally renounces his sexual urges, identifies with his father, and represses all relevant memories, which then become the nucleus of the superego. At adolescence, repressed sexual urges surface, are redirected toward adult partners, and the person generally achieves *genital sexuality.* In female children, the *Electra complex* develops, with love toward the father and rivalry toward the mother.

6. Freud tried to apply his theory of unconscious conflict to many areas of everyday life, including slips of the tongue, memory lapses, and dreams. He believed that all dreams are at bottom wish fulfillments. Since many of these wishes prompt anxiety, their full expression is *censored.* As a result, the underlying *latent dream* is transformed into the *manifest dream,* in which the forbidden urges emerge in a disguised, sometimes symbolic form.

7. The verdict on Freud's more specific hypotheses about the nature and origin of unconscious conflicts has not been too favorable. An important challenge came from the *neo-Freudians,* who emphasized social and cultural factors rather than biological ones. A related challenge came from *cultural anthropology,* which has shown that personality patterns typical of our own culture are by no means universal. In particular, there is no evidence for a universal *Oedipus complex,* independent of culture.

CHAPTER 11

Social Cognition and Emotion

The preceding chapters have explored the ways in which social behavior is shaped by our past. We began by considering certain social reactions that stem from an evolutionary past that predates our own by many eons; the built-in facets of filial, sexual, and aggressive behavior, and various signals such as the distress cry and the smile that seem to be part of our biological heritage (see Chapter 9). We then turned to the theories of Sigmund Freud, who was one of the first thinkers to pay serious attention to social patterns that are rooted in our own personal past (see Chapter 10). Whether his particular views about the role of childhood socialization are right or wrong is not the issue (for more detail on this, see Chapters 14 and 16). For now, we merely note that there is little doubt that both genetic makeup and socialization provide necessary preconditions for social life.

But these effects of our biological and personal past cannot by themselves account for our adult social behavior. They do not explain why we vote for one candidate rather than another, why we join or don't join a protest organization, why we help or ignore a stricken passerby, why we believe a rumor or discount it, why we buy one detergent and not another. These are the kinds of choices that are the stuff of social life. When millions of individuals make one of these choices rather than another, they affect the general condition of our social, political, or economic world.

The way in which these choices are made seems to depend more upon the *present* situation than upon factors in our (relatively distant) past. If we are convinced that a certain bank is failing, we withdraw our money; the particulars of our childhood history have relatively little effect. To be sure, we first have to be socialized into the cultural patterns of our world. A Mundugomor or an Arapesh would probably not understand our monetary system and would therefore not join in a run on the bank. But socialization provides only the initial entry into the social drama, especially in adulthood. Once we are upon that stage, our behavior depends upon the present situation as we see it now. Do we see others running to the teller's window? Is the bank insured? It is these situational factors in the present and our response to them that are the province of modern social psychology.

We react to any situation as we understand it to be The misunderstandings that may then occur can form the plot foundation of tragedy as well as comedy. In Shakespeare's Othello, *the hero strangles his wife because he wrongly believes she committed adultery. In the movie* Tootsie, *the hero disguises himself as a woman with resulting complications in his social relations. (From a production of* Othello *at the 1987 Stratford Festival in Ontario, Canada, with Howard Rollins and Wenna Shaw; photograph by Michael Cooper; and the 1982 film* Tootsie, *with Dustin Hoffman and Jessica Lange; courtesy Photofest)*

The main purpose of this and the following chapter is to give some sense of what modern social psychologists do and how they do it. To do this, we will organize our account around two interrelated questions. The present chapter asks how the social world affects our beliefs and attitudes. The next chapter asks how it affects our actions.

SOCIAL COGNITION AND SOCIAL REALITY

An individual's response to a social situation depends upon what he understands that situation to be. Romeo killed himself in front of Juliet's tomb because he thought that Juliet was dead; had he known that she was only drugged, the play would have had a happy ending. This simple point forms the basis for much of modern social psychology. But many modern social psychologists make an important further assertion: The way in which we interpret and try to comprehend such social events—that is, the nature of *social cognition*—is in principle no different from the way in which we interpret and try to comprehend any event whatsoever, whether social or not.

The Interpersonal Nature of Belief

Seen in this light, many facets of social psychology are simply an aspect of the psychology of thinking and cognition in general. But over and above this, social cognition has certain features that make it uniquely social. For there is no doubt that much of what we know, we know because of others. The primary medium of this cognitive interdependence is of course human language, which allows us to share our discoveries and pass them on to the next generation. As a result, we look at the world not just through our own eyes, but also through the eyes of others, and we form our beliefs on the basis of what we've heard them say or write.

But the shared aspects of human knowledge go deeper than this, for our very notion of physical reality is at least in part a matter of mutual agreement. This point was made very dramatically in a classic study performed by Solomon Asch (Asch, 1956).

In Asch's experiment, nine or ten subjects are brought together in a laboratory room and shown pairs of cards placed a few feet in front of them. On one card is a black line, say, 8 inches long. On the other card are three lines of varying lengths, say 6 1/4, 8, and 6 3/4 inches (Figure 11.1). The subjects are asked to make a sim-

11.1 The stimulus cards in Asch's social pressure experiment The cards are drawn to scale. In the actual experiment, they were generally placed on the ledge of a blackboard, separated by forty inches. (Asch, 1956)

A   B   C

11.2 The subject in a social pressure experiment *(A) The true subject (center) listens to the instructions. (B) On hearing the unanimous verdict of the others, he leans forward to look at the cards more carefully. (C) After twelve such trials, he explains that "he has to call them as he sees them." (Photographs by William Vandivert)*

ple perceptual judgment. They have to indicate which of the three lines on the one card is equal in length to the one line on the other card. Then the experimenter tells the subjects that this procedure is only a minor prelude to another study and casually asks them, in the interest of saving time, to indicate their judgments aloud by calling them out in turn (the three comparison lines are designated by the numbers 1, 2, and 3 printed underneath them). This procedure continues for a dozen or so pairs of cards.

Considering the sizable differences among the stimuli, the task is absurdly simple except for one thing: There is only one "real" subject. All of the others are the experimenter's secret confederates. They have arranged their seating order so that most of them will call out their judgments before the real subject's turn comes around. After the first few trials, they unanimously render false judgments on most of the ones thereafter. For example, the confederates might declare that a 6 1/4-inch line equals an 8-inch line, and so on, for a dozen more trials. What does the real subject do now? (See Figure 11.2.)

Asch found that the chances were less than one in four that the real subject would be fully independent and would stick to his guns on all trials on which the group disagreed with him (Figure 11.3). Most subjects yielded to the group on at least some occasions, in fine disregard of the evidence of their senses. When interviewed after the experiment, most of the yielding subjects made it clear that the group didn't really affect how they *saw* the lines. No matter what everyone else said, the 8-inch line still looked bigger than the 6 1/4-inch line. But the subjects wondered whether they were right, became worried about their vision and sanity, and were exceedingly embarrassed at expressing their deviance in public (Asch, 1952, 1956; Asch and Gleitman, 1953).

For our present purposes, our primary concern is not so much with what the subjects *did,* but rather with how they *felt.* In this regard, most of them were alike. Some yielded and some were independent (see Chapter 12), but assuming they did not suspect a trick (and few of them did), they were generally very much disturbed. Why all the furor? The answer is that Asch's procedure had violated a basic premise of the subjects' existence: However people may differ, they all share the same physical reality. Under the circumstances, it is small wonder that Asch's subjects were deeply alarmed by a discrepancy they had never previously encountered. (Needless to say, the whole experiment was carefully explained to them immediately afterwards.)

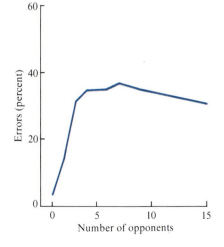

11.3 Social pressure and group size *The figure plots the extent to which the subject yielded as a function of the size of the group against him. In Asch's experiment, the effect seemed to reach its maximum with a group size of three, though other studies (such as Gerard, Wilhelmy, and Conolley, 1968) have found that conformity continues to rise beyond this point as the number of opponents increases. (After Asch, 1955)*

The belief that others see, feel, and hear pretty much as we do is a cognitive axiom of our everyday experience. When this axiom is violated, as it is in Asch's experiment, a vital prop is knocked out from under us, a prop so basic we never even realized that it was there.

Social Comparison

The Asch study shows what happens when the clear evidence of one's senses is contradicted by the verdict of a unanimous group. But suppose that our own perception does not provide a clear-cut answer. This would happen, for example, if the lines differed by only a small amount. If left to our own devices, we would try to obtain some further sensory evidence. We might look at the lines once more but from a different angle, or try to measure them with a ruler. But if we can't do that, then it's only reasonable to listen to what others have to say. Their judgment can then be used in lieu of further information provided by our own eyes or hands. If the others should now disagree with us, we might well change our own answer on their say-so. Several studies have shown that this is precisely what occurs in an Asch-type experiment in which the discrimination is fairly difficult. There is more yielding and very little emotional disturbance (Crutchfield, 1955; for further discussion of conformity effects, see Chapter 12, pp. 340–41).

This general line of reasoning may explain why people seek the opinion of others whenever they are confronted by a situation that they do not fully understand. To evaluate the situation, they need more information. If they cannot get it first hand, they will try to compare their own reactions to those of others (Festinger, 1954; Suls and Miller, 1977). The need for such *social comparison* is especially pronounced when the evaluations pertain to social issues, such as the qualifications of a political candidate or the pros and cons of fluoridating the water supply.

Cognitive Processes and Belief

The preceding discussion has shown that people try to make sense of the world they encounter. But how? In effect, they do this by looking for some consistency among their own experiences and memories and then turning to other people for comparison and confirmation. If all checks out, then well and good. But what if there is some incongruity? The Asch study showed what happens when there is a serious incongruity between one's own experiences (and the beliefs based upon them) and those reported by others. But suppose the incongruity is among the person's own experiences, beliefs, or actions? Many social psychologists believe that this will trigger some tendency to restore cognitive consistency—to reinterpret the situation so as to minimize whatever inconsistency may be there.

What kinds of mechanisms might explain this general tendency to reinterpret aspects of our experience so that they fit together sensibly? A very influential approach was developed by Leon Festinger who proposed that any perceived inconsistency among various aspects of knowledge, feelings, and behavior sets up an unpleasant internal state that he called *cognitive dissonance,* which people try to reduce whenever possible (Festinger, 1957).

One of the earliest examples is provided by a study of a sect that was awaiting the end of the world. The founder of the sect announced that she had received a message from the "Guardians" of outer space. On a certain day, there would be an enormous flood. Only the true believers were to be saved and would be picked up at midnight of the appointed day in flying saucers. (Technology has advanced considerably since the days of Noah's Ark.) On doomsday, the members of the

The interpersonal nature of reality   A scene from the 1939 film Gaslight, *with Charles Boyer and Ingrid Bergman, in which a scheming husband terrifies his young wife into doubting her own sanity. (Courtesy the Kobal Collection)*

(Drawing by Rea; © 1955, 1983, The New Yorker Magazine, Inc.)

sect huddled together, awaiting the predicted cataclysm. The arrival time of the flying saucers came and went; tension mounted. Finally, the leader of the sect received another message: To reward the faith of the faithful, the world was saved. Joy broke out, and the believers became more faithful than ever (Festinger, Riecken, and Schachter, 1956).

Given the failure of a clear-cut prophecy, one might have expected the very opposite. A disconfirmation of a predicted event should presumably lead one to abandon the beliefs that produced the prediction. But cognitive dissonance theory says otherwise. By abandoning the belief that there are Guardians, the person who had once held this belief would have to accept a painful dissonance between her present skepticism and her past beliefs and actions. Her prior faith would now appear extremely foolish. Some members of the sect had gone to such lengths as giving up their jobs or spending their savings; such acts would lose all meaning in retrospect without the belief in the Guardians. Under the circumstances, the dissonance was intolerable. It was reduced by a belief in the new message which bolstered the original belief. Since other members of the sect stood fast along with them, their conviction was strengthened all the more. They could now think of themselves not as fools, but as loyal, steadfast members of a courageous little band whose faith had saved the earth.

ATTITUDES

Social beliefs are accompanied by strong feelings. Take the conviction that abortion is murder—a far cry from the many beliefs we hold that are completely unencumbered by emotion, such as our nonchalant assurance that the sum of the angles of a triangle is 180 degrees. Emotionally tinged social views of the former kind are generally called attitudes. Since various people often have different attitudes, they tend to interpret many social situations differently; the same crowd may look like a group of peaceful demonstrators to one observer and like a rioting mob to another.

As modern social psychologists use the term, an ***attitude*** is a rather stable mental position held toward some idea, or object, or person. Examples are attitudes toward nuclear power, the legalization of marijuana, school integration, or packaged breakfast foods. Every attitude is a combination of beliefs, feelings, evaluations, and some predisposition to act accordingly. Thus, people who differ in their attitudes toward nuclear power will probably have different beliefs on the subject (e.g., "nuclear power plants are—or are not—unsafe"), will evaluate it differently (from extreme *pro* to extreme *con*), and these differences will make them more likely to take some actions rather than others (e.g., to support or protest the construction of a new nuclear plant).

Attitudes *Attitudes are a combination of beliefs, feelings, and evaluations, coupled with some predisposition to act accordingly. (Left: photograph by Sylvia Johnson/Woodfin Camp, 1989. Right: photograph by Susan McElhinney, 1980/Woodfin Camp)*

Attitudes and Behavior

Attitudes can be measured in a number of ways. The most widely used methods involve some form of self-report. For example, the subject might be given an ***attitude questionnaire*** with items that relate to the matter at hand. Thus, in a questionnaire on nuclear power and related issues, subjects might be given a statement such as: "Accidental explosions in nuclear plants pose some danger; but this risk is relatively small compared to the economic and social benefits of cheap and abundant energy." They would then be asked to select a number between, say, $+10$ and -10 to indicate the extent of their agreement or disagreement. The sum of a person's responses to a number of statements that all tap the same concerns may then provide a quantitative expression of that person's attitude.

Do attitudes as measured by self-report predict what people actually do? The question has led to controversy, for some earlier reports suggested that the relationship is much weaker than one might have thought. During the thirties when there was considerable prejudice against Asians, Richard LaPiere traveled through the country with a Chinese couple and stopped at over fifty hotels and motels and at nearly two hundred restaurants. All but one hotel gave them accommodations, and no restaurant refused them service. Later on the very same establishments received a letter that asked whether they would house or serve Chinese persons. Ninety-two percent of the replies were "No" (LaPiere, 1934). It appeared that there was a major inconsistency between people's attitudes as verbally expressed and their actual behavior.

The results of this and some related studies led some social psychologists to doubt whether the attitude concept is particularly useful. If attitudes don't predict behavior, what is the point of studying them in the first place? (Wicker, 1969). But upon further analysis, this pessimism proved to be unwarranted. For later studies showed that under many circumstances attitudes do indeed predict behavior. Thus voter preferences during the four presidential campaigns of 1952 to 1964 as expressed in preelection interviews were a pretty good predictor of later behavior in the voting booth: 85 percent of the persons interviewed voted in line with their previously expressed preference. For the most part, those who shifted had initial preferences that were rather weak (Kelley and Mirer, 1974).

It appears that attitudes often do predict behavior. But if so, how can we explain the fact that they don't always do so? An important factor is how specifically the attitude is defined. The more general one's definition, the less likely is it to predict a particular bit of behavior. A demonstration comes from a study on women's attitudes toward birth control. Positive attitudes toward birth control *in general* showed only a negligible correlation with the use of oral contraceptives during a two-year period. But attitudes toward using birth control pills *in particular* correlated quite well with their actual use during this period (Davidson and Jaccard, 1979).

Attitude Change

While attitudes have a certain resilience, their stability is threatened at every turn, especially in modern mass society where our attitudes and beliefs are under continual assault. Hundreds of commercials urge us to buy one product rather than another, political candidates clamor for our vote, and any number of organizations exhort us to fight for (or against) arms control, or legalized abortion, or environmental protection, and so on and so on. When we add these mass-produced appeals to the numerous private attempts at persuasion undertaken by our friends and relatives, it is hardly surprising that attitudes sometimes do change. Social psychologists have spent a great deal of effort in trying to understand how such attitude changes come about.

PERSUASIVE COMMUNICATIONS

A number of investigators have studied the effectiveness of so-called *persuasive communications.* These are messages that openly try to persuade us: to stop smoking, to outlaw abortion, to favor capital punishment, or—on a more humble level—to choose one brand of toothpaste rather than another. Among the factors that determine whether a given message has its desired effect are the person who sends the message and the message itself (Cialdini, Petty, and Cacioppo, 1981; McGuire, 1985).

The message source One factor that determines whether someone will change your mind on a given issue is who that someone is. To begin with, there is the element of *credibility.* Not surprisingly, communications have more of an effect if they are attributed to someone who is an acknowledged expert than to someone who is not. Thus a recommendation that antihistamines should be sold over the counter was more effective when ascribed to the *New England Journal of Medicine* than to a popular mass circulation magazine (Hovland and Weiss, 1952; Aronson, Turner, and Carlsmith, 1963).

Expertise is important, but so is *trustworthiness.* For the would-be persuader will have a much harder time if we believe that she has something to gain from persuading us (Walster, Aronson, and Abrahams, 1966). When a used car salesman tells you *not* to buy a car from his lot, you are likely to believe him. (Unless you believe that the other lot to which he refers you belongs to his brother-in-law.)

The message However important the messenger, the message she delivers is surely more important yet. What are the factors that determine whether that message will change attitudes? According to the so-called *elaboration-likelihood model* of persuasion, there are two routes to persuasion. One is the *central route to persuasion,* in which we follow the message with some care and mentally elaborate its arguments with yet further arguments and counterarguments of our own. We would take this route if the issue is one that matters to us and if we're not diverted by other matters. Here content and information are what matter, and strong arguments will indeed be more effective in changing our minds than will weak arguments. But the situation is quite different if the message comes by way

Attempts at persuasive communication
Two advertising messages that try to change consumer attitudes toward various products. (A) links a perfume to exotic glamour; (B) asserts that a certain bread will appeal to any ethnic group whatever. (Courtesy Guerlain; Best Foods Baking Group)

Another attempt to persuade *An American advertisement from around 1900. (Frontispiece from* The Wonderful World of American Advertising, 1865–1900 *by Leonard de Vries and Ilonka van Amstel, Chicago: Follett, 1972)*

of the ***peripheral route to persuasion.*** We'll be induced to take this route if we don't care much about the issue, or if the message isn't clearly heard because of background noise, or if we are otherwise distracted. If so, then content and arguments matter little. What counts instead is how or by whom or in what surroundings the message is presented (Petty and Cacioppo, 1985).

The so-called central route to persuasion involves reasoned thought. But just what is the peripheral route? According to some authors, it often represents a kind of mental shortcut. After all, there are only so many things we can pay attention to, and so we use some rules of thumb, or ***heuristics,*** to help us decide whether to accept or reject the message (Eagly and Chaiken, 1984; Chaiken, 1987). Such heuristics may include the speaker's apparent expertise ("experts know what they're talking about"), or likability ("nice people can be trusted"), or the sheer number or length of the arguments that are presented, regardless of how good they are ("the more arguments they give, the more likely that they are right"). Such heuristics in reacting to persuasive communications are reminiscent of heuristics in decision making; both are mental shortcuts we resort to because our cognitive capacity is limited (see Chapter 7, pp. 212–13, for a further discussion of heuristics).

COGNITIVE DISSONANCE AND ATTITUDE CHANGE

We've already seen that attitudes can affect behavior. But the relation can also go the other way. For in some situations, what an individual does will lead to a change in his attitudes. According to some social psychologists, this effect is produced by a tendency to reduce cognitive dissonance analogous to that which we've considered in the context of a change in beliefs.

Post-decision dissonance Suppose there is some inconsistency between a person's attitudes and her behavior. Suppose further that the behavior is an act she has already performed. How can she reconcile the inconsistency now? She can't change her behavior, for that's past and done with. All she can do is to readjust her present attitude.

Dissonance theorists point to a number of phenomena that demonstrate attitude changes that preserve some harmony between past acts and present attitudes. Some involve reevaluations that occur after some irrevocable decision has been made. Suppose a person has to choose between two alternatives: to attend one college rather than another, or to buy one make of automobile rather than another. If both options are attractive, the final decision will necessarily lead to dissonance—for whichever alternative is chosen means giving up the other. According to the theory, there will now be a tendency to reduce dissonance by reevaluating the two alternatives: the one that was finally chosen will seem more attractive and the one that was rejected will seem less attractive than it did before. A number of studies have given results in line with this prediction (e.g., Brehm, 1956; Knox and Inkster, 1968).

Justification of effort Some related findings concern retrospective explanations of prior efforts. People often make considerable sacrifices to attain a goal—backbreaking exertion to scale a mountain, years and years of study to become a cardiologist. Was it worth it? According to dissonance theory, the goal will be esteemed more highly the harder it was to reach. If it were not, there would be cognitive dissonance. Support comes from common observation of the effects of harsh initiation rites, such as fraternity hazing. After the ordeal is passed, the initiates seem to value their newly found membership all the more. Similar effects have been obtained in the laboratory. Subjects admitted to a discussion group after going through a fairly harsh screening test put a higher value on their new membership (Aronson and Mills, 1959; Gerard and Mathewson, 1966).

Forced compliance A related result is the effect of ***forced compliance.*** The basic idea is simple. Suppose someone agrees to give a speech in support of a view that is contrary to his own position, as in the case of a bartender arguing for prohibition. Will his public act change his private views? The answer seems to depend upon why he agreed to make the speech in the first place. If he was bribed by an enormous sum, there will be little effect. As he looks back upon his public denunciation of alcohol, he knows why he did what he did; $500 in cold cash is justification enough. But suppose he gave the speech with lesser urging and received only a trifling sum. If we later ask what he thinks about prohibition, we will find that he has begun to believe in his own speech. According to Festinger, the reason is the need to reduce cognitive dissonance. If the bartender asks himself why he took a public stand so contrary to his own attitudes, he can find no adequate justification; the few dollars he received are not enough. To reduce the dissonance, the compliant bartender does the only thing he can: He decides that what he said wasn't really all that different from what he believes.

A number of studies have demonstrated such forced compliance effects in the laboratory. In a classic experiment, subjects were asked to perform several extremely boring tasks, such as packing spools into a tray and then unpacking and turning one screw after another for a quarter turn. When they were finished, they were induced to tell another subject (who was about to engage in the same activities) that the tasks were really very interesting. They were paid either $1 or $20 for lying in this way. When later asked how enjoyable they themselves had found the tasks, the well-paid subjects said that they were boring, while the poorly paid subjects said that they were fairly interesting. This result is rather remarkable. One might have guessed that the well-paid liar would have been more persuaded by his own arguments than the poorly paid one. But contrary to this initial intuition—and in line with dissonance theory—the exact opposite was the case (Festinger and Carlsmith, 1959; see Figure 11.4). A number of other studies have performed variants on the original experiment with essentially the same results (e.g., Rosenfeld, Giacalone, and Tedeschi, 1984).

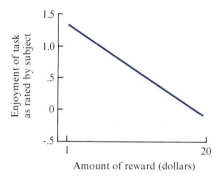

11.4 The effect of forced compliance on attitude *After being paid either $1 or $20 to tell someone that a boring task they had just performed was very interesting, subjects were asked to rate their own true attitude. As the figure shows, subjects who were only paid $1 gave a much higher rating than those paid $20. (After Festinger and Carlsmith, 1959)*

DISSONANCE RECONSIDERED

The reevaluation of prior decisions and the effect of forced compliance seem to be ways of reducing dissonance. But just what is the dissonance that is here reduced? In the early days of dissonance theory, dissonance was regarded as essentially equivalent to logical inconsistency, like the inconsistency between the belief that the sun moves around the earth and the belief that the sun is at the center of the solar system. But more recent evidence suggests that dissonance reduction is not always a cognitive matter. A number of studies indicate that we often try to reduce the dissonance between our acts and beliefs for more emotional reasons. One such factor is an effort to maintain a favorable picture of ourselves (Aronson, 1969; Steele and Liu, 1983; Cooper and Fazio, 1984).

Consider the retrospective reevaluation of whether some achievement was worth its cost. People who have made a great sacrifice to attain some goal will value it more than those who achieved the goal with little effort. The original interpretation was that this dissonance reduction was produced by a tendency toward logical consistency—the worth of the goal has to match its cost, just as the noun must fit the pronoun. But there is a noncognitive reason that is just as plausible. The effect may be caused by a desire to maintain a ***favorable self-picture.*** An individual who goes through a difficult initiation rite to join a club and later

---

* The term *forced compliance* was coined to describe the phenomenon when it was first demonstrated experimentally (Festinger and Carlsmith, 1959). It is a bit of a misnomer since the subject is not really "forced" to lie about his attitudes but is rather persuaded or coaxed. Modern social psychologists prefer the more accurate—if more clumsy—designation *counter-attitudinal advocacy.*

discovers that the club is rather dull might well feel like a fool. To avoid this, she adjusts her attitude to fit her own acts and overvalues her group membership.

Similar considerations apply to the effect of forced compliance. A subject who has argued for a position he doesn't hold will change his attitude to fit his arguments (assuming he wasn't paid too much for presenting them). The original interpretation of this effect was that it was an attempt to reduce a cognitive inconsistency. But the critical factor may have been emotional—a sense of guilt at having persuaded someone to spend an unpleasant hour at a boring task. If we can manage to change our own views just a bit (which is easier if we weren't paid too much for lying), we may salve our conscience (Cooper, Zanna, and Goethals, 1974).

Seen in this light, dissonance reduction is essentially equivalent to what Sigmund Freud called "rationalization" (see Chapter 10).

Attitude Stability

We've seen that attitudes can be changed—by certain forms of persuasion (if the source is credible and trustworthy and if the message is appropriate) and by tendencies toward cognitive consistency (especially with regard to acts we've already performed). But on balance, the overall picture is one of attitude stability rather than of attitude change. Attitudes can be altered, but it takes some doing. By and large, there seems to be a tendency to hold on to the attitudes one already has.

Why should this be so? One reason is cognitive consistency, which on the whole is a force to keep things as they are. As an example, take the general public's evaluation of televised presidential debates. Such confrontations may have an effect on those who are still undecided, but they seem to do little to shake the faith of those who are already committed. In the 1976 presidential debates between Gerald Ford and Jimmy Carter, the judgment of "who did the better job" depended largely on who did the judging. Those initially in favor of Carter were sure that he had won the debate; those originally in favor of Ford were no less certain that their candidate was the winner (Freedman, Sears, and Carlsmith, 1981).

Another reason for attitude stability is that people generally stay in the same social and economic environment. Their family, their friends and fellow workers, their social and economic situations tend to remain much the same over the years. Top-level executives know other top executives, and trade union members know other union members. On any one day, they may read or hear a speech that advocates a position contrary to their own, and they may even be affected. But on that evening and the day after, they will go back to the same old setting and will encounter the same old views that they had held before. Under the circumstances, it is hardly surprising that attitude stability is more common than attitude change. To be sure, there are striking events that may transform our

Attitude stability   Attitudes are generally resistant to change. One reason is that people generally stay in the same social environment, keeping company with others whose views of the world are essentially the same. (Photographs from left to right by Francis Laping/Black Star; Roger Sandler/Black Star; Christopher Morris/ Black Star)

attitudes completely—not just our own, but also those of everyone around us. An example is the news of the attack on Pearl Harbor on December 7, 1941. Without a doubt, this led to an instant and radical change in Americans' attitudes toward Japan. But by their very nature, such events—and the extreme changes in attitudes they produce—are rare.

PERCEIVING OTHERS

Thus far our discussion of how people interpret the social world has focused upon the way in which they try to harmonize various events with their beliefs and attitudes. A similar approach has been applied to find out how we form impressions of other people and how we try to understand why they do what they do.

Forming Impressions

Perceiving the characteristics of another person is in some ways analogous to perceiving certain stable attributes of a physical object, such as its shape or size. In our previous discussion of visual perception, we saw that to do this the observer must extract certain invariant properties from the stimulus pattern (see Chapter 5). He must abstract the crucial relationships within the stimulus input so that he can see the form of the object, say, a catlike shape. He must also disregard various features of the stimulus pattern that tend to obscure the stable characteristics of the object; examples are illumination, distance, and angle of regard. By doing all this, the observer attains perceptual constancy and can answer such life-and-death questions as whether he is dealing with a kitten nearby or a tiger far away.

Something analogous occurs when we perceive—or rather, infer—such attributes of a person as his violent temper or warmth, and so on. In effect, we are making a judgment as to what the person is "really" like, a judgment independent of the particular moment and occasion. His personal attributes (often called *traits)* are inferred invariant properties that seem to characterize his behavior in different situations. When we say that a person is irascible, we don't mean that he will utter an impolite expletive when someone deliberately steps on his toe. We mean that he will generally be short-tempered over a wide range of circumstances. To put it another way, the attempt to understand what another person is like boils down to an effort to note the *consistencies* in what he does over time and under different circumstances (see Chapter 16).

The question is how this consistency is abstracted from the few bits of behavior of the other person that are all we can actually observe.

Impressions of Others as Patterns

Several theorists assume that the processes whereby we try to understand another person are in many ways analogous to the way in which we perceive various attributes of physical objects. Consider visual form. This is a perceptual Gestalt that depends upon the *relation* among the elements of which the form is composed; thus, a triangle can be composed of dots or crosses and remain the same triangle (see Chapter 5). According to Solomon Asch, a similar principle describes our conceptions of other people. In his view, these conceptions of others are not a simple aggregate of the attributes we perceive them to have. Instead, they form an organized whole whose elements are interpreted in relation to the overall pattern (Asch, 1952).

Radical attitude change produced by striking events *Occasionally a rare and momentous event changes attitudes. An example is the opening of the Berlin Wall in the winter of 1989, which signaled the end of the Cold War. (Photograph by Michael Probst, UPI/Bettman Newsphotos)*

To test his hypothesis, Asch performed several studies of how people form impressions of others. His technique was to give subjects a list of attributes that they were told described the same person. Their task was to write a short sketch of the person so characterized and to rate this person on a checklist of antonyms (generous/ungenerous, good-natured/irritable). In one study, some subjects were given a list of seven traits: *intelligent, skillful, industrious, warm, determined, practical, cautious.* Other subjects received the same list except that *cold* was substituted for *warm.* The resulting sketches were quite different. The "warm person" was seen as "driven by the desire to accomplish something that would be of benefit" while the "cold person" was described as "snobbish . . . calculating and unsympathetic." The checklist results were in the same direction. The person described as warm was seen as generous, happy, and good-natured. The "cold person" was characterized by the appropriate antonyms (Asch, 1946).

According to Asch, the warm/cold trait acted as a focus around which the total impression of the person was organized. To use his term, it was a central trait that determined the perception of the whole. Other traits seemed to be of lesser importance. For example, it made little difference whether the list of traits included *polite* or *blunt.**

Solomon E. Asch   *(Courtesy Swarthmore College)*

Impressions of Others as Cognitive Constructions

Asch tried to understand impression formation by an analogy to perceptual patterning. A number of recent authors champion a view that is in many ways a modern version of Asch's approach, but they appeal to concepts derived from modern theories of memory and thinking rather than to principles of visual perception. In their view, our impressions of others are cognitive constructions based on various **schemas** (also known as **schemata**)—sets of organized expectations about the way in which different behaviors of people hang together. Such schemas cannot help but affect the way in which we perceive other people. If we believe that someone is outgoing and gregarious, we will also expect her to be relatively talkative. She may or may not be, but the pattern we perceive is partially imposed by our schema of what an outgoing and gregarious person is like. Such schemas about persons are sometimes called **implicit theories of personality** (Bruner and Tagiuri, 1954; Schneider, 1973).

A demonstration of how such cognitive constructions operate used subjects who read several lists of attributes. One described a person said to be an "extrovert," another a person who was an "introvert." On a later recognition test, subjects falsely recognized adjectives that had not been on the original list if they fit in with the appropriate label. Thus terms such as *spirited* and *boisterous* that had not been presented previously were misremembered as being part of the original list that described the extrovert; terms such as *shy* and *reserved* were falsely remembered as part of the list that described the introvert (Cantor and Mischel, 1979).

Phenomena of this kind suggest that the processes of **social cognition,** that is, the ways in which we gain knowledge of social events, are much like those of cognition in general. Suppose we briefly looked into a tool chest and were then shown a set of objects and asked which of them we had seen. We'd surely be more likely to misremember having seen a hammer than a baby bottle. Our cognitive

---

* The question of why and when some traits are central and others not has received considerable attention. According to Julius Wishner, the effect is partially dependent on the observer's beliefs about which traits go together with others (Wishner, 1960).

schema of a tool chest includes a hammer, just as our schema of an extrovert includes the attribute "boisterous."

SOCIAL COGNITION AND STEREOTYPES

The uncritical application of social schemas can lead to errors that have serious social consequences. This is particularly clear in the case of social *stereotypes,* when schemas are simplified and applied to whole groups. Such stereotypes are categories by means of which we try to simplify the complex world in which we live, so that we talk about Greeks, and Jews, and blacks (or student radicals, upwardly mobile Yuppies, or little old ladies in tennis shoes) as if they were all alike. Such group stereotypes are often negative, especially if they are applied to minority groups.

While the schema approach cannot explain how particular stereotypes come about, it has some suggestions for how they become perpetuated. One possible factor is *illusory correlation.* Many characteristics of the world are correlated; they go together more often than would occur by chance alone—clouds and rainfall, accidents and fire sirens, and so on. But some of the correlations we perceive are illusory, a creation of our minds rather than a real relationship in the world outside. Such illusory correlations come about because certain co-occurrences are more readily noted and remembered than are others. One reason may be because they are the ones that are expected.

Some evidence for this idea comes from a study in which subjects were presented with a number of statements that described members of different occupational groups, for example, "Doug, an accountant, is timid and thoughtful" or "Nancy, a waitress, is busy and talkative." Some of the characteristics were judged to fit the stereotype (e.g., accountant—perfectionist; stewardess—attractive; salesman—enthusiastic), while others did not. But the sentences were so constructed that each occupation was systematically paired with each kind of adjective, so that in fact no correlation was encountered. The subjects were later asked to estimate how often each adjective described each occupational group in the sentences they had just read. Their estimates indicated that they believed that accountants were more often described as timid than were waitresses, stewardesses more often as attractive than were librarians, and so on—a good example of an illusory correlation, suggesting how stereotypes can be maintained even in the face of contradictory evidence (Hamilton and Rose, 1980).

ATTRIBUTION

As previously pointed out, the attempt to understand what another person is like is really an attempt to find the pattern, the consistency, in what he does. An important step toward that end is to infer what *caused* his behavior on any particular occasion—for the meaning of any given act depends upon the cause. But what cause do we see in what the other person does? Consider a football player who violently bumps an opponent in the course of the game. If the bumping occurred while the play was in progress, not much is revealed about the bumper's personality; he was behaving according to the rules of the game. But if the bump occurred some seconds after the official blew his whistle and the play was over, the situation is different. Now the act is more revealing and may be *attributed* to a grudge or a nasty disposition. The bumpee will conclude that the bumper's action was *internally caused,* and will then self-righteously become a bumper when his own turn comes.

11.6
by the
Accor
subject
simply
to the
We see
dinosa
trigger
pound
respon

The Cognitive Arousal Theory of Emotion

In contrast to the James-Lange theory, which emphasizes the role of bodily feedback, an alternative account focuses on cognitive factors. After all, emotional experiences are usually initiated by certain external events—a letter with tragic news, a loved one's return. Events such as these bring grief or joy, but before they can possibly affect us emotionally they must be appraised and understood. Suppose we see a man who throws a spherical object toward us. Our emotional reaction will surely be different if we think the object is a ball than if we believe that it is a hand grenade. The emotion depends on some cognitive interpretation of the situation that in turn depends on what we see, what we know, and what we expect (Arnold, 1970).

Can a cognitive approach to emotion be combined with the James-Lange emphasis on bodily feedback? Proponents of Stanley Schachter's *cognitive arousal theory* believe that it can. As they see it, various stimuli may trigger a general state of autonomic arousal, but this arousal will provide only the raw materials for an emotional experience—a state of undifferentiated excitement and nothing more. This excitement is shaped into a specific emotional experience by cognitive appraisal and interpretation. In effect, this amounts to an attribution process. A person's heart beats rapidly and her hands are trembling—is it fear, rage, joyful anticipation, or a touch of the flu? If the individual has just been insulted, she will interpret her internal reactions as anger and will feel and act accordingly. If she is confronted by William James's bear, she will attribute her visceral excitement to the bear and experience fear. If she is at home in bed, she will probably assume that she is sick. In short, according to cognitive arousal theory, emotional experience is produced, not by autonomic arousal as such, but rather by the interpretation of this arousal in the light of the total situation as the subject sees it (Schachter and Singer, 1962; Schachter, 1964; Mandler, 1984; see Figure 11.7).

THE MISATTRIBUTION OF AROUSAL

To test this general conception, Schachter and Singer performed a now classic experiment in which subjects were autonomically aroused but did not know what caused the arousal. Toward this end, the subjects were injected with a drug that they believed to be a vitamin supplement but that was really adrenaline (epinephrine). Some subjects were informed of the drug's real effects, such as increase in heart rate, flushing, tremor, and so on. Other subjects were misinformed. They were told that the drug might have some side effects, such as numbness or itching, but they were not informed of its actual bodily consequences. After the drug had been administered, the subjects sat in the waiting room while waiting for what they thought was a test of vision. In actual fact, the main experiment was conducted in this waiting room with a confederate posing as another subject while the experimenter watched through a one-way screen. One condition was set up to produce anger. The confederate was sullen and irritable and eventually stalked out of the room. Another condition provided a context for euphoria. The confederate was ebullient and frivolous. He threw paper planes out of the window, played with a hula hoop, and tried to engage the subject in an improvised basketball game with paper balls. Following their stay in the waiting room, the subjects were asked to rate their emotional feelings (Schachter and Singer, 1962).

The critical question was whether the prior information about the drug's effects had influenced the subjects' reactions. Schachter and Singer reasoned that those subjects who had been correctly informed about the physiological consequences of the injection would show less of an emotional response than those

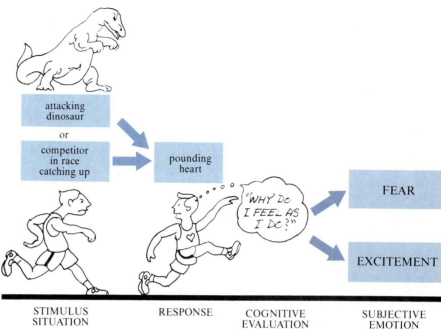

11.7 The sequence of events as conceived by Schachter and Singer's cognitive arousal theory of emotions *According to Schachter and Singer, subjectively experienced emotion is the result of an evaluation process in which the subject interprets his own bodily reactions in the light of the total situation. Any number of external stimuli (ranging from attacking dinosaurs to competition in a race) may lead to the same general bodily reaction pattern—running and increased heart rate. The subjective emotion depends upon what the subject attributes these bodily responses to. If he attributes them to a danger signal (the dinosaur) he will feel fear. If he attributes them to the race, he will feel excitement.*

who had been misinformed. The informed subjects could attribute their tremors and palpitations to the drug rather than to the external situation. In contrast, the misinformed subjects had to assume that their internal reactions were caused by something outside—the elation of the euphoric confederate or the sullenness of the angry one. Given this external attribution, their emotional state would be in line with the environmental context—euphoric or angry as the case might be. The results were more or less as predicted. The misinformed subjects in the euphoria condition described themselves as more joyful than their correctly informed counterparts and were somewhat more likely to join in the confederate's mad antics. Analogous results were obtained in the anger condition.

Beyond Cognitive Arousal Theory

Cognitive arousal theory has come in for some criticisms. A number of authors have pointed to various problems with the original Schachter and Singer study; some of the effects were rather small or inconclusive, and several later investigators did not succeed in replicating the full range of results predicted by cognitive arousal theory (Reisenzein, 1983). But the main point at issue goes beyond the details raised by that experiment. It concerns cognitive arousal theory's contention that visceral arousal can lead to any and all emotional experiences, depending upon the person's interpretation of the situation. Some later studies suggest that emotional experience is not quite as flexible as this. Thus injections of epinephrine may be more likely to lead to negative emotional experiences (such as fear and anger) than to positive ones (such as euphoria) regardless of the context in which they occur (Marshall and Zimbardo, 1979; Maslach, 1979; for a rebuttal, see Schachter and Singer, 1979).

The issue is by no means settled, but a plausible position is one that stands midway between the James-Lange and Schachter theories. As we saw, the Schachter-Singer approach starts out with the assumption that all human emotions have the same bodily underpinning. But this assumption can be questioned. Some investigators claim that there are differences in the autonomic patterns that

11.8   Six fundamental emotions *The photos depict the facial expressions that some investigators regard as characteristic of six fundamental human emotions: (A) happiness, (B) surprise, (C) sadness, (D) anger, (E) disgust, and (F) fear. (From Matsumoto and Ekman, 1989; photographs courtesy of David Matsumoto)*

A

B

C

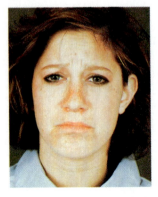

D

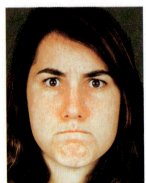

E

F

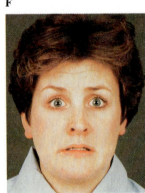

accompany such emotions as anger, sadness, and fear (e.g., Ax, 1953; Funkenstein, 1956; Schwartz, Weinberger, and Singer, 1981). Other investigators make similar claims but base them mainly on differences in facial expressions. According to these authors, these different bodily and facial patterns characterize a number of different ***fundamental emotions*** (Ekman, 1971, 1984; Izard, 1977). If so, the autonomic raw materials may not allow themselves to be shaped into virtually any emotional experience as Schacter and Singer had supposed.

FUNDAMENTAL EMOTIONS AND FACIAL EXPRESSION

The hypothesis that there are a few fundamental emotions that are revealed by distinctive patterns of facial expression goes back to Charles Darwin (Darwin, 1872b). Just how many of these elemental emotions are there? One account lists six: happiness, surprise, anger, sadness, disgust, and fear (Ekman, 1985; see Figure 11.8). Others offer different lists, numbering from eight to ten (e.g., Izard, 1971; Plutchik, 1980). But specific numbers aside, all theorists who subscribe to this general conception accept Darwin's original belief that these fundamental emotions represent several broad behavior patterns that serve vital adaptive functions. Thus, anger is thought to accompany impulses to destroy barriers, expressed by lowered brows, widened eyes, and open mouth with exposed teeth—signals to one's fellows that they better get out of one's way. Similarly for the expression of disgust (or in its milder form, contempt), which goes with riddance reactions such as vomiting, and so on, and is signaled by an expression in which the nose is wrinkled as if to shut out a smell and the lips are pursed and thrust forward as if to spit something out (Plutchik, 1970, 1984; Izard, 1977).

In a previous chapter, we've seen that the same expressive signals are used and recognized in many cultures, that they emerge at a very early age, that they are displayed in blind and deaf children who could not have learned them by observation, and that they must therefore be regarded as part of our built-in human heritage (see Chapter 9, pp. 278–80). But as we've also seen, this doesn't mean that they can't be overlaid by all sorts of learned ***display rules***—about when such signals may or may not be shown overtly. (For discussion, see Fridlund, 1990.)

FUNDAMENTAL EMOTIONS AND COGNITION

There are a number of problems about the way in which the fundamental emotion hypothesis explains how emotional experience arises. One concerns the fact that the number of fundamental emotions is rather small. The largest number that has been suggested is ten. But we surely can distinguish between many more emotional experiences than this—for example, between sadness, resignation, regret, grief, and despair, and between happiness, jubilation, rapture, and serene delight. But how can we do this if we possess at most ten different fundamental emotions?

The best guess is that further distinctions have to be made by just the kind of interpretive process that Schachter and Singer had described. A situation arouses the bodily states (and expressive reactions) corresponding to one of the fundamental emotions. This in turn produces an emotional experience—say of fear, or anger, or joy, or sadness. But its exact nature is then further shaped by the situation as the individual interprets it to be. And since the number of situations that the individual can face is countless, the number of emotional experiences that he can feel is countless as well—each with its own complexity and subtle shadings.

TAKING STOCK

On looking back, we should note that many of the phenomena we've considered in this chapter may involve the operation of either (or both) cognition and motivation or, to use two old-fashioned terms, reason and passion. Consider the effect of forced compliance. Is it caused by a force toward cognitive consistency (that is, dissonance reduction), or by an attempt to minimize guilt feelings? Or take the actor-observer bias in attribution. Is it produced by such cognitive factors as differential information and distinct perspectives or by the self-serving bias? Finally consider emotion. Here, if anywhere, motivational factors should be paramount. But we saw that even here—the very stronghold of passion—cognitive processes operate jointly with motivational ones to determine what we experience.

Both reason and passion determine what we think, and feel, and do. As we try to make sense of our social world, we try to be rational thinkers, although our cognitive limitations often force us to become lazy thinkers who rely on various mental shortcuts and schemas that may lead to errors and biases. But we are also persons with motives and passions and a need to maintain self-esteem, so that we are sometimes wishful thinkers rather than rational ones.

SUMMARY

1. Social behavior depends in part on how people interpret situations they encounter. The processes that lead to such interpretations are in many ways similar to those that underlie cognitive processes in general.

2. Our conception of what is real is heavily affected by confirmation from others, as shown by Asch's study on the effects of group pressure and by the need for *social comparison,* especially in ambiguous situations.

3. To make sense of the world, people look for *cognitive consistency.* According to *dissonance theory,* they will do what they can to reduce any inconsistency (dissonance) they perceive by reinterpreting information to fit in with their *beliefs, attitudes,* and actions.

4. The interpretation of the situations people encounter is affected by their *attitudes,* which tend to vary from one person to another. Attitudes are rather stable mental positions held toward some idea, object, or person, which combine beliefs, feelings, and predispositions to action.

5. Social psychologists have studied a number of approaches to changing attitudes. One concerns the effectiveness of *persuasive communications.* This depends in part on various characteristics of the message source, including its *trustworthiness* and *credibility.* It also depends on characteristics of the message itself. According to the *elaboration-likelihood model of persuasion,* strong arguments will be more likely to change attitudes if the mes-

sage comes in through the *central route* than if it enters through the *peripheral route,* where there is more reliance on rough-and-ready *heuristics.*

6. Another approach asserts that changes in attitude are often produced by an attempt to reduce *cognitive dissonance.* There is some evidence that the dissonance reduction effects observed in *justification of effort* and *forced compliance* studies are a way of protecting the individual's *self-picture* rather than a means to remove logical inconsistency.

7. While these various means for changing attitudes have some effect, attitudes tend to remain rather stable, in part because of *cognitive consistency,* which on the whole is a force for keeping things the way they are.

8. The way we perceive others is in some ways similar to the way we perceive and think of inanimate objects or events. Some theorists believe that *impressions of others* can be regarded as Gestalt patterns whose elements are interpreted in terms of the whole, thus accounting for the role of *central traits* in impression formation. More recent theorists emphasize the role of *social cognition,* which leads to the formation of *schemas* and *implicit theories of personality.*

9. *Attribution theory* tries to explain how we infer the causes of another person's behavior, attributing them either to *situational factors* or to *dispositional qualities.* In part, this process is quite rational and depends on the conditions in which the behavior in question is seen to occur. But in part, it leads to various errors. In judging others, we tend to make the *fundamental attribution error,* overestimating the role of dispositional and underestimating that of situational factors. This attribution bias is reversed when we ourselves are the actors rather than the observers. Reasons for the *actor-observer difference* include the fact that actors and observers have different perspectives. An additional reason is the *self-serving bias,* which tends to make people deny responsibility for their failures while taking credit for their successes.

10. According to *self-perception theory,* similar attribution processes determine how we perceive ourselves. In line with this theory is evidence that people realign their self-perception to fit their behavior.

11. An influential application of self-perception theory is Schachter and Singer's *cognitive arousal theory,* which is a revision of the *James-Lange theory of emotions.* Cognitive arousal theory argues that the emotion we feel is an interpretation of our own autonomic arousal in light of the situation to which we attribute it.

12. Many investigators doubt that one arousal process underlies all emotions. They suggest that there are some six to ten *fundamental emotions* that correspond to different *facial expressions.*

CHAPTER 12

Social Interaction

In the previous chapter, we discussed the ways in which we try to understand the social world around us. Our primary emphasis was on social cognition: our attitudes and how they are changed, our impressions of people, our interpretation of why they do what they do, and finally, the way that we ourselves interpret our own actions and experiences. In this chapter, our focus will be on action, or more precisely, *inter*action, as we ask how people deal with each other, influence each other, and act in groups.

We will consider three major kinds of interaction. Some are *one-on-one*, as when two friends have dinner or a customer tries to bargain with a used-car salesman. Others are *many-on-one*, as when a group of teenagers pressures one in their midst to wear the same clothes as all the others. Still another kind of interaction is *many-on-many*, as in riots or panics when many persons affect many others and are affected by them in turn.

RELATING TO OTHERS: ONE-ON-ONE INTERACTIONS

How do people interact on a one-on-one basis? To a large extent, the answer depends on the relationship the actors have with each other. We deal one way with comparative strangers, another with people we know and like, and yet another with those we know but don't like. But according to many social scientists, there are some common threads that run through most of our relationships, no matter how tenuous or strong they may be. We'll begin by looking at the ways in which we interact with comparative strangers.

Social Exchange

A number of theorists believe that one common principle that underlies the way people deal with others is ***social exchange.*** According to this view, each partner in a relationship gives something to the other and expects to receive something in

Social exchange *The photo shows fruit vendors in Beijing. The process of social exchange is most obvious when it is economic. (Photograph by Hiroji Kubota/Magnum Photos)*

return. Just what is exchanged depends on the relationship. If it is economic, as between buyers and sellers or employees and employers, the exchange will involve goods or labor for money. If it is between friends, lovers, or family members, the exchange will involve valued intangibles such as esteem, loyalty, and affection. According to social exchange theory, all (or at least, most) human relationships have this underlying give-and-take quality. If one partner gives but receives nothing in return, the relationship will disintegrate sooner or later (Kelley and Thibaut, 1978).

Reciprocity

The social exchange perspective is essentially economic, and thus quite appropriate to the realm of material transactions. In the marketplace, money provides a common standard by which the value of commodities can be assessed. As a result, the value of what is given and received can be compared. This is much harder (and perhaps impossible) to accomplish when the exchange involves such "commodities" as praise or loyalty, let alone love. Whether the social exchange approach applies to all social interactions is therefore a matter of debate, but that it applies to *some* is indubitable. One important example is the operation of the *reciprocity principle.* This is a basic rule that affects many aspects of social behavior. We feel that we somehow must repay whatever we have been given: a favor for a favor, a gift for a gift, a smile for a smile. As one author points out, this sense of social indebtedness is so deeply ingrained that it has been built into the vocabulary of several languages: thus, "much obliged" is a virtual synonym for "thank you" (Cialdini, 1984).

According to Robert Cialdini, the reciprocity principle can become a powerful tool of persuasion (Cialdini, 1984). Cialdini points out that incurring a favor necessarily leads to a sense of indebtedness. We feel that we must repay a donor, even if we never wanted his gift in the first place. As a result, we are sometimes manipulated into compliance, saying "yes" or buying some merchandise or making donations—all despite the fact that we never really wanted to. As an example, Cialdini describes the techniques of the Hare Krishna Society in soliciting donations. Members of this sect approach airport travellers and press a flower into

The gifts of the Magi   *The social exchange position can be stretched too far, for sometimes we give without expectation of return. (Courtesy S. Apollinare Nuovo, Ravenna)*

their hands. The traveller typically wants to return the unwanted gift, but the Krishna member will not take the flower back, insisting sweetly that "It is our gift to you." The member's next step is to request a donation to the society. Many travellers feel that under the circumstances they have no choice. Since they took the gift (no matter how unwillingly), they feel that they have to reciprocate. Their only defense—and many travellers resort to it—is to beware of Krishnas bearing gifts!

Still another kind of behavior often affected by the reciprocity rule is bargaining. The seller states his price. The potential buyer says "No." Now the seller makes a concession by offering the item (the house, the car, or whatever) at a lower price. This very concession exerts a pressure on the buyer to increase *her* offer; since he offered a concession, she feels that she ought to give a little on her side too.

The reciprocal concession effect has been the subject of several laboratory investigations. In one study, an experimenter approached persons walking on a university campus and first made a very large request. He asked them to work as unpaid volunteer counselors in a juvenile detention center for two hours a week over a two-year period. Not a single subject agreed. The experimenter then made a much smaller request: that they accompany a group of boys or girls from the juvenile detention center on a single two-hour trip to the zoo. When this smaller request came on the heels of the large request that had been refused, 50 percent of the subjects consented. In contrast, only 17 percent of the subjects acceded to the smaller request when this was not preceded by the prior, larger demand. In the first case, there was an apparent concession; in the second, there was not. The sheer fact that the experimenter seemed to make a concession was enough to make the subjects feel that they should now make a concession of their own (Cialdini et al., 1975). This method for achieving compliance has been dubbed the *door-in-the-face technique* by way of contrast to the *foot-in-the-door technique,* in which compliance with a small request makes the subject more likely to comply with the larger one (see Chapter 11, pp. 321–22). Both techniques take their names from the tricks of door-to-door salespeople (Cialdini, 1984).

Altruism

Social exchange theory suggests (and the reciprocity principle derived from it insists) that no one ever gets anything for nothing. There is no such thing as a free lunch. But this harsh judgment on human nature seems to be contradicted by the fact that people sometimes act unselfishly. Or do they?

There is ample evidence that people often fail to help others who are in distress. The widespread indifference of pedestrians to the beggars and the homeless all around them is by now a daily fact of American city life. The classic example of public apathy to a stranger's plight is the case of Kitty Genovese who was attacked and murdered on an early morning in 1964 on a street corner in Queens, New York. The assault lasted over half an hour, during which time she screamed and struggled while her assailant stabbed her repeatedly until she finally died. It later developed that thirty-eight of her neighbors had watched the episode from their windows. But none of them had come to her aid. No one even called the police (Rosenthal, 1964). What accounts for this appalling inactivity?

THE BYSTANDER EFFECT

One factor may be a lack of altruistic motivation. Perhaps people in a big city simply don't care about the fate of strangers, no matter how terrible it may be. But according to Bibb Latané and John Darley, the failure to help is often pro-

The bystander effect

duced by the way the people understand the situation. It's not that they don't care, but that they don't understand what should be done. Here as in many other contexts, social action (and interaction) is heavily affected by social cognition (see Chapter 11).

Ambiguity   Consider the passerby who sees a man lying unconscious on a city street. How can he tell whether the man is ill or is drunk? The situation is ambiguous. A similar confusion troubled some of the witnesses to the Genovese slaying. They later reported that they weren't quite sure what was going on. Perhaps it was a joke, a drunken bout, a lover's quarrel. If it was any of these, intervention might have proved very embarrassing.

Pluralistic ignorance   The situation is further complicated by the fact that the various witnesses to the Genovese tragedy realized that many others were seeing just what they did. For as they watched the drama on the street unfold, they saw the lights go on in many of the windows of the building. As a result there was **pluralistic ignorance.** Each of the witnesses looked to the others to decide whether there really was an emergency. Each was ignorant of the fact that the others were just as unsure as they. The sheer fact that the various witnesses could see each other through the windows reassured them that nothing urgent was going on.

Diffusion of responsibility   The fact that each observer knew that others observed the same event made it difficult to realize that the event was an emergency. But this fact had yet another consequence. It made intervention less probable even for those witnesses who did recognize (or at least suspect) that the situation *was* an emergency. For these persons were now faced with a **diffusion of responsibility.** No one thought that it was *his* responsibility to act. After all, while many of the observers might have felt some impulse to help, they also had self-centered motives that held them back. Some didn't want to get involved, others were afraid of the assailant, still others were apprehensive about dealing with the police. The conflict between the desire to help and to mind one's own business was finally resolved in favor of inaction through the knowledge that others witnessed the same event. Everyone assumed that since so many others saw just what they did, surely one of them would do something about it or had already done it (such as calling the police). As a result, no one did anything.

This general line of reasoning has been tested in a number of experiments. In one, subjects were asked to participate in what they thought was a group discussion about college life with either one, three, or five other persons. The subjects were placed in individual cubicles and took turns in talking to each other over an intercom system. In actuality, there was only one subject; all the other discussants were tape recordings. The discussion began as one of the (tape-recorded) confederates described some of his own personal problems, which included a tendency toward epileptic seizures in times of stress. When he began to speak again during the second round of talking, he feigned a seizure and gasped for help. The question was whether the subject would leave his own cubicle to assist the stricken victim (usually, by asking the experimenter's help). The results demonstrated the so-called **bystander effect:** the larger the size of the group that the subject is in (or thought he was in), the *less likely* he is to come to the victim's assistance (Darley and Latané, 1968; see Figure 12.1).

The bystander effect has been obtained in numerous other situations. In some, a fellow subject seems to have an asthma attack; in another, the experimenter appears to faint in an adjacent room; in still others, the laboratory fills with smoke. But whatever the emergency, the result is always the same: the larger the group the subject is in (or thinks he is in), the smaller the chance that he will take any ac-

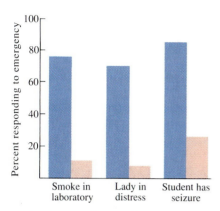

12.1 Group inhibition of bystander intervention in emergencies *When people are alone (in blue) they are more likely to respond in an emergency than when they are—or think they are—with others (in pink), in part because of diffusion of felt responsibility. (A) Percent of subjects who respond to smoke coming through a vent in the laboratory. (B) Percent of (male) subjects who came to the help of a female confederate who apparently had suffered a fall. (C) Percent of subjects who respond to a fellow subject who seems to have suffered a seizure. (Data from Darley, 1968; Latané and Rodin, 1969)*

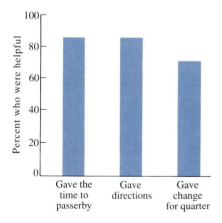

12.2 Small acts of helping in a large city *Various minor and prosaic acts of helping strangers are by no means uncommon even in a big city. (Data from Gerard, Wilhelmy, and Conolley, 1968)*

tion—in dramatic accord with the diffusion of responsibility hypothesis (Latané and Nida, 1981; Latané, Nida, and Wilson, 1981).*

THE COSTS OF HELPING

The work on the bystander effect indicates that people often don't recognize that a need for help exists and that even when they do, they may not act because they think that others will. But suppose the situation is not ambiguous and that responsibility for helping is not diffused? Will they then help a stranger in distress?

One factor that determines whether they will or won't is the physical or psychological cost to the prospective helper. The greater that cost, the smaller the chance that he will in fact help. In some cases, the cost is physical danger. In others, it is simply time and effort. In one study, students had to go from one campus building to another to give a talk. They were told to hurry, since they were already late. As they rushed to their appointments, these students passed by a shabbily dressed man who lay in a doorway groaning. Only 10 percent stopped to help the victim. Ironically enough, the students were members of a theological seminary, and the topic of their talk was the parable of the "Good Samaritan" who came to the aid of a man lying injured on a roadside. It appears that if the cost—here in time—is high enough, even theological students may not behave altruistically (Darley and Batson, 1973).

What is costly to one potential helper may not be equally so to another. Take physical danger. It is probably not surprising that bystanders who intervene in cases of assault are generally much taller, stronger, and better trained than bystanders who do not intervene, and are almost invariably men (Huston et al., 1981).

THE SELFISH BENEFITS OF UNSELFISHNESS

Providing help can yield benefits as well as costs. Some of the benefits are various signs of social approval, as in the case of a wealthy donor who is sure to make a lavish contribution as long as everyone watches. Other benefits have to do with avoiding embarrassment. Many city dwellers give two or three quarters to a beggar not because they want to help him but because it's easier to give than to say no. Occasionally the benefits of giving involve romance. In one study, the investigators posed as motorists in distress, trying to flag passing cars to provide help with a flat tire. The passing cars were much more likely to stop for a female than for a male, and the cars that stopped were generally driven by young men alone. The best guess is that the young men's altruism was not entirely unalloyed by sexual interest (West, Whitney, and Schnedler, 1975).

IS THERE ANY GENUINE ALTRUISM?

The preceding discussion paints a somewhat unflattering portrait of human nature. It seems that we often fail to help strangers in need of assistance and that when we do, our help is often rather grudging and calculating. But that picture is too one-sided. For while people can be callous and indifferent, they are also capable of true generosity and altruism (see Figure 12.2). People sometimes share

---

* Diffusion of responsibility may well explain a number of other phenomena of social interaction. One of these is *social loafing.* This describes the fact that when individuals work as a group on a common task, all doing the same thing, they often generate less effort than they would if they worked alone. An example is pulling at a rope. In one study, one man working alone pulled with an average force of 139 pounds, while groups of eight pulling together only averaged 546 pounds, which is less than four times the solo rate (Latané, Williams, and Harkins, 1979).

Altruism *Helping victims of a highway collapse during the San Francisco earthquake of 1989. (UPI/Bettmann Newsphotos)*

food, give blood, contribute to charities, and administer artificial respiration to accident victims. Yet more impressive are the unselfish deeds of living, genetically unrelated donors who have given one of their kidneys to a stranger who would otherwise have died (Sadler et al., 1971). And still others are commemorated by Jerusalem's Avenue of the Righteous, dedicated to the European Christians who sheltered Jews during the Nazi Holocaust, risking (and often giving) their own lives to save those to whom they gave refuge (London, 1970).

Such acts of altruism suggest that human behavior is not always selfish. This probably undermines the claim that *all* social interactions can be understood as a form of exchange. To be sure, acts of altruism in which the giver gets no benefits at all—no gratitude, no public acclaim—are fairly rare. The true miracle is that they exist at all. One aspect of our humanity is that we can go beyond the calls of social exchange and reciprocity.

Attraction

Thus far, we've primarily looked at social interactions with virtual strangers. What happens when the interactions are with people to whom we are closer and about whom we have stronger feelings? We'll begin by asking about the factors that attract us to others.

PROXIMITY

One of the most important determinants of attraction and liking is sheer *physical proximity.* By now, dozens of studies have documented the fact that if you want to predict who makes friends with whom, the first thing to ask is who is nearby. Students who live next to each other in a dormitory or sit next to each other in classes develop stronger relations than those who live only a bit farther away (Berscheid and Walster, 1978; Berscheid, 1985).

What holds for friendship also holds for mate selection. The statistics are rather impressive. For example, there is evidence that more than half of the couples who took out marriage licenses in Columbus, Ohio, during the summer of 1949 were persons who lived within sixteen blocks of each other when they went out on their first date (Clarke, 1952). Much the same holds for the probability that an engagement will ultimately lead to marriage; the farther apart the two live, the greater the chance that the engagement will be broken off (Berscheid and Walster, 1978).

Why should proximity be so important? One answer is that you can't like someone you've never met, and the chances of meeting that someone are much greater if he is nearby. But why should getting to know him make you like him?

One reason may be *familiarity.* There is a good deal of evidence that people tend to like what's more familiar. This seems to hold for just about any stimulus, whether it's a word in a foreign language, or a melody, or the name of a commercial product, or the photograph of a stranger's face—the more often it is seen or heard, the better it will be liked (Zajonc, 1968; Brickman and D'Amato, 1975; Moreland and Zajonc, 1982). The same familiarity process probably plays an important role in determining what we feel about other people. The hero of a well-known musical comedy explains his affection for the heroine by singing "I've grown accustomed to her face." In a more prosaic vein, the laboratory provides evidence that photographs of strangers' faces are judged to be more likable the

12.3 Familiarity and liking *The figure shows two versions of a rather well-known lady. Which do you like better—the one on the right or the one on the left? (Courtesy Documentation Photographique de la Réunion des Musées Nationaux)* (Please turn to p. 336.)

more often they have been seen (Jorgensen and Cervone, 1978). Another study applied this general idea to the comparison of faces and their mirror images. Which will be better liked? If familiarity is the critical variable, then our friends should prefer a photograph of our face to one of its mirror image, since they've seen the first much more often than the second. But we ourselves should prefer the mirror image, which for us is by far the more familiar. The results were as predicted by the familiarity hypothesis (Mita, Dermer, and Knight, 1977; see Figure 12.3).

SIMILARITY

Do people like others who are similar to themselves, or do they prefer those who are very different? To put it differently, which bit of folk wisdom is more nearly correct: "Birds of a feather flock together" or—perhaps in analogy with magnets —"Opposites attract." It appears that birds have more to teach us in this matter than magnets do, for the evidence suggests that, in general, people tend to like others who are similar to themselves. For example, elementary school students prefer other children who perform about as well as they do in academics, sports, and music (Tesser, Campbell, and Smith, 1984), and "best friends" in high school resemble each other in age, race, year in school, and high school grades (Kandel, 1978).

When it comes to marital choice and stability, objective attributes such as race, ethnic origin, social and educational level, family background, income, and religion clearly have an important effect. This also holds for such behavioral patterns as the degree of gregariousness and drinking and smoking habits. A widely cited study has shown that engaged couples in the United States are similar along all of these dimensions (Burgess and Wallin, 1943). The authors interpreted these findings as evidence for *homogamy*—a powerful tendency of like to marry like. A recent study has shown that homogamy plays a role in determining a couple's stability; couples who had stayed together after two-and-one-half years were more similar than those who had broken up (Hill, Rubin, and Peplau, 1976).

Is homogamy really produced by the effect of similarity on mutual liking? Or is it just a byproduct of proximity, of the fact that "few of us have an opportunity to meet, interact with, become attracted to, and marry, a person markedly dissimilar from ourselves"? (Berscheid and Walster, 1978, p. 87). The answer to this chicken-and-egg problem is as yet unknown. But whether similarity is a cause of the attraction, or is a side effect of some other factors that led to it initially, the end product is the same: like pairs with like, and no heiress ever marries the butler except in the movies. We're not really surprised to discover that when a princess kisses a frog he turns into a prince. What would really be surprising is to see the frog turn into a *peasant* whom the princess then marries all the same.

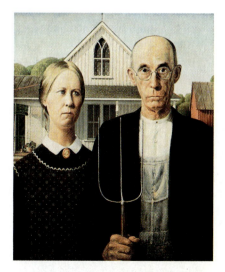

Homogamy American Gothic by *Grant Wood, 1930 (Photograph © 1989 The Art Institute of Chicago, all rights reserved)*

335

Revisiting Figure 12.3   The familiarity-leads-to-liking hypothesis would predict a preference for the right panel—a retouched photograph of the Mona Lisa (see p. 335). The panel on the left is a mirror image of that photograph, which is presumably the less familiar of the two.

PHYSICAL ATTRACTIVENESS

There is little doubt that for a given time and culture there is considerable agreement as to how physically attractive a particular man or woman is. Nor is there any doubt that this factor is overwhelmingly important in determining a person's appeal—or at least, his or her initial appeal—to members of the opposite sex. The vast sums of money spent on cosmetics, fashions, diets, and various forms of plastic surgery are one kind of testimony; our everyday experience is another. Under the circumstances, one may wonder whether there is any need to document the point experimentally, but in any case, such documentation does exist. In one study, the subjects were clients of a commercial video-dating service who selected partners after consulting files that included a photograph, background information, and detailed information about interests, hobbies, and personal ideals. When it came to the actual choice, the primary determinant was the photograph: both male and female clients selected on the basis of physical attractiveness (Green, Buchanan, and Heuer, 1984).

Matching for attractiveness   Physical attractiveness is clearly a very desirable quality. But if we all set our sights on only those who occupy the very top of this dimension, the world would soon be depopulated—there are simply not enough movie queens and matinee idols to go around. One would therefore assume that people behave in a more sensible fashion. They may well covet the most attractive of all possible mates, but they also have a fairly reasonable perception of their own social desirability (which is determined in part by their own physical attractiveness). In consequence, they will seek partners of roughly comparable social assets; while trying to get a partner who is most desirable, they also try to avoid rejection. This **matching hypothesis** predicts a strong correlation between the physical attractiveness of the two partners (Berscheid et al., 1971). This hypothesis is well supported by everyday observations ("They make such a fine couple!") and has been repeatedly documented in various empirical observations of dating couples, which show a remarkable similarity in the rated attractiveness of the two partners (Silverman, 1971; White, 1980).

What underlies physical attractiveness?   Our discussion has assumed that physical attractiveness is a given and that people pretty much agree on who is and who is not attractive. But why should this be? Why should one set of particular fea-

Attractiveness   People ornament themselves in virtually every culture but choose different ways for doing so (A) Balinese dancer (Photograph by George K. Fuller), (B) Ahka girl from a village in Thailand (Photograph by George K. Fuller), (C) Masai girl in Kenya (John Moss/ Photo Researchers)

B

C

A

Tattooed Maori man and woman *Some cultures employ tattooing as both ornamentation and a sign of enhanced prestige. Among the Maori of New Zealand, both men and women of sufficient social standing were heavily tattooed, with the chief's tattoos most lavish of all. (Top: from The New York Public Library, Astor, Lenox, and Tilden Foundations. Bottom: © Morri Manning/Black Star, 1978)*

tures, one set of bodily proportions, represent the apex of attractiveness for so many people in our time and culture? As yet we don't know.

So far we are only beginning to discover just what it is that constitutes physical attractiveness in our own culture. According to one study, American college men judge women as more attractive if their face has certain features that are perceived as "cute" and tend to be found in children, such as (relatively) large and widely separated eyes, a small nose, and a small chin. If this result holds up in other cultures (for which there is no evidence thus far), a sociobiologist might suggest that this is because perceived youthfulness is a sign of fertility. The trouble is that there are a number of other features judged to be attractive that are associated with maturity rather than immaturity; for example, wide cheekbones and narrow cheeks (Cunningham, 1986).

In any case, there is little reason to suppose that the standards of attractiveness —of face or body—are essentially the same across different times and places. To be sure, some similarities do exist. Signs of ill health and deformity (which might suggest a poor genetic bet) are considered unattractive in all cultures. The same holds for signs of advancing age (which generally signal lower fertility, especially in females). In addition, all cultures want males to look male and females to look female, although the specific cues that weigh in this judgment (and that are considered attractive) vary widely. Beyond this, however, the differences probably outweigh the similarities.

Consider the kind of female body build preferred by males. Are plump women more attractive than slim ones? You will probably agree with enthusiasm if you happen to be a Chukchi of Northeast Siberia or a Thonga of Mozambique. But your views will be very different if you are a Dobuan from New Guinea to whom corpulence is disgusting. While men in many cultures are especially attracted to women with wide hips and a broad pelvis (presumably an advantage for childbearing), men in one or two of the cultures on which data exist strongly dislike women with these bodily characteristics (Ford and Beach, 1951).

Love

Attraction tends to bring people closer together. If they are close enough, their relation may be that of "love." According to some authorities, psychologists might have been "wise to have abdicated responsibility for analysis of this term and left it to poets" (Reber, 1985). But wise or not, in recent years psychologists have tried to say some things about this strange state of mind that has puzzled both sages and poets throughout the ages.

Most investigators distinguish between two kinds of love. One is **romantic**—or **passionate—love,** the kind of love that one "falls into," that one is "in." The other is **companionate love,** a less violent state that emphasizes companionship and mutual trust and care.

ROMANTIC LOVE

Romantic love as an emotion Romantic love has been described as essentially passionate: "a wildly emotional state [in which] tender and sexual feelings, elation and pain, anxiety and relief, altruism and jealousy coexist in a confusion of feelings" (Berscheid and Walster, 1978). The extent to which the lovers feel that they are in the grip of an emotion they can't control is indicated by the very language in which they describe their love: They "fall in love," "are swept off their feet," and "can't stop themselves" (Solomon, 1981).

These tumultuous emotions are sharply focused on the beloved, who is almost always seen through a rosy glow. The lover constantly thinks about the beloved

337

and continually wants to be in his or her company, sometimes to the point of near obsession. Given this giddy mixture of erotic, irrational, obsessed passions and idealized fantasy, it's understandable why Shakespeare felt that lovers have much in common with both madmen and poets. They are a bit mad because their emotions are so turbulent and their thoughts and actions so obsessive; they are a bit poetic because they don't see their beloved as he or she really is but as an idealized fabrication of their own desires and imaginings.

The rocky course of romantic love   It has often been observed that romantic love thrives on obstacles. Shakespeare tells us that the "course of true love never did run smooth," but if it had, the resulting love may well have lacked in ardor. In part, this may be another example of the cognitive reinterpretation of arousal we have encountered in our previous discussion of emotions (see Chapter 11, pp. 324–25). The fervor of a wartime romance or of an extramarital affair is probably fed in part by danger and frustration, and many a lover's passion becomes all the more intense for being unrequited. In all these cases, there is increased arousal, whether through fear, frustration, or anxiety. This arousal continues to be interpreted as love, a cognitive appraisal that fits in perfectly with our ideas about romantic love, for these include suffering as well as rapture. An interesting demonstration of this phenomenon is the so-called **Romeo-and-Juliet effect** (named after Shakespeare's doomed couple whose parents violently opposed their love). This describes the fact that parental opposition tends to *intensify* the couple's romantic passion rather than to diminish it. In one study, couples were asked whether their parents interfered with their relationship. The greater this interference, the more deeply the couples fell in love (Driscoll, Davis, and Lipitz, 1972). The moral is that if parents want to break up a romance, their best bet is to ignore it. If the feuding Montagues and Capulets had simply looked the other way, Romeo and Juliet might well have become bored with each other by the end of the second act.

Rocky course of romantic love *Parental opposition tends to intensify Romeo and Juliet's passion. Pictured here is the balcony scene from Prokofiev's ballet,* Romeo and Juliet. *(From a 1990 performance by American Ballet Theater; photograph by Martha Swope)*

COMPANIONATE LOVE

It's widely agreed that romantic love tends to be a short-lived bloom. That wild and tumultuous state, with its intense emotional ups and downs, with its obsessions, fantasies, and idealizations, rarely if ever lasts forever. Eventually there are no further obstacles, no further surprises, no further room for fantasy and idealization. The adventure is over, and romantic love ebbs. Sometimes it turns into indifference (if not active dislike). Sometimes it is transformed into a related but gentler emotion—**companionate love.** This is sometimes defined as the "affection we feel for those with whom our lives are deeply intertwined." This is not to say that the earlier passion doesn't occasionally flare up again. But it no longer has the obsessive quality that it once had, where the lover is unable to think of anything but the beloved (Berscheid and Walster, 1978).

Companionate love *When passion and obsession ebb, the companionship and affection of companionate love, as shown here, may follow. (© Paul Fusco/Magnum)*

SOCIAL INFLUENCE: MANY-ON-ONE INTERACTIONS

Up to now, our discussion has focused upon one-on-one interactions: some between comparative strangers, others between friends and lovers. In such interactions, other people often affect what we do, as in the case of a salesman trying to sell a car to a potential customer or a would-be lover who tries to persuade his beloved to reciprocate his affections. But there are instances in which the interaction is more complex and in which the social effects come from many persons simultaneously.

Such situations are usually discussed under the general heading of *social influence.* In these cases, the interaction is of the form of many-on-one: the influence of many others converges upon one individual. In some cases, the influence of others may make us tailor our behavior to *conform* to theirs. In others, it will make us obey them and *comply* with their orders. And in still other instances, the others exert their influence upon us in an even simpler way—by their *mere presence* as an audience.

Social Facilitation: Social Influence by Mere Presence

It has long been known that the presence of other people has an effect on us. An example is laughter. Every comedian knows that laughter is contagious; each guffaw triggers another and then yet another, a fact that led to the use of canned TV laughter on the theory that if the home audience hears the (dubbed) laughs of others, they will laugh along (Wilson, 1985). Similar effects have been demonstrated by many investigators who compared people on various tasks that they performed either alone or in the presence of others. The initial results suggested that the social effect is always beneficial. When together with others who are engaged in the same task, people race bicycles faster, learn simple mazes more quickly, and perform more multiplication problems in the same period of time. Such effects have been grouped under the general title *social facilitation* (Allport, 1920).

Other studies, however, have indicated that the presence of others can sometimes be a hindrance instead of a help. While college students are faster at solving simple mazes when working together with others, they are considerably slower when the mazes are more complex (Hunt and Hillery, 1973; Zajonc, 1965, 1980). An audience can evidently inhibit as well as facilitate. How can such divergent results be reconciled?

According to Robert Zajonc, the explanation is that the presence of others leads to a state of increased drive or arousal. Such an increase would resolve the apparent contradiction if we assume that such increased arousal strengthens the tendency to perform highly *dominant* responses—the ones that seem to come "automatically." If so, then we should expect that the presence of others will improve performance when the dominant response is also the correct one—as in performing simple motor skills or learning simple mazes. But when the task gets harder—as in the case of complex mazes—then the dominant response is often incorrect. As a result, we should expect performance to get worse when others watch us, for now the dominant response (enhanced by increased arousal) will inhibit the less dominant but correct reaction. And this is just what happens.

As an example from ordinary life consider an accomplished professional actor. Such a person generally thrives in front of an audience—the bigger the audience, the happier he is. For him, the dominant responses are precisely those demanded by his role; he knows his part and how to make the most of it, and so the audience brings his performance to even higher peaks. But the situation is very different for an unpracticed young amateur who is still stumbling over his lines and unsure of his part. His dominant responses are inappropriate to what he ought to be doing, and so he coughs, gives an embarrassed smile, and takes a few undecided half steps. He becomes aroused by the audience, but this arousal makes his performance even worse than it would be otherwise (Zajonc, 1965, 1980).

Some evidence comes from observations of pool players in a college union building. When good players were watched by an audience of four others, their accuracy rose from 71 to 80 percent. But when poor players were observed, their accuracy became even worse than it was before, dropping from 35 to 25 percent (Michaels et al., 1982).

Social facilitation *Audiences generally enhance the performance of an accomplished professional. But the effect on novices is not always beneficial. (Photograph by Gale Zucker/Stock, Boston)*

Conformity   *(Photograph by G. Frank Radway)*

Conformity

Social facilitation (and inhibition) may well be the simplest form of social influence. It shows that our behavior is affected by the mere presence of others regardless of what they do. But in other forms of social influence what others do matters very much indeed. An important example is *conformity,* in which we go along with what other people think or do. We may regard ourselves as independent nonconformists, but in some situations we all conform whether in speech or dress or manner. In the last chapter, we saw that people may go along with a group even when the group is patently wrong, as in Asch's experiment when the subjects yielded to a majority that judged an 8-inch line to be equal to one whose length was 6 1/4 inches (Asch, 1952, 1955, 1956; see Chapter 11, pp. 306–8).

THE CAUSES OF CONFORMITY

Why do people conform? The evidence suggests that there are two main reasons. One is that they want to be right; another is that they want to be liked (or at least that they don't want to appear foolish).

One basis for following others is when we ourselves aren't sure what is right. In such cases, the group exerts influence because it provides information that we feel that we ourselves don't have. This holds for information about any difficult judgment, whether it is sensory, social, or moral. If we are nearsighted and aren't wearing glasses, we'll ask others to read distant street signs; if we are not sure of what to wear (or what to say, or who to vote for), we watch what others do to get some clues for how we ourselves should act. If people are made to believe that they are more competent and knowledgeable in some area than others are (for example, seeing hidden figures), they are less likely to conform (e.g., Wiesenthal et al., 1976; Campbell, Tesser, and Fairey, 1986).

One reason for going along with the crowd is that we believe the group is right. But on other occasions, our reason is not so much cognitive as motivational. For we sometimes conform even if we believe that we are right and the others are wrong. Consider the original Asch study in which a unanimous majority made a grossly incorrect judgment. The subject sees the world as it is, but he has every reason to believe that the others see it differently. If he now says what he believes, he can't help but be embarrassed; after all, the others will probably think that he's a fool and may then laugh at him. Under the circumstances, many subjects prefer to disguise what they really believe and go along.

THE EFFECT OF HAVING AN ALLY

A unanimous majority evidently exerts a powerful effect on a solitary individual that makes him want to conform. What happens when the individual is no longer alone?

To answer this question, Asch varied his experiment by having one of the confederates act as the subject's ally; all of the other confederates gave wrong answers while the ally's judgments were correct. Under these circumstances, the real subject yielded very rarely and was not particularly upset.

The moral seems simple enough: One person who believes as we do can sustain us against all others. But on closer examination, things were not quite as simple as that. For in another variation, the confederate again deviated from the majority, but he didn't do so by giving the correct answer. On the contrary, *he gave an answer that was even further from the truth than was the group's.* Thus, on a trial in which the correct answer was 6 1/4 inches and the group's answer was 6 3/4

The ally effect *Not being alone sustains one against a majority but also in other struggles, such as against evil witches and all-powerful wizards. (From the 1939 movie,* The Wizard of Oz, *with Judy Garland, Ray Bolger, Jack Haley, and Bert Lahr; courtesy Photofest)*

inches, the confederate's answer might be 8 inches. This response was obviously not arrayed on the side of the subject (or of truth), but it helped to liberate the subject even so. He now yielded very much less than when confronted by a unanimous majority. What evidently mattered was the group's unanimity; once this was broken, the subject felt that he could speak up without fear of embarrassment (Asch, 1952). Similar findings have been performed in other laboratories with essentially similar results (Allen and Levine, 1971; Allen, 1975).

One person who shares our view can sustain us against all others. But if we can't find a supporter, the next best thing is to find another person who also opposes the majority, even if *his* opposition comes from the other side than your own. Totalitarian systems have good reasons to stifle dissent of any kind, whether of the right or the left. The moment one voice is raised in dissent, the unanimity is broken and then others may (and often do) find the courage to express their own dissent, whatever its form.

Blind Obedience

There is another way of influencing the behavior of others that is much more direct than any we've considered thus far. It is by getting people to *obey* what we command them to do. Of particular interest is the case of **blind obedience** to orders that violate one's own conscience, actions in which the individual subordinates his own understanding of the situation to that of some authority.*

A certain degree of obedience is a necessary ingredient of living in a society. In any society, no matter how primitive, some individuals have authority over others, at least within a limited sphere. Obedience is particularly relevant as societies get more complex, where the spheres within which authority can be exerted become much more differentiated. Teachers assign homework, doctors order in-

* On the face of it, obedience seems to differ from the forms of social influence we have considered thus far because commands are usually delivered on a one-to-one basis: the student obeys the teacher, the automobile driver obeys the policeman. But at bottom, the interaction is not truly one-on-one, because the teacher and the policeman speak with the authority of the whole society behind them when they order us to hand in our homework or to pull over to the roadside. To the extent that this is so, obedience and conformity (and social facilitation and inhibition) are all instances of social influence.

travenous feedings, and policemen stop automobiles. The pupils, nurses, and motorists generally obey. Their obedience is based on an implicit recognition that the persons who issued the orders were operating within their legitimate domain of authority. If this domain is overstepped, obedience is unlikely. Policemen can't order motorists to recite lists of irregular French verbs or to take two aspirins and go to bed.

Some tendency to obey authority is thus a vital cement that holds society together; without it, there would be chaos. But the atrocities of this century—the Nazi death camps, the Cambodian massacres—give terrible proof that this disposition to obedience can also become a corrosive poison that destroys our sense of humanity. Some of these atrocities could not have been committed without the obedience of tens or hundreds of thousands and the acquiescence of many more.

OBEDIENCE: PERSONALITY STRUCTURE OR SITUATION?

What makes people obey and thus participate in any of the unspeakable acts of which history tells us? One interpretation is that some personalities are more prone to obey than others, that the crucial determinant is *within* the person rather than in the situation.

An influential version of the person-centered hypothesis was presented in the decade after World War II by a group of investigators who claimed to have discovered a personality type—the so-called *authoritarian personality*—that was predisposed toward totalitarian dogma and might thus be more ready to obey unquestioningly. Such persons were prejudiced against various minority groups and also held certain sentiments about authority, including submission to those above, harshness to those below, and general belief in the importance of power and dominance (Adorno et al., 1950). While these studies have been criticized on various theoretical and methodological grounds (e.g., Snyder and Ickes, 1985), some of their major claims seem to have a basis in fact. Minority prejudice probably does go together with authoritarian sentiments, and persons with such sentiments appear to be more obedient to authority, to vote for conservative law-and-order candidates, and to accept the attitudes of those in power (Brown, 1965; Elms and Milgram, 1966; Izzett, 1971; Poley, 1974).

Can the person-centered hypothesis explain the atrocities of recent times? Were those who obeyed the order to massacre countless innocents sick minds or abnormal personalities, completely different from the rest of us? Some of them probably were (Dicks, 1972). But the frightening fact is that many of these men seemed to be cast in a much more ordinary mold; what is horrifying about them is what they did and not who they were. An example is a convicted war criminal who had personally murdered dozens of persons. He obtained his position as a guard so as to get ahead in the world. According to the psychiatric interview, he was a rather average man who "could have lived his life in quieter days unnoticed, a respectable craftsman and probably harming nobody" (Dicks, 1972, p. 141). In a well-known account of the trial of Adolf Eichmann, the man who supervised the deportation of six million Jews to the Nazi gas chambers, the author comments on this grotesque "banality of evil": "The trouble with Eichmann was precisely that so many were like him, and that the many were neither perverted nor sadistic, that they were, and still are, terribly and terrifyingly normal" (Arendt, 1965, p. 276).

THE MILGRAM STUDY

The importance of situational factors in producing obedience is highlighted by the results of one of the best-known experiments of modern social psychology, a study conducted by Stanley Milgram (1963). Milgram's subjects were drawn

Obedience *The commandant of a concentration camp in Germany stands amid some of his prisoners who were burned or shot as the American army approached the camp during the last days of World War II. Most Nazis who held such positions insisted that they were "just following orders." (Courtesy United Press International)*

from a broad spectrum of socioeconomic and educational levels; they were recruited by a local newspaper ad offering $4.50 per hour to persons willing to participate in a study of memory. Milgram's subjects arrived at the laboratory where a white-coated experimenter told them that the study in which they were to take part concerned the effect of punishment on human learning.

The subjects were run in pairs and drew lots to determine who would be the "teacher" and who the "learner." The task of the learner was to master a list of paired associates. The task of the teacher was to present the stimuli, record the learner's answers, and—most important—to administer punishment whenever the learner responded incorrectly. The learner was conducted to a cubicle where the experimenter strapped him in a chair, to "prevent excess movement," and attached the shock electrodes to his wrist—all in full view of the teacher. After the learner was securely strapped in place, the teacher was brought back to the main experimental room and seated in front of an imposing-looking shock generator. The generator had 30 lever switches with labeled shock intensities, ranging from 15 volts to 450 volts in 15-volt increments. Below each of the levers there were also verbal descriptions ranging from "Slight Shock" to "Danger: Severe Shock." The labels below the last two levers were even more ominous; they were devoid of any verbal designation and were simply marked "XXX" (Figure 12.4).

The teacher presented the items that had to be memorized. He was instructed to move on to the next item on the list whenever the learner responded correctly but to administer a shock whenever an error was made. He was told to increase the level of punishment with each succeeding error, beginning with 15 volts and going up by one step for each error thereafter until 450 volts was reached. To get an idea what the learner experienced, the teacher first submitted to a sample shock of 45 volts, the third of the 30-step punishment series, which gave an unpleasant jolt. During the experiment, all communications between teacher and learner were conducted over an intercom, since the learner was out of sight, strapped to a chair in the experimental cubicle.

Needless to say, the shock generator never delivered any shocks (except for the initial sample) and the lot drawing was rigged so that the learner was always a confederate, played by a mild-mannered, middle-aged actor. The point of the experiment was simply to determine how far the subjects would go in obeying the experimenter's instructions. Since the learner made a fair number of errors, the shock level of the prescribed punishment kept on rising. By the time 120 volts was reached, the victim shouted that the shocks were becoming too painful. At 150 volts he demanded that he be let out of the experiment. At 180 volts, he cried out that he could no longer stand the pain. At 300 volts, he screamed that he would give no further answers and insisted that he be freed. On the next few shocks there were agonized screams. After 330 volts, there was silence.

The learner's responses were of course predetermined. But the real subjects—the teachers—did not know that, so they had to decide what to do. When the victim cried out in pain or refused to go on, the subjects usually turned to the experimenter for instructions. In response, the experimenter told the subjects that the experiment had to go on, indicated that he took full responsibility, and pointed out that "the shocks may be painful but there is no permanent tissue damage."

How far do subjects go in obeying the experimenter? When the study was described to several groups of judges, including a group of forty psychiatrists, all

12.4 The obedience experiment   *(A) The "shock generator" used in the experiment. (B) The learner is strapped into his chair and electrodes are attached to his wrist. (C) The teacher receives a sample shock. (D) The teacher breaks off the experiment. (Copyright 1965 by Stanley Milgram. From the film* Obedience, *distributed by the New York University Film Library)*

predicted considerable defiance. In their view, only a pathological fringe of at most 2 percent of the subjects would go to the maximum shock intensity. But these predictions were far off the mark. In fact, about 65 percent of Milgram's subjects continued to obey the experimenter to the bitter end. This proportion was unaffected even when the learner mentioned that he suffered from a mild heart condition. This isn't to say that the obedient subjects had no moral qualms. Quite the contrary, many of them were seriously upset. They bit their lips, twisted their hands, sweated profusely—and obeyed even so.

Is there a parallel between obedience in these artificial laboratory situations and obedience in the all-too-real nightmares of Nazi Germany or Cambodia? In some ways, there is no comparison, given the enormous disparities in scope and degree. But Milgram believes that some of the underlying psychological processes may be the same in both cases.

Being another person's agent   In Milgram's view, one of the crucial factors is a personal history in which there is a continual stress on obedience to legitimate authority, first within the family, then in the school, and still later within the institutional settings of the adult world. The good child does what he is told; the good employee may raise a question but will accept the boss's final decision; the good soldier is not even allowed to question why. As a result, all of us are well practiced in adopting the attitude of an agent who performs an action that is initiated by someone else. The responsibility belongs to that someone else, and not to us.

One way of reducing the sense of personal responsibility is to increase the psychological distance between one's own actions and their end result. This phenomenon was studied in Milgram's laboratory. In one variation, two teachers were used. One was a confederate who was responsible for administering the shocks; the other was the real subject who was asked to perform such subsidiary tasks as reading the stimuli over a microphone and recording the learner's responses. In this new role, the subject was still essential to the smooth functioning of the experimental procedure. If he stopped, the victim would receive no further shocks. But even so, the subject might be expected to feel further removed from the ultimate consequence of the procedure, like a minor cog in a bureaucratic machine. After all, *he* didn't do the actual shocking! Under these conditions, over 90 percent of the subjects went all the way (Milgram, 1963, 1965; see also Kilham and Mann, 1974).

If obedience is increased by decreasing the subject's sense of personal responsibility, does the opposite hold as well? To answer this question, Milgram *decreased* the psychological distance between what the subject did and its effect upon the victim. Rather than being out of sight in an experimental cubicle, the victim was now seated directly adjacent to the subject who was told to administer the shock in a brutally direct manner. He had to press the victim's hand upon a shock electrode, holding it down by force if necessary. (His own hand was encased in an insulating glove to protect it from the shock; see Figure 12.5). Now compliance dropped considerably, in analogy to the fact that it is easier to drop bombs on an unseen enemy than to plunge a knife into his body when he looks you in the eye. But even so, 30 percent of the subjects still reacted with perfect obedience.

Cognitive reinterpretations   To cope with the moral dilemma posed by compliance with immoral orders, the obedient person develops an elaborate set of cognitive devices to reinterpret the situation and his own part in it. One of the most common approaches is to put on psychic blinders and try to shut out the awareness that the victim is a living, suffering fellow being. According to one of Milgram's subjects, "You really begin to forget that there's a guy out there, even though you can hear him. For a long time I just concentrated on pressing the switches and reading the words" (Milgram, 1974, p. 38). This **dehumanization** of

12.5   Obedient subject pressing the learner's hand upon the shock electrode *(Copyright 1965 by Stanley Milgram. From the film* Obedience, *distributed by the New York University Film Library)*

the victim is a counterpart to the obedient person's self-picture as an agent of another's will, someone "who has a job to do" and who does it whether he likes it or not. The obedient person sees himself as an instrument; by the same token, he sees the victim as an object. In his eyes, both have become dehumanized (Bernard, Ottenberg, and Redl, 1965).

The cognitive reorientation by which a person no longer feels responsible for his own acts is not achieved in an instant. Usually, inculcation is gradual. The initial act of obedience is relatively mild and does not seriously clash with the person's own moral outlook. Escalation is gradual so that each step seems only slightly different from the one before. This of course was the pattern in Milgram's study. A similar program of progressive escalation was evidently used in the indoctrination of death-camp guards. The same is true for the military training of soldiers everywhere. Draftees go through "basic training," in part to learn various military skills, but much more important, to acquire the habit of instant obedience. Raw recruits are rarely asked to point their guns at another person and shoot. It's not only that they don't know how; most of them probably wouldn't do it.

CROWD BEHAVIOR: MANY-ON-MANY INTERACTIONS

In this chapter we've considered two broad classes of social interaction. The first involved *one-on-one* interactions between two persons who might be relative strangers or friends and lovers. In a second group, the interactions were of *many-on-one*—cases of social influence in which the impact of a number of others converged on an individual producing social facilitation or inhibition, conformity, or obedience. We now turn to a third class of social interactions in which the relation is *many-on-many.* These are group interactions in which a number of persons interact with a number of others simultaneously. An important example is **crowd behavior.***

There is little doubt that under some circumstances people in crowds behave differently from the way they do when alone. In riots or lynch mobs, they express aggression at a level of bestial violence that would be inconceivable if they acted in isolation. In other situations, crowds may become frantically fearful, as in panics that may sweep a tightly packed auditorium when someone shouts "Fire." Yet another example is provided by occasional reports of crowds that gather to watch some disturbed person on a high ledge of a tall building, and then taunt the would-be suicide and urge him to jump.

What does the crowd do to the individual to make him act so differently from his everyday self? In analogy to the attempt to explain blind obedience, we can distinguish between two contrasting views. One holds that the crowd transforms the individual completely so that he loses his individuality and becomes deindividuated and essentially irrational. Another position holds that crowd behavior is not quite as irrational as it appears at first, but that it can be explained—at least in part—as a function of the individual's cognitive appraisal of the total situation.

Deindividuation and Crowd Behavior

An early exponent of the deindividuation approach was Gustav Le Bon (1841–1931), a French writer of conservative leanings whose disdain for the masses was reflected in his theory of crowd behavior. According to Le Bon, persons in a

* The many-on-one and many-on-many distinction is not hard and fast. At bottom, most many-on-many interactions are probably composed of a large number of many-on-one interactions, as each member in a panicky crowd or a rioting mob is influenced by the collective force of the mass of others.

Deindividuation *(A) Some deindividuation effects are harmless. (B) Others represent a menace to a humane, democratic society. (Top: © 1983 by Michael Sheil/Black Star. Bottom: © Detroit Free Press, 1988, Pauline Lubens/Black Star)*

crowd become wild, stupid, and irrational, giving vent to primitive impulses that are normally suppressed. Their emotion spreads by a sort of contagion, and rises to an ever-higher pitch as more and more crowd members become affected. In consequence, fear becomes terror, hostility turns into murderous rage, and the crowd member becomes a savage barbarian—"a grain of sand among other grains of sand, which the wind stirs up at will" (Le Bon, 1895).

A number of social psychologists have tried to translate some of these ideas into modern terms. To them, the key to crowd behavior is *deindividuation,* a state in which an individual in a group loses the awareness of himself as a separate individual. This state is more likely to occur when there is a high level of arousal and anonymity. Deindividuation tends to disinhibit impulsive actions that are normally under restraint. Just what the impulses are that are disinhibited by deindividuation depends on the group and the situation. In a carnival, the (masked) revelers may join in wild orgies; in a lynch mob, the group members will kill and torture (Festinger, Pepitone, and Newcomb, 1952; Zimbardo, 1969; Diener, 1979).

To study deindividuation experimentally, one investigation focused on the effect of anonymity in children who were trick-or-treating on Halloween. Some came alone; others came in groups. Some were asked for their names by the adults in the homes they visited; others were not. All children were then given an opportunity to steal pennies or candy when the adult left the room on some pretext. The children were much more likely to steal if they came in groups and were anonymous. Thus an increase in wrongdoing may have occurred because anonymity made the child less aware of himself as a separate individual—that is, made him deindividuated—with a resulting disinhibition of petty thievery. But there may have been a simpler and perfectly rational reason: being anonymous, the child was less afraid of being caught (Diener et al., 1976).

Another illustration comes from a study of crowds that taunt would-be suicides. One investigator examined a number of cases in which crowds were present when a person threatened to jump off a building, bridge, or tower. In some of these cases, members of the crowd baited the victim—shouting "Jump," screaming obscenities, and in one case, throwing stones and debris at the rescue squad. In other cases, there was no baiting. Baiting was more common when the crowd was quite large and when the potential suicide occurred at or toward night time and thus under the cover of darkness—conditions that would enhance anonymity and deindividuation (Mann, 1981).

Cognitive Factors and the Panicky Crowd

Is crowd behavior really as irrational as the deindividuation approach suggests? To be sure, phenomena such as panics indicate that people in groups sometimes act in ways that have disastrous consequences which none of them foresaw or desired. This shows that crowd behavior can be profoundly maladaptive, but does it prove that the individual members of the crowd acted irrationally? Several social psychologists have argued that it does not (Brown, 1965). They point out that in certain situations, such as fires in crowded auditoriums, the optimum solution for all participants (that is, escape for all) can only come about if they all trust one another to behave cooperatively (that is, not to run for the exits). If this trust is lacking, each individual will do the next best thing given her motives and her expectations of what others will do. She will run to the exit because she is sure that everyone else will do the same, hoping that if she runs quickly enough she will get there before them. The trouble is that all others make the same assumption that she does, and so they all arrive more or less together, jam the exit, and perish.

Panic *In June of 1985, a riot broke out at a soccer match in Brussels resulting in the collapse of a stadium wall that killed 38 persons and injured more than 200 others. The photo gives a glimpse of the resulting panic. (Photograph by Eamonn McCabe, The Observer)*

According to this cognitive interpretation, intense fear as such will not produce crowd panic, contrary to Le Bon's assertion. What matters are people's beliefs about escape routes. If they think that the routes for escape (the theater exits) are open and readily accessible, they will not stampede. Nor will panic develop if all escape routes are thought to be completely blocked, as in a mine collapse or a submarine explosion. Such disasters may lead to terror or apathetic collapse; but there will be none of the chaos that characterizes a panicky crowd. For panic to occur, the exits from danger must be seen to be limited or closing. In that case, each individual may well think that he can escape only if he rushes ahead of the others. If everyone thinks this way, panic may ensue (Smelser, 1963).

THE PRISONER'S DILEMMA

Roger Brown believes that some facets of escape panic can be understood in terms of a problem taken from the mathematical theory of games (Brown, 1965). It is generally known as the ***prisoner's dilemma*** (Luce and Raiffa, 1957). Consider the hypothetical problem of two men arrested on suspicion of bank robbery. The district attorney needs a confession to guarantee conviction. He hits on a diabolical plan. He talks to each prisoner separately and offers each a simple choice—confess or stay silent. But he tells each man that the consequences will depend, not just on what he does, but also on his partner's choice. If both confess, he will recommend an intermediate sentence of, say, eight years in prison for each. If neither confesses, he will be unable to prosecute them for robbery but he will charge them with a lesser crime such as illegal possession of a gun and both will get one year in jail. But suppose one confesses and the other does not? In this case the two men will be dealt with very differently. The one who confesses will be treated with extra leniency for turning state's evidence; he will receive a suspended sentence and won't go to jail at all. But the one who remains silent will feel the full force of the law. The D.A. will recommend the maximum penalty of twenty years.

As the situation is set up, there are four possible combinations of what the prisoners may do. Both may remain silent; Prisoner A may confess while B does not;

Table 12.1   PAYOFF MATRIX FOR THE PRISONER'S DILEMMA

		Prisoner B:	
		Stays silent	Confesses
Prisoner A:	Stays silent	1 year for *A* 1 year for *B*	20 years for *A* No jail for *B*
	Confesses	No jail for *A* 20 years for *B*	8 years for *A* 8 years for *B*

B may confess while A does not; both may confess. Each of the four sets of decisions has a different consequence or *payoff* for each of the two prisoners. The four sets of decisions and the payoffs associated with each yield a so-called *payoff matrix* as shown in Table 12.1.

Given this payoff matrix, what can the prisoners do? If both remain silent, the consequence is reasonably good for each of them. But how can either be sure that his partner won't double-cross him? If A remains silent while B tells all, B is even better off than he would be if both kept quiet; he stays out of jail entirely, while poor, silent A gets twenty years. Can A take the chance that B will not confess? Conversely, can B take this chance on A? The best bet is that they will *both* confess. The D.A. will get his conviction, and both men will get eight years.

In a sense, the prisoners' behavior is maladaptive, for the outcome is far from optimal for each. But this doesn't mean that either of the two men behaved irrationally. On the contrary: Paradoxically enough, each picked the most rational course of action considering that he couldn't be sure how his partner would decide. Each individual acted as rationally as possible; the ironic upshot was an unsatisfactory outcome for each. In the best of all possible worlds they would have been able to trust each other, would have remained silent, and been in jail for a much shorter period.

THE PRISONER'S DILEMMA AND PANIC

The underlying logic of the prisoner's dilemma applies to various social interactions whose payoff matrix is formally analogous. Brown has shown how it pertains to panic. Here there are more than two participants, but the essential ingredients are much the same. Each individual in the burning auditorium has two choices—she can wait her turn to get to the exit or she can rush ahead. What are the probable outcomes? As in the case of the prisoners, they partially depend upon what others in the auditorium (especially those nearby) will do. If the individual rushes to the exit and everyone else does too, they will all probably suffer severe injuries and run some risk of death. If she takes her turn and others decorously do the same, the outcome is better; they will probably all escape, though they may suffer some minor injuries. The best outcome for the individual is produced if she ruthlessly pushes herself ahead of the others while the others continue to file out slowly. In this case *she* will surely escape without a blister, but the chances for the others to escape are lessened. Suppose the situation is reversed so that the individual waits her turn while everyone near her runs ahead? Now the others may very well get out without injury while she herself may die. These sets of decisions and their associated outcomes represent just another version of the prisoner's dilemma, which are shown in the payoff matrix of Table 12.2.

Given the payoff matrix of Table 12.2, most persons will probably opt to rush ahead rather than wait their turn. As in the case of the two prisoners, this solution

Beach pollution and the prisoner's dilemma *It's less costly in time and effort to throw waste into the ocean rather than to dispose of it properly. If everyone acts so as to achieve this personal payoff, however, the ultimate result is ocean and beach pollution, which will reduce the payoff for everyone. But unless everyone believes that all others will forego their own payoff in the interest of the ultimate good for all, they will not give up their own payoff, with the inevitable worst-for-all outcome. (Photo by Michael Baytof/ Black Star)*

Table 12.2   PAYOFF MATRIX FOR AN INDIVIDUAL *(I)* AND OTHERS *(O)* IN A
BURNING AUDITORIUM

		Others *(O)*:	
		Take turns	Rush ahead
Individual *(I)*:	Takes turn	Minor injuries for *I* Minor injuries for *O*	Increased chance of death for *I* No injuries for *O*
	Rushes ahead	No injuries for *I* Increased chance of death for *O*	Severe injuries for *I* Severe injuries for *O*

is grossly maladaptive, but from the point of view of each separate individual it is, sadly enough, quite rational. We again face the peculiar irony of the prisoner's dilemma. As Brown notes, "This irony about escape behavior . . . is always worked over by newspaper editorialists after panic occurs. 'If only everyone had stayed calm and taken his turn, then . . .' " (Brown, 1965, p. 741).

Brown's model of panic applies only if certain qualifications are met. As already noted, the danger must seem serious enough and the escape routes must appear to be inadequate. Another factor is the strength of certain social inhibitions. Most of us have been socialized to act with some modicum of respect for others; pushing ahead is socially disapproved and would therefore contribute a negative value to the relevant cells in the payoff matrix. The weight of this factor depends on the situation. If the fire seems minor enough, the embarrassment at behaving discourteously (or acting like a coward) might outweigh the fear of being the last to escape. If so, the payoff matrix will not be that of the prisoner's dilemma, and no panic will ensue.

Cognitive Factors and the Hostile Crowd

The preceding discussion has shown that there are reasons to suppose that at least some aspects of crowd panic can be explained by cognitive factors. Can the same be said about the behavior of violent crowds whose frenzy is turned either against defenseless victims (as in lynchings or pogroms) or against another group that fights back (as in many riots)?

A number of social psychologists believe that the answer is yes. Of course, the specific explanation must be different from those that handle panic. In a panic, the members of the crowd are essentially all competing with one another, while in a lynching or a rioting mob, the crowd members are united against others outside of their group. As a result, the conditions of the prisoner's dilemma don't apply. But some other cognitive factors seem to operate even here. As a result, the mob's behavior, horrible and even bestial as it is, is not quite as irrational as it may seem at first.

An example comes from a shameful page of American history—the lynching of blacks in the rural South.

THE MOTIVES FOR LYNCHING

What motives impelled the lynchers, who often tortured and mutilated their victims and finally burnt them alive? There is little doubt that one major purpose was socioeconomic: to maintain the unequal status of blacks. While lynching has an early history that goes back to the frontier days of the West, blacks did not become its primary victims until some time after the Civil War. From then on, lynching became a bloody instrument to maintain social and economic control over the newly freed slaves, to keep them "in their place." It was a response to threatening signs of defiance and assertion; the mere suspicion of an attack on a white person was often grounds enough. The horrible fate of the victim would then serve as a warning to other blacks. It is probably no accident that lynchings were comparatively uncommon in Southern counties run on the plantation system in which blacks worked as tenant farmers and wage hands. Here the caste system was so sharply drawn that whites saw little threat. Lynchings were more prevalent in poor rural communities in which blacks were a minority who often competed economically with lower-class whites (Brown, 1954).

OVERCOMING SOCIAL PROHIBITIONS

However intense the individual mob member's hatred, it would probably not suffice to make him kill and torture were he alone. There are various restraints on violence, some based on fear of retribution, others on internalized moral qualms. The presence of others somehow weakens these constraints. The question is how.

One factor is *anonymity* and the accompanying state of deindividuation we have discussed before. Another factor is the perception of unanimity which leads to *pluralistic ignorance* among the waverers in the crowd. In actuality, the crowd is not as homogeneous as it seems. But the waverers don't know that. They only hear the vociferous clamors for violence, assume they are alone in their opposition, and therefore go along, in ignorance of the fact that there are others who feel as they do.

Yet another effect of the appearance of unanimity is that it produces a sense of *diffusion of responsibility,* which leads to a diminished fear of retribution. When there are dozens of participants, it becomes harder to determine what each of them actually did. The same applies to each person's sense of guilt, which becomes diluted by the fact that there are so many others. (A similar diffusion effect is produced in a firing squad whose members know that only some of the rifles are loaded with real bullets while the rest contain blanks.)

THE HOSTILE CROWD AND THE APATHETIC CROWD

A final point: We've previously considered the failure of bystanders to help persons in distress, including such dramatic instances as the case of Kitty Genovese (see pp. 331–32). In effect, such bystanders can be considered as a crowd. The behavior that characterizes the members of this *apathetic crowd* is obviously very different from that found in violent and rioting crowds. But in several regards, the behavior of the two crowds is similar. As we've seen, they both exhibit pluralistic ignorance. An individual member of the lynch mob may have doubts and scruples, but he believes that no one else does, and so he goes along and joins the others. But something quite similar holds for the passive bystanders. They saw the other witnesses who didn't help and therefore assumed that help was not really needed.

Another similarity between the violent and the apathetic crowd is that they both involve a diffusion of responsibility. In both cases this diffusion helps to tip the scale against personal morality. In the violent crowd, it leads all mob members to act in a hideous act of *commission*—the lynching. In the crowd of apathetic onlookers, it makes all witnesses perform an unfeeling act of *omission* —the failure to help.

(Photograph by Susan Shapiro)

THE GENERALITY OF SOCIAL PSYCHOLOGY

In this and the preceding chapter we asked how the individual interprets the social world in which he lives and how he interacts with the other persons in it. This led to a survey of many topics, including the way we perceive the motives and acts of others as well as our own selves, how we interact with others, how we conform and obey, and how we behave in crowds.

As so often, we are left with many more questions than answers. Even so, it appears that social psychology has contributed to our understanding of social behavior. But how broadly applicable is this understanding? Does it bring us closer to an understanding of basic human nature, or is it necessarily limited to our own time and place?

For all we know, many of the assertions of modern social psychology hold true only for our own present-day culture. Perhaps consistency, attribution of motives, self-perception, obedience, diffusion of responsibility, and so on, are patterns of behavior that are specific to twentieth-century industrialized society, and don't describe how people act and think in other places and other times (e.g., Gergen, 1973; Jahoda, 1979).

But there are reasons to believe that human social nature is not entirely culture-specific. Such diverse political theorists as Aristotle, Hobbes, and Machiavelli are still read despite the fact that they lived many centuries ago and under very different political systems than our own; they wrote about characteristics of human social behavior that we can recognize even today. History provides many other examples of enduring social reactions. There are records of panics in Roman amphitheaters when the stands collapsed, of riots during sporting events in Byzantium, and of murderous mobs in medieval Europe. The cast and costumes differ, but the basic plots were much the same as now. Some of the ancients even used certain of our modern propaganda devices. When the city of Pompeii was destroyed by a volcano in 79 A.D., it was evidently in the midst of a municipal election. Modern archeologists have found some of the election slogans on the excavated walls: "Vote for Vatius, all the whoremasters vote for him" and "Vote for Vatius, all the wife-beaters vote for him." While the techniques of the anti-Vatius faction may be a bit crude for our modern taste, they certainly prove that the psychology of the smear campaign has a venerable history (Raven and Rubin, 1976).

Phenomena of this sort suggest that there are some invariant properties of human social behavior which can provide the foundation for a genuine science of social psychology.

SUMMARY

1. Social interactions can be classified as those that are *one-on-one*, those that are *many-on-one*, and those that are *many-on-many*. According to some theorists, all one-on-one interactions depend on *social exchange* as shown by the operation of the *reciprocity rule*.

2. In investigating *altruism*, social psychologists have found that people often fail to help others in an emergency. One reason is the *bystander effect*. The more people that are present, the less likely that any one of them will provide help, in part because of *pluralistic ignorance*, in part because of *diffusion of responsibility*.

3. Social psychologists have studied some of the factors that attract people to each other. They include *physical proximity, familiarity, similarity,* and *physical attractiveness*. There

is evidence in favor of the *matching hypothesis,* which predicts a strong correlation between the physical attractiveness of the two partners. *Love* is an especially close relation between two partners. Some authors distinguish between *romantic love,* in which the emotions are intensely focused, and *companionate love,* which is less turbulent and more long-lasting.

4. A number of many-on-one situations involve *social influence.* In some cases, all that matters is the mere presence of others, which produces *social facilitation and inhibition.*

5. Another case of social influence is *conformity.* One reason for conformity is *informational:* We may believe that the group has knowledge we don't possess. Another reason is *motivational:* We go along because we want to be liked.

6. Still another form of social influence is *obedience.* Blind obedience has sometimes been ascribed to factors within the person, as in studies on the *authoritarian personality.* But situational factors may be even more important, as shown by Milgram's obedience studies. His findings suggest that obedience depends on the psychological distance between one's own actions and their end result. When this distance is increased—by decreasing one's sense of responsibility, by *depersonalization*—obedience increases too.

7. In *many-on-many interactions,* a number of persons interact with a number of others simultaneously. An example is *crowd behavior,* as in panics or riots. According to one account, the behavior of such crowds is essentially irrational. According to another interpretation, it is not as irrational as it appears at first. The *prisoner's dilemma* shows that under certain conditions there can be collective irrationality even though all of the participants behave rationally as individuals.

8. Other forms of apparently irrational crowd behavior are violent *group hostility* and *apathy.* In violent crowds, there is *deindividuation,* a weakened sense of personal identity. But part of the explanation may lie in the way the individual members of the group interpret the situation. An important factor is *diffusion of responsibility,* which applies to both sins of commission (as in rioting mobs) and sins of omission (as in bystander apathy).

PART IV

Development

How do psychologists try to explain the phenomena they describe? Thus far, we've primarily dealt with two main approaches. One is concerned with mechanism—*it tries to understand how something works. A second approach focuses on* function—*it tries to explain what something is good for. But there is yet another approach to explanation in psychology which focuses on* development. *This approach deals with questions of history—it asks how a given state of affairs came into being.*

In the next two chapters, our concern will be with this developmental perspective on psychological phenomena. We will ask how various psychological processes arise in the organism's history—how we come to see and remember, reason and think, feel and act as we now do; how it is that we are no longer children, but for better or worse have become adults in mind as well as body.

CHAPTER 13

Physical and Cognitive Development

At the beginning of the nineteenth century, many thinkers became increasingly interested in all forms of progressive change. They lived at a time of dramatic upheavals—the French Revolution, which ushered in a period of continued political unrest, and the Industrial Revolution, which transformed the social and economic structure of Europe and North America. These massive changes suggested that human history is more than a mere chronicle of battles and successive dynasties, that it also reveals an underlying pattern of social development toward greater "progress" (Bury, 1932). Given this intellectual background, many scientists became interested in development wherever they saw it: in the history of the planet as it changed from a molten rock and formed continents and oceans; in the history of life as it evolved from simple early forms to myriad species of fossils and plants. One aspect of this intellectual movement was an increasing concern with the life history of individual organisms, starting from their embryonic beginnings and continuing as they develop toward maturity.

All animals develop, and so do we. The duckling becomes a duck, the kitten a cat, the human baby an adult. In this regard all humans are alike. It doesn't matter whether they are Gandhi or Hitler, Joan of Arc or Isaac Newton—they all started life as infants. Is there any common pattern in the progression that marks the developmental history of each human life? If so, what is it? The attempt to answer these questions is the province of developmental psychology.

Children as miniature adults *Children dressed as did the adults of their time and class as shown in this 1786 Dutch painting. (Helena van der Schalke, by G. ter Borch, Courtesy Rijksmuseum, Amsterdam)*

WHAT IS DEVELOPMENT?

There seem to be some characteristics that apply to many aspects of human development, at least in a very general way, whether it is *physical development*, the maturation of various bodily structures; *motor development*, the progressive attainment of various motor skills; *cognitive development*, the growth of the child's intellectual functioning; or *social development*, changes in the way the child deals

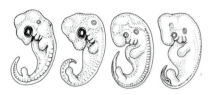

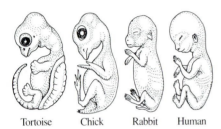

Tortoise   Chick   Rabbit   Human

13.1 Differentiation during embryonic development *The figure shows three stages in the embryonic development of four different vertebrates—tortoise, chick, rabbit, and human. At the first stage, all of the embryos are very similar to each other. As development proceeds, they diverge more and more. By the third stage, each embryo has taken on some of the distinctive characteristics of its own species. (From Keeton, 1980. Redrawn from Romanes, 1882)*

with others. According to many developmental psychologists, one such characteristic is **differentiation** as revealed in the physical development of the embryo and childhood behavior.

Development as Differentiation

The concept of differentiation grows out of some early discoveries in embryology, which charts the history of the individual organism as it develops from a single egg and assumes the complex shape and function of its adult form. The German biologist Karl Ernst von Baer (1792–1876) pointed out that embryological development involves a progressive change from the more general to the more particular, from the simpler to the more complex—in short, **differentiation.** In embryonic development, anatomical differentiation is directly apparent. Initially there is one cell, then several cell layers, then the crude beginnings of the major organ systems, until the different organs and their component parts gradually take shape. Von Baer argued that this is the reason why embryos of very different species are so similar at early stages of development and utterly dissimilar at later stages (see Figure 13.1). Initially, the embryo only manifests the very general body plan characteristic of a broad class of animals. Thus a very young chick embryo looks much like the embryo of any other vertebrate animal at a similar stage of its development. The embryonic structures that will eventually become wings are quite similar to those structures of a very young human embryo that will eventually become arms. As embryonic development proceeds, special features begin to emerge and the chick embryo begins to look like a bird, then like some kind of fowl, and still later like a chicken (Gould, 1977).

Von Baer's differentiation principle was initially regarded as a description of anatomical development and nothing else. But a number of psychologists suggested that a similar differentiation principle also applies to the development of behavior. Consider the development of grasping movements in human infants.

13.2 The development of manual skills *The diagram shows the progressive differentiation in the infant's use of the hand when holding an object. At 16 weeks of age, he reaches for the object but can't hold on to it. At 20 weeks, he grasps it using the hand as a whole, with no differentiated use of the fingers. Between 24 and 36 weeks, the fingers and thumb become differentiated in use, but the four fingers operate more or less as a whole. By 52 weeks of age, hand, thumb, and fingers are successfully differentiated to produce precise and effective pincer movements. (Adapted from Liebert, Polous, and Strauss, 1974) Photos illustrate the same point at 23, 28, and 58 weeks. (Photographs by Kathy Hirsh-Pasek)*

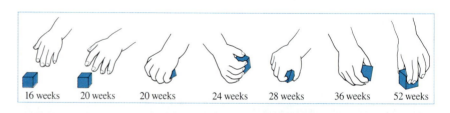

16 weeks   20 weeks   20 weeks   24 weeks   28 weeks   36 weeks   52 weeks

23 weeks

28 weeks

58 weeks

When reaching for a small block, they initially curl their entire hand around the block; still later, they oppose the thumb to all four fingers. By the time they are one year old, they can victoriously coordinate hand, thumb, and one or two fingers to pick up the block with an elegant pincer movement (although such ultimate triumphs of manual differentiation as picking up a tea cup while holding the little finger extended will probably have to wait until they are old enough to read a book on etiquette) (Halverson, 1931; see Figure 13.2).

Development as Growth

One of the most obvious characteristics of all development is growth. Organisms "grow up" as they change from a fertilized egg to a fetus, and after birth, they continue to grow in both sheer physical size and mental complexity.

GROWTH BEFORE BIRTH

Each human existence begins at conception when a sperm and egg cell unite to form the fertilized egg. This egg divides and redivides repeatedly and produces a

13.3   Early stages of human prenatal development   *(A) Six-week-old embryo, shown in its amniotic sac. It is three-fifths of an inch long, and its eyes, ears, and limbs are beginning to take shape but are still at a comparatively early stage of differentiation. For example, the hands have not yet differentiated into separate fingers. (B) Seven-week-old embryo, now nearly an inch long. Differentiation is further along as witness the presence of fingers. (C) Three-month-old fetus, three inches long. By now the fetus's features are recognizably human. Fingers and toes are fully formed, and there are external ears and eyelids. (D) Four-month-old fetus pushing against the amniotic sac. The fetus is more than six inches long, with all organs formed. (From Nilsson, 1974)*

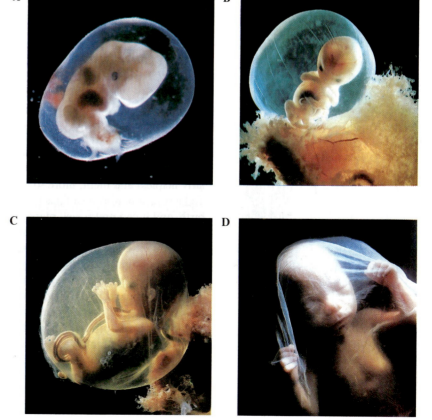

A

FETAL POSITION
0 month

CHIN UP
1 month

CHEST UP
2 months

REACH AND MISS
3 months

SIT WITH SUPPORT
4 months

SIT ON LAP
GRASP OBJECT
5 months

SIT ON HIGH CHAIR
GRASP DANGLING OBJECT
6 months

SIT ALONE
7 months

STAND WITH HELP
8 months

CREEP
10 months

WALK WHEN LED
11 months

PULL TO STAND
BY FURNITURE
12 months

CLIMB STAIR STEPS
13 months

STAND ALONE
14 months

WALK ALONE
15 months

13.6   The development of locomotion   *(A) The average age at which babies master locomotor skills, from holding their chins up to walking alone. These ages vary considerably. (From Shirley, 1961) (B) A pictorial record of these milestones in the life of one child. (Photographs courtesy of Kathy Hirsh-Pasek)*

B

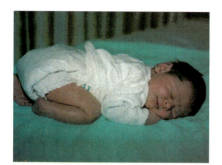

2 days

2 months

6 months

8 months

that each step in the sequence comes before the next. No baby can walk before he can crawl.

Somewhat similar progressions are found in aspects of intellectual development. An example is the acquisition of language (see Chapter 8). Here too there is an orderly sequence. Initially the baby coos, then he babbles, then he utters the first word or two, then he develops a small, first vocabulary but is limited to one-word sentences, then he increases his vocabulary and utters two-word sentences, after which both vocabulary and sentence complexity increase until they finally reach adult levels.

Developmental psychologists have mapped various other sequences in which important cognitive and social skills are acquired in the course of childhood. Some of them have tried to show that these various sequences are interrelated and indicate a succession of general stages of development. We will turn to these matters in later sections. For now, we only want to underline the main point—development generally proceeds by an orderly sequence of steps, and this holds for the growth of our minds as well as our bodies.

10 months

10 months

14 months

PIAGET'S THEORY OF COGNITIVE DEVELOPMENT

Thus far, our discussion of development has focused on physical growth and changes in motor behavior. But the child grows in mind as well as body—in what she knows, how she comes to know it, how she thinks about it, and in the fact that she can tell it to others (sometimes interminably so). This intellectual growth that accompanies the progress from infancy to adulthood is generally called *cognitive development.*

We will organize our discussion of the child's mental growth around the work of the Swiss psychologist Jean Piaget (1896–1980). Piaget's conceptions have aroused considerable controversy, but there is hardly a developmental psychologist who has not been greatly affected by them.

Piaget believed that mental growth involves major qualitative changes. This hypothesis is relatively recent. According to the eighteenth-century empiricists, the child's mental machinery is fundamentally the same as the adult's, the only difference being that the child has fewer associations. Nativists also minimized the distinction between the child's mind and the adult's, for they viewed the basic categories of time, space, number, and causality as given *a priori,* being part of the native equipment that all humans have at birth. Thus both empiricists and nativists regarded the child as much like an adult; the first saw him as an adult-in-training, the second as an adult-in-miniature. In contrast, Piaget and many other developmental psychologists usually look for qualitative differences and try to chart the orderly progression of human intellect as the child grows into an adult.

Piaget's original training was as a biologist, which may be one of the reasons why his conception of intellectual development bears many resemblances to the way an embryologist thinks of the development of anatomical structures. The human fetus doesn't just get larger between, say, two and seven months; its whole structure changes drastically. Piaget argued that mental development is characterized by similar qualitative changes. He proposed that there are four main stages of intellectual growth, whose overall thrust is toward an increasing emancipation from the here-and-now of the immediate, concrete present, to a conception of the world in increasingly symbolic and abstract terms. These stages are the period of *sensory-motor intelligence* (from birth to about two years), the *preoperational period* (two to seven years), the period of *concrete operations* (seven to eleven years), and the period of *formal operations* (eleven years and on). The age ranges are very approximate and successive stages are often thought to overlap and blend into each other.

Jean Piaget (Photograph by Yves DeBraine, Black Star)

Sensory-Motor Intelligence

According to Piaget, at first there is nothing but a succession of transient, unconnected sensory impressions and motor reactions. For mental life during the first few months contains neither past nor future, no distinction between stable objects and fleeting events, and no differentiation between the *me* and the *not me.* The critical achievement of the first two years is the development of these distinctions.

OBJECT PERMANENCE

Consider an infant holding a rattle. To an adult, the rattle is an object, a *thing,* of whose existence he has no doubt, whether he looks at it or briefly looks away. The adult is sure of its existence, for he is certain that he will see it once more when he

13.7 Object permanence *(A) A six-month-old looks intently at a toy. (B) But when the toy is hidden from view, the infant does not search for it. According to Piaget, this is because the infant does not as yet have the concept of object permanence. (Photograph by Doug Goodman 1986/Monkmeyer)*

looks at it again. But does the rattle exist as a thing in the same sense to the infant? Does the infant have the notion of ***object permanence***?

According to Piaget, there is little object permanence in the first few months of life. The infant may look at a new toy with evident delight, but if it disappears from view, he shows little concern (see Figure 13.7). It seems as if what's out of sight is also out of mind and does not really exist for the infant.

Needless to say, infants eventually come to live in a world whose objects do not capriciously appear and disappear with the movement of their eyes. At about eight months of age, they start to search for toys that have been hidden or that have fallen out of their cribs.

According to Piaget, the notion that objects exist on their own, and continue to exist even if they are not seen, heard, felt, or reached for, is a major accomplishment of the sensory-motor period. This notion emerges as the infant gradually interrelates his various sensory experiences and motor reactions. Eventually he coordinates the sensory spaces provided by the different modalities—of vision, hearing, touch, and bodily movement—into one real space in which all of the world's objects—himself included—exist.

SENSORY-MOTOR SCHEMAS

The newborn starts life with a rather limited repertoire of built-in reactions, such as gross bodily movements in response to distress, sucking and swallowing reflexes, and after a few days, certain orienting responses such as head and eye movements. These recurrent action patterns are the first mental elements—or ***schemas***—through which the infant organizes the world that impinges upon her. At first, these various schemas operate in isolation. A one-month-old infant can grasp a rattle and can also suck it or look at it. But she will perform these actions only if the stimulus object is directly applied to the relevant sensory surface. She will suck the rattle if it touches her mouth and will grasp it if it's pressed into her palm. But she is as yet unable to grasp whatever she's sucking or to look at whatever she's grasping. The coordination of all these patterns takes time and is not complete until she's about five months of age. How is this integration achieved?

According to Piaget, the answer lies in the joint action of the two processes that in his view are responsible for all facets of cognitive development: ***assimilation*** and ***accommodation***. At any given point, the child has to be able to interpret the environment in terms of the mental schemas he has at the time; the environment is *assimilated* to the schema. But the schemas necessarily change as the child continues to interact with the world around her; they *accommodate* themselves to the environment. In the case of the sucking response, the initial schema only applies to the nipple. But with time, the infant starts to suck other objects such as her rattle. Piaget would say that by doing this she has assimilated the rattle into her sucking schema. The rattle is now understood and dealt with as a "suckable." But the process does not stop there. After all, rattles are not the same as nipples; while both are suckable, they are not suckable in quite the same way. This necessarily leads to new discriminations. As a result, the sucking schema adjusts (that is, accommodates) to the new object to which it is applied. This process continues, with further assimilations followed by yet further accommodations, until finally looking, reaching, grasping, and sucking have all merged into one unified exploratory schema (Piaget, 1952).

BEGINNINGS OF REPRESENTATIONAL THOUGHT

The last phase of the sensory-motor period (about eighteen to twenty-four months) marks a momentous change in intellectual development. Children begin to conceive of objects and events that are not immediately present by representing (that is re-presenting) some prior experience with these to themselves. Such **representations** may be internalized actions, images, or words. But in all cases, they function as symbols that stand for whatever they may signify but are not equivalent to it.

One demonstration of this change is the achievement of full object permanence. At eighteen months or so, children actively search for absent toys and are surprised (and sometimes outraged) if they don't find them under the sofa cover where they saw the experimenter hide them; it is reasonable to infer that they have some internal representation of the sought-for-object. Even more persuasive is **deferred imitation** in which children imitate actions that occurred some time past, such as a playmate's temper tantrum observed a day ago. A related phenomenon is make-believe play, which is often based on deferred imitation.

The Preoperational Period

Given the tools of representational thought, the two-year-old has taken a gigantic step. A year ago, he could interact with the environment only through direct sensory or motor contact; now he can carry the whole world in his head. But while his mental world now contains stable objects and events that can be represented internally, it is still a far cry from the world of adults. The two-year-old has overcome the initial chaos of separate sensations and motor impressions, but only to exchange it for a chaos of ideas (that is, representations) that he is as yet unable to relate in any coherent way. The achievement of the next five years is the emergence of a reasonably well-ordered world of ideas. According to Piaget, this requires higher-order schemas that he calls **operations,** which allow the internal manipulation of ideas according to a stable set of rules. In his view, genuine operations do not appear until about seven or so, hence the term **preoperational** for the period from two to seven years.

FAILURE OF CONSERVATION

Conservation of quantity and number A revealing example of preoperational thought is the young child's failure to **conserve quantity.** One of Piaget's experimental procedures uses two identical glasses, *A* and *B*, which stand side by side and are filled with the same amount of some colored liquid such as orangeade. A child is asked whether there is more orangeade in one glass or in the other, and the experimenter obligingly adds a drop here and pours a drop there until his subject is completely satisfied that there is "the same to drink in this glass as in that." Four-year-olds can easily make this judgment.

The next step involves a new glass, *C*, which is much taller but also narrower than *A* and *B* (see Figure 13.8). While the child is watching, the experimenter

13.8 Conservation of liquid quantity
(A) Patrick, aged 4 years, 3 months, is asked by the experimenter, "Do we both have the same amount of juice to drink?" Patrick says yes. (B) The experimenter pours the juice from one of the beakers into a new, wider beaker. When now asked, "Which glass has more juice?" he points to the thinner one. (Photographs by Chris Massey)

A

B

13.9   Conservation of mass quantity
In parallel to the failure to conserve liquid quantity is the preschooler's failure to conserve mass. Tyler, aged 4 years, 5 months, is shown two balls of Play-doh which she adjusts until she is satisfied that there is the same amount of Play-doh in both. The experimenter takes one of the balls and rolls it into a long, thin "hot dog." When now asked which has more Play-doh in it, she points to the hot dog. (Photograph by Chris Massey)

pours the entire contents of glass *A* into glass *C*. He now points to *B* and *C*, and asks, "Is there more orangeade in this glass or in that?" For an adult, the question is almost too simple to merit an answer. The amounts are obviously identical, since *A* was completely emptied into *C*, and *A* and *B* were set to equality at the outset. But four- or five-year-olds don't see this. They insist that there is more orangeade in *C*. When asked for their reason, they explain that the liquid comes to a much higher level in *C*. They seem to think that the orangeade has somehow increased in quantity as it was transferred from one glass to another. They are too impressed by the visible changes in appearance that accompany each transfer (the changing liquid levels) to realize that there is an underlying reality (the quantity of liquid) that remains constant throughout.

By the time children are about seven years old, they respond much like adults. They hardly look at the two glasses, for their judgment needs little empirical support. "It's the same. It seems as if there's less because it's wider, but it's the same." The experimenter may continue with further glasses of different sizes and shapes, but the judgment remains what it was: "It's still the same because it always comes from the same glass." To justify their answer, the children point to the fact that one can always pour the liquid back into the original glass (that is, *A*) and thus obtain the same levels. They have obviously understood that the various transformations in the liquid's appearance are **reversible.** For every transformation that changes the way the liquid looks, there is another that restores its original appearance. Given this insight, children at this age recognize that there is an underlying attribute of reality, the quantity of liquid that remains constant (is *conserved*), throughout the various perceptual changes. (For comparable results with malleable solids like clay or plasticene, see Figure 13.9.)

A related phenomenon is **conservation of number.** The child is first shown a row of six evenly spaced bottles, each of which has a glass standing next to it. The child agrees that there are as many bottles as there are glasses. The experimenter now rearranges the six glasses by setting them out into a much longer row while leaving the six bottles as they were. Here the turning point comes a bit earlier, at about five or six. Up to that age, children generally assert that there are more glasses (or disks, or checkers, or whatever) because "they're more spread out" (see Figure 13.10). From about six on, there is conservation; the child has no doubt that there are just as many bottles in the tightly spaced row as there are glasses in the spread-out line. In all these conservation tasks, the older child's explanation emphasizes reversibility—liquid can be poured back in the taller glass, and the long line of glasses can be reassembled into a compact row.

Attending to several factors simultaneously   Why are preschool children unable to appreciate that the amount of a substance remains unaffected by changes of shape or that the number of objects in a given set does not vary with changes in the spatial arrangement? According to Piaget, part of the problem is the child's

13.10   Conservation of number   *(A) The experimenter points to two rows of checkers, one hers, the other Tyler's. She asks, "Do I have as many checkers as you?" and Tyler nods. (B) One row of checkers is spread out and the experimenter says, "Now, do we still have the same?" Tyler says no and points to the spread-out row, which she says has more. (Photographs by Chris Massey)*

A

B

inability to attend to all of the relevant dimensions simultaneously. Consider conservation of liquid quantity. To conserve, the children must first comprehend that there are two relevant factors: the height of the liquid column and the width. They must then appreciate that an *increase* in the column's height is accompanied by a *decrease* in its width. Initially, they center their attention only on the height and do not realize that the change in height is compensated for by a corresponding change in width. Later on, say at five, they may well attend to width on one occasion and to height on another (with corresponding changes in judgment). But to attend to both dimensions concurrently and to relate them properly requires a higher-order schema that reorganizes initially discrete perceptual experiences into one conceptual unit.

In Piaget's view, this reorganization occurs when the child focuses on the transformations from one experience into another, rather than on the individual transformations by themselves. The child sees that these transformations are effected by various reversible overt actions, such as pouring the contents of one glass into another. The overt action eventually becomes internalized as a reversible operation so that the child can mentally pour the liquid back and forth. The result is conservation of quantity (Piaget, 1952).

In summary, the preoperational child is the prisoner of his own immediate perceptual experience and tends to take appearance for reality. When a seven-year-old watches a magician, she can easily distinguish between her perception and her knowledge. She *perceives* that the rabbits come out of the hat, but she *knows* that they couldn't possibly do so. Her four-year-old brother has no such sophistication. He is delighted to see rabbits anytime and anywhere, and if they want to come out of a hat, why shouldn't they?

EGOCENTRISM

The inability of preoperational children to consider two physical dimensions simultaneously has a counterpart in their approach to the social world. They cannot understand another person's point of view, for they are as yet unable to recognize that different points of view exist. This characteristic of preoperational thought is often called **egocentrism.** As Piaget uses the term, it does not imply selfishness. It is not that children seek to benefit at the expense of others; it is rather that they haven't fully grasped that there are other selves.

An interesting demonstration of egocentrism involves a literal interpretation of "point of view." If two adults stand at opposite corners of a building, each knows that the other sees a different wall. But according to Piaget, preoperational children don't understand this. In one study, children were shown a three-dimensional model of a mountain scene. While the children viewed the scene from one position, a small doll was placed at various other locations around the model. The child's job was to decide what the doll saw from *its* vantage point (see Figure 13.11). To answer, the child had to choose one of several drawings that depicted different views of the mountain scene. Up to four years of age, the children didn't even understand the question. From four to seven years old, their response was fairly consistent—they chose the drawing that showed what *they* saw, regardless of where the doll was placed (Piaget and Inhelder, 1956).

13.11 The three-mountain test of egocentrism The child is asked to indicate what the doll sees. The results suggest that the child thinks the doll sees the scene just as she does, including the little house which is of course obstructed from the doll's vantage point. (After Piaget and Inhelder, 1967)

Concrete and Formal Operations

Seven-year-olds have acquired mental operations that allow them to abstract some of the essential attributes of reality such as number and substance. But according to Piaget, these operations are primarily applicable to the relations between concrete events (hence the term *concrete operations*). They do not really suffice when these relations must be considered entirely in the abstract. Eight- or nine-year-olds can perform various simple manipulations on specific numbers they are presented with, but they generally fail to understand that certain results will hold for any number whatsoever. They may realize that 4 is an even number and 4 + 1 is odd, and similarly for 6 and 6 + 1, 8 and 8 + 1, and so on, but they are by no means sure that the addition of 1 to any even number must always produce a number that is odd. According to Piaget, the comprehension of such highly abstract and formal relationships requires *formal operations,* operations of a higher order which emerge at about eleven or twelve years of age. Given formal operations, the child's thought can embrace the possible as well as the real. He can now entertain hypothetical possibilities, can deal with what *might be* no less than what *is.*

An illustration of the role of formal operations comes from a study in which children had to discover what makes a pendulum go fast or go slow. They were shown how to construct a pendulum by hanging some object from a string. They were also shown how to vary the length of the string, the weight of the suspended object, and the initial force that set the pendulum in motion. Children between seven and eleven typically varied several factors at a time. They might compare a heavy weight suspended from a long string with a light weight suspended from a short string, and would then conclude that a pendulum swings faster the shorter its length and the lighter its weight. Needless to say, their reasoning was faulty, for the way to determine whether a given factor (e.g., weight) has an effect is to hold all others (e.g., length) constant. Children below about eleven cannot do this, for they can operate only on the concretely given. They are unable to consider potential cause-and-effect relationships, which must first be deliberately excluded and then tested for later on. In contrast, older children can plan and execute an appropriate series of tests. Their mental operations proceed on a more formal plane so that they can grasp the notion of "other things being equal" (Inhelder and Piaget, 1958).

The period of formal operations is the last important milestone in the child's intellectual progression that Piaget and his co-workers have charted in some detail. Their account of the developmental steps that led up to this point has been enormously influential. But this doesn't mean that it has gone unchallenged. We will now consider some of the efforts to look at Piaget's description of human cognitive development with a more critical eye.

PERCEPTION IN INFANCY

One important challenge to Piaget's work concerns his views of what is given at the very start of life. A number of modern developmental psychologists contend that Piaget—who in this regard was much like the early British empiricists—had seriously underestimated the infant's native endowment. These critics deny that the infant's mind is the mere jumble of unrelated sensory impressions and motor reactions that Piaget had declared it to be, for they believe that some of the major categories by which adults organize the world—such as the concepts of space, time, objects, and causality—have primitive precursors in early life. They have buttressed their position by systematic studies of perception in very young infants. One line of evidence bears on a fundamental Piagetian (and empiricist) claim: the view that infants begin life with no conception that the world outside consists of real objects that exist independently of whether they are touched or seen.

A

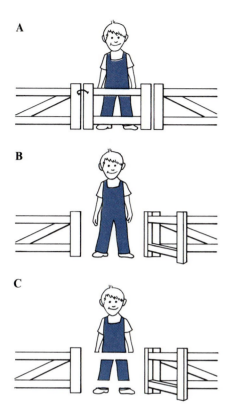

B

C

13.12 The perceptual effect of occlusion
*(A) A child occluded by a gate is perceived
as a whole person behind a gate, so that he
will look like (B) when the gate is opened,
rather than being perceived as (C) a child
with gaps in his body.*

Perceiving Occluded Objects

One series of studies hinged on the perceptual effect of ***occlusion.*** Consider Figure 13.12A, which shows an object that partially obscures (occludes) the view of an object behind it. When adults encounter this sight, they will surely perceive it as a boy behind a gate. They are completely certain that when the gate is opened so that the partial occlusion is removed, they will see a whole boy (Figure 13.12B) and would be utterly astounded if the opened gate revealed a boy with gaps in him (Figure 13.12C). This ability to perceive partly hidden objects as they really are is continually called upon in our everyday life, for most of the things we see are partly concealed by others in front of them. But even so, we perceive a world of complete objects rather than disjointed fragments (see Chapter 5).

What accounts for the adult's ability to perceive partly hidden objects? To some extent, it is surely a matter of learning. We know that people have no gaps in them, and that even if they do, they can't stand unsupported in mid-air. But does this mean that Piaget is correct and that the infant starts life with no idea at all that there are external objects outside? Some authors believe it does not. In their view, the infant comes equipped with some primitive concept of a physical world that contains unitary objects whose parts are connected and stay connected regardless of whether the object is partially hidden. Their evidence comes from experiments which show that under some conditions four-month-old infants seem to perceive occluded objects in much the same manner that adults do. Most of these experiments employed the ***habituation procedure*** (Figure 13.13).

In one such study, the infants were shown a rod that moved back and forth behind a solid block that occluded the rod's central portion (Figure 13.14A). This display was kept in view until the infants became bored (that is, habituated), and stopped looking at it. The question was whether the infant perceived a complete, unitary rod, despite the fact that this rod was partially hidden. To find out, the experimenters presented the infants with two new and unoccluded displays. One was an unbroken rod that moved back and forth (Figure 13.14B). The other con-

13.13 The habituation procedure *(A) A four-month-old's face, looking at a small slowly rotating pyramid in front of her (the pyramid can be seen in the mirror that is behind the infant and above her head). (B) Habituation: The infant becomes increasingly bored and looks away. (C) Dishabituation: The infant sees a new object (the rotating cube shown in the mirror) and looks again. This dishabituation effect provides evidence that the infant perceives a difference between the first and second stimulus (that is, the pyramid and the cube). (Photographs courtesy of Phillip Kellman)*

A

B

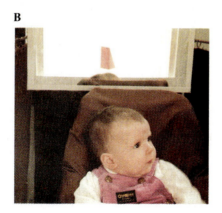

C

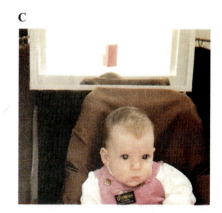

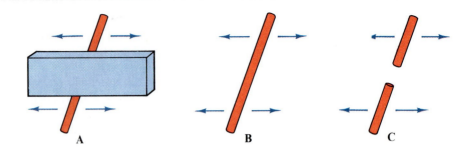

13.14   The perceptual effect of occlusion in early infancy   *Four-month-olds were shown a rod that moved back and forth behind an occluding block as shown in (A). After they became habituated to this display and stopped looking at it, they were shown two new displays, neither of which was occluded. (B) was an unbroken rod that moved back and forth. (C) was made of two aligned rod pieces that moved back and forth together. The infants spent much more time looking at (C) than at (B). (After Kellman and Spelke, 1983)*

sisted of two aligned rod pieces, that moved back and forth in unison (Figure 13.14C). If the infants saw the original display as a complete rod that moved behind the block, they would presumably regard the broken rod as a novel stimulus. If so, they would keep on looking at it for a longer time than at the (now unobstructed) complete rod. This is just what happened. The fact that the top and bottom of the rod in the original display were seen to move together behind the block apparently led to the perception that they were connected. This suggests that some notion of a real physical object exists even at four months of age (Kellman and Spelke, 1983; Kellman, Spelke, and Short, 1986).

Knowing about Objects

The preceding discussion suggests that very young infants have some conception that objects exist even though they are not fully seen. They evidently see objects rather than disjointed fragments. Do they also understand certain rock-bottom principles of the physical world, such as the fact that two objects can't occupy the same space at the same time?

To answer that question, four-and-a-half-month-olds were shown a miniature stage in the middle of which was a medium-sized yellow box. In front of the box was a screen that was hinged on a rod attached to the stage floor. Initially, that screen was laid flat so that the box behind it was clearly visible, but the screen was then rotated upwards like a drawbridge, hiding the box from view (Figure 13.15A). There were two conditions. In one condition, the screen rotated backwards until it reached the no longer visible box, stopped, and then rotated forwards and returned to its initial position at which point the box became visible again (Figure 13.15B). In the other condition, the screen rotated backwards until it reached the occluded box and then kept on going as though the box was no longer there. Once it finished the full 180 degree arc, it reversed direction and swiveled all the way backward at which point the box was revealed again (the box being surreptitiously removed and replaced as required; see Figure 13.15C; Baillargeon, Spelke, and Wasserman, 1985; Baillargeon, 1987).

To an adult, these two conditions present the observer with two radically different events. The first of these makes perfect physical sense: Since two objects can't occupy the same space at the same time, the screen necessarily stops when it en-

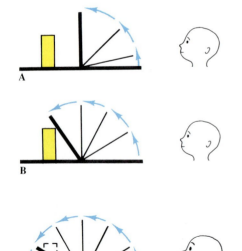

13.15   Knowing about objects   *A four-and-a-half-month-old infant is looking at a stage on which he sees an upright, brightly colored box. In front of the box is a screen that initially lies flat and then (A) starts to rotate upward. In the first condition (B), the screen stops rotating as soon as it hits the box. In the second condition (C), when the screen is at a point high enough to hide the box, the box is surreptitiously removed and the screen continues to rotate backwards. The infant seems to find this quite surprising as shown by the fact that he continues to look at the stage much longer than he did in the first condition. Infants evidently seem able to distinguish possible from impossible events. (After Baillargeon, 1987a)*

counters the solid box. But the second event is physically impossible: If one assumes the box is still where it was originally seen to be, the screen couldn't possibly pass through it.

This is all very well for adults, but do infants see the world the same way? The answer seems to be yes. They spent much less time looking at the stage in the first condition than they did in the second. In the first condition, the screen did what it "was supposed to": it came to a halt when it came up against the—presumably still present—solid box. But in the second condition, the screen behaved rather oddly, for it apparently passed through a solid object. The four-month-olds evidently found the second condition more surprising—or puzzling—than the first. This suggests that, Piaget notwithstanding, these young infants had some notion of object permanence, for they evidently believed that the yellow box they had seen before continued to exist even though it was now occluded. It also suggests that young infants have some notions of the principles that govern objects in space; they evidently know that two objects (here, the screen and the yellow box) can't occupy the same place at the same time.

Results of this kind do not really prove that some foundation for object perception is built in. After all, the subjects in these studies had already lived for four months, and some learning may well have occurred during this period. But the results make such a built-in basis far more plausible than had been previously supposed (Spelke, 1983). All in all, there is reason to believe that Piaget and the empiricists to the contrary, infants come remarkably well equipped to see the world as it really is.

THE PRESCHOOLER AND THE STAGE CONCEPT

The preceding discussion showed why many critics feel that Piaget has underestimated the infant's native cognitive endowments. If these critics are right, the starting point of mental growth is higher than that which Piaget assumed it to be. But what about the process of development from then on? As Piaget described it, cognitive development goes through several distinct *stages* that are in some ways analogous to the stages found in embryological development. This stage notion of development has been the subject of considerable debate. No one doubts that there is mental growth, that the child changes in the way she thinks as she gets older. But is this growth best described as a progression through successive stages?

The Meaning of Mental Stage

What do we mean by *stage?* There is one sense of the term that is essentially empty. Suppose someone announces that "Johnny is going through the thumb-sucking stage." This is just a cumbersome way of saying that Johnny is currently sucking his thumb, for it asserts nothing further. The same is true for a whole host of similar statements, such as "Jane is in the no-saying stage," or "Joey is in the covering-the-wall-with-crayons stage," which respectively inform us that Jane generally says "no" and that Joey crayons the wall, regrettable facts we already knew and to which nothing more is added by calling them stages.

When Piaget used the term *stage* he tried to say considerably more than this. In effect, he took the embryological analogy seriously. In this context, a developmental stage has two characteristics. One is that development at a given stage is more or less *consistent.* That is, the characteristics of a given embryological stage hold pretty much across the board—the development of the gastrointestinal tract is more or less on a par with the development of the circulatory system, and so on. A second characteristic is that embryological stages tend to be *discrete* rather than continuous. There is a qualitative difference between a tadpole and a frog; to be sure, the change from one to the other takes a while, but by the time the creature is a frog, its tadpole days are emphatically over. As Piaget is generally interpreted, his claim was that the same two characteristics—consistency and discreteness—apply to cognitive development. A number of critics have questioned whether they really do. For the most part, these critics have focused on the preschooler's abilities.

The Question of Discreteness

How discrete are developmental stages? As Piaget's account is often understood, many cognitive capacities that mark one period of development are totally absent at prior periods. Consider conservation of quantity or number. According to a simple discrete-stage hypothesis, these should be totally absent at an early age, say, five years old and younger. They are then thought to emerge, virtually full blown, when the curtain finally opens on the next act of the developmental drama, the period of concrete operations. A number of modern investigators disagree, for they deny that cognitive development is essentially all-or-none. As these critics see it, various cognitive achievements such as conservation have primitive precursors that appear several years earlier than the Piagetian calendar would predict (Gelman, 1978; Gelman and Baillargeon, 1983).

EGOCENTRISM REVISITED

One area of reevaluation concerns the concept of egocentrism. According to Piaget, young preschool children are unable to appreciate the difference between another's point of view and their own. But recent studies show that a modicum of this ability is found in children between two and four.

One study used a picture-showing task. Children from one to three years of age were asked to show a photograph to their mother who was seated opposite them. At two and a half and three years of age, all children turned the picture so that it faced the mother. But this implies that they had some conception of the difference between one person's angle of regard and another's. If they had been totally egocentric, they should have shown their mothers the back of the picture while continuing to look at it from the front (Lempers, Flavell, and Flavell, 1977).

A SECOND LOOK AT CONSERVATION

Another phenomenon whose reexamination suggests that preschoolers are less inept than Piaget supposed is conservation, especially conservation of number. We have previously described the standard Piagetian finding: When preschoolers are asked to compare two rows that contain the same number of, say, toy soldiers, they often say that the longer row contains more soldiers, in an apparent confusion of length and number. But recent studies show that children as young as three have surprising precursors of number conservation if the test conditions are suitably arranged.

In one procedure, the children were shown two toy plates, each with a row of toy mice attached with velcro. One plate might have two mice, while the other had three. One plate was designated the "winner," the other the "loser." Each plate was then covered by a can and shuffled around while the children were instructed to keep track of the winner—a small-fry version of the venerable shell game. After each trial, the plates were uncovered, and the children received a prize if they could correctly identify the winner and the loser. After several such

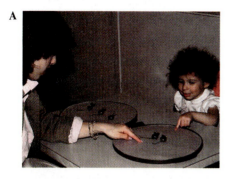

13.16 Gelman's mouse-plate test
(A) The experimenter points to the plate that has two mice and says it is the "winner" while three-year-old Carly watches. (B) After the experimenter covers the plates and rearranges them by a sleight-of-hand trick, (C) Carly points to the correct "winner" and then looks at the experimenter with surprise and says, "Hey—they're spreaded out!" (Photographs courtesy of Hilary Schmidt)

trials, the real test was conducted. The experimenter surreptitiously substituted a new plate for the original winner. In one case, the new plate contained the same number of mice as the original, but the row was made longer or shorter. In the other case, the row length stayed unchanged, but a mouse was added or subtracted. The results showed that spatial arrangement made little difference. But changes in number had dramatic consequences even at three and four years of age. The children were surprised, asked where the missing mouse was, and searched for it (Gelman, 1972; see Figure 13.16).

Phenomena of this kind argue against the notion that cognitive development proceeds by sudden, dramatic leaps. The achievements of the concrete-operational period do not come out of the blue. If we look carefully enough, we see that they have preludes in much earlier childhood years. It may well be true that there are stages of intellectual growth that have to be passed in an ordered sequence. But there are no neat demarcations between stages and no sharp transitions. The stages of cognitive development are not as all-or-none as the changes from tadpole to frog (let alone from frog to prince).

Sequence or Stages?

What can we conclude about Piaget's stages of mental development? The evidence as a whole suggests that the child's mental growth does not proceed as neatly as a simple stage theory might lead one to expect (Flavell, 1985).

Does this mean that Piaget's cognitive milestones have no psychological reality? Not really. The cognitive sequence may not be as neat as one might have wished, but there is little doubt that some such sequence exists. Consider the difference between seven-year-olds and preschoolers. Despite all the precursors of concrete operations at four or even earlier, there is no question that seven- and eight-year-olds have something preschoolers lack—the ability to apply their insights to a much wider range of problems (Fodor, 1972). Three-year-olds can tell the difference between two and three mice regardless of how they are spaced on the table. But they haven't fully grasped the underlying idea—that number and spatial arrangements are in principle independent and that this is so for all numbers and all spatial arrangements. As a result, they fail—and will continue to fail until they are six or seven years old—the standard Piagetian test for conservation of number in which they have to recognize that two rows of, say, nine buttons contain the same number of buttons, regardless of how the rows are expanded or compressed. This task baffles the preschool child, who finds the number in each row too large to count and gets confused. Seven-year-olds have no such problems. They can count higher, but that's not the issue. They know that there is no need to count, that the number of buttons in each row has to be identical, regardless of the way they are arranged. As a result, they can conserve number in general.

What holds for conservation of number holds for many other intellectual achievements that are generally associated with the first school years. Most of them have precursors, often at much earlier ages than Piaget led us to suppose. But these preschool abilities usually represent isolated pockets of knowledge that can't be applied very widely. The seven- or eight-year-old's understanding of physical, numerical, and social reality is considerably more general, so much so that it seems qualitatively different from what went on before. By simplifying the task in various ways, experimenters can induce preschoolers to perform more creditably. But the interesting fact remains that by the time the child is seven or eight years old, no such simplification is necessary. A seven- or eight-year-old conserves with barely a glance at the containers in which the liquid is sloshed around. He *knows* that the liquid quantity is unaffected no matter how the containers are shaped.

A

B

C

13.17 Development as maturation?
*(A) A butterfly emerging from its crysalis
and (B) walking are largely matters of
maturation. (C) Is the cognitive growth
that underlies a seven-and-a-half-year-old's
success in a Piagetian conservation task to
be understood in similar terms? (Photographs by Pat Lynch/Photo Researchers;
Ray Ellis/Photo Researchers; Chris
Massey)*

THE CAUSES OF COGNITIVE GROWTH

Thus far, we have looked at cognitive growth and seen that there is some question of how it might be best described (e.g., stage or sequence). We now turn to attempts at explanation. Trying to explain cognitive development has turned out to be even more difficult than trying to describe it (Siegler, 1989). As so often in the field of cognition, the attempts to come up with an adequate explanation have fluctuated between the two poles of the nature-nurture controversy.

The Nativist Approach: Maturation

Some investigators are inclined toward a nativist interpretation. There is of course no doubt that native endowment must play some role in cognitive development. The human infant begins life with a potential that is quite different from that of his near and distant cousins in the rest of the animal kingdom, and no amount of training and nurturing can ever erase these differences in the equipment with which the varying species begin. Worms won't count, platypuses won't form higher-order chunkings, and polar bears won't conserve liquid quantity, no matter what environments they are reared in. Our native equipment is thus a necessary precondition for all development. But can this endowment explain the orderly progression of cognitive development?

Some theorists believe that it can. They believe that development is largely driven by some form of physical *maturation,* a pre-programmed growth process based on changes in underlying neural structures that are relatively independent of environmental conditions. Maturation is obviously an important factor in motor development—for example, flying in sparrows and walking in humans. These are behavior patterns that are characteristic of all adult members of the species. They emerge as the organism matures, but their development is relatively unaffected by environmental changes (except those extreme enough to cripple or kill).

Could cognitive development be a matter of maturation (in part or whole), in the sense in which walking is (Figure 13.17)? There is good evidence for a maturational contribution during the first two years of life. There is a tenfold increase in the number of synaptic connections in the cortex between birth and twelve months of age, and a still further increase until about age two. Yet further changes last into the school years (Siegler, 1989).

A number of authors have argued that maturational changes of this kind underlie many aspects of human cognitive development. In their view, there is something inexorable about cognitive development, especially up to age seven or eight (Wohlwill, 1973). This view is buttressed by the fact that, at least in broad outline, mental growth seems rather similar in children of different cultures and nationalities. While children of different cultures master intellectual tasks such as conservation at somewhat different ages, they usually pass these landmarks in the same order. Thus Arab, Indian, Somali, and British children show the same progression from nonconservation of quantity to conservation (Hyde, 1959). This is reminiscent of physical maturation. Different butterflies may emerge from their chrysalis at slightly different times, but none is a butterfly first and a chrysalis second. The timing of the transitions may well be affected by environmental conditions: in humans, by culture; in butterflies, by temperature. But according to the maturational hypothesis, the order of the stages is determined by the genetic code.

The Empiricist Approach: Specific Learning

The simplest alternative to a maturation-centered approach is one that emphasizes learning by exposure to the environment. The most extreme version of this view is that of the empiricists who followed in the footsteps of John Locke (see Chapter 4). To them, the human mind starts out as a blank wax tablet, a *tabula rasa,* upon which experience gradually leaves its mark. But can such a radical empiricist position explain the systematic sequence of cognitive development that Piaget and other investigators have chronicled?

Piaget argued that simple learning theories of the kind espoused by the early empiricists—and by their modern heirs such as Pavlov and Skinner—will not do. According to such theories, learning is the acquisition of relatively specific skills —such as figure skating—that in principle could be mastered at any age. But this is precisely what Piaget denied. According to Piaget, four-year-olds cannot possibly be taught how to use a measuring cup correctly, no matter how attractive the reinforcements or how many the number of trials. He argued that four-year-olds lack the prerequisite concepts of number and quantity (which they cannot attain before the concrete-operational level), so that any attempt to teach them is as fruitless as trying to build the third story of a house without a second story underneath it. This view has obvious relevance to educational policy. If Piaget is right, then there is little point in efforts to teach children this or that aspect of the curriculum before they are "ready" for it.

In an attempt to test this claim, several investigators have tried to determine whether children can be trained to reach certain cognitive landmarks such as conservation ahead of schedule. The results are a bit ambiguous. Formerly, most investigators concluded that specific training has little impact. In some cases, conservation was speeded up by special coaching, but later checks revealed that the children had not really understood the underlying principles and quickly reverted to their previous, nonconserving ways (e.g., Smedslund, 1961). But some later studies showed more substantial effects. In some cases, these were brought about by mere observation; for example, six-year-old nonconservers who watched conservers perform showed subsequent conservation of mass or number (Botvin and Murray, 1975; Murray, 1978). But the best guess is that the children already had most of the necessary conceptual ingredients at the time they were "trained." If so, then training (or watching another child) did not really teach conservation; it only helped to uncover what was already there (Gold, 1978; Gelman and Baillargeon, 1983).

Related findings come from a study conducted in a Mexican village whose inhabitants made pottery and whose children helped and participated in this activity from early on. When tested for conservation of mass, these children turned out to be more advanced than their North American counterparts (or those studied by Piaget in Switzerland). Having spent much of their lives working at a potter's wheel, they were more likely to know that the amount of clay is the same whether it is rolled into a ball or stretched into a long, thin sausage (Price-Williams, Gordon, and Ramirez, 1969). But these effects of pottery making were relatively specific. They led to an advance on tests of conservation of mass but to little else. (For further discussion, see Greenfield, 1976; Price-Williams, 1981; Rogoff, Gauvain, and Ellis, 1984.)

All in all, there is little doubt that environment must play *some* role in cognitive development. To acquire liquid conservation, one presumably has to live in a world in which liquids exist. If a frozen planet like Jupiter had inhabitants whose cognitive potential was like our own, their young would never know that when water is poured from a wide jar into a tall, thin beaker the amount of

373

9. Trying to explain cognitive growth has turned out to be even more difficult and controversial than trying to describe it. The nativist approach assumes that development is largely driven by *maturation.* Empiricists assume that the answer is *specific learning.* Piaget himself rejected both empiricist and nativist extremes, arguing that development involves a constant interchange between organism and environment as the environment is *assimilated* to the child's current schema and the schema in turn *accommodates* itself to aspects of the environment. A current approach sees cognitive development as a change in *information processing* and argues that increased mental growth is based in part on the acquisition of better and larger *chunks* and of various *strategies* for thinking and remembering.

Memory Span

5
4
3
2
1

*13.18 M
(After Ca:*

CHAPTER 14

Social Development

In the preceding chapters we discussed physical and cognitive development: the ways in which we progress from embryos to full-grown adults, from crawling infants to energetic tricyclists, from babbling babes to sophisticated eight-year-olds who understand all about liquid conservation. But children don't just grow in size and thought; they also develop in their relations to other people. To find out how they do this is the task of psychologists who study *social development.*

Physical, cognitive, and social development pertain to different aspects of the human journey from birth to maturity. But even so, they are alike in one respect: In all three, we see an ever-increasing enlargement of the developing individual's universe. In biological development, the infant enlarges her physical horizons. As she grows in sheer size and strength, she develops the ability to move freely within her environment and becomes emancipated from her initial limitations in physical space. Cognitive development leads to an analogous expansion of horizons, but now of the mental rather than the physical world as the growing child comes to transcend the immediate here-and-now to live in a world of ever more abstract ideas.

In social development, there is a similar pattern of continued expansion. In the first months of life, the baby's social world is limited to just one person, usually the mother. In time, her social horizons become enlarged to include both parents, then the rest of the family, then young peers in the nursery and in school. As adolescence sets in, friends of the opposite sex assume more and more importance, sexuality begins in earnest, and the individual soon becomes a parent in her own right and starts the reproductive cycle all over again. But the expansion of the child's social world goes yet further. As she grows older, she comes to understand the system of social rules through which she is linked, not just to her own family circle, but to a larger social universe. A major concern of this chapter is to chart the course of this social expansion through which babes in arms grow into citizens of the world.

Attachment (Mother and Child, c. 1890, by Mary Cassatt; Courtesy Wichita Art Museum, Wichita, Kansas; the Roland P. Murdock Collection)

ATTACHMENT

Social development begins with the first human bond that is sometimes said to lay the foundations for all later relationships with others: the infant's **attachment** to the person who takes care of him.* The infant wants to be near his mother, and if unhappy, he is comforted by her sight, her sound, and her touch. In this regard, human children have much in common with the young of many other species. Rhesus infants cling to their mother's body, chicks follow the hen, and lambs run after the ewe. As the young grow older, they venture farther away from the mother, gaining courage for ever more distant explorations. But for quite a while, the mother continues to provide a secure home base, a place to run back to should unmanageable threats be encountered.

The Roots of Attachment

Until fairly recently, most theorists believed that the attachment to the mother is a secondary consequence of her association with basic creature satisfactions such as the alleviation of hunger, thirst, and pain. The most influential version of this approach was probably that of Sigmund Freud, who believed that the infant's upset at the mother's absence is based on the crass fear that his bodily needs would now go unsatisfied. The British psychiatrist John Bowlby has called this the "cupboard theory" of mother love; it boils down to the view that the first love object is the breast or the bottle (Bowlby, 1969, 1973).

IS THE NEED FOR THE MOTHER PRIMARY?

The cupboard theory of the infant's tie to his mother has been criticized on several grounds. One problem is the fact that babies often show great interest in other people, even those who have never fed them or satisfied their other bodily needs. They seem to enjoy seeing others smile or playing peek-a-boo. Does anyone seriously propose that infants want someone to play peek-a-boo with them because this game has previously been associated with food? It seems much more reasonable to assume that the infant comes predisposed to seek social satisfaction, which is rewarding in and of itself.

Another demonstration that love of mother goes beyond bodily needs comes from the work of Harry Harlow (1905–1981). Harlow raised newborn rhesus monkeys without their mothers. Each young monkey lived alone in a cage that contained two stationary figures. One of these models was built of wire; the other was made of soft terry cloth. The wire figure was equipped with a nipple that yielded milk, but no similar provision was made for the terry-cloth model. Even so, the monkey infants spent much more time on the terry-cloth "mother" than on the wire figure. The terry-cloth figure could be clung to and could provide what Harlow called "contact comfort" (Figure 14.1). This was especially clear when the infants were frightened. When placed in an unfamiliar room or faced with a mechanical toy that approached with clanking noises, they invariably rushed to the terry-cloth mother and clung to her tightly. The infants never sought similar solace from the wire mothers, who were their source of food and nothing more (Harlow, 1958).

14.1 The need for contact comfort A frightened rhesus monkey baby clings to its terry-cloth mother for comfort. (Photograph by Martin Rogers/Stock, Boston)

* Since the caregiver is typically the child's mother (she almost always was in earlier eras), we will from here on refer to the child's caregiver by the traditional term *mother,* despite the fact that the actual caregiver may well be another person, such as the father or a babysitter.

14.2 Contact comfort in humans
(*Photograph by Suzanne Szasz*)

These results are in complete opposition to the cupboard theory. The monkey infant evidently loves its mother (whether real or terry cloth), not because she feeds it, but because she feels so "comforting." Whether touch is equally important to human infants is as yet unclear, but very likely it plays some role. Frightened young humans run to their mothers and hug them closely just as rhesus infants do (Figure 14.2). Children also like stuffed, cuddly toys such as teddy bears, whom they hold tightly when they feel apprehensive. Perhaps Linus's security blanket is a kind of terry-cloth mother. It may or may not be; but contrary to the cupboard theory, it is emphatically not a substitute tablecloth.

BOWLBY'S THEORY OF ATTACHMENT

What is the alternative to the cupboard theory? According to John Bowlby, attachment results because infants are born with a number of interrelated built-in tendencies that make them seek direct contact with an adult (usually the mother).

One facet of attachment seeking is positive. The infant evidently enjoys being with his mother and interacting with her. From birth on, he is well-equipped for social interaction. He quickly comes to recognize and prefer his mother's voice and even her smell (MacFarlane, 1975; DeCasper and Fifer, 1980). If he is contented, he is generally calm, gurgles, and (starting at about six weeks) will produce a full-blown social smile. The mother—and other important adults—will happily reciprocate; when the baby smiles, they smile back. As the infant gets older and acquires some locomotor control, he will do whatever he can to be in the adult's company—reaching toward the mother and father to be picked up, crawling toward them, and so on (Campos et al., 1983).

Bowlby believes that attachment seeking has a second, more negative cause. This is a built-in fear of the unknown and unfamiliar, which is yet another reason why the young of most mammals and birds become attached and stay close to some object that has become familiar to them.

According to Bowlby, a built-in fear of the unfamiliar has a simple survival value. In prehistoric times, infants who lacked it would stray away from their mother and would be more likely to get lost and perish. In particular, they might well have fallen victim to predators, for beasts of prey tend to attack weak animals that are separated from their fellows.

Needless to say, infants don't know enough about the world to fear specific predators. But Bowlby argues that the built-in fear is initially quite unspecific. He conjectures that the fear aroused by the mother's absence is analogous to what psychiatrists call *free-floating anxiety.* This is a state in which the patient is desperately afraid but doesn't know what he is afraid of; he therefore becomes all the more afraid. Given this anxiety, even mild external threats become enormous to the child; the increased need for reassurance may lead to wild clinging and "childish" dependency, as in the dark or during a thunderstorm. This may occur even when the threat comes from the parents themselves. A child who is severely punished by his parents often becomes even more clinging and dependent than before. The parents caused the fear, but they are the ones who are approached for reassurance. This is analogous to the dog who licks the hand that whipped him. The whipping led to fear and pain, but whom can the dog approach for solace but his master?

IMPRINTING

According to Bowlby, the fear of the unfamiliar produces an attachment to a familiar object. In the real world of animals, this object is generally the mother. But it needn't be. Harlow's studies have already shown us that the focus of filial devo-

Imprinting in ducklings   *Imprinted ducklings following Konrad Lorenz. (Courtesy Nina Leen)*

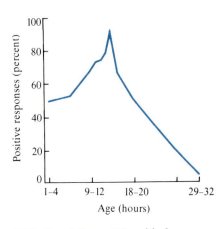

14.3   Imprinting and the critical period   *The curve shows the relation between imprinting and the age at which a duckling was exposed to a male moving model. The imprinting score represents the percentage of trials on which the duckling followed the model on a later test. (After Hess, 1958)*

tion is not rigidly determined by the genes, as witness the love borne for the terry-cloth mother.

A similar point is made by *imprinting* in birds, which has been studied extensively by the European ethologist Konrad Lorenz. Imprinting is a kind of learning that occurs very early in life and provides the basis for the chick's attachment to its mother. When a newly hatched duckling is first exposed to a moving stimulus, it will approach and follow this stimulus as soon as it is able to walk (at about twelve hours after hatching). If the duckling follows the object for about ten minutes, an attachment is formed; the bird is imprinted. In nature, the moving stimulus is the duckling's mother and all is well. But in the laboratory, it need not be. The duckling may be exposed to a moving duck on wheels, or to a rectangle sliding back and forth behind a glass window, or even to Konrad Lorenz's booted legs. In each case, the result is the same. The duckling becomes imprinted on the wooden duck or on the rectangle or on Lorenz; it follows one of these objects as if it were its mother, uttering piteous distress calls whenever it is not nearby. The real mother may quack enticingly so as to woo her lost offspring back, but to no avail; the imprinted duckling continues to follow the wooden duck or the moving rectangle or Lorenz (Hess, 1959, 1973).

Imprinting occurs most readily during a so-called *sensitive period* that in ducklings lasts for around two days, with a maximum sensitivity at some fifteen hours after hatching (Hess, 1959). Subsequent to this period, imprinting is difficult to achieve (see Figure 14.3). According to Lorenz, this phenomenon reflects a decline in the plasticity of some part of the young bird's brain—a decline that is somehow tied to a physiological clock (Gottlieb, 1961). Another possible explanation is that ducklings are difficult to imprint after the sensitive period is past because by then they have become thoroughly afraid of all new objects. When exposed to the wooden duck (or Lorenz's boots or a moving rectangle), the bird flees instead of following. Having lived for several days, it has learned something about what is familiar, and it can therefore appreciate—and fear—what is strange. Some evidence for this position comes from the fact that older ducklings can be imprinted on new objects if they are forced to remain in their presence for a while. One group of investigators exposed five-day-old ducklings to a moving rectangle. The ducklings tried to flee and huddled in a corner. After a while, their fear diminished. At this point, they began to follow the rectangle and gave distress calls when it was withdrawn. They had become imprinted even though they were long past the sensitive period (Hoffman, 1978; for still another account, see Bateson, 1984).

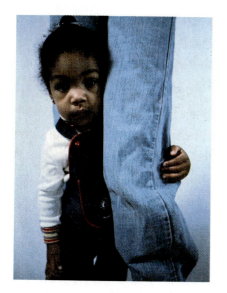

(Photograph by J. Blyenberg/Leo de Wys)

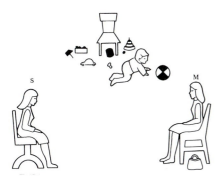

14.4 A diagrammatic sketch of the "Strange Situation" M indicates the mother, and S the stranger. (Adapted from Ainsworth, Blehar, Waters, and Wall, 1978, p. 34)

Separation and Loss

The attachment to the mother has a corollary: A separation from her evokes distress. During the first few months of life, the infant will accept a substitute, perhaps because there is as yet no clear-cut conception of the mother that differentiates her from all other persons. But from somewhere between six and eight months of age, the infant comes to know who his mother is; he now cries and fusses when he sees her leave. The age at which children begin to register this protest against separation is pretty much the same across such diverse cultures as African Bushmen in Botswana, U.S. city dwellers, Indians in a Guatemalan village, and members of an Israeli kibbutz (Kagan, 1976).

LONG SEPARATION AND PERMANENT LOSS

To the child, seeing the mother leave is bad enough, but it's even worse if she doesn't return shortly. Lengthy separations can have serious effects. Infants of seven months or older who are placed in a hospital for a short stay fret and protest and seem negative and frightened. After returning home, they remain anxious for a while, as if terrified of another separation. They continually cling to their mother, scream when left alone by her, are unusually afraid of strangers, and may even become suspicious of such familiar persons as fathers and siblings (Schaffer and Callender, 1959).

Similar effects are often seen in older children. One study dealt with two- and three-year-olds who were placed in a residential nursery for some weeks. During the first few days, they cried frequently and clung desperately to some favorite toy they had brought along. After a while their crying abated, but not their distress. They became apathetic and hostile and lost previously acquired bowel control (Heinicke and Westheimer, 1966).

ASSESSING ATTACHMENT

The reaction to separation provides a means for assessing the kind of attachment a particular infant has to his mother. A widely used procedure is the so-called "Strange Situation" devised by Mary Ainsworth and her colleagues for children of about one year of age (Figure 14.4). The child is first brought into an unfamiliar room that contains many toys, and he is given an opportunity to explore and play while the mother is present. After a while, a stranger enters, talks to the mother and then approaches the child. The next step is a brief separation—the mother goes out of the room, and leaves the child alone with the stranger. A reunion follows—the mother comes back and the stranger leaves (Ainsworth and Bell, 1970; Ainsworth, Blehar, Waters, and Wall, 1978).

The behavior of one-year-olds falls into several broad categories. One group (over two-thirds of the children in one of Ainsworth's studies) is described as "securely attached." As long as the mother is present, these children explore, play with the toys, and even make wary overtures to the stranger. They show some distress when the mother leaves, but greet her return with great enthusiasm. The remaining children show various behavior patterns that Ainsworth and her colleagues regard as signs of "insecure attachment." Some are described as "resistant." They don't explore even in the mother's presence, become intensely upset and very panicky when she leaves, and act emotionally ambivalent during the reunion, running to her to be picked up and then angrily struggling to get down. Others are described as "avoidant." They are distant and aloof from the very outset, show little distress when the mother leaves, and ignore her when she returns.

Ainsworth and other adherents of attachment theory believe that these behavior patterns reflect fairly stable characteristics, at least for the first few years of life. Thus children who were rated as securely attached in the Strange Situation at fifteen months of age were judged to be more outgoing, popular, and well-adjusted in nursery school at age three and a half (Waters, Wippman, and Sroufe, 1979).

ASSESSING THE ROLE OF THE FATHER

Ainsworth's general approach has provided a means for studying various other aspects of early social development. An example is the infant's relation to the father. Thus far, we've concentrated entirely on the child's attachment to the mother. Is the father left out in the cold? To find out, one investigator used the Strange Situation with fathers as well as mothers and found signs of distress when the father left and some clinging and touching when he returned (see Figure 14.5). It appears that the emotional life of the child is not exclusively wrapped up in the mother. But the mother seems to be more important, at least at an early age. There was more distress at the mother's departure than at the father's and more enthusiasm at her return (Kotelchuk, 1976).

Further evidence indicates that the attachments to the two parents have some different characteristics. A number of studies have shown that fathers are more likely to play with their infants (and young children) than mothers are. In addition, their play is more physical and vigorous; they may lift or bounce their babies or toss them in the air. In contrast, mothers generally play more quietly with their infants, and stress verbal rather than physical interactions. As a result, while the mother may be the parent the child is more likely to run to for care and comfort, the father is often the preferred playmate. This difference in the response to the two parents begins in early infancy, when there are more smiles for the mother and more giggles for the father. By the time the children are toddlers, two out of three pick the father as the one they want to play with. Mother is security and comfort; father is fun (Lamb, 1977; Clarke-Stewart, 1978; Parke, 1981).

How Crucial Is Early Experience?

What happens when the initial attachment of the child to the mother is not allowed to form? The effects are apparently drastic.

MOTHERLESS MONKEYS

We previously considered Harlow's studies on rhesus monkeys raised with substitute mothers made of terry cloth. Some later studies asked what happens when monkey infants are reared without any contact at all. The infants were isolated for periods that ranged from three months to one year. During this time, they lived in an empty steel chamber and saw no living creature, not even a human hand.

After their period of solitary confinement, the animals' reactions were observed in various test situations. A three-month isolation had comparatively little effect. But longer periods led to dramatic disturbances. The animals huddled in a corner of the cage, clasped themselves, and rocked back and forth. When they were brought together with normally reared age-mates, the results were pathetic. There was none of the active chasing and playful romping that is characteristic of monkeys at that age. Whenever the normals took an aggressive lunge at them, the monkeys reared in isolation were unable to fight back. They withdrew, huddled, rocked—and bit *themselves* (Figure 14.6).

A

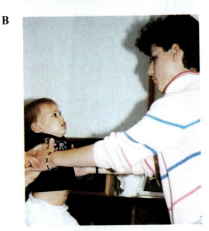

B

C

14.5 Stranger anxiety *An eleven-month-old taken from his father's lap by a stranger (Photograph by Stephanie Arch, courtesy Kathy Hirsh-Pasek)*

14.6 *Motherless monkeys* *An isolated monkey biting itself at the approach of a stranger. (Courtesy Harry Harlow, University of Wisconsin Primate Laboratory)*

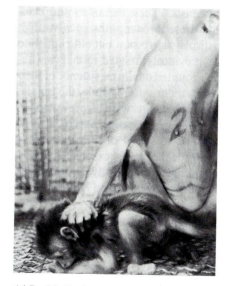

14.7 *Motherless monkeys as mothers* *Female monkeys raised in isolation may become mothers by artificial impregnation. They usually ignore their infants. Sometimes, as shown here, they abuse them. (Courtesy Harry Harlow, University of Wisconsin Primate Laboratory)*

This social inadequacy persisted into adolescence and adulthood. One manifestation was a remarkable incompetence in sexual and parental matters. Formerly isolated males were utterly inept in the business of reproduction: As Harlow put it, "Isolates may grasp other monkeys of either sex by the head and throat aimlessly, a semi-erotic exercise without amorous achievements." Formerly isolated females resisted the sexual overtures of normal males. Some were eventually impregnated, in many cases by artificial means. When these motherless monkeys became monkey mothers themselves, they seemed to have no trace of love for their offspring. In a few cases, there was horrible abuse. The mothers crushed the infant's head to the floor, chewed off its toes or fingers, or bit it to death (Figure 14.7). Early social deprivation had evidently played havoc with the animals' subsequent social and emotional development (Suomi and Harlow, 1971; Harlow and Harlow, 1972; Harlow and Novak, 1973).

HUMANS REARED IN INSTITUTIONS

Can we generalize from infant monkeys to human children? There is reason to suspect that there are some important similarities. It appears that human infants reared under conditions of comparative social isolation (although needless to say, not as drastic as that imposed on the monkeys) suffer somewhat analogous deficits.

The evidence comes from studies of infants reared in institutions. In many cases, they received perfectly adequate nutrition and bodily care; the problem was that there was very little social stimulation. In one institution the infants were kept in separate cubicles for the first eight months or so as a precaution against infectious disease. Their brief contacts with adults were restricted to the times when they were fed or diapered. Feeding took place in the crib with a propped-up bottle. There was little social give and take, little talk, little play, and little chance that the busy attendant would respond to any one baby's cry (Goldfarb, 1955; Provence and Lipton, 1962).

When these infants were compared to others who were raised normally, there were no differences for the first three or four months. Thereafter, the two groups diverged markedly. The institutionalized infants showed serious impairments in their social development. Some were insatiable in their incessant demands for individual love and attention. But the majority went in the opposite direction and

he thinks that he will be caught is not moral; he's merely prudent. One aim of socialization is to instill moral values that are **internalized,** so that the individual will shun transgressions because he feels that they are wrong and not because he is afraid of being punished.

Internalization A four-year-old reproaches her doll: "Bad girl! Didn't I tell you to keep out of the dirt?" In imitating how her mother scolds her, the child is taking the first steps toward internalizing the mother's prohibitions. (Photograph by Suzanne Szasz)

INTERNALIZATION AND THE SUPEREGO

What leads to the internalization of right and wrong? According to Freud, the primary agent of internalization is the **superego,** a component of the personality that controls various forbidden impulses by administering self-punishment in the form of guilt and anxiety (see Chapter 10). The child kicks his little brother, and the parents punish him. As a result, the forbidden act (or, for that matter, the mere thought of that act) becomes associated with anxiety. This in turn will make the boy feel a pang of anxiety the next time he starts to attack his younger brother. To stop this painful feeling, he must stop that which triggered it: the thought, let alone the execution, of the forbidden behavior. The superego is the sum total of all such internalized inhibitions, a remnant of our childhood that remains with us for the rest of our lives and makes sure that we commit no wrong. The external authorities that once punished our transgressions have long stopped watching the cookie jar. But they no longer have to because they now inhabit our minds, where we can no longer hide from them.

INTERNALIZATION AND MINIMAL SUFFICIENCY

This general view of the inhibition of forbidden acts makes certain predictions about the relation between child rearing and moral behavior. If the superego is a remnant of punishment administered during childhood, one might expect that the internalization of prohibition is most pronounced in children whose parents relied on sheer power in raising them—whether this power was exercised by the use of physical punishment, or deprivation of privileges, or threats of withdrawal of love and of abandonment. But this prediction turns out to be false. For a number of studies suggest that prohibitions are *less* internalized in children whose parents primarily relied on power in its various forms than in children whose parents took pains to explain just why a misdeed was wrong and why the child ought to behave differently. The children of power-asserting (autocratic) parents were more likely to cheat for a prize when they thought no one was looking, and they were less likely to feel guilt about their misdeeds or to confess them when confronted (Hoffman, 1970).

One proposal tries to deduce these and other phenomena of socialization from the so-called principle of **minimal sufficiency.** This states that a child will internalize a certain way of acting if there is just enough pressure to get her to behave in this new way, but not enough so that she feels she was forced to do so. This principle seems to fit a number of experimental findings. An example is a study in which children were prohibited from playing with a particularly attractive toy. For some children, the prohibition was backed with a mild threat (e.g., "I will be a little bit annoyed with you"); for others, the threat was severe (e.g., "I will be very upset and very angry with you"). When later tested in a rather different situation in which they thought they were unobserved, the mildly threatened children resisted temptation more than the severely threatened ones. The punishment led to internalization, but it did so only if it was *not* the most memorable part of the child's experience.

The same principle may help account for some of the effects of child rearing we've discussed in a prior section. We saw that the children of authoritative-reciprocal parents are more likely to internalize their parents' standards than the children of autocratic or permissive parents. This is in accord with the minimal

"They never pushed me. If I wanted to retrieve, shake hands, or roll over, it was entirely up to me."
(Drawing by Frascino; ©1971 The New Yorker Magazine, Inc.)

A

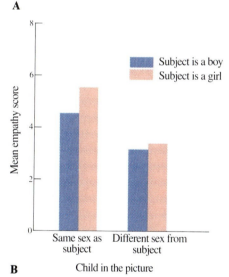

B

14.11 It is easier to empathize with those who are similar (A) Six- and seven-year-olds were presented with sequences of pictures such as this. After looking at each sequence, the child was asked "How do you feel?" Empathy was scored as a feeling that corresponded to that of the child in the picture (here, anger). (Courtesy of Norma Feshbach) (B) The children's empathy scores (the maximum score was 8). As the figure shows, the boys (in blue) felt greater empathy when the child in the picture was a boy than when it was a girl; the girls (in pink) felt more empathy when it was a girl than when it was a boy. (Adapted from Feshbach and Roe, 1968)

sufficiency hypothesis. Autocratic parents supply too much force to induce their children to behave in the appropriate way, so their children become outwardly compliant but will not change their inner attitudes. Permissive parents apply no force at all, so their children never change their behavior in the first place—they won't even comply outwardly, let alone internalize. But authoritative-reciprocal parents somehow manage to strike the proper balance. They apply a force just strong enough to get their children to change their behavior, but mild enough so that the children come to believe that they performed the moral act of their own free will (Lepper, 1983).*

Doing Good

Thus far, our discussion of moral action has dealt with the inhibition of forbidden acts. But moral action pertains to do's no less than to don'ts, to doing good as well as not committing evil. In a previous chapter we considered the fact that humans are capable of positive moral actions that call for some personal sacrifice and altruism (see Chapter 12). We now ask how this capacity develops in the child.

Thus far, we are still far from an answer. A number of studies show that even very young children try to help and comfort others, and occasionally share with them (Rheingold, Hay, and West, 1976; Radke-Yarrow, Zahn-Waxler, and Chapman, 1983). The question is why.

EMPATHY

Some evidence comes from studies of *empathy* in very young infants. Empathy is a direct emotional response to another person's emotions; we see a patient writhe in pain in a hospital bed, and we ourselves experience vicarious distress (Aronfreed, 1968; see also Chapter 12). Some precursors to such empathic reactions are found in the first two days of life. On hearing a newborn's cry, one-day-old infants cry too and their hearts beat faster (Simner, 1971; Sagi and Hoffman, 1976).

The newborn's response to another baby's cry is just the first step in the development of empathic feelings for others. Initially, there is probably no clear separation between "self" and "other," and the infant may not really know that he is reacting to *another* child's distress. Genuine empathy, in which one feels for another while yet perfectly aware that this other is not oneself, probably doesn't come much before the end of the first year. At about two years of age, children can put it in words: "Her eyes are crying—her sad" or "Janie crying, want mommy" (Bretherton, McNew, and Beeghly-Smith, 1981; see Figure 14.11).

FROM EMPATHIC DISTRESS TO UNSELFISH ACTION

The mere fact that one feels empathy doesn't mean that one will do anything about it. For to help one's fellows, one has to do more than just feel for them. One also has to act on this feeling. And one has to know how.

Consider a two-year-old girl who sees an adult in pain—say, an uncle who has cut his finger with a knife. In all likelihood, she will feel empathy and become distressed herself. But what will she do? A number of anecdotes suggest that she will give her uncle whatever *she* finds most comforting herself—for example, her favorite doll. While appreciating her kindly sentiments, the uncle would probably

* This is reminiscent of the effects of forced compliance on attitudes. As we saw in Chapter 11, subjects who are pressured into performing some action that runs counter to their own attitudes, will tend to change this attitude if the pressure (the threat or the bribe) is relatively small, but will not change the attitude if the pressure is large (Festinger and Carlsmith, 1959; Aronson and Carlsmith, 1963).

have preferred a band-aid or a stiff drink. But the child is as yet too young to take his perspective and doesn't realize that his needs are not the same as hers (Hoffman, 1977a, 1979, 1984).

As we develop, we become increasingly able to tell what other people are likely to feel in a given situation and how to help if help is needed. But even that is not enough to ensure that we will act unselfishly. For helping is only one means of getting rid of the empathic distress that is caused by the sight of another person's pain. There is an easier but more callous method: One can simply look away. This often occurs in the big city, with its many homeless and victims of violence, where empathy may seem a luxury one can no longer afford. It may also occur in war or other situations where people "harden their hearts" to become immune to the sufferings of others (see Chapter 12). Such examples indicate that while empathy is a likely precursor of altruism, it does not guarantee it.

Moral Reasoning

Thus far, our focus has been on the development of moral behavior. What about the development of moral thought? What happens to the child's conception of right and wrong as he grows up?

KOHLBERG'S STAGES OF MORAL REASONING

An influential account of moral reasoning was devised by Lawrence Kohlberg. His basic method was to confront subjects with a number of stories that pose a moral dilemma. An example is a story about a man whose wife will die unless treated with a very expensive drug that costs $2,000. The husband scraped together all the money he could, but it was not enough. He promised to pay the balance later, but the pharmacist still refused to give him the drug. In desperation, the husband broke into the pharmacy and stole the drug. The subjects were asked whether the husband's act was right or wrong and why (Kohlberg, 1969).

Kohlberg analyzed the subjects' answers and concluded that moral reasoning proceeds through a series of successive stages. Roughly speaking, there is a progression from a primitive morality guided by personal fear of punishment or desire for gain ("If you let your wife die, you'll get in trouble"), through stages in which right or wrong are defined by convention, by what people will say ("Your family will think you're an inhuman husband if you don't"), to the highest stage in which there are internalized moral principles that have become one's own ("If you didn't steal the drug, you wouldn't be blamed and you would have lived up to the outside rule of the law, but you wouldn't have lived up to your own standards of conscience"). As one might expect, there is a rough correlation between Kohlberg's levels and age. But even in adulthood only a small proportion of the subjects give answers that correspond to Kohlberg's highest level. In a recent study that made use of a revised set of Kohlberg's criteria, no subject below the age of twenty was judged to have reached Stage 5, and Stage 6 was not found at all (Colby, Kohlberg, Gibbs, and Lieberman, 1983; Colby and Kohlberg, 1986). Considering that Kohlberg considers this final stage to be the level that characterized such moral giants as Mahatma Gandhi and Dr. Martin Luther King, the failure of his subjects (and no doubt, most of us) to attain it, is probably not too surprising (Figure 14.12; Table 14.1).

MORAL REASONING IN MEN AND WOMEN

Are there sex differences in moral orientation? An influential discussion by Carol Gilligan suggests that there may be. In her view, men tend to see morality as a

14.12   *Level of moral reasoning as a function of age*   With increasing age, the level of moral reasoning changes. In this figure, the percent of all moral judgments made by children at various ages falls into one of three general categories defined by Kohlberg. At seven, virtually all moral judgments are in terms of avoiding punishment or gaining reward (Kohlberg's levels 1 and 2). At ten, about half the judgments are based on criteria of social approval and disapproval or of a—rigid—code of laws (Kohlberg's levels 3 and 4). From thirteen on, some of the children refer to more abstract rules—a generally agreed-upon social contract or a set of abstract ethical principles (Kohlberg's levels 5 and 6). (After Kohlberg, 1963)

Table 14.1 KOHLBERG'S STAGES OF MORAL REASONING

Stage of moral reasoning	Moral behavior is that which:
Preconventional morality	
Level 1	Avoids punishment
Level 2	Gains reward
Conventional morality	
Level 3	Gains approval and avoids disapproval of others
Level 4	Is defined by rigid codes of "law and order"
Postconventional morality	
Level 5	Is defined by a "social contract" generally agreed upon for the public good
Level 6	Is based on abstract ethical principles that determine one's own moral code

SOURCE: Adapted from Kohlberg, 1969.

matter of *justice,* ultimately based on abstract, rational principles by which all individuals can be treated fairly. As one eleven-year-old boy put it in describing the moral dilemmas posed by Kohlberg: "It's sort of like a math problem with humans." Women in contrast see morality in more concrete, social terms. To them, the focus is on *caring*—on compassion, on human relationships, on special responsibilities to those with whom one is intimately connected. Given these different emphases, one might expect women to score lower than men when moral reasoning is assessed by Kohlberg's yardstick. For as Gilligan sees it, Kohlberg's system has a built-in gender bias in which the moral outlook usually adopted by men is judged to be more advanced than that which is more characteristic of women. Kohlberg calls the highest steps on his moral staircase "postconventional morality," which is defined by just those abstract, rational principles that tend to fit in with the way in which men see the moral order. The moral outlook of women, on the other hand, with their emphasis on helping others, would be judged to be on one of Kohlberg's lower steps. Under the circumstances, it would not be surprising to find that women obtain lower scores on Kohlberg's tests than men (Gilligan, 1982).

Psychologists interested in moral reasoning were quick to ask whether men really do achieve "higher" levels of moral reasoning as defined by Kohlberg. It turns out that they don't. According to several authors, a systematic check of the work performed on the topic reveals no reliable sex differences in moral reasoning on Kohlberg's test; of 108 studies, only 8 showed a superiority of males over females (4 or 5 went in the opposite direction) (Brabeck, 1983; Walker, 1984; but see Baumrind, 1986). But if so, what remains of Gilligan's critique?

Gilligan states that she herself never said that women *can't* reason at Kohlberg's "highest" level; the point is that they usually *choose* not to do so. As she sees it, the female perspective emphasizes human relationships, attachments, and personal responsibilities rather than the abstract conceptions of rights and justice emphasized by the male perspective (Gilligan, 1986). That such a difference in emphases exists is suggested by various empirical findings, including the fact that girls seem to place a greater value on going out of one's way to help other people and show more emotional empathy than do boys (Hoffman, 1977b).

Is either perspective preferable to the other? Virtually everyone agrees that the answer is no and that an appropriate conception of morality must include both justice and compassion. As Kohlberg points out, both of these orientations are built into the New Testament's Golden Rule. That rule is formulated in two ways. One insists on justice: "Do unto others as you would have them do unto you." The other urges care and compassion: "Love thy neighbor as thyself" (Kohlberg and Candee, 1984).

MORAL REASONING AND MORAL CONDUCT

Are stages of moral reasoning related to ethical conduct? To some extent they may be. Thus a number of studies found that delinquents were at a lower stage of moral reasoning than nondelinquents of the same age and IQ. Other studies suggest that individuals at higher, principled levels of moral reasoning are less likely to cheat in an ambiguous situation in which they are unobserved and are more likely to maintain their position against the pressure of other people's views. But taken as a whole, the results suggest that the relation between moral reasoning and moral conduct is far from perfect (Blasi, 1980; Rest, 1983; Gibbs et al., 1986). To some extent, this result is reminiscent of the relatively low correlations between social attitudes and behavior we encountered in a previous chapter (see Chapter 11). Kohlberg's stages (just like attitudes) don't specifically pertain to conduct. They indicate whether an individual *describes* certain moral principles, but they don't tell us much about the individual's actual behavior, which may or may not be ruled by the moral principles he described (for discussion, see Rest, 1984; Blasi, 1984; Kohlberg, Levine, and Hewer, 1984).

THE DEVELOPMENT OF SEX AND GENDER

Thus far, our emphasis has been on social development considered as growth and expansion. But social development is more than that. Like physical and cognitive development, it involves growth, but this growth is not just a matter of increasing size. It is also accompanied by increasing differentiation. For as the child gets older, she becomes increasingly aware of the fact that people differ from each other and from herself. In so doing, she also gains a clearer conception of her own self and of her own personality—what she is really like, in her own eyes and in those of others.

Seen in this light, social development goes hand in hand with the development of a sense of personal identity. One of the most important examples of this is sexual identity—of being male or female and all that goes with it.

Biologically, sexual identity seems simple enough. It may refer to XX vs. XY chromosome pairs or to the external genitals. But what does it mean psychologically? It refers to three issues. One is *gender identity*—our inner sense of whether we are male or female. A second is *gender role*—a whole host of external behavior patterns that a given culture deems appropriate for each sex. A third is *sexual orientation*—the choice of a sexual partner, which is by and large—though of course not always—directed toward the opposite sex. Gender identity, gender role, and sexual orientation are among the most important determinants of a person's social existence.* How do they come about?

Gender Roles

Gender roles pervade all facets of social life. The induction into one or the other of these roles begins with the very first question that is asked when a human being enters the world: "Is it a boy or a girl?" As soon as the answer is supplied, the

Moral reasoning in men and women   The belief that men and women focus on different aspects of morality has ancient roots. A classical example is Sophocles's tragedy Antigone *which revolves around the irreconcilable conflict between Antigone, who insists on burying a slain brother, and her uncle Creon, the king, who issues a decree forbidding anyone from doing so on pain of death. To Antigone, the ultimate moral obligation is to the family; to Creon, it is to the state and its laws. (From a 1982 production at the New York Shakespeare Festival, with F. Murray Abraham and Lisa Banes; photograph by Martha Swope)*

* It has become customary to distinguish between *sex* and *gender*. The term *sex* is generally reserved for aspects of the male-female difference that pertain to reproductive functions (for example, ovaries versus testes, vagina versus penis) or that are likely to be linked to genetic factors (for example, differences in average height and muscular strength). It is also used to designate erotic feelings, inclinations, or practices (for example, heterosexual, homosexual). The term *gender* refers to social or psychological aspects of being seen as a man or woman or regarding oneself to be so. It is one thing to be a male, it is another to be a man. The same holds for being a female and being a woman (Stoller, 1968). A special note about the term *sex difference*. As here employed, this term will be used to designate male-female differences when no presupposition is made about either a biological or a cultural origin.

Social learning of gender roles
(Photograph by Suzanne Arms/ Jeroboam)

process of gender typing begins, and the infant is started along one of two quite different social paths. Some of the patterns of gender typing have probably changed in the wake of the women's movement of the sixties and seventies, but many differences in child rearing persist.

The stereotype is simple enough: The infant is dressed in either pink or blue; the child plays with either dolls or trucks; the adult woman's place is in the home, while the man's is in the marketplace—or the buffalo hunting grounds, or whatever. Society not only has different expectations about what the two sexes should *do*; it also has different conceptions of what they should *be*. In our own culture, the male has been expected to be more aggressive and tough, more restrained emotionally, and more interested in things than in people. The contrasting expectations for females are greater submissiveness, greater emotional expressiveness, and an interest in people rather than in things.

There is no doubt that these gender-role stereotypes have a considerable effect on the way we perceive people, even newborns and very young infants. In one study, mothers of young infants were asked to participate as subjects in an experiment on "how children play." The mothers were introduced to a six-month-old baby, little "Joey" or "Janie," and they were asked to play with him or her for a few minutes. In fact, the six-month-old was a "baby actor" who dressed up as a boy or girl regardless of its actual sex. The results showed that the subjects' behavior depended on whether they thought they were playing with "Joey" or "Janie." To "Joey" they offered toys such as a hammer or a rattle, while "Janie" was invariably presented with a doll. In addition, the subjects handled "Joey" and "Janie" differently physically. In dealing with "Joey," they often tended to bounce "him" about, thus stimulating the whole body. In contrast, their response to "Janie" was gentler and less vigorous (Smith and Lloyd, 1978).

Children soon behave as adults expect them to. Starting at about age one and a half, they begin to show gender-typed differences. By three years of age, they prefer different toys and play with peers of their own sex (Huston, 1983). As they grow older, they become increasingly aware of male and female stereotypes. In one study, both male and female children had to decide whether certain characteristics were more likely in a man or a woman. Over 90 percent of a group of U.S. eleven-year-olds thought that the adjectives *weak, emotional, appreciative, gentle, soft-hearted, affected, talkative, fickle,* and *mild* probably described a woman, and that the adjectives *strong, aggressive, disorderly, cruel, coarse, adventurous, independent, ambitious,* and *dominant* probably described a man. Boys and girls had just about the same gender-role stereotypes (Best et al., 1977).

There is little doubt that many of these gender-role stereotypes are reinforced by parents and peers. When young children play with toys that are judged to be inappropriate—as when a boy plays with a dollhouse—their parents are likely to express disapproval. This is especially so for fathers, who vehemently object to any such behavior in their sons. By and large, girls are allowed more latitude in such matters. A girl can be a tomboy and get away with it; a boy who is a sissy is laughed at (Langlois and Downs, 1980).

Constitutional Factors and Sex Differences

What accounts for the difference in current gender roles? We will consider both constitutional and social factors in an attempt to understand how biology and society conspire to make boys into men and girls into women.

Which of the differences between the sexes are based on constitutional differences? Apart from the obvious anatomical and physiological differences that pertain to reproduction, there are of course differences in average size, strength, and physical endurance. But what about *psychological* differences? There is no doubt that such differences do exist and that some of them fit cultural stereotypes. The question is whether any of these differences—in aggression, independence, emotional expressiveness, social sensitivity, and so on—are biologically given, whether they accompany the sexual anatomy the way menstruation goes along with a female XX chromosome pair.

Before proceeding, note two preliminary cautions. The first is that any psychological difference between the sexes is one of averages. The *average* three-year-old girl seems to be more dependent than her male counterpart; she is more likely to ask for help, to cling, and to seek affection (Emmerich, 1966). But this doesn't mean that the two groups don't overlap. For there are certainly many three-year-old girls who are *less* dependent than many three-year-old boys. After all, the same holds true even for many physical differences. There is no doubt that men are, on the average, taller than women. But it is equally clear that a considerable number of women are taller than many men.

A second caution concerns interpretation. Suppose we obtain a difference. What accounts for it? It might be a difference in biological predispositions. But it may also reflect the society in which the children are raised. In our society—as indeed, in many others—boys are encouraged to be independent, to be "little men," beginning at a very early age, and the obtained difference in dependency may simply reflect this cultural fact. Here, as in so many other areas, nature and nurture are difficult to disentangle.

AGGRESSION

If there is one sex difference that might well be constitutional in origin, at least in part, it is aggression. Males tend to be more active and assertive than females. This difference is apparent from the very outset; male infants are more irritable and physically active than female infants. At two or three, boys are much more likely to engage in rough-and-tumble play and mock fighting than are girls (a difference also seen in apes and monkeys; see Figure 14.13). By four or five, they are more ready to exchange verbal insults and to repel aggression by counterattack. The difference continues into adulthood. While acts of physical violence are relatively rare among both sexes, they are very much more common among men than women; thus among adolescents, arrests for violent crimes occur five times more often among males than females (Johnson, 1979). A similar pattern of results holds in different social classes and in such widely different cultural settings as Ethiopia, India, Kenya, Mexico, Okinawa, and Switzerland (Whiting and Whiting, 1975; Maccoby and Jacklin, 1974, 1980; Parke and Slaby, 1983).

It is probably not surprising that this sex difference is more pronounced for physical aggression than for other forms of aggression. When aggression is measured by rating the degree of verbal hostility or by asking how intense a shock a subject is willing to administer to another person, the difference is not as striking (Hyde, 1981). But even so, it is still quite marked.

The fact that this sex difference in aggression—especially in its physical manifestations—is found so early in life, is observed in so many different cultures, and is also seen in our primate relatives, suggests a constitutional origin—all the more so given the fact that aggressiveness is enhanced by the administration of male sex hormones (see Chapter 9).

PATTERN OF INTELLECTUAL APTITUDES

There is another psychological difference that is often said to be based on biological givens—a different pattern of intellectual abilities. On the average, men do better on tests of spatial and mathematical ability than do women (Figure 14.14; Maccoby and Jacklin, 1974, 1980; Halpern, 1986). Until fairly recently, it was generally believed that the reverse held for verbal abilities. But according to some

14.13 The development of rough-and-tumble play in male and female rhesus monkeys *Roughhouse play in two male and two female rhesus monkeys during the first year of life. The scores are based on both frequency and vigor of this activity, in which monkeys wrestle, roll, or sham bite—all presumably in play, since no one ever gets hurt. Roughhouse play is considerably more pronounced in males than in females, a difference that increases during the first year of life. (After Harlow, 1962)*

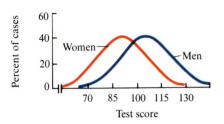

14.14 Sex differences in spatial ability
Results on a spatial-mathematical test which included questions such as "How many times between three and four o'clock do the hands of a clock make a straight line?" The curve plots the percentage of subjects who receive a particular score (with men in blue and women in red). As the curve shows, the men perform better than the women, though the two curves overlap considerably. (Data from Very, 1967, with test scores adjusted by a method called normalization)

recent studies, the superiority of women over men on verbal tasks may be much smaller than had previously been assumed (Hyde and Linn, 1988).

What accounts for the sex difference in cognitive aptitudes, especially in spatial-mathematical abilities? In part, it may simply reflect a difference in the way boys and girls are brought up. But various lines of evidence suggest that social factors are only part of the story. An example is a study of SAT scores in 40,000 male and female adolescents. The investigators found the usual sex difference on spatial and mathematical tasks even when they limited their comparison to boys and girls who had taken the same high school math courses and had expressed the same degree of interest in mathematics (Benbow and Stanley, 1983; Benbow, 1988).

A number of authors feel that such sex differences in mathematical aptitude are ultimately produced by a difference in certain spatial abilities. An example is the ability to visualize objects in space, which is often assessed by asking subjects to rotate a three-dimensional object in their imagination to decide whether it is a rotated version of another figure or whether it is its mirror image. Since a number of branches of mathematics rely on such abilities—for example, geometry, topology, trigonometry, and much of calculus—it does not seem too far-fetched to assume that the sex difference in this ability underlies those in quantitative aptitude and achievement (Burnett, Lane, and Dratt, 1979; Hunt, 1985a; Halpern, 1986).

A number of investigators have searched for a constitutional basis for the male-female difference in spatial abilities. Some believe that the key to the puzzle is in different maturation rates. There is some evidence that children who mature later tend to do better on spatial tests than children who mature earlier. An intriguing hypothesis is that this effect is related to the different functions of the two cerebral hemispheres. As we've previously seen, the right hemisphere is specialized for spatial tasks, the left for language (see Chapter 1). By making the assumption that the right hemisphere matures more slowly than the left, and that neurological maturation comes to an effective end at the time of puberty, we can account for most of the evidence. The usual male-female difference in cognitive orientation would then follow from the fact that girls generally reach puberty before boys. If so, their right (spatial) hemisphere is stopped at an earlier point of neurological organization (Waber, 1977, 1979).

Social Factors and Sex Differences

While some psychological sex differences may have biological roots, even more important is the way in which boys and girls are socialized. We will begin our discussion by taking a second look at the two characteristics for which there is some evidence of a biologically based sex difference: aggression and the discrepancy between spatial and verbal aptitudes. We'll see that even here there is some reasonable evidence that social effects augment and interact with whatever constitutional difference may have been there to start with.

ARE CONSTITUTIONALLY GIVEN DIFFERENCES REALLY CONSTITUTIONAL?

There may well be a greater initial predisposition toward aggression in boys than in girls, but cultural pressures serve to magnify whatever sex differences exist at the outset. Parents will generally allow (and even foster) a degree of aggressiveness in a boy that they would not countenance in a girl. Thus fathers often encourage their sons to fight back when another boy attacks them (Sears, Maccoby, and Levin, 1957). The result of such differential training is that the initial built-in bias toward a sex difference in behavior is considerably exaggerated.

401

Similar considerations may apply to the discrepancy between spatial and verbal aptitudes. In our society, girls are expected to do better in English than in math. This belief is shared by teachers, parents, and pupils, who all help to make it come true. As a result, even the girl who does have the appropriate genetic potential may do worse on spatial and mathematical tests than her ability warrants.

SEX REASSIGNMENT IN CHILDHOOD

The most dramatic examples of the effect of social factors in the determination of gender identity and gender role come from studies of children who at birth were declared to be of one sex but who were later reassigned to the other. This sometimes occurs if the newborn is a **hermaphrodite,** with reproductive organs that are anatomically ambiguous so that they are not exclusively male or female. In such cases, parents and physicians sometimes decide to reverse the initial sex assignment. Corrective surgery is undertaken, the sex is officially reassigned, and the child is raised accordingly. The results suggest that if the reassignment occurs early enough—according to some investigators, up to eighteen months, according to others, up to three or four years—the child adjusts to a remarkable degree. It becomes a he or a she, in part because this is how other people now regard it (Money and Ehrhardt, 1972).

The effects of reassignment   The reports of parents leave no doubt that the child is seen very differently before and after the reassignment. One case involved a child that was genetically male. It had a male's XY chromosome pair and testes. But the external genitals were otherwise more similar to a female's than to a male's. At birth the child was pronounced a boy, but the decision was reversed seventeen months later, at which time there was corrective surgery. According to the parents, there was an immediate change in the way the child was now treated. Even her three-year-old brother reacted differently and showed a "marked tendency to treat her much more gently. Whereas before he was just as likely to stick his foot out to trip her as he went by, he now wants to hold her hand to make sure she doesn't fall" (Money and Ehrhardt, 1972, p. 124).

A critical period for gender identity?   Until fairly recently, most practitioners felt that sex reassignment is virtually impossible after at most four or five years of age. This in turn led to the belief that there is a critical period for the establishment of gender identity (e.g., Money and Ehrhardt, 1972). But this view has been called into question by the discovery of a number of male children with a rare genetic disorder in three rural villages in the Dominican Republic. In the fetal stage, they are relatively insensitive to the effects of androgen. As a result, their external genitals at birth look much like a female's, and so they often are thought to be girls and raised as such. But puberty with its sudden upsurge in male hormone levels brings a dramatic change. The so-called girls develop male genitals, their voice deepens, and their torso becomes muscular. If sex reassignment after age four or five is really as difficult or traumatic as it has been said to be, there ought to be a psychological catastrophe. But in fact, the great majority of these adolescents come to adopt their new male identity with relatively little difficulty. They change their name and take up male occupations. While they are initially anxious about sexual relationships, they ultimately seem to be fairly successful. Thus fifteen out of sixteen such subjects eventually married or lived in common-law relationships (Imperato-McGinley et al., 1974; Imperato-McGinley et al., 1979).

It's hard to know how this surprising finding should be interpreted. The successful change in gender identity may be a result of the massive increase in androgen at puberty. It may also reflect the role of social factors, for these changes are by now accepted by the community and are common enough so that the villagers

Social factors and sex differences   Social effects augment constitutional differences. (Photograph by Roberta Intrater)

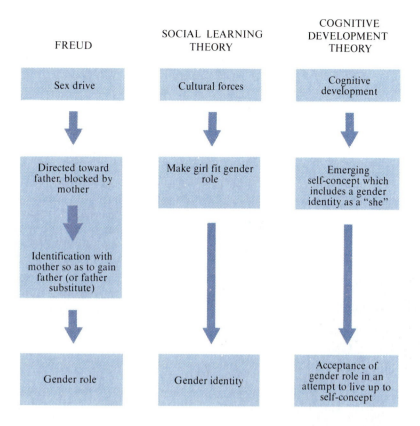

14.15 Three theories of sex typing
The figure summarizes the three major theories of sex typing (for females).

have coined a name for individuals with this condition: *machihembra* (first woman, then man). In any case, the phenomenon is an argument against the view that gender identity is essentially unchangeable after the age of five.

Theories of Gender Typing

Social factors are evidently of great importance in fashioning our sense of being men or women, and they shape our behavior accordingly. But exactly how do these social factors exert their effects? Each of the three main theories of socialization—psychoanalysis, social learning theory, and the cognitive developmental approach—has tried to come up with an answer (see Figure 14.15).

PSYCHOANALYTIC THEORY

According to Freud, the basic mechanism is *identification.* The child models himself or herself on the same-sex parent in an effort to become like him or her. In Freud's view, identification is the end product of the Oedipus conflict, which reaches its culmination at about age five or six. The little boy is unable to cope with the mounting anxieties aroused by his sexual longing for the mother and his resentment of the father. He therefore represses both incestuous love and patricidal hate. But his renunciation of the mother is only for the time being. He identifies with the all-powerful father in an effort to propitiate him (if I am like him, he won't want to hurt me) and also in the hope that he will thereby gain the mother's sexual love in some blissful future (if I am like him, she will love me). By means of this identification process, which Freud thought to be largely unconscious, the boy incorporates many aspects of the father's personality, including those that

403

pertain to gender role. By a roughly analogous process the little girl comes to identify with her mother.

SOCIAL LEARNING THEORY

A very different position is held by social learning theorists, who argue that gender role and gender identity do not arise from the sex drive. In their view, children behave in gender-appropriate ways for the simplest of possible reasons: They are rewarded if they do so and are punished if they don't. For the most part, they learn what each sex is supposed to do by *imitation.* But whom shall they imitate? They quickly discover that they must choose a model (usually the parent) of their own sex. The girl imitates her mother and is rewarded for rocking the baby (for the time being a doll may have to do), for prettying herself up, for becoming mother's little helper. The boy who imitates these maternal acts will be ridiculed and called a sissy. He will do better by imitating his father, who rewards him for doing boylike things (Mischel, 1970).

According to this view, the sex drive has little to do with the matter, and anatomy enters only indirectly. The penis and vagina are relevant only in determining whether the child is a boy or a girl in the parents' eyes. From this point on, differential rewards and punishments do the rest.

COGNITIVE DEVELOPMENTAL THEORY

Yet another proposal was offered by Lawrence Kohlberg, who regarded gender typing in the context of cognitive development. Kohlberg's emphasis was on the child's emerging awareness of his or her gender identity—the sense of being male or female. While social learning theory emphasizes what a boy and girl must learn to *do* to fit the role of man or woman, Kohlberg focuses on what a boy and girl must *understand* to recognize that they belong to the category man or woman (Kohlberg, 1966).

According to Kohlberg, the concept of gender is quite vague until the child is five or six years old. The four-year-old has only a shadowy notion of what the categories "male" and "female" mean. He has no real comprehension of how these categories pertain to genital anatomy. When presented with dolls that have either male or female genitals and either short or long hair and are asked to tell which are the boys and which the girls, preschoolers generally decide on the basis of hair length (McConaghy, 1979). A related phenomenon is the fact that four-year-olds don't really understand that gender is one of the permanent and (for all intents and purposes) unchangeable attributes of the self. Children develop a sense of gender identity by about age three. But it takes them another two years or so to achieve the concept of *gender constancy*—the recognition that being male and female is irrevocable. When shown a picture of a girl, four-year-olds say that she could be a boy if she wanted to, or if she wore a boy's haircut or wore a boy's clothes. But in Kohlberg's view, the problem is not with gender as such. For the majority of four-year-olds also say that a cat could be a dog if it wanted to, or if its whiskers were cut off. This suggests that the lack of gender constancy is just another reflection of the preschooler's failure to comprehend the underlying constancies of the universe. After all, children at this stage of cognitive development do not conserve liquid quantity, mass, or number (see Chapter 13).

According to Kohlberg, the child's identification with the parent of the same sex *follows* the acquisition of gender identity. Once they recognize that they are boys or girls, they will try to live up to their sense of gender identity, to act in a manner that befits their own self-concept. They will now look for appropriate models—and the most readily available ones are their mothers and fathers—that can show them how to get better and better at being a male or a female.

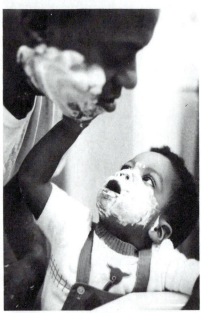

Male and female models (Top: *photograph by Suzanne Szasz.* Bottom: *photograph by Burk Uzzle/Woodfin Camp)*

Sexual Orientation

The majority of men and women are *heterosexual:* They seek a partner of the opposite sex. But for a significant minority, the sexual orientation is otherwise; their erotic and romantic feelings are directed primarily or exclusively toward members of their own sex. They are *homosexual,* or to use the currently popular terms, they are *gay men* and *lesbians.**

THE INCIDENCE OF HOMOSEXUALITY

According to a number of surveys made in the United States, about 4 percent of American males are predominantly homosexual (Kinsey, Pomeroy, and Martin, 1948; Gebhard, 1972). The comparable incidence of exclusive homosexuality among American women seems to be lower—about 1 to 2 percent (Kinsey et al., 1953; Gebhard, 1972). Clearly, a substantial number of men and women are erotically and romantically oriented toward a partner of their own sex, despite the fact that our society generally stigmatizes such behavior. This cultural taboo is by no means universal. According to one cross-cultural survey, two-thirds of the societies studied regarded homosexuality as normal and acceptable, at least for some persons and for some age groups (Ford and Beach, 1951). In a number of South Pacific cultures, homosexuality among young men is actually prescribed until they are married (Davenport, 1965; Stoller and Herdt, 1985). In a number of American Indian tribes, male homosexuals, or *berdaches,* were viewed with respect and sometimes reverence: They were regarded as persons with special spiritual and mystical gifts who sometimes took on the roles of shamans and visionaries (Williams, 1986). And our own Western heritage includes historical periods in which homosexual relations were glorified, as in classical Greece where Pericles, the great Athenian statesman, was regarded as a bit odd because he was *not* attracted to beautiful boys.

Homosexuality underlines the fact that sexual orientation, gender identity, and gender role are in principle independent. Virtually all gay males think of themselves as men and are so regarded by others; the analogous point holds for lesbians (Marmor, 1975).

WHAT CAUSES HOMOSEXUALITY?

What leads to homosexuality? So far, there is no clear answer. It may well be that this question simply represents the other side of the question, "What leads to heterosexuality?" This second question is rarely asked because most people take the heterosexual preference for granted. Yet if we knew how to explain the origin of heterosexuality, we would probably be much closer to an understanding of how homosexuality comes about.

Stating the two questions in this parallel form may help us see another point. People sometimes ask whether gay men and lesbians can somehow be transformed into heterosexual men and women.[†] The answer seems to be that such a

Homosexual behavior in antiquity
Among the ancient Greeks homosexual relations between men were widely practiced and accepted, as the mural from the Tomb of the Diver (c. 480 B.C.–470 B.C.), found in what was a Greek settlement in southern Italy, suggests. (Courtesy National Archaeological Museum, Paestum, Italy)

---

* The term *gay* is sometimes used as a generic adjective that can apply to both men and women, though this usage may be deplored by some lesbian authors.

† One may well ask why one would want to change a person's sexual orientation in the first place. One reason is an old and now quite discredited psychiatric view which holds that homosexuality is a pathological condition (e.g., Bieber et al., 1965). This position has long been abandoned, as indicated by the official stance of the American Psychiatric Association which no longer lists homosexuality as a psychiatric disorder.

A lesbian couple

(Top: *Photograph by Roberta Intrater;*
Bottom: *photograph by Michael
Nichols/Magnum*)

shallow human relationships. In early middle age, she has to develop a sense of personal creativity that extends beyond her own self. This includes a concern for others, for her work, for the community of which she is a part. And toward the end of life, there is a final crisis during which she has to come to terms with her own life and accept it for what it was, with a sense of integrity rather than of despair. Erikson eloquently sums up this final reckoning: "It is the acceptance of one's own and only life cycle as something that had to be and that, by necessity, permitted of no substitutes. . . . healthy children will not fear life if their elders have integrity enough not to fear death" (Erikson, 1963, pp. 268–69).

RECENT ATTEMPTS TO FIND COMMON STAGES

Erikson's developmental scheme is a literary and moving account of the human odyssey through life, but in what sense is it a true description? Are the crises he listed *the* crises through which all of us must pass, and are their characteristics what he described them to be? A number of modern investigators have studied adults at various stages of their lives to find out what, if any, patterns are common to a given time of life. By and large, most of them have described a number of developmental periods that resemble some of Erikson's "ages of man" (Gould, 1978; Levinson, 1978). Others have tried to find similarities between youthful patterns and adult fulfillment when the same person is interviewed some thirty years later (Vaillant, 1977; see Chapter 16).

A stage of adult development that has received considerable attention from both Erikson and later authors is the so-called "mid-life transition" (which sometimes amounts to a mid-life crisis), in which the individual reappraises what she has done with her life thus far and may reevaluate her marriage and her career. It is a period when the individual begins to see physical changes that show that the summer of life is over and its autumn has begun, a recognition that may occur earlier in women than in men (in part, because of the psychological impact of menopause). There is a shift in the way one thinks about time, from "How long have I lived?" to "How much time do I have left?" Some investigators point out that the middle-aged person is in the middle in more than one sense as she observes her children grow up and her own parents age and die:

It is as if there are two mirrors before me, each held at a partial angle. I see part of myself in my mother who is growing old, and part of her in me. In the other mirror I see part of myself in my daughter. . . . (Neugarten and Datan, quoted in Colarusso and Nemiroff, 1981, p. 124)

HOW UNIVERSAL ARE THE STAGES OF ADULT DEVELOPMENT?

There is enough consistency in the results obtained by various investigators of adult development to suggest that the stages and transitions they describe apply fairly widely to people in our time and place. But are they universal? When we considered various stage theories of child development, we asked whether these stages occur in all cultures. The same question can be asked about adult development. Is there a mid-life transition among the Arapesh? Does a Tchambuli man of fifty go through an agonizing reappraisal of what he's done with his life to date? If the answer is no, then we have to ask ourselves what the various stages described by Erikson and other students of the adult life span really are.

Thus far, there is little concrete evidence one way or the other, so we can only guess. Certain adult milestones are clearly biological. In all cultures, humans reach puberty, mate, have children, begin to age, go through female menopause or male climacteric, age still further, and finally die. But the kind of crises that

(Photograph by Eve Arnold, Magnum)

confront persons at different points of the life cycle surely depend on the society in which they live.

An example of the effect of social conditions on adult crises is the transition into old age. Over a century ago in the United States, different generations often lived close together as part of an extended family system. There was much less segregation by age than there is now; children, parents, and grandparents frequently lived under the same roof or close to each other in the same neighborhood. In times of economic hardship, older people contributed to the family's resources even when they were too old to work—by caring for the children of working mothers, helping with the housekeeping, and so on. But today, the elderly have no such recognized family role. They usually live apart, are effectively segregated from the rest of society, are excluded from the work force, and have lost their role as esteemed advisers. Given these changes, it follows that the transition into old age today is quite different from what it was 150 years ago. People still age as they did then—although the proportion of persons who live into their seventies has increased radically—but they view aging differently (Hareven, 1978).

Facts of this sort suggest that various aspects of the stages proposed by students of adult development may be quite specific to our society and can therefore not be said to be universal. But if so, can we say anything about the life cycle that goes beyond the narrow specifics of our own time and social condition? Perhaps the best suggestion comes from a lecture by Erikson in which he tried to define adulthood:

> . . . In youth you find out what you *care to do* and who you *care to be.* . . . In young adulthood you learn whom you *care to be with.* . . . In adulthood, however, you learn what and whom you can *take care of.* . . . (Erikson, 1974, p. 124)

The ages of man Jacob Blessing the Sons of Joseph *by Rembrandt, 1656 (Copyright by Staatliche, Kunstsammlungen Kassel. Photograph by M. Busing)*

Seen in this light, the later phases of the life cycle can perhaps be regarded as the culmination of the progressive expansion of the social world that characterizes the entire course of social development from early infancy on. In a way, it is a final expansion in which our concern turns from ourselves to others and from our own present to their future (and in some cases, the future of all humankind).

This may or may not be a good description of what genuine adulthood *is*. But it seems like an admirable prescription for what it *ought* to be.

SUMMARY

1. The infant's *socialization* begins with the first human bond he forms—his *attachment* to his mother (or other caregiver). Studies of infant humans and monkeys indicate that this attachment is not caused by the fact that the mother feeds them, but rather because she feels so "comforting." A separation from the mother generally leads to *separation anxiety*.

2. Developmental psychologists have tried to assess the quality of the child's attachment to the mother by observing the behavior of infants and young children in the "Strange Situation." There is some evidence that the quality of attachment at about fifteen months of age predicts behavior two years later, but there is some controversy as to whether this reflects a long-term effect of the early mother-child relationship or is based on other factors, such as persisting patterns in the mother-child relationship or some continuity of childhood temperament.

3. Some theorists have proposed that the attachment to the mother can only be formed during a *sensitive period* in early life, In part, this position derives from work on *imprinting* in birds. According to this view, if such an early attachment is not formed, later social development may be seriously impaired, as indicated by studies of motherless monkeys and children reared in institutions. But later work on monkey isolates and adopted children suggests that this impairment is not necessarily irrevocable.

4. The process of *socialization* continues with child rearing by the parents. Some important differences in the way children are reared depend on the dominant values of the culture of which the parents are a part. Modern attempts to explain the mechanisms that underlie socialization include *social learning theory,* which emphasizes *modeling,* and *cognitive developmental theory,* which emphasizes the role of understanding as opposed to imitation.

5. The evidence indicates that different modes of weaning or toilet training have little or no long-term effects. What seems to matter instead is the general home atmosphere, as shown by the effects of *autocratic, permissive,* and *authoritative-reciprocal* patterns of child rearing. On the other hand, how the parents treat the child is partially determined by the child's own characteristics, as suggested by studies on infant *temperament.*

6. One aspect of moral conduct concerns the *internalization* of prohibitions. According to some theorists, punishment is more likely to lead to such internalization if the threatened punishment fits the principle of *minimal sufficiency.* Another aspect of moral conduct involves altruistic acts. Studies of *empathy* suggest that some precursors of altruism may be present in early infancy.

7. The study of *moral reasoning* has been strongly affected by Piaget's cognitive developmental approach. An influential example is Kohlberg's analysis of progressive stages in moral reasoning. According to a later critique by Carol Gilligan, there are some important gender differences in moral orientation, with men emphasizing justice and women stressing human relationships and compassion.

8. Socialization plays a role in determining various senses of being male or female, including *gender identity, gender role,* and *sexual orientation.*

9. Certain psychological differences between the sexes may be based on biological differences. One is *aggression,* which tends to be more pronounced in men. Another is a tendency for males to perform better on spatial tests of mental ability than females do. Such biologically based differences—if any—are undoubtedly magnified by socially imposed gender roles. The importance of such roles is illustrated by the effects of *sex reassignment* in childhood.

10. Each of the three main theories of socialization—psychoanalysis, social learning theory, and cognitive developmental theory—tries to explain how social factors shape our sense of being male or female. Psychoanalysis asserts that the basic mechanism is *identification.* Social learning theory proposes that it is *imitation* of the parent of the same sex. Cognitive developmental theorists believe that identification comes after the child acquires gender identity, which presupposes an understanding of *gender constancy.* Some of these theoretical differences grow out of differences of emphasis. Psychoanalysis focuses on sexual orientation, social learning theory concentrates on gender role, and cognitive developmental theory is most interested in gender identity.

11. In the past, some psychiatrists regarded homosexuality as a psychological disorder, but this view is now discredited. Its causes are still unclear. Constitutional factors probably play a major role, but some aspects of early childhood learning may also be relevant.

12. Development continues after childhood is past. Some theorists, notably Erik Erikson, have tried to map later stages of development. One such stage is *adolescence,* which marks the transition into adulthood.

PART V

Individual Differences

People are different. They vary in bodily characteristics such as height, weight, strength, and hair color. They also vary along many psychological dimensions. They may be proud or humble, adventurous or timid, gregarious or withdrawn, intelligent or dull—the list of psychological distinctions is very large. Thus far such individual differences have not been our main concern. Our emphasis has been on attempts to find general psychological laws that apply to all persons, whether in physiological function, perception, memory, learning, or social behavior. To be sure, we have occasionally dealt with individual differences, as in the discussions of handedness, color blindness, and variations in imagery. But our focus was not on these differences as such; it was rather on what they could tell us about people in general—on how color blindness could help to explain the underlying mechanisms of color vision or how variations in child rearing might help us understand some aspects of socialization. In effect, our concern was with the nature of humankind, not with particular men and women.

We now change our emphasis and consider individual differences as a topic in its own right. We will first deal with the measurement of psychological attributes, specifically intelligence and personality traits. We will then turn to the discussion of psychopathology and attempts to treat it, a field in which the fact that people are in some ways different—sometimes all too different—is starkly clear.

CHAPTER 15

Intelligence: Its Nature and Measurement

In twentieth-century industrialized society, especially in the United States, the description of individual differences is a flourishing enterprise that has produced a multitude of psychological tests to assess various personal characteristics, especially those that pertain to intellectual aptitude. This effort is a relatively recent phenomenon, for until the turn of the century most psychologists preferred to study the "generalized human mind" without worrying about the fact that different minds are not identical.

As we will see, the interest in individual differences grew in part from an effort to apply evolutionary ideas to humanity itself. But even more important was the social climate of the times, which provided a fertile soil for such concerns. The study of individual differences makes little sense in a society in which each person's adult role is fully determined by the social circumstances of his or her birth. In a caste society there is no need for vocational counselors or personnel managers. In such a society farmers beget farmers, soldiers beget soldiers, and princes beget princes; there is no point in administering mental tests to assist in educational selection or job placement. The interest in *human differences* arises only if such differences matter, if there is a social system that will accommodate them.

In a complex, industrialized society like our own, with its many different socioeconomic niches and some mobility across them, we have the precondition for a systematic assessment of human characteristics. Such a society will try to find a means, however imperfect, for selecting the proper person to occupy the proper niche.

Mental tests were meant to supply this means. They were devised as an instrument to help in educational and occupational selection, for use in various forms of personal guidance and diagnosis. As such, they are often regarded as one of the major contributions of psychology to the world of practical affairs. However, for this very reason, the discussion of test results and applications necessarily touches upon social and political issues that go beyond the usual confines of scientific discourse. Under the circumstances, it is hardly surprising that some of the ques-

Francis Galton (1822–1911), a pioneer in the study of individual differences. (Courtesy National Library of Medicine)

tions raised by testing, especially intelligence testing, are often debated in an emotionally charged atmosphere. Should a student be denied admission to a college because of his or her scholastic aptitude test score? Are such tests fair to disadvantaged ethnic or racial groups? Are scores on such tests determined by heredity, by environment, by both? This chapter will not be able to provide definitive answers to all of these questions. Some involve judgments about social and political matters; others hinge on as yet unresolved issues of fact. Our primary purpose is to provide a background against which such questions can be evaluated.

MENTAL TESTS

Mental tests come in different varieties. Some are tests of **achievement;** they measure what an individual can do *now,* his present knowledge and competence in a given area—how well he understands computer language or how well he can draw. Other tests are tests of **aptitude;** they predict what an individual will be able to do *later,* given the proper training and the right motivation. An example is a test of mechanical aptitude, which tries to determine the likelihood that an individual will do well as an engineer after an appropriate training period. **Intelligence tests** are sometimes considered as tests of a very general cognitive aptitude, including the ability to benefit from schooling. Still another kind of test is a **test of personality,** which tries to assess an individual's characteristic behavior dispositions—whether she is generally outgoing or withdrawn, placid or moody, and so on.

We will begin our discussion by considering the nature of mental tests in general, regardless of what in particular they try to measure. But before we can describe the reasoning that underlies the construction and use of such tests, we must first take a detour to look at the general problem of variability and its measurement.

The Study of Variation

The study of how individuals vary from each other grew up in close association with the development of statistical methods. Until the nineteenth century, the term *statistics* meant little more than the systematic collection of various state records (*state*-istics) such as birth and death rates or the physical measurements of army recruits. In poring over such figures, the Belgian scientist Adolphe Quetelet (1796–1874) saw that many of them fell into a pattern. From this, he determined the **frequency distribution** of various sets of observations, that is, the frequency with which individual cases are distributed over different intervals along some measure. For example, he plotted the frequency distribution of the chest expansion of Scottish soldiers, noting the number of cases that fell into various intervals, from 33 to 33.9 inches, 34 to 34.9 inches, and so on (Table 15.1).

VARIABILITY

Two facts are immediately apparent. The scores tend to cluster around a central value. One of the most common measures of this central tendency is the **mean,** or average, which is obtained by summing all of the values and dividing by the total number of cases. But the clustering tendency is by no means perfect, for there is variability around the average. All Scottish soldiers are not alike, whether in their chest sizes or anything else. An important measure of variability in a distribution

Table 15.1 QUETELET'S DISTRIBUTIONS OF CHEST MEASURES OF SCOTTISH SOLDIERS

Measures of the chest in inches	Number of men per 10,000
33	4
34	31
35	141
36	322
37	732
38	1,305
39	1,867
40	1,882
41	1,628
42	1,148
43	645
44	160
45	87
46	38
47	7
48	2

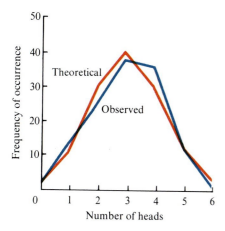

15.1   Theoretical and observed distribution of number of heads in 128 throws of six coins   *(After Anastasi, 1958)*

is the *variance (V)*. This is computed by taking the difference between each score and the mean, squaring this difference, and then taking the average of these squared differences. For many purposes, a more useful measure of variability is the *standard deviation (SD)* which is simply the square root of the variance.*

Quetelet's main contribution was the realization that, when put on a graph, the frequency distributions of various human physical attributes have a characteristic bell-shaped form. This symmetrical curve approximates the so-called *normal curve* which had already been studied by mathematicians in connection with games of chance. The normal curve describes the probability of obtaining certain combinations of chance events. Suppose, for example, that someone has the patience to throw six coins for over a hundred trials. How often will the coins fall to yield six heads, or five, four, three, two, one, or none? The expected distribution is shown in Figure 15.1, which also indicates what happened when a dedicated statistician actually performed the experiment. As more and more coins are thrown on any one trial, the expected distribution will approach the normal curve (Figure 15.2).

According to Quetelet, the variability found in many human characteristics can be explained in similar terms. He believed that nature aims at an ideal value —whether of height, weight, or chest size—but that it generally misses the mark, sometimes falling short and sometimes overshooting. The actual value of an attribute such as height depends upon a host of factors, some of which lead to an increase, others to a decrease. But each of these factors is independent, and their operation is determined by chance. Thus nature is in effect throwing a multitude of coins to determine any one person's height. Each head adds, say, a millimeter to the average, and each tail subtracts one. The result is a frequency distribution of heights that approximates a normal curve.

VARIABILITY AND DARWIN

After Darwin published his *Origin of Species,* variability within a species was suddenly considered in a new perspective. Darwin showed that it provides the raw material on which natural selection can work. Suppose that the average finch on a particular island has a fairly long and narrow beak. There is some variability; a few finches have beaks that are shorter and wider. These few would be able to crack certain hard seeds that the other finches could not open. If these hard seeds suddenly become the primary foodstuffs in the habitat, the short-beaked finches might find themselves at a reproductive advantage. They would outlive and thus

* For a fuller description of these and other statistical matters which will be referred to in this chapter, see the Appendix, "Statistics: The Collection, Organization, and Interpretation of Data."

15.2   The normal curve   *(A) The probability of the number of heads that will occur in a given number of coin tosses.(B) When the number of coins tossed approaches infinity, the resulting distribution is the normal curve. The fact that this curve describes the distribution of many physical and mental attributes suggests that these attributes are affected by a multitude of independent factors, some pulling one way and some another.*

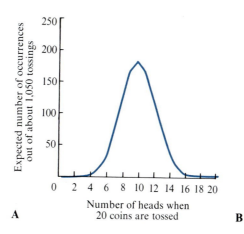

A

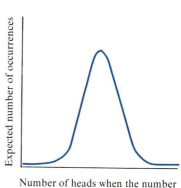

B

outbreed their long-beaked comrades and eventually a new species might be born (or more precisely, hatched). Seen in this light, variability is far from being an error of nature that missed the ideal mark as Quetelet had thought. On the contrary, it is the very stuff of which evolution is made (Figure 15.3).

CORRELATION

Could this line of reasoning be applied to variations in human characteristics? It might, if these characteristics could be shown to be hereditary, at least in part. This assumption seemed reasonable enough for physical attributes of the kind that Quetelet had tabulated, but is it appropriate for mental characteristics such as intellectual ability? A half-cousin of Darwin's, Francis Galton (1822–1911) spent much of his life trying to prove that it is. Most of the subsequent work in the area rests on the statistical methods he and his followers developed to test his assertions.

An important part of Galton's program called for the assessment of similarity among relatives. The trouble is that such relationships are not perfect. Children tend to be like their parents, but only to some extent. The problem was to find some measure of this relationship. Put more generally, the question was how one could determine whether a variation along one characteristic could be accounted for by a variation along another. The two characteristics might be the height of a father and that of his son. They might also be characteristics within the same individual such as a person's height and the same person's weight.

Take as an example an individual's weight. How is this related to his height? The first step is to construct a *scatter diagram* in which one axis represents weight and the other height. Each person will be represented by one point corresponding to his position along the weight and height axes (see Figure 15.4A). Inspection of the scatter diagram reveals that the two variables are related, for they covary: that is, as height goes up, so does weight. But this covariation, or *correlation,* is far from perfect. We can draw a *line of best fit* through the points in the scatter diagram, which allows us to make the best prediction of a person's weight given his height. But this prediction is relatively crude, for there is considerable variability around the line of best fit.

Galton and his students developed a mathematical expression that summarizes both the direction and the strength of the relationship between the two measures. This is the *correlation coefficient* which varies between + 1.00 and − 1.00 and is symbolized by the letter *r.* The plus or minus sign of the correlation coefficient indicates the direction of the relationship. In the case of height and

15.3   Darwin's finches   *In 1835 Charles Darwin visited the Galapagos Islands in the Pacific Ocean and observed a number of different species of finches. They eventually provided an important stimulus to his theory of natural selection, as he supposed that "one species had been taken and modified for different ends." The figure shows two of these finches. One has a rather narrow beak and is a woodpecker-like bird that lives in trees and feeds on insects. The other is a large-beaked seed-eater. (After Lack, 1953)*

15.4   Correlation   *(A) A scatter diagram of the heights and weights of 50 male undergraduates. Note that the points fall within an ellipse which indicates the variation around the line of best fit. The correlation for these data was +.70. (Technically, there are two lines of best fit. One predicts weight from height; the other predicts height from weight. The line shown on the diagram is an average of these two.) (B) A scatter diagram of the test performances of 70 students in an introductory psychology course. The diagram plots number of errors in a midterm against number of correct answers on the final. The correlation was −.53. If errors (or correct answers) had been plotted on both exams, the correlation would of course have been positive.*

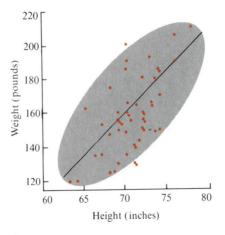

A

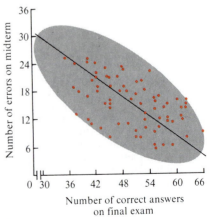

B

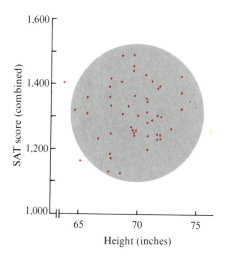

15.5 A correlation of zero *A scatter diagram of the scholastic aptitude scores and the heights of 50 undergraduate males. Not surprisingly, there was no relation as shown by the fact that the points fall within a circle. The correlation was +.05, which for all essential purposes is equivalent to zero.*

weight this direction is positive: as height increases so does weight (15.4A). With other measures, the direction is negative: as the score on one measure increases, the score on the other declines (Figure 15.4B).

The strength of the correlation is expressed by its absolute value (that is, its value regardless of sign). A correlation of $r = .00$ indicates no relation whatsoever. An example might be the relation between a student's height and his scholastic aptitude score. If we plot the scatter diagram, the points will be arranged in a circle. There is no way of predicting a student's scholastic aptitude from his height, so there is no single line of best fit (Figure 15.5).

As the absolute value of r increases, the dots on the scatter diagram form an ellipse around the line of best fit. As the correlation goes up, the ellipse gets thinner and thinner. The thinner the ellipse, the less error there is as we try to predict the value of one variable (say, weight) when given the value of the other (say, height). When the absolute value of r reaches 1.00 (whether $+1.00$ or -1.00), the ellipse finally becomes a straight line. There is no more variation at all around the line of best fit; the correlation is perfect and prediction is error-free. However, such perfect correlations are virtually never encountered in actual practice; even in the physical sciences there is bound to be some error of measurement.

While correlations are a useful index of the degree to which two variables are related, they have a limitation. The fact that two variables are correlated says nothing about the underlying causal relationship between them. Sometimes, there is none at all. Examples are correlations that are produced by some third factor. The number of umbrellas one sees on a given day is surely correlated with the number of people who wear raincoats. A Martian observing the human scene might conclude that umbrella-carrying causes raincoat-wearing or vice versa; our own earthly wisdom tells us that both are caused by rain.

Evaluating Mental Tests

While the correlation techniques developed by Galton and his students were initially meant to investigate the extent to which relatives resemble each other, they were soon extended to other problems. One important application was to mental testing for which they provided the underlying statistical methodology.

A mental test is meant to be an objective yardstick to assess some psychological trait or capacity on which people differ (for example, artistic and mechanical aptitude; see Figure 15.6). But how can one tell that a given test actually accomplishes this objective?

RELIABILITY

One important criterion of the adequacy of a test is its *reliability*, the consistency with which it measures what it measures. Consider a spring balance. If the spring is in good condition, the scale will give virtually identical readings when the same object is repeatedly weighed. But if the spring is gradually losing its elasticity, repeated weighings will give different values. If it does this, we throw away the scale. It has proved to be unreliable.

The same logic underlies test reliability. One way of assessing this is by administering the same test twice to the same group of subjects. The correlation between test and retest scores will then be an index of the test's reliability.

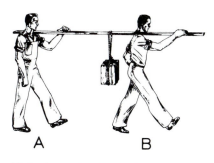

15.6 A test of mechanical comprehension *One of the items asks, "Which man carries more weight?" (Sample item from the Bennett Test of Mechanical Comprehension; courtesy The Psychological Corporation)*

423

One trouble with the *test-retest method* is that the performance on the retest may be affected by what the subject learned the first time around. For example, some people may look up the answers to questions they missed. To avoid this problem, testers sometimes develop *alternative forms* of a test; if the two alternate forms are exactly equivalent, reliability can be assessed by using one form on one occasion and another on a second. Since any two halves of a single test can be considered "alternate forms," reliability is often measured by the *split-half technique* (correlating subjects' scores on, say, all of the odd items with their scores on all of the even items). If both halves correlate highly, we consider the test reliable; if they don't, we regard it as unreliable.

Most standard psychological tests now in use have *reliability coefficients* (that is, test-retest or split-half correlations) in the .90s or in the high .80s. Tests with lower reliability are of little practical use in making decisions about individuals.

VALIDITY

High reliability alone does not guarantee that a test is a good measuring rod. Even more critical is a test's *validity,* which is most simply defined as the extent to which it measures what it is supposed to measure.

Again consider the spring scale. If the spring is made of good steel, the scale may be highly reliable. But suppose someone decides to use this scale to measure *length.* This bizarre step will produce an instrument of high reliability but virtually no validity. It measures some attribute very precisely and consistently but that attribute is not length. As a test of length, the scale is invalid.

In the case of the scale, we can readily define the physical attribute that it is meant to measure and this lets us assess validity. But how can we define the psychological attribute that a mental test tries to assess?

Predictive validity   One approach is to consider the test as a *predictor* of future performance. If a test claims to measure scholastic aptitude, a score on that test should predict later school or college performance. The same holds for tests of vocational aptitude, which ought to predict how persons later succeed on the job. One index of a test's validity is the success with which it makes such predictions. This is usually measured by the correlation between the test score and some appropriate *criterion.* For scholastic aptitude, a common criterion is the grade-point average the student later attains. For vocational aptitude, it is some measure of later job proficiency. For example, aptitude tests for salespersons might be validated against their sales records.

Validity coefficients (that is, the correlations between test scores and criteria) for scholastic aptitude are generally in the neighborhood of .50 or .60, which means that the prediction is far from perfect. This is hardly surprising. For one thing, the tests probably don't provide a perfect index of one's "capacity" (ignoring for the time being just what this capacity might be). But even if they did, we would not expect validity coefficients of 1.00, for we all know that school grades depend on many factors in addition to ability (for example, motivation).

Construct validity   Predictive validity is not the only way of assessing whether a test measures what it claims to measure. Another approach is to establish that the test has *construct validity* (Cronbach and Meehl, 1955). This is the extent to which the performance on the test fits into a theoretical scheme—or construct—about the attribute the test tries to measure. For example, suppose someone tries to develop a test to assess behavioral tendencies toward depression (see Chapter 17). The validity of such a test would not be established by correlating it with any *one* factor, such as feelings of helplessness. Instead, the investigator would try to relate the test to a whole network of hypotheses about depression. To the extent that the results do indeed fit into this larger pattern, they confer construct validity on the test.

STANDARDIZATION

To evaluate a test, we need one further item of information in addition to its reliability and validity. We have to know something about the group on which the test was **standardized.** A person's test score by itself provides little information. It can, however, be interpreted by comparing it with the scores obtained by other people. These other scores provide the **norms** against which an individual's test scores are evaluated. To obtain these norms, the test is first administered to a large sample of the population on which the test is to be used. This initial group is the **standardization sample.**

A crucial requirement in using tests is the comparability between the subjects who are tested and the standardization sample that yields the norms. If these two are drawn from different populations, the test scores may not be interpretable. Consider a scholastic aptitude test standardized on ten-year-olds in 1920. Its norms will surely not apply today to ten-year-olds whose schooling undoubtedly differs in many ways. There will be no way of evaluating a particular test score, for the comparison is with ten-year-olds today rather than seventy years ago.

A similar issue crops up when tests are administered to persons whose cultural backgrounds are different from that of the standardization sample. This problem is by no means hypothetical; examples are the cultural differences between ethnic and racial groups and between rural and urban dwellers. Some test items clearly discriminate in favor of one group or another. When urban schoolchildren were asked questions like "What is the largest river in the United States?" or "How can banks afford to pay interest on the money you deposit?" they did considerably better than rural schoolchildren of the same age. The difference was reversed for questions like "Name a vegetable that grows above ground" or "Why does seasoned wood burn more easily than green wood?" (Shimberg, 1929).

Using Tests for Selection

Suppose we have a test of good reliability and reasonable validity. How can it be used? One important application in our society is as a selection device. A well-known example is an aptitude test for pilot training developed by the Army Air Force during World War II. A large number of separate subtests were constructed for this purpose, including tests of motor coordination, reaction time, perceptual skills, and general intellectual ability. These subtests were administered to over 185,000 men who went through pilot training. The initial question was how each of these subtests correlated with the criterion—success or failure in training. The scores of each subtest were then weighted to produce a composite score that gave the best estimate of the criterion. The use of this composite pilot aptitude test score led to an appreciable improvement in trainee selection. Without the test, the failure rate was 24 percent. By using the test, the failure rate was cut to 10 percent. This was accomplished by setting a **cutoff score** on the test below which no applicant was accepted (Flanagan, 1947).

Given a reasonable validity coefficient, the use of tests evidently helps to reduce the number of selection errors. The overall number of such errors declines as the validity coefficient of the test increases. But some errors will always be present, for validity coefficients are never at 1.00; in fact, most vocational aptitude testers count themselves lucky if they manage to obtain validity correlations of .40 or .50.

INTELLIGENCE TESTING

What is *intelligence?* In a crude sense, of course, we all have some notion of what the term refers to. The dictionary is full of adjectives that distinguish levels of intellectual functioning such as *bright* and *dull, quick-witted* and *slow.* Intelligence tests try to get at some attribute (or attributes) that roughly corresponds to such distinctions. But the test constructors did not begin with a precise conception of what it was they wanted to test. There was no consensus as to a definition of intelligence, and those definitions that were offered were usually so broad and all-inclusive as to be of little use. Intelligence was said to be a capacity, but what is it a capacity for? Is it for learning, for transfer, for abstract thinking, or judgment, comprehension, reason, or perhaps all of these? There was no agreement. Edward Thorndike suggested a first approximation according to which intelligence was to be defined "as the quality of mind . . . in respect to which Aristotle, Plato, Thucydides, and the like, differed most from Athenian idiots of their day." While this seemed sensible enough, it hardly went beyond the intuitive notions people had long before psychologists appeared on the scene (Thorndike, 1924).

Measuring Intelligence

Given the difficulty in defining intelligence, devising tests for this hard-to-define attribute was an undertaking of a rather different sort from constructing a specialized aptitude test for prospective pilots. The pilot aptitude test has a rather clear-cut validity criterion. But what is the best validity criterion for intelligence tests? Since the nature of intelligence is unclear, we can't be sure of what the appropriate validity criterion might be.

Our theoretical ignorance notwithstanding, we do have intelligence tests, and many of them. They were developed to fulfill certain practical needs. We may not understand exactly what it is that they assess, but the test consumers—schools, armies, industries—want them even so. The fact is that for many practical purposes these tests work quite well.

TESTING INTELLIGENCE IN CHILDREN

The pioneering step was taken by a French psychologist, Alfred Binet (1857–1911). As so often in the field of individual differences, the impetus came from the world of practical affairs. By the turn of the century, compulsory elementary education was the rule among the industrialized nations. Large numbers of schoolchildren had to be dealt with and some of them seemed mentally retarded. If they were indeed retarded, it appeared best to send them to special schools. But mere backwardness was not deemed sufficient to justify this action; perhaps a child's prior education had been poor, or perhaps the child suffered from some illness. In 1904, the French minister of public instruction appointed a special committee, including Binet, and asked it to look into this matter. The committee concluded that there was a need for an objective diagnostic instrument to assess each child's intellectual state. Much of what we now know about the measurement of intelligence comes from Binet's efforts to satisfy this need.

Intelligence as a general cognitive capacity   Binet and his collaborator, Théophile Simon, started with the premise that intelligence is a rather general attribute

Alfred Binet   (Courtesy National Library of Medicine)

that manifests itself in many spheres of cognitive functioning. This view led them to construct a test that ranged over many areas. It included tasks that varied in both content and difficulty—copying a drawing, repeating a string of digits, recognizing coins and making change, explaining absurdities. The child's performance on all these subtests yielded a composite score. Later studies showed that this composite measure correlated with the child's school grades and with the teacher's evaluations of the child's intelligence.

The intelligence quotient, IQ Binet made another assumption about intelligence. He believed that it develops with age until maturity is reached. Here too his ideas fit our intuitive notions. We know that an average group of six-year-olds is no intellectual match for an average group of eight-year-olds. It's not just that they know less; they're not as smart. This conception provided the basis for the test's scoring system.

Binet and Simon first gave their test to a special standardization group composed of children of varying ages whose test performance provided the norms. Binet and Simon noted which items were passed by the average six-year-old, and so on. (Items that were passed by younger but not by older children were excluded.)

The resulting classification of the test items generated a ladder of tasks in which each rung corresponds to a number of subtests that were successfully passed by the average child of a given age. Testing a child's intelligence was thus tantamount to a determination of how high the child could ascend this ladder before the tasks finally became too difficult. The rung she attained indicated her **mental age** (usually abbreviated MA). If she successfully coped with all items passed by the average eight-year-old and failed all those passed by the average nine-year-old, her MA was said to be eight years. Appropriate scoring adjustments were made when the performance pattern did not work out quite as neatly; for example, if a child passed all items at the seven-year-old level, 75 percent of those at the eight-year-old level, 30 percent of those at the nine-year-old level, and none beyond, then her mental age was judged to be 8.3.

The MA assesses an absolute level of cognitive capacity. To determine whether a child is "bright" or "dull" one has to compare her MA with her chronological age (CA). To the extent that her MA exceeds her CA, we regard the child as "bright" or advanced; the opposite is true if the MA is below the CA. But a particular lag or advance clearly has different import depending upon the child's age. A six-year-old with an MA of three is obviously more retarded than a ten-year-old with an MA of seven. To cope with this difficulty, a German psychologist, William Stern (1871–1938), proposed the use of a ratio measure, the **intelligence quotient** or **IQ.** This is computed by dividing the MA by the CA. The resulting quotient is multiplied by 100 to get rid of decimal points. Thus,

$$IQ = \frac{MA}{CA} \times 100.$$

By definition, an IQ of 100 indicates average intelligence; it means that the child's MA is equivalent to his CA and thus to the average score attained by his age-mates in the standardization sample. By the same token, an IQ greater than 100 indicates that the child is above average, an IQ of less than 100 that he is below average.

Stern's quotient measure has various drawbacks. The major problem is that the top rung of Binet's mental age ladder was sixteen (in some later revisions of the Stanford-Binet the ceiling was higher). In some ways this makes good sense, for intelligence does not grow forever any more than height does. But since CAs keep on rising beyond the MA ceiling, the IQ (defined as a quotient) cannot help but decline. Consider the IQ of an adult. If her CA is 48 and her MA is 16, the use of the standard computation results in an IQ of 33 ($16/48 \times 100 = 33$), a score that indicates severe mental retardation—an obvious absurdity.

Eventually a new approach was adopted. In the last analysis, an intelligence score indicates how an individual stands in relation to an appropriate comparison sample—his own age-mates. The intelligence quotient expresses this comparison as a ratio, but there are more direct measures of getting at the same thing. One example is an individual's ***percentile rank;*** that is, the proportion of persons in his comparison group whose score is below his. A more commonly used measure that provides the same information is the ***deviation IQ.*** We will not go into the details of how this measure is arrived at; suffice it to say that an IQ of 100 indicates a score equal to the average of the comparison sample (and thus a percentile rank of 50); that for most standard tests, IQs of 85 and 115 indicate percentile ranks of about 16 and 84, and IQs of 70 and 130 percentile ranks of 2 and 98.

TESTING INTELLIGENCE IN ADULTS

Although the Binet scales were originally meant for children, demands soon arose for the diagnosis of adults' intelligence. One reason was that the Binet scale had not been standardized on an adult population so that there were no appro-

---

COMPREHENSION	INFORMATION
1. Why should we obey traffic laws and speed limits?	1. Who wrote *Huckleberry Finn?*
2. Why are antitrust laws necessary?	2. Where is Finland?
3. Why should we lock the doors and take the keys to our car when leaving the car parked?	3. At what temperature does paper burn?
4. What does this saying mean: "Kill two birds with one stone."	4. What is entomology?

ARITHMETIC	
1. How many 15¢ stamps can you buy for a dollar?	3. A man bought a used stereo system for ¾ of what it cost new. He paid $225 for it. How much did it cost new?
2. How many hours will it take a cyclist to travel 60 miles if he is going 12 miles an hour?	4. Six men can finish a job in ten days. How many men will be needed to finish the job in two and a half days?

A. Verbal tests

B. Picture completion

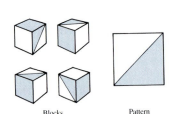

C. Block design

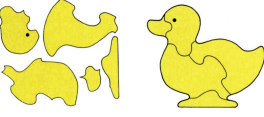

D. Object assembly

15.7   Test items similar to some in the Wechsler Adult Intelligence Scale   (A) Verbal tests. These include tests of information, comprehension, and arithmetic. (B) Picture completion. The task is to note the missing part. (C) Block design. The materials consist of four blocks, which are all blue on some sides, all white on other sides, and half blue and half white on the rest of the sides. The subject is shown a pattern and has to arrange the four blocks to produce this design. (D) Object assembly. The task is to arrange the cut-up pieces to form a familiar object. (Courtesy The Psychological Corporation)

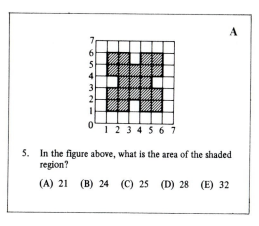

5. In the figure above, what is the area of the shaded region?

    (A) 21   (B) 24   (C) 25   (D) 28   (E) 32

25. LINGUISTICS : LANGUAGE :: **B**
     (A) statistics : sociology
     (B) ceramics : clay
     (C) gymnastics : health
     (D) dynamics : motion
     (E) economics : warfare

15.8 Two items from the Scholastic Aptitude Test (SAT) (Courtesy of The College Entrance Examination Board and the Educational Testing Service)

priate norms. Such considerations led David Wechsler to construct an intelligence test for adults—the Wechsler Adult Intelligence Scale (Wechsler, 1958).

Performance versus verbal tests   One of Wechsler's objections to the Binet scales was that they were too heavily loaded with items that require verbal skills. Wechsler argued that there are intellectual abilities that are not predominantly verbal (a view that has found later confirmation in studies of hemispheric function; see Chapter 1).

To cope with this, Wechsler divided his test into a verbal and a performance subtest. The verbal test includes items that assess general information, vocabulary, comprehension, and arithmetic. The performance test includes tasks that require the subject to assemble the cut-up parts of a familiar object so as to form the appropriate whole, to complete an incomplete drawing, or to rearrange a series of pictures so that they are in the proper sequence and tell a story (Figure 15.7).

Wechsler's employment of verbal and performance subtests proved so popular that he developed several extensions of his test for use with children: the Wechsler Intelligence Scale for Children (or WISC) for ages five to fifteen, and the Wechsler Preschool and Primary Scale of Intelligence (WPPSI) for ages four to six.

Group tests   Both the Binet and the Wechsler scales are administered individually. This has the advantage of permitting a more careful evaluation of the person who is tested. But there is the obvious drawback that individual testing is a lengthy and expensive business. If the object is to assess a large number of persons —army recruits, potential employees in large industrial organizations, myriads of children in a city's schools, college applicants—the cost of administering tests individually becomes prohibitive.

Such economic facts of life led to the development of group tests of various cognitive and scholastic aptitudes, usually of the paper-and-pencil multiple-choice format. Some examples are the Scholastic Aptitude Test (SAT) taken by most college applicants, and the Graduate Record Examination, a more difficult version of the SAT designed for applicants to graduate schools (Figure 15.8). A test that emphasizes abstract, nonverbal intellectual ability is the Progressive Matrices Test (Figure 15.9).

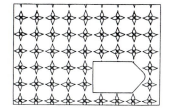

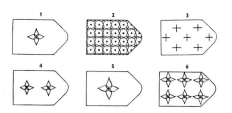

15.9 An example item from the Raven Progressive Matrices Test   The task is to select the alternative that fits into the empty slot above. (Courtesy J. C. Raven Limited)

In recent years, a new test for children has come to prominence, the ***Kaufman Assessment Battery for Children (K-ABC).*** Like virtually all intelligence tests, this is an outgrowth of those devised by Binet and Wechsler. But it has two novel aspects. To begin with, its construction is based on some modern formulations that try to understand intelligence within the conceptual framework of information processing (see Chapters 6, 7, and 13). Some of its subtests assess the child's capacity for sequential cognitive processing, for example, his ability to recall a number of digits in the same sequence as he heard them or to copy the exact sequence in which the examiner tapped the table with his hand. Others assess his ability to process simultaneously presented information; for example, his ability to select the picture that best completes a visual analogy or to recall the location of items arranged randomly on a page. Another novelty is that the test gives particular attention to the assessment of handicapped children and is appropriate for cultural and linguistic minorities. Toward that end, it includes a nonverbal scale with questions that are presented in pantomime and have to be answered with various motor gestures. This scale is particularly useful for testing children who cannot speak English (or can't speak it well) or who are hearing-impaired, and its scores seem to be less affected by sociocultural conditions than those of the Stanford-Binet or of Wechsler's scales for children (Anastasi, 1984, 1985; Coffman, 1985; Kaufman, Kamphaus, and Kaufman, 1985; Page, 1985).

An Area of Application: Mental Retardation

Binet's original purpose was to design an instrument for the diagnosis of mental retardation. How well did he and his followers succeed? On the whole, the tests seem to perform this function rather well, at least as a first step toward diagnosis. The usual demarcation for retardation is an IQ of about 70 or below. Thus defined, about 2.5 percent of the population of the United States would be regarded as retarded (Grossman, 1983). But the test performance is not the only criterion. Equally important are social and cultural competence, the ability to learn and cope with the demands of society, to take care of oneself, to earn a living. This competence obviously depends in part upon the nature of the society in which a person lives. A complex technological culture like ours puts a higher premium on various intellectual skills than does an agrarian society. Someone classified as mildly retarded in twentieth-century America probably would have managed perfectly well in, say, feudal Europe.

CLASSIFYING RETARDATION

A widely used classification system distinguishes several degrees of retardation: "mild" (IQ of approximately 50–55 to 70), "moderate" (35–40 to 50–55), "severe" (20–25 to 35–40), and "profound" (20–25 and below). The more severe the retardation, the less frequently it occurs: In 100 retarded persons, one would expect that the degree of retardation would be "mild" in 90, "moderate" in 6, "severe" in 3, and "profound" in 1 of the cases (Robinson and Robinson, 1970).

Table 15.2 presents a description of the general level of intellectual functioning in each of the categories at various ages. The table shows that mentally retarded persons do not have to be excluded from useful participation in society. This is especially true for those whose degree of retardation is mild, and they account for almost 90 percent of all the cases. If provided with appropriate education and training, such persons can ultimately achieve an acceptable level of adjustment in adult life (Tyler, 1965).

Table 15.2   CHARACTERISTICS OF THE MENTALLY RETARDED*

Degree of retardation	IQ range	Level of functioning at school age (6–20 years)	Level of functioning in adulthood (21 years and over)
Mild	50–55 to approx. 70	Can learn academic skills up to approximately sixth-grade level by late teens; can be guided toward social conformity.	Can usually achieve social and vocational skills adequate to maintain self-support, but may need guidance and assistance when under unusual social or economic stress.
Moderate	35–40 to 50–55	Can profit from training in social and occupational skills; unlikely to progress beyond second-grade level in academic subjects; may learn to travel alone in familiar places.	May achieve self-maintenance in unskilled or semiskilled work under sheltered conditions; needs supervision and guidance when under mild social or economic stress.
Severe	20–25 to 35–40	Can talk or learn to communicate; can be trained in elemental health habits; profits from systematic habit training.	May contribute partially to self-maintenance under complete supervision; can develop self-protection skills at a minimum useful level in controlled environment.
Profound	below 20–25	Some motor development present; may respond to minimal or limited training in self-help.	Some motor and speech development; may achieve very limited self-care; needs nursing care.

* Descriptive terms and score intervals are from a classificatory system recommended by the American Association for Mental Deficiency.
Source: Grossman, 1983, p. 13.

THE CAUSES OF RETARDATION

Retardation is not a condition that has one single cause, but it can reflect any number of underlying factors, some of which are as yet unknown. Some forms of retardation are produced by certain known genetic disorders or by aberrations in the chromosome structure (see p. 439). Others are produced by brain damage suffered in the womb, during delivery, or after birth. Still others may reflect the composite effects of hundreds of genes. And yet others may be the result of impoverished environmental conditions, especially during early life (Edgerton, 1979). One of the most important of these is severe malnutrition during the first two years or so of infancy (an all too common condition among infants of the very poor and of those in underdeveloped countries), which produces a profound and lasting depression of intellectual functioning (Birch et al., 1971; Stoch et al., 1982).

THE PSYCHOMETRIC APPROACH TO INTELLIGENCE

We have seen that there is no consensus on a definition of intelligence and thus no clear-cut validity criterion for a test that claims to measure it. But even so, many psychologists would agree that such instruments as the Stanford-Binet and the Wechsler tests do distinguish people in ways that have a rough correspondence with our intuitive conceptions of the term *intelligence.* There is no doubt that with appropriate modifications, either scale would easily differentiate between Aristotle and the Athenian village idiot. Can we get any further than this?

According to one group of investigators, the starting point for further inquiries into the nature of intelligence is just the fact that intelligence tests do make some distinctions between people that fit our initial sense of what intelligence is about. These investigators believe that we can refine our knowledge of the nature of intelligence by a careful further study of these distinctions. This line of reasoning underlies the **psychometric approach** to the study of intelligence. In effect, it amounts to a bootstrap operation. One looks at the results the measuring instrument provides in order to find out what the instrument really measures.

The Structure of Mental Abilities

When we use the term *intelligence,* we imply that it is a unitary ability. But is it really? In principle, one could imagine several kinds of mental ability that are quite unrelated. Perhaps different intellectual tasks draw on distinctly different cognitive gifts. It may also be that the truth is in between. Perhaps human intellectual abilities are composed of both general and more particular capacities. How can we decide among these alternatives?

All we have to go on are people's scores on various tests. These scores presumably reflect some underlying abilities—perhaps one, perhaps several. But these underlying capacities are not observable directly; they can only be inferred. Students of psychometrics have tried to perform this inference by looking at the intercorrelations among different tests.

To get an intuitive idea of this general approach, consider a man who looks at a lake and sees what appear to be serpentlike parts:

A

He can entertain various hypotheses. One is that all visible parts belong to one huge sea monster (a hypothesis that is analogous to the assumption that there is a unitary intellectual ability):

B

He might also assume that there are several such beasts (analogous to separate mental abilities):

C

Or finally, he might believe that there are as many sea animals as there are visible parts (analogous to the hypothesis that every test measures a totally different ability):

D

How can he choose among these alternatives, given that he has no way of peering below the waters? His best bet is to wait and watch how the serpentine parts change over time and space. If he does this, he can find out which parts go together. If all parts move jointly (B), the most reasonable interpretation is that they all belong to one huge sea monster. (For the purposes of our example, we will assume sea serpents are severely arthritic and are unable to move their body portions separately.) If the first part goes with the second, while the third goes with the fourth (C), there are presumably two smaller creatures. If all parts move separately (D), the best bet is that there are as many sea serpents as there are visible parts. In effect, our sea-serpent watcher has studied a correlation pattern on the basis of which he can infer the invisible structure (or structures) under the surface.

SPEARMAN AND THE CONCEPT OF "GENERAL INTELLIGENCE"

The psychometric equivalent of the joint movements of sea-serpent portions is the correlation pattern among different tests of mental abilities. As an example, consider the correlations among four subtests of the Wechsler Adult Scale: Information *(I)*, comprehension *(C)*, arithmetic *(A)*, and vocabulary *(V)*. These intercorrelations are all quite high. The correlation between *I* and *C* is .70, that between *I* and *A* is .66, and so on. These results can be presented in the form of a *correlation matrix,* in which the intercorrelations can be read off directly (Table 15.3).

Table 15.3   CORRELATION MATRIX OF FOUR SUBTESTS ON THE WECHSLER ADULT SCALE

	I	*C*	*A*	*V*
I (Information)	—	.70	.66	.81
C (Comprehension)		—	.49	.73
A (Arithmetic)			—	.59
V (Vocabulary)				—

NOTE: The matrix shows the correlation of each subtest with each of the other three. Note that the left-to-right diagonal (which is here indicated by the dashes) can't have any entries because it is made up of the cells that describe the correlation of each subtest with itself. The cells below the dashes are left blank because they would be redundant.
SOURCE: From Wechsler, 1958.

An inspection of this correlation matrix suggests that there is a common factor that runs through all four of these subtests. The positive correlations indicate that people with a greater fund of information are also people who are likely to get higher scores in comprehension, who are probably better at arithmetic, and who generally have a larger vocabulary. Given the fact that all of these measures are correlated, it is plausible to assume that they share something in common, that they all measure the same underlying attribute. This was exactly the conclusion reached by the English psychologist Charles Spearman (1863–1945), who developed the first version of *factor analysis,* a statistical technique by which one can "extract" this common factor that all of the various tests share. In his view, this factor was best described as *general intelligence,* or *g,* a mental attribute that is called upon in any intellectual task a person has to perform.

Spearman pointed out that this *g*-factor alone cannot explain the intercorrelations among mental tests. If test performance were determined by *g* and only *g,* then the correlations between any two subtests should be perfect except for errors of measurement. But in fact the intercorrelations fall far short of this. To explain

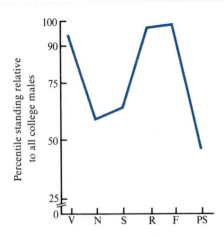

15.10 An ability profile based on group factors *An ability profile for a hypothetical male college student considering a career in architecture. The profile indicates his percentile scores on some important group factors. These are V (verbal ability—e.g., vocabulary, synonyms), N (numerical ability—e.g., arithmetic), S (spatial ability—e.g., reassembling cut-up objects), R (reasoning—e.g., interference problems), F (word fluency—e.g., give as many five-letter words as you can that start with T), and PS (perceptual speed—e.g., rapid visual recognition). As the profile shows, the student is quite superior on the verbal and reasoning factors, but only average on the spatial and perceptual factors. Under the circumstances, a counselor might suggest a shift in career plans.*

15.11 Drawing ability in an "idiot savant" *A drawing by Nadia, a severely retarded child with remarkable drawing ability. This horse was drawn when she was 4 years old. (From Selfe, 1977)*

why this is so, Spearman proposed that any test taps not only *g* but also some other ability, *s*, that is completely specific to the particular test used. Thus performance on an arithmetic subtest depends in part on *g* and in part on numerical skills *(s)* that are specific to that subtest. Since people vary along both general intelligence, *g*, and these different specific factors, the *s*'s, the intercorrelations among different tests cannot be perfect (Spearman, 1927; for further discussion, see Baron, 1985).

Group-factor theories Spearman's theory of intelligence is sometimes described as "monarchic." As he saw it, there is one and only one underlying factor, *g*, that reigns supreme over all intellectual functions. But his position was soon challenged by other investigators who argued that the intercorrelations among test scores are better explained by a set of underlying mental abilities than by one overarching *g*-factor. Spearman called this **group-factor theory** an "oligarchic" conception of intelligence, since it viewed intelligence as just the composite of separate abilities without a sovereign capacity that enters into each (see Figure 15.10). L. L. Thurstone (1887–1955), who originated most of the concepts and techniques that underlie this approach, regarded these group factors as the "primary mental abilities." Some of the most important of these are spatial, numerical, verbal, and reasoning abilities.

THE NOTION OF MULTIPLE INTELLIGENCES

A distant cousin of group-factor theory is Howard Gardner's concept of multiple intelligences (Gardner, 1983). Like Thurstone, Gardner believes that there are several essential, independent mental capacities. Gardner lists six such abilities (which he calls "intelligences"): linguistic, logical-mathematical, spatial, musical, bodily-kinesthetic, and personal intelligence. The first three are familiar enough, for they are assessed by most standard intelligence scales (and emerged as primary factors in Thurstone's analyses), and everyone knows pretty much what's meant by musical ability. By bodily-kinesthetic intelligence, Gardner refers to the ability to learn and create complex motor patterns, as in dancers and skilled athletes. By personal intelligence, he refers to the ability to understand others and oneself.

One line of evidence for Gardner's claim that these "intelligences" are largely independent of each other comes from studies of different brain lesions, which may affect some abilities (e.g., language) while leaving others unimpaired (e.g., mathematical ability). Thus certain lesions will make a person unable to recognize drawings (spatial intelligence), while others will make him unable to perform a sequence of movements (bodily-kinesthetic intelligence), and still others will produce major changes in personality (personal intelligence).

Further arguments for Gardner's theory of multiple intelligences comes from the study of certain mentally retarded persons who have some remarkable talent that seems out of keeping with their low level of general intelligence.* Some display unusual artistic talent (see Figure 15.11). Others are calendar calculators; they are able to come up promptly with the right answer if asked questions like, "What was the date of the third Monday in 1682?" Still others have unusual mechanical talents, such as the ability to build a functional full-sized merry-go-round or scale models of ships. And yet others have unusual musical skills as in the case of a woman who could play "Happy Birthday" in the style of different composers (Hill, 1978).

Some of the evidence Gardner cites in support of his general contention of independent intelligences can be questioned, however. That Beethoven and Mi-

* In earlier literature, such cases are often called *idiot savants.*

chelangelo represent the absolute top of musical and artistic ability is self-evident, but a glance at the letters and diaries of these giants indicates that their verbal and logical intelligence was also far from negligible, which argues against the view that these various capacities are independent.

Whatever the ultimate verdict on Gardner's theory, there is no doubt that he has performed a very valuable service by drawing attention to a whole set of abilities that are all too often ignored by our society, which values (and perhaps overvalues) the kind of intelligence that helps people succeed in our educational system. That these various abilities should be highly esteemed is undeniable, but this doesn't mean that the same term—intelligence—should be applied to all of them.

Intelligence and Age

Factor analysts have tried to get some insight into the nature of intelligence (now referring to intelligence as Binet and Wechsler used the term) by studying how scores on various subtests correlate with each other. Another psychometric approach is to relate test performance to other attributes on which people vary. An obvious candidate is age, which after all provided the basis on which the first intelligence tests were standardized.

Many investigators have tried to plot the growth of intelligence from middle childhood to old age. To do so, they administered the same test to people in different age groups matched by sex and socioeconomic level. Figure 15.12 presents a composite curve based on several such studies. The figure should hearten the young and bring gloom to all who are past age twenty. There is a sharp increase in mental ability between ages ten and twenty, and an accelerating decline thereafter.

Does intelligence really decline after twenty? Later investigators (perhaps prompted by the fact that they were over thirty) concluded that the situation could not be as bleak as that. They argued that the steep decline in intelligence could have resulted from an artifact, a by-product of an irrelevant factor: on the average, the older age groups had a lower level of education. Such a difference might have been present even if the groups were matched by years of schooling, for curricula have probably improved over time. One way of getting around this difficulty is through a ***longitudinal*** study in which the same persons are tested at different ages. The results of such longitudinal studies suggest that age (or at least middle age) is not as deleterious to mental functioning as it had seemed at first (Schaie and Strother, 1968; Schaie, 1979). There is a continued *rise* on tests for verbal meaning, for reasoning, and for educational aptitude until about age fifty. After this, there is a moderate decline (Figure 15.13).

Fluid and crystallized intelligence Further work has shown that the age curve of intelligence depends on just what abilities are being tested. Many facets of verbal abilities show little decline until age seventy. The results of tests of vocabulary are even more encouraging to those of later years; there is no drop in vocabulary even at age eighty-five (Blum, Jarvik, and Clark, 1970). In contrast, nonverbal abilities that are tapped by such tests as the Progressive Matrices decline earlier, usually around age forty (Green, 1969). The most pronounced drops are found for tests that depend on quick recall, especially when there is no memory organization that can help retrieval. An example is the word fluency test in which the subject has two minutes to write down as many words as he can think of that start with a particular letter. Such mental calisthenics are best left to the young; declines in

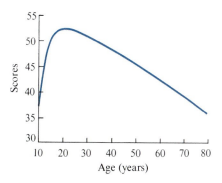

15.12 Mental test scores as related to age *The scores are based on comparisons of different age groups. They are expressed in units that allow comparisons of different tests and are based on averaged results of three different studies. (After Jones and Kaplan, 1945)*

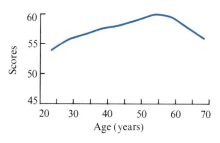

15.13 Mental test scores as related to age when studied by a variation of the longitudinal method *The scores, which cover a fifty-year age range, were obtained over a seven-year period from several adult populations, the youngest of which was twenty at the beginning of the study and the oldest in their sixties. (After Schaie and Strother, 1968)*

word fluency are very steep and are seen as early as thirty (Schaie and Strother, 1968).

Some authors believe that the different age curves obtained for different subtests of intelligence scales reflect an important distinction between two underlying intellectual abilities (Cattell, 1963). One is *fluid intelligence,* which is the ability to deal with essentially new problems. The other is *crystallized intelligence,* which is the repertoire of information, cognitive skills, and strategies acquired by the application of fluid intelligence to various fields.

Examples of tasks that emphasize fluid intelligence are scrambled sentences and number series. Consider the set of words shown below:

tree pick an climbed man our apple the to

When a person is asked to rearrange these words so as to make a meaningful sentence, she can't just rely on what she has previously learned but has to reason it out. The same holds for number series, such as the one below in which the task is to find the number that is next in the series:

3   8   12   15   17

In contrast, tasks that primarily rely on crystallized intelligence are exemplified by tests of vocabulary (e.g., what is *amenuensis*?) or of calculation (e.g., $6 \times 7 - 4 \times 5 = ?$).

According to the theory, fluid intelligence declines with age, beginning in middle adulthood or earlier. But crystallized intelligence does not drop off. On the contrary, it will continue to grow until old age if the person is in an intellectually stimulating environment. From the point of view of actual functioning in middle age and beyond, the drop in the one ability may be more than compensated for by the increase in the other.* The older person has "appropriated the collective intelligence of the culture for his own use" (Horn and Cattell, 1967). By so doing, he has not only amassed a store of knowledge larger than the one he had when he was younger, but he has also developed better ways of organizing this knowledge, of approaching problems, and of filing new information away for later use.

NATURE, NURTURE, AND IQ

While it is far from clear just what intelligence tests really measure, this state of affairs has not deterred psychologists—nor indeed, the general public—from making intelligence-test performance one of the major foci of the nature-nurture controversy, debating it with a stormy passion rarely found in any other area of the discipline (see Block and Dworkin, 1976; Eysenck vs. Kamin, 1981; Fancher, 1987).

Some Political Issues

The vehemence of the debate over intelligence-test performance is understandable considering that mental testing is a field in which the concerns of the scientist impinge drastically upon those of the practical world. In our society, those who are well off tend to do better on intelligence tests than those who are disadvantaged. The same holds for their children. What accounts for this difference? There is some tendency for social groups to be biased in favor of different answers to this question. This bias was especially marked some seventy years ago when

* Some of these issues are still a matter of debate (see Horn and Donaldson, 1976; Baltes and Schaie, 1976).

"Immigration Restriction. Prop Wanted."

Anti-immigration sentiment in the United States *A cartoon that appeared in the January 23, 1903, issue of the* Philadelphia Inquirer *calling for more restrictive immigration laws. (Courtesy of the New York Public Library)*

the prevailing social climate was much more conservative. Then—and to a lesser extent even now—advantaged groups were more likely to believe that intelligence is largely inherited. This assertion was certainly comforting to those who benefited from the status quo since it suggested they got what they "deserved."

In contrast, spokesmen for the disadvantaged took a different view. To begin with, they often disparaged the tests themselves, arguing that the tests are not fair to their own subculture. In addition, they argued that intellectual aptitudes are much more determined by nurture than nature. In their view, differences in intelligence, especially those between different ethnic and racial groups, are determined predominantly by environmental factors such as early home background and schooling. Seen in this light, the children of the poor obtain lower test scores, not because they inherit deficient genes, but rather because they inherit poverty.

These contrasting views lead to different prescriptions for social policy. An example of the impact of a hereditarian bias is the rationale behind the U.S. immigration policy between the two World Wars. The Immigration Act of 1924 set definite quotas to minimize the influx of what were thought to be biologically "weaker stocks," specifically those from Southern and Eastern Europe. To prove the genetic intellectual inferiority of these immigrants, a congressional committee pointed to their army intelligence-test scores, which were indeed substantially below those attained by Americans of Northern European ancestry.

In actual fact, the differences were primarily related to the length of time that the immigrants had been in the United States prior to the test; their average test scores rose with every year and became indistinguishable from native-born Americans after twenty years of residence in the United States. This result undermines the hypothesis of a hereditary difference in intelligence between, say, Northern and Eastern Europeans. But the congressional proponents of differential immigration quotas did not analyze the results so closely. They had their own reasons for restricting immigration, such as fears of competition from cheap labor. The theory that the excluded groups were innately inferior provided a convenient justification for their policies (Kamin, 1974).

A more contemporary example of the relation between psychological theory and social policy is the argument over the value of compensatory education programs for preschool children from disadvantaged backgrounds. Such programs have been said to be failures because they often don't lead to improvement in later scholastic performance. Assuming this is true (and it may well not be), the question is why. A highly controversial paper by Arthur Jensen suggested that the difference in the intellectual performance of the advantaged and the disadvantaged groups is partially caused by a genetic difference between the groups. Given this hereditarian position, Jensen argued that environmental alterations can at best mitigate the group difference; they cannot abolish it (Jensen, 1969).

Jensen's thesis has been vehemently debated on many counts, some of which we will discuss below. For now, we will only note that the failure of any given program (assuming it was really a failure) does not prove the hereditarians' claim. Perhaps the preschool experience that was provided was not of the right sort; perhaps it was inadequate to counteract the overwhelming effects of ghetto life (Hunt, 1961). In any case, there is by now a growing consensus that Jensen and others have underestimated the effectiveness of preschool education on school performance in later years (Zigler and Berman, 1983). Such preschool experiences may or may not raise the childrens' intelligence-test scores.* But further

---

* Some preschool experiences apparently do seem to raise intelligence-test scores, both here and in underdeveloped regions elsewhere in the world, especially if they are accompanied by health measures, nutritional supplements, and various efforts to help the mother through job training, remedial education, and the like (e.g., McKay et al., 1978; Garber and Heber, 1982). Other programs were less successful, especially when evaluated some years after the preschool experience (see Coleman et al., 1966; Bronfenbrenner, 1975).

analyses have shown that, regardless of their effect on IQ scores, many such programs have had positive effects on the childrens' school performance in later years. Thus low-income children who have participated in such programs seem to perform more acceptably in later grades (from fourth to twelfth grades) than children who had no such experience; they were less likely to be held back in grade, less likely to drop out of school, and so on (Lazar and Darlington, 1982).

Genetic Factors

Thus far, our emphasis has been on the social and political aspects of the nature-nurture issue in intelligence, the considerations that bias people to take one or another side of the issue. But while it is interesting to know what people prefer to believe about the world, our primary concern is with what the world is really like. What is the evidence about the contributions of heredity and environment in producing differences *within* groups (for instance, among American whites) and *between* groups (for instance, between American whites and blacks)?

GENETIC TRANSMISSION

Before turning to the relationship between intelligence-test performance and genetic endowment, we must say a few words about the mechanisms that underlie the transmission of genetic characteristics from one generation to the next.

The mechanism of genetic transmission   Each organism starts life with a genetic blueprint, a set of instructions that steers its development from fertilized cell to mature animal or plant. The genetic commands are contained in the ***chromosomes*** in the cell's nucleus. In organisms that reproduce sexually, the chromosomes come in corresponding pairs, with one member of each pair contributed by each parent. In humans, there are twenty-three such chromosome pairs.

Every chromosome stores thousands of genetic commands each of which is biologically engraved in a ***gene,*** the unit of hereditary transmission. Any given gene is located at a particular place on a given chromosome. Since chromosomes come in pairs, both members of each pair have corresponding loci at which there are genes that carry instructions about the same bodily characteristic (for example, eye color). These two related genes—one contributed by each parent—may or may not be identical. Consider eye color. If both the genes for eye color are identical (blue-blue or brown-brown), there is no problem; the eye color will follow suit. But suppose they are different. Now the overt expression of the genetic blueprint depends upon still other relationships between the two members of the gene pair. In humans, the brown-eyed gene is ***dominant;*** it will exert its effect regardless of whether the other member of the gene pair calls for brown or blue eyes. In contrast, the blue-eyed gene is ***recessive.*** This recessive blue-eyed gene will lead to blue eyes only if there is an identical (that is, blue-eyed) gene on the corresponding locus of the paired chromosome. (See Figure 15.14.)

Phenotype and genotype   A key distinction in any discussion of hereditary transmission is that between ***phenotype*** and ***genotype.*** The phenotype corresponds to the overt appearance of the organism—its visible structure and behavior. But this phenotype is by no means equivalent to the organism's genotype, which describes the set of the relevant genes. There are several ways in which a genotype may be kept from overt (that is, phenotypic) expression. One depends on gene dominance; as we've seen, if one member of a gene pair is dominant while the other is recessive, the first will mask the effects of the second. Another way in which an underlying genotype may be held back from outer manifestation is through the

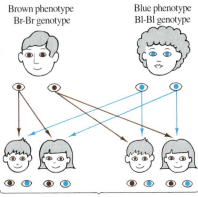

15.14   Phenotype and genotype in the transmission of eye color   Eye color of the children of a brown-eyed and a blue-eyed parent if the brown-eyed parent's genotype is brown-brown. All of the children's eyes (phenotypes) will be brown, although their genotypes will be brown-blue. In the figure, genotypes are indicated by a pair of schematic eye-color genes under each face.

Brown phenotype
Br-Br genotype

Blue phenotype
Bl-Bl genotype

Brown phenotype
Br-Bl genotype

interaction between the genotype and its environment. This interaction is especially important during the early stages in the organism's development since a particular genetic command can only be executed if certain physical characteristics (oxygen concentration, hormone levels, temperature) both inside and outside of the developing body are within a certain range.

As an example, consider the dark markings on the paws, tail, and eartips of a Siamese cat. These markings are not present at birth, but they appear gradually as the kitten matures. The genealogical records kept by cat breeders leave no doubt that these markings in the mature animal are determined by heredity. But this does not mean that they emerge independently of the environment. The dark markings will only appear if the kitten's extremities are kept at their normal temperature, which happens to be lower than that of the rest of the animal's body. If the extremities are deliberately warmed during early kittenhood by such devices as leggings and tail- and earmuffs, they will not turn darker—in apparent defiance of the creature's genotype (Ilyin and Ilyin, 1930).

This example underlines the fact that genes do not operate in a vacuum. They are instructions to a developing organism, instructions that will be followed only within a given range of environmental conditions. It therefore makes no sense to talk of heredity alone or environment alone, for there is no trait that does not depend upon both. There can be no organism without a genotype, and this genotype cannot ever express itself independently of the environment.

The inheritance of behavior　There is ample evidence that many behavioral attributes are affected by hereditary makeup. An important example of a psychological characteristic that is determined by a single gene is a severe form of mental retardation, ***phenylketonuria*** or ***PKU.*** In the United States, about one baby in every fifteen thousand is born with this defect. PKU is caused by a deficiency in an enzyme that allows the body to transform ***phenylalanine,*** an amino acid (a building block of proteins), into another amino acid. When this enzyme is missing, phenylalanine is converted into a toxic agent that accumulates in the infant's bloodstream and damages his developing nervous system. Analyses of the incidence of PKU among the siblings of afflicted children and among others in their family trees indicate that this disorder is produced by a single recessive gene.

Although PKU is of genetic origin, it can be treated by appropriate environmental intervention. The trick is a special diet that contains very little phenylalanine. If this diet is introduced at an early enough age, retardation can be minimized, or even eliminated.

This result demonstrates the fallacy of the popular belief that what is inborn is necessarily unchangeable. The genes lay down certain biochemical instructions that determine the development of a particular organ system. If we understand the genetic command clearly enough, we may eventually find ways to circumvent it. In the case of PKU, we are already on the way to doing so (McClearn and DeFries, 1973).

Polygenic inheritance　Most of the preceding discussion concerned hereditary traits that are for the most part produced by the action of one gene pair. Such characteristics are usually all-or-none, such as being brown-eyed or blue-eyed. But what about attributes that vary continuously, such as height or intelligence, which partially depend on genetic factors? The answer is ***polygenic inheritance,*** in which the trait is controlled not by one but by many gene pairs. Take height. Some gene pairs pull toward increased stature, others toward lesser stature; the individual's ultimate genetic potential for height (for now, ignoring environmental effects) is then determined by the combined action of all the height-controlling gene pairs. To the extent that intelligence (or any other psychological attribute that varies continuously) is partially determined by hereditary factors, the same logic applies to it.

Genetic effects on behavior　*(Drawing by Shanahan; © 1989 The New Yorker Magazine, Inc.)*

GENETICS AND IQ

How can we find out whether differences in human intelligence (at least as measured by intelligence-test performance) have a genetic basis? To do so, we have to infer the underlying genotypes from the observable phenotypic behavior. One strategy is to examine the similarities between relatives, an approach that dates back to Francis Galton. Galton found that eminence (which he measured by reputation) runs in families; eminent men were more likely to have eminent relatives than the average person (Galton, 1869). Similar results have been repeatedly obtained with intelligence-test scores. For example, the correlation between the IQs of children and parents, or between the IQs of siblings, runs in the neighborhood of .45 (Bouchard and McGue, 1981). From Galton's perspective, such findings document the inheritance of mental ability. But the environmentalist has a ready reply. Consider eminence. The relatives of an eminent person obviously share his or her social, educational, and financial advantages. As a result, there is a similarity of environmental background, as well as an overlapping set of genes. The same argument applies to the interpretation of the correlations between the IQs of close relatives.

A similar problem arises in another connection. IQs tend to be fairly stable; the ten-year-old with an IQ of 130 will probably get a roughly similar score at age fifteen. Supporters of the genetic theory of intelligence have often argued that this constancy of the IQ shows that intelligence tests measure an inborn capacity, "native intelligence," which is an essentially unalterable characteristic of an individual and is genetically based. This argument has been used as a justification of such educational practices as early assignment to one or another school track. But IQ constancy is no proof that intelligence is fixed or inborn. To the extent that this constancy occurs, it only demonstrates that a child tends to maintain his relative standing among his age-mates over time. This may be because of a genetically given attribute that remains unchanged with age. But it may also be because the child's environmental advantages stay pretty much the same as time goes on. If a child is born in a slum, the odds are pretty good that she will still be there at twelve; the same holds if she is born in a palace. Once again, the evidence is inconclusive.

During the last fifty years, psychologists have developed a variety of research designs that were meant to disentangle hereditary and environmental factors. We will consider two main attempts to accomplish this end: (1) the study of twins, and (2) the study of adopted children.

Twin studies   **Identical twins** originate from a single fertilized egg that splits into two exact replicas which then develop into two genetically identical individuals (see Figure 15.15). In contrast, **fraternal twins** arise from two different fertilized eggs. Each of two eggs in the female reproductive tract is fertilized by a different sperm cell. Under the circumstances, the genetic similarity between fraternal twins is no greater than that between ordinary siblings. Since this is so, a comparison between identical twins and fraternal twins of the same sex is of considerable interest, if one is willing to assume that the twins' environments are no more similar if they are identical than if they are fraternal. Given this premise, it follows that if identical twins turn out to be more similar on some trait than fraternals, one can conclude that this trait is in part genetically determined.

One review summarizes the results of several dozens of studies. The overall result shows that the correlation between the IQs of identical twins is substantially larger than that between the IQs of fraternal twins. Based on roughly 10,000 twin pairs in all, the average correlations are .86 for identicals and .60 for fraternals (Bouchard and McGue, 1981). Some further findings on familial similarity in IQ scores are presented in Table 15.4.

15.15 Identical twins *Photographs of a pair of identical twins taken at 18 months, 5, 15, and 50 years. (Photographs courtesy of Franklin A. Bryan)*

On the face of it, this pattern of results seems like clear-cut evidence for a genetic component in the determination of IQ. But a number of criticisms have been leveled at these and related studies. One argument bears on the assumption that the similarity in the environments of identical and fraternal twins is essentially equal. But is it really? Since identical twins look alike, there may be a tendency to treat them the same way. Ultimately, parents and teachers may develop the same expectations for them. In contrast, fraternal twins are no more or less similar in appearance than ordinary siblings and may thus evoke a more differentiated reaction from others. If this is so, the comparison of the IQ correlations between identical and fraternal twins is not as neat a test of the nature-nurture issue as it seemed at first (Anastasi, 1971; Kamin, 1974).

In a study designed to meet this criticism, over three hundred twins were classified as identical or fraternal according to two criteria. One was by a comparison of twelve blood-type characteristics. This is a reliable and objective method for assessing genotype identity. To be judged identical, both members of a twin pair must correspond on all of the twelve indices. Another criterion involved the subjects' own belief in whether they are identical or fraternal. This belief is presumably based on how similar the twins think they are and how similarly they feel that they are treated. In a sizable number of twins this subjective judgment did

Table 15.4 CORRELATIONS BETWEEN THE IQS OF FAMILY MEMBERS

Identical twins reared together	.86
Fraternal twins reared together	.60
Siblings reared together	.47
Child and natural parent by whom child is reared	.42
Child and biological mother separated from the child by adoption	.31
Child and unrelated adoptive mother	.17

SOURCE: Data on twins, siblings, and children reared with natural parents from Bouchard and McGue, 1981; data on adopted children from Horn, Loehlin, and Willerman, 1979.

441

not correspond to the biological facts as revealed by the blood tests. Which of the two ways of classifying a twin is a better predictor of the similarity in intelligence-test scores? The results suggest that the primary determinant is the true genotype. When the classification was by blood tests, there was the usual effect; identical twins scored more similarly than did fraternals. But when the classification was based on the twins' own judgments, this effect was markedly reduced. This result suggests that the greater intellectual similarity of identical as compared to fraternal twins is not an artifact of different environments. The best guess is that the effect occurs because intelligence-test performance is in part genetically determined (Scarr and Carter-Saltzman, 1979).

Adopted children Another line of evidence comes from studies of adopted children. One study was based on three hundred children who were adopted immediately after birth (Horn, 1983; Horn, Loehlin, and Willerman, 1979, 1982). When these children were later tested, the correlation between their IQs and those of their *biological* mothers (whom they had never seen) was greater than the corresponding correlation between their IQs and those of their *adoptive* mothers (.28 versus .15). Other investigators have shown that this pattern persists into adolescence. When the adopted child is tested at age fourteen, the correlation between his IQ and that of the biological mother's education is greater than that between the child's IQ and the educational level of the adoptive mother (.31 versus .04; Skodak and Skeels, 1949).

Environmental Factors

There is evidently a genetic component that helps determine differences in intelligence-test performance. But heredity alone does not account for all of the variance. Environmental factors also play a role.

Some of the evidence comes from an inspection of the same kind of data that demonstrate the importance of heredity: the similarities between members of the same family. The IQs of adopted children correlate .17 with those of their (genetically unrelated) adoptive mothers. To be sure, this correlation is fairly low and smaller than that between these same children and their *biological* mothers (.31), but even so, it demonstrates that the similarity in environments exerts some effect. Another argument for the role of environment comes from the fact that the correlation between the IQ scores of *fraternal* twins seems to be a bit higher than the correlation of scores between ordinary siblings (.60 versus .47). While the similarity in the hereditary makeup of fraternal twins is no greater than that of ordinary siblings, that of their environments obviously is; if there were any changes in the family circumstances (changed economic circumstances, death of a parent, divorce), they hit both twins at the same age.

IMPOVERISHED ENVIRONMENTS

Further evidence for environmental factors comes from studies of the effects of impoverished environments. Examples of what impoverished environments can do come from children who worked on canal boats in England during the 1920s and hardly attended school at all or who lived in remote regions of the Kentucky mountains. An environmentalist would argue that these are poor conditions for the development of the intellectual skills tapped by intelligence tests. If so, exposure to such an environment should have a cumulatively adverse effect; the longer the child remains in the environment, the more depressed his IQ should be. This is precisely what was found. There was a sizable *negative* correlation be-

Environmental deprivation A migratory family from Texas in 1940 living in a trailer in an open field without water or sanitation. The evidence suggests that the longer a child lives under such conditions the more depressed his IQ will be. (Photograph by Dorothea Lange; courtesy the National Archives)

tween IQ and age. The older the child, the longer he had been in the impoverished environment, and thus the lower his IQ (Gordon, 1923; Asher, 1935).

ENRICHED ENVIRONMENTS

Impoverishing the environment is evidently harmful. Enriching it has the opposite effect. An example is a community in East Tennessee that was quite isolated from the U.S. mainstream in 1930 but became less and less so during the following decade, with the introduction of schools, roads, and radios. Between 1930 and 1940, the average IQ of individuals in this community rose by 10 points, from 82 to 92 (Wheeler, 1942).

Further evidence comes from adoption studies. We have previously seen that they show the importance of genetic factors. But they also document the contribution of environment. One group of investigators studied the mean IQs of adopted children, most of whom were placed in foster homes before they were three months old. At age four, their mean IQ was 112, at age thirteen it was 117. The authors argue that these values are considerably higher than the mean IQ that would have been predicted for this group of children, given the fact that the occupational and educational levels of the biological parents were known to be below average. Since the adopting parents were above average on these indices as well as on IQ, it seems only natural to assume that the home background they provided led to an increase in the IQs of their adopted children (Skodak and Skeels, 1945, 1947, 1949). Similar results have been obtained in several other studies, both in France and in the United States (Schiff et al., 1982; Scarr and Weinberg, 1983).

Group Differences in IQ

Thus far, we have focused on IQ differences *within* groups and have considered the nature-nurture debate as it pertained to these. But the real fury of the controversy rages over another issue—the differences in average IQ that are found between groups, such as different socioeconomic classes or racial-ethnic groups.

Numerous studies have shown that the average score of American blacks is about 10 to 15 IQ points below the average of the white population (Loehlin,

Characters in 16th and 17th century Italy's Commedia dell' arte (A) Pantalone, the rich, stingy, old merchant, who is invariably deceived by his servants, his children, and his young wife. (B) Pulcinella, a sly and boisterous comic. (Courtesy Casa Goldoni, Venezia; photographs by Paul Smit, Imago)

In their comic drama, the Greeks and the Romans tended to think of people as *types*, a tradition that has continued in various forms to the present day. Their comedy created a large cast of stock characters, including the handsome hero, the pretty young maiden, the restless wife, her jealous husband, the angry old man, the sly servant, the panderer, the kind-hearted prostitute, the boastful soldier, the pedant, and so on. Many of these types were resurrected in later times and other countries. An example is the comic theater of Renaissance Italy, the *commedia dell' arte,* which boasted a large stable of such stock characters, each invariably played by the same actor, and always with a mask that indicated who he was. While modern movie and television actors usually don't wear masks (the Lone Ranger is one exception), they often represent stock characters even so. The hero and villain of the Western and the busybody and conniving schemer of the television soap opera are only a few of some of the instantly recognizable types.

Over the ages, there have been many discussions of the appropriate conception of dramatic and literary character. One concerned the use of type characters in drama and literature. Some critics argued that such characterizations are necessarily flat and two-dimensional and could not possibly do justice to an individual; in reality, even the most passionate lover is not just passionate, for he surely has other attributes as well. They therefore felt that drama and literature should avoid all such stock characters and instead only present fully rounded, complex characters, such as Hamlet, who are essentially like no one else. Such rounded characters are as difficult to describe perfectly as a person in real life and are therefore capable of surprising us (Forster, 1927). But other critics disagreed and felt that while simplified types could not possibly do full justice to any individual, they accomplished another and equally important aim: They showed what all people of a certain kind have in common rather than that which distinguishes them as individuals (Johnson, 1765).

Other arguments concerned the relative importance of internal versus external forces in determining what a character does. Some critics insisted that all dramatic action ultimately springs from within and grows out of the character's own essential nature, while others disagreed and pointed to the role of the external situation, as in the case of realistic modern dramas, such as *Death of a Salesman,* whose heroes do what they do because their social or economic situation forces them to. Yet another issue concerns the character's self-knowledge. Do her actions spring from goals of which she is aware, or is she reacting to unconscious forces that she herself does not recognize? (Bentley, 1983).

Some of these arguments between different schools of drama and literature are mirrored in current debates between different psychological theories of personality. As we will see, the drama of types is a distant cousin of modern **trait theory,** which holds that personality is best understood by the description and analysis of underlying personality traits (see pp. 459–72). The insistence that characters be rounded and to some extent unpredictable would be congenial to a **humanistic approach** to personality, which maintains that what is most important about people is how they achieve their own selfhood and actualize their human potentialities (see pp. 484–89). The insistence that a character's action is prompted by external circumstances is related to some formulations of the **behavioral approach** (sometimes called the behavioral-cognitive approach), which defines personality differences by the way in which different people act and think about their actions, and insists that these acts and thoughts are produced by the situation that the individuals face now or have faced on previous occasions (see pp. 479–84). And the belief that characters may act because of unconscious impulses is of course a dominant view of **psychodynamic theory,** which argues that the crucial aspects of personality stem from deeply buried, unconscious conflicts and desires (see Chapter 10 and pp. 473–79).

We will refer to some of the issues raised by the representation of dramatic character in this chapter, because they will provide us with a useful metaphorical framework within which to approach our present topic.

Before turning to theories of personality, we must first consider some of the methods by which differences in personality have been assessed.

ASSESSING PERSONALITY

There is an implicit assumption that underlies Theophrastus's sketches and any drama that uses character types, and that assumption is shared by most subsequent authors who have concerned themselves with personality: The personality patterns ascribed to their characters were assumed to be essentially consistent from time to time and from situation to situation. The hero was generally heroic, the villain villainous, and the garrulous man kept on talking regardless of who listened (or rather, tried not to listen). Some of the traits by which modern students of personality describe people are more subtle than those that define the stock characters of the classical or Renaissance stage, but for many investigators the key postulate of this *trait theory* still exists. They assume that these traits characterize a person's behavior in a variety of situations. This is just another way of saying that a knowledge of an individual's personality traits will permit us to predict what he is likely to do, even in situations in which we have never observed him (Allport, 1937).

Personality tests were devised in an attempt to supply the information that makes such prediction possible. In a way, they are analogous to an actor's audition; the director asks him to try out for a part by reading a page or two from a scene. Such an audition is a test that tries to determine (by no means perfectly) whether the actor *can play* a certain part. In contrast, a personality test is a test that tries to determine (again, far from perfectly) whether a person *is* that part.

Structured Personality Tests

As in the case of intelligence measurement, the impetus for the development of personality tests came from the world of practical affairs. But the parallel is even closer than that, for both kinds of tests began as instruments to determine certain undesirable conditions. Binet's test was originally designed to identify mentally retarded children. The first personality test had a parallel diagnostic aim. It was

Masks in modern theater *Masks are sometimes employed in modern drama in an allusion to their early use in classical times. (From a 1986 production of Harrison Birtwhistle's opera* The Mask of Orpheus *at the English National Opera; © Catherine Ashmore, London)*

Character types in the Nō drama of Japan *In the traditional Nō drama of Japan, character is indicated by a mask. The mask shown in the figure is that of a mystical old man with godlike powers. Before donning the mask, the actor who performs this part must go through various rituals of purification, because after he puts it on, the actor "becomes" the god. (Photograph by George Dineen/ Photo Researchers)*

meant to identify emotionally disturbed U.S. Army recruits during World War I. This test was an "adjustment inventory" consisting of a list of questions that dealt with various symptoms or problem areas (for instance, "Do you daydream frequently?" and "Do you wet your bed?"). If the subject reported many such symptoms, he was singled out for further psychiatric examination (Cronbach, 1970a).

The parallel between tests of intelligence and those of personality ends when we turn to the question of how these tests are validated. Binet and his successors had various criteria of validity: teachers' evaluations, academic performance, and, perhaps most important, chronological age. It turns out that validity criteria are much harder to come by in the field of personality measurement.

THE MMPI: CRITERION GROUPS FROM THE CLINIC

To provide an objective validity criterion, some later investigators turned to the diagnostic categories developed in clinical practice. Their object was to construct a test that could assess a person's similarity to this or the other psychiatric criterion group—hysterics, depressed patients, schizophrenics, and so on. The best-known test of this sort is the **Minnesota Multiphasic Personality Inventory,** or **MMPI,** which first appeared in 1940 and is still one of the most widely used personality tests on the current scene, both in clinical practice and research (Lanyon and Goldstein, 1982). It was called multiphasic because it was developed to assess a number of psychiatric patterns simultaneously.

Constructing the MMPI   The authors of the MMPI began by compiling a large set of test items taken from previously published inventories, from psychiatric examination forms, and from their own clinical hunches. These items were then administered to several patient groups with different diagnoses as well as to a group of normal subjects. The next step was to eliminate all items that did not discriminate between the patients and the normal controls and to retain those items that did. The end result was the MMPI in substantially its present form—an inventory of 550 items, the responses to which can be analyzed by reference to ten major scales. The score on each of these scales indicates how the subject's answers compare with those of the relevant criterion group (Table 16.1).

Table 16.1   SOME MMPI SCALES WITH REPRESENTATIVE EXAMPLE ITEMS*

Scale	Criterion group	Example items
Depression	Patients with intense unhappiness and feelings of hopelessness	"I often feel that life is not worth the trouble."
Paranoia	Patients with unusual degree of suspiciousness, together with feelings of persecution and delusions of grandeur	"Several people are following me everywhere."
Schizophrenia	Patients with a diagnosis of schizophrenia, characterized by bizarre or highly unusual thoughts or behavior, by withdrawal, and in many cases by delusions and hallucinations	"I seem to hear things that other people cannot hear."
Psychopathic deviance	Patients with marked difficulties in social adjustment, with histories of delinquency and other asocial behaviors	"I often was in trouble in school, although I do not understand for what reasons."

* In the example items here shown, the response appropriate to the scale is "True." For many other items, the reverse is true. Thus, answering "False" to the item "I liked school" would contribute to the person's score on the psychopathic deviance scale.

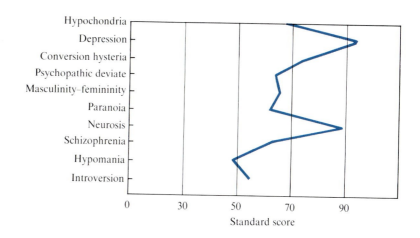

16.1 MMPI profile *The profile is of an adult male seeking help in a community health center. The scales are those described in Table 16.1. The scores are based on the performance of the standardization group. Scores above 70 will occur in about 2.5 percent of the cases; scores above 80 in about .1 percent. The profile strongly suggests considerable depression and neurotic anxiety. (After Lanyon and Goldstein, 1971)*

Using the MMPI In actual practice, interpreting an MMPI record is a complicated business. Clinicians don't merely look at the absolute scores obtained on any one scale. Instead, they consider the various scale values in relation to each other. This is most easily done by inspecting **score profiles** which present the scores on every scale in graphic form (Figure 16.1). An example is the interpretation of scores on the so-called depression scale. This consists of items that differentiated a group of patients diagnosed to be in a depressive state from normal persons. But a high score on this scale alone tells little more than that the patient is very unhappy. If we want to know more about the nature of this disturbance, we have to look at the profile as a whole (Meehl, 1956).

Validity scales One trouble with self-administered personality inventories is that the subjects can easily misrepresent themselves. To cope with this and related problems, the originators of the MMPI added a set of further items that make up several so-called validity scales. One is a simple lying scale. It contains items like "I gossip a little at times" and "Once in a while I laugh at a dirty joke." The assumption is that a person who denies a large number of such statements is either a saint (and few of those take personality tests) or is lying. Another validity scale consists of a number of bizarre statements like "There are persons who are trying to steal my thoughts and ideas" and "My soul sometimes leaves my body." To be sure, some of these statements are accepted by severely disturbed psychiatric patients, but even they endorse only a small proportion of them. As a result, we can be reasonably sure that a person who checks an unusually large number of such items is either careless, or has misunderstood the instructions, or is trying to fake psychiatric illness. If the score on these and similar validity scales is too high, the test record is discarded as invalid.

THE CPI: CRITERION GROUPS FROM NORMAL LIFE

While the MMPI can be employed to test normal subjects, it has some limitations when used in this way. The main problem is that the criterion groups that defined the scales were composed of psychiatric patients. This prompted the development of several new inventories constructed according to the same logic that led to the MMPI, but with normal rather than with pathological criterion groups. One of the best known of these is the *California Psychological Inventory,* or *CPI.* The CPI is especially aimed at high school and college students. It tests for various personality traits such as dominance, sociability, responsibility, sense of well-being, and so on.

As an example of how scales for these and other traits were derived, consider *dominance.* High school and college students were asked to name the most and the least dominant persons within their social circles. The persons who com-

cover, to find a useful framework within which to describe such differences, and to discover how they come about. In their efforts to answer these questions, they appeal to several so-called "personality theories."

Most of the theories of personality that have been developed thus far aren't really theories in the conventional sense. They are not specific enough to make the clear-cut predictions that would help us choose between them. What they are instead are different orientations from which the subject of personality is approached. We will begin with the *trait* approach, which tries to describe individuals by a set of characterizing attributes.

Trait theory is first of all an attempt to be descriptive. It tries to find some way to characterize people by reference to some underlying basic traits. But just which traits are basic? The comic dramas of classical and Renaissance days—and modern trait theory—imply not merely that a particular person has a characteristic personality, but that this personality can be categorized along with those of others who are in some ways equivalent. But what are the categories along which people should be grouped together? The early playwrights (and many film makers) picked a few attributes that were easy to characterize and caricature—the tight-lipped silence of the Western hero who speaks only with his guns, the virtuous chastity of the eternal heroine, the cowardice of the braggart soldier (who in Shakespeare's hands transcends his type and becomes Falstaff). But are these the personality traits that are really primary for the description of human personality?

The trait theorists' search for an answer is a bit like an attempt to find a few general principles that underlie the multitude of masks on, say, an Italian Renaissance stage. At first glance, these masks are very different, as different as the many persons we encounter in real life. Is there a way to classify these masks according to a few basic dimensions? Put another way, can we classify human personality by reference to a few fundamental traits?

The Search for the Right Taxonomy

In a way, much the same question is faced during the early stages of any science. At this point, a major task is the development of a useful *taxonomy,* or classification system. Consider the early biologists. They recognized that the various creatures differ in a multitude of ways—their size and color, the absence or the presence of a skeleton, the number and kind of appendages, and so on. The biologists had to decide which of these distinctions provided the most useful classification categories. Exactly the same issue faces the psychologist who studies personality differences. The dictionary lists 18,000 trait names (Allport and Odbert, 1936). But without some kind of taxonomy, how can we decide which of these are basic traits and important for classifying all people?

CLASSIFICATION THROUGH LANGUAGE

One step towards a taxonomy of personality traits grew out of an examination of the language used to describe personality attributes (Allport and Odbert, 1936). Advocates of this procedure argue that the adjectives used to describe people embody the accumulated observations of many previous generations. A systematic sifting of trait words would then give clues about individual differences whose description has been important enough to withstand the test of time (Goldberg, 1982).

This line of reasoning led to the development of a widely used personality inventory by Raymond Cattell (1957). Cattell's starting point was a set of 4,500 terms taken from the 18,000 trait words in an unabridged dictionary. This list

The seven dwarfs as character types   Doc, Sleepy, Grumpy, Dopey, Sneezy, Happy and Bashful. (From Walt Disney's Snow White; *courtesy the Kobal Collection*)

Table 16.2   THE NORMAN FIVE-FACTOR TAXONOMY OF PERSONALITY TRAITS

Factor names	Scale dimensions
Extroversion	Talkative/Silent Frank, open/Secretive Adventurous/Cautious Sociable/Reclusive
Agreeableness	Good-natured/Irritable Not jealous/Jealous Mild, gentle/Headstrong Cooperative/Negativistic
Conscientiousness	Fussy, tidy/Careless Responsible/Undependable Scrupulous/Unscrupulous Persevering/Quitting, fickle
Emotional stability	Poised/Nervous, tense Calm/Anxious Composed/Excitable Not hypochondriacal/Hypochondriacal
Culture	Artistically sensitive/Artistically insensitive Intellectual/Unreflective, narrow Polished, refined/Crude, boorish Imaginative/Simple, direct

SOURCE: Adapted from Norman, 1963.

was drastically reduced by throwing out difficult or uncommon words and eliminating synonyms. Finally 171 trait names were left. A group of judges was then asked to rate subjects by using these terms. Their ratings were subsequently factor analyzed by using methods similar to those employed in the study of intelligence-test performance—that is, by finding out which items correlated highly with one another while correlating little or not at all with others. The resulting item clusters were then inspected to see what they had in common, yielding what Cattell thought were some sixteen primary dimensions of personality (Cattell, 1966).

Later work by other investigators managed to reduce the number of primary dimensions to a smaller set. A widely quoted study by Warren Norman featured five major dimensions of personality: extroversion (sometimes called extraversion), emotional stability, agreeableness, conscientiousness, and cultural sensitivity. Norman's model is hierarchical in the sense that several lower-level traits (for example tidy/careless, persevering/fickle) can be regarded as manifestations of a higher-order factor (here, conscientiousness; see Table 16.2, from Norman, 1963).

NEUROTICISM AND EXTROVERSION/INTROVERSION

While many later studies have come up with five-factor descriptions of personality that are quite similar to Norman's (see Goldberg, 1981; Brody, 1988), others have suggested that the underlying dimensions may be fewer. The most influential alternative is that proposed by Hans Eysenck, who tried to encompass personality differences in a space defined by just two dimensions: neuroticism/emotional stability and extroversion/introversion (which correspond to two of Norman's dimensions).

Neuroticism is equivalent to emotional instability and maladjustment. It is assessed by affirmative answers to questions like "Do you ever feel 'just miserable' for no good reason at all?" And "Do you often feel disgruntled?" ***Extroversion-***

introversion are terms that refer to the main direction of a person's energies, toward the outer world of material objects and other people or toward the inner world of one's own thoughts and feelings. The extrovert is sociable, impulsive, and enjoys new experiences, while the introvert tends to be more solitary, cautious, and slow to change. Extroversion is indicated by affirmative answers to questions such as "Do you like to have many social engagements?" and "Would you rate yourself as a happy-go-lucky individual?"

As Eysenck sees it, neuroticism and extroversion-introversion are independent dimensions. To be sure, both introverts and many neurotics have something in common: They are both unsociable and withdrawn. But, in Eysenck's view, their lack of sociability has different roots. The healthy introverts are not afraid of social activities: They simply do not like them. In contrast, neurotically shy persons keep to themselves because of fear: They want to be with others but are afraid of joining them.

Eysenck points to an interesting relation between his own two-dimensional space and the venerable four-fold classification of temperaments proposed by the ancient Greek physician Hippocrates (ca. 400 B.C.). Hippocrates believed that there are four human temperaments that correspond to four different personality types: *sanguine* (cheerful and active), *melancholic* (gloomy), *choleric* (angry and violent), and *phlegmatic* (calm and passive). He believed that these temperaments reflected an excess of one of four bodily humors; thus sanguine persons were thought to have relatively more blood, melancholy persons to have an excess of black bile, phlegmatic persons to have an excess of phlegm, and choleric persons an excess of yellow bile (see Figure 16.7). Today the humor theory is a mere historical curiosity, but Hippocrates's four-fold classification is in some ways still with us. For the four quadrants of Eysenck's two-dimensional space seem to fit Hippocrates's four temperamental types. The category introverted and stable corresponds to phlegmatic, introverted and unstable to melancholic, extroverted and stable to sanguine, and extroverted and unstable to choleric (Eysenck and Rachman, 1965; see Figure 16.8).

Traits versus Situations

Different trait theorists may argue about the kind and number of trait dimensions with which to describe personality. Yet on one thing they all agree: There are personality traits that are stable and enduring properties of the individual. But during the last two decades, this basic credo has come under serious attack. One reason was the predictive validity of personality tests. For while tests such as the MMPI and the CPI predict behavior, they don't predict it all that accurately. Critics of the trait approach suggest that the tests don't do as well as one might wish because that which they are trying to measure—a set of stable personality traits—isn't really there. To put it another way, perhaps there is no real consistency in the way people behave at different times and in different situations.

THE DIFFICULTIES OF TRAIT THEORY

The concept of stable personality traits was seriously challenged by Walter Mischel, whose survey of the research literature led him to conclude that people behave much less consistently than a trait theory would predict (Mischel, 1968). A

16.7 An early taxonomy of personality   A medieval illustration of one of the earliest attempts to classify human personality, Hippocrates's four temperaments: sanguine (cheerful and active), melancholic (gloomy), choleric (angry and violent), and phlegmatic (calm and passive). (Courtesy the Bettmann Archive)

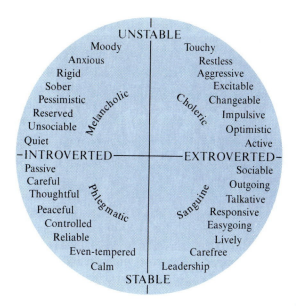

16.8 Eysenck's two-dimensional classification of personality Two dimensions of personality—neuroticism (emotional instability) and extroversion-introversion—define a space into which various trait terms may be fitted. Eysenck points out that the four quadrants of this space seem to fit Hippocrates's temperaments. Introverted and stable—phlegmatic; introverted and unstable—melancholic; extroverted and stable—sanguine; extroverted and unstable—choleric. (Eysenck and Rachman, 1965)

classic study concerns honesty in children (Hartshorne and May, 1928). Grade-school children were given the opportunity to lie, cheat, or steal in a wide variety of settings: in athletic events, in the classroom, at home, alone, or with peers. The important finding was that the child who was dishonest in one situation (cheating on a test) was not necessarily dishonest in another setting (an athletic contest). There was some consistency, but it was rather unimpressive; a later reanalysis of the results came up with an average intercorrelation of +.30 (Burton, 1963). The correlations were greater the greater the similarity between the two situations in which honesty was assessed. Honesty in one classroom situation was more consistent with honesty in another classroom situation than with honesty assessed at home.

Mischel argued that a similar lack of cross-situational consistency is found for many other behavior patterns. Examples are aggression, dependency, rigidity, and reactions to authority. The intercorrelations among different measures of what seems to be the same trait are often low and sometimes nonexistent. In Mischel's view, the fact that personality tests have relatively low validities is just another demonstration of the same phenomenon. A personality test taps behavior in one situation while the validity criterion of that test assesses behavior in an-

Traits versus situations Do the fighters punch each other because they want to win the prize money (situation) or because they are angry men (trait)? The blows probably hurt just as much either way. (George Bellows, Stag at Sharkey's, 1909, courtesy The Cleveland Museum of Art, Hinman B. Hurlbut Collection)

Aggression in boys and men *The same trait is often (though not always) expressed differently at different ages. (Left: Photograph by Wayne Miller/Magnum. Right: Photograph by Paul Kennedy/Leo de Wys)*

The criterion of consistency Another issue concerns the criterion of cross-situational consistency. A number of authors argue that behavioral inconsistency is often more apparent than real, for two reactions that are at first glance quite dissimilar may turn out to be a manifestation of the same underlying trait when examined more closely (e.g., Moskowitz, 1982; Buss and Craik, 1983; Rorer and Widiger, 1983).

Some good examples come from the study of development. Consider aggression. In males, aggression is fairly consistent between childhood and adolescence, but it takes different overt forms at different ages. Young boys pummel each other with their fists; young men rarely do more than shout in anger (Kagan and Moss, 1962). Another example concerns the distinction between the attributes *happy/outgoing* and *somber/reserved.* When different judges were asked to assess this trait in persons first studied at age six and then again at age fifteen, their ratings were quite similar, yielding correlations of about +.60. This consistency disappeared, however, when the judges were asked to rate overt behavior only. But as the author saw it, this result made sense. The five-year-old who is reserved and somber shows this by a low level of physical vitality. At ten, the same underlying attribute manifests itself as cautiousness and emotional vulnerability. Still later, during adolescence, this basic pattern goes together with a sense of inferiority (Bronson, 1966).

Here, as in so many other aspects of behavior, a superficial difference disguises a deeper sameness. At a surface level, the two sentences *John eats the apple* and *The apple is eaten by John* are obviously different. But at a deeper level, they are in many ways alike and mean much the same thing.

THE INTERACTION BETWEEN PERSON AND SITUATION

A number of psychologists feel that the debate between situationists and trait theorists has focused on the wrong distinction. As originally formulated, the question was whether an individual's actions are better predicted by the situation or by his or her own personal characteristics. But there is a third alternative: the critical factor may be the ***interaction*** between person and situation (e.g., Magnusson and Endler, 1977).

An example of such an interaction is provided by a study in which subjects were asked to describe their usual reaction to various threats (Endler and Hunt, 1969). Some of these perils involved loss of self-esteem (failing an examination), others physical danger (being on a high ledge on a mountaintop), still others a threat whose nature was still unclear (getting a police summons). The results showed that both individual differences and situations affected behavior to some extent. Some people seemed more generally fearful than others, and some situations ("being approached by cars racing abreast") evoked more fear than others ("sitting in a restaurant").

But even more important than these effects were the results of the person-by-situation interaction. Put in other words, people tend to be frightened (or angered or reassured) by different things. A simple situationism is evidently untenable; the man who is terrified of heights may well be a passionate scuba diver. This finding undercuts the usefulness of general traits such as "anxiety." To predict behavior better, such traits should be qualified; for example, "anxiety in an interpersonal setting," "anxiousness when facing physical danger," "anxiety in the face of the unknown." By this utilization of the person-by-situation interaction, the notion of stable personality differences can be maintained. But there is a price, for the process of qualification may be endless. Consider interpersonal anxiety. It probably depends on whether the situation involves members of the same or the opposite sex. If it does, should we subdivide the trait still further? The end result can only be an enormous proliferation of ever more finely drawn traits.

CONSISTENCY AS A TRAIT

By now there is general agreement that, when properly defined, traits do exist. We've seen that a major criterion for determining whether such traits are present is cross-situational consistency in behavior. But recently, psychologists have come to realize that consistency itself—the degree to which people do much the same thing in different situations—varies from person to person! To the extent that this is true, cross-situational consistency may be regarded as a trait in its own right.

Some people are more consistent than others   Most of us are affected by both our personal characteristics and by the demands of the situation. But the extent to which one or the other of these predominates varies from person to person. It goes without saying that there are some social situations that affect most people equally and allow little play for personal variations. At a funeral, everyone is quiet and restrained. But at a picnic, differences in sociability and energy level will be readily apparent (Price and Bouffard, 1974; Monson, Hesley, and Chernick, 1982). What about situations that are more ambiguous? Here some people will tend to behave much more consistently than others.

Self-monitoring   One of the factors that determines the extent to which people adjust their behavior to fit the social situation is the degree to which they try to control the impression they make on others, so that they can be "the right person

The extremes of the self-monitoring scale   (A) Woody Allen as the high self-monitor, Zelig, the man who can fit in with anybody, anywhere, anytime. (B) Woody Allen as the hero of most of his other movies who remains Woody Allen, the ultimate low self-monitor, who stays true to himself regardless of the situation. (Pictured with Calvin Coolidge and Herbert Hoover in Zelig, 1983, courtesy the Kobal Collection; with Diane Keaton in Annie Hall, 1977, courtesy Photofest)

A

B

in the right place at the right time." The tendency to do this is assessed by the *self-monitoring scale,* developed by Mark Snyder (for some representative items, see Table 16.3). High self-monitors care a great deal about the appearance of the self they project in a given social situation. By constantly adjusting to the situation, they are necessarily inconsistent; they'll act like cultured highbrows when with art lovers, and boisterous sports fans when with a group of college athletes. In effect, they always seem to ask themselves: "How can I be the person this situation calls for?" In contrast, low self-monitors are much less interested in how they appear to others. They want to be themselves whatever the social climate in which they find themselves. As a result, their behavior is much more consistent from situation to situation (Snyder, 1987).

Table 16.3   SOME REPRESENTATIVE ITEMS FROM THE SELF-MONITORING SCALE

1. I can look anyone in the eye and tell a lie with a straight face (if for a right end). (True)*

2. In different situations and with different people, I often act like very different persons. (True)

3. I have trouble changing my behavior to suit different people and different situations. (False)

4. I can only argue for ideas which I already believe. (False)

* In the items shown, the key after each question is in the direction of self-monitoring. Thus high self-monitors would presumably answer "True" to questions 1 and 2, and "False" to questions 3 and 4.
SOURCE: Snyder, 1987.

On the face of it, the high self-monitor seems to cut a rather less admirable figure than his low self-monitoring counterpart. But as Snyder points out, whether such value judgments apply depends on the way in which the self-monitoring pattern fits into the rest of the individual's life. The high self-monitor is probably rather pleasant to be with, and his diplomatic skill and adaptability may well be an asset in dealing with the many roles created by a complex society such as ours. The virtues of the low self-monitor are even more apparent; there's much to be said for the man of integrity who is the same today as he'll be tomorrow and to himself is true. But at the extremes, neither approach is particularly appealing. An extremely high self-monitor may very well be a shallow, unprincipled poseur. And an extremely low self-monitor may manage to turn the virtues of his pattern into vices as consistent adherence to principle becomes blind and stubborn rigidity. To march to the music of a different drummer is not necessarily admirable. It depends on what the music is (Snyder, 1987).

Consistency and mental disorder   When insensitivity to the situation becomes extreme enough, we are in the realm of mental disorder. Mentally disturbed persons are generally less (usually much less) responsive to the demands of a situation than are normal people. As a result, they show more behavioral consistency across situations. Normal people smile about births and cry about deaths; psychiatrically depressed patients may cry about both. The same applies to other forms of mental illness. The patients' responses are governed more by factors within themselves—depressions, violent elations, delusions—than by the situation that confronts them. As a result, their behavior is often viewed by others as inappropriate to the occasion (which is one of the reasons why they are in the psychiatric ward). But in consequence, they also manifest more cross-situational consistency than do the rest of us (for some relevant findings, see Moos, 1969).

In the light of all this, what can we say about the assumption that there is an underlying unity in how any one individual acts and thinks and feels, a basic consistency that we call personality? The evidence indicates that this assumption —which goes back to the ancient dramatists and before—still stands.

We all have an intuitive belief in something like "person constancy," a phenomenon analogous to "object constancy" in perception (see Chapter 5). A chair is perceived as a stable object whose size remains the same whether we are near to it or far away and whose shape remains unchanged regardless of our visual orientation. These constancies are not illusions; they reflect a genuine stability in the external world. The stability of persons is in some ways analogous. For we somehow manage to peer through a welter of ever-changing situations to perceive an individual's behavioral consistency. The constancy of personality is not as sturdy as that of chairs, but it has some reality even so.

To be sure, this constancy is far from perfect. We change from day to day; we're grouchy on Monday because of a headache and cheery on Tuesday because of a sunny sky. We also change from year to year—with age, experience, and various shifts of fortune. A number of psychologists suspect that we underestimate the extent to which such changes occur. In observing others, we form a notion of their personality. In observing ourselves, we form a so-called *self-concept*—a set of ideas about who we ourselves are. (For more detail, see pp. 321 and 485–86.) But in their view, our perception of the personality of others, as well as our own self-concept, are at bottom mental constructions, and as such they are subject to error. One such error is the tendency to see more uniformity and coherence than is actually there, to exaggerate person constancy in others and in ourselves (Shweder, 1975; Nisbett and Wilson, 1977; Nisbett, 1980; Kihlstrom and Cantor, 1984).

But the fact that there are errors in our perception of persons, doesn't mean that their personality is entirely in our own eyes. After all, there are visual illusions, but their existence does not disprove the fact that by and large we see the world as it really is. What holds for the world of vision probably holds for person perception as well, and this is probably why trait theory has continued to have so much appeal (Kenrick and Funder, 1988). Person constancy is a fact. Jane remains Jane whether she is at home or at the office, whether it is today or yesterday or the day after tomorrow. And at some level she is different from Carol and Margaret and five billion other humans alive today, for her personality—just like theirs—is unique.

Traits and Biology

To the extent that person constancy exists, we are probably justified in holding on to some version of the trait approach. People vary in their characteristic modes of behavior, and their variations can be described and assessed, however imperfectly, by the trait vocabulary. But how do such variations arise?

Thus far, we've talked about traits as if they were merely descriptive labels for broad groups of behavior patterns. But most trait theorists go further. In their view, traits are general predispositions to behave in one way or another that are ultimately rooted in the individual's biological makeup.

PERSONALITY AND TEMPERAMENT

A number of modern investigators believe that personality traits grow out of the individual's *temperament,* a characteristic reaction pattern of the individual that

Person constancy and caricature Most artists have always believed that there is a constancy of behavioral as well as of bodily features, as illustrated in this 1743 print by William Hogarth. (Detail from "Characters and Caricaturas," subscription ticket for Marriage à la Mode; reproduced by courtesy of the Trustees of the British Museum)

is present from a rather early age. Like Hippocrates who coined the term some 2500 years ago, they believe that such temperamental patterns are largely genetic and constitutional in origin (though they obviously don't share his archaic ideas of their underlying humoral basis). Such characteristic behavior patterns may begin in the first few months of life. An example comes from a study of 141 children, observed for about a decade following birth:

> Donald exhibited an extremely high activity level almost from birth. At three months . . . he wriggled and moved about a great deal while asleep in his crib. At six months he "swam like a fish" while being bathed. At twelve months he still squirmed constantly while he was being dressed or washed. . . . At two years he was "constantly in motion, jumping and climbing." At three, he would "climb like a monkey and run like an unleashed puppy". . . . By the time he was seven, Donald was encountering difficulty in school because he was unable to sit still long enough to learn anything. . . . (Thomas, Chess, and Birch, 1970, p. 104)

More recent investigators have tried to describe temperament within the framework of traditional trait classifications. An example is a temperament scale developed by Buss and Plomin that includes two major dimensions called sociability and emotionality (Buss and Plomin, 1984). According to Buss and Plomin, these two traits represent the core components of the main axes of Eysenck's system—extroversion and neuroticism/emotional stability. They feel that in young children, extroversion is best represented by sociability (which presumably affects the attachment bond between mother and child, reactions to strangers, and the like) while neuroticism/emotional instability is mainly represented by a greater tendency to be fearful (anxiety and guilt are reactions that come in later years). In line with these views, both sociability and emotionality show a fair degree of stability over the first twenty years of life, as demonstrated by correlations of +.48 between fearfulness at age five and in adulthood, and of +.53 between sociability at age six and at age fifteen (Bronson, 1966, 1967).

PERSONALITY AND THE GENES

Consistencies of this sort suggest the operation of genetic factors. Such hereditary effects are no news to animal breeders. Different strains of dogs show marked differences in temperament produced by centuries of breeding: Basset hounds are calm, terriers are excitable and aggressive, while spaniels become easily attached to people and are very peaceable (Scott and Fuller, 1965; see Figure 16.9). We wouldn't expect to find such enormous differences in human temperaments; for-

16.9   Temperamental differences in different breeds of dogs   *(A) Basset hounds are calm (Photograph by Wilfong Photographic/Leo de Wys, Inc.), (B) terriers are excitable, and (C) spaniels are very sociable and affectionate. (Photographs by H. Reinhard/Bruce Coleman)*

A

B

C

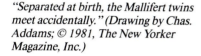

"Separated at birth, the Mallifert twins meet accidentally." (Drawing by Chas. Addams; © 1981, The New Yorker Magazine, Inc.)

tunately, there are no people breeders interested in creating pure-bred human strains. But some fairly sizable genetic effects on human personality exist even so.

The evidence comes from the same methods that have been used to study hereditary effects in the determination of intelligence—the study of twins. In just about all cases, identical twins turn out to be more alike than fraternal twins on various personality attributes (e.g., Buss and Plomin, 1984; Zuckerman, 1987). In one study, a personality questionnaire was administered to over 12,000 pairs of twins in Sweden. The results showed average correlations of +.50 between identical twins on scores both of extroversion and of neuroticism. The corresponding correlations for fraternal twins were +.21 and +.23 (Floderus-Myrhed, Pedersen, and Rasmuson, 1980). Given these findings, there is little doubt that hereditary factors make a sizable contribution to differences in personality makeup.

PERSONALITY AND PHYSIOLOGICAL AROUSAL

To say that personality traits are in part inherited is to say that they have some physical basis. But just what is this physical basis? Here the search for an answer has just begun.

An interesting approach comes from attempts to link certain personality traits to aspects of neurophysiological arousal. The pioneer in this area has been Hans Eysenck, who has tried to relate the extroversion-introversion dimension to many phenomena outside of the personality domain.

Extroversion and the arousal system As Eysenck sees it, introversion corresponds to a higher level of central nervous system arousal than does extroversion; in effect, introverts are thought to be more awake than extroverts. As a result, they are less distractible and better able to attend to the task at hand (Harkins and Green, 1975). A related finding is that introverts are more reactive to external stimuli than extroverts are; according to Eysenck, this is one of the reasons why they shy away from the world while extroverts embrace it enthusiastically. Thus introverts have lower pain tolerance (Bartol and Costello, 1976) and when studying prefer a lower noise level and fewer opportunities for socializing (Campbell and Hawley, 1982). On the other hand, extroverts prefer to be stimulated; they

A

B

C

Some people seek sensations whether in the air, on land, or on water. (Photographs from left to right by Guy Sauvage, Vandystadt/Photo Researchers; Gianfranco Gorgoni/Leo de Wys; Cirotteau-Lambolez, Vandystadt/Photo Researchers)

Others prefer a more quiet existence. (Photograph by Alan Carey/The Image Works)

seek diversion from job routine, enjoy going on trips without planned routes, and are more active sexually, both in terms of frequency and of number of different partners (Wilson, 1978). They need external stimulation more than do the naturally aroused introverts.

Sensation seeking A related topic concerns *sensation seeking.* This is the tendency to seek varied and novel experiences, to look for thrills and adventure, and to be highly susceptible to boredom, as shown by affirmative answers to items such as: "I would like to try parachute jumping," "I sometimes like to do 'crazy' things just to see the effect on others," and "I wish I didn't have to waste so much of a day sleeping" (Zuckerman, 1979). Marvin Zuckerman, who developed the scales that contained these items, has provided convincing evidence of their validity. People who score at the high end of these scales are more likely to participate in risky sports such as scuba diving, get more restless in a monotonous confined situation, are less likely to be afraid of snakes, and drive at faster speeds than people at the lower end (Zuckerman, 1983).

A final bit of validation comes from a study on "streaking," a popular fad of the 1970s, whose practitioners took off their clothes and then ran, walked, or bicycled naked through some public area. When students were asked whether they had ever considered streaking (or had in fact streaked), their answer showed a substantial correlation with the sensation-seeking scales (Bacon, 1974, quoted in Zuckerman, 1979).*

According to Zuckerman, the biological basis of sensation seeking is similar to that which Eysenck suggested for extroversion. In Zuckerman's view, sensation seekers are people who are underaroused in certain systems of the brain, specifically those whose neurotransmitter is norepinephrine (usually abbreviated NE). One of his lines of evidence comes from a study in which the level of NE in the spinal fluid was correlated with various measures on personality scales. The results showed a negative correlation: the greater the sensation-seeking tendency, the lower the NE level (Zuckerman et al., 1983). This fits in with the general hypothesis. Persons whose NE level is low are presumably underactive in their NE systems. In effect, they are underaroused; as a result they seek thrills and take risks to jog their depleted and sluggish NE systems into greater activity.

---

* While sensation seeking is related to extroversion, it is not identical with it. It focuses on the liveliness and intolerance of boredom that characterize extroversion, but seems to have little to do with the sociability, which is another aspect of that trait.

THE PSYCHODYNAMIC APPROACH

We've seen that trait theory tries to explain differences in human personality by reference to certain basic trait dimensions, some of which may well be based on genetic predispositions. But there are several alternative approaches to personality that take another tack entirely. One such alternative is the *psychodynamic approach.*

Adherents of the psychodynamic approach do not deny that some people are more sociable than others, or more impulsive, or emotionally labile, or whatever. But they feel that explaining such tendencies as the expression of a personality trait is rather superficial. In their view, what people do and say—and even what they consciously think—is only the tip of the iceberg. As they see it, human acts and thoughts are just the outer expression of a whole set of motives and desires that are often derived from early childhood experiences, that lie buried underneath the surface, that are generally pitted against each other, and that are for the most part unknown to the person himself. They believe that to understand a person is to understand these hidden psychological forces (often called *dynamics*) that make him an individual divided against himself.

We've previously seen that the trait approach bears a certain similarity to dramatic forms that employ stock characters such as the comedies of the classical age. In such plays, everything was exactly what it appeared to be. Once the character entered, the audience knew pretty much what to expect. If he wore the mask of the cowardly soldier, he would brag and run away; if he wore the mask of the miserly old man, he would jealously guard his money. In contrast, the psychodynamic perspective is related to a more modern approach to drama in which nothing is quite what it seems. In playing a character, actors who follow this approach may pay more attention to the so-called *subtext* (the unspoken thoughts and musings that go through the character's head while he speaks his lines) than the *text* itself (the actual lines the playwright put into the character's mouth). And many actors are interested in a still deeper subtext, which consists of thoughts and wishes of which the character is generally unaware.

Text and subtext   In many plays, what the characters leave unspoken (the subtext) is often more important than what they say (the text). (From a 1988 production of Anton Chekhov's The Cherry Orchard, *directed by Peter Brook, starring Natasha Perry and Erland Josephson)*

The dramatic presentation of inner conflicts   *In some cases, actors play a character who is not fully aware of her own subtext, so she, like one of Freud's patients, is really lying to herself. An example is Blanche, in this scene from Tennessee Williams's play* A Streetcar Named Desire. *She is both sexually attracted and repelled by her brutal brother-in-law Stanley. (From the stage version of* A Streetcar Named Desire, *1947, with Marlon Brando and Jessica Tandy; photograph courtesy of the Museum of the City of New York)*

Personality Structure and Development: The Freudian Account

All current versions of the psychodynamic approach are ultimately derived from the views of Sigmund Freud, the founder of psychoanalysis (1856–1939). We've already described Freud's general conceptions in a previous chapter (see Chapter 10), in which we saw that his theory of personality is a virtually all-embracing conception that encompasses phenomena as diverse as childhood development, neurotic symptoms, and psychoanalytic therapy. Since our present concern is with differences in personalities, we will only present a brief review of psychodynamic conceptions that bear on this issue.

Freud's ideas grew out of studies of emotionally disturbed individuals whose symptoms seemed to reflect certain emotionally charged thoughts or wishes that these patients had shoved out of consciousness (or to use his term, *repressed*). In his view, all human beings experience *unconscious conflicts* that originate in childhood and that influence later personality. He believed that many aspects of these conflicts are at bottom the same for us all.

Freud distinguished among three subsystems of the human personality that are usually locked in unconscious three-way combat: the *id,* a collection of blind instinctual strivings that scream out for immediate satisfaction; the *ego,* a set of partially conscious reaction patterns that try to mediate between the needs of the id and the realities of the actual world; and the *superego,* which corresponds to the internalized commands and prohibitions of the parents and punishes any transgressions with sharp pangs of guilt.

According to Freud, the fundamental principle of unconscious conflict is defense against anxiety. He believed that as parents reprimand the child for various forbidden thoughts or deeds, these thoughts or deeds become connected to anxiety. To ward off this unpleasant state, the child represses the thoughts, or memories, or desires that triggered the anxiety and shoves them out of consciousness. Repression is often supplemented by a number of other *defense mechanisms* against anxiety, including reaction formation, displacement, rationalization, and projection (see Chapter 10, pp. 292–93).

PSYCHOSEXUAL DEVELOPMENT IN CHILDHOOD

Freud believed that all of us begin life as a collection of blind, instinctual pleasure-seeking tendencies. This pleasure is obtained by the stimulation of the so-called *erogenous zones:* the mouth, anus, and the genitals. As the child develops, the relative importance of the three zones changes. Initially, there is the *oral stage,* during which the main focus is on the mouth and on the satisfactions of sucking, eating, and eventually biting, obtained in the course of feeding. Some time later, the emphasis shifts, and the child becomes concerned with matters related to toilet training during the *anal stage.*

At about four or five years of age, during the *phallic stage,* the primary stress is on the pleasure obtained from stimulation of the genitals and on the resolution of the Oedipus complex (see Chapter 10). At this point, the little boy directs his infantile sexual longings toward his mother, jealously hates his father, comes to fear his retribution, and finally shoves the entire set of conflicts out of consciousness and identifies with the father. (The little girl exhibits a symmetrical pattern: sexual desire for the father, rivalry and eventual identification with the mother.)

Following the furor of the Oedipal events, both girls and boys go through the six or seven years of the *latency period,* during which their sexuality lies dormant until it is reawakened beginning at puberty. With advancing adolescence, the last phase of psychosexual development brings the *genital stage,* in which the crude

Acting with the subtext Certain modern approaches to acting such as those developed by New York's Actor's Studio emphasize the importance of subtexts. The photo shows a scene from the film, Godfather PART II, *featuring Lee Strasberg, the late head of the Actor's Studio, and Al Pacino, one of its illustrious graduates. In the scene, a gangster overlord plans a deadly double-cross of another, while telling him: "You're a wise and considerate young man." (From* Godfather, PART II, *1974; courtesy the Kobal Collection)*

instinctual id-derived urges are transformed into mature sexual love, where the social and physical gratification of one's sexual partner plays a vital part.

ADULT PERSONALITY DIFFERENCES AS REMNANTS OF CHILDHOOD PATTERNS

While the psychodynamic approach (and Freud's theory in particular) makes many assertions about the nature of human personality in general, it has rather less to say about the way in which people (especially "normal" people) differ from each other. One influential conception goes back to Freud: the idea that adult patterns can be understood and classified as remnants of reactions at one or another stage of childhood psychosexual development.

The theory To develop, the child has to move from one stage to the next. But there are obstacles to smooth progression, for each change will necessarily produce some frustration as the child has to give up some earlier forms of gaining pleasure (for example, upon weaning). Certain reactions to the frustrations that occur at each changeover point may have lasting consequences. One such reaction is *fixation,* which refers to a lingering attachment to an earlier stage of pleasure seeking even after a new stage has been attained. Some remnants of the earlier pattern may hang on for a while, such as thumb-sucking in weaned infants. Another mode of response to frustration during development is *reaction formation,* a mechanism of defense through which the forbidden impulse that was pushed out of consciousness is replaced by its very opposite.

Freud believed that residues of early fixations and reaction formations continue into adulthood and lay the foundation for later personality patterns. An example is the so-called *anal character,* a personality that he thought was derived from severe conflicts during toilet training (Freud, 1908; Abraham, 1927). Since toilet training often begins before the child is physically capable of voluntary sphincter control, it is a difficult task. One result may be considerable anxiety, which in turn leads to a reaction formation in which the child inhibits rather than relaxes his bowels. This broadens and becomes manifest in more symbolic terms. The child becomes compulsively clean and orderly ("I must not soil myself").

Freud believed that there are several other such effects. One is obstinacy. The child asserts himself by holding back on his potty ("You can't make me if I don't want to"), a stubbornness which may become a more generalized "no." Another characteristic is stinginess. According to Freud, this is a form of withholding, a re-

Personality traits in art *The traits that Freud regarded as the defining attributes of the anal character—obstinancy, compulsive orderliness, and stinginess—are often held up to scorn and ridicule as in Charles Dickens's miserly Scrooge. But when viewed in a more benign light, these same traits—now labeled steadfastness, efficiency, and frugality—can be regarded as praiseworthy characteristics of the rising middle classes in Europe, as in this group portrait of 17th-century Dutch officials of the clothmakers' guild. (*The Syndics, *1662, by Rembrandt; courtesy of the Rijksmuseum, Amsterdam)*

fusal to part with what is one's own (that is, one's feces). This refusal generalizes, and the child becomes obsessed with property rights and jealously hoards his possessions. Freud believed that excessive conflicts during the anal stage may lead to an adult personality that displays the three symptomatic attributes of the anal character—compulsive orderliness, stubbornness, and stinginess.

The evidence   What is the evidence on the role of early childhood events in producing differences in adult personality? Some interesting results come from a work directed at Freud's theory of the anal character.

The evidence indicates that the critical "anal traits"—neatness, obstinacy, and parsimony—do in fact correlate to a significant extent (Fisher and Greenberg, 1977). In one such study, a number of undergraduates were asked to rate their own and their friends' characteristics. Their ratings showed that the three critical traits do indeed form a coherent cluster. Those students who judged themselves (or were judged by others) to be obstinate were also those who tended to be orderly and a bit stingy. More important, the students with these "anal" characteristics tended to have mothers with similar attributes, as shown by questionnaires administered to the mothers. These results seem to vindicate Freud's theory, since it appears that anal children have anal mothers. But a further finding runs counter to the theory. The mothers were asked at what age they toilet-trained their children. There was no correlation whatever between this factor and the personality traits that define the anal character (Beloff, 1957).

This result fits in with other studies on the effects of toilet training. There is little evidence that shows any long-term effects growing out of toilet-training practices, either in our own or other cultures (Orlansky, 1949). For example, there seems to be no relation between the severity of toilet training in different cultures and the degree of hoarding or economic competition (Cohen, 1953). There is thus little evidence for Freud's claim that the toilet is a prep school for becoming a banker or a captain of industry.

Personality and Patterns of Defense: Psychoanalysis after Freud

A related approach to the description and analysis of personality differences is by reference to the dominant patterns of defense. Psychodynamic theorists believe that anxiety is an inevitable part of human existence and that some defenses against anxiety will therefore be found in everyone. What makes people different is the pattern of defenses they have erected. A number of authors have tried to describe some of the characteristic patterns observed in nineteenth-century Western society. Many of these theorists belong to a group of psychoanalytic dissidents often grouped together under the loose label *neo-Freudians.* By and large, the neo-Freudians accepted Freud's general views on internal conflicts but had different ideas as to what these conflicts were about. Their main argument with Freud was in their insistence that the description of our inner conflicts should be in social and interpersonal rather than biological terms (see Chapter 10).

PATTERNS OF NEUROTIC CONFLICT

A major figure of the neo-Freudian movement was Karen Horney (1885–1952), who argued that many people in our society suffer from *basic anxiety*—an "all-pervading feeling of being alone and helpless in a hostile world" (Horney, 1937, p. 89). Horney believed that this anxious feeling should not be traced to childhood struggles with infantile sexual conflicts. She felt that instead its roots are in our culture, which often makes incompatible demands on the individual.

According to Karen Horney, the neurotics' basic anxiety leads them to the frantic pursuit of various goals, sought less for themselves than as a way to deaden this anxiety. Some neurotics try to assuage their anxiety by seeking love, others by seeking prestige or possessions, still others by withdrawing from any genuine emotional involvements, and yet others by deadening it with alcohol or drugs (Horney, 1937, 1945, 1950). Such efforts often fail, but they generally persist and harden into enduring patterns of personality. The question is why. Horney's answer is that the neurotic conflict creates a self-perpetuating *vicious circle.*

An example of such a vicious circle is the neurotic search for love. If a man needs a woman's love to deaden his sense of basic anxiety, his demands for affection will be unconditional and excessive. But if so, they can't possibly be fulfilled. The slightest failure to accede to his wishes will be interpreted as a rebuff and rejection. This will increase his feelings of anxiety, which will make him even more desperate for affectionate reassurance, which will further increase the chances of rebuff, and so on. Add the fact that such rebuffs—whether real or imagined—lead to hostility, which he can't possibly acknowledge lest he lose her altogether. Add the further fact that since his basic anxiety makes him devalue himself, he may well begin to devalue her. How could she be as wonderful as he thought at first, if she loves *him?* As Groucho Marx once said, "I wouldn't want to belong to any club that would accept me as a member." All of these further factors combine to enhance the love-seeking neurotic's sense of anxiety, which then refuels his desperate need for love and affection.

COPING PATTERNS AND MENTAL HEALTH

The patterns we have just described characterize people with emotional conflicts that in some cases are quite serious. But can they help us understand normal persons? Psychodynamically oriented theorists would say that they can. For in their view, unconscious conflict and defense mechanisms are found in so-called normal persons as well as in persons with profound emotional disorders; what distinguishes the two is the extent to which those conflicts are appropriately resolved.

Several investigators have studied the characteristic patterns of defense using normal persons. Much of this work was influenced by an emerging new movement in psychoanalysis, called *ego psychology,* whose initial impetus probably came from Freud's daughter Anna Freud (1895–1982) and whose leaders include Heinz Hartmann (1894–1970), as well as Erik Erikson (1902–   ) whose work we've encountered in a previous chapter (see Chapter 14). Adherents of this posi-

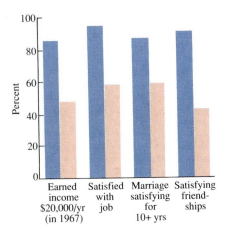

16.10 Maturity of defense mechanisms and life adjustment *Adult success at work and love, as shown by men with predominantly mature (blue) and immature (pink) adaptive styles. (After Vaillant, 1971)*

tion share the neo-Freudian concern with cultural factors and interpersonal factors. But they add a further element by stressing the healthy aspects of the self as it tries to *cope* with the world—to deal with reality as it is rather than to distort it or hide away from it (Freud, A., 1946; Hartmann, 1964).

To find out how coping patterns are employed over the course of the life span, a number of investigators have performed *longitudinal studies,* that is, studies in which the same person is examined at different ages. Longitudinal studies that cover a span of twenty to thirty years represent an arduous undertaking; subjects drop out of the study for any number of reasons, and the investigators who begin the study are rarely the ones who finally complete it. In longitudinal studies of personality, the raw material is usually in the form of interview records conducted at different points in time. These records are later rated for various characteristics, such as certain personality traits, or the use of this or another mechanism of defense.

An example of such a longitudinal study is George Vaillant's analysis of the case reports of ninety-four male college graduates studied at different points in their life span. They were extensively interviewed at age nineteen and then again at thirty-one, and yet again at forty-seven. Vaillant studied the predominant patterns of defense—that is, ways of coping—each man used at these three ages. He classified these coping patterns according to their level of psychological maturity. At the bottom of the hierarchy were mechanisms that are often found in early childhood and during serious psychiatric breakdown—for example, denial or gross distortions of external reality. Further up the ladder were patterns often seen in adolescence and in disturbed adults—for example, projection, hypochondria, and irrational, emotional outbursts, "acting out." Still higher were the mechanisms studied by Freud and seen in many adults—repression, isolation, reaction formation, and the like. At the top of the hierarchy were coping patterns that Vaillant had seen in "healthy" adolescents and adults—for example, humor, suppression (a conscious effort to push anxiety-evoking thoughts out of mind, at least for the time being, as opposed to repression, which is an unconscious process), and altruism (in which one tries to give to others what one might wish to receive oneself).

Vaillant's findings are simple enough. It's not particularly surprising (though certainly reassuring), that as his subjects grew older, their coping mechanisms generally became more mature. There was growth and change, but there was also some continuity; men whose coping patterns were better integrated at nineteen, were—somewhat—more likely to have mature patterns in their forties, which then predicted various objective indices—satisfaction in marriage, rewarding friendships, more gratifying jobs, and better physical health (see Figure 16.10). As so often, it is by no means clear just what in those men's lives was cause and what was effect; but regardless of whether the mature coping defenses produced success in marriage and career or vice versa, it is worth knowing that the two tend to be correlated (Vaillant, 1974, 1976, 1977).

COPING AND THE UNCONSCIOUS

On the face of it, the preceding discussion of adaptive patterns may appear rather distant from the orientation of psychodynamic theorists, especially as represented by Freud. After all, Freud emphasized unconscious processes that operated in a murky underground of which we are unaware. In contrast, the coping responses of normal people seem much more ordinary, and they are at least sometimes in plain view. Is there any relation between these two?

Ego-oriented psychoanalysts—and most modern psychologists—would answer yes. For whatever their many differences, the defense mechanisms of the neurotic and the shoulder-shrugging reaction of the mature adult who refuses to worry about things he can't help anyway have one thing in common—they are both ways of trying to cope with and adapt to the strains and stresses of existence.

The fact that some of these adaptive reactions are fully conscious while others are not doesn't necessarily mean that there is a sharp break between them. For a number of psychologists have pointed out that what Freud called unconscious mechanisms may be regarded as ways of not attending (Erdelyi and Goldberg, 1979; Bowers, 1984; Erdelyi, 1985). The person who is in favor of a particular political candidate is much more likely to attend to arguments on his behalf than to arguments that favor his opponent. The first he will tend to remember; the second he is likely to forget. Similarly, the woman who has just suffered a painful divorce may prefer not to think about her ex-husband. When some topic comes up that starts to remind her about him, she will deliberately try to think about something else and may forget what it was that started the new train of thought. This method of turning away from one's own pain may not be as exotic as the complicated repressive maneuvers of Freud's patients, but it belongs to the same family.

Most of us physically avoid some situations we would rather not face; by the same token, some of us mentally avoid (that is, don't attend to) sights or thoughts or memories we find unpleasant or frightening. Seen in this light, the so-called unconscious mechanisms lose some of their mystery. They are just one more way of coping with the world.

A BEHAVIORAL APPROACH TO PERSONALITY

Repertory roles   Lawrence Olivier is often regarded as the prototype of the repertory actor who could play any part. He once said that "in finding a character . . . I do it from the outside in," an approach quite different from that of the Actor's Studio. (A) As Hamlet (from the 1948 film he directed), (B) As Archie Rice, a cheap music hall entertainer (from the 1960 film, The Entertainer*), (C) as the Mahdi, the fanatical leader of a nineteenth-century Sudanese sect (from the 1966 film* Khartoum*). (Courtesy Photofest)*

Both trait theory and the psychodynamic approach try to explain the differences in what people do by reference to something that is within them: The one appeals to stable and perhaps built-in internal predispositions (that is, traits), the other to hidden conflicts and desires. The trait approach argues that people do what they do because of who they are: The jovial backslapper is the life of the party because he is an extreme extrovert. The psychodynamic approach argues that they do what they do because of what they want (even though they rarely know it): The backslapper clowns and laughs because he is covering up his own sense of emptiness (or his buried Oedipal conflicts or whatever). But there is an alternative view that takes issue with both trait theory and the psychodynamic orientation. This is the behavioral approach (sometimes called the behavioral-cognitive approach).

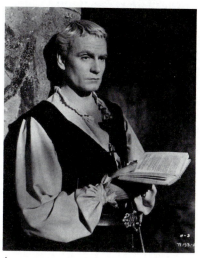

A

B

C

In contrast to trait and psychodynamic theory, the **behavioral approach*** asserts that human actions are determined from without: They are reactions to the external forces that impinge upon the person. This approach holds that people do what they do because of the situation in which they find themselves or in which they have found themselves on previous occasions. The life of the party acts his part precisely because he is *at* a party, a situation in which he will be reinforced for being outgoing and boisterous, as he has no doubt been reinforced on many previous occasions. This general view is obviously related to the situationist critique of trait theory we considered earlier (see pp. 462–65). It is a position that is traditionally associated with **behaviorism,** a very influential theoretical outlook that dominated American psychology for the first half of this century, emphasizing the role of environment and of learning, and insisting that people, no less than animals, must be studied objectively—from the outside (see Chapter 3).

If the trait approach can be likened to dramatic productions with character types who wear one mask that defines them throughout, the behavioral view corresponds to the dramatic approach of a repertory company in which every member takes many parts. Today he plays one role, tomorrow he learns to play another, depending upon the play. Nor is the way he plays them determined by anything from inside. Actors of the behavioral school don't worry about inner motivations or subtle subtexts. If required to enact an emotion, they don't try to feel it themselves. They will instead pay a great deal of attention to its visible bodily manifestations; they will tremble or sway or clench their fists or breathe more rapidly, depending upon the particular emotion they want to enact. For in their view, all that matters is their outer behavior, because that's all the audience ever hears or sees. Here again, they are much like behavior theorists, who believe that the only way to understand people is by studying them objectively—from the outside.

Social Learning Theory

Our primary interest is in a relatively modern version of behaviorism that takes a more cognitive approach to issues of personality and accepts terms like "expectation" and "belief" as a matter of course. Those who subscribe to this modified approach to personality are often called **social learning theorists,** including such figures as Albert Bandura and Walter Mischel.

At first glance, one might well think that social learning theorists would downplay the role of personality differences in predicting human behavior. For it was they (most prominently, Walter Mischel) who had attacked trait theory by arguing that differences between situations are more important than differences between persons in determining what people do. But by now, virtually everyone—whether trait or social learning theorist—has abandoned the extremes of the trait-situation controversy and agrees that both persons and situations matter, as well as the interaction between the two (see pp. 462–69). Thus social learning theorists do accept the notion of personality differences after all. But what are the terms in which they express that notion?

In essence, they believe that many of the personal qualities that characterize different people are essentially cognitive: different ways of seeing the world, thinking about it, and interacting with it, acquired in the course of an individual's history. Mischel lists some of the cognitive qualities on which people may differ.

Is personality coherent? Some early versions of the behavioral-cognitive approach argued that the consistency of personality is an illusion. (Nude Descending a Staircase by Marcel Duchamp, 1912; courtesy Philadelphia Museum of Art/Louise and Walter Arensberg Collection)

---

* This is sometimes called the *behavioral-cognitive* approach, since many recent adherents of the behavioral position assign increasing importance to cognitive factors such as expectations and beliefs.

One concerns the individual's *competencies*—the kinds of things a person can do and understand. Another concerns her *encoding strategies*—the way she tends to interpret situations. A third refers to her *expectancies*—her beliefs about what follows what: what acts will produce what outcomes, what events will lead to what consequences, and so on. A fourth difference concerns her *subjective values*—which outcomes she values. A final difference involves what Mischel calls *self-regulatory systems*—the way in which a person regulates her own behavior by various self-imposed goals and plans (Mischel, 1973, 1984).

CONTROL

We will consider only a few of the cognitive categories along which personalities may differ. One concerns a certain kind of expectancy: people's beliefs about the control they can exert on the world around them. But before discussing what different individuals *believe* about control, a few words are in order about the fact that just about all of them generally seem to *desire* it.

In a previous discussion, we saw that animals and babies behave as if they want to have a sense of control over their lives. Babies smile if an overhead mobile turns around because they made it turn; if it turns around regardless of what they do, they stop smiling. Dogs can cope with electric shocks if they can escape them; other dogs who get the same number of shocks no matter what they do, will suffer from learned helplessness (see Chapter 3). What holds for animals and babies also holds for human adults. They too prefer control.

A widely cited illustration is a series of studies of elderly persons in a nursing home. Patients on one floor of a nursing home were given small houseplants to take care of, and they were also asked to choose the time at which they wanted to participate in some of the nursing home activities (for example, visiting friends, watching television, planning social events). Patients on another floor were also given plants but with the understanding that they would be tended by the staff. They also participated in the same activities as the first group of patients, but at times chosen by the staff rather than by them. The results were clear-cut. According to both nurses and the patients' own report, the patients who were allowed to exert control were more active and felt better than the patients who lacked this control; this difference was still apparent a year later (Langer and Rodin, 1976; Rodin and Langer, 1977).

ATTRIBUTIONAL STYLE

The actual control an individual exercises over vital events in her life is important. But no less important is the extent to which she *believes* that these events are under her control. These beliefs are intimately related to her *attributional style,* a characteristic pattern in designating the causes of whatever good or bad fortunes may befall her. This style can be measured by a specially constructed *Attributional Style Questionnaire (ASQ),* in which a subject is asked to imagine herself in a number of situations (for example, failing a test) and to indicate what would have caused those events if they had happened to her (Peterson et al., 1982).

Much of the interest in attributional style comes from its use in predicting whether a person is likely to suffer from depression, a psychological disorder that can range from a mild case of "feeling blue" to an intense, chronic, and ultimately hospitalizable condition characterized by utter dejection, apathy, hopelessness, and such physical symptoms as loss of appetite and sleeplessness (for details, see Chapter 17). Being prone to depression is correlated with a tendency to attribute unfortunate events to internal, global, and stable causes—that is, to causes that refer to something within the person, that will generalize to other situ-

Loss of control   Patients in a Florida nursing home. (Photograph by Michael Heron, 1983/Woodfin Camp)

Delay of gratification

ations, and that will continue over time (for example, being unattractive or unintelligent) (Peterson and Seligman, 1984).*

According to proponents of this approach, the internal-global-stable attributional style for unfortunate events creates a predisposition that makes the person vulnerable to depression. This vulnerability will then be transformed into the actual disorder by a stressful event. (For a further discussion of the predisposition-stress approach to mental disorders, see Chapter 17.) To test this hypothesis, the investigators administered the Attributional Style Questionnaire to students enrolled in a large college class and also assessed the students' mood both before a mid-term exam and at several points thereafter (Metalsky et al., 1982; Metalsky, Halberstadt, and Abramson, 1987). The question was how a poor grade would affect the students' mood. The results were in line with the vulnerability-stress conception. A lasting depressive mood reaction was primarily found in students who had the appropriate internal-global-stable attributional style (the vulnerability) and also received a poor grade (the stress).

SELF-CONTROL

Expectancies about control represent one category of personality differences that social learning theorists have considered. Another concerns differences in patterns of self-regulation, especially self-control. Control refers to an individual's ability to do what he wants to do. Self-control refers to his ability to *refrain from doing* some of the things he wants to do (or doing some things he would rather not do) in order to get what he really wants some time in the future.†

An important example of self-control is **delay of gratification.** Much of our ordinary life requires us to postpone immediate rewards for the sake of some more important reward in the future. Some of the postponements involve delays of years or even decades, as in the case of a student who plans a career as a neurosurgeon or a fledgling politician who wants to become president. Others are reckoned in shorter intervals, such as waiting for a paycheck at the end of the week, or waiting one's turn in a cafeteria line. Many authors have pointed out that it's hard to imagine any culture that does not require some such system of self-imposed delays, whether they involve food or sex and reproduction. Farmers have to sow before they reap, and most cultures have elaborate rule systems that prescribe the when and where of sexuality and procreation (e.g., Freud, 1930; Mischel, 1986).

What is often called "will power" is presumably just this ability to forgo some immediate gratification in order to pursue some ultimate goal. According to popular wisdom, some people have this ability to a greater degree than others. But do they really? That is, is this ability consistent over time and across different situations?

Delay of gratification in young children   Walter Mischel and his associates have studied this ability in young children and have shown that it is related to a number of personality attributes in later life (Mischel, 1974, 1984). Their subjects were children between four and five years of age who were shown two treats, one of which they had previously said they preferred to the other (for example, two marshmallows or two pretzels versus one). To obtain the more desirable treat, they had to wait for an interval of about fifteen minutes. If they didn't want to wait or grew tired of waiting during the delay interval, they were given the less de-

---

* This attributional account of depression is a reformulation of an earlier model of depression based on helplessness (e.g., Seligman, 1975).

† Some manifestations of self-control involve forgoing a particular gratification altogether for the sake of some other reward or avoiding some aversive state of affairs. An example is giving up smoking.

sirable treat immediately but then had to forgo the more desirable one. The results showed that the length of time the children were able to wait depended on just what happened during that period. If the marshmallows were hidden from view, the subjects waited ten times longer than if they were visibly exposed (Mischel, Ebbesen, and Zeiss, 1972).

Further study showed that the mere physical presence or absence of the rewards was not the primary factor. What really mattered was what the children did and thought during the interval. If they looked at the marshmallow, or—even worse—thought about eating it, they usually succumbed and stopped waiting. But they could delay if they found (or were shown) some way of distracting their attention from the desired treat—for example, by thinking of some "fun things," such as Mommy pushing them on a swing. They could also delay if they thought about the desired objects in some way other than consuming them—for example, by focusing on the pretzels' shape and color rather than on their crunchy taste. By mentally transforming the goals in this fashion, the children managed to have their cake (or pretzel) and ultimately eat it too. By the time they were seven or eight, some of the children seemed to understand their own cognitive strategies for achieving self-control. One child explained why one mustn't look at the marshmallows: "If she's looking at them all the time, it will make her hungry . . . and she'd want to [stop waiting] . . ." (Mischel and Baker, 1975; Mischel and Moore, 1980; Mischel and Mischel, 1983; Mischel, 1984).

As Mischel points out, such results suggest that "will power" is not really the grimly heroic quality it is often said to be. At least in children, the trick is not in buckling up and bearing what's difficult and aversive, but in transforming what's unpleasant into what is pleasant, while yet sticking to the task at hand (Mischel, 1986).

Childhood delay and adolescent competence These various findings show that whether a child delays gratification depends on how he construes the situation. But it apparently also depends on some qualities in the child himself. The best evidence comes from follow-up studies that have demonstrated some remarkable correlations between the children's ability to delay at four years of age and some of their characteristics ten years later as rated by their parents. The results showed that the ability to tolerate lengthy delay of gratification in early childhood augurs well for later development. It correlates significantly with academic and social competence and with general coping ability in adolescence. Thus subjects who delayed longer in early childhood were judged to be more verbally fluent, attentive, self-reliant, and capable of thinking ahead, and less likely to go to pieces under stress than were subjects whose delay times were shorter (Mischel, Shoda, and Peake, 1988; see Figure 16.11).

Why should a four-year-old's willingness to wait fifteen minutes to get two pretzels rather than one be an indicator of such important personal characteristics as academic and social competence a full decade later? So far, we can only guess. One possibility is that some of the same cognitive characteristics that underlie this deceptively simple waiting task in childhood are similar to those demanded by successful performance in the more serious undertakings of adolescence and adulthood. To succeed in school, the student must be able to subordinate short-term goals to long-term purposes. Much the same is true of her social relations. The person who is at the whim of every momentary impulse will probably be unable to keep friendships, sustain commitments, or participate in any kind of team play, for reaching any long-term goal inevitably means some renunciation of lesser goals that beckon in the interval, whether in childhood or later life. One possibility is that there is some built-in disposition that underlies the child's behavior and also the adult's. But it may also be that the common personal quality is produced by learning. Some children may acquire certain general

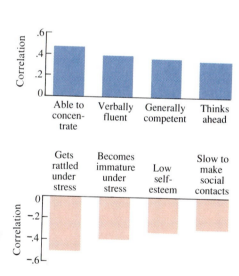

16.11   Childhood delay and adolescent competence   *The figure indicates the relation between the ability to delay gratification at age four or five and personality traits at about age sixteen by showing correlations between various personality traits of the adolescents as rated by their parents and the length of time they delayed gratification as preschoolers. Bars in blue show positive correlations; bars in pink show negative correlations. (Data from Mischel, 1984)*

cognitive skills (say, at keeping their attention on distant goals without getting too frustrated in the bargain) that they can continue to apply to more complex goal-directed efforts as they get older.

THE HUMANISTIC APPROACH

Some thirty years ago, a new perspective on human motivation and personality gained some prominence: the so-called ***humanistic approach.*** According to its adherents, neither trait theorists, psychodynamic theorists, or behaviorists have much to say about healthy, striving human beings. Psychoanalysts look at people as if they are all emotional cripples, behaviorists regard them as if they are blind, unthinking robots, and trait theorists see them as material to file in sterile pigeon-holes. Humanistic psychologists believe that all of these views have lost sight of what is truly human about human beings. Healthy humans want to feel free to choose and determine their own lives rather than to exist as mere pawns pushed around by stimuli from without and unconscious impulses from within. They seek more than food and sex and safety, strive for more than mere adjustment—they want to grow, to develop their potentialities, to become ***self-actualized.***

Returning to our theatrical analogy, the humanistic approach can be likened to certain modern movements in theater that emphasize spontaneity and improvisation. Actors who belong to this school insist that what is most important is genuine, authentic feeling. At least in principle (though rarely in actual practice), such actors might depart from the playwright's words and the director's stagings, to provide the audience and themselves with a sense of freedom and spontaneity. To the extent that this occurs, there is no mask left at all; the actor and the part have become one.

Improvisation   *Some actors are famed for their ability to improvise on the spur of the moment. An example is Robin Williams, who improvised many of his lines in the film* Good Morning Vietnam, *1987. (Courtesy the Kobal Collection)*

The Major Features of the Humanistic Movement

According to Abraham Maslow (1908–1970), the humanistic movement represents a kind of "third force" in American psychology—the other two being behaviorism and psychoanalysis. For expositional purposes, we will begin by presenting some of the major features of this movement with a minimum of editorial comment before discussing them more critically.

A POSITIVE VIEW OF HUMAN MOTIVATION

A major contrast between humanistic psychologists and the behaviorists and psychoanalysts that they oppose is in their contrasting conception of human motivation. According to Maslow, behaviorists and psychoanalysts see human beings as engaged in a never-ending struggle to remove some internal tension or make up for some deficit. The result is an essentially pessimistic and negative conception of human nature. Seen in this light, people always want to get away from something (pain, hunger, sexual tension) rather than to gain something positive. This perspective necessarily led to an emphasis on the physiological needs—hunger, thirst, escape from pain, sex. Maslow called these ***deficiency needs;*** in all these cases, we experience a lack and want to fill it. According to Maslow, an analogous deficiency sometimes underlies the so-called "social needs," such as the desire for prestige or security; an example is the woman who "hungers" for the admiration of all men around her and feels empty without it. But as Maslow pointed out, release from pain and tension does not account for everything we strive for. We sometimes seek things for their own sake, as a positive goal in themselves rather than as a means to remove a noxious state. There is the joy of solving a puzzle, the exhilaration of galloping on a horse, the ecstasy of fulfilled love, the quiet rapture in the contemplation of great art and music or a beautiful sunrise. All of these are experiences that human beings seek, and it is these positive, enriching experiences—rather than the filled stomach or the sexual release at orgasm—that make us most distinctively human. A hungry rat and a sexually aroused monkey seek food and orgasmic release pretty much as we do, but the joy of Beethoven's Ninth Symphony is ours alone. Maslow insisted that to understand what is truly human, psychologists must consider motives that go beyond the deficiency needs (Maslow, 1968).

Maslow proposed that there is a *hierarchy of needs,* in which the lower-order physiological needs are at the bottom, safety needs are further up, the need for attachment and love is still higher, and the desire for esteem is yet higher. At the very top of the hierarchy is the striving for *self-actualization*—the desire to realize oneself to the fullest (of which more later). (See Figure 16.12.)

Maslow believed that people will only strive for higher-order needs (say, seek esteem or artistic achievement) when lower-order needs (such as hunger) are satisfied. By and large this is plausible enough; the urge to write poetry generally takes a backseat if one hasn't eaten for days. But as Maslow pointed out, there are exceptions. Some artists starve rather than give up their poetry or their painting, and some martyrs proclaim their faith regardless of pain or suffering. But to the extent that Maslow's assumption holds, the motive at the very top of his hierarchy—that is, the drive toward self-actualization—will become a primary concern only when all the other needs beneath are satisfied.

THE SELF IN HUMANISTIC PSYCHOLOGY

Before trying to describe what Maslow and other humanistic psychologists mean by self-actualization, we should say a word about the self that is (or is not) being actualized. We've previously encountered some issues related to the self; social psychologists study it under the headings of self-perception theory and self-pres-

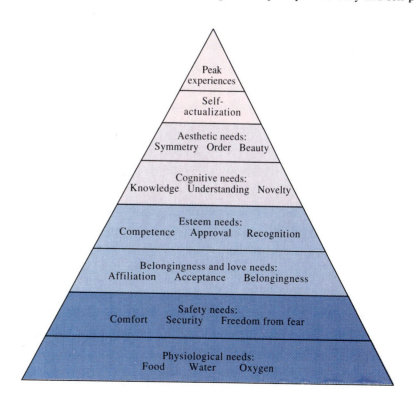

16.12 Maslow's hierarchy of needs
People will strive for higher-order needs (esteem or artistic achievement) generally after lower-order needs (hunger, safety) have been satisfied. (After Maslow, 1954)

entation (pp. 321–22), and Freud and Piaget treat it as a developmental matter since they believe that the "ego" emerges from an earlier diffuse state in which there is no self at all (pp. 290–91 and 361). To humanistic psychologists, the self is even more important, for one of their primary concerns is with subjective experience—with what the individual thinks and feels right here and now. According to Carl Rogers (1902–1987), who was a major figure in the humanistic movement, a crucial facet of this subjective experience is the *self* or *self-concept.* This self-concept is developed in early childhood and eventually comes to include one's sense of oneself as an agent who takes (or doesn't take) actions and makes (or doesn't make) decisions—the "I." It also includes one's sense of oneself as a kind of object that is seen and thought about and liked or disliked—the "me" (Rogers, 1959, 1961).

In the course of his work in clinical counseling, Rogers came to feel that an important condition for adult mental health is a solid sense of personal self-worth. Rogers believed that to achieve this the child requires ***unconditional positive regard***—the sense of being accepted and loved without condition or reservation. But such a prescription for child rearing is difficult to follow. For the parents can (and no doubt must) disapprove of some of the things the child does; they are unlikely to applaud when little Janie spills ketchup all over the new living room rug. They could still show Janie their unconditional positive regard by making it clear that while they certainly don't love *her behavior* they do and always will love *her.* But this is much easier said than done. Most parents probably do set some conditions on their love, no matter how subtly, indicating that they'll love her if she'll do well at school, or if she acts like a nice girl, or whatever. Rogers believed that the likely upshot is that the child will suppress some aspect of herself in order to feel loved and accepted. And this in turn may lead to a sense of confusion and disquiet, and a doubt of one's real self-worth.

SELF-ACTUALIZATION

Given a reasonable sense of self-worth and the satisfaction of the lower-level needs, the stage is set for the motive at the very top of Maslow's hierarchy of needs, the desire for self-actualization. Maslow and other humanistic psychologists describe this as the desire to realize one's potentialities, to fulfill oneself, to become what one can become (Maslow, 1968, 1970). But exactly what does this mean?

Maslow gave some examples by presenting case histories of a number of persons that he and his collaborators regarded as "self-actualized." Some of them were actual persons that he had interviewed; others were historical figures (for example, Thomas Jefferson and Ludwig van Beethoven) or recent luminaries (such as Eleanor Roosevelt and Albert Einstein), whose lives were studied by means of historical or other documents. Unlike most other investigators in the field, Maslow was not interested in these subjects' specific attributes or behavior patterns; all he looked for were some overall patterns that he felt were shared by them all. As Maslow saw it, these self-actualizers had many admirable characteristics. Among other things, they were realistically oriented, accepted themselves and others, were spontaneous, cared more about the problems they were working on than about themselves, had intimate relationships with a few people rather than superficial relationships with many, and had democratic values—all in all, an admirable list of human qualities (Maslow, 1968, 1970).

According to Maslow, one characteristic of self-actualized persons is that they are more likely to have so-called ***peak experiences*** than other people. Peak experiences are profound and deeply felt moments in a person's life, in which there is a "feeling of great ecstasy and awe . . . with the conviction that something extremely important and valuable had happened . . ." (Maslow, 1970, p. 164). Such

"I'm quite fulfilled. I always wanted to be a chicken." (Drawing by Joseph Farris; © 1989, The New Yorker Magazine, Inc.)

Self-actualization shown through self-portraits To actualize one's self may take a whole lifetime. Some great artists have given us a graphic record of the process at different points in their life, as in these self-portraits by Rembrandt. One was created at the age of 34, when he was very successful and saw himself as a Renaissance gentleman artist and virtuoso. The other was painted at about age 60, when he tried to reaffirm his identity through his art and portrayed himself as a painter holding the tools of his craft (Wright, 1982). (Left: Self-Portrait at the Age of 34; *courtesy National Gallery.* Right: Portrait of the Artist; *courtesy English Heritage, The Iveagh Bequest)*

moments might come while with a lover, or while watching the sea or a sunset, or while listening to music or watching a play—but regardless of when and where they occur, they seem to have some important and lasting effects on the individual who thereafter is likely to see himself and others in a more spontaneous and healthier way.

Evaluating the Humanistic Approach

What can we say by way of evaluating the humanistic approach to personality? We should begin by asking about its empirical and conceptual foundations.

EMPIRICAL AND CONCEPTUAL DIFFICULTIES

Consider Rogers's account of the origins of the feeling of self-worth. Is it really true that unconditional positive regard and empathic understanding are essential for the development of self-worth? We've previously noted the enormous difficulties in drawing any conclusions about the effects of child rearing on later personality development (see Chapter 14). Under the circumstances, Rogers's description of the parent-child relationships that lead to feelings of adequate or inadequate self-worth seems rather oversimplified.

Similar qualifications apply to a number of other assertions made by the proponents of the humanistic approach. How do we know that self-actualizers are in fact as Maslow described them to be—for example, realistically oriented, accepting of themselves and others, spontaneous, problem-centered, democratic, and so on? Or that peak experiences have lasting and often beneficial effects on later life? Or that self-actualizers have more such peak experiences than other people? As yet, there is no real evidence that would allow us to decide.

An even more serious criticism is the fact that many of the core conceptions of the humanistic approach are exceedingly unclear. Just what is meant by self-actualization, or by "letting yourself go and being yourself," or by unconditional positive regard, or by a peak experience? Since these terms are so vaguely defined, it is difficult to know how to evaluate any assertions about them.

Consider Maslow's study of self-actualizers. Maslow chose a number of persons as exemplars, including a number of prominent and historical figures. But by what criteria did he select them? Among the historical figures he chose were Thomas Jefferson, Abraham Lincoln (in his later years), Eleanor Roosevelt, and

Albert Einstein. Most of us would agree that these were admirable and creative persons, and we can understand what is meant when someone says that they fulfilled their potentialities and "actualized themselves." But why can't the same term be applied to many other individuals, some of whom are far from admirable and may be veritable monsters? What about Al Capone, or Napoleon, or even Adolf Hitler? It's very likely that these persons felt that they had become what they were meant to become (at least until Alcatraz, or St. Helena, or the final days in the Berlin bunker). But if so, why shouldn't we regard *them* as self-actualized? Given their belief that human growth has an inherent tendency toward good rather than evil, Maslow and Rogers would presumably rule out—by definition—moral monsters such as Capone or Hitler. But this line of reasoning can certainly be questioned. The development of personality may be a growth process, but this alone is not enough grounds for optimism. Given soil, sun, and water, a rose seedling will indeed become a rose. But if the seedling is a thistle, it may self-actualize and become a thistle.

HUMANISTIC PSYCHOLOGY AS A PROTEST MOVEMENT

It appears that many of the major tenets of the humanistic approach to personality rest on rather shaky foundations. But if so, why should we take it seriously? One answer is that the humanistic approach is best considered as a protest movement. It reacts against both behaviorism and psychoanalysis because it regards them as representatives of a sterile mechanism that treats people as marionettes pushed and pulled by forces from without and within. It reacts against trait psychology because it regards this approach as devoted to an endless cataloguing that reduces humans to mere ciphers. And it reacts against the general focus of much contemporary psychology, which it regards as narrow and pessimistic, oriented toward human sickness and deficiency rather than health and upward striving.

In some ways, the humanistic approach to personality is reminiscent of some prior movements in the political and literary spheres. Some two hundred years ago, the Romantic poets in England and Germany elevated feeling over reason, celebrated individualism and natural man, and deplored the effects of eighteenth-century science and technology. Some, such as William Blake and Samuel Coleridge, sought peak experiences in mystical visions or in opium dreams. Others railed against the cold, mechanical science that had left the universe dry and bare. An example is John Keats's lament that "Newton has destroyed all the poetry of the rainbow by reducing it to the prismatic colors" (Abrams, 1953, p. 303). And many of them agreed with the social philosopher Jean Jacques Rousseau (1712–1778), whose writings helped to shape the French and American Revolutions, that "man is by nature good, and . . . only our institutions have made him bad!" (in Durant and Durant, 1967, p. 19).

The similarity between these sentiments and many of the themes of the humanistic psychologists is clear enough. The Romantics protested against what they regarded as a cold, mechanical approach to nature and politics; the humanistic psychologists lodge similar complaints against contemporary approaches to psychology.

To be sure, the Romantic poets did much more than protest; they also made lasting contributions to literature. And Rousseau influenced the political landscape of Europe for a century after his death. Is there a corresponding positive contribution of humanistic psychology? Some critics feel that the humanists' concepts are as yet too vague and their assertions as yet too unproven to count as serious positive scientific accomplishments (e.g., Smith, 1950). Others argue that the humanists often serve as moral advocates rather than dispassionate scientists. They tell us what personality *should* be rather than what it *is*.

Romanticism in the arts *The romantic artists of the early nineteenth century stressed the full expression of the emotions. An example is this painting by Caspar David Friedrich. (*Man and Woman Gazing at the Moon; *courtesy Staatliche Museen Preussicher Kulturbesitz, Nationalgalerie, Berlin)*

But there is one accomplishment of which we can be sure. The humanistic psychologists remind us of many phenomena that other approaches to the study of personality have largely ignored. People do strive for more than food and sex or prestige; they read poetry, listen to music, fall in love, have occasional peak experiences, try to actualize themselves. Whether the humanistic psychologists have really helped us to understand these elusive phenomena better than we did before is debatable. But there is no doubt that what they have done is to insist that these phenomena are there, that they constitute a vital aspect of what makes us human, and that they must not be ignored. By so insisting, they remind us of the unfinished tasks that a complete psychology of personality must ultimately deal with.

TAKING STOCK

We've considered a number of approaches to personality. One is the trait approach, which tries to describe personality by reference to a few basic characteristics, many of which have a built-in basis. Another is the behavioral approach, which focuses on the individual's outwardly observable acts, and argues that these acts are produced by the situation that the individual faces now or has faced on previous occasions. Yet another is the psychodynamic approach, which centers on submerged feelings, unconscious conflicts, and desires. And still another is the humanistic approach, which asks how people achieve their own selfhood and realize their human potentialities.

Today there are relatively few theorists who would espouse any of these approaches in their most extreme form. By now, most adherents of the behavioral approach have shifted to a more cognitive conception of the subject matter, most psychodynamic theorists see unconscious defenses and conscious coping mechanisms as parts of a continuum, and virtually everyone grants that what people do depends on both traits and situations.

But even so, some important differences in approach clearly remain. This is probably fortunate. For these different theoretical orientations reflect different perspectives on the same subject matter, each of which has some validity. Some aspects of personality are clearly built in (trait theory); others are learned (social learning theory); some reflect buried conflicts (psychodynamic theory); others reveal the need for self-actualization (humanistic approach).

In this regard, the different perspectives on personality are again similar to different approaches to the presentation of character in literature or on the stage. Is the human drama best described by the use of a number of stock types, perhaps designated by a few well-chosen masks, or by well-rounded characters that are like themselves alone and no others? There is no simple yes or no, for people are both similar to and different from each other. Is character best described by the Classicists, who stress human reason, or by the Romantics, who emphasize feeling? Again there is no answer, for both emotion and rationality are part of our very nature. Should actors portray the inner life and concentrate on what lies behind the mask, or should they focus on the outward mask since that is what the audience sees? Here too there is no answer, for we all have both an inner and an outer life.

We are similar to others but we are also different. We are pulled by outer and inner forces, but we are also free to make our own choices. We are rational, but we are also impelled by feeling. We are both the masks we wear and something else beneath. Each of the approaches to personality—and to dramatic character —focuses on one or another of these aspects of our nature. Each of these aspects exists. And to that extent each of the approaches is valid.

SUMMARY

1. People differ in their predominant desires, in their characteristic feelings, and in their typical modes of expressing these desires and feelings. All of these distinctions fall under the general heading of *personality differences.* The four main attempts to understand these differences are the *trait approach, the psychodynamic approach,* the *behavioral-cognitive approach,* and the *humanistic approach* to personality.

2. One approach to personality assessment is by *objective personality inventories.* An example is the *Minnesota Multiphasic Personality Inventory,* or *MMPI.* It assesses traits by means of a number of different *scales,* each of which measures the extent to which a person's answers approximate those of a particular psychiatric *criterion group.* In actual practice, MMPI records are interpreted by inspecting the person's *score profile,* including his response to various *validity scales.* A number of other personality inventories such as the *California Psychological Inventory,* or *CPI,* were constructed in an analogous manner but using normal rather than pathological criterion groups.

3. The validity of personality inventories has been evaluated by using indices of *predictive validity.* The results show that while these tests predict, they predict not too well, for their *validity coefficients* are relatively low. When the evaluation is based on *construct validity,* the results look more promising.

4. A very different way of assessing personality is by means of *projective techniques.* Two prominent examples are the *Rorschach inkblot test* and the *Thematic Apperception Test,* or *TAT.* While these tests are often used in clinical practice, they have been criticized because of their relatively low predictive validity.

5. The *trait approach* to personality tries to describe individuals by a set of characterizing attributes. One of the first tasks of such an approach is to find an appropriate *taxonomy* for personality traits. Many investigators have tried to develop such a taxonomy by the method of *factor analysis.* One of the most influential of these attempts is Eysenck's scheme which is based on two main dimensions—*neuroticism* and *extroversion-introversion.*

6. The concept of stable personality traits has been seriously challenged by critics who claim that people behave much less consistently than a trait theory would lead one to predict. One alternative is *situationism,* which claims that human behavior is largely determined by the situation in which the individual finds himself. While most observers have concluded that there is strong support for behavioral *consistency over time,* there is still disagreement over the degree to which there is behavioral *consistency across situations.* Many commentators argue that behavioral consistencies will show up best if one looks at the *interaction* between person and situation.

7. Some people tend to be more inconsistent than others. To the extent that people modify their behavior to fit the social situation, they will behave inconsistently; the tendency to do so is assessed by the *self-monitoring scale.*

8. While some trait theorists view traits as merely descriptive categories, others see them as predispositions to behave in one way or another that are ultimately rooted in the individual's biological makeup. Some evidence for this view grows out of studies of *temperament,* a characteristic reaction pattern of an individual that is present from early childhood on.

9. There is evidence that some personality traits have a hereditary basis. Evidence comes from twin studies, which show that the correlations on traits such as dominance, sociability, self-acceptance, and self-control are considerably higher in identical than in fraternal twins.

10. Some investigators have tried to link certain personality traits to aspects of neurophysiological arousal. According to Hans Eysenck, introversion corresponds to a higher level of central nervous system arousal than does extroversion. As a result, introverts prefer lower levels of physical and social stimulation, while extroverts prefer to enhance their

level of stimulation. Much the same may hold for the trait of *sensation seeking,* which is thought to relate to underarousal of certain regions of the brain.

11. The *psychodynamic approach* is derived from Sigmund Freud's psychoanalytic theories, which emphasize *unconscious conflicts.* Many of these conflicts can be understood as defenses against *anxiety,* many of which have their origin during *psychosexual development* in early childhood. In Freud's view, differences in adult personality can be understood as residues of early *fixations* and *reaction formations.* An example is the *anal character,* whose attributes include compulsive neatness, obstinacy, and stinginess.

12. Later psychodynamic theorists who take a *neo-Freudian* orientation focus on interpersonal rather than biological forces in the individual and are more interested in the individual's present situation than in his childhood past. An example is Karen Horney, who studied self-perpetuating vicious circles in adult neurotic conflicts. Several modern psychodynamic theorists have studied characteristic patterns of defense and coping in normal persons, including patterns that are relatively immature and unhealthy (such as denial, projection, reaction formation) and patterns that are comparatively healthy and mature (e.g., humor, suppression). *Longitudinal studies* suggest that these patterns show considerable consistency over an individual's lifetime.

13. In contrast to the trait and psychodynamic approaches, the *behavioral approach* asserts that people do what they do because of the situation that they are in or have been in on previous occasions. An influential modern version of this approach is *social learning theory,* which is interested in what people think as well as in what they do, and is sometimes called the *behavioral-cognitive approach.* Social learning theorists have studied a number of cognitive characteristics along which personalities differ, such as the beliefs people have about the *control* they can exert on the world around them. One difference concerns their characteristic *attributional style*—the causes to which a person tends to attribute events that happen to her. Some of the interest in attributional style comes from its use in predicting depression.

14. While control refers to a person's ability to do what he wants to do, *self-control* refers to his ability to refrain from doing what he wants to do in order to get something he wants even more. There is evidence that four-year-olds who are able to tolerate delay of gratification for the sake of a more desirable reward show more social and academic competence in adolescence.

15. Another major orientation to personality is the *humanistic approach,* which maintains that what is most important about people is how they achieve their own selfhood and actualize their human potentialities. The humanistic approach emphasizes what it considers positive human motives such as *self-actualization* and positive personal events such as *peak experiences* rather than what it calls *deficiency needs.* A major concern of humanistic psychologists is the *self.* In their view, given the appropriate conditions, people will grow so as to realize their potential, which is for good rather than evil. Rogers believed that children will only achieve a solid sense of personal self-worth if they have experienced a sense of *unconditional positive regard.*

CHAPTER 17

Psychopathology

In the preceding chapter, we considered differences in human personality traits. We now turn to conditions in which such differences go beyond the range of normal functioning and take on the appearance of psychological disorder. The study of such disorders is the province of ***psychopathology*** or, as it is sometimes called, ***abnormal psychology.*** There is considerable debate about how the subject matter of abnormal psychology is to be defined. Is it simply a problem of statistical deviance, of behavior that is markedly different from the norm? Or should we take the term *psychopathology* more literally and regard its manifestations as something akin to illness? But if these manifestations are illnesses, of what kind are they? Are they caused by some bodily disorder, such as a defect in brain function or a biochemical imbalance? Or are they better conceived of as *mental* illnesses whose origin is psychological, such as a learned defense against anxiety?

As we shall see, there is no one answer to these questions. The reason is that the various conditions that are generally subsumed under the rubric of psychopathology are a very mixed lot. For some, the term *illness* seems quite appropriate; for others, this is not so clear. In any case, there is little doubt that many of the conditions that come to the attention of the psychopathologist—the psychiatrist, the clinical psychologist, or other mental-health specialists—often cause considerable anguish and and may seriously impair the afflicted person's functioning.

We will begin our discussion by considering some of the historical roots of our conceptions of what "madness" is and how it should be dealt with.

DIFFERENT CONCEPTIONS OF MADNESS

Mental disorders existed for many millennia before psychiatrists appeared on the scene. Early mythological and religious writings are proof enough. The Greek hero, Ajax, slew a flock of sheep which he mistook for his enemies; King Saul of Judea alternated between bouts of murderous frenzy and suicidal depressions; and the Babylonian King Nebuchadnezzar walked on all fours in the belief that

An early example of mental disorder
King Nebuchadnezzar as depicted by William Blake (1795). (Courtesy the Tate Gallery, London)

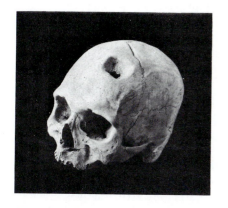

17.1 Trephining   A trephined prehistoric skull found in Peru. The patient apparently survived the operation for a while, for there is some evidence of bone healing. (Courtesy The American Museum of Natural History)

he was a wolf. Such phenomena were evidently not isolated instances. According to the Bible, young David feigned madness while seeking refuge from his enemies at the court of a Philistine king. This king had obviously encountered insanity before and upbraided his servants, "Do I lack madmen, that you have brought this fellow to play the madman in my presence?"

Insanity as Demonic Possession

What leads to mental disorder? One of the earliest theories held that the afflicted person was possessed by evil spirits. It followed that the cure for the malady was to drive the devils out. If the patient was lucky, the exorcism procedures were fairly mild; the unruly demons were calmed by music or were chased away by prayers and religious rites. More often the techniques were less benign. One approach was to provide a physical escape hatch for the devils. According to some anthropologists, this may explain why Stone Age men sometimes cut large holes into their fellows' skulls; many such *trephined* skulls have been found, often with signs that the patient managed to survive the operation (Figure 17.1). The plausibility of this hypothesis is enhanced by the fact that trephining is still performed by some preliterate tribes, and for much the same reasons (Stewart, 1957). Yet another idea was to make things as uncomfortable for the devil as possible so as to induce him to escape. Accordingly, the patient was chained, immersed in boiling hot or ice-cold baths, or starved, flogged, or tortured. That such procedures usually drove the patient into worse and worse derangement is hardly surprising.

According to some medical historians, the demonological approach to mental disorder reached its culmination during the witch hunts of the sixteenth and seventeenth centuries (Zilboorg and Henry, 1941). This was a period marked by a host of social, political, and religious upheavals, of wars, famines, and pestilence, all of which triggered a search for scapegoats whose punishment might alleviate these ills. Persons accused of witchcraft were doomed to this role; according to most theological authorities of the times they had become possessed by striking a

17.2 Witch hunts in sixteenth-century Europe *Witches about to be burned at the stake. (Courtesy the Bettmann Archive)*

bargain with the devil, which gave them power to cause effects ranging from plagues and floods to sexual impotence and the souring of milk (Figure 17.2).

Since such people were clearly a menace to society, no measures were too stern to deal with them. As a result, there was an unrelenting series of witch hunts that involved most of Europe and whose bonfires claimed about 500,000 lives (Harris, 1974). Some of these unfortunates were undoubtedly deranged in one way or another; many were senile, some suffered from various delusions, from hysteria, or mania, and so on. Some may have experienced hallucinations under the influence of LSD-like drugs, taken either wittingly or by accident. Such hallucinogenic substances are now known to occur in grains that have been invaded by a certain fungus; it is quite possible that the girls whose visions sparked the Salem witchcraft trials had eaten bread made of such hallucinogenic rye (Caporael, 1976). But many of those accused of witchcraft seem not to have suffered from any mental disorder. Some may have participated in various local cults derived from pagan origins that orthodox Christianity condemned as a form of Satanism. Others probably fell prey to some neighbor's avarice, since a considerable proportion of a condemned person's property was awarded to his or her accuser (Kors and Peters, 1972).

Insanity as a Disease

The demonological theory of mental disorder is a thing of the past. Even in its heyday there was an alternative view which held that such conditions were produced by natural causes and could be regarded as a kind of disease. But this belief did not necessarily lead to a more humane treatment of the afflicted. It might have done so if a ready cure had been available, but until recently, there was little hope of that. As a result, the "madmen" were treated with little sympathy, for they seemed to have no common bond with the rest of humanity, and there was little likelihood that they ever would have. They were seen as a nuisance at best and a menace at worst. In either case, the interests of society seemed best served by "putting them away."

To this end, a number of special hospitals were established throughout Europe. But until the beginning of the nineteenth century (and in some cases, much later still), most of these were hospitals in name only. Their real function was to serve as a place of confinement in which all kinds of social undesirables were segregated from the rest of humankind—criminals, idlers, old people, epileptics, incurables of all sorts, and the mentally disturbed (Rosen, 1966). After they had been in the "hospital" for a few years, it became hard to distinguish among them. Their treatment was barbaric. One author describes conditions in the major mental hospital for Parisian women at the end of the eighteenth century: "Madwomen seized by fits of violence are chained like dogs at their cell doors, and separated from keepers and visitors alike by a long corridor protected by an iron grille; through this grille is passed their food and the straw on which they sleep; by means of rakes, part of the filth that surrounds them is cleaned out" (Foucault, 1965, p. 72).

To most of their contemporaries, this treatment seemed only natural; after all, the so-called madmen were like dangerous animals and had to be caged. But since such animals are interesting to watch, some of the hospitals took on another function—they became a zoo. At London's Bethlehem hospital (whose name was slurred until it was popularly known as Bedlam), the patients were exhibited to anyone curious enough to pay the required penny per visit. In 1814, there were 96,000 such visits (Figure 17.3).

A number of reformers gradually succeeded in eliminating the worst of these practices. Historians have given much of the credit to the French physician,

17.3 The mentally disturbed on exhibit *An eighteenth-century depiction of a tour of Bedlam. (The Madhouse, 1735/1763, William Hogarth; courtesy the Bettmann Archive)*

Philippe Pinel (1745–1826), who was put in charge of the Parisian hospital system in 1793 when the Revolution was at its height. Pinel wanted to remove the inmates' chains and fetters, but the government gave its permission only grudgingly (Figure 17.4). A high functionary argued with Pinel, "Citizen, are you mad yourself that you want to unchain these animals?" (Zilboorg and Henry, 1941, p. 322).

MENTAL DISORDER AS AN ORGANIC ILLNESS

Pinel and other reformers sounded one main theme: Madness is a disease. By this assertion, they transformed the inmates from prisoners to patients for whom a cure had to be found. To find such a cure, one first had to discover the cause of the disease (or rather, diseases, since it was already known that there were several varieties of mental disorder). Today, almost two hundred years after Pinel, we are still searching for the causes of most of them.

At least initially, the notion of mental disorder as an illness implied a bodily cause, most likely some disease of the brain. Proponents of this *somatogenic* hypothesis (from *soma,* "body") could point to such relevant discoveries as the effects of cerebral strokes in impairing speech (see Chapter 1). But the somatogenic position gained its greatest impetus at the end of the nineteenth century from the

17.4 Pinel ordering the removal of the inmates' fetters *A nineteenth-century painting by Charles Muller. (Courtesy the Bettmann Archive)*

discovery of the organic cause of a once widely prevalent severe and debilitating disorder, *general paresis.* It is characterized by a general decline in physical and psychological functions, culminating in marked personality aberrations that may include childish delusions ("I am the Prince of Wales") or wild hypochondriacal depressions ("My heart has stopped beating"). Without treatment, there is increasing deterioration, progressive paralysis, and death within a few years (Dale, 1975).

By the end of the nineteenth century, the conviction had grown that general paresis has its roots in a syphilitic infection contracted many years prior to the appearance of overt symptoms. In some untreated syphilitics (according to recent estimates, perhaps 5 percent), the infection seems to be cured, but the spirochete that caused it remains, invading and damaging the nervous system. Experimental proof came in 1897. Several paretic patients were inoculated with matter taken from syphilitic sores, but none of them developed any of the earlier symptoms of syphilis.* This was a clear sign that they had contracted the disease previously. Once the cause of the disease was known, the discovery of its cure and prevention was just a matter of time. The preferred modern treatment is with penicillin. Its effectiveness is unquestioned. While general paresis at one time accounted for more than 10 percent of all admissions to mental hospitals, as of 1970 it accounted for less than 1 percent (Dale, 1975).

The conquest of general paresis reinforced the beliefs of somatogenicists that ultimately all mental disorders would be traced to some organic cause. They could point to some successes. Several psychoses had been explained as brain malfunctions. In the case of senile patients, the cause is atrophy of cortical cells; in the case of chronic alcoholics, the cause is a change in cerebral structures brought on by the dietary deficits that often accompany alcoholism. The question was whether this view could account for all mental disorders.

MENTAL DISORDER AS A PSYCHOLOGICAL ILLNESS

The achievements of the somatogenic approach were very impressive, but by the end of the nineteenth century it became clear that it could not include the full spectrum of mental disorders. One of the main stumbling blocks was a condition then known as *hysteria,* which we have already encountered in our discussion of psychoanalysis (see Chapter 10).

The story of hysteria (which is now called a *conversion disorder,* see p. 520) is part of the background that led to Freud's theories. For now, we will only reiterate the key discoveries. Hysteria featured a variety of symptoms that seemed to be organic but really were not, for example, paralyzed limbs that moved perfectly well during hypnosis. This suggested that hysteria is a *psychogenic* disorder, that is, a disorder whose origin is psychological rather than organic. A number of cases studied by French hypnotists of the nineteenth century seemed to have their origins in traumatic incidents. A patient trapped in a derailed railroad car developed hysterical paralysis of his legs; the legs were actually in perfect physical condition, but the patient's belief that they were crushed ultimately produced his hysterical symptoms. Freud's theories were cast in a similar psychogenic mold, but they were much more elaborate, focusing on repressed sexual fantasies in early childhood that threatened to break into consciousness and could only be held back by drastic defense maneuvers, of which the somatic symptom was one (see Chapter 10).

A

B

Psychogenically induced seizures In late eighteenth-century France, a number of so-called hysterical patients suffered from psychogenically induced seizures that had a characteristic pattern. The illustrations above show some stages of this pattern, one of which resembled an epileptic seizure (A), another called the "clown period" (B). Some authors suspect that the behavior of these patients was caused by the fact that they were extremely suggestible: They could sense what their physicians expected them to do and behaved appropriately. (Drawings by Paul Richter, 1885; published in Gilman, 1982)

* Modern medical and scientific practitioners are considerably more sensitive than our forebears to the ethical issues raised by this and similar studies. Today such a procedure would require the patients' informed consent.

Exactly what produced the hysteria is not our present concern. The important point is that by the turn of the century most theorists had become convinced that the disorder was psychogenic. This was another way of saying that there are illnesses that have mental *causes* as well as mental *symptoms.*

THE PATHOLOGY MODEL

Whatever their views about the somatogenic or psychogenic origins of mental disorders, most psychiatrists agree on one thing—these conditions are illnesses. They are called *mental* illnesses because their primary symptoms are psychological, but they are illnesses all the same, in some ways analogous to such nonpsychiatric illnesses as tuberculosis and diabetes. Given this assumption, it was only logical to propose that one should try to understand (and treat) such diseases according to the same broad set of rules by means of which we try to understand disease in general.

Just what are these rules? We will here class them together under a very general category that we'll call the **pathology model.** (Different practitioners subscribe to different subcategories of this model, of which more below.) According to the pathology model, various overt symptoms are produced by an underlying cause—the disease or pathology. The main object of the would-be healer is to remove the underlying pathology. After this is done, the symptoms will presumably disappear. As here used, the term *pathology model* makes no particular assumption about the kind of pathology that underlies a particular mental disorder. It might be somatogenic or psychogenic or perhaps a little of both.

Subcategories of the Pathology Model

There are a number of different approaches to psychopathology, which can be regarded as subcategories of the pathology model. We will briefly present a few of these. As we will see, some of these models are probably more appropriate to some forms of mental disorder than to others.

THE MEDICAL MODEL

Some authors endorse the **medical model,** a particular version of the pathology model, which makes certain further assumptions. To begin with, it assumes that the underlying pathology is organic. Its practitioners therefore employ various forms of somatic therapy such as drugs. In addition, it takes for granted that the would-be healers are members of the medical profession (Siegler and Osmond, 1974).

THE PSYCHOANALYTIC MODEL

Adherents of the **psychoanalytic model** follow the general conception of psychopathology developed by Sigmund Freud and other psychoanalysts. In their view, the symptoms of mental disorder are produced by psychogenic causes. The underlying pathology is a constellation of unconscious conflicts and various defenses against anxiety, often rooted in early childhood experience. Treatment is by some form of psychotherapy based on psychoanalytic principles, which allows the patient to gain insight into his own inner conflicts and thus removes the root of the pathology.

THE LEARNING MODEL

The *learning model* tends to view mental disorders as the result of some form of maladaptive learning. According to some practitioners (usually called *behavior therapists*), these faulty learning patterns are best described and treated by the laws of classical and instrumental conditioning. According to others (often called *cognitive therapists*), they are more properly regarded as faulty modes of thinking that can be dealt with by changing the way in which the patient thinks about himself and his situation.

Mental Disorder as Pathology

To get a better understanding of how mental disorder is viewed from the perspective of the general pathology model, we must first ask what is meant by disease in general. A moment's reflection tells us that the concept of disease is both a scientific and an evaluative notion. To say that measles and rickets are diseases is to say something about the kinds of causes that produce such conditions—infections, dietary insufficiencies, and so on. But it also says that such conditions are undesirable. They produce pain and disability, and sometimes they lead to death. Speaking most generally, they are conditions that interfere with the organism's proper functioning as a biological system.

The extension of the disease concept to the psychological realm is based on certain parallels between the effects of psychopathology and those of nonpsychiatric, organic disorders. Where ordinary organic illnesses are often associated with physical pain, many mental disorders are accompanied by psychological distress in the form of anxiety or depression. (Some may lead to death, as in the case of suicidal depression.) But the most important criterion is the interference with proper psychological functioning. The mentally disordered person may be unable to form or maintain gratifying relationships with others. Or she may be unable to work effectively. Or she may be unable to relax and play. According to advocates of the pathology model of mental disorder, the inability to function properly in these psychological areas is the behavioral analogue of the malfunctions in such biological domains as respiration, circulation, digestion, and so on, that characterize ordinary organic illnesses.

Classifying Mental Disorders

The ways in which we decide what is and what is not a mental disorder are by no means settled. But no less controversial is the issue of classifying these disorders. How do we decide whether two patients have the same disorder or two different ones?

As in other branches of medicine, the diagnostic process begins with a consideration of the overt *symptoms*. In nonpsychiatric disorders, these might be such complaints as fever or chest pains. Examples of symptoms in psychopathology would be anxiety or a profound sense of worthlessness. The trouble is that an individual symptom is rarely enough for diagnosis; fever occurs in a multitude of organic illnesses, and anxiety is found in many different mental disorders. As a result, the diagnostician often looks for a pattern of symptoms that tend to go together, a so-called *syndrome*. An example of such a syndrome in psychopathology is a set of symptoms that includes disorganization of thinking, withdrawal from others, and hallucinations. This syndrome is characteristic of schizophrenia.

By groupings of this kind, psychiatrists have set up a taxonomy of mental disorders. The entire list covers an enormous range that includes mental deficiency, senile deterioration, schizophrenia, mood disorders such as bipolar disorder and

Emil Kraepelin (1855–1925) The major figure in psychiatric classification, Kraepelin distinguished between two groups of severe mental disorders, schizophrenia and manic-depressive psychosis (now called bipolar mood disorder). (Courtesy Historical Pictures Service)

Insanity as seen by an artist This painting undoubtedly shows aspects of what Francisco Goya saw when he visited an insane asylum in Spain, but it may also have been affected by the then current views of the classification of mental disorder. Most early descriptions included the raving maniac (here the nude men wrestling in the center), the hopeless melancholic (the despairing figures on the left), and those with grotesque delusions (the men with crowns demanding allegiance from their subjects). *(The Insane Asylum, c1810, Francisco Goya, Accademia S. Fernando, Madrid; courtesy Art Resource)*

depression, phobias, conversion disorders, and drug addiction, to mention only the most prominent.

Until about fifteen years ago, most psychiatrists believed that many of these conditions could be subsumed under two broad super-categories, *neurosis* and *psychosis.* They applied the term *neurosis* to any disorder whose main characteristic was thought to be anxiety or the defense against anxiety. Neurotic patients might be severely handicapped by their symptoms and were often in great distress, but they had not lost contact with reality no matter how miserable they might feel. In contrast, the term *psychosis* was applied to conditions such as schizophrenia in which the patients' thoughts, moods, and deeds were grossly disturbed and no longer met the demands of reality (DSM-II, 1968).

Today, the terms *psychosis* and *neurosis* are no longer widely used in psychiatric classification. A major reason for this change was the psychiatrists' desire to classify conditions by observable symptoms rather than by their inferred causes. The new taxonomy is embodied in the new diagnostic manual of their profession, DSM-III-R (1987). Both it and its immediate predecessor (DSM-III, 1980) depart from earlier manuals in a number of ways. The most important is a greater stress on the *description* of disorders rather than on theories about their underlying causes. As a result, a number of disorders that had formerly been grouped together because of a—psychoanalytically inspired—belief that they are at bottom alike are now classified under different headings (for example, various conditions that were once regarded as subcategories of neurosis; see pp. 515–21). One consequence of these changes in procedure has been a considerable increase in diagnostic reliability (Matarazzo, 1983; DSM-III-R, 1987).

Given these changes in official taxonomy, the terms *neurosis* and *psychosis* have become rather passé. But we will nevertheless use these two terms in the present account, at least in an informal way. To avoid them altogether is difficult, given the fact that they have by now become part of common parlance. The same holds for a number of other terms that are no longer used in official diagnosis, for example *sociopath, hysteria,* and some others.

Explaining Disorder: Diathesis, Stress, and Pathology

Adherents of the pathology model believe that all—or at least many—mental disorders will ultimately prove to result from underlying causes, some organic and others psychological, that mirror the pathological processes found in other diseases. But since many of these pathologies are still unknown, how can we evaluate the assertion that they are actually there? One approach is to analyze a disease that is already well understood. This can then provide a standard against which the claims of the model's advocates can be judged. Our illustrative example will be an organic illness, diabetes.

The first step in the analysis of this, as of other medical disorders, is to look at the overt symptoms. In diabetes, these include declining strength, a marked increase in the quantity of urine passed, enormous thirst, and, in many cases, voracious appetite. The next step is to look for the underlying physiological pathology of which this syndrome is a manifestation. This pathology was discovered to be a disorder of carbohydrate metabolism which is produced by an insufficient secretion of insulin (see Chapter 2). These pathological conditions represent the immediate cause of the symptoms. But a full understanding of the disease requires a further step, an inquiry into the more remote causes that led to the present pathology.

When the causal chain is traced backward, two general factors emerge. One is a predisposition (technically called a *diathesis*) toward the illness. The other is a set of environmental conditions which *stress* the system and precipitate the defective insulin mechanism; for example, obesity. In diabetes, the diathesis is based on genetic factors that create a marked susceptibility to the disease, which is then triggered by precipitating stress.

The treatment follows from the analysis of the cause-and-effect relations. Since the diabetic's pancreas does not secrete enough insulin, this substance must be supplied from the outside. Further control of the faulty metabolism is then imposed by an appropriate diet (Dolger and Seeman, 1985).

The preceding discussion illustrates the so-called *diathesis-stress* conception that has proved helpful in the understanding of many organic as well as mental disorders. Many of these conditions result from the interaction of a diathesis that makes the individual potentially vulnerable to a particular disorder, and some form of environmental stress that transforms the potentiality into actuality. Just what the diathesis is that creates the vulnerability depends on the particular disorder. In many cases, as in diabetes, it is based on genetic constitution. In others, it may be produced by various social and psychological factors, such as chronic feelings of worthlessness.

Figure 17.5 provides a schematic summary of our discussion of diabetes, a nonpsychiatric ailment. The figure gives us an idea of what the analysis of a disease looks like when the disease is reasonably well understood. This is the framework we will use when we ask whether a particular mental disorder is an illness, and if so, in what sense. How such disorders are treated will be taken up in the next chapter.

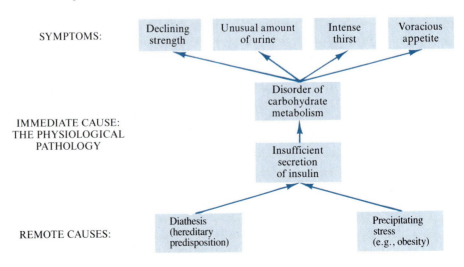

17.5   The pathology model as applied to diabetes

SYMPTOMS:

Declining strength | Unusual amount of urine | Intense thirst | Voracious appetite

Disorder of carbohydrate metabolism

IMMEDIATE CAUSE: THE PHYSIOLOGICAL PATHOLOGY

Insufficient secretion of insulin

REMOTE CAUSES:

Diathesis (hereditary predisposition) | Precipitating stress (e.g., obesity)

SCHIZOPHRENIA

One of the most serious conditions in the whole field of psychopathology is **schizophrenia** (from the Greek *schizo,* "split," and *phrene,* "mind").* The term was coined in 1911 by the Swiss psychiatrist Eugen Bleuler (1857–1939) to designate what he regarded as the main attribute of this disorder—a fragmentation of mental functions (Bleuler, 1911).

Schizophrenia is quite prevalent. According to one estimate, about one in a hundred Americans will need treatment for this disorder at some period during his or her lifetime, typically between the ages of fifteen and forty. At any one time about four hundred thousand persons are hospitalized with this condition, accounting for about half of all of the beds in the country's mental hospitals (Babigian, 1975).

Many investigators believe that schizophrenia is a disease, in the straightforward, somatogenic, sense of the term. To evaluate this position, we will discuss the disorder within the same framework we used when we considered the interpretation of the organic disease, diabetes—the symptom pattern, the underlying pathology, the less immediate causes such as genetic predisposition, and the precipitating factors.

The Symptoms

The fragmentation of mental life characteristic of schizophrenia can be seen in disorders of cognition, of motivation and emotion, and of social relationships. Few patients who are diagnosed as schizophrenics show all of these signs. Until fairly recently, this led to considerable disagreements in diagnosis, since different clinicians used different yardsticks to determine how many symptoms had to be present and to what degree. With the advent of DSM-III and DSM-III-R, which both introduced a number of objective criteria for the diagnosis (e.g., a gross distortion in the perception of reality, symptoms present for at least six months, and so on), such discrepancies were minimized.

DISORDERS OF COGNITION

Disturbance of thought   A key symptom is a pervasive thought disturbance. The schizophrenic doesn't "think straight"; he can't maintain one unified guiding thought, but rather skips from one idea to the next. An example is a fragment of a letter written by one of Bleuler's patients:

> I am writing on paper. The pen I am using is from a factory called "Perry & Co." This factory is in England. I assume this. Behind the name of Perry Co., the city of London is inscribed; but not the city. The city of London is in England. I know this from my school-days. Then, I always liked geography. My last teacher in that subject was Professor August A. He was a man with black eyes. I also like black eyes. There are also blue and gray eyes and other sorts too. I have heard it said that snakes have green eyes. All people have eyes. There are some, too, who are blind. These blind people are led about by a boy. (Bleuler, 1911, p. 17)

Disturbance of attention   Such examples show that the schizophrenic may have difficulty in suppressing irrelevant ideas that come from within. Similar prob-

Eugen Bleuler   *(Courtesy National Library of Medicine)*

---

* This etymological derivation is responsible for a widespread confusion between schizophrenia, and *multiple (or split) personality.* While both fall under the general rubric of psychopathology, the two conditions are quite different.

Paintings by schizophrenics *Paintings by schizophrenics often have an odd, eerie quality. In many cases, the usual artistic conventions are disregarded, and the picture includes written comments, digits, and other idiosyncratic material. (A) Saint-Adolf-Grand-Grand-God-Father (1915), a painting by Adolf W., who was institutionalized in early adulthood and elaborated a fantastic autobiography that featured himself as Saint Adolf II, a young god who travels through space and has many adventures. (B) Guardian Angels by Else B., an institutionalized schizophrenic. In all her works, the legs of angels are painted as though they had fused at the top, to make sure that "nothing happens there." (Prinzhorn, 1972; courtesy Galerie Rothe Heidelberg)*

lems arise with irrelevant stimuli that assail her from without. We have seen that in ordinary perception one focuses on some aspects of the world while de-emphasizing others. We somehow filter out the irrelevant stimuli so that we can follow a conversation without being continually distracted by other people's voices or radiator clankings or whatever (see Chapter 5). But schizophrenics seem to be less efficient in attending selectively. They hear (and see and feel) too much, perhaps because they can't exclude what is extraneous. Some patients (only mildly disordered or recovered) describe what this feels like:

> During the last while back I have noticed that noises all seem louder to me than they were before. It's as if someone turned up the volume. . . . I notice it most with background noises. . . . Now they seem to be just as loud and sometimes louder than the main noises that are going on. . . . it makes it difficult to keep your mind on something when there's so much going on that you can't help listening to. (McGhie and Chapman, 1961, p. 105)

LOSING CONTACT

A common facet of schizophrenia is a withdrawal from contact with other people. In some patients this withdrawal begins quite early; they have had few friends and little or no adolescent sexual experience. What brings on this withdrawal is still unknown. One possibility is that it is a defense against the overstimulation to which they are exposed because of their inability to filter out the irrelevant. Another possibility is that it grows out of pathological family relations during childhood and adolescence.

Whatever the reason that led up to it, the schizophrenic's withdrawal from social contacts has drastic consequences. The individual starts to live in a private world of his own, a condition that becomes increasingly worse. The withdrawal from others provides fewer and fewer opportunities for *social-reality testing* in which one's own ideas are checked against those of others and corrected when necessary. As a result, the schizophrenic's ideas become ever more idiosyncratic, until the patient may have trouble communicating with others even if he wants to; they may very well rebuff him because they can't understand him and think he's "weird." The result is further withdrawal, which leads to further idiosyncracy, still further withdrawal, and so on. The final consequence of this vicious cycle is a condition in which the patient can no longer distinguish between his own thoughts and fantasies and external reality. He has lost contact.

ELABORATING THE PRIVATE WORLD

The private world of some schizophrenics is organized in elaborate detail. They have strange beliefs, and may see and hear things that aren't there.

Delusions Once having initiated the break with the social world, many schizophrenics develop *ideas of reference.* They begin to believe that external events are specially related to them, personally. The patient observes some strangers talking and concludes that they are talking about *her;* she sees people walk by and decides that they are following *her;* she hears a radio commercial and is sure that it contains a specially disguised message aimed at *her.* Eventually, these ideas become systematized in the form of false beliefs or *delusions.* Such delusions are especially common in a subcategory called *paranoid schizophrenia.*

An example of paranoid schizophrenia is a delusion of persecution. The patient is sure that *they*—the Communists or the FBI or the members of the American Medical Association or whoever—are spying on him and plotting against him. This delusion gradually expands as the patient gathers further evidence that convinces him that his wife and children, the ward psychiatrist, and the man in the bed near the door, are all part of the conspiracy.

Hallucinations Delusions result from misinterpretations of real events. In contrast, **hallucinations** are perceived experiences that occur in the absence of actual sensory stimulation. This phenomenon is fairly common in schizophrenia. The patient "hears" voices, or, less commonly, "sees" various persons or objects. The voices may be of God, the devil, relatives, or neighbors. If the patient can make out what they say, she hears that they are talking about her, sometimes threateningly and sometimes obscenely.

Some authors believe that such hallucinations reflect an inability to distinguish between one's own memory images and perceptual experiences that originate from without. The patients may be talking to themselves, but they will then interpret their own inner speech as originating from outside. They "heard themselves talk" and thought they heard voices (McGuigan, 1966; Green and Preston, 1981).

DISORDERS OF MOTIVATION AND EMOTION

Thus far our focus has been on the schizophrenic's thoughts. When we look at his motives and feelings, we find similar evidence of disruption and fragmentation. In the early phase of the disorder, there is often a marked emotional oversensitivity in which the slightest rejection may trigger an extreme response. As time goes on, this sensitivity declines. In many patients it dips below normal until there is virtual indifference to their own fate or that of others. This apathy is especially pronounced in long-term schizophrenics, who stare vacantly, their faces expressionless, and answer questions in a flat and toneless voice.

In some cases, emotional reaction is preserved but the emotion is strikingly inappropriate to the situation. A patient may break into happy laughter at the news of a brother's death "because she was so pleased at receiving letters with black borders"; another becomes enraged when someone says hello (Bleuler, 1911).

DISORDERS OF BEHAVIOR

Given the disruptions in the schizophrenics' thoughts, motives, and feelings, it is hardly surprising that there are often concomitant disorders in how they act. Some patients—in a subtype called **catatonic schizophrenia**—exhibit very unusual motor reactions that may be extremely violent and excited or stuporous and frozen. When in the stuporous state, the patients remain virtually motionless for long periods of time. They may be standing or sitting, or they may adopt some unusual posture that they will often maintain for hours on end (Figure 17.6).

According to some theorists, the patients' immobility is a secondary reaction to their basic disturbance of thought and attention. The schizophrenic is overstimulated as it is, but this stimulation becomes even greater when she is in motion. So she stops moving, in sheer self-defense. As one patient put it, "I did not want to move, because if I did everything changed around me and upset me horribly so I remained still to hold on to a sense of permanence" (quoted in Broen, 1968, p. 138).

17.6 Patient with a diagnosis of catatonic schizophrenia who spent virtually all waking hours in this crouched position (Photograph by Bill Bridges/Globe Photos)

Subcategories of Schizophrenia

Psychiatrists have tried to distinguish among several subtypes of schizophrenia that are defined by the kind of symptoms that are predominant. A recent proposal is based on a distinction between positive and negative symptoms. *Positive symptoms* are those that involve what the patients *do* (and see and think) that normal persons don't: hallucinations, delusions, bizarre behaviors. In contrast, **negative symptoms** are those that involve a *lack* of normal functioning: apathy, poverty of speech, emotional blunting, and the inability to experience pleasure or sociability. As we will see later, a classification based on this distinction may help to account for which patients will benefit from drug therapy and which of them suffer from cerebral atrophy (see p. 505; Opler et al., 1984; Andreasen, 1985; Crow, 1985).

The Search for the Underlying Pathology

We have described the various symptoms that define schizophrenia. As in diabetes or in any other organic disease, the next step is to look for the underlying malfunction from which these symptoms spring. To begin with, one has to specify the underlying *psychological malfunction* of which the symptoms are a manifestation. This done, then—if there is reason to suspect that the disorder is somatogenic—one searches for the organic pathology of which this psychological malfunction is an expression.

WHAT IS THE PSYCHOLOGICAL DEFICIT?

A widely held view is that the schizophrenic's primary trouble is cognitive. The details of the proposed explanations vary, but most of them agree that the patient's major deficit is an inability to keep things in proper focus. Normal people focus in both space and time. They perceive objects without being distracted by extraneous stimuli; they execute plans without interference by irrelevant responses. Not so the schizophrenic who has considerable difficulty in holding onto one line of thought or action and is forever lured off the main path (Chapman and Chapman, 1973; Patterson et al., 1986).

Given this deficit, the patient's many disturbances of language and thought follow. His speech is marked by one tangent after another; sometimes the sheer sound of a word is enough to trigger a series of rhyming associations, as in "How are you today by the bay as a gay, doctor?" (Davison and Neale, 1986, p. 338). His inability to disregard irrelevant attributes leads to strange conceptualizations in which incongruous items are grouped together. One patient explained that Jesus, cigar boxes, and sex are all identical. This was because all three are encircled—the head of Jesus by a halo, a cigar box by the tax band, and a woman by a man's sexually interested glance (Von Domarus, 1944).

It may be that some of the other major symptoms of schizophrenia such as delusions and hallucinations are yet further consequences of the basic thought disturbance. Bleuler believed that these symptoms are the elaborations of the private world of a person who has lost contact with other people and can no longer distinguish between his private fantasies and external reality.

WHAT IS THE ORGANIC PATHOLOGY?

Many investigators believe that the psychological deficits that underlie schizophrenia are an expression of an organic pathology. They have focused on two possible kinds of malfunctions. One involves the disordered functioning of certain neurotransmitters in the nervous system. The other emphasizes abnormalities and lesions in the patients' brains (Meltzer, 1987).

Malfunctioning neurotransmitters Many investigators believe that the underlying organic pathology involves some malfunction of neurotransmitters, the sub-

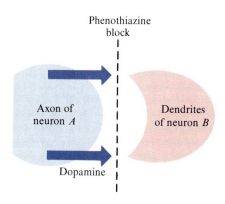

17.7   The dopamine-block hypothesis of phenothiazine action

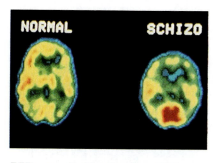

PET scans of schizophrenics *PET scans comparing the normal and the schizophrenic brain reveal certain abnormalities of brain structure and increased metabolic activity in different areas of the schizophrenic's brain.*

stances whose secretion by one neuron may either trigger or inhibit an impulse in another neuron on the other side of the synapse. A likely candidate is ***dopamine.*** This is one of the ***catecholamines,*** transmitters liberated by neurons, which have an arousing function in various parts of the brain. According to the dopamine hypothesis, many neurons in the schizophrenic's brain have become oversensitive to dopamine. One line of evidence comes from the effect of the ***phenothiazines.*** Phenothiazines are known to block dopamine at the synapse (Figure 17.7). This dopamine blockade is more pronounced in some phenothiazine drugs than in others. As predicted by the dopamine hypothesis, the stronger the blockade, the more therapeutic the drug (Snyder, 1976).

If a decrease of dopamine activity makes schizophrenics better, an increase should presumably make them worse. This is indeed the case. One group of investigators injected small doses of a drug that increases dopamine activity into the veins of schizophrenics who were in a comparatively mild state. Within a minute, the patients' symptoms became wild and extreme. One started to shred a pad of paper, announcing that he had been sending and receiving messages from ancient Egypt. Others became catatonic (Davis, 1974).

Anatomical deficits   Recent technological breakthroughs in assessing brain abnormalities in living patients, such as PET scans (see Chapter 1), show that some schizophrenics suffer from certain abnormalities of brain structure. One such abnormality is an enlargement of the ventricles—the hollow cavities filled with cerebrospinal fluid that form the core of the brain—which suggests an atrophy of brain tissue (Andreasen et al., 1986; Meltzer, 1987). Such findings seem to support the view that the underlying biological pathology of schizophrenia consists of some kind of anatomical deficit.

The two-syndrome hypothesis   Both the dopamine hypothesis and the anatomical-deficit hypothesis face a problem: Each fits some schizophrenics, but not all. Thus, many schizophrenic patients respond to the dopamine-blocking drugs, but a number do not. Similarly, a significant number of schizophrenics show signs of cerebral atrophy, but many do not. Some authors have tried to handle these facts by proposing the ***two-syndrome hypothesis*** of schizophrenia (Crow, 1982, 1985). According to this view, schizophrenia is really a composite of two underlying pathologies—known as Type I and Type II—that correspond to the positive and negative symptom subcategories we have discussed before (see pp. 503–4). Type I is caused by a malfunction of neurotransmitters (especially dopamine) and produces such "positive" symptoms of schizophrenia as delusions, hallucinations, and thought disorders. Type II is produced by cerebral damage and atrophy and leads to "negative" symptoms such as flat affect, social withdrawal, and apathy. Support for this view comes from the fact that, by and large, patients with mostly positive symptoms tend to respond well to phenothiazines and show no cerebral damage. The reverse holds for patients with mostly negative symptoms. They are generally not improved by phenothiazine treatment and are more likely to show signs of cerebral damage (Crow, 1980, 1985).

More Remote Causes of Schizophrenia

We have considered several analyses of the basic pathology in schizophrenia, including hypotheses about the underlying psychological deficit and some guesses about organic malfunctions. These hypotheses about pathological processes—at either the psychological or the physiological level—are about the *immediate causes* of the disorder. The next question concerns causes that are less immediate and further back in time. As we have seen in our discussion of diabetes, any attempt to understand a disease involves both a consideration of its immediate causes (a metabolic malfunction brought on by insulin insufficiency) and a search for causes that are more remote (genetic factors, environmental effects) that might suggest a possible diathesis-stress interpretation. We will follow the same approach in our discussion of schizophrenia.

HEREDITARY PREDISPOSITION

Does schizophrenia have a hereditary basis? This question has been studied by the same means used to assess the role of heredity in other human traits such as intelligence. The basic approach is to consider family resemblance. In schizophrenia, as in intelligence, this resemblance is considerable. For example, the likelihood that a person who has a schizophrenic sibling is schizophrenic himself or will eventually become so is about 8 percent; this compares to a 1 percent risk of schizophrenia in the general population (Rosenthal, 1970). But again, as in the area of intelligence, such family resemblances don't settle anything about the nature-nurture issue, for they can be interpreted either way. For more conclusive evidence we have to turn to the familiar methodological standbys that are used to disentangle the contributions of heredity and environment—studies of twins and of adopted children. A widely used method focuses on twins, one of whom is schizophrenic. The question is whether the schizophrenic's twin is schizophrenic as well. The probability of this event, technically called *concordance,* is 44 percent if the twins are identical, compared to only 9 percent if they are fraternal (Gottesman and Shields, 1972, 1982; Gottesman, McGuffin, and Farmer, 1987; see Figure 17.8). Further evidence comes from adoption studies. Children born to schizophrenic mothers and placed in foster homes within a week or so after birth are more likely to become schizophrenic than persons in a matched control group of adoptees born to normal mothers (Heston, 1966; Kety, 1983; Kendler and Gruenberg, 1984).

ENVIRONMENTAL STRESS

The preceding discussion indicates that schizophrenia has a genetic basis. But there is no doubt that environment also plays a role. One line of evidence comes from identical twins. Their concordance for schizophrenia is considerable, but is much less than 100 percent. Since identical twins have the same genotype, there

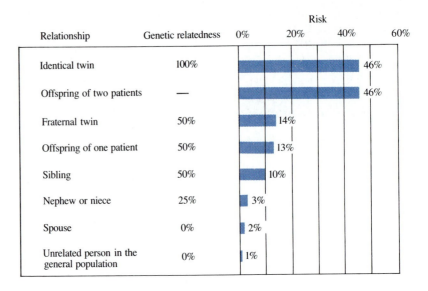

17.8   Genetic factors in schizophrenia
Risk estimates for schizophrenia as a function of relationship to a schizophrenic patient. (From Nicol and Gottesman, 1983, p. 399)

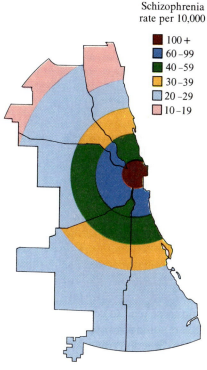

Schizophrenia
rate per 10,000

■ 100 +
■ 60 –99
■ 40 –59
■ 30 –39
■ 20 –29
■ 10 –19

17.9   The prevalence of schizophrenia in different regions of a city   *A map of Chicago (1922–1934) represented by a series of concentric zones. The center zone is the business and amusement area, which is without residents except for some transients and vagabonds. Surrounding this center is a slum region inhabited largely by unskilled laborers. Further out are more stable regions: a zone largely populated by skilled workers, followed by zones of middle- and upper-middle-class apartment dwellers and, furthest out, the upper-middle-class commuters. The map shows clearly that the incidence of schizophrenia increases the closer one gets to the city's center. (After Faris and Dunham, 1939)*

must be some nongenetic factors that also have a say in the determination of who becomes schizophrenic and who does not.

What are these nongenetic factors? As yet, there is no consensus. We will consider a few lines of evidence that relate to various potentially stress-producing situations. Some involve the person's social class and economic condition; others concern his family. According to many modern investigators, these and other stress-producing environmental factors may bring out the latent pathology in a person with a genetic predisposition toward schizophrenia and will eventually precipitate the actual disorder, much as obesity or continued emotional stress precipitates diabetes. The stronger the diathesis, the less stress would presumably be required to convert the predisposition into actuality (Meehl, 1962; Gottesman and Shields, 1982).

Social class   In searching for environmental causes, sociologically minded investigators have focused upon social class. They have found a sizable relationship. The proportion of schizophrenics is much higher at the bottom of the socioeconomic hierarchy than it is at the top. According to one study, the ratio is 9 to 1 (Hollingshead and Redlich, 1958). The prevalence of schizophrenia is highest in the poorest and most dilapidated areas of the city and diminishes progressively as one moves outward toward the higher status regions (Figure 17.9). This general relation between social class and schizophrenia has been found in city after city, from New York, Omaha, New Haven, and Milwaukee in the United States to Oslo, Helsinki, London, and Taiwan abroad (Kohn, 1968).

Pathology in the family   Other investigators have concentrated upon the schizophrenic's family. They paint a gloomy picture. As they describe them, schizophrenics' mothers are rejecting, cold, dominating, and prudish, while their fathers are detached, humorless, weak, and passive (Arieti, 1959). Later studies concentrated on the relationships within the family. In general, they found a high degree of instability (Lidz et al., 1957).

Schizophrenics evidently come from a less benign family background than do normal children. But this does not prove that the familial environment is a *cause* of the patient's disorder. It may also be an *effect*. After all, having a schizophrenic in the family is surely quite disturbing. Several studies of parent-child interactions suggest that something of this sort may indeed play a role (Mishler and Waxler, 1968; Liem, 1974). In one of these studies, the investigators observed mothers who had both a schizophrenic and a healthy daughter (Mishler and Waxler, 1968). When observed with their schizophrenic daughters, the mothers seemed unresponsive and aloof. But when observed with their healthy daughters, the mothers behaved more normally. This suggests that their unresponsiveness was not a general characteristic of their personality (and thus perhaps a *cause* of their child's disorder), but it was instead a reaction to the schizophrenic daughter (and thus an *effect* of the child's disorder upon the mother's behavior).

Family environment as a factor in therapy and relapse   The preceding discussion suggests that poor familial relations may not cause the patient's illness. But some further findings show that they have much to do with keeping him from getting well. The evidence comes from studies of schizophrenic patients who had recovered well enough to be discharged from the hospital and who went back to live with their parents or spouses. The investigators interviewed these family members at the time of the patient's breakdown to determine how they felt about him: the extent to which they were critical, hostile, or emotionally overinvolved and manifested these negative feelings to the patient. The more intense the degree of these so-called "expressed emotions," the greater the chance that the patient would eventually relapse and have to be readmitted to the mental hospital. On re-

creased when the patients became manic (Muscettola et al., 1984; Schildkraut, Green, and Mooney, 1985).

Further confirmation comes from the effect of two kinds of **antidepressant drugs:** the **tricyclics** and the **monoamine oxidase (MAO) inhibitors.** Both of these drugs have some success in relieving depression, and both increase the amount of norepinephrine and serotonin available for synaptic transmission.

Psychogenic Factors

The organic pathology—whatever it may turn out to be—might account for the extremes of some patients' moods, the fact that they are speeded up or slowed down in virtually all respects. But can it explain *what* the patient thinks or does, the manic's glow of overweening satisfaction and the depressive's hopeless despair and self-loathing? How does an inadequate supply of norepinephrine or serotonin lead to the belief that one is the "most inferior person in the world"?

MOOD OR COGNITION?

What comes first, mood or cognition? The question is again one of cause and effect. Theorists who regard the disorder as primarily somatogenic believe that what the patient thinks *follows* from her mood. If a transmitter insufficiency (or some other biochemical state) makes her feel sluggish and gloomy, she looks for reasons to explain her own mood. Eventually she will find them; the world is no good and neither is she. The end result is that her cognitions match her feelings. (For an analogous approach to the nature of emotional feelings in normal persons, see Chapter 11.)

Does this approach really do justice to the phenomenon? Theorists who believe in a psychogenic explanation think not. They grant that mood disorders—especially those that are bipolar—may involve a constitutional predisposition toward mood excess, but they insist that psychological factors play a vital role in at least some cases of depression. In their view, the patient's view that she and the world are no good comes first and her depression comes second—as an *effect* of these cognitions rather than as their cause.

BECK'S COGNITIVE THEORY OF DEPRESSION

This cognitive view underlies a very influential approach to the understanding and treatment of depression developed by Aaron Beck (Beck, 1967, 1976). Beck believes that the patient's condition can be traced to a trio of intensely negative and irrational beliefs about himself, about his future, and about the world around him: that he is worthless, that his future is bleak, and that whatever happens around him is sure to turn out to be for the worst. According to Beck, these beliefs form the core of a negative cognitive schema in terms of which the patient interprets whatever happens to him. Facing minor setbacks, the depressive makes mountains out of molehills (insisting that he has ruined his car when he's only scratched a fender); facing major accomplishments he makes molehills out of mountains (insisting that he's inept even though he's just won an important professional prize). To counteract this system of essentially irrational beliefs, Beck has developed a psychological treatment called **cognitive therapy** by means of which the patients are made to confront and overcome the essential irrationality of their beliefs, which we will discuss in a later section (Beck, 1967; Beck et al., 1979; see Chapter 18).

Sorrow   *(Vincent Van Gogh, 1882; courtesy Vincent Van Gogh Foundation/ National Museum Vincent Van Gogh, Amsterdam)*

Depression and despair *Edward Adamson, a professional artist, founded a studio in a British mental hospital for the use of the institutionalized patients. Many of their works forcefully express these patients' depression and despair, as in the case of this painting entitled* Cri de Coeur *or "Cry from the heart." (*Cri de Coeur, *by Martha Smith; reproduced from Adamson, 1984)*

Where Beck's cognitive theory grew out of clinical observations of depressed patients, a related cognitive account, proposed by Martin Seligman, had its source in studies of animal learning. The initial findings that led to Seligman's approach concerned **learned helplessness,** first observed in the animal laboratory (Seligman, 1975; see Chapter 3).

Learned helplessness and depression When normal dogs are placed in a shuttle-box in which they have to jump from one compartment to another in order to escape an electric shock, they learn to do so with little difficulty. This is in contrast with a second group of dogs who have first been exposed to a series of painful shocks about which they could do absolutely nothing. When this second group was later placed in the shuttlebox, their performance was drastically different from that of normal dogs. They did not look for some means of escape. Nor did they ever find the correct response—jumping over the hurdle. Instead, they simply gave up; they lay down, whimpered, and passively accepted their fate. They had learned to become helpless (Seligman, Maier, and Solomon, 1971).

Seligman argued that learned helplessness in animals is in many ways similar to at least some forms of depression. Like the helpless dogs, depressed patients have given up. They just sit there, passively, unable to take any initiative that might help them cope. Some further similarities concern the effects of antidepressant drugs. As we've seen, these drugs alleviate the symptoms of many depressed patients. It turns out that they have a similar effect on animals rendered helpless; the helplessness disappears, and the animals behave much like normal animals (Porsolt, LePichon, and Jalfre, 1977).

Seligman supposed that the essential similarity between the helpless dogs and the depressed people is the expectation that one's own acts are of no avail. In dogs, the cause was a series of inescapable shocks that the animals could do nothing about. In humans, the precipitating factor may be some personal catastrophe —rejection, bankruptcy, physical disease, the death of a loved one. In some persons, this may lead to a generalized sense of impotence, a belief that there is nothing one can do to shape one's own destiny, that one is a passive victim with no control over events—that one is helpless.

Attributional style and depression The helplessness interpretation of depression runs into a number of problems. To begin with, it can't explain why being helpless doesn't necessarily lead to depression. People who are about to undergo an operation are helpless in the sense of being utterly dependent on their surgeons, but if they believe they will recover they will generally not become depressed. A further problem is the depressive's self-hatred. If he thinks that he is helpless, then why does he blame himself? (Abramson and Sackheim, 1977). Considerations of this sort led to a revised version of the helplessness theory, which proposed that what really matters is the individual's **attributional style,** the way in which he habitually tries to explain events—especially bad events—that happen to him (see also Chapter 16, pp. 481–82). Does he attribute unfortunate events to internal, global, and stable causes—that is, to causes that refer to something within himself, that will generalize to other situations, and that will continue over time (for example, being unattractive or unintelligent)? If so, he has an attributional style that will predispose him to depression (Abramson, Seligman, and Teasdale, 1978). There is good evidence that this despondent explanatory style is indeed characteristic of depressed persons (as shown by results with the Attributional Style Questionnaire described in Chapter 16, p. 481; Peterson and Seligman, 1984).

A recent extension of this general approach focuses on hopelessness. Its main point is that in some cases of depression, hopelessness is a major cause rather than a symptom. If the patient believes that he has absolutely nothing to look forward to and that the future is utterly bleak, he will probably start a downward spiral that will eventually have bodily manifestations and end in a full-fledged depression. The precise differences between this and related psychogenic views (such as Beck's and other offshoots of the learned helplessness approach) are still being spelled out (Alloy, Hartlage, and Abramson, 1988; Abramson, Metalsky, and Alloy, 1989).

The male-female ratio in depression Conceptions derived from the learned helplessness theory and related views may help us understand an important fact about major depressions. They are about twice as common in women as in men, even when incomes and socioeconomic levels are held constant. What accounts for this difference? While hormonal factors, such as drops in estrogen and progesterone levels during the premenstrual period, the postpartum period, and menopause may play a role, they are at best only part of the picture. One guess is that the sex ratio is produced by culturally produced differences in the way men and women are taught to cope with difficult life situations. The culture expects men to be self-reliant and active, while women are supposed to be more passive and dependent. To the extent that this is true, men learn that they have control over their fate, while women gradually learn to feel much less able to determine what happens to them—the very condition that presumably leads to learned helplessness and depression. A further factor may be a difference in the way the culture determines how men and women deal with their own moods. According to a recent study, when men are depressed, they try to distract themselves: "I avoid thinking of reasons why I'm depressed," or "I do something physical." In contrast, women who are depressed seem to dwell on their despondency: "I try to determine why I'm depressed," "I talk to other people about my feelings," and "I cry to relieve the tension." The result of these different ways of dealing with one's own feelings is that the initial depression is more likely to escalate and last longer in women than in men (Nolen-Hoeksema, 1987).

Depression in women *Major depressions are about twice as common in women as in men. (Photograph by Mark Antman/ The Image Works)*

Mood Disorders and the Diathesis-Stress Conception

Mood disorders are often preceded by some stressful event—marital difficulties, difficulties at work, serious physical illness, or a death in the family (Leff, Roatsch, and Bunney, 1970; Paykel, 1982). But it's clear that environmental stress cannot be the whole story. After all, there are many people who suffer major setbacks and serious losses but who don't fall into a depressive collapse. There is evidently a diathesis—some people are more prone to mood disorders than others—and the stressful event precipitates it. This diathesis may be based on biological factors—such as an insufficiency of available norepinephrine or serotonin. But the predisposition may well be psychological in nature—such as a negative view of oneself or the world or a depressive attributional style. In either case, the diathesis makes the individual more vulnerable to later stress.

Seen in this light, psychological and biological factors are intermingled, so that the distinction between somatogenic and psychogenic origins becomes somewhat blurred. Negative cognitions and learned helplessness can produce a depletion of norepinephrine and serotonin, but the causal chain can also run the other way around. Either way, there will be a predisposition for later depression, which will be manifested in both behavior and in biochemistry.

ANXIETY DISORDERS

In major depressions, the primary symptom is a profoundly dejected mood: The patient believes that his condition *is* awful and that there is no hope that it will ever get better. In another group of conditions, the ***anxiety disorders,*** the primary symptoms are anxiety or defenses against anxiety: The patient fears that something awful *will* happen to him. While such symptoms often cause serious distress and impair the person's functioning, they generally do not render him incapable of coping with external reality. In the terms of an earlier nomenclature, he is a neurotic, not a psychotic.

Phobias

A relatively common anxiety disorder is a ***phobia,*** which is characterized by an intense and irrational fear of some object or situation. During the nineteenth century, some of these irrational fears were catalogued and assigned high-sounding Greek or Latin names. Examples are fear of high places (acrophobia), or open places (agoraphobia), or enclosed places (claustrophobia), or of crowds (ocholophobia), or germs (mysophobia), or cats (ailurophobia)—the list is potentially endless. The crucial point in the definition is that the fear must be *irrational,* that there really is no danger or that the danger is exaggerated out of all proportion. An African villager who lives at the outskirts of the jungle and is worried about leopards has an understandable fear; a San Francisco apartment dweller with a similar fear has a phobia. In many cases, this irrationality is quite apparent to the sufferer, who knows that the fear is groundless but continues to be afraid all the same.

In phobia, the irrational fear exerts an enormous effect on every aspect of the sufferer's life, for he is always preoccupied with his phobia. On the face of it, it is not entirely clear why this should be so. Why can't the phobic simply avoid the situations that frighten him? If he is afraid of leopards and snakes, he should stay

Phobias *An artist's conception of (A) the fear of dirt, and (B) the fear of open spaces. (Paintings by Vassos)*

A   B

515

Compulsive hand washing in literature   *A scene from the Old Vic's 1956 production of* Macbeth *with Coral Browne. It shows Lady Macbeth walking in her sleep and scrubbing imaginary blood off her hands, as she relives the night in which she and her husband murdered the king. (Courtesy of the Performing Arts Research Center, The New York Public Library)*

away from the zoo; if he is terrified of heights, he should refrain from visits to the top of the Sears Tower. Some phobias may be minor enough to be handled this easily, but most cannot. In many cases this is because the phobia tends to expand. The fear of leopards becomes a fear of the part of the city where the zoo is located, of all cats and catlike things, or of all spotted objects, and so on. Other phobias may be more wide-ranging to begin with. An example is *agoraphobia* (from a Greek word meaning "fear of the marketplace"), which is sometimes described as a fear of open places but is essentially a fear of being in places from which escape would be difficult.*

What is the mechanism that underlies phobias? One notion goes back to John Locke who believed that such fears are produced by a chance association of ideas, as when a child is told stories about goblins that come by night and is forever after terrified of the dark (Locke, 1690). Several modern authors express much the same idea in the language of conditioning theory. In their view, phobias result from classical conditioning; the conditioned stimulus is the feared object (e.g., cats), and the response is the autonomic upheaval (increased heart rate, cold sweat, and so on) characteristic of fear (Wolpe, 1958).

A number of phobias may indeed develop in just this fashion. Examples include fear of dogs after dog bites, fear of heights after a fall down a flight of stairs, and fear of cars or driving after a serious automobile accident (Marks, 1969). Conditioning theorists can readily explain why phobias acquired in this manner expand and spread to new stimuli. The fear response is initially conditioned to a particular stimulus. If this stimulus subsequently occurs in a new context, the fear will be evoked and thus conditioned to a whole set of new stimuli. An example is a woman who developed a fear of anesthetic masks after experiencing a terrifying sensation of suffocation while being anesthetized. This same sense of suffocation reoccurred later when she was in a stuffy, crowded elevator. This in turn led to a dread of elevators, whether empty or crowded. The phobia generalized to any and all situations in which she could not leave at will, even playing cards (Wolpe, 1958, p. 98).

Obsessive-Compulsive Disorders

In phobias, anxiety is aroused by external objects or situations. In contrast, anxiety in *obsessive-compulsive disorders* is produced by internal events—persistent thoughts or wishes that intrude into consciousness and cannot be stopped. An example of such an *obsession* is a mother who has recurrent thoughts of strangling her children. To ward off the anxiety produced by such obsessions, the patient often feels compelled to perform a variety of ritualistic acts. Such *compulsions* are attempts to counteract the anxiety-producing impulse that underlies the obsessive thought; in Freud's terms, a way of *undoing* what should not have been done. Examples of such compulsions are ritualistic cleaning, handwashing, and incessant counting. The mother with uncontrollable thoughts of committing infanticide might feel compelled to count her children over and over again, as if to check that they are all there, that she hasn't done away with any. The obsessive-compulsive patient is aware that his behavior is irrational, but he can't help himself even so. Lady Macbeth knew that "what's done cannot be undone," but she nevertheless continued to wash the invisible blood off her hands.

Minor and momentary obsessional thoughts or compulsions are commonplace. After all, most people have had the occasional feeling that they ought to check whether the door is locked even when they are perfectly sure that it is. But

---

* In many cases, agoraphobia accompanies panic disorder (see pp. 517–19).

in obsessive-compulsive disorders, such thoughts and acts are the patient's major preoccupation and are crippling:

> A man in his 30's, fearing lest he push a stranger off the subway platform in the path of an oncoming train, was compelled to keep his arms and hands glued rigidly to his sides. . . . [He] was on one occasion obsessed with the idea that, despite his stringent precautions, he had, after all, inadvertently knocked someone off the subway platform. He struggled with himself for weeks to dispel what he rationally knew was a foolish notion but was at length compelled to call the transport authority to reassure himself that there had not in fact been any such accident. The same patient was for a time preoccupied with the concern that, when he walked on the streets, he was dislodging manhole covers so that strangers passing by would fall into the sewer and be injured. Whenever he passed a manhole in the company of friends, he would be compelled to count his companions to make sure that none was missing. (Nemiah, 1985, p. 913)

Generalized Anxiety Disorders

In the anxiety disorders we have discussed thus far, anxiety is relatively focused, for it occurs in response to a fairly specific condition. In phobia, anxiety is aroused by the feared object; in obsessive-compulsive disorder, it is aroused by a thought or the belief that one hasn't performed some important act. In contrast, there are several conditions in which anxiety is not related to anything in particular, but isn't any less upsetting for all that.

In *generalized anxiety disorders,* anxiety is all-pervasive, or free-floating. The patient is constantly tense and worried, feels inadequate, is oversensitive, can't concentrate or make decisions, and suffers from insomnia. This state of affairs is generally accompanied by any number of physiological concomitants—rapid heart rate, irregular breathing, excessive sweating, and chronic diarrhea.

According to a psychoanalytic interpretation, generalized anxiety disorders show what happens when there are no defenses against anxiety or when those defenses are too weak and collapse, so that unacceptable impulses are able to break into consciousness and to precipitate anxiety reactions.

Conditioning theorists offer another account. In their view, a generalized anxiety condition is much like a phobia. The difference is that anxiety is conditioned to a very broad range of stimuli so that avoidance is virtually impossible (Wolpe, 1958). The trouble is that the stimuli to which anxiety is said to be conditioned are not easily specified. Since this is so, the conditioning interpretation of this disorder is hard to evaluate.

Panic Disorder

Panic disorder is like generalized anxiety disorder in being characterized by anxiety that is not directed at anything in particular. The difference is in the frequency and intensity of the anxiety. Patients with panic disorder don't suffer from the nagging, chronic tensions and worries that beset persons with generalized anxiety disorder. But when anxiety strikes them, it strikes with a vengeance.

Panic disorder is characterized by sudden storms of overwhelming anxiety. The patient suffers sudden attacks that come out of the blue and bring terrifying bodily symptoms that she doesn't understand: labored breathing, choking, dizziness, tingling in the hands and feet, sweating, trembling, heart palpitations, and chest pain. These bodily sensations are accompanied by feelings of intense apprehension, terror, and a sense of impending doom. The patient often has an intense experience of unreality and fears that she is losing control, is going insane, or is

The Scream   *(Edvard Munch, 1893; courtesy Nasjonalgalleriet, Oslo)*

about to die. Panic disorder is diagnosed if such attacks occur once a week or more often; based on that criterion, it is found in about 1 percent of the population (Myers et al., 1984).

What accounts for panic disorder? Some authors hold to a cognitive theory of the condition. They believe that it is produced by a vicious cycle that begins with a misinterpretation of certain bodily reactions to fear. In fear reactions, the sympathetic nervous system produces a number of circulatory and respiratory responses such as quicker heartbeats and faster and shallower breathing. This is normal enough, but the person with the panic disorder overreacts to her own internal sensations. She believes that the shortness of breath and quickened heartbeat are a sign of an impending heart attack. This makes her more fearful, which intensifies the bodily reactions, which makes her even more fearful, and so on, spiraling upward toward the full-blown attack. This pattern becomes even worse after the patient has her first panic attack, for now every normal anxiety reaction becomes a potential signal of a further panic (Clark, 1986).

How can we explain the patient's unusual misinterpretation of her own internal signals? One possibility is that these signals are physiologically unusual to begin with. In normal persons, there is a neurochemical system that dampens the sympathetic emergency reaction after it occurs; without this sympathetic dampening, we'd all be in a continual state of stress. There is evidence that this dampening effect is deficient in patients with panic disorders (Nesse et al., 1984). Further evidence indicates that there is some genetic predisposition, as shown by a 31 percent concordance for the disorder in identical twins compared to a zero concordance in fraternals (Torgersen, 1983).

In light of these facts, should we regard panic disorder as somatogenic or psychogenic? The answer is that it is both. There may well be an underlying organic pathology, perhaps based on a genetic predisposition: some chemical abnormality of the brain that makes for overintense sympathetic reactions that last too long. A behavioral (that is psychogenic) pathology is built upon that: a repeated misinterpretation of the sympathetic signals. This leads to a vicious cycle in which organic and behavioral reactions go hand in hand to spiral into a panic attack, after which there is a further psychogenic process (the fear of further attacks) that leads to still further escalation.

Anxiety Disorders and the Pathology Model

Anxiety disorders (as well as many other conditions) were until recently considered as subclasses of a larger category, the neuroses. Their symptoms vary widely, and so they are now grouped separately for diagnostic purposes. But are at least some of them similar in sharing a common underlying diagnostic pathology?

ANXIETY AS A POSSIBLE UNDERLYING CAUSE

Many modern practitioners follow Freud in believing that there is a pathology that underlies phobias and obsessive-compulsive disorders, but that it is behavioral (that is, mental) rather than organic. In their view, the symptoms of these disorders are primarily a defense against some intolerable anxiety. This view fits some of these conditions rather well. For example, compulsive acts can be understood as responses that block an anxiety-related obsessive thought, even if only temporarily. But in phobias, let alone the other anxiety disorders, the role of the symptom in defending the patient against anxiety is a matter of debate.

Suppose a person has a crippling phobia about water that makes it hard for him to drink, wash, and so on. A psychoanalyst would argue that this water phobia is only the visible part of the disorder. To understand this symptom, we have to dig deeper and find out what the patient is "really" afraid of, what water stands for in his private symbolism. But a behavior theorist would probably take a different tack. He would argue that the patient's trouble is a conditioned fear of water, no more and no less, and that there are no hidden conflicts of which this fear of water is a devious manifestation. In his view, the symptom *is* the disease, and it is the removal of this symptom toward which treatment—or as he would call it, ***behavior therapy***—should be directed.

MORE REMOTE CAUSES

Whatever their theoretical differences, most theorists agree that in common with other psychopathological conditions, most anxiety disorders have remote as well as immediate causes.

On the face of it, one might well suspect that the various anxiety disorders are partially based on a genetic predisposition. After all, we know that temperaments differ from birth on and that emotionality (which Eysenck called neuroticism) is heritable (see Chapter 16, pp. 469–71). Under the circumstances, one wouldn't be surprised to find a genetic component in phobias (perhaps some people get conditioned more readily to fear-arousing stimuli) or in generalized anxiety disorder (perhaps some are more tense and worrisome to begin with). But thus far, the only anxiety condition for which a genetic component has been established is panic disorder, although there are some indications that a hereditary contribution may be involved for some of the others (e.g., Carey and Gottesman, 1981).

A diathesis can be genetic and organically based. But such a predisposition can also rest on prior (and presumably learned) patterns of thinking and reacting as in the attributional style of depressives. In phobias and certain anxiety attacks, the immediate cause of the disorder is a stressful event in the just preceding past: a traumatic episode that led to a phobia, or a marital breakup that initiated an anxiety attack. But upon investigation, it often turns out that the patient had some prior adjustment problems. At least in part, the trauma may have served to evoke some earlier reactions to anxiety acquired in the more distant past. An example is psychiatric breakdown during combat. Soldiers who collapse under relatively minor stress are more likely to have a history of prior psychiatric difficulty, signs of serious maladjustment during childhood, and so on (Slater, 1943).

CONVERSIONS AND DISSOCIATIVE DISORDERS

The defense reactions set up in many of the anxiety disorders are cumbersome and never work completely. Thus patients with obsessive-compulsive patterns are always encumbered with guilt and vacillation. But there is another group of disorders in which the person seems to do a better job at managing anxiety. Some are *conversion disorders* in which the patient "converts" a psychological conflict into an apparent bodily symptom. Others are *dissociative disorders* in which a whole set of mental processes is split off from the rest of the individual's consciousness. Freud believed that these are conditions in which the primary defense seems to be repression. In both disorders, the individual pushes all anxiety-evoking materials out of consciousness. This allows him to deny that there is anything to be anxious about.

Conversion Disorders

Historically, *conversion disorders* (or to use an earlier term, *conversion hysterias*) represented the first and most dramatic arguments for the psychogenic approach to psychopathology and were the initial foundation on which psychoanalytic theory was built. According to Freud, persons with these disorders resolve some intolerable conflict by developing a hysterical ailment, such as being unable to see or hear or move an arm even though there is nothing organically wrong with them (see Chapter 10).* The soldier who is terrified of going into battle but cannot face the idea of being a coward may become hysterically paralyzed. This allows him to give in to his impulse of refusing to march. But it also lets him do so without guilt or shame—he is not marching because he *cannot* march.

Dissociative Disorders

Another way in which a person can deny responsibility for some acts (or thoughts or wishes) is by insisting that they were never committed, or at least not by him. This approach is characteristic of *dissociative reactions.* In these disorders, a whole set of mental events—acts, thoughts, feelings, memories—is shoved out of ordinary consciousness. One example is psychogenic *amnesia* in which the individual is unable to remember some period of his life, or sometimes all events prior to the onset of the amnesia, including his own identity. In other cases, the dissociation involves a *fugue state,* in which the individual wanders away from home, and then, days, weeks, or even years thereafter, suddenly realizes that he is in a strange place, doesn't know how he got there, and has total amnesia for the entire period.

---

* The term "conversion" was coined by Freud who believed that the repressed energies that power the patient's unconscious conflict are converted into a somatic symptom much as a steam engine converts thermal energy into mechanical energy. Until recently, this condition was called *conversion hysteria.* The authors of DSM-III dropped the term *hysteria* because of its erroneous implication that it is a disorder found only in women. (The term *hysteria* is derived from the Greek *hystera,* meaning *womb.*)

Still more drastic are cases of *multiple personality.* Here the dissociation is so massive that it results in two or more separate personalities. The second—and sometimes third or fourth—personality is built upon a nucleus of memories that already had some prior separate status. An example is a shy and inhibited person who has had fantasies of being carefree and outgoing from childhood on. These memories eventually take on the characteristics of a separate self. Once formed, the new self may appear quite suddenly, as in the famous case of Eve White:

> After a tense moment of silence, her hands dropped. There was a quick, reckless smile and, in a bright voice that sparkled, she said, "Hi there, Doc." . . . There was in the newcomer a childishly daredevil air, an erotically mischievous glance, a face marvelously free from the habitual signs of care, seriousness, and underlying distress, so long familiar in her predecessor. This new and apparently carefree girl spoke casually of Eve White and her problems, always using *she* or *her* in every reference, always respecting the strict bounds of a separate identity. When asked her own name she immediately replied, "Oh, I'm Eve Black." (Thigpen and Cleckley, 1957, as described in Coleman, 1972, p. 246)

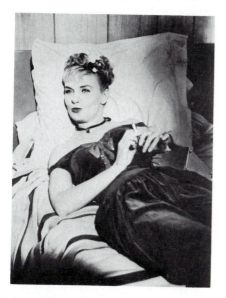

A movie recreation of a case of multiple personality Joanne Woodward in The Three Faces of Eve *portraying Eve White (top) and Eve Black (bottom). (Courtesy the Museum of Modern Art/Film Stills Archive)*

Factors That Underlie Conversions and Dissociative Conditions

The cause of conversion and dissociative symptoms is still obscure. Freud believed that such symptoms are a defense against anxiety. Conditioning theorists hold a similar position, translated into their own conceptual framework. But this anxiety hypothesis only accounts for the patient's motives. It may explain why he wants not to see or not to walk or to develop an alternate personality; it does not explain how he accomplishes these feats, especially the wholesale alterations of consciousness that characterize dissociations.

Some authors suggest that such phenomena may represent an unusual form of self-dramatization in which the person acts *as if* she were blind or *as if* she were Eve Black without any consciousness that any playacting is going on (Ziegler, Imboden, and Rodgers, 1963; Sarbin and Allen, 1968). According to this view, the patient is like an actor who becomes so involved in his role that he is no longer aware that he is on stage. In actuality, of course, no actor ever completely forgets that he is playing a part; if he did, he would be unable to leave the stage when the play calls for his exit. But by the same token, no patient is ever completely paralyzed or blind and so on; his "paralyzed" leg still responds to reflex stimulation and will probably serve quite well in emergencies such as a fire.

Whether dissociations and conversion reactions are a defense against anxiety or an unconscious kind of playacting, most investigators suspect that they have roots in earlier patterns of behavior that set the stage for the full-blown disorder under later conditions of stress. An example is provided by cases of multiple personality. Those with this disorder often seem to have histories of severe abuse in childhood (Bliss, 1980; Putnam et al., 1986). According to one investigator, such patients were unusually adept at self-hypnosis during early childhood and created a new personality during their hypnotic trance as a form of escape from the threatening traumatic event (Bliss, 1980).

PSYCHOPHYSIOLOGICAL DISORDERS

Thus far, our concern has been with psychopathological disorders whose primary symptoms are psychological. But certain other conditions can lead to genuine organic damage. For example, peptic ulcer or asthma may be produced by organic causes, as in the case of an asthmatic allergic reaction. Yet they may also be produced (or aggravated) by emotional factors. If so, they are called *psychophysiological conditions* (or, to use an older term, *psychosomatic disorders*).* But whether their origin is organic or mental makes no difference to the victim: They are equally real in either case.

In this regard, the symptoms of a psychophysiological condition are quite different from the somatic complaints of a patient with a conversion disorder. That patient's paralysis of the legs may disappear after his underlying conflict is resolved; after all, his locomotor machinery is still intact. But the patient with a psychophysiological ulcer (or asthma, or high blood pressure) has a disorder that plays for keeps. His ulcer will bleed and hurt just as much as an ulcer caused by a gastric disease, and if it perforates his stomach wall he will suffer the same case of peritonitis and, if he dies, his death will be no less final.

Essential Hypertension

Several psychophysiological disorders involve the circulatory system. One is *essential hypertension.* This is a chronic elevation of blood pressure that can lead to serious disability and premature death. While some cases of hypertension result from various organic pathologies, essential hypertension is at least partially psychogenic (Lipowski, 1975; Harrell, 1980).

THE EFFECT OF CONTINUED AUTONOMIC AROUSAL

Blood pressure is the pressure exerted by the blood as the heart pumps it through the body's arteries. One way in which this pressure can rise is by the constriction of the arteries. This occurs in fight-or-flight emergencies, as when a zebra suddenly sees a hungry lion (see Chapter 2). The sympathetic branch of the autonomic nervous system is aroused and, among other things, this leads to the contraction of the muscles of the arterial walls. The effect is much like squeezing on a water hose. There is an immediate increase in the force of the liquid spurting out. As a result, the skeletal muscle, and the heart muscles themselves, get blood more quickly—a vital necessity in life-or-death situations that call for sudden, violent exertions.

Such extraordinary measures are all very well for zebras trying to get away from lions. The emergency really does call for increased muscular effort; when it is over, the muscles inform the nervous system that they no longer need the same supply of food. When this happens, the circulatory system soon returns to normal. The situation is quite different for us today. We rarely encounter emergencies that call for violent muscular effort. But our lives are filled with any number of fear- and anger-producing situations. An unfair grade, a neighbor's snub, a near-miss on the superhighway—all these trigger the sympathetic emergency reaction, even though a sudden spurt of muscular energy is of no avail. But our autonomic nervous system doesn't know that. And so we are put on an emergency basis, some of us more than others, but all to some extent. As a result, our blood pressure goes up, again and again, in the daily stress of living. Since the emergency does not lead to any extra muscular effort, the autonomic nervous system never gets the proper message that signals the end of the emergency. As a result, the blood pressure remains up for a while after the incident has passed.

In some people, continued autonomic overactivity eventually takes its toll—the elevated blood pressure no longer comes down to normal. One reason is a gradual thickening of the arterial muscle walls. This, together with an increased sensitivity to stimulation, makes these muscles overreact to normal neural im-

---

* In DSM-III-R, they are listed under "psychological factors affecting physical conditions."

pulses. As a result, they are in an almost continual state of constriction. The more constricted they are, the thicker and more sensitive they get. The ultimate effect of this vicious cycle is **hypertension,** a condition that afflicts twenty-three million Americans and represents a major public health problem. Among its relatively minor symptoms are headaches and dizziness. If serious and prolonged, the disorder leads to lesions in the arteries that supply the kidneys, the brain, and the heart. The final results include kidney failure, cerebral stroke, coronary disease, and heart attacks (Lipowski, 1975).

HYPERTENSION AND EMOTIONAL STRESS

Hypertension is evidently a residue of continued sympathetic arousal. Thus, we would expect its incidence to go up with increasing emotional stress. This is indeed the case. For example, there was a marked increase in the rate of hypertension among the inhabitants of Leningrad during the siege and bombardment of that city during World War II (Henry and Cassel, 1969). Similar effects are produced by socioeconomic stress. Hypertension is much more common among blacks than whites in the United States; and it is especially prevalent in metropolitan regions marked by high population density, poverty, and crime (Lipowski, 1975). Still other studies show that hypertension is more prevalent among persons whose occupations impose unusual emotional stress. An example is provided by air-traffic controllers, especially those who work in airports in which traffic density is high (Cobb and Rose, 1973; Rose, Jenkins, and Hurst, 1978).

In all of these cases, the critical element is not environmental stress as such, but rather the individual's reaction to it. What the besieged citizen of Leningrad, the unemployed inner-city black, and the overburdened air-traffic controller have in common is unremitting sympathetic arousal; they are continually afraid or angry or harassed, and eventually their bodies pay the price in the form of hypertension (Figure 17.12).

Coronary Heart Disease

Coronary heart disease is a progressively increasing blockage of the arteries that supply blood to the heart muscles. This may result in severe chest pains (angina), indicating that the muscles in a certain region of the heart don't get enough oxygen to maintain their current work load. It may also result in the death of some portion of the heart muscle tissue (a "heart attack") that received no oxygen at all. There are a number of biological factors that increase the risk of coronary heart disease such as cholesterol level, obesity, smoking, and gender (men are more prone to the disease than women). But in addition, psychopathologists have identified certain characteristic behavior patterns that provide a major additional risk factor.

THE TYPE A PERSONALITY

One such behavior pattern characterizes the so-called **Type A personality.** People with this pattern are highly competitive, hard-driving people who are always in a hurry and are irritable, impatient, and hostile. In the words of the two cardiologists, Friedman and Rosenman, who first described this pattern, such individuals are "aggressively involved in a chronic, incessant struggle to achieve more and more in less and less time, and if required to do so, against the opposing efforts of other things or other persons" (Friedman and Rosenman, 1974, p. 67). The so-called **Type B personality** is best defined by way of contrast; Type B's are less hurried and more easygoing, less competitive, and more friendly than their Type A

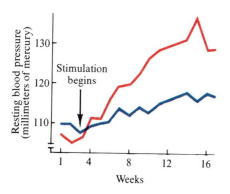

17.12   Chronic autonomic arousal and hypertension   *A group of rats was exposed to continued electrical stimulation of the hypothalamic defense area. The electric stimulation was mild; it merely produced alerting reactions such as sniffing. But the stimulation was chronic, with one stimulus every minute for 12 hours every day over the better part of a four-month period. The figure shows the average resting blood pressure of the rats in this group (red) compared to the blood pressure of a control group that suffered no hypothalamic stimulation (blue). The toll exacted by the continued defense reaction is shown by the difference between the two groups after four months. (After Folkow and Rubenstein, 1966)*

counterparts. The Type A person fumes vehemently when stuck in a traffic jam; the Type B individual shrugs his shoulders philosophically and calmly listens to a radio broadcast of a baseball game. Needless to say, many people are not extreme A or B types, but fall somewhere in between.

A common method for assessing the degree of Type A behavior is a questionnaire that contains items such as "Has your spouse or friend ever told you that you eat too fast?" and "Do you ever set deadlines for yourself at work or at home?" (Jenkins, Rosenman, and Friedman, 1967). Another method is a standardized clinical situation in which the interviewer intentionally creates a stressful atmosphere to elicit signs of impatience or hostility. For example, the interviewer may deliberately pause and stall while asking a question to determine whether the person he is assessing will interrupt him or give an answer before the question is completed (Rosenman, 1978).

Several large-scale studies have shown that persons with a Type A pattern are more likely to contract coronary heart disease than Type B individuals. In one such study, over 3,000 men with no sign of coronary heart disease were evaluated to determine their A-B behavior type. The single best predictor of whether these men developed coronary heart disease during the subsequent eight years was their original A-B assessment: Type A's were twice as likely to become victims than Type B's. Could this be because Type A's smoked more, or had higher blood pressure, or had higher cholesterol levels? The answer was no, for the relation between behavior pattern and heart disease held up even when these other risk factors were statistically held constant (Rosenman et al., 1975). Further work showed that the same relation held for women. Compared to men, women—whether Type A or Type B—are much less likely to suffer coronary heart disease, for reasons that are still a matter of debate. But compared to Type B women, Type A women are more at risk; they are two to three times more likely to suffer a heart attack, and this regardless of whether they are working women or not (Haynes, Feinleib, and Kannel, 1980).

"I don't care if they are moving better over there. This is the fast lane. This is where I live." (Drawing by Handelsman; © 1983, The New Yorker Magazine, Inc.)

IMPATIENCE OR HOSTILITY

It appears that some characteristic that is associated with the Type A personality predicts heart disease. But just what is the crucial part of this behavior complex? Is it the Type A person's impatience, or his relentless need for achievement, or his irritability? Some recent investigations suggest that these different components of the behavior pattern are not as tightly linked—to each other or to the disease—as they were initially thought to be (Mathews, 1982). In the opinion of many investigators, the major contributor to the cardiac disorder is a combination of continual anger and chronic distrust of other people that is found in some—but by no means all—Type A's. Those who say yes to questions like "Most people are honest chiefly through fear of being caught" or "When someone does me a wrong I feel I should pay him back if I can, just for the principle of the thing" are more likely to fall victim to cardiac disease than those who do not. Other facets of the Type A pattern, such as the sense of hurry and competitiveness, seem to be of lesser importance (Williams, 1987; Krantz et al., 1988; Barefoot et al., 1989).

The Diathesis-Stress Concept and Psychophysiological Disorders

Emotional stress can lead to hypertension or coronary heart disease, but it can also lead to various other psychophysiological disorders such as peptic ulcers. Is there any way to predict which disorder will be produced in any one person by stress? What determines whether "she will eat her heart out" or "whether she'll tie her stomach into knots?" The answer is diathesis and stress.

There is reason to believe that the susceptibility to a given psychophysiological disorder depends on a preexisting somatic diathesis that may be of genetic origin. Given enough emotional stress, the body will cave in at its most vulnerable point.

Some evidence for this view comes from studies which show that elevated blood pressure tends to run in families, in mice as well as men. In humans, a blood-pressure correlation between children and parents is seen as early as infancy. The best guess is that there is a genetic factor which is partially responsible for the initial blood-pressure elevation. This may bias the individual to respond to stress with his arterial muscles rather than with his lungs or stomach. If the stress is prolonged enough, the individual will become a hypertensive rather than an asthmatic or an ulcer patient (Henry and Cassel, 1969).

A CATEGORIZING REVIEW

We have looked at a number of different mental disorders. The pathology model provides a convenient framework to review the way in which these disorders are generally considered today. This review is summarized in Table 17.1, which classifies disorders by the nature of their main symptoms and of their presumed underlying pathology (which in many cases is still controversial). Either the main symptoms or the pathology or both, can be organic. But they can also be mental, that is, defined by behavioral rather than by organic attributes.

Table 17.1   A CLASSIFICATION OF SOME MENTAL DISORDERS

		Symptoms	
		Primarily organic	Primarily mental
Presumed underlying disorder	Primarily organic	Diabetes Measles Rickets	General paresis Schizophrenia* Bipolar disorders*
	Primarily mental	Psycho- physiological disorders	Phobias Obsessive-compulsive disorders Dissociative disorders

* Whether the underlying pathology of these disorders is primarily organic or psychogenic is still a matter of debate. In some cases, such as panic disorders, organic and behavioral causes are so intertwined that it's impossible to say which is primary.

THE SOCIOLOGICAL CRITIQUE OF THE PATHOLOGY MODEL

Thus far, our focus has been on the psychological and biological aspects of mental disorder. But psychopathological conditions can also be looked at from a sociological perspective that emphasizes how disordered people are viewed and dealt with by society. This sociological approach has led to several influential attacks on the pathology model.

What Society Does to Those It Calls Mad

The sociological critique of the pathology model is among other things a form of social protest. One of its recurrent themes is that mentally disordered persons are treated as outcasts, even today. Social historians point out that this has been their

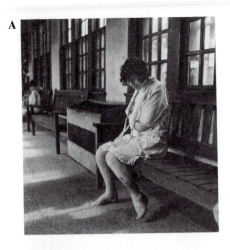

A

B

C

17.13 The condition of mental patients *The shameful conditions that held through the mid-forties in many state hospitals are illustrated by (A) a woman in a Cleveland state hospital in 1946, and (B) male patients in a Philadelphia mental hospital in 1946, sitting naked on refuse-covered floors. (C) Conditions have improved considerably, but in many cases, the mental hospital is still more of a custodial than a therapeutic institution, and the patients' life there is often empty and barren. (Photographs by Jerry Cooke/Life; and Ken Heyman)*

role since before medieval times. During the 1700s, madmen were caged like beasts. Although their fate has improved considerably in modern times, even today they are still largely exiles from the rest of the world.

Some critics of the way in which mental disorder is dealt with in modern society accuse psychiatrists of acting more like jailors than like physicians. Many mentally disordered people are relegated to mental hospitals whose function is custodial rather than therapeutic (see Figure 17.13). Until fairly recently, the inmates of such institutions had few legal rights, especially if they were committed. In 1949, only 10 percent of the admissions to mental hospitals in the United States were voluntary. Today, this proportion is much higher, but involuntary institutionalizations are still more common than voluntary ones. A number of recent patients' rights campaigns have led to the establishment of more stringent safeguards on commitment procedures. But while such measures have curbed some abuses, they have not changed the fact that mentally disturbed people are still more or less banished and live under a social stigma that is hard to remove.

Whom Does Society Call Mad?

The treatment society metes out to mentally disordered persons is grim even with enlightened attitudes. The sociological critics of the pathology model ask who the people are who are treated in this way. To the mental health practitioner, the answer is obvious: those who demonstrate mental illness by a variety of signs and symptoms. The sociological critics reply that in many ways the causal chain works in reverse; sometimes the label creates the symptoms. The fact that a person is called mentally ill makes others see and treat him differently. Eventually, the labeled individual may change his own self-perception; then he and others will behave so as to make the label fit better and better.

To the extent that this is true, it is a demonstration of a self-fulfilling prophecy. This sometimes has paradoxical effects. To the hospital authorities—attendants, nurses, psychiatrists—the very fact that a person is an inmate is virtual proof that there must be something wrong with her. If a mental patient proclaims her sanity, this is merely evidence that she is even more deranged than anyone had suspected; she doesn't even "have insight." The patient has a better chance of getting discharged if she first admits that she is sick. She can then announce that she is getting better; now the authorities will tend to look at her more kindly, for she is obviously "responding to treatment" (Goffman, 1961).

MENTAL ILLNESS AS A MYTH

Some critics maintain that the key to mental disorder is the label; without this, there would be no disorder at all. A prominent exponent of this position is psychiatrist Thomas Szasz. According to Szasz, mental illness is a myth (Szasz, 1974). He and other critics charge that it is merely a term by which we designate people whose behavior deviates from the norms of their society but does not fall into any of the recognized categories of nonconformity. They are neither criminals, nor prostitutes, nor heretics, nor revolutionaries, and so on. To account for their deviance, only one explanation is left—they are mentally ill (Scheff, 1966). Seen in this light, mental disorder is not a condition that is inherent in the individual; instead, it depends upon how the individual is seen by others. According to this position, madness (like beauty) is in the eye of the beholder.

BEING SANE IN INSANE PLACES

Proponents of labeling theory often appeal to the results of a study by David Rosenhan to support their position. Rosenhan arranged to have himself and seven other normal persons admitted as patients to various psychiatric hospitals across the country. Each of these "pseudopatients" came to the hospital with the same complaint—he or she heard voices that said "empty," "hollow," or "thud." They employed a pseudonym and sometimes misrepresented their professions, but in all other respects they reported their own life histories and their true present circumstances. All pseudopatients were admitted to the psychiatric ward, all but one with the diagnosis of schizophrenia. Once on the ward, the pseudopatients' behavior was completely normal. They said that they no longer heard voices and that they felt perfectly fine.

There was not a single case in which a hospital staff member detected the deception. The fact that pseudopatients behaved quite normally did not help, for whatever they did was generally interpreted in line with the original diagnosis. For example, all of the pseudopatients took extensive notes. At first, they did so surreptitiously, but they soon found out that there was no need for circumspection. The note-taking was seen as just one further manifestation of the disorder. A typical nurse's report read, "Patient engaged in writing behavior." No one ever asked what was written and why; presumably it was an aspect of being schizophrenic.

Prior to the study, all of the pseudopatients had agreed that they would try to get discharged without outside help by convincing the hospital staff that they were sane, but without admitting the original deception. They found that it was easier to get in than out. On the average, it took nineteen days; in one case, it took fifty-two. When they were finally discharged, it was with the diagnosis "Schizophrenia, in remission." In lay terms, this means that there are no symptoms, at least for now. The validity of the original diagnosis was never questioned (Rosenhan, 1973).

The Rosenhan findings show that a diagnostic label may reinforce a preexisting conception of what a patient is like. But do they really show that the distinc-

Are those whom society calls mad merely those of whom society disapproves? The film One Flew over the Cuckoo's Nest *with Jack Nicholson dramatizes this question. (Courtesy the Museum of Modern Art/Film Stills Archives)*

Madness as label *The influential physician-anatomist Sir Charles Bell made this drawing after a visit to Bedlam in 1805 to illustrate the nature of "madness." The drawing reflects the then prevailing concept of the "madman" as a wild and ferocious being, reduced to the state of a lower animal. (Charles Bell's "Madness" from his* Essays on the Anatomy of Expression in Painting, *1806)*

tion between sane and insane depends *only* upon the label and that mental illness is a myth?

The answer is no. Consider the situation from the psychiatrist's point of view. A patient had auditory hallucinations on entering the hospital. This symptom promptly disappears. What are the psychiatrists to do? The idea of deception never occurs to them. (After all, who would be paranoid enough to suspect that it was all part of a psychological experiment?) Under the circumstances, they must conclude that the patient is or was suffering from some psychotic disorder, probably schizophrenia, and should be kept under further observation. The fact that the patient's later acts are interpreted in terms of the original diagnosis is now quite understandable. He did hear voices a few days ago, so his present sanity is probably more apparent than real. Seen in this light, the psychiatrists' acts seem quite understandable (Wishner, 1974; Spitzer, 1976).

Social Deviance

It is rather ironic that the sociological critics of the pathology model have concentrated most of their fire on a mental disorder which the pathology model handles reasonably well, namely schizophrenia. A similar critique might have found more appropriate targets had it been directed at certain other diagnostic categories that also huddle under the psychiatric umbrella. The psychiatric classification system includes a number of human conditions that are certainly deviant and usually undesirable, such as antisocial personality, alcoholism, drug addiction, and various sexual deviations. But it is by no means clear that all of these are really mental disorders. Nor is it clear that the pathology model is the most appropriate framework within which they should be viewed.

Society calls some forms of deviance criminal while calling others mad, and it has set up institutions to deal with each—the judicial system for the first and the mental health system for the second. In actual fact, the two classifications overlap and both shade off into normality. Figure 17.14 is an attempt to provide a graphic description of how the terms "normal," "bad," and "mad" are usually applied. Some kinds of persons can be classified unambiguously: you and I (definitely "normal," or at least, so we hope), a professional criminal ("bad"), and a severe

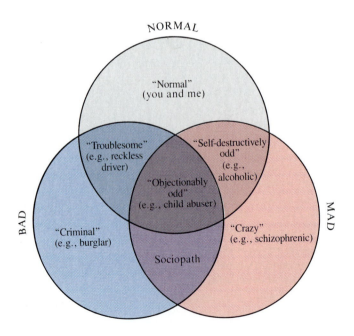

17.14 The three labels, BAD, MAD, and NORMAL, and some labels for their areas of overlap *(After Stone, 1975)*

case of schizophrenia ("mad"). But there are also areas of overlap. Some people occupy a gray area between normality and lawlessness. An example might be a person who is a habitual reckless driver. Others are on the boundary between mental disorder and normality. An example would be a person with a serious drinking problem. Still others are in the region of overlap between criminality and mental disorder. They are somehow both "mad" and "bad" at the same time. Our present concern is with one such group of individuals, the so-called **antisocial personalities,** or, as they have also been called, **sociopaths.***

THE SOCIOPATH

The clinical picture　The sociopath is an individual who gets into continual trouble with others and with society. He is grossly selfish, callous, impulsive, and irresponsible. His—or, somewhat less frequently, her—difficulties generally start with truancy from school, runaway episodes, and a "wild adolescence" marked by belligerence and precocious sexual experience and promiscuity (Robins, 1966). Later on there are various minor scrapes that often escalate into increasingly serious legal and social offenses. But the distinguishing characteristics of sociopathy go deeper than this. One feature is the lack of any genuine feeling of love or loyalty for any person or any group. Another characteristic is that there is relatively little guilt or anxiety. As a result, the sociopath is a creature of the present whose primary object is to gratify the impulses he feels now, with little concern about the future and even less remorse about the past.

All of this is another way of saying that sociopaths are not truly socialized. They are not pack animals; they are genuine loners. They are often quite adept at the outward skills of social living; they are frequently charming and of greater than average intelligence. In these regards, sociopaths are quite different from ordinary criminals and delinquents. These too are in conflict with established society, but unlike sociopaths, they generally have a society of their own, such as a juvenile gang or a crime syndicate, whose code they try to honor and to which they have some sense of loyalty.

Some possible causes of sociopathy　What accounts for the inadequate socialization that characterizes sociopaths? A number of investigators have focused on the sociopath's lack of concern about the future consequences of his actions. Sociopaths are comparatively fearless. This is especially true when the danger is far off. One investigator told sociopaths and normal persons that they would receive a shock at the end of a ten-minute period. The subjects' apprehensiveness was assessed by their galvanic skin response (GSR). As the time grew closer, the control subjects grew increasingly nervous. In contrast, the sociopaths showed little anticipatory fear (Lippert and Senter, 1966). If future pain had just as little import when the sociopath was young, his inadequate socialization becomes partially comprehensible. Whoever tried to teach him the don'ts of childhood had no effective deterrents (Figure 17.15).

The strange fearlessness of sociopaths has been observed by several writers who have noted their "extraordinary poise," their "smooth sense of physical being," and their "relative serenity" under conditions that would produce agitation in most of us (Cleckley, 1976). How does this difference between sociopaths and normals come about? Several investigators believe that there is a difference in some underlying physiological functions. One line of evidence concerns the EEG (electrical recordings from the brain; see Chapter 2). It appears that a fairly high

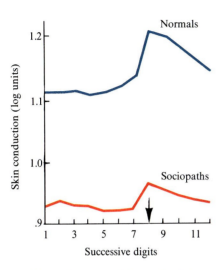

17.15　Anticipation of electric shock in normals and sociopaths　*Normals and sociopaths were repeatedly presented with a series of 12 consecutive digits from 1 to 12. Whenever the digit 8 appeared, the subjects suffered an electric shock. To determine whether there were any differences in anticipatory anxiety prior to the advent of shock, the galvanic skin response (GSR) was measured. The results are shown in units of log conductance (a measure of GSR activity) for each of the 12 digits in the series. The sociopaths showed a much lower base-response level. In addition, they showed less anticipatory reaction to the digits just prior to the critical digit. (After Hare, 1965)*

---

　* An earlier designation was **psychopath.** Some versions of this term are still in current use. An example is the MMPI scale which attempts to measure *psychopathic deviance.*

CHAPTER 18

Treatment of Psychopathology

What can be done about mental disorders? There is no scarcity of proposed remedies, each with its own adherents. Some rely on biological interventions such as drugs. Others approach the condition at the psychological level; the classical example is psychoanalysis. But until recently the proven accomplishments of these interventions were relatively modest. This was hardly surprising. Since not too much was known about the causes of many of the mental disorders, one could not really expect to know much more about their cure. But of late, the outlook has become more optimistic. There are no miracle cures, but at least some of the disorders seem to respond reasonably well to certain biological and/or psychological treatments.

SOMATIC THERAPIES

One approach to treatment is through various manipulations of the body. Such **somatic therapies** constitute medicine's classical attack on any disease. Thus, once mental disorder was cast as an illness, it was only natural to try to heal it with the traditional tools of the physician's trade. But in fact, until fairly recently, most such attempts were unsuccessful. In some cases, the would-be cures were worse than the disease. We already mentioned a very early example: trephining, the removal of sections of the skull, a prehistoric practice that persisted into medieval times. Other early procedures involved a relentless succession of bloodlettings and purgatives, all in the hope of restoring a proper harmony among the bodily humors. Later developments were hardly milder. For example, Benjamin Rush (1745–1813), one of the signers of the Declaration of Independence and the acknowledged father of American psychiatry, dunked patients into hot or cold water and kept them under just short of drowning, or twirled them on special devices at speeds that often led to unconsciousness (Figure 18.1). Such methods were said to reestablish the balance between bodily and mental functions. They almost certainly had no such salutary effects, although they were probably welcomed by hospital attendants since such methods undoubtedly terrified the inmates and thus helped to "keep order" (Mora, 1975).

B

C

A

18.1 Early methods for treating mental disorder (A) A crib for violent patients. (Courtesy Historical Pictures Service) (B) A centrifugal-force bed. (Courtesy National Library of Medicine) (C) A swinging device. (Courtesy Culver Pictures)

Drug Therapies

The bleak outlook for somatic therapy did not appreciably brighten until the beginning of this century. The first step was the conquest of general paresis, a progressive deterioration of physical and psychological functioning, by an attack on the syphilitic infection that caused it (see Chapter 17). But the major breakthrough has come only during the last thirty years or so with the discovery of a number of drugs that seem to control, or at least to alleviate, the symptoms of schizophrenia and affective disorders.

MAJOR PSYCHIATRIC DRUGS

Antipsychotic drugs In the last chapter, we saw that one of the major arguments offered by adherents of a biochemical theory of schizophrenia is the effectiveness of certain drugs such as chlorpromazine (Thorazine), which belong to a family called the **phenothiazines.** Chlorpromazine and its pharmacological relatives tend to reduce many of the major positive symptoms of schizophrenia, such as thought disorder and hallucinations. These drugs blockade synaptic receptors in pathways of the brain that are sensitive to **dopamine,** and it is this blockade that is generally thought to produce the therapeutic effects.

The impact of the phenothiazines and related antipsychotic drugs (together with that of drugs aimed at affective disorders) upon psychiatric practice has been enormous. The discovery of these drugs lent further support to a new social policy that stressed discharge rather than long-term hospitalization. This deinstitutionalization program, prompted by both humane and economic considerations, led to the Community Mental Health Center Act of 1963. The result was a drastic reduction in the total hospital population. In 1955, there were 559,000 patients in the state mental hospitals in the United States; in 1984, at any given time there were about 132,000. The new drugs made it possible to discharge schizophrenic patients more quickly than ever before. According to one estimate, prior to the introduction of these drugs, two out of three schizophrenic patients spent most of their lives in the state asylum. Today their average stay is about two months (Lamb, 1984; Davis, 1985a; see Figure 18.2).

It has sometimes been argued that drugs like chlorpromazine are not really antipsychotic agents at all but are merely fancy sedatives that quiet patients down. This view does not square with the facts. While chlorpromazine and other phenothiazines alleviate schizophrenic symptoms, such powerful sedatives as phenobarbital have no such effect. They put the patient to sleep, but when he wakes up, his delusions and hallucinations will be just as they were before. Still other evidence suggests that the phenothiazines have a **specific drug effect.** They work on

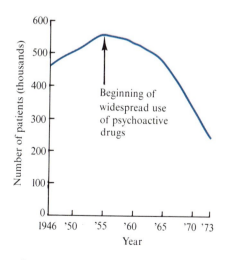

18.2 Number of residents in state and local government mental hospitals between 1946 and 1973 in the United States (Based on data from U.S. Public Health Service)

the symptoms that characterize schizophrenia but have no effect on symptoms that are not specific to that disorder. For example, they help to clear up the patient's disordered thought but have little effect on depression or anxiety. It is thus hardly surprising that chlorpromazine and other phenothiazines do *not* calm down normal persons or patients with anxiety disorders (Davis, 1985a).

Antidepressants   Shortly after the introduction of the antipsychotic agents, two major groups of drugs were found that acted as ***antidepressants: monoamine oxidase (MAO) inhibitors*** and ***tricyclics.*** Of these, the tricyclics—such as ***imipramine*** (Tofranil)—are the most widely used; they tend to be more effective and have fewer side effects. The therapeutic effectiveness of such antidepressants seems to be due to the fact that they increase the amount of norepinephrine and serotonin available for synaptic transmission. These drugs can be very effective in counteracting depression, but not all of them work for all patients. It appears that different patients have somewhat different biochemical deficits and thus require different antidepressant medication. There is some evidence that there are some "biological markers" (usually obtained through blood tests) that may help to match the proper antidepressant drug to the particular patient (Maugh, 1981; Davis, 1985b).

Lithium   Another pharmacological development is the use of lithium salts such as ***lithium carbonate*** in the treatment of bipolar disorder. Most manic episodes subside within five or ten days after the patients start lithium therapy. There is some further evidence that the drug can also forestall the depressive episodes in bipolar disorder. Just what accounts for these effects is largely unknown. According to one hypothesis, lithium limits the availability of norepinephrine, an effect opposite to that of the antidepressant drugs. This might explain its role in counteracting mania, but it sheds no light on how it forestalls depression in bipolar patients (Fieve, 1975; Gerbino, Oleshansky, and Gershon, 1978; Georgotas, 1985).

EVALUATING A DRUG

How can we assess the effectiveness of a drug? We will consider how this is done in detail, for some of the issues raised by drug evaluation methods are not limited to tests of drug therapy. In principle, they apply to the evaluation of any therapeutic procedure whatever, including psychotherapy.

Suppose we want to find out whether a given drug, say, chlorpromazine, has the curative effects its advocates claim. The most obvious approach is to administer the drug to a group of schizophrenic patients for some period and then make a before-and-after assessment. In fact, many of the clinical studies reported in the literature are of just this kind. But a little reflection shows that this procedure is not adequate.

Controlling for spontaneous improvement   One problem with the simple before-and-after test is that it ignores the possibility that the patient's condition would have cleared up without treatment, whether permanently or just for a while. Such spontaneous improvements occur in many disorders. To control for this factor, one has to compare two groups of patients drawn from the same population. One group would receive the drug for, say, six weeks; a control group would not. Both groups would be judged at the start and the end of the study (and perhaps during periods in between). Initially, they ought to be equivalent. The question is whether they will be judged to be different when the six weeks are up.

Controlling for placebo effects   Suppose that after six weeks the patients who were given chlorpromazine seem to be less disoriented and withdrawn than the untreated controls. The fact that the untreated control group improved less or not at all rules out the possibility that this change for the better was produced by spontaneous improvement. So can we now conclude that the lessening of schizophrenic symptoms was caused by the drug as such? The answer is no, for we have not controlled for the possibility that the result is a so-called *placebo effect.*

In medicine, the term *placebo* refers to some inert (that is, medically neutral) substance that is administered to a patient who believes that this substance has certain therapeutic powers, although it actually has none. Numerous studies have shown that, given this belief, a sizable proportion of patients suffering from many disorders will show some kind of improvement after ingesting what are actually sugar pills or receiving injections of harmless salt solutions. Such placebo effects probably account for many of the cures of ancient physicians whose medications included such items as crocodile dung, swine teeth, and moss scraped from the skull of a man who died a violent death (Shapiro, 1971).

Given the power of the placebo effect, how can we be sure that the improvement in the drug-treated group of our example is caused by the properties of the drug itself? Perhaps a sugar pill—or a bit of crocodile dung—would have done as well. To rule out this possibility, we must administer a placebo to the control patients. They will thus no longer be "untreated." On the contrary, they will receive the same attention, will be told the same thing, and will be given the same number of pills at the same time as the patients in the true drug group. There will be only one difference between the two groups: the control patients will swallow pills that, unbeknownst to them, contain only inert materials. As a result of this stratagem, we achieve simultaneous control for two factors—spontaneous improvement and placebo effects. Now that these two factors are controlled, a difference in the way the two groups appear after treatment can finally be attributed to the effect of the drug itself. Figure 18.3 shows the results of such a study, comparing the effects of chlorpromazine and a placebo control after one, three, and six weeks of treatment. As the figure shows, chlorpromazine is clearly superior. But as the figure also shows, some slight improvement is found in the placebo group as well, thus highlighting the need for such a control in the evaluation of drug effectiveness.

What explains placebo effects? Some of them may be the result of *endorphins,* chemicals produced by the brain itself which act like opiates and reduce pain (see Chapter 1). Evidence for this view comes from a study in which pain was reduced by a placebo medication that the patients believed was a pain reliever. But this relief stopped as soon as the patients received a dose of a drug that is known to counteract the effects of any opiate (Levine, Gordon, and Fields, 1979).

Controlling for the doctor's expectations By definition, a placebo control implies that all of the patients in the group think that they are being treated with the real drug. But to guarantee this desired state of ignorance, the doctors—and the nurses and attendants—must also be kept in the dark about who is getting a placebo and who the real drug, for the true information may affect their ratings of the patients' progress. If they believe in the drug's effectiveness, they may exaggerate signs of improvement in members of the drug-treated group.

The staff members' knowledge may also have a more indirect effect. They may unwittingly communicate it to the patients, perhaps by observing the drug-treated ones more closely or by being less concerned if a placebo-treated patient fails to take her morning pill. By such signals, the patients may find out whether the doctors expect them to get better or not. If so, there is no genuine placebo control. To guard against such confounding effects of expectation, modern drug evaluators use the *double-blind technique* in which neither the staff members nor the patients know who is assigned to which group. The only ones who know are the investigators who run the study.

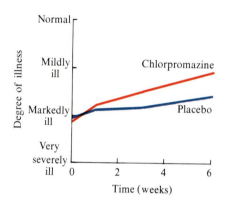

18.3 Controlling for placebo effects
Severity of illness over a six-week period during which patients were treated with either chlorpromazine or a placebo.

Some adverse effects of deinstitutionalization *Some of the homeless in American cities may be persons discharged from mental hospitals who are unable to make an adjustment to the world outside. (Photograph by Herlinde Koelbl/Leo de Wys)*

LIMITATIONS OF DRUG THERAPY

The preceding discussion may have suggested that present-day psychiatric drugs are an unqualified boon which provide a definite cure for schizophrenia or mood disorders. But as of yet, this is far from the case.

To begin with, these drugs often have side effects. For example, the phenothiazines may produce various disruptions of autonomic functioning that range from chronic dryness of the mouth to blurred vision, difficulty in urination, and cardiac irregularities. In addition, there are sometimes disturbances of posture and involuntary movement, with symptoms such as tremors, a shuffling gait, and a curiously inexpressive, masklike face. Individuals react differently to the drugs. For some, the side effects are great; for others, they are minimal.

These side effects can be regarded simply as a cost exacted by the drugs. But how great are the drugs' benefits? Critics of drug therapy contend that currently the beneficial results of drug therapy are still quite limited. This is especially so for the antipsychotic drugs. To be sure, the phenothiazines have made it possible to discharge schizophrenic patients much sooner than in pre-drug days. But this doesn't mean that these patients are cured. For one thing, they often have to stay on a ***maintenance dose*** of the drug outside of the hospital, which they often prefer not to do given the drug's unpleasant side effects.

But even with a maintenance dose, there is no guarantee that the discharged patients will become normal members of the community. Those with mood disorders often will, but the outlook is much less favorable for schizophrenics, especially those whose social adjustment was poor before they developed psychotic symptoms. Such patients will probably only make a marginal adjustment to the external world. The original proponents of deinstitutionalization meant to provide the newly discharged schizophrenic patient with a whole array of community services: outpatient facilities, halfway houses, special residential facilities, and appropriate counseling to help the discharged patient reenter the world outside. But these facilities turned out to be much less adequate than originally envisaged. There were simply too few of them, and many of those that did exist did not provide enough of the required help. As a result, many discharged patients relapsed, were readmitted to the hospital, were discharged again, and then relapsed and reentered the hospital yet again, producing a "revolving door phenomenon" (Rosenhan and Seligman, 1989). Others eked out a marginal existence in less than ideal board-and-care homes, while still others became drifters and joined the swelling ranks of the homeless. According to a recent report, some 40 percent of New York City's homeless people suffer persistent mental disorder or have a history of mental illness (Golden, 1990). Such findings make it clear that while the antipsychotic drugs help to alleviate the symptoms of schizophrenia, they do not provide a cure. Given the current inadequacy—and in many cases, the complete lack—of appropriate community services, this poses a serious problem for the ultimate success of the deinstitutionalization policy (Jones, 1983; Lamb, 1984; Westermeyer, 1987).

Despite these serious limitations, the modern drug therapies are a major step forward. This is especially clear in the case of lithium and the antidepressants, which sometimes do for patients with mood disorders what insulin does for patients with diabetes: While they don't cure the disease, they sometimes do a fine job of controlling it. But the antipsychotic drugs also represent an important advance. They have restored some patients to normal functioning and have allowed those who would otherwise have spent much of their lives in hospital wards to manage, however imperfectly, in a family or community setting. No less important is the fact that these drugs—especially the phenothiazines—have completely changed the atmosphere of mental hospitals, in particular those maintained by the states. Until a few decades ago, straitjackets were common, as were feces-smeared and shriek-filled wards; today, such things are comparatively rare because the drugs diminish the more violent symptoms of many mental ailments. As a result, the mental hospital can function as a therapeutic center. It can provide important social and psychological services, including some forms of psychotherapy, all of which would have been unthinkable in the "snake pit" settings of former times.

Other Somatic Therapies

PSYCHOSURGERY

Until the advent of the major psychiatric drugs, psychiatrists relied on several other somatic therapies, all of which involved more drastic assaults on the nervous system. Some of these consisted of brain surgery. An example is *prefrontal lobotomy,* in which the neurological connections between the thalamus and the frontal lobes are severed, in whole or in part. This operation was meant to liberate the patient's thoughts from the pathological influence of his emotions, on the dubious neurological assumption that thought and emotion are localized in the frontal lobes and the thalamus respectively.

Evaluations of these surgical procedures have come up with largely ambiguous results (Robbin, 1958). Furthermore, there is a serious possibility that such operations produce some impairment of higher intellectual functions, such as foresight and the ability to sustain attention. Therefore these procedures are now used only rarely in the United States. Irreversible damage to the brain is a stiff price to pay, whatever the therapeutic benefits. If one can't even be sure that such benefits exist, the price appears exorbitant (Maher, 1966).

CONVULSIVE TREATMENTS

Other attempts at somatic therapy involve the deliberate production of massive convulsive seizures. Today, the most widely used form of the convulsive method is *electroconvulsive shock treatment,* or *ECT.* A current of moderate intensity is passed between two electrodes attached to each side of the patient's forehead; it is applied for about half a second. The result is immediate loss of consciousness, followed by a convulsive seizure similar to that seen in epilepsy (Figure 18.4). When

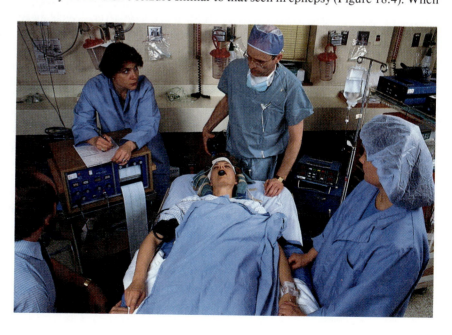

18.4   Patient about to undergo electroconvulsive shock treatment   (Photograph by James D. Wilson/Woodfin Camp)

this treatment first came into use, patients sometimes suffered serious bruises or bone fractures while thrashing about during their convulsions. To prevent this, modern practitioners usually administer muscle relaxants prior to the treatment (Redlich and Freedman, 1966).

While ECT was originally meant as a treatment of schizophrenia, appropriate evaluation studies soon showed that its area of primary effectiveness is depression. Here, its efficacy is considerable. It may well be more effective than any MAO inhibitor or tricyclic, and it works for a sizable proportion of patients who don't respond to any antidepressant drug (Janicak et al., 1985). In addition, it seems to act more quickly than the drugs usually do (Weiner, 1984b, 1985).

Despite these advantages, the use of ECT is highly controversial. The main reason is the possibility of brain damage. After all, a current intensity great enough to set off a convulsion may well be sufficient to injure nervous tissue; the danger is all the greater since ECT is usually administered to the patient repeatedly. According to some critics there is memory impairment, which in some cases lasts for months or even longer (Squire, 1977; Breggin, 1979; for discussion, see Weiner, 1984a, 1984b). Under the circumstances, ECT is generally used only after drug therapy has failed or when there seems to be a serious chance of suicide. In the latter case, the fast-acting quality of ECT treatment may be an overriding advantage. This has prompted several attempts to minimize possible tissue damage. One is to apply the current in very brief pulses to just one cerebral hemisphere (typically, the nondominant one), which apparently lessens memory impairment and other side effects but does not diminish the therapeutic effect (Inglis, 1969; Welch et al., 1982; Squire and Zouzounis, 1986).

What accounts for the therapeutic effects of ECT? As yet, we have little more than speculations. According to one hypothesis, ECT leads to heightened activation of certain neural pathways, which increases the availability of norepinephrine and serotonin in the brain (Weiner, 1984b, 1985).

PSYCHOTHERAPY

Biological manipulations represent one approach to the treatment of psychopathology. But as we have already seen, there is another approach to the treatment of such disorders that forgoes all ministrations to the patient's body but instead relies on psychological means alone. Such attempts to treat mental disturbance by psychological rather than somatic methods are here grouped together under the general label *psychotherapy.*

There are many different approaches to psychotherapy. A major difference among them is in their theories about the nature of psychopathology. Some of these theories see psychopathology from a psychoanalytic perspective and emphasize unconscious conflicts; others are based on behavior theories of animal conditioning; yet others take a cognitive approach and insist that mental disorder grows out of faulty thinking; while still others take a humanistic outlook and are concerned with free will and the need to imbue life with coherent meaning. Given these different perspectives on psychopathology, it is hardly surprising that the techniques of therapy of these different approaches differ also.

We will distinguish among five subtypes of psychotherapy conducted with individual patients: (1) orthodox psychoanalysis, (2) modern offshoots of psychoanalysis, (3) behavior therapy, (4) cognitive therapy, and (5) humanistic approaches to psychotherapy.*

* Many practitioners use the term *psychotherapy* to describe only a subset of the full range of psychological treatments. The problem is that these subsets are different for different writers. Freudian

An early attempt at psychotherapy The biblical King Saul was subject to severe bouts of rage and depression but was apparently calmed by listening to young David playing the harp. (Rembrandt's David Playing the Harp Before Saul; *photograph © Foundation Johan Maurits van Nassau. Courtesy Mauritshuis, The Hague, inv. nr 621)*

Classical Psychoanalysis

Classical psychoanalysis is the method Freud developed at the start of this century. According to some writers, this technique is the ancestor of virtually all forms of modern psychotherapy, whether they acknowledge this heritage or not (London, 1964).

As we have previously seen, Freud's basic assumption was that his patients' ills (in his terms, their neuroses) stemmed from unconscious defenses against unacceptable urges that date back to early childhood. The neurotic has drawn a mental blanket over his head and is unable to see either the outer or the inner world as it really is. His symptoms are an indirect manifestation of his unconscious conflicts (see Chapter 10). To overcome his neurosis, the patient must drop the blanket, must achieve access to his buried thoughts and wishes, and gain insight into why he buried them. By so doing, he will master the internal conflicts that crippled him for so long. Once these are resolved, his symptoms will presumably wither away by themselves. In effect, Freud's prescription for the neuroses is the victory of reason over passion: "Where id was, there shall ego be."

THE RECOVERY OF UNCONSCIOUS MEMORIES

Free association The origin of psychoanalytic technique dates back to Freud's attempts to treat hysteria by helping the patient recover some emotionally charged memories (see Chapter 10). Initially, Freud and his then collaborator, Josef Breuer, probed for these memories while their patients were hypnotized.

---

psychoanalysts speak of psychotherapy when they want to describe briefer, and in their view, more diluted versions of psychoanalysis. Conversely, behavior therapists use the term to embrace virtually all forms of psychological treatment that try to help patients gain insight into their own inner thoughts and wishes rather than deal with the undesirable behavior patterns by themselves. The result of these divergent usages is considerable terminological confusion. The usage here adopted treats the term as a simple nonevaluative category label that embraces all forms of psychological treatment and makes no further statements about their methods, theories, or therapeutic effectiveness (White and Watt, 1973).

A picture of Freud's consultation room
In classical psychoanalysis, the patient reclines on the couch while the analyst sits behind him, out of sight. Freud adopted this method to avoid influencing the patient's flow of associations by his own facial expressions. He also had a personal motive: "I cannot bear to be gazed at for eight hours a day." (Freud, 1913; photograph by Edmund Engelman)

Later on it became clear that such memories could be dug up even in the normal waking state by the method of *free association.* The patient was asked to say whatever came into his mind, and sooner or later the relevant memory was likely to emerge. Various forms of *resistance,* usually unconscious, by which the patient tried to derail a given train of thought—by changing the topic, forgetting what he was about to say, and so on—often gave important clues that the patient was about to remember something he had previously tried to forget.

In popularized movie or TV versions, this dredging up of forgotten memories is often presented as the essence of psychoanalysis. The distraught heroine finally remembers a childhood scene in which she was spanked for a little sister's misdeed, suddenly a weight lifts from her shoulders, she rises from the couch reborn, is ready to face life and love serenely, and will live happily—or at least unneurotically—ever after. But as Freud described it, what actually happens is much less dramatic. The discovery of the patient's unconscious conflicts comes bit by bit, as a memory surfaces here, a dream or a slip of the tongue suggests a meaning there, and as the analyst offers an occasional interpretation of the resistances that crop up in a given session. To help the patient see how all of these strands of her mental life are woven together is one of the analyst's main tasks.

EMOTIONAL INSIGHT

Psychoanalysts want their patients to attain insight into the motives of which they were formerly unaware, but they don't want that insight to be merely intellectual. The patient must regain access, not just to various repressed thoughts and memories, but also and more importantly, to the feelings that go along with them. Freud was emphatic that recollections without emotions have little therapeutic effect. Genuine self-discovery is only achieved when the patient rids himself of the repressive forces that had kept the insights from him, and this typically requires a good deal of emotional involvement. Without this involvement, the psychoanalytic process is an intellectual exercise rather than a therapy (Freud, 1913).

Catharsis   What would produce the necessary emotional involvement? Originally, Freud put his faith in the *catharsis* that accompanied the recovery of certain long-lost memories. When these surfaced, a host of associated emotions followed in their wake and were explosively discharged in fits of sobbing or in bursts of sharp anger. Such an emotional release is generally experienced as a kind of relief. It turned out, however, that dramatic reactions of this kind were fairly rare. Moreover, even when they did occur, their benefits proved rather short-lived; after a while, the symptoms reappeared. If emotions are a necessary ingredient of analytic therapy, they have to be evoked by another means.

Transference Freud believed that the major means for providing the necessary emotional component is the **transference** relationship in which the patient responds to the analyst in increasingly personal terms. He reacts to him as he had reacted to the major figures in his own life, and he will therefore love or hate the analyst as he had loved or hated his mother, father, siblings, and, more recently, his lovers and friends. All of these feelings are transferred to the analyst, as a kind of emotional reliving of the unresolved problems of the patient's childhood.

Freud argued that this transference relation can be a powerful therapeutic tool. It lets the analyst hold up a mirror to the patient, to show him how he really feels and acts toward the important people in his life. As an example, take a person who expresses violent anger at the psychiatrist, and then is immediately seized by a feeling of total terror. What is going on? A psychoanalytic interpretation is that the patient had equated the analyst with his own tyrannical father. Having transgressed against him, he could not help but expect some awful retribution. But needless to say, the analyst will not retaliate. Instead, he may say something mildly reassuring, such as "That was hard to get out, wasn't it?" After that he will probably interpret the patient's outburst and subsequent fear and will point out the discrepancy between the actual present and the long-dead past.

Modern Versions of Psychoanalysis

A sizable number of present-day psychotherapists still use techniques that bear Freud's imprint. Although some practice psychoanalysis just as Freud did, this is becoming less frequent. The majority of practitioners have modified Freud's theories and procedures in various ways. Most of them subscribe to *neo*-Freudian views or to related approaches such as ego psychology. Their emphasis is on interpersonal and cultural factors rather than on psychosexual development, and on the patient's problems in the present rather than on the origin of these problems in his early past (see Chapters 10 and 16). But like Freud, they believe that the key to what they call neurosis is unconscious conflict and that therapy requires emotional insight into these processes as they affect the patient's present.

Behavior Therapy

Not all psychotherapists use techniques that are as directly affected by psychoanalytic thinking as those we have just described. The last two or three decades have seen the emergence of two major movements. Both are reactions against psychoanalysis, but for reasons that are diametrically opposed. The first is **behavior therapy,** which maintains that the theoretical notions underlying psychoanalysis are vague and untestable, while its therapeutic effectiveness is a matter of doubt. The other group consists of various **humanistic therapies,** which regard psychoanalysis as too mechanistic and too atomistic in its approach. Freud, who had a fine sense of irony, would have been wryly amused to find himself in the middle of this two-front war in which one side accuses him of being too scientific and the other of not being scientific enough.

Behavior therapists hold that the condition Freud called neurosis is caused by maladaptive learning and that its remedy is a form of reeducation. Taken by it-

"Don't worry. Fantasies about devouring the doctor are perfectly normal." (Drawing by Lorenz; © 1991 The New Yorker Magazine, Inc.)

self, this view is hardly original. What makes it different is that the behavior therapists take the emphasis on learning and relearning much more seriously than anyone had before them. They see themselves as applied scientists whose techniques for reeducating troubled people are adapted from principles of learning and conditioning discovered in the laboratories of Pavlov, Thorndike, and Skinner (see Chapter 3).

Like the learning theorists to whom they trace their descent, behavior therapists have a basically tough-minded and pragmatic outlook. They emphasize overt, observable behavior rather than hypothetical underlying causes, such as unconscious thoughts and wishes, which they regard as hard to define and even harder to observe. Their concern is with what a person does, especially if it causes him distress. If so, the behavior therapists want to modify such behaviors—to get the agoraphobic over his fear of open places, to help the compulsive overcome his hand-washing rituals that threaten to rub his skin away. To accomplish these ends, behavior therapists resort to various techniques for learning and unlearning —extinction of fear responses, conditioning of incompatible reactions, or whatever. But their treatment does not include any attempt to have the patient gain insight into the origin of these symptoms. As these therapists see it, such insights into the past have no therapeutic effect, even if they happen to be valid. What is wrong is the patient's behavior in the here and now, and it is this that has to be righted.

FLOODING AND IMPLOSION

One group of behavior therapists utilizes techniques based on concepts drawn from classical conditioning. The major target of these therapists is unrealistic fear or anxiety, as in the case of a morbid fear of heights. Their basic hypothesis is that this fear is a classically conditioned response that is evoked by various eliciting stimuli such as looking down a flight of stairs or being on a rooftop (see Chapters 3 and 17).

The most obvious way of removing the classically conditioned connection is through *extinction.* Imagine a rat that has been shocked on seeing a flashing light. To extinguish the fear, all we have to do is to present the conditioned stimulus (the light) without the unconditioned stimulus (the shock). But this is easier said than done, for the animal has learned to avoid the fear-arousing stimulus and runs away as soon as the light starts flashing. As a result, it can't "test reality" and discover that the formerly dangerous stimulus no longer signals shock. Therefore, its fear won't extinguish. What holds for the rat, also holds for the person with a phobia. He is afraid of snakes, or of dogs, or of open spaces. His fear makes him avoid these stimuli, which is why he can't ever find out that his terrors are unjustified.

One way of getting the rat (or the phobic) to test reality is to make him expose himself to the flashing light (or the snakes or open spaces). If the rat is forced to remain in the compartment in which it was formerly shocked and is repeatedly presented with the flashing light that is now no longer followed by shock, its fear of the light will eventually disappear (Baum, 1970). Much the same holds for phobic patients who are trained by a method called *flooding.* In this procedure, phobic patients agree to stay in the presence of the fear-arousing stimulus for a period of time. In one study, agoraphobics went through several sessions in which they had to go out into the street and walk alone until they could no longer manage. A few such sessions led to marked improvement as judged by both client and therapist (Emmelkamp and Wessels, 1975).

In flooding, the treatment procedure is carried out *in vivo,* that is, in actual real life. But real-life exposure to threatening stimuli is often impossible or impractical. It's not all that easy to bring snakes and dogs (let alone swimming pools or skyscrapers) into the therapist's office to do flooding therapy on people who are terrified of snakes, or dogs, or water, or high places. Under the circumstances, the next best thing is to flood *in vitro*—not in real life, but in a simulation. (*In vitro* literally means "in glass," that is, in a test tube.) In behavior therapy, in vitro methods generally refer to the use of imagery. The patient will be asked to *imagine* the fearful situations. (And there is excellent evidence that imagined terrors arouse quite a bit of anxiety.) A particularly dramatic version of flooding in vitro is called *implosion therapy.* Here, the patient must imagine the most terrifying situations he could possibly conceive. The woman with a fear of dogs must imagine herself surrounded by half a dozen snarling Dobermans; the man who is plagued by an obsessive fear of contamination that he tries to allay by endless washing rituals must imagine himself immersed in a stinking sewer (Stampfl and Levis, 1967). One therapist described the case of Mary, a patient who was so terrified of water that she wore a life preserver when she took a bath. This patient was asked to imagine that she was taking a bath in a bottomless tub, without a life preserver: "See yourself vividly, clearly, slipping, slipping, slipping under the water. You can't breathe—feel the water—down, down, down. You open your mouth and water pours in." In the first session and for some sessions thereafter, Mary was terrified. But as the sessions were repeated, the anxiety diminished; Mary had faced the worst, but since nothing had happened to her, her fear gradually extinguished (Stampfl, 1975).

SYSTEMATIC DESENSITIZATION

While flooding and implosion lead to considerable improvement with various anxiety conditions (such as phobias and some obsessive-compulsive disorders), they may not work for all patients. In the view of some critics, flooding and implosion can be much like throwing a child into a swimming pool to get him over his fear of water. It's fine if it works, but if it doesn't, the child's fear will be greater than ever before. For confronting fears head on is a dangerous business, especially in vivo. One of the patients in the agoraphobic study just described hid out in the cellar rather than being sent into the street for ninety minutes (Emmelkamp and Wessels, 1975).

Some of these problems are avoided by the most widely used behavioral therapeutic technique for unlearning fears today, *systematic desensitization,* developed by the psychiatrist Joseph Wolpe. Its basic idea is to connect the stimuli that now evoke fear to a new response that is incompatible with fear and that will therefore displace it (Wolpe, 1958). The competing response is *muscular relaxation,* a pervasive untensing of the body's musculature that is presumably incompatible with the autonomic and skeletal reactions that underlie the fear response. To acquire this relaxation pattern, the patient learns to focus his full attention on each of his major muscle groups by first tensing and then untensing them. After several training sessions, the patient can achieve this state of relaxation whenever the therapist asks him to. Once this point is reached, the goal is to condition the relaxation to the fear-evoking stimuli, whether snakes, open spaces, or high rooftops (see Figure 18.5).

To establish the desired link between relaxation and the fear-evoking situations, the patient is asked to imagine these situations as vividly as possible while in deep relaxation. Such imagined encounters have enough reality for most patients to evoke a reasonable amount of anxiety (Wolpe and Lazarus, 1966). To make sure that this anxiety is not excessive, Wolpe adopted a policy of deliberate gradualism, in which the therapist sneaks up on the fear response, step by step. He first asks the patient to construct an *anxiety hierarchy* in which feared situations are arranged from least to most anxiety-provoking. The patient starts out by imagining the first scene in the hierarchy (for example, being on the first floor of

A

$S_{stairs, etc.}$ ⟶ R_{fear}

B

$S_{stairs, etc.}$ ⟶ R_{fear}
⟶ $R_{relaxation}$

C

$S_{stairs, etc.}$ ⟶ $R_{relaxation}$

18.5 Systematic desensitization (A) The state of affairs in phobia. Various stimuli such as flights of stairs arouse the response of fear. (B) These stimuli are conditioned to the response of relaxation. As this connection becomes stronger, the connection between the stimulus and the fear response is weakened. (C) The state of affairs when counterconditioning is complete. The relaxation response has completely displaced the old fear response.

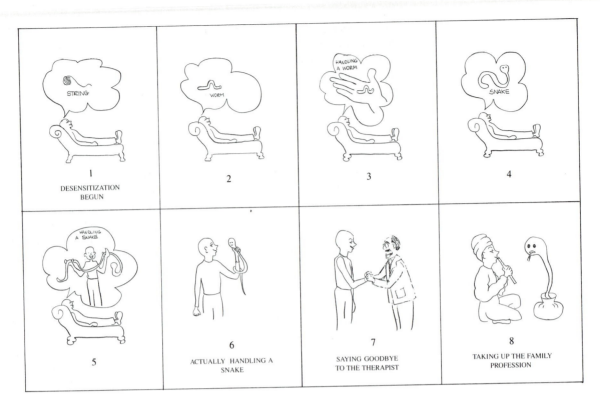

Desensitization *(Courtesy of Henry Gleitman and Mary Bullock)*

the Empire State Building). He imagines this scene while in a state of deep relaxation. He will stay with this scene—imagining and relaxing—until he no longer feels any qualms. After this, the next scene is imagined and thoroughly counterconditioned, and so on, until the patient finally can imagine the most frightening scene of all (leaning over the railing of the observation tower above the 102nd floor) and still be able to relax.

While the desensitization method is most directly applicable to simple phobias, many behavior therapists believe that it is useful whenever anxiety is a major factor in the disorder and when the stimuli that trigger this disorder are known. Examples are sexual disturbances such as impotence and frigidity (Brady, 1985).

AVERSION THERAPY

Another behavior therapy technique, *aversion therapy,* tries to attach negative feelings to stimulus situations that are initially very attractive so that the patient will no longer want to approach them. The object of this endeavor is to eliminate behavior patterns that both patient and therapist regard as undesirable. Examples are overeating, excessive drinking, or engaging in certain sexual deviations such as exhibitionism.

The basic procedure of aversion therapy is very simple. One pairs the stimulus that one wants to render unpleasant with some obnoxious unconditioned stimulus. An example is aversion therapy for excessive drinking. The patient takes a sip of alcohol while under the effect of a nausea-producing drug. He tastes the liquor while he desperately wants to vomit.

Whether aversion therapy works is debatable. No one doubts that it works in the therapist's office; the question is whether it is effective outside, when the shocking device is no longer attached or the nausea-producing drugs are no longer administered (Rachman and Teasdale, 1969; Emmelkamp, 1986). There is some suggestion that the nausea-producing procedure has lasting effects in some cases of alcoholism. According to one review, two-thirds of alcoholics treated in this manner remained abstinent for a year, one-third for three years (Wiens and Menustik, 1983). In effect, the patients acquired a learned taste aversion so that the actual taste and smell of alcohol became repellent.

OPERANT TECHNIQUES

Most of the behavior therapies we've discussed so far are based on classical conditioning. As such, they try to alter the significance of various stimulus events, as in making a patient realize that snakes are not really threatening. Another set of behavioral therapies is derived from the principles of instrumental conditioning and emphasizes the relation between acts and consequences (see Chapter 3). Its theme is the same as that which underlies the entire operant approach—the control of behavior through reinforcement.

An example of this approach is the use of *token economies* in certain hospital wards, some of which house patients that have been given up as hopeless. These tokens function much as money does in our economy; they can be exchanged for desirable items such as snacks or watching TV. But again, like money, they must be earned by the patient, perhaps by making his own bed, or being neatly dressed, or performing various ward chores. The overall effect seems to be salutary. While the patients are certainly not cured, they become less apathetic and the general ward atmosphere is much improved (Ayllon and Azrin, 1968).

Cognitive-Behavioral Therapies

Desensitization, flooding, and aversion therapies focus on behaviors that are more or less overt and try to modify them by techniques based on the principles of simple learning. In desensitization, flooding, and implosion, the emphasis is on some external stimulus (such as heights) that is connected with anxiety, a connection the therapy tries to sever. In aversion therapy, it is on some overt response (such as excessive drinking), a response the therapy tries to eliminate. But what treatment is appropriate when the patient's problems cannot be so readily described by referring to fear-evoking stimuli or to overt, undesirable responses? There are many patients whose difficulties stem from anxiety that is triggered by their own thoughts and feelings. An example is the obsessive-compulsive whose own obsessional thoughts lead to intense anxiety that can only be relieved by ever more frantic compulsive rituals. Here the critical features of the disorder derive from covert rather than overt sources—thoughts and feelings that go on "within the patient's head." How does a behavior-oriented approach to therapy handle cases such as these?

A number of therapists deal with such problems by a frontal attack on the way the patient thinks. They try to replace the patient's irrational beliefs and attitudes that caused his emotional stress by a more appropriate mode of thinking that is in better accord with reality. This general form of therapy goes under various labels. A relatively recent version is *cognitive therapy,* originally developed as a treatment for depression by the psychiatrist Aaron Beck (Beck, 1967).

On the face of it, the goal of all cognitive approaches seems similar to the psychoanalytic quest for emotional insight. But cognitive therapists see themselves as more closely allied to behavior therapy. While they make little use of conditioning principles and concentrate on what the patients think rather than on what they do overtly, their techniques share many of the characteristics of behavior therapy. They are extremely *directive.* They are primarily concerned with the patient in the here and now rather than with her history, and they focus on beliefs that affect what the patient does and feels.

THE MAJOR TECHNIQUES OF COGNITIVE THERAPY

The basic technique of cognitive therapists is to confront the patients with the contradictions inherent in their maladaptive beliefs. To accomplish this end, the therapist adopts an active, dominant role throughout the proceedings, and—like many modern behavior therapists—gives the patient "homework assignments." One such task is to discover certain irrational thoughts that come in the form of certain illogical phrases and sentences the patients say to themselves, such as, "it's all my fault," and "if no one loves me, I'm no good," and so on. Such automatic and ultimately self-defeating thoughts may explain why patients sometimes feel unaccountably upset. A certain stimulus—for example, seeing an old acquaintance across the street—leads to a wave of anxiety. The patient doesn't know why this stimulus led to the emotional response, but the therapist can help the patient fill the mental gap. Seeing the old friend triggered an automatic and irrational thought that led to the anxiety:

> The anxiety seemed incomprehensible until [the patient] "played back" his thoughts: "If I greet Bob, he may not remember me. He may snub me, it has been so long, he may not know who I am. . . ." (Ellis, 1962, quoted in Beck, 1985, p. 1436)

The job of the therapist is to help the patient to identify the automatic thought and to recognize its irrationality. After all, Bob may very well remember him. And if he doesn't, it may be because Bob's memory is faulty. But suppose the patient is right, and Bob never liked him in the first place and might well have snubbed him. Is that the end of the world? Is it really necessary to be liked by everybody? Once these irrational beliefs are ferreted out, the patients have to tell themselves repeatedly that they are false. If he can stop himself from such self-defeating automatisms, he will feel better, which will allow him to function at a higher level, which will make him feel better still, leading to a beneficent cycle of emotional improvement.

Humanistic Therapies

A number of practitioners charge that behavior therapy (and to a lesser extent, psychoanalysis) describes human beings too atomistically, explains them too mechanistically, and treats them too manipulatively. These *humanistic therapists* try to deal with the individual at a more global level, not as a bundle of conditioned fear responses to be extinguished, nor as a collection of warring, unconscious strivings to be resolved, but rather as a whole person, who must be "encountered and understood" in his own "living, suffering actuality."

CLIENT-CENTERED THERAPY

One example of a humanistically oriented approach is ***client-centered therapy*** (Rogers, 1951, 1970). This psychotherapeutic system was initially developed by the psychologist Carl Rogers (1902–1987) during the early 1940s. One of its main premises is that the process of personality development is akin to growth. In this view, Rogers followed theorists like Abraham Maslow (1908–1970) and other adherents of a humanistic approach to personality in believing that all persons have a native impulse toward the full realization of their human potentialities (Maslow, 1968; see Chapter 16, pp. 484–87). In this sense, he held that human nature is inherently good. But, alas, such self-actualization is fairly rare, for personality growth is often stunted. There are many people who dislike themselves, are out of touch with their own feelings, and are unable to reach out to others as genuine fellow beings. Rogers's remedy was to provide the appropriate psychological soil in which personal growth could resume; this soil was the therapeutic relationship.

Rogers initially tried to achieve this client-centered quality by a variety of **nondirective techniques** (Rogers, 1942). He would never advise or interpret directly, but would only try to clarify what the client really felt, by echoing or restating what the client himself seemed to say or feel.

In later formulations, Rogers decided that there is no way of being truly nondirective. Despite one's best intentions one can't help but convey some evaluation with even the blandest nod. But more important, Rogers came to believe that the main contribution of the therapist does not lie in any particular approach or technique; it is rather to supply the one crucial condition of successful therapy, *himself* or *herself,* as a genuinely involved, participating fellow person. The Rogerian therapist's main job is to let the client know that she understands how the world looks through *his* eyes; that she can empathize with his wishes and feelings; and, most important of all, that she accepts and values him as a human being. In Rogers's view, this awareness that another person unconditionally accepts and esteems him, ultimately helps the client to accept and esteem himself (Rogers, 1961). Perhaps this is just a modern restatement of the old idea that love can redeem us all.*

EXISTENTIAL THERAPY

Rogers's approach to therapy is distinctively American in its optimistic faith in an almost limitless human capacity for growth and self-improvement. Another humanistic approach to therapy originates in Europe and takes a more somber view. This is **existential therapy,** a movement that echoes some of the major themes sounded by a group of philosophers called **existentialists.** Existential therapists are primarily concerned with what they regard as the major emotional sickness of our times, an inability to endow life with meaning. In their view, this condition is a by-product of the rootless, restless anonymity of twentieth-century Western life; it is especially prevalent in modern Europe, in the wake of the despair that followed two bloody world wars and the Nazi terror. It is marked by a sense that one is alienated, lost, and dehumanized; that one is nothing but a cog in a huge, impersonal machine; and that one's existence is meaningless. According to existential therapists, this feeling that everything is pointless is a common facet of many modern emotional disorders. It is this, rather than the specific symptoms of the disorders —the phobias, the obsessions, and the like—that they want to rectify (Ofman, 1985).

Like practitioners of most other schools, existential therapists stress the role of the therapeutic relationship in affecting the changes they want to bring about. In their view, the key element of this relationship is what they call the **encounter** in which two individuals meet as genuine persons of whose independent human existence neither has any doubt. According to existential therapists, the experience derived from this encounter will ultimately transfer to the way in which the patient sees himself and others (May, 1958).

In the past, the task that existential therapists set themselves was generally held to be the province of clergymen. It was priests and parsons and rabbis who tried to help people find some meaning in their existence. They did so within a reli-

Existential therapy (Hand with Reflecting Sphere, *1935, by M. C. Escher;* © *M. C. Escher Heirs, c/o Cordon Art, Baarn, Holland)*

---

* Rogers's humanistic approach has often been attacked by behavior therapists who regard him as "antiscientific." Under the circumstances, it is somewhat ironic that Rogers was one of the pioneers of psychotherapy evaluation, the first major figure in the field of psychotherapy who looked for evidence that his techniques were actually having some effect.

gious framework that defined the spiritual dimension of human life. As religious values have eroded, other social institutions have stepped in and have tried to take the clergy's place. One of these is modern humanistic psychotherapy, especially the existentialist school. It is no accident that an influential book by a prominent existential therapist bears the title *The Doctor and the Soul* (Frankl, 1966).

Some Common Themes

The various forms of psychotherapy differ in some important regards in what they try to do. The psychoanalytically oriented therapists' primary focus is on *understanding.* Their aim is to help the patient realize what is behind his thoughts and actions so that he can face his unconscious conflicts and overcome them. Behavior therapists emphasize *doing.* They try to help their patients eliminate undesirable responses and extinguish irrational fears. Cognitive-behavioral therapists are most concerned with *thinking.* They want to enable their patients to overcome patterns of irrational and self-defeating thoughts. Humanistic therapists stress *feeling.* Their hope is to help their clients come to terms with who they really are by accepting what they want and feel in the here-and-now.

These differences among the various therapeutic schools are real enough. But of late there have been trends toward a rapprochement between the different schools of therapy. Thus, some psychoanalytically oriented practitioners have come to use techniques that were formerly the exclusive preserve of behavior therapists; for example, modeling and "homework" assignments (Wachtel, 1977, 1982). And on the other side, many behavior therapists have come to realize that the client-therapist relation is an important part of treatment, that something like Freud's "transference" comes into play even in therapies such as flooding or desensitization, which are based on classical conditioning concepts (Lazarus, 1971, 1981).

But quite apart from such trends toward an eclectic approach to therapy, there are some underlying common themes that run through the beliefs and practices of all the contending schools, despite all of their divergences.

EMOTIONAL DEFUSING

All psychotherapies aim at some kind of emotional reeducation. They try to help the patient rid himself of various intense and unrealistic fears. To this end, these fears, and other strong emotions such as anger, are evoked during the therapeutic session. Since this happens in the presence of an accepting, noncondemning therapist, the fear is weakened.

INTERPERSONAL LEARNING

All major schools stress the importance of interpersonal learning and follow Freud in believing that the therapeutic relationship is an important tool in bringing this about. This relationship shows the patient how she generally reacts to others and also provides a vehicle through which she can discover and rehearse new and better ways for doing so.

INSIGHT

Most psychotherapists try to help their patients achieve greater self-knowledge, though the various therapeutic schools differ in what kind of self-knowledge they try to bring about. For psychoanalysts, the crucial emotional insights the patient

A
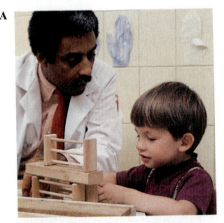

B

Play therapy, an extension of psychotherapy adapted for children (A) In play therapy, the therapist tries to help the child understand and express his feelings about his parents and other family members through play with various toys. (B) Puppets are sometimes used to act out problems, as in this example of a therapy session with victims of child abuse. (Top: photograph by Michal Heron, 1979/ Monkmeyer Press. Bottom: photograph by Bart Bartholomew, 1984/Black Star)

must acquire refer to his own past; for Rogerians, they concern his feelings in the present; for behavior therapists, the relevant self-understanding is the correct identification of the stimuli to which his fear has been conditioned.

THERAPY AS A STEP-BY-STEP PROCESS

There is general agreement that therapy is a gradual affair and that this is so regardless of whether the therapy emphasizes cognitive insight, feelings, or behaviors. There are few sudden flashes of insight or emotional understanding which change a patient overnight. Instead, each newfound insight and freshly acquired skill must be laboriously applied in one life situation after another before the patient can call it her own.

THERAPY AS A SOCIALLY ACCEPTED PRACTICE

Most psychotherapists operate within a social context that gives them the status of officially designated healers for emotional ills. As a result, the stage is set for a number of nonspecific gains of psychotherapy. One is an intimate, confiding relation with another person. This alone may be a boon to some persons who have no close bonds to anyone and for whom psychotherapy may amount to what one author calls "the purchase of friendship" (Schofield, 1964). Another nonspecific gain is the hope that one will get better. This may lead the patient to think better of himself, which may lead to small successes in the outside world, which may fuel further hope and increase the chances of yet other successes.

EVALUATING THERAPEUTIC OUTCOME

We have just surveyed what different kinds of therapists do. We now ask whether what they do does any good. This question often arouses indignant protests from therapists and patients alike. For many of them feel utterly certain that they help or have been helped; they therefore see no point in questioning what to them is obvious. But their testimonials alone are not convincing. For one thing, both patients and therapists have a serious stake in believing that psychotherapy works. If it doesn't, the patient has wasted his money and the therapist has wasted his time. Under the circumstances, neither may be the most objective judge in assessing whether there was a significant change. But even granting that change occurred, what caused this change? Was it produced by the therapeutic situation, or would it have come about in any case? And, assuming that the therapy did play a role, was the improvement caused by the therapy as such or was it produced by nonspecific, placebo-like factors such as hope, expectations of cure, and the decision to "turn over a new leaf"?

Does Psychotherapy Work?

Much of the impetus for discussions of psychotherapeutic outcomes came from a sharp attack on the efficacy of psychoanalysis and similar "insight therapies" launched by the British psychologist Hans Eysenck (Eysenck, 1961). Eysenck surveyed some two dozen articles that reported the number of neurotic patients who improved or failed to improve after psychotherapy. Overall, about 60 percent improved, a result that might be considered fairly encouraging. But Eysenck argued that there was really nothing to cheer about. According to Eysenck's analysis, the spontaneous recovery rate in neurotics who received *no* treatment was, if anything, even higher—about 70 percent. If so, psychotherapy apparently has no curative effects.

In retrospect, it appears that Eysenck's appraisal was unduly harsh. In particular, he evidently overestimated the rate of spontaneous improvement. According to one review, the median rate of patients who get better without therapy is around 30 percent compared to an average improvement rate of 60 percent for neurotic patients who received psychotherapy, a difference that constitutes what the author called "some modest evidence that psychotherapy 'works'" (Bergin, 1971, p. 229; see also Luborsky, Singer, and Luborsky, 1975).

META-ANALYSES OF THERAPY OUTCOME

More recent analyses of the research literature provide an even more optimistic picture. For the most part, they are based on a new statistical technique called *meta-analysis* by means of which the results of many different studies can be combined. In a comprehensive analysis of this kind, Smith, Glass, and Miller reviewed 475 different studies, comprising 25,000 patients in all (Smith, Glass, and Miller, 1980). By averaging across the 475 studies reviewed in their analysis, Smith, Glass, and Miller concluded that the "average person who receives therapy is better off at the end of it than 80 percent of the persons who do not" (Smith, Glass, and Miller, 1980, p. 87). Later analyses that used somewhat more stringent criteria in eliminating studies that were methodologically suspect yielded similar results (e.g., Andrews and Harvey, 1981; Shapiro and Shapiro, 1982). Still further studies have shown that these improvements continue to be found when patients are studied months or years after treatment (Nicholson and Berman, 1983).

COMPARING DIFFERENT THERAPIES

The preceding discussion indicates that patients who receive psychotherapy will —on the average—be better off than patients who do not. To the extent that this is so, psychotherapy works. But as we've seen, there are any number of different psychotherapies: psychodynamic, humanistic, behavioral, cognitive, and so on. Do any of them get better results than the others? This question has been asked by several investigators. Their answer is unlikely to provide comfort for the adherents of any one school of psychotherapy. Most studies of psychotherapeutic outcomes suggest that the differences in the effectiveness of the various psychotherapies are slight or nonexistent. This view is sometimes called the *Dodo Bird verdict* after the Dodo Bird in *Alice in Wonderland* who organized a race between various Wonderland creatures and concluded that "Everyone has won and all must have prizes" (Luborsky, Singer, and Luborsky, 1975). While a few reviewers feel that the behavioral and cognitive therapies have a slight advantage (e.g., Shapiro and Shapiro, 1982), many others judge that the outcome similarities far outweigh the differences (e.g., Smith, Glass, and Miller, 1980; Sloane et al., 1975).

EXTENSIONS OF PSYCHOTHERAPY

In Freud's time, psychotherapy was still considered a somewhat arcane art, practiced by a few initiates and limited to a selected group of well-educated adult patients. Since then, psychotherapy has been broadened and extended to cover increasingly more terrain. One set of extensions widened the patient population to include children, retarded persons, various kinds of sociopaths, and psychotics. Another extension was a shift from the original one-therapist, one-patient formula to various modes of **group therapy** that feature all conceivable permutations: one therapist and several patients, several therapists and several patients, several patients and no therapist, and so on.

Group Therapy

One reason for treating patients in groups is that there simply aren't enough trained therapists for all the people who want their services; seeing clients in groups is one way of making the supply fit the demand. But the appeal of group therapy may have some deeper reasons as well. For instance, the new therapeutic groups seem to fill a void, at least temporarily, left by the weakening of family and religious ties in modern urbanized society.

SHARED-PROBLEM GROUPS

One approach is to organize a group of people all of whom have the same problem. They may all be alcoholics, or drug addicts, or ex-convicts. The members meet, share relevant advice and information, help newcomers along, exhort and support each other in their resolve to overcome their handicaps. The classic example is *Alcoholics Anonymous,* which provides the alcoholic with a sense that he is not alone and helps him weather crises without suffering a relapse. In such we-are-all-in-the-same-boat groups, the primary aim of the group is to *manage* the problem that all members share. No specific therapy is provided for emotional problems that are unique to any one individual.

THERAPY GROUPS

The rules of the game are very different in groups explicitly organized for the purpose of **group therapy.** Here, a group of selected patients, usually around ten, are

(Drawing by Whitney Darrow, Jr.; © 1976, The New Yorker Magazine, Inc.)

"When Jud accuses Zack, here, of hostility toward his daughter, like he seems to every session, why, it's plain to me he's only rationalizing his own lack of gumption in standing up to a stepson who's usurping the loyalty of his second wife. The way he lit into him just now shows he's got this here guilt identification with Zack's present family constellation. Calling Zack egotistical ain't nothing but a disguise mechanism for concealing his secret envy of Zack's grit and all-around starch, and shows mighty poor ego boundaries of his own, it appears to me."

treated together under the guidance of a trained therapist. This form of therapy may have some advantages that individual treatment lacks. According to its proponents, in group therapy the therapist does not really treat the members of the group; instead, he helps them to treat each other. The specific techniques of the therapist may vary from psychoanalytically oriented insight therapy to various forms of behavior therapy to Rogerian client-centered approaches. But whatever techniques the therapist favors, the treatment of each group member really begins as he realizes that he is not all that different from the others. He learns that there are other people who are painfully shy, who have hostile fantasies about their parents, or whatever. Further benefits come from a sense of group belongingness, of support, and of encouragement. But most important of all is the fact that the group provides a ready-made laboratory in interpersonal relations. The patient can discover just what he does that rubs others the wrong way, how he can relate to certain kinds of people more effectively, and so on (Sadock, 1975).

Marital and Family Therapy

In the therapy groups we've considered thus far, the members are almost always strangers before the sessions begin. This is in marked contrast to what happens in *marital and family therapy.* Here the persons seeking help have known each other very well (sometimes only too well) before they enter therapy.

In recent years, family therapy has become a major therapeutic movement (Satir, 1967; Minuchin, 1974; Kerr and Bowen, 1988). It is probably no coincidence that this growth has occurred during a time of turmoil in American families, evidenced by spiraling divorce rates and increasing numbers of single-parent households.

Family and marital therapists regard the family as an emotional unit that can influence the onset and continuing symptoms of many mental disorders and social problems. Seen from this perspective, the key to marital and family distress is not necessarily in the pathology of any individual spouse or family member. It is rather in the relationships within the family system: between the husband and wife or the various members of the family. In a dislocated shoulder, both the upper arm and shoulder socket may be perfectly sound, but until their mutual relationship is appropriately readjusted, there will necessarily be pain and the shoulder won't be able to function. Many marital (or couple) and family therapists feel that their task is in principle similar to that of the orthopedist who resets the dislocated shoulder: They try to help the couple or the family readjust their interrelations.

"We're not living happily ever after."
(Drawing by Chas. Addams; © 1959, 1987, The New Yorker Magazine, Inc.)

The Expansion of Therapeutic Goals

Group methods and other extensions made psychotherapy available to a much larger number of people. But did all of them really need it? The answer depends on what one believes the goals of therapy to be.

To Freud, the matter was simple. Most of the neurotics he saw were incapable of any kind of healthy life. They were crippled by terrorizing phobias or all-consuming compulsions and were thus unable to work and love. Freud wanted to cure these pathologies so that his patients could once again deal with their everyday existence. But he never regarded this cure as equivalent to happiness or fulfillment or the discovery of a meaning in life. These the patients had to find for themselves, and they might very well fail to do so even when no longer saddled with their neuroses.

Later therapists broadened the treatment goals. This is especially true of humanistic therapists such as Rogers. To be sure, Rogerian therapists try to remove or alleviate their clients' distress. But their ambitions go further. They aim at more than a cure (the goal of psychoanalysts, at least in their early days) and at more than the modification of unwanted behavior patterns (the goal of behavior therapists). Their ultimate object is to help their clients to "grow" and to "realize their human potentialities." But with this expansion of the therapeutic goal, there is a concomitant widening of the group to which the therapeutic enterprise may be said to apply. Now therapy can be appropriate for just about anyone, regardless of whether he suffers some form of psychopathology or does not (Orne, 1975). After all, who among us can claim to have achieved his full potential?

A CENTURY OF THERAPY

Where does all of this leave us? What can we say today about the treatment of mental disorder about a hundred years after the discovery that general paresis is caused by syphilis and after Freud and Breuer conducted their classic studies of hysteria?

All in all, we can say that the last century has shown a great deal of progress.

Let's begin with psychotherapy. The first thing to say is that there is little doubt that psychotherapy produces some nonspecific benefits. It helps people by providing someone in whom they can confide, who can give advice about troubling matters, who listens to them, and who instills new hope and the expectation that they will get better. The critic may reply that such gains merely reflect placebo effects and similar matters. According to this view, the benefits are not produced by any specific psychotherapeutic technique but might just as easily have been provided by a wise uncle or an understanding family doctor. Even if this were true—and it is certainly not the whole story—the point may not be relevant. For wise uncles are in short supply today. The extended family in which uncles, nieces, and grandparents lived in close proximity is largely a thing of the past. The same is true of the family doctor, who has vanished from the scene, together with his bedside manner. All of this suggests that psychotherapy has come to fill a social vacuum. Some of its effect may well be placebo-like, but a placebo may be better than nothing. And for the present, the psychotherapeutic professions seem to be the officially designated dispensers of such placebos.

But this is by no means all. For over and above placebos there are some genuine specific psychotherapeutic effects that produce improvement, though rarely a complete cure. The specific ingredients that bring these effects about have not been identified with certainty but they probably include emotional defusing, interpersonal learning, and some insight—all acquired within the therapeutic situation and somehow transferred to the patient's life beyond.

How about somatic therapies? Here too there has been progress. The antipsychotic drugs alleviate some of the worst symptoms of schizophrenia, the antidepressants (and where appropriate, electroconvulsive therapy) do the same for depression, and lithium salts do a good job in controlling manic episodes in bipolar disorder. These advances are far from what one might wish. The drugs don't begin to effect a cure and generally have side effects. But we're farther along than we were a hundred years ago.

How far is far? As so often, it depends on where we look. If we look back and compare our current practices with those at the time of the American Revolution when Benjamin Rush dunked his patients into ice cold water or whirled them around until they were unconscious, we've come a long way. But if we look ahead to some diagnostic manual of the future in which schizophrenia, mood disorders, anxiety states, and all the rest of the current DSM-III-R entries have neatly catalogued therapies that are sure to work, we must recognize that we have a much longer way to go. But considering how much progress was made in the last hundred years, there is certainly room for hope.

SUMMARY

1. One major form of treatment of mental disorder is by *somatic therapies.* Of these, the most widely used are *drug therapies. Antipsychotic drugs* such as *phenothiazines* are helpful in alleviating the major symptoms of schizophrenia; *antidepressants,* including the *MAO inhibitors* and *tricyclics,* counteract depression; and *lithium carbonate* is useful in cases of bipolar mood disorders, especially in forestalling manic episodes.

2. The effectiveness of drug treatment—as indeed of all therapies—requires careful evaluation procedures that control for *spontaneous improvement* and *placebo effects,* and that also guard against both the physicians' and the patients' expectations by use of *double-blind techniques.* Such studies have demonstrated genuine effects of certain psychiatric drugs, some of which are quite specific to a particular disorder. But thus far these drugs have not produced complete cures, especially in schizophrenia. Without a *maintenance dose,* a discharged patient may relapse; even with it, his adjustment may be only marginal.

3. Other somatic therapies include *frontal lobotomy,* a procedure now widely suspect, and *electroconvulsive shock treatment (ECT)* in cases of severe and potentially suicidal depression.

4. Another approach to mental disorder, *psychotherapy,* relies on psychological means alone. It derives from *classical psychoanalysis.* Psychoanalysts try to help their patients to recover repressed memories and wishes so that they can overcome crippling internal conflicts. Their tools are *free association* and the *interpretation* of the patient's *resistance.* The goal is emotional rather than mere intellectual insight, an achievement made possible by an analysis of the *transference* relationship between analyst and patient.

5. Many modern psychoanalysts practice modified variants of Freud's technique. They generally place greater emphasis on interpersonal and social problems in the present than on psychosexual matters in the past. They also tend to take a more active role in helping the patient extend the therapeutic experience to the world outside.

6. A different approach is taken by *behavior therapists* whose concern is with unwanted, overt behaviors rather than with hypothetical underlying causes. Many of the behavior therapists' techniques are derived from the principles of classical and instrumental conditioning. Therapies based on classical conditioning include *flooding and implosion,* which attempt to extinguish the patient's fear by evoking the fear response in full force. Others are *systematic desensitization,* which tries to *countercondition* the patient's fear by a policy of gradualism. Yet another is *aversion therapy,* in which undesirable behaviors, thoughts, and desires are coupled with unpleasant stimuli. Therapies based on operant conditioning principles include the use of *token economies,* in which patients are systematically reinforced for desirable behaviors.

7. Some recent offshoots of behavior therapy share its concrete and *directive* orientation but not its emphasis on conditioning. One example is *cognitive therapy,* which tries to change the way the patient thinks about his situation.

8. Another group of practitioners, the *humanistic therapists,* charge that both behavior therapy and psychoanalysis are too mechanistic and manipulative and that they fail to deal with their patients as "whole persons." An example of such a humanistic approach is Rogers's *client-centered therapy,* which is largely *nondirective,* and is based on the idea that therapy is a process of personal growth. A related approach is *existential therapy,* whose goal is to help patients recognize the importance of personal responsibility and free choice, and to assist them in discovering some meaning in life.

9. In recent years, many investigators have assessed the effectiveness of psychotherapies through a statistical technique called *meta-analysis,* by means of which the results of many different studies can be combined. The results of such analyses indicate that all therapies are moderately effective and that they are effective to about the same extent (the *Dodo Bird verdict*).

10. The last few decades have seen an enormous extension of psychotherapy. One extension is of method. An example is *group therapy* in which patients are treated in groups rather than individually. Another example is *family (and marital) therapy,* whose practitioners believe that family distress is not in the pathology of any one individual but in the relationships within the family system and who therefore try to rectify these faulty relationships. Another extension concerns the *therapeutic goals.* While the original purpose of psychotherapy was to cure pathology, some practitioners gradually broadened this goal to include personal growth and the discovery of meaning in life.

Epilogue

We have come to the end of our journey. We have traveled through the sprawling fields of psychology, a loosely federated intellectual empire that stretches from the domains of the biological sciences on one border to those of the social sciences on the other. We have gone from one end of psychology to another. What have we learned?

In looking back over our journey, there is little doubt that we have encountered many more questions than answers. To be sure, very much more is known today about mind and behavior than was known in the days of, say, Thorndike and Köhler, let alone those of Descartes, Locke, and Kant. For by now, psychology has assuredly become a science, and in fact, a science of quite respectable accomplishments. But this does not change the fact that what we know today is just a small clearing in a vast jungle of ignorance. As we come to know more, the clearing expands, but so does the circumference that borders on the uncharted wilderness.

What can we say? We can point at what we know and congratulate ourselves. Or we can consider what we do not know and bemoan our ignorance. Perhaps a wiser course is one recommended by Sigmund Freud on thinking about some aspects of human intellectual history (Freud, 1917).

Freud suggested a parallel between the psychological growth of each human child and the intellectual progress of humanity as a whole. As he saw it, the infant is initially possessed by an all-pervading sense of his own power and importance. He cries and his parents come to change or feed or rock him, and so he feels that he is the cause of whatever happens around him, the sole center of a world that revolves around him alone. But this happy delusion of his own omnipotence cannot last forever. Eventually the growing infant discovers that he is not the hub of the universe. This recognition may come as a cruel blow, but he will ultimately be the better for it. For the child cannot become strong and capable without some awareness that he is not so as yet, without first accepting the fact that he can't have his way just by wishing. His first achievements will be slight—as he lifts his own cup or a bit later says his first word—but they are real enough and will lay the foundation for his later mastery of his environment.

Freud thought that a similar theme underlies the growth of humankind's awareness of the world in which we live. On two crucial occasions in our history, we had to give up some cherished beliefs in our own power and importance. With Copernicus, we had to cede our place in the center of the physical universe: The sun doesn't circle us but we the sun. With Darwin, we had to perform a similar abdication in the biological sphere: We are not specially created but are descended from other animals. Each of these intellectual revolutions ran into vehement opposition, in large part because each represented a gigantic blow to humanity's self-love and pride. They made us face our own ignorance and insignificance. But however painful it may have been initially, each recognition of our weakness ultimately helped us gain more strength; each confession of ignorance eventually led to deeper understanding. The Copernican revolution forced us to admit our minute place in the celestial scheme of things, but this admission was the first step in a journey of ever-increasing physical horizons, a journey that in our own time brought human beings to the moon. The Darwinian revolution made us aware that we are just one biological species among millions, the product of the same evolutionary process that brought forth sea urchins and penguins as well as us. But this awareness opened the way for continually expanding explorations of the biological universe, explorations that have already given us much greater control of our own bodily condition and of the fragile environment in which humans and other species exist.

In this century we have had to suffer yet another blow to our self-pride. We learned that we are not sure of what goes on in our own minds. Modern psychology, for all its accomplishments, has made it utterly clear that thus far we know even less about our own mental processes and behavior than we know about the physical and biological world around us. Here, too, we have to confess that we are weak and ignorant. We can only hope that this confession will have some of the effects of our previous admissions, that here again strength will grow out of weakness and knowledge out of folly and ignorance. If so, we may finally understand why we think and do what we think and do, so that we may ultimately master our inner selves as we have learned to master the world around us.

There are few goals in science that are worthier than this.

Statistics: The Collection, Organization, and Interpretation of Data

By Neil A. Macmillan

A large body of psychological knowledge has been summarized in this book, and a good part of the discussion was devoted to the ways in which this knowledge was obtained. But there are certain methodological issues that were dealt with only in passing. These concern *statistical methods,* the ways in which investigators gather, organize, and interpret collections of numerical data.

Suppose some investigators want to find out whether three-year-old boys are more aggressive than three-year-old girls. To answer this question is a very big job. To start with, the investigators will have to come up with some appropriate measure of aggression. They will then have to select the subjects. The investigators presumably want to say something about three-year-olds in general, not just the particular three-year-olds in their study. To make sure that this can be done, they have to select their subjects appropriately. Even more important, their groups of boys and girls must be as comparable as possible, so that one can be reasonably sure that any differences between the two groups is attributable to the difference in sex rather than to other factors (such as intellectual development, social class, and so on).

The investigators are now ready to collect their data. But having collected them, they will have to find some way of organizing these data in a meaningful way. Suppose the study used two groups of, say, 50 boys and 50 girls, each observed on 10 separate occasions. This means that the investigators will end up with at least 1,000 separate numerical entries (say, number of aggressive acts for each child on each occasion), 500 for the boys and 500 for the girls. Something has to be done to reduce this mass of numbers into some manageable, summarized form. This is usually accomplished by some process of averaging scores.

The next step involves statistical interpretation. Suppose the investigators find that the average aggression score is greater for the boys than for the girls (it probably will be). Can they be sure that the difference between the groups is large enough not to be dismissed as a fluke, a chance event? For it is just about certain that the data contain *variability*. The children in each group will not perform equally; furthermore, the same child may very well behave differently on one occasion than another. As a result, the scores in the two groups will almost surely overlap; that is, some girls will get a higher aggression score than some boys. Could it be that the difference *between* the groups (that is, the difference between the two averages) is an accidental chance product of the variability that is seen to hold *within* the two groups? One of the key functions of statistical methods is to deal with questions of this sort, to help us draw useful and general conclusions about organisms despite the unavoidable variability in their behavior.

The preceding example indicates the main tasks to which statistical methods have been applied. In this appendix, we will sketch the logic that underlies these methods as psychologists use them.

DESCRIBING THE DATA

The data with which statistics deals are numerical, so a preliminary step in statistical analysis is the reduction of the actual results of a study to numbers. Much of the power of statistics results from the fact that numbers (unlike responses to a questionnaire, videotapes of social interactions, or lists of words recalled by a subject in a memory experiment) can be manipulated with the rules of arithmetic. As a result, scientists prefer to use response measures that are in numerical form. Consider our hypothetical study of aggression and sex. The investigators who watched the subjects might rate their aggression in various situations (from, say, "extremely aggressive" to "extremely docile") or they might count the number of aggressive acts (say, hitting or insulting another child), and so on. This operation of assigning numbers to observed events (usually, a subject's responses) is called *scaling.*

There are several types of scales that will concern us. They differ by the arithmetical operations that can be performed upon them.

Categorical and Ordinal Scales

Sometimes the scores assigned to individuals are merely *categorical* (also called *nominal.*) For example, when respondents to a poll are asked to name the television channel they watch most frequently, they might respond "4," "2," or "13." These numbers serve only to group the responses into categories. They can obviously not be subjected to any arithmetic operations.

Ordinal numbers convey more information, in that their relative magnitude is meaningful—not arbitrary, as in the case of categorical scales. If individuals are asked to list the ten people they most admire, the number 1 can be assigned to the most admired person, 2 to the runner-up, and so on. The smaller the number assigned, the more the person is admired. Notice that no such statement can be made of television channels: Channel 4 is not more anything than channel 2, just different from it.

Scores which are ordinally scaled cannot, however, be added or subtracted. The first two persons on the most-admired list differ in admirability by 1; so do the last two. Yet the individual who has done the ranking may admire the first person far more than the other nine, all of whom might be very similar in admirability; in other words, given an ordinal scale, differences of 1 are not necessarily equal psychologically. Imagine a child who, given this task, lists his mother first, followed by the starting lineup of the Chicago Cubs baseball team. In this example, the difference of 8 between person 2 and person 10 probably represents a smaller difference in judged admirability than the difference of 1 obtained between persons 1 and 2 (at least so the mother hopes).

Interval Scales

Scales in which equal differences between scores, or intervals, *can* be treated as equal units are called *interval scales.* Reaction time is a common psychological variable which is usually treated as an interval scale. In some memory experiments, a subject must respond as quickly as possible to each of several words, some of which he has seen earlier in the experiment; the task is to indicate whether each word has appeared before by pressing one of two buttons. An unknown, but possibly constant, part of the reaction time is simply the time required to press the response button; the rest is the time required for the decision-making process:

$$\text{reaction time} = \text{decision time} + \text{button-press time} \tag{1}$$

Suppose a subject requires an average of 2 seconds to respond to nouns, 3 seconds for verbs, and 4 seconds for adjectives. The difference in decision time between nouns and verbs ($3 - 2 = 1$ second) is the same as the difference in decision time between verbs and adjectives ($4 - 3 = 1$ second). We can make this statement—which in turn suggests various hypotheses about the factors that underlie such differences—precisely because reaction time can be regarded as an interval scale.

Ratio Scales

Scores based on an interval scale allow subtraction and addition. But they do not necessarily allow multiplication and division. Consider the centigrade scale of temperature. There is no doubt that the difference between 10 and 20 degrees centigrade is equal to that between 30 and 40 degrees centigrade. But can one say that 20 degrees centigrade is *twice* as high a temperature as 10 degrees centigrade? The answer is no, for the centigrade scale of temperature is only an interval scale. It is not a *ratio scale* which allows statements such as 10 feet is 1/5 as long as 50 feet, or 15 pounds is 3 times as heavy as 5 pounds. To make such statements one needs a true zero point. Such a ratio scale with a zero point does exist for temperature—the Kelvin absolute temperature scale, whose zero point is about -273 degrees centigrade.

   Some psychological variables can be described by a ratio scale. This is true of various forms of sensory intensity—brightness, loudness, and so on. For example, it makes sense to say that the rock music emanating from your neighbor's apartment is four times as loud as your roommate singing in the shower. But there are many psychological variables which cannot be so readily described in ratio terms. Let's go back to reaction time. This cannot be considered a ratio scale for the decision process. In our previous example we saw that the reaction time for adjectives was 4 seconds, while that for nouns was 2 seconds. But we cannot say that the 4-second response represents twice as much *decision* time as the 2-second response, because of the unknown time required to press the response button. Since this time is unknown, we have no zero point.

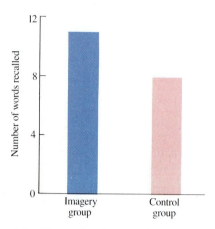

A.1   The results of an experiment on memorizing   *Subjects in the imagery group, who formed visual images of the words they were to memorize, recalled an average of 11 words. Subjects in the control group, who received no special instructions, recalled an average of 8 words.*

The fact that very few variables are ratio scaled does not, of course, prevent people from describing ordinal- or interval-scaled variables in ratio terms. A claim by an advertiser that drug *A* is "twice as effective" as drug *B* may mean that *A* works twice as fast, or for twice the time, or is successfl on twice as many people, or requires only half the dose. A potential consumer needs to know the advertiser's meaning of "effective" to evaluate the claim. Similarly, a 4-second reaction time in the word-recognition experiment is certainly twice as long as a 2-second reaction time; there is no harm in saying so, as long as it is understood that we are not talking about the decision time but rather about the total reaction time.

COLLECTING THE DATA

The kinds of scales we have just discussed concern the ways in which psychological variables are described in numerical terms. The point of most psychological investigations is to see how such variables are related to various factors that may produce them. Psychologists—and most other scientists—employ three major methodological tools to achieve this end: the experiment, the observational study, and the case study.

The Experiment

An *experiment* is a study in which the experimenter deliberately manipulates one or more variables to determine the effect of this manipulation on another variable. As an example, consider an experiment conducted to determine whether visual imagery aids memory. Participants in the experiment listen to a list of words, which they are instructed to memorize; later they are asked to recall as many words as possible. Two groups of subjects are chosen. One is the *experimental group;* this is the group to which the experimenter's manipulation is applied. It consists of subjects who are instructed to form visual images that connect each word to the preceding word. Other subjects form the *control group,* a group to which the experimenter's manipulation is not applied. These control subjects are not given imagery instructions. Many experiments have more than one experimental group (in this example, different groups might be told to do their visual imagining in different ways), or more than one control group (here, a second control group might be instructed to rehearse by repeating each word over and over).

Like many other experiments, this one can be thought of as a situation in which the experimenter varies something (here the instructions given to the subjects) and observes the effect of this variation on certain responses of the subjects (the number of words they correctly recall). The variable which is manipulated by the experimenter (imagery instructions) is called the *independent variable.* The subject's response (number of words recalled) is called the *dependent variable,* since the investigator wants to know whether it is dependent upon his manipulation of the independent variable. Speaking loosely, independent variables are sometimes regarded as causes, dependent variables as effects.

The results of our experiment are graphically presented in Figure A.1. The values of the independent variable are indicated on the horizontal, or *x*-axis, and the values of the dependent variable on the vertical, or *y*-axis. The figure displays the average number of items recalled for subjects who used visual imagery in memorizing and for those who did not. We will have more to say about this experiment presently.

Observational Studies

Much psychological research departs from the experimental method in that investigators do not produce the effects directly, but only observe them. They do not so much design the experiment as discover it. Such an investigation is called an *observational study.* Consider the question "What is the effect of prenatal malnutrition on IQ?" This question can only be answered by locating children whose mothers were malnourished during pregnancy and measuring their IQs; to deliberately provide pregnant women with inadequate diets is obviously worse than unethical. But even though the investigators do not manipulate the mother's diet (or indeed, anything else), some of the methodological terms used before can still be applied. We can consider the mother's diet as the independent variable, and the child's IQ as the dependent variable. A group analogous to the experimental group would consist of children whose mothers were malnourished during pregnancy. An analogue to the control group is a group of children whose mothers' diet was adequate.

Observatinal studies like this one are sometimes called "experiments of nature." Because nature does not always provide exactly those control groups which the investigator might have wished for, observational studies can be difficult to interpret. For example, children whose mothers were malnourished during pregnancy are often born into environments which might also be expected to have negative effects on IQ. Women whose diet is inadequate during pregnancy are likely to be poor; they are therefore less likely to provide some of the physical advantages (like good food and health care) and educational advantages (like books and nursery schools) which may well be helpful in developing intelligence.

The Case Study

In many areas of psychology, conclusions are based on only one person who is studied intensively. Such an investigation is called a *case study.* Individuals who display unusual psychological or physiological characteristics, such as rare forms of color blindness, exceptionally good or poor memory, or brain injuries, can sometimes provide information about normal vision, memory, or brain function that would be difficult or impossible to obtain from normal individuals. Take the patient known as H.M., who suffered severe amnesia after brain surgery (see Chapter 7). Before the operation his memory was normal; afterward he could remember virtually nothing about events that occurred after the operation. This patient has been extensively studied because of his unusual memory disorder. Since his amnesia is apparently the result of the destruction of a particular structure in the brain, the hippocampus, a comparison of H.M.'s performance with that of normal individuals allows us to make inferences about the role of the hippocampus in normal memory.

Some of the most famous case studies in psychology are those described by Sigmund Freud, whose extensive psychoanalytic interviews of his patients led him to develop theories of dreams, defense mechanisms, and other psychological processes (see Chapter 12).

SELECTING THE SUBJECTS

How does one select the subjects for a psychological study? To answer this question, we have to consider the difference between a population and a sample.

Sample and Population

Psychologists—again like other scientists—usually want to make statements about a larger group of persons (or animals) than the particular subjects they happen to use in their study. They want their conclusions to apply to a given *population:* all members of a given group—say, all three-year-old boys, all schizophrenic patients, all U.S. voters, and in some cases, all humans. But they obviously can't study all members of the population. As a result, they have to select a *sample,* that is, a subset of the population they are interested in. Their hope is that the results found in the sample can be generalized to the population from which the sample is drawn.

It is important to realize that generalizations from a given sample to a particular population can only be made if the sample is representative (that is, typical) of the population to which one wants to generalize. Suppose one does a study on memory by using college students. Can one generalize the results to adults in general? Strictly speaking one cannot, for college students are on the average younger than the population at large and are more accustomed to memorizing things. Under the circumstances, the safest course may be to restrict one's generalizations to the population of college students.

Most experimenters would probably argue that college students don't differ too greatly from the general population (at least in memory skills), so that results obtained with them do apply in general, at least approximately. But there are many cases in which inadequate sampling leads to gross blunders. The classic example is a 1936 poll which predicted that Franklin D. Roosevelt would lose the presidential election. In fact, he won by a landslide. This massive error was produced by a *biased sample*—all persons polled were selected from telephone directories. But in 1936 having a telephone was much more likely among persons of higher than of lower socioeconomic status. As a result, the sample was not representative of the voting population as a whole. Since socioeconomic level affected voting preference, the poll predicted falsely.

Random and Stratified Samples

To ensure that one can generalize from sample to population, investigators use a *random sample.* This is a sample in which every member of the population has an equal chance of being picked—as in a jury drawn by lot from all the voters of a given district (if none are disqualified or excuse themselves). The random sampling procedure applies with special force to the assignment of subjects in an experiment. Here every effort has to be made to assign subjects randomly to the various experimental or control groups.

For some purposes, even a random sample may not be good enough. While every member of the population has an equal chance of being selected, the sample may still turn out to be atypical by chance alone. This danger of chance error becomes less and less the greater the size of the sample. But if one is forced to use a small sample (and one often is because of lack of time or money), other sampling procedures may be necessary. Suppose we want to take a poll to determine the attitudes of American voters toward legalized abortion. We can expect peoples' attitudes to differ depending on (at least) their age, sex, and religion. If the sample is fairly small, it is important that each subgroup of the population be (randomly) sampled in proportion to its size. This procedure is called *stratified sampling,* and is common in studying psychological traits or attitudes which vary greatly among different subgroups of the population.

Sampling Responses

The distinction between sample and population does not only apply to subjects. It also applies to the subjects' responses. Consider the investigators who studied aggressive behavior in 50 three-year-old boys. Each of these boys was observed on 10 occasions. Those 10 occasions can be regarded as a sample of all such occasions, just as the 50 boys can be regarded as a sample of all three-year-old boys (or at least of all middle-class U.S. boys). The investigators will surely want to generalize from this sample of occasions to the population of all such occasions. To make sure that such a generalization is warranted, one has to see to it that the occasions are not atypical—that the child isn't especially tired, or sick, and so on.

ORGANIZING THE DATA: DESCRIPTIVE STATISTICS

We have considered the ways in which psychologists describe the data provided by their subjects by assigning numbers to them (scaling) and the ways in which they collect these data in the first place (experiments, observational studies, case studies). Our next task is to see how these data are organized.

The Frequency Distribution

Suppose we have designed and performed an experiment such as the imagery study described previously. The data will not automatically arrange themselves in the form shown in Figure A.1. Instead, investigators will first be faced with a list of numbers, the scores (number of words recalled correctly) for each subject in a given group. For example, if there were 10 subjects in the control group, their scores (in words correct) might have been

$$8, 11, 6, 7, 5, 9, 5, 9, 9, 11$$

A first step in organizing the data is to list all the possible scores and the frequency with which they occurred, as shown in Table A.1. Such an arrangement is called a *frequency distribution.*

A.2 Histogram In a histogram, a frequency distribution is graphically represented by a series of rectangles. The location of each rectangle on the x-axis indicates a score value, while its height shows how often that score value occurred.

Table A.1 FREQUENCY DISTRIBUTION

Score	Frequency
11	2
10	0
9	3
8	1
7	1
6	1
5	2

The frequency distribution can be expressed graphically. A common means for doing this is a *histogram* which depicts the frequency distribution by a series of contiguous rectangles (Figure A.2). The values of the dependent variable (here, number of words recalled) are shown by the location of each rectangle on the horizontal or *x*-axis. The frequency of each score is shown on the vertical or *y*-axis, that is, by the height of each rectangle. This is simple enough for our example, but in practice graphic presentation often requires a further step. The number of possible values the dependent variable can assume is often very large. As a result, exactly equal values rarely occur, as when reaction times are measured to the nearest millisecond (thousandth of a second). To get around this, the scores are generally grouped by intervals for purposes of graphic display. The histogram might then plot the frequency of all reaction times between, say, 200 and 225 milliseconds, between 226 and 250 milliseconds, and so on.

Measures of Central Tendency

A frequency distribution is a more concise description of the result of the experiment than the raw list of scores from which it was derived, but for many purposes we may want a description that is even more concise. We often wish to summarize an entire distribution by a single, central score; such a score is called a *measure of central tendency*. Three measures of central tendency are commonly used to express this central point of a distribution: the mode, the median, and the mean.

The *mode* is simply the score that occurs most frequently. In our example, the mode is 9. More subjects (to be exact, 3) recalled 9 words than recalled any other number of words.

The *median* is the point that divides the distribution into two equal halves, when the scores are arranged in increasing order. To find the median in our example, we first list the scores:

$$5, 5, 6, 7, 8, 9, 9, 9, 11, 11$$
$$\uparrow$$

Since there are 10 scores, the median lies between the fifth and sixth scores, that is, between 8 and 9, as indicated by the arrow. Any score between 8 and 9 would divide the distribution into two equal halves, but it is conventional to choose the number in the center of the interval between them, that is, 8.5. When there is an odd number of scores this problem does not arise.

The third measure of central tendency, the *mean (M),* is the familiar arithmetic average. If N stands for the number of scores, then

$$M = \frac{\text{sum of scores}}{N}$$

$$= \frac{5 + 5 + 6 + 7 + 8 + 9 + 9 + 9 + 11 + 11}{10} = \frac{80}{10} = 8.0$$

Of these three measures, the mode is the least helpful, because the modes of two samples from the same population can differ greatly even if the samples have very similar distributions. If one of the 3 subjects who recalled 9 words recalled only 5 instead, the mode would have been 5 rather than 9. But the mode does have its uses. For example, in certain elections, the candidate with the most votes —the modal candidate—wins.

The median and the mean differ most in the degree to which they are affected by extreme scores. If the highest score in our sample were changed from 11 to 111, the median would be unaffected, whereas the mean would jump from 8.0 to 18.0. Most people would find the median (which remains 8.5) a more compelling "average" than the mean in such a situation, since most of the scores in the distribution are close to the median, but are not close to the mean (18.0).

Distributions with extreme values at one end are said to be *skewed.* A classic example is income, since there are only a few high incomes but many low ones. Suppose we sample 10 individuals from a neighborhood, and find their yearly incomes (in thousands of dollars) to be:

5, 5, 5, 5, 10, 10, 10, 20, 20, 1,000

The median income for this sample is 10 ($10,000), since both the fifth and sixth scores are 10, and this value reflects the income of the typical individual. The mean income for this sample, however, is $(5 + 5 + 5 + 5 + 10 + 10 + 10 + 20 + 20 + 1,000)/10 = 109$, or $109,000. A politician who wants to demonstrate that his neighborhood has prospered might—quite honestly—use these data to claim that the average (mean) income is $109,000. If, on the other hand, he wished to plead for financial aid, he might say—with equal honesty—that the average (median) income is only $10,000. There is no single "correct" way to find an "average" in this situation, but it is obviously important to know which average (that is, which measure of central tendency) is being used.

When deviations in either direction from the mean are equally frequent, the distribution is said to be **symmetric.** In such distributions, the mean and the median are equal. Many psychological variables have symmetric distributions, but for variables with skewed distributions, like income, measures of central tendency must be chosen with care.

Measures of Variability

In reducing an entire frequency distribution to an average score, we have discarded a lot of very useful information. Suppose we (or the National Weather Service) measure the temperature every day for a year in various cities, and construct a frequency distribution for each city. The mean of this distribution tells us something about the city's climate. That it does not tell us everything is shown by the fact that the mean temperature in both San Francisco and Albuquerque is 56 degrees Fahrenheit. But the climates of the two cities nonetheless differ considerably, as indicated in Table A.2.

Table A.2   TEMPERATURE DATA FOR TWO CITIES (DEGREES FAHRENHEIT)

City	Lowest month	Mean	Highest month	Range
Albuquerque, New Mexico	35	56	77	42
San Francisco, California	48	56	63	15

The weather displays much more variability in the course of a year in Albuquerque than in San Francisco. A simple measure of variability is the **range,** the highest score minus the lowest. The range of temperatures in San Francisco is 15, while in Albuquerque it is 42.

A shortcoming of the range as a measure of variability is that it reflects the values of only two scores in the entire sample. As an example, consider the following distributions of ages in two college classes:

Distribution *A:* 19, 19, 19, 19, 19, 20, 25
Distribution *B:* 17, 17, 17, 20, 23, 23, 23

Each distribution has a mean of 20. Intuitively, distribution *A* has less variability, since all scores but one are very close to the mean. Yet the range of scores is the same (6) in both distributions. The problem arises because the range is determined by only two of the seven scores in each distribution.

A better measure of variability would incorporate every score in the distribution rather than just two scores. One might think that the variability could be measured by the average difference between the various scores and the mean, that is, by:

$$\frac{\text{sum of (score} - M)}{N}$$

This hypothetical measure is unworkable, however, because some of the scores are greater than the mean and some are smaller, so that the numerator is a sum of both positive and negative terms. (In fact, it turns out that the sum of the positive terms equals the sum of the negative terms, so that the expression shown above always equals zero.) The solution to this problem is simply to square all the terms in the numerator, thus making them all positive.* The resulting measure of variability is called the *variance (V):*

$$V = \frac{\text{sum of (score} - M)^2}{N} \tag{2}$$

The calculation of the variance for the control group in the memorization experiment is shown in Table A.3. As the table shows, the variance is obtained by subtracting the mean (M, which equals 8) from each score, squaring each result, adding all the squared terms, and dividing the resulting sum by the total number of scores (N, which equals 10), yielding a value of 4.4.

Table A.3 CALCULATING VARIANCE

Score	Score − mean	(Score − mean)²
8	$8 - 8 = 0$	$0^2 = 0$
11	$11 - 8 = 3$	$3^2 = 9$
6	$6 - 8 = -2$	$(-2)^2 = 4$
7	$7 - 8 = -1$	$(-1)^2 = 1$
5	$5 - 8 = -3$	$(-3)^2 = 9$
9	$9 - 8 = 1$	$1^2 = 1$
5	$5 - 8 = -3$	$(-3)^2 = 9$
9	$9 - 8 = 1$	$1^2 = 1$
9	$9 - 8 = 1$	$1^2 = 1$
11	$11 - 8 = 3$	$3^2 = 9$

Because deviations from the mean are squared, the variance is expressed in units different from the scores themselves. If our dependent variable were a distance, measured in centimeters, the variance would be expressed in square centimeters. As we will see in the next section, it is convenient to have a measure of variability which can be added to or subtracted from the mean; such a measure ought to be expressed in the same units as the original scores. To accomplish this end, we employ another measure of variability, the *standard deviation,* or *SD.* The standard deviation is derived from the variance (V); it is obtained by taking

* An alternative solution would be to sum the absolute value of (score − M), that is, consider only the magnitude of this difference for each score, not the sign. The resulting statistic, called the *average deviation,* is little used, however, primarily because absolute values are not too easily dealt with in certain mathematical terms that underlie statistical theory. As a result, statisticians prefer to transform negative into positive numbers by squaring them.

the square root of the variance. Thus

$$SD = \sqrt{V}$$

In our example, SD is about 2.1, the square root of the variance which is 4.4.

Converting Scores to Compare Them

Suppose a person takes two tests. One measures her memory span—how many digits she can remember after one presentation. The other test measures her running ability—how fast she can run 100 yards. It turns out that she can remember 8 digits and runs 100 yards in 17 seconds. Is there any way to decide whether she can remember digits better (or worse or equally well) than she can run 100 years? On the face of it, the question seems absurd; it seems to be like comparing apples and oranges. But in fact, there is a way, for we can ask where each of these two scores is located on the two frequency distributions of other persons (presumably women of the same age) who are given the same two tasks.

PERCENTILE RANKS

One way of doing this is by transforming each of the two scores into *percentile ranks.* The percentile rank of a score indicates the percentage of all scores that lie below that given score. Let's assume that 8 digits is the 78th percentile, which means that 78 percent of the relevant comparison group remembers fewer digits. Let's further assume that a score of 17 seconds in the 100-yard dash is the 53rd percentile of the same comparison group. We can now answer the question with which we started. Our subject can remember digits better than she can run 100 yards. By converting into percentile ranks we have rendered incompatible scores compatible, allowing us to compare the two.

STANDARD SCORES

For many statistical purposes there is an even better method of comparing scores or of interpreting the meaning of individual scores. This is to express them by reference to the mean and standard deviation of the frequency distribution of which they are part, by converting them into *standard scores* (often called *z-scores*).

Suppose you take a test that measures aptitude for accounting and are told your score is 36. In itself, this number cannot help you decide whether to pursue or avoid a career in accounting. To interpret your score you need to know both the average score and how variable the scores are. If the mean is 30, you know you are above average, but how far above average is 6 points? This might be an extreme score, or one attained by many, depending on the variability of the distribution.

Let us suppose that the standard deviation of the distribution is 3. Your score of 36 is therefore 2 standard deviations (6 points) above the mean (30). A score which is expressed this way, as so many standard deviations from the mean, is called a standard score, or z-score. The formula for calculating a z-score is:

$$z = \frac{(\text{score} - M)}{SD} \tag{3}$$

Your aptitude of 36 has a z-score of $(36 - 30)/3 = 2$; that is, your score is 2 standard deviations above the mean.

The use of z-scores allows one to compare scores from different distributions. Still unsure whether to become an accountant, you take a screen test to help you decide whether to be an actor. Here your score is 60. This is a larger number than the 36 you scored on the earlier test, but it may not reveal much acting aptitude. Suppose the mean score on the screen test is 80, the standard deviation 20; then your z-score is $(60 - 80)/20 = -1$. In acting aptitude, you are 1 standard deviation below the mean (that is, $z = -1$); in accounting aptitude, 2 standard deviations above (that is, $z = +2$). The use of z-scores makes your relative abilities clear.

Notice that scores below the mean have negative z-scores, as in the last example. A z-score of 0 corresponds to a score which equals the mean.

Percentile rank and a z-score give similar information, but one cannot be converted into the other unless we know more about the distribution than just its mean and standard deviation. In many cases this information is available, as we shall now see.

The Normal Distribution

Frequency histograms can have a wide variety of shapes, but many variables of psychological interest have a **normal distribution** (often called **normal curve**), which is a symmetric distribution of the shape shown in Figure A.3. The graph is smooth, unlike the histogram in Figure A.2, because it approximates the distribution of scores from a very large sample. The normal curve is bell-shaped, with most of its scores near the mean; the farther a score is from the mean, the less likely it is to occur. Among the many variables whose distributions are approximately normal are IQ, scholastic aptitude test scores (SAT), and women's heights (see Table A.4).*

A.3 Normal distribution *Values taken from any normally distributed variable (such as those presented in Table A.4) can be converted to z-scores by the formula $z = (score - mean)/(standard\ deviation)$. The figure shows graphically the proportions that fall between various values of z.*

Table A.4   NORMALLY DISTRIBUTED VARIABLES

Variable	Mean	Standard deviation	-2	-1	0	1	2
						z-scores	
IQ	100	15	70	85	100	115	130
SAT	500	100	300	400	500	600	700
Height (women)	160 cm	5 cm	150	155	160	165	170

* Men's heights are also normally distributed, but the distribution of the heights of all adults is not. Such a distribution would have two peaks, one for the modal height of each sex, and would thus be shaped quite differently from the normal curve. Distributions with two modes are called **bimodal.**

These three variables, IQ, SAT score, and height, obviously cannot literally have the "same" distribution, since their means and standard deviations are different (Table A.4 gives plausible values for them). In what sense, then, can they all be said to be normal? The answer is that the distribution of z-scores for all these variables is the same. For example, an IQ of 115 is 15 points, or 1 standard deviation, above the IQ mean of 100; a height of 165 centimeters is 5 centimeters, or 1 standard deviation, above the height mean of 160 centimeters. Both scores, therefore, have z-scores of 1. Furthermore, the percentage of heights between 160 and 165 centimeters is the same as the percentage of IQ scores between 100 and 115, that is, it is 34 percent. This is the percentage of scores which lie between the mean and one standard deviation above the mean for any normally distributed variable.

THE PERCENTILE RANK OF A z-SCORE

When a variable is known to have a normal distribution, a z-score can be converted directly into a percentile rank. A z-score of 1 has a percentile rank of 84, that is, 34 percent of the scores lie between the mean and $z = 1$, and (because the distribution is symmetric) 50 percent of the scores lie below the mean. A z-score of -1 corresponds, in a normal distribution, to a percentile rank of 16: only 16 percent of the scores are lower. These relationships are illustrated in Figure A.3 and Table A.4.

HOW THE NORMAL CURVE ARISES

Why should variables such as height or IQ scores—and many others—form distributions that have this particular shape? Mathematicians have shown that whenever a given variable is the sum of many smaller variables, its distribution will be close to that of the normal curve. An example is height. Height can be thought of as the sum of the contributions of the many genes (and some environmental factors) which influence this trait; it therefore satisfies the general condition.

The basic idea is that the many different factors that influence a given measure (such as the genes for height) operate independently. A given gene will pull height up or push it down; the direction in which it exerts its effort is a matter of chance. If the chances are equal either way, then a good analogy to this situation is a person who tosses a coin repeatedly and counts the number of times the coin comes up heads. In this analogy, a head corresponds to a gene that tends to increase height, a tail to a gene that tends to diminish it. The more often the genetic coin falls heads, the taller the person will be.

What will the distribution of the variable "number of heads" be? Clearly, it depends on the number of tosses. If the coin is tossed only once, then there will be either 0 heads or 1 head, and these are equally likely. The resulting distribution is shown in the top panel of Figure A.4.

If the number of tosses (which we will call N) is 2, then 0, 1, or 2 heads can arise. However, not all these outcomes are equally likely: 0 heads come up only if the sequence tail-tail (TT) occurs; 2 heads only if head-head (HH) occurs; but 1 head results from either HT or TH. The distribution of heads for $N = 2$ is shown in the second panel of Figure A.4. The area above 1 head has been subdivided into two equal parts, one for each possible sequence containing a single head.*

As N increases, the distribution of the number of heads looks more and more like the normal distribution, as the subsequent panels of Figure A.4 show. When N becomes as large as the number of factors that determine height, the distribution of the number of heads is virtually identical to the normal distribution. Similar arguments justify the assumption of normality for many psychological variables.

DESCRIBING THE RELATION BETWEEN TWO VARIABLES: CORRELATION

The basic problem facing psychological investigators is to account for observed differences in some variable they are interested in. Why, for example, do some people display better memory than others? The experimental approach to the problem, described earlier, is to ask whether changes in an independent variable produce systematic changes in the dependent variable. In the memory experiment, we asked whether subjects using visual imagery as an aid to memorizing would recall more words on the average than those who did not. In an observa-

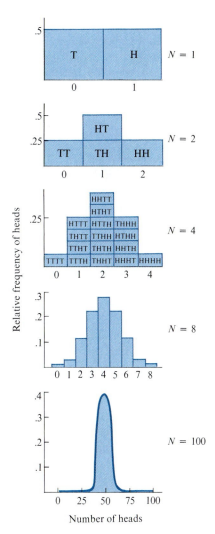

T = Tail
H = Head

A.4 Histograms showing expected number of heads in tossing a fair coin N times *In successive panels, N = 1, 2, 4, and 8. The bottom panel illustrates the case when N = 100 and shows a smoothed curve.*

* The distribution of the number of heads is called the **binomial distribution,** because of its relation to the binomial theorem: the number of head-tail sequences which can lead to k heads is the $(k + 1)$st coefficient of $(a + b)^N$.

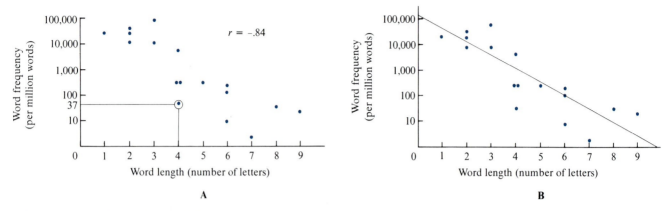

A.5 Scatter plot of a negative correlation between word length and word frequency

tional study, however, our approach must be different, for in such a study we do not manipulate the variables. What is often done here is to observe the relationship between two—sometimes more—variables as they occur naturally, in the hope that differences in one variable can be attributed to differences in a second.

Positive and Negative Correlation

Imagine that a taxicab company wants to identify drivers who will earn relatively large amounts of money (for themselves and, of course, for the company). The company's officers make the plausible guess that one relevant factor is the driver's knowledge of the local geography, so they devise an appropriate test of street names, routes from place to place, and so on, and administer the test to each driver. The question is whether this test score is related to the driver's job performance as measured by his weekly earnings. To decide, one has to find out whether the test score and the earnings are ***correlated***—that is, whether they tend to vary together.

In the taxicab example, the two variables will probably be ***positively correlated*** —as one variable (test score) increases, the other (earnings) will generally increase too. But other variables may be ***negatively correlated***—when one increases, the other will tend to decrease. An example is a phenomenon called Zipf's law, which states that words that occur frequently in a language tend to be relatively short. The two variables word length and word frequency are negatively correlated, since one variable tends to increase as the other decreases.

Correlational data are often displayed in a ***scatter plot*** (or scatter diagram), in which values of one variable are shown on the horizontal axis and variables of the other on the vertical axis. Figure A.5*A* is a scatter plot of word frequency versus word length for the words in this sentence.* Each word is represented by a single point. An example is provided by the word *plot,* which is 4 letters long and occurs with a frequency of 37 times per million words of English text (and is represented by the circled dot). The points on the graph display a tendency to decrease on one variable as they increase on the other, although the relation is by no means perfect. It is helpful to draw a straight line through the various points in a scatter plot which comes as close as possible to all of them (Figure A.5*B*). The line is called a ***line of best fit,*** and it indicates the general trend of the data. Here, the line slopes downward because the correlation between the variables is negative.

---

* There is no point for the "word" A.5*A* in this sentence. The frequencies of the other words are taken from H. Kucera and W. N. Francis, *Computational Analysis of Present-Day American English* (Providence, R. I.: Brown University Press, 1967).

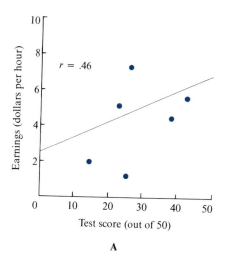

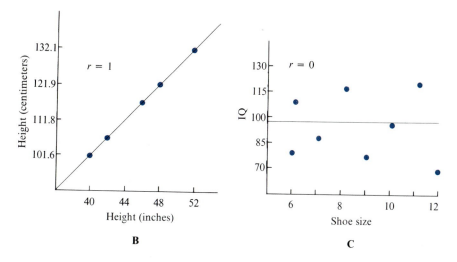

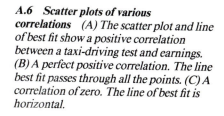

A	B	C

A.6   Scatter plots of various correlations   *(A) The scatter plot and line of best fit show a positive correlation between a taxi-driving test and earnings. (B) A perfect positive correlation. The line best fit passes through all the points. (C) A correlation of zero. The line of best fit is horizontal.*

The three panels of Figure A.6 are scatter plots showing the relation between other pairs of variables. In Figure A.6*A* hypothetical data from the taxicab example show that there is a positive correlation between test score and earnings (since the line of best fit slopes upward), but that test score is not a perfect predictor of on-the-job performance (since the points are fairly widely scattered around the line). Points above the line represent individuals who earn more than their test score would lead one to predict, points below the line individuals who earn less.

The examples in Figures A.5 and A.6*A* each illustrate moderate correlations; panels *B* and *C* of Figure A.6 are extreme cases. Figure A.6*B* shows data from a hypothetical experiment conducted in a fourth-grade class to illustrate the relation between metric and English units of length. The heights of five children are measured twice, once in inches and once in centimeters; each point on the scatter plot gives the two height measurements for one child. All the points in the figure fall on the line of best fit, because height in centimeters always equals 2.54 times height in inches. The two variables, height in centimeters and height in inches, are perfectly correlated—one can be perfectly predicted from the other. Once you know your height in inches, there is no information to be gained by measuring yourself with a meterstick.

Figure A.6*C* presents a relation between IQ and shoe size. These variables are unrelated to each other; people with large shoes have neither a higher nor a lower IQ than people with small ones. The line of best fit is therefore horizontal, because the best guess of an individual's IQ is the same no matter what his or her shoe size—it is the mean IQ of the population.

The Correlation Coefficient

Correlations are often described by a ***correlation coefficient,*** denoted ***r,*** a number that can vary from +1.00 to −1.00 which expresses the strength and the direction of the correlation. For positive correlations, *r* is positive; for negative correlations, it is negative; for variables which are completely uncorrelated, $r = 0$. The largest positive value *r* can have is +1.00, which represents a perfect correlation (as in Figure A.6*B*); the largest possible negative value is −1.00, which is also a perfect correlation. The closer the points in a scatter plot come to falling on the line of best fit, the nearer *r* will be to +1.00 or −1.00, and the more confident we can be in predicting scores on one variable from scores on the other. The values of *r* for the scatter plots in Figures A.5 and A.6*A* are given on the figures.

The method for calculating r between two variables, X and Y, is shown in Table A.5. The formula is

$$r = \frac{\text{sum } (z_x z_y)}{N} \tag{4}$$

The variable z_x is the z-score corresponding to X; z_y is the z-score corresponding to Y. To find r, each X and Y score must first be converted to a z-score by subtracting the mean and then dividing by the standard deviation. Then the product of z_x and z_y is found for each pair of scores. The average of these products (the sum of the products divided by N, the number of pairs of scores) is the correlation coefficient r.

Table A.5   CALCULATION OF THE CORRELATION COEFFICIENT

1. Data (from Figure A.6A).

Test score (X)	Earnings (Y)
45	6
25	2
15	3
40	5
25	6
30	8

2. Find the mean and standard deviation for X and Y.

For X, mean = 30, standard deviation = 10
For Y, mean = 5, standard deviation = 2

3. Convert each X and each Y to a z-score, using $z = \dfrac{(\text{score} - M)}{SD}$

X	Y	z-score for X (z_x)	z-score for Y (z_y)	$z_x z_y$
45	6	1.5	0.5	0.75
25	2	−0.5	−1.5	0.75
15	3	−1.5	−1.0	1.50
40	5	1.0	0.0	0.00
25	6	−0.5	0.5	−0.25
30	8	0.0	1.5	0.00
				2.75

4. Find the product $z_x z_y$ for each pair of scores.

5. $r = \dfrac{\text{sum } (z_x z_y)}{N} = \dfrac{2.75}{6} = .46$

Figure A.7 illustrates why this procedure yields positive values of r for positively related variables and negative values of r for negatively related variables. For positively correlated variables, most points are either above or below the mean on both variables. If they are above the mean, both z_x and z_y will be positive; if they are below, both z_x and z_y will be negative. (This follows from the definition of a z-score.) In either case the product $z_x z_y$ will be positive, so r will be positive. For negatively correlated variables, most points which are above the mean on one variable are below the mean on the other—either z_x is positive and z_y is negative, or vice versa. The product $z_x z_y$ is therefore negative, and so is r.

z_x and z_y are both positive, so $z_x z_y$ is positive

z_x is negative, z_y is positive, so $z_x z_y$ is negative

Z_y

Z_x

z_x and z_y are both negative, so $z_x z_y$ is positive

Z_y

Z_x

z_x is positive, z_y is negative, so $z_x z_y$ is negative

A.7 Correlation coefficients *(A) Two positively correlated variables. Most of the points lie in the upper right and lower left quadrants, where $z_x z_y$ is positive, so r is positive. (B) Two negatively correlated variables. Most of the points lie in the upper left and lower right quadrants, where $z_x z_y$ is negative, so r is negative.*

Interpreting and Misinterpreting Correlations

It is tempting, but false, to assume that if two variables are correlated, one is the cause of the other. There is a positive correlation between years of education and annual income in the population of North American adults; many people, including some educators, argue from these data that students should stay in school as long as possible in order to increase their eventual earning power. The difficulty with this reasoning is not the existence of counterexamples (such as Andrew Carnegie, the American industrialist and millionaire who never finished high school), which merely show that the correlation is less than 1.00. It is rather that it is difficult to infer causality from this correlation because both variables are correlated with yet a third variable. Years of schooling and income as an adult are not only correlated with each other, they are also correlated with a third variable—the parents' income. Given this fact, can we make any assertions about what causes adult income? Perhaps income is determined by one's education (it probably is, in part). But perhaps the relationship between income and education is a spurious byproduct of the parents' income. Perhaps this third factor partially determines both one's education and one's income, and there is no real causal connection between the two.

Another demonstration of the fact that correlation is not equivalent to causation occurs while waiting for a bus or a subway whose schedule is unknown. There is a negative correlation between the number of minutes a rider will have to wait for the next subway and the number of people waiting when the rider enters the station: the more people who are waiting, the sooner the subway will arrive. This negative correlation is fairly substantial, but even so, one would hardly try to cut down one's waiting time by arriving at the station with fifty friends. Here, the third, causal variable (time since the last train or bus left) is fairly obvious.* But even when it is harder to imagine just what the third variable might be, it is still possible that such a third variable exists and is responsible for the correlation. As a result, correlations can never provide solid evidence of a causal link.

* I thank Barry Schwartz for this example.

INTERPRETING DATA: INFERENTIAL STATISTICS

We have seen that a psychologist collecting data encounters variability. In memory experiments, for example, different individuals recall different numbers of items, and the same person is likely to perform differently when tested twice. An investigator wishes to draw general conclusions from data in spite of this variability, or to discover the factors that are responsible for it.

Accounting for Variability

As an example of how variability may be explained, consider a person shooting a pistol at a target. Although he always aims at the bull's eye, the shots scatter around it (Figure A.8*A*). Assuming that the mean is the bull's eye, the variance of these shots is the average squared deviation of the shots from the center; suppose this variance is 100.

Now we set about explaining the variance. If the shooting was done outdoors, the wind may have increased the spread; moving the shooter to an indoor shooting range produces the tighter grouping shown in Figure A.8*B*. The new variance is 80, a reduction of 20 percent—this means that the wind accounts for 20 percent of the original variance. Some of the variance may result from the unsteady hand of the shooter, so we now mount the gun. This yields a variance of 50 (Figure A.8*C*), a reduction of 50 percent, so 50 percent of the variance can be attributed to the shaky hand of the shooter. To find out how much of the variance can be accounted for by both the wind and the shaking, we mount the gun *and* move it indoors; now we may find a variance of only 30 (Figure A.8*D*). This means we

A. Outdoors, no mount. Variance = 100.

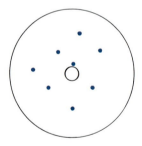

C. Outdoors, mount. Variance = 50.

A.8   Results of target shooting under several conditions   In each case, the bull's eye is the mean and the variance is the average squared deviation of the shots from the bull's eye. (A) Outdoors, no mount. Variance = 100. (B) Indoors, no mount. Variance = 80. (C) Outdoors, mount. Variance = 50. (D) Indoors, mount. Variance = 30.

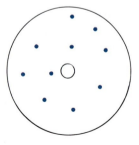

B. Indoors, no mount. Variance = 80.

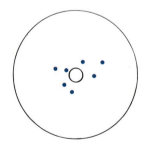

D. Indoors, mount. Variance = 30.

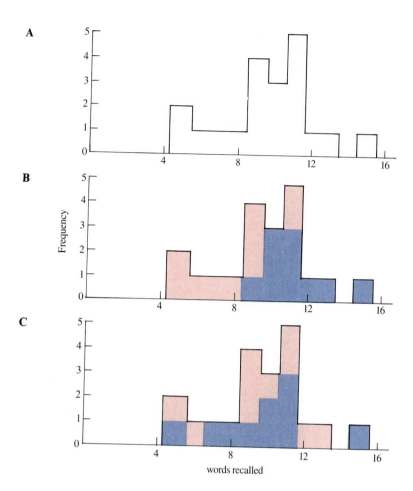

A.9 Accounting for variance in an experiment on memorizing *(A) The distribution of number of words recalled is shown for all 20 subjects lumped together; the variance of this distribution is 6.25. (B) The distributions of the experimental and control groups are displayed separately. The number of words recalled by the group that received imagery instructions is shown in color; the number recalled by the control group that received no special instructions is shown in gray. Within each of these groups, the variance is about 4.00. (C) The distribution of number of words recalled is plotted separately for men and women regardless of how they were instructed. Color indicates the number of words recalled by women, gray the number of men. The variance is 6.25.*

have explained 70 percent of the variance, leaving 30 percent unaccounted for.* Not all changes in the situation will reduce the variance. For example, if we find that providing the shooter with earmuffs leaves the variance unchanged, we know that none of the original variance was due to the noise of the pistol.

VARIANCE AND EXPERIMENTS

Figure A.9 shows how this approach can be applied to the experiment on visual imagery described earlier (see page A5). Figure A.9*A* shows the distribution of scores for all 20 subjects in the experiment lumped together; the total variance of this overall distribution is 6.25. But as we saw, 10 of these subjects had been instructed to use visual imagery in memorizing, whereas another 10 control subjects were given no special instructions. How much of the overall variance can be accounted for by the difference in these instructions? In Figure A.9*B,* the distributions are no longer lumped together. They are instead presented as two separate histograms; the subjects who received imagery instructions are shown in color while those who did not are indicated in gray. As the figure shows, there is less variability within either the imagery group or the control group than in the overall distribution that lumped both kinds of subjects together. While the variance in the overall distribution is 6.25, the variance within the two subgroups averages to only 4.0. We conclude that the difference between the instructions the subjects were given accounted for 36 percent of the variance, and that 64 percent (4 ÷ 6.25) still remains unexplained.

* I am grateful to Paul Rozin for suggesting this example.

Figure A.9*C* shows a situation in which an independent variable (in this case, sex) accounts for little or none of the variance. In this figure, the subjects' scores are again presented as two separate histograms; one for the scores of the men (regardless of whether they were instructed to use imagery or not), and the other for the scores of the women (again, regardless of the instructions they received). The men's scores are shown in gray; the women's, in color. Now the variance of the two subgroups (that is, men vs. women) averages to 6.25, a value identical to that found for the overall distribution. We conclude that the subject's sex accounts for none of the overall variance in memorizing performance.

VARIANCE AND CORRELATION

The technique of explaining the variance in one variable by attributing it to the effect of another variable can also be applied to correlational studies. Here, the values of one variable are explained (that is, accounted for) when the values of the other variable are known. Recall the taxicab example. In it a correlation of .46 was found between taxi drivers' earnings and their scores on a screening test. Since the correlation is neither perfect nor zero, some but not all of the variance in job performance can be explained by the aptitude test scores. The greater the magnitude of the correlation coefficient, r, the more variance is accounted for. The rule is that the proportion of variance which is explained equals r^2: If $r = .46$, one variable accounts for $(.46)^2 = .21$ of the variance of the other. (Just why this proportion is r^2 is beyond the scope of this discussion.) To put this another way, suppose all the cab drivers were identical on the one variable, their performance on the geographical text. This means that the variance on that variable would be zero. As a result, the variability on the second variable, earnings, would be reduced. The formula tells us by how much. The original variance on earnings can be determined from the data in Table A.5. It is 4. Its correlation with the geography test is .46. Since the effect of this variable, the geography test, is completely controlled, the variability on earnings will be $4 - (.46)^2 \times 4 = 3.16$. The drop in the variance from 4 to 3.16 is a reduction of 21 percent. The aptitude test does help us to predict taxicab earnings, for it accounts for 21 percent of the variance. But a good deal of the variance, 79 percent, is still unexplained.

Hypothesis Testing

Much behavioral research attempts to answer two-alternative questions. Does the amount of food a person eats depend on the effort required to eat it? Can people learn while they are sleeping? Is drug X more effective than aspirin? Each of these questions suggests an experiment, and the procedures described in the previous section could be used to discover how much of the variance in the dependent variable could be accounted for by the independent variable. But how can the results of such experiments lead to simple yes-or-no answers to the questions that inspired them?

TESTING HYPOTHESES ABOUT SINGLE SCORES

We will begin by testing a hypothesis about single scores. Consider the problem in interpreting a lie-detector test. In such a test, a person is asked a series of questions and various measures of physiological arousal are taken as he answers. An answer that is accompanied by an unusually high degree of arousal is taken as possible evidence that the person is lying. The question is how high is "unusually high?"

To answer this question we will first rephrase it. Can we reject the hypothesis that the given score came from the distribution of responses the same individual gave to neutral questions? (An example is "Is your name Fred?") Suppose the average arousal score to such control questions is 50, that the standard deviation of these neutral responses is 10, and that the arousal scores are normally distributed. We now look at the arousal score to the critical item. Let us say that this is 60. How likely is it that this score is from a sample drawn by chance from the population of responses to neutral questions? To find out, we convert it to a z-score, by computing its distance from the mean and dividing it by the standard deviation. The resulting z-score is $(60 - 50)/10$ or 1. Since the distribution is normal, Figure A.3 tells us that 16 percent of this person's arousal scores would be as high or higher than this. Under the circumstances we don't feel justified in rejecting the hypothesis that the score in question comes from the distribution of neutral responses. Put another way, we don't feel justified in accusing the person of lying. Our feelings might be different if the score were 70 or above. For now the z-score is $(70 - 50)/10$, or 2 standard deviations above the mean of the neutral distribution. The chances that a score this high or higher is from a sample drawn from the population of neutral responses is only 2 in a 100. We might now feel more comfortable in rejecting the hypothesis that this score is simply a chance event. We are more likely to assume that it is drawn from another distribution—in short, that the person is lying.

In this example we had to decide between two hypotheses. We look at a given score (or a set of scores) obtained under a particular experimental condition (in this case, a loaded question). One hypothesis is that the experimental condition has no effect, that the score is merely a reflection of the ordinary variability around the mean of a control condition (in this case, neutral questions). This is the so-called **null hypothesis,** the hypothesis that there really is no effect. The **alternative hypothesis** is that the null hypothesis is false, that the score is far enough away from the control mean so that we can assume that the same experimental condition has some effect. To decide between these two hypotheses, the data are expressed as a z-score, which in the context of hypothesis testing is called a **critical ratio.** Behavioral scientists generally accept a critical ratio of 2 as a cutting point. If this ratio is 2 or greater, they generally reject the null hypothesis and assume there is an effect of the experimental condition. (Such critical ratios of 2 or more are said to be **statistically significant,** which is just another way of saying that the null hypothesis can be rejected.) Critical ratios of less than 2 are considered too small to allow the rejection of the null hypothesis.

This general procedure is not foolproof. It is certainly possible for a subject in the lie-detection example to have an arousal score of 70 (a critical ratio of 2) or higher even though he is telling the truth. According to Figure A.3, this will happen about 2 percent of the time, and the person administering the test will erroneously "detect" a lie. Raising the cutoff value to the critical ratio of 3 or 4 would make such errors less common, but would not eliminate them entirely; furthermore, such a high critical value might mean failure to discover any lies the subject does utter. One of the important consequences of the variability in psychological data can be seen here: the investigator who has to decide between two interpretations of the data (the null hypothesis and the alternative hypothesis) cannot be correct all the time.

TESTING HYPOTHESES ABOUT MEANS

In the preceding discussion, our concern was with hypotheses about single scores. We now turn to the more commonly encountered problems in which the hypotheses involve means.

In many experiments, the investigator compares two or more groups—subjects tested with or without a drug, with or without imagery instructions, and so on. Suppose we get a difference between the two groups. How do we decide whether the difference is genuine rather than a mere chance fluctuation?

Let us return to the experiment in which memory for words was tested with and without instructions to imagine the items visually. To simplify the exposition, we will here consider a modified version of the experiment in which the same subjects serve in both the imagery and the nonimagery conditions. Each subject memorizes a list of 20 words without instructions, then memorizes a second list of 20 words under instructions to visualize. What we want to know is whether the subjects show any improvement with imagery instructions. There is no separate control group in this experiment, but, because a subject's score in the imagery condition can be compared with his score in the uninstructed condition, each subject provides his own control.

Table A.6 gives data for the 10 subjects in the experiment. For each subject, the table lists the number of words recalled without imagery instructions, the number recalled with such instructions, and the improvement (the difference between the two scores). The mean improvement overall is 3 words, from a mean of 8 words recalled without imagery to a mean of 11 words with imagery. But note that this does not hold for all subjects. For example, for Fred and Hortense, the "improvement" is negative—they both do better without imagery instructions. The question is whether we can conclude that there is an imagery facilitation effect overall. Put in other words, is the difference between the two conditions statistically significant?

Table A.6 NUMBER OF ITEMS RECALLED WITH AND WITHOUT IMAGERY INSTRUCTION, FOR 10 SUBJECTS

Subject	Score with imagery	Score without imagery	Improvement
Alphonse	11	5	6
Betsy	15	9	6
Cheryl	11	5	6
Davis	9	9	0
Earl	13	6	7
Fred	10	11	−1
Germaine	11	8	3
Hortense	10	11	−1
Imogene	8	7	1
Jerry	12	9	3
Mean	11	8	3

$$\text{Variance of improvement scores} = \frac{\text{sum of (score} - 3)^2}{10} = 8.8$$

$$\text{Standard deviation of improvement scores} = \sqrt{8.8} = 2.97$$

To show how this question is answered, we will follow much the same logic as that used in the analysis of the lie-detection problem. We have a mean—the average difference score of 10 subjects. What we must realize is that this mean—3—is really a sample based on the one experiment with 10 subjects we have just run. Suppose we had run the experiment again, with another set of 10 subjects—not just once, but many times. Each such repetition of the experiment would yield its own mean. And each of these means would constitute another sample. But what is the population to which these samples refer? It is the set of all of these means— the average differences between imagery and nonimagery instructions obtained in each of the many repetitions of the experiment we might possibly perform. And the mean of these means—a kind of grand mean—is the mean of the population. Any conclusions we want to draw from our experiment are really assertions about this population mean. If we say that the difference we found is statistically significant, we are asserting that the population mean is a difference score which is greater than zero (and in the same direction as in the sample). Put another way, we are asserting that the difference we found is not just a fluke but is real and would be obtained again and again if we repeated the experiment, thus rejecting the null hypothesis.

The null hypothesis amounts to the claim that the mean we actually obtained could have been drawn by chance from a distribution of sample means (that is, the many means of the possible repetitions of our experiment) around a population mean of zero. To test this claim, we have to compute a critical ratio that can tell us how far from zero our own mean actually is. Like all critical ratios, this is a z-score which expresses the distance of a score from a mean in units of the standard deviation (the SD). Thus, $z = (\text{score} - M)/SD$. In our present case, the score is our obtained mean (that is, 3); the mean is the hypothetical population mean of zero (assumed by the null hypothesis). But what is the denominator? It is the standard deviation of the distribution of sample means, the means of the many experiments we might have done.

The standard deviation of such a distribution of sample means is called the *standard error* of the mean *(SE).* Its value is determined by two factors: the standard deviation of the sample and the size of that sample. Specifically,

$$SE = \frac{SD}{\sqrt{N-1}}$$

$$(5)$$

It is clear that the variability of a mean (and this is what the standard error measures) goes down with the increasing sample size. (Why this factor turns out to be $\sqrt{N-1}$ is beyond the scope of this discussion.) A clue as to why comes from the consideration of the effects of an atypical score. Purely by chance, a sample may include an extreme case. But the larger the size of that sample, the less the effect of on extreme case on the average. If a sample of 3 persons includes a midget, the average height will be unusually far from the population mean. But in a sample of 3,000, one midget will not affect the average very markedly.

We can now conclude our analysis of the results of the memorization experiment. The critical ratio to be evaluated is:

$$\text{Critical Ratio} = \frac{\text{obtained sample mean} - \text{population mean}}{SE}$$

Since the population mean is assumed to be zero (by the null hypothesis), this expression becomes:

$$\text{Critical Ratio} = \frac{\text{obtained sample mean}}{SE}$$

This critical ratio expresses the mean difference between the two experimental conditions in units of the variability of the sample mean, that is, the standard error.* To compute the standard error, we first find the standard deviation of the

---

* There are several simplifications in this account. One is that the critical ratio described here does not have an exactly normal distribution. When the sample size is large, this effect is unimportant, but for small samples (like the one in the example) they can be material. To deal with these and related problems, statisticians often utilize measures that refer to distributions other than the normal one. An example is the *t*-test, a kind of critical ratio based on the so-called *t*-distribution.

improvement scores; this turns out to be 2.97, as shown in Table A.6. Then equation (5) tells us

$$SE = \frac{SD}{\sqrt{N-1}} = \frac{2.97}{\sqrt{10-1}} = .99$$

The critical ratio is now the obtained mean difference divided by the standard error, or $3/.99 = 3.03$. This is clearly larger than 2.0, so we conclude that the observed difference in memory between the imagery and control conditions is much too great to be attributed to chance factors. Thus using visual imagery evidently does improve recall.

CONFIDENCE INTERVALS

In statistical hypothesis testing we ask whether a certain sample mean could be drawn by chance from a distribution of sample means around some assumed population mean. (When testing the null hypothesis, this assumed population mean is zero.) But there is another way of phrasing this question. Can we be reasonably confident that the mean of the population falls within a certain specified interval? If we know the standard error of the mean, the answer is yes. We have already seen that about 2 percent of the scores in a normal distribution are more than two standard deviations above, and about 2 percent are lower than two standard deviations below the mean of that distribution. Since this is so, we can conclude that the chances are roughly 4 in 100 that the population mean is within an interval whose largest value is two standard errors above the sample mean and whose lowest value is two standard errors below. Because we can be fairly (96 percent) confident that the actual population mean will fall within this specified range, it is often called the *confidence interval.*

As an example, consider the prediction of political elections. During election campaigns, polling organizations report the current standing of various candidates by statements such as the following: "In a poll of 1,000 registered voters, 57 percent favored candidate Smith; the margin of error was 3 percent." This margin of error is the confidence interval around the proportion (that is, ± 3 percent).

To determine this confidence interval, the pollsters compute the standard error of the proportion they found. (In this case, .57). This standard error is analogous to the standard error of a mean we discussed in the previous section. Given an N of 1,000, this standard error happens to be .015.* Since $2 \times .015$ is .03 or 3 percent, the appropriate confidence interval for our example is the interval from 54 to 60 percent. Under the circumstances, candidate Smith can be fairly confident that she has the support of at least 50 percent of the electorate since 50 percent is well *below* the poll's confidence interval (see Figure A.10).

Some Implications of Statistical Inference

The methods of testing hypotheses and estimating confidence intervals which we have just described are routinely employed in evaluating the results of psycholog-

---

* The standard error of a proportion (e.g., the proportion of polled voters who express pro-X sentiments) is analogous to the standard error of the mean, and measures the precision with which our sample proportion estimates the population proportion. The formula for the standard error of a proportion p is:

$$SE_P = \sqrt{\frac{p \times (1-p)}{N}} \tag{7}$$

In our example, $p = .57$ and $N = 1,000$, so $SE_P = .015$.

ical research. But they have several characteristics that necessarily affect the interpretation of all such results.

THE PROBABILISTIC NATURE OF HYPOTHESIS TESTING AND CONFIDENCE INTERVALS

Since there is always some unexplained variance in any psychological study, there is always some probability that the conclusions are wrong as applied to the population. If we use a confidence interval of ± 2 SE, the chances that the population mean (or proportion, or whatever) falls outside of that interval are less than 4 or 5 in 100. Do we want to be more confident than this? If so, we might use a confidence interval of ± 3 SE where the equivalent chance is only 1 in 1,000. The same holds for critical ratios. We can say that a critical ratio of 2 means that a difference is statistically significant, but that only means that the chances are less than 2 in 100 that the difference as large or larger than this arose by chance. If we want to be more certain than this, we must insist that the critical ratio be larger—perhaps 3 (a chance factor of 1 in 2,000) or 4 (5 in 100,000), and so on. As long as there is some unexplained variance, there is some chance of error.

The probabilistic nature of statistical reasoning has another consequence. Even if we can come to a correct conclusion about the mean of a population (or a proportion, as in polls), we cannot generalize to individuals. Thus a study which shows that men have higher scores than women on spatial relations tests is not inconsistent with the existence of brilliant female artists or architects. Sample means for the two groups can differ significantly, even though there is considerable overlap in the two distributions of scores.

THE CONSERVATIVE NATURE OF HYPOTHESIS TESTING

Another characteristic of statistical hypothesis testing is that it is essentially conservative. This is because of the great stress placed on the null hypothesis in reaching a decision: one has to be quite sure that the null hypothesis is false before one entertains the alternative hypothesis. There are other imaginable strategies for reaching statistical decisions, but the conservative one has a perfectly rational basis. Let's suppose that some independent variable *does* produce a difference between two groups that is quite genuine and not the result of chance, but that the critical ratio is too low to reject the null hypothesis. If so, we will have falsely concluded that no difference exists in the population. As a result, we will have failed to discover a small effect. But what of it? If the effect is interesting enough, someone else may well attempt a similar experiment and manage to find the difference we didn't uncover. On the other hand, suppose we "discover" that some inde-

A.10 A candidate's poll results and their confidence intervals *The results of a mythical poll conducted for a no-less-mythical presidential candidate Smith by randomly sampling 200 persons in each of five regions of the U.S. The figure shows the pro-Smith proportions in each region, together with the confidence intervals around them, and indicates that she is ahead in all five samples. But there are two regions where she cannot be confident that she is ahead in the population—the South and the Southwest, where the confidence intervals of the pro-Smith proportion dip below 50 percent.*

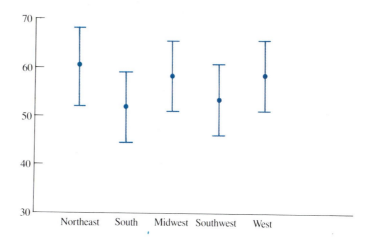

pendent variable has an effect when it actually does not (that is, the null hypothesis is true). By falsely rejecting the null hypothesis, we will have added an inaccurate "fact" to the store of scientific knowledge, and run the risk of leading other investigators into a blind alley.

THE ROLE OF SAMPLE SIZE

A last point concerns the role of sample size in affecting the interpretations of results. The larger the sample, the smaller the standard error and the smaller the confidence interval around the mean or the proportion. This can have major effects on hypothesis testing.

Suppose that, in the population, a certain independent variable produces a very small difference. As an example, suppose that the population difference between men and women on a certain test of spatial relations is 1 percent. We would probably be unable to reject the null hypothesis (that there is no sex difference on the test) with samples of moderate size. But if the sample size were sufficiently increased, we could reject the null hypothesis. For such a sizable increase in N would lead to a decrease in the standard errors of the sample means, which in turn would lead to an increase in the critical ratio. Someone who read a report of this experiment would now learn that, by using thousands of subjects, we had discovered a "significant" difference of 1 percent. A fair reaction to this bit of intelligence would be that the null hypothesis can indeed be rejected, but that the *psychological* significance of this finding is rather slight. The moral is simple. Statistical significance is required before a result can be considered reliable, but this statistical significance does not guarantee that the effect discovered is of psychological significance or of any practical importance.

SUMMARY

1. Statistical methods concern the ways in which investigators describe, gather, organize, and interpret collections of numerical data. A crucial concern of statistical endeavors is to deal with the variability that is encountered in all research.

2. An early step in the process is *scaling,* a procedure for assigning numbers to psychological responses. Scales can be *categorical, ordinal, interval,* or *ratio scales.* These differ in the degree to which they can be subjected to arithmetical operations.

3. There are three main methods for conducting psychological research: by means of an *experiment,* an *observational study,* and a *case study.* In an experiment, the investigator manipulates one variable, the *independent variable,* to see how it affects the subject's response, the *dependent variable.* In an observational study, the investigator does not manipulate any variables directly but rather observes them as they occur naturally. A case study is an investigation in which one person is studied in depth.

4. An important distinction in psychological research is that between *sample* and *population.* The population is the entire group about which the investigator wants to draw conclusions. The sample is the subset (usually small) of that population that is actually tested. Generalizations from sample to population are only possible if the one is representative of the other. This requires the use of *random samples.* In some cases a special version of the random sample, the *stratified sample,* may be employed.

5. A first step in organizing the data is to arrange them in a *frequency distribution,* often displayed in graphic form, as in a *histogram.* Frequency distributions are characterized by a *central tendency* and by *variability* around this central tendency. The common measure of central tendency is the *mean,* though sometimes another measure, the *median,* may be preferable, as in cases when the distribution is *skewed.* Important measures of variability are the *variance* and the *standard deviation.*

6. One way of comparing two scores drawn from different distributions is to convert both into *percentile ranks.* Another is to transform them into *z-scores,* which express the distance of a score from its mean in standard deviation units. The percentile rank of a *z*-score can be computed if the shape of that score's distribution is known. An important example is the *normal distribution,* graphically displayed by the *normal curve* which describes the distribution of many psychological variables and is basic to much of statistical reasoning.

7. In observational studies, the relation between variables is often expressed in the form of a *correlation* which may be positive or negative. It is measured by the *correlation coefficient,* a number that can vary from $+1.00$ to -1.00. While correlations reflect the extent to which two variables vary together, they do not necessarily indicate that one of them causes the other.

8. A major task of any investigator is to explain the variability of some dependent variable, usually measured by the variance. One means for doing so is to see whether that variance is reduced when a certain independent variable is controlled. If so, this independent variable is said to account for some of the variability of the dependent variable.

9. One of the main functions of statistical methods is to help test hypotheses about population given information about the sample. An important example is the difference between mean scores obtained under two different conditions. Here the investigator has to decide between the *null hypothesis* which asserts that the difference was obtained by chance, and the *alternative hypothesis* which asserts that the difference is genuine and exists in the population. The decision is made by dividing the obtained mean difference by the *standard error,* a measure of the variability of that mean difference. If the resulting ratio, called the *critical ratio,* is large enough, the null hypothesis is rejected, the alternative hypothesis is accepted, and the difference is said to be *statistically significant.* A related way of making statistical decisions is by using a *confidence interval,* or margin of error. This is based on the variability of the scores from a sample and determines the interval within which the population mean or proportion probably falls.

Glossary

absolute threshold The lowest intensity of some stimulus that produces a response.

accommodation (1) The process by which the lens is thickened or flattened to focus on an object. (2) In Piaget's theory of development, one of the twin processes that underlies cognitive development. *See* assimilation and accommodation.

accommodative distortion Retrospective alterations of memory to fit a schema. *See also* schema.

acetylcholine A neurotransmitter found in many parts of the nervous system. Among many other functions, it serves as an excitatory transmitter at the synaptic junctions between muscle fibers and motor neurons.

action potential A brief change in the electrical potential of an axon, which is the physical basis of the nervous impulse.

active memory *See* short-term memory.

active sleep (or REM sleep) A stage of sleep during which the EEG is similar to that of waking during which there are rapid eye movements (REMs) and during which dreams occur.

actor-observer difference The difference in attributions made by actors who describe their own actions and observers who describe another person's. The former emphasizes external, situational causes; the latter, internal, dispositional factors. *See also* attribution theory, fundamental attribution error, self-serving bias.

adaptive value In biological terms, the extent to which an attribute increases the likelihood of viable offspring.

additive color mixture Mixing colors by stimulating the eye with two sets of wavelengths simultaneously (e.g., by focusing filtered light from two projectors on the same spot). *See also* subtractive color mixture.

adrenaline *See* epinephrine.

affective disorders *See* mood disorders.

afferent nerves Sensory nerves that carry messages to the brain.

agnosia A serious disturbance in the organization of sensory information produced by lesions in certain cortical association areas. An example is visual agnosia in which the patient can see, but often does not recognize what it is that he sees.

alarm call Special, genetically programmed cry that impels members of a given species to seek cover. A biological puzzle, since it suggests a form of altruism in which the individual appears to endanger his own survival. *See also* altruism.

algorithm In both human and computer problem solving, a procedure in which all of the operations are specified step-by-step. *See also* heuristics.

all-or-none law Describes the fact that once a stimulus exceeds threshold, further increases do not increase the amplitude of the action potential.

alpha blocking The disruption of the alpha rhythm by visual stimulation or by active thought with the eyes closed.

alpha waves Fairly regular EEG waves, between eight to twelve per second, characteristic of a relaxed, waking state, usually with eyes closed.

alternative hypothesis In statistics, the hypothesis that the null hypothesis is false, that an obtained difference is so far from zero that one has to assume that the mean difference in the population is greater than zero and that the experimental condition has some effect. *See also* null hypothesis.

altruism (1) Acting so as to elevate the interests and welfare of others above one's own. (2) As used by sociobiologists, any behavior pattern that benefits individuals who are not one's own offspring (e.g., an alarm call). According to the kin-selection hypothesis, such altruism has biological survival value because the altruist's beneficiaries tend to be close relatives who carry a high proportion of his or her own genes. According to the reciprocal altruism hypothesis, altruism is based on the expectation that today's giver will be tomorrow's taker. *See also* alarm call.

Alzheimer's disease A degenerative brain disorder characterized by increasing memory loss followed by increasing disorientation culminating in total physical and mental helplessness and death. One of the major sites of the destruction is a pathway of acetylcholine-releasing cells leading from the base of the forebrain to the cortex and hippocampus. *See also* acetylcholine.

ambiguity (in sentence meaning) The case in which a sentence has two meanings. (For example, "These missionaries are ready to eat" overheard in a conversation between two cannibals.)

American Sign Language (ASL) The manual-visual language system of deaf persons in America.

anal character According to Freud, a personality type that derives from serious conflicts during the anal stage and is distinguished by three symptomatic traits: compulsive orderliness, stubbornness, and stinginess. *See also* anal stage.

anal stage In psychoanalytic theory, the stage of psychosexual devel-

A29

opment during which the focus of pleasure is on activities related to elimination.

androgen Any male sex hormone.

anorexia nervosa An eating disorder that primarily afflicts young women and that is characterized by an exaggerated concern with being overweight and by compulsive dieting, sometimes to the point of self-starvation. *See also* bulimia and obesity.

anterograde amnesia A memory deficit suffered after some brain damage. It is an inability to learn and remember any information imparted after the injury, with little effect on memory for information acquired previously. *See also* retrograde amnesia.

antidepressant drugs Drugs that alleviate depressive symptoms, presumably because they increase the availability of certain neurotransmitters (especially norepinephrine and serotonin) at synaptic junctions. The two major classes are monoamine oxidase (MAO) inhibitors and tricyclics. Of these, the tricyclics, such as imipramine, are the most widely used.

antidiuretic hormone (ADH) A hormone secreted by one of the parts of the pituitary gland. This hormone instructs the kidneys to reabsorb more of the water that passes through them. *See also* pituitary gland.

antisocial personality Also called psychopath or sociopath. The term describes persons who get into continual trouble with society, are indifferent to others, impulsive, with little concern for the future or remorse about the past.

anxiety An emotional state akin to fear. According to Freud, many mental illnesses center around anxiety and on attempts to ward it off by various unconscious mechanisms.

anxiety disorders *See* phobia, generalized anxiety disorder, obsessive-compulsive disorders.

anxiety hierarchy *See* systematic desensitization.

aphagia Refusal to eat (and in an extreme version, to drink) brought about by lesion of the lateral hypothalamus.

aphasia A disorder of language produced by lesions in certain association areas of the cortex. A lesion in Broca's area leads to expressive aphasia, one in Wernicke's area to receptive aphasia.

apparent movement The perception of movement produced by stimuli that are stationary but flash on and off at appropriate time intervals.

apraxia A serious disturbance in the organization of voluntary action produced by lesions in certain cortical association areas, often in the frontal lobes.

artificial intelligence A field that draws on concepts from both cognitive psychology and computer science to develop artificial systems that display some aspects of human-like intelligence. Examples are computer programs that recognize patterns or solve certain kinds of problems.

assimilation and accommodation In Piaget's theory, the twin processes by means of which cognitive development proceeds. Assimilation is the process whereby the environment is interpreted in terms of the schemas the child has at the time. Accommodation is the way the child changes his schemas as he continues to interact with the environment.

association areas Regions of the cortex that are not projection areas. They tend to be involved in the integration of sensory information or of motor commands.

association A linkage between two psychological processes as a result of past experience in which the two have occurred together. A broad term that subsumes conditioning and association of ideas among others.

attachment The tendency of the young of many species to stay in close proximity to an adult, usually their mother. *See also* imprinting.

attention A collective label for all the processes by which we perceive selectively.

attitude A fairly stable, evaluative disposition that makes a person think, feel, or behave positively or negatively about some person, group, or social issue.

attribution theory A theory about the process by which we try to explain a person's behavior, attributing it to situational factors or to inferred dispositional qualities or both.

attributional style The characteristic manner in which a person explains good or bad fortunes that befall him. A particular attributional style in which bad fortunes are generally attributed to internal, global, and stable causes may create a predisposition that makes a person vulnerable to depression. *See also* depression.

authoritarian personality A cluster of personal attributes (e.g., submission to persons above and harshness to those below) and social attitudes (e.g., prejudice against minority groups), which is sometimes held to constitute a distinct personality.

automatization A process whereby components of a skilled activity become subsumed under a higher-order organization and are run off automatically.

autonomic nervous system (ANS) A part of the nervous system that controls the internal organs, usually not under voluntary control.

availability heuristic A rule of thumb often used to make probability estimates, which depends on the frequency with which certain events readily come to mind. This can lead to errors since very vivid events will be remembered out of proportion to their actual frequency of occurrence.

aversion therapy A form of behavior therapy in which the undesirable response leads to an aversive stimulus (e.g., the patient shocks himself every time he reaches for a cigarette).

avoidance learning Instrumental learning in which the response averts an aversive stimulus before it occurs. This poses a problem: What is the reinforcement for this kind of learning? *See also* punishment training, escape learning.

axon Part of a neuron that transmits impulses to other neurons or effectors.

backward pairing A classical conditioning procedure in which the conditioned stimulus (CS) follows the unconditioned stimulus (US). *See also* forward pairing, simultaneous pairing.

base rate *See* representativeness heuristic.

basilar membrane *See* cochlea.

behavior therapy A general approach to psychological treatment which (1) holds that the disorders to which it addresses itself are produced by maladaptive learning and must be remedied by reeducation, (2) proposes techniques for this reeducation based on principles of learning and conditioning, (3) focuses on the maladaptive behaviors as such rather than on hypothetical unconscious processes of which they may be expressions.

behavioral-cognitive approach to personality An approach that defines personality differences by the way in which different people act and think about their actions. It tends to emphasize situational determinants and prior learning in trying to explain how such differences come about.

belongingness in learning The fact that the ease with which associations are formed depends upon the items to be associated. Thus, in classical conditioning some conditioned stimulus-unconditioned stimulus (CS-US) combinations are more effective than others (e.g., learned taste aversions).

bidirectional activation models Models of pattern recognition in which elements are activated as well as inhibited from both lower levels (bottom-up processing) and higher levels (top-down processing).

bipolar disorder Mood disorder in which the patient swings from one emotional extreme to another, experiencing both manic and depressive episodes. Formerly called manic-depressive psychosis.

blocking   An effect produced when two conditioned stimuli, *A* and *B*, are both presented together with the unconditioned stimulus (US). If stimulus *A* has previously been associated with the unconditioned stimulus while *B* has not, the formation of an association between stimulus *B* and the US will be impaired (that is, blocked).

bottom-up processes   *See* top-down processes.

brightness   A perceived dimension of visual stimuli—the extent to which they appear light or dark.

brightness contrast   The perceiver's tendency to exaggerate the physical difference in the light intensities of two adjacent regions. As a result, a gray patch looks brighter on a black background, darker on a white background.

British empiricism   A school of thought that holds that all knowledge comes by way of empirical experience, that is, through the senses.

Broca's area   *See* aphasia.

bulimia   A milder form of eating disorder characterized by repeated binge-and-purge bouts. In contrast to anorexics, bulimics tend to be of roughly normal weight. *See also* anorexia nervosa, obesity.

bystander effect   The phenomenon that underlies many examples of failing to help strangers in distress: The larger the group a person is in (or thinks he is in), the less likely he is to come to the stranger's assistance. One reason is diffusion of responsibility (no one thinks it is *his* responsibility to act).

case study   An observational study in which one person is studied intensively.

CAT scan (Computerized Axial Tomography)   A technique for examining brain structure in living humans by constructing a composite X-ray picture based on views from all different angles.

catatonic schizophrenia   A subcategory of schizophrenia. Its main symptoms are peculiar motor patterns such as periods in which the patient is immobile and maintains strange positions for hours on end.

catecholamines   A family of neurotransmitters that have an activating function, including epinephrine, norepinephrine, and dopamine.

categorical scale   A scale that divides the responses into categories that are not numerically related. *See also* interval scale, ordinal scale, ratio scale.

catharsis   An explosive release of hitherto dammed-up emotions that is sometimes believed to have therapeutic effects.

censorship in dreams   *See* Freud's theory of dreams.

central nervous system (CNS)   The brain and spinal cord.

central route to persuasion   *See* elaboration-likelihood model of persuasion.

central tendency   The tendency of scores in a frequency distribution to cluster around a central value. *See also* median, mean, and variability.

central trait   A trait that is associated with many other attributes of the person who is being judged. Warm and cold are central because they are important in determining overall impressions.

cerebellum   Two small hemispheres that form part of the hindbrain and control muscular coordination and equilibrium.

cerebral cortex   The outermost layer of the gray matter of the cerebral hemispheres.

cerebral hemispheres   Two hemispherical structures that comprise the major part of the forebrain in mammals and serve as the main coordinating center of the nervous system.

childhood amnesia   The failure to remember the events of our very early childhood. This is sometimes ascribed to massive change in retrieval cues, sometimes to different ways of encoding memories in early childhood.

chlorpromazine   *See* phenothiazines.

chromosomes   Structures in the nucleus of each cell that contain the genes, the units of hereditary transmission. A human cell has 46 chromosomes, arranged in 23 pairs. One of these pairs consists of the sex chromosomes. In males, one member of the pair is an X-chromosome, the other a Y-chromosome. In females, both members are X-chromosomes. *See also* gene.

chunking   A process of reorganizing (or recoding) materials in memory that permits a number of items to be packed into a larger unit.

classical conditioning   A form of learning in which a hitherto neutral stimulus, the conditioned stimulus (CS), is paired with an unconditioned stimulus (US) regardless of what the animal does. In effect, what has to be learned is the relation between these two stimuli. *See also* instrumental conditioning.

client-centered therapy   A humanistic psychotherapy developed by Carl Rogers. *See also* humanistic therapies.

closure   A factor in visual grouping. The perceptual tendency to fill in gaps in a figure so that it looks closed.

cochlea   Coiled structure in the inner ear that contains the basilar membrane whose deformation by sound-produced pressure stimulates the auditory receptors.

cognitive dissonance   An inconsistency among some experiences, beliefs, attitudes, or feelings. According to dissonance theory, this sets up an unpleasant state that people try to reduce by reinterpreting some part of their experiences to make them consistent with the others.

cognitive arousal theory of emotions   A theory proposed by Schachter and Singer which asserts that emotions are an interpretation of our own autonomic arousal in the light of the situation to which we attribute it. *See also* attribution theory.

cognitive map   *See* cognitive theory.

cognitive theory   A conception of human and animal learning which holds that both humans and animals acquire items of knowledge (cognitions) such as what is where (cognitive map) or what leads to what (expectancy). This contrasts with theories of instrumental learning such as Thorndike's or Skinner's which assert that learning consists of the strengthening or weakening of particular response tendencies.

cognitive therapy   An approach to therapy that tries to change some of the patient's habitual modes of thinking. It is related to behavior therapy because it regards such thought patterns as a form of behavior.

common sense   As used in the discussion of artificial intelligence, the term refers to an understanding of what is relevant to a problem and what is not.

complementary colors   Two colors that, when additively mixed with each other in the right proportions, produce the sensation of gray.

compulsions   *See* obsessive-compulsive disorders.

concept   A class or category that subsumes a number of individual instances. An important way of relating concepts is through propositions, which make some assertion that relates a subject (e.g., *chickens*) and a predicate (e.g., *lay eggs*).

concordance   The probability that a person who stands in a particular family relationship to a patient (e.g., an identical twin) has the same disorder as the patient.

concrete operational period   In Piaget's theory, the period from ages six or seven to about eleven. At this time, the child has acquired mental operations that allow her to abstract some essential attributes of reality such as number and substance, but these operations are as yet applicable only to concrete events and cannot be considered entirely in the abstract.

conditioned reflex   *See* conditioned response.

conditioned reinforcer   An initially neutral stimulus that acquires reinforcing properties through pairing with another stimulus that is already reinforcing.

conditioned response (CR) A response elicited by some initially neutral stimulus, the conditioned stimulus (CS), as a result of pairings between that CS and an unconditioned stimulus (US). This CR is typically not identical with the unconditioned response though it often is similar to it. *See also* conditioned stimulus, unconditioned response, unconditioned stimulus.

conditioned stimulus (CS) In classical conditioning, the stimulus that comes to elicit a new response by virtue of pairings with the unconditioned stimulus (US). *See also* conditioned response, unconditioned response, unconditioned stimulus.

cones Visual receptors that respond to relatively greater light intensities and give rise to chromatic (color) sensations. *See also* rods.

confidence interval An interval around a sample mean or proportion within which the population mean or proportion is likely to fall. In common practice, the largest value of the interval is 2 standard errors above the mean or proportion, and the smallest value is 2 standard errors below it.

confirmation bias The tendency to seek evidence to confirm one's hypothesis rather than to look for evidence to see whether the hypothesis is false.

conservation In Piaget's theory, the understanding that certain attributes such as substance and number remain unchanged despite various transformations (e.g., liquid conservation, the realization that the amount of liquid remains the same when poured from a tall, thin beaker into a wide jar).

construct validity The extent to which performance on a test fits into a theoretical scheme about the attribute the test tries to measure.

content morphemes Morphemes that carry the main burden of meaning (e.g., *strange*). This is in contrast to function morphemes that add details to the meaning but also serve various grammatical purposes (e.g., the suffixes *s* and *er*, the connecting words *and, or, if,* and so on).

context effects *See* top-down processes.

contiguity The togetherness in time of two events, which is sometimes regarded as the condition that leads to association.

contingency A relation between two events in which one is dependent upon another. If the contingency is greater than zero, then the probability of event *A* will be greater when event *B* is present than when it is absent.

convergence The movement of the eyes as they swivel toward each other to focus upon an object.

conversion disorders Formerly called conversion hysteria. A condition in which there are physical symptoms that seem to have no physical basis. They instead appear to be linked to psychological factors and are often believed to serve as a means of reducing anxiety. *See also* hysteria.

conversion hysteria *See* conversion disorders.

corpus callosum A bundle of fibers that connects the two cerebral hemispheres.

correlation The tendency of two variables to vary together. If one goes up as the other goes up, the correlation is positive; if one goes up as the other goes down, the correlation is negative.

correlation coefficient A number, referred to as *r,* that expresses both the size and the direction of a correlation, varying from +1.00 (perfect positive correlation) through 0.00 (absence of any correlation) to −1.00 (perfect negative correlation).

counterconditioning A procedure for weakening a classically conditioned CR by connecting the stimuli that presently evoke it to a new response that is incompatible with the CR.

criterion groups Groups whose test performance sets the validity criterion for certain tests (e.g., the Minnesota Multiphasic Personality Inventory, MMPI, which uses several psychiatric criterion groups to define most of its subscales).

critical period Period in the development of an organism when it is particularly sensitive to certain environmental influences. Outside of this period, the same environmental influences have little effect (e.g., the period during which a duckling can be imprinted). After embryonic development, this phenomenon is rarely all-or-none. As a result, most developmental psychologists prefer the term *sensitive period*.

critical ratio A *z*-score used for testing the null hypothesis. It is obtained by dividing an obtained mean difference by the standard error (SE) so that critical ratio = obtained mean difference/SE. If this ratio is large enough, the null hypothesis is rejected and the difference is said to be statistically significant. *See also* standard error of the mean.

crystallized intelligence The repertoire of information, cognitive skills, and strategies acquired by the application of fluid intelligence to various fields. This is said to increase with age, in some cases into old age. *See also* fluid intelligence.

cultural anthropology A branch of anthropology that compares the similarities and differences among human cultures.

culture fairness of a test The extent to which test performance does not depend upon information or skills provided by one culture but not another.

curare A drug that completely paralyzes the skeletal musculature but does not affect visceral reactions.

cutoff score A score on a test used for selection below which no individual is accepted.

decay A possible factor in forgetting, producing some loss of the stored information through erosion by some as yet unknown physiological process.

decision making The process of forming probability estimates of events and utilizing them to choose between different courses of action.

declarative knowledge Knowing "that" (e.g., someone's name) as contrasted with procedural knowledge, which is knowing "how" (e.g., riding a bicycle).

deductive reasoning Reasoning in which one tries to determine whether some statement logically follows from certain premises, as in the analysis of syllogisms. This is in contrast with inductive reasoning in which one observes a number of particular instances and tries to determine a general rule that covers them all.

defense mechanism In psychoanalytic theory, a collective term for a number of reactions that try to ward off or lessen anxiety by various unconscious means. *See also* displacement, projection, rationalization, reaction formation, repression.

definition (of a word) A set of necessary and sufficient features shared by all members of a category, which are the criteria for membership in that category.

deindividuation A weakened sense of personal identity in which self-awareness is merged in the collective goals of a group.

delay of gratification The postponement of immediate satisfaction in order to achieve a more important reward later on, a process that plays an important role in some behavioral-cognitive approaches to personality.

delusion Systematized false beliefs, often of grandeur or persecution.

demand characteristics (of an experiment) The cues that tell a subject what the experimenter expects of him.

dendrites A typically highly branched part of a neuron that receives impulses from receptors or other neurons and conducts them toward the cell body and axon.

dependent variable *See* experiment.

depolarization A drop of the membrane potential of a neuron from its resting potential. The basis of neural excitation.

depression A state of deep and pervasive dejection and hopelessness, accompanied by apathy and a feeling of personal worthlessness.

descriptive rules *See* prescriptive rules.

deviation IQ A measure of intelligence test performance based on an individual's standing relative to his own age-mates (e.g., an IQ of 100 is average, and IQs of 70 and 130 correspond to percentile ranks of 2 and 98 respectively). *See also* Intelligence Quotient.

diathesis *See* diathesis-stress conception.

diathesis-stress conception The belief that many organic and mental disorders arise from an interaction between a diathesis (a predisposition toward the illness) and some form of precipitating environmental stress.

dichotic listening A procedure by which each ear receives a different message while the listener is asked to attend to one.

difference threshold The amount by which a given stimulus must be increased or decreased so that the subject can perceive a just noticeable difference (j.n.d.).

differentiation A progressive change from the general to the particular and from the simpler to the more complex that characterizes embryological development. According to some theorists, the same pattern holds for the development of behavior after birth.

diffusion of responsibility *See* bystander effect.

directed thinking Thinking that is aimed at the solution of a problem.

discrimination A process of learning to respond to certain stimuli that are reinforced and not to others that are unreinforced.

disinhibition An increase of some reaction tendency by the removal of some inhibiting influence upon it (e.g., the increased strength of a frog's spinal reflexes after decapitation).

displacement In psychoanalytic theory, a redirection of an impulse from a channel that is blocked into another, more available outlet (e.g., displaced aggression, as in a child who hits a sibling when punished by her parents).

display Term used by ethologists to describe genetically programmed responses that serve as stimuli for the reaction of others of the same species and, thus, serve as the basis of a communication system (e.g., mating rituals).

dissociative disorders Disorders in which a whole set of mental events is stored out of ordinary consciousness. These include psychogenic amnesia, fugue states, and cases of multiple personality.

dissonance theory *See* cognitive dissonance.

distal stimulus An object or event outside (e.g., a tree) as contrasted to the proximal stimulus (e.g., the retinal image of the tree), which is the pattern of physical energies that originates from the distal stimulus and impinges on a sense organ.

dominant gene *See* gene.

dopamine (DA) A neurotransmitter involved in various brain structures, including those that control motor action. Some authors believe that one subtype of schizophrenia is produced by an oversensitivity to dopamine in some parts of the brain.

dopamine hypothesis of schizophrenia Asserts that schizophrenics are oversensitive to the neurotransmitter dopamine and are therefore in a state of overarousal. Evidence for this view comes from the fact that the phenothiazines, which alleviate schizophrenic symptoms, block dopamine transmission. *See also* phenothiazines.

double-blind technique A technique for evaluating drug effects independent of the effects produced by the expectations of patients (placebo effects) and of physicians. This is done by assigning patients to a drug group or a placebo group with both patients and staff members in ignorance of who is assigned to which group. *See also* placebo effect.

drive-reduction theory A theory that claims that all built-in rewards are at bottom reductions of some noxious bodily state. The theory has difficulty in explaining motives in which one seeks stimulation, such as sex and curiosity.

DSM-III The diagnostic manual of the American Psychiatric Association adopted in 1980. A major distinction between it and its predecessor is that it categorizes mental disorders by their descriptive characteristics rather than by theories about their underlying cause. Thus a number of disorders that were formerly grouped together under the general heading "neurosis" (e.g., phobias, conversion disorders) are now classified under separate headings. *See also* conversion disorders, neurosis, phobia.

DSM-III-R The current diagnostic manual of the American Psychiatric Association adopted in 1987, a relatively minor revision of its predecessor, DSM-III.

effectors Organs of action; in humans, muscles and glands.

efferent nerves Nerves that carry messages to the effectors.

ego In Freud's theory, a set of reactions that try to reconcile the id's blind pleasure strivings with the demands of reality. These lead to the emergence of various skills and capacities that eventually become a system that can look at itself—an "I." *See also* id and superego.

egocentrism In Piaget's theory, a characteristic of preoperational children, an inability to see another person's point of view.

eidetic memory A rather rare kind of memory characterized by relatively long-lasting and detailed images of scenes that can be scanned as if they were physically present.

elaboration-likelihood model of persuasion A theory that asserts that the factors that make for persuasion depend on the extent to which the arguments of the persuasive message are thought about (elaborated). If they are seriously thought about, the central route to persuasion will be used, and attitude change will depend on the nature of the arguments. If they are not seriously considered, the peripheral route to persuasion will be used, and attitude change will depend on more peripheral factors.

Electra complex *See* Oedipus complex.

electroconvulsive shock treatment (ECT) A somatic treatment, mostly used for cases of severe depression, in which a brief electric current is passed through the brain to produce a convulsive seizure.

electroencephalogram (EEG) A record of the summed activity of cortical cells picked up by wires placed on the skull.

embryo The earliest stage in a developing animal. In humans, up to about eight weeks after conception.

empathic concern A feeling of sympathy and concern for the sufferings of another coupled with the desire to relieve this suffering. *See also* vicarious distress.

encoding The form in which some information is stored.

encoding specificity principle The hypothesis that retrieval is most likely if the context at the time of recall approximates that during the original encoding.

endocrine system The system of ductless glands whose secretions are released directly into the bloodstream and affect organs elsewhere in the body (e.g., adrenal gland).

endorphin A drug produced within the brain itself whose effects and chemical composition are similar to such pain-relieving opiates as morphine.

epinephrine (adrenaline) A neurotransmitter released into the bloodstream by the adrenal medulla whose effects are similar to those of sympathetic activation (e.g., racing heart).

episodic memory Memory for particular events in one's own life (e.g., I missed the train this morning). *See also* generic memory.

erogenous zones In psychoanalytic theory, the mouth, anus, and genitals. These regions are particularly sensitive to touch. According to Freud, the various pleasures associated with each of them have a common element, which is sexual.

escape learning Instrumental learning in which reinforcement consists of the reduction or cessation of an aversive stimulus (e.g., electric shock). *See also* punishment training, avoidance learning.

essential hypertension *See* psychophysiological disorders.

estrogen A female sex hormone that dominates the first half of the female cycle through ovulation.

estrus In most mammalian animals, the period in the cycle when the female is sexually receptive (in heat).

ethology A branch of biology that studies the behavior of animals under natural conditions.

existential therapy A humanistic therapy that emphasizes people's free will and tries to help them achieve a personal outlook to give meaning to their lives.

expectancy *See* cognitive theory.

experiment A study in which the investigator manipulates one (or more than one) variable (the independent variable) to determine its effect on the subject's response (the dependent variable).

expert systems Computer problem-solving programs with a very narrow scope that only deal with problems in a limited domain of knowledge (e.g., the diagnosis of infectious diseases).

explicit memory Memory retrieval in which there is awareness of remembering at the time of retrieval. *See also* implicit memory.

expressive movements Movements of the face and body in animals and humans that seem to express emotion. They are usually regarded as built-in social displays.

externality hypothesis The hypothesis that some and perhaps all obese people are relatively unresponsive to their own internal hunger state but are much more susceptible to signals from without.

extinction In classical conditioning, the weakening of the tendency of CS to elicit CR by unreinforced presentations of CS. In instrumental conditioning, a decline in the tendency to perform the instrumental response brought about by unreinforced occurrences of that response.

extroversion-introversion In Eysenck's system, a trait dimension that refers to the main direction of a person's energies; toward the outer world of objects and other people (extroversion) or toward the inner world of one's own thoughts and feelings (introversion).

factor analysis A statistical method for studying the interrelations among various tests, the object of which is to discover what the tests have in common and whether these commonalities can be ascribed to one or several factors that run through all or some of these tests.

false alarm *See* payoff matrix.

familiarity effect The fact that increased exposure to a stimulus tends to make that stimulus more likable.

family resemblance structure Overlap of features among members of a category of meaning such that few if any of the members of the category have all of the features but all members have some of them.

family therapy A general term for a number of therapies that treat the family (or a couple), operating on the assumption that the key to family or marital distress is not necessarily in the pathology of any individual spouse or family member but is rather in the interrelationships within the family or marriage system.

feature detectors Neurons in the retina or brain that respond to specific features of the stimulus such as movement, orientation, and so on.

Fechner's law The assertion that the strength of a sensation is proportional to the logarithm of physical stimulus intensity.

feedback system A system in which some action produces a consequence that affects (feeds back on) the action. In negative feedback, the consequence stops or reverses the action (e.g., thermostat-controlled furnace). In positive feedback, the consequence strengthens the action (e.g., rocket that homes in on airplanes).

fetus A later stage in embryonic development. In humans, from about eight weeks until birth.

figure-ground organization The segregation of the visual field into a part (the figure) that stands out against the rest (the ground).

fixed-action patterns Term used by ethologists to describe stereotyped, species-specific behaviors triggered by genetically programmed releasing stimuli.

flashbulb memories Vivid, detailed, and apparently accurate memories said to be produced by unexpected and emotionally important events.

flooding A form of behavior therapy based on concepts derived from classical conditioning in which the patient exposes himself to whatever he is afraid of, thus extinguishing his fear. *See also* implosion therapy.

fluid intelligence The ability, which is said to decline with age, to deal with essentially new problems. *See also* crystallized intelligence.

forced compliance effect An individual persuaded to act or speak publicly in a manner contrary to his own beliefs may change his own views in the direction of the public action. But this will happen only if his reward for the false public pronouncement is relatively small. If the reward is large, there is no dissonance and hence no attitude change. *See also* cognitive dissonance.

forebrain In mammals, the bulk of the brain. Its foremost region includes the cerebral hemispheres; its rear includes the thalamus and hypothalamus.

forward pairing A classical conditioning procedure in which the conditioned stimulus (CS) precedes the unconditioned stimulus (US). This contrasts with simultaneous pairing, in which CS and US are presented simultaneously, and backward pairing, in which CS follows US. *See also* classical conditioning, conditioned stimulus, unconditioned stimulus.

framing A heuristic that affects the subjective desirability of an event by changing the standard of reference for judging the desirability of that event.

fraternal twins Twins that arise from two different eggs that are (simultaneously) fertilized by different sperm cells. Their genetic similarity is no different than that between ordinary siblings. *See also* identical twins.

free association Method used in psychoanalytic therapy in which the patient is to say anything that comes to her mind, no matter how apparently trivial, unrelated, or embarrassing.

free recall A test of memory that asks for as many items in a list as a subject can recall regardless of order.

frequency distribution An arrangement in which scores are tabulated by the frequency in which they occur.

Freud's theory of dreams A theory that holds that at bottom all dreams are attempts to fulfill a wish. The wish fulfillment is in the latent dream, which represents the sleeper's hidden desires. This latent dream is censored and reinterpreted to avoid anxiety. It reemerges in more acceptable form as the manifest dream, the dream the sleeper remembers upon awakening.

frontal lobe A lobe in each cerebral hemisphere that includes the motor projection area.

function morphemes Consists of all the "little" words and morphemes whose function is grammatical (e.g., *the, and, who, -ed, -s,* etc.). This is in contrast to the content morphemes, which consist of all the nouns, adjectives, verbs, and adverbs of the language and which carry the major meanings in sentences.

functional fixedness A set to think of objects in terms of their normal function.

fundamental attribution error The tendency to attribute behaviors to dispositional qualities while underrating the role of the situation. *See also* actor-observer difference, attribution theory, self-serving bias.

fundamental emotions According to some theorists, a small set of elemental, built-in emotions revealed by distinctive patterns of facial expression. *See also* facial feedback hypothesis.

galvanic skin response (GSR) A drop in the electrical resistance of the skin, widely used as an index of autonomic reaction.

gender constancy The recognition that being male or female is to all intents and purposes irrevocable.

gender identity The inner sense of being male or female. *See also* gender role, sexual orientation.

gender role The set of external behavior patterns a given culture deems appropriate for each sex. *See also* gender identity, sexual orientation.

gene The unit of hereditary transmission, located at a particular place in a given chromosome. Both members of each chromosome pair have corresponding locations at which there are genes that carry instructions about the same characteristic (e.g., eye color). If one member of a gene pair is dominant and the other is recessive, the dominant gene will exert its effect regardless of what the recessive gene calls for. The characteristic called for by the recessive gene will only be expressed if the other member of the gene pair is also recessive. *See also* chromosomes.

general paresis A psychosis characterized by progressive decline in cognitive and motor function culminating in death, reflecting a deteriorating brain condition produced by syphilitic infection.

generalization gradient The curve that shows the relationship between the tendency to respond to a new stimulus and its similarity to the original conditioned stimulus (CS).

generalized anxiety disorder A mental disorder (formerly called anxiety neurosis) whose primary characteristic is an all-pervasive, "free-floating" anxiety. A member of the diagnostic category "anxiety disorders," which also includes phobias and obsessive-compulsive disorders. *See also* phobia, obsessive-compulsive disorders.

generic memory Memory for items of knowledge as such (e.g., The capital of France is Paris), independent of the occasion on which they are learned. *See also* episodic memory.

genital stage In psychoanalytic theory, the stage of psychosexual development reached in adult sexuality in which sexual pleasure involves not only one's own gratification but also the social and bodily satisfaction brought to another person.

genotype The genetic blueprint of an organism which may or may not be overtly expressed by its phenotype. *See also* phenotype.

Gestalt An organized whole such as a visual form or a melody.

Gestalt psychology A theoretical approach that emphasizes the role of organized wholes (Gestalten) in perception and other psychological processes.

glove anesthesia A condition sometimes seen in conversion disorders, in which there is an anesthesia of the entire hand with no loss of feeling above the wrist. This symptom makes no organic sense given the anatomical arrangement of the nerve trunks and indicates that the condition has a psychological basis.

glucose A form of sugar that is the major source of energy for most bodily tissues. If plentiful, much of it is converted into glycogen and stored away.

glycogen A stored form of metabolic energy derived from glucose. To be used, it must first be converted back into glucose.

good continuation A factor in visual grouping. Contours tend to be seen in such a way that their direction is altered as little as possible.

gradient of reinforcement The curve that describes the declining effectiveness of reinforcement, with increasing delay between the response and the reinforcer.

group-factor theory of intelligence A factor-analytic approach to intelligence test performance which argues that intelligence is the composite of separate abilities (group factors such as verbal ability, spatial ability, etc.) without a sovereign capacity that enters into each. *See also* factor analysis, Spearman's theory of general intelligence.

group therapy Psychotherapy of several persons at one time.

habituation A decline in the tendency to respond to stimuli that have become familiar. While short-term habituation dissipates in a matter of minutes, long-term habituation may persist for days or weeks.

habituation procedure A widely used method for studying infant perception. After some exposure to a visual stimulus, an infant becomes habituated and stops looking at it. The extent to which a new stimulus leads to renewed interest and resumption of looking is taken as a measure of the extent to which the infant regards this new stimulus as different from the old one to which she became habituated.

hallucination Perceived experiences that occur in the absence of actual sensory stimulation.

hermaphrodite A person whose reproductive organs are anatomically ambiguous so that they are not exclusively male or female.

heterosexuality A sexual orientation leading to a choice of sexual partners of the opposite sex.

heuristics In both human and computer problem solving, a procedure that has often worked in the past and is likely, but not certain, to work again. *See also* algorithm.

hierarchical organization Organization in which narrower categories are subsumed under broader ones, which are subsumed under still broader ones, and so on. Often expressed in the form of a tree diagram.

hierarchy of needs According to Maslow, human needs are arranged in a hierarchy with physiological needs such as hunger at the bottom, safety needs further up, the need for attachment and love still higher, and the desire for esteem yet higher. At the very top of the hierarchy is the striving for self-actualization. By and large, people will only strive for the higher-order needs when the lower ones are fulfilled. *See* self-actualization.

higher-order conditioning In classical conditioning, a procedure by which a new stimulus comes to elicit the conditioned response (CR) by virtue of being paired with an effective conditioned stimulus (CS) (e.g., first pairings of tone and food, then pairings of bell and tone, until finally the bell elicits salivation by itself).

hindbrain The most primitive portion of the brain, which includes the medulla and the cerebellum.

hippocampus A structure in the temporal lobe that constitutes an important part of the limbic system. One of its functions seems to involve memory.

histogram A graphic rendering of a frequency distribution that depicts the distribution by a series of contiguous rectangles. *See also* frequency distribution.

homeostasis The body's tendency to maintain the conditions of its internal environment by various forms of self-regulation.

homogamy The tendency of like to marry like.

homosexuality A sexual orientation leading to a choice of partners of the same sex.

hue A perceived dimension of visual stimuli whose meaning is close to the term *color* (e.g., red, blue).

humanistic approach to personality Asserts that what is most important about people is how they achieve their selfhood and actualize their potentialities. *See also* behavioral-cognitive approach, psychodynamic approach, trait theory.

humanistic therapies Methods of treatment that emphasize personal growth and self-fulfillment. They try to be relatively nondirective since their emphasis is on helping the clients achieve the capacity for making their own choices. *See also* nondirective techniques.

hyperphagia Voracious, chronic overeating brought about by lesion of the ventromedial region of the hypothalamus.

hyperpolarization A rise of the membrane potential of a neuron from its resting potential. The basis of neural inhibition. *See also* depolarization.

hypnosis A temporary, trancelike state that can be induced in normal persons. During hypnosis, various hypnotic or posthypnotic suggestions sometimes produce effects that resemble some of the symptoms of conversion disorders. *See also* conversion disorders.

hypothalamus A small structure at the base of the brain that plays a vital role in the control of the autonomic nervous system, of the endocrine system, and of the major biological drives.

hysteria An older term for a group of presumably psychogenic disorders that included conversion disorders and dissociative disorders. Since DSM-III, it is no longer used as a diagnostic category, in part because of an erroneous implication that the condition is more prevalent in women (Greek *hystera*—womb). *See also* conversion disorders, dissociative disorders, glove anesthesia.

id In Freud's theory, a term for the most primitive reactions of human personality, consisting of blind strivings for immediate biological satisfaction regardless of cost. *See also* ego and superego.

ideas of reference A characteristic of some mental disorders, notably schizophrenia, in which the patient begins to think that external events are specially related to him personally (e.g., "People walk by and follow me").

identical twins Twins that originate from a single fertilized egg that then splits into two exact replicas that develop into two genetically identical individuals. *See also* fraternal twins.

identification In psychoanalytic theory, a mechanism whereby a child models himself or herself (typically) on the same-sex parent in an effort to become like him or her.

ill-defined problems *See* well-defined problems.

imipramine *See* antidepressant drugs.

implicit memory Memory retrieval in which there is no awareness of remembering at the time of retrieval. *See also* explicit memory.

implicit theories of personality Beliefs about the way in which different patterns of behavior of people hang together and why they do so.

implosion therapy A form of behavior therapy related to flooding in which the patient exposes herself to whatever she is afraid of in its most extreme form, but does so in imagination rather than in real life (e.g., a person afraid of dogs has to imagine herself surrounded by a dozen snarling Dobermans). *See* flooding.

imprinting A learned attachment that is formed at a particular period in life (the critical period) and is difficult to reverse (e.g., the duckling's acquired tendency to follow whatever moving stimulus it encounters twelve to twenty-four hours after hatching).

incidental learning Learning without trying to learn (e.g, as in a study in which subjects judge a speaker's vocal quality when she recites a list of words and are later asked to produce as many of the words as they can recall). *See also* intentional learning.

independent variable *See* experiment.

induced movement Perceived movement of an objectively stationary stimulus that is enclosed by a moving framework.

inductive reasoning Reasoning in which one observes a number of particular instances and tries to determine a general rule that covers them all.

information processing A general term for the presumed operations whereby the crude raw materials provided by the senses are refashioned into items of knowledge. Among these operations are perceptual organization, comparison with items stored in memory, and so on.

insightful learning Learning by understanding the relations between components of the problem; often contrasted with "blind trial and error" and documented by wide and appropriate transfer if tested in a new situation.

instrumental conditioning Also called operant conditioning. A form of learning in which a reinforcer (e.g., food) is given only if the animal performs the instrumental response (e.g., pressing a lever). In effect, what has to be learned is the relationship between the response and the reinforcer. *See* classical conditioning.

insulin A hormone with a crucial role in utilization of nutrients. One of its functions is to help promote the conversion of glucose into glycogen.

Intelligence Quotient (IQ) A ratio measure to indicate whether a child's mental age (MA) is ahead or behind her chronological age (CA); specifically IQ = 100 × MA/CA. *See also* deviation IQ, mental age.

intentional learning Learning when informed that there will be a later test of learning. *See also* incidental learning.

interference theory of forgetting The assertion that items are forgotten because they are somehow interfered with by other items learned before or after.

internalization The process whereby moral codes are adopted by the child so that they control his behavior even where there are no external rewards or punishments.

interneurons Neurons that receive impulses and transmit them to other neurons.

interval scale A scale in which equal differences between scores can be treated as equal so that the scores can be added or subtracted. *See also* categorical scale, ordinal scale, ratio scale.

introversion *See* extroversion-introversion.

invariant Some aspect of the proximal stimulus pattern that remains unchanged despite various transformations of the stimulus.

isolation A mechanism of defense in which anxiety arousing memories are retained but without the emotion that accompanied them.

James-Lange theory of emotions A theory that asserts that the subjective experience of emotion is the awareness of one's own bodily reactions in the presence of certain arousing stimuli.

just noticeable difference (j.n.d.) *See* difference threshold.

kin-selection hypothesis *See* altruism.

kinesthesis A general term for sensory information generated by receptors in the muscles, tendons, and joints which informs us of our skeletal movement.

Korsakoff syndrome A brain disorder characterized by serious memory disturbances. The most common cause is extreme and chronic alcohol use.

labeling theory of mental disorders The assertion that the label "mental illness" acts as a self-fulfilling prophecy that perpetuates the condition once the label has been applied. In its extreme form, it asserts that the concept is a myth, mental illness being merely the term by which we designate social deviance that does not fall into other, recognized categories of deviance.

latency General term for the interval before some reaction occurs.

latency period In psychoanalytic theory, a stage in psychosexual development in which sexuality lies essentially dormant, roughly from ages five to twelve.

latent dream *See* Freud's theory of dreams.

latent learning Learning that occurs without being manifested by performance.

lateral hypothalamus A region of the hypothalamus which is said to be a "hunger center" and to be in an antagonistic relation to a supposed "satiety center," the ventromedial region of the hypothalamus.

lateral inhibition The tendency of adjacent neural elements of the visual system to inhibit each other; it underlies brightness contrast and the accentuation of contours. *See also* brightness contrast.

lateralization An asymmetry of function of the two cerebral hemispheres. In most right-handers, the left hemisphere is specialized for language functions, while the right hemisphere is better at various visual and spatial tasks.

law of effect A theory that asserts that the tendency of a stimulus to evoke a response is strengthened if the response is followed by reward and is weakened if the response is not followed by reward. Applied to instrumental learning, this theory states that as trials proceed, incorrect bonds will weaken while the correct bond will be strengthened.

learned helplessness A condition created by exposure to inescapable aversive events. This retards or prevents learning in subsequent situations in which escape or avoidance is possible.

learned helplessness theory of depression The theory that depression is analogous to learned helplessness effects produced in the laboratory by exposing subjects to uncontrollable aversive events.

learning curve A curve in which some index of learning (e.g., the number of drops of saliva in Pavlov's classical conditioning experiment) is plotted against trials or sessions.

learning model As defined in the text, a subcategory of the pathology model that (1) views mental disorders as the result of some form of faulty learning and (2) believes that these should be treated by behavior therapists according to the laws of classical and instrumental conditioning or by cognitive therapists who try to affect faulty modes of thinking. *See also* behavior therapy, cognitive therapy, medical model, pathology model, psychoanalytic model.

learning set The increased ability to solve various problems, especially in discrimination learning, as a result of previous experience with problems of a similar kind.

lexical access The process of recognizing and understanding a word, which is presumably achieved by making contact (accessing) with the word in the mental lexicon.

lightness constancy The tendency to perceive the lightness of an object as more or less the same despite the fact that the light reflected from these objects changes with the illumination that falls upon them.

limbic system A set of brain structures including a relatively primitive portion of the cerebral cortex and parts of the thalamus and hypothalamus; it is believed to be involved in the control of emotional behavior and motivation.

line of best fit A line drawn through the points in a scatter diagram; it yields the best prediction of one variable when given the value of the other variable.

lithium carbonate A drug used in the treatment of mania and bipolar disorders.

lobotomy *See* prefrontal lobotomy.

long-term habituation *See* habituation.

long-term memory Sometimes called passive memory. Those parts of the memory system that are currently dormant and inactive, but

have enormous storage capacity. According to the stage theory of memory, information can only enter into the long-term store if it first passes through short-term memory and remains in it for some period of time. *See also* short-term memory, stage theory of memory.

longitudinal study A developmental study in which the same person is tested at various ages.

mania Hyperactive state with marked impairment of judgment, usually accompanied by intense euphoria.

manifest dream *See* Freud's theory of dreams.

marital therapy *See* family therapy.

matching hypothesis The hypothesis that persons of a given level of physical attractiveness will seek out partners of a roughly similar level.

matching to sample A procedure in which an organism has to choose one of two alternative stimuli that is the same as a third sample stimulus.

maturation A programmed growth process based on changes in underlying neural structures that are relatively unaffected by environmental conditions (e.g., flying in sparrows and walking in humans).

mean (M) The most commonly used measure of the central tendency of a frequency distribution. It is the arithmetical average of all the scores. If M is the mean and N the number of cases, then $M = $ sum of the scores/N. *See also* central tendency, median.

medial forebrain bundle (MFB) A bundle of fibers that runs through the base of the forebrain and parts of the hypothalamus. Electric stimulation of this bundle is usually rewarding.

median A measure of the central tendency of a frequency distribution. It is the point that divides the distribution into two equal halves when the scores are arranged in ascending order. *See also* central tendency and mean.

medical model As defined in the text, a subcategory of the pathology model that (1) holds that the underlying pathology is organic and that (2) the treatment should be conducted by physicians. *See also* learning model, pathology model, psychoanalytic model.

medulla The rearmost portion of the brain, just adjacent to the spinal cord. It includes centers that help to control respiration and muscle tone.

memory span The number of items a person can recall after just one presentation.

memory trace The change in the nervous system left by an experience that is the physical basis of its retention in memory. What this change is, is still unknown.

mental age (MA) A score devised by Binet to represent a child's test performance. It indicates the chronological age at which 50 percent of the children in that age group will perform. If the child's MA is greater than his chronological age (CA), he is ahead of his age mentally; if his MA is lower than his CA, he lags behind.

mental retardation Usually defined as an IQ of about 70 and below.

mental set The predisposition to perceive (or remember or think of) one thing rather than another.

meta-analysis A statistical technique by means of which the results of many different techniques can be combined. Has been useful in studies on the outcome of psychotherapy.

metacognition A general term for knowledge about knowledge, as in knowing that we do or don't remember something.

midbrain Part of the brain which includes some lower centers for sensory-motor integration (e.g., eye movements) and part of the reticular formation.

middle ear An antechamber to the inner ear which amplifies sound-produced vibrations of the eardrum and imparts them to the cochlea. *See also* cochlea.

Minnesota Multiphasic Personality Inventory (MMPI) *See* criterion groups.

mnemonics Deliberate devices for helping memory. Many of them utilize imagery such as the method of pegs and method of loci.

monoamine oxidase (MAO) inhibitors *See* antidepressant drugs.

monocular depth cues Various features of the visual stimulus that indicate depth, even when viewed with one eye (e.g., linear perspective and motion parallax).

mood disorders A group of disorders (formerly called affective disorders) whose primary characteristic is a disturbance of mood and that is characterized by two emotional extremes—the energy of mania, or the despair or lethargy of depression, or both. *See also* bipolar disorder, depression, mania, unipolar disorder.

morpheme The smallest significant unit of meaning in a language (e.g., the word *boys* has two morphemes, *boy* and *s*).

Motherese A whimsical term for the speech pattern that mothers and other adults generally employ when talking to infants.

motor projection areas *See* projection areas.

nalaxone A drug that inhibits the effect of morphine and similar opiates and blocks the pain alleviation ascribed to endorphins.

nativism The view that some important aspects of perception and of other cognitive processes are innate.

natural selection The explanatory principle that underlies Darwin's theory of evolution. Some organisms produce offspring that are able to survive and reproduce while other organisms of the same species do not. Thus organisms with these hereditary attributes will eventually outnumber organisms who lack these attributes.

negative feedback *See* feedback system.

negative symptoms of schizophrenia Symptoms that involve a lack of normal functioning, such as apathy, poverty of speech, and emotional blunting. *See* positive symptoms of schizophrenia.

neo-Freudians A group of theorists who accept the psychoanalytic conception of unconscious conflict but who differ with Freud in (1) describing these conflicts in social terms rather than in terms of particular bodily pleasures or frustrations, and (2) maintaining that many of these conflicts arise from the specific cultural conditions under which the child was reared rather than being biologically preordained.

nerve impulse *See* action potential.

network models Theories of cognitive organization, especially of semantic memory, that assert that items of information are represented by a system of nodes linked through associative connections. *See also* node.

neuron A nerve cell.

neurosis In psychoanalytic theory, a broad term for mental disorders whose primary symptoms are anxiety or what seem to be defenses against anxiety. Since the adoption of DSM-III, the term has been dropped as the broad diagnostic label it once was. Various disorders that were once diagnosed as subcategories of neurosis (e.g., phobia, conversion disorders, dissociative disorders) are now classified as separate disorders.

neuroticism A trait dimension that refers to emotional instability and maladjustment.

neurotransmitters Chemicals liberated at the terminal end of an axon which travel across the synapse and have an excitatory or inhibitory effect on an adjacent neuron (e.g., norepinephrine).

node A point in a network on which a number of connections converge.

nondirective techniques A set of techniques for psychological treatment developed by Carl Rogers. As far as possible, the counselor refrains from offering advice or interpretation but only tries to clarify the patient's own feelings by echoing him or restating what he says.

nonsense syllable Two consonants with a vowel between that do not form a word. Used to study associations between relatively meaningless items.

norepinephrine (NE) The neurotransmitter by means of which the sympathetic fibers exert their effect on internal organs. It is also the neurotransmitter of various arousing systems in the brain.

normal curve A symmetrical, bell-shaped curve that describes the probability of obtaining various combinations of chance events. It describes the frequency distributions of many physical and psychological attributes of humans and animals.

normal distribution A frequency distribution whose graphic representation has a symmetric, bell-shaped form—the normal curve. Its characteristics are often referred to when investigators test statistical hypotheses and make inferences about the population from a given sample.

null hypothesis The hypothesis that an obtained difference is merely a chance fluctuation from a population in which the true mean difference is zero. *See also* alternative hypothesis.

obesity A condition of marked overweight in animals and humans; it is produced by a large variety of factors including metabolic factors (oversecretion of insulin) and behavioral conditions (overeating, perhaps produced by nonresponsiveness to one's own internal state).

object permanence The conviction that an object remains perceptually constant over time and exists even when it is out of sight. According to Piaget, this does not develop until infants are age eight months or more.

observational study A study in which the investigator does not manipulate any of the variables but simply observes their relationship as they occur naturally.

obsessions *See* obsessive-compulsive disorders.

obsessive-compulsive disorders A disorder whose symptoms are obsessions (persistent and irrational thoughts or wishes) and compulsions (uncontrollable, repetitive acts), which seem to be defenses against anxiety. A member of a diagnostic category called anxiety disorders, which also includes generalized anxiety disorder and phobias. *See also* generalized anxiety disorder, phobia.

occipital lobe A lobe in each cerebral hemisphere that includes the visual projection area.

Oedipus complex In psychoanalytic theory, a general term for a whole cluster of impulses and conflicts that occur during the phallic phase, at around age five. In boys, a fantasied form of intense sexual love is directed at the mother, which is soon followed by hate and fear of the father. As the fear mounts, the sexual feelings are pushed underground and the boy identifies with the father. An equivalent process in girls is called the Electra complex.

operant conditioning *See* instrumental conditioning.

operant In Skinner's system, an instrumental response. *See also* instrumental conditioning.

opponent-process theory of color vision A theory of color vision that asserts that there are three pairs of color antagonists: red-green, blue-yellow, and white-black. Excitation of one member of a pair automatically inhibits the other member.

opponent-process theory of motivation A theory that asserts that the nervous system has the general tendency to counteract any deviation from the neutral point of the pain-pleasure dimension. If the original stimulus is maintained, there is an attenuation of the emotional state one is in; if it is withdrawn, the opponent process reveals itself, and the emotional state swings sharply in the opposite direction.

oral stage In psychoanalytic theory, the earliest stage of psychosexual development during which the primary source of bodily pleasure is stimulation of the mouth and lips, as in sucking at the breast.

ordinal scale A scale in which responses are rank-ordered by relative magnitude but in which the intervals between successive ranks are not necessarily equal. *See also* categorical scale, interval scale, ratio scale.

orienting response In classical conditioning, an animal's initial reaction to a new stimulus (e.g., turning toward it and looking attentive).

paired-associate method A procedure in which subjects learn to provide particular response terms to various stimulus items.

panic disorder A disorder characterized by sudden anxiety attacks in which there are bodily symptoms such as choking, dizziness, trembling, and chest pains, accompanied by feelings of intense apprehension, terror, and a sense of impending doom.

parallel search The simultaneous comparison of a target stimulus to several items in memory. *See also* serial search.

paranoid schizophrenia A subcategory of schizophrenia. Its dominant symptom is a set of delusions, which are often elaborately systematized, usually of grandeur or persecution.

parasympathetic system A division of the autonomic nervous system which serves vegetative functions and conserves bodily energies (e.g., slowing heart rate). Its action is antagonistic to that of the sympathetic system.

parietal lobe A lobe in each cerebral hemisphere that includes the somatosensory projection area.

partial reinforcement A condition in which a response is reinforced only some of the time.

partial-reinforcement effect The fact that a response is much harder to extinguish if it was acquired during partial rather than continuous reinforcement.

passive memory *See* long-term memory.

pathology model A term adopted in the text to describe a general conception of mental disorders which holds that (1) one can generally distinguish between symptoms and underlying causes, and (2) these causes may be regarded as a form of pathology. *See also* learning model, medical model, psychoanalytic model.

pattern recognition The process by which the perceptual system matches the form of a figure against a figure stored in memory.

payoff matrix In a detection experiment, a table that shows the costs and benefits for each of the four possible outcomes: a hit, reporting the stimulus when it is present; a correct negative, reporting it as absent when it is in fact absent; a miss, failing to report it when it is present; and a false alarm, reporting it as present when it is not.

peak experience Profound and deeply felt moments in a person's life, sometimes said to be more common in self-actualized persons than in others. *See* self-actualization.

percentile rank The percentage of all the scores in a distribution that lie below a given score.

perceptual adaptation The gradual adjustment to various distortions of the perceptual world, as in wearing prisms that tilt the entire visual world in one direction.

perceptual defense The tendency to perceive anxiety-related stimuli less readily than neutral stimuli.

perceptual differentiation Learning to perceive features of stimulus patterns that were not perceptible at first. A phenomenon central to the theory of perceptual learning proposed by J. J. Gibson and E. J. Gibson.

perceptual parsing The process of grouping the various visual elements of a scene appropriately, deciding which elements go together and which do not.

period of formal operations In Piaget's theory, the period from about age eleven on, when genuinely abstract mental operations can be undertaken (e.g., the ability to entertain hypothetical possibilities).

peripheral route to persuasion *See* elaboration-likelihood model of persuasion.

person-by-situation interaction The fact that the effect of a situational variable may depend on the person. Thus some people may on average be equally fearful, but while one is afraid of meeting people but unafraid of large animals, another may be afraid of large animals but be unafraid of meeting people. *See also* situationism.

personality inventories Paper-and-pencil tests of personality that ask questions about feelings or customary behavior. *See also* projective techniques.

PET scan (Positron Emission Tomography) A technique for examining brain structure and function in intact humans by recording the degree of metabolic activity of different regions of the brain.

phallic stage In psychoanalytic theory, the stage of psychosexual development during which the child begins to regard his or her genitals as a major source of gratification.

phenothiazines A group of drugs, including chlorpromazine, that seem to be effective in alleviating the major symptoms of schizophrenia.

phenotype The overt appearance and behavior of an organism, regardless of its genetic blueprint. *See also* genotype.

phenylketonuria (PKU) A severe form of mental retardation determined by a single gene. This disorder can be treated by means of a special diet (if detected early enough), despite the fact that the disorder is genetic.

pheromones Special chemicals secreted by many animals, which trigger particular reactions in members of the same species.

phobia One of a group of mental disorders called anxiety disorders that is characterized by an intense and, at least on the surface, irrational fear. *See also* generalized anxiety disorder, obsessive-compulsive disorders.

phoneme The smallest significant unit of sound in a language. In English, it corresponds roughly to a letter of the alphabet (e.g., *apt, tap,* and *pat* are all made up of the same phonemes).

phonology The rules in a language that govern the sequence in which phonemes can be arranged.

phrase A sequence of words within a sentence that function as a unit (e.g., *The ball/rolled/down the hill*).

phrase structure The organization of sentences into phrases. Underlying structure is the phrase organization that describes the meaning of parts of the sentence, such as doer, action, and done-to.

pituitary gland An endocrine gland heavily influenced by the hypothalamus. A master gland because many of its secretions trigger hormone secretions in other glands.

placebo In medical practice, a term for a chemically inert substance that the patient believes will help him.

placebo effect A beneficial effect of a treatment administered to a patient who believes it has therapeutic powers even though it has none.

pluralistic ignorance A situation in which individuals in a group don't know that there are others in the group who share their feelings.

polyandry A mating system in which one female monopolizes the reproductive efforts of several males.

polygenic inheritance Inheritance of an attribute whose expression is controlled not by one but by many gene pairs.

polygyny A mating system in which one male monopolizes the reproductive efforts of several females.

population The entire group of subjects (or test trials) about which the investigator wants to draw conclusions. *See also* sample.

positive feedback *See* feedback system.

positive symptoms of schizophrenia Symptoms that center on what these patients do (or think or perceive) that normals don't, for example, hallucinations, delusions, and bizarre behaviors. *See* negative symptoms of schizophrenia.

predicate *See* concept.

predictive validity A measure of a test's validity based on the correlation between the test score and some criterion of behavior the test predicted (e.g., a correlation between a scholastic aptitude test and college grades).

prefrontal lobotomy A somatic treatment for severe mental disorders which surgically cuts the connections between the thalamus and the frontal lobes.

preoperational period In Piaget's theory, the period from about ages two to six during which children come to represent actions and objects internally but cannot systematically manipulate these representations or relate them to each other; the child is therefore unable to conserve quantity across perceptual transformations and also is unable to take points of view other than her own.

prescriptive rules Rules prescribed by "authorities" about how people *ought* to speak and write that often fail to conform to the facts about natural talking and understanding. This is in contrast to the structural principles of a language that describe (rather than prescribe) the principles according to which native speakers of a language actually arrange their words into sentences. Sentences formed according to these principles are called well-formed or grammatical.

prestige suggestion Approving some statement because a high-prestige person has approved it.

primacy effect In free recall, the superiority of the items in the first part of a list compared to those in the middle.

prisoner's dilemma A particular arrangement of payoffs in a two-person situation in which each individual has to choose between two alternatives without knowing the other's choice. The payoff structure is so arranged that the optimal strategy for each person depends upon whether he can trust the other or not. If trust is possible, the payoffs for each will be considerably higher than if there is no trust.

proactive inhibition Disturbance of recall of some material by other material learned previously. *See* retroactive inhibition.

procedural knowledge *See* declarative knowledge.

progesterone A female sex hormone that dominates the latter phase of the female cycle during which the uterus walls thicken to receive the embryo.

projection In psychoanalytic theory, a mechanism of defense in which various forbidden thoughts and impulses are attributed to another person rather than the self, thus warding off some anxiety (e.g., "I hate you" becomes "You hate me").

projection areas Regions of the cortex that serve as receiving stations for sensory information or as dispatching stations for motor commands.

projective techniques Devices for assessing personality by presenting relatively unstructured stimuli that elicit subjective responses of various kinds. Their advocates believe that such tasks allow the person to "project" her own personality into her reactions (e.g., the TAT and the Rorschach inkblot test). *See also* personality inventories.

proposition *See* concept.

prosopagnosia The inability to recognize faces produced by a brain lesion.

prototype The typical example of a category of meaning (e.g., robin is a prototypical bird).

proximal stimulus *See* distal stimulus.

psychoanalysis (1) A theory of human personality formulated by Freud whose key assertions include unconscious conflict and psychosexual development. (2) A method of therapy that draws heavily on this theory of personality. Its main aim is to have the patient gain insight into his own, presently unconscious, thoughts and feelings. Therapeutic tools employed toward this end include free association, interpretation, and the appropriate use of the transference relationship between patient and analyst. *See also* free association, transference.

psychoanalytic model As defined in the text, a subcategory of the pathology model which holds that (1) the underlying pathology is a constellation of unconscious conflicts and defenses against anxiety, usually rooted in early childhood and (2) treatment should be by some form of psychotherapy based on psychoanalytic principles.

psychodynamic approach of personality An approach to personality originally derived from psychoanalytic theory that asserts that personality differences are based on unconscious (dynamic) conflicts within the individual.

psychogenic disorders Disorders whose origins are psychological rather than organic (e.g., phobias). *See also* somatogenic mental disorders.

psychometric approach to intelligence An attempt to understand the nature of intelligence by studying the pattern of results obtained on intelligence tests.

psychopath *See* antisocial personality.

psychopathology The study of psychological disorders.

psychophysics The field that tries to relate the characteristics of physical stimuli to the sensory experience they produce.

psychophysiological disorders In these disorders (formerly called psychosomatic), the primary symptoms involve genuine organic damage whose ultimate cause is psychological (e.g., essential hypertension, a condition of chronic high blood pressure brought about by the bodily concomitant of chronic emotional stress).

psychosexual development In psychoanalytic theory, the description of the progressive stages in the way the child gains his main source of pleasure as he grows into adulthood, defined by the zone of the body through which this pleasure is derived (oral, anal, genital) and by the object toward which this pleasurable feeling is directed (mother, father, adult sexual partner). *See also* anal stage, genital stage, oral stage, phallic stage.

psychosis A broad category that describes some of the more severe mental disorders in which the patient's thoughts and deeds no longer meet the demands of reality.

psychosocial crises In Erik Erikson's theory, a series of crises through which all persons must pass as they go through their life cycle (e.g., the identity crisis during which adolescents or young adults try to establish the separation between themselves and their parents).

psychotherapy As used here, a collective term for all forms of treatment that use psychological rather than somatic means.

punishment training An instrumental training procedure in which a response is suppressed by having its occurrence followed by an aversive event. *See also* avoidance learning, escape learning.

quiet sleep Stages 2 to 4 of sleep during which there are no rapid eye movements and during which the EEG shows progressively less cortical arousal. Also known as non-REM sleep.

random sample *See* sample.

ratio scale An interval scale in which there is a true zero point, thus allowing ratio statements (e.g., this sound is twice as loud as the other). *See also* categorical scale, interval scale, ordinal scale.

ratio schedule A schedule of reinforcement in which reinforcement is delivered after a certain number of responses. In a fixed-ratio schedule, the subject has to produce a specified number of responses for every reinforcement; in a variable-ratio schedule this number varies irregularly.

rationalization In psychoanalytic theory, a mechanism of defense by means of which unacceptable thoughts or impulses are reinterpreted in more acceptable and thus less anxiety-arousing terms (e.g., the jilted lover who convinces himself he never loved her anyway).

reaction formation In psychoanalytic theory, a mechanism of defense in which a forbidden impulse is turned into its opposite (e.g., hate toward a sibling becomes exaggerated love).

reaction time The interval between the presentation of a signal and the observer's response to that signal.

recall A task in which some item must be produced from memory. *See* recognition.

recency effect In free recall, the recall superiority of the items at the end of the list compared to those in the middle. *See* primacy effect (in recall).

receptive field The retinal area in which visual stimulation affects a particular cell's firing rate.

receptors A specialized cell that can respond to various physical stimuli and transduce them.

recessive gene *See* gene.

reciprocal altruism *See* altruism.

reciprocal inhibition The arrangement by which excitation of some neural system is accompanied by inhibition of that system's antagonist (as in antagonistic muscles).

reciprocity principle A basic rule of many social interactions that decrees that one must repay whatever one has been given.

recoding Changing the form in which some information is stored.

recognition A task in which a stimulus has to be identified as having been previously encountered in some context or not. *See also* recall.

reference The relations between words or sentences and objects or events in the world (e.g., "ball" refers to ball).

reflex A simple, stereotyped reaction in response to some stimulus (e.g., limb flexion in withdrawal from pain).

reinforced trial In classical conditioning, a trial on which the CS is accompanied by the US. In instrumental conditioning, a trial in which the instrumental response is followed by reward, cessation of punishment, or other reinforcement.

reinforcement In classical conditioning, the procedure by which the US is made contingent on the CS. In instrumental conditioning, the procedure by which some sought-after outcome is made contingent upon some instrumental response.

releasing stimulus Term used by ethologists to describe a stimulus which is genetically programmed to elicit a fixed-action pattern (e.g., a long, thin, red-tipped beak which elicits a herring gull chick's begging response). *See also* fixed-action patterns.

reliability The consistency with which a test measures what it measures, as assessed, for example, by the test-retest method.

REM sleep *See* active sleep.

repetition priming An increase in the likelihood that a word is identified, recognized, or recalled by recent exposure to that item, which may occur without explicit awareness.

representational thought In Piaget's theory, thought that is internalized and includes mental representations of prior experiences with objects and events.

representativeness heuristic A rule of thumb in estimating the probability that an object (or event) belongs to a certain category based on the extent to which it resembles the prototype of that category regardless of the base rate at which it occurs. *See also* prototype.

repression In psychoanalytic theory, a mechanism of defense by means of which thoughts, impulses, or memories that give rise to anxiety are pushed out of consciousness.

resistance In psychoanalysis, a collective term for the patient's failures to associate freely and say whatever enters his head.

response bias A preference for one or another response in a psychophysical experiment, independent of the stimulus situation.

response suppression The inhibition of a conditioned response by conditioned fear.

restrained-eating hypothesis The hypothesis that the oversensitivity of obese persons to external cues is caused by the disinhibition of conscious restraints on eating. *See also* externality hypothesis, setpoint hypothesis.

restructuring A reorganization of a problem, often rather sudden, which seems to be a characteristic of creative thought.

retention The survival of the memory trace over some interval of time.

reticular activating system (RAS) A system that includes the upper portion of the reticular formation and its ascending branches to much of the brain. Its effect is to arouse the brain.

reticular formation A network of neurons extending throughout the midbrain with ramifications to higher parts of the brain. This plays an important role in sleep and arousal.

retina The structure that contains the visual receptors and several layers of neurons further up along the pathway to the brain.

retinal image The image of an object that is projected on the retina. Its size increases with the size of that object and decreases with its distance from the eye.

retrieval The process of searching for some item in memory and of finding it. If retrieval fails, this may or may not mean that the relevant memory trace is not present; it simply may be inaccessible.

retrieval cue A stimulus that helps to retrieve a memory trace.

retroactive inhibition Disturbance of recall of some material by other material learned subsequently. *See also* proactive inhibition.

retrograde amnesia A memory deficit suffered after head injury or concussion in which the patient loses memory of some period prior to the injury. *See also* anterograde amnesia.

reuptake A mechanism by which a neurotransmitter is drawn back into the presynaptic terminal that released it.

rods Visual receptors that respond to relatively lower light intensities and give rise to achromatic (colorless) sensations. *See also* cones.

Rorschach inkblot test A projective technique that requires the person to look at inkblots and say what she sees in them.

safety signal A stimulus that signals the absence of an electric shock (or another negative reinforcer) in a situation in which such shocks are sometimes delivered. *See also* contingency.

sample A subset of a population selected by the investigator for study. A random sample is one so constructed that each member of the population has an equal chance to be picked. A stratified sample is one so constructed that every relevant subgroup of the population is randomly sampled in proportion to its size. *See also* population.

saturation A perceived dimension of visual stimuli that describes the "purity" of a color—the extent to which it is rich in hue (e.g., green rather than olive).

scaling A procedure for assigning numbers to a subject's responses. *See also* categorical scale, interval scale, ordinal scale, ratio scale.

schedule of reinforcement A rule that determines the occasions when a response is reinforced. Examples are ratio and interval schedules.

schema (1) In theories of memory and thinking, a term that refers to a general cognitive structure in terms of which information can be organized. (2) In Piaget's theory of development, a mental pattern.

schizophrenia A group of severe mental disorders characterized by at least some of the following: marked disturbance of thought, withdrawal, inappropriate or flat emotions, delusions, and hallucinations. *See also* catatonic schizophrenia, paranoid schizophrenia.

score profile *See* test profile.

script A subcase of a schema, which describes a characteristic scenario of behaviors in a particular setting such as a restaurant script. *See also* schema.

seasonal depressive disorder A mood disorder with a seasonal pattern, with depressions that start in the late fall when the days become shorter and end when the days lengthen in the spring.

self-perception theory The assertion that we don't know ourselves directly but rather infer our own states and dispositions by an attribution process analogous to that which we use when we try to explain the behavior of other persons. *See also* attribution theory.

self-actualization A major concern of Maslow and other adherents of the humanistic approach, it is the realization of one's potentialities so that one becomes what one can become. *See also* hierarchy of needs, peak experience.

self-monitoring Monitoring one's own behavior so that it fits the situation.

self-perception theory A theory that asserts that we do not know our own attitudes and feelings directly but must infer them by observing our own behavior and then performing much the same attribution processes that we employ when trying to understand the behavior of others.

self-serving bias The tendency to deny responsibility for failures but take credit for successes. *See also* attribution theory, fundamental attribution error, actor-observer difference.

semantic feature The smallest significant unit of meaning within a word (e.g., male, human, and adult are semantic features of the word "man").

semantic memory The component of generic memory that concerns the meaning of words and concepts.

semantics The organization of meaning in language.

sensation According to the British empiricists, the primitive experiences that the senses give us (e.g., green, bitter).

sensation seeking The tendency to seek novel experiences, look for thrills and adventure, and be highly susceptible to boredom.

sensitive period *See* critical period.

sensory adaptation The decline in sensitivity found in most sensory systems after continuous exposure to the same stimulus.

sensory code The rule (code) by which the nervous system represents sensory characteristics of the stimulus. An example is firing frequency, which is the general code for increased stimulus intensity.

sensory coding The process by which the nervous system translates various aspects of the stimulus into dimensions of our sensory experience.

sensory-motor intelligence In Piaget's theory, intelligence during the first two years of life, which consists mainly of sensations and motor impulses with, at first, little in the way of internalized representations.

sensory projection areas *See* projection areas.

serial search The successive comparison of a target stimulus to different items in memory. *See also* parallel search.

serotonin (5HT) A neurotransmitter involved in many of the mechanisms of sleep and emotional arousal.

set *See* mental set.

setpoint A general term for the level at which negative feedback tries to maintain the system. An example is the setting of a thermostat. *See also* setpoint hypothesis.

setpoint hypothesis The hypothesis that different persons have different setpoints for weight. *See also* setpoint.

sexual orientation The direction of a person's choice of a sexual partner, which may be heterosexual or homosexual. *See also* gender identity, gender role.

sexual dimorphism A condition that describes a species in which there is a marked difference in the size and/or form of the two sexes as in the case of deer (antlers) or peacocks (long tail feathers).

shape constancy The tendency to perceive the shape of objects as more or less the same despite the fact that the retinal image of these objects changes its shape as we change the angle of orientation from which we view them.

shaping An instrumental learning procedure through which an animal (or human) is trained to perform a rather difficult response by reinforcing successive approximations to that response.

short-term memory Also called active memory and working memory. A part of the memory system that is currently activated, but has relatively little cognitive capacity. According to the stage theory of memory, information can only enter into the long-term store if it first passes through short-term memory and remains in it for some period of time. *See also* short-term memory, stage theory of memory.

short-term habituation *See* habituation.

signal-detection theory A theory that provides the conceptual background for separating response bias and sensitivity in a detection experiment. *See also* payoff matrix.

simultaneous pairing A classical conditioning procedure in which the conditioned stimulus (CS) and the unconditioned stimulus (US) are presented simultaneously. *See also* backward pairing, forward pairing.

situational factors *See* attribution theory.

situationism The view that human behavior is largely determined by the characteristics of the situation rather than those of the person. *See also* trait theory.

size constancy The tendency to perceive the size of objects as more or less the same despite the fact that the retinal image of these objects changes in size whenever we change the distance from which we view them.

social comparison A process of reducing uncertainty about one's own beliefs and attitudes by comparing them to those of others.

social exchange theory A theory that asserts that each partner in a social relationship gives something to the other and expects to get something in return.

social facilitation The tendency to perform better in the presence of others than when alone. This facilitating effect works primarily for simple and/or well-practiced tasks.

social learning theory A theoretical approach to socialization and personality that is midway between behavior theories such as Skinner's and cognitive approaches. It stresses learning by observing others who serve as models for the child's behavior. The effect of the model may be to allow learning by imitation and also may be to show the child whether a response he already knows should or should not be performed.

socialization The process whereby the child acquires the patterns of behavior characteristic of her society.

sociobiology A recent theoretical movement in biology that tries to trace social behavior to genetically based predispositions; an approach that has led to some controversy when extended to humans.

sociopath *See* antisocial personality.

somatic therapies A collective term for any treatment of mental disorders by means of some organic manipulation. This includes drug administration, any form of surgery, convulsive treatments, etc.

somatogenic mental disorders Mental disorders that are produced by an organic cause. This is the case for some disorders (e.g., general paresis) but almost surely not for all (e.g., phobias). *See also* psychogenic disorders.

sound waves Successive pressure variations in the air that vary in amplitude and wave length.

Spearman's theory of general intelligence (g) Spearman's account, based on factor analytic studies, ascribes intelligence test performance to one underlying factor, general intelligence *(g)*, which is tapped by all subtests, and a large number of specific skills (*s*'s), which depend on abilities specific to each subtest. *See also* factor analysis, group-factor theory.

split brain A condition in which the corpus callosum and some other fibers are cut so that the two cerebral hemispheres are isolated.

spontaneous recovery An increase in the tendency to perform an extinguished response after a time interval in which neither conditioned stimulus (CS) nor unconditioned stimulus (US) are presented.

spreading activation model A memory model that assumes that elements in a semantic memory network are activated the smaller the distance between them.

stage theory of memory A theoretical approach that asserts that there are several memory stores. One is short-term memory, which holds information for fairly short intervals and has a small capacity; another is long-term memory, which holds information for very long periods and has a vast capacity. According to the theory, information will only enter into long-term memory if it has been in short-term memory for a while. *See also* long-term memory, short-term memory.

standard deviation (SD) A measure of the variability of a frequency distribution, which is the square root of the variance. If V is the variance and SD the standard deviation, then $SD = \sqrt{V}$. *See also* variance.

standard error of the mean A measure of the variability of the mean whose value depends both on the standard deviation *(SD)* of the distribution and the number of cases in the sample *(N)*. If SE is the standard error, then $SE = SD/\sqrt{N-1}$.

standard score (z-score) A score that is expressed as a deviation from the mean in standard deviation units, which allows a comparison of scores drawn from different distributions. If M is the mean and SD the standard deviation, then $z = (\text{score} - M)/SD$.

standardization group The group against which an individual's test score is evaluated.

stimulus Anything in the environment that the organism can detect and respond to.

stimulus generalization In classical conditioning, the tendency to respond to stimuli other than the original conditioned stimulus (CS). The greater the similarity between the CS and the new stimulus, the greater this tendency will be. An analogous phenomenon in instrumental conditioning is a response to stimuli other than the original discriminative stimulus.

Stroop effect A marked decrease in the speed of naming the colors in which various color names (such as green, red, etc.) are printed when the colors and the names are different. An important example of automatization.

structural principles (of language) *See* prescriptive rules.

subtractive color mixture Mixing colors by subtracting one set of wavelengths from another set (as in mixing colors on a palette or superimposing two colored filters). *See also* additive color mixture.

superego In Freud's theory, a set of reaction patterns within the ego that represent the internalized rules of society and that control the ego by punishing with guilt. *See also* ego and id.

surface structure *See* phrase structure.

sympathetic system A division of the autonomic nervous system which mobilizes the body's energies for emergencies (e.g., increasing

heart rate). Its action is antagonistic to that of the parasympathetic system.

symptoms The outward manifestations of an underlying pathology.

synapse The juncture between the axon of one neuron and the dendrite or cell body of another.

syndrome A pattern of symptoms that tend to go together.

systematic desensitization A behavior therapy that tries to remove anxiety connected to various stimuli by a gradual process of counterconditioning to a response incompatible with fear, usually muscular relaxation. The stimuli are usually evoked as mental images according to an anxiety hierarchy whereby the less frightening stimuli are counterconditioned before the more frightening ones.

taste buds The receptor organs for taste.

taxonomy A classification system.

temperament In modern usage, a characteristic level of reactivity and energy, often thought to be based on constitutional factors.

temporal lobe A lobe in each cerebral hemisphere, which includes the auditory projection area.

territory Term used by ethologists to describe a region a particular animal stakes out as its own. The territory holder is usually a male, but in some species the territory is held by a mating pair or by a group.

test profile A graphic indication of an individual's performance on several components of a test. This is often useful for guidance or clinical evaluation because it indicates which abilities or traits are relatively high or low in that person.

testosterone The principal male sex hormone (androgen) in mammals.

texture gradient A distance cue based on changes in surface texture that depend on the distance of the observer.

thalamus A part of the lower portion of the forebrain that serves as a major relay and integration center for sensory information.

Thematic Apperception Test (TAT) A projective technique in which persons are shown a set of pictures and asked to write a story about each.

threshold Some value a stimulus must reach to produce a response.

tip-of-the-tongue phenomenon The condition in which one keeps on feeling on the verge of retrieving a word or name but continues to be unsuccessful even so.

token economy An arrangement for operant behavior modification in hospital settings. Certain responses (e.g., talking to others) are reinforced with tokens which can be exchanged for desirable items.

tolerance *See* opponent-process theory of motivation.

top-down processes Processes in form recognition, which begin with higher units and then work down to smaller units (e.g., from phrases to words to letters). This is in contrast with bottom-up processes, which start with smaller component parts and then gradually build up to the higher units on top (e.g., from letters to words to phrases). One demonstration of top-down processing is provided by context effects in which knowledge or expectations affect what one sees.

trace consolidation hypothesis The hypothesis that newly acquired traces undergo a gradual change that makes them more and more resistant to any disturbance.

trait *See* trait theory.

trait theory The view that people differ in regard to a number of underlying attributes (traits) that partially determine behavior and that are presumed to be essentially consistent from time to time and situation to situation. It tends toward the view that many such traits are based on genetic predispositions. *See also* behavioral-cognitive approach, humanistic approach, psychodynamic approach, situationism.

transduction   The process by which a receptor translates some physical stimulus (e.g., light or pressure) to give rise to an action potential in another neuron.

transfer of training   The effect of having learned one task on learning another. If learning the first task helps in learning the second, the transfer is called positive. If it impedes in learning the second, the transfer is said to be negative.

transference   In psychoanalysis, the patient's tendency to transfer emotional reactions that were originally directed to one's own parents (or other crucial figures in one's early life) and redirect them toward the analyst.

transposition   The phenomenon whereby visual and auditory patterns (i.e., figures and melodies) remain the same even though the parts of which they are composed are changed.

tricyclics   *See* antidepressant drugs.

two-syndrome hypothesis of schizophrenia   The hypothesis that schizophrenia is a composite of two different syndromes, Type I and Type II. According to the hypothesis, Type I is produced by a malfunction of transmitters, especially dopamine, and produces primarily positive symptoms, while Type II is caused by cerebral damage and atrophy and leads to negative symptoms.

Type A personality   A personality type characterized by extreme impatience, competitiveness, and vehement aggressiveness when thwarted. *See also* Type B personality.

Type B personality   In contrast to the Type A personality, characterized by a more easygoing, less hurried, less competitive, and friendlier behavior pattern. *See also* Type A personality.

unconditioned reflex   *See* unconditioned response.

unconditioned response (UR)   In classical conditioning, the response that is elicited by the unconditioned stimulus without prior training. *See* conditioned response, conditioned stimulus, unconditioned stimulus.

unconditioned stimulus (US)   In classical conditioning, the stimulus that elicits the unconditioned response and the presentation of which acts as reinforcement. *See* conditioned response, conditioned stimulus, unconditioned response.

unconscious inference   A process postulated by Helmholtz to explain certain perceptual phenomena such as size constancy. An object is perceived to be in the distance and is therefore unconsciously perceived or inferred to be larger than it appears to be retinally. *See also* size constancy.

unipolar disorder   Mood disorder (usually depression) in which there is no back-and-forth swing between the two emotional extremes.

validity   The extent to which a test measures what it is supposed to measure. *See also* construct validity, incremental validity, predictive validity.

variability   The tendency of scores in a frequency distribution to scatter away from the central value. *See also* central tendency, standard deviation, variance.

variance (V)   A measure of the variability of a frequency distribution. It is computed by finding the difference between each score and the mean, squaring the result, adding all the squared deviations obtained in this manner, and dividing it by the number of cases. If V is the variance, M the mean, and N the number of scores, then $V = \text{sum of } (\text{score} - M)^2 / N$.

vasoconstriction   The constriction of the capillaries brought on by activation of the sympathetic division of the autonomic nervous system in response to excessive cold.

vasodilatation   The dilating of the capillaries brought on by activation of the parasympathetic division of the autonomic nervous system in response to excessive heat.

ventromedial region of the hypothalamus   An area in the hypothalamus that is said to be a "satiety center" and in an antagonistic relation to a supposed "hunger center," the lateral hypothalamus.

vestibular senses   A set of receptors that provide information about the orientation and movements of the head, located in the semicircular canals and the vestibular sacs of the inner ear.

vicarious distress   The distress produced by witnessing the suffering of another. This is a less reliable motive for helping that person than empathic concern. *See also* empathic concern.

vicarious reinforcement   According to social learning theorists, a form of reinforcement said to occur when someone watches a model being rewarded or punished.

visual cliff   A device for assessing depth perception in young organisms; it consists of a glass surface that extends over an apparently deep side (the cliff) and an apparently shallow side.

Weber's law   The observation that the size of the difference threshold is proportional to the intensity of the standard stimulus.

well-defined problems   Problems in which there is a clear-cut way for deciding whether a proposed solution is correct. This is in contrast to ill-defined problems in which it is not clear what a correct solution might be.

Wernicke's area   *See* aphasia.

wish fulfillment in dreams   *See* Freud's theory of dreams.

withdrawal effects   *See* opponent-process theory of motivation.

working memory   *See* short-term memory.

z-score   *See* standard score.

References

ABRAHAM, K. 1927. The influence of oral eroticism on character formation. In Abraham, K., *Selected papers,* pp. 393–406. London: Hogarth Press.

ABRAMS, M. H. 1953. *The mirror and the lamp: Romantic theory and the critical tradition.* New York: Oxford University Press.

ABRAMSON, L. Y.; METALSKY, G. I.; AND ALLOY, L. B. 1989. Hopelessness depression: A theory-based subtype of depression. *Psychological Review* 96:358–72.

ABRAMSON, L. Y.; SELIGMAN, M. E. P.; AND TEASDALE, J. D. 1978. Learned helplessness in humans: Critique and reformulation. *Journal of Abnormal Psychology* 87:49–74.

ABRAMSON, L. Y., AND SACKHEIM, H. A. 1977. A paradox in depression: Uncontrollability and self-blame. *Psychological Bulletin* 84: 835–51.

ADAMSON, E. 1984. *Art as healing.* London: Coventure Ltd.

ADOLPH, E. F. 1947. Urges to eat and drink in rats. *American Journal of Physiology* 151:110–25.

ADORNO, T. W.; FRENKEL-BRUNSWIK, E.; LEVINSON, D. J.; AND SANFORD, R. N. 1950. *The authoritarian personality.* New York: Harper & Row.

AINSWORTH, M. D. S., AND BELL, S. M. 1970. Attachment, exploration, and separation: Illustrated by the behavior of one-year-olds in a strange situation. *Child Development* 41:49–67.

AINSWORTH, M. D. S.; BLEHAR, M. C.; WATERS, E.; AND WALL, S. 1978. *Patterns of attachment.* Hillsdale, N.J.: Erlbaum.

ALBA, J. W., AND HASHER, W. 1983. Is memory schematic? *Psychological Bulletin* 93:203–31.

ALEXANDER, B. K., AND HADAWAY, B. F. 1982. Opiate addiction: The case for an adaptive orientation. *Psychological Bulletin* 92:367–81.

ALLARD, F.; GRAHAM, S.; AND PAARSALU, M. E. 1980. Perception in sport: Basketball. *Journal of Sport Psychology* 2:14–21.

ALLEN, M. 1976. Twin studies of affective illness. *Archives of General Psychiatry* 33:1476–78.

ALLEN, V. L. 1975. Social support for non-conformity. In L. Berkowitz (Ed.), *Advances in experimental social psychology,* vol. 8. New York: Academic Press.

ALLEN, V. L., AND LEVINE, J. M. 1971. Social support and conformity: The role of independent assessment. *Journal of Experimental Social Psychology* 7:48–58.

ALLOY, L. B.; HARTLAGE, S.; AND ABRAMSON, L. Y. 1988. Testing the cognitive-diathesis stress theories of depression: Issues of research design, conceptualization, and assessment. In Alloy, L. B. (Ed.), *Cognitive processes in depression.* New York: Guilford.

ALLPORT, F. 1920. The influence of the group upon association and thought. *Journal of Experimental Psychology* 3:159–82.

ALLPORT, G. W. 1937. *Personality: A psychological interpretation.* New York: Henry Holt.

ALLPORT, G. W., AND ODBERT, H. S. 1936. Trait-names: A psychological study. *Psychological Monographs* 47(Whole No. 211).

AMOORE, J. E.; JOHNSON, J. W., JR.; AND RUBIN, M. 1964. The sterochemical theory of odor. *Scientific American* 210:42–49.

ANASTASI, A. 1958. *Differential psychology,* 3rd ed. New York: Macmillan.

ANASTASI, A. 1971. More on heritability: Addendum to the Hebb and Jensen interchange. *American Psychologist* 26:1036–37.

ANASTASI, A. 1984. The K-ABC in historical perspective. *Journal of Special Education* 18:357–66.

ANASTASI, A. 1985. Review of Kaufman's Assessment Battery for Children. *Ninth Mental Measurements Yearbook,* vol. 1, pp. 769–71.

ANDERSON, J. R. 1990. *Cognitive psychology and its implications,* 3rd ed. San Francisco: Freeman.

ANDERSON, R. C., AND PICHERT, J. 1978. Recall of previously unrecallable information following a shift in perspective. *Journal of Verbal Learning and Verbal Behavior* 17:1–12.

ANDREASEN, N. C. 1985. Positive vs. negative schizophrenia: A critical evaluation. *Schizophrenia Bulletin* 1985:380–89.

ANDREASEN, N. C.; NASRALLAH, H. A.; DUNN, V.; OLSEN, S. C.; GROVE, W. M.; EHRHARDT, J. C.; COFFMAN, J. A.; AND CROSSETT, I. H. W. 1986. Structural abnormalities in the frontal system in schizophrenia: A magnetic resonance imaging study. *Archives of General Psychiatry* 43:136–44.

ANDRES, R. 1980. Influence of obesity on longevity in the aged. In Borek, C.; Fenoglio, C. M.; and King, D. W. (Eds.), *Aging, cancer, and cell membranes,* pp. 230–46. New York: Thieme-Stratton.

ANDREWS, G., AND HARVEY, R. 1981. Does psychotherapy benefit neurotic patients? A reanalysis of the Smith, Glass, and Miller data. *Archives of General Psychiatry* 38:1203–1208.

ANREP, G. V. 1920. Pitch discrimination in the dog. *Journal of Physiology* 53:367–85.

APPEL, L. F.; COOPER, R. G.; MCCARRELL, N.; SIMS-KNIGHT, J.; YUSSEN, S. R.; AND FLAVELL, J. H. 1972. The development of the distinction between perceiving and memorizing. *Child Development* 43:1365–81.

ARANOFF, M. 1976. *Word-formation in generative grammar* (Linguistic Inquiry Monograph 1). Cambridge, Mass.: MIT Press.

ARENDT, H. 1965. *Eichmann in Jerusalem: A report on the banality of evil.* New York: Viking Press.

ARIETI, S. 1959. Schizophrenia: The manifest symptomatology, the psychodynamic and formal mechanisms. In Arieti, S. (Ed.), *Amer-

ican handbook of psychiatry, vol. 1, pp. 455–84. New York: Basic Books.

ARMSTRONG, S. L.; GLEITMAN, L. R.; AND GLEITMAN, H. 1983. What some concepts might not be. *Cognition* 13:263–308.

ARNOLD, M. B. 1970. Perennial problems in the field of emotion. In Arnold, M. B. (Ed.), *Feelings and emotion: The Loyola symposium.* New York: Academic Press.

ARONFREED, J. 1968. *Conduct and conscience.* New York: Academic Press.

ARONFREED, J. 1969. The problem of imitation. In Lipsett, L. P., and Reese, H. W. (Eds.), *Advances in child development and behavior,* vol. 4. New York: Academic Press.

ARONSON, E., AND CARLSMITH, J. M. 1963. The effect of the severity of threat on the devaluation of forbidden behavior. *Journal of Abnormal and Social Psychology* 66:584–88.

ARONSON, E., AND MILLS, J. 1959. The effect of severity of initiation on liking for a group. *Journal of Abnormal and Social Psychology* 59:177–81.

ARONSON, E.; TURNER, J. A.; AND CARLSMITH, J. M. 1963. Communicator credibility and communication discrepancy as determinants of opinion change. *Journal of Abnormal and Social Psychology* 67:31–36.

ASCH, S. E. 1946. Forming impressions of personality. *Journal of Abnormal and Social Psychology* 41:258–90.

ASCH, S. E. 1952. *Social psychology.* New York: Prentice-Hall.

ASCH, S. E. 1955. Opinions and social pressure. *Scientific American* 193:31–35.

ASCH, S. E. 1956. Studies of independence and conformity: A minority of one against a unanimous majority. *Psychological Monographs* 70 (9, Whole No. 416).

ASCH, S. E., AND GLEITMAN, H. 1953. Yielding to social pressure as a function of public or private commitment. Unpublished manuscript.

ASHER, E. J. 1935. The inadequacy of current intelligence tests for testing Kentucky Mountain children. *Journal of Genetic Psychology* 46:480–86.

ASLIN, R. N. 1987. Visual and auditory development in infancy. In Osofsky, J. D. (Ed.), *Handbook of infant development,* 2nd ed., pp. 5–97. New York: Wiley.

ATKINSON, J. W., AND MCCLELLAND, D. C. 1948. The projective expression of needs. II. The effect of different intensities of the hunger drive on thematic apperception. *Journal of Experimental Psychology* 38:643–58.

ATKINSON, R. C., AND SHIFFRIN, R. M. 1968. Human memory: A proposed system and its control. In Spence, K. W., and Spence, J. T. (Eds.), *The psychology of learning and motivation,* vol. 2, pp. 89–105. New York: Academic Press.

AX, A. F. 1953. The physiological differentiation of fear and anger in humans. *Psychosomatic Medicine* 15:433–42.

AYLLON, T., AND AZRIN, N. H. 1968. *The token economy: A motivational system for therapy and rehabilitation.* New York: Appleton-Century-Crofts.

BABIGIAN, H. M. 1975. Schizophrenia: Epidemiology. In Freedman, A. M.; Kaplan, H. I.; and Sadock, B. J. (Eds.), *Comprehensive textbook of psychiatry—II,* vol. 1, pp. 860–66. Baltimore: Williams & Wilkins.

BADDELEY, A. D. 1976. *The psychology of human memory.* New York: Basic Books.

BADDELEY, A. D. 1978. The trouble with levels: A reexamination of Craik and Lockhart's framework for memory research. *Psychological Review* 85:139–52.

BADDELEY, A. D. 1986. *Working memory.* Oxford: Clarendon Press.

BAHRICK, H. P. 1984. Semantic memory content in permastore: 50 years of memory for Spanish learned in school. *Journal of Experimental Psychology: General* 113:1–29.

BAILLARGEON, R. 1987. Object permanence in 3½- and 4½-month-old infants. *Developmental Psychology* 23:655–664.

BAILLARGEON, R.; SPELKE, E. S.; AND WASSERMAN, S. 1985. Object permanence in five-month-old infants. *Cognition* 20: 191–208.

BALL, W., AND TRONICK, E. 1971. Infant responses to impending collision: optical and real. *Science* 171:818–20.

BALTES, P. B.; REESE, H. W.; AND LIPSITT, L. P. 1980. Life-span developmental psychology. In Rosenzweig, M. R., and Porter, L. W. (Eds.), *Annual Review of Psychology* 31:65–110.

BALTES, P. B., AND SCHAIE, K. W. 1976. On the plasticity of intelligence in adulthood and old age. *American Psychologist* 31: 720–25.

BANDURA, A. 1965. Influence of models' reinforcement contingencies on the acquisition of imitative responses. *Journal of Personality and Social Psychology* 1:589–95.

BANDURA, A.; ROSS, D.; AND ROSS, S. A. 1963. Imitation of film-mediated aggressive models. *Journal of Abnormal and Social Psychology* 66:3–11.

BANDURA, A., AND WALTERS, R. H. 1963. *Social learning and personality development.* New York: Holt, Rinehart & Winston.

BAREFOOT, J. C.; DODGE, K. A.; PETERSON, B. L.; DAHLSTROM, W. G.; AND WILLIAMS, R. B. 1989. The Cook-Medley Hostility Scale: Item content and ability to predict survival. *Psychosomatic Medicine* 51:46–57.

BARLOW, H. B., AND HILL, R. M. 1963. Evidence for a physiological explanation of the waterfall illusion and figural after-effects. *Nature* 200:1345–47.

BARNETT, S. A. 1963. *The rat: A study in behavior.* Chicago: Aldine.

BARON, J. 1985. What kinds of intelligence components are fundamental? In Chipman, S. F.; Segal, J. W.; and Glaser, R. (Eds.), *Thinking and learning skills. Vol. 2: Research and open questions.* Hillsdale, N.J.: Erlbaum.

BARRERA, M. E., AND MAURER, D. 1981. Recognition of mother's photographed face by the three-month-old infant. *Child Development* 52:714–16.

BARTOL, C. R., AND COSTELLO, N. 1976. Extraversion as a function of temporal duration of electric shock: An exploratory study. *Perceptual and Motor Skills* 42:1174.

BATES, E. 1976. *Language and context: The acquisition of pragmatics.* New York: Academic Press.

BATES, E., AND MACWHINNEY, B. 1982. Functionalist approaches to grammar. In Wanner, E., and Gleitman, L. (Eds.), *Language acquisition: State of the art.* New York: Cambridge University Press.

BATESON, P. P. G. 1984. The neural basis of imprinting. In Marler, P., and Terrace, H. S. (Eds.), *The biological basis of learning,* pp. 325–39. Dahlem-Konferenzen. Berlin: Springer.

BAUM, W. M. 1970. Extinction of avoidance response following response prevention. *Psychological Bulletin* 74:276–84.

BAUMRIND, D. 1967. Child care practices anteceding three patterns of preschool behavior. *Genetic Psychology Monographs* 75: 43–88.

BAUMRIND, D. 1971. Current patterns of parental authority. *Genetic Psychology Monographs* 1.

BAUMRIND, D. 1977. Socialization determinants of personal agency. Paper presented at the biennial meetings of the Society for Research in Child Development, New Orleans. (Cited in Maccoby, E. E. 1980. *Social development.* New York: Harcourt Brace Jovanovich.)

BAUMRIND, D. 1986. Sex differences in moral reasoning: Response to Walker's (1984) conclusion that there are none. *Child Development* 57:511–21.

BAYER, E. 1929. Beitrge zur Zweikomponententheorie des Hungers. *Zeitschrift der Psychologie* 112:1–54.

BECK, A. T. 1967. *Depression: Causes and treatment.* Philadelphia: University of Pennsylvania Press.

BECK, A. T. 1976. *Cognitive therapy and the emotional disorders.* New York: International Universities Press.

BECK, A. T. 1985. Cognitive therapy. In Kaplan, H. I., and Sadock, J. (Eds.), *Comprehensive textbook of psychiatry,* 4th ed. Baltimore: Williams & Wilkins.

BECK, A. T.; RUSH, A. J.; SHAW, B. F.; AND EMERY, G. 1979. *Cognitive therapy of depression.* New York: Guilford Press.

BÉKÉSY, G. VON. 1957. The ear. *Scientific American* 197:66–78.

BELL, A. P.; WEINBERG, M. S.; AND HAMMERSMITH, S. K. 1981. *Sexual preference: Its development in men and women.* Bloomington, Ind.: Indiana University Press.

BELL, R. Q. 1968. A reinterpretation of the direction of effects in studies of socialization. *Psychological Review* 75:81–95.

BELL, R. Q., AND HARPER, L. V. 1977. *Child effects on adults.* Hillsdale, N.J.: Erlbaum.

BELLAK, L. 1986. *The thematic apperception test, the children's apperception test, and the senior apperception test in clinical use,* 4th ed. Orlando, Fla.: Academic Press.

BELLUGI, U. 1971. Simplification in children's language. In Huxley, R., and Ingram, E., (Eds.), *Language acquisition: Models and methods.* New York: Academic Press.

BELOFF, H. 1957. The structure and origin of the anal character. *Genetic Psychology Monographs* 55:141–72.

BEM, D. J. 1967. Self-perception: An alternative interpretation of cognitive dissonance phenomena. *Psychological Review* 74:183–200.

BEM, D. J. 1972. Self-perception theory. In Berkowitz, L. (Ed.), *Advances in experimental social psychology,* vol. 6, pp. 2–62. New York: Academic Press.

BENBOW, C. P. 1988. Sex differences in mathematical reasoning ability in intellectually talented preadolescents: Their nature, effects, and possible causes. *Behavior and Brain Sciences* 11:169–232.

BENBOW, C. P., AND STANLEY, J. C. 1983. Sex differences in mathematical reasoning: More facts. *Science* 222:1029–31.

BENTLEY, E. 1983. *The life of the drama.* New York: Atheneum.

BERGIN, A. 1971. The evaluation of therapeutic outcomes. In Bergin, A. E. and Garfield, S. L. (Eds.), *Handbook of psychotherapy and behavior change: An empirical analysis.* New York: Wiley.

BERMANT, G., AND DAVIDSON, J. M. 1974. *Biological bases of sexual behavior.* New York: Harper & Row.

BERNARD, V. W.; OTTENBERG, P.; AND REDL, F. 1965. Dehumanization: A composite psychological defense in relation to modern war. In Schwebel, M. (Ed.), *Behavioral science and human survival,* pp. 64–82. Palo Alto, Calif.: Science and Behavior Books.

BERNHEIM, K. W., AND LEWINE, R. R. J. 1979. *Schizophrenia: Symptoms, causes, treatments.* New York: Norton.

BERSCHEID, E. 1985. Interpersonal attraction. In Lindzey, G., and Aronson, E. (Eds.), *Handbook of social psychology,* vol. 2, pp. 413–84. New York: Academic Press.

BERSCHEID, E.; DION, K.; WALSTER, E.; AND WALSTER, G. W. 1971. Physical attractiveness and dating choice: A test of the matching hypothesis. *Journal of Experimental Social Psychology* 7:173–89.

BERSCHEID, E., AND WALSTER, E. H. 1978. *Interpersonal attraction,* 2nd ed. Reading, Mass.: Addison-Wesley.

BEST, D. L.; WILLIAMS, J. E.; CLOUD, J. M.; DAVIS, S. W.; ROBERTSON, L. S.; EDWARDS, J. R.; GILES, E.; AND FOWLES, J. 1977. Development of sex-trait stereotypes among young children in the United States, England, and Ireland. *Child Development* 48:1375–84.

BIGELOW, A. 1987. Early words of blind children. *Journal of Child Language* 14(1):1–22.

BIRCH, H. G.; PIÑEIRO, C.; ALCADE, E.; TOCA, T.; AND CRAVIOTA, J. 1971. Relation of kwashiokor in early childhood and intelligence at school age. *Pediatric Research* 5:579–92.

BJÖRKLUND, A., AND STENEVI, U. 1984. Intracerebral implants: Neuronal replacement and reconstruction of damaged circuitries. *Annual Review of Neuroscience* 7:279–308.

BJÖRKLUND, A.; STENEVI, U.; SCHMIDT, R. H.; DUNNETT, S. B.; AND GAGE, F. H. 1983. Intracerebral grafting of neuronal suspensions I. Introduction and general methods of preparation. *Acta Physiologica Scandinavica Supplement* 522:1–8.

BLAKEMORE, C. 1977. *Mechanics of the mind.* New York: Cambridge University Press.

BLASI, A. 1980. Bridging moral cognition and moral action: A critical review of the literature. *Psychological Bulletin* 88:1–45.

BLASI, A. 1984. Moral identity: Its role in moral functioning. In Kurtines, W. M., and Gewirtz, L. (Eds.), *Morality, moral behavior, and moral development,* pp. 128–39. New York: Wiley.

BLEULER, E. 1911. *Dementia praecox, or the group of schizophrenias.* English translation by Zinkin, J., and Lewis, N. D. New York: International Universities Press, 1950.

BLISS, E. L. 1980. Multiple personalities: Report of fourteen cases with implications for schizophrenia and hysteria. *Archives of General Psychiatry* 37:1388–97.

BLOCK, J. 1971. *Lives through time.* Berkeley, Calif.: Bancroft Books.

BLOCK, J. 1977. Advancing the psychology of personality: Paradigmatic shift or improving the quality of research. In Magnusson, D., and Endler, N. S. (Eds.), *Personality at the crossroads,* pp. 37–64. New York: Wiley.

BLOCK, N.J., AND DWORKIN, G. 1976. *The IQ controversy: Critical readings.* New York: Pantheon.

BLOOM, F. E. 1983. The endorphins: A growing family of pharmacologically pertinent peptides. *Annual Review of Pharmacology and Toxicology* 23:151–70.

BLOOM, F. E.; LAZERSON, A.; AND HOFSTADTER, L. 1988. *Brain, mind, and behavior.* New York: Freeman.

BLOOM, K. 1988. Quality of adult vocalizations affects the quality of infant vocalizations. *Journal of Child Language* 15(1):469–80.

BLOOM, L. 1970. *Language development: Form and function in emerging grammars.* Cambridge, Mass.: MIT Press.

BLOOM, P. 1990. Syntactic distinctions in child language. *Journal of Child Language* 17(2):343–56.

BLUM, G. S. 1949. A study of the psychoanalytic theory of psychosexual development. *Genetic Psychology Monographs* 39:3–99.

BLUM, G. S. 1950. *The Blacky pictures.* New York: Psychological Corporation.

BLUM, J. E.; JARVIK, L. F.; AND CLARK, E. T. 1970. Rate of change on selective tests of intelligence: A twenty-year longitudinal study. *Journal of Gerontology* 25:171–76.

BODEN, M. 1977. *Artificial intelligence and natural man.* New York: Basic Books.

BODNAR, R. J.; KELLY, D. D.; BRUTUS, M.; AND GLUSMAN, M. 1980. Stress-induced analgesia: Neural and hormonal determinants. *Neuroscience and biobehavioral reviews* 4:87–100.

BOGEN, J. E. 1969. The other side of the brain II: An appositional mind. *Bulletin of the Los Angeles Neurological Societies* 34:135–62.

BOGEN, J. E.; FISHER, E. D.; AND VOGEL, P. J. 1965. Cerebral commissurotomy: A second case report. *Journal of the American Medical Association* 194:1328–29.

BOLLES, R. C., AND FANSELOW, M. S. 1982. Endorphins and behavior. *Annual Review of Psychology* 33:87–102.

BOOTH, D. A. 1980. Acquired behavior controlling energy and output. In Stunkard, A. J. (Ed.), *Obesity,* pp. 101–43. Philadelphia: Saunders.

BORING, E. G. 1930. A new ambiguous figure. *American Journal of Psychology* 42:444–45.

BORING, E. G. 1964. Size constancy in a picture. *American Journal of Psychology* 77:494–98.

BORNSTEIN, M. H. 1985. Perceptual development. In Bornstein, M. H., and Lamb, M. E. (Eds.), *Developmental psychology: An advanced textbook,* pp. 81–132. Hillsdale, N.J.: Erlbaum.

BOTVIN, G. J., AND MURRAY, F. B. 1975. The efficacy of peer modelling and social conflict in the acquisition of conservation. *Child Development* 46:796–97.

BOUCHARD, C.; TREMBLAY, A.; DESPRÈS, J-P.; NADEAU, A.; LUPIEN, P. L.; THÈRIAULT, G.; DUSSAULT, J.; MOORJANI, S.; PINAULT, S. M.; AND FOURNIER, G. 1990. The response to long-term overfeeding in identical twins. *New England Journal of Medicine* 322:1477–82.

BOUCHARD, T. J., JR., AND MCGUE, M. 1981. Familial studies of intelligence: A review. *Science* 212:1055–59.

BOWER, G. H. 1970. Analysis of a mnemonic device. *American Scientist* 58:496–510.

BOWER, G. H.; BLACK, J. B.; AND TURNER, T. J. 1979. Scripts in memory for text. *Cognitive Psychology* 11:177–220.

BOWER, T. G. R. 1966. Slant perception and shape constancy in infants. *Science* 151:832–34.

BOWERS, K. S. 1984. On being unconsciously influenced and informed. In Bowers, K. S., and Meichenbaum, D. (Eds.), *The unconscious reconsidered.* New York: Wiley.

BOWLBY, J. 1969. *Attachment and loss: Vol. 1. Attachment.* New York: Basic Books.

BOWLBY, J. 1973. *Separation and loss.* New York: Basic Books.

BOWMAKER, J. K., AND DARTNALL, H. J. A. 1980. Visual pigments and rods and cones in a human retina. *Journal of Physiology* 298:501–11.

BRABECK, M. 1983. Moral judgement: Theory and research on differences between males and females. *Developmental Review* 3:274–91.

FANCHER, R. E. 1987. *The intelligence men: Makers of the IQ controversy*. New York: Norton.

FANT, L. G. 1972. *Ameslan: An introduction to American Sign Language*. Silver Springs, Md.: National Association of the Deaf.

FANTZ, R. L. 1957. Form preferences in newly hatched chicks. *Journal of Comparative and Physiological Psychology* 50:422–30.

FANTZ, R. L. 1961. The origin of form perception. *Scientific American* 204:66–72.

FANTZ, R. L. 1970. Visual perception and experience in infancy: Issues and approaches. In National Academy of Science, *Early experience and visual information processing in perceptual and reading disorders*, pp. 351–81. New York: National Academy of Science.

FARIS, R. E. L., AND DUNHAM, H. W. 1939. *Mental disorders in urban areas*. Chicago: University of Chicago Press.

FEDER, H. H. 1984. Hormones and sexual behavior. *Annual Review of Psychology* 35:165–200.

FELDMAN, H.; GOLDIN-MEADOW, S.; AND GLEITMAN, L. R. 1978. Beyond Herodotus: The creation of language by linguistically deprived deaf children. In Lock, A. (Ed.), *Action, gesture, and symbol: The emergence of language*. London: Academic Press.

FERSTER, C. B., AND SKINNER, B. F. 1957. *Schedules of reinforcement*. New York: Appleton-Century-Crofts.

FERSTER, D. 1981. A comparison of binocular depth mechanisms in areas 17 and 18 of the cat visual cortex. *Journal of Physiology* 311:623–55.

FESHBACH, N., AND ROE, K. 1968. Empathy in six- and seven-year-olds. *Child Development* 39:133–45.

FESTINGER, L. 1954. A theory of social comparison processes. *Human Relations* 7:117–40.

FESTINGER, L. 1957. *A theory of cognitive dissonance*. Evanston, Ill.: Row, Peterson.

FESTINGER, L., AND CARLSMITH, J. M. 1959. Cognitive consequences of forced compliance. *Journal of Abnormal and Social Psychology* 58:203–10.

FESTINGER, L.; PEPITONE, A.; AND NEWCOMB, T. 1952. Some consequences of deindividuation in a group. *Journal of Abnormal and Social Psychology* 47:387–89.

FESTINGER, L.; RIECKEN, H.; AND SCHACHTER, S. 1956. *When prophecy fails*. Minneapolis: University of Minnesota Press.

FIEVE, R. R. 1975. Lithium (antimanic) therapy. In Freedman, A. M.; Kaplan, H. I.; and Sadock, B. J. (Eds.), *Comprehensive textbook of psychiatry*, vol. 2, pp. 1982–87. Baltimore: Williams & Wilkins.

FIGLER, M. 1972. The relation between eliciting stimulus strength and habituation of the threat display in male Siamese fighting fish, *Betta splendens*. *Behavior* 42:63–96.

FILLMORE, C. 1968. The case for case. In Bach, E., and Harms, R. (Eds.), *Universals in linguistic theory*. New York: Holt, Rinehart and Winston.

FINE, A. 1986. Transplantation in the central nervous system. *Scientific American* (August issue, pp. 52–58).

FISHER, S., AND GREENBERG, R. P. 1977. *The scientific credibility of Freud's theory and therapy*. New York: Basic Books.

FITZGERALD, F. T. 1981. The problem of obesity. *Annual Review of Medicine* 32:221–31.

FLANAGAN, J. C. 1947. Scientific development of the use of human resources: Progress in the Army Air Forces. *Science* 105:57–60.

FLAVELL, J. H. 1970. Developmental studies of mediated memory. In Reese, H. W., and Lipsitt, L. P. (Eds.), *Advances in child development and behavior*, vol. 5. New York: Academic Press.

FLAVELL, J. H. 1977. *Cognitive development*. Englewood Cliffs, N.J.: Prentice-Hall.

FLAVELL, J. H. 1985. *Cognitive development*, 2nd ed. Englewood Cliffs, N.J.: Prentice-Hall.

FLAVELL, J. H.; FLAVELL, E. R.; AND GREEN, F. L. 1983. Development of the appearance-reality distinction. *Cognitive Psychology* 15:95–120.

FLAVELL, J. H., AND WELLMAN, H. M. 1977. Metamemory. In Kail, R. V., Jr., and Hagen, J. W. (Eds.), *Perspectives on the development of memory and cognition*, pp. 3–34. Hillsdale, N.J.: Erlbaum.

FLODERUS-MYRHED, B.; PEDERSEN, N.; AND RASMUSON, L. 1980. Assessment of heritability for personality, based on a short form of the Eysenck Personality Inventory: A study of 12,898 twin pairs. *Behavior Genetics* 10:153–62.

FLYNN, J.; VANEGAS, H.; FOOTE, W.; AND EDWARDS, S. 1970. Neural mechanisms involved in a cat's attack on a rat. In Whalen, R. F.; Thompson, M.; Verzeano, M.; and Weinberger, N. (Eds.), *The neural control of behavior*. New York: Academic Press.

FLYNN, S. 1987. *A parameter-setting model of L2 acquisition: Experimental studies in anaphora*. Dordrecht: Reidel.

FODOR, J. A. 1972. Some reflections on L. S. Vygotsky's *Thought and language*. *Cognition* 1:83–95.

FODOR, J. A. 1983. *The modularity of mind*. Cambridge, Mass.: MIT Press, Bradford Books.

FODOR, J. A. 1988. *Psychosemantics*. Cambridge, Mass.: MIT Press.

FOLKOW, B., AND RUBENSTEIN, E. H. 1966. Cardiovascular effects of acute and chronic stimulations of the hypothalamic defense area in the rat. *Acta Physiologica Scandinavica* 68:48–57.

FORD, C. S., AND BEACH, F. A. 1951. *Patterns of sexual behavior*. New York: Harper & Row.

FORSTER, E. M. 1927. *Aspects of the novel*. New York: Harcourt, Brace, and World.

FOUCAULT, M. 1965. *Madness and civilization*. New York: Random House.

FOUTS, R. S.; HIRSCH, A. D.; AND FOUTS, D. H. 1982. Cultural transmission of a human language in a chimpanzee mother-infant relationship. In Fitzgerald, H. E.; Mullins, J. A.; and Gage, P. (Eds.), *Child nurturance: Vol. 3, Studies of development in nonhuman primates*, pp. 159–69. New York: Plenum.

FRANKL, V. E. 1966. *The doctor and the soul*. New York: Knopf.

FREED, W. J.; DE MEDICACELLI, L.; AND WYATT, R. J. 1985. Promoting functional plasticity in the damaged nervous system. *Science* 227:1544–52.

FREEDMAN, D. G. 1971. Behavioral assessment in infancy. In Stoeling, G. B. A., and Van Der Weoff Ten Bosch, J. J. (Eds.), *Normal and abnormal development of brain and behavior*, pp. 92–103. Leiden: Leiden University Press.

FREEDMAN, J. L., AND FRASER, S. C. 1966. Compliance without pressure: The foot-in-the-door technique. *Journal of Personality and Social Psychology* 4:195–202.

FREEDMAN, J. L.; SEARS, D. O.; AND CARLSMITH, J. M. 1981. *Social psychology*, 4th ed. Englewood Cliffs, N.J.: Prentice-Hall.

FREEMAN, D. 1983. *Margaret Mead and Samoa: The making and unmaking of an anthropological myth*. Canberra: Australian National University Press.

FREGE, G. (1892/1952). On sense and reference, In Geach, P., and Black, M. (Eds.), *Philosophical writings of Gottlob Frege*. Oxford: Oxford University Press.

FRENCH, J. D. 1957. The reticular formation. *Scientific American* 196:54–60.

FREUD, A. 1946. *The ego and the mechanisms of defense*. London: Hogarth Press.

FREUD, S. 1900. The interpretation of dreams. In Strachey, J., trans. and ed., *The complete psychological works*, vols. 4–5. New York: Norton, 1976.

FREUD, S. 1901. The psychopathology of everyday life. Translated by Tyson, A. New York: Norton, 1971.

FREUD, S. 1905. Three essays on the theory of sexuality. In Strachey, J., trans. and ed., *The complete psychological works*, vol. 7. New York: Norton, 1976.

FREUD, S. 1908. Character and anal eroticism. In Rieff, P. (Ed.), *Collected papers of Sigmund Freud: Character and culture*. New York: Collier Books, 1963.

FREUD, S. 1911. Psychoanalytic notes upon an autobiographical account of a case of paranoia (dementia paranoides). In Strachey, J., trans. and ed., *The complete psychological works*, vol. 12. New York: Norton, 1976.

FREUD, S. 1913. *Further recommendations in the technique of psychoanalysis*. In Strachey, J., trans. and ed., *The complete psychological works*, vol. 12. New York: Norton, 1976.

FREUD, S. 1917. *A general introduction to psychoanalysis*. Translated by Riviere, J. New York: Washington Square Press, 1952.

FREUD, S. 1923. *The ego and the id*. Translated by Riviere, J. New York: Norton, 1962.

FREUD, S. 1926. *Inhibitions, symptoms, and anxiety.* Translated by Strachey, J. New York: Norton.

FREUD, S. 1930. *Civilization and its discontents.* Translated by Strachey, J. New York: Norton, 1961.

FREUD, S., AND BREUER, J. 1895. Studies on hysteria. In Strachey, J., trans. and ed., *The complete psychological works,* vol. 2. New York: Norton, 1976.

FRIDLUND, A. J. 1990. Evolution and facial action in reflex, social motive, and paralanguage. In Ackles, P. K.; Jennings, J. R.; and Coles, M. G. H. (Eds.), *Advances in psychophysiology,* vol. 4. Greenwich, Conn.: JAI Press.

FRIDLUND, A. J.; EKMAN, P.; AND OSTER, H. 1983. Facial expression of emotion: Review of literature, 1970–1983. In Siegman, A. (Ed.), *Nonverbal behavior and communication.* Hillsdale, N.J.: Erlbaum.

FRIEDMAN, M., AND ROSENMAN, R. H. 1974. *Type A behavior.* New York: Knopf.

FRIEDMAN, M. I., AND STRICKER, E. M. 1976. The physiological psychology of hunger: A physiological perspective. *Psychological Review* 83:409–31.

FRISBY, J. P. 1980. *Seeing: Illusion, brain and mind.* New York: Oxford University Press.

FRISHBERG, N. 1975. Arbitrariness and iconicity: Historical change in American Sign Language. *Language* 51:696–719.

FROMKIN, V.; KRASHEN, S.; CURTISS, S.; RIGLER, D.; AND RIGLER, M. 1974. The development of language in Genie: A case of language acquisition beyond the "critical period." *Brain and Language* 1:81–107.

FUNKENSTEIN, D. H. 1956. Norepinephrine-like and epinephrine-like substances in relation to human behavior. *Journal of Mental Diseases* 124:58–68.

GAGE, F. H., AND BJÖRKLUND, A. 1986. Cholinergic septal grafts into the hippocampal formation improve spatial learning and memory in aged rats by an atropine-sensitive mechanism. *Journal of Neuroscience* 6:2837–47.

GALLAGAN, R. 1987. Intonation with single words: purposive and grammatical use. *Journal of Child Language* 14:1–22.

GALLISTEL, C. R. 1973. Self-stimulation: The neurophysiology of reward and motivation. In Deutsch, J. A. (Ed.), *The physiological basis of memory,* pp. 175–267. New York: Academic Press.

GALLISTEL, C. R. 1983. Self-stimulation. In Deutsch, J. A. (Ed.), *The physiological basis of memory,* pp. 269–349. New York: Academic Press.

GALTON, F. 1869. *Hereditary genius: An inquiry into its laws and consequences.* London: Macmillan.

GARBER, H., AND HEBER, R. 1982. Modification of predicted cognitive development in high-risk children through early intervention. In Detterman, D. K., and Sternberg, R. J. (Eds.), *How and how much can intelligence be increased?,* pp. 121–40. Norwood, N.J.: Ablex.

GARCIA, J., AND KOELLING, R. A. 1966. The relation of cue to consequence in avoidance learning. *Psychonomic Science* 4:123–24.

GARDNER, H. 1983. *Frames of mind: The theory of multiple intelligences.* New York: Basic Books.

GARDNER, R. A., AND GARDNER, B. T. 1969. Teaching sign language to a chimpanzee. *Science* 165:664–72.

GARDNER, R. A., AND GARDNER, B. T. 1975. Early signs of language in child and chimpanzee. *Science* 187:752–53.

GARDNER, R. A., AND GARDNER, B. T. 1978. Comparative psychology and language acquisition. *Annals of the New York Academy of Science* 309:37–76.

GAZZANIGA, M. S. 1967. The split brain in man. *Scientific American* 217:24–29.

GAZZANIGA, M. S. 1970. *The bisected brain.* New York: Appleton-Century-Crofts.

GAZZANIGA, M. S. 1983. Right hemisphere language following brain bisection: A 20-year perspective. *American Psychologist* 38:525–37.

GEBHARD, P. H. Incidence of overt homosexuality in the United States and in Western Europe. In Livingood, J. M. (Ed.) 1972. *National Institute of Mental Health (U.S.) Task Force on Homosexuality:*

Final report and background papers. Rockville, Md.: National Institute of Mental Health. DHEW Publication No. (HSM) 72–9116.

GELMAN, R. 1972. Logical capacity of very young children: Number invariance rules. *Child Development* 43:75–90.

GELMAN, R. 1978. Cognitive development. *Annual Review of Psychology* 29:297–332.

GELMAN, D. 1989. The brain killer. *Newsweek* (December 18):54–56.

GELMAN, R., AND BAILLARGEON, R. 1983. A review of some Piagetian concepts. In Mussen, P. (Ed.), *Carmichael's manual of child psychology: Vol 3. Cognitive development* (Markman, E. M., and Flavell, J. H., volume editors), pp. 167–230. New York: Wiley.

GEORGOTAS, A. 1985. Affective disorders: Pharmacotherapy. In Kaplan, H. I., and Sadock, J. (Eds.), *Comprehensive textbook of psychiatry,* 4th ed. Baltimore: Williams & Wilkins.

GERARD, H. B., AND MATHEWSON, G. C. 1966. The effects of severity of initiation on liking for a group: A replication. *Journal of Experimental Social Psychology* 2:278–87.

GERARD, H. B.; WILHELMY, R. A.; AND CONOLLEY, E. S. 1968. Conformity and group size. *Journal of Personality and Social Psychology* 8:79–82.

GERBINO, L.; OLESHANSKY, M.; AND GERSHON, S. 1978. Clinical use and mode of action of lithium. In Killiam, F. K. (Ed.), *Psychopharmacology: A generation of progress,* pp. 1261–75. New York: Raven.

GERGEN, K. 1973. Social psychology as history. *Journal of Personality and Social Psychology* 26:309–20.

GERKEN, L.; LANDAU, B.; AND REMEZ, R. 1990. Function morphemes in young children's speech perception and production. *Developmental Psychology* 26(2):204–16.

GERSHON, E. S.; NURNBERGER, J. I., JR.; BERRETTINI, W. H.; AND GOLDIN, L. R. 1985. Affective disorders: Genetics. In Kaplan, H. I., and Sadock, J. (Eds.), *Modern synopsis of comprehensive textbook of psychiatry,* 4th ed. Baltimore: Williams & Wilkins.

GESCHWIND, N. 1970. The organization of language and the brain. *Science* 170:940–44.

GESCHWIND, N. 1972. Language and the brain. *Scientific American* 226:76–83.

GESCHWIND, N. 1975. The apraxias: Neural mechanisms of disorders of learned movement. *American Scientist* 63:188–95.

GIBBS, J., AND SMITH, G. P. 1984. The neuroendocrinology of postprandial satiety. In Martini, L., and Ganong, W. F. (Eds.), *Frontiers in neuroendocrinology,* vol. 8. New York: Raven.

GIBBS, J. C.; CLARK, P. M.; JOSEPH, J. A.; GREEN, J. L.; GOODRICK, T. S.; AND MAKOWSKI, D. G. 1986. Relations between moral judgment, moral courage, and field independence. *Child Development* 57:1040–43.

GIBSON, E. J. 1969. *Principles of perceptual learning and development.* New York: Appleton-Century-Crofts.

GIBSON, J. J. 1950. *The perception of the visual world.* Boston: Houghton Mifflin.

GIBSON, J. J. 1966. *The senses considered as perceptual systems.* Boston: Houghton Mifflin.

GIBSON, J. J. 1979. *The ecological approach to visual perception.* Boston: Houghton Mifflin.

GICK, M. L., AND HOLYOAK, K. J. 1980. Analogical problem solving. *Cognitive Psychology* 12:306–55.

GICK, M. L., AND HOLYOAK, K. J. 1983. Schema induction and analogical transfer. *Cognitive Psychology* 15:1–38.

GILLIGAN, C. 1982. *In a different voice: Psychological theory and women's development.* Cambridge, Mass.: Harvard University Press.

GILLIGAN, C. 1986. Profile of Carol Gilligan. In Scarr, S.; Weinberg, R. A.; and Levine, A. 1986. *Understanding development,* pp. 488–91. New York: Harcourt Brace Jovanovich.

GILMAN, S. 1982. *Seeing the insane.* New York: Wiley.

GINZBERG, L. 1909. *The legends of the Jews,* vol. 1. Translated by Szold, H. Philadelphia: Jewish Publication Society of America.

GLADUE, B. A.; GREEN, R.; AND HELLMAN, R. E. 1984. Neuroendocrine responses to estrogen and sexual orientation. *Science* 225:1496–98.

GLANZER, M., AND CUNITZ, A. 1966. Two storage mechanisms in free recall. *Journal of Verbal Learning and Verbal Behavior* 5:531–60.

GLEITMAN, H. 1963. Place-learning. *Scientific American* 209:116–22.

GLEITMAN, H. 1971. Forgetting of long-term memories in animals. In Honig, W. K., and James, P. H. R. (Eds.), *Animal memory*, pp. 2–46. New York: Academic Press.

GLEITMAN, H. 1985. Some trends in the study of cognition. In Koch, S., and Leary, D. E. (Eds.), *A century of psychology as science*, pp. 420–36. New York: McGraw-Hill.

GLEITMAN, L. R. 1986. Biological dispositions to learn language. In Demopolous, W., and Marras, A. (Eds.), *Language learning and concept acquisition*. Norwood, N.J.: Ablex.

GLEITMAN, L. R. 1990. Structural sources of verb learning. *Language Acquisition* 1:1–54.

GLEITMAN, L. R.; GLEITMAN, H.; AND SHIPLEY, E. F. 1972. The emergence of the child as grammarian. *Cognition* 1(2):137–64.

GLEITMAN, L. R., AND WANNER, E. 1982. Language acquisition: The state of the art. In Wanner, E., and Gleitman, L. (Eds.), *Language acquisition: The state of the art*. New York: Cambridge University Press.

GLUCKSBERG, S. 1962. The influence of strength of drive on functional fixedness and perceptual recognition. *Journal of Experimental Psychology* 63:36–41.

GODDEN, D. R., AND BADDELEY, A. D. 1975. Context-dependent memory in two natural environments: On land and underwater. *British Journal of Psychology* 66:325–31.

GOFFMAN, E. 1961. *Asylums*. Chicago: Aldine.

GOLD, R. 1978. On the meaning of nonconservation. In Lesgold, A. M.; Pellegrino, J. W.; Fokkema, S. D.; and Glaser, R. (Eds.), *Cognitive psychology and instruction*. New York: Plenum.

GOLDBERG, L. R. 1981. Developing a taxonomy of trait-descriptive terms. In Fiske, D. W. (Ed.), *Problems with language imprecision*, pp. 43–66. San Francisco: Jossey-Bass.

GOLDBERG, L. R. 1982. From ace to zombie: Some explorations in the language of personality. In Spielberger, C., and Butcher, J. N. (Eds.), *Advances in personality assessment*, vol. 1. Hillsdale, N.J.: Erlbaum.

GOLDFARB, W. 1955. Emotional and intellectual consequences of psychological deprivation in infancy: A reevaluation. In Hock, P. H., and Zubin, J. (Eds.), *Psychopathology of childhood*. New York: Grune and Stratton.

GOLDIN-MEADOW, S. 1982. Fragile and resilient properties of language learning. In Wanner, E., and Gleitman, L. R. (Eds.), *Language acquisition: State of the art*. New York: Cambridge University Press.

GOLDIN-MEADOW, S., AND MYLANDER, C. 1983. Gestural communication in deaf children: The non-effects of parental input. *Science* 221:372–74.

GOLDSTEIN, E. B. 1984. *Sensation and perception*, 2nd ed. Belmont, Calif.: Wadsworth.

GOLDSTEIN, E. B. 1989. *Sensation and perception*, 3rd ed. Belmont, Calif.: Wadsworth.

GOMBRICH, E. H. 1961. *Art and illusion*. Princeton, N.J.: Bollingen Series, Princeton University Press.

GORDON, H. 1923. Mental and scholastic tests among retarded children. *Educational Pamphlet*, no. 44. London: Board of Education.

GOTTESMAN, I. I.; McGUFFIN, P.; AND FARMER, A. 1987. Clinical genetics as clues to the "real" genetics of schizophrenia (a decade of modest gains while playing for time). *Schizophrenia Bulletin* 13:23–47.

GOTTESMAN, I. I., AND SHIELDS, J. 1972. *Schizophrenia and genetics: A twin study vantage point*. New York: Academic Press.

GOTTESMAN, I. I., AND SHIELDS, J. 1982. *Schizophrenia: The epigenetic puzzle*. New York: Cambridge University Press.

GOTTLIEB, G. 1961. Developmental age as a baseline for determination of the critical period for imprinting. *Journal of Comparative and Physiological Psychology* 54:422–27.

GOUGH, H. G. 1975. *California psychological inventory: Manual*, rev. ed. Palo Alto, Calif.: Consulting Psychologists Press (original edition, 1957).

GOULD, S. J. 1977. *Ontogeny and phylogeny*. Cambridge, Mass.: Harvard University Press.

GOULD, S. J. 1978. Sociobiology: The art of storytelling. *New Scientist* 80:530–33.

GRAF, P., AND MANDLER, G. 1984. Activation makes words more accessible, but not necessarily more retrievable. *Journal of Verbal Learning and Verbal Behavior* 23:553–68.

GRAF, P.; MANDLER, G.; AND HADEN, P. 1982. Simulating amnesic symptoms in normal subjects. *Science* 218:1243–44.

GRAF, P.; MANDLER, G.; AND SQUIRE, L. R. 1984. The information that amnesic patients don't forget. *Journal of Experimental Psychology: Learning, Memory, and Cognition* 10:164–78.

GRAF, P., AND SCHACTER, D. L. 1985. Implicit and explicit memory for new associations in normal and amnesic subjects. *Journal of Experimental Psychology: Learning, Memory, and Cognition* 11:501–18.

GRAHAM, C. H., AND HSIA, Y. 1954. Luminosity curves for normal and dichromatic subjects including a case of unilateral color blindness. *Science* 120:780.

GRAY, S. 1977. Social aspects of body image: Perception of normalcy of weight and affect of college undergraduates. *Perceptual and Motor Skills* 45:1035–40.

GREEN, D. M. 1976. *An introduction to hearing*. New York: Academic Press.

GREEN, D. M., AND SWETS, J. A. 1966. *Signal detection theory and psychophysics*. New York: Wiley.

GREEN, P., AND PRESTON, M. 1981. Reinforcement of vocal correlates of auditory hallucinations by auditory feedback: A case study. *British Journal of Psychiatry* 139:204–208.

GREEN, R. 1969. Age-intelligence relationships between ages sixteen and sixty-four: A rising trend. *Developmental Psychology* 1:618–27.

GREEN, S. K.; BUCHANAN, D. R.; AND HEUER, S. K. 1984. Winners, losers, and choosers: A field investigation of dating initiation. *Personality and Social Psychology Bulletin* 10:502–11.

GREGORY, R. L. 1963. Distortion of visual space as inappropriate constancy scaling. *Nature* 199:678–80.

GREGORY, R. L. 1966. Visual illusions. In Foss, B. (Ed.), *New horizons in psychology*. Baltimore: Penguin Books.

GREVEN, P. J., JR. 1970. *Four generations: Population, land, and family in colonial Andover, Massachusetts*. Ithaca: N.Y.: Cornell University Press.

GREVERT, P., AND GOLDSTEIN, A. 1985. Placebo analgesia, naloxone, and the role of endogenous opioids. In White, L.; Turks, B.; and Schwartz, G. E. (Eds.), *Placebo*, pp. 332–51. New York: Guilford.

GRICE, H. P. 1968. Utterer's meaning, sentence-meaning and word-meaning. *Foundations of Language* 4:225–42.

GRIMSHAW, J. 1981. Form, function, and the language acquisition device. In Baker, C., and McCarthy, J. (Eds.), *The logical problem of language acquisition*. Cambridge, Mass.: MIT Press.

GROSSMAN, H. J. (Ed.). 1983. *Manual on terminology and classification in mental retardation*, rev. ed. Washington, D. C.: American Association for Mental Deficiency.

GROVES, P. M., AND REBEC, G. V. 1988. *Introduction to biological psychology*, 3rd ed. Dubuque, Iowa: W. C. Brown.

GUTTMAN, N., AND KALISH, H. I. 1956. Discriminability and stimulus generalization. *Journal of Experimental Psychology* 51:79–88.

GUYTON, A. C. 1981. *Textbook of medical physiology*. Philadelphia: Saunders.

HABER, R. N. 1969. Eidetic images. *Scientific American* 220:36–44.

HALL, C. S. 1953. A cognitive theory of dream symbols. *Journal of General Psychology* 48:169–86.

HALL, E. T. 1959. *The silent language*. New York: Doubleday.

HALPERN, D. F. 1986. *Sex differences in cognitive abilities*. Hillsdale, N.J.: Erlbaum.

HALVERSON, H. M. 1931. An experimental study of prehension infants by means of systematic cinema records. *Genetic Psychology Monographs* 47:47–63.

HAMILTON, D. L., AND ROSE, T. L. 1980. Illusory correlation and the maintenance of stereotypic beliefs. *Journal of Personality and Social Psychology* 39:832–45.

HAMILTON, W. D. 1964. The genetical evolution of social behavior. *Journal of Theoretical Biology* 7:1–51.

HARE, R. D. 1965. Temporal gradients of fear arousal in psychopaths. *Journal of Abnormal Psychology* 70:422–45.

HARE, R. D. 1978. A research scale for the assessment of psychopathy in criminal populations. *Personality and Individual Differences* 1:111–19.

HAREVEN, T. K. 1978. The last stage: Historical adulthood and old age. In Erikson, E. H. (Ed.), *Adulthood*, pp. 201–16. New York: Norton.

HARKINS, S., AND GREEN, R. G. 1975. Discriminability and criterion differences between extraverts and introverts during vigilance. *Journal of Research in Personality* 9:335–40.

HARLOW, H. F. 1949. The formation of learning sets. *Psychological Review* 56:51–65.

HARLOW, H. F. 1950. Learning and satiation of response in intrinsically motivated complex puzzle performance in monkeys. *Journal of Comparative and Physiological Psychology* 43:289–94.

HARLOW, H. F. 1958. The nature of love. *American Psychologist* 13:673–85.

HARLOW, H. F. 1959. Learning set and error factor theory. In Koch, S. (Ed.), *Psychology: A study of a science*, vol. 2, pp. 492–537. New York: McGraw-Hill.

HARLOW, H. F. 1962. The heterosexual affectional system in monkeys. *American Psychologist* 17:1–9.

HARLOW, H. F., AND HARLOW, M. K, 1972. The young monkeys. *Readings in Psychology Today*, 2nd ed. Albany, N.Y.: Delmar Publishers, CRM Books.

HARLOW, H. F., AND NOVAK, M. A. 1973. Psychopathological perspectives. *Perspectives in Biology and Medicine* 16:461–78.

HARRELL, J. P. 1980. Psychological factors and hypertension: A status report. *Psychological Bulletin* 87:482–501.

HARRIS, G. W., AND MICHAEL, R. P. 1964. The activation of sexual behavior by hypothalamic implants of estrogen. *Journal of Physiology* 171:275–301.

HARRIS, M. 1974. *Cows, pigs, wars, and witches.* New York: Random House.

HARTMANN, H. 1964. *Essays on ego psychology: Selected problems in psychoanalytic theory.* New York: International Universities Press.

HARTSHORNE, H., AND MAY, M. A. 1928. *Studies in the nature of character*, vol. 1. New York: Macmillan.

HARVEY, L. O., JR., AND LEIBOWITZ, H. 1967. Effects of exposure duration, cue reduction, and temporary monocularity on size matching at short distances. *Journal of the Optical Society of America* 57:249–53.

HASE, H. D., AND GOLDBERG, L. R. 1967. Comparative validities of different strategies of constructing personality inventory scales. *Psychological Bulletin* 67:231–48.

HAYNES, S. G.; FEINLEIB, M.; AND KANNEL, W. B. 1980. The relationship of psychosocial factors to coronary heart disease in the Framingham study: Eight years incidence in coronary heart disease. *American Journal of Epidemiology* 3:37–85.

HAYES, C. 1952. *The ape in our house.* London: Gollacz.

HEALY, A. F., AND MILLER, G. A. 1970. The verb as the main determinant of sentence meaning. *Psychonomic Science* 20:372.

HEARST, E. 1972. Psychology across the chessboard. In *Readings in Psychology Today*, 2nd ed. Albany, N.Y.: Delmar Publishers, CRM Books.

HEDIGER, H. 1968. *The psychology and behavior of animals in zoos and circuses.* New York: Dover.

HEIDER, F. 1958. *The psychology of interpersonal relationships.* New York: Wiley.

HEINICKE, C., AND WESTHEIMER, I. 1966. *Brief separations.* London: Longmans, Green.

HELLEKSON, C. J.; KLINE, J. A.; AND ROSENTHAL, N. E. 1986. Phototherapy for seasonal affective disorder in Alaska. *American Journal of Psychiatry* 143:1035–37.

HELMHOLTZ, H. 1909. *Wissenschaftliche Abhandlungen, II,* pp. 764–843.

HENLE, M. 1962. On the relation between logic and thinking. *Psychological Review* 69:366–78.

HENRY, J. P., AND CASSEL, J. C. 1969. Psychosocial factors in essential hypertension. *American Journal of Epidemiology* 90:171.

HERING, E. 1920. *Outlines of a theory of the light sense,* pp. 150–51. Edited by Hurvich, L. M., and Jameson, D. Cambridge, Mass.: Harvard University Press.

HERMAN, C. P., AND POLIVY, J. 1980. Restrained eating. In Stunkard, A. J. (Ed.), *Obesity,* pp. 208–25. Philadelphia: Saunders.

HERMAN, C. P., AND MACK, D. 1975. Restrained and unrestrained eating. *Journal of Personality* 43:647–60.

HESS, E. H. 1959. Imprinting. *Science* 130:133–41.

HESS, E. H. 1973. *Imprinting: Early experience and the developmental psychobiology of attachment.* New York: Van Nostrand.

HESTON, L. L. 1966. Psychiatric disorders in foster home reared children of schizophrenic mothers. *British Journal of Psychiatry* 112:819–25.

HILL, A. L. 1978. Savants: Mentally retarded individuals with specific skills. In N. R. Ellis (Ed.), *International Review of Research in Mental Retardation,* vol. 9. New York: Academic Press.

HILL, C. T.; RUBIN, L.; AND PEPLAU, L. A. 1976. Breakups before marriage: The end of 103 affairs. *Journal of Social Issues* 32:147–68.

HIRSCHFELD, AND CROSS, C. K. 1981. Epidemiology of affective disorders. *Archives of General Psychiatry* 39:3546

HIRSH-PASEK, K.; GOLINKOFF, R.; FLETCHER; DEGASPE-BEAUBIEN; AND CAULEY. 1985. In the beginning: one-word speakers comprehend word order. Paper presented at Boston Child Language Conference, October, 1985.

HOBBES, T. 1651. *Leviathan.* Baltimore: Penguin Books, 1968.

HOBSON, J. A. 1988. *The dreaming brain.* New York: Basic Books.

HOCHBERG, J. E. 1978a. *Perception,* 2nd ed. Englewood Cliffs, N.J.: Prentice-Hall.

HOCHBERG, J. E. 1978b. Art and perception. In Carterette, E. C., and Friedman, M. P. (Eds.), *Handbook of perception,* vol. 10, pp. 225–55. New York: Academic Press.

HOCHBERG, J. E. 1980. Pictorial functions and perceptual structures. In Hagen, M. A. (Ed.), *The perception of pictures,* vol. 2, pp. 47–93. New York: Academic Press.

HOCHBERG, J. 1981. On cognition in perception: Perceptual coupling and unconscious inference. *Cognition* 10:127–34.

HOCHBERG, J. 1988. Visual perception. In Atkinson, R. C.; Herrnstein, R. J.; Lindzey, G.; and Luce, R. D. (Eds.), *Stevens' handbook of experimental psychology: Vol. 1. Perception and motivation.* rev. ed., pp. 195–276. New York: Wiley.

HODGKIN, A. L., AND HUXLEY, A. F. 1939. Action potentials recorded from inside nerve fiber. *Nature* 144:710–11.

HOEBEL, B. G. AND TEITELBAUM, P. 1976. Weight regulation in normal and hyperphagic rats. *Journal of Physiological and Comparative Psychology* 61:189–93.

HOFFMAN, H. S. 1978. Experimental analysis of imprinting and its behavioral effects. *The Psychology of Learning and Motivation* 12:137.

HOFFMAN, H. S., AND FLESHLER, M. 1964. An apparatus for the measurement of the startle response in the rat. *American Journal of Psychology* 77:307–308.

HOFFMAN, L. W. 1974. Effects of maternal employment on the child. A review of the research. *Developmental Psychology* 10:204–28.

HOFFMAN, M. L. 1970. Moral development. In Mussen, P. H., (Ed.), *Carmichael's manual of child psychology,* 3rd. ed., vol. 2, pp. 457–558. New York: Wiley.

HOFFMAN, M. L. 1977a. Empathy, its development and prosocial implications. In Keasey, C. B. (Ed.), *Nebraska Symposium on Motivation* 25:169–217.

HOFFMAN, M. L. 1977b. Sex differences in empathy and related behaviors. *Psychological Bulletin* 84:712–22.

HOFFMAN, M. L. 1979. Development of moral thought, feeling, and behavior. *American Psychologist* 34:295–318.

HOFFMAN, M. L. 1984. Empathy, its limitations, and its role in a comprehensive moral theory. In Kurtines, W. M., and Gewirtz, L. (Eds.), *Morality, moral behavior, and moral development,* pp. 283–302. New York: Wiley.

HÖHN, E. O. 1969. The phalarope. *Scientific American* 220:104.

HOLDING, D. H. 1985. *The psychology of chess skill.* N.J.: Erlbaum.

HOLDING, D. H., AND REYNOLDS, R. I. 1982. Recall or evaluation of chess positions as determinants of chess skill. *Memory and Cognition* 10:237–42.

HOLLINGSHEAD, A. B., AND REDLICH, F. C. 1958. *Social class and mental illness: A community study.* New York: Wiley.

HOLT, R. R. 1978. *Methods in clinical psychology: Vol. 1. Projective assessment.* New York: Plenum.

HOLWAY, A. F., AND BORING, E. G. 1947. Determinants of apparent visual size with distance variant. *American Journal of Psychology* 54:21–37.

HOOLEY, J. M. 1985. Expressed emotion: A review of the critical literature. *Clinical Psychology Review* 5:119–39.

HORN, J. L., AND CATTELL, R. B. 1967. Age differences in fluid and crystallized intelligence. *Acta Psychologica* 26:107–29.

HORN, J. L., AND DONALDSON, G. 1976. On the myth of intellectual decline in adulthood. *American Psychologist* 31:701–19.

HORN, J. M. 1983. The Texas Adoption Project: Adopted children and their biological and adoptive parents. *Child Development* 54:268–75.

HORN, J. M.; LOEHLIN, J. C.; AND WILLERMAN, L. 1979. Intellectual resemblance among adoptive and biological relatives: The Texas Adoption Project. *Behavior Genetics* 13:459–71.

HORN, J. M.; LOEHLIN, J. C.; AND WILLERMAN, L. 1982. Aspects of the inheritance of intellectual abilities. *Behavior Genetics* 12:479–516.

HORNE, R. L., AND PICARD, R. S. 1979. Psychosocial risk factors for lung cancer. *Psychosomatic Medicine* 41:503–14.

HORNEY, K. 1937. *The neurotic personality of our time.* New York: Norton.

HORNEY, K. 1945. *Our inner conflicts.* New York: Norton.

HORNEY, K. 1950. *New ways in psychoanalysis.* New York: Norton.

HOVLAND, C. I., AND WEISS, W. 1952. The influence of source credibility on communication effectiveness. *Public Opinion Quarterly* 15:635–50.

HOWARD, D. V. 1983. *Cognitive psychology.* New York: Macmillan.

HRDY, S. B., AND WILLIAMS, G. C. 1983. Behavioral biology and the double standard. In Wasser, S. K., (Ed.), *The social behavior of female vertebrates,* pp. 3–17. New York: Academic Press.

HUBEL, D. H. 1963. The visual cortex of the brain. *Scientific American* 209:54–62.

HUBEL, D. H., AND WIESEL, T. N. 1959. Receptive fields of single neurons in the cat's visual cortex. *Journal of Physiology* 148:574–91.

HUBEL, D. H., AND WIESEL, T. N. 1970. Stereoscopic vision in the macaque monkey. Nature 225:41–42.

HUBEL, D. H., AND WIESEL, T. N. 1979. Brain mechanisms of vision. *Scientific American* 241:150–68.

HULL, C. L. 1943. *Principles of behavior.* New York: Appleton-Century-Crofts.

HUMPHREY, G. 1951. *Thinking: An introduction to its experimental psychology.* New York: Wiley.

HUMPHREYS, L. G. 1939. The effect of random alternation of reinforcement on the acquisition and extinction of conditioned eyelid reactions. *Journal of Experimental Psychology* 25:141–58.

HUNT, E. 1985. The correlates of intelligence. In D. K. Detterman (Ed.), *Current topics in human intelligence,* vol. 1. Norwood, N.J.: Ablex.

HUNT, J. M. 1961. *Intelligence and experience.* New York: Ronald Press.

HUNT, P., AND HILLERY, J. M. 1973. Social facilitation in a coaction setting: An examination of the effects over learning trials. *Journal of Experimental Social Psychology* 9:563–71.

HURVICH, L. M. 1981. *Color vision.* Sunderland, Mass.: Sinauer Assoc.

HURVICH, L. M., AND JAMESON, D. 1957. An opponent-process theory of color vision. *Psychological Review* 64:384–404.

HURVICH, L. M., AND JAMESON, D. 1974. Opponent processes as a model of neural organization. *American Psychologist* 29:88–102.

HUSTON, A. C. 1983. Sex-typing. In Mussen, P. (Ed.), *Carmichael's manual of child psychology: Vol. 4. Socialization, personality, and social development,* pp. 387–468. (Hetherington, E. M., volume editor). New York: Wiley.

HUSTON, T. L.; RUGGIERO, M.; CONNER, R.; AND GEIS, G. 1981. Bystander intervention into crime: A study based on naturally occurring episodes. *Social Psychology Quarterly* 44:14–23.

HUTTENLOCHER, J.; SMILEY, P.; AND CHARNEY, R. 1983. Emergence of action categories in the child: Evidence from verb meanings. *Psychological Review* 90:72–93.

HUTTENLOCHER, P. R. 1979. Synaptic density in human frontal cortex—developmental changes and effects of aging. *Brain Research* 163:195–205.

HYDE, D. M. 1959. An investigation of Piaget's theories of the development of the concept of number. Unpublished doctoral dissertation. University of London. (Quoted in Flavell, J. H., *The developmental psychology of Jean Piaget,* p. 383. New York: Van Nostrand Reinhold).

HYDE, J. S. 1981. How large are cognitive gender differences? A meta-analysis using w^2 and d. *American Psychologist* 36:892–901.

HYDE, J. S., AND LYNN, M. C. 1988. Gender differences in verbal ability: A meta-analysis. *Psychological Bulletin* 104:53–69.

ILYIN, N. A., AND ILYIN, V. N. 1930. Temperature effects on the color of the Siamese cat. *Journal of Heredity* 21:309–18.

IMPERATO-MCGINLEY, J.; GUERRERO, L.; GAUTIER, T.; AND PETERSON, R. E. 1974. Steroid 5-alpha reductase deficiency in man: An inherited form of male pseudohermaphroditism. *Science* 186:1213–15.

IMPERATO-MCGINLEY, J.; PETERSON, R. E.; GAUTIER, T.; AND STURLA, E. 1979. Androgens and the evolution of male-gender identity among male pseudohermaphrodites with 5-alpha reductase deficiency. *The New England Journal of Medicine* 300:1233–37.

INGLIS, J. 1969. Electrode placement and the effect of ECT on mood and memory in depression. *Canadian Psychiatric Association Journal* 14:463–471.

INGVAR, D. H., AND LASSEN, N. A. 1979. Activity distribution in the cerebral cortex in organic dementia as revealed by measurements of regional cerebral blood flow. *Bayer Symposium VII. Brain function in old age,* 268–77.

INHELDER, B. AND PIAGET, J. 1958. *The growth of logical thinking from childhood to adolescence.* New York: Basic Books.

IZARD, C. E. 1977. *Human emotions.* New York: Plenum.

IZZETT, R. 1971. Authoritarianism and attitudes toward the Vietnam War as reflected in behavioral and self-report measures. *Journal of Personality and Social Psychology* 17:145–48.

JACKENDOFF, R. 1987. The status of thematic relations in linguistic theory. *Linguistic Inquiry* 18(3):369–411.

JACOBS, A. 1955. Formation of new associations to words selected on the basis of reaction-time-GSR combinations. *Journal of Abnormal and Social Psychology* 51:371–77.

JACOBY, L. L., AND DALLAS, M. 1981. On the relationship between autobiographical memory and perceptual learning. *Journal of Experimental Psychology: General* 3:306–40.

JACOBY, L. L., AND WITHERSPOON, D. 1982. Remembering without awareness. *Canadian Journal of Psychology* 36:300–24.

JAHODA, G. 1979. A cross-cultural perspective on experimental social psychology. *Personality and Social Psychology Bulletin* 5:142–48.

JAMES, W. 1890. *Principles of psychology.* New York: Henry Holt.

JAMESON, D. 1975. From contrast to assimilation in art and in the eye. *Leonardo* 8:125–31.

JAMESON, D., AND HURVICH, L. M.. 1975. From contrast to assimilation: In art and in the eye. *Leonardo* 8:125–31.

JANICAK, P. G.; DAVIS, J. M.; GIBBONS, R. D.; ERICKSEN, S.; CHANG, S.; AND GALLAGHER, P. 1985. Efficacy of ECT: A meta-analysis. *American Journal of Psychiatry* 142:297–302.

JANIS, I. L.; MAHL, G. G.; KAGAN, J.; AND HOLT, R. R. 1969. *Personality: Dynamics, development and assessment.* New York: Harcourt, Brace and World.

JENCKS, C.; SMITH, M.; ACLAND, H.; BANE, M. J.; COHEN, D.; GINTIS, H.; HEYNS, B.; AND MICHELSON, S. 1972. *Inequality: A reassessment of the effect of family and schooling in America.* New York: Basic Books.

JENKINS, C. D.; ROSENMAN, R. H.; AND FRIEDMAN, M. 1967. Development of an objective psychological test for the determination of the coronary prone behavior pattern in employed men. *Journal of Chronic Disease* 20:371–79.

JENKINS, J. G., AND DALLENBACH, K. M. 1924. Oblivescence during sleep and waking. *American Journal of Psychology* 35:605–12.

JENSEN, A. R. 1965. Scoring the Stroop test. *Acta Psychologica* 24:398–408.

JENSEN, A. R. 1969. How much can we boost I. Q. and scholastic achievement? *Harvard Educational Review* 39:1–123.

JENSEN, A. R. 1973. *Educability and group differences.* New York: Harper & Row.

JENSEN, A. R. 1985. The nature of the black-white difference on various psychometric tests: Spearman's hypothesis. *Behavioral and Brain Sciences* 8:193–263.

JOHNSON, J., AND NEWPORT, E. 1989. Critical period efforts in second-language learning: The influence of maturational state on the acquisition of English as a second language. *Cognitive Psychology* 21:60–90.

JOHNSON, R. E. 1979. *Juvenile delinquency and its origins.* New York: Cambridge University Press.

JOHNSON, S. 1765. Shakespeare criticism. In Danziger, M. K. (Ed.), *Samuel Johnson on literature.* New York: Ungar, 1979.

JONES, E. 1954. *Hamlet and Oedipus.* New York: Doubleday.

JONES, E. E., AND NISBETT, R. E. 1972. The actor and the observer: Divergent perceptions of the cause of behavior. In Jones, E. E.; Karouse, D. E.; Kelley, H. H.; Nisbett, R. E.; Valins, S.; and Weiner, B. (Eds.), *Attribution: Perceiving the causes of behavior.* Morristown, N.J.: General Learning Press.

JONES, H. E., AND KAPLAN, O. J. 1945. Psychological aspects of mental disorders in later life. In Kaplan, O. J. (Ed.), *Mental disorders in later life*, pp. 69–115. Stanford, Calif.: Stanford University Press.

JONES, R. E. 1983. Street people and psychiatry: An introduction. *Hospital Community Psychiatry* 34:807–11.

JONIDES, J. 1980. Toward a model of the mind's eye's movement. *Canadian Journal of Psychology* 34:103–12.

JONIDES, J. 1983. Further toward a model of the mind's eye's movement. *Bulletin of the Psychonomic Society* 21:247–50.

JONIDES, J., AND BAUM, D. R. 1978. Cognitive maps as revealed by distance estimates. Paper presented at the 18th annual meeting of the Psychonomic Society. Washington, D.C.

JORGENSEN, B. W., AND CERVONE, J. C. 1978. Affect enhancement in the pseudo recognition task. *Personality and Social Psychology Bulletin* 4:285–88.

JOSHI, A. K. 1983. Varieties of cooperative responses in question-answer systems. In Keifer, F. (Ed.), *Questions and answers*, pp. 229–40. Amsterdam: D. Reidel Publishing Co.

JOSSELSON, R. 1980. Ego development in adolescence. In Adelson, J. (Ed.), *Handbook of adolescent psychology*, pp. 188–211. New York: Wiley.

JOUVET, M. 1967. The stages of sleep. *Scientific American* 216:62–72.

JULESZ, B. 1978. Perceptual limits of texture discrimination and their implications to figure-ground separation. In Leeuwenberg, E. and Buffart, H. (Eds.), *Formal theories of perception*, pp. 205–16. New York: Wiley.

JULIEN, R. M. 1985. *A primer of drug action*, 4th ed. New York: Freeman.

JUSCZYK, P. 1985. On characterizing the development of speech perception. In Mehler, J., and Fox, R. (Eds.), *Neonate cognition: Beyond the blooming buzzing confusion.* Hillsdale, N.J.: Erlbaum.

KAGAN, J. 1976. Emergent themes in human development. *American Scientist* 64:186–96.

KAGAN, J.; KEARSLEY, R. B.; AND ZELAZO, P. R. 1978. *Infancy: Its place in human development.* Cambridge, Mass.: Harvard University Press.

KAGAN, J., AND MOSS, H. A. 1962. *Birth to maturity: The Fels study of psychological development.* New York: Wiley.

KAHNEMAN, D., AND TVERSKY, A. 1972. Subjective probability: A judgment of representativeness. *Cognitive Psychology* 3:430–54.

KAHNEMAN, D., AND TVERSKY, A. 1973. On the psychology of prediction. *Psychological Review* 80:237–51.

KALAT, J. W. 1984. *Biological psychology*, 2nd ed. Belmont, Calif.: Wadsworth.

KALLMAN, F. J. 1952. Comparative twin study of genetic aspects of male homosexuality. *Journal of Mental and Nervous Diseases* 15:283–98.

KAMIN, L. J. 1965. Temporal and intensity characteristics of the conditioned stimulus. In Prokasy, W. F. (Ed.), *Classical conditioning.* New York: Appleton-Century-Crofts.

KAMIN, L. J. 1969. Predictability, surprise, attention and conditioning. In Campbell, B. A., and Church, R. M. (Eds.), *Punishment and aversive behavior*, pp. 279–96. New York: Appleton-Century-Crofts.

KAMIN, L. J. 1974. *The science and politics of I. Q.* New York: Wiley.

KANDEL, D. 1978. Similarity in real-life adolescent friendship pairs. *Journal of Personality and Social Psychology* 36:306–12.

KANIZSA, G. 1976. Subjective contours. *Scientific American* 234:48–52.

KATZ, B. 1952. The nerve impulse. *Scientific American* 187:55–64.

KATZ, J. J. 1972. *Semantic theory.* New York: Harper & Row.

KATZ, J. J., AND FODOR, J. A. 1963. The structure of a semantic theory. *Language* 39:170–210.

KATZ, N.; BAKER, E.; AND MACNAMARA, J. 1974. What's in a name? A study of how children learn common and proper names. *Child Development* 45:469–73.

KAUFMAN, A. S.; KAMPHAUS; R. W.; AND KAUFMAN, N. L. 1985. The Kaufman Assessment Battery for Children (K-ABC). In Newmark, C. S. (Ed.), *Major psychological assessment instruments.* Boston: Allyn and Bacon.

KAUFMAN, L., AND ROCK, I. 1962. The moon illusion. *Scientific American* 207:120–30.

KEELE, S. W. 1982. Learning and control of coordinated motor patterns: The programming perspective. In Kelso, J. A. S. (Ed.), *Human motor behavior*, pp. 143–60. Hillsdale, N.J.: Erlbaum.

KEESEY, R. E., AND PAWLEY, T. L. 1986. The regulation of body weight. *Annual Review of Psychology* 37:109–34.

KEETON, W. T. 1972 AND 1980. *Biological science*, 2nd and 3rd eds. New York: Norton.

KEETON, W. T., AND GOULD, J. L. 1986. *Biological science*, 4th ed. New York: Norton.

KEIL, F. C., AND BATTERMAN, N. 1984. A characteristic-to-defining shift in the development of word meaning. *Journal of Verbal Learning and Verbal Behavior* 23:221–36.

KELLER, H. 1955. *Teacher: Anne Sullivan Macy.* Westport, Conn.: Greenwood Press.

KELLEY, H. H. 1967. Attribution theory in social psychology. In Levine, D. (Ed.), *Nebraska Symposium on Motivation*, pp. 192–238. Lincoln, Neb.: University of Nebraska Press.

KELLEY, H. H., AND MICHELA, J. L. 1980. Attribution theory and research. *Annual Review of Psychology* 31:457–501.

KELLEY, H., AND THIBAUT, J. W. 1978. *Interpersonal relations: A theory of interdependence.* New York: Wiley-Interscience.

KELLEY, S., AND MIRER, T. W. 1974. The simple act of voting. *American Political Science Review* 68:572–91.

KELLMAN, P. J., AND SPELKE, E. S. 1983. Perception of partially occluded objects in infancy. *Cognitive Psychology* 15:483–524.

KELLMAN, P. J.; SPELKE, E. S.; AND SHORT, K. R. 1986. Infant perception of object unity from translatory motion in depth and vertical translation. *Child Development* 57:72–86.

KENDLER, K. S., AND GRUENBERG, A. M. 1984. An independent analysis of the Danish adoption study of schizophrenia: VI. The relationship between psychiatric disorders as defined by DSM-III in the relatives and adoptees. *Archives of General Psychiatry* 41:555–64.

KENRICK, D. T., AND FUNDER, D. C. 1988. Profiting from controversy: Lessons from the person-situation debate. *American Psychologist* 43:23–34.

KERR, M. E., AND BOWEN, M. 1988. *Family evaluation.* New York: Norton.

KESSEL, E. L. 1955. The mating activities of balloon flies. *Systematic Zoology* 4:97–104.

KETY, S. S. 1983. Mental illness in the biological and adoptive relatives of schizophrenic adoptees: Findings relevant to genetic and environmental factors in etiology. *Journal of American Psychiatry* 140:720–27.

KIHLSTROM, J. F., AND CANTOR, N. 1984. Mental representations of the self. In Berkowitz, L. (Ed.), *Advances in experimental social psychology*, vol. 17, pp. 1–47. New York: Academic Press.

KILHAM, W., AND MANN, L. 1974. Level of destructive obedience as a function of transmitter and executant roles in the Milgram obedience paradigm. *Journal of Personality and Social Psychology* 29:696–702.

KIMBLE, G. A. 1961. *Hilgard and Marquis' conditioning and learning.* New York: Appleton-Century-Crofts.

KING, H. E. 1961. Psychological effects of excitation in the limbic system. In Sheer, D. E. (Ed.), *Electrical stimulation of the brain.* Austin: University of Texas Press.

KINSEY, A. C.; POMEROY, W. B.; AND MARTIN, C. E. 1948. *Sexual behavior in the human male.* Philadelphia: Saunders.

KINSEY, A.; POMEROY, W.; MARTIN, C.; AND GEBHARD, P. 1953. *Sexual behavior in the human female.* Philadelphia: Saunders.

KITCHER, P. 1985. *Vaulting ambition: Sociobiology and the quest for human nature.* Cambridge, Mass: M. I. T. Press.

KITTRIE, N. N. 1971. *The right to be different: Deviance and enforced therapy.* Baltimore: Penguin Books.

KLEINMUNTZ, B. 1982. *Personality and psychological assessment.* New York: St. Martin's Press.

KLEITMAN, N. 1960. Patterns of dreaming. *Scientific American* 203:82–88.

KLIMA, E.; AND BELLUGI, U.; WITH BATTISON, R.; BOYES-BRAEM, P.; FISCHER, S.; FRISHBERG, N.; LANE, H.; LENTZ, E. M.; NEWKIRK, D.; NEWPORT, E.; PEDERSEN, C.; AND SIPLE, P. 1979. *The signs of language.* Cambridge, Mass.: Harvard University Press.

KLINEBERG, O. 1940. *Social psychology.* New York: Henry Holt.

KLOPFER, B.; AINSWORTH, M.; KLOPFER, W. G.; AND HOLT, R. R. 1954. *Developments in the Rorschach technique.* Yonkers, N.Y.: World Book.

KLOPFER, P. H. 1974. *An introduction to animal behavior: Ethology's first century.* Englewood Cliffs, N.J.: Prentice-Hall.

KNITTLE, J. L., AND HIRSCH, J. 1968. Effect of early nutrition on the development of the rat epididymal fat pads: Cellularity and metabolism. *Journal of Clinical Investigations* 47:2091.

KNOX, R. E., AND INKSTER, J. A. 1968. Postdecision dissonance at post-time. *Journal of Personality and Social Psychology* 8:319–23.

KOHLBERG, L. 1963. Development of children's orientations toward a moral order. *Vita Humana* 6:11–36.

KOHLBERG, L. 1966. A cognitive developmental analysis of children's sex-role concepts and attitudes. In Maccoby, E. E. (Ed.), *The development of sex differences,* pp. 82–171. Stanford, Calif.: Stanford University Press.

KOHLBERG, L. 1969. Stage and sequence: The cognitive developmental approach to socialization. In Goslin, D. A. (Ed.), *Handbook of socialization theory of research,* pp. 347–480. Chicago: Rand McNally.

KOHLBERG, L. AND CANDEE, D. 1984. The relationship of moral judgment to moral action. In Kurtines, W. M., and Gewirtz, L. (Eds.), *Morality, moral behavior, and moral development,* pp. 52–73. New York: Wiley.

KOHLBERG, L.; LEVINE, C.; AND HEWER, A. 1984. Synopses and detailed replies to critics. In Kohlberg, L. (Ed.), *The psychology of moral development: The nature and validity of moral stages,* pp. 320–86. San Francisco: Harper & Row.

KÖHLER, W. 1925. *The mentality of apes.* New York: Harcourt Brace and World.

KOHN, M. L. 1968. Social class and schizophrenia: A critical review. In Rosenthal, D., and Kety, S. S. (Eds.), *The transmission of schizophrenia,* pp. 155–74. London: Pergamon.

KOLB, B., AND MILNER, B. 1981. Performance of complex art and facial movements after focal brain lesions. *Neuropsychologia* 19:491–503.

KOLB, B., AND WHISHAW, I. Q. 1980. *Fundamentals of human neuropsychology.* San Francisco: Freeman.

KOLB, B., AND WHISHAW, I. 1990. *Fundamentals of human neuropsychology,* 3rd ed. San Francisco: Freeman.

KOLODNY, R.; MASTERS, W.; HENDRYX, J.; AND TORO, G. 1971. Plasma testosterone and semen analysis in male homosexuals. *New England Journal of Medicine* 285:1170–74.

KORIAT, A., AND LIEBLICH, I. 1974. What does a person in a TOT state know that a person in a "Don't Know" state doesn't know? *Memory and Cognition* 2:647–55.

KORS, A. C., AND PETERS, E. 1972. *Witchcraft in Europe:1100–1700. A documentary history.* Philadelphia: University of Pennsylvania Press.

KOSSLYN, S. M. 1980. *Image and mind.* Cambridge, Mass.: Harvard University Press.

KOSSLYN, S. M. 1984. *Ghosts in the mind's machine.* New York: Norton.

KOSSLYN, S. M.; BALL, T. M.; AND REISSER, B. J. 1978. Visual images preserve metric spatial information: Evidence from studies of image scanning. *Journal of Experimental Psychology: Human Perception and Performance* 4:1–20.

KOTELCHUK, M. 1976. The infant's relationship to the father: Some experimental evidence. In Lamb, M. (Ed.), *The role of the father in child development.* New York: Wiley.

KRANTZ, D. S.; CONTRADA, R. J.; HILL, D. R.; AND FRIEDLER, E. 1988. Environmental stress and behavioral antecedents of coronary heart disease. *Journal of Consulting and Clinical Psychology* 56: 333–41.

KRASHEN, S. 1981. Second language acquisition and second language learning. London: Pergamon Press.

KREBS, J. R. 1982. Territorial defence in the great tit. *Parus Major L. Ecology* 52:2–22.

KREBS, J. R., AND DAVIES, N. B. 1987. *An introduction to behavioral ecology,* 2nd ed. Boston: Blackwell Scientific Publications.

KRECH, D., AND CRUTCHFIELD, R. 1958. *Elements of psychology.* New York: Knopf.

KUCZAJ, S. A. 1977. The acquisition of regular and irregular past tense forms. *Journal of Verbal Learning and Verbal Behavior* 16: 589–600.

KUFFLER, S. W. 1953. Discharge pattern and functional organization of mammalian retina. *Journal of Neurophysiology* 16:37–68.

KUPFER, D. J.; FOSTER, F. G.; AND REICH, L. 1976. EEG sleep changes as predictors in depression. *American Journal of Psychiatry* 133:622.

KUZNICKI, J. T., AND McCUTCHEON, N. B. 1979. Cross enhancement of the sour taste of single human taste papillae. *Journal of Experimental Psychology* 198:68–89.

LA BERGE, D. 1975. Acquisition of automatic processing in perceptual and associative learning. In Rabbitt, P. M. A., and Dormic, S. (Eds.), *Attention and performance,* vol. 5. London: Academic Press.

LABOV, W. 1970. The logic of nonstandard English. In Williams, F. (Ed.), *Language and poverty: Perspectives on a theme,* pp. 153–89. Chicago: Markham.

LACK, D. 1953. Darwin's finches. *Scientific American* 188: 66–72.

LAMB, H. R. 1984. Deinstitutionalization and the homeless mentally ill. *Hospital Community Psychiatry* 35:899–907.

LAMB, M. E. 1977. Father-infant and mother-infant interaction in the first year of life. *Child Development* 48:167–81.

LANDAU, B., AND GLEITMAN, L. R. 1985. *Language and experience: Evidence from the blind child.* Cambridge, Mass.: Harvard University Press.

LANDAU, B.; SMITH, L.; AND JONES, S. 1988. The importance of shape in early lexical learning. *Cognitive Development* 3:299–321.

LANDIS, C., AND HUNT, W. A. 1932. Adrenalin and emotion. *Psychological Review* 39:467–85.

LANGER, E. J., AND RODIN, J. 1976. The effects of choice and enhanced personal responsibility for the aged: A field experiment in an institutional setting. *Journal of Personality and Social Psychology* 34: 191–98.

LANGLOIS, J. H., AND DOWNS, A. C. 1980. Mothers, fathers, and peers as socialization agents of sex-typed play behaviors in young children. *Child Development* 51:1237–1347.

LANYON, R. I., AND GOLDSTEIN, L. D. 1971. *Personality assessment.* New York: Wiley.

LANYON, R. I., AND GOLDSTEIN, L. D. 1982. *Personality assessment.* 2nd ed. New York: Wiley.

LaPiere, R. 1934. Attitudes versus actions. *Social Forces* 13:230–37.

Lash, J. P. 1980. *Helen and Teacher: The story of Helen Keller and Anne Sullivan Macy.* New York: Delacorte Press.

Lashley, K. S. 1930. The mechanism of vision:1. A method for rapid analysis of pattern-vision in the rat. *Journal of Genetic Psychology* 37:453–60.

Lashley, K. S. 1951. The problem of serial order in behavior. In Jeffress, L. A. (Ed.), *Cerebral mechanisms in behavior, the Hixon Symposium.* New York: Wiley.

Lasky, J. J.; Hover, G. L.; Smith, P. A.; Bostian, D. W.; Duffendeck, S. C.; and Nord, C. L. 1959. Post-hospital adjustment as predicted by psychiatric patients and by their staff. *Journal of Consulting Psychology* 23:213–18.

Lassen, N. A.; Ingvar, D. H.; and Skinhoj, E. 1978. Brain function and blood flow. *Scientific American* 239:62–71.

Latané, B., and Nida, S. 1981. Group size and helping. *Psychological Bulletin* 89:308–24.

Latané, B.; Nida, S. A.; and Wilson, D. W. 1981. The effects of group size on helping behavior. In Rushton, J. P., and Sorrentino, R. M. (Eds.), *Altruism and helping behavior: Social, personality, and developmental perspectives.* Hillsdale, N.J.: Erlbaum.

Latané, B., and Rodin, J. 1969. A lady in distress: Inhibiting effects of friends and strangers on bystander intervention. *Journal of Experimental Social Psychology.* 5:189–202.

Latané, B.; Williams, K.; and Harkins, S. 1979. Many hands make light the work: The causes and consequences of social loafing. *Journal of Personality and Social Psychology* 37:822–32.

Lau, R. R., and Russell, D. 1980. Attributions in the sports pages. *Journal of Personality and Social Psychology* 39:29–38.

Layzer, D. 1972. Science or superstition: A physical scientist looks at the I. Q. controversy. *Cognition* 1:265–300.

Lazar, I. and Darlington, R. 1982. Lasting effects of early education: A report from the Consortium for Longitudinal Studies. *Monographs of the Society for Research in Child Development* 47 (2–3, Serial No. 195).

Lazarus, A. A. 1971. *Behavior therapy and beyond.* New York: McGraw-Hill.

Lazarus, A. A. 1981. *The practice of multi-modal therapy.* New York: McGraw-Hill.

Le Bon, G. 1895. *The crowd.* New York: Viking Press, 1960.

Leask, J.; Haber, R. N.; and Haber, R. B. 1969. Eidetic imagery in children: II. Longitudinal and experimental results. *Psychonomic Monograph Supplements* 3(Whole No. 35):25–48.

Leeper, R. W. 1935. A study of a neglected portion of the field of learning: The development of sensory organization. *Journal of Genetic Psychology* 46:41–75.

Leff, M. J.; Roatsch, J. F.; and Bunney, W. E., Jr. 1970. Environmental factors preceding the onset of severe depressions. *Psychiatry* 33:298–311.

Lefkowitz, M. M.; Blake, R. R.; and Mouton, J. S. 1955. Status factors in pedestrian violation of traffic signals. *Journal of Abnormal and Social Psychology* 51:704–706.

Leibowitz, H.; Brislin, R.; Perlmutter, L.; and Hennessy, R. 1969. Ponzo perspective illusion as a manifestation of space perception. *Science* 166:1174–76.

Lempers, J. S.; Flavell, E. R.; and Flavell, J. H. 1977. The development in very young children of tacit knowledge concerning visual perception. *Genetic Psychology Monographs* 95:3–53.

Lenneberg, E. H. 1967. *Biological foundations of language.* New York: Wiley.

Lepper, M. R. 1983. Social control processes, attributions of motivation, and the internalization of social values. In Higgins, E. T.; Ruble, D. N.; and Hartup, W. W. (Eds.), *Social cognition and social behavior: Developmental perspectives.* New York: Cambridge University Press.

Levine, J. D.; Gordon, N. C.; and Fields, H. L. 1979. The role of endorphins in placebo analgesia. In Bonica, J. J.; Liebesking, J. C.; and Albe-Fessard, D. (Eds.), *Advances in pain research and therapy,* vol. 3. New York: Raven.

Levinson, D. J. 1978. *The seasons of a man's life.* New York: Knopf.

Levy, J. 1983. Language, cognition, and the right hemisphere: A response to Gazzaniga. *American Psychologist* 38:538–41.

Lewandowsky, S.; Dunn, J. C.; and Kirsner, K. (Eds.). 1989. *Implicit memory: Theoretical issues.* Hillsdale, N.J.: Erlbaum.

Lewis, E. R. et al. 1969. Study of neural organization in aplysia with the scanning electron microscope. *Science* 165:1140–43.

Lewontin, R. C. 1976. Race and intelligence. In Block, N. J., and Dworkin, G. (Eds.), *The IQ controversy,* pp. 78–92. New York: Pantheon.

Lewy, A.; Sack, L.; Miller, S.; and Hoban, T. M. 1987. Antidepressant and circadian-phase shifting effects of light. *Science* 235: 352–54.

Lickley, J. D. 1919. *The nervous system.* New York: Longman.

Lidz, T.; Cornelison, A.; Fleck, S.; and Terry, D. 1957. The intrafamilial environment of schizophrenic patients: II. Marital schism and marital skew. *American Journal of Psychiatry* 114:241–48.

Lieberman, P. L. 1975. *On the origins of language.* New York: Macmillan.

Liebert, R. M.; Poulos, R. W.; and Strauss, G. D. 1974. *Developmental psychology.* Englewood Cliffs, N.J.: Prentice-Hall.

Liem, J. H. 1974. Effects of verbal communications of parents and children: A comparison of normal and schizophrenic parents. *Journal of Consulting and Clinical Psychology* 42:438–50.

Lindsay, P. H., and Norman, D. A. 1977. *Human information processing,* 2nd ed. New York: Academic Press.

Lindsley, D. B. 1960. Attention, consciousness, sleep, and wakefulness. In *Handbook of physiology: vol. 3, sect. 1, Neurophysiology.* Washington, D. C.: American Physiological Society.

Lindsley, D. B.; Schreiner, L. H.; Knowles, W. B.; and Magoun, H. W. 1950. Behavioral and EEG changes following chronic brain stem lesions in the cat. *Electroencephalography and Clinical Neurophysiology* 2:483–98.

Lipowski, Z. J. 1975. Psychophysiological cardiovascular disorders. In Freedman, A. M.; Kaplan, H. I.; and Sadock, B. J. (Eds.), *Comprehensive textbook of psychiatry,* vol. 2, pp. 1660–68. Baltimore: Williams & Wilkins.

Lippert, W. W., and Senter, R. J. 1966. Electrodermal responses in the sociopath. *Psychonomic Science* 4:25–26.

Liske, E., and Davis, W. J. 1984. Sexual behavior of the Chinese praying mantis. *Animal Behavior* 32:916.

Little, K. B., and Shneidman, E. S. 1959. Congruencies among interpretations of psychological test and anamnestic data. *Psychological Monographs* 73 (Whole No. 476).

Locke, J. 1690. *An essay concerning human understanding.* Edited by A. D. Woozley. Cleveland: Meridian Books, 1964.

Loehlin, J. C.; Lindzey, G.; and Spuhler, J. N. 1975. *Race difference in intelligence.* San Francisco: Freeman.

Loewi, O. 1960. An autobiographical sketch. *Perspectives in Biological Medicine* 4:2–35.

Loftus, E. F. 1973. Activation of semantic memory. *American Journal of Psychology* 86:331–37.

Loftus, E. F. 1975. Leading questions and the eyewitness report. *Cognitive Psychology* 7:560–72.

Loftus, E. F., and Zanni, G. 1975. Eyewitness testimony: The influence of the wording of a question. *Bulletin of the Psychonomic Society* 5:86–88.

Logan, G. D. 1988. Toward an instance theory of automatization. *Psychological Review* 95:492–527.

Logue, A. W. 1979. Taste aversion and the generality of the laws of learning. *Psychological Bulletin* 86:276–96.

Logue, A. W. 1986. *The psychology of eating and drinking.* New York: Freeman.

London, P. 1964. *The modes and morals of psychotherapy.* New York: Holt, Rinehart & Winston.

London, P. 1970. The rescuers: Motivational hypotheses about Christians who saved Jews from the Nazis. In Macauley, J., and Berkowitz, L. (Eds.), *Altruism and helping behvaior.* New York: Academic Press.

Lorenz, K. Z. 1966. *On aggression.* London: Methuen.

Luborsky, L. I.; Singer, B.; and Luborsky, L. 1975. Comparative studies of psychotherapies. *Archives of General Psychiatry* 20:84–88.

LUCE, R. D., AND RAIFFA, H. 1957. *Games and decisions.* New York: Wiley.

LUCHINS, A. S. 1942. Mechanization in problem-solving: The effect of Einstellung. *Psychological Monographs* 54 (Whole No. 248).

LURIA, A. R. 1966. *Higher cortical functions in man.* New York: Basic Books.

MACCOBY, E. E. 1980. *Social development.* New York: Harcourt Brace Jovanovich.

MACCOBY, E. E., AND JACKLIN, C. N. 1974. *The psychology of sex differences.* Stanford, Calif.: Stanford University Press.

MACCOBY, E. E., AND JACKLIN, C. N. 1980. Sex differences in aggression: A rejoinder and reprise. *Child Development* 51:964–80.

MACCOBY, E. E., AND MARTIN, J. A. 1983. Socialization in the context of the family: Parent-child interaction. In Mussen, P. H. (Ed.), *Carmichael's manual of child psychology: Vol. 4. Socialization, personality and social development* (Hetherington, M. E., volume editor), pp. 1–102. New York: Wiley.

MACFARLANE, A. 1975. Olfaction in the development of social preferences in the human neonate. *Parent-infant interaction.* Amsterdam: CIBA Foundation Symposium.

MACNEILAGE, P. 1972. Speech physiology. In Gilbert, J. (Ed.), *Speech and cortical functioning.* New York: Academic Press.

MACNICHOL, E. F., JR. 1964. Three-pigment color vision: *Scientific American* 211:48–56.

MAGNUS, O., AND LAMMERS, J. 1956. The amygdaloid-nuclear complex. *Folia Psychiatrica Neurologica et Neurochirurgico Neerlandica* 59:552–82.

MAGNUSSON, D., AND ENDLER, N. S. 1977. Interactional psychology: Present status and future prospects. In Magnusson, D., and Endler, N. S. (Eds.), *Personality at the crossroads,* pp. 3–31. New York: Wiley.

MAGOUN, H. W.; HARRISON, F.; BROBECK, J. R.; AND RANSON, S. W. 1938. Activation of heat loss mechanisms by local heating of the brain. *Journal of Neurophysiology* 1:101–14.

MAHER, B. A. 1966. *Principles of psychopathology.* New York: McGraw-Hill.

MAHONEY, M. J. 1976. *Scientist as subject: The psychological imperative.* Cambridge, Mass.: Ballinger.

MAIER, S. F.; LAUDENSLAGER, M. L.; AND RYAN, S. M. 1985. Stressor controllability, immune function, and endogenous opiates. In Bush, F., and Overmier, J. B. (Eds.), *Affect, conditioning, and cognition.* Hillsdale, N.J.: Erlbaum.

MAIER, S. F.; SELIGMAN, M. E. P.; AND SOLOMON, R. L. 1969. Pavlovian fear conditioning and learned helplessness: Effects on escape and avoidance behavior of (a) the CS-US contingency and (b) the independence of the US and voluntary responding. In Campbell, B. A., and Church, R. M. (Eds.), *Punishment and aversive behavior,* pp. 299–342. New York: Appleton-Century-Crofts.

MALINOWSKI, B. 1927. *Sex and repression in savage society.* New York: Meridian, 1955.

MANDLER, G. 1975. *Mind and emotion.* New York: Wiley.

MANDLER, G. 1984. *Mind and body: Psychology of emotion and stress.* New York: Norton.

MANN, F.; BOWSHER, D.; MUMFORD, J.; LIPTON, S.; AND MILES, J. 1973. Treatment of intractable pain by acupuncture. *Lancet* 2:57–60.

MANN, L. 1981. The baiting crowd in episodes of threatened suicide. *Journal of Personality and Social Psychology* 41:703–709.

MARATSOS, M. 1982. The child's construction of grammatical categories. In Wanner, E. and Gleitman, L. R. (Eds.) *Language acquisition: the state of the art.* New York: Cambridge University Press.

MARKMAN, E. M., AND HUTCHINSON, J. E. 1984. Children's sensitivity to constraints on word meaning: Taxonomic vs. thematic relations. *Cognitive Psychology* 16:1–27.

MARKS, I. M. 1969. *Fears and phobias.* New York: Academic Press.

MARLER, P. R. 1970. A comparative approach to vocal learning: Song development in white-crowned sparrows. *Journal of Comparative and Physiological Psychology Monographs* 71(No. 2, Part 2):1–25.

MARR, D. 1976. Early processing of visual information. *Philosophical Transactions of the Royal Society of London,* Series B, 275:483–524.

MARSHALL, D. A., AND MOULTON, D. G. 1981. Olfactory sensitivity to α-ionine in humans and dogs. *Chemical Senses* 6:53–61.

MARSHALL, G. D., AND ZIMBARDO, P. G. 1979. Affective consequences of inadequately explained physiological arousal. *Journal of Personality and Social Psychology* 37:970–88.

MARSLEN-WILSON, W. D., AND TEUBER, H. L. 1975. Memory for remote events in anterograde amnesia: Recognition of public figures from news photographs. *Neuropsychologia* 13:353–64.

MASLACH, C. 1979. Negative emotional biasing of unexplained physiological arousal. *Journal of Personality and Social Psychology* 37:953–69.

MASLOW, A. H. 1954. *Motivation and personality.* New York: Harper & Row.

MASLOW, A. H. 1968. *Toward a psychology of being,* 2nd ed. Princeton, N.J.: Van Nostrand.

MASLOW, A. H. 1970. *Motivation and personality,* 2nd ed. New York: Harper.

MATARAZZO, J. D. 1983. The reliability of psychiatric and psychological diagnosis. *Clinical Psychology Review* 3:103–45.

MATHEWS, K. A. 1982. Psychological perspectives on the type A behavior pattern. *Psychological Bulletin* 91:293–323.

MATSUMOTO, D., AND EKMAN, P. 1989. Japanese and Caucasian Facial Expressions of Emotion. JACFEE.

MAUGH, T. M. 1981. Biochemical markers identify mental states. *Science* 214:39–41.

MAY, R. 1958. Contributions of existential psychotherapy. In May, R.; Angel, E.; and Ellenberger, H. F. (Eds.), *Existence,* pp. 37–91. New York: Basic Books.

MAYER, D. J.; PRICE, D. D.; RAFII, A.; AND BARBER, J. 1976. Acupuncture hypalgesia: Evidence for activation of a central control system as a mechanism of action. In Bonica, J. J., and Albe-Fessard, D. (Eds.), *Advances in pain research and therapy,* vol. 1. New York: Raven Press.

MAYER, D. J. 1979. Endogenous analgesia systems: Neural and behavioral mechanisms. In Bonica, J. J. et al. (Eds.), *Advances in pain research and therapy,* vol. 3. New York: Raven.

MAYER, J. 1955. Regulation of energy intake and body weight: The glucostatic theory and the lipostatic hypothesis. *Annals of the New York Academy of Sciences* 63:15–43.

MAYES, A. R. 1988. *Human organic memory disorders.* New York: Cambridge University Press.

MAYNARD-SMITH, J. 1965. The evolution of alarm calls. *American Naturalist* 100:637–50.

MCBURNEY, D. H.; LEVINE, J. M.; AND CAVANAUGH, P. H. 1977. Psychophysical and social ratings of human body odor. *Personality and Social Psychology Bulletin* 3:135–38.

MCBURNEY, D. H., AND SHICK, T. R. 1971. Taste and water taste of twenty-six compounds for man. *Perception and Psychophysics* 10:249–52.

MCCLEARN, G. E., AND DEFRIES, J. C. 1973. *Introduction to behavioral genetics.* San Francisco: Freeman.

MCCLELLAND, D. C. 1975. *Power: The inner experience.* New York: Irvington.

MCCLELLAND, D. C.; ATKINSON, J. W.; CLARK, R. A.; AND LOWELL, E. L. 1953. *The achievement motive.* New York: Appleton.

MCCLINTOCK, M. K. 1971. Menstrual synchrony and suppression. *Nature* 229:244–45.

MCCLINTOCK, M. K., AND ADLER, N. T. 1978. The role of the female during copulation in wild and domestic Norway rats (*Rattus Norvegicus*). *Behaviour* 67:67–96.

MCCLOSKEY, M.; WIBLE, C. G.; AND COHEN, N.J. 1988. Is there a special flashbulb-memory mechanism? *Journal of Experimental Psychology: General* 117:171–81.

MCCONAGHY, M. J. 1979. Gender constancy and the genital basis of gender: Stages in the development of constancy by gender identity. *Child Development* 50:1223–26.

MCEWEN, B. S.; BIEGON, A.; DAVIS, P. G.; KREY, L. C.; LUINE, V. N.; MCGINNIS, M.; PADEN, C. M.; PARSONS, B.; AND RAINBOW, T. C. 1982. Steroid hormones: Humoral signals which alter brain cell properties and functions. *Recent Progress in Brain Research* 38:41–83.

MCGHIE, A., AND CHAPMAN, J. 1961. Disorders of attention and perception in early schizophrenia. *British Journal of Medical Psychology* 34:103–16.

McGuigan, F. J. 1966. Covert oral behavior and auditory hallucinations. *Psychophysiology* 3:421–28.

McGuire, W. J. 1985. The nature of attitude and attitude change. In Lindzey, G., and Aronson, E. (Eds.), *Handbook of social psychology*, 3rd ed., vol. 2. New York: Random House.

McKay, H.; Sinisterra, L.; McKay, A., Gomez, H.; and Lloreda, P. 1978. Improving cognitive ability in chronically deprived children. *Science* 200:270–78.

McKenzie, B. E.; Tootell, H. E.; and Day, R. H. 1980. Development of size constancy during the 1st year of human infancy. *Developmental Psychology* 16:163–74.

Mead, G. H. 1934. *Mind, self, and society.* Chicago: University of Chicago Press.

Mead, M. 1935. *Sex and temperament in three primitive societies.* New York: Morrow.

Mead, M. 1937. *Cooperation and competition among primitive peoples.* New York: McGraw-Hill.

Mead, M. 1939. *From the South Seas: Studies of adolescence and sex in primitive societies.* New York: Morrow.

Meehl, P. E. 1956. Profile analysis of the MMPI in differential diagnosis. In Welsh, G. S., and Dahlstrom, W. G. (Eds.), *Basic readings on the MMPI in psychology and medicine*, pp. 291–97. Minneapolis: University of Minnesota Press.

Meehl, P. E. 1959. Some ruminations on the validation of clinical procedures. *Canadian Journal of Psychology* 13:102–28.

Meehl, P. D. 1962. Schizotaxia, schizotypy, schizophrenia. *American Psychologist* 17:827–38.

Meltzer, H. Y. 1987. Biological studies in schizophrenia. *Schizophrenia Bulletin* 13:77–111.

Melzack, R. 1973. *The puzzle of pain.* New York: Basic Books.

Mendlewicz, J., and Rainer, J. D. 1977. Adoption study supporting genetic transmission in manic-depressive illness. *Nature* 268:327–29.

Menyuk, P. 1977. *Language and maturation.* Cambridge, Mass.: MIT Press.

Menzel, E. W. 1973. Chimpanzee spatial memory organization. *Science* 182:943–45.

Menzel, E. W. 1978. Cognitive maps in chimpanzees. In Hulse, S. H.; Fowler, H.; and Honig, W. K. (Eds.), *Cognitive processes in animal behavior*, pp. 375–422. Hillsdale, N.J.: Erlbaum.

Metalsky, G. I.; Abramson, L. Y.; Seligman, M. E. P.; Semmel; and Peterson, C. 1982. Attributional style and life events in the classroom: Vulnerability and invulnerability to depressive mood reactions. *Journal of Personality and Social Psychology* 43:612–17.

Metalsky. G. I.; Halberstadt, L. J.; and Abramson, L. Y. 1987. Vulnerability to depressive mood reactions: Toward a more powerful test of the diathesis-stress and causal mediation components of the reformulated theory of depression. *Journal of Personality and Social Psychology* 52:386–93.

Michael, R. P., and Keverne, E. B. 1968. Pheromones in the communication of sexual status in primates. *Nature* 218:746–49.

Michaels, J. W.; Blommel, J. M.; Brocato, R. M.; Linkous, R. A.; and Rowe, J. S. 1982. Social facilitation and inhibition in a natural setting. *Replications in Social Psychology* 2:21–24.

Milgram, S. 1963. Behavioral study of obedience. *Journal of Abnormal and Social Psychology* 67:371–78.

Milgram, S. 1965. Some conditions of obedience and disobedience to authority. *Human Relations* 18:57–76.

Milgram, S. 1974. *Obedience to authority.* New York: Harper & Row.

Miller, G. A. 1956. The magical number seven plus or minus two: Some limits in our capacity for processing information. *Psychological Review* 63:81–97.

Miller, G., and Gildea, P. 1987. How children learn words. *Scientific American* 257:94–99.

Miller, G., and Johnson-Laird, P. 1976. *Language and perception.* Cambridge, Mass.: Harvard University Press.

Miller, N. E.; Bailey, C. J.; and Stevenson, J. A. F. 1950. Decreased "hunger" but increased food intake resulting from hypothalamic lesions. *Science* 112:256–59.

Milner, B. 1966. Amnesia following operation on the temporal lobes. In Whitty, C. W. M., and Zangwill, O. L. (Eds.), *Amnesia*, pp. 109–33. London: Butterworth.

Milner, B.; Corkin, S.; and Teuber, H. L. 1968. Further analysis of the hippocampal syndrome:14-year follow-up study of H. M. *Neuropsychologia* 6:215–34.

Minuchin, S. 1974. *Families and family therapy.* Cambridge, Mass.: Harvard University Press.

Mischel, W. 1968. *Personality and assessment.* New York: Wiley.

Mischel, W. 1970. Sex-typing and socialization. In Mussen, P. H. (Ed.), *Carmichael's manual of child development*, vol. 1. New York: Wiley.

Mischel, W. 1973. Towards a cognitive social learning reconceptualization of personality. *Psychological Review* 80:252–83.

Mischel, W. 1974. Processes in delay of gratification. In Berkowitz, L. (Ed.), *Advances in experimental social psychology*, vol. 7. New York: Academic Press.

Mischel, W. 1979. On the interface of cognition and personality: Beyond the person-situation debate. *American Psychologist* 34:740–54.

Mischel, W. 1984. Convergences and challenges in the search for consistency. *American Psychologist* 39:351–64.

Mischel, W. 1986. *Introduction to personality*, 4th ed. New York: Holt, Rinehart & Winston.

Mischel, W., and Baker, N. 1975. Cognitive appraisals and transformations in delay behavior. *Journal of Personality and Social Psychology* 31:254–61.

Mischel, W.; Ebbesen, E. B.; and Zeiss, A. R. 1972. Cognitive and attentional mechanisms in delay of gratification. *Journal of Personality and Social Psychology* 21:204–18.

Mischel, W., and Mischel, H. N. 1983. Development of children's knowledge of self-control strategies. *Child Development* 54:603–19.

Mischel, W.; Shoda, Y.; and Peake, P. K. 1988. The nature of adolescent competencies predicted by preschool delay of gratification. *Journal of Personality and Social Psychology* 54:687–96.

Mischel, W., and Moore, B. 1980. The role of ideation in voluntary delay for symbolically presented awards. *Cognitive Therapy and Research* 4:211–21.

Miselis, R. R., and Epstein, A. N. 1970. Feeding induced by 2-deoxy-D-glucose injections into the lateral ventrical of the rat. *The Physiologist* 13:262.

Mishkin, M., and Appenzeller, T. 1987. The anatomy of memory. *Scientific American* 256:80–89.

Mishler, E. G., and Waxler, N. E. 1968. Family interaction and schizophrenia: Alternative frameworks of interpretation. In Rosenthal, D., and Kety, S. S. (Eds.), *The transmission of schizophrenia*, pp. 213–22. New York: Pergamon.

Mita, T. H.; Dermer, M.; and Knight, J. 1977. Reversed facial images and the mere exposure hypothesis. *Journal of Personality and Social Psychology* 35:597–601.

Mitroff, I. I. 1974. *The subjective side of science.* Amsterdam: Elsevier.

Money, J., and Ehrhardt, A. A. 1972. *Man and woman, boy and girl.* Baltimore: Johns Hopkins University Press.

Monson, T. C.; Hesley, J. W.; and Chernick, L. 1982. Specifying when personality traits can and cannot predict behavior: An alternative to abandoning the attempt to predict single-act criteria. *Journal of Personality and Social Psychology* 43:385–99.

Moore, J. W. 1972. Stimulus control: Studies of auditory generalization in rabbits. In Black, A. H., and Prokasy, W. F. (Eds.), *Classical conditioning II: Current research and theory*, pp. 206–30. New York: Appleton-Century-Crofts.

Moos, R. H. 1969. Sources of variance in responses to questionnaires and in behavior. *Journal of Abnormal Psychology* 74:405–12.

Mora, G. 1975. Historical and theoretical trends in psychiatry. In Freedman, A. M.; Kaplan, H. I.; and Sadock, B. J. (Eds.), *Comprehensive textbook of psychiatry*, vol. 1, pp. 1–75. Baltimore: Williams & Wilkins.

Moray, N. 1959. Attention in dichotic listening: Affective cues and the influence of instructions. *Quarterly Journal of Experimental Psychology* 11:56–60.

MORELAND, R. L., AND ZAJONC, R. B. 1982. Exposure effects in person perception: Familiarity, similarity, and attraction. *Journal of Experimental Social Psychology* 18:395–415.

MORGAN, C. D., AND MURRAY, H. A. 1935. A method for investigating fantasies: The thematic apperception test. *Archives of Neurological Psychiatry* 34:289–306.

MORGAN, J., AND TRAVIS, L. 1989. Limits on negative information in language input. *Journal of Child Language* 16(3):531–52.

MORRIS, D. 1967. *The naked ape.* New York: McGraw-Hill.

MOSCOVITCH, M., AND ROZIN, P. 1989. Disorders of the nervous system and psychopathology. In Rosenhan, D. L., and Seligman, M. E. P. *Abnormal psychology,* 2nd ed., pp. 558–602. New York: Norton.

MOSKOWITZ, D. W. 1982. Coherence and cross-situational generality in personality: A new analysis of old problems. *Journal of Personality and Social Psychology* 43:754–68.

MULFORD, R. 1986. First words of the blind child. In Smith, M., and Locke, J. (Eds.), *The emergent lexicon: The child's development of a linguistic vocabulary.* New York: Academic Press.

MURDOCK, B. 1962. The serial position effect of free recall. *Journal of Experimental Psychology* 64:482–88.

MURRAY, F. B. 1978. Teaching strategies and conservation training. In Lesgold, A. M.; Pellegrino, J. W.; Fekkeman, D.; and Glaser, R. (Eds.), *Cognitive psychology and instruction,* vol. 1. New York: Plenum.

MUSCETTOLA, G.; POTTER, W. Z.; PICKAR, D.; AND GOODWIN, F. K. 1984. Urinary 3-methoxy-4-hydroxyphenylglycol and major affective disorders. *Archives of General Psychiatry* 41:337–42.

MUUSS, R. E. 1970. Puberty rites in primitive and modern societies. *Adolescence* 5:109–28.

MYERS, J. K.; WEISSMAN, M. M.; TISCHLERM, G. L.; HOLZER, C. E.; LEAF, P. J.; ORVASCHEL, H. A.; ANTHONY, J. C.; BOYD, J. H.; BURKE, J. D.; KRAMER, M.; AND STOLTZMAN, R. 1984. Six-month prevalance of psychiatric disorders in three communities:1980–1982. *Archives of General Psychiatry* 41:959–67.

NADEL, L. AND ZOLA-MORGAN, S. 1984. Infantile amnesia: a neurobiological perspective. In Muscovitch, M. (Ed.) *Infant memory.* New York: Plenum Press.

NAUTA, W. J. H., AND FEIRTAG, M. 1986. *Fundamental neuroanatomy.* New York: Freeman.

NEISSER, U. 1967. *Cognitive psychology.* New York: Appleton-Century-Crofts.

NEISSER, U. 1982. *Memory observed.* San Francisco: Freeman.

NEISSER, U. 1986. Remembering Pearl Harbor: Reply to Thompson and Cowan. *Cognition* 23:285–86.

NEISSER, U. 1989. Domains of memory. In Solomon, P. R.; Goethals, G. R.; Kelley, C. M.; and Stephens, B. R. (Eds.), *Memory: Interdisciplinary approaches,* pp. 67–83. New York: Springer Verlag.

NELSON, K. 1973. Structure and strategy in learning to talk. *Monographs of the Society for Research in Child Development* 38:(1–2, Serial No. 149).

NEMIAH, J. C. 1985. Obsessive-compulsive disorder (Obsessive-compulsive neurosis). In Kaplan, H. I., and Sadock, J. (Eds.), *Comprehensive textbook of psychiatry,* 4th ed. Baltimore: Williams & Wilkins.

NESSE, F. M.; CAMERON, O. G.; CURTIS, G. C.; McCANN, D. S.; AND HUBER-SMITH, M. J. 1984. Adrenergic function in patients with panic anxiety. *Archives of General Psychiatry* 41:771–76.

NEWELL, A., AND SIMON, H. A. 1972. *Human problem solving.* Englewood Cliffs, N.J.: Prentice-Hall.

NEWELL, A., AND ROSENBLOOM, P. S. 1981. Mechanisms of skill acquisition and the law of practice. In Anderson, J. R. (Ed.), *Cognitive skills and their acquisition,* pp. 1–55. Hillsdale, N.J.: Erlbaum.

NEWMEYER, F. 1983. *Linguistic theory in America,* New York: Academic Press.

NEWPORT, E. L. 1984. Constraints on learning: Studies in the acquisition of American Sign Language. *Papers and Reports on Child Language Development* 23:1–22. Stanford, Calif.: Stanford University Press.

NEWPORT, E. 1990. Maturational constraints on language learning. *Cognitive Science* 14:11–28.

NEWPORT, E. L., AND ASHBROOK, E. F. 1977. The emergence of semantic relations in American Sign Language. *Papers and Reports in Child Language Development* 13.

NICHOLSON, R. A., AND BERMAN, J. S. 1983. Is follow-up necessary in evaluating psychotherapy? *Psychological Bulletin* 93:261–78.

NICOL, S. E., AND GOTTESMAN, I. I. 1983. Clues to the genetics and neurobiology of schizophrenia. *American Scientist* 71:398–404.

NILSSON, L. 1974. *Behold man.* Boston: Little, Brown.

NISBETT, R. E. 1968. Taste, deprivation, and weight determinants of eating behavior. *Journal of Personality and Social Psychology* 10:107–16.

NISBETT, R. E. 1972. Eating behavior and obesity in man and animals. *Advances in Psychosomatic Medicine* 7:173–93.

NISBETT, R. E. 1980. The trait construct in lay and professional psychology. In Festinger, L. (Ed.), *Retrospections on social psychology,* pp. 109–30. New York: Oxford University Press.

NISBETT, R., AND ROSS, L. 1980. *Human inference: Strategies and shortcomings of social judgment.* Englewood Cliffs, N.J.: Prentice-Hall.

NISBETT, R. E., AND WILSON, T. D. 1977. Telling more than we can know: Verbal reports on mental processes. *Psychological Review* 84:231–59.

NOLEN-HOEKSEMA, S. 1987. Sex differences in unipolar depression: Evidence and theory. *Psychological Bulletin* 101:259–82.

NORMAN, W. T. 1963. Toward an adequate taxonomy of personality attributes: Replicated factor structure in peer nomination personality ratings. *Journal of Abnormal and Social Psychology* 66:574–83.

NOTTEBOHM, F. 1987. Plasticity in adult avian central nervous system: Possible relations between hormones, learning, and brain repair. In Plum, F. (Ed.), *Higher functions of the nervous system: Section I, Vol. 5. Handbook of physiology.* Washington, D. C.: American Physiological Society.

NOVAK, M. A., AND HARLOW, H. F. 1975. Social recovery of monkeys isolated for the first year of life: I. Rehabilitation and therapy. *Developmental Psychology* 11:453–65.

O'KEEFE, J., AND NADEL, L. 1978. *The hippocampus as a cognitive map.* Oxford: Clarendon Press.

ODIORNE, J. M. 1957. Color changes. In Brown, M. E. (Ed.), *The physiology of fishes,* vol. 2. New York: Academic Press.

OFMAN, W. V. 1985. Existential psychotherapy. In Kaplan, H. I., and Sadock, J. (Eds.), *Comprehensive textbook of psychiatry,* 4th ed, pp. 1438–43. Baltimore: Williams & Wilkins.

OLDS, J., AND MILNER, P. 1954. Positive reinforcement produced by electrical stimulation of septal areas and other regions of rat brains. *Journal of Comparative and Physiological Psychology* 47:419–27.

OLTON, D. S. 1978. Characteristics of spatial memory. In Hulse, S. H., Fowler, H., and Honig, W. K. (Eds.), *Cognitive processes in animal behavior,* pp. 341–73. Hillsdale, N.J.: Erlbaum.

OLTON, D. S. 1979. Mazes, maps, and memory. *American Psychologist* 34:583–96.

OLTON, D. S., AND SAMUELSON, R. J. 1976. Remembrance of places passed: Spatial memory in rats. *Journal of Experimental Psychology: Animal Behavior Processes* 2:97–116.

OLWEUS, D. 1980. Familial and temperamental determinants of aggressive behavior in adolescent boys: A causal analysis. *Developmental Psychology* 16:644–66.

OPLER, L. A.; KAY, S. R.; ROSADO, V.; AND LINDENMAYER, J. P. 1984. Positive and negative symptoms in chronic schizophrenic patients. *Journal of Nervous and Mental Diseases* 172:317–25.

ORLANSKY, H. 1949. Infant care and personality. *Psychological Bulletin* 46:1–48.

ORNE, M. T. 1975. Psychotherapy in contemporary America: Its development and context. In Arieti, S. (Ed.), *American handbook of psychiatry,* 2nd ed., vol. 5, pp. 1–33. New York: Basic Books.

OSOFSKY, J. D., AND DANZGER, B. 1974. Relationships between neo-natal characteristics and mother-infant characteristics. *Developmental Psychology* 10:124–30.

PACKER, C. 1977. Reciprocal altruism in olive baboons. *Nature* 265:441–43.

PAGE, E. B. 1985. Review of Kaufman's Assessment Battery for Children. *Ninth mental measurements yearbook,* vol. 1., pp. 773–77.

PARKE, R. D. 1981. *Fathers.* Cambridge, Mass.: Harvard University Press.

PARKE, R. D., AND SLABY, R. G. 1983. The development of aggression. In Mussen, P. H. (Ed.), *Carmichael's manual of child psychology: Vol. 4. Socialization, personality and social development* (Hetherington, M. E., volume editor), pp. 547–642. New York: Wiley.

PASCALE-LEONE, J. 1978. Compounds, confounds and models in developmental information processing: A reply to Trabasso and Foellinger. *Journal of Experimental Child Psychology* 26:18–40.

PATIENCE, A., AND SMITH, J. W. 1986. Derek Freeman and Samoa: The making and unmaking of a biobehavioral myth. *American Anthropologist* 88:157–61.

PATTERSON, T.; SPOHN, H. E.; BOGIA, D. P.; AND HAYES, K. 1986. Thought disorder in schizophrenia: Cognitive and neuroscience approaches. *Schizophrenia Bulletin* 12:460–72.

PAVLOV, I. 1927. *Conditioned reflexes.* Oxford, England: Oxford University Press.

PAVLOV, I. 1928. *Lectures on conditioned reflexes,* vol 1. New York: International Publishers Co., Inc.

PAYKEL, E. S. 1982. Life events and early environment. In Paykel, E. S. (Ed.), *Handbook of affective disorders.* New York: Guilford.

PEEKE, H. V. S. 1984. Habituation and the maintenance of territorial boundaries. In Peeke, H. V. S., and Petrinovich, L. (Eds.), *Habituation, sensitization and behavior,* pp. 393–422. New York: Academic Press.

PENFIELD, W. 1975. *The mystery of the mind.* Princeton, N.J.: Princeton University Press.

PENFIELD, W., AND RASMUSSEN, T. 1950. *The cerebral cortex of man.* New York: Macmillan.

PENFIELD, W., AND ROBERTS, L. 1959. *Speech and brain mechanisms.* Princeton, N.J.: Princeton University Press.

PERIN, C. T. 1943. A quantitative investigation of the delay of reinforcement gradient. *Journal of Experimental Psychology* 32:37–51.

PETERSON, C.; SEMMEL, A.; VON BAEYER, C.; ABRAMSON, L. Y.; METALSKY, G. I.; AND SELIGMAN, M. E. P. 1982. The Attributional Style Questionnaire. *Cognitive Therapy and Research* 6:287–99.

PETERSON, C., AND SELIGMAN, M. E. P. 1984. Causal explanations as a risk factor for depression: Theory and evidence. *Psychological Review* 91:341–74.

PIAGET, J. 1952. *The origins of intelligence in children.* New York: International University Press.

PIAGET, J., AND INHELDER, B. 1967. *The child's conception of space.* New York: Norton.

PILLARD, R. C., AND WEINREICH, J. D. 1986. Evidence of familial nature of male homosexuality. *Archives of General Psychiatry* 43:808–12.

PILLEMER, D. B. 1984. Flashbulb memories of the assassination attempt on President Reagan. *Cognition* 16:63–80.

PINKER, S. 1984. *Language learnability and language development.* Cambridge, Mass: Harvard University Press.

PINKER, S. 1989. *Learnability and cognition: The acquisition of argument structure.* Cambridge, Mass: MIT Press.

PINKER, S., AND PRINCE, A. 1988. On language and connectionism: Analysis of a parallel distributed processing model of language acquisition. *Cognition* 28(1):73–194.

PLUTCHIK, R. 1970. Emotions, evolution, and adaptive processes. In Arnold, M. B. (Ed.), *Feelings and emotions: The Loyola symposium.* New York: Academic Press.

PLUTCHIK, R. 1980. The evolutionary context. In Plutchik, R., and Kellerman, H. (Eds.), *Emotion: Theory, research and experience,* vol. 1. New York: Academic Press.

PLUTCHIK, R. 1984. Emotions: A general psychoevolutionary approach. In Scherer, K., and Ekman, P. *Approaches to emotion.* Hillsdale, N.J.: Erlbaum.

POGGIO, G. F., AND FISCHER, B. 1978. Binocular interaction and depth sensitivity in striate and prestriate cortex of behaving rhesus monkey. *Journal of Neurophysiology* 40:1392–1405.

POLEY, W. 1974. Dimensionality in the measurement of authoritarian and political attitudes. *Canadian Journal of Behavioral Science* 6:83–94.

PORAC, C. AND COREN, S. 1981. Lateral preferences and human behavior. New York: Springer-Verlag.

PORSOLT, R. D.; LEPICHON, M.; AND JALFRE, M. 1977. Depression: A new animal model sensitive to antidepressant treatments. *Nature* 266:730–32.

POSTAL, P. M. 1968. Epilogue. In Jacobs, R. A., and Rosenbaum, P. S., *English transformational grammar,* pp. 253–89. Waltham, Mass.: Blaisdell.

PREMACK, D. 1976. *Intelligence in ape and man.* Hillsdale, N.J.: Erlbaum.

PREMACK, A., AND PREMACK, D. 1983. *The mind of an ape.* New York: Norton.

PREMACK, D. AND PREMACK, A. J. 1972. Teaching language to an ape. *Scientific American* 227:92–99.

PRICE, R. H., AND BOUFFARD, B. L. 1974. Behavioral appropriateness and situational constraint. *Journal of Personality and Social Psychology* 30:579–86.

PRICE-WILLIAMS, D. R. 1981. Concrete and formal operations. In Munroe, R. H.; Munroe, R. L.; and Whiting, B. B. (Eds.), *Handbook of cross-cultural development,* pp. 403–22. New York: Garland.

PRICE-WILLIAMS, D., GORDON, W., AND RAMIREZ, M. 1969. Skill and conservation: A study of pottery-making children. *Developmental Psychology* 1:769.

PRINCE, E. 1981. Toward a taxonomy of given-new information. In P. Cole (Ed.), *Syntax and semantics 9 Pragmatics.* New York: Academic Press.

PRINZHORN, H. 1972. *Artistry of the mentally ill.* New York: Springer-Verlag.

PROVENCE, S., AND LIPTON, R. C. 1962. *Infants in institutions.* New York: International Universities Press.

PUTNAM, F. W.; GUROFF, J. J.; SILBERMAN, E. K.; BARBAN, L.; AND POST, R. M. 1986. The clinical phenomenology of multiple personality disorder: Review of 100 recent cases. *Journal of Clinical Psychiatry* 47:285–93.

PUTNAM, H. 1975. The meaning of "meaning." In Gunderson, K. (Ed.), *Language, mind, and knowledge.* Minneapolis: University of Minnesota Press.

QUAY, H. C. 1965. Psychopathic personality as pathological stimulation seeking. *American Journal of Psychiatry* 122:180–83.

QUAY, L. C. 1971. Language, dialect, reinforcement, and the intelligence test performance of Negro children. *Child Development* 42:5–15.

RACHMAN, S. J., AND TEASDALE, J. 1969. Aversion therapy: An appraisal. In Franks, C. M. (Ed.), *Behavior therapy: Appraisal and status,* pp. 279–320. New York: McGraw-Hill.

RADFORD, A. 1988. *Transformational grammar: A first course* New York: Cambridge University Press.

RADKE-YARROW, M.; ZAHN-WAXLER, C.; AND CHAPMAN, M. 1983. Children's prosocial dispositions and behavior. In Mussen, P. E. (Ed.), *Carmichael's manual of child psychology: Vol. 4. Socialization, personality, and social development* (Hetherington, E. M., volume editor), pp. 469–546. New York: Wiley.

RAINER, J. D.; MESNIKOFF, A.; KOLB, L. C.; AND CARR, A. 1960. Homosexuality and heterosexuality in identical twins. *Psychosomatic Medicine* 22:251–58.

RAPPAPORT, M., AND LEVIN, B. 1988. What to do with roles. In W. Wilkins (Ed), *Syntax and semantics: Vol. 21. Thematic relations.* San Diego: Academic Press.

RAVEN, B. H., AND RUBIN, J. Z. 1976. *Social psychology: People in groups.* New York: Wiley.

RAYNER, K. 1978. Eye movements in reading and information processing. *Psychological Bulletin* 85:618–60.

REBER, A. S. 1985. *The Penguin dictionary of psychology.* New York: Viking Penguin.

REDLICH, F. C., AND FREEDMAN, D. X. 1966. *The theory and practice of psychiatry.* New York: Basic Books.

REISENZEIN, R. 1983. The Schachter theory of emotions: Two decades later. *Psychological Bulletin* 94:239–64.

RESCORLA, R. A. 1966. Predictability and number of pairings in Pavlovian fear conditioning. *Psychonomic Science* 4:383–84.

RESCORLA, R. A. 1967. Pavlovian conditioning and its proper control procedures. *Psychological Review* 74:71–80.

RESCORLA, R. A. 1980. *Pavlovian second-order conditioning.* Hillsdale, N.J.: Erlbaum.

RESCORLA, R. A. 1988. Behavioral studies of Pavlovian conditioning. *Annual Review of Neuroscience* 11: 329–52.

REST, J. R. 1983. Morality. In Mussen, P. E. (Ed.), *Carmichael's manual of child psychology: Vol. 4. Socialization, personality, and social development* (Hetherington, E. M., volume editor). New York: Wiley.

REST, J. R. 1984. The major components of morality. In Kurtines, W. M., and Gewirtz, L. (Eds.), *Morality, moral behavior, and moral development.* New York: Wiley.

REVLIN, R., AND LEIRER, V. O. 1980. Understanding quantified categorical expressions. *Memory and Cognition* 8:447–58.

REVUSKY, S. H. 1971. The role of interference in association over a delay. In Honig, W. K., and James, H. R. (Eds.), *Animal memory.* New York: Academic Press.

REVUSKY, S. 1977. Learning as a general process with an emphasis on data from feeding experiments. In Milgram, N. W.; Krames, L.; and Alloway, T. H. (Eds.), *Food aversion learning,* pp. 1–51. New York: Plenum.

REYNOLDS, G. S. 1968. *A primer of operant conditioning.* Glenview, Ill.: Scott, Foresman.

RHEINGOLD, H. L.; HAY, D. F.; AND WEST, M. J. 1976. Sharing in the second year of life. *Child Development* 47:1148–58.

RICHARDS, W. 1977. Lessons in constancy from neurophysiology. In Epstein, W. W. (Ed.), *Stability and constancy in visual perception: Mechanisms and processes,* pp. 421–36. New York: Wiley.

ROBBIN, A. A. 1958. A controlled study of the effects of leucotomy. *Journal of Neurology, Neurosurgery and Psychiatry* 21:262–69.

ROBBINS, S. J. 1990. Mechanisms underlying spontaneous recovery in autoshaping. *Journal of Experimental Psychology: Animal Behavior Processes* 16:235–49.

ROBINS, L. R. 1966. *Deviant children grown up: A sociological and psychiatric study of sociopathic personality.* Baltimore: Williams & Wilkins.

ROBINSON, H. B. AND ROBINSON, N. M. 1970. Mental retardation. In Mussen, P. H. (Ed.), *Carmichael's manual of child psychology: Vol. 2,* (3d ed.), pp. 615–66. New York: Wiley.

ROCK, I. 1975. *An introduction to perception.* New York: Macmillan.

ROCK, I. 1977. In defense of unconscious inference. In Epstein, W. W. (Ed.), *Stability and constancy in visual perception: Mechanisms and processes,* pp. 321–74. New York: Wiley.

ROCK, I. 1983. *The logic of perception.* Cambridge, Mass.: MIT Press.

ROCK, I. 1986. The description and analysis of object and event perception. In Boff, K. R.; Kauffman, L.; and Thomas, J. P. (Eds.), *Handbook of perception and human performance: Vol. 2. Cognitive processes and performance,* pp. 1–71. New York: Wiley.

ROCK, I., AND KAUFMAN, L. 1962. The moon illusion, II. *Science* 136:1023–31.

RODIN, J. 1980. The externality theory today. In Stunkard, A. J. (Ed.), *Obesity,* pp. 226–39. Philadelphia: Saunders.

RODIN, J. 1981. Current status of the internal-external hypothesis for obesity. What went wrong? *American Psychologist* 36:361–72.

RODIN, J., AND LANGER, E. J. 1977. Long-term effects of a control-relevant intervention with the institutionalized aged. *Journal of Personality and Social Psychology* 35:897–902.

ROEDER, K. D. 1935. An experimental analysis of the sexual behavior of the praying mantis. *Biological Bulletin* 69:203–20.

ROEDER, L. 1967. *Nerve cells and insect behavior.* Cambridge, Mass.: Harvard University Press.

ROGERS, C. R. 1942. *Counseling and psychotherapy: New concepts in practice.* Boston: Houghton Mifflin.

ROGERS, C. R. 1951 and 1970. *Client-centered therapy: Its current practice, implications, and theory,* 1st and 2nd eds. Boston: Houghton Mifflin.

ROGERS, C. R. 1959. A theory of therapy, personality, and interpersonal relationships as developed in the client-centered framework. In Koch, S. (Ed.), *Psychology: A study of a science,* vol. 3. New York: McGraw-Hill.

ROGERS, C. R. 1961. *On becoming a person: A therapist's view of psychotherapy.* Boston: Houghton Mifflin.

ROGOFF, B.; GAUVAIN, M.; AND ELLIS, S. 1984. Development viewed in its cultural context. In Bornstein, M. H., and Lamb, M. E. (Eds.), *Developmental psychology: An advanced textbook.* Hillsdale, N.J.: Erlbaum.

ROMANES, G. J. 1882. *Animal intelligence.* London: Kegan Paul.

RORER, L. G., AND WIDIGER, T. A. 1983. Personality structure and assessment. In Rosenzweig, M. R., and Porter, L. W. (Eds.), *Annual Review of Psychology* 34:431–63.

ROSCH, E. H. 1973a. Natural categories. *Cognitive Psychology* 4:328–50.

ROSCH, E. H. 1973b. On the internal structure of perceptual and semantic categories. In Moore, T. E. (Ed.), *Cognitive development and the acquisition of language.* New York: Academic Press.

ROSCH, E. H., AND MERVIS, C. B. 1975. Family resemblances: Studies in the internal structure of categories. *Cognitive Psychology* 7:573–605.

ROSE, R. M.; JENKINS, C. D.; AND HURST, M. W. 1978. *Air traffic controller health change study.* Report to the Federal Aviation Administration. Cited in Davison and Neale, 1986.

ROSEN, G. 1966. *Madness in society.* Chicago: University of Chicago Press.

ROSENFELD, P.; GIACALONE, R. A.; AND TEDESCHI, J. T. 1984. Cognitive dissonance and impression management explanations for effort justification. *Personality and Social Psychology Bulletin* 10: 394–401.

ROSENHAN, D. L. 1973. On being sane in insane places. *Science* 179:250–58.

ROSENHAN, D. L., AND SELIGMAN, M. E. P. 1989. *Abnormal Psychology,* 2nd ed. New York: Norton.

ROSENMAN, R. H. 1978. The interview method of assessment of the coronary-prone behavior pattern. In Dembrowski, T. M.; Weiss, S. M.; Shields, J. L. et al. (Eds.), *Coronary-prone behavior.* New York: Springer.

ROSENMAN, R. H.; BRAND, R. J.; JENKINS, C. D.; FRIEDMAN, M.; AND STRAUS, R. 1975. Coronary heart disease in the Western Collaborative Group Study: Final follow-up experience of 8½ years. *Journal of the American Medical Association* 233:872–77.

ROSENTHAL, A. M. 1964. *Thirty-eight witnesses.* New York: McGraw-Hill.

ROSENTHAL, D. 1970. *Genetic theory and abnormal behavior.* New York: McGraw-Hill.

ROSENTHAL, N. E.; CARPENTER, C. J.; JAMES, S. P.; PARRY, B. L.; ROGERS, S. L. B.; AND WEHER, T. A. 1986. Seasonal affective disorder in children and adolescents. *American Journal of Psychiatry* 143:356–58.

ROSENTHAL, N. E.; SACK, D. A.; GILLIN, J. C.; LEWY, A. J.; GOODWIN, F. K.; DAVENPORT, Y.; MUELLER, P. S.; NEWSOME, D. A.; AND WEHR, T. A. 1984. Seasonal affective disorder: A description of the syndrome and preliminary findings with light therapy. *Archives of General Psychiatry* 41:72–80.

ROSENZWEIG, M. R., AND LEIMAN, A. L. 1982. *Physiological psychology.* Lexington, Mass.: Heath.

ROSENZWEIG, M. R., AND LEIMAN, A. L. 1989. *Physiological psychology,* 2nd ed. New York: Random House.

ROSS, J., AND LAWRENCE, K. Q. 1968. Some observations on memory artifice. *Psychonomic Science* 13:107–108.

ROSS, L. 1977. The intuitive psychologist and his shortcomings: Distortions in the attribution process. In Berkowitz, L. (Ed.), *Advances in experimental social psychology,* vol. 10. New York: Academic Press.

ROSS, L.; AMABILE, T. M.; AND STEINMETZ, J. L. 1977. Social roles, social control, and biases in social perception processes. *Journal of Experimental Social Psychology* 35:817–29.

ROZIN, P. 1976a. The evolution of intelligence and access to the cognitive unconscious. In Stellar, E., and Sprague, J. M. (Eds.), *Progress in psychobiology and physiological psychology,* vol. 6. New York: Academic Press.

ROZIN, P. 1976b. The psychobiological approach to human memory. In Rosenzweig, M. R., and Bennett, E. L., *Neural mechanisms of learning and memory,* pp. 3–48. Cambridge, Mass.: MIT Press.

ROZIN, P., AND KALAT, J. W. 1971. Specific hungers and poison avoidance as adaptive specializations of learning. *Psychological Review* 78:459–86.

RUMBAUGH, D. M. (Ed.). 1977. *Language learning by a chimpanzee: The Lana Project.* New York: Academic Press.

RUMELHART, D., AND MCCLELLAND, J. 1986. On learning the past tenses of English verbs. In McClelland, J.; Rumelhart, D.; and the PDP Research Group (Eds.), *Parallel distributed processing: Explorations in the microstructure of cognition,* vol. I. Cambridge, Mass: MIT Press.

RUSSEK, M. 1971. Hepatic receptors and the neurophysiological mechanisms controlling feeding behavior. In Ehrenpreis, S. (Ed.), *Neurosciences research,* vol. 4. New York: Academic Press.

RUSSELL, G. V. 1961. Interrelationship within the limbic and centrencephalic systems. In Sheer, D. E. (Ed.), *Electrical stimulation of the brain,* pp. 167–81. Austin, Tex.: University of Texas Press.

RUSSELL, M. J. 1976. Human olfactory communication. *Nature* 260:520–22.

RUSSELL, M. J.; SWITZ, G. M.; AND THOMPSON, K. 1980. Olfactory influence on the human menstrual cycle. *Pharmacology, Biochemistry, and Behavior* 13:737–38.

SACHS, J., AND TRUSWELL, L. 1978. Comprehension of two-word instructions by children in the one-word stage. *Journal of Child Language* 5:17–24.

SACKS, O. 1985. *The man who mistook his wife for a hat.* New York: Harper & Row.

SADLER, H. H.; DAVISON, L.; CARROLL, C.; AND KOUNTZ, S. L. 1971. The living, genetically unrelated, kidney donor. *Seminars in Psychiatry* 3:86–101.

SADOCK, B. J. 1975. Group psychotherapy. In Freedman, A. M.; Kaplan, H. I.; and Sadock, B. J. (Eds.), *Comprehensive textbook of psychiatry,* vol. 2, pp. 1850–76. Baltimore: Williams & Wilkins.

SAGHIR, M. T., AND ROBINS, E. 1973. *Male and female homosexuality.* Baltimore: Williams & Wilkins.

SAGI, A., AND HOFFMAN, M. L. 1976. Empathic distress in the newborn. *Developmental Psychology* 12:175–76.

SALAPATEK, P. 1975. Pattern perception in early infancy. In Cohen, L. B., and Salapatek, P. (Eds.), *Infant perception: From sensation to cognition,* vol. 1, pp. 133–248. New York: Academic Press.

SALAPATEK, P., AND KESSEN, W. 1966. Visual scanning of triangles by the human newborn. *Journal of Experimental Child Psychology* 3:113–22.

SARASON, S. B. 1973. Jewishness, blackness, and the nature-nurture controversy. *American Psychologist* 28:926–71.

SARBIN, T. R., AND ALLEN, V. L. 1968. Role theory. In Lindzey, G., and Aronson, E. (Eds.), *The handbook of social psychology,* 2nd ed., vol. 1, pp. 488–567. Reading, Mass.: Addison-Wesley.

SARNOFF, C. 1957. *Medical aspects of flying motivation—a fear-of-flying case book.* Randolph Air Force Base, Texas: U. S. Air Force, Air University, School of Aviation Medicine.

SATINOFF, E. 1964. Behavioral thermoregulation in response to local cooling of the rat brain. *American Journal of Physiology* 206:1389–94.

SATIR, V. 1967. *Conjoint family therapy,* rev. ed. Palo Alto, Calif.: Science and Behavior Books.

SAVAGE-RUMBAUGH, E.; MCDONALD, D.; SEVCIK, R.; HOPKINS, W.; AND RUPERT, E. 1986. Spontaneous symbol acquisition and communicative use by pygmie chimpanzees. *Journal of Experimental Psychology: General* 115:211–235.

SAVAGE-RUMBAUGH, E.; RUMBAUGH, D.; SMITH, S.; AND LAWSON, J. 1980. Reference: The linguistic essential. *Science* 210:922–25.

SAVAGE-RUMBAUGH, S. 1987. A new look at ape language: Comprehension of vocal speech and syntax. *Nebraska Symposium on Motivation* 35:201–55.

SCARR, S., AND CARTER-SALTZMAN, L. 1979. Twin method: Defense of a critical assumption. *Behavior Genetics* 9:527–42.

SCARR, S., AND CARTER-SALTZMAN, L. 1982. Genetics and intelligence. In Sternberg, R. J. (Ed.), *Handbook of human intelligence,* pp. 792–896. New York: Cambridge University Press.

SCARR, S., AND MCCARTNEY, K. 1983. How people make their own environments: A theory of genotype-environment effects. *Child Development* 54:424–35.

SCARR, S., AND WEINBERG, R. A. 1976. IQ test performance of black children adopted by white families. *American Psychologist* 31:726–39.

SCARR, S., AND WEINBERG, R. A. 1983. The Minnesota adoption studies genetic differences and malleability. *Child Development* 54:260–67.

SCHACHER, S. 1981. Determination and differentiation in the development of the nervous system. In Kandel, E. R., and Schwartz, J. H. (Eds.), *Principles of neural science.* New York: Elsevier North Holland.

SCHACHTEL, E. G. 1947. On memory and childhood amnesia. *Psychiatry* 10:1–26.

SCHACHTER, S. 1964. The interaction of cognitive and physiological determinants of emotional state. In Berkowitz, L. (Ed.), *Advances in Experimental Social Psychology,* pp. 49–80. New York: Academic Press.

SCHACHTER, S. 1971. Some extraordinary facts about obese humans and rats. *American Psychologist* 26:129–44.

SCHACHTER, S., AND RODIN, J. 1974. *Obese humans and rats.* Washington, D. C.: Erlbaum-Halstead.

SCHACHTER, S., AND SINGER, J. 1962. Cognitive, social and physiological determinants of emotional state. *Psychological Review* 69:379–99.

SCHACHTER, S., AND SINGER, J. E. 1979. Comments on the Maslach and Marshall-Zimbardo experiments. *Journal of Personality and Social Psychology* 37:989–95.

SCHACTER, D. L. 1987. Implicit memory: History and current status. *Journal of Experimental Psychology: Learning, Memory, and Cognition* 13:501–18.

SCHAFFER, H. R., AND CALLENDER, W. M. 1959. Psychological effects of hospitalization in infancy. *Pediatrics* 24:528–39.

SCHAIE, K. W. 1979. The primary mental abilities in adulthood: An exploration in the development of psychometric intelligence. In Baltes, P. B., and Brim, O. G., Jr. (Eds.), *Life-span development and behavior,* vol. 2. New York: Academic Press.

SCHAIE, K., AND STROTHER, C. 1968. A cross-sequential study of age changes in cognitive behavior. *Psychological Bulletin* 70:671–80.

SCHANK, R. C., AND ABELSON, R. 1977. *Scripts, plans, goals, and understanding.* Hillsdale, N.J.: Erlbaum.

SCHEERER, M. 1963. Problem solving. *Scientific American* 208:118–28.

SCHEERER, M.; GOLDSTEIN, K.; AND BORING, E. G. 1941. A demonstration of insight: The horse-rider puzzle. *American Journal of Psychology* 54:437–38.

SCHEFF, T. 1966. *Being mentally ill: A sociological theory.* Chicago: Aldine.

SCHIFF, M.; DUYME, M.; DUMARET, A.; AND TOMKIEWICZ, S. 1982. How much *could* we boost scholastic achievement and IQ scores? A direct answer from a French adoption study. *Cognition* 12:165–96.

SCHIFF, W. 1965. Perception of impending collision. *Psychological Monographs* 79:1–26.

SCHIFFMAN, H. R. 1976. *Sensation and perception: An integrated approach.* New York: Wiley.

SCHIFFRIN, D. 1988. Conversational analysis. In F. Newmeyer (Ed.), *Linguistics: The Cambridge survey: Vol. IV. The socio-cultural context.* Cambridge: Cambridge University Press.

SCHILDKRAUT, J. J. 1965. The catecholamine hypothesis of affective disorders: A review of supporting evidence. *American Journal of Psychiatry* 122:509–22.

SCHILDKRAUT, J. J.; GREEN, A. I.; AND MOONEY, J. J. 1985. Affective disorders: Biochemical aspects. In Kaplan, H. I.; and Sadock, J. (Eds.), *Comprehensive textbook of psychiatry,* 4th ed. Baltimore: Williams & Wilkins.

SCHNEIDER, D. J. 1973. Implicit personality theory: A review. *Psychological Bulletin* 79:294–309.

SCHNEIDER, D. J.; HASTORF, A. H.; AND ELLSWORTH, P. C. 1979. *Person perception,* 2nd ed. Reading, Mass.: Addison-Wesley.

SCHOFIELD, W. 1964. *Psychotherapy: The purchase of friendship.* Englewood Cliffs, N.J.: Prentice-Hall.

SCHWAB, E. C., AND NUSBAUM, H. C. (Eds.). 1986. *Pattern recognition by humans and machines,* vol. 2. New York: Academic Press.

SCHWARTZ, B. 1989. *Psychology of learning and behavior,* 3rd ed. New York: Norton.

SCHWARTZ, B., AND REISBERG, D. 1991. *Psychology of learning and memory.* New York: Norton.

SCHWARTZ, G. E.; WEINBERGER, D. A.; AND SINGER, J. A. 1981. Cardiovascular differentiation of happiness, sadness, anger, and fear following imagery and exercise. *Psychosomatic Medicine* 43:343–64.

SCOTT, J. P., AND FULLER, J. L. 1965. *Genetics and the social behavior of the dog.* Chicago: University of Chicago Press.

SEARLE, J. R. 1969. *Speech acts: An essay in the philosophy of language.* New York: Cambridge University Press.

SEARS, R. R.; MACCOBY, E. E.; AND LEVIN, H. 1957. *Patterns of child rearing.* Evanston, Ill.: Row, Peterson.

SEIDENBERG, M. S., AND PETITTO, L. A. 1979. Signing behavior in apes: A critical review. *Cognition* 7:177–215.

SELFE, L. 1977. *Nadia: A case of extraordinary drawing ability in an autistic child.* New York: Academic Press.

SELFRIDGE, O. G. 1959. Pandemonium: A paradigm for learning. In Blake, D. V., and Uttley, A. M. (Eds.), *Proceedings of the Symposium on the Mechanisation of Thought Processes.* London: HM Stationary Office.

SELIGMAN, M. E. P. 1968. Chronic fear produced by unpredictable electric shock. *Journal of Comparative and Physiological Psychology* 66:402–11.

SELIGMAN, M. E. P. 1970. On the generality of the laws of learning. *Psychological Review* 77:406–18.

SELIGMAN, M. E. P. 1975. *Helplessness: On depression, development, and death.* San Francisco: Freeman.

SELIGMAN, M. E. P., AND MAIER, S. F. 1967. Failure to escape traumatic shock. *Journal of Experimental Psychology* 74:1–9.

SELIGMAN, M. E. P.; MAIER, S. F.; AND SOLOMON, R. L. 1971. Unpredictable and uncontrollable aversive events. In Brush, F. R. (Ed.), *Aversive conditioning and learning.* New York: Academic Press.

SELLS, P. 1985. *Lectures on contemporary syntactic theories.* Stanford, Calif.: Center for the Study of Language and Information.

SENDAK, M. 1979. *Higglety pigglety pop! or There must be more to life.* New York: Harper & Row.

SHALTER, M. D. 1984. Predator-prey behavior and habituation. In Peeke, H. V. S., and Petrinovich, L. (Eds.), *Habituation, sensitization and behavior,* pp. 423–58. New York: Academic Press.

SHAPIRO, A. K. 1971. Placebo effects in medicine, psychotherapy, and psychoanalysis. In Bergin, A. E., and Garfield, S. L. (Eds.), *Handbook of psychotherapy and behavior change,* pp. 439–73. New York: Wiley.

SHAPIRO, D. A., AND SHAPIRO, D. 1982. Meta-analysis of comparative therapy outcome studies: A replication and refinement. *Psychological Bulletin* 92:581–604.

SHEFFIELD, F. D., AND ROBY, T. B. 1950. Reward value of a nonnutritive sweet taste. *Journal of Comparative and Physiological Psychology* 43:471–81.

SHEINGOLD, K., AND TENNEY, Y. J. 1982. Memory for a salient childhood event. In Neisser, U. (Ed.), *Memory observed,* pp. 201–12. San Francisco: Freeman.

SHEKELLE, R. B.; RAYNOR, W. J.; OSTFELD, A. M.; GARRON, D. C.; BIELIAVSKAS, L. A.; LIV, S. C.; MALIZA, C.; AND PAUL, O. 1981. Psychological depression and the 17-year risk of cancer. *Psychosomatic Medicine* 43:117–25.

SHERMAN, P. W. 1977. Nepotism and the evolution of alarm calls. *Science* 197:1246–54.

SHERRICK, C. E., AND CHOLEWIAK, R. W. 1986. Cutaneous sensitivity. In Boff, K. R.; Kaufman, L.; and Thomas, J. P. (Eds.), *Handbook of perception and human performance,* Chapter 12. New York: Wiley.

SHERRINGTON, C. S. 1906. *The integrative action of the nervous system,* 2nd ed. New Haven, Conn.: Yale University Press, 1947.

SHIFFRIN, R. M., AND SCHNEIDER, W. 1977. Controlled and automatic human information processing: II. Perceptual learning, automatic attending, and a general theory. *Psychological Review* 84: 127–90.

SHIMBERG, M. E. 1929. An investigation into the validity of norms with special reference to urban and rural groups. In *Archives of Psychology,* No. 104.

SHIPLEY, E. F.; KUHN, I. F.; AND MADDEN, E. C. 1983. Mothers' use of superordinate terms. *Journal of Child Language* 10:571–88.

SHIPLEY, E. F.; SMITH, C. S.; AND GLEITMAN, L. R. 1969. A study in the acquisition of language: Free responses to commands. *Language* 45:322–42.

SHIRLEY, M. M. 1961. *The first two years: A study of twenty-five babies.* Minneapolis: University of Minnesota Press.

SHORTLIFFE, E. H.; AXLINE, S. G.; BUCHANAN, B. G.; MERIGAN, T. C.; AND COHEN, N. S. 1973. An artificial intelligence program to advise physicians regarding antimicrobial therapy. *Computers and Biomedical Research* 6:544–60.

SHUEY, A. 1966. *The testing of Negro intelligence.* New York: Social Science Press.

SHWEDER, R. A. 1975. How relevant is an individual difference theory of personality? *Journal of Personality* 43:455–85.

SIEGEL, R. K. 1984. Changing patterns of cocaine use: Longitudinal observations, consequences, and treatment. In Grabowski, J. (Ed.), *Cocaine: Pharmacology, effects, and treatment of abuse,* pp. 92–110. NIDA Research Monograph 50.

SIEGEL, S. 1983. Classical conditioning, drug tolerance, and drug dependence. In Israel, Y.; Glaser, F. B.; Kalant, H.; Popham, R. E.; Schmidt, W.; and Smart, R. G. (Eds.), *Research advances in alcohol and drug problems,* vol. 7. New York: Plenum.

SIEGLER, R. S. 1989. Mechanisms of cognitive development. In Rosenzweig, M. R., and Porter, L. W. (Eds.), *Annual Review of Psychology* 40:353–79.

SIEGLER, M., AND OSMOND, H. 1974. *Models of madness, models of medicine.* New York: Harper & Row.

SILK, J. B. 1986. Social behavior in evolutionary perspective. In Smuts, B. B.; Cheney, D. L.; Seyfarth, R. M.; Wrangham, R. W.; and Struhsaker, T. T. (Eds.), *Primate societies.* Chicago: University of Chicago Press.

SILVERMAN, I. 1971. Physical attractiveness and courtship. Cited in Hatfield, E., and Walster, G. W. *A new look at love.* Reading, Mass.: Addison-Wesley, 1981.

SIMNER, M. L. 1971. Newborn's response to the cry of another infant. *Developmental Psychology* 5:136–50.

SIMS, E. A. 1986. Energy balance in human beings: The problems of plentitude. *Vitamins and hormones: Research and applications* 43:1–101.

SINCLAIR, H. 1970. The transition from sensory-motor behavior to symbolic activity. *Interchange* 1:119–26.

SINCLAIR, H. 1973. Language acquisition and cognitive development. In Moore, T. E. (Ed.), *Cognitive development and the acquisition of language.* New York: Academic Press.

SJÖSTRÖM, L. 1980. Fat cells and body weight. In Stunkard, A. J. (Ed.), *Obesity.* pp. 72–100. Philadelphia: Saunders.

SKEELS, H. 1966. Adult status of children with contrasting early life experiences. *Monograph of the Society for Research in Child Development* 31 (No. 3).

SKINNER, B. F. 1938. *The behavior of organisms.* New York: Appleton-Century-Crofts.

SKODAK, M., AND SKEELS, H. M. 1949. A final follow-up study of children in adoptive homes. *Journal of Genetic Psychology* 75: 85–125.

SLATER, E. 1943. The neurotic constitution. *Journal of Neurological Psychiatry* 6:1–16.

SLOANE, R. B.; STAPLES, F. R.; CRISTOL, A. H.; YORKSTON, N.J.; AND WHIPPLE, K. 1975. *Psychotherapy vs. behavior therapy.* Cambridge, Mass.: Harvard University Press.

SMEDSLUND, J. 1961. The acquisition of conservation of substance and weight in children. *Scandinavia Journal of Psychology* 2:11–20.

SMELSER, N. J. 1963. *Theory of collective behavior.* New York: Free Press, Macmillan.

SMITH, C., AND LLOYD, B. 1978. Maternal behavior and perceived sex of infant: Revisited. *Child Development* 49:1263–65.

SMITH, D. G. 1981. The association between rank and reproductive success of male rhesus monkeys. *American Journal of Primatology* 1:83–90.

SMITH, E. E., AND MEDIN, D. L. 1981. *Categories and concepts.* Cambridge, Mass.: Harvard University Press.

SMITH, M. B. 1950. The phenomenological approach in personality theory: Some critical remarks. *Journal of Abnormal and Social Psychology* 45:516–22.

SMITH, M. L.; GLASS, G. V.; AND MILLER, R. L. 1980. *The benefits of psychotherapy.* Baltimore: Johns Hopkins Press.

SMITH, S. M. 1979. Remembering in and out of context. *Journal of Experimental Psychology: Human Learning and Memory* 5: 460–71.

SNOW, C., AND HOEFNAGEL-HOHLE, M. 1978. The critical period for language acquisition: Evidence from second language learning. *Child Development* 49:1114–28.

SNYDER, M. 1987. *Public appearances/private realities.* New York: Freeman.

SNYDER, M., AND CUNNINGHAM, M. R. 1975. To comply or not comply: Testing the self-perception explanation of the "foot-in-the-door" phenomenon. *Journal of Personality and Social Psychology* 31:64–67.

SNYDER, M., AND ICKES, W. 1985. Personality and social behavior. In Lindzey, G., and Aronson, E. (Eds.), *Handbook of Social Psychology,* 3rd ed., vol. 2. New York: Random House.

SNYDER, S. H. 1976. The dopamine hypothesis of schizophrenia. *American Journal of Psychiatry* 133:197–202.

SNYDER, S. H., AND CHILDERS, S. R. 1979. Opiate receptors and opioid peptides. *Annual Review of Neuroscience* 2:35–64.

SOLOMON, R. C. 1981. The love lost in clichés. *Psychology Today,* October 1981, pp. 83–85, 87–88.

SOLOMON, R. L. 1980. The opponent-process theory of acquired motivation: The costs of pleasure and the benefits of pain. *American Psychologist* 35:691–712.

SOLOMON, R. L., AND CORBIT, J. D. 1974. An opponent-process theory of motivation: I. Temporal dynamics of affect. *Psychological Review* 81:119–45.

SOLOMON, R. L., AND WYNNE, L. C. 1953. Traumatic avoidance learning: Acquisition in normal dogs. *Psychological Monographs* 67 (Whole No. 354).

SPEARMAN, C. 1927. *The abilities of man.* London: Macmillan.

SPELKE, E. S. 1983. Perception of unity, persistence, and identity: Thoughts on infants' conceptions of objects. In Meehler, J. (Ed.), *Infant and neonate cognition.* Hillsdale, N.J.: Erlbaum.

SPERBER, D., AND WILSON, D. 1986. *Relevance: Communication and cognition.* Oxford: Blackwell.

SPERRY, R. W. 1974. Lateral specialization in the surgically separated hemispheres. In Schmitt, F. O., and Worden, F. G. (Eds.), *The Neuroscience Third Study Program.* Cambridge, Mass.: MIT Press.

SPERRY, R. W. 1982. Some effects of disconnecting the cerebral hemispheres. *Science* 217:1223–26.

SPIES, G. 1965. Food versus intracranial self-stimulation reinforcement in food deprived rats. *Journal of Comparative and Physiological Psychology* 60:153–57.

SPITZER, R. L. 1976. More on pseudoscience in science and the case for psychiatric diagnosis. *Archives of General Psychiatry* 33:459–70.

SPOONER, A., AND KELLOGG, W. N. 1947. The backward conditioning curve. *American Journal of Psychology* 60:321–34.

SPRINGER, S. P., AND DEUTSCH, G. 1981. *Left brain, right brain.* San Francisco: Freeman.

SQUIRE L. R. 1977. ECT and memory loss. *American Journal of Psychiatry* 134:997–1001.

SQUIRE, L. R. 1986. Mechanisms of memory. *Science* 232:1612–19.

SQUIRE, L. R. 1987. *Memory and brain.* New York: Oxford University.

SQUIRE, L. R., AND COHEN, N. J. 1979. Memory and amnesia: Resistance to disruption develops for years after learning. *Behavioral Biology and Neurology* 25:115–25.

SQUIRE, L. R., AND COHEN, N. J. 1982. Remote memory, retrograde amnesia, and the neuropsychology of memory. In Cermak, L. S. (Ed.), *Human memory and amnesia,* pp. 275–304. Hillsdale, N.J.: Erlbaum.

SQUIRE, L. R., AND ZOUZOUNIS, J. A. 1986. ECT and memory: Brief pulse versus sine wave. *American Journal of Psychiatry* 143: 596–601.

STACHER, G.; BAUER, H.; AND STEINRINGER, H. 1979. Cholecystokinin decreases appetite and activation evoked by stimuli arising from preparation of a meal in man. *Physiology and Behavior* 23:325–31.

STAMPFL, T. G. 1975. Implosive therapy: Staring down your nightmares. *Psychology Today* 8:66–68.

STAMPFL, T. G., AND LEVIS, D. J. 1967. Essentials of implosive therapy: A learning-theory-based psychodynamic behavior therapy. *Journal of Abnormal Psychology* 72:496–503.

STARK, L., AND ELLIS, S. 1981. Scanpaths revisited: Cognitive models direct active looking. In Fisher, D.; Monty, R.; and Senders, I. (Eds.), *Eye movements: Cognition and visual perception,* pp. 193–226. Hillsdale, N.J.: Erlbaum.

STEELE, C. M., AND LIU, T. J. 1983. Dissonance processes as self-affirmation. *Journal of Personality and Social Psychology* 45:5–19.

STEINER, J. E. 1974. The gustafacial response: Observation on normal and anencephalic newborn infants. In Bosma, F. J. (Ed.), *Fourth symposium on oral sensation and perception: Development in the fetus and infant* (DHEW Publication No. NIH 73–546). Washington, D. C.: U. S. Government Printing Office.

STEINER, J. E. 1977. Facial expressions of the neonate infant indicating the hedonics of food-related chemical stimuli. In Weiffenbach, J. M. (Ed.), *Taste and development: The genesis of sweet preference* (DHEW Publication No. NIH 77–1068), pp. 173–88. Washington, D. C.: U. S. Government Printing Office.

STELLAR, E. 1954. The physiology of motivation. *Psychological Review* 61:5–22.

STELLAR, J. R., AND STELLAR, E. 1985. *The neurobiology of motivation and reward.* New York: Springer Verlag.

STERNBACH, R. A. 1963. Congenital insensitivity to pain: A review. *Psychological Bulletin* 60:252–64.

STERNBERG, R. J., AND GARDNER, M. K. 1983. Unities in inductive reasoning. *Journal of Experimental Psychology: General* 112: 80–116.

STERNBERG, S. 1969. Memory-scanning: Mental processes revealed by reaction-time experiments. *American Scientist* 57:421–57.

STERNBERG, S. 1970. Memory-scanning: Mental processes revealed by reaction time experiments. In Antrobus, J. S., *Cognition and affect,* pp. 13–58. Boston: Little,Brown.

STEVENS, A., AND COUPE, P. 1978. Distortions in judged spatial relations. *Cognitive Psychology* 10:422–37.

STEWART, T. D. 1957. Stone age surgery: A general review, with emphasis on the New World. *Annual Review of the Smithsonian Institution.* Washington, D. C.: Smithsonian Institute.

STOKOE, W. C., JR. 1960. Sign language structure: An outline of the visual communication systems. *Studies in Linguistics Occasional Papers* 8.

STOLLER, R. J. 1968. *Sex and gender: On the development of masculinity and femininity.* New York: Science House.

STOLLER, R. J. AND HERDT, G. H. 1985. Theories of origins of male homosexuality: A cross-cultural look. *Archives of General Psychiatry* 42:399–404.

STONE, A. 1975. *Mental health and law: A system in transition.* (DHEW Publication No. 75176). Washington, D.C.: U. S. Government Printing Office.

STORMS, M. D. 1973. Videotape and the attribution process: Reversing actors' and observers' points of view. *Journal of Personality and Social Psychology* 27:165–75.

STRICKER, E. M. 1973. Thirst, sodium appetite, and complementary physiological contributions to the regulation of intravascular fluid volume. In Epstein, A. N.; Kissilef, H. R.; and Stellar, E., (Eds.), *The neurophysiology of thirst: New findings and advances in concepts.* Washington, D.C.: Winston.

STRICKER, E. M., AND ZIGMOND, M. J. 1976. Recovery of function after damage to catecholamine-containing neurons: A neurochemical model for the lateral hypothalamic syndrome. In Sprague, J. M., and Epstein, A. N. (Eds.), *Progress in psychobiology and physiological psychology,* vol. 6, pp. 121–88. New York: Academic Press.

STROOP, J. R. 1935. Studies of interference in serial verbal reactions. *Journal of Experimental Psychology* 18:643–62.

STUART, R. B., AND MITCHELL, C. 1980. Self-help groups in the control of body weight. In Stunkard, A. J. (Ed.), *Obesity*, pp. 354–55. Philadelphia: Saunders.

STUNKARD, A. J. 1975. Obesity. In Freedman, A. M.; Kaplan, H. I.; and Sadock, B. J. (Eds.), *Comprehensive textbook of psychiatry —II*, vol. 2, pp. 1648–54. Baltimore: Williams & Wilkins.

STUNKARD, A. 1980. Psychoanalysis and psychotherapy. In Stunkard, A. J. (Ed.), *Obesity*, pp. 355–68. Philadelphia: Saunders.

SULS, J. M., AND MILLER, R. L. (Eds.). 1977. *Social comparison processes: Theoretical and empirical perspectives.* New York: Washington Hemisphere Publishing Co.

SUOMI, S. J. 1989. Personal communication.

SUOMI, S. J., AND HARLOW, H. F. 1971. Abnormal social behavior in young monkeys. In Helmuth, J. (Ed.), *Exceptional infant: Studies in abnormalities,* vol. 2, pp. 483–529. New York: Brunner/Mazel.

SUOMI, S., AND HARLOW, H. 1972. Social rehabilitation of isolate-reared monkeys. *Developmental Psychology* 6:487–96.

SUPALLA, T. 1986. The classifier system in American Sign Language. In Craig, C. (Ed.), *Noun classes and categorization: Typological studies in language,* vol. 7. Amsterdam: John Benjamins.

SUPALLA, I., AND NEWPORT, E. L. 1978. How many seats in a chair? The derivation of nouns and verbs in American Sign Language. In Siple, P. (Ed.), *Understanding language through sign language research.* New York: Academic Press.

SYMONS, D. 1979. *The evolution of human sexuality.* New York: Oxford University Press.

SZASZ, T. S. 1974. *The myth of mental illness: Foundations of a theory of personal conduct,* rev. ed. New York: Harper & Row.

TANNER, J. M. 1970. Physical growth. In Mussen, P. H. (Ed.), *Carmichael's manual of child psychology,* 3rd ed., pp. 77–105. New York: Wiley.

TAYLOR, S. E., AND FISKE, S. T. 1975. Point of view and perceptions of causality. *Journal of Personality and Social Psychology* 32:439–45.

TEITELBAUM, P. 1955. Sensory control of hypothalamic hyperphagia. *Journal of Comparative and Physiological Psychology* 48: 156–63.

TEITELBAUM, P. 1961. Disturbances in feeding and drinking behavior after hypothalamic lesions. In Jones, M. R. (Ed.), *Nebraska Symposium on Motivation,* pp. 39–65. Lincoln, Neb.: University of Nebraska Press.

TEITELBAUM, P., AND EPSTEIN, A. N. 1962. The lateral hypothalamic syndrome: Recovery of feeding and drinking after lateral hypothalamic lesions. *Psychological Review* 69:74–90.

TERRACE, H. S. 1979. *Nim.* New York: Knopf.

TERRACE, H. S.; PETITTO, L. A.; SANDERS, D. L.; AND BEVER, T. G. 1979. Can an ape create a sentence? *Science* 206:891–902.

TERVOORT, B. T. 1961. Esoteric symbolism in the communication behavior of young deaf children. *American Annals of the Deaf* 106:436–80.

TESSER, A.; CAMPBELL, J.; AND SMITH, M. 1984. Friendship choice and performance: Self-evaluation maintenance in children. *Journal of Personality and Social Psychology* 46:561–74.

THOMAS, A.; CHESS, S.; AND BIRCH, H. G. 1970. The origin of personality. *Scientific American* 223:102–109.

THOMPSON, C. P., AND COWAN, T. 1986. Flashbulb memories: A nicer recollection of a Neisser recollection. *Cognition* 22:199–200.

THOMPSON, R. F. 1973. *Introduction to biopsychology.* San Francisco: Albion Publishing Co.

THORNDIKE, E. L. 1898. Animal intelligence: An experimental study of the associative processes in animals. *Psychological Monographs* 2 (Whole No. 8).

THORNDIKE, E. L. 1911. *Animal intelligence: Experimental studies.* New York: Macmillan.

THORNDIKE, E. L. 1924. The measurement of intelligence: Present status. *Psychological Review* 31:219–52.

TINBERGEN, N. 1951. *The study of instinct.* Oxford, England: Clarendon.

TIZARD, B., AND HODGES, J. 1978. The effect of early institutional rearing on the development of eight-year-old children. *Journal of Child Psychology and Psychiatry* 19:98–118.

TOLMAN, E. C. 1932. *Purposive behavior in animals and men.* New York: Appleton-Century-Crofts.

TOLMAN, E. C. 1948. Cognitive maps in rats and men. *Psychological Review* 55:189–208.

TOLMAN, E. C., AND GLEITMAN, H. 1949. Studies in learning and motivation: I. Equal reinforcements in both end-boxes, followed by shock in one end-box. *Journal of Experimental Psychology* 39:810–19.

TOLMAN, E. C., AND HONZIK, C. H. 1930. Introduction and removal of reward, and maze performance in rats. *University of California Publications in Psychology* 4:257–75.

TORGERSEN, S. 1983. Genetic factors in anxiety disorders. *Archives of General Psychiatry* 40:1085–89.

TORGERSEN, S. 1986. Genetic factors in moderately severe and mild affective disorders. *Archives of General Psychiatry* 43:222–26.

TREISMAN, A. M. 1964. Selective attention in man. *British Medical Bulletin* 20:12–16.

TRIVERS, R. L. 1971. The evolution of reciprocal altruism. *Quarterly Review of Biology* 46:35–57.

TRIVERS, R. L. 1972. Parental investment and sexual selection. In Campbell, B. (Ed.), *Sexual selection and the descent of man,* pp. 139–79. Chicago: Aldine.

TULVING, E. 1972. Episodic and semantic memory. In Tulving, E., and Donaldson, W. (Eds.), *Organization and memory.* New York: Academic Press.

TULVING, E., AND OSLER, S. 1968. Effectiveness of retrieval cues in memory for words. *Journal of Experimental Psychology* 77: 593–601.

TULVING, E., AND PEARLSTONE, Z. 1966. Availability versus accessability of information in memory for words. *Journal of Verbal Learning and Verbal Behavior* 5:381–91.

TULVING, E.; SCHACTER, D. L.; AND STARK, H. A. 1982. Priming effects in word-fragment completion are independent of recognition memory. *Journal of Experimental Psychology: Learning, Memory, and Cognition* 8:336–42.

TULVING, E., AND THOMSON, D. M. 1973. Encoding specificity and retrieval processes in episodic memory. *Psychological Review* 80: 352–73.

TURING, A. M. 1950. Computing machinery and intelligence. *Mind* 59:433–60.

TURNER, A. M., AND GREENOUGH, W. T. 1985. Differential rearing effects on rat visual cortex synapses. I. Synaptic and neuronal density and synapses per neuron. *Brain Research* 329:195–203.

TVERSKY, A., AND KAHNEMAN, D. 1973. Availability: A heuristic for judging frequency and probability. *Cognitive Psychology* 5: 207–32.

TVERSKY, A., AND KAHNEMAN, D. 1974. Judgment under uncertainty: Heuristics and biases. *Science* 125:1124–31.

TYLER, L. E. 1965. *The psychology of human differences.* New York: Appleton-Century-Crofts.

URWIN, C. 1983. Dialogue and cognitive functioning in the early language development of three blind children. In Mills, A. E. (Ed.), *Language acquisition in the blind child.* London: Croom Helm.

VAILLANT, G. E. 1971. Theoretical hierarchy of adaptive ego mechanisms. *Archives of General Psychiatry* 24:107–18.

VAILLANT, G. E. 1974. Natural history of male psychological health. II. Some antecedents of health adult adjustment. *Archives of General Psychiatry* 31:15–22.

VAILLANT, G. E. 1976. Natural history of male psychological health. V: Relation of choice of ego mechanisms of defense to adult adjustment. *Archives of General Psychiatry* 33:535–45.

VAILLANT, G. E. 1977. *Adaptation to life.* Boston: Little, Brown & Co.

VALENTA, J. G., AND RIGBY, M. K. 1968. Discrimination of the odor of stressed rats. *Science* 161:599–601.

VANDELL, D. L.; HENDERSON, V. K.; AND WILSON, K. S. 1988. A longitudinal study of children with day care experiences of varying quality. *Child Development* 59:1286–92.

VAULTIN, R. G., AND BERKELEY, M. A. 1977. Responses of single cells in cat visual cortex to prolonged stimulus movement: Neural correlates of visual aftereffects. *Journal of Neurophysiology* 40: 1051–65.

VERAA, R. P., AND GRAFSTEIN, B. 1981. Cellular mechanisms

for recovery from nervous system injury: A conference report. *Experimental Neurology* 71:6–75.

VERY, P. S. 1967. Differential factor structure in mathematical ability. *Genetic Psychology Monographs* 75:169–208.

VISINTAINER, M.; VOLPICELLI, J. R.; AND SELIGMAN, M. E. P. 1982. Tumor rejection in rats after inescapable or escapable shock. *Science* 216:437–39.

VOLPICELLI, J. 1989. Psychoactive substance use disorders. In Rosenhan, D. L., and Seligman, M. E. P. *Abnormal psychology,* 2nd ed. New York: Norton.

VON DOMARUS, E. 1944. The specific laws of logic in schizophrenia. In Kasanin, J. (Ed.), *Language and thought in schizophrenia.* Berkeley, Calif.: University of California Press.

WABER, D. P. 1977. Sex differences in mental abilities, hemispheric lateralization, and rate of physical growth at adolescence. *Developmental Psychology* 13:29–38.

WABER, D. P. 1979. Cognitive abilities and sex-related variations in the maturation of cerebral cortical functions. In Wittig, M. A., and Petersen, A. C. (Eds.), *Sex-related differences in cognitive functioning,* pp. 161–89. New York: Academic Press.

WACHTEL, P. L. 1977. *Psychoanalysis and behavior therapy: Toward an integration.* New York: Basic Books.

WACHTEL, P. L. 1982. What can dynamic therapies contribute to behavior therapy? *Behavior Therapy* 13:594–609.

WALD, G. 1950. Eye and camera. *Scientific American* 183:32–41.

WALDFOGEL, S. 1948. The frequency and affective character of childhood memories. *Psychological Monographs,* vol. 62 (Whole No. 291).

WALK, R. 1978. Depth perception and experience. In Walk, R., and Pick, H. (Eds.), *Perception and experience.* New York: Plenum.

WALK, R. D., AND GIBSON, E. J. 1961. A comparative and analytical study of visual depth perception. *Psychological Monographs* 75 (Whole No. 519).

WALKER, L. J. 1984. Sex differences in the development of moral reasoning: A critical review. *Child Development* 55:677–91.

WALLACH, H. 1948. Brightness constancy and the nature of achromatic colors. *Journal of Experimental Psychology* 38:310–24.

WALSTER, E.; ARONSON, E.; AND ABRAHAMS, D. 1966. On increasing the persuasiveness of a low prestige communicator. *Journal of Experimental Social Psychology* 2:325–42.

WALTERS, J. R., AND SEYFARTH, R. M. 1986. Conflict and cooperation. In Smuts, B. B.; Cheney, D. L.; Seyfarth, R. M.; Wrangham, R. W.; and Struhsaker, T. T. (Eds.), *Primate societies.* Chicago: University of Chicago Press.

WARD, I. L. 1984. The prenatal stress syndrome: Current status. *Psychoneuroendocrinology* 9:3–11.

WARREN, R. M. 1970. Perceptual restorations of missing speech sounds. *Science* 167:392–93.

WASON, P. C. 1960. On the failure to eliminate hypotheses in a conceptual task. *Quarterly Journal of Experimental Psychology* 12:129–40.

WASON, P. C. 1966. Reasoning. In Foss, B. M. (Ed.), *New horizons in psychology,* vol. 1., pp. 135–51. Harmondsworth, England: Penguin Books.

WASON, P. C. 1968. On the failure to eliminate hypotheses—A second look. In Wason, P. C., and Johnson-Laird, P. N. (Eds.), *Thinking and reasoning.* Harmondsworth, England: Penguin Books.

WASON, P. C., AND JOHNSON-LAIRD, P. N. 1972. *Psychology of reasoning.* London: B. T. Batsford, Ltd.

WATERS, E.; WIPPMAN, J.; AND SROUFE, L. A. 1979. Attachment, positive affect, and competence in the peer group: Two studies in construct validation. *Child Development* 50:821–29.

WATKINS, L. R., AND MAYER, D. J. 1982. Organization of endogenous opiate and nonopiate pain control systems. *Science* 216:1185–92.

WATSON, J. S. 1967. Memory and "contingency analysis" in infant learning. *Merrill-Palmer Quarterly* 13:55–76.

WAUGH, N. C., AND NORMAN, D. A. 1965. Primary memory. *Psychological Review* 72:89–104.

WECHSLER, D. 1958. *The measurement and appraisal of adult intelligence,* 4th ed. Baltimore: Williams & Wilkins.

WEINER, R. D. 1984a. Does electroconvulsive therapy cause brain damage? (with peer commentary). *The Behavioral and Brain Sciences* 7:1–54.

WEINER, R. D. 1984b. Convulsive therapy:50 years later. *American Journal of Psychiatry* 141:1078–79.

WEINER, R. D. 1985. Convulsive therapies. In Kaplan, H. I., and Sadock, J. (Eds.), *Comprehensive textbook of psychiatry,* 4th ed. Baltimore: Williams & Wilkins.

WEINGARTNER, H., AND PARKER, E. S. (Eds.). 1984. *Memory consolidation: Psychobiology of cognition.* Hillsdale, N.J.: Erlbaum.

WEINSTOCK, S. 1954. Resistance to extinction of a running response following partial reinforcement under widely spaced trials. *Journal of Comparative and Physiological Psychology* 47:318–22.

WEISBERG, R. W., AND ALBA, J. W., 1981. An examination of the alleged role of "fixation" in the solution of several "insight" problems. *Journal of Experimental Psychology: General* 110:169–92.

WEISKRANTZ, L., AND WARRINGTON, E. K. 1979. Conditioning in amnesic patients. *Neuropsychologia* 18:177–84.

WEISS, J. M. 1970. Somatic effects of predictable and unpredictable shock. *Psychosomatic Medicine* 32:397–408.

WEISS, J. M. 1977. Psychological and behavioral influences on gastrointestinal lesions in animal models. In Maser, J. D., and Seligman, M. E. P. (Eds.), *Psychopathology: Experimental models,* pp. 232–69. San Francisco: Freeman.

WEISS, B., AND LATIES, V. G. 1961. Behavioral thermoregulation. *Science* 133:1338–44.

WEISSMAN, M., AND BOYD, J. H. 1985. Affective disorders: Epidemiology. In Kaplan, H. I., and Sadock, J. (Eds.), *Modern synopsis of comprehensive textbook of psychiatry,* 4th ed. Baltimore: Williams & Wilkins.

WEISSTEIN, N., AND WONG, E. 1986. Figure-ground organization and the spatial and temporal responses of the visual system. In Schwab, E. C., and Nusbaum, H. C. (Eds.), *Pattern recognition by humans and machines,* vol. 2. New York: Academic Press.

WELCH, C. A.; WEINER, R. D.; WEIR, D.; CAHILL, J. F.; ROGERS, H. J.; DAVIDSON, J.; MILLER, R. D.; AND MANDEL, M. R. 1982. Efficacy of ECT in the treatment of depression: Wave form and electrode placement considerations. *Psychopharmacological Bulletin* 18:31–34.

WELKER, W. I.; JOHNSON, J. I.; AND PUBOLS, B. H. 1964. Some morphological and physiological characteristics of the somatic sensory system in raccoons. *American Zoologist* 4:75–94.

WELLMAN, H. M.; RITTER, K.; AND FLAVELL, J. H. 1975. Deliberate memory behavior in the delayed reactions of very young children. *Developmental Psychology* 11:780–87.

WENDER, P. H.; KETY, S. S.; ROSENTHAL, D.; SCHULSINGER, F.; AND ORTMAN, J. 1986. Psychiatric disorders in the biological relatives of adopted individuals with affective disorders. *Archives of General Psychiatry* 43:923–29.

WERKER, J., AND TEES, R. 1984. Cross-language speech perception: Evidence for perceptual reorganization during the first year of life. *Infant Behavior and Development* 7:49–63.

WERTHEIMER, M. 1912. Experimentelle Studien über das Gesehen von Bewegung. *Zeitschrift frPsychology* 61:161–265.

WERTHEIMER, M. 1923. Untersuchungen zur Lehre von der Gestalt, II. *Psychologische Forschung* 4:301–50.

WERTHEIMER, M. 1945. *Productive thinking.* New York: Harper.

WERTHEIMER, M. 1961. Psychomotor coordination of auditory and visual space at birth. *Science* 134:1692.

WEST, S. G.; WHITNEY, G.; AND SCHNEDLER, R. 1975. Helping a motorist in distress: The effects of sex, race, and neighborhood. *Journal of Personality and Social Psychology,* 31:691–98.

WESTERMEYER, J. 1987. Public health and chronic mental illness. *American Journal of Public Health* 77:667–68.

WHEELER, L. R. 1942. A comparative study of the intelligence of East Tennessee mountain children. *Journal of Educational Psychology* 33:321–34.

WHITE, G. L. 1980. Physical attractiveness and courtship progress. *Journal of Personality and Social Psychology* 39:660–68.

WHITE, R. W., AND WATT, N. F. 1973. *The abnormal personality,* 4th ed. New York: Ronald Press.

WHITE, S. H., AND PILLEMER, D. B. 1979. Childhood amnesia and the development of a functionally accessible memory system. In Kihlstrom, J. F., and Evans, F. J. (Eds.), *Functional disorders of memory.* Hillsdale, N.J.: Erlbaum.

WHITING, J. W. M., AND WHITING, B. B. 1975. *Children of six cultures: A psychocultural analysis.* Cambridge, Mass.: Harvard University Press.

WICKELGREN, W. A. 1974. *How to solve problems.* San Francisco: Freeman.

WICKER, A. W. 1969. Attitudes versus action: The relationship of verbal and overt behavioral responses to attitude objects. *Journal of Social Issues* 25:41–78.

WIENS, A. N., AND MENUSTIK, C. E. 1983. Treatment outcome and patient characteristics in an aversion therapy program for alcoholism. *American Psychologist* 38:1089–96.

WIESENTHAL, D. L.; ENDLER, N. S.; COWARD, T. R.; AND EDWARDS, J. 1976. Reversibility of relative competence as a determinant of conformity across different perceptual tasks. *Representative Research in Social Psychology* 7:319–42.

WILCOXIN, H. C.; DRAGOIN, W. B.; AND KRAL, P. A. 1971. Illness-induced aversions in rat and quail: Relative salience of visual and gustatory cues. *Science* 171:826–28.

WILLIAMS, C. D. 1959. The elimination of tantrum behavior by extinction procedures. *Journal of Abnormal and Social Psychology* 59:269.

WILLIAMS, G. C. 1966. *Adaptation and natural selection.* Princeton, N.J.: Princeton University Press.

WILLIAMS, H. L.; TEPAS, D. I.; AND MORLOCK, H. C. 1962. Evoked responses to clicks and electroencephalographic stages of sleep in man. *Science* 138:685–86.

WILLIAMS, M. D., AND HOLLAN, J. D. 1982. The process of retrieval from very long-term memory. *Cognitive Science* 5:87–119.

WILLIAMS, R. B. 1987. Psychological factors in coronary artery disease: Epidemiological evidence. *Circulation* 76 (suppl I) 117–23.

WILLIAMS, W. L. 1986. *The spirit and the flesh: sexual diversity in American Indian culture.* Boston: Beacon Press.

WILSON, D. H.; REEVES, A. G.; GAZZANIGA, M. S.; AND CULVER, C. 1977. Cerebral commissurotomy for the control of intractable seizures. *Neurology* 27:708–15.

WILSON, E. O. 1978. *On human nature.* Cambridge, Mass; Harvard University Press.

WILSON, E. O. 1975. *Sociobiology.* Cambridge, Mass.: Harvard University Press.

WILSON, G. 1978. Introversion/extraversion. In London, H., and Exner, J. (Eds.), *Dimensions of personality.* New York: Wiley.

WILSON, G. 1985. *The psychology of the performing arts.* London and Sydney: Croom Helm.

WILSON, G. T. 1980. Behavior modification and the treatment of obesity. In Stunkard, A. J. (Ed.), *Obesity*, pp. 325–44. Philadelphia: Saunders.

WISE, R. A., AND BOZARTH, M. A. 1987. A psychomotor stimulant theory of addiction. *Psychological Review* 94:469–92.

WISHNER, J. 1960. Reanalysis of "impressions of personality." *Psychological Review* 67:96–112.

WISHNER, J. 1974. *Psychopathology: Defective concept or defective practice?* Invited address delivered at the XVIII International Congress of Applied Psychology, Montreal, Canada.

WITTGENSTEIN, L. 1953. *Philosophical investigations.* Trans. by Anscombe, G. E. M. Oxford, England: Blackwell.

WOHLWILL, J. H. 1973. *The study of behavioral development.* New York: Academic Press.

WOLLEN, K. A.; WEBER, A.; AND LOWRY, D. 1972. Bizarreness versus interaction of mental images as determinants of learning. *Cognitive Psychology* 3:518–23.

WOLPE, J. 1958. *Psychotherapy by reciprocal inhibition.* Stanford, Calif.: Stanford University Press.

WOLPE, J., AND LAZARUS, A. A. 1966. *Behavior therapy techniques: A guide to the treatment of neuroses.* Elmsford, N.Y.: Pergamon.

WOLPERT, E. A., AND TROSMAN, H. 1958. Studies in psychophysiology of dreams: I. Experimental evocation of sequential dream episodes. *Archives of Neurology and Psychiatry* 79:603–606.

WOODWORTH, R. S. 1938. *Experimental psychology.* New York: Holt.

WRIGHT, C. 1982. Rembrandt: Self-portraits. London: Gordon Fraser.

WYERS, E. J.; PEEKE, H. V. S.; AND HERZ, M. J. 1973. Behavioral habituation in invertebrates. In Peeke, H. V. S., and Herz, M. J. (Eds.), *Habituation: Vol. 1. Behavioral studies.* New York: Academic Press.

YANDO, R.; SEITZ, V.; AND ZIGLER, E. 1978. *Imitation: A developmental perspective.* Hillsdale, N.J.: Erlbaum.

YARBUS, A. L. 1967. Eye movements and vision. Trans. by Riggs, L. A. New York: Plenum Press.

YARROW, L. J. 1961. Maternal deprivation: Toward an empirical and conceptual reevaluation. *Psychological Bulletin* 58:459–90.

YARROW, L. J., AND GOODWIN, M. S. 1973. The immediate impact of separation reactions of infants to a change in mother figures. In Stone, L. J.; Smith, T. J.; and Murphy, L. B. (Eds.), *The competent infant.* New York: Basic Books.

YERKES, R. M., AND MORGULIS, S. 1909. Method of Pavlov in animal psychology. *Psychological Bulletin* 6:264.

YONAS, A. 1981. Infants' response to optical information for collision. In Aslin, R. N.; Alberts, J. R.; and Petersen, M. R. (Eds.), *Development of perception*, pp. 313–34. New York: Academic Press.

YUSSEN, S. R., AND LEVY, V. M. 1975. Developmental changes in predicting one's own span of memory. *Journal of Experimental Child Psychology* 19:502–508.

ZAIDEL, E. 1976. Auditory vocabulary of the right hemisphere following brain bisection or hemidecortication. *Cortex* 12:191–211.

ZAIDEL, E. 1983. A response to Gazzaniga: Language in the right hemisphere. *American Psychologist* 38:542–46.

ZAJONC, R. B. 1965. Social facilitation. *Science* 149:269–74.

ZAJONC, R. B. 1968. Attitudinal effects of mere exposure. *Journal of Personality and Social Psychology Monograph Supplement* 9:1–27.

ZAJONC, R. B. 1980. Copresence. In Paulus, P. (Ed.), *The psychology of group influence.* Hillsdale, N.J.: Erlbaum.

ZIEGLER, F. J.; IMBODEN, J. B.; AND RODGERS, D. A. 1963. Contemporary conversion reactions: III. Diagnostic considerations. *Journal of the American Medical Association* 186:307–11.

ZIGLER, E., AND BERMAN, W. 1983. Discerning the future of early childhood intervention. *American Psychologist* 38:894–906.

ZIGLER, E., AND CHILD, I. L. 1969. Socialization. In Lindzey, G., and Aronson, E. (Eds.), *The handbook of social psychology,* vol. 3, pp. 450–589. Reading, Mass.: Addison-Wesley.

ZIGLER, E. F.; LAMB, M. E.; AND CHILD, I. L. 1982. *Socialization and personality development,* 2nd ed. New York: Oxford University Press.

ZILBOORG, G., AND HENRY, G. W. 1941. *A history of medical psychology.* New York: Norton.

ZIMBARDO, P. G. 1969. The human choice: Individuation, reason, and order versus deindividuation, impulse and chaos. In Arnold, W. J. and Levine, E. (Eds.), *Nebraska Symposium on Motivation,* pp. 237–308. Lincoln, Neb.: University of Nebraska Press.

ZUBIN, J.; ERON, L. D.; AND SHUMER, F. 1965. *An experimental approach to projective techniques.* New York: Wiley.

ZUCKERMAN, M. 1979. *Sensation seeking: Beyond the optimum level of arousal.* Hillsdale, N.J.: Erlbaum.

ZUCKERMAN, M. 1983. A biological theory of sensation seeking. In Zuckerman, M. (Ed.), *Biological bases of sensation seeking, impulsivity, and anxiety.* Hillsdale, N.J.: Erlbaum.

ZUCKERMAN, M. 1987. All parents are environmentalists until they have their second child. Peer commentary on Plomin, R., and Daniels, D. Why are children from the same family so different from one another? *Behavioral and Brain Sciences* 10:38–39.

ZUCKERMAN, M.; BALLENGER, J. C.; JIMERSON, D. C.; MURPHY, D. L.; AND POST, R. M. 1983. A correlational test in humans of the biological models of sensation seeking and anxiety. In Zuckerman, M. (Ed.), *Biological bases of sensation seeking, impulsivity, and anxiety*, pp. 229–48. Hillsdale, N.J.: Erlbaum.

ZUCKERMAN, M.; KLORMAN, R.; LARRANCE, D.; AND SPIEGEL, N. H. 1981. Facial, autonomic, and subjective components of emotion: The facial feedback hypothesis versus the externalizer-internalizer distinction. *Journal of Personality and Social Psychology* 41:929–44.

ZUGER, B. 1984. Early effeminate behavior in boys. *Journal of Nervous and Mental Disease* 172:90–96.

Acknowledgments and Copyrights

FIGURES

1.1 Photograph by Michael Abbey/Photo Researchers. **1.2** Photograph by Dr. John Mazziotta, UCLA School of Medicine/Science Photo Library/Photo Researchers **1.4B** Nilsson, Lennart, *Behold Man.* Boston: Little, Brown & Company, 1974. Reproduced by permission of the publisher. **1.5** Copyright Guigoz/Dr. A. Privat/Petit Format/Science Source/Photo Researchers **1.9** Eccles, J. C., *The Understanding of the Brain.* New York: McGraw-Hill, 1973. Adapted by permission of the publisher. **1.13** Roeder, K., *Nerve Cells and Insect Behavior,* p. 198. Cambridge, MA: Harvard University Press, 1972. Adapted by permission of the publisher. **1.15** Bloom, F. E., Lazerson, A., and Hofstadter, L., *Brain, Mind and Behavior.* New York: Freeman, 1988. Adapted by permission of WNET/Thirteen. **1.16** *Physiological Psychology,* 2nd ed., by Mark Rosenzweig and Arnold Leiman. Copyright 1989 by Random House. Reprinted by permission of McGraw-Hill. **1.17** Blakemore, C., *Mechanics of the Mind,* p. 42. New York: Cambridge University Press, 1977. Reprinted by Permission of the publisher. **1.20** Lickley, J. D., *The Nervous System.* Essex, England: Longman, 1919. Reprinted by permission of the publisher. **1.21A** Photograph by Biophoto Associates/Photo Researchers. **1.21B** Keeton, W. T., *Biological Science,* 3rd ed. New York: W. W. Norton & Company, Inc., 1980. Copyright 1980, 1979, 1972, 1967 by W. W. Norton & Company. Used with permission. **1.24** Bloom, F. E., Lazerson, A., and Hofstadter, L., *Brain, Mind and Behavior.* New York: Freeman, 1988. Adapted by permission of WNET/Thirteen. **1.25** Adapted by permission of Macmillan Publishing Co., Inc., from *The Cerebral Cortex of Man* by Wilder Penfield and Theodore Rasmussen. Copyright 1950 by Macmillan Publishing Co., Inc., renewed 1978 by Theodore Rasmussen. **1.26** Cobb, S., *Foundations of Neuropsychiatry.* Baltimore, MD: William & Wilkins, 1941. Adapted by permission of the publisher. **1.27** NIH/SPL/Photo Researchers, Inc. **1.28** Photograph by Dr. John Mazziotta et al./Photo Researchers **1.29** From *Higher Cortical Functions in Man* by Aleksandr Romanovich Luria. Copyright 1966, 1979 Consultants Bureau Enterprises, Inc. and Basic Books, Inc. Reprinted by permission of Basic Books, Inc., New York. **1.30** Photograph by M. Sakka, Courtesy Musée de L'Homme et Musée Depuytren, Paris. **1.33** Adapted from Gazzaniga, M. S., The split brain in man, *Scientific American* 217 (August 1967): 27. Copyright 1967 by Scientific American. All rights reserved. **1.35** Courtesy of Neils A. Lassen. **1.36** Adapted from Coyle, J. T., Price, D., and Delong, M. R., Alzheimer's disease: A disorder of cholinergic innervation, *Science* 219 (1983): 1184–90. Copyright 1983 by the American Association for the Advancement of Science (AAAS). Reproduced by permission of the AAAS and the author.

2.3 Keeton, W. T., and Gould, J. L., *Biological Science,* 4th ed. New York: W. W. Norton & Company, Inc., 1986. Copyright 1986, 1980, 1979, 1972, 1967 by W. W. Norton & Company. Used with permission. **2.5** Photographs courtesy of Jacob Steiner. **2.6** Courtesy Neal E. Miller, Rockefeller University. **2.7** Adapted from Bouchard, C., Tremblay, A., Desprès, J. P., Nadeau, A., Lupien, P. L., Theriault, G., Dussault, J., Moorjani, S., Pinault, S. M., and Fournier, G., "The response to long-term overfeeding in identical twins," *New England Journal of Medicine* (1990) 322: pp. 1477–1482. Reprinted by permission of the publisher. **2.8** Adapted from Nisbett, R. E., "Taste deprivation and weight determinants of eating behavior," *Journal of Personality and Social Psychology* 10 (1968): 107–16. Copyright by the American Psychological Association. Adapted by permission of the author. **2.9** Herman, H. C., and Mack, D., "Restrained and unrestrained eating," *Journal of Personality* vol. 43 (1975): 647–60. Adapted by permission of Duke University Press. **2.10** Andres, R., "Influence of obesity on longevity in the aged," in Borek, C., Fenoglio, C. M., and King, D. W., (eds.) *Aging, Cancer and Cell Membranes,* pp. 230–46. New York: Thieme-Stratton, 1980. **2.11** Reprinted by permission of Hawthorne Properties (Elsevier-Dutton Publishing Co., Inc.) from *Bodily Changes in Pain, Hunger, Fear and Rage* by W. B. Cannon. Copyright 1929 by Appleton-Century Co,; 1957 by W. B. Cannon.

2.12 Copyright Walter Chandoha, 1991. **2.13** Bloom, F. E., Lazerson, A., and Hofstadter, L., *Brain, Mind and Behavior.* New York: Freeman, 1988. Adapted by permission of WNET/Thirteen. **2.17** Courtesy of William C. Dement. **2.18** Adapted from Kleitman, N., Patterns of dreaming, *Scientific American* 203 (November 1960): 82–88. Copyright 1960 by Scientific American, Inc. All rights reserved. **2.19** Photography courtesy of the University of Wisconsin Primate Laboratory.

3.4 Pavlov, I. P., *Lectures on conditioned reflexes,* vol. 1. New York: International Publishers Company, Inc., 1928. Adapted by permission of the International Publishers Company, Inc. **3.5** Moore, J. W., "Stimulus control: studies of auditory generalization in rabbits," in Black, A. H., and Prokasy, W. F. (eds.), *Classical Conditioning II: Current Theory and Research.* Copyright 1972 by Prentice-Hall, Inc., Englewood Cliffs, N.J. Adapted by permission of the publisher. **3.10A** Photograph by Mike Salisbury. **3.10B** Photograph by Susan M. Hogue. **3.12** From *A Primer of Operant Conditioning* by G. S. Reynolds. Copyright 1968 by Scott, Foresman & Co. Reprinted by permission of the publisher. **3.13** Photographs courtesy of Animal Behavior Enterprises, Inc. **3.14** Courtesy Yerkes Regional Primate Research Center of Emory University. **3.16, 3.17, 3.18** Ferster, C. B., and Skinner, B. F., *Schedules of Reinforcement,* c. 1957, pp. 56, 146, 399. Englewood Cliffs, NJ: Prentice-Hall, Inc., 1957. Adapted by permission of the author. **3.22** Spooner, A., and Kellogg, W. N., "The backward conditioning curve," *American Journal of Psychology* 60 (1947): 321–34. Copyright 1941 by the Board of Trustees of the University of Illinois. Used with permission of the publisher. **3.23** Rescorla, R. A., Predictability and number of pairings in Pavlovian fear conditioning, *Psychonomic Science* 4 (1966): 383–84. **3.25** Colwill, R. M., and Rescorla, R. A., "Postconditioning devaluation of a reinforcer affects instrumental responding," *Journal of Experimental Psychology: Animal Behavioral Process* 11 (1985): 120–132. Copyright 1985 by the American Psychological Association. Adapted by permission of the publisher and the author. **3.27** Maier, S. F., Seligman, M. E. P., and Solomon, R. L., Pavlovian fear conditioning and learned helplessness: effects on escape and avoidance behavior of (a) the CS-US contingency and (b) the independence of the US and voluntary responding, in Campbell, B. A., and Church, R. M. (eds.) *Punishment and Aversive Behavior,* p. 328. Copyright 1969 by Prentice-Hall, Inc., Englewood Cliffs, N.J. Adapted by permission of the publisher. **3.29** Olton, D. S., and Samuelson, R. J., "Remembrance of places passed: Spatial memory in rats," *Journal of Experimental Psychology: Animal Behavior Processes* 2 (1976): 97–116. Copyright 1976 by the American Psychological Association. Reprinted by permission of the publisher. **3.30** Kohler, W., *The Mentality of Apes.* London: Routledge and Kegan Paul Ltd., 1925. Reprinted by permission of the publisher. **3.33** Figure adapted from *Why Chimps Can Read* by A. J. Premack. Copyright 1976 by Ann J. Premack. Reprinted by permission of HarperCollins Publishers.

4.2 *The School of Athens* by Raphael, 1505; Stanza della Segnatura, Vatican; courtesy Scala/Art Resource, New York. **4.3A** Krech, D., and Crutchfield, R., *Elements of Psychology.* New York: Knopf, Inc., 1958. Adapted by permission of Hilda Krech. **4.3B** Adapted from *Biological Psychology,* 2nd ed., by James W. Kalat. Copyright 1984 by Wadsworth, Inc. **4.4** Adapted from Carlson, N. R., *Physiology of Behavior,* 3rd ed. Boston: Allyn and Bacon, 1986. Reprinted by permission of the publisher. **4.6** Gibson, J. J., *The Senses Considered as Perceptual Systems,* p. 80, Fig. 5.4. Boston: Houghton Mifflin Company, 1966. Reprinted by permission of the publisher. **4.7** Thompson, R. F., *Introduction to Biopsychology.* San Rafael, CA: Albion Publishing Company, 1973. Adapted by permission of the publisher. **4.8, 4.9A, 4.10A** Lindsay, P. H., and Norman, D. A., *Human Information Processing,* 2nd edition, pp. 126, 133, 136. New York: Academic Press, 1977. Adapted by permission of the author and Harcourt Brace Jovanovich. **4.9B, 4.10B, 4.12** Coren, S., and Ward, L. M., *Sensation and Per-*

ception, 3rd ed. San Diego: Harcourt Brace Jovanovich, 1989. Adapted by permission of the author and publisher. **4.11** Adapted from Wald, G., Eye and camera, *Scientific American* 183 (August 1950): 33. Copyright 1950 by Scientific American, Inc. All rights reserved. **4.13, 4.14** Cornsweet, T. M., *Visual Perception,* pp. 140, 276. New York: Academic Press, 1970. Adapted by permission of the author and Harcourt Brace Jovanovich. **4.16** Hering, E., *Outlines of a theory of the light sense,* 1920, (translated by Hurvich, L. M., and Jameson, D., 1964), pp. 150–151. Cambridge, MA: Harvard University Press, 1964. Adapted by permission of the publisher. **4.21A** Hurvich, L. M., *Color Vision.* Sunderland, MA: Sinauer Associates Publications, 1981. Reprinted by permission of the publisher. **4.21B** Courtesy of Munsell Color, 2441 N. Calvert Street, Baltimore, MD 21218 USA. **4.24** Detail and full use of Georges Seurat's *The Channel of Gravelines, Petit Fort Philippe,* 1890, oil on canvas, 45.195. Copyright 1991 Indianapolis Museum of Art, gift of Mrs. James W. Fesler in memory of Daniel W. and Elizabeth C. Marmon. **4.29** Hurvich, L. M., *Color Vision.* Sunderland, MA: Sinauer Associates Publications, 1981. Reprinted by permission of the publisher. **4.30** DeValois, R. C., and DeValois, K. K., *Neural Coding of Color,* in Carterette, E. C., and Friedman, M. P., eds. *Handbook of Perception,* vol. 5. New York: Academic Press, 1975. Adapted by permission of the publisher.

5.1 Julian Hochberg, *Perception,* 2nd ed., p. 56. Englewood Cliffs, NJ: Prentice-Hall, Inc., 1978. Adapted by permission of the publisher. **5.2** Photograph by Roberta Intrater. **5.5** Photographs by Hans Wallach and Robert Gillmor. **5.6** Figures 40 and 41 from *The Perception of the Visual World* by James J. Gibson. Copyright 1978, 1950 by Houghton Mifflin Company. Used with permission. **5.7** Coren, S., and Ward, L. M., *Sensation and Perception,* 3rd ed., p. 103. San Diego: Harcourt Brace Jovanovich, 1989. Adapted by permission of the author and publisher. **5.8** Courtesy of Richard D. Walk. **5.10** Duncker, K., Uber induzierte Bewegung, *Psychologische Forschung* 12 (1929): 180–259. Adapted by permission of Springer-Verlag, Inc. **5.11** Fagan, J. F., Infants' recognition of invariant features of faces, *Child Development* 47 (1976): 627–638. Copyright 1976 by The Society for Research in Child Development, Inc. **5.12** Adapted from Hubel, D. H., The visual cortex of the brain, *Scientific American* 209 (November 1963): 54–58. Copyright 1963 by Scientific American, Inc. All rights reserved. **5.13** Photograph by Jeffrey Grosscup. **5.16** Salvador Dali's *The Trojan War;* courtesy Esquire. **5.20** From Kanizsa, G., Subjective contours, *Scientific American* 234 (1976): 48–52. Copyright 1976 by Scientific American, Inc. All rights reserved. **5.22** Goldstein, E. B., *Sensation and Perception,* 2nd ed. Belmont, CA: Wadsworth, Inc., 1984. Adapted by permission of the publisher. **5.23** Selfridge, O. G., Pattern recognition and modern computers, in *Proceedings of Western Joint Computer Conference,* Los Angeles, Calif., 1955. **5.24** Boring, E. G., 1930. A new ambiguous figure, *American Journal of Psychology* 42 (1930): 444–45; and Leeper, R. W., A study of a neglected portion of the field of learning: The development of sensory organization, *Journal of Genetic Psychology* 46 (1935): 41–75. Reproduced by permission of Lucy D. Boring. **5.25** Photograph by Ronald James. **5.26** Yarbus, A. L., *Eye Movements and Vision,* pp. 179–85. Translated by Riggs, R. A. New York: Plenum Press, 1967. Copyright 1967 by Plenum Press. Reprinted by permission of the publisher. **5.27, 5.28** Photographs by Jeffrey Grosscup. **5.29** Adapted by permission of Macmillan Publishing Co., Inc., from *An Introduction to Perception* by Irvin Rock. Copyright 1975 by Irvin Rock. **5.31** Gibson, J. J., *The Perception of the Visual World.* Copyright 1978, 1950 by Houghton Mifflin Company. Used with permission. **5.32** Rock, I., and Kaufman, L., The moon illusion, II, *Science* 136 (June 1962): 1023–31, Figure 22. Copyright 1962 by the American Association for the Advancement of Science. Reprinted by permission of the publisher. **5.32B** Drawings by Debra Mackay. **5.33** Coren, S., and Girgus, J. S., *Seeing Is Deceiving,* 1978. Hillsdale, N.J.: Lawrence Erlbaum Associates, Inc. Reprinted by permission of the publisher. **5.35** Courtesy the Egyptian Museum, Cairo. **5.36** *The Annunciation* by Crivelli; courtesy the National Gallery, London. **5.37** *Bend in the Epte River, near Giverny* by Claude Monet; courtesy Philadelphia Museum of Art; the William L. Elkins Collection. **5.38** *Violin and Grapes* by Pablo Picasso. The Museum of Modern Art, New York; Mrs. David M. Levy Bequest. **5.39** Private Collection, Italy.

6.1 Waugh, N. C., and Norman, D. A., Primary memory, *Psychological Review* 72 (1965) 89–104. Copyright 1965 by the American Psychological Association. Adapted by permission of the publisher. **6.2, 6.4** Murdock, B., The serial position effect of free recall, *Journal of Experimental Psychology* 64 (1962): 482–88. Copyright 1962 by the American Psychological Association. Adapted by permission of the publisher. **6.3** Glanzer, M., and Cunitz, A., Two storage mechanisms in free recall, *Journal of Verbal Learning and Verbal Behavior* 5 (1966): 351–60. Copyright 1966 by the Academic Press, Inc. Adapted by permission of the author and publisher. **6.5** Ericsson, K. A., Chase, W. G., and Faloon, S., Acquisition of a memory skill, *Science* 208 (June 1980): 1181–82. Copyright 1980 by the American Association for the Advancement of Science. Adapted by permission of the publisher. **6.6** Bower, G. H., Analysis of a mneumonic device, *American Scientist* 58 (1970): 446–510. Adapted by permission of *American Scientist,* journal of Sigma Xi, The Scientific Research Society. **6.7** Godden, D. R., and Baddeley, A. D., Context-dependent memory in two natural environments: On land and underwater, *British Journal of Psychology* 66 (1975): 325–331. Reprinted by permission of the British Psychological Society and the author. **6.10** Sternberg, S., Memory scanning: mental processes revealed by reaction time experiments, in Antrobus, J. S., *Cognition and Effect,* pp. 13–58. Boston, MA: Little, Brown and Company, 1970. Adapted by permission of the author. **6.12** Collins, A. M., and Loftus, E. F., A spreading activation theory of semantic processing, *Psychological Review* 82 (1975): 407–28. Copyright 1975 by the American Psychological Association. **6.13** Illustration by Marjorie Torrey; from Lewis Carroll's *Alice in Wonderland,* illustrated by Marjorie Torrey. Copyright 1955 by Random House, Inc. Reprinted by permission of the publisher. **6.14** Kosslyn, S. M., Ball, T. M., and Reiser, V. J., Visual images preserve metric spatial information: Evidence from studies of image scanning, *Journal of Experimental Psychology: Human Perception and Performance* 4 (1978): 47–60. Copyright 1978 by the American Psychological Association. Adapted by permission of the publisher. **6.17** Bahrick, H. P., Semantic memory content in parameters: Fifty years of memory for Spanish learned in school, *Journal of Experimental Psychology: General* 113 (1984): 1–29. Copyright 1984 by the American Psychological Association. Adapted by permission of the publisher. **6.19A** Kolb, B., and Whishaw, I. Q., *Fundamentals of Human Neuropsychology,* 2nd ed., figure 20–5, p. 485. San Francisco: W.H. Freeman and Company, 1980, 1985. Adapted by permission of the publisher. **6.19B** Milner, B., Corkin, S., and Teuber, H. L., Further analysis of the hippocampal amnesic syndrome: Fourteen-year follow-up of H.M., *Psychologia* 6 (1968): 215–34.

7.7 Adapted from Duncker, K., On problem solving, *Psychological Monographs,* Whole No. 270 (1945): 1–113. **7.12, 7.17** Scheerer, M., Goldstein, K., and Boring, E. G., A demonstration of insight: The horse-rider puzzle, *American Journal of Psychology* 54 (1941): 437–38. Copyright 1941 by the Board of Trustees of the University of Illinois. Used with permission of the publisher. **7.13** Photographs by Jeffrey Grosscup. **7.14** Wickelgren, W. A., *How to Solve Problems.* San Francisco: W.H. Freeman and Company, 1974. Reprinted by permission of the publisher. **7.18** Engraving by Walter H. Ruff; courtesy The Granger Collection, New York. **7.20** Reproduced from Lewis Carroll's *Alice in Wonderland,* original illustrations by John Tenniel; in color for this edition by Martina Selway. Secaucus, NJ: Castle Books, Reprinted courtesy of Book Sales, Inc. **7.21** Photograph by Owen Franken/Stock Boston.

8.3 Reproduced from Lewis Carroll's *Alice in Wonderland,* original illustrations by John Tenniel; in color for this edition by Martina Selway. Secaucus, NJ: Castle Books, Reprinted courtesy of Book Sales, Inc. **8.4** Courtesy Sharon Armstrong. **8.7A** Photograph by Philip Morse, University of Wisconsin. **8.7B** Eimas, P. D., Siqueland, E. R., Jusczyk, P., and Vigorito, J., Speech Perception in Infants, *Science* 171 (22 January 1971): 303–6. Copyright 1971 by the American Association for the Advancement of Science. **8.9** Courtesy of Roberta Golinkoff. **8.11** *Higglety Pigglety Pop! or There Must Be More To Life,* by Maurice Sendak. New York: HarperCollins. Copyright 1967 by Maurice Sendak. **8.12** Brown, R., Cazden, C., and Bellugi-Klima, U., The child's grammar from 1 to 3, in Hill, J. P., ed., *Minnesota Symposium on Child Psychology.* Minneapolis, MN: The University of Minnesota Press. Copyright 1969 by the University of Minnesota. **8.14** Photographs courtesy of AP/Wide World Photos. **8.15** Frishberg, N., Arbitrariness and iconicity: Historical change in American Sign Language, *Language* 51 (1975): 696–719. **8.16** Drawings courtesy Noel Yovovich. **8.17** Drawings courtesy Robert Thacker. **8.19** Marler, P. R., A comparative approach to vocal learning: Song development in white crowned sparrows, *Journal of Comparative and Physiological Psychology Monograph* 71 (May 1970): (No. 2, Part 2), pp. 1–25. Copyright 1970 by the American Psychological Association. **8.20** Johnson, J., and Newport, E., Critical period effects in second language learning: The influence of maturational state on the acquisition of English as a second language, *Cognitive Psychology* 21 (1989): 60–99. Copyright 1989 by Academic Press, Inc. Adapted by permission of the publisher. **8.21** Photographs courtesy of David Premack.

9.1 Keeton, W. T., and Gould, J. L., *Biological Science,* 4th ed. New York: W. W. Norton & Company, Inc., 1986. Copyright 1986, 1980, 1979, 1972, 1967 by W. W. Norton & Company. Used with permission. **9.2** Barnett, S. A., *The Rat: A Study in Behavior,* pp. 86–89. Chicago: The University of Chicago Press, 1963. Reprinted by permission of the publisher. **9.3** Photographs by Leonard Lee Rue III/Bruce Coleman **9.4A** Photograph by Joseph T. Collins/Photo Researchers. **9.4B** Photograph by Wolfgang Bayer/Bruce Coleman **9.5A** Courtesy L. T. Nash, Arizona State University **9.5B** Courtesy of Bruce Coleman. **9.6** Photograph by Allan D. Cruickshank, 1978/Photo Researchers. **9.7** Photograph by Mitch Reardon/Photo Researchers. **9.8** Photograph by Garry D. McMichael, 1987/Photo Researchers. **9.9A** Photograph by Philip Green. **9.9B** Photograph by Bob and Clara Calhoun/Bruce Coleman. **9.9C** Photograph by Jeff Foott/Bruce Coleman. **9.10** Klopfer, P. H., *An Introduction to Animal Behavior: Ethology's First Century,* 2nd ed., p. 208. Englewood Cliffs, NJ: Prentice-Hall, Inc., 1974. Adapted by permission of the publisher. **9.11** Hohn, E. O., The phalarope, *Scientific American* 220 (June 1969): 104. Copyright 1969 by Scientific American, Inc. All rights reserved. **9.12** Bermant, G., and Davidson, J. M., *Biological Bases of Sexual Behavior.* New York: Harper and Row, 1974. In turn adapted from data of Davidson, J. M., Rodgers, C. H., Smith, E. R., and Bloch, G. J., Relative threshholds of behavioral and somatic responses to estrogen, *Physiology and Behavior* 3 (1968): 227–29. Copyright 1968, Pergamon Press, Ltd. **9.13A** Photograph by Pat and Tom Leeson/Photo Reseachers. **9.13B** Nina Leen/Life Magazine. Copyright Time

Warner, Inc. **9.14** Photographs courtesy of Ian Wyllie, Monks Wood Experiment Station. **9.15** Copyright Paul Eckman, 1971. **9.16** Photograph by Wayne Lankinen/Bruce Coleman. **9.17** Photograph by George D. Lepp/Bio-Tec Images.

11.1 Asch, S. E., Studies of independence and conformity: A minority of one against a unanimous majority, *Psychological Monographs* 70 (9, Whole No. 416), 1956. Copyright 1956 by the American Psychological Association. **11.2** Photographs by William Vandivert. **11.4** Festinger, L., and Carlsmith, J. M., Cognitive consequences of forced compliance, *Journal of Abnormal and Social Psychology* 58 (1959): 203–10. Copyright 1959 by the American Psychological Association. Reprinted by permission of the author. **11.8** Photographs courtesy of David Matsumoto.

12.3 Leonardo da Vinci's *La Jaconde* (Mona Lisa), Louvre, Paris; photograph courtesy of Service Photographique de la Reunion des Musées Nationaux. **12.4, 12.5** Copyright 1965 by Stanley Milgram. From the film *Obedience,* distributed by Pennsylvania State University, Audio-Visual Services.

13.1 Keeton, W. T., and Gould, J. L., *Biological Science,* 4th ed. New York: W. W. Norton & Company, Inc., 1986. Copyright 1986, 1980, 1979, 1972, 1967 by W. W. Norton & Company. Used with permission. **13.2** Liebert, R. M., Poulos, R. W., and Strauss, G. D., *Developmental Psychology,* Fig. III–10, p. 81. Englewood Cliffs, NJ: Prentice-Hall, Inc., 1974. Originally adapted from H. M. Halverston, printed by The Journal Press, 1931. Photographs by Kathy Hirsh-Pasek. **13.3** Nilsson, Lennart, *Behold Man.* Boston: Little, Brown & Company, 1974. **13.4** Tanner, J. M., Physical growth, in *Carmichael's Manual of Child Psychology,* 3rd ed., vol. 1, Mussen, P. H., ed., Figure 6, p. 85. New York: John Wiley & Sons, Inc., 1970. **13.5** Conel, J. L., *The Postnatal Development of the Human Cortex,* vols. 1, 3, 5. Cambridge, MA: Harvard University Press, 1939, 1947, 1955. **13.6** Shirley, M. M., *The First Two Years: A Study of Twenty-five Babies,* vol. II. Minneapolis, MN: The University of Minnesota Press, 1933, 1961. Photographs courtesy of Kathy Hirsh-Pasek. **13.7** Photographs by Doug Goodman, 1986/Monkmeyer. **13.8, 13.9, 13.10** Photographs by Chris Massey. **13.11** Piaget, J., and Inhelder, B., *The Child's Conception of Space.* Atlantic Highlands, NJ: Humanities Press International, Inc., 1967. Adapted by permission of the publisher and Routledge & Kegan Paul Ltd. **13.13** Photographs by Phillip Kellman. **13.14** Kellman, P. J., and Spelke, E. S., Perception of partially occluded objects in infancy, *Cognitive Psychology* 15 (1983): 483–524. Copyright 1983 by the Academic Press. **13.15** Baillargeon, R., Object permanence in 3-1/2 and 4-1/2 month old infants, *Developmental Psychology* 23 (1987): 655–64. Adapted by permission of the author and the American Psychological Association. **13.16** Photographs courtesy of Hilary Schmidt. **13.17A** Photographs by Pat Lynch/Photo Researchers. **13.17B** Photograph by Ray Ellis/Photo Researchers. **13.17C** Photograph by Chris Massey. **13.18** Case, R., Intellectual development from birth to adulthood: A neo-Piagetian interpretation, in Siegler, R., ed., *Children's Thinking: What Develops.* Hillsdale, NJ: Lawrence Erlbaum Associates, Inc., 1978. Reprinted by permission of the publisher.

14.1 Photograph by Martin Rogers/Stock Boston. **14.2** Photograph by Suzanne Szasz. **14.4** Ainsworth, M., Blehar, M., Waters, E., and Wall, S., *Patterns of Attachment,* p. 34. Hillsdale, NJ: Lawrence Erlbaum Associates, Inc., 1978. Reprinted by permission of the publisher. **14.5** Photographs by Kathy Hirsh-Pasek. **14.6, 14.7, 14.8** Courtesy Harry Harlow, University of Wisconsin Primate Laboratory. **14.9** Photograph by Michal Heron/Woodfin Camp. **14.10** Bandura, A., Ross, D., and Ross, S. A., Imitation of film-mediated aggressive models, *Journal of Abnormal and Social Psychology* 66 (1963): 8. Copyright 1963 by the American Psychological Association. Reprinted by permission of the author. **14.11** Feshbach, N., and Roe, K., Empathy in six- and seven-year olds, *Child Development* 39 (1968): 133–45. Reprinted by permission of The Society for Research in Child Development, Inc. **14.12** Kohlberg, L., Development of children's orientation towards a moral order in sequence in the development of moral thought, *Vita Humana* 6 (1963): 11–36. Adapted by permission of S. Karger AG, Basel. **14.16** Tanner, J. M., Physical growth, in Mussen, P. H., ed., *Carmichael's Manual of Child Psychology,* 3rd ed., vol. 1, Figure 6, p. 85. New York: John Wiley & Sons, Inc., 1970. Reprinted by permission of the publisher. **14.17A** Photograph by Blair Seitz, 1986/Photo Researchers. **14.17B** Photograph by Thomas D. W. Friedmann/Photo Researchers.

15.1 From Ann Anastasi, *Different Psychology,* 3rd ed., p. 57. Copyright 1958 by Macmillan Publishing Co. Inc. Adapted with permission of the publisher. **15.6** Sample item from the Bennett Test of Mechanical Comprehension. Copyright 1967, 1968 by The Psychological Corporation. Reproduced with permission. **15.7** Adapted by permission from the Wechsler Adult Intelligence Scale—Revised. Copyright 1955, 1981 by The Psychological Corporation. All rights reserved. **15.8** SAT questions selected from *10 SAT's,* College Entrance Examinations Board (1983). Reprinted by permission of Educational Testing Service, the copyright owner of the test questions. **15.9** From the Raven Standard Progressive Matrices, by permission of J. C. Raven Limited. **15.11** Selfe, S., *Nadia: A Case of Extraordinary Drawing Ability in an Autistic Child,* New York: Academic Press, 1977. Reprinted by permission of the publisher and Lorna

Selfe. **15.12** Jones, H. E., and Kaplan, O. J., Psychological aspects of mental disorders in later life, in Kaplan, O. J., ed., *Mental Disorders in Later Life,* 72. Stanford, CA: Stanford University Press, 1945. Adapted by permission of the publisher. **15.13** Schaie, K., and Strother, C., A cross-sequential study of age changes in cognitive behavior, *Psychological Bulletin* 70 (1968): 671–80. Copyright 1968 by the American Psychological Association. Reprinted by permission of the author. **15.15** Photographs courtesy of Dr. Franklin A. Bryan.

16.1 Lanyon, R. I., and Goodstein, L. D., *Personality Assessment,* p. 79. New York: John Wiley & Sons, Inc., 1971. Adapted by permission of the publisher. **16.5** Courtesy Leopold Bellak; reproduced by permission of C. P. S., Inc. Box 83, Larchmont, NY 10538, from The Children's Apperception Test (C. A. T.). **16.6** Courtesy Dr. Gerald S. Blum and Psychodynamic Instruments, Ann Arbor, Michigan. **16.7** Courtesy The Bettmann Archive. **16.8** Eysnck, H. J., and Rachman, S., *The Causes and Cures of Neurosis,* p. 16. San Diego, CA: Robert R. Knapp, 1965. **16.9A** Photograph by Wilfong Photographic/Leo de Wys. **16.9B and C** Photographs by H. Reinhard/Bruce Coleman. **16.12** "Hierarchy of Needs," from *Motivation and Personality* by Abraham H. Maslow. Copyright 1954 by Harper & Row, Publishers, Inc. Copyright 1970 by Abraham H. Maslow. Reprinted by permission of HarperCollins Publishers.

17.1 Negative #31568. Courtesy Department of Library Services, The American Museum of Natural History. **17.2** Courtesy The Bettmann Archive. **17.3** William Hogarth's *The Madhouse,* 1735/1763; courtesy The Bettmann Archive. **17.4** Charles Muller's *Pinel Ordering the Removal of the Inmates' Fetters;* courtesy The Bettmann Archive. **17.6** Photograph by Bill Bridges/Globe Photos. **17.8** Nicol, S. E., and Gottesman, I. I., Clues to the genetics and neurobiology of schizophrenia, *American Scientist* 71 (1983): 398–404. Reprinted by permission of *American Scientist,* journal of Sigma Xi, The Scientific Research Society. **17.9** Data from Faris, R. E. L., and Dunham, H. W., *Mental Disorders in Urban Areas.* Chicago: University of Chicago Press, 1939. Adapted by permission of the author. **17.11** Rosenthal, N. E., Sack, D. A., Gillin, J. C., Lewy, A. J., Goodwin, F. K., Davenport, Y., Mueller, P. S., Newsome, D. A., and Wehr, T. A., Seasonal affective disorder: A description of the syndrome and preliminary findings with light therapy. *Archives of General Psychiatry* 41 (1984): 72–80. Copyright 1984 by the American Medical Association. **17.12** Folkow, B., and Rubenstein, E. H., Cardiovascular effects of acute and chronic stimulations of the hypothalmic defense area in the rat, *Acta Physiologica Scandinavica* 68 (1966): 48–57. Adapted by permission of Acta Physiologica Scandinavica. **17.13A** Photograph by Jerry Cooke/Life Magazine, copyright Time Warner, Inc. **17.13B and C** Photographs by Ken Heyman/Life Magazine, copyright Time Warner, Inc. **17.14** Stone, A., Mental health and law: A system in transition, U.S. Department of Health, Education and Welfare, #75176, p. 7, 1975.

18.1A Courtesy Historical Pictures Service. **18.1B** Courtesy National Library of Medicine. **18.1C** Courtesy Culver Pictures. **18.4** Photograph by James D. Wilson/Woodfin Camp.

TABLES

14.1 Adapted from Kohlberg, L., Classification of moral judgment into levels and stages of development, in Sizer, Theodore R., *Religion and Public Education,* pp. 171–73. Copyright © 1967 Houghton Mifflin Company. Used with permission. **14.2** Erikson, E. H., *Childhood and Society.* New York: W. W. Norton & Company, Inc., 1963. Adapted by permission. **15.3** Wechsler, D., *The Measurement and Appraisal of Adult Intelligence,* 4th ed. Baltimore, MD: The Williams & Wilkins Co., 1958. Copyright 1958 by David Wechsler. Used by permission of Ruth Wechsler, executor David Wechsler estate. Table adapted from the Manual for the Wechsler Adult Intelligence Scale. Copyright 1955 by The Psychological Corporation. **16.2** Norman, W. T., Toward an adequate taxonomy of personality attributes: Replicated factor structure in peer nomination personality ratings, *Journal of Abnormal and Social Psychology* 66 (1963): 577. Copyright 1963 by the American Psychological Association. Adapted by permission of the author.

UNNUMBERED PHOTOS AND ART

2 *Top* Courtesy of Kaiser Porcelain Ltd. *Bottom* Bugelski, B. R., and Alampay, D. A., The role of frequency in developing perceptual sets, *Canadian Journal of Psychology* 15 (1961): 205–211. Adapted by permission of the Canadian Psychological Association. **3** *Left* Courtesy of Richard D. Walk. *Right* Courtesy of William Vandivert. **4** *Top Left* Photograph by Keith Gunnar/Bruce Coleman. *Top Center* Photograph by B. Caster/Bruce Coleman. *Top Right* Photograph by William E. Ferguson. *Bottom Left* Photograph by George H. Harrison/Grant Heilman. *Bottom Right* Photograph by Suzanne Szasz. **5** Collection of Robert H.

Helmick; courtesy Brooke Alexander, New York. **6** *Top* Courtesy Historical Pictures Service, Chicago. *Bottom* Courtesy The Warder Collection. **7** (Part Opener I) Detail from George Bellows' *Dempsey and Firpo.* 1924, oil on canvas, 51 × 63-1/4″. Collection of Whitney Museum of American Art. Purchased with funds from Gertrude Vanderbilt Whitney 31.95. **16** Nilsson, Lennart, *Behold Man.*

Boston: Little, Brown & Company, 1974. Reprinted by permission of the publisher. **21** Lewis, E. R., Everhart, T. E., and Zeevi, Y. Y., Studying neural organization in aplysia with the scanning electron microscope, *Science* 165 (12 September 1969): 1140–43. Copyright 1969 by the American Association for the Advancement of Science. Reprinted by permission of the publisher and author. **22** Photograph by Borys Malkin/Anthro Photo. **31** *Left* Radiography Department, Royal Victoria Infirmary, Newcastle-upon-Tyne. Photo by Simon Fraser/Science Photo Library/Photo Researchers. *Right* Photograph by Grant LeDuc, 1988/Monkmeyer. **43** Theodore Gericault's *The Raft of the Medusa,* 1818–19, The Louvre; copyright Service Photographique de la Reunion des Musée Nationaux. **51.** Photograph courtesy of Black Star, New York. **55** *Left The Venus of Willendorf;* courtesy Naturhistorisches Museum, Vienna. *Center* Peter Paul Rubens' *The Three Graces;* copyright Museo del Prado, Madrid. *Right* Photograph by Mauro Carraro/Gamma Liaison Network. **62** *Jacob's Ladder,* from the Lambeth Bible; courtesy the Archbishop of Canterbury and the Trustees of Lambeth Palace Library. **63** *Left* Photograph by Georg Gerster/Photo Researchers. *Center* Photograph by Jose A. Fernandez/Woodfin Camp. *Right* Courtesy The Kobal Collection. **66** Courtesy of Dr. M. E. Olds. **71** Photograph by Toni Angermayer/Photo Researchers. **72** Courtesy Sovfoto. **77** Courtesy The Granger Collection, New York. **79** Photograph by Nina Leen/Life Magazine, copyright Time Warner, Inc. **87** Photograph by Erika Stone. **87** Courtesy Psychology Department, University of California, Berkeley. **96** Photographs by Lincoln P. Brower. **99.** *Top* Courtesy The Warder Collection. *Bottom* Kohler, W., *The Mentality of Apes.* London: Routledge and Kegan Paul Ltd., 1925. Reprinted by permission of Routledge. **105** (Part Opener II) Edgar Degas, *Portrait of E. Duranty,* 1879. The Burrell Collection, Glasgow Museums. **108** Detail from *The Bermuda Group* by John Smibert; courtesy Yale University Art Gallery; gift of Isaac Lothrop of Plymouth, MA. **123** Courtesy Nobel Stiftelsen. **132** Photographs by Fritz Goro. **141** Claude Monet's *Terrace at Sainte-Adresse,* oil on canvas, 38-5/8 × 51-1/8″; reproduced by permission of the Metropolitan Museum of Art, New York; purchased with special contributions and purchase funds given or bequeathed by friends of the Museum, 1967. **146** Photograph courtesy Omikron. **151** *Left* Courtesy U.S. Government. *Right* Ferrell Grehan/Photo Researchers. **172** Salvador Dali's *The Persistence of Memory,* 1931, oil on canvas, 9-1/2 × 13″; Collection, The Museum of Modern Art, New York; given anonymously. **177** Paul Cezanne's *The Cardplayers;* courtesy Metropolitan Museum of Art, bequest of Stephen C. Clark, 1960. **178** Photograph courtesy of The Kobal Collection. **180** Photograph courtesy of The Kobal Collection. **181** Photograph by Nina Leen/Life Magazine, copyright Time Warner, Inc. **192** Photograph by Suzanne Szasz. **193** Photographs courtesy of The Bettmann Archive. **200** Rembrandt's *Aristotle with a Bust of Homer,* oil on canvas, 56-1/2 × 53-3/4″; courtesy The Metropolitan Museum of Art, purchased with special funds and gifts of friends of the Museum, 1961. **201** Pablo Picasso's *Portrait of Amboise Vollard,* 1909, Puskin Museum, Moscow; courtesy Scala/Art Resource, New York. **212** Courtesy Melvin L. Prueitt, C-6, Los Alamos National Laboratory. **219** From a British National Theatre production of *Galileo* by Bertolt Brecht; photograph by Zoe Dominic. **226** Pieter Brueghel the Elder, *Turmbau zu Babel (Tower of Babel);* courtesy Kunsthistorisches Museum, Vienna. **227** *My Fair Lady;* photograph by Leonard McCombe/Life Magazine, copyright Time Warner, Inc. **228** *Top* William

Blake's *Adam Naming the Beasts;* courtesy The Stirling Maxwell Collection, Pollak House, Glasgow Museums. *Bottom* Henri Rousseau's *The Sleeping Gypsy,* 1897, oil on canvas, 51″ × 6′7″; Collection, The Museum of Modern Art, New York. Gift of Mrs. Simon Guggenheim. **232** By permission. From Webster's Ninth New Collegiate Dictionary. Copyright 1991 by Merriam-Webster Inc., publisher of the Merriam-Webster dictionaries. **233, 235** Reproduced from Lewis Carroll's *Alice in Wonderland,* original illustrations by John Tenniel; in color for this edition by Martina Selway. Secaucus, NJ: Castle Books. Reprinted courtesy of Book Sales, Inc. **237** Lewis Carroll's *Through the Looking Glass,* illustrated by Tenniel, courtesy of General Research Division, The New York Public Libary, Astor, Lenox, and Tilden Foundations. **238** Photograph by Erika Stone. **244** Photograph by Roberta Grobel Intrater. **250** Photograph by Larry Morris/New York Times Photography; courtesy American Foundation for the Blind, New York. **251** Photograph by Larry Morris/New York Times Photography; courtesy American Foundation for the Blind, New York. **254** Photographs courtesy of Herbert Terrace. **259** (Part Opener III) Detail from Renoir's *A Luncheon at Bougival (Un dejeuner à Bougival),* 1880–81, oil on canvas, 51 × 68″; courtesy The Phillips Collection, Washington, DC. **261** Painting by John Michael

Wright; courtesy The Granger Collection, New York. **262** Painting by J. Collier; courtesy of The National Portrait Gallery, London. **262** Photograph by G. K. Brown/Ardea London Ltd. **263** Photograph by Brian M. Rogers/Biofotos. **266** *Top* Stouffer Pro ductions/Animals Animals. *Bottom* Robert W. Hernandez/Photo Researchers. **274** Photograph by Robert W. Hernandez/Photo Researchers. **275** Copyright Carol Rosegg/Martha Swope Photography, Inc. **276** Photograph by Roy P. Fontaine. **283** Courtesy of Photofest. **284** Francisco de Zurbaran's *St. Serapion,* 1628, oil on canvas, 47-9/16 × 41″: courtesy of Wadsworth Atheneum, Hartford. The Ella Gallup Sumner and Mary Caitlin Sumner Collection. **288** Gravure's *Jean M. Charcot—A Clinical Lecture at the Salpetriere;* courtesy The Bettmann Archive. **291** Photograph by Nobby Clark. **293** Reproduced from Walter Crane's *The Baby's Own Aesop,* engraved and printed by Edmund Evans; reproduced from the Print Collection, Miriam & Ira D. Wallach Division of Art, Prints and Photographs, The New York Public Library, Astor, Lenox, and Tilden Foundations. **295** Courtesy Billy Rose Theatre Collection, The New York Public Library at Lincoln Center, Astor, Lenox, and Tilden Foundations. **299** Henry Fuseli's *The Nightmare;* courtesy The Detroit Institute of Arts. **301** Courtesy The American Museum of Natural History. **302** Photograph courtesy Mary Evans/Freud copyrights. **303** Courtesy Wide World Photos. **306** *Top left* Photograph by Michael Copper/Stratford Festival. *Top right* Courtesy Photofest. *Bottom* Courtesy Swathmore College. **308** Courtesy The Kobal Collection. **310** *Left* Copyright Sylvia Johnson/Woodfin Camp *Right* Copyright Susan McElhinney/Woodfin Camp. **311** *Top* Mitsouko. Guerlain, Paris. *Bottom* Best Foods Baking Group. **312** Frontispiece from *The Wonderful World of American Advertising, 1865–1900,* by Leonard de Vries and Ilonka van Amstel. Chicago: Follett, 1972. **314** *Left* Photograph by Francis Laping/Black Star. *Center* Roger Sandler/Black Star. *Right* Christopher Morris/Black Star. **315** Photograph by Michael Probst/UPI, Bettmann Newsphotos. **318** Courtesy AP/Wide World Photos. **319** Courtesy The Kobal Collection **320** Courtesy Reuters/Bettmann Newphotos. **321** Photograph by Suzanne Szasz. **322** Copyright Lee Snider/Photo Images; courtesy New York Gilbert & Sullivan Players. **329** Photograph by Hiroji Kubota/Magnum Photos. **330** *The Gifts of the Magi,* Basilica of Sant Apollinare Nuovo, Ravenna; courtesy Giorgio la Pira. **334** UPI/Bettmann Newsphotos. **335** Grant Wood, American, 1892–1942, *American Gothic,* 1930, oil on beaver board, 76 × 63.3 cm, Art Institute of Chicago, Friends of American Art Collection, 1930.934; photograph copyright 1990, The Art Institute of Chicago. All rights reserved. **336** *Left and center* Photographs by George K. Fuller. *Right* Photograph by John Moss/Photo Researchers. **337** *Top* Photograph from

Subject Index

flooding in, 544–45
for mood disorders, 543–47
systematic desensitization in, 545–46
beliefs:
changes in, forced compliance and, 395*n*
cognitive consistency and, 308–9
control and, 481
interpersonal nature of, 306–8
response bias and, 113–14
see also attitudes
belongingness effect, 95–97
Bethlehem hospital (Bedlam), 494
binocular depth cues, 141–42
binomial distributions, A13*n*
biological constraints, 95
bipolar cells, 125
bipolar disorder, 509, 511, 536, 555
birds:
altruism in, 280–81
brain size of, 12*n*
courtship and mating rituals of, 3–4, 272
critical periods in, 252
defense behaviors of, 265
displays of, 264, 280–81
fixed-action patterns in, 264
imprinting in, 382
learned food aversions in, 96, 97
mate selection of, 272
parent-child bonding in, 276
temperature regulation in, 45
territoriality in, 265–66
young, gaping response in, 277
bitter tastes, 49, 117
blacks:
hypertension in whites vs., 523
IQ of whites vs., 443–47
black-white system, 135, 136
Blacky test, psychoanalytic theory of
development and, 458
blindness:
color, 137
emotional expression and, 279
language learning and, 249–50
in one eye, depth perception and, 142–43
blind obedience, 341–45
cognitive reinterpretations in, 344–45
personality structure and, 342
and reduction of personal responsibility, 344
situational factors in, 342–45
blind spots, 125
blocking, in classical conditioning, 90–91
blood, flow of, to brain, 2
bloodlettings, 534
blood pressure, 522–23
high, *see* hypertension
psychological disorders and, 522–23
bluffs, 267
bonding, *see* attachment, mother-child;
male-female bond
bottom-up processes, in perception,
153–55, 187
bower birds, courtship and mating rituals
of, 3–4
brain, 25–40
abnormalities of, 505
activity of, during sleep, 60
anatomy of, 26–29
blood flow in, 2
convulsive treatments and, 539–40
electrical stimulation of, 1–2
growth of, 358
injury, recovery from, 37–39
language areas of, 33–34, 36–37, 251

lateralization of, 34–37
localization of function in, 31–32, 39–40
of male songbirds, 12*n*
malfunctions of, 496
of newborns, 358
pain alleviation and, 23–24
prefrontal lobotomy and, 539
split, 35–36
see also cerebral cortex; cerebral
hemispheres; hypothalmus
brain stem, 26
brightness:
of color, 130, 131
light intensity and, 124
opponent-process theory and, 136
brightness contrast, 127–29, 133, 164
lateral inhibition and, 128–29
lightness constancy and, 160–61
opponent-process theory and, 136
Broca's area, 34, 37, 251
bulimia, 54
bundles of semantic features, 233
bystander effect, 331–33

California Psychological Inventory (CPI),
453, 454
camouflage, good continuation and, 150
cancer, learned helplessness and, 94–95
caring, moral reasoning and, 397
case studies, A5
castration anxiety, 294–95
catatonic schizophrenia, 503
catecholamines, 505
catharsis, 288, 542–43
CAT scans (Computerized Axial Tomography), 31
cats in puzzle box, 78
CCK (cholecystokinin), 48
Cedar Waxwings, gaping in, 277
cell bodies, 12, 13, 16, 20, 15*n*
central excitatory state, 47
central nervous system (CNS), 26–29
see also brain; cerebral cortex; cerebral
hemispheres
central route to persuasion, 311, 312
central tendency, measures of, A8–A9
central traits, 316
CER (conditioned emotional response), 76
cerebellum, 26
cerebral cortex, 27–28, 29–40
activation of, 59–60
amnesia due to lesions in, 194
aphasia due to damage in, 33–34, 251
association areas of, 31–34
disorders of, 31–34
dreaming and, 62
lateralization of, 34–37
localization of function in, 31–32, 39–40
motor areas of, 29–30, 34, 37
projection areas of, 29–31, 34, 37
recovery from injury of, 37–39
sensory areas of, 30–31
cerebral hemispheres, 26, 27–28
lateralization of, 34–37
and sexual differences in maturation, 401
chaining, in problem solving, 201–2, 203–4
chess playing, 205
memory in, 375
child development, *see* cognitive development; development; language
learning; psychosexual development;
social development
childhood amnesia, 192
child rearing, 388–93, 486

in institutions, 385–86
moral conduct and, 393–96
patterns of, 391–93
reinforcement in, 389
children:
beginnings of representational thought in,
362–63
concrete and formal operations in,
365–66
conservation of number and quantity in,
363–65, 370–71, 373
delay of gratification in, 482–84
deprived of access to some meanings,
249–50
egocentrism in, 365, 370
intelligence testing of, 426–28
isolated, 246
as limited mental processors, 374
maturation of, 372
memory development in, 374, 375–76
motor development in, 359–60
as novices, 375
physical growth in, 358–59
as poor strategists, 375–76
temperamental differences in, 393
wild, 245–46
see also adolescence; attachment,
mother-child; infants; newborns
Children's Apperception Test, 458
chimpanzees:
insightful behavior in, 99–102
language learning and, 253–55
symbol manipulation in, 101–2
chlorpromazine, 22–23, 535, 537
cholecystokinin (CCK), 48
choleric personality, 462
chromatic colors, 129–30
chromosomes, 438
chunking:
cognitive development and, 374–76
in memory organization, 176, 178,
374–76
mental images and, 179
in problem solving, 202–6
classical conditioning, 71–77
acquisition of conditioned responses in,
73–74
arbitrariness vs. belongingness in,
95–97
behavior therapy based on, 543–48, 550
and biological constraints on learning,
95–98
blocking in, 90–91
cognitive view of, 87–91
contiguity in, 88, 89–90, 97
contingency in, 89–90, 93
discrimination in, 75
extensions of, 76–77
extinction in, 74–75
fear in, 76–77
generalization in, 75
higher-order conditioning in, 74
instrumental conditioning vs., 77, 79–81
major phenomena of, 73–75
Pavlov's discovery of, 72–73
phobias and, 86–87, 515–16
temporal relations in, 88–89
terms of, defined, 71–72
classical theory of concept meaning, 201
client-centered therapy, 548–49
closure, in perceptual grouping, 150
CNS (central nervous system), 26–29
see also brain; cerebral cortex; cerebral
hemispheres

dancing flies, courtship and mating rituals of, 272
dark adaptation, 126
data, research:
  collection of, A1, A4–A5
  description of, A2–A4
  interpretation of, A2, A18–A26
  organization of, A1, A7–A13
day-care centers, 387
deafness, language learning and, 247–49
death, 412
decay, of memory trace, 190–91
decibels, 120
decision making, 220–23
  availability heuristic in, 221–23
  cognitive shortcuts for estimating probabilities in, 220–22
  framing in, 222–23
  representativeness heuristic in, 221
declarative knowledge, 196
deductive reasoning, 217–218, 220
Deep Thought chess program, 213
deer, alarm calls of, 281
defense, patterns of, 476–79
defense mechanisms, 292–93
  displacement, 292
  evidence of, 298–99
  isolation, 293
  projection, 293
  psychodynamic approach to personality and, 474, 478–79
  rationalization, 293
  reaction formation, 292–93, 475
  repression, 289, 292, 295, 298–99, 301, 474, 478
defense reactions, 265
deferred imitation, 363
deficiency needs, 484
definitional theory of word meaning, 232–33, 234
dehumanization of victims, 344–45
deindividuation, 345–46, 350
deinstitutionalization policy, 535, 538
delayed reinforcement, 83, 85–86
delay of gratification, 482–84
delay of reward principle, 83
delusions, in schizophrenia, 23, 502–3, 504
demonic possession, insanity as, 493–94
dendrites, 12, 15n, 20
depressant drugs, 65
depression, 509–11, 515
  attributional style and, 481–82, 513–14, 519
  Beck's cognitive theory of, 512
  colvulsive treatments for, 540
  drug therapies for, 512, 513, 536, 540, 555
  learned helplessness and, 94, 513, 514, 482n
  MMPI and, 452, 453
  sex differences in, 514
  suicide and, 510
deprivation, see social deprivation
depth cues, 141–44
  binocular, 141–42
  monocular, 142–43
  in perceptual illusions, 162–63
  pictorial, 109–10, 142–43, 165
depth perception, 141–45
  in infants, 3, 144–45
  through motion, 143–44
descriptive rules of language, 227
desensitization, systematic, 545–46, 547

detection experiments, 115
development, 6, 355–78
  in adolescence, 407, 408–11
  in adulthood, 408, 411–14
  characteristics of, 355–56
  as differentiation, 356–57, 358
  in embryo, 356–58, 359, 369–70
  as growth, 357–59
  human, slow rate of, 358–59
  as maturation, 372
  motor, 355, 356–57, 359–60, 361–63, 372
  as orderly progression, 359–60
  physical, 355, 356–59
  as progressive change, 355
  psychosexual, 293–96, 302
  sensory, 359, 361–63
  see also cognitive development; social development
deviation:
  average, A10n
  standard (SD), 421, A10–A11, A23
deviation IQ, 428
diabetes, 500
Diagnostic and Statistical Manual of Mental Disorders (Revised) (DSM-III-R), 499, 501, 556
diaphragms, in eyes, 125
diathesis-stress conception, 500, 514, 524–25
  see also pathology model of psychopathology
dichotic listening, 157
differences, individual, 6
difference threshold, 112
differentiation:
  behavior and, 356–57
  in embryonic development, 356–57, 358
  perceptual, 149
diffusion of responsibility, 332–33
directed action, 42–43
  in newborns, 362
discrimination learning, 75, 80–81
  in monkeys, 101
disease, definition of, 498
disinhibition, in neuron excitation, 18–19
displacement, in psychoanalytic theory, 292
displays, 3–4
  alarm calls, 280–81
  in animal behavior, 264, 267, 271, 272, 278, 280–81
  in courtship and mating rituals, 271–72
  evolutionary origin of, 272
  and expression of emotions in humans, 278–80
  feigning injury and, 280
  motives in, 278
  preparatory movements and, 278
  releasing stimuli and, 264
  rules of, 326
  of sex differences, 271
  threat, 267, 278
dispositional factors, in attribution of traits, 318–21
dispositional quality, 319
dissociative disorders, 520–21
dissonance theory, 308–9, 312–14, 322n
distal stimuli, 108, 140, 158
distance, perceived size and, 158–59, 161–62
distance cues, pictorial, 109–10
distance sense, smell as, 119
distress calls, 276–77

distibutions, statistical, A7–A11
  binomial, A13n
  frequency, A7–A14
  and measures of central tendency, A8–A9
  normal, A12–A13
  skewed, A8–A9
  symmetric, A9
  t, A23n
Dodo Bird verdict, 552
dogs, babyness cues in, 278
dominance hierarchies, 268
dominant genes, 438
door-in-the-face technique, 331
dopamine (DA), 21, 22–23, 505
double-blind technique, 537
dreams:
  Freud's theory of, 296–97, 299–300
  function of, 62
  REM sleep and, 62
  symbolism in, 297, 299, 300
  wish fulfillment in, 296–97, 300
  see also sleep
drive, 59
drive-reduction theory of motivation, 63–64
drugs, 64–66
  addiction to, 65–66, 530
  agonist, 22
  antagonist, 22
  antipsychotic, 22–23, 535–36, 538, 555
  arousal level and, 65
  depressant, 65
  neurotransmitter activity affected by, 22–23
  opponent-process theory and, 66
  stimulant, 65
  tolerance to, 65, 66
  withdrawl from, 65, 66
drug therapies, 497, 535–39
  doctors' expectations and, 537
  evaluation of, 536–37
  limitations of, 538–39
  for mood disorders, 511, 513, 535–56, 538
  placebo effects and, 536–37
  for schizophrenia, 505, 535, 538, 555
  side effects of, 538
  spontaneous improvement and, 536
dual-center theory of hypothalamic control, 49–50
duct glands, 24n
duodenum, 48
duplexity theory of vision, 126
dynamics, 473

eardrums, 121
ears:
  anatomy of, 120–21
  vestibular senses and, 115
  see also hearing
eating, see feeding
eating disorders, hypothalamic lesions and, 50
EEGs, see electroencephalograms
effectors, 11, 13
efferent nerves, 11, 16, 18, 26
effort, justification of, 312, 322n
ego, 290–91, 474, 486
egocentrism, 365, 370
ego psychology, 477, 478–79
Egyptian art, 164, 165
eidetic imagery, 189
eight ages of man, Erikson on, 408, 412

elaboration-likelihood model, 311
elderly, 413, 481
Electra complex, 296
electrical potentials, resting and action, 13–14, 20
electroconvulsive shock treatment (ECT), 539–40, 555
electroencephalograms (EEGs):
    during sleep, 60
    of sociopaths, 529–30
embryonic development:
    differentiation in, 356–58
    orderly progression of, 359
    stages of, 357–58, 369–70
embryos, 272
emergency reaction, 56–58, 522
    central controls in, 57–58
    habituation and, 71
    negative effects of, 58
eminence, genetic factors in, 440
emotional defusing, 550
emotional insight, 542–43, 550–51
emotionality, 470, 519
emotional stress, 523
emotions:
    arousal and, 324–25
    catharsis and, 288, 542–43
    cognitive arousal theory of, 324–27
    culture and, 279–80
    disorders of, in schizophrenia, 503
    displays and, 4
    expression of, 278–80, 507
    facial expressions and, 279, 326
    fundamental, 326–27
    James-Lange theory of, 322–23, 324
    opponent-process theory and, 66
    romantic love and, 337–38
    subjective experience of, 322–27
    universality of, 278–79
empathy, 395–96
empiricism:
    cognitive development and, 361, 373–74
    perception and, 158–60, 161, 162, 165
    sensory experience and, 107–10
    thinking and, 199–200, 201
    see also nativism
encoding, 172, 173–79, 184
    specificity of, 180
encoding strategies, 481
encounters, 549
endocrine glands, 24
endorphins, 23–24, 537
environment, 480
    behavior as reaction to, 11
    cognitive development and, 373–74
    genotype vs. phenotype and, 438–39
    intelligence and, 436–38, 440–43, 444–46
    internal, homeostasis and, 44–54, 55, 58
    language learning and, 245–51
    schizophrenia and, 506–8
    sociopathy and, 530
    temperament and, 393
epilepsy, 35, 40, 194
epinephrine (adrenalin), 56, 57
    emotional experience and, 324–25
episodic memory, 187
equipotentiality principle, 95, 97
erogenous zones, 294, 474
escape learning, 86
escape reaction, see emergency reaction
essential hypertension, see hypertension
estrogen, 273, 514
estrus, 273

ethology, 263–64
    see also animal behavior
evolution:
    animal learning and, 77–78
    and variability within species, 421–22
    see also natural selection
excitation, reflex response and, 17–18
existential therapy, 549–50
expectancies, 481
experimental groups, A4
experiments, A4
    variance and, A19–A20
expert systems, artificial intelligence and, 213–14
explicit memory, 182, 192, 196–97
expressive aphasia, 33–34
expressive movements, 278–79
extensor muscles, 18
externality hypothesis of obesity, 52
extinction, 80
    of avoidance learning, 87
    in classical conditioning, 74–75, 544
    partial-reinforcement effect and, 84–85
    reconditioning and, 74
extroversion, 461–62, 470, 471–72
eye movements:
    in perceptual selection, 155–56
    rapid (REM), 61–62
    vestibular senses and, 115
eyes, anatomy of, 124–25
    see also retinas; vision
eyewitness testimony, memory distortions in, 185–86

facial expressions, emotions and, 279, 326
factor analysis, 433
    of personality traits, 460–62
false alarms, in signal-detection experiments, 114
familiarity, liking and, 334–35
family:
    culture and, 302
    schizophrenia and, 507–8
    see also attachment, mother-child; child rearing; children; infants; newborns
family resemblance structure, 234
family therapy, 554
fathers:
    assessing role of, 384
    of sociopaths, 530
    see also child rearing; family; parents
fat metabolism, 50
favorable self-picture, 313–14
fear:
    conditioned, 76–77, 90–91
    emergency reaction and, 55–58
    pheromones as signal of, 119
    of strangers, 383, 470
    of unfamiliar, mother-child attachment and, 381
    see also phobias
feature analysis, 147, 152–53
feature detectors, 147, 152
Fechner's law, 113
feedback systems, 43–44
feeding, 47–54
    anorexia nervosa and bulimia in, 54
    child rearing and, 391–92
    dual-center theory of, 49–50
    fat metabolism and, 50
    hypothalamic control centers in, 49–50
    internal signals for, 48
    obesity and, 51–54

receptors for, 47–48
    signals for, 47–49
fetuses, 357, 358
fighting, ritualized, 267
    see also aggression
figure-ground differentiation, 149
filter theory of attention, 157
finches, natural selection and, 421–22
fixation, 206–7, 475
fixation point, 156
fixed action patterns, 264
fixed-interval (FI) schedules of reinforcement, 84
fixed-ratio (FR) schedules of reinforcement, 83–84, 85
flashbulb memories, 193–94
flexor muscles, 18
flight-or-fight reaction, see emergency reaction
flooding, 544–45
fluid intelligence, 435–36
food, conflicts over, 262
    see also feeding
foot-in-the-door technique, 331
forced compliance, 313, 322n, 395n
forebrain, 26, 27–29
forgetting, 190–94
    and change of retrieval cues, 192
    decay in, 190–91
    interference in, 191
    from long-term memory, 190–92
    occurrence of, 192–94
    from short-term memory, 174–75
    theories of, 190–92
forgetting curves, 190
formal operations period, 361, 365–66
form equivalence, 152
form perception, 146–54, 164
    elements of, 146–47
    feature detectors in, 147
    figure-ground differentiation in, 149
    innate factors in, 147
    pattern recognition in, 151–54
    perceptual grouping in, 150
    perceptual segregation in, 148–50
    size and shape constancy in, 161–62
forward pairing, in conditioning, 88
foveas, 125, 126, 156
framing, 222–23
fraternal twins, personality traits shared by, 471
free association, 289, 541–42
free-floating anxiety, 381
free recall, 175–76
frequency, of sound waves, 120, 121, 123
frequency distributions, 420, A7–A11
    central tendency of, A8–A9
    graphic representation of, A7–A8
    variability of, A9–A11
Freudian slips, 296
frontal lobes, 27, 29, 34
fugue state, 520
functional fixedness, 208
function morphemes, 231, 240
fundamental attribution error, 318–19
fundamental emotions, 326–27

galvanic skin response (GSR), 57
ganglion cells, 125
gaping, in young birds, 277
gender, 398–407
    cognitive developmental theory and, 404
    constitutional factors and, 399–401

thinking, thought *(cont.)*
  repression of, 292
  spatial, 215–17
  see also problem solving
thirst, 46–47
threat, reaction to, *see* emergency reaction
threat displays, 267, 278
three-mountain test of egocentrism, 365
threshold:
  absolute, in sensory processes, 111–12,
    113–14, 126
  of neuron impulse, 15
tip-of-the-tongue phenomenon, 181–82
toilet training, 294, 391–92, 474, 475–76
token economies, 547
tolerance, in drug use, 65, 66
tombloys, 399
tongue, taste sensitivity of, 116, 117
top-down processes, in perception, 153–55,
  184, 187
touch, sense of, 116
trace consolidation, 195
train of thought, 201
traits, *see* personality traits
trait theory of personality, 450, 451, 459–72
  defense of, 465–66
  difficulties with, 462–65
transduction, 13, 111, 123
  in cochlea, 122–23
  in eyes, 124–25
transfer, in learning, 100
transference, 543, 550
transmission for chimpanzee communication, 254
transposition of form or pattern, 152
treatment of psychopathology, 534–57
  convulsive treatments, 539–40
  drug therapies, 497, 511, 513, 535–39,
    540
  institutionalization in, 494–95, 526
  psychosurgery, 539
  spontaneous improvements and, 536,
    551–52
  see also psychotherapy
tree diagrams, 235–36
trephining, 493, 534
tricyclics, 536, 540
Trobriand Islanders, family patterns of, 302
trustworthiness, persuasive communications
  and, 311
twins, identical vs. fraternal, 440–42
twin studies:
  on genetic contribution to intelligence,
    440–42, 471
  on homosexuality, 406
  on mood disorders, 511
  on personality, 471
  on schizophrenia, 506
  on sociopathy, 530
two-syndrome hypothesis of schizophrenia,
  505
Type A personality, 523–24
Type B personality, 523–24

ulcers, 521–22, 524
unconditional positive regard, 486
unconditioned responses (UR), 73, 87

unconditioned stimuli (US), 73–74, 77, 80,
  82, 87
  belongingness and, 95–97
  blocking of, 90
  contingency of CS and, 89–90
  defined, 73
  fear and, 76
  learned taste aversions and, 97
  temporal relations between CS and, 88
unconscious:
  psychoanalysis and, 289, 290–97, 302–3,
    541
  recovery of memories in, 296, 298–99,
    541–42
  use of term, 298
unconscious conflict, 290–97, 302–3, 474
  antagonists of, 290–91
  evidence for, 298–99
  nature of, 291–93
  in normal life, 296–97
  origins of, 293–96
  social vs. biological factors in, 300–301
unconscious inference, in perception, 159
unconscious mechanisms, 478–79
unipolar mood disorders, 509
unique colors, 130
unreinforced vs. reinforced trials, 74
unselfishness, 333, 395–96

vagus nerve, 19
validity:
  of mental tests, 424–25
  of personality tests, 452, 454–55, 458–59,
    462
validity coefficients, 424, 425
validity scales, in MMPI, 452, 453
variability, A2
  accounting for, A18–A20
  correlation and, 422–23
  measures for, A9–A11
  natural selection and, 421–22
variable-interval (VI) schedules of reinforcement, 84
variable ratio (VR) schedules of reinforcement, 84, 85
variables:
  dependent, A4
  independent, A4
  normal distribution of, A12–A13
variance (V), 421, A10–A11
  correlation and, A20
  experiments and, A4, A19–A20
vasoconstriction, 45, 46
vasodilation, 45, 46
ventromedial hypothalamic region, 49–50
verbal memory, 178–79
verbal skills, sexual differences and,
  400–401
verb phrases, 235
vesicles, 20
vestibular senses, 115
vicious circle, neurotic conflict and, 477
virginity, loss of, 410
visible spectrum, 124, 130
vision, 124–37
  acuity, 125–26
  adaptation phenomena in, 127, 134
  brightness contrast in, 127–29, 133, 136,
    160–61

color, 129–37
distal and proximal stimuli in, 108, 155,
  158–59
duplexity theory of, 126
eye anatomy and, 124–25
in infancy, 359
lateral inhibition in, 128–29
light as stimulus in, 124
perceptual grouping in, 150
peripheral, 126, 155–56
receptors in, 125–27, 128–29, 134–35,
  136
selective, 156–57
semicircular canal system and, 115
visual pigments in, 127
Weber fraction for, 112–13
see also perception
visual cliff, 3, 143, 144–45
visual memory, 188–90
visual pigments, 127
visual projection area, 31
visual search procedure, 156
visual segregation, 148–49
visual sensations, 124, 128
vocabulary, chimpanzees' acquisition of,
  254
vocal apparatus, phonemes and, 229–30

waking, 59–60
warmth sensations, 116
wavelength:
  of light, 124
  of sound waves, 120, 121
weaning, 391, 392
Weber fraction, 112–13
Weber's law, 112–13
Wechsler Adult Intelligence Scale, 429, 430,
  433
Wernicke's area, 34, 251
will power, 482
wish fulfillment, in dreams, 296–97, 300
withdrawal, from drug use, 65, 66
withdrawal, social, as symptom of schizophrenia, 502
wolves, appeasement signals in, 267
words:
  in abstract thought, 200–201
  classes, 244–45
  combining definitional and prototype
    descriptions in, 234
  definitional theory of meaning in,
    232–33
  meaning as reference in, 232
  into meaningful sentences, 234–36
  meaning of, 232–34, 240, 244–45
  morphemes and, 230–31
  mothers' aids to learning of, 244
  perceptual and conceptual biases of,
    244
  prototype theory of meaning in, 233–
    34
working backwards, problem solving and,
  208, 211
working memory, 177–78, 182–84

Zipf's law, A14
z-scores, A11–A13, A23
zygotes, 270